W9-CDO-154

THE HISTORIES AND POEMS

OF

WILLIAM SHAKESPEARE

THE HISTORIES
AND POEMS
OF
WILLIAM
SHAKESPEARE

THE MODERN LIBRARY

NEW YORK

1995 Modern Library Edition

Jacket photograph courtesy of The Granger Collection, New York

Printed on recycled, acid-free paper

Library of Congress Cataloging-in-Publication Data
Shakespeare, William, 1564–1616.
The histories and poems of William Shakespeare.
p.   cm.
ISBN 0-679-60143-0
1. Great Britain—History—1066–1687—Drama.   2. Great Britain—
Kings and rulers—Drama.   3. Historical drama, English.   I. Title.
PR2762   1995
822.3\3—dc20   94-34173

Manufactured in the United States of America

2 4 6 8 9 7 5 3 1

CONTENTS

THE LIFE AND DEATH
OF KING JOHN

SCENE

Sometimes in England, and sometimes in France

THE LIFE AND DEATH OF
KING JOHN

ACT ONE

SCENE ONE

A Room of State in the Palace.

*Enter King John, Queen Elinor, Pembroke, Essex,
Salisbury, and Others, with Chatillon*

KING JOHN. Now, say, Chatillon, what would France with
us?

CHATILLON. Thus, after greeting, speaks the King of France,
In my behaviour, to the majesty,
The borrow'd majesty of England here.

ELINOR. A strange beginning; 'borrow'd majesty!'

KING JOHN. Silence, good mother; hear the embassy.

CHATILLON. Philip of France, in right and true behalf
Of thy deceased brother Geffrey's son,
Arthur Plantagenet, lays most lawful claim
To this fair island and the territories,
To Ireland, Poictiers, Anjou, Touraine, Maine;
Desiring thee to lay aside the sword
Which sways usurpingly these several titles,
And put the same into young Arthur's hand,
Thy nephew and right royal sovereign.

KING JOHN. What follows if we disallow of this?

CHATILLON. The proud control of fierce and bloody war,
To enforce these rights so forcibly withheld.

KING JOHN. Here have we war for war, and blood for blood,
Controlment for controlment: so answer France.

CHATILLON. Then take my king's defiance from my mouth,
The furthest limit of my embassy.

KING JOHN. Bear mine to him, and so depart in peace:
Be thou as lightning in the eyes of France;
For ere thou canst report I will be there,

The thunder of my cannon shall be heard.
So, hence! Be thou the trumpet of our wrath
And sullen presage of your own decay.
An honourable conduct let him have:
Pembroke, look to 't. Farewell, Chatillon.

Exeunt Chatillon and Pembroke

ELINOR. What now, my son! have I not ever said
How that ambitious Constance would not cease
Till she had kindled France and all the world
Upon the right and party of her son?
This might have been prevented and made whole
With very easy arguments of love,
Which now the manage of two kingdoms must
With fearful bloody issue arbitrate.

KING JOHN. Our strong possession and our right for us.

ELINOR. Your strong possession much more than your right,
Or else it must go wrong with you and me:
So much my conscience whispers in your ear,
Which none but heaven and you and I shall hear.

Enter a Sheriff, who whispers to Essex

ESSEX. My liege, here is the strangest controversy,
Come from the country to be judg'd by you,
That e'er I heard: shall I produce the men?

KING JOHN. Let them approach.   *Exit Sheriff*
Our abbeys and our priories shall pay
This expedition's charge.

Re-enter Sheriff, with Robert
Faulconbridge and Philip, his bastard Brother
          What men are you?

THE BASTARD. Your faithful subject I, a gentleman
Born in Northamptonshire, and eldest son,
As I suppose, to Robert Faulconbridge,
A soldier, by the honour-giving hand
Of Cœur-de-Lion knighted in the field.

KING JOHN. What art thou?

ROBERT. The son and heir to that same Faulconbridge.

KING JOHN. Is that the elder, and art thou the heir?
You came not of one mother then, it seems.

THE BASTARD. Most certain of one mother, mighty king,
That is well known: and, as I think, one father:
But for the certain knowledge of that truth
I put you o'er to heaven and to my mother:

Of that I doubt, as all men's children may.

ELINOR. Out on thee, rude man! thou dost shame thy mother
And wound her honour with this diffidence.

THE BASTARD. I, madam? no, I have no reason for it;
That is my brother's plea and none of mine;
The which if he can prove, a' pops me out
At least from fair five hundred pound a year:
Heaven guard my mother's honour and my land!

KING JOHN. A good blunt fellow. Why, being younger born,
Doth he lay claim to thine inheritance?

THE BASTARD. I know not why, except to get the land.
But once he slander'd me with bastardy:
But whe'r I be as true-begot or no,
That still I lay upon my mother's head;
But that I am as well-begot, my liege,—
Fair fall the bones that took the pains for me!—
Compare our faces and be judge yourself.
If old Sir Robert did beget us both,
And were our father, and this son like him;
O old Sir Robert, father, on my knee
I give heaven thanks I was not like to thee!

KING JOHN. Why, what a madcap hath heaven lent us here!

ELINOR. He hath a trick of Cœur-de-Lion's face:
The accent of his tongue affecteth him.
Do you not read some tokens of my son
In the large composition of this man?

KING JOHN. Mine eye hath well examined his parts,
And finds them perfect Richard. Sirrah, speak:
What doth move you to claim your brother's land?

THE BASTARD. Because he hath a half-face, like my father.
With half that face would he have all my land;
A half-fac'd groat five hundred pound a year!

ROBERT. My gracious liege, when that my father liv'd,
Your brother did employ my father much,—

THE BASTARD. Well, sir, by this you cannot get my land:
Your tale must be how he employ'd my mother.

ROBERT. And once dispatch'd him in an embassy
To Germany, there with the emperor
To treat of high affairs touching that time.
The advantage of his absence took the king,
And in the mean time sojourn'd at my father's;
Where how he did prevail I shame to speak,

But truth is truth: large lengths of seas and shores
Between my father and my mother lay,—
As I have heard my father speak himself,—
When this same lusty gentleman was got.
Upon his death-bed he by will bequeath'd
His lands to me, and took it on his death
That this my mother's son was none of his;
An if he were, he came into the world
Full fourteen weeks before the course of time.
Then, good my liege, let me have what is mine,
My father's land, as was my father's will.

KING JOHN. Sirrah, your brother is legitimate;
Your father's wife did after wedlock bear him,
And if she did play false, the fault was hers;
Which fault lies on the hazards of all husbands
That marry wives. Tell me, how if my brother,
Who, as you say, took pains to get this son,
Had of your father claim'd this son for his?
In sooth, good friend, your father might have kept
This calf bred from his cow from all the world;
In sooth he might: then, if he were my brother's,
My brother might not claim him; nor your father,
Being none of his, refuse him: this concludes;
My mother's son did get your father's heir;
Your father's heir must have your father's land.

ROBERT. Shall then my father's will be of no force
To dispossess that child which is not his?

THE BASTARD. Of no more force to dispossess me, sir,
Than was his will to get me, as I think.

ELINOR. Whether hadst thou rather be a Faulconbridge
And like thy brother, to enjoy thy land,
Or the reputed son of Cœur-de-Lion,
Lord of thy presence and no land beside?

THE BASTARD. Madam, an if my brother had my shape,
And I had his, Sir Robert his, like him;
And if my legs were two such riding-rods,
My arms such eel-skins stuff'd, my face so thin
That in mine ear I durst not stick a rose
Lest men should say, 'Look, where three-farthings goes!'
And, to his shape, were heir to all this land,
Would I might never stir from off this place,
I 'd give it every foot to have this face:

I would not be Sir Nob in any case.

ELINOR. I like thee well; wilt thou forsake thy fortune,
Bequeath thy land to him, and follow me?
I am a soldier and now bound to France.

THE BASTARD. Brother, take you my land, I 'll take my chance.
Your face hath got five hundred pounds a year,
Yet sell your face for five pence and 'tis dear.
Madam, I 'll follow you unto the death.

ELINOR. Nay, I would have you go before me thither.

THE BASTARD. Our country manners give our betters way.

KING JOHN. What is thy name?

THE BASTARD. Philip, my liege, so is my name begun;
Philip, good old Sir Robert's wife's eldest son.

KING JOHN. From henceforth bear his name whose form thou
    bearest:
Kneel thou down Philip, but arise more great;
Arise Sir Richard, and Plantagenet.

THE BASTARD. Brother by the mother's side, give me your
    hand:
My father gave me honour, yours gave land.
Now blessed be the hour, by night or day,
When I was got, Sir Robert was away!

ELINOR. The very spirit of Plantagenet!
I am thy grandam, Richard: call me so.

THE BASTARD. Madam, by chance but not by truth; what
    though?
Something about, a little from the right,
    In at the window, or else o'er the hatch:
Who dares not stir by day must walk by night,
    And have is have, however men do catch.
Near or far off, well won is still well shot,
    And I am I, howe'er I was begot.

KING JOHN. Go, Faulconbridge: now hast thou thy desire;
A landless knight makes thee a landed squire.
Come, madam, and come, Richard: we must speed
For France, for France, for it is more than need.

THE BASTARD. Brother, adieu: good fortune come to thee!
For thou wast got i' the way of honesty.
                                    Exeunt all but the Bastard
A foot of honour better than I was,
But many a many foot of land the worse.
Well, now can I make any Joan a lady.

'Good den, Sir Richard!' 'God-a-mercy, fellow!'
And if his name be George, I 'll call him Peter;
For new-made honour doth forget men's names:
'Tis too respective and too sociable
For your conversion. Now your traveller,
He and his toothpick at my worship's mess,
And when my knightly stomach is suffic'd,
Why then I suck my teeth, and catechize
My picked man of countries: 'My dear sir,'—
Thus, leaning on mine elbow, I begin,—
'I shall beseech you,'—that is question now;
And then comes answer like an absey-book:
'O, sir,' says answer, 'at your best command;
At your employment; at your service, sir':
'No, sir,' says question, 'I, sweet sir, at yours':
And so, ere answer knows what question would,
Saving in dialogue of compliment,
And talking of the Alps and Apennines,
The Pyrenean and the river Po,
It draws toward supper in conclusion so.
But this is worshipful society
And fits the mounting spirit like myself;
For he is but a bastard to the time,
That doth not smack of observation;
And so am I, whether I smack or no;
And not alone in habit and device,
Exterior form, outward accoutrement,
But from the inward motion to deliver
Sweet, sweet, sweet poison for the age's tooth:
Which, though I will not practise to deceive,
Yet, to avoid deceit, I mean to learn;
For it shall strew the footsteps of my rising.
But who comes in such haste in riding-robes?
What woman-post is this? hath she no husband
That will take pains to blow a horn before her?

   Enter Lady Faulconbridge and James Gurney

O me! it is my mother. How now, good lady!
What brings you here to court so hastily?
LADY FAULCONBRIDGE. Where is that slave, thy brother?
 where is he,
That holds in chase mine honour up and down?
THE BASTARD. My brother Robert? old Sir Robert's son?

Colbrand the giant, that same mighty man?
Is it Sir Robert's son that you seek so?

LADY FAULCONBRIDGE. Sir Robert's son! Ay, thou unrever-
end boy,
Sir Robert's son: why scorn'st thou at Sir Robert?
He is Sir Robert's son, and so art thou.

THE BASTARD. James Gurney, wilt thou give us leave awhile?

GURNEY. Good leave, good Philip.

THE BASTARD.   Philip! sparrow! James,
There's toys abroad: anon I'll tell thee more. *Exit Gurney*
Madam, I was not old Sir Robert's son:
Sir Robert might have eat his part in me
Upon Good-Friday and ne'er broke his fast.
Sir Robert could do well: marry, to confess,
Could he get me? Sir Robert could not do it:
We know his handiwork: therefore, good mother,
To whom am I beholding for these limbs?
Sir Robert never holp to make this leg.

LADY FAULCONBRIDGE. Hast thou conspired with thy brother
too,
That for thine own gain shouldst defend mine honour?
What means this scorn, thou most untoward knave?

THE BASTARD. Knight, knight, good mother, Basilisco-like.
What! I am dubb'd; I have it on my shoulder.
But, mother, I am not Sir Robert's son;
I have disclaim'd Sir Robert and my land;
Legitimation, name, and all is gone.
Then, good my mother, let me know my father;
Some proper man, I hope; who was it, mother?

LADY FAULCONBRIDGE. Hast thou denied thyself a Faulcon-
bridge?

THE BASTARD. As faithfully as I deny the devil.

LADY FAULCONBRIDGE. King Richard Cœur-de-Lion was thy
father:
By long and vehement suit I was seduc'd
To make room for him in my husband's bed.
Heaven lay not my transgression to my charge!
Thou art the issue of my dear offence,
Which was so strongly urg'd past my defence.

THE BASTARD. Now, by this light, were I to get again,
Madam, I would not wish a better father.
Some sins do bear their privilege on earth,

And so doth yours; your fault was not your folly:
Needs must you lay your heart at his dispose,
Subjected tribute to commanding love,
Against whose fury and unmatched force
The aweless lion could not wage the fight,
Nor keep his princely heart from Richard's hand.
He that perforce robs lions of their hearts
May easily win a woman's. Ay, my mother,
With all my heart I thank thee for my father!
Who lives and dares but say thou didst not well
When I was got, I'll send his soul to hell.
Come, lady, I will show thee to my kin;
   And they shall say, when Richard me begot,
If thou hadst said him nay, it had been sin:
   Who says it was, he lies: I say, 'twas not.   *Exeunt*

ACT TWO

SCENE ONE

France. Before the Walls of Angiers.

Enter, on one side, the Duke of Austria, and Forces; on the other, Philip, King of France, and Forces, Lewis, Constance, Arthur, and Attendants

KING PHILIP. Before Angiers well met, brave Austria.
Arthur, that great forerunner of thy blood,
Richard, that robb'd the lion of his heart
And fought the holy wars in Palestine,
By this brave duke came early to his grave:
And, for amends to his posterity,
At our importance hither is he come,
To spread his colours, boy, in thy behalf,
And to rebuke the usurpation
Of thy unnatural uncle, English John:
Embrace him, love him, give him welcome hither.
ARTHUR. God shall forgive you Cœur-de-Lion's death
The rather that you give his offspring life,
Shadowing their right under your wings of war.
I give you welcome with a powerless hand,
But with a heart full of unstained love:
Welcome before the gates of Angiers, duke.
PHILIP. A noble boy! Who would not do thee right?
AUSTRIA. Upon thy cheek lay I this zealous kiss,
As seal to this indenture of my love,
That to my home I will no more return
Till Angiers, and the right thou hast in France,
Together with that pale, that white-fac'd shore,
Whose foot spurns back the ocean's roaring tides
And coops from other lands her islanders,
Even till that England, hedg'd in with the main,
That water-walled bulwark, still secure
And confident from foreign purposes,

Even till that utmost corner of the west
Salute thee for her king: till then, fair boy,
Will I not think of home, but follow arms.
CONSTANCE. O! take his mother's thanks, a widow's thanks,
Till your strong hand shall help to give him strength
To make a more requital to your love.
AUSTRIA. The peace of heaven is theirs that lift their swords
In such a just and charitable war.
PHILIP. Well then, to work: our cannon shall be bent
Against the brows of this resisting town.
Call for our chiefest men of discipline,
To cull the plots of best advantages:
We 'll lay before this town our royal bones,
Wade to the market-place in Frenchmen's blood,
But we will make it subject to this boy.
CONSTANCE. Stay for an answer to your embassy,
Lest unadvis'd you stain your swords with blood.
My Lord Chatillon may from England bring
That right in peace which here we urge in war;
And then we shall repent each drop of blood
That hot rash haste so indirectly shed.

Enter Chatillon

PHILIP. A wonder, lady! lo, upon thy wish,
Our messenger, Chatillon, is arriv'd!
What England says, say briefly, gentle lord;
We coldly pause for thee; Chatillon, speak.
CHATILLON. Then turn your forces from this paltry siege
And stir them up against a mightier task.
England, impatient of your just demands,
Hath put himself in arms: the adverse winds,
Whose leisure I have stay'd, have given him time
To land his legions all as soon as I;
His marches are expedient to this town,
His forces strong, his soldiers confident.
With him along is come the mother-queen,
An Ate, stirring him to blood and strife;
With her her niece, the Lady Blanch of Spain;
With them a bastard of the king's deceas'd;
And all the unsettled humours of the land,
Rash, inconsiderate, fiery voluntaries,
With ladies' faces and fierce dragons' spleens,
Have sold their fortunes at their native homes,

Bearing their birthrights proudly on their backs,
To make a hazard of new fortunes here.
In brief, a braver choice of dauntless spirits
Than now the English bottoms have waft o'er
Did never float upon the swelling tide,
To do offence and scathe in Christendom.

Drums heard within

The interruption of their churlish drums
Cuts off more circumstance: they are at hand,
To parley or to fight; therefore prepare.

PHILIP. How much unlook'd for is this expedition!
AUSTRIA. By how much unexpected, by so much
We must awake endeavour for defence,
For courage mounteth with occasion:
Let them be welcome then, we are prepar'd.

Enter King John, Elinor,
Blanch, the Bastard, Lords, and Forces

KING JOHN. Peace be to France, if France in peace permit
Our just and lineal entrance to our own;
If not, bleed France, and peace ascend to heaven,
Whiles we, God's wrathful agent, do correct
Their proud contempt that beats his peace to heaven.
PHILIP. Peace be to England, if that war return
From France to England, there to live in peace.
England we love; and, for that England's sake
With burden of our armour here we sweat:
This toil of ours should be a work of thine;
But thou from loving England art so far
That thou hast under-wrought his lawful king,
Cut off the sequence of posterity,
Out-faced infant state, and done a rape
Upon the maiden virtue of the crown.
Look here upon thy brother Geffrey's face:
These eyes, these brows, were moulded out of his;
This little abstract doth contain that large
Which died in Geffrey, and the hand of time
Shall draw this brief into as huge a volume.
That Geffrey was thy elder brother born,
And this his son; England was Geffrey's right
And this is Geffrey's. In the name of God
How comes it then that thou art call'd a king,
When living blood doth in these temples beat,

Which owe the crown that thou o'ermasterest?

KING JOHN. From whom hast thou this great commission,
France,
To draw my answer from thy articles?

PHILIP. From that supernal judge, that stirs good thoughts
In any breast of strong authority,
To look into the blots and stains of right:
That judge hath made me guardian to this boy:
Under whose warrant I impeach thy wrong,
And by whose help I mean to chastise it.

KING JOHN. Alack! thou dost usurp authority.

PHILIP. Excuse; it is to beat usurping down.

ELINOR. Who is it thou dost call usurper, France?

CONSTANCE. Let me make answer; thy usurping son.

ELINOR. Out, insolent! thy bastard shall be king,
That thou mayst be a queen, and check the world!

CONSTANCE. My bed was ever to thy son as true
As thine was to thy husband, and this boy
Liker in feature to his father Geffrey
Than thou and John in manners; being as like
As rain to water, or devil to his dam.
My boy a bastard! By my soul I think
His father never was so true begot:
It cannot be an if thou wert his mother.

ELINOR. There's a good mother, boy, that blots thy father.

CONSTANCE. There's a good grandam, boy, that would blot
thee.

AUSTRIA. Peace!

THE BASTARD.   Hear the crier.

AUSTRIA.   What the devil art thou?

THE BASTARD. One that will play the devil, sir, with you,
An a' may catch your hide and you alone.
You are the hare of whom the proverb goes,
Whose valour plucks dead lions by the beard.
I'll smoke your skin-coat, an I catch you right.
Sirrah, look to 't; i' faith, I will, i' faith.

BLANCH. O! well did he become that lion's robe,
That did disrobe the lion of that robe.

THE BASTARD. It lies as sightly on the back of him
As great Alcides' shows upon an ass:
But, ass, I'll take that burden from your back,
Or lay on that shall make your shoulders crack.

AUSTRIA. What cracker is this same that deafs our ears
  With this abundance of superfluous breath?
  King Philip, determine what we shall do straight.
PHILIP. Women and fools, break off your conference.
  King John, this is the very sum of all:
  England and Ireland, Anjou, Touraine, Maine,
  In right of Arthur do I claim of thee.
  Wilt thou resign them and lay down thy arms?
KING JOHN. My life as soon: I do defy thee, France.
  Arthur of Britaine, yield thee to my hand;
  And out of my dear love I 'll give thee more
  Than e'er the coward hand of France can win.
  Submit thee, boy.
ELINOR.   Come to thy grandam, child.
CONSTANCE. Do, child, go to it grandam, child;
  Give grandam kingdom, and it grandam will
  Give it a plum, a cherry, and a fig:
  There 's a good grandam.
ARTHUR.   Good my mother, peace!
  I would that I were low laid in my grave:
  I am not worth this coil that 's made for me.
ELINOR. His mother shames him so, poor boy, he weeps.
CONSTANCE. Now shame upon you, whe'r she does or no!
  His grandam's wrongs, and not his mother's shames,
  Draw those heaven-moving pearls from his poor eyes,
  Which heaven shall take in nature of a fee;
  Ay, with these crystal beads heaven shall be brib'd
  To do him justice and revenge on you.
ELINOR. Thou monstrous slanderer of heaven and earth!
CONSTANCE. Thou monstrous injurer of heaven and earth!
  Call not me slanderer; thou and thine usurp
  The dominations, royalties, and rights
  Of this oppressed boy: this is thy eld'st son's son,
  Infortunate in nothing but in thee:
  Thy sins are visited in this poor child;
  The canon of the law is laid on him,
  Being but the second generation
  Removed from thy sin-conceiving womb.
KING JOHN. Bedlam, have done.
CONSTANCE.   I have but this to say,
  That he 's not only plagued for her sin,
  But God hath made her sin and her the plague

On this removed issue, plagu'd for her,
And with her plague, her sin; his injury
Her injury, the beadle to her sin,
All punish'd in the person of this child,
And all for her. A plague upon her!

ELINOR. Thou unadvised scold, I can produce
A will that bars the title of thy son.

CONSTANCE. Ay, who doubts that? a will! a wicked will;
A woman's will; a canker'd grandam's will!

PHILIP. Peace, lady! pause, or be more temperate:
It ill beseems this presence to cry aim
To these ill-tuned repetitions.
Some trumpet summon hither to the walls
These men of Angiers; let us hear them speak
Whose title they admit, Arthur's or John's.

Trumpet sounds. Enter Citizens upon the Walls.

FIRST CITIZEN. Who is it that hath warn'd us to the walls?

PHILIP. 'Tis France, for England.

KING JOHN.   England for itself.
You men of Angiers, and my loving subjects,—

PHILIP. You loving men of Angiers, Arthur's subjects,
Our trumpet call'd you to this gentle parle,—

KING JOHN. For our advantage; therefore hear us first.
These flags of France, that are advanced here
Before the eye and prospect of your town,
Have hither march'd to your endamagement:
The cannons have their bowels full of wrath,
And ready mounted are they to spit forth
Their iron indignation 'gainst your walls:
All preparation for a bloody siege
And merciless proceeding by these French
Confronts your city's eyes, your winking gates;
And but for our approach those sleeping stones,
That as a waist do girdle you about,
By the compulsion of their ordinance
By this time from their fixed beds of lime
Had been dishabited, and wide havoc made
For bloody power to rush upon your peace.
But on the sight of us your lawful king,—
Who painfully with much expedient march
Have brought a countercheck before your gates,
To save unscratch'd your city's threaten'd cheeks—

Behold, the French amaz'd vouchsafe a parle;
And now, instead of bullets wrapp'd in fire,
To make a shaking fever in your walls,
They shoot but calm words folded up in smoke,
To make a faithless error in your ears:
Which trust accordingly, kind citizens,
And let us in, your king, whose labour'd spirits,
Forwearied in this action of swift speed,
Crave harbourage within your city walls.
PHILIP. When I have said, make answer to us both.
Lo! in this right hand, whose protection
Is most divinely vow'd upon the right
Of him it holds, stands young Plantagenet,
Son to the elder brother of this man,
And king o'er him and all that he enjoys:
For this down-trodden equity, we tread
In warlike march these greens before your town,
Being no further enemy to you
Than the constraint of hospitable zeal,
In the relief of this oppressed child,
Religiously provokes. Be pleased then
To pay that duty which you truly owe
To him that owes it, namely, this young prince;
And then our arms, like to a muzzled bear,
Save in aspect, have all offence seal'd up;
Our cannons' malice vainly shall be spent
Against the invulnerable clouds of heaven;
And with a blessed and unvex'd retire,
With unhack'd swords and helmets all unbruis'd,
We will bear home that lusty blood again
Which here we came to spout against your town,
And leave your children, wives, and you, in peace.
But if you fondly pass our proffer'd offer,
'Tis not the roundure of your old-fac'd walls
Can hide you from our messengers of war,
Though all these English and their discipline
Were harbour'd in their rude circumference.
Then tell us, shall your city call us lord,
In that behalf which we have challeng'd it?
Or shall we give the signal to our rage
And stalk in blood to our possession?

FIRST CITIZEN. In brief, we are the King of England's
    subjects:
  For him, and in his right, we hold this town.
KING JOHN. Acknowledge then the king, and let me in.
FIRST CITIZEN. That can we not; but he that proves the king,
    To him will we prove loyal: till that time
    Have we ramm'd up our gates against the world.
KING JOHN. Doth not the crown of England prove the king?
    And if not that, I bring you witnesses,
    Twice fifteen thousand hearts of England's breed,—
THE BASTARD. Bastards, and else.
KING JOHN. To verify our title with their lives.
PHILIP. As many and as well-born bloods as those,—
THE BASTARD. Some bastards too.
PHILIP. Stand in his face to contradict his claim.
FIRST CITIZEN. Till thou compound whose right is worthiest,
    We for the worthiest hold the right from both.
KING JOHN. Then God forgive the sins of all those souls
    That to their everlasting residence,
    Before the dew of evening fall, shall fleet,
    In dreadful trial of our kingdom's king!
PHILIP. Amen, Amen! Mount, chevaliers! to arms!
THE BASTARD. Saint George, that swing'd the dragon, and
    e'er since
    Sits on his horse back at mine hostess' door,
    Teach us some fence! (*To Austria*) Sirrah, were I at home,
    At your den, sirrah, with your lioness,
    I would set an ox-head to your lion's hide,
    And make a monster of you.
AUSTRIA.   Peace! no more.
THE BASTARD. O! tremble, for you hear the lion roar.
KING JOHN. Up higher to the plain; where we 'll set forth
    In best appointment all our regiments.
THE BASTARD. Speed then, to take advantage of the field.
PHILIP. It shall be so; (*To Lewis*) and at the other hill
    Command the rest to stand. God, and our right!   *Exeunt*
        Alarums and excursions; then a retreat.
    Enter a French Herald, with trumpets, to the gates
FRENCH HERALD. You men of Angiers, open wide your gates,
    And let young Arthur, Duke of Britaine, in,
    Who, by the hand of France this day hath made
    Much work for tears in many an English mother,

Whose sons lie scatter'd on the bleeding ground;
Many a widow's husband grovelling lies,
Coldly embracing the discolour'd earth;
And victory, with little loss, doth play
Upon the dancing banners of the French,
Who are at hand, triumphantly display'd,
To enter conquerors and to proclaim
Arthur of Britaine England's king and yours.

Enter English Herald, with trumpets

ENGLISH HERALD. Rejoice, you men of Angiers, ring your
    bells;
King John, your king and England's, doth approach,
Commander of this hot malicious day.
Their armours, that march'd hence so silver-bright,
Hither return all gilt with Frenchmen's blood;
There stuck no plume in any English crest
That is removed by a staff of France;
Our colours do return in those same hands
That did display them when we first march'd forth;
And, like a jolly troop of huntsmen, come
Our lusty English, all with purpled hands
Dy'd in the dying slaughter of their foes.
Open your gates and give the victors way.

FIRST CITIZEN. Heralds, from off our towers we might
    behold,
From first to last, the onset and retire
Of both your armies; whose equality
By our best eyes cannot be censured:
Blood hath bought blood, and blows have answer'd blows;
Strength match'd with strength, and power confronted
    power:
Both are alike; and both alike we like.
One must prove greatest: while they weigh so even,
We hold our town for neither, yet for both.

Re-enter the two Kings, with their powers, severally

KING JOHN. France, hast thou yet more blood to cast away?
Say, shall the current of our right run on?
Whose passage, vex'd with thy impediment,
Shall leave his native channel and o'erswell
With course disturb'd even thy confining shores,
Unless thou let his silver water keep
A peaceful progress to the ocean.

PHILIP. England, thou hast not sav'd one drop of blood,
    In this hot trial, more than we of France;
    Rather, lost more: and by this hand I swear,
    That sways the earth this climate overlooks,
    Before we will lay down our just-borne arms,
    We 'll put thee down, 'gainst whom these arms we bear,
    Or add a royal number to the dead,
    Gracing the scroll that tells of this war's loss
    With slaughter coupled to the name of kings.
THE BASTARD. Ha, majesty! how high thy glory towers
    When the rich blood of kings is set on fire!
    O! now doth Death line his dead chaps with steel;
    The swords of soldiers are his teeth, his fangs;
    And now he feasts, mousing the flesh of men,
    In undetermin'd differences of kings.
    Why stand these royal fronts amazed thus?
    Cry 'havoc!' kings; back to the stained field,
    You equal-potents, fiery-kindled spirits!
    Then let confusion of one part confirm
    The other's peace; till then, blows, blood, and death!
KING JOHN. Whose party do the townsmen yet admit?
PHILIP. Speak, citizens, for England; who 's your king?
FIRST CITIZEN. The King of England, when we know the
        king.
PHILIP. Know him in us, that here hold up his right.
KING JOHN. In us, that are our own great deputy,
    And bear possession of our person here,
    Lord of our presence, Angiers, and of you.
FIRST CITIZEN. A greater power than we denies all this;
    And, till it be undoubted, we do lock
    Our former scruple in our strong-barr'd gates,
    Kings of ourselves; until our fears, resolv'd,
    Be by some certain king purg'd and depos'd.
THE BASTARD. By heaven, these scroyles of Angiers flout
        you, kings,
    And stand securely on their battlements
    As in a theatre, whence they gape and point
    At your industrious scenes and acts of death.
    Your royal presences be rul'd by me:
    Do like the mutines of Jerusalem,
    Be friends awhile and both conjointly bend
    Your sharpest deeds of malice on this town.

By east and west let France and England mount
Their battering cannon charged to the mouths,
Till their soul-fearing clamours have brawl'd down
The flinty ribs of this contemptuous city:
I'd play incessantly upon these jades,
Even till unfenced desolation
Leave them as naked as the vulgar air.
That done, dissever your united strengths,
And part your mingled colours once again;
Turn face to face and bloody point to point;
Then, in a moment, Fortune shall cull forth
Out of one side her happy minion,
To whom in favour she shall give the day,
And kiss him with a glorious victory.
How like you this wild counsel, mighty states?
Smacks it not something of the policy?

KING JOHN. Now, by the sky that hangs above our heads,
I like it well. France, shall we knit our powers
And lay this Angiers even with the ground;
Then after fight who shall be king of it?

THE BASTARD. An if thou hast the mettle of a king,
Being wrong'd as we are by this peevish town,
Turn thou the mouth of thy artillery,
As we will ours, against these saucy walls;
And when that we have dashed them to the ground,
Why then defy each other, and, pell-mell,
Make work upon ourselves, for heaven or hell.

PHILIP. Let it be so. Say, where will you assault?

KING JOHN. We from the west will send destruction
Into this city's bosom.

AUSTRIA. I from the north.

PHILIP.   Our thunder from the south
Shall rain their drift of bullets on this town.

THE BASTARD. O, prudent discipline! From north to south
Austria and France shoot in each other's mouth:
I 'll stir them to it. Come, away, away!

FIRST CITIZEN. Hear us, great kings: vouchsafe a while to
stay,
And I shall show you peace and fair-fac'd league;
Win you this city without stroke or wound;
Rescue those breathing lives to die in beds,
That here come sacrifices for the field.

Persever not, but hear me, mighty kings.
KING JOHN. Speak on with favour: we are bent to hear.
FIRST CITIZEN. That daughter there of Spain, the Lady
    Blanch,
  Is near to England. Look upon the years
  Of Lewis the Dauphin and that lovely maid.
  If lusty love should go in quest of beauty,
  Where should he find it purer than in Blanch?
  If zealous love should go in search of virtue,
  Where should he find it purer than in Blanch?
  If love ambitious sought a match of birth,
  Whose veins bound richer blood than Lady Blanch?
  Such as she is, in beauty, virtue, birth,
  Is the young Dauphin every way complete:
  If not complete of, say he is not she;
  And she again wants nothing, to name want,
  If want it be not that she is not he:
  He is the half part of a blessed man,
  Left to be finished by such a she;
  And she a fair divided excellence,
  Whose fulness of perfection lies in him.
  O! two such silver currents, when they join,
  Do glorify the banks that bound them in;
  And two such shores to two such streams made one,
  Two such controlling bounds shall you be, kings,
  To these two princes if you marry them.
  This union shall do more than battery can
  To our fast-closed gates; for at this match,
  With swifter spleen than powder can enforce,
  The mouth of passage shall we fling wide ope,
  And give you entrance; but without this match,
  The sea enraged is not half so deaf,
  Lions more confident, mountains and rocks
  More free from motion, no, not death himself
  In mortal fury half so peremptory,
  As we to keep this city.
THE BASTARD.   Here's a stay,
  That shakes the rotten carcase of old Death
  Out of his rags! Here's a large mouth, indeed,
  That spits forth death and mountains, rocks and seas,
  Talks as familiarly of roaring lions
  As maids of thirteen do of puppy-dogs.

What cannoneer begot this lusty blood?
He speaks plain cannon fire, and smoke and bounce;
He gives the bastinado with his tongue;
Our ears are cudgell'd; not a word of his
But buffets better than a fist of France.
'Zounds! I was never so bethump'd with words
Since I first call'd my brother's father dad.

ELINOR. (*Aside to King John*) Son, list to this conjunction,
    make this match;
Give with our niece a dowry large enough;
For by this knot thou shalt so surely tie
Thy now unsur'd assurance to the crown,
That yon green boy shall have no sun to ripe
The bloom that promiseth a mighty fruit.
I see a yielding in the looks of France;
Mark how they whisper: urge them while their souls
Are capable of this ambition,
Lest zeal, now melted by the windy breath
Of soft petitions, pity and remorse,
Cool and congeal again to what it was.

FIRST CITIZEN. Why answer not the double Majesties
This friendly treaty of our threaten'd town?

PHILIP. Speak England first, that hath been forward first
To speak unto this city: what say you?

KING JOHN. If that the Dauphin there, thy princely son,
Can in this book of beauty read 'I love,'
Her dowry shall weigh equal with a queen:
For Anjou, and fair Touraine, Maine, Poictiers,
And all that we upon this side the sea,—
Except this city now by us besieg'd,—
Find liable to our crown and dignity,
Shall gild her bridal bed and make her rich
In titles, honours, and promotions,
As she in beauty, education, blood,
Holds hand with any princess of the world.

PHILIP. What sayst thou, boy? look in the lady's face.

LEWIS. I do, my lord; and in her eye I find
A wonder, or a wondrous miracle,
The shadow of myself form'd in her eye;
Which, being but the shadow of your son
Becomes a sun, and makes your son a shadow:
I do protest I never lov'd myself

Till now infixed I beheld myself,
Drawn in the flattering table of her eye.

Whispers with Blanch

THE BASTARD. Drawn in the flattering table of her eye!
    Hang'd in the frowning wrinkle of her brow!
And quarter'd in her heart! he doth espy
    Himself love's traitor: this is pity now,
That hang'd and drawn and quarter'd, there should be
In such a love so vile a lout as he.

BLANCH. My uncle's will in this respect is mine:
If he see aught in you that makes him like,
That anything he sees, which moves his liking,
I can with ease translate it to my will;
Or if you will, to speak more properly,
I will enforce it easily to my love.
Further I will not flatter you, my lord,
That all I see in you is worthy love,
Than this: that nothing do I see in you,
Though churlish thoughts themselves should be your
    judge,
That I can find should merit any hate.

KING JOHN. What say these young ones? What say you, my
    niece?

BLANCH. That she is bound in honour still to do
What you in wisdom still vouchsafe to say.

KING JOHN. Speak then, Prince Dauphin; can you love this
    lady?

LEWIS. Nay, ask me if I can refrain from love;
For I do love her most unfeignedly.

KING JOHN. Then do I give Volquessen, Touraine, Maine,
Poictiers, and Anjou, these five provinces,
With her to thee; and this addition more,
Full thirty thousand marks of English coin.
Philip of France, if thou be pleas'd withal,
Command thy son and daughter to join hands.

PHILIP. It likes us well. Young princes, close your hands.

AUSTRIA. And your lips too; for I am well assur'd
That I did so when I was first assur'd.

PHILIP. Now, citizens of Angiers, ope your gates,
Let in that amity which you have made;
For at Saint Mary's chapel presently
The rites of marriage shall be solemniz'd.

Is not the Lady Constance in this troop?
I know she is not; for this match made up
Her presence would have interrupted much:
Where is she and her son? tell me, who knows.

LEWIS. She is sad and passionate at your highness' tent.

PHILIP. And, by my faith, this league that we have made
Will give her sadness very little cure.
Brother of England, how may we content
This widow lady? In her right we came;
Which we, God knows, have turn'd another way,
To our own vantage.

KING JOHN.   We will heal up all;
For we 'll create young Arthur Duke of Britaine
And Earl of Richmond; and this rich fair town
We make him lord of. Call the Lady Constance:
Some speedy messenger bid her repair
To our solemnity: I trust we shall,
If not fill up the measure of her will,
Yet in some measure satisfy her so,
That we shall stop her exclamation.
Go we, as well as haste will suffer us,
To this unlook'd-for unprepared pomp.

                    Exeunt all except the Bastard
                    The Citizens retire from the walls

THE BASTARD. Mad world! mad kings! mad composition!
John, to stop Arthur's title in the whole,
Hath willingly departed with a part;
And France, whose armour conscience buckled on,
Whom zeal and charity brought to the field
As God's own soldier, rounded in the ear
With that same purpose-changer, that sly devil,
That broker, that still breaks the pate of faith,
That daily break-vow, he that wins of all,
Of kings, of beggars, old men, young men, maids,
Who having no external thing to lose
But the word 'maid,' cheats the poor maid of that,
That smooth-fac'd gentleman, tickling Commodity,
Commodity, the bias of the world;
The world, who of itself is peized well,
Made to run even upon even ground,
Till this advantage, this vile-drawing bias,
This sway of motion, this Commodity,

Makes it take head from all indifferency,
From all direction, purpose, course, intent:
And this same bias, this Commodity,
This bawd, this broker, this all-changing word,
Clapp'd on the outward eye of fickle France,
Hath drawn him from his own determin'd aid,
From a resolv'd and honourable war,
To a most base and vile-concluded peace.
And why rail I on this Commodity?
But for because he hath not woo'd me yet.
Not that I have the power to clutch my hand
When his fair angels would salute my palm;
But for my hand, as unattempted yet,
Like a poor beggar, raileth on the rich.
Well, whiles I am a beggar, I will rail,
And say there is no sin but to be rich;
And being rich, my virtue then shall be
To say there is no vice but beggary.
Since kings break faith upon Commodity,
Gain, be my lord, for I will worship thee!   *Exit*

ACT THREE

SCENE ONE

France. The French King's Tent.

Enter Constance, Arthur, and Salisbury

CONSTANCE. Gone to be married! gone to swear a peace!
  False blood to false blood join'd! gone to be friends!
  Shall Lewis have Blanch, and Blanch those provinces?
  It is not so; thou hast misspoke, misheard;
  Be well advis'd, tell o'er thy tale again:
  It cannot be; thou dost but say 'tis so.
  I trust I may not trust thee, for thy word
  Is but the vain breath of a common man:
  Believe me, I do not believe thee, man;
  I have a king's oath to the contrary.
  Thou shalt be punish'd for thus frighting me,
  For I am sick and capable of fears;
  Oppress'd with wrongs, and therefore full of fears;
  A widow, husbandless, subject to fears;
  A woman, naturally born to fears;
  And though thou now confess thou didst but jest,
  With my vex'd spirits I cannot take a truce,
  But they will quake and tremble all this day.
  What dost thou mean by shaking of thy head?
  Why dost thou look so sadly on my son?
  What means that hand upon that breast of thine?
  Why holds thine eye that lamentable rheum,
  Like a proud river peering o'er his bounds?
  Be these sad signs confirmers of thy words?
  Then speak again; not all thy former tale,
  But this one word, whether thy tale be true.
SALISBURY. As true as I believe you think them false
  That give you cause to prove my saying true.
CONSTANCE. O! if thou teach me to believe this sorrow,
  Teach thou this sorrow how to make me die;

And let belief and life encounter so
As doth the fury of two desperate men
Which in the very meeting fall and die.
Lewis marry Blanch! O boy! then where art thou?
France friend with England, what becomes of me?
Fellow, be gone! I cannot brook thy sight:
This news hath made thee a most ugly man.
SALISBURY. What other harm have I, good lady, done,
But spoke the harm that is by others done?
CONSTANCE. Which harm within itself so heinous is
As it makes harmful all that speak of it.
ARTHUR. I do beseech you, madam, be content.
CONSTANCE. If thou, that bidd'st me be content, wert grim,
Ugly and slanderous to thy mother's womb,
Full of unpleasing blots and sightless stains,
Lame, foolish, crooked, swart, prodigious,
Patch'd with foul moles and eye-offending marks,
I would not care, I then would be content;
For then I should not love thee, no, nor thou
Become thy great birth, nor deserve a crown.
But thou art fair; and at thy birth, dear boy,
Nature and Fortune join'd to make thee great:
Of Nature's gifts thou mayst with lilies boast
And with the half-blown rose. But Fortune, O!
She is corrupted, chang'd, and won from thee:
She adulterates hourly with thine uncle John,
And with her golden hand hath pluck'd on France
To tread down fair respect of sovereignty
And made his majesty the bawd to theirs.
France is a bawd to Fortune and King John,
That strumpet Fortune, that usurping John!
Tell me, thou fellow, is not France forsworn?
Envenom him with words, or get thee gone
And leave those woes alone which I alone
Am bound to underbear.
SALISBURY.   Pardon me, madam,
I may not go without you to the kings.
CONSTANCE. Thou mayst, thou shalt: I will not go with thee.
I will instruct my sorrows to be proud;
For grief is proud and makes his owner stoop.
To me and to the state of my great grief
Let kings assemble; for my grief 's so great

That no supporter but the huge firm earth
Can hold it up: here I and sorrows sit;
Here is my throne, bid kings come bow to it.

Seats herself on the ground
Enter King John, King Philip, Lewis, Blanch,
Elinor, the Bastard, Duke of Austria, and Attendants

PHILIP. 'Tis true, fair daughter; and this blessed day
Ever in France shall be kept festival:
To solemnize this day the glorious sun
Stays in his course and plays the alchemist,
Turning with splendour of his precious eye
The meagre cloddy earth to glittering gold:
The yearly course that brings this day about
Shall never see it but a holiday.

CONSTANCE. (*Rising*) A wicked day, and not a holy day!
What hath this day deserv'd? what hath it done
That it in golden letters should be set
Among the high tides in the calendar?
Nay, rather turn this day out of the week,
This day of shame, oppression, perjury:
Or, if it must stand still, let wives with child
Pray that their burdens may not fall this day,
Lest that their hopes prodigiously be cross'd:
But on this day let seamen fear no wrack;
No bargains break that are not this day made;
This day all things begun come to ill end;
Yea, faith itself to hollow falsehood change!

PHILIP. By heaven, lady, you shall have no cause
To curse the fair proceedings of this day:
Have I not pawn'd to you my majesty?

CONSTANCE. You have beguil'd me with a counterfeit
Resembling majesty, which, being touch'd and tried,
Proves valueless: you are forsworn, forsworn;
You came in arms to spill mine enemies' blood,
But now in arms you strengthen it with yours:
The grappling vigour and rough frown of war
Is cold in amity and painted peace,
And our oppression hath made up this league.
Arm, arm, you heavens, against these perjur'd kings!
A widow cries; be husband to me, heavens!
Let not the hours of this ungodly day
Wear out the day in peace; but, ere sunset,

Set armed discord 'twixt these perjur'd kings!
Hear me! O, hear me!

AUSTRIA.   Lady Constance, peace!

CONSTANCE. War! war! no peace! peace is to me a war.
O, Lymoges! O, Austria! thou dost shame
That bloody spoil; thou slave, thou wretch, thou coward!
Thou little valiant, great in villany!
Thou ever strong upon the stronger side!
Thou Fortune's champion, that dost never fight
But when her humorous ladyship is by
To teach thee safety! thou art perjur'd too,
And sooth'st up greatness. What a fool art thou,
A ramping fool, to brag and stamp and swear
Upon my party! Thou cold-blooded slave,
Hast thou not spoke like thunder on my side?
Been sworn my soldier? bidding me depend
Upon thy stars, thy fortune, and thy strength?
And dost thou now fall over to my foes?
Thou wear a lion's hide! doff it for shame,
And hang a calf's-skin on those recreant limbs.

AUSTRIA. O! that a man should speak those words to me.

THE BASTARD. And hang a calf's-skin on those recreant
       limbs.

AUSTRIA. Thou dar'st not say so, villain, for thy life.

THE BASTARD. And hang a calf's-skin on those recreant
       limbs.

KING JOHN. We like not this; thou dost forget thyself.

                         Enter Pandulph

PHILIP. Here comes the holy legate of the pope.

PANDULPH. Hail, you anointed deputies of heaven!
To thee, King John, my holy errand is.
I Pandulph, of fair Milan cardinal,
And from Pope Innocent the legate here,
Do in his name religiously demand
Why thou against the Church, our holy mother,
So wilfully dost spurn; and, force perforce,
Keep Stephen Langton, chosen Archbishop
Of Canterbury, from that holy see?
This, in our foresaid holy father's name,
Pope Innocent, I do demand of thee.

KING JOHN. What earthly name to interrogatories
Can task the free breath of a sacred king?

Thou canst not, cardinal, devise a name
So slight, unworthy and ridiculous,
To charge me to an answer, as the pope.
Tell him this tale; and from the mouth of England
Add thus much more: that no Italian priest
Shall tithe or toil in our dominions;
But as we under heaven are supreme head,
So under him that great supremacy,
Where we do reign, we will alone uphold,
Without the assistance of a mortal hand:
So tell the pope; all reverence set apart
To him, and his usurp'd authority.

PHILIP. Brother of England, you blaspheme in this.

KING JOHN. Though you and all the kings of Christendom
Are led so grossly by this meddling priest,
Dreading the curse that money may buy out;
And, by the merit of vile gold, dross, dust,
Purchase corrupted pardon of a man,
Who in that sale sells pardon from himself;
Though you and all the rest so grossly led
This juggling witchcraft with revenue cherish,
Yet I alone, alone do me oppose
Against the pope, and count his friends my foes.

PANDULPH. Then, by the lawful power that I have,
Thou shalt stand curs'd and excommunicate:
And blessed shall he be that doth revolt
From his allegiance to a heretic;
And meritorious shall that hand be call'd,
Canonized and worshipp'd as a saint,
That takes away by any secret course
Thy hateful life.

CONSTANCE.   O! lawful let it be
That I have room with Rome to curse awhile.
Good father cardinal, cry thou amen
To my keen curses; for without my wrong
There is no tongue hath power to curse him right.

PANDULPH. There's law and warrant, lady, for my curse.

CONSTANCE. And for mine too: when law can do no right,
Let it be lawful that law bar no wrong.
Law cannot give my child his kingdom here,
For he that holds his kingdom holds the law:
Therefore, since law itself is perfect wrong,

How can the law forbid my tongue to curse?

PANDULPH. Philip of France, on peril of a curse,
Let go the hand of that arch-heretic,
And raise the power of France upon his head,
Unless he do submit himself to Rome.

ELINOR. Look'st thou pale, France? do not let go thy hand.

CONSTANCE. Look to that, devil, lest that France repent,
And by disjoining hands, hell lose a soul.

AUSTRIA. King Philip, listen to the cardinal.

THE BASTARD. And hang a calf's-skin on his recreant limbs.

AUSTRIA. Well, ruffian, I must pocket up these wrongs,
Because—

THE BASTARD. Your breeches best may carry them.

KING JOHN. Philip, what sayst thou to the cardinal?

CONSTANCE. What should he say, but as the cardinal?

LEWIS. Bethink you, father; for the difference
Is purchase of a heavy curse from Rome,
Or the light loss of England for a friend:
Forego the easier.

BLANCH.   That's the curse of Rome.

CONSTANCE. O Lewis, stand fast! the devil tempts thee here,
In likeness of a new untrimmed bride.

BLANCH. The Lady Constance speaks not from her faith,
But from her need.

CONSTANCE.   O! if thou grant my need,
Which only lives but by the death of faith,
That need must needs infer this principle,
That faith would live again by death of need:
O! then, tread down my need, and faith mounts up;
Keep my need up, and faith is trodden down.

KING JOHN. The king is mov'd, and answers not to this.

CONSTANCE. O! be remov'd from him, and answer well.

AUSTRIA. Do so, King Philip: hang no more in doubt.

THE BASTARD. Hang nothing but a calf's-skin, most sweet
lout.

PHILIP. I am perplex'd, and know not what to say.

PANDULPH. What canst thou say but will perplex thee more,
If thou stand excommunicate and curs'd?

PHILIP. Good reverend father, make my person yours,
And tell me how you would bestow yourself.
This royal hand and mine are newly knit,
And the conjunction of our inward souls

Married in league, coupled and link'd together
With all religious strength of sacred vows;
The latest breath that gave the sound of words
Was deep-sworn faith, peace, amity, true love,
Between our kingdoms and our royal selves;
And even before this truce, but new before,
No longer than we well could wash our hands
To clap this royal bargain up of peace,
Heaven knows, they were besmear'd and overstain'd
With slaughter's pencil, where revenge did paint
The fearful difference of incensed kings:
And shall these hands, so lately purg'd of blood,
So newly join'd in love, so strong in both,
Unyoke this seizure and this kind regreet?
Play fast and loose with faith? so jest with heaven,
Make such unconstant children of ourselves,
As now again to snatch our palm from palm,
Unswear faith sworn, and on the marriage-bed
Of smiling peace to march a bloody host,
And make a riot on the gentle brow
Of true sincerity? O! holy sir,
My reverend father, let it not be so!
Out of your grace, devise, ordain, impose
Some gentle order, and then we shall be bless'd
To do your pleasure and continue friends.

PANDULPH. All form is formless, order orderless,
Save what is opposite to England's love.
Therefore to arms! be champion of our Church,
Or let the Church, our mother, breathe her curse,
A mother's curse, on her revolting son.
France, thou mayst hold a serpent by the tongue,
A chafed lion by the mortal paw,
A fasting tiger safer by the tooth,
Than keep in peace that hand which thou dost hold.

PHILIP. I may disjoin my hand, but not my faith.

PANDULPH. So mak'st thou faith an enemy to faith:
And like a civil war sett'st oath to oath,
Thy tongue against thy tongue. O! let thy vow
First made to heaven, first be to heaven perform'd;
That is, to be the champion of our Church.
What since thou swor'st is sworn against thyself,
And may not be performed by thyself;

For that which thou hast sworn to do amiss
Is not amiss when it is truly done;
And being not done, where doing tends to ill,
The truth is then most done not doing it.
The better act of purposes mistook
Is to mistake again; though indirect,
Yet indirection thereby grows direct,
And falsehood falsehood cures, as fire cools fire
Within the scorched veins of one new-burn'd.
It is religion that doth make vows kept;
But thou hast sworn against religion
By what thou swear'st, against the thing thou swear'st,
And mak'st an oath the surety for thy truth
Against an oath: the truth thou art unsure
To swear, swears only not to be forsworn;
Else what a mockery should it be to swear!
But thou dost swear only to be forsworn;
And most forsworn, to keep what thou dost swear.
Therefore thy later vows against thy first
Is in thyself rebellion to thyself;
And better conquest never canst thou make
Than arm thy constant and thy nobler parts
Against these giddy loose suggestions:
Upon which better part our prayers come in,
If thou vouchsafe them; but, if not, then know
The peril of our curses light on thee
So heavy as thou shalt not shake them off,
But in despair die under their black weight.

AUSTRIA. Rebellion, flat rebellion!
THE BASTARD.   Will 't not be?
Will not a calf's-skin stop that mouth of thine?
LEWIS. Father, to arms!
BLANCH.   Upon thy wedding-day?
Against the blood that thou hast married?
What! shall our feast be kept with slaughter'd men?
Shall braying trumpets and loud churlish drums,
Clamours of hell, be measures to our pomp?
O husband, hear me! ay, alack! how new
Is husband in my mouth; even for that name,
Which till this time my tongue did ne'er pronounce,
Upon my knee I beg, go not to arms
Against mine uncle.

CONSTANCE.   O! upon my knee,
 Made hard with kneeling, I do pray to thee,
 Thou virtuous Dauphin, alter not the doom
 Forethought by heaven.

BLANCH. Now shall I see thy love: what motive may
 Be stronger with thee than the name of wife?

CONSTANCE. That which upholdeth him that thee upholds,
 His honour: O! thine honour, Lewis, thine honour.

LEWIS. I muse your Majesty doth seem so cold,
 When such profound respects do pull you on.

PANDULPH. I will denounce a curse upon his head.

PHILIP. Thou shalt not need. England, I 'll fall from thee.

CONSTANCE. O fair return of banish'd majesty!

ELINOR. O foul revolt of French inconstancy!

KING JOHN. France, thou shalt rue this hour within this hour.

THE BASTARD. Old Time the clock-setter, that bald sexton
  Time,
 Is it as he will? well then, France shall rue.

BLANCH. The sun 's o'ercast with blood: fair day, adieu!
 Which is the side that I must go withal?
 I am with both: each army hath a hand;
 And in their rage, I having hold of both,
 They whirl asunder and dismember me.
 Husband, I cannot pray that thou mayst win;
 Uncle, I needs must pray that thou mayst lose;
 Father, I may not wish the fortune thine;
 Grandam, I will not wish thy wishes thrive:
 Whoever wins, on that side shall I lose;
 Assured loss before the match be play'd.

LEWIS. Lady, with me; with me thy fortune lies.

BLANCH. There where my fortune lives, there my life dies.

KING JOHN. Cousin, go draw our puissance together.

            Exit the Bastard

 France, I am burn'd up with inflaming wrath;
 A rage whose heat hath this condition,
 That nothing can allay, nothing but blood,
 The blood, and dearest-valu'd blood of France.

PHILIP. Thy rage shall burn thee up, and thou shalt turn
 To ashes, ere our blood shall quench that fire:
 Look to thyself, thou art in jeopardy.

KING JOHN. No more than he that threats. To arms let 's hie!

                Exeunt

SCENE TWO

The Same. Plains near Angiers.

Alarums; excursions. Enter the Bastard, with the
Duke of Austria's head

THE BASTARD. Now, by my life, this day grows wondrous
     hot;
     Some airy devil hovers in the sky
     And pours down mischief. Austria's head lie there,
     While Philip breathes.
                    Enter King John, Arthur, and Hubert
KING JOHN. Hubert, keep this boy. Philip, make up.
     My mother is assailed in our tent,
     And ta'en, I fear.
THE BASTARD.   My lord, I rescu'd her;
     Her Highness is in safety, fear you not:
     But on, my liege; for very little pains
     Will bring this labour to a happy end.   *Exeunt*

SCENE THREE

The Same.

Alarums; excursions; retreat. Enter King John, Elinor,
Arthur, the Bastard, Hubert, and Lords

KING JOHN. (*To Elinor*) So shall it be; your Grace shall stay
     behind
     So strongly guarded. (*To Arthur*) Cousin, look not sad:
     Thy grandam loves thee; and thy uncle will
     As dear be to thee as thy father was.
ARTHUR. O! this will make my mother die with grief.
KING JOHN. (*To the Bastard*) Cousin, away for England!
     haste before;
     And, ere our coming, see thou shake the bags
     Of hoarding abbots; set at liberty
     Imprison'd angels: the fat ribs of peace
     Must by the hungry now be fed upon:
     Use our commission in his utmost force.

THE BASTARD. Bell, book, and candle shall not drive me back
    When gold and silver becks me to come on.
    I leave your Highness. Grandam, I will pray,—
    If ever I remember to be holy,—
    For your fair safety; so I kiss your hand.
ELINOR. Farewell, gentle cousin.
KING JOHN.   Coz, farewell.

Exit the Bastard

ELINOR. Come hither, little kinsman; hark, a word.

She takes Arthur aside

KING JOHN. Come hither, Hubert. O my gentle Hubert,
    We owe thee much: within this wall of flesh
    There is a soul counts thee her creditor,
    And with advantage means to pay thy love:
    And, my good friend, thy voluntary oath
    Lives in this bosom, dearly cherished.
    Give me thy hand. I had a thing to say,
    But I will fit it with some better time.
    By heaven, Hubert, I am almost asham'd
    To say what good respect I have of thee.
HUBERT. I am much bounden to your Majesty.
KING JOHN. Good friend, thou hast no cause to say so yet;
    But thou shalt have; and creep time ne'er so slow,
    Yet it shall come for me to do thee good.
    I had a thing to say, but let it go:
    The sun is in the heaven, and the proud day,
    Attended with the pleasures of the world,
    Is all too wanton and too full of gawds
    To give me audience: if the midnight bell
    Did, with his iron tongue and brazen mouth,
    Sound on into the drowsy race of night;
    If this same were a churchyard where we stand,
    And thou possessed with a thousand wrongs;
    Or if that surly spirit, melancholy,
    Had bak'd thy blood and made it heavy-thick,
    Which else runs tickling up and down the veins,
    Making that idiot, laughter, keep men's eyes
    And strain their cheeks to idle merriment,
    A passion hateful to my purposes;
    Or if that thou couldst see me without eyes,
    Hear me without thine ears, and make reply
    Without a tongue, using conceit alone,

Without eyes, ears, and harmful sound of words;
Then, in despite of brooded watchful day,
I would into thy bosom pour my thoughts:
But ah! I will not: yet I love thee well;
And, by my troth, I think thou lov'st me well.

HUBERT. So well, that what you bid me undertake,
Though that my death were adjunct to my act,
By heaven, I would do it.

KING JOHN.   Do not I know thou wouldst?
Good Hubert! Hubert, Hubert, throw thine eye
On yon young boy: I 'll tell thee what, my friend,
He is a very serpent in my way;
And wheresoe'er this foot of mine doth tread
He lies before me: dost thou understand me?
Thou art his keeper.

HUBERT.   And I 'll keep him so
That he shall not offend your Majesty.

KING JOHN. Death.

HUBERT.   My lord?

KING JOHN.   A grave.

HUBERT.   He shall not live.

KING JOHN.   Enough.
I could be merry now. Hubert, I love thee;
Well, I 'll not say what I intend for thee:
Remember. Madam, fare you well:
I 'll send those powers o'er to your Majesty.

ELINOR. My blessing go with thee!

KING JOHN.   For England, cousin; go:
Hubert shall be your man, attend on you
With all true duty. On toward Calais, ho!   *Exeunt*

SCENE FOUR

The Same. The French King's Tent.

Enter King Philip, Lewis, Pandulph, and Attendants

PHILIP. So, by a roaring tempest on the flood,
A whole armado of convicted sail
Is scatter'd and disjoin'd from fellowship.

PANDULPH. Courage and comfort! all shall yet go well.

PHILIP. What can go well when we have run so ill?

Are we not beaten? Is not Angiers lost?
Arthur ta'en prisoner? divers dear friends slain?
And bloody England into England gone,
O'erbearing interruption, spite of France?
LEWIS. What he hath won that hath he fortified:
So hot a speed with such advice dispos'd,
Such temperate order in so fierce a cause,
Doth want example: who hath read or heard
Of any kindred action like to this?
PHILIP. Well could I bear that England had this praise,
So we could find some pattern of our shame.
                    Enter Constance
Look, who comes here! a grave unto a soul;
Holding the eternal spirit, against her will,
In the vile prison of afflicted breath.
I prithee, lady, go away with me.
CONSTANCE. Lo now! now see the issue of your peace.
PHILIP. Patience, good lady! comfort, gentle Constance!
CONSTANCE. No, I defy all counsel, all redress,
But that which ends all counsel, true redress,
Death, death: O, amiable lovely death!
Thou odoriferous stench! sound rottenness!
Arise forth from the couch of lasting night,
Thou hate and terror to prosperity,
And I will kiss thy detestable bones,
And put my eyeballs in thy vaulty brows,
And ring these fingers with thy household worms,
And stop this gap of breath with fulsome dust,
And be a carrion monster like thyself:
Come, grin on me; and I will think thou smil'st
And buss thee as thy wife! Misery's love,
O! come to me.
PHILIP.   O fair affliction, peace!
CONSTANCE. No, no, I will not, having breath to cry:
O! that my tongue were in the thunder's mouth!
Then with a passion would I shake the world,
And rouse from sleep that fell anatomy
Which cannot hear a lady's feeble voice,
Which scorns a modern invocation.
PANDULPH. Lady, you utter madness, and not sorrow.
CONSTANCE. Thou art not holy to belie me so;
I am not mad: this hair I tear is mine;

My name is Constance; I was Geffrey's wife;
Young Arthur is my son, and he is lost!
I am not mad: I would to heaven I were!
For then 'tis like I should forget myself:
O! if I could, what grief should I forget.
Preach some philosophy to make me mad,
And thou shalt be canoniz'd, cardinal;
For being not mad but sensible of grief,
My reasonable part produces reason
How I may be deliver'd of these woes,
And teaches me to kill or hang myself:
If I were mad, I should forget my son,
Or madly think a babe of clouts were he.
I am not mad: too well, too well I feel
The different plague of each calamity.

PHILIP. Bind up those tresses. O! what love I note
In the fair multitude of those her hairs:
Where but by chance a silver drop hath fallen,
Even to that drop ten thousand wiry friends
Do glue themselves in sociable grief;
Like true, inseparable, faithful loves,
Sticking together in calamity.

CONSTANCE. To England, if you will.

PHILIP.   Bind up your hairs.

CONSTANCE. Yes, that I will; and wherefore will I do it?
I tore them from their bonds, and cried aloud
'O! that these hands could so redeem my son,
As they have given these hairs their liberty!'
But now I envy at their liberty,
And will again commit them to their bonds,
Because my poor child is a prisoner.
And, father cardinal, I have heard you say
That we shall see and know our friends in heaven.
If that be true, I shall see my boy again;
For since the birth of Cain, the first male child,
To him that did but yesterday suspire,
There was not such a gracious creature born.
But now will canker-sorrow eat my bud
And chase the native beauty from his cheek,
And he will look as hollow as a ghost,
As dim and meagre as an ague's fit,
And so he 'll die; and, rising so again,

When I shall meet him in the court of heaven
I shall not know him: therefore never, never
Must I behold my pretty Arthur more.
PANDULPH. You hold too heinous a respect of grief.
CONSTANCE. He talks to me, that never had a son.
PHILIP. You are as fond of grief as of your child.
CONSTANCE. Grief fills the room up of my absent child,
Lies in his bed, walks up and down with me,
Puts on his pretty looks, repeats his words,
Remembers me of all his gracious parts,
Stuffs out his vacant garments with his form:
Then have I reason to be fond of grief.
Fare you well: had you such a loss as I,
I could give better comfort than you do.
I will not keep this form upon my head
When there is such disorder in my wit.
O Lord! my boy, my Arthur, my fair son!
My life, my joy, my food, my all the world!
My widow-comfort, and my sorrows' cure!   *Exit*
PHILIP. I fear some outrage, and I 'll follow her.   *Exit*
LEWIS. There 's nothing in this world can make me joy:
Life is as tedious as a twice-told tale,
Vexing the dull ear of a drowsy man;
And bitter shame hath spoil'd the sweet world's taste,
That it yields nought but shame and bitterness.
PANDULPH. Before the curing of a strong disease,
Even in the instant of repair and health,
The fit is strongest: evils that take leave,
On their departure most of all show evil.
What have you lost by losing of this day?
LEWIS. All days of glory, joy, and happiness.
PANDULPH. If you had won it, certainly you had.
No, no; when Fortune means to men most good,
She looks upon them with a threatening eye.
'Tis strange to think how much King John hath lost
In this which he accounts so clearly won.
Are not you griev'd that Arthur is his prisoner?
LEWIS. As heartily as he is glad he hath him.
PANDULPH. Your mind is all as youthful as your blood.
Now hear me speak with a prophetic spirit;
For even the breath of what I mean to speak
Shall blow each dust, each straw, each little rub,

Out of the path which shall directly lead
Thy foot to England's throne; and therefore mark.
John hath seiz'd Arthur; and it cannot be,
That whiles warm life plays in that infant's veins
The misplac'd John should entertain an hour,
One minute, nay, one quiet breath of rest.
A sceptre snatch'd with an unruly hand
Must be as boisterously maintain'd as gain'd;
And he that stands upon a slippery place
Makes nice of no vile hold to stay him up:
That John may stand, then Arthur needs must fall;
So be it, for it cannot be but so.

LEWIS. But what shall I gain by young Arthur's fall?

PANDULPH. You, in the right of Lady Blanch your wife,
May then make all the claim that Arthur did.

LEWIS. And lose it, life and all, as Arthur did.

PANDULPH. How green you are and fresh in this old world!
John lays you plots; the times conspire with you;
For he that steeps his safety in true blood
Shall find but bloody safety and untrue.
This act so evilly borne shall cool the hearts
Of all his people and freeze up their zeal,
That none so small advantage shall step forth
To check his reign, but they will cherish it;
No natural exhalation in the sky,
No scope of nature, no distemper'd day,
No common wind, no customed event,
But they will pluck away his natural cause
And call them meteors, prodigies, and signs,
Abortives, presages, and tongues of heaven,
Plainly denouncing vengeance upon John.

LEWIS. May be he will not touch young Arthur's life,
But hold himself safe in his prisonment.

PANDULPH. O! sir, when he shall hear of your approach,
If that young Arthur be not gone already,
Even at that news he dies; and then the hearts
Of all his people shall revolt from him
And kiss the lips of unacquainted change,
And pick strong matter of revolt and wrath
Out of the bloody fingers' ends of John.
Methinks I see this hurly all on foot:
And, O! what better matter breeds for you

Than I have nam'd. The bastard Faulconbridge
Is now in England ransacking the Church,
Offending charity: if but a dozen French
Were there in arms, they would be as a call
To train ten thousand English to their side;
Or as a little snow, tumbled about,
Anon becomes a mountain. O noble Dauphin!
Go with me to the king. 'Tis wonderful
What may be wrought out of their discontent
Now that their souls are topful of offence.
For England go; I will whet on the king.
LEWIS. Strong reasons make strong actions. Let us go:
If you say ay, the king will not say no.   *Exeunt*

ACT FOUR

SCENE ONE

Northampton. A Room in the Castle.

Enter Hubert and Two Attendants

HUBERT. Heat me these irons hot; and look thou stand
  Within the arras. When I strike my foot
  Upon the bosom of the ground, rush forth,
  And bind the boy which you shall find with me
  Fast to the chair. Be heedful. Hence, and watch.
FIRST ATTENDANT. I hope your warrant will bear out the
    deed.
HUBERT. Uncleanly scruples! fear not you: look to 't.
                                        Exeunt Attendants
  Young lad, come forth; I have to say with you.
                          Enter Arthur
ARTHUR. Good-morrow, Hubert.
HUBERT.   Good-morrow, little prince.
ARTHUR. As little prince,—having so great a title
  To be more prince,—as may be. You are sad.
HUBERT. Indeed, I have been merrier.
ARTHUR.   Mercy on me!
  Methinks nobody should be sad but I:
  Yet I remember, when I was in France,
  Young gentlemen would be as sad as night,
  Only for wantonness. By my christendom,
  So I were out of prison and kept sheep,
  I should be as merry as the day is long;
  And so I would be here, but that I doubt
  My uncle practises more harm to me:
  He is afraid of me, and I of him.
  Is it my fault that I was Geffrey's son?
  No, indeed, is 't not; and I would to heaven
  I were your son, so you would love me, Hubert.
HUBERT. (*Aside*) If I talk to him with his innocent prate

He will awake my mercy which lies dead:
Therefore I will be sudden and dispatch.

ARTHUR. Are you sick, Hubert? you look pale to-day:
In sooth, I would you were a little sick,
That I might sit all night and watch with you:
I warrant I love you more than you do me.

HUBERT. (*Aside*) His words do take possession of my
   bosom.
Read here, young Arthur.   *Showing a paper*
                    (*Aside*) How now, foolish rheum!
Turning dispiteous torture out of door!
I must be brief, lest resolution drop
Out at mine eyes in tender womanish tears.
Can you not read it? Is it not fair writ?

ARTHUR. Too fairly, Hubert, for so foul effect.
Must you with hot irons burn out both mine eyes?

HUBERT. Young boy, I must.

ARTHUR.   And will you?

HUBERT.   And I will.

ARTHUR. Have you the heart? When your head did but ache,
I knit my handkercher about your brows,—
The best I had, a princess wrought it me,—
And I did never ask it you again;
And with my hand at midnight held your head,
And like the watchful minutes to the hour,
Still and anon cheer'd up the heavy time,
Saying, 'What lack you?' and, 'Where lies your grief?'
Or, 'What good love may I perform for you?'
Many a poor man's son would have lain still,
And ne'er have spoke a loving word to you;
But you at your sick-service had a prince.
Nay, you may think my love was crafty love,
And call it cunning: do an if you will.
If heaven be pleas'd that you must use me ill,
Why then you must. Will you put out mine eyes?
These eyes that never did nor never shall
So much as frown on you?

HUBERT.   I have sworn to do it;
And with hot irons must I burn them out.

ARTHUR. Ah! none but in this iron age would do it!
The iron of itself, though heat red-hot,
Approaching near these eyes, would drink my tears,

And quench this fiery indignation
Even in the matter of mine innocence;
Nay, after that, consume away in rust,
But for containing fire to harm mine eye.
Are you more stubborn-hard than hammer'd iron?
An if an angel should have come to me
And told me Hubert should put out mine eyes,
I would not have believ'd him; no tongue but Hubert's.

HUBERT. (*Stamps*) Come forth.

   Re-enter Attendants, with cord, irons, &c.

Do as I bid you do.

ARTHUR. O! save me, Hubert, save me! my eyes are out
Even with the fierce looks of these bloody men.

HUBERT. Give me the iron, I say, and bind him here.

ARTHUR. Alas! what need you be so boisterous-rough?
I will not struggle; I will stand stone-still.
For heaven's sake, Hubert, let me not be bound!
Nay, hear me, Hubert: drive these men away,
And I will sit as quiet as a lamb;
I will not stir, nor wince, nor speak a word,
Nor look upon the iron angerly.
Thrust but these men away, and I 'll forgive you,
Whatever torment you do put me to.

HUBERT. Go, stand within: let me alone with him.

FIRST ATTENDANT. I am best pleas'd to be from such a deed.

        Exeunt Attendants

ARTHUR. Alas! I then have chid away my friend.
He hath a stern look, but a gentle heart.
Let him come back, that his compassion may
Give life to yours.

HUBERT.   Come, boy, prepare yourself.

ARTHUR. Is there no remedy?

HUBERT.   None, but to lose your eyes.

ARTHUR. O heaven! that there were but a mote in yours,
A grain, a dust, a gnat, a wandering hair,
Any annoyance in that precious sense;
Then feeling what small things are boisterous there,
Your vile intent must needs seem horrible.

HUBERT. Is this your promise? Go to, hold your tongue.

ARTHUR. Hubert, the utterance of a brace of tongues
Must needs want pleading for a pair of eyes:
Let me not hold my tongue; let me not, Hubert:

Or Hubert, if you will, cut out my tongue,
So I may keep mine eyes: O! spare mine eyes,
Though to no use but still to look on you:
Lo! by my troth, the instrument is cold
And would not harm me.

HUBERT.   I can heat it, boy.

ARTHUR. No, in good sooth; the fire is dead with grief,
Being create for comfort, to be us'd
In undeserv'd extremes: see else yourself;
There is no malice in this burning coal;
The breath of heaven hath blown his spirit out
And strew'd repentant ashes on his head.

HUBERT. But with my breath I can revive it, boy.

ARTHUR. An if you do you will but make it blush
And glow with shame of your proceedings, Hubert:
Nay, it perchance will sparkle in your eyes;
And like a dog that is compell'd to fight,
Snatch at his master that doth tarre him on.
All things that you should use to do me wrong
Deny their office: only you do lack
That mercy which fierce fire and iron extends,
Creatures of note for mercy-lacking uses.

HUBERT. Well, see to live; I will not touch thine eyes
For all the treasure that thine uncle owes:
Yet am I sworn and I did purpose, boy,
With this same very iron to burn them out.

ARTHUR. O! now you look like Hubert, all this while
You were disguised.

HUBERT.   Peace! no more. Adieu.
Your uncle must not know but you are dead;
I 'll fill these dogged spies with false reports:
And pretty child, sleep doubtless and secure,
That Hubert for the wealth of all the world
Will not offend thee.

ARTHUR.   O heaven! I thank you, Hubert.

HUBERT. Silence! no more, go closely in with me:
Much danger do I undergo for thee.   *Exeunt*

SCENE TWO

The Same. A Room of State in the Palace.

Enter King John, crowned; Pembroke, Salisbury, and other Lords. The King takes his state

KING JOHN. Here once again we sit, once again crown'd,
　And look'd upon, I hope, with cheerful eyes.
PEMBROKE. This 'once again,' but that your Highness
　　pleas'd,
　Was once superfluous: you were crown'd before,
　And that high royalty was ne'er pluck'd off,
　The faiths of men ne'er stained with revolt;
　Fresh expectation troubled not the land
　With any long'd-for change or better state.
SALISBURY. Therefore, to be possess'd with double pomp,
　To guard a title that was rich before,
　To gild refined gold, to paint the lily,
　To throw a perfume on the violet,
　To smooth the ice, or add another hue
　Unto the rainbow, or with taper-light
　To seek the beauteous eye of heaven to garnish,
　Is wasteful and ridiculous excess.
PEMBROKE. But that your royal pleasure must be done,
　This act is as an ancient tale new told,
　And in the last repeating troublesome,
　Being urg'd at a time unseasonable.
SALISBURY. In this the antique and well-noted face
　Of plain old form is much disfigured;
　And, like a shifted wind unto a sail,
　It makes the course of thoughts to fetch about,
　Startles and frights consideration,
　Makes sound opinion sick and truth suspected,
　For putting on so new a fashion'd robe.
PEMBROKE. When workmen strive to do better than well
　They do confound their skill in covetousness;
　And oftentimes excusing of a fault
　Doth make the fault the worse by the excuse:
　As patches set upon a little breach
　Discredit more in hiding of the fault

Than did the fault before it was so patch'd.

SALISBURY. To this effect, before you were new-crown'd,
We breathed our counsel: but it pleas'd your Highness
To overbear it, and we are all well pleas'd;
Since all and every part of what we would
Doth make a stand at what your Highness will.

KING JOHN. Some reasons of this double coronation
I have possess'd you with and think them strong;
And more, more strong,—when lesser is my fear,—
I shall indue you with: meantime but ask
What you would have reform'd that is not well;
And well shall you perceive how willingly
I will both hear and grant you your requests.

PEMBROKE. Then I,—as one that am the tongue of these
To sound the purposes of all their hearts,—
Both for myself and them,—but, chief of all,
Your safety, for the which myself and them
Bend their best studies,—heartily request
The enfranchisement of Arthur; whose restraint
Doth move the murmuring lips of discontent
To break into this dangerous argument:
If what in rest you have in right you hold,
Why then your fears,—which, as they sad attend
The steps of wrong,—should move you to mew up
Your tender kinsman, and to choke his days
With barbarous ignorance, and deny his youth
The rich advantage of good exercise?
That the time's enemies may not have this
To grace occasions, let it be our suit
That you have bid us ask his liberty;
Which for our goods we do no further ask
Than whereupon our weal, on you depending,
Counts it your weal he have his liberty.

Enter Hubert

KING JOHN. Let it be so: I do commit his youth
To your direction. Hubert, what news with you?

Taking him apart

PEMBROKE. This is the man should do the bloody deed:
He show'd his warrant to a friend of mine:
The image of a wicked heinous fault
Lives in his eye; that close aspect of his
Does show the mood of a much troubled breast;

And I do fearfully believe 'tis done,
What we so fear'd he had a charge to do.

SALISBURY. The colour of the king doth come and go
Between his purpose and his conscience,
Like heralds 'twixt two dreadful battles set:
His passion is so ripe it needs must break.

PEMBROKE. And when it breaks, I fear will issue thence
The foul corruption of a sweet child's death.

KING JOHN. We cannot hold mortality's strong hand:
Good lords, although my will to give is living,
The suit which you demand is gone and dead:
He tells us Arthur is deceas'd to-night.

SALISBURY. Indeed we fear'd his sickness was past cure.

PEMBROKE. Indeed we heard how near his death he was
Before the child himself felt he was sick:
This must be answer'd, either here or hence.

KING JOHN. Why do you bend such solemn brows on me?
Think you I bear the shears of destiny?
Have I commandment on the pulse of life?

SALISBURY. It is apparent foul play; and 'tis shame
That greatness should so grossly offer it:
So thrive it in your game! and so, farewell.

PEMBROKE. Stay yet, Lord Salisbury; I 'll go with thee,
And find the inheritance of this poor child,
His little kingdom of a forced grave.
That blood which ow'd the breadth of all this isle,
Three foot of it doth hold: bad world the while!
This must not be thus borne: this will break out
To all our sorrows, and ere long I doubt.   *Exeunt Lords*

KING JOHN. They burn in indignation. I repent:
There is no sure foundation set on blood,
No certain life achiev'd by others' death.

                    Enter a Messenger

A fearful eye thou hast: where is that blood
That I have seen inhabit in those cheeks?
So foul a sky clears not without a storm:
Pour down thy weather: how goes all in France?

MESSENGER. From France to England. Never such a power
For any foreign preparation
Was levied in the body of a land.
The copy of your speed is learn'd by them;
For when you should be told they do prepare,

The tidings come that they are all arriv'd.

KING JOHN. O! where hath our intelligence been drunk?
Where hath it slept? Where is my mother's care
That such an army could be drawn in France,
And she not hear of it?

MESSENGER.   My liege, her ear
Is stopp'd with dust: the first of April died
Your noble mother; and, as I hear, my lord,
The Lady Constance in a frenzy died
Three days before: but this from rumour's tongue
I idly heard; if true or false I know not.

KING JOHN. Withhold thy speed, dreadful occasion!
O! make a league with me, till I have pleas'd
My discontented peers. What! mother dead!
How wildly then walks my estate in France!
Under whose conduct came those powers of France
That thou for truth giv'st out are landed here?

MESSENGER. Under the Dauphin.

KING JOHN.   Thou hast made me giddy
With these ill tidings.

          Enter the Bastard, and Peter of Pomfret
                          Now, what says the world
To your proceedings? do not seek to stuff
My head with more ill news, for it is full.

THE BASTARD. But if you be afeard to hear the worst,
Then let the worst unheard fall on your head.

KING JOHN. Bear with me, cousin, for I was amaz'd
Under the tide; but now I breathe again
Aloft the flood, and can give audience
To any tongue, speak it of what it will.

THE BASTARD. How I have sped among the clergymen,
The sums I have collected shall express.
But as I travell'd hither through the land,
I find the people strangely fantasied,
Possess'd with rumours, full of idle dreams,
Not knowing what they fear, but full of fear.
And here's a prophet that I brought with me
From forth the streets of Pomfret, whom I found
With many hundreds treading on his heels;
To whom he sung, in rude harsh-sounding rimes,
That, ere the next Ascension-day at noon,
Your Highness should deliver up your crown.

KING JOHN. Thou idle dreamer, wherefore didst thou so?
PETER. Foreknowing that the truth will fall out so.
KING JOHN. Hubert, away with him; imprison him:
  And on that day at noon, whereon, he says,
  I shall yield up my crown, let him be hang'd.
  Deliver him to safety, and return,
  For I must use thee.   *Exit Hubert, with Peter*
                O my gentle cousin,
  Hear'st thou the news abroad, who are arriv'd?
THE BASTARD. The French, my lord; men's mouths aɪe full of
    it:
  Besides, I met Lord Bigot and Lord Salisbury,
  With eyes as red as new-enkindled fire,
  And others more, going to seek the grave
  Of Arthur, whom they say is kill'd to-night
  On your suggestion.
KING JOHN.   Gentle kinsman, go,
  And thrust thyself into their companies.
  I have a way to win their loves again;
  Bring them before me.
THE BASTARD.   I will seek them out.
KING JOHN. Nay, but make haste; the better foot before.
  O! let me have no subject enemies
  When adverse foreigners affright my towns
  With dreadful pomp of stout invasion.
  Be Mercury, set feathers to thy heels,
  And fly like thought from them to me again.
THE BASTARD. The spirit of the time shall teach me speed.
KING JOHN. Spoke like a sprightful noble gentleman.
                          Exit the Bastard
  Go after him; for he perhaps shall need
  Some messenger betwixt me and the peers;
  And be thou he.
MESSENGER.   With all my heart, my liege.   *Exit*
KING JOHN. My mother dead!
              Re-enter Hubert
HUBERT. My lord, they say five moons were seen to-night:
  Four fixed, and the fifth did whirl about
  The other four in wondrous motion.
KING JOHN. Five moons!
HUBERT.   Old men and beldams in the streets
  Do prophesy upon it dangerously:

Young Arthur's death is common in their mouths;
And when they talk of him, they shake their heads
And whisper one another in the ear;
And he that speaks, doth gripe the hearer's wrist
Whilst he that hears makes fearful action,
With wrinkled brows, with nods, with rolling eyes.
I saw a smith stand with his hammer, thus,
The whilst his iron did on the anvil cool,
With open mouth swallowing a tailor's news;
Who, with his shears and measure in his hand,
Standing on slippers,—which his nimble haste
Had falsely thrust upon contrary feet,—
Told of a many thousand warlike French,
That were embattailed and rank'd in Kent.
Another lean unwash'd artificer
Cuts off his tale and talks of Arthur's death.

KING JOHN. Why seek'st thou to possess me with these fears?
Why urgest thou so oft young Arthur's death?
Thy hand hath murder'd him: I had a mighty cause
To wish him dead, but thou hadst none to kill him.

HUBERT. No had, my lord! why, did you not provoke me?

KING JOHN. It is the curse of kings to be attended
By slaves that take their humours for a warrant
To break within the bloody house of life,
And on the winking of authority
To understand a law, to know the meaning
Of dangerous majesty, when, perchance, it frowns
More upon humour than advis'd respect.

HUBERT. Here is your hand and seal for what I did.

KING JOHN. O! when the last account 'twixt heaven and
    earth
Is to be made, then shall this hand and seal
Witness against us to damnation.
How oft the sight of means to do ill deeds
Makes ill deeds done! Hadst not thou been by,
A fellow by the hand of nature mark'd,
Quoted and sign'd to do a deed of shame,
This murder had not come into my mind;
But taking note of thy abhorr'd aspect,
Finding thee fit for bloody villany,
Apt, liable to be employ'd in danger,
I faintly broke with thee of Arthur's death;

And thou, to be endeared to a king,
Made it no conscience to destroy a prince.
HUBERT. My lord,—
KING JOHN. Hadst thou but shook thy head or made a pause
When I spake darkly what I purposed,
Or turn'd an eye of doubt upon my face,
As bid me tell my tale in express words,
Deep shame had struck me dumb, made me break off,
And those thy fears might have wrought fears in me:
But thou didst understand me by my signs
And didst in signs again parley with sin;
Yea, without stop, didst let thy heart consent,
And consequently thy rude hand to act
The deed which both our tongues held vile to name.
Out of my sight, and never see me more!
My nobles leave me; and my state is brav'd,
Even at my gates, with ranks of foreign powers:
Nay, in the body of this fleshly land,
This kingdom, this confine of blood and breath,
Hostility and civil tumult reigns
Between my conscience and my cousin's death.
HUBERT. Arm you against your other enemies,
I 'll make a peace between your soul and you.
Young Arthur is alive: this hand of mine
Is yet a maiden and an innocent hand,
Not painted with the crimson spots of blood.
Within this bosom never enter'd yet
The dreadful motion of a murderous thought;
And you have slander'd nature in my form,
Which, howsoever rude exteriorly,
Is yet the cover of a fairer mind
Than to be butcher of an innocent child.
KING JOHN. Doth Arthur live? O! haste thee to the peers,
Throw this report on their incensed rage,
And make them tame to their obedience.
Forgive the comment that my passion made
Upon thy feature; for my rage was blind,
And foul imaginary eyes of blood
Presented thee more hideous than thou art.
O! answer not; but to my closet bring
The angry lords, with all expedient haste.
I conjure thee but slowly; run more fast.   *Exeunt*

SCENE THREE

The Same. Before the Castle.

Enter Arthur, on the Walls

ARTHUR. The wall is high; and yet will I leap down.
  Good ground, be pitiful and hurt me not!
  There s few or none do know me; if they did,
  This ship-boy's semblance hath disguis'd me quite.
  I am afraid; and yet I 'll venture it.
  If I get down, and do not break my limbs,
  I 'll find a thousand shifts to get away:
  As good to die and go, as die and stay.   *Leaps down*
  O me! my uncle's spirit is in these stones:
  Heaven take my soul, and England keep my bones!   *Dies*
       Enter Pembroke, Salisbury, and Bigot
SALISBURY. Lords, I will meet him at Saint Edmundsbury.
  It is our safety, and we must embrace
  This gentle offer of the perilous time.
PEMBROKE. Who brought that letter from the cardinal?
SALISBURY. The Count Melun, a noble lord of France;
  Whose private with me of the Dauphin's love,
  Is much more general than these lines import.
BIGOT. To-morrow morning let us meet him then.
SALISBURY. Or rather than set forward; for 'twill be
  Two long days' journey, lords, or e'er we meet.
       Enter the Bastard
THE BASTARD. Once more to-day well met, distemper'd
    lords!
  The King by me requests your presence straight.
SALISBURY. The king hath dispossess'd himself of us:
  We will not line his thin bestained cloak
  With our pure honours, nor attend the foot
  That leaves the print of blood where'er it walks.
  Return and tell him so: we know the worst.
THE BASTARD. Whate'er you think, good words, I think, were
    best.
SALISBURY. Our griefs, and not our manners, reason now.
THE BASTARD. But there is little reason in your grief;
  Therefore 'twere reason you had manners now.

PEMBROKE. Sir, sir, impatience hath his privilege.

THE BASTARD. 'Tis true; to hurt his master, no man else.

SALISBURY. This is the prison.   *Seeing Arthur*
        What is he lies here?

PEMBROKE. O death, made proud with pure and princely
    beauty!

The earth had not a hole to hide this deed.

SALISBURY. Murder, as hating what himself hath done,

Doth lay it open to urge on revenge.

BIGOT. Or when he doom'd this beauty to a grave,

Found it too precious-princely for a grave.

SALISBURY. Sir Richard, what think you? Have you beheld,

Or have you read, or heard? or could you think?

Or do you almost think, although you see,

That you do see? Could thought, without this object,

Form such another? This is the very top,

The height, the crest, or crest unto the crest,

Of murder's arms: this is the bloodiest shame,

The wildest savagery, the vilest stroke,

That ever wall-eyed wrath or staring rage

Presented to the tears of soft remorse.

PEMBROKE. All murders past do stand excus'd in this:

And this, so sole and so unmatchable,

Shall give a holiness, a purity,

To the yet unbegotten sin of times;

And prove a deadly bloodshed but a jest,

Exampled by this heinous spectacle.

THE BASTARD. It is a damned and a bloody work;

The graceless action of a heavy hand,

If that it be the work of any hand.

SALISBURY. If that it be the work of any hand!

We had a kind of light what would ensue:

It is the shameful work of Hubert's hand;

The practice and the purpose of the king:

From whose obedience I forbid my soul,

Kneeling before this ruin of sweet life,

And breathing to his breathless excellence

The incense of a vow, a holy vow,

Never to taste the pleasures of the world,

Never to be infected with delight,

Nor conversant with ease and idleness,

Till I have set a glory to this hand,

By giving it the worship of revenge.

PEMBROKE.
BIGOT.   } Our souls religiously confirm thy words.

Enter Hubert

HUBERT. Lords, I am hot with haste in seeking you:
Arthur doth live: the king hath sent for you.

SALISBURY. O! he is bold and blushes not at death.
Avaunt, thou hateful villain! get thee gone.

HUBERT. I am no villain.

SALISBURY. (*Drawing his sword*) Must I rob the law?

THE BASTARD. Your sword is bright, sir; put it up again.

SALISBURY. Not till I sheathe it in a murderer's skin.

HUBERT. Stand back, Lord Salisbury, stand back, I say:
By heaven, I think my sword 's as sharp as yours.
I would not have you, lord, forget yourself,
Nor tempt the danger of my true defence;
Lest I, by marking of your rage, forget
Your worth, your greatness, and nobility.

BIGOT. Out, dunghill! dar'st thou brave a nobleman?

HUBERT. Not for my life; but yet I dare defend
My innocent life against an emperor.

SALISBURY. Thou art a murderer.

HUBERT.   Do not prove me so;
Yet I am none. Whose tongue soe'er speaks false,
Not truly speaks; who speaks not truly, lies.

PEMBROKE. Cut him to pieces.

THE BASTARD.   Keep the peace, I say.

SALISBURY. Stand by, or I shall gall you, Faulconbridge.

THE BASTARD. Thou wert better gall the devil, Salisbury:
If thou but frown on me, or stir thy foot,
Or teach thy hasty spleen to do me shame,
I 'll strike thee dead. Put up thy sword betime:
Or I 'll so maul you and your toasting-iron,
That you shall think the devil is come from hell.

BIGOT. What wilt thou do, renowned Faulconbridge?
Second a villain and a murderer?

HUBERT. Lord Bigot, I am none.

BIGOT.   Who kill'd this prince?

HUBERT. 'Tis not an hour since I left him well:
I honour'd him, I lov'd him; and will weep
My date of life out for his sweet life's loss.

SALISBURY. Trust not those cunning waters of his eyes,

For villany is not without such rheum;
And he, long traded in it, makes it seem
Like rivers of remorse and innocency.
Away with me, all you whose souls abhor
The uncleanly savours of a slaughter-house;
For I am stifled with this smell of sin.

BIGOT. Away toward Bury; to the Dauphin there!

PEMBROKE. There tell the king he may inquire us out.

Exeunt Lords

THE BASTARD. Here 's a good world! Knew you of this fair
　　work?
Beyond the infinite and boundless reach
Of mercy, if thou didst this deed of death,
Art thou damn'd, Hubert.

HUBERT. 　　　　　　　　Do but hear me, sir.

THE BASTARD. Ha! I 'll tell thee what;
Thou art damn'd as black—nay, nothing is so black;
Thou art more deep damn'd than Prince Lucifer:
There is not yet so ugly a fiend of hell
As thou shalt be, if thou didst kill this child.

HUBERT. Upon my soul,—

THE BASTARD. 　　　　　　If thou didst but consent
To this most cruel act, do but despair;
And if thou want'st a cord, the smallest thread
That ever spider twisted from her womb
Will serve to strangle thee; a rush will be a beam
To hang thee on; or wouldst thou drown thyself,
Put but a little water in a spoon,
And it shall be as all the ocean,
Enough to stifle such a villain up.
I do suspect thee very grievously.

HUBERT. If I in act, consent, or sin of thought,
Be guilty of the stealing that sweet breath
Which was embounded in this beauteous clay,
Let hell want pains enough to torture me.
I left him well.

THE BASTARD. 　　　Go, bear him in thine arms.
I am amaz'd, methinks, and lose my way
Among the thorns and dangers of this world.
How easy dost thou take all England up!
From forth this morsel of dead royalty,
The life, the right and truth of all this realm

Is fled to heaven; and England now is left
To tug and scramble and to part by the teeth
The unow'd interest of proud swelling state.
Now for the bare-pick'd bone of majesty
Doth dogged war bristle his angry crest,
And snarleth in the gentle eyes of peace:
Now powers from home and discontents at home
Meet in one line; and vast confusion waits,—
As doth a raven on a sick-fallen beast,—
The imminent decay of wrested pomp.
Now happy he whose cloak and ceinture can
Hold out this tempest. Bear away that child
And follow me with speed: I 'll to the king:
A thousand businesses are brief in hand,
And heaven itself doth frown upon the land.   *Exeunt*

ACT FIVE

SCENE ONE

The Same. A Room in the Palace.

Enter King John, Pandulph with the crown, and Attendants

KING JOHN. Thus have I yielded up into your hand
   The circle of my glory.
PANDULPH. (*Giving John the crown*) Take again
   From this my hand, as holding of the pope,
   Your sovereign greatness and authority.
KING JOHN. Now keep your holy word: go meet the French,
   And from his Holiness use all your power
   To stop their marches 'fore we are inflam'd.
   Our discontented counties do revolt,
   Our people quarrel with obedience,
   Swearing allegiance and the love of soul
   To stranger blood, to foreign royalty.
   This inundation of mistemper'd humour
   Rests by you only to be qualified:
   Then pause not; for the present time 's so sick,
   That present medicine must be minister'd,
   Or overthrow incurable ensues.
PANDULPH. It was my breath that blew this tempest up
   Upon your stubborn usage of the pope;
   But since you are a gentle convertite,
   My tongue shall hush again this storm of war
   And make fair weather in your blustering land.
   On this Ascension-day, remember well,
   Upon your oath of service to the pope,
   Go I to make the French lay down their arms.   *Exit*
KING JOHN. Is this Ascension-day? Did not the prophet
   Say that before Ascension-day at noon
   My crown I should give off? Even so I have:
   I did suppose it should be on constraint;

But, heaven be thank'd, it is but voluntary.
Enter the Bastard

THE BASTARD. All Kent hath yielded; nothing there holds out
But Dover Castle: London hath receiv'd,
Like a kind host, the Dauphin and his powers:
Your nobles will not hear you, but are gone
To offer service to your enemy;
And wild amazement hurries up and down
The little number of your doubtful friends.

KING JOHN. Would not my lords return to me again
After they heard young Arthur was alive?

THE BASTARD. They found him dead and cast into the streets,
An empty casket, where the jewel of life
By some damn'd hand was robb'd and ta'en away.

KING JOHN. That villain Hubert told me he did live.

THE BASTARD. So, on my soul, he did, for aught he knew.
But wherefore do you droop? why look you sad?
Be great in act, as you have been in thought;
Let not the world see fear and sad distrust
Govern the motion of a kingly eye:
Be stirring as the time; be fire with fire;
Threaten the threatener, and outface the brow
Of bragging horror: so shall inferior eyes,
That borrow their behaviours from the great,
Grow great by your example and put on
The dauntless spirit of resolution.
Away! and glister like the god of war
When he intendeth to become the field:
Show boldness and aspiring confidence.
What! shall they seek the lion in his den
And fright him there? and make him tremble there?
O! let it not be said. Forage, and run
To meet displeasure farther from the doors,
And grapple with him ere he comes so nigh.

KING JOHN. The legate of the pope hath been with me
And I have made a happy peace with him;
And he hath promis'd to dismiss the powers
Led by the Dauphin.

THE BASTARD.   O inglorious league!
Shall we, upon the footing of our land,
Send fair-play orders and make compromise,
Insinuation, parley and base truce

To arms invasive? shall a beardless boy,
A cocker'd silken wanton, brave our fields,
And flesh his spirit in a warlike soil,
Mocking the air with colours idly spread,
And find no check? Let us, my liege, to arms:
Perchance the cardinal cannot make your peace;
Or if he do, let it at least be said
They saw we had a purpose of defence.
KING JOHN. Have thou the ordering of this present time.
THE BASTARD. Away then, with good courage! yet, I know,
Our party may well meet a prouder foe.   *Exeunt*

SCENE TWO

A Plain, near St. Edmundsbury. The French Camp.

*Enter, in arms, Lewis, Salisbury, Melun, Pembroke,
Bigot, and Soldiers*

LEWIS. My Lord Melun, let this be copied out,
And keep it safe for our remembrance.
Return the precedent to these lords again;
That, having our fair order written down,
Both they and we, perusing o'er these notes,
May know wherefore we took the sacrament,
And keep our faiths firm and inviolable.
SALISBURY. Upon our sides it never shall be broken.
And, noble Dauphin, albeit we swear
A voluntary zeal, an unurg'd faith
To your proceedings; yet, believe me, prince,
I am not glad that such a sore of time
Should seek a plaster by contemn'd revolt,
And heal the inveterate canker of one wound
By making many. O! it grieves my soul
That I must draw this metal from my side
To be a widow-maker! O! and there
Where honourable rescue and defence
Cries out upon the name of Salisbury.
But such is the infection of the time,
That, for the health and physic of our right,
We cannot deal but with the very hand
Of stern injustice and confused wrong.

And is 't not pity, O my grieved friends!
That we, the sons and children of this isle,
Were born to see so sad an hour as this;
Wherein we step after a stranger, march
Upon her gentle bosom, and fill up
Her enemies' ranks,—I must withdraw and weep
Upon the spot of this enforced cause,—
To grace the gentry of a land remote,
And follow unacquainted colours here?
What, here? O nation! that thou couldst remove;
That Neptune's arms, who clippeth thee about,
Would bear thee from the knowledge of thyself,
And gripple thee unto a pagan shore;
Where these two Christian armies might combine
The blood of malice in a vein of league,
And not to spend it so unneighbourly!

LEWIS. A noble temper dost thou show in this;
And great affections wrestling in thy bosom
Do make an earthquake of nobility.
O! what a noble combat hast thou fought
Between compulsion and a brave respect.
Let me wipe off this honourable dew,
That silverly doth progress on thy cheeks:
My heart hath melted at a lady's tears,
Being an ordinary inundation;
But this effusion of such manly drops,
This shower, blown up by tempest of the soul,
Startles mine eyes, and makes me more amaz'd
Than had I seen the vaulty top of heaven
Figur'd quite o'er with burning meteors.
Lift up thy brow, renowned Salisbury,
And with a great heart heave away this storm:
Commend these waters to those baby eyes
That never saw the giant world enrag'd;
Nor met with fortune other than at feasts,
Full warm of blood, of mirth, of gossiping.
Come, come; for thou shalt thrust thy hand as deep
Into the purse of rich prosperity
As Lewis himself: so, nobles, shall you all,
That knit your sinews to the strength of mine.
          Enter Pandulph, attended
And even there, methinks, an angel spake:

Look, where the holy legate comes apace,
To give us warrant from the hand of heaven,
And on our actions set the name of right
With holy breath.

PANDULPH.   Hail, noble Prince of France!
The next is this: King John hath reconcil'd
Himself to Rome; his spirit is come in
That so stood out against the holy Church,
The great metropolis and see of Rome.
Therefore thy threatening colours now wind up,
And tame the savage spirit of wild war,
That, like a lion foster'd up at hand,
It may lie gently at the foot of peace,
And be no further harmful than in show.

LEWIS. Your Grace shall pardon me; I will not back:
I am too high-born to be propertied,
To be a secondary at control,
Or useful serving-man and instrument
To any sovereign state throughout the world.
Your breath first kindled the dead coals of wars
Between this chastis'd kingdom and myself,
And brought in matter that should feed this fire;
And now 'tis far too huge to be blown out
With that same weak wind which enkindled it.
You taught me how to know the face of right,
Acquainted me with interest to this land,
Yea, thrust this enterprise into my heart;
And come you now to tell me John hath made
His peace with Rome? What is that peace to me?
I, by the honour of my marriage-bed,
After young Arthur, claim this land for mine;
And, now it is half-conquer'd, must I back
Because that John hath made his peace with Rome?
Am I Rome's slave? What penny hath Rome borne,
What men provided, what munition sent,
To underprop this action? is 't not I
That undergo this charge? who else but I,
And such as to my claim are liable,
Sweat in this business and maintain this war?
Have I not heard these islanders shout out,
'Vive le roy!' as I have bank'd their towns?
Have I not here the best cards for the game

To win this easy match play'd for a crown?
And shall I now give o'er the yielded set?
No, no, on my soul, it never shall be said.

PANDULPH. You look but on the outside of this work.

LEWIS. Outside or inside, I will not return
Till my attempt so much be glorified
As to my ample hope was promised
Before I drew this gallant head of war,
And cull'd these fiery spirits from the world,
To outlook conquest and to win renown
Even in the jaws of danger and of death.   *Trumpet sounds*
What lusty trumpet thus doth summon us?
              Enter the Bastard, attended

THE BASTARD. According to the fair play of the world,
Let me have audience; I am sent to speak:
My holy Lord of Milan, from the king
I come, to learn how you have dealt for him;
And, as you answer, I do know the scope
And warrant limited unto my tongue.

PANDULPH. The Dauphin is too wilful-opposite,
And will not temporize with my entreaties:
He flatly says he 'll not lay down his arms.

THE BASTARD. By all the blood that ever fury breath'd,
The youth says well. Now hear our English king;
For thus his royalty doth speak in me.
He is prepar'd; and reason too he should:
This apish and unmannerly approach,
This harness'd masque and unadvised revel,
This unhair'd sauciness and boyish troops,
The king doth smile at; and is well prepar'd
To whip this dwarfish war, these pigmy arms,
From out the circle of his territories.
That hand which had the strength, even at your door,
To cudgel you and make you take the hatch;
To dive, like buckets, in concealed wells;
To crouch in litter of your stable planks;
To lie like pawns lock'd up in chests and trunks;
To hug with swine; to seek sweet safety out
In vaults and prisons; and to thrill and shake,
Even at the crying of your nation's crow,
Thinking this voice an armed Englishman:
Shall that victorious hand be feebled here

That in your chambers gave you chastisement?
No! Know, the gallant monarch is in arms,
And like an eagle o'er his aiery towers,
To souse annoyance that comes near his nest.
And you degenerate, you ingrate revolts,
You bloody Neroes, ripping up the womb
Of your dear mother England, blush for shame:
For your own ladies and pale-visag'd maids
Like Amazons come tripping after drums,
Their thimbles into armed gauntlets change,
Their neelds to lances, and their gentle hearts
To fierce and bloody inclination.

LEWIS. There end thy brave, and turn thy face in peace;
We grant thou canst outscold us: fare thee well;
We hold our time too precious to be spent
With such a brabbler.

PANDULPH.   Give me leave to speak.

THE BASTARD. No, I will speak.

LEWIS.   We will attend to neither.
Strike up the drums; and let the tongue of war
Plead for our interest and our being here.

THE BASTARD. Indeed, your drums, being beaten, will cry
out;
And so shall you, being beaten. Do but start
An echo with the clamour of thy drum,
And even at hand a drum is ready brac'd
That shall reverberate all as loud as thine;
Sound but another, and another shall
As loud as thine rattle the welkin's ear
And mock the deep-mouth'd thunder: for at hand,—
Not trusting to this halting legate here,
Whom he hath us'd rather for sport than need,—
Is warlike John; and in his forehead sits
A bare-ribb'd death, whose office is this day
To feast upon whole thousands of the French.

LEWIS. Strike up our drums, to find this danger out.

THE BASTARD. And thou shalt find it, Dauphin, do not doubt.

Exeunt

SCENE THREE

The Same. A Field of Battle.

Alarums. Enter King John and Hubert

KING JOHN. How goes the day with us? O! tell me, Hubert.
HUBERT. Badly, I fear. How fares your Majesty?
KING JOHN. This fever, that hath troubled me so long,
Lies heavy on me: O! my heart is sick.
                    Enter a Messenger
MESSENGER. My lord, your valiant kinsman, Faulconbridge,
Desires your Majesty to leave the field,
And send him word by me which way you go.
KING JOHN. Tell him, toward Swinstead, to the abbey there.
MESSENGER. Be of good comfort: for the great supply
That was expected by the Dauphin here,
Are wrack'd three nights ago on Goodwin sands.
This news was brought to Richard but even now.
The French fight coldly, and retire themselves.
KING JOHN. Ay me! this tyrant fever burns me up,
And will not let me welcome this good news.
Set on toward Swinstead: to my litter straight;
Weakness possesseth me, and I am faint.   *Exeunt*

SCENE FOUR

The Same. Another Part of the Same.

Enter Salisbury, Pembroke, Bigot, and Others

SALISBURY. I did not think the king so stor'd with friends.
PEMBROKE. Up once again; put spirit in the French:
If they miscarry we miscarry too.
SALISBURY. That misbegotten devil, Faulconbridge,
In spite of spite, alone upholds the day.
PEMBROKE. They say King John, sore sick, hath left the field.
            Enter Melun wounded, and led by Soldiers
MELUN. Lead me to the revolts of England here.
SALISBURY. When we were happy we had other names.
PEMBROKE. It is the Count Melun.

SALISBURY.   Wounded to death.

MELUN. Fly, noble English; you are bought and sold;
　　Unthread the rude eye of rebellion,
　　And welcome home again discarded faith.
　　Seek out King John and fall before his feet;
　　For if the French be lords of this loud day,
　　He means to recompense the pains you take
　　By cutting off your heads. Thus hath he sworn,
　　And I with him, and many moe with me
　　Upon the altar at Saint Edmundsbury;
　　Even on that altar where we swore to you
　　Dear amity and everlasting love.

SALISBURY. May this be possible? May this be true?

MELUN. Have I not hideous death within my view,
　　Retaining but a quantity of life,
　　Which bleeds away, even as a form of wax
　　Resolveth from his figure 'gainst the fire?
　　What in the world should make me now deceive,
　　Since I must lose the use of all deceit?
　　Why should I then be false, since it is true
　　That I must die here and live hence by truth?
　　I say again, if Lewis do win the day,
　　He is forsworn, if e'er those eyes of yours
　　Behold another day break in the east:
　　But even this night, whose black contagious breath
　　Already smokes about the burning crest
　　Of the old, feeble, and day-wearied sun,
　　Even this ill night, your breathing shall expire,
　　Paying the fine of rated treachery
　　Even with a treacherous fine of all your lives,
　　If Lewis by your assistance win the day.
　　Commend me to one Hubert with your king;
　　The love of him, and this respect besides,
　　For that my grandsire was an Englishman,
　　Awakes my conscience to confess all this.
　　In lieu whereof, I pray you, bear me hence
　　From forth the noise and rumour of the field,
　　Where I may think the remnant of my thoughts
　　In peace, and part this body and my soul
　　With contemplation and devout desires.

SALISBURY. We do believe thee: and beshrew my soul
　　But I do love the favour and the form

Of this most fair occasion, by the which
We will untread the steps of damned flight,
And like a bated and retired flood,
Leaving our rankness and irregular course,
Stoop low within those bounds we have o'erlook'd,
And calmly run on in obedience,
Even to our ocean, to our great King John.
My arm shall give thee help to bear thee hence,
For I do see the cruel pangs of death
Right in thine eye. Away, my friends! New flight;
And happy newness, that intends old right.
                              Exeunt, leading off Melun

SCENE FIVE

The Same. The French Camp.

Enter Lewis and his Train

LEWIS. The sun of heaven methought was loath to set,
    But stay'd and made the western welkin blush,
    When the English measur'd backward their own ground
    In faint retire. O! bravely came we off,
    When with a volley of our needless shot,
    After such bloody toil, we bid good-night,
    And wound our tottering colours clearly up,
    Last in the field, and almost lords of it!
                    Enter a Messenger
MESSENGER. Where is my prince, the Dauphin?
LEWIS.   Here: what news?
MESSENGER. The Count Melun is slain; the English lords,
    By his persuasion, are again fall'n off;
    And your supply, which you have wish'd so long,
    Are cast away and sunk, on Goodwin sands.
LEWIS. Ah, foul shrewd news! Beshrew thy very heart!
    I did not think to be so sad to-night
    As this hath made me. Who was he that said
    King John did fly an hour or two before
    The stumbling night did part our weary powers?
MESSENGER. Whoever spoke it, it is true, my lord.
LEWIS. Well; keep good quarter and good care to-night:
    The day shall not be up so soon as I,
    To try the fair adventure of to-morrow.   *Exeunt*

SCENE SIX

*An open Place in the neighbourhood
of Swinstead Abbey.*

Enter the Bastard and Hubert, severally

HUBERT. Who 's there? speak, ho! speak quickly, or I shoot.

THE BASTARD. A friend. What art thou?

HUBERT.   Of the part of England.

THE BASTARD. Whither dost thou go?

HUBERT. What 's that to thee? Why may not I demand
   Of thine affairs as well as thou of mine?

THE BASTARD. Hubert, I think?

HUBERT.   Thou hast a perfect thought:
   I will upon all hazards well believe
   Thou art my friend, that know'st my tongue so well.
   Who art thou?

THE BASTARD.   Who thou wilt: and if thou please,
   Thou mayst befriend me so much as to think
   I come one way of the Plantagenets.

HUBERT. Unkind remembrance! thou and eyeless night
   Have done me shame: brave soldier, pardon me,
   That any accent breaking from thy tongue
   Should 'scape the true acquaintance of mine ear.

THE BASTARD. Come, come; sans compliment, what news
   abroad?

HUBERT. Why, here walk I in the black brow of night,
   To find you out.

THE BASTARD.   Brief, then; and what 's the news?

HUBERT. O! my sweet sir, news fitting to the night,
   Black, fearful, comfortless, and horrible.

THE BASTARD. Show me the very wound of this ill news:
   I am no woman: I 'll not swound at it.

HUBERT. The king, I fear, is poison'd by a monk:
   I left him almost speechless; and broke out
   To acquaint you with this evil, that you might
   The better arm you to the sudden time
   Than if you had at leisure known of this.

THE BASTARD. How did he take it? who did taste to him?

HUBERT. A monk, I tell you; a resolved villain,

Whose bowels suddenly burst out: the king
Yet speaks, and peradventure may recover.

THE BASTARD. Whom didst thou leave to tend his majesty?

HUBERT. Why, know you not? the lords are all come back,
And brought Prince Henry in their company;
At whose request the king hath pardon'd them,
And they are all about his Majesty.

THE BASTARD. Withhold thine indignation, mighty heaven,
And tempt us not to bear above our power!
I 'll tell thee, Hubert, half my power this night,
Passing these flats, are taken by the tide;
These Lincoln Washes have devoured them:
Myself, well-mounted, hardly have escap'd.
Away before! conduct me to the king;
I doubt he will be dead or ere I come.   *Exeunt*

SCENE SEVEN

The Orchard of Swinstead Abbey.

Enter Prince Henry, Salisbury, and Bigot

PRINCE HENRY. It is too late: the life of all his blood
Is touch'd corruptibly; and his pure brain,—
Which some suppose the soul's frail dwelling-house,—
Doth, by the idle comments that it makes,
Foretell the ending of mortality.
                    Enter Pembroke

PEMBROKE. His Highness yet doth speak; and holds belief
That, being brought into the open air,
It would allay the burning quality
Of that fell poison which assaileth him.

PRINCE HENRY. Let him be brought into the orchard here.
Doth he still rage?   *Exit Bigot*

PEMBROKE.   He is more patient
Than when you left him: even now he sung.

PRINCE HENRY. O, vanity of sickness! fierce extremes
In their continuance will not feel themselves.
Death, having prey'd upon the outward parts,
Leaves them invisible; and his siege is now
Against the mind, the which he pricks and wounds
With many legions of strange fantasies,

Which, in their throng and press to that last hold,
Confound themselves. 'Tis strange that death should sing.
I am the cygnet to this pale faint swan,
Who chants a doleful hymn to his own death,
And from the organ-pipe of frailty sings
His soul and body to their lasting rest.

SALISBURY. Be of good comfort, prince; for you are born
To set a form upon that indigest
Which he hath left so shapeless and so rude.

Re-enter Bigot and Attendants, carrying King John in a chair

KING JOHN. Ay, marry, now my soul hath elbow-room;
It would not out at windows, nor at doors.
There is so hot a summer in my bosom
That all my bowels crumble up to dust:
I am a scribbled form, drawn with a pen
Upon a parchment, and against this fire
Do I shrink up.

PRINCE HENRY.   How fares your Majesty?

KING JOHN. Poison'd, ill-fare; dead, forsook, cast off;
And none of you will bid the winter come
To thrust his icy fingers in my maw;
Nor let my kingdom's rivers take their course
Through my burn'd bosom; nor entreat the north
To make his bleak winds kiss my parched lips
And comfort me with cold. I do not ask you much:
I beg cold comfort; and you are so strait
And so ingrateful you deny me that.

PRINCE HENRY. O! that there were some virtue in my tears,
That might relieve you.

KING JOHN.   The salt in them is hot.
Within me is a hell; and there the poison
Is as a fiend confin'd to tyrannize
On unreprievable condemned blood.

Enter the Bastard

THE BASTARD. O! I am scalded with my violent motion
And spleen of speed to see your Majesty.

KING JOHN. O cousin! thou art come to set mine eye:
The tackle of my heart is crack'd and burn'd,
And all the shrouds wherewith my life should sail
Are turned to one thread, one little hair;
My heart hath one poor string to stay it by,
Which holds but till thy news be uttered;

And then all this thou seest is but a clod
And module of confounded royalty.

THE BASTARD. The Dauphin is preparing hitherward,
Where heaven he knows how we shall answer him:
For in a night the best part of my power,
As I upon advantage did remove,
Were in the Washes all unwarily
Devoured by the unexpected flood.   *The King dies*

SALISBURY. You breathe these dead news in as dead an ear.
My liege! my lord! But now a king, now thus.

PRINCE HENRY. Even so must I run on, and even so stop.
What surety of the world, what hope, what stay,
When this was now a king, and now is clay?

THE BASTARD. Art thou gone so? I do but stay behind
To do the office for thee of revenge,
And then my soul shall wait on thee to heaven,
As it on earth hath been thy servant still.
Now, now, you stars, that move in your right spheres,
Where be your powers? Show now your mended faiths,
And instantly return with me again,
To push destruction and perpetual shame
Out of the weak door of our fainting land.
Straight let us seek, or straight we shall be sought:
The Dauphin rages at our very heels.

SALISBURY. It seems you know not then so much as we.
The Cardinal Pandulph is within at rest,
Who half an hour since came from the Dauphin,
And brings from him such offers of our peace
As we with honour and respect may take,
With purpose presently to leave this war.

THE BASTARD. He will the rather do it when he sees
Ourselves well sinewed to our defence.

SALISBURY. Nay, it is in a manner done already;
For many carriages he hath dispatch'd
To the sea-side, and put his cause and quarrel
To the disposing of the cardinal:
With whom yourself, myself, and other lords,
If you think meet, this afternoon will post
To consummate this business happily.

THE BASTARD. Let it be so. And you, my noble prince,
With other princes that may best be spar'd,
Shall wait upon your father's funeral.

PRINCE HENRY. At Worcester must his body be interr'd;·
  For so he will'd it.
THE BASTARD.   Thither shall it then.
  And happily may your sweet self put on
  The lineal state and glory of the land!
  To whom, with all submission, on my knee,
  I do bequeath my faithful services
  And true subjection everlastingly.
SALISBURY. And the like tender of our love we make,
  To rest without a spot for evermore.
PRINCE HENRY. I have a kind soul that would give you
    thanks,
  And knows not how to do it but with tears.
THE BASTARD. O! let us pay the time but needful woe
  Since it hath been beforehand with our griefs.
  This England never did, nor never shall,
  Lie at the proud foot of a conqueror,
  But when it first did he'p to wound itself.
  Now these her princes are come home again,
  Come the three corners of the world in arms,
  And we shall shock them. Nought shall make us rue,
  If England to itself do rest but true.   *Exeunt*

THE TRAGEDY OF KING RICHARD THE SECOND

CAST OF CHARACTERS

KING RICHARD THE SECOND
JOHN OF GAUNT, *Duke of Lancaster* } *Uncles to*
EDMUND OF LANGLEY, *Duke of York* } *the King*
HENRY, *surnamed* BOLINGBROKE, *Duke of Hereford,*
    Son to John of Gaunt; afterwards King Henry IV
DUKE OF AUMERLE, *Son to the Duke of York*
THOMAS MOWBRAY, *Duke of Norfolk*
DUKE OF SURREY
EARL OF SALISBURY
LORD BERKELEY

BUSHY }
BAGOT } *Servants to King Richard*
GREEN }

EARL OF NORTHUMBERLAND
HENRY PERCY, *surnamed* HOTSPUR, *his Son*
LORD ROSS
LORD WILLOUGHBY
LORD FITZWATER
BISHOP OF CARLISLE
ABBOT OF WESTMINSTER
LORD MARSHAL
SIR PIERCE OF EXTON
SIR STEPHEN SCROOP
Captain of a Band of Welshmen

QUEEN TO KING RICHARD
DUCHESS OF GLOUCESTER
DUCHESS OF YORK
Lady attending on the Queen

Lords, Heralds, Officers, Soldiers, Gardeners, Keep-
er, Messenger, Groom, and other Attendants

SCENE
England and Wales

THE TRAGEDY OF KING RICHARD THE SECOND

ACT ONE

SCENE ONE

London. A Room in the Palace.

*Enter King Richard, attended; John of **Gaunt**, and other Nobles*

KING RICHARD. Old John of Gaunt, time-honour'd **Lancaster**,
Hast thou, according to thy oath and band,
Brought hither Henry Hereford thy bold son,
Here to make good the boisterous late appeal,
Which then our leisure would not let us hear,
Against the Duke of Norfolk, Thomas Mowbray?
GAUNT. I have, my liege.
KING RICHARD. Tell me, moreover, hast thou sounded **him,**
If he appeal the duke on ancient malice,
Or worthily, as a good subject should,
On some known ground of treachery in him?
GAUNT. As near as I could sift him on that argument,
On some apparent danger seen in him
Aim'd at your Highness, no inveterate malice.
KING RICHARD. Then call them to our presence: face to face,
And frowning brow to brow, ourselves will hear
The accuser and the accused freely speak:

Exeunt some Attendants

High-stomach'd are they both, and full of ire,
In rage deaf as the sea, hasty as fire.
Re-enter Attendants, with Bolingbroke and Mowbray
BOLINGBROKE. Many years of happy days befall
My gracious sovereign, my most loving liege!
MOWBRAY. Each day still better other's happiness
Until the heavens, envying earth's good hap,
Add an immortal title to your crown!
KING RICHARD. We thank you both: yet one but flatters **us,**

As well appeareth by the cause you come;
Namely, to appeal each other of high treason.
Cousin of Hereford, what dost thou object
Against the Duke of Norfolk, Thomas Mowbray?

BOLINGBROKE. First,—heaven be the record to my speech!—
In the devotion of a subject's love,
Tendering the precious safety of my prince,
And free from other misbegotten hate,
Come I appellant to this princely presence.
Now, Thomas Mowbray, do I turn to thee,
And mark my greeting well; for what I speak
My body shall make good upon this earth,
Or my divine soul answer it in heaven.
Thou art a traitor and a miscreant;
Too good to be so and too bad to live,
Since the more fair and crystal is the sky,
The uglier seem the clouds that in it fly.
Once more, the more to aggravate the note,
With a foul traitor's name stuff I thy throat;
And wish, so please my sovereign, ere I move,
What my tongue speaks, my right drawn sword may
     prove.

MOWBRAY. Let not my cold words here accuse my zeal:
'Tis not the trial of a woman's war,
The bitter clamour of two eager tongues,
Can arbitrate this cause betwixt us twain;
The blood is hot that must be cool'd for this:
Yet can I not of such tame patience boast
As to be hush'd and nought at all to say.
First, the fair reverence of your Highness curbs me
From giving reins and spurs to my free speech;
Which else would post until it had return'd
These terms of treason doubled down his throat.
Setting aside his high blood's royalty,
And let him be no kinsman to my liege,
I do defy him, and I spit at him;
Call him a slanderous coward and a villain:
Which to maintain I would allow him odds,
And meet him, were I tied to run afoot
Even to the frozen ridges of the Alps,
Or any other ground inhabitable,
Wherever Englishman durst set his foot.

Meantime let this defend my loyalty:
By all my hopes, most falsely doth he lie.
BOLINGBROKE. Pale trembling coward, there I throw my
    gage,
Disclaiming here the kindred of the king;
And lay aside my high blood's royalty,
Which fear, not reverence, makes thee to except:
If guilty dread have left thee so much strength
As to take up mine honour's pawn, then stoop:
By that, and all the rites of knighthood else,
Will I make good against thee, arm to arm,
What I have spoke, or thou canst worse devise.
MOWBRAY. I take it up; and by that sword I swear,
Which gently laid my knighthood on my shoulder,
I 'll answer thee in any fair degree,
Or chivalrous design of knightly trial:
And when I mount, alive may I not light,
If I be traitor or unjustly fight!
KING RICHARD. What doth our cousin lay to Mowbray's
    charge?
It must be great that can inherit us
So much as of a thought of ill in him.
BOLINGBROKE. Look, what I speak, my life shall prove it
    true;
That Mowbray hath receiv'd eight thousand nobles
In name of lendings for your Highness' soldiers,
The which he hath detain'd for lewd employments,
Like a false traitor and injurious villain.
Besides I say and will in battle prove,
Or here or elsewhere to the furthest verge
That ever was survey'd by English eye,
That all the treasons for these eighteen years
Complotted and contrived in this land,
Fetch from false Mowbray their first head and spring.
Further I say and further will maintain
Upon this bad life to make all this good,
That he did plot the Duke of Gloucester's death,
Suggest his soon-believing adversaries,
And consequently, like a traitor coward,
Sluic'd out his innocent soul through streams of blood:
Which blood, like sacrificing Abel's, cries,
Even from the tongueless caverns of the earth,

To me for justice and rough chastisement;
And, by the glorious worth of my descent,
This arm shall do it, or this life be spent.

KING RICHARD. How high a pitch his resolution soars!
Thomas of Norfolk, what sayest thou to this?

MOWBRAY. O! let my sovereign turn away his face
And bid his ears a little while be deaf,
Till I have told this slander of his blood
How God and good men hate so foul a liar.

KING RICHARD. Mowbray, impartial are our eyes and ears:
Were he my brother, nay, my kingdom's heir,—
As he is but my father's brother's son,—
Now, by my sceptre's awe I make a vow,
Such neighbour nearness to our sacred blood
Should nothing privilege him, nor partialize
The unstooping firmness of my upright soul.
He is our subject, Mowbray; so art thou:
Free speech and fearless I to thee allow.

MOWBRAY. Then, Bolingbroke, as low as to thy heart,
Through the false passage of thy throat, thou liest.
Three parts of that receipt I had for Calais
Disburs'd I duly to his Highness' soldiers;
The other part reserv'd I by consent,
For that my sovereign liege was in my debt
Upon remainder of a dear account,
Since last I went to France to fetch his queen.
Now swallow down that lie. For Gloucester's death,
I slew him not; but to mine own disgrace
Neglected my sworn duty in that case.
For you, my noble Lord of Lancaster,
The honourable father to my foe,
Once did I lay an ambush for your life,
A trespass that doth vex my grieved soul;
But ere I last receiv'd the sacrament
I did confess it, and exactly begg'd
Your Grace's pardon, and I hope I had it.
This is my fault: as for the rest appeal'd,
It issues from the rancour of a villain,
A recreant and most degenerate traitor;
Which in myself I boldly will defend,
And interchangeably hurl down my gage
Upon this overweening traitor's foot,

To prove myself a loyal gentleman
Even in the best blood chamber'd in his bosom.
In haste whereof, most heartily I pray
Your Highness to assign our trial day.

KING RICHARD. Wrath-kindled gentlemen, be rul'd by me;
Let's purge this choler without letting blood:
This we prescribe, though no physician;
Deep malice makes too deep incision:
Forget, forgive; conclude and be agreed,
Our doctors say this is no month to bleed.
Good uncle, let this end where it begun;
We 'll calm the Duke of Norfolk, you your son.

GAUNT. To be a make-peace shall become my age:
Throw down, my son, the Duke of Norfolk's gage.

KING RICHARD. And, Norfolk, throw down his.

GAUNT.   When, Harry, when?
Obedience bids I should not bid again.

KING RICHARD. Norfolk, throw down, we bid; there is no
boot.

MOWBRAY. Myself I throw, dread sovereign, at thy foot.
My life thou shalt command, but not my shame:
The one my duty owes; but my fair name,—
Despite of death that lives upon my grave,—
To dark dishonour's use thou shalt not have.
I am disgrac'd, impeach'd, and baffled here,
Pierc'd to the soul with slander's venom'd spear,
The which no balm can cure but his heart-blood
Which breath'd this poison.

KING RICHARD.   Rage must be withstood:
Give me his gage: lions make leopards tame.

MOWBRAY. Yea, but not change his spots: take but my
shame,
And I resign my gage. My dear dear lord,
The purest treasure mortal times afford
Is spotless reputation; that away,
Men are but gilded loam or painted clay.
A jewel in a ten-times-barr'd-up chest
Is a bold spirit in a loyal breast.
Mine honour is my life; both grow in one;
Take honour from me, and my life is done:
Then, dear my liege, mine honour let me try;
In that I live and for that will I die.

KING RICHARD. Cousin, throw down your gage: do
    you begin.
BOLINGBROKE. O! God defend my soul from such deep sin.
    Shall I seem crest-fall'n in my father's sight,
    Or with pale beggar-fear impeach my height
    Before this out-dar'd dastard? Ere my tongue
    Shall wound mine honour with such feeble wrong,
    Or sound so base a parle, my teeth shall tear
    The slavish motive of recanting fear,
    And spit it bleeding in his high disgrace,
    Where shame doth harbour, even in Mowbray's face.
                                                Exit Gaunt
KING RICHARD. We were not born to sue, but to command:
    Which since we cannot do to make you friends,
    Be ready, as your lives shall answer it,
    At Coventry, upon Saint Lambert's day:
    There shall your swords and lances arbitrate
    The swelling difference of your settled hate:
    Since we cannot atone you, we shall see
    Justice design the victor's chivalry.
    Marshal, command our officers-at-arms
    Be ready to direct these home alarms.   *Exeunt*

SCENE TWO

The Same. A Room in the Duke of Lancaster's Palace.

Enter Gaunt and Duchess of Gloucester

GAUNT. Alas! the part I had in Woodstock's blood
    Doth more solicit me than your exclaims,
    To stir against the butchers of his life.
    But since correction lieth in those hands
    Which made the fault that we cannot correct,
    Put we our quarrel to the will of heaven;
    Who, when they see the hours ripe on earth,
    Will rain hot vengeance on offenders' heads.
DUCHESS. Finds brotherhood in thee no sharper spur?
    Hath love in thy old blood no living fire?
    Edward's seven sons, whereof thyself art one,
    Were as seven vials of his sacred blood,
    Or seven fair branches springing from one root:

Some of those seven are dried by nature's course,
Some of those branches by the Destinies cut;
But Thomas, my dear lord, my life, my Gloucester,
One vial full of Edward's sacred blood,
One flourishing branch of his most royal root,
Is crack'd, and all the precious liquor spilt;
Is hack'd down, and his summer leaves all faded,
By envy's hand and murder's bloody axe.
Ah, Gaunt! his blood was thine: that bed, that womb,
That metal, that self-mould, that fashion'd thee
Made him a man; and though thou liv'st and breath'st,
Yet art thou slain in him: thou dost consent
In some large measure to thy father's death
In that thou seest thy wretched brother die,
Who was the model of thy father's life.
Call it not patience, Gaunt; it is despair:
In suffering thus thy brother to be slaughter'd
Thou showest the naked pathway to thy life,
Teaching stern murder how to butcher thee:
That which in mean men we entitle patience
Is pale cold cowardice in noble breasts.
What shall I say? to safeguard thine own life,
The best way is to venge my Gloucester's death.
GAUNT. God's is the quarrel; for God's substitute,
His deputy anointed in his sight,
Hath caus'd his death; the which if wrongfully,
Let heaven revenge, for I may never lift
An angry arm against his minister.
DUCHESS. Where then, alas! may I complain myself?
GAUNT. To God, the widow's champion and defence.
DUCHESS. Why then, I will. Farewell, old Gaunt.
Thou go'st to Coventry, there to behold
Our cousin Hereford and fell Mowbray fight:
O! sit my husband's wrongs on Hereford's spear,
That it may enter butcher Mowbray's breast.
Or if misfortune miss the first career,
Be Mowbray's sins so heavy in his bosom
That they may break his foaming courser's back,
And throw the rider headlong in the lists,
A caitiff recreant to my cousin Hereford!
Farewell, old Gaunt: thy sometimes brother's wife
With her companion grief must end her life.

GAUNT. Sister, farewell; I must to Coventry.
  As much good stay with thee as go with me!
DUCHESS. Yet one word more. Grief boundeth where it falls,
  Not with the empty hollowness, but weight:
  I take my leave before I have begun,
  For sorrow ends not when it seemeth done.
  Commend me to my brother, Edmund York.
  Lo! this is all: nay, yet depart not so;
  Though this be all, do not so quickly go;
  I shall remember more. Bid him—ah, what?—
  With all good speed at Plashy visit me.
  Alack! and what shall good old York there see
  But empty lodgings and unfurnish'd walls,
  Unpeopled offices, untrodden stones?
  And what hear there for welcome but my groans?
  Therefore commend me; let him not come there,
  To seek out sorrow that dwells every where.
  Desolate, desolate will I hence, and die:
  The last leave of thee takes my weeping eye.   *Exeunt*

SCENE THREE

*Open Space, near Coventry. Lists set out, and a Throne.
Heralds, &c., attending.*

Enter the Lord Marshal and Aumerle

MARSHAL. My Lord Aumerle, is Harry Hereford arm'd?
AUMERLE. Yea, at all points, and longs to enter in.
MARSHAL. The Duke of Norfolk, sprightfully and bold,
  Stays but the summons of the appellant's trumpet.
AUMERLE. Why then, the champions are prepar'd, and stay
  For nothing but his Majesty's approach.
    *Flourish. Enter King Richard, who takes his seat
on his Throne; Gaunt, Bushy, Bagot, Green, and Others,
who take their places. A trumpet is sounded, and answered
by another trumpet within. Then enter Mowbray, in armour,
      defendant, preceded by a Herald*
KING RICHARD. Marshal, demand of yonder champion
  The cause of his arrival here in arms:
  Ask him his name, and orderly proceed
  To swear him in the justice of his cause.

MARSHAL. In God's name, and the king's, say who thou art,
And why thou com'st thus knightly clad in arms,
Against what man thou comest, and what thy quarrel.
Speak truly, on thy knighthood and thine oath;
As so defend thee heaven and thy valour!

MOWBRAY. My name is Thomas Mowbray, Duke of Norfolk,
Who hither come engaged by my oath,—
Which God defend a knight should violate!—
Both to defend my loyalty and truth
To God, my king, and his succeeding issue,
Against the Duke of Hereford that appeals me;
And, by the grace of God and this mine arm,
To prove him, in defending of myself,
A traitor to my God, my king, and me:
And as I truly fight, defend me heaven!   *He takes his seat*
                    Trumpet sounds. Enter Bolingbroke,
          appellant, in armour, preceded by a Herald

KING RICHARD. Marshal, ask yonder knight in arms,
Both who he is and why he cometh hither
Thus plated in habiliments of war;
And formally, according to our law,
Depose him in the justice of his cause.

MARSHAL. What is thy name? and wherefore com'st thou
    hither,
Before King Richard in his royal lists?
Against whom comest thou? and what's thy quarrel?
Speak like a true knight, so defend thee heaven!

BOLINGBROKE. Harry of Hereford, Lancaster, and Derby,
Am I; who ready here do stand in arms,
To prove by God's grace and my body's valour,
In lists, on Thomas Mowbray, Duke of Norfolk,
That he's a traitor foul and dangerous,
To God of heaven, King Richard, and to me:
And as I truly fight, defend me heaven!

MARSHAL. On pain of death, no person be so bold
Or daring-hardy as to touch the lists,
Except the marshal and such officers
Appointed to direct these fair designs.

BOLINGBROKE. Lord Marshal, let me kiss my sovereign's
    hand,
And bow my knee before his Majesty:
For Mowbray and myself are like two men

That vow a long and weary pilgrimage;
Then let us take a ceremonious leave
And loving farewell of our several friends.

MARSHAL. The appellant in all duty greets your Highness,
And craves to kiss your hand and take his leave.

KING RICHARD. (*Descends from his throne*) We will descend
and fold him in our arms.
Cousin of Hereford, as thy cause is right,
So be thy fortune in this royal fight!
Farewell, my blood; which if to-day thou shed,
Lament we may, but not revenge thee dead.

BOLINGBROKE. O! let no noble eye profane a tear
For me, if I be gor'd with Mowbray's spear.
As confident as is the falcon's flight
Against a bird, do I with Mowbray fight.
My loving lord, I take my leave of you;
Of you, my noble cousin, Lord Aumerle;
Not sick, although I have to do with death,
But lusty, young, and cheerly drawing breath.
Lo! as at English feasts, so I regreet
The daintiest last, to make the end most sweet:
O thou, the earthly author of my blood,
Whose youthful spirit, in me regenerate,
Doth with a twofold vigour lift me up
To reach at victory above my head,
Add proof unto mine armour with thy prayers,
And with thy blessings steel my lance's point,
That it may enter Mowbray's waxen coat,
And furbish new the name of John a Gaunt,
Even in the lusty haviour of his son.

GAUNT. God in thy good cause make thee prosperous!
Be swift like lightning in the execution;
And let thy blows, doubly redoubled,
Fall like amazing thunder on the casque
Of thy adverse pernicious enemy:
Rouse up thy youthful blood, be valiant and live.

BOLINGBROKE. Mine innocency and Saint George to thrive!
He takes his seat

MOWBRAY. (*Rising*) However God or fortune cast my lot,
There lives or dies, true to King Richard's throne,
A loyal, just, and upright gentleman.
Never did captive with a freer heart

Cast off his chains of bondage and embrace
His golden uncontroll'd enfranchisement,
More than my dancing soul doth celebrate
This feast of battle with mine adversary.
Most mighty liege, and my companion peers,
Take from my mouth the wish of happy years.
As gentle and as jocund as to jest,
Go I to fight: truth has a quiet breast.

KING RICHARD. Farewell, my lord: securely I espy
Virtue with valour couched in thine eye.
Order the trial, marshal, and begin.

The King and the Lords return to their seats

MARSHAL. Harry of Hereford, Lancaster, and Derby,
Receive thy lance; and God defend the right!

BOLINGBROKE. (*Rising*) Strong as a tower in hope, I cry
'amen.'

MARSHAL. (*To an Officer*) Go bear this lance to Thomas,
Duke of Norfolk.

FIRST HERALD. Harry of Hereford, Lancaster, and Derby,
Stands here for God, his sovereign, and himself,
On pain to be found false and recreant,
To prove the Duke of Norfolk, Thomas Mowbray,
A traitor to his God, his king, and him;
And dares him to set forward to the fight.

SECOND HERALD. Here standeth Thomas Mowbray, Duke of
Norfolk,
On pain to be found false and recreant,
Both to defend himself and to approve
Henry of Hereford, Lancaster, and Derby,
To God, his sovereign, and to him, disloyal;
Courageously and with a free desire,
Attending but the signal to begin.

MARSHAL. Sound, trumpets; and set forward, combatants.

A charge sounded

Stay, stay, the king hath thrown his warder down.

KING RICHARD. Let them lay by their helmets and their
spears,
And both return back to their chairs again:
Withdraw with us; and let the trumpets sound
While we return these dukes what we decree.

A long flourish

(*To the Combatants*) Draw near,

And list what with our council we have done.
For that our kingdom's earth should not be soil'd
With that dear blood which it hath fostered;
And for our eyes do hate the dire aspect
Of civil wounds plough'd up with neighbours' swords;
And for we think the eagle-winged pride
Of sky-aspiring and ambitious thoughts,
With rival-hating envy, set on you
To wake our peace, which in our country's cradle
Draws the sweet infant breath of gentle sleep;
Which so rous'd up with boisterous untun'd drums,
With harsh-resounding trumpets' dreadful bray,
And grating shock of wrathful iron arms,
Might from our quiet confines fright fair peace
And make us wade even in our kindred's blood:
Therefore, we banish you our territories:
You, cousin Hereford, upon pain of life,
Till twice five summers have enrich'd our fields,
Shall not regreet our fair dominions,
But tread the stranger paths of banishment.

BOLINGBROKE. Your will be done: this must my comfort be,
That sun that warms you here shall shine on me;
And those his golden beams to you here lent
Shall point on me and gild my banishment.

KING RICHARD. Norfolk, for thee remains a heavier doom,
Which I with some unwillingness pronounce:
The sly slow hours shall not determinate
The dateless limit of thy dear exile;
The hopeless word of 'never to return'
Breathe I against thee, upon pain of life.

MOWBRAY. A heavy sentence, my most sovereign liege,
And all unlook'd for from your Highness' mouth:
A dearer merit, not so deep a maim
As to be cast forth in the common air,
Have I deserved at your Highness' hands.
The language I have learn'd these forty years,
My native English, now I must forego;
And now my tongue's use is to me no more
Than an unstringed viol or a harp,
Or like a cunning instrument cas'd up,
Or, being open, put into his hands
That knows no touch to tune the harmony:

Within my mouth you have engaol'd my tongue,
Doubly portcullis'd with my teeth and lips;
And dull, unfeeling, barren ignorance
Is made my gaoler to attend on me.
I am too old to fawn upon a nurse,
Too far in years to be a pupil now:
What is thy sentence then but speechless death,
Which robs my tongue from breathing native breath?
KING RICHARD. It boots thee not to be compassionate:
After our sentence plaining comes too late.
MOWBRAY. Then, thus I turn me from my country's light,
To dwell in solemn shades of endless night.   *Retiring*
KING RICHARD. Return again, and take an oath with thee.
Lay on our royal sword your banish'd hands;
Swear by the duty that you owe to God—
Our part therein we banish with yourselves—
To keep the oath that we administer:
You never shall,—so help you truth and God!—
Embrace each other's love in banishment;
Nor never look upon each other's face;
Nor never write, regreet, nor reconcile
This lowering tempest of your home-bred hate;
Nor never by advised purpose meet
To plot, contrive, or complot any ill
'Gainst us, our state, our subjects, or our land.
BOLINGBROKE. I swear.
MOWBRAY. And I, to keep all this.
BOLINGBROKE. Norfolk, so far, as to mine enemy:—
By this time, had the king permitted us,
One of our souls had wander'd in the air,
Banish'd this frail sepulchre of our flesh,
As now our flesh is banish'd from this land:
Confess thy treasons ere thou fly the realm;
Since thou hast far to go, bear not along
The clogging burden of a guilty soul.
MOWBRAY. No, Bolingbroke: if ever I were traitor,
My name be blotted from the book of life,
And I from heaven banish'd as from hence!
But what thou art, God, thou, and I do know;
And all too soon, I fear, the king shall rue.
Farewell, my liege. Now no way can I stray;
Save back to England, all the world's my way.   *Exit*

KING RICHARD. Uncle, even in the glasses of thine eyes
  I see thy grieved heart: thy sad aspect
  Hath from the number of his banish'd years
  Pluck'd four away.—(*To Bolingbroke*) Six frozen winters
    spent,
  Return with welcome home from banishment.
BOLINGBROKE. How long a time lies in one little word!
  Four lagging winters and four wanton springs
  End in a word: such is the breath of kings.
GAUNT. I thank my liege, that in regard of me
  He shortens four years of my son's exile;
  But little vantage shall I reap thereby:
  For, ere the six years that he hath to spend
  Can change their moons and bring their times about,
  My oil-dried lamp and time-bewasted light
  Shall be extinct with age and endless night;
  My inch of taper will be burnt and done,
  And blindfold death not let me see my son.
KING RICHARD. Why, uncle, thou hast many years to live.
GAUNT. But not a minute, king, that thou canst give:
  Shorten my days thou canst with sullen sorrow,
  And pluck nights from me, but not lend a morrow;
  Thou canst help time to furrow me with age,
  But stop no wrinkle in his pilgrimage;
  Thy word is current with him for my death,
  But dead, thy kingdom cannot buy my breath.
KING RICHARD. Thy son is banish'd upon good advice,
  Whereto thy tongue a party-verdict gave:
  Why at our justice seem'st thou then to lower?
GAUNT. Things sweet to taste prove in digestion sour.
  You urg'd me as a judge; but I had rather
  You would have bid me argue like a father.
  O! had it been a stranger, not my child,
  To smooth his fault I should have been more mild:
  A partial slander sought I to avoid,
  And in the sentence my own life destroy'd.
  Alas! I look'd when some of you should say,
  I was too strict to make mine own away;
  But you gave leave to my unwilling tongue
  Against my will to do myself this wrong.
KING RICHARD. Cousin, farewell; and, uncle, bid him so:
  Six years we banish him, and he shall go.

Flourish. Exeunt King Richard and Train

AUMERLE. Cousin, farewell: what presence must not know,
From where you do remain let paper show.

MARSHAL. My lord, no leave take I; for I will ride,
As far as land will let me, by your side.

GAUNT. O! to what purpose dost thou hoard thy words,
That thou return'st no greeting to thy friends?

BOLINGBROKE. I have too few to take my leave of you,
When the tongue's office should be prodigal
To breathe the abundant dolour of the heart.

GAUNT. Thy grief is but thy absence for a time.

BOLINGBROKE. Joy absent, grief is present for that time.

GAUNT. What is six winters? they are quickly gone.

BOLINGBROKE. To men in joy; but grief makes one hour ten.

GAUNT. Call it a travel that thou tak'st for pleasure.

BOLINGBROKE. My heart will sigh when I miscall it so,
Which finds it an inforced pilgrimage.

GAUNT. The sullen passage of thy weary steps
Esteem as foil wherein thou art to set
The precious jewel of thy home return.

BOLINGBROKE. Nay, rather, every tedious stride I make
Will but remember me what a deal of world
I wander from the jewels that I love.
Must I not serve a long apprenticehood
To foreign passages, and in the end,
Having my freedom, boast of nothing else
But that I was a journeyman to grief?

GAUNT. All places that the eye of heaven visits
Are to a wise man ports and happy havens.
Teach thy necessity to reason thus;
There is no virtue like necessity.
Think not the king did banish thee,
But thou the king. Woe doth the heavier sit,
Where it perceives it is but faintly borne.
Go, say I sent thee forth to purchase honour,
And not the king exil'd thee; or suppose
Devouring pestilence hangs in our air,
And thou art flying to a fresher clime.
Look, what thy soul holds dear, imagine it
To lie that way thou go'st, not whence thou com'st.
Suppose the singing birds musicians,
The grass whereon thou tread'st the presence strew'd,

The flowers fair ladies, and thy steps no more
Than a delightful measure or a dance;
For gnarling sorrow hath less power to bite
The man that mocks at it and sets it light.

BOLINGBROKE. O! who can hold a fire in his hand
By thinking on the frosty Caucasus?
Or cloy the hungry edge of appetite
By bare imagination of a feast?
Or wallow naked in December snow
By thinking on fantastic summer's heat?
O, no! the apprehension of the good
Gives but the greater feeling to the worse:
Fell sorrow's tooth doth never rankle more
Than when it bites, but lanceth not the sore.

GAUNT. Come, come, my son, I 'll bring thee on thy way.
Had I thy youth and cause, I would not stay.

BOLINGBROKE. Then, England's ground, farewell; sweet
    soil, adieu:
My mother, and my nurse, that bears me yet!
Where'er I wander, boast of this I can,
Though banish'd, yet a true-born Englishman.   *Exeunt*

SCENE FOUR

London. A Room in the King's Castle.

*Enter King Richard, Bagot, and Green at one door;
Aumerle at another*

KING RICHARD. We did observe. Cousin Aumerle,
How far brought you high Hereford on his way?

AUMERLE. I brought high Hereford, if you call him so,
But to the next highway, and there I left him.

KING RICHARD. And say, what store of parting tears were
    shed?

AUMERLE. Faith, none for me; except the north-east wind,
Which then blew bitterly against our faces,
Awak'd the sleeping rheum, and so by chance
Did grace our hollow parting with a tear.

KING RICHARD. What said our cousin when you parted with
    him?

AUMERLE. 'Farewell':
    And, for my heart disdained that my tongue
    Should so profane the word, that taught me craft
    To counterfeit oppression of such grief
    That words seem'd buried in my sorrow's grave.
    Marry, would the word 'farewell' have lengthen'd hours
    And added years to his short banishment,
    He should have had a volume of farewells;
    But, since it would not, he had none of me.
KING RICHARD. He is our cousin, cousin; but 'tis doubt,
    When time shall call him home from banishment,
    Whether our kinsman come to see his friends.
    Ourself and Bushy, Bagot here and Green
    Observ'd his courtship to the common people,
    How he did seem to dive into their hearts
    With humble and familiar courtesy,
    What reverence he did throw away on slaves,
    Wooing poor craftsmen with the craft of smiles
    And patient underbearing of his fortune,
    As 'twere to banish their affects with him
    Off goes his bonnet to an oyster-wench;
    A brace of draymen bid God speed him well,
    And had the tribute of his supple knee,
    With 'Thanks, my countrymen, my loving friends';
    As were our England in reversion his,
    And he our subjects' next degree in hope.
GREEN. Well, he is gone; and with him go these thoughts.
    Now for the rebels which stand out in Ireland;
    Expedient manage must be made, my liege,
    Ere further leisure yield them further means
    For their advantage and your Highness' loss.
KING RICHARD. We will ourself in person to this war.
    And, for our coffers with too great a court
    And liberal largess are grown somewhat light,
    We are enforc'd to farm our royal realm;
    The revenue whereof shall furnish us
    For our affairs in hand. If that come short,
    Our substitutes at home shall have blank charters;
    Whereto, when they shall know what men are rich,
    They shall subscribe them for large sums of gold,
    And send them after to supply our wants;
    For we will make for Ireland presently.

Enter Bushy

Bushy, what news?

BUSHY. Old John of Gaunt is grievous sick, my lord,
Suddenly taken, and hath sent post-haste
To entreat your Majesty to visit him.

KING RICHARD. Where lies he?

BUSHY. At Ely House.

KING RICHARD. Now, put it, God, in his physician's mind
To help him to his grave immediately!
The lining of his coffers shall make coats
To deck our soldiers for these Irish wars.
Come, gentlemen, let's all go visit him:
Pray God we may make haste, and come too late.

ALL. Amen.   *Exeunt*

ACT TWO

SCENE ONE

London. An Apartment in Ely House.

Gaunt on a couch; the Duke of York and Others standing by him

GAUNT. Will the king come, that I may breathe my last
  In wholesome counsel to his unstaid youth?
YORK. Vex not yourself, nor strive not with your breath;
  For all in vain comes counsel to his ear.
GAUNT. O! but they say the tongues of dying men
  Enforce attention like deep harmony:
  Where words are scarce, they are seldom spent in vain,
  For they breathe truth that breathe their words in pain.
  He that no more must say is listen'd more
    Than they whom youth and ease have taught to glose;
  More are men's ends mark'd than their lives before:
    The setting sun, and music at the close,
  As the last taste of sweets, is sweetest last,
  Writ in remembrance more than things long past:
  Though Richard my life's counsel would not hear,
  My death's sad tale may yet undeaf his ear.
YORK. No; it is stopp'd with other flattering sounds,
  As praises of his state: then there are fond
  Lascivious metres, to whose venom sound
  The open ear of youth doth always listen:
  Report of fashions in proud Italy,
  Whose manners still our tardy apish nation
  Limps after in base imitation.
  Where doth the world thrust forth a vanity,—
  So it be new there 's no respect how vile,—
  That is not quickly buzz'd into his ears?
  Then all too late comes counsel to be heard,
  Where will doth mutiny with wit's regard.
  Direct not him whose way himself will choose:

'Tis breath thou lack'st, and that breath wilt thou lose.
GAUNT. Methinks I am a prophet new inspir'd,
    And thus expiring do foretell of him:
    His rash fierce blaze of riot cannot last,
    For violent fires soon burn out themselves;
    Small showers last long, but sudden storms are short;
    He tires betimes that spurs too fast betimes;
    With eager feeding food doth choke the feeder:
    Light vanity, insatiate cormorant,
    Consuming means, soon preys upon itself.
    This royal throne of kings, this scepter'd isle,
    This earth of majesty, this seat of Mars,
    This other Eden, demi-paradise,
    This fortress built by Nature for herself
    Against infection and the hand of war,
    This happy breed of men, this little world,
    This precious stone set in the silver sea,
    Which serves it in the office of a wall,
    Or as a moat defensive to a house,
    Against the envy of less happier lands;
    This blessed plot, this earth, this realm, this England,
    This nurse, this teeming womb of royal kings,
    Fear'd by their breed and famous by their birth,
    Renowned for their deeds as far from home,—
    For Christian service and true chivalry,—
    As is the sepulchre in stubborn Jewry
    Of the world's ransom, blessed Mary's Son:
    This land of such dear souls, this dear, dear land,
    Dear for her reputation, through the world,
    Is now leas'd out,—I die pronouncing it,—
    Like to a tenement, or pelting farm:
    England, bound in with the triumphant sea,
    Whose rocky shore beats back the envious siege
    Of watery Neptune, is now bound in with shame,
    With inky blots, and rotten parchment bonds:
    That England, that was wont to conquer others,
    Hath made a shameful conquest of itself.
    Ah! would the scandal vanish with my life,
    How happy then were my ensuing death.
        Enter King Richard and Queen;
    Aumerle, Bushy, Green, Bagot, Ross, and Willoughby
YORK. The king is come: deal mildly with his youth;

For young hot colts, being rag'd, do rage the more.
QUEEN. How fares our noble uncle, Lancaster?
KING RICHARD. What comfort, man? How is 't with aged
    Gaunt?
GAUNT. O! how that name befits my composition;
    Old Gaunt indeed, and gaunt in being old:
    Within me grief hath kept a tedious fast;
    And who abstains from meat that is not gaunt?
    For sleeping England long time have I watch'd;
    Watching breeds leanness, leanness is all gaunt.
    The pleasure that some fathers feed upon
    Is my strict fast, I mean my children's looks;
    And therein fasting hast thou made me gaunt.
    Gaunt am I for the grave, gaunt as a grave,
    Whose hollow womb inherits nought but bones.
KING RICHARD. Can sick men play so nicely with their
    names?
GAUNT. No; misery makes sport to mock itself:
    Since thou dost seek to kill my name in me,
    I mock my name, great king, to flatter thee.
KING RICHARD. Should dying men flatter with those that live?
GAUNT. No, no; men living flatter those that die.
KING RICHARD. Thou, now a-dying, sayst thou flatterest me.
GAUNT. O, no! thou diest, though I the sicker be.
KING RICHARD. I am in health, I breathe, and see thee ill.
GAUNT. Now, he that made me knows I see thee ill;
    Ill in myself to see, and in thee seeing ill.
    Thy death-bed is no lesser than thy land
    Wherein thou liest in reputation sick:
    And thou, too careless patient as thou art,
    Committ'st thy anointed body to the cure
    Of those physicians that first wounded thee:
    A thousand flatterers sit within thy crown,
    Whose compass is no bigger than thy head;
    And yet, incaged in so small a verge,
    The waste is no whit lesser than thy land.
    O! had thy grandsire, with a prophet's eye,
    Seen how his son's son should destroy his sons,
    From forth thy reach he would have laid thy shame,
    Deposing thee before thou wert possess'd,
    Which art possess'd now to depose thyself.
    Why, cousin, wert thou regent of the world,

It were a shame to let this land by lease;
But for thy world enjoying but this land,
Is it not more than shame to shame it so?
Landlord of England art thou now, not king:
Thy state of law is bondslave to the law,
And—

KING RICHARD. And thou a lunatic lean-witted fool,
Presuming on an ague's privilege,
Dar'st with thy frozen admonition
Make pale our cheek, chasing the royal blood
With fury from his native residence.
Now, by my seat's right royal majesty,
Wert thou not brother to great Edward's son,—
This tongue that runs so roundly in thy head
Should run thy head from thy unreverent shoulders.

GAUNT. O! spare me not, my brother Edward's son,
For that I was his father Edward's son.
That blood already, like the pelican,
Hast thou tapp'd out and drunkenly carous'd:
My brother Gloucester, plain well-meaning soul,—
Whom fair befall in heaven 'mongst happy souls!—
May be a precedent and witness good
That thou respect'st not spilling Edward's blood:
Join with the present sickness that I have;
And thy unkindness be like crooked age,
To crop at once a too-long wither'd flower.
Live in thy shame, but die not shame with thee!
These words hereafter thy tormentors be!
Convey me to my bed, then to my grave:
Love they to live that love and honour have.

Exit, borne out by his Attendants

KING RICHARD. And let them die that age and sullens have;
For both hast thou, and both become the grave.

YORK. I do beseech your Majesty, impute his words
To wayward sickliness and age in him:
He loves you, on my life, and holds you dear
As Harry, Duke of Hereford, were he here.

KING RICHARD. Right, you say true: as Hereford's love, so
his;
As theirs, so mine; and all be as it is.

Enter Northumberland

NORTHUMBERLAND. My liege, old Gaunt commends him to
     your Majesty.
KING RICHARD. What says he?
NORTHUMBERLAND. Nay, nothing; all is said:
     His tongue is now a stringless instrument;
     Words, life, and all, old Lancaster hath spent.
YORK. Be York the next that must be bankrupt so!
     Though death be poor, it ends a mortal woe.
KING RICHARD. The ripest fruit first falls, and so doth he:
     His time is spent; our pilgrimage must be.
     So much for that. Now for our Irish wars.
     We must supplant those rough rug-headed kerns,
     Which live like venom where no venom else
     But only they have privilege to live.
     And for these great affairs do ask some charge,
     Towards our assistance we do seize to us
     The plate, coin, revenues, and moveables,
     Whereof our uncle Gaunt did stand possess'd.
YORK. How long shall I be patient? Ah! how long
     Shall tender duty make me suffer wrong?
     Not Gloucester's death, nor Hereford's banishment,
     Not Gaunt's rebukes, nor England's private wrongs,
     Nor the prevention of poor Bolingbroke
     About his marriage, nor my own disgrace,
     Have ever made me sour my patient cheek,
     Or bend one wrinkle on my sovereign's face.
     I am the last of noble Edward's sons,
     Of whom thy father, Prince of Wales, was first;
     In war was never lion rag'd more fierce,
     In peace was never gentle lamb more mild,
     Than was that young and princely gentleman.
     His face thou hast, for even so look'd he,
     Accomplish'd with the number of thy hours;
     But when he frown'd, it was against the French,
     And not against his friends; his noble hand
     Did win what he did spend, and spent not that
     Which his triumphant father's hand had won:
     His hands were guilty of no kindred's blood,
     But bloody with the enemies of his kin.
     O Richard! York is too far gone with grief,
     Or else he never would compare between.
KING RICHARD. Why, uncle, what's the matter?

YORK.   O! my liege.
Pardon me, if you please; if not, I, pleas'd
Not to be pardon'd, am content withal.
Seek you to seize and gripe into your hands
The royalties and rights of banish'd Hereford?
Is not Gaunt dead, and doth not Hereford live?
Was not Gaunt just, and is not Harry true?
Did not the one deserve to have an heir?
Is not his heir a well-deserving son?
Take Hereford's rights away, and take from Time
His charters and his customary rights;
Let not to-morrow then ensue to-day;
Be not thyself; for how art thou a king
But by fair sequence and succession?
Now, afore God,—God forbid I say true!—
If you do wrongfully seize Hereford's rights,
Call in the letters-patent that he hath
By his attorneys-general to sue
His livery, and deny his offer'd homage,
You pluck a thousand dangers on your head,
You lose a thousand well-disposed hearts,
And prick my tender patience to those thoughts
Which honour and allegiance cannot think.
KING RICHARD. Think what you will: we seize into our hands
His plate, his goods, his money, and his lands.
YORK. I 'll not be by the while: my liege, farewell:
What will ensue hereof, there 's none can tell;
But by bad courses may be understood
That their events can never fall out good.   *Exit*
KING RICHARD. Go, Bushy, to the Earl of Wiltshire straight:
Bid him repair to us to Ely House
To see this business. To-morrow next
We will for Ireland; and 'tis time, I trow:
And we create, in absence of ourself,
Our uncle York Lord Governor of England;
For he is just, and always lov'd us well.
Come on, our queen: to-morrow must we part;
Be merry, for our time of stay is short.   *Flourish*
    Exeunt King, Queen, Bushy, Aumerle, Green, and Bagot
NORTHUMBERLAND. Well, lords, the Duke of Lancaster is
    dead.
ROSS. And living too; for now his son is duke.

WILLOUGHBY. Barely in title, not in revenue.

NORTHUMBERLAND. Richly in both, if justice had her right.

ROSS. My heart is great; but it must break with silence,
Ere 't be disburden'd with a liberal tongue.

NORTHUMBERLAND. Nay, speak thy mind; and let him ne'er
speak more
That speaks thy words again to do thee harm!

WILLOUGHBY. Tends that thou 'dst speak to the Duke of
Hereford?
If it be so, out with it boldly, man;
Quick is mine ear to hear of good towards him.

ROSS. No good at all that I can do for him,
Unless you call it good to pity him,
Bereft and gelded of his patrimony.

NORTHUMBERLAND. Now, afore God, 'tis shame such wrongs
are borne
In him, a royal prince, and many more
Of noble blood in this declining land.
The king is not himself, but basely led
By flatterers; and what they will inform,
Merely in hate, 'gainst any of us all,
That will the king severely prosecute
'Gainst us, our lives, our children, and our heirs.

ROSS. The commons hath he pill'd with grievous taxes,
And quite lost their hearts: the nobles hath he fin'd
For ancient quarrels, and quite lost their hearts.

WILLOUGHBY. And daily new exactions are devis'd;
As blanks, benevolences, and I wot not what:
But what, o' God's name, doth become of this?

NORTHUMBERLAND. Wars have not wasted it, for warr'd he
hath not,
But basely yielded upon compromise
That which his ancestors achiev'd with blows.
More hath he spent in peace than they in wars.

ROSS. The Earl of Wiltshire hath the realm in farm.

WILLOUGHBY. The king's grown bankrupt, like a broken man.

NORTHUMBERLAND. Reproach and dissolution hangeth over
him.

ROSS. He hath not money for these Irish wars,
His burdenous taxations notwithstanding,
But by the robbing of the banish'd duke.

NORTHUMBERLAND. His noble kinsman: most degenerate
king!

But, lords, we hear this fearful tempest sing,
Yet seek no shelter to avoid the storm;
We see the wind sit sore upon our sails,
And yet we strike not, but securely perish.
ROSS. We see the very wrack that we must suffer;
And unavoided is the danger now,
For suffering so the causes of our wrack.
NORTHUMBERLAND. Not so: even through the hollow eyes of
     death
I spy life peering; but I dare not say
How near the tidings of our comfort is.
WILLOUGHBY. Nay, let us share thy thoughts, as thou dost
     ours.
ROSS. Be confident to speak, Northumberland:
We three are but thyself: and, speaking so,
Thy words are but as thoughts; therefore, be bold.
NORTHUMBERLAND. Then thus: I have from Port le Blanc, a
     bay
In Brittany, receiv'd intelligence
That Harry Duke of Hereford, Rainold Lord Cobham,
That late broke from the Duke of Exeter,
His brother, Archbishop late of Canterbury,
Sir Thomas Erpingham, Sir John Ramston,
Sir John Norbery, Sir Robert Waterton, and Francis
     Quoint,
All these well furnish'd by the Duke of Britaine,
With eight tall ships, three thousand men of war,
Are making hither with all due expedience,
And shortly mean to touch our northern shore.
Perhaps they had ere this, but that they stay
The first departing of the king for Ireland.
If then we shall shake off our slavish yoke,
Imp out our drooping country's broken wing,
Redeem from broking pawn the blemish'd crown,
Wipe off the dust that hides our sceptre's gilt,
And make high majesty look like itself,
Away with me in post to Ravenspurgh;
But if you faint, as fearing to do so,
Stay and be secret, and myself will go.
ROSS. To horse, to horse! urge doubts to them that fear.
WILLOUGHBY. Hold out my horse, and I will first be there.
                                        Exeunt

SCENE TWO

The Same. A Room in the Palace.

Enter Queen, Bushy, and Bagot

BUSHY. Madam, your Majesty is too much sad:
　　You promis'd, when you parted with the king,
　　To lay aside life-harming heaviness,
　　And entertain a cheerful disposition.
QUEEN. To please the king I did; to please myself
　　I cannot do it; yet I know no cause
　　Why I should welcome such a guest as grief,
　　Save bidding farewell to so sweet a guest
　　As my sweet Richard: yet, again, methinks,
　　Some unborn sorrow, ripe in fortune's womb,
　　Is coming towards me, and my inward soul
　　With nothing trembles; at some thing it grieves
　　More than with parting from my lord the king.
BUSHY. Each substance of a grief hath twenty shadows
　　Which show like grief itself, but are not so.
　　For sorrow's eye, glazed with blinding tears,
　　Divides one thing entire to many objects;
　　Like perspectives, which rightly gaz'd upon
　　Show nothing but confusion; ey'd awry
　　Distinguish form: so your sweet Majesty,
　　Looking awry upon your lord's departure,
　　Finds shapes of grief more than himself to wail;
　　Which, look'd on as it is, is nought but shadows
　　Of what it is not. Then, thrice-gracious queen,
　　More than your lord's departure weep not: more's not
　　　　seen;
　　Or if it be, 'tis with false sorrow's eye,
　　Which for things true weeps things imaginary.
QUEEN. It may be so; but yet my inward soul
　　Persuades me it is otherwise: howe'er it be,
　　I cannot but be sad, so heavy sad,
　　As, though in thinking on no thought I think,
　　Makes me with heavy nothing faint and shrink.
BUSHY. 'Tis nothing but conceit, my gracious lady.
QUEEN. 'Tis nothing less: conceit is still deriv'd

From some forefather grief; mine is not so,
For nothing hath begot my something grief;
Or something hath the nothing that I grieve:
'Tis in reversion that I do possess;
But what it is, that is not yet known; what
I cannot name; 'tis nameless woe, I wot.

Enter Green

GREEN. God save your Majesty! and well met, gentlemen:
I hope the king is not yet shipp'd for Ireland.

QUEEN. Why hop'st thou so? 'tis better hope he is,
For his designs crave haste, his haste good hope:
Then wherefore dost thou hope he is not shipp'd?

GREEN. That he, our hope, might have retir'd his power,
And driven into despair an enemy's hope,
Who strongly hath set footing in this land:
The banish'd Bolingbroke repeals himself,
And with uplifted arms is safe arriv'd
At Ravenspurgh.

QUEEN.   Now God in heaven forbid!

GREEN. Ah! madam, 'tis too true: and that is worse,
The Lord Northumberland, his son young Henry Percy,
The Lords of Ross, Beaumond, and Willoughby,
With all their powerful friends, are fled to him.

BUSHY. Why have you not proclaim'd Northumberland
And all the rest of the revolted faction traitors?

GREEN. We have: whereupon the Earl of Worcester
Hath broke his staff, resign'd his stewardship,
And all the household servants fled with him
To Bolingbroke.

QUEEN. So, Green, thou art the midwife to my woe,
And Bolingbroke my sorrow's dismal heir:
Now hath my soul brought forth her prodigy,
And I, a gasping new-deliver'd mother,
Have woe to woe, sorrow to sorrow join'd.

BUSHY. Despair not, madam.

QUEEN.   Who shall hinder me?
I will despair, and be at enmity
With cozening hope: he is a flatterer,
A parasite, a keeper-back of death,
Who gently would dissolve the bands of life,
Which false hope lingers in extremity.

Enter York

GREEN. Here comes the Duke of York.

QUEEN. With signs of war about his aged neck:
O! full of careful business are his looks.
Uncle, for God's sake, speak comfortable words.

YORK. Should I do so, I should belie my thoughts:
Comfort 's in heaven; and we are on the earth,
Where nothing lives but crosses, cares, and grief.
Your husband, he is gone to save far off,
Whilst others come to make him lose at home:
Here am I left to underprop his land,
Who, weak with age, cannot support myself.
Now comes the sick hour that his surfeit made;
Now shall he try his friends that flatter'd him.

Enter a Servant

SERVANT. My lord, your son was gone before I came.

YORK. He was? Why, so! go all which way it will!
The nobles they are fled, the commons they are cold,
And will, I fear, revolt on Hereford's side.
Sirrah, get thee to Plashy, to my sister Gloucester;
Bid her send me presently a thousand pound.
Hold, take my ring.

SERVANT. My lord, I had forgot to tell your lordship:
To-day, as I came by, I called there;
But I shall grieve you to report the rest.

YORK. What is 't, knave?

SERVANT. An hour before I came the duchess died.

YORK. God for his mercy! what a tide of woes
Comes rushing on this woeful land at once!
I know not what to do: I would to God,—
So my untruth had not provok'd him to it,—
The king had cut off my head with my brother's
What! are there no posts dispatch'd for Ireland?
How shall we do for money for these wars?
Come, sister,—cousin, I would say,—pray, pardon me.—
Go, fellow, get thee home; provide some carts
And bring away the armour that is there.   *Exit Servant*
Gentlemen, will you go muster men? If I know
How or which way to order these affairs
Thus thrust disorderly into my hands,
Never believe me. Both are my kinsmen:

The one is my sovereign, whom both my oath
And duty bids defend; the other again
Is my kinsman, whom the king hath wrong'd,
Whom conscience and my kindred bids to right.
Well, somewhat we must do. Come, cousin,
I 'll dispose of you. Gentlemen, go muster up your men,
And meet me presently at Berkeley Castle.
I should to Plashy too:
But time will not permit. All is uneven,
And every thing is left at six and seven.

Exeunt York and Queen

BUSHY. The wind sits fair for news to go to Ireland,
But none returns. For us to levy power
Proportionable to the enemy
Is all unpossible.

GREEN. Besides, our nearness to the king in love
Is near the hate of those love not the king.

BAGOT. And that 's the wavering commons; for their love
Lies in their purses, and whoso empties them,
By so much fills their hearts with deadly hate.

BUSHY. Wherein the king stands generally condemn'd.

BAGOT. If judgment lie in them, then so do we,
Because we ever have been near the king.

GREEN. Well, I 'll for refuge straight to Bristol Castle;
The Earl of Wiltshire is already there.

BUSHY. Thither will I with you; for little office
Will the hateful commons perform for us,
Except like curs to tear us all to pieces.
Will you go along with us?

BAGOT. No; I will to Ireland to his Majesty.
Farewell: if heart's presages be not vain,
We three here part that ne'er shall meet again.

BUSHY. That 's as York thrives to beat back Bolingbroke.

GREEN. Alas, poor duke! the task he undertakes
Is numbering sands and drinking oceans dry:
Where one on his side fights, thousands will fly.
Farewell at once; for once, for all, and ever.

BUSHY. Well, we may meet again.

BAGOT.   I fear me, never.   *Exeunt*

SCENE THREE

The Wolds in Gloucestershire.

Enter Bolingbroke and Northumberland, with Forces

BOLINGBROKE. How far is it, my lord, to Berkeley now?
NORTHUMBERLAND. Believe me, noble lord,
  I am a stranger here in Gloucestershire:
  These high wild hills and rough uneven ways
  Draw out our miles and make them wearisome;
  But yet your fair discourse hath been as sugar,
  Making the hard way sweet and delectable.
  But I bethink me what a weary way
  From Ravenspurgh to Cotswold will be found
  In Ross and Willoughby, wanting your company
  Which, I protest, hath very much beguil'd
  The tediousness and process of my travel:
  But theirs is sweeten'd with the hope to have
  The present benefit which I possess;
  And hope to joy is little less in joy
  Than hope enjoy'd: by this the weary lords
  Shall make their way seem short, as mine hath done
  By sight of what I have, your noble company.
BOLINGBROKE. Of much less value is my company
  Than your good words. But who comes here?
                Enter Henry Percy
NORTHUMBERLAND. It is my son, young Harry Percy,
  Sent from my brother Worcester, whencesoever.
  Harry, how fares your uncle?
HENRY PERCY. I had thought, my lord, to have learn'd his
    health of you.
NORTHUMBERLAND. Why, is he not with the queen?
HENRY PERCY. No, my good lord; he hath forsook the court,
  Broken his staff of office, and dispers'd
  The household of the king.
NORTHUMBERLAND.   What was his reason?
  He was not so resolv'd when last we spake together.
HENRY PERCY. Because your lordship was proclaimed
    traitor.
  But he, my lord, is gone to Ravenspurgh,

    To offer service to the Duke of Hereford,
    And sent me over by Berkeley to discover
    What power the Duke of York had levied there;
    Then with direction to repair to Ravenspurgh.

NORTHUMBERLAND. Have you forgot the Duke of Hereford,
    boy?

HENRY PERCY. No, my good lord; for that is not forgot
    Which ne'er I did remember: to my knowledge
    I never in my life did look on him.

NORTHUMBERLAND. Then learn to know him now: this is the
    duke.

HENRY PERCY. My gracious lord, I tender you my service,
    Such as it is, being tender, raw, and young,
    Which elder days shall ripen and confirm
    To more approved service and desert.

BOLINGBROKE. I thank thee, gentle Percy; and be sure
    I count myself in nothing else so happy
    As in a soul remembering my good friends;
    And as my fortune ripens with thy love,
    It shall be still thy true love's recompense:
    My heart this covenant makes, my hand thus seals it.

NORTHUMBERLAND. How far is it to Berkeley? and what stir
    Keeps good old York there with his men of war?

HENRY PERCY. There stands the castle, by yon tuft of trees,
    Mann'd with three hundred men, as I have heard;
    And in it are the Lords of York, Berkeley, and Seymour;
    None else of name and noble estimate.

Enter Ross and Willoughby

NORTHUMBERLAND. Here come the Lords of Ross and
    Willoughby,
    Bloody with spurring, fiery-red with haste.

BOLINGBROKE. Welcome, my lords. I wot your love pursues
    A banish'd traitor; all my treasury
    Is yet but unfelt thanks, which, more enrich'd,
    Shall be your love and labour's recompense.

ROSS. Your presence makes us rich, most noble lord.

WILLOUGHBY. And far surmounts our labour to attain it.

BOLINGBROKE. Evermore thanks, the exchequer of the poor;
    Which, till my infant fortune comes to years,
    Stands for my bounty. But who comes here?

Enter Berkeley

NORTHUMBERLAND. It is my Lord of Berkeley, as I guess.

BERKELEY. My Lord of Hereford, my message is to you.
BOLINGBROKE. My lord, my answer is—to Lancaster;
    And I am come to seek that name in England;
    And I must find that title in your tongue
    Before I make reply to aught you say.
BERKELEY. Mistake me not, my lord; 'tis not my meaning
    To raze one title of your honour out:
    To you, my lord, I come, what lord you will,
    From the most gracious regent of this land,
    The Duke of York, to know what pricks you on
    To take advantage of the absent time
    And fright our native peace with self-born arms.

                Enter York, attended

BOLINGBROKE. I shall not need transport my words by you:
    Here comes his Grace in person.

                         My noble uncle!   *Kneels*

YORK. Show me thy humble heart, and not thy knee,
    Whose duty is deceivable and false.
BOLINGBROKE. My gracious uncle—
YORK. Tut, tut!
    Grace me no grace, nor uncle me no uncle:
    I am no traitor's uncle; and that word 'grace'
    In an ungracious mouth is but profane.
    Why have those banish'd and forbidden legs
    Dar'd once to touch a dust of England's ground?
    But then, more 'why?' why have they dar'd to march
    So many miles upon her peaceful bosom,
    Frighting her pale-fac'd villages with war
    And ostentation of despised arms?
    Com'st thou because the anointed king is hence?
    Why, foolish boy, the king is left behind,
    And in my loyal bosom lies his power.
    Were I but now the lord of such hot youth
    As when brave Gaunt thy father, and myself,
    Rescu'd the Black Prince, that young Mars of men,
    From forth the ranks of many thousand French,
    O! then, how quickly should this arm of mine,
    Now prisoner to the palsy, chastise thee
    And minister correction to thy fault!
BOLINGBROKE. My gracious uncle, let me know my fault:
    On what condition stands it and wherein?
YORK. Even in condition of the worst degree,

In gross rebellion and detested treason:
Thou art a banish'd man, and here art come
Before the expiration of thy time,
In braving arms against thy sovereign.

BOLINGBROKE. As I was banish'd, I was banish'd Hereford;
But as I come, I come for Lancaster.
And, noble uncle, I beseech your Grace
Look on my wrongs with an indifferent eye:
You are my father, for methinks in you
I see old Gaunt alive: O! then, my father,
Will you permit that I shall stand condemn'd
A wandering vagabond; my rights and royalties
Pluck'd from my arms perforce and given away
To upstart unthrifts? Wherefore was I born?
If that my cousin king be King of England,
It must be granted I am Duke of Lancaster.
You have a son, Aumerle, my noble kinsman;
Had you first died, and he been thus trod down,
He should have found his uncle Gaunt a father,
To rouse his wrongs and chase them to the bay.
I am denied to sue my livery here,
And yet my letters-patent give me leave:
My father's goods are all distrain'd and sold,
And these and all are all amiss employ'd.
What would you have me do? I am a subject,
And challenge law: attorneys are denied me,
And therefore personally I lay my claim
To my inheritance of free descent.

NORTHUMBERLAND. The noble duke hath been too much
abus'd.

ROSS. It stands your Grace upon to do him right.

WILLOUGHBY. Base men by his endowments are made great.

YORK. My lords of England, let me tell you this:
I have had feeling of my cousin's wrongs,
And labour'd all I could to do him right;
But in this kind to come, in braving arms,
Be his own carver and cut out his way,
To find out right with wrong, it may not be;
And you that do abet him in this kind
Cherish rebellion and are rebels all.

NORTHUMBERLAND. The noble duke hath sworn his coming
is

But for his own; and for the right of that
We all have strongly sworn to give him aid;
And let him ne'er see joy that breaks that oath!
YORK. Well, well, I see the issue of these arms:
I cannot mend it, I must needs confess,
Because my power is weak and all ill left;
But if I could, by him that gave me life,
I would attach you all and make you stoop
Unto the sovereign mercy of the king;
But since I cannot, be it known to you
I do remain as neuter. So, fare you well;
Unless you please to enter in the castle
And there repose you for this night.
BOLINGBROKE. An offer, uncle, that we will accept:
But we must win your Grace to go with us
To Bristol Castle; which they say is held
By Bushy, Bagot, and their complices,
The caterpillars of the commonwealth,
Which I have sworn to weed and pluck away.
YORK. It may be I will go with you; but yet I 'll pause;
For I am loath to break our country's laws.
Nor friends nor foes, to me welcome you are:
Things past redress are now with me past care.   *Exeunt*

SCENE FOUR

A Camp in Wales.

Enter Salisbury and a Captain

CAPTAIN. My Lord of Salisbury, we have stay'd ten days,
And hardly kept our countrymen together,
And yet we hear no tidings from the king;
Therefore we will disperse ourselves: farewell.
SALISBURY. Stay yet another day, thou trusty Welshman:
The king reposeth all his confidence in thee.
CAPTAIN. 'Tis thought the king is dead: we will not stay.
The bay-trees in our country are all wither'd
And meteors fright the fixed stars of heaven,
The pale-fac'd moon looks bloody on the earth
And lean-look'd prophets whisper fearful change,
Rich men look sad and ruffians dance and leap,

The one in fear to lose what they enjoy,
The other to enjoy by rage and war:
These signs forerun the death or fall of kings.
Farewell: our countrymen are gone and fled,
As well assur'd Richard their king is dead.   *Exit*
SALISBURY. Ah, Richard! with the eyes of heavy mind
I see thy glory like a shooting star
Fall to the base earth from the firmament.
Thy sun sets weeping in the lowly west,
Witnessing storms to come, woe, and unrest.
Thy friends are fled to wait upon thy foes,
And crossly to thy good all fortune goes.   *Exit*

ACT THREE

SCENE ONE

Bristol. Bolingbroke's Camp.

*Enter Bolingbroke, York, Northumberland, Henry Percy,
Willoughby, Ross; Officers behind, with
Bushy and Green, prisoners*

BOLINGBROKE. Bring forth these men.
Bushy and Green, I will not vex your souls—
Since presently your souls must part your bodies—
With too much urging your pernicious lives,
For 'twere no charity; yet, to wash your blood
From off my hands, here in the view of men
I will unfold some causes of your deaths.
You have misled a prince, a royal king,
A happy gentleman in blood and lineaments,
By you unhappied and disfigur'd clean:
You have in manner with your sinful hours
Made a divorce betwixt his queen and him,
Broke the possession of a royal bed,
And stain'd the beauty of a fair queen's cheeks
With tears drawn from her eyes by your foul wrongs.
Myself, a prince by fortune of my birth,
Near to the king in blood, and near in love
Till you did make him misinterpret me,
Have stoop'd my neck under your injuries,
And sigh'd my English breath in foreign clouds,
Eating the bitter bread of banishment;
Whilst you have fed upon my signories,
Dispark'd my parks, and felled my forest woods,
From mine own windows torn my household coat,
Raz'd out my impress, leaving me no sign,
Save men's opinions and my living blood,
To show the world I am a gentleman.

This and much more, much more than twice all this,
Condemns you to the death. See them deliver'd over
To execution and the hand of death.

BUSHY. More welcome is the stroke of death to me
Than Bolingbroke to England. Lords, farewell.

GREEN. My comfort is, that heaven will take our souls
And plague injustice with the pains of hell.

BOLINGBROKE. My Lord Northumberland, see them
    dispatch'd.   *Exeunt Northumberland*
                      and Others, with Bushy and Green

Uncle, you say the queen is at your house;
For God's sake, fairly let her be entreated:
Tell her I send to her my kind commends;
Take special care my greetings be deliver'd.

YORK. A gentleman of mine I have dispatch'd
With letters of your love to her at large.

BOLINGBROKE. Thanks, gentle uncle. Come, lords, away,
To fight with Glendower and his complices:
Awhile to work, and after holiday.   *Exeunt*

SCENE TWO

The Coast of Wales. A Castle in view.

*Flourish: drums and trumpets. Enter King Richard, the
Bishop of Carlisle, Aumerle, and Soldiers*

KING RICHARD. Barkloughly Castle call they this at hand?

AUMERLE. Yea, my lord. How brooks your Grace the air,
After your late tossing on the breaking seas?

KING RICHARD. Needs must I like it well: I weep for joy
To stand upon my kingdom once again.
Dear earth, I do salute thee with my hand,
Though rebels wound thee with their horses' hoofs:
As a long-parted mother with her child
Plays fondly with her tears and smiles in meeting,
So, weeping, smiling, greet I thee, my earth,
And do thee favour with my royal hands.
Feed not thy sovereign's foe, my gentle earth,
Nor with thy sweets comfort his ravenous sense;
But let thy spiders, that suck up thy venom,
And heavy-gaited toads lie in their way,

Doing annoyance to the treacherous feet
Which with usurping steps do trample thee.
Yield stinging nettles to mine enemies;
And when they from thy bosom pluck a flower,
Guard it, I pray thee, with a lurking adder
Whose double tongue may with a mortal touch
Throw death upon thy sovereign's enemies.
Mock not my senseless conjuration, lords:
This earth shall have a feeling and these stones
Prove armed soldiers, ere her native king
Shall falter under foul rebellion's arms.

CARLISLE. Fear not, my lord: that Power that made you king
Hath power to keep you king in spite of all.
The means that heaven yields must be embrac'd,
And not neglected; else, if heaven would,
And we will not, heaven's offer we refuse,
The proffer'd means of succour and redress.

AUMERLE. He means, my lord, that we are too remiss;
Whilst Bolingbroke, through our security,
Grows strong and great in substance and in friends.

KING RICHARD. Discomfortable cousin! know'st thou not
That when the searching eye of heaven is hid
Behind the globe, and lights the lower world,
Then thieves and robbers range abroad unseen,
In murders and in outrage bloody here;
But when, from under this terrestrial ball
He fires the proud tops of the eastern pines
And darts his light through every guilty hole,
Then murders, treasons, and detested sins,
The cloak of night being pluck'd from off their backs,
Stand bare and naked, trembling at themselves?
So when this thief, this traitor, Bolingbroke,
Who all this while hath revell'd in the night
Whilst we were wandering with the antipodes,
Shall see us rising in our throne, the East,
His treasons will sit blushing in his face,
Not able to endure the sight of day,
But self-affrighted tremble at his sin.
Not all the water in the rough rude sea
Can wash the balm from an anointed king;
The breath of worldly men cannot depose
The deputy elected by the Lord.

For every man that Bolingbroke hath press'd
To lift shrewd steel against our golden crown,
God for his Richard hath in heavenly pay
A glorious angel: then, if angels fight,
Weak men must fall, for heaven still guards the right.

Enter Salisbury

Welcome, my lord: how far off lies your power?

SALISBURY. Nor near nor further off, my gracious lord,
Than this weak arm: discomfort guides my tongue
And bids me speak of nothing but despair.
One day too late, I fear me, noble lord,
Hath clouded all thy happy days on earth.
O! call back yesterday, bid time return,
And thou shalt have twelve thousand fighting men:
To-day, to-day, unhappy day too late,
O'erthrows thy joys, friends, fortune, and thy state;
For all the Welshmen, hearing thou wert dead,
Are gone to Bolingbroke, dispers'd and fled.

AUMERLE. Comfort, my liege! why looks your Grace so pale?

KING RICHARD. But now, the blood of twenty thousand men
Did triumph in my face, and they are fled;
And till so much blood thither come again
Have I not reason to look pale and dead?
All souls that will be safe, fly from my side;
For time hath set a blot upon my pride.

AUMERLE. Comfort, my liege! remember who you are.

KING RICHARD. I had forgot myself. Am I not king?
Awake, thou sluggard majesty! thou sleepest.
Is not the king's name twenty thousand names?
Arm, arm, my name! a puny subject strikes
At thy great glory. Look not to the ground,
Ye favourites of a king: are we not high?
High be our thoughts: I know my uncle York
Hath power enough to serve our turn. But who comes
    here?

Enter Sir Stephen Scroop

SCROOP. More health and happiness betide my liege
Than can my care-tun'd tongue deliver him!

KING RICHARD. Mine ear is open and my heart prepar'd:
The worst is worldly loss thou canst unfold.
Say, is my kingdom lost? why, 'twas my care;
And what loss is it to be rid of care?

Strives Bolingbroke to be as great as we?
Greater he shall not be: if he serve God
We 'll serve him too, and be his fellow so:
Revolt our subjects? that we cannot mend;
They break their faith to God as well as us:
Cry woe, destruction, ruin, loss, decay;
The worst is death, and death will have his day.

SCROOP. Glad am I that your Highness is so arm'd
To bear the tidings of calamity.
Like an unseasonable stormy day
Which makes the silver rivers drown their shores,
As if the world were all dissolv'd to tears,
So high above his limits swells the rage
Of Bolingbroke, covering your fearful land
With hard bright steel and hearts harder than steel.
White-beards have arm'd their thin and hairless scalps
Against thy majesty; and boys, with women's voices,
Strive to speak big, and clap their female joints
In stiff unwieldy arms against thy crown;
Thy very beadsmen learn to bend their bows
Of double-fatal yew against thy state;
Yea, distaff-women manage rusty bills
Against thy seat: both young and old rebel,
And all goes worse than I have power to tell.

KING RICHARD. Too well, too well thou tell'st a tale so ill.
Where is the Earl of Wiltshire? where is Bagot?
What is become of Bushy? where is Green?
That they have let the dangerous enemy
Measure our confines with such peaceful steps?
If we prevail, their heads shall pay for it.
I warrant they have made peace with Bolingbroke.

SCROOP. Peace have they made with him, indeed, my lord.

KING RICHARD. O villains, vipers, damn'd without
      redemption!
Dogs, easily won to fawn on any man!
Snakes, in my heart-blood warm'd, that sting my heart!
Three Judases, each one thrice worse than Judas!
Would they make peace? terrible hell make war
Upon their spotted souls for this offence!

SCROOP. Sweet love, I see, changing his property,
Turns to the sourest and most deadly hate.
Again uncurse their souls; their peace is made

    With heads and not with hands: those whom you curse
    Have felt the worst of death's destroying wound
    And lie full low, grav'd in the hollow ground.

AUMERLE. Is Bushy, Green, and the Earl of Wiltshire dead?

SCROOP. Yea, all of them at Bristol lost their heads.

AUMERLE. Where is the duke my father with his power?

KING RICHARD. No matter where. Of comfort no man speak:
    Let 's talk of graves, of worms, and epitaphs;
    Make dust our paper, and with rainy eyes
    Write sorrow on the bosom of the earth;
    Let 's choose executors and talk of wills:
    And yet not so—for what can we bequeath
    Save our deposed bodies to the ground?
    Our lands, our lives, and all are Bolingbroke's,
    And nothing can we call our own but death,
    And that small model of the barren earth
    Which serves as paste and cover to our bones.
    For God's sake, let us sit upon the ground
    And tell sad stories of the death of kings:
    How some have been deposed, some slain in war,
    Some haunted by the ghosts they have depos'd,
    Some poison'd by their wives, some sleeping kill'd;
    All murder'd: for within the hollow crown
    That rounds the mortal temples of a king
    Keeps Death his court, and there the antick sits,
    Scoffing his state and grinning at his pomp;
    Allowing him a breath, a little scene,
    To monarchize, be fear'd, and kill with looks,
    Infusing him with self and vain conceit
    As if this flesh which walls about our life
    Were brass impregnable; and humour'd thus
    Comes at the last, and with a little pin
    Bores through his castle wall, and farewell king!
    Cover your heads, and mock not flesh and blood
    With solemn reverence: throw away respect,
    Tradition, form, and ceremonious duty,
    For you have but mistook me all this while:
    I live with bread like you, feel want,
    Taste grief, need friends: subjected thus,
    How can you say to me I am a king?

CARLISLE. My lord, wise men ne'er sit and wail their woes,
    But presently prevent the ways to wail.

To fear the foe, since fear oppresseth strength,
Gives in your weakness strength unto your foe,
And so your follies fight against yourself.
Fear and be slain; no worse can come to fight:
And fight and die is death destroying death;
Where fearing dying pays death servile breath.

AUMERLE. My father hath a power; inquire of him
And learn to make a body of a limb.

KING RICHARD. Thou chid'st me well. Proud Bolingbroke, I
    come
To change blows with thee for our day of doom.
This ague-fit of fear is over-blown;
An easy task it is, to win our own.—
Say, Scroop, where lies our uncle with his power?
Speak sweetly, man, although thy looks be sour.

SCROOP. Men judge by the complexion of the sky
    The state and inclination of the day;
So may you by my dull and heavy eye,
    My tongue hath but a heavier tale to say.
I play the torturer, by small and small
To lengthen out the worst that must be spoken.
Your uncle York is join'd with Bolingbroke,
And all your northern castles yielded up,
And all your southern gentlemen in arms
Upon his party.

KING RICHARD.   Thou hast said enough.
    (To Aumerle) Beshrew thee, cousin, which didst lead me
    forth
Of that sweet way I was in to despair!
What say you now? What comfort have we now?
By heaven, I 'll hate him everlastingly
That bids me be of comfort any more.
Go to Flint Castle: there I'll pine away;
A king, woe's slave, shall kingly woe obey.
That power I have, discharge; and let them go
To ear the land that hath some hope to grow,
For I have none: let no man speak again
To alter this, for counsel is but vain.

AUMERLE. My liege, one word.

KING RICHARD.   He does me double wrong,
That wounds me with the flatteries of his tongue.
Discharge my followers; let them hence away,
From Richard's night to Bolingbroke's fair day.   *Exeunt*

SCENE THREE

Wales. Before Flint Castle.

Enter, with drum and colours, Bolingbroke and Forces;
York, Northumberland, and Others

BOLINGBROKE. So that by this intelligence we learn
The Welshmen are dispers'd and Salisbury
Is gone to meet the king, who lately landed
With some few private friends upon this coast.

NORTHUMBERLAND. The news is very fair and good, my lord:
Richard not far from hence hath hid his head.

YORK. It would beseem the Lord Northumberland
To say 'King Richard': alack the heavy day
When such a sacred king should hide his head!

NORTHUMBERLAND. Your Grace mistakes; only to be brief
Left I his title out.

YORK.   The time hath been,
Would you have been so brief with him, he would
Have been so brief with you, to shorten you,
For taking so the head, your whole head's length.

BOLINGBROKE. Mistake not, uncle, further than you should.

YORK. Take not, good cousin, further than you should,
Lest you mistake the heavens are o'er our heads.

BOLINGBROKE. I know it, uncle; and oppose not myself
Against their will. But who comes here?

                    Enter Henry Percy
Welcome, Harry: what, will not this castle yield?

HENRY PERCY. The castle royally is mann'd, my lord,
Against thy entrance.

BOLINGBROKE. Royally!
Why, it contains no king?

HENRY PERCY.   Yes, my good lord,
It doth contain a king: King Richard lies
Within the limits of yon lime and stone;
And with him are the Lord Aumerle, Lord Salisbury,
Sir Stephen Scroop; besides a clergyman
Of holy reverence; who, I cannot learn.

NORTHUMBERLAND. O! belike it is the Bishop of Carlisle.

BOLINGBROKE. (*To Northumberland*) Noble lord,
    Go to the rude ribs of that ancient castle,
    Through brazen trumpet send the breath of parley
    Into his ruin'd ears, and thus deliver:
    Henry Bolingbroke
    On both his knees doth kiss King Richard's hand,
    And sends allegiance and true faith of heart
    To his most royal person; hither come
    Even at his feet to lay my arms and power,
    Provided that my banishment repeal'd,
    And lands restor'd again be freely granted.
    If not, I 'll use the advantage of my power,
    And lay the summer's dust with showers of blood
    Rain'd from the wounds of slaughter'd Englishmen:
    The which, how far off from the mind of Bolingbroke
    It is, such crimson tempest should bedrench
    The fresh green lap of fair King Richard's land,
    My stooping duty tenderly shall show.
    Go, signify as much, while here we march
    Upon the grassy carpet of this plain.
    Let 's march without the noise of threatening drum,
    That from the castle's totter'd battlements
    Our fair appointments may be well perus'd.
    Methinks King Richard and myself should meet
    With no less terror than the elements
    Of fire and water, when their thundering shock
    At meeting tears the cloudy cheeks of heaven.
    Be he the fire, I 'll be the yielding water:
    The rage be his, while on the earth I rain
    My waters; on the earth, and not on him.
    March on, and mark King Richard how he looks.
        A Parley sounded, and answered by a
Trumpet within. Flourish. Enter on the Walls, King Richard,
    the Bishop of Carlisle, Aumerle, Scroop, and Salisbury
HENRY PERCY. See, see, King Richard doth himself appear,
    As doth the blushing discontented sun
        From out the fiery portal of the East,
    When he perceives the envious clouds are bent
    To dim his glory and to stain the track
    Of his bright passage to the Occident.
YORK. Yet looks he like a king: behold, his eye,

As bright as is the eagle's, lightens forth
Controlling majesty: alack, alack, for woe,
That any harm should stain so fair a show!
KING RICHARD. (*To Northumberland*) We are amaz'd; and
    thus long have we stood
To watch the fearful bending of thy knee,
Because we thought ourself thy lawful king:
And if we be, how dare thy joints forget
To pay their awful duty to our presence?
If we be not, show us the hand of God
That hath dismiss'd us from our stewardship;
For well we know, no hand of blood and bone
Can gripe the sacred handle of our sceptre,
Unless he do profane, steal, or usurp.
And though you think that all, as you have done,
Have torn their souls by turning them from us,
And we are barren and bereft of friends;
Yet know, my master, God omnipotent,
Is mustering in his clouds on our behalf
Armies of pestilence; and they shall strike
Your children yet unborn and unbegot,
That lift your vassal hands against my head
And threat the glory of my precious crown.
Tell Bolingbroke,—for yond methinks he is,—
That every stride he makes upon my land
Is dangerous treason: he is come to open
The purple testament of bleeding war;
But ere the crown he looks for live in peace,
Ten thousand bloody crowns of mothers' sons
Shall ill become the flower of England's face,
Change the complexion of her maid-pale peace
To scarlet indignation, and bedew
Her pastures' grass with faithful English blood.
NORTHUMBERLAND. The King of Heaven forbid our lord the
    king
Should so with civil and uncivil arms
Be rush'd upon! Thy thrice-noble cousin,
Harry Bolingbroke, doth humbly kiss thy hand;
And by the honourable tomb he swears,
That stands upon your royal grandsire's bones,
And by the royalties of both your bloods,
Currents that spring from one most gracious head,

And by the buried hand of warlike Gaunt,
And by the worth and honour of himself,
Comprising all that may be sworn or said,
His coming hither hath no further scope
Than for his lineal royalties and to beg
Enfranchisement immediate on his knees:
Which on thy royal party granted once,
His glittering arms he will commend to rust,
His barbed steeds to stables, and his heart
To faithful service of your Majesty.
This swears he, as he is a prince, is just;
And, as I am a gentleman, I credit him.

KING RICHARD. Northumberland, say, thus the king returns:
His noble cousin is right welcome hither;
And all the number of his fair demands
Shall be accomplish'd without contradiction:
With all the gracious utterance thou hast
Speak to his gentle hearing kind commends.

    Northumberland retires to Bolingbroke

(*To Aumerle*) We do debase ourself, cousin, do we not,
To look so poorly and to speak so fair?
Shall we call back Northumberland and send
Defiance to the traitor, and so die?

AUMERLE. No, good my lord; let 's fight with gentle words,
Till time lend friends and friends their helpful swords.

KING RICHARD. O God! O God! that e'er this tongue of mine,
That laid the sentence of dread banishment
On yond proud man, should take it off again
With words of sooth. O! that I were as great
As is my grief, or lesser than my name,
Or that I could forget what I have been,
Or not remember what I must be now.
Swell'st thou, proud heart? I 'll give thee scope to beat,
Since foes have scope to beat both thee and me.

AUMERLE. Northumberland comes back from Bolingbroke.

KING RICHARD. What must the king do now? Must he
  submit?
The king shall do it: must he be depos'd?
The king shall be contented: must he lose
The name of king? o' God's name, let it go:
I 'll give my jewels for a set of beads,
My gorgeous palace for a hermitage,

My gay apparel for an almsman's gown,
My figur'd goblets for a dish of wood,
My sceptre for a palmer's walking-staff,
My subjects for a pair of carved saints,
And my large kingdom for a little grave,
A little little grave, an obscure grave;
Or I 'll be buried in the king's highway,
Some way of common trade, where subjects' feet
May hourly trample on their sovereign's head;
For on my heart they tread now whilst I live;
And buried once, why not upon my head?
Aumerle, thou weep'st, my tender-hearted cousin!
We 'll make foul weather with despised tears;
Our sighs and they shall lodge the summer corn,
And make a dearth in this revolting land.
Or shall we play the wantons with our woes,
And make some pretty match with shedding tears?
As thus; to drop them still upon one place,
Till they have fretted us a pair of graves
Within the earth; and, there inlaid: 'There lies
Two kinsmen digg'd their graves with weeping eyes.
Would not this ill do well? Well, well, I see
I talk but idly and you laugh at me.
Most mighty prince, my Lord Northumberland,
What says King Bolingbroke? will his Majesty
Give Richard leave to live till Richard die?
You make a leg, and Bolingbroke says ay.

NORTHUMBERLAND. My lord, in the base court he doth attend
    To speak with you; may 't please you to come down?

KING RICHARD. Down, down, I come; like glistering Phaethon,
Wanting the manage of unruly jades.
In the base court? Base court, where kings grow base,
To come at traitors' calls and do them grace.
In the base court? Come down? Down, court! down, king!
For night-owls shriek where mounting larks should sing.

                                        Exeunt from above

BOLINGBROKE. What says his Majesty?

NORTHUMBERLAND.   Sorrow and grief of heart
    Makes him speak fondly, like a frantic man:
    Yet he is come.

Enter King Richard, and his Attendants

BOLINGBROKE. Stand all apart,
  And show fair duty to his Majesty.   *Kneeling*
  My gracious lord,—

KING RICHARD. Fair cousin, you debase your princely knee
  To make the base earth proud with kissing it:
  Me rather had my heart might feel your love
  Than my unpleas'd eye see your courtesy.
  Up, cousin, up; your heart is up, I know,
  Thus high at least, although your knee be low.

BOLINGBROKE. My gracious lord, I come but for mine own.

KING RICHARD. Your own is yours, and I am yours, and all.

BOLINGBROKE. So far be mine, my most redoubted lord,
  As my true service shall deserve your love.

KING RICHARD. Well you deserve: they well deserve to have
  That know the strong'st and surest way to get.
  Uncle, give me your hand: nay, dry your eyes;
  Tears show their love, but want their remedies.
  Cousin, I am too young to be your father,
  Though you are old enough to be my heir.
  What you will have I 'll give, and willing too;
  For do we must what force will have us do.
  Set on towards London. Cousin, is it so?

BOLINGBROKE. Yea, my good lord.

KING RICHARD.   Then I must not say no.
                                  Flourish. Exeunt

SCENE FOUR

Langley. The Duke of York's Garden.

Enter the Queen and two Ladies

QUEEN. What sport shall we devise here in this garden,
  To drive away the heavy thought of care?

FIRST LADY. Madam, we 'll play at bowls.

QUEEN. 'Twill make me think the world is full of rubs,
  And that my fortune runs against the bias.

FIRST LADY. Madam, we 'll dance.

QUEEN. My legs can keep no measure in delight
  When my poor heart no measure keeps in grief:
  Therefore, no dancing, girl; some other sport.

FIRST LADY. Madam, we 'll tell tales.

QUEEN. Of sorrow or of joy?

FIRST LADY.   Of either, madam.

QUEEN. Of neither, girl:
> For if of joy, being altogether wanting,
> It doth remember me the more of sorrow;
> Or if of grief, being altogether had,
> It adds more sorrow to my want of joy:
> For what I have I need not to repeat,
> And what I want it boots not to complain.

FIRST LADY. Madam, I 'll sing.

QUEEN.   'Tis well that thou hast cause;
> But thou shouldst please me better wouldst thou weep.

FIRST LADY. I could weep, madam, would it do you good.

QUEEN. And I could sing, would weeping do me good,
> And never borrow any tear of thee.
> But stay, here come the gardeners:
> Let 's step into the shadow of these trees.
> My wretchedness unto a row of pins,
> They 'll talk of state; for every one doth so
> Against a change: woe is forerun with woe.

Queen and Ladies retire

Enter a Gardener and two Servants

GARDENER. Go, bind thou up yon dangling apricocks,
> Which, like unruly children, make their sire
> Stoop with oppression of their prodigal weight:
> Give some supportance to the bending twigs.
> Go thou, and like an executioner,
> Cut off the heads of too fast growing sprays,
> That look too lofty in our commonwealth:
> All must be even in our government.
> You thus employ'd, I will go root away
> The noisome weeds, that without profit suck
> The soil's fertility from wholesome flowers.

FIRST SERVANT. Why should we in the compass of a pale
> Keep law and form and due proportion,
> Showing, as in a model, our firm estate,
> When our sea-walled garden, the whole land,
> Is full of weeds, her fairest flowers chok'd up,
> Her fruit-trees all unprun'd, her hedges ruin'd,
> Her knots disorder'd, and her wholesome herbs
> Swarming with caterpillars?

GARDENER.   Hold thy peace:
  He that hath suffer'd this disorder'd spring
  Hath now himself met with the fall of leaf;
  The weeds that his broad-spreading leaves did shelter,
  That seem'd in eating him to hold him up,
  Are pluck'd up root and all by Bolingbroke;
  I mean the Earl of Wiltshire, Bushy, Green.

FIRST SERVANT. What! are they dead?

GARDENER.   They are; and Bolingbroke
  Hath seiz'd the wasteful king. O! what pity is it
  That he hath not so trimm'd and dress'd his land
  As we this garden. We at time of year
  Do wound the bark, the skin of our fruit-trees,
  Lest, being over-proud with sap and blood,
  With too much riches it confound itself:
  Had he done so to great and growing men,
  They might have liv'd to bear and he to taste
  Their fruits of duty: superfluous branches
  We lop away that bearing boughs may live:
  Had he done so, himself had borne the crown,
  Which waste of idle hours hath quite thrown down.

FIRST SERVANT. What! think you then the king shall be
  depos'd?

GARDENER. Depress'd he is already, and depos'd
  'Tis doubt he will be: letters came last night
  To a dear friend of the good Duke of York's,
  That tell black tidings.

QUEEN. O! I am press'd to death through want of speaking.
                                 Coming forward
  Thou, old Adam's likeness, set to dress this garden,
  How dares thy harsh rude tongue sound this unpleasing
  news?
  What Eve, what serpent, hath suggested thee
  To make a second fall of cursed man?
  Why dost thou say King Richard is depos'd?
  Dar'st thou, thou little better thing than earth,
  Divine his downfall? Say, where, when, and how
  Cam'st thou by these ill tidings? speak, thou wretch.

GARDENER. Pardon me, madam: little joy have I
  To breathe these news, yet what I say is true.
  King Richard, he is in the mighty hold
  Of Bolingbroke; their fortunes both are weigh'd:

In your lord's scale is nothing but himself,
And some few vanities that make him light;
But in the balance of great Bolingbroke,
Besides himself, are all the English peers,
And with that odds he weighs King Richard down.
Post you to London and you 'll find it so;
I speak no more than every one doth know.

QUEEN. Nimble mischance, that art so light of foot,
Doth not thy embassage belong to me,
And am I last that knows it? O! thou think'st
To serve me last, that I may longest keep
Thy sorrow in my breast. Come, ladies, go,
To meet at London London's king in woe.
What! was I born to this, that my sad look
Should grace the triumph of great Bolingbroke?
Gardener, for telling me these news of woe,
Pray God the plants thou graft'st may never grow.

Exeunt Queen and Ladies

GARDENER. Poor queen! so that thy state might be no worse,
I would my skill were subject to thy curse.
Here did she fall a tear; here, in this place,
I 'll set a bank of rue, sour herb of grace;
Rue, even for ruth, here shortly shall be seen,
In the remembrance of a weeping queen.   *Exeunt*

ACT FOUR

SCENE ONE

London. Westminster Hall.

The Lords spiritual on the right side of the throne: the Lords temporal on the left; the Commons below. Enter Boling-broke, Aumerle, Surrey, Northumberland, Henry Percy, Fitzwater, another Lord, the Bishop of Carlisle, the Abbot of Westminster, and Attendants. Officers behind with Bagot

BOLINGBROKE. Call forth Bagot.
　　Now, Bagot, freely speak thy mind;
　　What thou dost know of noble Gloucester's death,
　　Who wrought it with the king, and who perform'd
　　The bloody office of his timeless end.
BAGOT. Then set before my face the Lord Aumerle.
BOLINGBROKE. Cousin, stand forth, and look upon that man.
BAGOT. My Lord Aumerle, I know your daring tongue
　　Scorns to unsay what once it hath deliver'd.
　　In that dead time when Gloucester's death was plotted,
　　I heard you say, 'Is not my arm of length,
　　That reacheth from the restful English court
　　As far as Calais, to my uncle's head?'
　　Amongst much other talk, that very time,
　　I heard you say that you had rather refuse
　　The offer of a hundred thousand crowns
　　Than Bolingbroke's return to England;
　　Adding withal, how blest this land would be
　　In this your cousin's death.
AUMERLE. 　　　　　　　　　Princes and noble lords,
　　What answer shall I make to this base man?
　　Shall I so much dishonour my fair stars,
　　On equal terms to give him chastisement?
　　Either I must, or have mine honour soil'd

With the attainder of his slanderous lips.
There is my gage, the manual seal of death,
That marks thee out for hell: I say thou liest,
And will maintain what thou hast said is false
In thy heart-blood, though being all too base
To stain the temper of my knightly sword.

BOLINGBROKE. Bagot, forbear; thou shalt not take it up.

AUMERLE. Excepting one, I would he were the best
In all this presence that hath mov'd me so.

FITZWATER. If that thy valour stand on sympathies,
There is my gage, Aumerle, in gage to thine:
By that fair sun which shows me where thou stand'st,
I heard thee say, and vauntingly thou spak'st it,
That thou wert cause of noble Gloucester's death.
If thou deny'st it twenty times, thou liest;
And I will turn thy falsehood to thy heart,
Where it was forged, with my rapier's point.

AUMERLE. Thou darest not, coward, live to see that day.

FITZWATER. Now, by my soul, I would it were this hour.

AUMERLE. Fitzwater, thou art damn'd to hell for this.

HENRY PERCY. Aumerle, thou liest; his honour is as true
In this appeal as thou art all unjust;
And that thou art so, there I throw my gage,
To prove it on thee to the extremest point
Of mortal breathing: seize it if thou dar'st.

AUMERLE. And if I do not may my hands rot off
And never brandish more revengeful steel
Over the glittering helmet of my foe!

LORD. I task the earth to the like, forsworn Aumerle;
And spur thee on with full as many lies
As may be holla'd in thy treacherous ear
From sun to sun: there is my honour's pawn;
Engage it to the trial if thou dar'st.

AUMERLE. Who sets me else? by heaven, I 'll throw at all:
I have a thousand spirits in one breast,
To answer twenty thousand such as you.

SURREY. My Lord Fitzwater, I do remember well
The very time Aumerle and you did talk.

FITZWATER. 'Tis very true: you were in presence then;
And you can witness with me this is true.

SURREY. As false, by heaven, as heaven itself is true.

FITZWATER. Surrey, thou liest.

SURREY.   Dishonourable boy!
  That lie shall lie so heavy on my sword
  That it shall render vengeance and revenge,
  Till thou the lie-giver and that lie do lie
  In earth as quiet as thy father's skull.
  In proof whereof, there is my honour's pawn:
  Engage it to the trial if thou darest.

FITZWATER. How fondly dost thou spur a forward horse!
  If I dare eat, or drink, or breathe, or live,
  I dare meet Surrey in a wilderness,
  And spit upon him, whilst I say he lies,
  And lies, and lies: there is my bond of faith
  To tie thee to my strong correction.
  As I intend to thrive in this new world,
  Aumerle is guilty of my true appeal:
  Besides, I heard the banish'd Norfolk say
  That thou, Aumerle, didst send two of thy men
  To execute the noble duke at Calais.

AUMERLE. Some honest Christian trust me with a gage.
  That Norfolk lies, here do I throw down this,
  If he may be repeal'd to try his honour.

BOLINGBROKE. These differences shall all rest under gage
  Till Norfolk be repeal'd: repeal'd he shall be,
  And though mine enemy, restor'd again
  To all his lands and signories; when he 's return'd,
  Against Aumerle we will enforce his trial.

CARLISLE. That honourable day shall ne'er be seen.
  Many a time hath banish'd Norfolk fought
  For Jesu Christ in glorious Christian field,
  Streaming the ensign of the Christian cross
  Against black pagans, Turks, and Saracens;
  And toil'd with works of war, retir'd himself
  To Italy; and there at Venice gave
  His body to that pleasant country's earth,
  And his pure soul unto his captain Christ,
  Under whose colours he had fought so long.

BOLINGBROKE. Why, bishop, is Norfolk dead?

CARLISLE. As surely as I live, my lord.

BOLINGBROKE. Sweet peace conduct his sweet soul to the
    bosom
  Of good old Abraham! Lords appellants,
  Your differences shall all rest under gage

Till we assign you to your days of trial.
Enter York, attended

YORK. Great Duke of Lancaster, I come to thee
From plume-pluck'd Richard; who with willing soul
Adopts thee heir, and his high sceptre yields
To the possession of thy royal hand.
Ascend his throne, descending now from him;
And long live Henry, of that name the fourth!
BOLINGBROKE. In God's name, I 'll ascend the regal throne.
CARLISLE. Marry, God forbid!
Worst in this royal presence may I speak,
Yet best beseeming me to speak the truth.
Would God that any in this noble presence
Were enough noble to be upright judge
Of noble Richard! then, true noblesse would
Learn him forbearance from so foul a wrong.
What subject can give sentence on his king?
And who sits here that is not Richard's subject?
Thieves are not judg'd but they are by to hear,
Although apparent guilt be seen in them;
And shall the figure of God's majesty,
His captain, steward, deputy elect,
Anointed, crowned, planted many years,
Be judg'd by subject and inferior breath,
And he himself not present? O! forfend it, God,
That in a Christian climate souls refin'd
Should show so heinous, black, obscene a deed.
I speak to subjects, and a subject speaks,
Stirr'd up by God thus boldly for his king.
My Lord of Hereford here, whom you call king,
Is a foul traitor to proud Hereford's king;
And if you crown him, let me prophesy,
The blood of English shall manure the ground
And future ages groan for this foul act;
Peace shall go sleep with Turks and infidels,
And in this seat of peace tumultuous wars
Shall kin with kin and kind with kind confound;
Disorder, horror, fear and mutiny
Shall here inhabit, and this land be call'd
The field of Golgotha and dead men's skulls.
O! if you rear this house against this house,
It will the woefullest division prove

That ever fell upon this cursed earth.
Prevent it, resist it, let it not be so,
Lest child, child's children, cry against you 'woe!'
NORTHUMBERLAND. Well have you argu'd, sir; and, for your
    pains,
Of capital treason we arrest you here.
My Lord of Westminster, be it your charge
To keep him safely till his day of trial.
May it please you, lords, to grant the commons' suit.
BOLINGBROKE. Fetch hither Richard, that in common view
He may surrender; so we shall proceed
Without suspicion.
YORK.   I will be his conduct.   *Exit*
BOLINGBROKE. Lords, you that here are under our arrest,
Procure your sureties for your days of answer.
    (*To Carlisle*) Little are we beholding to your love,
And little look'd for at your helping hands.

                Re-enter York, with King Richard,
                and Officers bearing the Crown, &c.

KING RICHARD. Alack! why am I sent for to a king
Before I have shook off the regal thoughts
Wherewith I reign'd? I hardly yet have learn'd
To insinuate, flatter, bow, and bend my limbs:
Give sorrow leave awhile to tutor me
To this submission. Yet I well remember
The favours of these men: were they not mine?
Did they not sometime cry, 'All haill' to me?
So Judas did to Christ: but he, in twelve,
Found truth in all but one; I, in twelve thousand, none.
God save the king! Will no man say, amen?
Am I both priest and clerk? well then, amen.
God save the king! although I be not he;
And yet, amen, if heaven do think him me.
To do what service am I sent for hither?
YORK. To do that office of thine own good will
Which tired majesty did make thee offer,
The resignation of thy state and crown
To Henry Bolingbroke.
KING RICHARD. Give me the crown. Here, cousin, seize the
    crown;
Here cousin,
On this side my hand and on that side thine.

Now is this golden crown like a deep well
That owes two buckets filling one another;
The emptier ever dancing in the air,
The other down, unseen and full of water:
That bucket down and full of tears am I,
Drinking my griefs, whilst you mount up on high.

BOLINGBROKE. I thought you had been willing to resign.

KING RICHARD. My crown, I am; but still my griefs are mine.
You may my glories and my state depose,
But not my griefs; still am I king of those.

BOLINGBROKE. Part of your cares you give me with your
crown.

KING RICHARD. Your cares set up do not pluck my cares
down.
My care is loss of care, by old care done;
Your care is gain of care, by new care won.
The cares I give I have, though given away;
They tend the crown, yet still with me they stay.

BOLINGBROKE. Are you contented to resign the crown?

KING RICHARD. Ay, no; no, ay; for I must nothing be;
Therefore no no, for I resign to thee.
Now mark me how I will undo myself:
I give this heavy weight from off my head,
And this unwieldy sceptre from my hand,
The pride of kingly sway from out my heart;
With mine own tears I wash away my balm,
With mine own hands I give away my crown,
With mine own tongue deny my sacred state,
With mine own breath release all duteous rites:
All pomp and majesty I do forswear;
My manors, rents, revenues, I forego;
My acts, decrees, and statutes I deny:
God pardon all oaths that are broke to me!
God keep all vows unbroke are made to thee!
Make me, that nothing have, with nothing griev'd,
And thou with all pleas'd, that hast all achiev'd!
Long mayst thou live in Richard's seat to sit,
And soon lie Richard in an earthy pit!
God save King Henry, unking'd Richard says,
And send him many years of sunshine days!
What more remains?

NORTHUMBERLAND. (*Offering a paper*) No more, but that
      you read
   These accusations and these grievous crimes
   Committed by your person and your followers
   Against the state and profit of this land;
   That, by confessing them, the souls of men
   May deem that you are worthily depos'd.
KING RICHARD. Must I do so? and must I ravel out
   My weav'd-up follies? Gentle Northumberland,
   If thy offences were upon record,
   Would it not shame thee in so fair a troop
   To read a lecture of them? If thou wouldst,
   There shouldst thou find one heinous article,
   Containing the deposing of a king,
   And cracking the strong warrant of an oath,
   Mark'd with a blot, damn'd in the book of heaven.
   Nay, all of you that stand and look upon me,
   Whilst that my wretchedness doth bait myself,
   Though some of you with Pilate wash your hands,
   Showing an outward pity; yet you Pilates
   Have here deliver'd me to my sour cross,
   And water cannot wash away your sin.
NORTHUMBERLAND. My lord, dispatch; read o'er these
      articles.
KING RICHARD. Mine eyes are full of tears, I cannot see:
   And yet salt water blinds them not so much
   But they can see a sort of traitors here.
   Nay, if I turn mine eyes upon myself,
   I find myself a traitor with the rest;
   For I have given here my soul's consent
   To undeck the pompous body of a king;
   Made glory base and sovereignty a slave,
   Proud majesty a subject, state a peasant.
NORTHUMBERLAND. My lord,—
KING RICHARD. No lord of thine, thou haught insulting man,
   Nor no man's lord; I have no name, no title,
   No, not that name was given me at the font,
   But 'tis usurp'd: alack the heavy day!
   That I have worn so many winters out,
   And know not now what name to call myself.
   O! that I were a mockery king of snow,
   Standing before the sun of Bolingbroke,

> To melt myself away in water-drops.
> Good king, great king,—and yet not greatly good,
> An if my word be sterling yet in England,
> Let it command a mirror hither straight,
> That it may show me what a face I have,
> Since it is bankrupt of his majesty.

BOLINGBROKE. Go some of you and fetch a looking-glass.

> *Exit an Attendant*

NORTHUMBERLAND. Read o'er this paper while the glass
> doth come.

KING RICHARD. Fiend! thou torment'st me ere I come to hell.

BOLINGBROKE. Urge it no more, my Lord Northumberland.

NORTHUMBERLAND. The commons will not then be satisfied.

KING RICHARD. They shall be satisfied: I 'll read enough
> When I do see the very book indeed
> Where all my sins are writ, and that 's myself.

> *Re-enter Attendant, with a glass*

> Give me the glass, and therein will I read.
> No deeper wrinkles yet? Hath sorrow struck
> So many blows upon this face of mine
> And made no deeper wounds? O, flattering glass!
> Like to my followers in prosperity,
> Thou dost beguile me. Was this face the face
> That every day under his household roof
> Did keep ten thousand men? Was this the face
> That like the sun did make beholders wink?
> Was this the face that fac'd so many follies,
> And was at last out-fac'd by Bolingbroke?
> A brittle glory shineth in this face:
> As brittle as the glory is the face;

> *Dashes the glass against the ground*

> For there it is, crack'd in a hundred shivers.
> Mark, silent king, the moral of this sport,
> How soon my sorrow hath destroy'd my face.

BOLINGBROKE. The shadow of your sorrow hath destroy'd
> The shadow of your face.

KING RICHARD.   Say that again.
> The shadow of my sorrow! Ha! let 's see:
> 'Tis very true, my grief lies all within;
> And these external manners of laments
> Are merely shadows to the unseen grief

That swells with silence in the tortur'd soul;
There lies the substance: and I thank thee, king,
For thy great bounty, that not only givest
Me cause to wail, but teachest me the way
How to lament the cause. I 'll beg one boon,
And then be gone and trouble you no more.
Shall I obtain it?

BOLINGBROKE.   Name it, fair cousin.

KING RICHARD. 'Fair cousin'! I am greater than a king;
For when I was a king, my flatterers
Were then but subjects; being now a subject,
I have a king here to my flatterer.
Being so great, I have no need to beg.

BOLINGBROKE. Yet ask.

KING RICHARD. And shall I have?

BOLINGBROKE. You shall.

KING RICHARD. Then give me leave to go.

BOLINGBROKE. Whither?

KING RICHARD. Whither you will, so I were from your sights.

BOLINGBROKE. Go, some of you convey him to the Tower.

KING RICHARD. O, good! convey? conveyers are you all,
That rise thus nimbly by a true king's fall.

Exeunt King Richard and Guard

BOLINGBROKE. On Wednesday next we solemnly set down
Our coronation: lords, prepare yourselves.

*Exeunt all except the Bishop of
Carlisle, the Abbot of Westminster, and Aumerle*

ABBOT. A woeful pageant have we here beheld.

CARLISLE. The woe 's to come; the children yet unborn
Shall feel this day as sharp to them as thorn.

AUMERLE. You holy clergyman, is there no plot
To rid the realm of this pernicious blot?

ABBOT. My lord,
Before I freely speak my mind herein,
You shall not only take the sacrament
To bury mine intents, but also to effect
Whatever I shall happen to devise.
I see your brows are full of discontent,
Your hearts of sorrow, and your eyes of tears:
Come home with me to supper; I will lay
A plot shall show us all a merry day.   *Exeunt*

ACT FIVE

SCENE ONE

London. A Street leading to the Tower.

Enter the Queen and Ladies

QUEEN. This way the king will come; this is the way
    To Julius Cæsar's ill-erected tower,
    To whose flint bosom my condemned lord
    Is doom'd a prisoner by proud Bolingbroke.
    Here let us rest, if this rebellious earth
    Have any resting for her true king's queen.
                Enter King Richard and Guard
    But soft, but see, or rather do not see,
    My fair rose wither: yet look up, behold,
    That you in pity may dissolve to dew,
    And wash him fresh again with true-love tears.
    Ah! thou, the model where old Troy did stand,
    Thou map of honour, thou King Richard's tomb,
    And not King Richard; thou most beauteous inn,
    Why should hard-favour'd grief be lodg'd in thee,
    When triumph is become an alehouse guest?
KING RICHARD. Join not with grief, fair woman, do not so,
    To make my end too sudden: learn, good soul,
    To think our former state a happy dream;
    From which awak'd, the truth of what we are
    Shows us but this. I am sworn brother, sweet,
    To grim Necessity, and he and I
    Will keep a league till death. Hie thee to France,
    And cloister thee in some religious house:
    Our holy lives must win a new world's crown,
    Which our profane hours here have stricken down.
QUEEN. What! is my Richard both in shape and mind
    Transform'd and weaken'd! Hath Bolingbroke depos'd
    Thine intellect? hath he been in thy heart?
    The lion dying thrusteth forth his paw

And wounds the earth, if nothing else, with rage
To be o'erpower'd; and wilt thou, pupil-like,
Take thy correction mildly, kiss the rod,
And fawn on rage with base humility,
Which art a lion and a king of beasts?
KING RICHARD. A king of beasts, indeed; if aught but beasts,
I had been still a happy king of men.
Good sometime queen, prepare thee hence for France,
Think I am dead, and that even here thou tak'st,
As from my death-bed, my last living leave.
In winter's tedious nights sit by the fire
With good old folks, and let them tell thee tales
Of woeful ages, long ago betid;
And ere thou bid good-night, to quit their grief,
Tell thou the lamentable tale of me,
And send the hearers weeping to their beds:
For why, the senseless brands will sympathize
The heavy accent of thy moving tongue,
And in compassion weep the fire out;
And some will mourn in ashes, some coal-black,
For the deposing of a rightful king.
                    Enter Northumberland, attended
NORTHUMBERLAND. My lord, the mind of Bolingbroke is
      chang'd;
You must to Pomfret, not unto the Tower.
And, madam, there is order ta'en for you;
With all swift speed you must away to France.
KING RICHARD. Northumberland, thou ladder wherewithal
The mounting Bolingbroke ascends my throne,
The time shall not be many hours of age
More than it is, ere foul sin gathering head
Shall break into corruption. Thou shalt think,
Though he divide the realm and give thee half,
It is too little, helping him to all;
And he shall think that thou, which know'st the way
To plant unrightful kings, wilt know again,
Being ne'er so little urg'd, another way
To pluck him headlong from the usurped throne.
The love of wicked friends converts to fear;
That fear to hate, and hate turns one or both
To worthy danger and deserved death.

NORTHUMBERLAND. My guilt be on my head, and there an
    end.
  Take leave and part; for you must part forthwith.
KING RICHARD. Doubly divorc'd! Bad men, ye violate
  A twofold marriage; 'twixt my crown and me,
  And then, betwixt me and my married wife.
  Let me unkiss the oath 'twixt thee and me;
  And yet not so, for with a kiss 'twas made.
  Part us, Northumberland: I towards the north,
  Where shivering cold and sickness pines the clime;
  My wife to France: from whence, set forth in pomp,
  She came adorned hither like sweet May,
  Sent back like Hallowmas or short'st of day.
QUEEN. And must we be divided? must we part?
KING RICHARD. Ay, hand from hand, my love, and heart
    from heart.
QUEEN. Banish us both and send the king with me.
NORTHUMBERLAND. That were some love but little policy.
QUEEN. Then whither he goes, thither let me go.
KING RICHARD. So two, together weeping, make one woe.
  Weep thou for me in France, I for thee here;
  Better far off than near, be ne'er the near.
  Go, count thy way with sighs, I mine with groans.
QUEEN. So longest way shall have the longest moans.
KING RICHARD. Twice for one step I 'll groan, the way being
    short,
  And piece the way out with a heavy heart.
  Come, come, in wooing sorrow let 's be brief,
  Since, wedding it, there is such length in grief.
  One kiss shall stop our mouths, and dumbly part;
  Thus give I mine, and thus take I thy heart.   *They kiss*
QUEEN. Give me mine own again; 'twere no good part
  To take on me to keep and kill thy heart.   *They kiss again*
  So, now I have mine own again, be gone,
  That I may strive to kill it with a groan.
KING RICHARD. We make woe wanton with this fond delay:
  Once more, adieu; the rest let sorrow say.   *Exeunt*

SCENE TWO

The Same. A Room in the Duke of York's Palace.

Enter York and his Duchess

DUCHESS. My lord, you told me you would tell the rest,
When weeping made you break the story off,
Of our two cousins coming into London.
YORK. Where did I leave?
DUCHESS.   At that sad stop, my lord,
Where rude misgovern'd hands, from windows' tops,
Threw dust and rubbish on King Richard's head.
YORK. Then, as I said, the duke, great Bolingbroke,
Mounted upon a hot and fiery steed,
Which his aspiring rider seem'd to know,
With slow but stately pace kept on his course,
While all tongues cried, 'God save thee, Bolingbroke!'
You would have thought the very windows spake,
So many greedy looks of young and old
Through casements darted their desiring eyes
Upon his visage, and that all the walls
With painted imagery had said at once
'Jesu preserve thee! welcome, Bolingbroke!'
Whilst he, from one side to the other turning,
Bare-headed, lower than his proud steed's neck,
Bespake them thus, 'I thank you, countrymen':
And thus still doing, thus he pass'd along.
DUCHESS. Alack, poor Richard! where rode he the whilst?
YORK. As in a theatre, the eyes of men,
After a well-grac'd actor leaves the stage,
Are idly bent on him that enters next,
Thinking his prattle to be tedious;
Even so, or with much more contempt, men's eyes
Did scowl on Richard: no man cried, 'God save him';
No joyful tongue gave him his welcome home;
But dust was thrown upon his sacred head,
Which with such gentle sorrow he shook off,
His face still combating with tears and smiles,
The badges of his grief and patience,
That had not God, for some strong purpose, steel'd

The hearts of men, they must perforce have melted,
And barbarism itself have pitied him.
But heaven hath a hand in these events,
To whose high will we bound our calm contents.
To Bolingbroke are we sworn subjects now,
Whose state and honour I for aye allow.

DUCHESS. Here comes my son Aumerle.

YORK.   Aumerle that was;
But that is lost for being Richard's friend,
And, madam, you must call him Rutland now.
I am in parliament pledge for his truth
And lasting fealty to the new made king.

Enter Aumerle

DUCHESS. Welcome, my son: who are the violets now
That strew the green lap of the new come spring?

AUMERLE. Madam, I know not, nor I greatly care not:
God knows I had as lief be none as one.

YORK. Well, bear you well in this new spring of time,
Lest you be cropp'd before you come to prime.
What news from Oxford? hold those justs and triumphs?

AUMERLE. For aught I know, my lord, they do.

YORK. You will be there, I know.

AUMERLE. If God prevent it not, I purpose so.

YORK. What seal is that that hangs without thy bosom?
Yea, look'st thou pale? let me see the writing.

AUMERLE. My lord, 'tis nothing.

YORK.   No matter then, who sees it:
I will be satisfied; let me see the writing.

AUMERLE. I do beseech your Grace to pardon me:
It is a matter of small consequence,
Which for some reasons I would not have seen.

YORK. Which for some reasons, sir, I mean to see.
I fear, I fear,—

DUCHESS.   What should you fear?
'Tis nothing but some bond he 's enter'd into
For gay apparel 'gainst the triumph day.

YORK. Bound to himself! what doth he with a bond
That he is bound to? Wife, thou art a fool.
Boy, let me see the writing.

AUMERLE. I do beseech you, pardon me; I may not show it.

YORK. I will be satisfied; let me see it, I say.

Snatches it, and reads

Treason! foul treason! villain! traitor! slave!

DUCHESS. What is the matter, my lord?

YORK. Ho! who is within there?

Enter a Servant

Saddle my horse.

God for his mercy! what treachery is here!

DUCHESS. Why, what is it, my lord?

YORK. Give me my boots, I say; saddle my horse.
  Now, by mine honour, by my life, my troth,
  I will appeach the villain.   *Exit Servant*

DUCHESS.   What 's the matter?

YORK. Peace, foolish woman.

DUCHESS. I will not peace. What is the matter, Aumerle?

AUMERLE. Good mother, be content; it is no more
  Than my poor life must answer.

DUCHESS.   Thy life answer!

YORK. Bring me my boots: I will unto the king.

Re-enter Servant with boots

DUCHESS. Strike him, Aumerle. Poor boy, thou art amaz'd.
  (*To Servant*) Hence, villain! never more come in my
      sight.   *Exit Servant*

YORK. Give me my boots, I say.

DUCHESS. Why, York, what wilt thou do?
  Wilt thou not hide the trespass of thine own?
  Have we more sons, or are we like to have?
  Is not my teeming date drunk up with time?
  And wilt thou pluck my fair son from mine age,
  And rob me of a happy mother's name?
  Is he not like thee? is he not thine own?

YORK. Thou fond, mad woman,
  Wilt thou conceal this dark conspiracy?
  A dozen of them here have ta'en the sacrament,
  And interchangeably set down their hands,
  To kill the king at Oxford.

DUCHESS.   He shall be none;
  We 'll keep him here: then, what is that to him?

YORK. Away, fond woman! were he twenty times
  My son, I would appeach him.

DUCHESS.   Hadst thou groan'd for him
  As I have done, thou 'dst be more pitiful.
  But now I know thy mind: thou dost suspect
  That I have been disloyal to thy bed,

And that he is a bastard, not thy son:
Sweet York, sweet husband, be not of that mind:
He is as like thee as a man may be,
Not like to me, nor any of my kin,
And yet I love him.

YORK.   Make way, unruly woman!   *Exit*
DUCHESS. After, Aumerle! Mount thee upon his horse;
Spur post, and get before him to the king,
And beg thy pardon ere he do accuse thee.
I 'll not be long behind; though I be old,
I doubt not but to ride as fast as York:
And never will I rise up from the ground
Till Bolingbroke have pardon'd thee. Away! be gone.
                                    Exeunt

SCENE THREE

Windsor. A Room in the Castle.

Enter Bolingbroke as King; Henry Percy, and other Lords

BOLINGBROKE. Can no man tell of my unthrifty son?
'Tis full three months since I did see him last.
If any plague hang over us, 'tis he.
I would to God, my lords, he might be found:
Inquire at London, 'mongst the taverns there,
For there, they say, he daily doth frequent,
With unrestrained loose companions,
Even such, they say, as stand in narrow lanes
And beat our watch and rob our passengers;
While he, young wanton and effeminate boy,
Takes on the point of honour to support
So dissolute a crew.

HENRY PERCY. My lord, some two days since I saw the
      prince,
And told him of these triumphs held at Oxford.

BOLINGBROKE. And what said the gallant?

HENRY PERCY. His answer was: he would unto the stews,
And from the common'st creature pluck a glove,
And wear it as a favour; and with that
He would unhorse the lustiest challenger.

BOLINGBROKE. As dissolute as desperate; yet through both,

I see some sparkles of a better hope,
Which elder days may happily bring forth.
But who comes here?

Enter Aumerle

AUMERLE.   Where is the king?

BOLINGBROKE.   What means
Our cousin, that he stares and looks so wildly?

AUMERLE. God save your Grace! I do beseech your Majesty,
To have some conference with your Grace alone.

BOLINGBROKE. Withdraw yourselves, and leave us here
    alone.   *Exeunt Henry Percy and Lords*
What is the matter with our cousin now?

AUMERLE. (*Kneels*) For ever may my knees grow to the
    earth,
My tongue cleave to my roof within my mouth,
Unless a pardon ere I rise or speak.

BOLINGBROKE. Intended or committed was this fault?
If on the first, how heinous e'er it be,
To win thy after-love I pardon thee.

AUMERLE. Then give me leave that I may turn the key,
That no man enter till my tale be done.

BOLINGBROKE. Have thy desire.   *Aumerle locks the door*

YORK. (*Within*) My liege, beware! look to thyself;
Thou hast a traitor in thy presence there.

BOLINGBROKE. (*Drawing*) Villain, I 'll make thee safe.

AUMERLE. Stay thy revengeful hand; thou hast no cause to
    fear.

YORK. (*Within*) Open the door, secure, foolhardy king:
Shall I for love speak treason to thy face?
Open the door, or I will break it open.

                              Bolingbroke unlocks
                        the door; and afterwards relocks it
                              Enter York

BOLINGBROKE. What is the matter, uncle? speak;
Recover breath; tell us how near is danger,
That we may arm us to encounter it.

YORK. Peruse this writing here, and thou shalt know
The treason that my haste forbids me show.

AUMERLE. Remember, as thou read'st, thy promise pass'd:
I do repent me; read not my name there;
My heart is not confederate with my hand.

YORK. 'Twas, villain, ere thy hand did set it down.

I tore it from the traitor's bosom, king;
Fear, and not love, begets his penitence.
Forget to pity him, lest thy pity prove
A serpent that will sting thee to the heart.

BOLINGBROKE. O heinous, strong, and bold conspiracy!
O loyal father of a treacherous son!
Thou sheer, immaculate, and silver fountain,
From whence this stream through muddy passages
Hath held his current and defil'd himself!
Thy overflow of good converts to bad,
And thy abundant goodness shall excuse
This deadly blot in thy digressing son.

YORK. So shall my virtue be his vice's bawd,
And he shall spend mine honour with his shame,
As thriftless sons their scraping fathers' gold.
Mine honour lives when his dishonour dies,
Or my sham'd life in his dishonour lies:
Thou kill'st me in his life; giving him breath,
The traitor lives, the true man 's put to death.

DUCHESS. (*Within*) What ho, my liege! for God's sake let
    me in.

BOLINGBROKE. What shrill-voic'd suppliant makes this eager
    cry?

DUCHESS. (*Within*) A woman, and thine aunt, great king;
    'tis I.
Speak with me, pity me, open the door:
A beggar begs, that never begg'd before.

BOLINGBROKE. Our scene is alter'd from a serious thing,
And now chang'd to 'The Beggar and the King.'
My dangerous cousin, let your mother in:
I know she 's come to pray for your foul sin.

                              Aumerle unlocks the door

YORK. If thou do pardon, whosoever pray,
More sins, for this forgiveness, prosper may.
This fester'd joint cut off, the rest rests sound;
This, let alone, will all the rest confound.

                              Enter Duchess

DUCHESS. O king! believe not this hard-hearted man:
Love, loving not itself, none other can.

YORK. Thou frantic woman, what dost thou make here?
Shall thy old dugs once more a traitor rear?

DUCHESS. Sweet York, be patient.   *Kneels*
                    Hear me, gentle liege.
BOLINGBROKE. Rise up, good aunt.
DUCHESS.   Not yet, I thee beseech.
   For ever will I walk upon my knees,
   And never see day that the happy sees,
   Till thou give joy: until thou bid me joy,
   By pardoning Rutland, my transgressing boy.
AUMERLE. Unto my mother's prayers I bend my knee.
                                        Kneels
YORK. Against them both my true joints bended be. *Kneels*
   Ill mayst thou thrive if thou grant any grace!
DUCHESS. Pleads he in earnest? look upon his face;
   His eyes do drop no tears, his prayers are in jest;
   His words come from his mouth, ours from our breast:
   He prays but faintly and would be denied;
   We pray with heart and soul and all beside:
   His weary joints would gladly rise, I know;
   Our knees shall kneel till to the ground they grow:
   His prayers are full of false hypocrisy;
   Ours of true zeal and deep integrity.
   Our prayers do out-pray his; then let them have
   That mercy which true prayer ought to have.
BOLINGBROKE. Good aunt, stand up.
DUCHESS.   Nay, do not say 'stand up';
   But 'pardon' first, and afterwards 'stand up.'
   An if I were thy nurse, thy tongue to teach,
   'Pardon' should be the first word of thy speech.
   I never long'd to hear a word till now;
   Say 'pardon,' king; let pity teach thee how:
   The word is short, but not so short as sweet;
   No word like 'pardon,' for kings' mouths so meet.
YORK. Speak it in French, king; say, 'pardonnez moy.'
DUCHESS. Dost thou teach pardon pardon to destroy?
   Ah! my sour husband, my hard-hearted lord,
   That sett'st the word itself against the word.
   Speak 'pardon' as 'tis current in our land;
   The chopping French we do not understand.
   Thine eye begins to speak, set thy tongue there,
   Or in thy piteous heart plant thou thine ear,
   That hearing how our plaints and prayers do pierce,
   Pity may move thee pardon to rehearse.

BOLINGBROKE. Good aunt, stand up.

DUCHESS.   I do not sue to stand;
Pardon is all the suit I have in hand.

BOLINGBROKE. I pardon him, as God shall pardon me.

DUCHESS. O happy vantage of a kneeling knee!
Yet am I sick for fear: speak it again;
Twice saying 'pardon' doth not pardon twain,
But makes one pardon strong.

BOLINGBROKE.   With all my heart
I pardon him.

DUCHESS.   A god on earth thou art.

BOLINGBROKE. But for our trusty brother-in-law and the
abbot,
With all the rest of that consorted crew,
Destruction straight shall dog them at the heels.
Good uncle, help to order several powers
To Oxford, or where'er these traitors are:
They shall not live within this world, I swear,
But I will have them, if I once know where.
Uncle, farewell: and cousin too, adieu:
Your mother well hath pray'd, and prove you true.

DUCHESS. Come, my old son: I pray God make thee new.
                                        Exeunt

SCENE FOUR

Another Room in the Castle.

Enter Exton and a Servant

EXTON. Didst thou not mark the king, what words he spake?
'Have I no friend will rid me of this living fear?'
Was it not so?

SERVANT.   Those were his very words.

EXTON. 'Have I no friend?' quoth he: he spake it twice,
And urg'd it twice together, did he not?

SERVANT. He did.

EXTON. And speaking it, he wistly looked on me,
As who should say, 'I would thou wert the man
That would divorce this terror from my heart';
Meaning the king at Pomfret. Come, let's go:
I am the king's friend, and will rid his foe.   *Exeunt*

SCENE FIVE

Pomfret. The Dungeon of the Castle.

Enter King Richard

KING RICHARD. I have been studying how I may compare
    This prison where I live unto the world:
    And for because the world is populous,
    And here is not a creature but myself,
    I cannot do it; yet I 'll hammer it out.
    My brain I 'll prove the female to my soul;
    My soul the father: and these two beget
    A generation of still-breeding thoughts,
    And these same thoughts people this little world
    In humours like the people of this world,
    For no thought is contented. The better sort,
    As thoughts of things divine, are intermix'd
    With scruples, and do set the word itself
    Against the word:
    As thus: 'Come, little ones'; and then again,
    'It is as hard to come as for a camel
    To thread the postern of a needle's eye.'
    Thoughts tending to ambition, they do plot
    Unlikely wonders; how these vain weak nails
    May tear a passage through the flinty ribs
    Of this hard world, my ragged prison walls;
    And, for they cannot, die in their own pride.
    Thoughts tending to content flatter themselves
    That they are not the first of fortune's slaves,
    Nor shall not be the last; like silly beggars
    Who sitting in the stocks refuge their shame,
    That many have and others must sit there:
    And in this thought they find a kind of ease,
    Bearing their own misfortune on the back
    Of such as have before endur'd the like.
    Thus play I in one person many people,
    And none contented: sometimes am I king;
    Then treason makes me wish myself a beggar,
    And so I am: then crushing penury
    Persuades me I was better when a king;

Then am I king'd again; and by and by
Think that I am unking'd by Bolingbroke,
And straight am nothing: but whate'er I be,
Nor I nor any man that but man is
With nothing shall be pleas'd, till he be eas'd
With being nothing. Music do I hear?   *Music*
Ha, ha! keep time. How sour sweet music is
When time is broke and no proportion kept!
So is it in the music of men's lives.
And here have I the daintiness of ear
To check time broke in a disorder'd string;
But for the concord of my state and time
Had not an ear to hear my true time broke.
I wasted time, and now doth time waste me;
For now hath time made me his numbering clock:
My thoughts are minutes, and with sighs they jar
Their watches on unto mine eyes, the outward watch,
Whereto my finger, like a dial's point,
Is pointing still, in cleansing them from tears.
Now sir, the sound that tells what hour it is
Are clamorous groans, that strike upon my heart,
Which is the bell: so sighs and tears and groans
Show minutes, times, and hours; but my time
Runs posting on in Bolingbroke's proud joy,
While I stand fooling here, his Jack o' the clock.
This music mads me: let it sound no more;
For though it have holp madmen to their wits,
In me it seems it will make wise men mad.
Yet blessing on his heart that gives it me!
For 'tis a sign of love, and love to Richard
Is a strange brooch in this all-hating world.
                    Enter a Groom of the Stable
GROOM. Hail, royal prince!
KING RICHARD.   Thanks, noble peer;
The cheapest of us is ten groats too dear.
What art thou? and how comest thou hither, man,
Where no man never comes but that sad dog
That brings me food to make misfortune live?
GROOM. I was a poor groom of thy stable, king,
When thou wert king; who, travelling towards York,
With much ado at length have gotten leave
To look upon my sometimes royal master's face.

O! how it yearn'd my heart when I beheld
In London streets, that coronation day
When Bolingbroke rode on roan Barbary,
That horse that thou so often hast bestrid,
That horse that I so carefully have dress'd.

KING RICHARD. Rode he on Barbary? Tell me, gentle friend,
How went he under him?

GROOM. So proudly as if he disdain'd the ground.

KING RICHARD. So proud that Bolingbroke was on his back!
That jade hath eat bread from my royal hand;
This hand hath made him proud with clapping him.
Would he not stumble? Would he not fall down,—
Since pride must have a fall,—and break the neck
Of that proud man that did usurp his back?
Forgiveness, horse! why do I rail on thee,
Since thou, created to be aw'd by man,
Wast born to bear? I was not made a horse;
And yet I bear a burden like an ass,
Spur-gall'd and tir'd by jauncing Bolingbroke.
                Enter Keeper, with a dish

KEEPER. (*To the Groom*) Fellow, give place; here is no
longer stay.

KING RICHARD. If thou love me, 'tis time thou wert away.

GROOM. What my tongue dares not, that my heart shall say.
                                                    Exit

KEEPER. My lord, will 't please you to fall to?

KING RICHARD. Taste of it first, as thou art wont to do.

KEEPER. My lord, I dare not: Sir Pierce of Exton,
Who lately came from the king, commands the contrary.

KING RICHARD. The devil take Henry of Lancaster, and thee!
Patience is stale, and I am weary of it. *Strikes the Keeper*

KEEPER. Help, help, help!
                Enter Exton and Servants, armed

KING RICHARD. How now! what means death in this rude
assault?
Villain, thine own hand yields thy death's instrument.
                Snatching a weapon and killing one
Go thou and fill another room in hell.
                He kills another: then Exton strikes him down
That hand shall burn in never-quenching fire
That staggers thus my person. Exton, thy fierce hand
Hath with the king's blood stain'd the king's own land,

Mount, mount, my soul! thy seat is up on high,
Whilst my gross flesh sinks downward, here to die.   *Dies*
EXTON. As full of valour as of royal blood:
Both have I spilt; O! would the deed were good;
For now the devil, that told me I did well,
Says that this deed is chronicled in hell.
This dead king to the living king I 'll bear.
Take hence the rest and give them burial here.   *Exeunt*

SCENE SIX

Windsor. An Apartment in the Castle.

*Flourish. Enter Bolingbroke and York, with Lords
and Attendants*

BOLINGBROKE. Kind uncle York, the latest news we hear
Is that the rebels have consum'd with fire
Our town of Cicester in Gloucestershire;
But whether they be ta'en or slain we hear not.
                    Enter Northumberland
Welcome, my lord. What is the news?
NORTHUMBERLAND. First, to thy sacred state wish I all hap-
    piness.
The next news is: I have to London sent
The heads of Salisbury, Spencer, Blunt, and Kent.
The manner of their taking may appear
At large discoursed in this paper here.
BOLINGBROKE. We thank thee, gentle Percy, for thy pains,
And to thy worth will add right worthy gains.
                    Enter Fitzwater
FITZWATER. My lord, I have from Oxford sent to London
The heads of Brocas and Sir Bennet Seely,
Two of the dangerous consorted traitors
That sought at Oxford thy dire overthrow.
BOLINGBROKE. Thy pains, Fitzwater, shall not be forgot;
Right noble is thy merit, well I wot.
            Enter Henry Percy, with the Bishop of Carlisle
HENRY PERCY. The grand conspirator, Abbot of West-
    minster,
With clog of conscience and sour melancholy,
Hath yielded up his body to the grave;

But here is Carlisle living, to abide
Thy kingly doom and sentence of his pride.
BOLINGBROKE. Carlisle, this is your doom:
Choose out some secret place, some reverend room,
More than thou hast, and with it joy thy life;
So, as thou livest in peace, die free from strife:
For though mine enemy thou hast ever been,
High sparks of honour in thee have I seen.

Enter Exton, with Attendants bearing a coffin
EXTON. Great king, within this coffin I present
Thy buried fear: herein all breathless lies
The mightiest of thy greatest enemies,
Richard of Bordeaux, by me hither brought.
BOLINGBROKE. Exton, I thank thee not; for thou hast
wrought
A deed of slander with thy fatal hand
Upon my head and all this famous land.
EXTON. From your own mouth, my lord, did I this deed.
BOLINGBROKE. They love not poison that do poison need,
Nor do I thee: though I did wish him dead,
I hate the murderer, love him murdered.
The guilt of conscience take thou for thy labour,
But neither my good word nor princely favour:
With Cain go wander through the shade of night,
And never show thy head by day nor light.
Lords, I protest, my soul is full of woe,
That blood should sprinkle me to make me grow:
Come, mourn with me for that I do lament,
And put on sullen black incontinent.
I 'll make a voyage to the Holy Land,
To wash this blood off from my guilty hand.
March sadly after; grace my mournings here,
In weeping after this untimely bier.   *Exeunt*

THE FIRST PART OF KING HENRY THE FOURTH

CAST OF CHARACTERS

KING HENRY THE FOURTH

HENRY, *Prince of Wales* }
JOHN OF LANCASTER } *Sons to the King*

EARL OF WESTMORELAND
SIR WALTER BLUNT
THOMAS PERCY, *Earl of Worcester*
HENRY PERCY, *Earl of Northumberland*
HENRY PERCY, *surnamed* HOTSPUR, *his son*
EDMUND MORTIMER, *Earl of March*
RICHARD SCROOP, *Archbishop of York*
ARCHIBALD, *Earl of Douglas*
OWEN GLENDOWER
SIR RICHARD VERNON
SIR JOHN FALSTAFF
SIR MICHAEL, *a Friend to the Archbishop of York*
POINS
GADSHILL
PETO
BARDOLPH

LADY PERCY, *Wife to Hotspur, and Sister to Mortimer*
LADY MORTIMER, *Daughter to Glendower, and Wife to Mortimer*
MISTRESS QUICKLY, *Hostess of the Boar's Head Tavern in Eastcheap*

Lords, Officers, Sheriff, Vintner, Chamberlain, Drawers, Two Carriers, Travellers, and Attendants

SCENE

England

THE FIRST PART OF KING HENRY THE FOURTH

ACT ONE

SCENE ONE

London. The Palace.

Enter King Henry, Westmoreland, and Others

KING HENRY. So shaken as we are, so wan with care,
Find we a time for frighted peace to pant,
And breathe short-winded accents of new broils
To be commenc'd in stronds afar remote.
No more the thirsty entrance of this soil
Shall daub her lips with her own children's blood;
No more shall trenching war channel her fields,
Nor bruise her flowerets with the armed hoofs
Of hostile paces: those opposed eyes,
Which, like the meteors of a troubled heaven,
All of one nature, of one substance bred,
Did lately meet in the intestine shock
And furious close of civil butchery,
Shall now, in mutual well-beseeming ranks,
March all one way, and be no more oppos'd
Against acquaintance, kindred, and allies:
The edge of war, like an ill-sheathed knife,
No more shall cut his master. Therefore, friends,
As far as to the sepulchre of Christ,—
Whose soldier now, under whose blessed cross
We are impressed and engag'd to fight,—
Forthwith a power of English shall we levy,
Whose arms were moulded in their mothers' womb
To chase these pagans in those holy fields
Over whose acres walk'd those blessed feet
Which fourteen hundred years ago were nail'd
For our advantage on the bitter cross.

But this our purpose is a twelvemonth old,
And bootless 'tis to tell you we will go:
Therefore we meet not now. Then let me hear
Of you, my gentle cousin Westmoreland,
What yesternight our council did decree
In forwarding this dear expedience.

WESTMORELAND. My liege, this haste was hot in question
And many limits of the charge set down
But yesternight; when all athwart there came
A post from Wales loaden with heavy news;
Whose worst was, that the noble Mortimer,
Leading the men of Herefordshire to fight
Against the irregular and wild Glendower,
Was by the rude hands of that Welshman taken,
And a thousand of his people butchered;
Upon whose dead corpse there was such misuse,
Such beastly shameless transformation
By those Welshwomen done, as may not be
Without much shame re-told or spoken of.

KING HENRY. It seems then that the tidings of this broil
Brake off our business for the Holy Land.

WESTMORELAND. This match'd with other like, my gracious
    lord;
For more uneven and unwelcome news
Came from the North and thus it did import:
On Holy-rood day, the gallant Hotspur there,
Young Harry Percy and brave Archibald,
That ever-valiant and approved Scot,
At Holmedon met,
Where they did spend a sad and bloody hour;
As by discharge of their artillery,
And shape of likelihood, the news was told;
For he that brought them, in the very heat
And pride of their contention did take horse,
Uncertain of the issue any way.

KING HENRY. Here is a dear and true industrious friend,
Sir Walter Blunt, new lighted from his horse,
Stained with the variation of each soil
Betwixt that Holmedon and this seat of ours;
And he hath brought us smooth and welcome news.
The Earl of Douglas is discomfited;
Ten thousand bold Scots, two and twenty knights,

Balk'd in their own blood did Sir Walter see
On Holmedon's plains: of prisoners Hotspur took
Mordake the Earl of Fife, and eldest son
To beaten Douglas, and the Earls of Athol,
Of Murray, Angus, and Menteith.
And is not this an honourable spoil?
A gallant prize? ha, cousin, is it not?
WESTMORELAND. In faith,
    It is a conquest for a prince to boast of.
KING HENRY. Yea, there thou mak'st me sad and mak'st me
    sin
In envy that my lord Northumberland
Should be the father to so blest a son,
A son who is the theme of honour's tongue;
Amongst a grove the very straightest plant;
Who is sweet Fortune's minion and her pride:
Whilst I, by looking on the praise of him,
See riot and dishonour stain the brow
Of my young Harry. O! that it could be prov'd
That some night-tripping fairy had exchang'd
In cradle-clothes our children where they lay,
And call'd mine Percy, his Plantagenet.
Then would I have his Harry, and he mine.
But let him from my thoughts. What think you, coz,
Of this young Percy's pride? The prisoners,
Which he in this adventure hath surpris'd,
To his own use he keeps, and sends me word,
I shall have none but Mordake Earl of Fife.
WESTMORELAND. This is his uncle's teaching, this is
    Worcester,
Malevolent to you in all aspects;
Which makes him prune himself, and bristle up
The crest of youth against your dignity.
KING HENRY. But I have sent for him to answer this;
And for this cause a while we must neglect
Our holy purpose to Jerusalem.
Cousin, on Wednesday next our council we
Will hold at Windsor; so inform the lords:
But come yourself with speed to us again;
For more is to be said and to be done
Than out of anger can be uttered.
WESTMORELAND. I will, my liege.   *Exeunt*

SCENE   TWO

The Same. An Apartment of the Prince's.

Enter the Prince and Falstaff

FALSTAFF. Now, Hal, what time of day is it, lad?

PRINCE. Thou art so fat-witted, with drinking of old sack, and unbuttoning thee after supper, and sleeping upon benches after noon, that thou hast forgotten to demand that truly which thou wouldst truly know. What a devil hast thou to do with the time of the day? unless hours were cups of sack, and minutes capons, and clocks the tongues of bawds, and dials the signs of leaping-houses, and the blessed sun himself a fair hot wench in flame-colour'd taffeta, I see no reason why thou shouldst be so superfluous to demand the time of the day.

FALSTAFF. Indeed, you come near me now, Hal; for we that take purses go by the moon and the seven stars, and not by Phœbus, he, 'that wandering knight so fair.' And, I prithee, sweet wag, when thou art king,—as, God save thy Grace,—Majesty, I should say, for grace thou wilt have none,—

PRINCE. What! none?

FALSTAFF. No, by my troth; not so much as will serve to be prologue to an egg and butter.

PRINCE. Well, how then? come, roundly, roundly.

FALSTAFF. Marry, then, sweet wag, when thou art king, let not us that are squires of the night's body be called thieves of the day's beauty: let us be Diana's foresters, gentlemen of the shade, minions of the moon; and let men say, we be men of good government, being governed as the sea is, by our noble and chaste mistress the moon, under whose countenance we steal.

PRINCE. Thou sayest well, and it holds well too; for the fortune of us that are the moon's men doth ebb and flow like the sea, being governed as the sea is, by the moon. As for proof now: a purse of gold most resolutely snatched on Monday night and most dissolutely spent on Tuesday morning; got with swearing 'Lay by'; and spent with crying 'Bring in': now in as low an ebb as the foot of the

ladder, and by and by in as high a flow as the ridge of the
gallows.

FALSTAFF. By the Lord, thou sayest true, lad. And is not
my hostess of the tavern a most sweet wench?

PRINCE. As the honey of Hybla, my old lad of the castle.
And is not a buff jerkin a most sweet robe of durance?

FALSTAFF. How now, how now, mad wag! what, in thy
quips and thy quiddities? what a plague have I to do with
a buff jerkin?

PRINCE. Why, what a pox have I to do with my hostess of
the tavern?

FALSTAFF. Well, thou hast called her to a reckoning many
a time and oft.

PRINCE. Did I ever call for thee to pay thy part?

FALSTAFF. No; I 'll give thee thy due, thou hast paid all
there.

PRINCE. Yea, and elsewhere, so far as my coin would stretch;
and where it would not, I have used my credit.

FALSTAFF. Yea, and so used it that, were it not here ap-
parent that thou art heir apparent,—But, I prithee, sweet
wag, shall there be gallows standing in England when
thou art king, and resolution thus fobbed as it is with the
rusty curb of old father antick the law? Do not thou, when
thou art king, hang a thief.

PRINCE. No; thou shalt.

FALSTAFF. Shall I? O rare! By the Lord, I 'll be a brave
judge.

PRINCE. Thou judgest false already; I mean, thou shalt have
the hanging of the thieves and so become a rare hangman.

FALSTAFF. Well, Hal, well; and in some sort it jumps with
my humour as well as waiting in the court, I can tell you.

PRINCE. For obtaining of suits?

FALSTAFF. Yea, for obtaining of suits, whereof the hangman
hath no lean wardrobe. 'Sblood, I am as melancholy as a
gib cat, or a lugged bear.

PRINCE. Or an old lion, or a lover's lute.

FALSTAFF. Yea, or the drone of a Lincolnshire bagpipe.

PRINCE. What sayest thou to a hare, or the melancholy of
Moor-ditch?

FALSTAFF. Thou hast the most unsavoury similes, and art,
indeed, the most comparative, rascalliest, sweet young
prince; but, Hal, I prithee, trouble me no more with van-

ity. I would to God thou and I knew where a commodity
of good names were to be bought. An old lord of the coun-
cil rated me the other day in the street about you, sir, but
I marked him not; and yet he talked very wisely, but I re-
garded him not; and yet he talked wisely, and in the street
too.

PRINCE. Thou didst well; for wisdom cries out in the streets,
and no man regards it.

FALSTAFF. O! thou hast damnable iteration, and art indeed
able to corrupt a saint. Thou hast done much harm upon
me, Hal; God forgive thee for it! Before I knew thee, Hal,
I knew nothing; and now am I, if a man should speak
truly, little better than one of the wicked. I must give over
this life, and I will give it over; by the Lord, an I do not,
I am a villain: I 'll be damned for never a king's son in
Christendom.

PRINCE. Where shall we take a purse to-morrow, Jack?

FALSTAFF. Zounds! where thou wilt, lad, I 'll make one; an
I do not, call me a villain and baffle me.

PRINCE. I see a good amendment of life in thee; from pray-
ing to purse-taking.

Enter Poins, at a distance

FALSTAFF. Why, Hal, 'tis my vocation, Hal; 'tis no sin for a
man to labour in his vocation. Poins! Now shall we know
if Gadshill have set a match. O! if men were to be saved
by merit, what hole in hell were hot enough for him? This
is the most omnipotent villain that ever cried 'Stand!' to a
true man.

PRINCE. Good-morrow, Ned.

POINS. Good-morrow, sweet Hal. What says Monsieur Re-
morse? What says· Sir John Sack-and-Sugar? Jack! how
agrees the devil and thee about thy soul, that thou soldest
him on Good-Friday last for a cup of Madeira and a cold
capon's leg?

PRINCE. Sir John stands to his word, the devil shall have his
bargain; for he was never yet a breaker of proverbs: he
will give the devil his due.

POINS. Then art thou damned for keeping thy word with the
devil.

PRINCE. Else he had been damned for cozening the devil.

POINS. But my lads, my lads, to-morrow morning, by four
o'clock, early at Gadshill! There are pilgrims going to

Canterbury with rich offerings, and traders riding to Lon-
don with fat purses: I have vizards for you all; you have
horses for yourselves. Gadshill lies tonight in Rochester;
I have bespoke supper to-morrow night in Eastcheap: we
may do it as secure as sleep. If you will go I will stuff your
purses full of crowns; if you will not, tarry at home and be
hanged.

FALSTAFF. Hear ye, Yedward: if I tarry at home and go not,
I 'll hang you for going.

POINS. You will, chops?

FALSTAFF. Hal, wilt thou make one?

PRINCE. Who, I rob? I a thief? not I, by my faith.

FALSTAFF. There 's neither honesty, manhood, nor good fel-
lowship in thee, nor thou camest not of the blood royal,
if thou darest not stand for ten shillings.

PRINCE. Well then, once in my days I 'll be a madcap.

FALSTAFF. Why, that 's well said.

PRINCE Well, come what will, I 'll tarry at home.

FALSTAFF. By the Lord, I 'll be a traitor then, when thou art
king.

PRINCE. I care not.

POINS. Sir John, I prithee, leave the prince and me alone:
I will lay him down such reasons for this adventure that
he shall go.

FALSTAFF. Well, God give thee the spirit of persuasion and
him the ears of profiting, that what thou speakest may
move, and what he hears may be believed, that the true
prince may, for recreation sake, prove a false thief; for the
poor abuses of the time want countenance. Farewell: you
shall find me in Eastcheap.

PRINCE. Farewell, thou latter spring! Farewell, All-hallown
summer!   *Exit Falstaff*

POINS. Now, my good sweet honey lord, ride with us to-
morrow: I have a jest to execute that I cannot manage
alone. Falstaff, Bardolph, Peto, and Gadshill shall rob
those men that we have already waylaid; yourself and I
will not be there; and when they have the booty, if you
and I do not rob them, cut this head from my shoulders.

PRINCE. But how shall we part with them in setting forth?

POINS. Why, we will set forth before or after them, and ap-
point them a place of meeting, wherein it is at our pleas-
ure to fail; and then will they adventure upon the exploit

themselves, which they shall have no sooner achieved but
we 'll set upon them.

PRINCE. Yea, but 'tis like that they will know us by our
horses, by our habits, and by every other appointment, to
be ourselves.

POINS. Tut! our horses they shall not see, I 'll tie them in the
wood; our vizards we will change after we leave them;
and, sirrah, I have cases of buckram for the nonce, to
inmask our noted outward garments.

PRINCE. Yea, but I doubt they will be too hard for us.

POINS. Well, for two of them, I know them to be as true-
bred cowards as ever turned back; and for the third, if he
fight longer than he sees reason, I 'll forswear arms. The
virtue of this jest will be, the incomprehensible lies that
this same fat rogue will tell us when we meet at supper:
how thirty, at least, he fought with; what wards, what
blows, what extremities he endured; and in the reproof
of this lies the jest.

PRINCE. Well, I 'll go with thee: provide us all things neces-
sary and meet me to-morrow night in Eastcheap; there
I 'll sup. Farewell.

POINS. Farewell, my lord.   *Exit*

PRINCE. I know you all, and will awhile uphold
The unyok'd humour of your idleness:
Yet herein will I imitate the sun,
Who doth permit the base contagious clouds
To smother up his beauty from the world,
That when he please again to be himself,
Being wanted, he may be more wonder'd at,
By breaking through the foul and ugly mists
Of vapours that did seem to strangle him.
If all the year were playing holidays,
To sport would be as tedious as to work;
But when they seldom come, they wish'd for come,
And nothing pleaseth but rare accidents.
So, when this loose behaviour I throw off,
And pay the debt I never promised,
By how much better than my word I am
By so much shall I falsify men's hopes;
And like bright metal on a sullen ground,
My reformation, glittering o'er my fault,
Shall show more goodly and attract more eyes

Than that which hath no foil to set it off.
I 'll so offend to make offence a skill;
Redeeming time when men think least I will.   *Exit*

SCENE THREE

The Same. The Palace.

*Enter King Henry, Northumberland, Worcester, Hotspur,
Sir Walter Blunt, and Others*

KING HENRY. My blood hath been too cold and temperate,
  Unapt to stir at these indignities,
  And you have found me; for accordingly
  You tread upon my patience: but, be sure,
  I will from henceforth rather be myself,
  Mighty, and to be fear'd, than my condition,
  Which hath been smooth as oil, soft as young down,
  And therefore lost that title of respect
  Which the proud soul ne'er pays but to the proud.
WORCESTER. Our house, my sovereign liege, little deserves
  The scourge of greatness to be us'd on it;
  And that same greatness too which our own hands
  Have holp to make so portly.
NORTHUMBERLAND. My lord,—
KING HENRY. Worcester, get thee gone; for I do see
  Danger and disobedience in thine eye.
  O, sir, your presence is too bold and peremptory,
  And majesty might never yet endure
  The moody frontier of a servant brow.
  You have good leave to leave us; when we need
  Your use and counsel we shall send for you.
                                        Exit Worcester
  (*To Northumberland*) You were about to speak.
NORTHUMBERLAND.   Yea, my good lord.
  Those prisoners in your Highness' name demanded,
  Which Harry Percy here at Holmedon took,
  Were, as he says, not with such strength denied
  As is deliver'd to your Majesty:
  Either envy, therefore, or misprision
  Is guilty of this fault and not my son.
HOTSPUR. My liege, I did deny no prisoners:

But I remember, when the fight was done,
When I was dry with rage and extreme toil,
Breathless and faint, leaning upon my sword,
Came there a certain lord, neat, and trimly dress'd,
Fresh as a bridegroom; and his chin, new reap'd,
Show'd like a stubble-land at harvest-home:
He was perfumed like a milliner,
And 'twixt his finger and his thumb he held
A pouncet-box, which ever and anon
He gave his nose and took't away again;
Who therewith angry, when it next came there,
Took it in snuff: and still he smil'd and talk'd;
And as the soldiers bore dead bodies by,
He call'd them untaught knaves, unmannerly,
To bring a slovenly unhandsome corpse
Betwixt the wind and his nobility.
With many holiday and lady terms
He question'd me; among the rest, demanded
My prisoners in your Majesty's behalf.
I then all smarting with my wounds being cold,
To be so pester'd with a popinjay,
Out of my grief and my impatience
Answer'd neglectingly, I know not what,
He should, or he should not; for he made me mad
To see him shine so brisk and smell so sweet
And talk so like a waiting-gentlewoman
Of guns, and drums, and wounds,—God save the mark!—
And telling me the sovereign'st thing on earth
Was parmaceti for an inward bruise;
And that it was great pity, so it was,
This villanous saltpetre should be digg'd
Out of the bowels of the harmless earth,
Which many a good tall fellow had destroy'd
So cowardly; and but for these vile guns,
He would himself have been a soldier.
This bald unjointed chat of his, my lord,
I answer'd indirectly, as I said;
And I beseech you, let not his report
Come current for an accusation
Betwixt my love and your high majesty.

BLUNT. The circumstance consider'd, good my lord,
Whatever Harry Percy then had said

To such a person and in such a place,
At such a time, with all the rest re-told,
May reasonably die and never rise
To do him wrong, or any way impeach
What then he said, so he unsay it now.
KING HENRY. Why, yet he doth deny his prisoners,
But with proviso and exception,
That we at our own charge shall ransom straight
His brother-in-law, the foolish Mortimer;
Who, on my soul, hath wilfully betray'd
The lives of those that he did lead to fight
Against the great magician, damn'd Glendower,
Whose daughter, as we hear, the Earl of March
Hath lately married. Shall our coffers then
Be emptied to redeem a traitor home?
Shall we buy treason, and indent with fears,
When they have lost and forfeited themselves?
No, on the barren mountains let him starve;
For I shall never hold that man my friend
Whose tongue shall ask me for one penny cost
To ransom home revolted Mortimer.
HOTSPUR. Revolted Mortimer!
He never did fall off, my sovereign liege,
But by the chance of war: to prove that true
Needs no more but one tongue for all those wounds,
Those mouthed wounds, which valiantly he took,
When on the gentle Severn's sedgy bank,
In single opposition, hand to hand,
He did confound the best part of an hour
In changing hardiment with great Glendower.
Three times they breath'd and three times did they drink,
Upon agreement, of swift Severn's flood,
Who then, affrighted with their bloody looks,
Ran fearfully among the trembling reeds,
And hid his crisp head in the hollow bank
Blood-stained with these valiant combatants.
Never did base and rotten policy
Colour her working with such deadly wounds;
Nor never could the noble Mortimer
Receive so many, and all willingly:
Then let him not be slander'd with revolt.

KING HENRY. Thou dost belie him, Percy, thou dost belie
 him:
 He never did encounter with Glendower:
 I tell thee.
 He durst as well have met the devil alone
 As Owen Glendower for an enemy.
 Art thou not asham'd? But, sirrah, henceforth
 Let me not hear you speak of Mortimer:
 Send me your prisoners with the speediest means,
 Or you shall hear in such a kind from me
 As will displease you. My Lord Northumberland,
 We license your departure with your son.
 Send us your prisoners, or you'll hear of it.
     Exeunt King Henry, Blunt, and Train
HOTSPUR. An if the devil come and roar for them,
 I will not send them: I will after straight
 And tell him so; for I will ease my heart,
 Albeit I make a hazard of my head.
NORTHUMBERLAND. What! drunk with choler? stay, and
 pause awhile:
 Here comes your uncle.
     Re-enter Worcester
HOTSPUR. Speak of Mortimer!
 'Zounds! I will speak of him; and let my soul
 Want mercy if I do not join with him:
 In his behalf I'll empty all these veins,
 And shed my dear blood drop by drop i' the dust,
 But I will lift the down-trod Mortimer
 As high i' the air as this unthankful king,
 As this ingrate and canker'd Bolingbroke.
NORTHUMBERLAND. Brother, the king hath made your
 nephew mad.
WORCESTER. Who struck this heat up after I was gone?
HOTSPUR. He will, forsooth, have all my prisoners;
 And when I urg'd the ransom once again
 Of my wife's brother, then his cheek look'd pale,
 And on my face he turn'd an eye of death,
 Trembling even at the name of Mortimer.
WORCESTER. I cannot blame him: was he not proclaim'd
 By Richard that dead is, the next of blood?
NORTHUMBERLAND. He was; I heard the proclamation:
 And then it was when the unhappy king,—

Whose wrongs in us God pardon!—did set forth
Upon his Irish expedition;
From whence he, intercepted, did return
To be depos'd, and shortly murdered.

WORCESTER. And for whose death we in the world's wide mouth
Live scandaliz'd and foully spoken of.

HOTSPUR. But, soft! I pray you, did King Richard then
Proclaim my brother Edmund Mortimer
Heir to the crown?

NORTHUMBERLAND.   He did; myself did hear it.

HOTSPUR. Nay, then I cannot blame his cousin king,
That wish'd him on the barren mountains starve.
But shall it be that you, that set the crown
Upon the head of this forgetful man,
And for his sake wear the detested blot
Of murd'rous subornation, shall it be,
That you a world of curses undergo,
Being the agents, or base second means,
The cords, the ladder, or the hangman rather?
O! pardon me that I descend so low,
To show the line and the predicament
Wherein you range under this subtle king.
Shall it for shame be spoken in these days,
Or fill up chronicles in time to come,
That men of your nobility and power,
Did gage them both in an unjust behalf,
As both of you—God pardon it!—have done,
To put down Richard, that sweet lovely rose,
And plant this thorn, this canker, Bolingbroke?
And shall it in more shame be further spoken,
That you are fool'd, discarded, and shook off
By him for whom these shames ye underwent?
No; yet time serves wherein you may redeem
Your banish'd honours, and restore yourselves
Into the good thoughts of the world again;
Revenge the jeering and disdain'd contempt
Of this proud king, who studies day and night
To answer all the debt he owes to you,
Even with the bloody payment of your deaths.
Therefore, I say,—

WORCESTER.   Peace, cousin! say no more:

And now I will unclasp a secret book,
And to your quick-conceiving discontents
I 'll read you matter deep and dangerous,
As full of peril and adventurous spirit
As to o'er-walk a current roaring loud,
On the unsteadfast footing of a spear.

HOTSPUR. If he fall in, good-night! or sink or swim:
Send danger from the east unto the west,
So honour cross it from the north to south,
And let them grapple: O! the blood more stirs
To rouse a lion than to start a hare.

NORTHUMBERLAND. Imagination of some great exploit
Drives him beyond the bounds of patience.

HOTSPUR. By heaven methinks it were an easy leap
To pluck bright honour from the pale-fac'd moon,
Or dive into the bottom of the deep,
Where fathom-line could never touch the ground,
And pluck up drowned honour by the locks;
So he that doth redeem her thence might wear
Without corrival all her dignities:
But out upon this half-fac'd fellowship!

WORCESTER. He apprehends a world of figures here,
But not the form of what he should attend.
Good cousin, give me audience for a while.

HOTSPUR. I cry you mercy.

WORCESTER.   Those same noble Scots
That are your prisoners,—

HOTSPUR.   I 'll keep them all;
By God, he shall not have a Scot of them:
No, if a Scot would save his soul, he shall not:
I 'll keep them, by this hand.

WORCESTER.   You start away,
And lend no ear unto my purposes.
Those prisoners you shall keep.

HOTSPUR.   Nay, I will; that 's flat:
He said he would not ransom Mortimer;
Forbade my tongue to speak of Mortimer;
But I will find him when he lies asleep,
And in his ear I 'll holla 'Mortimer!'
Nay,
I 'll have a starling shall be taught to speak
Nothing but 'Mortimer,' and give it him,

To keep his anger still in motion.

WORCESTER. Hear you, cousin; a word.

HOTSPUR. All studies here I solemnly defy,
  Save how to gall and pinch this Bolingbroke:
  And that same sword-and-buckler Prince of Wales,
  But that I think his father loves him not,
  And would be glad he met with some mischance,
  I would have him poison'd with a pot of ale.

WORCESTER. Farewell, kinsman: I will talk to you
  When you are better temper'd to attend.

NORTHUMBERLAND. Why, what a wasp-stung and impatient
    fool
  Art thou to break into this woman's mood,
  Tying thine ear to no tongue but thine own!

HOTSPUR. Why, look you, I am whipp'd and scourg'd with
    rods,
  Nettled, and stung with pismires, when I hear
  Of this vile politician, Bolingbroke.
  In Richard's time,—what do ye call the place?—
  A plague upon 't—it is in Gloucestershire;—
  'Twas where the madcap duke his uncle kept,
  His uncle York; where I first bow'd my knee
  Unto this king of smiles, this Bolingbroke,
  'Sblood!
  When you and he came back from Ravenspurgh.

NORTHUMBERLAND. At Berkeley Castle.

HOTSPUR. You say true.
  Why, what a candy deal of courtesy
  This fawning greyhound then did proffer me!
  Look, 'when his infant fortune came to age,'
  And 'gentle Harry Percy,' and 'kind cousin.'
  O! the devil take such cozeners. God forgive me!
  Good uncle, tell your tale, for I have done.

WORCESTER. Nay, if you have not, to 't again;
  We 'll stay your leisure.

HOTSPUR.   I have done, i' faith.

WORCESTER. Then once more to your Scottish prisoners.
  Deliver them up without their ransom straight,
  And make the Douglas' son your only mean
  For powers in Scotland; which, for divers reasons
  Which I shall send you written, be assur'd,
  Will easily be granted. (*To Northumberland*) You, my
    lord,

Your son in Scotland being thus employ'd,
Shall secretly into the bosom creep
Of that same noble prelate well belov'd,
The Archbishop.

HOTSPUR. Of York, is it not?

WORCESTER. True; who bears hard
His brother's death at Bristol, the Lord Scroop.
I speak not this in estimation,
As what I think might be, but what I know
Is ruminated, plotted and set down;
And only stays but to behold the face
Of that occasion that shall bring it on.

HOTSPUR. I smell it.
Upon my life it will do wondrous well.

NORTHUMBERLAND. Before the game 's afoot thou still lett'st
slip.

HOTSPUR. Why, it cannot choose but be a noble plot:
And then the power of Scotland and of York,
To join with Mortimer, ha?

WORCESTER.   And so they shall.

HOTSPUR. In faith, it is exceedingly well aim'd.

WORCESTER. And 'tis no little reason bids us speed,
To save our heads by raising of a head;
For, bear ourselves as even as we can,
The king will always think him in our debt,
And think we think ourselves unsatisfied,
Till he hath found a time to pay us home.
And see already how he doth begin
To make us strangers to his looks of love.

HOTSPUR. He does, he does: we 'll be reveng'd on him.

WORCESTER. Cousin, farewell: no further go in this,
Than I by letters shall direct your course.
When time is ripe,—which will be suddenly,—
I 'll steal to Glendower and Lord Mortimer;
Where you and Douglas and our powers at once,—
As I will fashion it,—shall happily meet,
To bear our fortunes in our own strong arms,
Which now we hold at much uncertainty.

NORTHUMBERLAND. Farewell, good brother: we shall thrive,
I trust.

HOTSPUR. Uncle, adieu: O! let the hours be short,
Till fields and blows and groans applaud our sport! *Exeunt*

ACT TWO

SCENE ONE

Rochester. An Inn-Yard.

Enter a Carrier, with a lanthorn in his hand

FIRST CARRIER. Heigh-ho! An 't be not four by the day I 'll be hanged: Charles' Wain is over the new chimney, and yet our horse not packed. What, ostler!

OSTLER. (*Within*) Anon, anon.

FIRST CARRIER. I prithee, Tom, beat Cut's saddle, put a few flocks in the point; the poor jade is wrung in the withers out of all cess.

Enter another Carrier

SECOND CARRIER. Peas and beans are as dank here as a dog, and that is the next way to give poor jades the bots; this house is turned upside down since Robin Ostler died.

FIRST CARRIER. Poor fellow! never joyed since the price of oats rose; it was the death of him.

SECOND CARRIER. I think this be the most villanous house in all London road for fleas: I am stung like a tench.

FIRST CARRIER. Like a tench! by the mass, there is ne'er a king christen could be better bit than I have been since the first cock.

SECOND CARRIER. Why, they will allow us ne'er a jordan, and then we leak in the chimney; and your chamber-lie breeds fleas like a loach.

FIRST CARRIER. What, ostler! come away and be hanged, come away.

SECOND CARRIER. I have a gammon of bacon and two razes of ginger, to be delivered as far as Charingcross.

FIRST CARRIER. Godsbody! the turkeys in my pannier are quite starved. What, ostler! A plague on thee! hast thou never an eye in thy head? canst not hear? An 'twere not as good a deed as drink to break the pate on thee, I am a very villain. Come, and be hanged! hast no faith in thee?

Enter Gadshill

GADSHILL. Good-morrow, carriers. What 's o'clock?

FIRST CARRIER. I think it be two o'clock.

GADSHILL. I prithee, lend me thy lanthorn, to see my gelding in the stable.

FIRST CARRIER. Nay, by God, soft: I know a trick worth two of that, i' faith.

GADSHILL. I prithee, lend me thine.

SECOND CARRIER. Ay, when? canst tell? Lend me thy lanthorn, quoth a'? marry, I 'll see thee hanged first.

GADSHILL. Sirrah carrier, what time do you mean to come to London?

SECOND CARRIER. Time enough to go to bed with a candle, I warrant thee. Come, neighbour Mugs, we 'll call up the gentlemen: they will along with company, for they have great charge. *Exeunt Carriers*

GADSHILL. What, ho! chamberlain!

CHAMBERLAIN. (*Within*) 'At hand, quoth pick-purse.'

GADSHILL. That 's even as fair as, 'at hand, quoth the chamberlain'; for thou variest no more from picking of purses than giving direction doth from labouring; thou layest the plot how.

Enter Chamberlain

CHAMBERLAIN. Good morrow, Master Gadshill. It holds current that I told you yesternight: there 's a franklin in the wild of Kent hath brought three hundred marks with him in gold: I heard him tell it to one of his company last night at supper; a kind of auditor; one that hath abundance of charge too, God knows what. They are up already and call for eggs and butter: they will away presently.

GADSHILL. Sirrah, if they meet not with Saint Nicholas' clerks, I 'll give thee this neck.

CHAMBERLAIN. No, I 'll none of it: I prithee, keep that for the hangman; for I know thou worship'st Saint Nicholas as truly as a man of falsehood may.

GADSHILL. What talkest thou to me of the hangman? If I hang I 'll make a fat pair of gallows; for if I hang, old Sir John hangs with me, and thou knowest he 's no starveling. Tut! there are other Troyans that thou dreamest not of, the which for sport sake are content to do the profession some grace; that would, if matters should be looked into, for their own credit sake make all whole. I am joined with no foot-land-rakers, no long-staff sixpenny strikers, none of these mad mustachio-purple-hued malt-worms; but with nobility and tranquillity, burgomasters and great oneyers such as can hold in, such as will strike sooner than speak, and speak sooner than drink, and drink sooner than pray: and yet I lie; for they pray continually to their saint, the commonwealth; or, rather, not pray to her, but prey on her, for they ride up and down on her and make her their boots.

CHAMBERLAIN. What! the commonwealth their boots? will she hold out water in foul way?

GADSHILL. She will, she will; justice hath liquored her. We steal as in a castle, cock-sure; we have the receipt of fern-seed, we walk invisible.

CHAMBERLAIN. Nay, by my faith, I think you are more beholding to the night than to fern-seed for your walking invisible.

GADSHILL. Give me thy hand: thou shalt have a share in our purchase, as I am a true man.

CHAMBERLAIN. Nay, rather let me have it, as you are a false thief.

GADSHILL. Go to; 'homo' is a common name to all men. Bid the ostler bring my gelding out of the stable. Farewell, you muddy knave.   *Exeunt*

SCENE TWO

The Road by Gadshill.

Enter the Prince and Poins

POINS. Come, shelter, shelter: I have removed Falstaff's horse, and he frets like a gummed velvet.

PRINCE. Stand close.

Enter Falstaff

FALSTAFF. Poins! Poins, and be hanged! Poins!

PRINCE. Peace, ye fat-kidneyed rascal! What a brawling dost thou keep!

FALSTAFF. Where 's Poins, Hal?

PRINCE. He is walked up to the top of the hill: I 'll go seek him.   *Pretends to seek Poins, and retires*

FALSTAFF. I am accursed to rob in that thief's company; the

rascal hath removed my horse and tied him I know not where. If I travel but four foot by the squire further afoot I shall break my wind. Well, I doubt not but to die a fair death for all this, if I 'scape hanging for killing that rogue. I have forsworn his company hourly any time this two-and-twenty years, and yet I am bewitched with the rogue's company. If the rascal have not given me medicines to make me love him, I 'll be hanged: it could not be else: I have drunk medicines. Poins! Hal! a plague upon you both! Bardolph! Peto! I 'll starve ere I 'll rob a foot further. An 'twere not as good a deed as drink to turn true man and leave these rogues, I am the veriest varlet that ever chewed with a tooth. Eight yards of uneven ground is threescore and ten miles afoot with me, and the stony-hearted villains know it well enough. A plague upon 't when thieves cannot be true one to another! (*They whistle*) Whew! A plague upon you all! Give me my horse, you rogues; give me my horse and be hanged.

PRINCE. (*Coming forward*) Peace, ye fat-guts! lie down: lay thine ear close to the ground, and list if thou canst hear the tread of travellers.

FALSTAFF. Have you any levers to lift me up again, being down? 'Sblood! I 'll not bear mine own flesh so far afoot again for all the coin in thy father's exchequer. What a plague mean ye to colt me thus?

PRINCE. Thou liest: thou art not colted; thou art uncolted.

FALSTAFF. I prithee, good Prince Hal, help me to my horse, good king's son.

PRINCE. Out, you rogue! shall I be your ostler?

FALSTAFF. Go, hang thyself in thine own heir apparent garters! If I be ta'en I 'll peach for this. An I have not ballads made on you all, and sung to filthy tunes, let a cup of sack be my poison: when a jest is so forward, and afoot too! I hate it.

Enter Gadshill

GADSHILL. Stand.

FALSTAFF. So I do, against my will.

POINS. O! 'tis our setter: I know his voice.

Enter Bardolph and Peto

BARDOLPH. What news?

GADSHILL. Case ye, case ye; on with your vizards: there 's

money of the king's coming down the hill; 'tis going to the
king's exchequer.

FALSTAFF. You lie, you rogue; 'tis going to the king's tavern.

GADSHILL. There 's enough to make us all.

FALSTAFF. To be hanged.

PRINCE. Sirs, you four shall front them in the narrow lane;
Ned Poins and I will walk lower: if they 'scape from your
encounter then they light on us.

PETO. How many be there of them?

GADSHILL. Some eight or ten.

FALSTAFF. 'Zounds! will they not rob us?

PRINCE. What! a coward, Sir John Paunch?

FALSTAFF. Indeed, I am not John of Gaunt, your grand-
father; but yet no coward, Hal.

PRINCE. Well, we leave that to the proof.

POINS. Sirrah Jack, thy horse stands behind the hedge:
when thou needst him there thou shalt find him. Farewell,
and stand fast.

FALSTAFF. Now cannot I strike him if I should be hanged.

PRINCE. (*Aside to Poins*) Ned, where are our disguises?

POINS. Here, hard by; stand close. *Exeunt Prince and Poins*

FALSTAFF. Now my masters, happy man be his dole, say I:
every man to his business.

Enter Travellers

FIRST TRAVELLER. Come, neighbour; the boy shall lead our
horses down the hill; we 'll walk afoot awhile, and ease
our legs.

THIEVES. Stand!

TRAVELLERS. Jesu bless us!

FALSTAFF. Strike; down with them; cut the villains' throats:
ah! whoreson caterpillars! bacon-fed knaves! they hate us
youth: down with them; fleece them.

TRAVELLERS. O! we are undone, both we and ours for ever.

FALSTAFF. Hang ye, gorbellied knaves, are ye undone? No,
ye fat chuffs; I would your store were here! On, bacons,
on! What! ye knaves, young men must live. You are
grand-jurors are ye? We 'll jure ye, i' faith.

> *Here they rob and bind them. Exeunt*
> *Re-enter the Prince and Poins*

PRINCE. The thieves have bound the true men. Now could
thou and I rob the thieves and go merrily to London, it

would be argument for a week, laughter for a month, and
a good jest for ever.

POINS. Stand close; I hear them coming.

Re-enter Thieves

FALSTAFF. Come, my masters; let us share, and then to
horse before day. An the Prince and Poins be not two ar-
rant cowards, there 's no equity stirring: there 's no more
valour in that Poins than in a wild duck.

PRINCE. Your money!

POINS. Villains!

As they are sharing, the Prince and Poins
set upon them. They all run away; and Falstaff, after a
blow or two, runs away too, leaving the booty behind

PRINCE. Got with much ease. Now merrily to horse:
The thieves are scatter'd and possess'd with fear
So strongly that they dare not meet each other;
Each takes his fellow for an officer.
Away, good Ned. Falstaff sweats to death
And lards the lean earth as he walks along:
Were 't not for laughing I should pity him.

POINS. How the rogue roar'd! *Exeunt*

SCENE THREE

Warkworth. A Room in the Castle.

Enter Hotspur, reading a letter

'But for mine own part, my lord, I could be well con-
tented to be there, in respect of the love I bear your
house.'
He could be contented; why is he not then? In respect of
the love he bears our house: he shows in this he loves his
own barn better than he loves our house. Let me see some
more.
'The purpose you undertake is dangerous;—'
Why, that 's certain: 'tis dangerous to take a cold, to sleep,
to drink; but I tell you, my lord fool, out of this nettle,
danger, we pluck this flower, safety.
'The purpose you undertake is dangerous; the friends
you have named uncertain; the time itself unsorted; and

your whole plot too light for the counterpoise of so great
an opposition.'

Say you so, say you so? I say unto you again, you are a
shallow cowardly hind, and you lie. What a lack-brain is
this! By the Lord, our plot is a good plot as ever was laid;
our friends true and constant: a good plot, good friends,
and full of expectation; an excellent plot, very good
friends. What a frosty-spirited rogue is this! Why, my
Lord of York commends the plot and the general course
of the action. 'Zounds! an I were now by this rascal, I
could brain him with his lady's fan. Is there not my father,
my uncle, and myself? Lord Edmund Mo timer, my Lord
of York, and Owen Glendower? Is there not besides the
Douglas? Have I not all their letters to meet me in arms
by the ninth of the next month, and are they not some of
them set forward already? What a pagan rascal is this! an
infidel! Ha! you shall see now in very sincerity of fear and
cold heart, will he to the king and lay open all our pro-
ceedings. O! I could divide myself and go to buffets, for
moving such a dish of skim milk with so honourable an
action. Hang him! let him tell the king; we are prepared. I
will set forward to-night.

Enter Lady Percy

How now, Kate! I must leave you within these two hours.
LADY PERCY. O, my good lord! why are you thus alone?
For what offence have I this fortnight been
A banish'd woman from my Harry's bed?
Tell me, sweet lord, what is 't that takes from thee
Thy stomach, pleasure, and thy golden sleep?
Why dost thou bend thine eyes upon the earth,
And start so often when thou sitt'st alone?
Why hast thou lost the fresh blood in thy cheeks,
And given my treasures and my rights of thee
To thick-eyed musing and curst melancholy?
In thy faint slumbers I by thee have watch'd,
And heard thee murmur tales of iron wars,
Speak terms of manage to thy bounding steed,
Cry, 'Courage! to the field!' And thou hast talk'd
Of sallies and retires, of trenches, tents,
Of palisadoes, frontiers, parapets,
Of basilisks, of cannon, culverin,
Of prisoners' ransom, and of soldiers slain,

And all the currents of a heady fight.
Thy spirit within thee hath been so at war,
And thus hath so bestirr'd thee in thy sleep,
That beads of sweat have stood upon thy brow,
Like bubbles in a late-disturbed stream;
And in thy face strange motions have appear'd,
Such as we see when men restrain their breath
On some great sudden hest. O! what portents are these?
Some heavy business hath my lord in hand.
And I must know it, else he loves me not.

HOTSPUR. What, ho!

Enter Servant

     Is Gilliams with the packet gone?

SERVANT. He is, my lord, an hour ago.

HOTSPUR. Hath Butler brought those horses from the
  sheriff?

SERVANT. One horse, my lord, he brought even now.

HOTSPUR. What horse? a roan, a crop-ear, is it not?

SERVANT. It is, my lord.

HOTSPUR.   That roan shall be my throne.
 Well, I will back him straight: O, Esperance!
 Bid Butler lead him forth into the park. *Exit Servant*

LADY PERCY. But hear you, my lord.

HOTSPUR. What sayst thou, my lady?

LADY PERCY. What is it carries you away?

HOTSPUR. Why, my horse, my love, my horse.

LADY PERCY. Out, you mad-headed ape!
 A weasel hath not such a deal of spleen
 As you are toss'd with. In faith,
 I 'll know your business, Harry, that I will.
 I fear my brother Mortimer doth stir
 About his title, and hath sent for you
 To line his enterprise. But if you go—

HOTSPUR. So far afoot, I shall be weary, love.

LADY PERCY. Come, come, you paraquito, answer me
 Directly unto this question that I ask.
 In faith, I 'll break thy little finger, Harry,
 An if thou wilt not tell me all things true.

HOTSPUR. Away.
 Away, you trifler! Love! I love thee not,
 I care not for thee, Kate: this is no world
 To play with mammets and to tilt with lips:

We must have bloody noses and crack'd crowns,
And pass them current too. God 's me, my horse!
What sayst thou, Kate? what wouldst thou have with me?
LADY PERCY. Do you not love me? do you not, indeed?
Well, do not, then; for since you love me not,
I will not love myself. Do you not love me?
Nay, tell me if you speak in jest or no.
HOTSPUR. Come, wilt thou see me ride?
And when I am o' horseback, I will swear
I love thee infinitely. But hark you, Kate;
I must not have you henceforth question me
Whither I go, nor reason whereabout.
Whither I must, I must; and, to conclude,
This evening must I leave you, gentle Kate.
I know you wise; but yet no further wise
Than Harry Percy's wife: constant you are,
But yet a woman: and for secrecy,
No lady closer; for I well believe
Thou wilt not utter what thou dost not know;
And so far will I trust thee, gentle Kate.
LADY PERCY. How! so far?
HOTSPUR. Not an inch further. But, hark you, Kate:
Whither I go, thither shall you go too;
To-day will I set forth, to-morrow you.
Will this content you, Kate?
LADY PERCY.   It must, of force.   *Exeunt*

SCENE FOUR

Eastcheap. A Room in the Boar's Head Tavern.

Enter the Prince and Poins

PRINCE. Ned, prithee, come out of that fat room, and lend
me thy hand to laugh a little.
POINS. Where hast been, Hal?
PRINCE. With three or four loggerheads amongst three or
four score hogsheads. I have sounded the very base string
of humility. Sirrah, I am sworn brother to a leash of draw-
ers, and can call them all by their christen names, as Tom,
Dick, and Francis. They take it already upon their salva-
tion, that though I be but Prince of Wales, yet I am the

king of courtesy; and tell me flatly I am no proud Jack,
like Falstaff, but a Corinthian, a lad of mettle, a good boy,
—by the Lord, so they call me,—and when I am King of
England, I shall command all the good lads in Eastcheap.
They call drinking deep, dyeing scarlet; and when you
breathe in your watering, they cry 'hem!' and bid you play
it off. To conclude, I am so good a proficient in one quar-
ter of an hour, that I can drink with any tinker in his own
language during my life. I tell thee, Ned, thou hast lost
much honour that thou wert not with me in this action.
But, sweet Ned,—to sweeten which name of Ned, I give
thee this pennyworth of sugar, clapped even now into my
hand by an underskinker, one that never spake other
English in his life than—'Eight shillings and sixpence,' and
—'You are welcome,' with this shrill addition,—'Anon,
anon, sir! Score a pint of bastard in the Half-moon,' or so.
But, Ned, to drive away the time till Falstaff come, I
prithee do thou stand in some by-room, while I question
my puny drawer to what end he gave me the sugar; and
do thou never leave calling 'Francis!' that his tale to me
may be nothing but 'Anon.' Step aside, and I 'll show thee
a precedent.

POINS. Francis!
PRINCE. Thou art perfect.
POINS. Francis!   *Exit Poins*

Enter Francis

FRANCIS. Anon, anon, sir. Look down into the Pomgarnet,
Ralph.
PRINCE. Come hither, Francis.
FRANCIS. My lord.
PRINCE. How long hast thou to serve, Francis?
FRANCIS. Forsooth, five years, and as much as to—
POINS. (*Within*) Francis!
FRANCIS. Anon, anon, sir.
PRINCE. Five years! by'r lady a long lease for the clinking of
pewter. But, Francis, darest thou be so valiant as to play
the coward with thy indenture and show it a fair pair of
heels and run from it?
FRANCIS. O Lord, sir! I 'll be sworn upon all the books in
England, I could find in my heart—
POINS. (*Within*) Francis!
FRANCIS. Anon, sir.

PRINCE. How old art thou, Francis?

FRANCIS. Let me see—about Michaelmas next I shall be—

POINS. (*Within*) Francis!

FRANCIS. Anon, sir. Pray you, stay a little, my lord.

PRINCE. Nay, but hark you, Francis. For the sugar thou gavest me, 'twas a pennyworth, was 't not?

FRANCIS. O Lord, sir! I would it had been two.

PRINCE. I will give thee for it a thousand pound: ask me when thou wilt and thou shalt have it.

POINS. (*Within*) Francis!

FRANCIS. Anon, anon.

PRINCE. Anon, Francis? No, Francis; but to-morrow, Francis; or, Francis, o' Thursday; or, indeed, Francis, when thou wilt. But, Francis!

FRANCIS. My lord?

PRINCE. Wilt thou rob this leathern-jerkin, crystal-button, knot-pated, agate-ring, puke-stocking, caddis-garter, smooth-tongue, Spanish-pouch,—

FRANCIS. O Lord, sir, who do you mean?

PRINCE. Why then, your brown bastard is your only drink; for, look you, Francis, your white canvas doublet will sully. In Barbary, sir, it cannot come to so much.

FRANCIS. What, sir?

POINS. (*Within*) Francis!

PRINCE. Away, you rogue! Dost thou not hear them call?

Here they both call him; the
Drawer stands amazed, not knowing which way to go
Enter Vintner

VINTNER. What! standest thou still, and hearest such a calling? Look to the guests within. (*Exit Francis*) My lord, old Sir John, with half a dozen more, are at the door: shall I let them in?

PRINCE. Let them alone awhile, and then open the door. (*Exit Vintner*) Poins!

Re-enter Poins

POINS. Anon, anon, sir.

PRINCE. Sirrah, Falstaff and the rest of the thieves are at the door: shall we be merry?

POINS. As merry as crickets, my lad. But hark ye; what cunning match have you made with this jest of the drawer? come, what 's the issue?

PRINCE. I am now of all humours that have show'd them-

selves humours since the old days of goodman Adam to
the pupil age of this present twelve o'clock at midnight.
(*Francis crosses the stage, with wine*) What 's o'clock,
Francis?

FRANCIS. Anon, anon, sir.   *Exit*

PRINCE. That ever this fellow should have fewer words than
a parrot, and yet the son of a woman! His industry is up-
stairs and down-stairs; his eloquence the parcel of a reck-
oning. I am not yet of Percy's mind, the Hotspur of the
North; he that kills me some six or seven dozen of Scots
at a breakfast, washes his hands, and says to his wife, 'Fie
upon this quiet life! I want work.' 'O my sweet Harry,'
says she, 'how many hast thou killed to-day?' 'Give my
roan horse a drench,' says he, and answers, 'Some four-
teen,' an hour after, 'a trifle, a trifle.' I prithee call in Fal-
staff: I 'll play Percy, and that damned brawn shall play
Dame Mortimer his wife. 'Rivo!' says the drunkard. Call
in ribs, call in tallow.

Enter Falstaff, Gadshill, Bardolph, Peto, and Francis

POINS. Welcome, Jack; where hast thou been?

FALSTAFF. A plague of all cowards, I say, and a vengeance
too! marry, and amen! Give me a cup of sack, boy. Ere I
lead this life long, I 'll sew nether-stocks and mend them
and foot them too. A plague of all cowards! Give me a cup
of sack, rogue.—Is there no virtue extant?   *He drinks*

PRINCE. Didst thou never see Titan kiss a dish of butter—
pitiful-hearted Titan, that melted at the sweet tale of the
sun? if thou didst then behold that compound.

FALSTAFF. You rogue, here 's lime in this sack too: there is
nothing but roguery to be found in villanous man: yet a
coward is worse than a cup of sack with lime in it, a vil-
lanous coward! Go thy ways, old Jack; die when thou wilt.
If manhood, good manhood, be not forgot upon the face
of the earth, then am I a shotten herring. There live not
three good men unhanged in England, and one of them is
fat and grows old: God help the while! a bad world, I say.
I would I were a weaver; I could sing psalms or anything.
A plague of all cowards, I say still.

PRINCE. How now, wool-sack! what mutter you?

FALSTAFF. A king's son! If I do not beat thee out of thy king-
dom with a dagger of lath, and drive all thy subjects afore

thee like a flock of wild geese, I 'll never wear hair on my
face more. You Prince of Wales!

PRINCE. Why, you whoreson round man, what 's the matter?

FALSTAFF. Are you not a coward? answer me to that; and
Poins there?

POINS. 'Zounds! ye fat paunch, an ye call me coward, I 'll
stab thee.

FALSTAFF. I call thee coward! I 'll see thee damned ere I call
thee coward; but I would give a thousand pound I could
run as fast as thou canst. You are straight enough in the
shoulders; you care not who sees your back: call you that
backing of your friends? A plague upon such backing!
give me them that will face me. Give me a cup of sack: I
am a rogue if I drunk to-day.

PRINCE. O villain! thy lips are scarce wiped since thou
drunkest last.

FALSTAFF. All 's one for that. (*He drinks*) A plague of all
cowards, still say I.

PRINCE. What 's the matter?

FALSTAFF. What 's the matter? there be four of us here have
ta'en a thousand pound this day morning.

PRINCE. Where is it, Jack? where is it?

FALSTAFF. Where is it! taken from us it is: a hundred upon
poor four of us.

PRINCE. What, a hundred, man?

FALSTAFF. I am a rogue, if I were not at half-sword with a
dozen of them two hours together. I have 'scap'd by mir-
acle. I am eight times thrust through the doublet, four
through the hose; my buckler cut through and through;
my sword hacked like a hand-saw: ecce signum! I never
dealt better since I was a man: all would not do. A plague
of all cowards! Let them speak: if they speak more or less
than truth, they are villains and the sons of darkness.

PRINCE. Speak, sirs; how was it?

GADSHILL. We four set upon some dozen,—

FALSTAFF. Sixteen, at least, my lord.

GADSHILL. And bound them.

PETO. No, no, they were not bound.

FALSTAFF. You rogue, they were bound, every man of them;
or I am a Jew else, an Ebrew Jew.

GADSHILL. As we were sharing, some six or seven fresh men
set upon us,—

FALSTAFF. And unbound the rest, and then come in the other.

PRINCE. What, fought ye with them all?

FALSTAFF. All! I know not what ye call all; but if I fought
not with fifty of them, I am a bunch of radish: if there
were not two or three and fifty upon poor old Jack, then
am I no two-legged creature.

PRINCE. Pray God you have not murdered some of them.

FALSTAFF. Nay, that 's past praying for: I have peppered
two of them: two I am sure I have paid, two rogues in
buckram suits. I tell thee what, Hal, if I tell thee a lie, spit
in my face, call me horse. Thou knowest my old ward;
here I lay, and thus I bore my point. Four rogues in buck-
ram let drive at me,—

PRINCE. What, four? thou saidst but two even now.

FALSTAFF. Four, Hal; I told thee four.

POINS. Ay, ay, he said four.

FALSTAFF. These four came all a-front, and mainly thrust at
me. I made me no more ado but took all their seven points
in my target, thus.

PRINCE. Seven? why, there were but four even now.

FALSTAFF. In buckram.

POINS. Ay, four, in buckram suits.

FALSTAFF. Seven, by these hilts, or I am a villain else.

PRINCE. Prithee, let him alone; we shall have more anon.

FALSTAFF. Dost thou hear me, Hal?

PRINCE. Ay, and mark thee too, Jack.

FALSTAFF. Do so, for it is worth the listening to. These nine
in buckram that I told thee of,—

PRINCE. So, two more already.

FALSTAFF. Their points being broken,—

POINS. Down fell their hose.

FALSTAFF. Began to give me ground; but I followed me
close, came in foot and hand and with a thought seven of
the eleven I paid.

PRINCE. O monstrous! eleven buckram men grown out of
two.

FALSTAFF. But, as the devil would have it, three misbegot-
ten knaves in Kendal-green came at my back and let drive
at me; for it was so dark, Hal, that thou couldst not see thy
hand.

PRINCE. These lies are like the father that begets them; gross
as a mountain, open, palpable. Why, thou clay-brained

guts, thou knotty-pated fool, thou whoreson, obscene, greasy tallow-ketch,—

FALSTAFF. What, art thou mad? art thou mad? is not the truth the truth?

PRINCE. Why, how couldst thou know these men in Kendal-green, when it was so dark thou couldst not see thy hand? come, tell us your reason: what sayest thou to this?

POINS. Come, your reason, Jack, your reason.

FALSTAFF. What, upon compulsion? 'Zounds! an I were at the strappado, or all the racks in the world, I would not tell you on compulsion. Give you a reason on compulsion! if reasons were as plenty as blackberries I would give no man a reason upon compulsion, I.

PRINCE. I 'll be no longer guilty of this sin: this sanguine coward, this bed-presser, this horseback-breaker, this huge hill of flesh;—

FALSTAFF. 'Sblood, you starveling, you elf-skin, you dried neat's-tongue, you bull's pizzle, you stock-fish! O! for breath to utter what is like thee; you tailor's yard, you sheath, you bow-case, you vile standing tuck;—

PRINCE. Well, breathe awhile, and then to it again; and when thou hast tired thyself in base comparisons, hear me speak but this.

POINS. Mark, Jack.

PRINCE. We two saw you four set on four and you bound them, and were masters of their wealth. Mark now, how a plain tale shall put you down. Then did we two set on you four, and, with a word, out-faced you from your prize, and have it; yea, and can show it you here in the house. And, Falstaff, you carried your guts away as nimbly, with as quick dexterity, and roared for mercy, and still ran and roared, as ever I heard bull-calf. What a slave art thou, to hack thy sword as thou hast done, and then say it was in fight! What trick, what device, what starting-hole canst thou now find out to hide thee from this open and apparent shame?

POINS. Come, let 's hear, Jack; what trick hast thou now?

FALSTAFF. By the Lord, I knew ye as well as he that made ye. Why, hear you, my masters: was it for me to kill the heir apparent? Should I turn upon the true prince? Why, thou knowest I am as valiant as Hercules; but beware instinct; the lion will not touch the true prince. Instinct is a

great matter, I was a coward on instinct. I shall think the
better of myself and thee during my life; I for a valiant
lion, and thou for a true prince. But, by the Lord, lads, I
am glad you have the money. Hostess, clap to the doors:
watch to-night, pray to-morrow. Gallants, lads, boys,
hearts of gold, all the titles of good fellowship come to
you! What! shall we be merry? shall we have a play ex-
tempore?

PRINCE. Content; and the argument shall be thy running
away.

FALSTAFF. Ah! no more of that, Hal, an thou lovest me!

Enter Mistress Quickly

QUICKLY. O Jesu! my lord the prince!

PRINCE. How now, my lady the hostess! what sayest thou to
me?

QUICKLY. Marry, my lord, there is a nobleman of the court at
door would speak with you: he says he comes from your
father.

PRINCE. Give him as much as will make him a royal man,
and send him back again to my mother.

FALSTAFF. What manner of man is he?

QUICKLY. An old man.

FALSTAFF. What doth gravity out of his bed at midnight?
Shall I give him his answer?

PRINCE. Prithee, do, Jack.

FALSTAFF. Faith, and I'll send him packing.   *Exit*

PRINCE. Now, sirs: by 'r lady, you fought fair; so did you,
Peto; so did you, Bardolph: you are lions too, you ran
away upon instinct, you will not touch the true prince; no,
fie!

BARDOLPH. Faith, I ran when I saw others run.

PRINCE. Faith, tell me now in earnest, how came Falstaff's
sword so hacked?

PETO. Why he hacked it with his dagger, and said he would
swear truth out of England but he would make you be-
lieve it was done in fight, and persuaded us to do the like.

BARDOLPH. Yea, and to tickle our noses with spear-grass to
make them bleed, and then to beslubber our garments
with it and swear it was the blood of true men. I did that I
did not this seven year before; I blushed to hear his mon-
strous devices.

PRINCE. O villain! thou stolest a cup of sack eighteen years

ago, and wert taken with the manner, and ever since thou
hast blushed extempore. Thou hadst fire and sword on thy
side, and yet thou rannest away. What instinct hadst
thou for it?

BARDOLPH. (*Pointing to his face*) My lord, do you see these
meteors? do you behold these exhalations?

PRINCE. I do.

BARDOLPH. What think you they portend?

PRINCE. Hot livers and cold purses.

BARDOLPH. Choler, my lord, if rightly taken.

PRINCE. No, if rightly taken, halter.—

Re-enter Falstaff

Here comes lean Jack, here comes bare-bone.—How now,
my sweet creature of bombast! How long is 't ago, Jack,
since thou sawest thine own knee?

FALSTAFF. My own knee! when I was about thy years, Hal,
I was not an eagle's talon in the waist; I could have crept
into any alderman's thumb-ring. A plague of sighing and
grief! it blows a man up like a bladder. There 's villanous
news abroad: here was Sir John Bracy from your father:
you must to the court in the morning. That same mad fel-
low of the North, Percy, and he of Wales, that gave Amai-
mon the bastinado and made Lucifer cuckold, and swore
the devil his true liegeman upon the cross of a Welsh hook
—what a plague call you him?

POINS. Owen Glendower.

FALSTAFF. Owen, Owen, the same; and his son-in-law Mor-
timer and old Northumberland; and that sprightly Scot of
Scots, Douglas, that runs o' horseback up a hill perpen-
dicular.

PRINCE. He that rides at high speed and with his pistol kills
a sparrow flying.

FALSTAFF. You have hit it.

PRINCE. So did he never the sparrow.

FALSTAFF. Well, that rascal hath good mettle in him; he will
not run.

PRINCE. Why, what a rascal art thou then to praise him so
for running?

FALSTAFF. O' horseback, ye cuckoo! but, afoot he will not
budge a foot.

PRINCE. Yes, Jack, upon instinct.

FALSTAFF. I grant ye, upon instinct. Well, he is there

too, and one Mordake, and a thousand blue-caps more. Worcester is stolen away to-night; thy father's beard is turned white with the news: you may buy land now as cheap as stinking mackerel.

PRINCE. Why then, it is like, if there come a hot June and this civil buffeting hold, we shall buy maidenheads as they buy hob-nails, by the hundreds.

FALSTAFF. By the mass, lad, thou sayest true; it is like we shall have good trading that way. But tell me, Hal, art thou not horribly afeard? thou being heir apparent, could the world pick thee out three such enemies again as that fiend Douglas, that spirit Percy, and that devil Glendower? Art thou not horribly afraid? doth not thy blood thrill at it?

PRINCE. Not a whit, i' faith; I lack some of thy instinct.

FALSTAFF. Well, thou wilt be horribly chid to-morrow when thou comest to thy father: if thou love me, practise an answer.

PRINCE. Do thou stand for my father, and examine me upon the particulars of my life.

FALSTAFF. Shall I? content: this chair shall be my state, this dagger my sceptre, and this cushion my crown.

PRINCE. Thy state is taken for a joint-stool, thy golden sceptre for a leaden dagger, and thy precious rich crown for a pitiful bald crown!

FALSTAFF. Well, an the fire of grace be not quite out of thee, now shalt thou be moved. Give me a cup of sack to make mine eyes look red, that it may be thought I have wept; for I must speak in passion, and I will do it in King Cambyses' vein.   *Drinks*

PRINCE. Well, here is my leg.   *Makes a bow*

FALSTAFF. And here is my speech. Stand aside, nobility.

QUICKLY. O Jesu! This is excellent sport, i' faith!

FALSTAFF. Weep not, sweet queen, for trickling tears are vain.

QUICKLY. O, the father! how he holds his countenance.

FALSTAFF. For God's sake, lords, convey my tristful queen, For tears do stop the flood-gates of her eyes.

QUICKLY. O Jesu! he doth it as like one of these harlotry players as ever I see!

FALSTAFF. Peace, good pint-pot! peace, good tickle-brain! Harry, I do not only marvel where thou spendest thy time, but also how thou art accompanied: for though the camomile, the more it is trodden on the faster it grows, yet youth, the more it is wasted the sooner it wears. That thou art my son, I have partly thy mother's word, partly my own opinion; but chiefly, a villanous trick of thine eye and a foolish hanging of thy nether lip, that doth warrant me. If then thou be son to me, here lies the point; why, being son to me, art thou so pointed at? Shall the blessed sun of heaven prove a micher and eat blackberries? a question not to be asked. Shall the son of England prove a thief and take purses? a question to be asked. There is a thing, Harry, which thou hast often heard of, and it is known to many in our land by the name of pitch: this pitch, as ancient writers do report, doth defile; so doth the company thou keepest; for, Harry, now I do not speak to thee in drink, but in tears, not in pleasure but in passion, not in words only, but in woes also. And yet there is a virtuous man whom I have often noted in thy company, but I know not his name,

PRINCE. What manner of man, an it like your majesty?

FALSTAFF. A goodly portly man, i' faith, and a corpulent; of a cheerful look, a pleasing eye, and a most noble carriage; and, as I think, his age some fifty, or by 'r lady, inclining to threescore; and now I remember me, his name is Falstaff: if that man should be lewdly given, he deceiveth me; for, Harry, I see virtue in his looks. If then the tree may be known by the fruit, as the fruit by the tree, then, peremptorily I speak it, there is virtue in that Falstaff: him keep with, the rest banish. And tell me now, thou naughty varlet, tell me, where hast thou been this month?

PRINCE. Dost thou speak like a king? Do thou stand for me, and I 'll play my father.

FALSTAFF. Depose me? if thou dost it half so gravely, so majestically, both in word and matter, hang me up by the heels for a rabbit-sucker or a poulter's hare.

PRINCE. Well, here I am set.

FALSTAFF. And here I stand. Judge, my masters.

PRINCE. Now, Harry! whence come you?

FALSTAFF. My noble lord, from Eastcheap.

PRINCE. The complaints I hear of thee are grievous.

FALSTAFF. 'Sblood, my lord, they are false: nay, I 'll tickle ye for a young prince, i' faith.

PRINCE. Swearest thou, ungracious boy? henceforth ne'er look on me. Thou art violently carried away from grace: there is a devil haunts thee in the likeness of a fat old man; a tun of man is thy companion. Why dost thou converse with that trunk of humours, that bolting-hutch of beastliness, that swoln parcel of dropsies, that huge bombard of sack, that stuffed cloak-bag of guts, that roasted Manning-tree ox with the pudding in his belly, that reverend vice, that grey iniquity, that father ruffian, that vanity in years? Wherein is he good but to taste sack and drink it? wherein neat and cleanly but to carve a capon and eat it? wherein cunning but in craft? wherein crafty but in villany? wherein villanous but in all things? wherein worthy but in nothing?

FALSTAFF. I would your Grace would take me with you: whom means your Grace?

PRINCE. That villanous abominable misleader of youth, Falstaff, that old white-bearded Satan.

FALSTAFF. My lord, the man I know.

PRINCE. I know thou dost.

FALSTAFF. But to say I know more harm in him than in myself were to say more than I know. That he is old, the more the pity, his white hairs do witness it; but that he is, saving your reverence, a whoremaster, that I utterly deny. If sack and sugar be a fault, God help the wicked! If to be old and merry be a sin, then many an old host that I know is damned: if to be fat be to be hated, then Pharaoh's lean kine are to be loved. No, my good lord; banish Peto, banish Bardolph, banish Poins; but for sweet Jack Falstaff, kind Jack Falstaff, true Jack Falstaff, valiant Jack Falstaff, and therefore more valiant, being, as he is, old Jack Falstaff, banish not him thy Harry's company: banish not him thy Harry's company: banish plump Jack, and banish all the world.

PRINCE. I do, I will.   *A knocking heard*
            Exeunt Mistress Quickly, Francis, and Bardolph
                    Re-enter Bardolph, running

BARDOLPH. O! my lord, my lord, the sheriff with a most monstrous watch is at the door.

FALSTAFF. Out, ye rogue! Play out the play: I have much to say in the behalf of that Falstaff.
                    Re-enter Mistress Quickly

QUICKLY. O Jesu! my lord, my lord!

PRINCE. Heigh, heigh! the devil rides upon a fiddle-stick: what's the matter?

QUICKLY. The sheriff and all the watch are at the door: they are come to search the house. Shall I let them in?

FALSTAFF. Dost thou hear, Hal? never call a true piece of gold a counterfeit: thou art essentially mad without seeming so.

PRINCE. And thou a natural coward without instinct.

FALSTAFF. I deny your major. If you will deny the sheriff, so; if not, let him enter: if I become not a cart as well as another man, a plague on my bringing up! I hope I shall as soon be strangled with a halter as another.

PRINCE. Go, hide thee behind the arras: the rest walk up above. Now, my masters, for a true face and good conscience.

FALSTAFF. Both which I have had; but their date is out, and therefore I'll hide me.

Exeunt all but the Prince and Peto

PRINCE. Call in the sheriff.

Enter Sheriff and Carrier

Now, master sheriff, what's your will with me?

SHERIFF. First, pardon me, my lord. A hue and cry
Hath follow'd certain men unto this house.

PRINCE. What men?

SHERIFF. One of them is well known, my gracious lord,
A gross fat man.

CARRIER.   As fat as butter.

PRINCE. The man, I do assure you, is not here,
For I myself at this time have employ'd him.
And, sheriff, I will engage my word to thee,
That I will, by to-morrow dinner-time,
Send him to answer thee, or any man,
For anything he shall be charg'd withal:
And so let me entreat you leave the house.

SHERIFF. I will, my lord. There are two gentlemen
Have in this robbery lost three hundred marks.

PRINCE. It may be so: if he have robb'd these men,
He shall be answerable; and so farewell.

SHERIFF. Good-night, my noble lord.

PRINCE. I think it is good-morrow, is it not?

SHERIFF. Indeed, my lord, I think it be two o'clock.

Exeunt Sheriff and Carrier

PRINCE. This oily rascal is known as well as Paul's. Go, call him forth.

PETO. Falstaff! Fast asleep behind the arras, and snorting like a horse.

PRINCE. Hark, how hard he fetches breath. Search his pockets. (*He searcheth his pockets, and findeth certain papers*) What hast thou found?

PETO. Nothing but papers, my lord.

PRINCE. Let 's see what they be: read them.

PETO. 'Item, A capon   2s. 2d.
    Item, Sauce   4d.
    Item, Sack, two gallons   5s. 8d.
    Item, Anchovies and sack after supper 2s. 6d.
    Item, Bread   ob.'

PRINCE. O monstrous! but one half-pennyworth of bread to this intolerable deal of sack! What there is else, keep close; we 'll read it at more advantage. There let him sleep till day. I 'll to the court in the morning. We must all to the wars, and thy place shall be honourable. I 'll procure this fat rogue a charge of foot; and, I know, his death will be a march of twelve-score. The money shall be paid back again with advantage. Be with me betimes in the morning; and so good-morrow, Peto.

PETO. Good-morrow, good my lord.   *Exeunt*

ACT THREE

SCENE ONE

Bangor. A Room in the Archdeacon's House.

Enter Hotspur, Worcester, Mortimer, and Glendower

MORTIMER. These promises are fair, the parties sure,
  And our induction full of prosperous hope.
HOTSPUR. Lord Mortimer, and cousin Glendower,
  Will you sit down?
  And uncle Worcester: a plague upon it!
  I have forgot the map.
GLENDOWER.   No, here it is.
  Sit, cousin Percy; sit, good cousin Hotspur;
  For by that name as oft as Lancaster
  Doth speak of you, his cheek looks pale and with
  A rising sigh he wishes you in heaven.
HOTSPUR. And you in hell, as often as he hears
  Owen Glendower spoke of.
GLENDOWER. I cannot blame him: at my nativity
  The front of heaven was full of fiery shapes,
  Of burning cressets; and at my birth
  The frame and huge foundation of the earth
  Shak'd like a coward.
HOTSPUR. Why, so it would have done at the same season, if
  your mother's cat had but kittened, though yourself had
  never been born.
GLENDOWER. I say the earth did shake when I was born.
HOTSPUR. And I say the earth was not of my mind,
  If you suppose as fearing you it shook.
GLENDOWER. The heavens were all on fire, the earth did
    tremble.
HOTSPUR. O! then the earth shook to see the heavens on fire,
  And not in fear of your nativity.
  Diseased nature oftentimes breaks forth

In strange eruptions; oft the teeming earth
Is with a kind of colic pinch'd and vex'd
By the imprisoning of unruly wind
Within her womb; which, for enlargement striving,
Shakes the old beldam earth, and topples down
Steeples and moss-grown towers. At your birth
Our grandam earth, having this distemperature,
In passion shook.

GLENDOWER.   Cousin, of many men
I do not bear these crossings. Give me leave
To tell you once again that at my birth
The front of heaven was full of fiery shapes,
The goats ran from the mountains, and the herds
Were strangely clamorous to the frighted fields.
These signs have mark'd me extraordinary;
And all the courses of my life do show
I am not in the roll of common men.
Where is he living, clipp'd in with the sea
That chides the banks of England, Scotland, Wales,
Which calls me pupil, or hath read to me?
And bring him out that is but woman's son
Can trace me in the tedious ways of art
And hold me pace in deep experiments.

HOTSPUR. I think there 's no man speaks better Welsh.
I 'll to dinner.

MORTIMER. Peace, cousin Percy! you will make him mad.

GLENDOWER. I can call spirits from the vasty deep.

HOTSPUR. Why, so can I, or so can any man;
But will they come when you do call for them?

GLENDOWER. Why, I can teach thee, cousin, to command
The devil.

HOTSPUR. And I can teach thee, coz, to shame the devil
By telling truth: tell truth and shame the devil.
If thou have power to raise him, bring him hither,
And I 'll be sworn I have power to shame him hence.
O! while you live, tell truth and shame the devil!

MORTIMER. Come, come;
No more of this unprofitable chat.

GLENDOWER. Three times hath Henry Bolingbroke made
head
Against my power; thrice from the banks of Wye
And sandy-bottom'd Severn have I sent him

Bootless home and weather-beaten back.

HOTSPUR. Home without boots, and in foul weather too!
How 'scapes he agues, in the devil's name?

GLENDOWER. Come, here 's the map: shall we divide our
    right
According to our threefold order ta'en?

MORTIMER. The archdeacon hath divided it
Into three limits very equally.
England, from Trent and Severn hitherto,
By south and east, is to my part assign'd:
All westward, Wales beyond the Severn shore,
And all the fertile land within that bound,
To Owen Glendower: and, dear coz, to you
The remnant northward, lying off from Trent.
And our indentures tripartite are drawn,
Which being sealed interchangeably,
A business that this night may execute,
To-morrow, cousin Percy, you and I
And my good Lord of Worcester will set forth
To meet your father and the Scottish power,
As is appointed us, at Shrewsbury.
My father Glendower is not ready yet,
Nor shall we need his help these fourteen days.
    (*To Glendower*) Within that space you may have drawn
    together
Your tenants, friends, and neighbouring gentlemen.

GLENDOWER. A shorter time shall send me to you, lords;
And in my conduct shall your ladies come,
From whom you now must steal and take no leave;
For there will be a world of water shed
Upon the parting of your wives and you.

HOTSPUR. Methinks my moiety, north from Burton here,
In quantity equals not one of yours:
See how this river comes me cranking in,
And cuts me from the best of all my land
A huge half-moon, a monstrous cantle out.
I 'll have the current in this place damm'd up,
And here the smug and silver Trent shall run
In a new channel, fair and evenly:
It shall not wind with such a deep indent,
To rob me of so rich a bottom here.

GLENDOWER. Not wind! it shall, it must; you see it doth.

MORTIMER. Yea, but
    Mark how he bears his course, and runs me up
    With like advantage on the other side;
    Gelding the opposed continent as much,
    As on the other side it takes from you.

WORCESTER. Yea, but a little charge will trench him here,
    And on this north side win this cape of land;
    And then he runs straight and even.

HOTSPUR. I 'll have it so; a little charge will do it.

GLENDOWER. I will not have it alter'd.

HOTSPUR.   Will not you?

GLENDOWER. No, nor you shall not.

HOTSPUR.   Who shall say me nay?

GLENDOWER. Why, that will I.

HOTSPUR.   Let me not understand you then:
    Speak it in Welsh.

GLENDOWER. I can speak English, lord, as well as you,
    For I was train'd up in the English court;
    Where, being but young, I framed to the harp
    Many an English ditty lovely well,
    And gave the tongue an helpful ornament;
    A virtue that was never seen in you.

HOTSPUR. Marry, and I 'm glad of it with all my heart.
    I had rather be a kitten, and cry mew
    Than one of these same metre ballad-mongers;
    I had rather hear a brazen canstick turn'd,
    Or a dry wheel grate on the axle-tree;
    And that would set my teeth nothing on edge,
    Nothing so much as mincing poetry:
    'Tis like the forc'd gait of a shuffling nag.

GLENDOWER. Come, you shall have Trent turn'd.

HOTSPUR. I do not care: I 'll give thrice so much land
    To any well-deserving friend;
    But in the way of bargain, mark you me,
    I 'll cavil on the ninth part of a hair.
    Are the indentures drawn? shall we be gone?

GLENDOWER. The moon shines fair, you may away by night:
    I 'll haste the writer and withal
    Break with your wives of your departure hence:
    I am afraid my daughter will run mad,
    So much she doteth on her Mortimer. *Exit*

MORTIMER. Fie, cousin Percy! how you cross my father!

HOTSPUR. I cannot choose: sometimes he angers me
    With telling me of the moldwarp and the ant,
    Of the dreamer Merlin and his prophecies,
    And of a dragon, and a finless fish,
    A clip-wing'd griffin, and a moulten raven,
    A couching lion, and a ramping cat,
    And such a deal of skimble-skamble stuff
    As puts me from my faith. I 'll tell thee what;
    He held me last night at least nine hours
    In reckoning up the several devils' names
    That were his lackeys: I cried 'hum!' and 'well, go to.'
    But mark'd him not a word. O! he 's as tedious
    As a tired horse, a railing wife;
    Worse than a smoky house. I had rather live
    With cheese and garlick in a windmill, far,
    Than feed on cates and have him talk to me
    In any summer-house in Christendom.
MORTIMER. In faith, he is a worthy gentleman,
    Exceedingly well read, and profited
    In strange concealments, valiant as a lion
    And wondrous affable, and as bountiful
    As mines of India. Shall I tell you, cousin?
    He holds your temper in a high respect,
    And curbs himself even of his natural scope
    When you do cross his humour; faith, he does.
    I warrant you, that man is not alive
    Might so have tempted him as you have done,
    Without the taste of danger and reproof:
    But do not use it oft, let me entreat you.
WORCESTER. In faith, my lord, you are too wilful-blame;
    And since your coming hither have done enough
    To put him quite beside his patience.
    You must needs learn, lord, to amend this fault:
    Though sometimes it show greatness, courage, blood,—
    And that 's the dearest grace it renders you,—
    Yet oftentimes it doth present harsh rage,
    Defect of manners, want of government,
    Pride, haughtiness, opinion, and disdain:
    The least of which haunting a nobleman
    Loseth men's hearts and leaves behind a stain
    Upon the beauty of all parts besides,
    Beguiling them of commendation.

HOTSPUR. Well, I am school'd; good manners be your speed!
  Here come our wives, and let us take our leave.
          Re-enter Glendower, with the Ladies
MORTIMER. This is the deadly spite that angers me,
  My wife can speak no English, I no Welsh.
GLENDOWER. My daughter weeps; she will not part with
    you:
  She 'll be a soldier too: she 'll to the wars.
MORTIMER. Good father, tell her that she and my aunt
    Percy,
  Shall follow in your conduct speedily.
                    Glendower speaks to Lady
        Mortimer in Welsh, and she answers him in the same
GLENDOWER. She 's desperate here; a peevish self-will'd
  harlotry, one that no persuasion can do good upon.
                    She speaks to Mortimer in Welsh
MORTIMER. I understand thy looks: that pretty Welsh
  Which thou pour'st down from these swelling heavens
  I am too perfect in; and, but for shame,
  In such a parley would I answer thee.   *She speaks again*
  I understand thy kisses and thou mine,
  And that 's a feeling disputation:
  But I will never be a truant, love,
  Till I have learn'd thy language; for thy tongue
  Makes Welsh as sweet as ditties highly penn'd,
  Sung by a fair queen in a summer's bower,
  With ravishing division, to her lute.
GLENDOWER. Nay, if you melt, then will she run mad.
                                    She speaks again
MORTIMER. O! I am ignorance itself in this.
GLENDOWER. She bids you
  Upon the wanton rushes lay you down
  And rest your gentle head upon her lap,
  And she will sing the song that pleaseth you,
  And on your eyelids crown the god of sleep,
  Charming your blood with pleasing heaviness,
  Making such difference 'twixt wake and sleep
  As is the difference between day and night
  The hour before the heavenly-harness'd team
  Begins his golden progress in the east.
MORTIMER. With all my heart I 'll sit and hear her sing:
  By that time will our book, I think, be drawn.

GLENDOWER. Do so;
And those musicians that shall play to you
Hang in the air a thousand leagues from hence,
And straight they shall be here: sit, and attend.

HOTSPUR. Come, Kate, thou art perfect in lying down:
come, quick, quick, that I may lay my head in thy lap.

LADY PERCY. Go, ye giddy goose.

Glendower speaks some Welsh words, and music is heard

HOTSPUR. Now I perceive the devil understands Welsh;
And 'tis no marvel he is so humorous.
By 'r lady, he 's a good musician.

LADY PERCY. Then should you be nothing but musical for
you are altogether governed by humours. Lie still, ye
thief, and hear the lady sing in Welsh.

HOTSPUR. I had rather hear Lady, my brach, howl in Irish.

LADY PERCY. Wouldst thou have thy head broken?

HOTSPUR. No.

LADY PERCY. Then be still.

HOTSPUR. Neither; 'tis a woman's fault.

LADY PERCY. Now, God help thee!

HOTSPUR. To the Welsh lady's bed.

LADY PERCY. What 's that?

HOTSPUR. Peace! she sings.

A Welsh song sung by Lady Mortimer

HOTSPUR. Come, Kate, I 'll have your song too.

LADY PERCY. Not mine, in good sooth.

HOTSPUR. Not yours, 'in good sooth'! Heart! you swear like a
comfit-maker's wife! Not you, 'in good sooth'; and, 'as
true as I live'; and, 'as God shall mend me'; and, 'as sure
as day':
And giv'st such sarcenet surety for thy oaths,
As if thou never walk'dst further than Finsbury.
Swear me, Kate, like a lady as thou art,
A good mouth-filling oath; and leave 'in sooth,'
And such protest of pepper-gingerbread,
To velvet-guards and Sunday-citizens.
Come, sing.

LADY PERCY. I will not sing.

HOTSPUR. 'Tis the next way to turn tailor or be red-breast
teacher. An the indentures be drawn, I 'll away within
these two hours; and so, come in when ye will.   *Exit*

GLENDOWER. Come, come, Lord Mortimer; you are as slow

      As hot Lord Percy is on fire to go.
      By this our book is drawn; we will but seal,
      And then to horse immediately.
MORTIMER. With all my heart.   *Exeunt*

                    SCENE TWO

            London. A Room in the Palace.

        Enter King Henry, the Prince, and Lords

KING HENRY. Lords, give us leave; the Prince of Wales and I
      Must have some private conference: but be near at hand,
      For we shall presently have need of you.   *Exeunt Lords*
      I know not whether God will have it so,
      For some displeasing service I have done,
      That, in his secret doom, out of my blood
      He 'll breed revengement and a scourge for me;
      But thou dost in thy passages of life
      Make me believe that thou art only mark'd
      For the hot vengeance and the rod of heaven
      To punish my mistreadings. Tell me else,
      Could such inordinate and low desires,
      Such poor, such bare, such lewd, such mean attempts,
      Such barren pleasures, rude society,
      As thou art match'd withal and grafted to,
      Accompany the greatness of thy blood
      And hold their level with thy princely heart?
PRINCE. So please your Majesty, I would I could
      Quit all offences with as clear excuse
      As well as I am doubtless I can purge
      Myself of many I am charg'd withal:
      Yet such extenuation let me beg,
      As, in reproof of many tales devis'd,
      Which oft the ear of greatness needs must hear,
      By smiling pick-thanks and base newsmongers,
      I may, for some things true, wherein my youth
      Hath faulty wander'd and irregular,
      Find pardon on my true submission.
KING HENRY. God pardon thee! yet let me wonder, **Harry**,
      At thy affections, which do hold a wing
      Quite from the flight of all thy ancestors.

Thy place in council thou hast rudely lost,
Which by thy younger brother is supplied,
And art almost an alien to the hearts
Of all the court and princes of my blood.
The hope and expectation of thy time
Is ruin'd, and the soul of every man
Prophetically do forethink thy fall.
Had I so lavish of my presence been,
So common-hackney'd in the eyes of men,
So stale and cheap to vulgar company,
Opinion, that did help me to the crown,
Had still kept loyal to possession
And left me in reputeless banishment,
A fellow of no mark nor likelihood.
By being seldom seen, I could not stir,
But like a comet I was wonder'd at;
That men would tell their children, 'This is he';
Others would say, 'Where? which is Bolingbroke?'
And then I stole all courtesy from heaven,
And dress'd myself in such humility
That I did pluck allegiance from men's hearts,
Loud shouts and salutations from their mouths,
Even in the presence of the crowned king.
Thus did I keep my person fresh and new;
My presence, like a robe pontifical,
Ne'er seen but wonder'd at: and so my state,
Seldom but sumptuous, showed like a feast,
And won by rareness such solemnity.
The skipping king, he ambled up and down
With shallow jesters and rash bavin wits,
Soon kindled and soon burnt; carded his state,
Mingled his royalty with capering fools,
Had his great name profaned with their scorns,
And gave his countenance, against his name,
To laugh at gibing boys and stand the push
Of every beardless vain comparative;
Grew a companion to the common streets,
Enfeoff'd himself to popularity;
That, being daily swallow'd by men's eyes,
They surfeited with honey and began
To loathe the taste of sweetness, whereof a little
More than a little is by much too much.

So, when he had occasion to be seen,
He was but as the cuckoo is in June,
Heard, not regarded; seen, but with such eyes
As, sick and blunted with community,
Afford no extraordinary gaze,
Such as is bent on sun-like majesty
When it shines seldom in admiring eyes;
But rather drows'd and hung their eyelids down,
Slept in his face, and render'd such aspect
As cloudy men use to their adversaries,
Being with his presence glutted, gorg'd, and full.
And in that very line, Harry, stand'st thou;
For thou hast lost thy princely privilege
With vile participation: not an eye
But is aweary of thy common sight,
Save mine, which hath desir'd to see thee more;
Which now doth that I would not have it do,
Make blind itself with foolish tenderness.

PRINCE. I shall hereafter, my thrice gracious lord,
Be more myself.

KING HENRY.   For all the world,
As thou art to this hour was Richard then
When I from France set foot at Ravenspurgh;
And even as I was then is Percy now.
Now, by my sceptre and my soul to boot,
He hath more worthy interest to the state
Than thou the shadow of succession;
For of no right, nor colour like to right,
He doth fill fields with harness in the realm,
Turns head against the lion's armed jaws,
And, being no more in debt to years than thou,
Leads ancient lords and reverend bishops on
To bloody battles and to bruising arms.
What never-dying honour hath he got
Against renowned Douglas! whose high deeds,
Whose hot incursions and great name in arms,
Holds from all soldiers chief majority,
And military title capital,
Through all the kingdoms that acknowledge Christ.
Thrice hath this Hotspur, Mars in swathling clothes,
This infant warrior, in his enterprises
Discomfited great Douglas; ta'en him once,

Enlarged him and made a friend of him,
To fill the mouth of deep defiance up
And shake the peace and safety of our throne.
And what say you to this? Percy, Northumberland,
The Archbishop's Grace of York, Douglas, Mortimer
Capitulate against us and are up.
But wherefore do I tell these news to thee?
Why, Harry, do I tell thee of my foes,
Which art my near'st and dearest enemy?
Thou that art like enough, through vassal fear,
Base inclination, and the start of spleen,
To fight against me under Percy's pay,
To dog his heels, and curtsy at his frowns,
To show how much thou art degenerate.

PRINCE. Do not think so; you shall not find it so:
And God forgive them, that so much have sway'd
Your Majesty's good thoughts away from me!
I will redeem all this on Percy's head,
And in the closing of some glorious day
Be bold to tell you that I am your son;
When I will wear a garment all of blood
And stain my favours in a bloody mask,
Which, wash'd away, shall scour my shame with it:
And that shall be the day, whene'er it lights,
That this same child of honour and renown,
This gallant Hotspur, this all-praised knight,
And your unthought-of Harry chance to meet.
For every honour sitting on his helm,—
Would they were multitudes, and on my head
My shames redoubled!—for the time will come
That I shall make this northern youth exchange
His glorious deeds for my indignities.
Percy is but my factor, good my lord,
To engross up glorious deeds on my behalf;
And I will call him to so strict account
That he shall render every glory up,
Yea, even the slightest worship of his time,
Or I will tear the reckoning from his heart.
This, in the name of God, I promise here:
The which, if he be pleas'd I shall perform,
I do beseech your Majesty may salve
The long-grown wounds of my intemperance:

If not, the end of life cancels all bands,
And I will die a hundred thousand deaths
Ere break the smallest parcel of this vow.

KING HENRY. A hundred thousand rebels die in this:
Thou shalt have charge and sovereign trust herein.

Enter Sir Walter Blunt

How now, good Blunt! thy looks are full of speed.

BLUNT. So hath the business that I come to speak of.
Lord Mortimer of Scotland hath sent word
That Douglas and the English rebels met,
The eleventh of this month at Shrewsbury.
A mighty and a fearful head they are,—
If promises be kept on every hand,—
As ever offer'd foul play in a state.

KING HENRY. The Earl of Westmoreland set forth to-day,
With him my son, Lord John of Lancaster;
For this advertisement is five days old.
On Wednesday next, Harry, you shall set forward;
On Thursday we ourselves will march: our meeting
Is Bridgenorth; and Harry, you shall march
Through Gloucestershire; by which account,
Our business valued, some twelve days hence
Our general forces at Bridgenorth shall meet.
Our hands are full of business: let 's away;
Advantage feeds him fat while men delay.   *Exeunt*

SCENE THREE

Eastcheap. A Room in the Boar's Head Tavern.

Enter Falstaff and Bardolph

FALSTAFF. Bardolph, am I not fallen away vilely since this
last action? do I not bate? do I not dwindle? Why, my skin
hangs about me like an old lady's loose gown; I am with-
ered like an old apple-john. Well, I 'll repent, and that sud-
denly, while I am in some liking; I shall be out of heart
shortly, and then I shall have no strength to repent. An I
have not forgotten what the inside of a church is made of,
I am a peppercorn, a brewer's horse: the inside of a
church! church! Company, villanous company, hath been
the spoil of me.

BARDOLPH. Sir John, you are so fretful, you cannot live long.

FALSTAFF. Why, there is it: come, sing me a bawdy song; make me merry. I was as virtuously given as a gentleman need to be; virtuous enough: swore little; diced not above seven times a week; went to a bawdy-house not above once in a quarter—of an hour; paid money that I borrowed three or four times; lived well and in good compass; and now I live out of all order, out of all compass.

BARDOLPH. Why, you are so fat, Sir John, that you must needs be out of all compass, out of all reasonable compass, Sir John.

FALSTAFF. Do thou amend thy face, and I 'll amend my life: thou art our admiral, thou bearest the lanthorn in the poop, but 'tis in the nose of thee: thou art the Knight of the Burning Lamp.

BARDOLPH. Why, Sir John, my face does you no harm.

FALSTAFF. No, I 'll be sworn; I make as good use of it as many a man doth of a Death's head, or a memento mori: I never see thy face but I think upon hell-fire and Dives that lived in purple; for there he is in his robes, burning, burning. If thou wert any way given to virtue, I would swear by thy face; my oath should be, 'By this fire, that 's God's angel': but thou art altogether given over, and wert indeed, but for the light in thy face, the son of utter darkness. When thou rannest up Gadshill in the night to catch my horse, if I did not think thou hadst been an ignis fatuus or a ball of wildfire, there 's no purchase in money. O! thou art a perpetual triumph, an everlasting bonfire-light. Thou hast saved me a thousand marks in links and torches, walking with thee in the night betwixt tavern and tavern: but the sack that thou hast drunk me would have bought me lights as good cheap at the dearest chandler's in Europe. I have maintained that salamander of yours with fire any time this two-and-thirty years; God reward me for it!

BARDOLPH. 'Sblood, I would my face were in your belly.

FALSTAFF. God-a-mercy! so should I be sure to be heart-burned.

Enter Mistress Quickly

How now, Dame Partlet the hen! have you inquired yet who picked my pocket?

QUICKLY. Why, Sir John, what do you think, Sir John? Do you think I keep thieves in my house? I have searched, I have inquired, so has my husband, man by man, boy by boy, servant by servant: the tithe of a hair was never lost in my house before.

FALSTAFF. You lie, hostess: Bardolph was shaved and lost many a hair; and I 'll be sworn my pocket was picked. Go to, you are a woman; go.

QUICKLY. Who, I? No; I defy thee: God's light! I was never called so in my own house before.

FALSTAFF. Go to, I know you well enough.

QUICKLY. No, Sir John; you do not know me, Sir John: I know you, Sir John: you owe me money, Sir John, and now you pick a quarrel to beguile me of it: I bought you a dozen of shirts to your back.

FALSTAFF. Dowlas, filthy dowlas: I have given them away to bakers' wives, and they have made bolters of them.

QUICKLY. Now, as I am a true woman, holland of eight shillings an ell. You owe money here besides, Sir John, for your diet and by-drinkings, and money lent you, four-and-twenty pound.

FALSTAFF. He had his part of it; let him pay.

QUICKLY. He! alas! he is poor; he hath nothing.

FALSTAFF. How! poor? look upon his face; what call you rich? let them coin his nose, let them coin his cheeks. I 'll not pay a denier. What! will you make a younker of me? shall I not take mine ease in mine inn but I shall have my pocket picked? I have lost a seal-ring of my grandfather's worth forty mark.

QUICKLY. O Jesu! I have heard the prince tell him, I know not how oft, that that ring was copper.

FALSTAFF. How! the prince is a Jack, a sneak-cup; 'sblood! an he were here, I would cudgel him like a dog, if he would say so.

Enter the Prince and Poins, marching. Falstaff
meets them, playing on his truncheon like a fife

How now, lad! is the wind in that door, i' faith? must we all march?

BARDOLPH. Yea, two and two, Newgate fashion.

QUICKLY. My lord, I pray you, hear me.

PRINCE. What sayest thou, Mistress Quickly? How does thy husband? I love him well, he is an honest man.

QUICKLY. Good my lord, hear me.

FALSTAFF. Prithee, let her alone, and list to me.

PRINCE. What sayest thou, Jack?

FALSTAFF. The other night I fell asleep here behind the arras and had my pocket picked: this house is turned bawdy-house; they pick pockets.

PRINCE. What didst thou lose, Jack?

FALSTAFF. Wilt thou believe me, Hal? three or four bonds of forty pound a-piece, and a seal-ring of my grand-father's.

PRINCE. A trifle; some eight-penny matter.

QUICKLY. So I told him, my lord; and I said I heard your Grace say so: and, my lord, he speaks most vilely of you, like a foul-mouthed man as he is, and said he would cudgel you.

PRINCE. What! he did not?

QUICKLY. There 's neither faith, truth, nor womanhood in me else.

FALSTAFF. There 's no more faith in thee than in a stewed prune; nor no more truth in thee than in a drawn fox; and for womanhood, Maid Marian may be the deputy's wife of the ward to thee. Go, you thing, go.

QUICKLY. Say, what thing? what thing?

FALSTAFF. What thing! why, a thing to thank God on.

QUICKLY. I am no thing to thank God on, I would thou shouldst know it; I am an honest man's wife; and, setting thy knighthood aside, thou art a knave to call me so.

FALSTAFF. Setting thy womanhood aside, thou art a beast to say otherwise.

QUICKLY. Say, what beast, thou knave thou?

FALSTAFF. What beast! why, an otter.

PRINCE. An otter, Sir John! why, an otter?

FALSTAFF. Why? she 's neither fish nor flesh; a man knows not where to have her.

QUICKLY. Thou art an unjust man in saying so: thou or any man knows where to have me, thou knave thou!

PRINCE. Thou sayest true, hostess; and he slanders thee most grossly.

QUICKLY. So he doth you, my lord; and said this other day you ought him a thousand pound.

PRINCE. Sirrah! do I owe you a thousand pound?

FALSTAFF. A thousand pound, Hal! a million: thy love is worth a million; thou owest me thy love.

QUICKLY. Nay, my lord, he called you Jack, and said he would cudgel you.

FALSTAFF. Did I, Bardolph?

BARDOLPH. Indeed, Sir John, you said so.

FALSTAFF. Yea; if he said my ring was copper.

PRINCE. I say 'tis copper: darest thou be as good as thy word now?

FALSTAFF. Why, Hal, thou knowest, as thou art but man, I dare; but as thou art prince, I fear thee as I fear the roaring of the lion's whelp.

PRINCE. And why not as the lion?

FALSTAFF. The king himself is to be feared as the lion: dost thou think I'll fear thee as I fear thy father? nay, an I do, I pray God my girdle break!

PRINCE. O! if it should, how would thy guts fall about thy knees But, sirrah, there's no room for faith, truth, or honesty in this bosom of thine; it is all filled up with guts and midriff. Charge an honest woman with picking thy pocket! Why, thou whoreson, impudent, embossed rascal, if there were any thing in thy pocket but tavern reckonings, memorandums of bawdy-houses, and one poor pennyworth of sugar-candy to make thee long-winded; if thy pocket were enriched with any other injuries but these, I am a villain. And yet you will stand to it, you will not pocket up wrong. Art thou not ashamed?

FALSTAFF. Dost thou hear, Hal? thou knowest in the state of innocency Adam fell; and what should poor Jack Falstaff do in the days of villany? Thou seest I have more flesh than another man, and therefore more frailty. You confess then, you picked my pocket?

PRINCE. It appears so by the story.

FALSTAFF. Hostess, I forgive thee. Go make ready breakfast; love thy husband, look to thy servants, cherish thy guests: thou shalt find me tractable to any honest reason: thou seest I am pacified. Still! Nay prithee, be gone. (*Exit Mistress Quickly*) Now, Hal, to the news at court: for the robbery, lad, how is that answered?

PRINCE. O! my sweet beef, I must still be good angel to thee: the money is paid back again.

FALSTAFF. O! I do not like that paying back; 'tis a double labour.

PRINCE. I am good friends with my father and may do any
thing.

FALSTAFF. Rob me the exchequer the first thing thou dost,
and do it with unwashed hands too.

BARDOLPH. Do, my lord.

PRINCE. I have procured thee, Jack, a charge of foot.

FALSTAFF. I would it had been of horse. Where shall I find
one that can steal well? O! for a fine thief, of the age of
two-and-twenty, or thereabouts; I am heinously unpro-
vided. Well, God be thanked for these rebels; they offend
none but the virtuous: I laud them, I praise them.

PRINCE. Bardolph!

BARDOLPH. My lord?

PRINCE. Go bear this letter to Lord John of Lancaster,
To my brother John; this to my Lord of Westmoreland.
Go, Poins, to horse, to horse! for thou and I
Have thirty miles to ride ere dinner-time.
Jack, meet me to-morrow in the Temple-hall
At two o'clock in the afternoon:
There shalt thou know thy charge, and there receive
Money and order for their furniture.
The land is burning; Percy stands on high;
And either we or they must lower lie.
                    Exeunt the Prince, Poins, and Bardolph

FALSTAFF. Rare words! brave world! Hostess, my breakfast;
come!
   O! I could wish this tavern were my drum.   *Exit*

ACT FOUR

SCENE ONE

The Rebel Camp near Shrewsbury.

Enter Hotspur, Worcester, and Douglas

HOTSPUR. Well said, my noble Scot: if speaking truth
In this fine age were not thought flattery,
Such attribution should the Douglas have,
As not a soldier of this season's stamp
Should go so general current through the world.
By God, I cannot flatter; do defy
The tongues of soothers; but a braver place
In my heart's love hath no man than yourself.
Nay, task me to my word; approve me, lord.

DOUGLAS. Thou art the king of honour:
No man so potent breathes upon the ground
But I will beard him.

HOTSPUR.   Do so, and 'tis well.

Enter a Messenger, with letters

What letters hast thou there? (*To Douglas*) I can but
thank you.

MESSENGER. These letters come from your father.

HOTSPUR. Letters from him! why comes he not himself?

MESSENGER. He cannot come, my lord: he 's grievous sick.

HOTSPUR. 'Zounds! how has he the leisure to be sick
In such a justling time? Who leads his power?
Under whose government come they along?

MESSENGER. His letters bear his mind, not I, my lord.

WORCESTER. I prithee, tell me, doth he keep his bed?

MESSENGER. He did, my lord, four days ere I set forth;
And at the time of my departure thence
He was much fear'd by his physicians.

WORCESTER. I would the state of time had first been whole
Ere he by sickness had been visited:
His health was never better worth than now.

HOTSPUR. Sick now! droop now! this sickness doth infect
   The very life-blood of our enterprise;
   'Tis catching hither, even to our camp.
   He writes me here, that inward sickness——
   And that his friends by deputation could not
   So soon be drawn; nor did he think it meet
   To lay so dangerous and dear a trust
   On any soul remov'd but on his own.
   Yet doth he give us bold advertisement,
   That with our small conjunction we should on,
   To see how fortune is dispos'd to us;
   For, as he writes, there is no quailing now,
   Because the king is certainly possess'd
   Of all our purposes. What say you to it?
WORCESTER. Your father's sickness is a maim to us.
HOTSPUR. A perilous gash, a very limb lopp'd off:
   And yet, in faith, 'tis not; his present want
   Seems more than we shall find it. Were it good
   To set the exact wealth of all our states
   All at one cast? to set so rich a main
   On the nice hazard of one doubtful hour?
   It were not good; for therein should we read
   The very bottom and the soul of hope,
   The very list, the very utmost bound
   Of all our fortunes.
DOUGLAS.   Faith, and so we should;
   Where now remains a sweet reversion:
   We may boldly spend upon the hope of what
   Is to come in:
   A comfort of retirement lives in this.
HOTSPUR. A rendezvous, a home to fly unto,
   If that the devil and mischance look big
   Upon the maidenhead of our affairs.
WORCESTER. But yet, I would your father had been here.
   The quality and hair of our attempt
   Brooks no division. It will be thought
   By some, that know not why he is away,
   That wisdom, loyalty, and mere dislike
   Of our proceedings, kept the earl from hence.
   And think how such an apprehension
   May turn the tide of fearful faction
   And breed a king of question in our cause;

For well you know we of the offering side
Must keep aloof from strict arbitrement,
And stop all sight-holes, every loop from whence
The eye of reason may pry in upon us:
This absence of your father's draws a curtain,
That shows the ignorant a kind of fear
Before not dreamt of.

HOTSPUR.   You strain too far.
I rather of his absence make this use:
It lends a lustre and more great opinion,
A larger dare to our great enterprise,
Than if the earl were here; for men must think,
If we without his help can make a head
To push against the kingdom, with his help
We shall o'erturn it topsy-turvy down.
Yet all goes well, yet all our joints are whole.

DOUGLAS. As heart can think: there is not such a word
Spoke of in Scotland as this term of fear.

Enter Sir Richard Vernon

HOTSPUR. My cousin Vernon! welcome, by my soul.

VERNON. Pray God my news be worth a welcome, lord.
The Earl of Westmoreland, seven thousand strong,
Is marching hitherwards; with him Prince John.

HOTSPUR. No harm: what more?

VERNON.   And further, I have learn'd,
The king himself in person is set forth,
Or hitherwards intended speedily,
With strong and mighty preparation.

HOTSPUR. He shall be welcome too. Where is his son,
The nimble-footed madcap Prince of Wales,
And his comrades, that daff'd the world aside,
And bid it pass?

VERNON.   All furnish'd, all in arms,
All plum'd like estridges that wing the wind,
Baited like eagles having lately bath'd,
Glittering in golden coats, like images,
As full of spirit as the month of May,
And gorgeous as the sun at midsummer,
Wanton as youthful goats, wild as young bulls.
I saw young Harry, with his beaver on,
His cushes on his thighs, gallantly arm'd,
Rise from the ground like feather'd Mercury,

And vaulted with such ease into his seat,
As if an angel dropp'd down from the clouds,
To turn and wind a fiery Pegasus
And witch the world with noble horsemanship.

HOTSPUR. No more, no more: worse than the sun in March
This praise doth nourish agues. Let them come;
They come like sacrifices in their trim,
And to the fire-ey'd maid of smoky war
All hot and bleeding will we offer them:
The mailed Mars shall on his altar sit
Up to the ears in blood. I am on fire
To hear this rich reprisal is so nigh
And yet not ours. Come, let me taste my horse,
Who is to bear me like a thunderbolt
Against the bosom of the Prince of Wales:
Harry to Harry shall, hot horse to horse,
Meet and ne'er part till one drop down a corse.
O! that Glendower were come.

VERNON.   There is more news:
I learn'd in Worcester, as I rode along,
He cannot draw his power these fourteen days.

DOUGLAS. That's the worst tidings that I hear of yet.

WORCESTER. Ay, by my faith, that bears a frosty sound.

HOTSPUR. What may the king's whole battle reach unto?

VERNON. To thirty thousand.

HOTSPUR.   Forty let it be:
My father and Glendower being both away,
The powers of us may serve so great a day.
Come, let us take a muster speedily:
Doomsday is near; die all, die merrily.

DOUGLAS. Talk not of dying: I am out of fear
Of death or death's hand for this one half year.   *Exeunt*

SCENE TWO

A public Road near Coventry.

Enter Falstaff and Bardolph

FALSTAFF. Bardolph, get thee before to Coventry; fill me a
bottle of sack: our soldiers shall march through: we'll to
Sutton-Co'fil' to-night.

BARDOLPH. Will you give me money, captain?

FALSTAFF. Lay out, lay out.

BARDOLPH. This bottle makes an angel.

FALSTAFF. An if it do, take it for thy labour; and if it make twenty, take them all, I 'll answer the coinage. Bid my Lieutenant Peto meet me at the town's end.

BARDOLPH. I will, captain: farewell.   *Exit*

FALSTAFF. If I be not ashamed of my soldiers, I am a soused gurnet. I have misused the king's press damnably. I have got, in exchange of a hundred and fifty soldiers, three hundred and odd pounds. I press me none but good householders, yeomen's sons; inquire me out contracted bachelors, such as had been asked twice on the banns; such a commodity of warm slaves, as had as lief hear the devil as a drum; such as fear the report of a caliver worse than a struck fowl or a hurt wild-duck. I pressed me none but such toasts-and-butter, with hearts in their bellies no bigger than pins' heads, and they have bought out their services; and now my whole charge consists of ancients, corporals, lieutenants, gentlemen of companies, slaves as ragged as Lazarus in the painted cloth, where the glutton's dogs licked his sores; and such as indeed were never soldiers, but discarded unjust serving-men, younger sons to younger brothers, revolted tapsters and ostlers trade-fallen, the cankers of a calm world and a long peace; ten times more dishonorable ragged than an old faced ancient: and such have I, to fill up the rooms of them that have bought out their services, that you would think that I had a hundred and fifty tattered prodigals, lately come from swine-keeping, from eating draff and husks. A mad fellow met me on the way and told me I had unloaded all the gibbets and pressed the dead bodies. No eye hath seen such scarecrows. I 'll not march through Coventry with them, that 's flat: nay, and the villains march wide betwixt the legs, as if they had gyves on; for, indeed I had the most of them out of prison. There 's but a shirt and a half in all my company; and the half shirt is two napkins tacked together and thrown over the shoulders like a herald's coat without sleeves; and the shirt, to say the truth, stolen from my host at Saint Alban's, or the red-nose innkeeper of Daventry. But that 's all one; they 'll find linen enough on every hedge.

Enter the Prince and Westmoreland

PRINCE. How now, blown Jack! how now, quilt!

FALSTAFF. What, Hal! How now, mad wag! what a devil
dost thou in Warwickshire? My good Lord of Westmore-
land, I cry you mercy: I thought your honour had already
been at Shrewsbury.

WESTMORELAND. Faith, Sir John, 'tis more than time that I
were there, and you too; but my powers are there already.
The king, I can tell you, looks for us all: we must away all
night.

FALSTAFF. Tut, never fear me: I am as vigilant as a cat to
steal cream.

PRINCE. I think to steal cream indeed, for thy theft hath al-
ready made thee butter. But tell me, Jack, whose fellows
are these that come after?

FALSTAFF. Mine, Hal, mine.

PRINCE. I did never see such pitiful rascals.

FALSTAFF. Tut, tut; good enough to toss; food for powder,
food for powder; they 'll fill a pit as well as better: tush,
man, mortal men, mortal men.

WESTMORELAND. Ay, but, Sir John, methinks they are ex-
ceeding poor and bare; too beggarly.

FALSTAFF. Faith, for their poverty, I know not where they
had that; and for their bareness, I am sure they never
learned that of me.

PRINCE. No, I 'll be sworn; unless you call three fingers on
the ribs bare. But sirrah, make haste: Percy is already in
the field.

FALSTAFF. What, is the king encamped?

WESTMORELAND. He is, Sir John: I fear we shall stay too
long.

FALSTAFF. Well,
To the latter end of a fray and the beginning of a feast
Fits a dull fighter and a keen guest.　　　　　*Exeunt*

SCENE THREE

The Rebel Camp near Shrewsbury.

Enter Hotspur, Worcester, Douglas, and Vernon

HOTSPUR. We 'll fight with him to-night.

WORCESTER.   It may not be.

DOUGLAS. You give him then advantage.

VERNON.   Not a whit.

HOTSPUR. Why say you so? looks he not for supply?

VERNON. So do we.

HOTSPUR.   His is certain, ours is doubtful.

WORCESTER. Good cousin, be advis'd: stir not to-night.

VERNON. Do not, my lord.

DOUGLAS.   You do not counsel well:
  You speak it out of fear and cold heart.

VERNON. Do me no slander, Douglas: by my life,—
  And I dare well maintain it with my life,—
  If well-respected honour bid me on,
  I hold as little counsel with weak fear
  As you, my lord, or any Scot that this day lives:
  Let it be seen to-morrow in the battle
  Which of us fears.

DOUGLAS.   Yea, or to-night.

VERNON.   Content.

HOTSPUR. To-night, say I.

VERNON. Come, come, it may not be. I wonder much,
  Being men of such great leading as you are,
  That you foresee not what impediments
  Drag back our expedition: certain horse
  Of my cousin Vernon's are not yet come up:
  Your uncle Worcester's horse came but to-day;
  And now their pride and mettle is asleep,
  Their courage with hard labour tame and dull,
  That not a horse is half the half of himself.

HOTSPUR. So are the horses of the enemy
  In general, journey-bated and brought low:
  The better part of ours are full of rest.

WORCESTER. The number of the king exceedeth ours:
  For God's sake, cousin, stay till all come in.

                        The trumpet sounds a parley

Enter Sir Walter Blunt

BLUNT. I come with gracious offers from the king,
If you vouchsafe me hearing and respect.
HOTSPUR. Welcome, Sir Walter Blunt; and would to God
You were of our determination!
Some of us love you well; and even those some
Envy your great deservings and good name,
Because you are not of our quality,
But stand against us like an enemy.
BLUNT. And God defend but still I should stand so,
So long as out of limit and true rule
You stand against anointed majesty.
But, to my charge. The king hath sent to know
The nature of your griefs, and whereupon
You conjure from the breast of civil peace
Such bold hostility, teaching his duteous land
Audacious cruelty. If that the king
Have any way your good deserts forgot,—
Which he confesseth to be manifold,—
He bids you name your griefs; and with all speed
You shall have your desires with interest,
And pardon absolute for yourself and these
Herein misled by your suggestion.
HOTSPUR. The king is kind; and well we know the king
Knows at what time to promise, when to pay.
My father and my uncle and myself
Did give him that same royalty he wears;
And when he was not six-and-twenty strong,
Sick in the world's regard, wretched and low,
A poor unminded outlaw sneaking home,
My father gave him welcome to the shore;
And when he heard him swear and vow to God
He came but to be Duke of Lancaster,
To sue his livery and beg his peace,
With tears of innocency and terms of zeal,
My father, in kind heart and pity mov'd,
Swore him assistance and perform'd it too.
Now when the lords and barons of the realm
Perceiv'd Northumberland did lean to him,
The more and less came in with cap and knee;
Met him in boroughs, cities, villages,
Attended him on bridges, stood in lanes,

Laid gifts before him, proffer'd him their oaths,
Gave him their heirs as pages, follow'd him
Even at the heels in golden multitudes.
He presently, as greatness knows itself,
Steps me a little higher than his vow
Made to my father, while his blood was poor,
Upon the naked shore at Ravenspurgh;
And now, forsooth, takes on him to reform
Some certain edicts and some strait decrees
That lie too heavy on the commonwealth,
Cries out upon abuses, seems to weep
Over his country's wrongs; and by this face,
This seeming brow of justice, did he win
The hearts of all that he did angle for;
Proceeded further; cut me off the heads
Of all the favourites that the absent king
In deputation left behind him here,
When he was personal in the Irish war.

BLUNT. Tut, I came not to hear this.

HOTSPUR.   Then to the point.
In short time after, he depos'd the king;
Soon after that, depriv'd him of his life;
And, in the neck of that, task'd the whole state;
To make that worse, suffer'd his kinsman March—
Who is, if every owner were well plac'd,
Indeed his king—to be engag'd in Wales,
There without ransom to lie forfeited;
Disgrac'd me in my happy victories;
Sought to entrap me by intelligence;
Rated my uncle from the council-board;
In rage dismiss'd my father from the court;
Broke oath on oath, committed wrong on wrong;
And in conclusion drove us to seek out
This head of safety; and withal to pry
Into his title, the which we find
Too indirect for long continuance.

BLUNT. Shall I return this answer to the king?

HOTSPUR. Not so, Sir Walter: we 'll withdraw awhile.
Go to the king; and let there be impawn'd
Some surety for a safe return again,
And in the morning early shall my uncle
Bring him our purposes; and so farewell.

BLUNT. I would you would accept of grace and love.
HOTSPUR. And may be so we shall.
BLUNT.   Pray God, you do!

Exeunt

SCENE FOUR

York. A Room in the Archbishop's Palace.

Enter the Archbishop of York and Sir Michael

ARCHBISHOP. Hie, good Sir Michael; bear this sealed brief
  With winged haste to the Lord Marshal;
  This to my cousin Scroop, and all the rest
  To whom they are directed. If you knew
  How much they do import, you would make haste.
SIR MICHAEL. My good lord,
  I guess their tenour.
ARCHBISHOP.   Like enough you do.
  To-morrow, good Sir Michael, is a day
  Wherein the fortune of ten thousand men
  Must bide the touch; for, sir, at Shrewsbury,
  As I am truly given to understand,
  The king with mighty and quick-raised power
  Meets with Lord Harry: and, I fear, Sir Michael,
  What with the sickness of Northumberland,—
  Whose power was in the first proportion,—
  And what with Owen Glendower's absence thence,
  Who with them was a rated sinew too,
  And comes not in, o'er-rul'd by prophecies,—
  I fear the power of Percy is too weak
  To wage an instant trial with the king.
SIR MICHAEL. Why, my good lord, you need not fear:
  There is the Douglas and Lord Mortimer.
ARCHBISHOP. No, Mortimer is not there.
SIR MICHAEL. But there is Mordake, Vernon, Lord Harry
      Percy,
  And there's my Lord of Worcester, and a head
  Of gallant warriors, noble gentlemen.
ARCHBISHOP. And so there is; but yet the king hath drawn
  The special head of all the land together:
  The Prince of Wales, Lord John of Lancaster,

The noble Westmoreland, and warlike Blunt;
And many moe corrivals and dear men
Of estimation and command in arms.
SIR MICHAEL. Doubt not, my lord, they shall be well
    oppos'd.
ARCHBISHOP. I hope no less, yet needful 'tis to fear;
And, to prevent the worst, Sir Michael, speed:
For if Lord Percy thrive not, ere the king
Dismiss his power, he means to visit us,
For he hath heard of our confederacy,
And 'tis but wisdom to make strong against him:
Therefore make haste. I must go write again
To other friends; and so farewell, Sir Michael.   *Exeunt*

ACT FIVE

SCENE ONE

The King's Camp near Shrewsbury.

Enter King Henry, the Prince, John of Lancaster, Sir Walter Blunt, and Sir John Falstaff

KING HENRY. How bloodily the sun begins to peer
Above yon busky hill! the day looks pale
At his distemperature.
PRINCE.   The southern wind
Doth play the trumpet to his purposes,
And by his hollow whistling in the leaves
Foretells a tempest and a blustering day.
KING HENRY. Then with the losers let it sympathize,
For nothing can seem foul to those that win.

Trumpet sounds

Enter Worcester and Vernon

How now, my Lord of Worcester! 'tis not well
That you and I should meet upon such terms
As now we meet. You have deceiv'd our trust,
And made us doff our easy robes of peace,
To crush our old limbs in ungentle steel:
This is not well, my lord; this is not well.
What say you to it? will you again unknit
This churlish knot of all-abhorred war,
And move in that obedient orb again
Where you did give a fair and natural light,
And be no more an exhal'd meteor,
A prodigy of fear and a portent
Of broached mischief to the unborn times?
WORCESTER. Hear me, my liege.
For mine own part, I could be well content
To entertain the lag-end of my life
With quiet hours; for I do protest
I have not sought the day of this dislike.

KING HENRY. You have not sought it! how comes it, then?

FALSTAFF. Rebellion lay in his way, and he found it.

PRINCE. Peace, chewet, peace!

WORCESTER. It pleas'd your Majesty to turn your looks
Of favour from myself and all our house;
And yet I must remember you, my lord,
We were the first and dearest of your friends.
For you my staff of office did I break
In Richard's time; and posted day and night
To meet you on the way, and kiss your hand,
When yet you were in place and in account
Nothing so strong and fortunate as I.
It was myself, my brother, and his son,
That brought you home and boldly did outdare
The dangers of the time. You swore to us,
And you did swear that oath at Doncaster,
That you did nothing purpose 'gainst the state,
Nor claim no further than your new-fall'n right,
The seat of Gaunt, dukedom of Lancaster.
To this we swore our aid: but, in short space
It rain'd down fortune showering on your head,
And such a flood of greatness fell on you,
What with our help, what with the absent king,
What with the injuries of a wanton time,
The seeming sufferances that you had borne,
And the contrarious winds that held the king
So long in his unlucky Irish wars,
That all in England did repute him dead:
And from this swarm of fair advantages
You took occasion to be quickly woo'd
To gripe the general sway into your hand;
Forgot your oath to us at Doncaster;
And being fed by us you us'd us so
As that ungentle gull, the cuckoo's bird,
Useth the sparrow: did oppress our nest,
Grew by our feeding to so great a bulk
That even our love durst not come near your sight
For fear of swallowing; but with nimble wing
We were enforc'd, for safety's sake, to fly
Out of your sight and raise this present head;
Whereby we stand opposed by such means
As you yourself have forg'd against yourself

By unkind usage, dangerous countenance,
And violation of all faith and troth
Sworn to us in your younger enterprise.

KING HENRY. These things indeed you have articulate,
Proclaim'd at market-crosses, read in churches,
To face the garment of rebellion
With some fine colour that may please the eye
Of fickle changelings and poor discontents,
Which gape and rub the elbow at the news
Of hurlyburly innovation:
And never yet did insurrection want
Such water-colours to impaint his cause;
Nor moody beggars, starving for a time
Of pellmell havoc and confusion.

PRINCE. In both our armies there is many a soul
Shall pay full dearly for this encounter,
If once they join in trial. Tell your nephew,
The Prince of Wales doth join with all the world
In praise of Henry Percy: by my hopes,
This present enterprise set off his head,
I do not think a braver gentleman,
More active-valiant or more valiant-young,
More daring or more bold, is now alive
To grace this latter age with noble deeds.
For my part, I may speak it to my shame,
I have a truant been to chivalry;
And so I hear he doth account me too;
Yet this before my father's Majesty—
I am content that he shall take the odds
Of his great name and estimation,
And will, to save the blood on either side,
Try fortune with him in a single fight.

KING HENRY. And, Prince of Wales, so dare we venture thee,
Albeit considerations infinite
Do make against it. No, good Worcester, no,
We love our people well; even those we love
That are misled upon your cousin's part;
And, will they take the offer of our grace,
Both he and they and you, yea, every man
Shall be my friend again, and I'll be his.
So tell your cousin, and bring me word
What he will do; but if he will not yield,

Rebuke and dread correction wait on us,
And they shall do their office. So, be gone:
We will not now be troubled with reply;
We offer fair, take it advisedly.

Exeunt Worcester and Vernon

PRINCE. It will not be accepted, on my life.
The Douglas and the Hotspur both together
Are confident against the world in arms.

KING HENRY. Hence, therefore, every leader to his charge;
For, on their answer, will we set on them;
And God befriend us, as our cause is just!

Exeunt King Henry, Blunt, and John of Lancaster

FALSTAFF. Hal, if thou see me down in the battle, and be-
stride me, so; 'tis a point of friendship.

PRINCE. Nothing but a colossus can do thee that friendship.
Say thy prayers, and farewell.

FALSTAFF. I would it were bed-time, Hal, and all well.

PRINCE. Why, thou owest God a death.   *Exit*

FALSTAFF. 'Tis not due yet: I would be loath to pay him
before his day. What need I be so forward with him that
calls not on me? Well, 'tis no matter; honour pricks me on.
Yea, but how if honour prick me off when I come on? how
then? Can honour set to a leg? No. Or an arm? No. Or take
away the grief of a wound? No. Honour hath no skill in
surgery then? No. What is honour? a word. What is that
word, honour? Air. A trim reckoning! Who hath it? he that
died o' Wednesday. Doth he feel it? No. Doth he hear it?
No. It is insensible, then? Yea, to the dead. But will it not
live with the living? No. Why? Detraction will not suffer
it. Therefore I 'll none of it: honour is a mere scutcheon;
and so ends my catechism.   *Exit*

SCENE TWO

The Rebel Camp near Shrewsbury.

Enter Worcester and Vernon

WORCESTER. Oh, no! my nephew must not know, Sir
    Richard,
The liberal kind offer of the king.

VERNON. 'Twere best he did.

WORCESTER.　　　　　　　　Then are we all undone.

　It is not possible, it cannot be,
The king should keep his word in loving us;
He will suspect us still, and find a time
To punish this offence in other faults:
Suspicion all our lives shall be stuck full of eyes;
For treason is but trusted like the fox,
Who, ne'er so tame, so cherish'd, and lock'd up,
Will have a wild trick of his ancestors.
Look how we can, or sad or merrily,
Interpretation will misquote our looks,
And we shall feed like oxen at a stall,
The better cherish'd, still the nearer death.
My nephew's trespass may be well forgot,
It hath the excuse of youth and heat of blood;
And an adopted name of privilege,
A hare-brain'd Hotspur, govern'd by a spleen.
All his offences live upon my head
And on his father's: we did train him on;
And, his corruption being ta'en from us,
We, as the spring of all, shall pay for all.
Therefore, good cousin, let not Harry know
In any case the offer of the king.

VERNON.　Deliver what you will, I 'll say 'tis so.
　Here comes your cousin.

　Enter Hotspur and Douglas; Officers and Soldiers behind

HOTSPUR.　My uncle is return'd: deliver up
　My Lord of Westmoreland. Uncle, what news?

WORCESTER.　The king will bid you battle presently.

DOUGLAS.　Defy him by the Lord of Westmoreland.

HOTSPUR.　Lord Douglas, go you and tell him so.

DOUGLAS.　Marry, and shall, and very willingly.　　　　*Exit*

WORCESTER.　There is no seeming mercy in the king.

HOTSPUR.　Did you beg any? God forbid!

WORCESTER.　I told him gently of our grievances,
　Of his oath-breaking; which he mended thus,
　By now forswearing that he is forsworn:
　He calls us rebels, traitors; and will scourge
　With haughty arms this hateful name in us.

　Re-enter Douglas

DOUGLAS.　Arm, gentlemen! to arms! for I have thrown
　A brave defiance in King Henry's teeth,

And Westmoreland, that was engag'd, did bear it;
Which cannot choose but bring him quickly on.

WORCESTER. The Prince of Wales stepp'd forth before the
    king,
And, nephew, challeng'd you to single fight.

HOTSPUR. O! would the quarrel lay upon our heads,
And that no man might draw short breath to-day
But I and Harry Monmouth. Tell me, tell me,
How show'd his tasking? seem'd it in contempt?

VERNON. No, by my soul; I never in my life
Did hear a challenge urg'd more modestly,
Unless a brother should a brother dare
To gentle exercise and proof of arms.
He gave you all the duties of a man,
Trimm'd up your praises with a princely tongue,
Spoke your deservings like a chronicle,
Making you ever better than his praise,
By still dispraising praise valu'd with you;
And, which became him like a prince indeed,
He made a blushing cital of himself,
And chid his truant youth with such a grace
As if he master'd there a double spirit
Of teaching and of learning instantly.
There did he pause. But let me tell the world,
If he outlive the envy of this day,
England did never owe so sweet a hope,
So much miscontru'd in his watonness.

HOTSPUR. Cousin, I think thou art enamoured
On his follies: never did I hear
Of any prince so wild a libertine.
But be he as he will, yet once ere night
I will embrace him with a soldier's arm,
That he shall shrink under my courtesy.
Arm, arm, with speed! And, fellows, soldiers, friends,
Better consider what you have to do,
Than I, that have not well the gift of tongue,
Can lift your blood up with persuasion.

Enter a Messenger

MESSENGER. My lord, here are letters for you.

HOTSPUR. I cannot read them now.
O gentlemen! the time of life is short;
To spend that shortness basely were too long,

If life did ride upon a dial's point,
Still ending at the arrival of an hour.
An if we live, we live to tread on kings;
If die, brave death, when princes die with us!
Now, for our consciences, the arms are fair,
When the intent of bearing them is just.

Enter another Messenger

MESSENGER. My lord, prepare; the king comes on apace.
HOTSPUR. I thank him that he cuts me from my tale,
For I profess not talking. Only this,—
Let each man do his best: and here draw I
A sword, whose temper I intend to stain
With the best blood that I can meet withal
In the adventure of this perilous day.
Now, Esperance! Percy! and set on.
Sound all the lofty instruments of war,
And by that music let us all embrace;
For, heaven to earth, some of us never shall
A second time do such a courtesy.

The trumpets sound. They embrace, and exeunt

SCENE THREE

Between the Camps.

*Excursions and Parties fighting. Alarum to the Battle. Then
enter Douglas and Sir Walter Blunt, meeting*

BLUNT. What is thy name, that in the battle thus
Thou crossest me? what honour dost thou seek
Upon my head?
DOUGLAS.   Know then, my name is Douglas;
And I do haunt thee in the battle thus
Because some tell me that thou art a king.
BLUNT. They tell thee true.
DOUGLAS. The Lord of Stafford dear to-day hath bought
Thy likeness; for, instead of thee, King Harry,
This sword hath ended him: so shall it thee,
Unless thou yield thee as my prisoner.
BLUNT. I was not born a yielder, thou proud Scot;
And thou shalt find a king that will revenge
Lord Stafford's death.   *They fight, and Blunt is slain*

Enter Hotspur

HOTSPUR. O, Douglas! hadst thou fought at Holmedon thus,
I never had triumph'd upon a Scot.

DOUGLAS. All 's done, all 's won: here breathless lies the
king.

HOTSPUR. Where?

DOUGLAS. Here.

HOTSPUR. This, Douglas! no; I know this face full well;
A gallant knight he was, his name was Blunt;
Semblably furnish'd like the king himself.

DOUGLAS. A fool go with thy soul, whither it goes!
A borrow'd title hast thou bought too dear:
Why didst thou tell me that thou wert a king?

HOTSPUR. The king hath many marching in his coats.

DOUGLAS. Now, by my sword, I will kill all his coats;
I 'll murder all his wardrobe, piece by piece,
Until I meet the king.

HOTSPUR.   Up, and away!
Our soldiers stand full fairly for the day.   *Exeunt*

Alarums. Enter Falstaff

FALSTAFF. Though I could 'scape shot-free at London, I
fear the shot here; here 's no scoring but upon the pate.
Soft! who art thou? Sir Walter Blunt: there 's honour for
you! here 's no vanity! I am as hot as molten lead, and as
heavy too: God keep lead out of me! I need no more
weight than mine own bowels. I have led my ragamuffins
where they are peppered: there 's not three of my hun-
dred and fifty left alive, and they are for the town's end,
to beg during life. But who comes here?

Enter the Prince

PRINCE. What! stand'st thou idle here? lend me thy sword:
Many a nobleman lies stark and stiff
Under the hoofs of vaunting enemies,
Whose deaths are unreveng'd: prithee, lend me thy
sword.

FALSTAFF. O Hal! I prithee, give me leave to breathe awhile.
Turk Gregory never did such deeds in arms as I have done
this day. I have paid Percy, I have made him sure.

PRINCE. He is, indeed; and living to kill thee. I prithee, lend
me thy sword.

FALSTAFF. Nay, before God, Hal, if Percy be alive, thou
gett'st not my sword; but take my pistol, if thou wilt.

PRINCE. Give it me. What! is it in the case?

FALSTAFF. Ay, Hal; 'tis hot, 'tis hot: there 's that will sack
a city.   *The Prince draws out a bottle of sack*

PRINCE. What! is 't a time to jest and dally now?
                    Throws it at him, and exit

FALSTAFF. Well, if Percy be alive, I 'll pierce him. If he do
come in my way, so: if he do not, if I come in his willingly,
let him make a carbonado of me. I like not such grinning
honour as Sir Walter hath: give me life; which if I can
save, so; if not, honour comes unlooked for, and there 's an
end.   *Exit*

SCENE FOUR

Another Part of the Field.

*Alarums. Excursions. Enter King Henry, the Prince, John
of Lancaster, and Westmoreland*

KING HENRY. I prithee,
Harry, withdraw thyself; thou bleed'st too much.
Lord John of Lancaster, go you with him.

LANCASTER. Not I, my lord, unless I did bleed too.

PRINCE. I beseech your Majesty, make up,
Lest your retirement do amaze your friends.

KING HENRY. I will do so.
My lord of Westmoreland, lead him to his tent.

WESTMORELAND. Come, my lord, I 'll lead you to your tent.

PRINCE. Lead me, my lord? I do not need your help:
And God forbid a shallow scratch should drive
The Prince of Wales from such a field as this,
Where stain'd nobility lies trodden on,
And rebels' arms triumph in massacres!

LANCASTER. We breathe too long: come, cousin Westmore-
land,
Our duty this way lies: for God's sake, come.
                Exeunt John of Lancaster and Westmoreland

PRINCE. By God, thou hast deceiv'd me, Lancaster;
I did not think thee lord of such a spirit:
Before, I lov'd thee as a brother, John;
But now, I do respect thee as my soul.

KING HENRY. I saw him hold Lord Percy at the point

With lustier maintenance than I did look for
Of such an ungrown warrior.

PRINCE.   O! this boy
Lends mettle to us all.   *Exit*

Alarums. Enter Douglas

DOUGLAS. Another king! they grow like Hydra's heads:
I am the Douglas, fatal to all those
That wear those colours on them: what art thou,
That counterfeit'st the person of a king?

KING HENRY. The king himself; who, Douglas, grieves at
    heart
So many of his shadows thou hast met
And not the very king. I have two boys
Seek Percy and thyself about the field:
But, seeing thou fall'st on me so luckily,
I will assay thee; so defend thyself.

DOUGLAS. I fear thou art another counterfeit;
And yet, in faith, thou bear'st thee like a king:
But mine I am sure thou art, whoe'er thou be,
And thus I win thee.

They fight. King Henry being in danger, re-enter the Prince

PRINCE. Hold up thy head, vile Scot, or thou art like
Never to hold it up again! the spirits
Of valiant Shirley, Stafford, Blunt, are in my arms:
It is the Prince of Wales that threatens thee,
Who never promiseth but he means to pay.

                              They fight: Douglas flies

Cheerly, my lord: how fares your Grace?
Sir Nicholas Gawsey hath for succour sent,
And so hath Clifton: I 'll to Clifton straight.

KING HENRY. Stay, and breathe awhile.
Thou hast redeem'd thy lost opinion,
And show'd thou mak'st some tender of my life,
In this fair rescue thou hast brought to me.

PRINCE. O God! they did me too much injury
That ever said I hearken'd for your death.
If it were so, I might have let alone
The insulting hand of Douglas over you;
Which would have been as speedy in your end
As all the poisonous potions in the world,
And sav'd the treacherous labour of your son.

KING HENRY. Make up to Clifton: I 'll to Sir Nicholas
 Gawsey.   *Exit*

Enter Hotspur

HOTSPUR. If I mistake not, thou art Harry Monmouth.
PRINCE. Thou speak'st as if I would deny my name.
HOTSPUR. My name is Harry Percy.
PRINCE.   Why, then, I see
 A very valiant rebel of that name.
 I am the Prince of Wales; and think not, Percy,
 To share with me in glory any more:
 Two stars keep not their motion in one sphere;
 Nor can one England brook a double reign,
 Of Harry Percy and the Prince of Wales.
HOTSPUR. Nor shall it, Harry; for the hour is come
 To end the one of us; and would to God
 Thy name in arms were now as great as mine!
PRINCE. I 'll make it greater ere I part from thee;
 And all the budding honours on thy crest
 I 'll crop, to make a garland for my head.
HOTSPUR. I can no longer brook thy vanities. *They fight*

Enter Falstaff

FALSTAFF. Well said, Hal! to it, Hal! Nay, you shall find no
 boy's play here, I can tell you.

Re-enter Douglas; he fights with
Falstaff, who falls down as if he were dead, and exit Douglas.
Hotspur is wounded, and falls

HOTSPUR. O, Harry! thou hast robb'd me of my youth.
 I better brook the loss of brittle life
 Than those proud titles thou hast won of me;
 They wound my thoughts worse than thy sword my flesh:
 But thought 's the slave of life, and life time's fool;
 And time, that takes survey of all the world,
 Must have a stop. O! I could prophesy,
 But that the earthy and cold hand of death
 Lies on my tongue. No, Percy, thou art dust,
 And food for—   *Dies*
PRINCE. For worms, brave Percy. Fare thee well, great
 heart!
 Ill-weav'd ambition, how much art thou shrunk!
 When that this body did contain a spirit,
 A kingdom for it was too small a bound;

But now, two paces of the vilest earth
Is room enough: this earth, that bears thee dead,
Bears not alive so stout a gentleman.
If thou wert sensible of courtesy,
I should not make so dear a show of zeal:
But let my favours hide thy mangled face,
And, even in thy behalf, I 'll thank myself
For doing these fair rites of tenderness.
Adieu, and take thy praise with thee to heaven!
Thy ignominy sleep with thee in the grave,
But not remember'd in thy epitaph!

He spies Falstaff on the ground

What! old acquaintance! could not all this flesh
Keep in a little life? Poor Jack, farewell!
I could have better spar'd a better man.
O! I should have a heavy miss of thee
If I were much in love with vanity.
Death hath not struck so fat a deer to-day,
Though many dearer, in this bloody fray.
Embowell'd will I see thee by and by:
Till then in blood by noble Percy lie.   *Exit*

FALSTAFF. (*Rising*) Embowelled! if thou embowel me to-
day, I 'll give you leave to powder me and eat me too,
to-morrow. 'Sblood! 'twas time to counterfeit, or that hot
termagant Scot had paid me scot and lot too. Counterfeit?
I lie, I am no counterfeit: to die, is to be a counterfeit; for
he is but the counterfeit of a man, who hath not the life
of a man; but to counterfeit dying, when a man thereby
liveth, is to be no counterfeit, but the true and perfect
image of life indeed. The better part of valour is discre-
tion; in the which better part, I have saved my life.
'Zounds! I am afraid of this gunpowder Percy though he
be dead: how, if he should counterfeit too and rise? By my
faith, I am afraid he would prove the better counterfeit.
Therefore I 'll make him sure; yea, and I 'll swear I killed
him. Why may not he rise as well as I? Nothing confutes
me but eyes, and nobody sees me: therefore, sirrah (*stab-
bing him*), with a new wound in your thigh come you
along with me.   *He takes Hotspur on his back*
          Re-enter the Prince and John of Lancaster

PRINCE. Come, brother John; full bravely hast thou flesh'd
Thy maiden sword.

LANCASTER.   But, soft! whom have we here?
Did you not tell me this fat man was dead?
PRINCE. I did; I saw him dead,   •
Breathless and bleeding on the ground.
Art thou alive? or is it fantasy
That plays upon our eyesight? I prithee, speak;
We will not trust our eyes without our ears:
Thou art not what thou seem'st.
FALSTAFF. No, that 's certain; I am not a double man: but
if I be not Jack Falstaff, then am I a Jack. There is Percy
(*throwing the body down*): if your father will do me any
honour, so; if not, let him kill the next Percy himself. I
look to be either earl or duke, I can assure you.
PRINCE. Why, Percy I killed myself, and saw thee dead.
FALSTAFF. Didst thou? Lord, lord! how this world is given
to lying. I grant you I was down and out of breath, and so
was he; but we rose both at an instant, and fought a long
hour by Shrewsbury clock. If I may be believed, so; if not,
let them that should reward valour bear the sin upon their
own heads. I 'll take it upon my death, I gave him this
wound in the thigh: if the man were alive and would deny
it, 'zounds, I would make him eat a piece of my sword.
LANCASTER. This is the strangest tale that e'er I heard.
PRINCE. This is the strangest fellow, brother John.
Come, bring your luggage nobly on your back:
For my part, if a lie may do thee grace,
I 'll gild it with the happiest terms I have.
                              A retreat is sounded
The trumpet sounds retreat; the day is ours.
Come, brother, let us to the highest of the field,
To see what friends are living, who are dead.
                    Exeunt the Prince and John of Lancaster
FALSTAFF. I 'll follow, as they say, for reward. He that re-
wards me, God reward him! If I do grow great, I 'll grow
less; for I 'll purge, and leave sack, and live cleanly, as a
nobleman should do.   *Exit*

SCENE FIVE

Another Part of the Field.

The trumpets sound. Enter King Henry, the Prince,
John of Lancaster, Westmoreland, and Others, with
Worcester and Vernon prisoners

KING HENRY. Thus ever did rebellion find rebuke.
Ill-spirited Worcester! did we not send grace,
Pardon, and terms of love to all of you?
And wouldst thou turn our offers contrary?
Misuse the tenour of thy kinsman's trust?
Three knights upon our party slain to-day,
A noble earl and many a creature else
Had been alive this hour,
If like a Christian thou hadst truly borne
Betwixt our armies true intelligence.
WORCESTER. What I have done my safety urg'd me to;
And I embrace this fortune patiently,
Since not to be avoided it falls on me.
KING HENRY. Bear Worcester to the death and Vernon too:
Other offenders we will pause upon.
                    Exeunt Worcester and Vernon, guarded
How goes the field?
PRINCE. The noble Scot, Lord Douglas, when he saw
The fortune of the day quite turn'd from him,
The noble Percy slain, and all his men
Upon the foot of fear, fled with the rest;
And falling from a hill he was so bruis'd
That the pursuers took him. At my tent
The Douglas is, and I beseech your Grace
I may dispose of him.
KING HENRY.   With all my heart.
PRINCE. Then, brother John of Lancaster, to you
This honourable bounty shall belong.
Go to the Douglas, and deliver him
Up to his pleasure, ransomless, and free:
His valour shown upon our crests to-day
Hath taught us how to cherish such high deeds,
Even in the bosom of our adversaries.

LANCASTER. I thank your Grace for this high courtesy,
Which I shall give away immediately.
KING HENRY. Then this remains, that we divide our power.
You, son John, and my cousin Westmoreland
Towards York shall bend you with your dearest speed,
To meet Northumberland and the prelate Scroop,
Who, as we hear, are busily in arms:
Myself and you, son Harry, will towards Wales,
To fight with Glendower and the Earl of March.
Rebellion in this land shall lose his sway,
Meeting the check of such another day:
And since this business so fair is done,
Let us not leave till all our own be won.   *Exeunt*

THE SECOND PART OF KING HENRY THE FOURTH

(*continued on next page*)

SHALLOW *and* SILENCE, *Country Justices*
DAVY, *Servant to Shallow*
MOULDY, SHADOW, WART, FEEBLE, *and* BULLCALF,
 Recruits
FANG *and* SNARE, *Sheriff's Officers*
A Porter
A Dancer, Speaker of the Epilogue

LADY NORTHUMBERLAND
LADY PERCY
MISTRESS QUICKLY, *Hostess of a tavern in East-
 cheap*
DOLL TEARSHEET

Lords and Attendants; Officers, Soldiers, Messenger,
Drawers, Beadles, Grooms, &c.

SCENE
England

INDUCTION

Warkworth. Before Northumberland's Castle.

Enter Rumour, painted full of tongues

RUMOUR. Open your ears; for which of you will stop
  The vent of hearing when loud Rumour speaks?
  I, from the Orient to the drooping West,
  Making the wind my post-horse, still unfold
  The acts commenced on this ball of earth:
  Upon my tongues continual slanders ride,
  The which in every language I pronounce,
  Stuffing the ears of men with false reports.
  I speak of peace, while covert enmity
  Under the smile of safety wounds the world:
  And who but Rumour, who but only I,
  Make fearful musters and prepar'd defence,
  Whilst the big year, swoln with some other grief
  Is thought with child by the stern tyrant war,
  And no such matter? Rumour is a pipe
  Blown by surmises, jealousies, conjectures,
  And of so easy and so plain a stop
  That the blunt monster with uncounted heads,
  The still-discordant wavering multitude,
  Can play upon it. But what need I thus
  My well-known body to anatomize
  Among my household? Why is Rumour here?
  I run before King Harry's victory;
  Who in a bloody field by Shrewsbury
  Hath beaten down young Hotspur and his troops,
  Quenching the flame of bold rebellion
  Even with the rebels' blood. But what mean I
  To speak so true at first? my office is
  To noise abroad that Harry Monmouth fell
  Under the wrath of noble Hotspur's sword,

And that the king before the Douglas' rage
Stoop'd his anointed head as low as death.
This have I rumour'd through the peasant towns
Between the royal field of Shrewsbury
And this worm-eaten hold of ragged stone,
Where Hotspur's father, old Northumberland,
Lies crafty-sick. The posts come tiring on,
And not a man of them brings other news
Than they have learn'd of me: from Rumour's tongues
They bring smooth comforts false, worse than true
 wrongs.   *Exit*

THE SECOND PART OF KING HENRY THE FOURTH

ACT ONE

SCENE ONE

Warkworth. Before Northumberland's Castle.

Enter Lord Bardolph

LORD BARDOLPH. Who keeps the gate here? ho!
                          The Porter opens the gate
                             Where is the earl?
PORTER. What shall I say you are?
LORD BARDOLPH.   Tell thou the earl
  That the Lord Bardolph doth attend him here.
PORTER. His lordship is walk'd forth into the orchard:
  Please it your honour knock but at the gate,
  And he himself will answer.
           Enter Northumberland
LORD BARDOLPH.   Here comes the earl.
                            Exit Porter
NORTHUMBERLAND. What news, Lord Bardolph? every min-
  ute now
  Should be the father of some stratagem.
  The times are wild; contention, like a horse
  Full of high feeding, madly hath broke loose
  And bears down all before him.
LORD BARDOLPH.   Noble earl,
  I bring you certain news from Shrewsbury.
NORTHUMBERLAND. Good, an God will!
LORD BARDOLPH.   As good as heart can wish.
  The king is almost wounded to the death;
  And, in the fortune of my lord your son,
  Prince Harry slain outright; and both the Blunts
  Kill'd by the hand of Douglas; young Prince John
  And Westmoreland and Stafford fled the field.
  And Harry Monmouth's brawn, the hulk Sir John,

Is prisoner to your son: O! such a day,
So fought, so follow'd, and so fairly won,
Came not till now to dignify the times
Since Cæsar's fortunes.

NORTHUMBERLAND.　　　How is this deriv'd?
Saw you the field? came you from Shrewsbury?

LORD BARDOLPH. I spake with one, my lord, that came from
　thence;
A gentleman well bred and of good name,
That freely render'd me these news for true.

NORTHUMBERLAND. Here comes my servant Travers, whom
　I sent
On Tuesday last to listen after news.

LORD BARDOLPH. My lord, I over-rode him on the way;
And he is furnish'd with no certainties
More than he haply may retail from me.

Enter Travers

NORTHUMBERLAND. Now, Travers, what good tidings come
　with you?

TRAVERS. My lord, Sir John Umfrevile turn'd me back
With joyful tidings; and, being better hors'd,
Out-rode me. After him came spurring hard
A gentleman, almost forspent with speed,
That stopp'd by me to breathe his bloodied horse.
He ask'd the way to Chester; and of him
I did demand what news from Shrewsbury.
He told me that rebellion had bad luck,
And that young Harry Percy's spur was cold.
With that he gave his able horse the head,
And, bending forward struck his armed heels
Against the panting sides of his poor jade
Up to the rowel-head, and, starting so,
He seem'd in running to devour the way,
Staying no longer question.

NORTHUMBERLAND.　　　Ha! Again:
Said he young Harry Percy's spur was cold?
Of Hotspur, Coldspur? that rebellion
Had met ill luck?

LORD BARDOLPH.　　My lord, I 'll tell you what:
If my young lord your son have not the day,
Upon mine honour, for a silken point
I 'll give my barony: never talk of it.

NORTHUMBERLAND. Why should the gentleman that rode
    by Travers
    Give then such instances of loss?
LORD BARDOLPH.   Who, he?
    He was some hilding fellow that had stolen
    The horse he rode on, and, upon my life,
    Spoke at a venture. Look, here comes more news.
             Enter Morton
NORTHUMBERLAND. Yea, this man's brow, like to a title-leaf,
    Foretells the nature of a tragic volume:
    So looks the strond, whereon the imperious flood
    Hath left a witness'd usurpation.
    Say, Morton, didst thou come from Shrewsbury?
MORTON. I ran from Shrewsbury, my noble lord;
    Where hateful death put on his ugliest mask
    To fright our party.
NORTHUMBERLAND.   How doth my son and brother?
    Thou tremblest, and the whiteness in thy cheek
    Is apter than thy tongue to tell thy errand.
    Even such a man, so faint, so spiritless,
    So dull, so dead in look, so woe-begone,
    Drew Priam's curtain in the dead of night,
    And would have told him half his Troy was burn'd;
    But Priam found the fire ere he his tongue,
    And I my Percy's death ere thou report'st it.
    This thou wouldst say, 'Your son did thus and thus;
    Your brother thus; so fought the noble Douglas';
    Stopping my greedy ear with their bold deeds:
    But in the end, to stop mine ear indeed,
    Thou hast a sigh to blow away this praise,
    Ending with 'Brother, son, and all are dead.'
MORTON. Douglas is living, and your brother, yet;
    But, for my lord your son,—
NORTHUMBERLAND.   Why, he is dead.—
    See, what a ready tongue suspicion hath!
    He that but fears the thing he would not know
    Hath by instinct knowledge from others' eyes
    That what he fear'd is chanced. Yet speak, Morton:
    Tell thou thy earl his divination lies,
    And I will take it as a sweet disgrace
    And make thee rich for doing me such wrong.
MORTON. You are too great to be by me gainsaid;

Your spirit is too true, your fears too certain.

NORTHUMBERLAND. Yet, for all this, say not that Percy's
    dead.
  I see a strange confession in thine eye:
  Thou shak'st thy head, and hold'st it fear or sin
  To speak a truth. If he be slain, say so;
  The tongue offends not that reports his death:
  And he doth sin that doth belie the dead,
  Not he which says the dead is not alive.
  Yet the first bringer of unwelcome news
  Hath but a losing office, and his tongue
  Sounds ever after as a sullen bell,
  Remember'd knolling a departing friend.

LORD BARDOLPH. I cannot think, my lord, your son is dead.

MORTON. I am sorry I should force you to believe
  That which I would to God I had not seen;
  But these mine eyes saw him in bloody state,
  Rendering faint quittance, wearied and outbreath'd,
  To Harry Monmouth; whose swift wrath beat down
  The never-daunted Percy to the earth,
  From whence with life he never more sprung up.
  In few, his death,—whose spirit lent a fire
  Even to the dullest peasant in his camp,—
  Being bruited once, took fire and heat away
  From the best-temper'd courage in his troops;
  For from his metal was his party steel'd;
  Which once in him abated, all the rest
  Turn'd on themselves, like dull and heavy lead:
  And as the thing that 's heavy in itself,
  Upon enforcement flies with greatest speed,
  So did our men, heavy in Hotspur's loss,
  Lend to this weight such lightness with their fear
  That arrows fled not swifter toward their aim
  Than did our soldiers, aiming at their safety,
  Fly from the field. Then was that noble Worcester
  Too soon ta'en prisoner; and that furious Scot,
  The bloody Douglas, whose well-labouring sword
  Had three times slain the appearance of the king,
  'Gan vail his stomach, and did grace the shame
  Of those that turn'd their backs; and in his flight,
  Stumbling in fear, was took. The sum of all
  Is, that the king hath won, and hath sent out

A speedy power to encounter you, my lord,
Under the conduct of young Lancaster
And Westmoreland. This is the news at full.
NORTHUMBERLAND. For this I shall have time enough to
    mourn.
In poison there is physic; and these news,
Having been well, that would have made me sick,
Being sick, have in some measure made me well:
And as the wretch, whose fever-weaken'd joints,
Like strengthless hinges, buckle under life,
Impatient of his fit, breaks like a fire
Out of his keeper's arms, even so my limbs,
Weaken'd with grief, being now enrag'd with grief,
Are thrice themselves. Hence, therefore, thou nice crutch!
A scaly gauntlet now, with joints of steel
Must glove this hand: and hence, thou sickly quoif!
Thou art a guard too wanton for the head
Which princes, flesh'd with conquest, aim to hit.
Now bind my brows with iron; and approach
The ragged'st hour that time and spite dare bring
To frown upon the enrag'd Northumberland!
Let heaven kiss earth! now let not nature's hand
Keep the wild flood confin'd! let order die!
And let this world no longer be a stage
To feed contention in a lingering act;
But let one spirit of the first-born Cain
Reign in all bosoms, that, each heart being set
On bloody courses, the rude scene may end,
And darkness be the burier of the dead!
TRAVERS. This strained passion doth you wrong, my lord.
LORD BARDOLPH. Sweet earl, divorce not wisdom from
    your honour.
MORTON. The lives of all your loving complices
Lean on your health; the which, if you give o'er
To stormy passion must perforce decay.
You cast the event of war, my noble lord,
And summ'd the account of chance, before you said,
'Let us make head.' It was your presurmise
That in the dole of blows your son might drop:
You knew he walk'd o'er perils, on an edge,
More likely to fall in than to get o'er;

You were advis'd his flesh was capable
Of wounds and scars, and that his forward spirit
Would lift him where most trade of danger rang'd:
Yet did you say, 'Go forth'; and none of this,
Though strongly apprehended, could restrain
The stiff-borne action: what hath then befallen,
Or what hath this bold enterprise brought forth,
More than that being which was like to be?

LORD BARDOLPH. We all that are engaged to this loss
Knew that we ventur'd on such dangerous seas
That if we wrought out life 'twas ten to one;
And yet we ventur'd, for the gain propos'd
Chok'd the respect of likely peril fear'd;
And since we are o'erset, venture again.
Come, we will all put forth, body and goods.

MORTON. 'Tis more than time: and, my most noble lord,
I hear for certain, and do speak the truth,
The gentle Archbishop of York is up,
With well-appointed powers: he is a man
Who with a double surety binds his followers.
My lord your son had only but the corpse',
But shadows and the shows of men to fight;
For that same word, rebellion, did divide
The action of their bodies from their souls;
And they did fight with queasiness, constrain'd,
As men drink potions, that their weapons only
Seem'd on our side: but, for their spirits and souls,
This word, rebellion, it had froze them up,
As fish are in a pond. But now the bishop
Turns insurrection to religion:
Suppos'd sincere and holy in his thoughts,
He 's follow'd both with body and with mind,
And doth enlarge his rising with the blood
Of fair King Richard, scrap'd from Pomfret stones;
Derives from heaven his quarrel and his cause;
Tells them he doth bestride a bleeding land,
Gasping for life under great Bolingbroke;
And more and less do flock to follow him.

NORTHUMBERLAND. I knew of this before; but, to speak
    truth,
This present grief had wip'd it from my mind.

Go in with me; and counsel every man
The aptest way for safety and revenge:
Get posts and letters, and make friends with speed:
Never so few, and never yet more need.   *Exeunt*

SCENE TWO

London. A Street.

*Enter Sir John Falstaff, with his Page bearing his
sword and buckler*

FALSTAFF. Sirrah, you giant, what says the doctor to my
water?

PAGE. He said, sir, the water itself was a good healthy
water; but, for the party that owed it, he might have more
diseases than he knew for.

FALSTAFF. Men of all sorts take a pride to gird at me: the
brain of this foolish-compounded clay, man, is not able to
invent anything that tends to laughter, more than I in-
vent or is invented on me: I am not only witty in myself,
but the cause that wit is in other men. I do here walk be-
fore thee like a sow that hath overwhelmed all her litter
but one. If the prince put thee into my service for any
other reason than to set me off, why then I have no judg-
ment. Thou whoreson mandrake, thou art fitter to be worn
in my cap than to wait at my heels. I was never manned
with an agate till now; but I will set you neither in gold
nor silver, but in vile apparel, and send you back again to
your master, for a jewel; the juvenal, the prince your mas-
ter, whose chin is not yet fledged. I will sooner have a
beard grow in the palm of my hand than he shall get one
on his cheek; and yet he will not stick to say, his face is a
face-royal: God may finish it when he will, it is not a hair
amiss yet: he may keep it still as a face-royal, for a barber
shall never earn sixpence out of it; and yet he will be
crowing as if he had writ man ever since his father was a
bachelor. He may keep his own grace, but he is almost out
of mine, I can assure him. What said Master Dombledon
about the satin for my short cloak and my slops?

PAGE. He said, sir, you should procure him better assurance than Bardolph; he would not take his bond and yours: he liked not the security.

FALSTAFF. Let him be damned like the glutton! may his tongue be hotter! A whoreson Achitophel! a rascally yea-forsooth knave! to bear a gentleman in hand, and then stand upon security. The whoreson smooth-pates do now wear nothing but high shoes, and bunches of keys at their girdles; and if a man is thorough with them in honest taking up, then they must stand upon security. I had as lief they would put ratsbane in my mouth as offer to stop it with security. I looked a' should have sent me two and twenty yards of satin, as I am a true knight, and he sends me security. Well, he may sleep in security; for he hath the horn of abundance, and the lightness of his wife shines through it: and yet cannot he see, though he have his own lanthorn to light him. Where 's Bardolph?

PAGE. He 's gone into Smithfield to buy your worship a horse.

FALSTAFF. I bought him in Paul's, and he 'll buy me a horse in Smithfield: an I could get me but a wife in the stews, I were manned, horsed, and wived.

Enter the Lord Chief Justice and Servant

PAGE. Sir, here comes the nobleman that committed the prince for striking him about Bardolph.

FALSTAFF. Wait close; I will not see him.

CHIEF JUSTICE. What 's he that goes there?

SERVANT. Falstaff, an 't please your lordship.

CHIEF JUSTICE. He that was in question for the robbery?

SERVANT. He, my lord; but he hath since done good service at Shrewsbury, and, as I hear, is now going with some charge to the Lord John of Lancaster.

CHIEF JUSTICE. What, to York? Call him back again.

SERVANT. Sir John Falstaff!

FALSTAFF. Boy, tell him I am deaf.

PAGE. You must speak louder, my master is deaf.

CHIEF JUSTICE. I am sure he is, to the hearing of anything good. Go, pluck him by the elbow; I must speak with him.

SERVANT. Sir John!

FALSTAFF. What! a young knave, and beg! Is there not wars? is there not employment? doth not the king lack subjects? do not the rebels want soldiers? Though it be a shame to be on any side but one, it is worse shame to beg than to be on the worst side, were it worse than the name of rebellion can tell how to make it.

SERVANT. You mistake me, sir.

FALSTAFF. Why, sir, did I say you were an honest man? setting my knighthood and my soldiership aside, I had lied in my throat if I had said so.

SERVANT. I pray you, sir, then set your knighthood and your soldiership aside, and give me leave to tell you you lie in your throat if you say I am any other than an honest man.

FALSTAFF. I give thee leave to tell me so! I lay aside that which grows to me! If thou gett'st any leave of me, hang me: if thou takest leave, thou wert better be hanged. You hunt counter: hence! avaunt!

SERVANT. Sir, my lord would speak with you.

CHIEF JUSTICE. Sir John Falstaff, a word with you.

FALSTAFF. My good lord! God give your lordship good time of day. I am glad to see your lordship abroad; I heard say your lordship was sick: I hope, your lordship goes abroad by advice. Your lordship, though not clean past your youth, hath yet some smack of age in you, some relish of the saltness of time; and I most humbly beseech your lordship to have a reverend care of your health.

CHIEF JUSTICE. Sir John, I sent for you before your expedition to Shrewsbury.

FALSTAFF. An 't please your lordship, I hear his Majesty is returned with some discomfort from Wales.

CHIEF JUSTICE. I talk not of his Majesty. You would not come when I sent for you.

FALSTAFF. And I hear, moreover, his Highness is fallen into this same whoreson apoplexy.

CHIEF JUSTICE. Well, heaven mend him! I pray you, let me speak with you.

FALSTAFF. This apoplexy is, as I take it, a kind of lethargy, an 't please your lordship; a kind of sleeping in the blood, a whoreson tingling.

CHIEF JUSTICE. What tell you me of it? be it as it is.

FALSTAFF. It hath its original from much grief, from study and perturbation of the brain. I have read the cause of his effects in Galen: it is a kind of deafness.

CHIEF JUSTICE. I think you are fallen into the disease, for you hear not what I say to you.

FALSTAFF. Very well, my lord, very well: rather, an 't please you, it is the disease of not listening, the malady of not marking, that I am troubled withal.

CHIEF JUSTICE. To punish you by the heels would amend the attention of your ears; and I care not if I do become your physician.

FALSTAFF. I am as poor as Job, my lord, but not so patient: your lordship may minister the potion of imprisonment to me in respect of poverty; but how I should be your patient to follow your prescriptions, the wise may make some dram of a scruple, or indeed a scruple itself.

CHIEF JUSTICE. I sent for you, when there were matters against you for your life, to come speak with me.

FALSTAFF. As I was then advised by my learned counsel in the laws of this land-service, I did not come.

CHIEF JUSTICE. Well, the truth is, Sir John, you live in great infamy.

FALSTAFF. He that buckles him in my belt cannot live in less.

CHIEF JUSTICE. Your means are very slender, and your waste is great.

FALSTAFF. I would it were otherwise: I would my means were greater and my waist slenderer.

CHIEF JUSTICE. You have misled the youthful prince.

FALSTAFF. The young prince hath misled me: I am the fellow with the great belly, and he my dog.

CHIEF JUSTICE. Well, I am loath to gall a new-healed wound: your day's service at Shrewsbury hath a little gilded over your night's exploit on Gadshill: you may thank the unquiet time for your quiet o'er-posting that action.

FALSTAFF. My lord!

CHIEF JUSTICE. But since all is well, keep it so: wake not a sleeping wolf.

FALSTAFF. To wake a wolf is as bad as to smell a fox.

CHIEF JUSTICE. What! you are as a candle, the better part burnt out.

FALSTAFF. A wassail candle, my lord; all tallow: if I did say of wax, my growth would approve the truth.

CHIEF JUSTICE. There is not a white hair on your face but should have his effect of gravity.

FALSTAFF. His effect of gravy, gravy, gravy.

CHIEF JUSTICE. You follow the young prince up and down, like his ill angel.

FALSTAFF. Not so, my lord; your ill angel is light, but I hope he that looks upon me will take me without weighing: and yet, in some respects, I grant, I cannot go, I cannot tell. Virtue is of so little regard in these costermonger times that true valour is turned bear-herd: pregnancy is made a tapster, and hath his quick wit wasted in giving reckonings: all the other gifts appertinent to man, as the malice of this age shapes them, are not worth a gooseberry. You that are old consider not the capacities of us that are young; you measure the heat of our livers with the bitterness of your galls; and we that are in the vaward of our youth, I must confess, are wags too.

CHIEF JUSTICE. Do you set down your name in the scroll of youth, that are written down old with all the characters of age? Have you not a moist eye, a dry hand, a yellow cheek, a white beard, a decreasing leg, an increasing belly? Is not your voice broken, your wind short, your chin double, your wit single, and every part about you blasted with antiquity, and will you yet call yourself young? Fie, fie, fie, Sir John!

FALSTAFF. My lord, I was born about three of the clock in the afternoon, with a white head, and something a round belly. For my voice, I have lost it with hollaing, and singing of anthems. To approve my youth further, I will not: the truth is, I am only old in judgment and understanding; and he that will caper with me for a thousand marks, let him lend me the money, and have at him! For the box o' the ear that the prince gave you, he gave it like a rude prince, and you took it like a sensible lord. I have checked him for it, and the young lion repents; marry, not in ashes and sackcloth, but in new silk and old sack.

CHIEF JUSTICE. Well, God send the prince a better companion!

FALSTAFF. God send the companion a better prince! I cannot rid my hands of him.

CHIEF JUSTICE. Well, the king hath severed you and Prince Harry. I hear you are going with Lord John of Lancaster against the archbishop and the Earl of Northumberland.

FALSTAFF. Yea; I thank your pretty sweet wit for it. But

look you pray, all you that kiss my Lady Peace at home,
that our armies join not in a hot day; for, by the Lord, I
take but two shirts out with me, and I mean not to sweat
extraordinarily: if it be a hot day, and I brandish any thing
but my bottle, I would I might never spit white again.
There is not a dangerous action can peep out his head but
I am thrust upon it. Well, I cannot last ever. But it was al-
ways yet the trick of our English nation, if they have a
good thing, to make it too common. If you will needs say I
am an old man, you should give me rest. I would to God
my name were not so terrible to the enemy as it is: I were
better to be eaten to death with rust than to be scoured to
nothing with perpetual motion.

CHIEF JUSTICE. Well, be honest, be honest; and God bless
your expedition.

FALSTAFF. Will your lordship lend me a thousand pound to
furnish me forth?

CHIEF JUSTICE. Not a penny; not a penny; you are too im-
patient to bear crosses. Fare you well; commend me to my
cousin Westmoreland.   *Exeunt Chief Justice and Servant*

FALSTAFF. If I do, fillip me with a three-man beetle. A man
can no more separate age and covetousness than he can
part young limbs and lechery; but the gout galls the one,
and the pox pinches the other; and so both the degrees
prevent my curses. Boy!

PAGE. Sir!

FALSTAFF. What money is in my purse?

PAGE. Seven groats and twopence.

FALSTAFF. I can get no remedy against this consumption of
the purse: borrowing only lingers and lingers it out, but
the disease is incurable. Go bear this letter to my Lord of
Lancaster; this to the prince; this to the Earl of West-
moreland; and this to old Mistress Ursula, whom I have
weekly sworn to marry since I perceived the first white
hair on my chin. About it: you know where to find me.
(*Exit Page*) A pox of this gout! or, a gout of this pox! for
the one or the other plays the rogue with my great toe.
'Tis no matter if I do halt; I have the wars for my colour,
and my pension shall seem the more reasonable. A good
wit will make use of anything; I will turn diseases to com-
modity.   *Exit*

SCENE THREE

York. A Room in the Archbishop's Palace.

Enter the Archbishop of York, the Lords Hastings,
Mowbray, and Bardolph

ARCHBISHOP. Thus have you heard our cause and known our
   means;
  And, my most noble friends, I pray you all,
  Speak plainly your opinions of our hopes:
  And first, Lord Marshal, what say you to it?
MOWBRAY. I well allow the occasion of our arms;
  But gladly would be better satisfied
  How in our means we should advance ourselves
  To look with forehead bold and big enough
  Upon the power and puissance of the king.
HASTINGS. Our present musters grow upon the file
  To five-and-twenty thousand men of choice;
  And our supplies live largely in the hope
  Of great Northumberland, whose bosom burns
  With an incensed fire of injuries.
LORD BARDOLPH. The question, then, Lord Hastings,
  standeth thus:
  Whether our present five-and-twenty thousand
  May hold up head without Northumberland.
HASTINGS. With him, we may.
LORD BARDOLPH.   Ay, marry, there 's the point:
  But if without him we be thought too feeble,
  My judgment is, we should not step too far
  Till we had his assistance by the hand;
  For in a theme so bloody-fac'd as this,
  Conjecture, expectation, and surmise
  Of aids incertain should not be admitted.
ARCHBISHOP. 'Tis very true, Lord Bardolph; for, indeed
  It was young Hotspur's case at Shrewsbury.
LORD BARDOLPH. It was, my lord; who lin'd himself with
  hope,
  Eating the air on promise of supply,
  Flattering himself with project of a power
  Much smaller than the smallest of his thoughts;

And so, with great imagination
Proper to madmen, led his powers to death,
And winking leap'd into destruction.

HASTINGS. But, by your leave, it never yet did hurt
To lay down likelihoods and forms of hope.

LORD BARDOLPH. Yes, if this present quality of war,—
Indeed the instant action,—a cause on foot,
Lives so in hope, as in an early spring
We see the appearing buds; which, to prove fruit,
Hope gives not so much warrant as despair
That frosts will bite them. When we mean to build,
We first survey the plot, then draw the model;
And when we see the figure of the house,
Then must we rate the cost of the erection;
Which if we find outweighs ability,
What do we then but draw anew the model
In fewer offices, or at last desist
To build at all? Much more, in this great work,—
Which is almost to pluck a kingdom down
And set another up,—should we survey
The plot of situation and the model,
Consent upon a sure foundation,
Question surveyors, know our own estate,
How able such a work to undergo,
To weigh against his opposite; or else,
We fortify in paper, and in figures,
Using the names of men instead of men:
Like one that draws the model of a house
Beyond his power to build it; who, half through,
Gives o'er and leaves his part-created cost
A naked subject to the weeping clouds,
And waste for churlish winter's tyranny.

HASTINGS. Grant that our hopes, yet likely of fair birth,
Should be still-born, and that we now possess'd
The utmost man of expectation;
I think we are a body strong enough,
Even as we are, to equal with the king.

LORD BARDOLPH. What! is the king but five-and-twenty
thousand?

HASTINGS. To us no more; nay, not so much, Lord Bardolph.
For his divisions, as the times do brawl,
Are in three heads: one power against the French,

And one against Glendower; perforce, a third
Must take up us: so is the unfirm king
In three divided, and his coffers sound
With hollow poverty and emptiness.

ARCHBISHOP. That he should draw his several strengths together
And come against us in full puissance,
Need not be dreaded.

HASTINGS.   If he should do so,
He leaves his back unarm'd, the French and Welsh
Baying him at the heels: never fear that.

LORD BARDOLPH. Who is it like should lead his forces hither?

HASTINGS. The Duke of Lancaster and Westmoreland;
Against the Welsh, himself and Harry Monmouth:
But who is substituted 'gainst the French
I have no certain notice.

ARCHBISHOP.   Let us on
And publish the occasion of our arms.
The commonwealth is sick of their own choice;
Their over-greedy love hath surfeited.
A habitation giddy and unsure
Hath he that buildeth on the vulgar heart.
O thou fond many! with what loud applause
Didst thou beat heaven with blessing Bolingbroke
Before he was what thou wouldst have him be:
And being now trimm'd in thine own desires,
Thou, beastly feeder, art so full of him
That thou provok'st thyself to cast him up.
So, so, thou common dog, didst thou disgorge
Thy glutton bosom of the royal Richard,
And now thou wouldst eat thy dead vomit up,
And howl'st to find it. What trust is in these times?
They that, when Richard liv'd, would have him die,
Are now become enamour'd on his grave:
Thou, that threw'st dust upon his goodly head,
When through proud London he came sighing on
After the admired heels of Bolingbroke,
Cry'st now, 'O earth! yield us that king again,
And take thou this!' O, thoughts of men accurst!
Past and to come seem best; things present worst.

MOWBRAY. Shall we go draw our numbers and set on?

HASTINGS. We are time's subjects, and time bids be gone.

                                        Exeunt

ACT TWO

SCENE ONE

London. A Street.

*Enter Mistress Quickly: Fang, and his Boy, with her;
and Snare following*

QUICKLY. Master Fang, have you entered the exion?

FANG. It is entered.

QUICKLY. Where 's your yeoman? Is it a lusty yeoman? will
a' stand to 't?

FANG. Sirrah, where 's Snare?

QUICKLY. O Lord, ay! good Master Snare.

SNARE. Here, here.

FANG. Snare, we must arrest Sir John Falstaff.

QUICKLY. Yea, good Master Snare; I have entered him and
all.

SNARE. It may chance cost some of us our lives, for he will
stab.

QUICKLY. Alas the day! take heed of him: he stabbed me in
mine own house, and that most beastly. In good faith, he
cares not what mischief he doth, if his weapon be out: he
will foin like any devil; he will spare neither man, woman,
nor child.

FANG. If I can close with him I care not for his thrust.

QUICKLY. No, no, I neither: I 'll be at your elbow.

FANG. An I but fist him once; an a' come but within my
vice,—

QUICKLY. I am undone by his going; I warrant you, he 's an
infinitive thing upon my score. Good Master Fang, hold
him sure: good Master Snare, let him not 'scape. A' comes
continuantly to Pie-corner—saving your manhoods—to
buy a saddle; and he 's indited to dinner to the Lubber's
Head in Lumbert Street, to Master Smooth's the silkman:
I pray ye, since my exion is entered, and my case so
openly known to the world, let him be brought in to his

answer. A hundred mark is a long one for a poor lone woman to bear; and I have borne, and borne, and borne; and have been fubbed off, and fubbed off, and fubbed off, from this day to that day, that it is a shame to be thought on. There is no honesty in such dealing; unless a woman should be made an ass, and a beast, to bear every knave's wrong. Yonder he comes; and that arrant malmsey-nose knave, Bardolph, with him. Do your offices, do your offices, Master Fang and Master Snare; do me, do me, do me your offices.

Enter Sir John Falstaff, Page, and Bardolph

FALSTAFF. How now! whose mare 's dead? what 's the matter?

FANG. Sir John, I arrest you at the suit of Mistress Quickly.

FALSTAFF. Away, varlets! Draw, Bardolph: cut me off the villain's head; throw the quean in the channel.

QUICKLY. Throw me in the channel! I 'll throw thee in the channel. Wilt thou? wilt thou? thou bastardly rogue! Murder, murder! Ah, thou honeysuckle villain! wilt thou kill God's officers and the king's? Ah, thou honey-seed rogue! thou art a honey-seed, a man-queller, and a woman-queller.

FALSTAFF. Keep them off, Bardolph.

FANG. A rescue! a rescue!

QUICKLY. Good people, bring a rescue or two! Thou wo't, wo't thou? thou wo't, wo't ta? do, do, thou rogue! do, thou hemp-seed!

FALSTAFF. Away, you scullion! you rampallian! you fustilarian! I 'll tickle your catastrophe.

Enter the Lord Chief Justice, attended

CHIEF JUSTICE. What is the matter? keep the peace here, ho!

QUICKLY. Good my lord, be good to me! I beseech you, stand to me!

CHIEF JUSTICE. How now, Sir John! what! are you brawling here?
Doth this become your place, your time and business?
You should have been well on your way to York.
Stand from him, fellow: wherefore hang'st upon him?

QUICKLY. O, my most worshipful lord, an 't please your Grace, I am a poor widow of Eastcheap, and he is arrested at my suit.

CHIEF JUSTICE. For what sum?

QUICKLY. It is more than for some, my lord; it is for all, all I have. He hath eaten me out of house and home; he hath put all my substance into that fat belly of his: but I will have some of it out again, or I will ride thee o' nights like the mare.

FALSTAFF. I think I am as like to ride the mare if I have any vantage of ground to get up.

CHIEF JUSTICE. How comes this, Sir John? Fie! what man of good temper would endure this tempest of exclamation? Are you not ashamed to enforce a poor widow to so rough a course to come by her own?

FALSTAFF. What is the gross sum that I owe thee?

QUICKLY. Marry, if thou wert an honest man, thyself and the money too. Thou didst swear to me upon a parcel-gilt goblet, sitting in my Dolphin-chamber, at the round table, by a seacoal fire, upon Wednesday in Wheeson week, when the prince broke thy head for liking his father to a singing-man of Windsor, thou didst swear to me then, as I was washing thy wound, to marry me and make me my lady thy wife. Canst thou deny it? Did not goodwife Keech, the butcher's wife, come in then and call me gossip Quickly? coming in to borrow a mess of vinegar; telling us she had a good dish of prawns; whereby thou didst desire to eat some, whereby I told thee they were ill for a green wound? And didst thou not, when she was gone down stairs, desire me to be no more so familiarity with such poor people: saying that ere long they should call me madam? And didst thou not kiss me and bid me fetch thee thirty shillings? I put thee now to thy book-oath: deny it if thou canst.

FALSTAFF. My lord, this is a poor mad soul; and she says up and down the town that her eldest son is like you. She hath been in good case, and the truth is, poverty hath distracted her. But for these foolish officers, I beseech you I may have redress against them.

CHIEF JUSTICE. Sir John, Sir John, I am well acquainted with your manner of wrenching the true cause the false way. It is not a confident brow, nor the throng of words that come with such more than impudent sauciness from you, can thrust me from a level consideration; you have, as it appears to me, practised upon the easy-yielding spirit of this woman, and made her serve your uses both in purse and in person.

QUICKLY. Yea, in troth, my lord.

CHIEF JUSTICE. Prithee, peace. Pay her the debt you owe her, and unpay the villany you have done her: the one you may do with sterling money, and the other with current repentance.

FALSTAFF. My lord, I will not undergo this sneap without reply. You call honourable boldness impudent sauciness: if a man will make curtsy, and say nothing, he is virtuous. No, my lord, my humble duty remembered, I will not be your suitor: I say to you, I do desire deliverance from these officers, being upon hasty employment in the king's affairs.

CHIEF JUSTICE. You speak as having power to do wrong: but answer in the effect of your reputation, and satisfy the poor woman.

FALSTAFF. Come hither, hostess.   *Taking her aside*

Enter Gower

CHIEF JUSTICE. Now, Master Gower! what news?

GOWER. The king, my lord, and Harry Prince of Wales
Are near at hand: the rest the paper tells.   *Gives a letter*

FALSTAFF. As I am a gentleman.

QUICKLY. Nay, you said so before.

FALSTAFF. As I am a gentleman. Come, no more words of it.

QUICKLY. By this heavenly ground I tread on, I must be fain to pawn both my plate and the tapestry of my dining-chambers.

FALSTAFF. Glasses, glasses, is the only drinking: and for thy walls, a pretty slight drollery, or the story of the Prodigal, or the German hunting in water-work, is worth a thousand of these bed-hangings and these fly-bitten tapestries. Let it be ten pound if thou canst. Come, an it were not for thy humours, there is not a better wench in England. Go, wash thy face, and draw thy action. Come, thou must not be in this humour with me; dost not know me? Come, come, I know thou wast set on to this.

QUICKLY. Prithee, Sir John, let it be but twenty nobles: i faith, I am loath to pawn my plate, so God save me, la!

FALSTAFF. Let it alone; I 'll make other shift: you 'll be a fool still.

QUICKLY. Well, you shall have it, though I pawn my gown.

I hope you 'll come to supper. You 'll pay me all together?

FALSTAFF. Will I live? (*To Bardolph*) Go, with her, with her; hook on, hook on.

QUICKLY. Will you have Doll Tearsheet meet you at supper?

FALSTAFF. No more words; let 's have her.

Exeunt Mistress Quickly, Bardolph, Officers, and Page

CHIEF JUSTICE. I have heard better news.

FALSTAFF. What 's the news, my good lord?

CHIEF JUSTICE. Where lay the king last night?

GOWER. At Basingstoke, my lord.

FALSTAFF. I hope, my lord, all 's well: what is the news, my lord?

CHIEF JUSTICE. Come all his forces back?

GOWER. No; fifteen hundred foot, five hundred horse,
Are march'd up to my Lord of Lancaster,
Against Northumberland and the archbishop.

FALSTAFF. Comes the king back from Wales, my noble lord?

CHIEF JUSTICE. You shall have letters of me presently.
Come, go along with me, good Master Gower.

FALSTAFF. My lord!

CHIEF JUSTICE. What 's the matter?

FALSTAFF. Master Gower, shall I entreat you with me to dinner?

GOWER. I must wait upon my good lord here; I thank you, good Sir John.

CHIEF JUSTICE. Sir John, you loiter here too long, being you are to take soldiers up in counties as you go.

FALSTAFF. Will you sup with me, Master Gower?

CHIEF JUSTICE. What foolish master taught you these manners, Sir John?

FALSTAFF. Master Gower, if they become me not, he was a fool that taught them me. This is the right fencing grace, my lord; tap for tap, and so part fair.

CHIEF JUSTICE. Now the Lord lighten thee! thou art a great fool.   *Exeunt*

SCENE TWO

The Same. Another Street.

Enter the Prince and Poins

PRINCE. Before God, I am exceeding weary.

POINS. Is it come to that? I had thought weariness durst not have attached one of so high blood.

PRINCE. Faith, it does me, though it discolours the complexion of my greatness to acknowledge it. Doth it not show vilely in me to desire small beer?

POINS. Why, a prince should not be so loosely studied as to remember so weak a composition.

PRINCE. Belike then my appetite was not princely got; for, by my troth, I do now remember the poor creature, small beer. But, indeed, these humble considerations make me out of love with my greatness. What a disgrace is it to me to remember thy name, or to know thy face to-morrow! or to take note how many pair of silk stockings thou hast; viz. these, and those that were thy peach-coloured ones! or to bear the inventory of thy shirts; as, one for superfluity, and one other for use! But that the tennis-court-keeper knows better than I, for it is a low ebb of linen with thee when thou keepest not racket there; as thou hast not done a great while, because the rest of thy low-countries have made a shift to eat up thy holland: and God knows whether those that bawl out the ruins of thy linen shall inherit his kingdom; but the mid-wives say the children are not in the fault; whereupon the world increases, and kindreds are mightily strengthened.

POINS. How ill it follows, after you have laboured so hard, you should talk so idly! Tell me, how many good young princes would do so, their fathers being so sick as yours at this time is?

PRINCE. Shall I tell thee one thing, Poins?

POINS. Yes, faith, and let it be an excellent good thing.

PRINCE. It shall serve among wits of no higher breeding than thine.

POINS. Go to; I stand the push of your one thing that you will tell.

PRINCE. Marry, I tell thee, it is not meet that I should be sad, now my father is sick: albeit I could tell to thee,—as to one it pleases me, for fault of a better, to call my friend, —I could be sad, and sad indeed too.

POINS. Very hardly upon such a subject.

PRINCE. By this hand, thou thinkest me as far in the devil's book as thou and Falstaff for obduracy and persistency: let the end try the man. But I tell thee my heart bleeds inwardly that my father is so sick; and keeping such vile company as thou art hath in reason taken from me all ostentation of sorrow.

POINS. The reason?

PRINCE. What wouldst thou think of me if I should weep?

POINS. I would think thee a most princely hypocrite.

PRINCE. It would be every man's thought; and thou art a blessed fellow to think as every man thinks: never a man's thought in the world keeps the road-way better than thine: every man would think me a hypocrite indeed. And what accites your most worshipful thought to think so?

POINS. Why, because you have been so lewd and so much engraffed to Falstaff.

PRINCE. And to thee.

POINS. By this light, I am well spoke on; I can hear it with mine own ears: the worst that they can say of me is that I am a second brother and that I am a proper fellow of my hands; and these two things I confess I cannot help. By the mass, here comes Bardolph.

Enter Bardolph and Page

PRINCE. And the boy that I gave Falstaff: a' had him from me Christian; and look, if the fat villain have not transformed him ape.

BARDOLPH. God save your Grace!

PRINCE. And yours, most noble Bardolph.

BARDOLPH. (*To the Page*) Come, you virtuous ass, you bashful fool, must you be blushing? wherefore blush you now? What a maidenly man-at-arms are you become! Is it such a matter to get a pottle-pot's maidenhead?

PAGE. A' calls me even now, my lord, through a red lattice, and I could discern no part of his face from the window: at last, I spied his eyes, and methought he had made two holes in the ale-wife's new petticoat, and peeped through.

PRINCE. Hath not the boy profited?

BARDOLPH. Away, you whoreson upright rabbit, away!

PAGE. Away, you rascally Althea's dream, away!

PRINCE. Instruct us, boy; what dream, boy?

PAGE. Marry, my lord, Althea dreamed she was delivered of a firebrand; and therefore I call him her dream.

PRINCE. A crown's worth of good interpretation. There it is, boy.   *Gives him money*

POINS. O! that this good blossom could be kept from cankers. Well, there is sixpence to preserve thee.

BARDOLPH. An you do not make him be hanged among you, the gallows shall have wrong.

PRINCE. And how doth thy master, Bardolph?

BARDOLPH. Well, my lord. He heard of your Grace's coming to town: there 's a letter for you.

POINS. Delivered with good respect. And how doth the martlemas, your master?

BARDOLPH. In bodily health, sir.

POINS. Marry, the immortal part needs a physician; but that moves not him: though that be sick, it dies not.

PRINCE. I do allow this wen to be as familiar with me as my dog; and he holds his place, for look you how he writes.

POINS. 'John Falstaff, knight,'—every man must know that, as oft as he has occasion to name himself: even like those that are akin to the king, for they never prick their finger but they say, 'There is some of the king's blood spilt.' 'How comes that?' says he that takes upon him not to conceive. The answer is as ready as a borrower's cap, 'I am the king's poor cousin, sir.'

PRINCE. Nay, they will be kin to us, or they will fetch it from Japhet. But to the letter:

POINS. 'Sir John Falstaff, knight, to the son of the king nearest his father, Harry Prince of Wales, greeting.' Why, this is a certificate.

PRINCE. Peace!

POINS. 'I will imitate the honourable Romans in brevity': sure he means brevity in breath, short-winded.—'I commend me to thee, I commend thee, and I leave thee. Be not too familiar with Poins; for he misuses thy favours so much that he swears thou art to marry his sister Nell. Repent at idle times as thou mayest, and so farewell.

Thine, by yea and no,—which is as much as to say, as thou usest him, JACK FALSTAFF, with my familiars;

JOHN, with my brothers and sisters, and SIR JOHN
with all Europe.'
My lord, I 'll steep this letter in sack and make him eat it.

PRINCE. That 's to make him eat twenty of his words. But do
you use me thus, Ned? must I marry your sister?

POINS. God send the wench no worse fortune! but I never
said so.

PRINCE. Well, thus we play the fools with the time, and the
spirits of the wise sit in the clouds and mock us. Is your
master here in London?

BARDOLPH. Yes, my lord.

PRINCE. Where sups he? doth the old boar feed in the old
frank?

BARDOLPH. At the old place, my lord, in Eastcheap.

PRINCE. What company?

PAGE. Ephesians, my lord, of the old church.

PRINCE. Sup any women with him?

PAGE. None, my lord, but old Mistress Quickly and Mistress
Doll Tearsheet.

PRINCE. What pagan may that be?

PAGE. A proper gentlewoman, sir, and a kinswoman of my
master's.

PRINCE. Even such kin as the parish heifers are to the town
bull. Shall we steal upon them, Ned, at supper?

POINS. I am your shadow, my lord; I 'll follow you.

PRINCE. Sirrah, you boy, and Bardolph; no word to your
master that I am yet come to town: there 's for your si-
lence.   *Gives money*

BARDOLPH. I have no tongue, sir.

PAGE. And for mine, sir, I will govern it.

PRINCE. Fare ye well; go.   *Exeunt Bardolph and Page*
This Doll Tearsheet should be some road.

POINS. I warrant you, as common as the way between Saint
Alban's and London.

PRINCE. How might we see Falstaff bestow himself to-night
in his true colours, and not ourselves be seen?

POINS. Put on two leathern jerkins and aprons, and wait
upon him at his table as drawers.

PRINCE. From a god to a bull! a heavy descension! it was
Jove's case. From a prince to a prentice! a low transforma-
tion! that shall be mine; for in every thing the purpose
must weigh with the folly. Follow me, Ned.   *Exeunt*

SCENE THREE

Warkworth. Before Northumberland's Castle.

*Enter Northumberland, Lady Northumberland,
and Lady Percy*

NORTHUMBERLAND. I pray thee, loving wife, and gentle
    daughter,
  Give even way unto my rough affairs:
  Put not you on the visage of the times,
  And be like them to Percy troublesome.
LADY NORTHUMBERLAND. I have given over, I will speak no
    more:
  Do what you will; your wisdom be your guide.
NORTHUMBERLAND. Alas! sweet wife, my honour is at pawn;
  And, but my going, nothing can redeem it.
LADY PERCY. O! yet for God's sake, go not to these wars.
  The time was, father, that you broke your word
  When you were more endear'd to it than now;
  When your own Percy, when my heart's dear Harry,
  Threw many a northward look to see his father
  Bring up his powers; but he did long in vain.
  Who then persuaded you to stay at home?
  There were two honours lost, yours and your son's:
  For yours, the God of heaven brighten it!
  For his, it stuck upon him as the sun
  In the grey vault of heaven; and by his light
  Did all the chivalry of England move
  To do brave acts: he was indeed the glass
  Wherein the noble youth did dress themselves:
  He had no legs that practis'd not his gait;
  And speaking thick, which nature made his blemish,
  Became the accents of the valiant;
  For those that could speak low and tardily,
  Would turn their own perfection to abuse,
  To seem like him: so that, in speech, in gait,
  In diet, in affections of delight,
  In military rules, humours of blood,
  He was the mark and glass, copy and book,
  That fashion'd others. And him, O wondrous him!

O miracle of men! him did you leave,—
Second to none, unseconded by you,—
To look upon the hideous god of war
In disadvantage; to abide a field
Where nothing but the sound of Hotspur's name
Did seem defensible: so you left him.
Never, O! never, do his ghost the wrong
To hold your honour more precise and nice
With others than with him: let them alone.
The marshal and the archbishop are strong:
Had my sweet Harry had but half their numbers,
To-day might I, hanging on Hotspur's neck,
Have talk'd of Monmouth's grave.

NORTHUMBERLAND.   Beshrew your heart,
Fair daughter! you do draw my spirits from me
With new lamenting ancient oversights.
But I must go and meet with danger there,
Or it will seek me in another place,
And find me worse provided.

LADY NORTHUMBERLAND.   O! fly to Scotland,
Till that the nobles and the armed commons
Have of their puissance made a little taste.

LADY PERCY. If they get ground and vantage of the king,
Then join you with them, like a rib of steel,
To make strength stronger; but, for all our loves,
First let them try themselves. So did your son;
He was so suffer'd: so came I a widow;
And never shall have length of life enough
To rain upon remembrance with mine eyes,
That it may grow and sprout as high as heaven,
For recordation to my noble husband.

NORTHUMBERLAND. Come, come, go in with me. 'Tis with
    my mind
As with the tide swell'd up unto its height,
That makes a still-stand, running neither way:
Fain would I go to meet the archbishop,
But many thousand reasons hold me back.
I will resolve for Scotland: there am I,
Till time and vantage crave my company.   *Exeunt*

SCENE FOUR

*London. A Room in the Boar's Head Tavern,
in Eastcheap.*

Enter two Drawers

FIRST DRAWER. What the devil hast thou brought there?
apple-johns? thou knowest Sir John cannot endure an
apple-john.

SECOND DRAWER. Mass, thou sayst true. The prince once set
a dish of apple-johns before him, and told him there were
five more Sir Johns; and, putting off his hat, said, 'I will
now take my leave of these six dry, round, old withered
knights.' It angered him to the heart; but he hath forgot
that.

FIRST DRAWER. Why then, cover, and set them down: and
see if thou canst find out Sneak's noise; Mistress Tearsheet
would fain hear some music. Dispatch: the room where
they supped is too hot; they 'll come in straight.

SECOND DRAWER. Sirrah, here will be the prince and Master
Poins anon; and they will put on two of our jerkins and
aprons; and Sir John must not know of it: Bardolph hath
brought word.

FIRST DRAWER. By the mass, here will be old utis: it will be
an excellent stratagem.

SECOND DRAWER. I 'll see if I can find out Sneak.   *Exit*

Enter Mistress Quickly and Doll Tearsheet

QUICKLY. I' faith, sweetheart, methinks now you are in an
excellent good temperality: your pulsidge beats as ex-
traordinarily as heart would desire; and your colour, I
warrant you, is as red as any rose; in good truth, la! But, i'
faith, you have drunk too much canaries, and that 's a
marvellous searching wine, and it perfumes the blood ere
one can say, What 's this? How do you now?

DOLL. Better than I was: hem!

QUICKLY. Why, that 's well said; a good heart 's worth gold.
Lo! here comes Sir John.

Enter Falstaff, singing

FALSTAFF. 'When Arthur first in court'--Empty the jordan.

(*Exit First Drawer*)—'And was a worthy king.' How now, Mistress Doll!

QUICKLY. Sick of a calm: yea, good sooth.

FALSTAFF. So is all her sect; an they be once in a calm they are sick.

DOLL. You muddy rascal, is that all the comfort you give me?

FALSTAFF. You make fat rascals, Mistress. Doll.

DOLL. I make them! gluttony and diseases make them; I make them not.

FALSTAFF. If the cook help to make the gluttony, you help to make the diseases, Doll: we catch of you, Doll, we catch of you; grant that, my poor virtue, grant that.

DOLL. Ay, marry; our chains and our jewels.

FALSTAFF. 'Your brooches, pearls, and owches':—for to serve bravely is to come halting off, you know: to come off the breach with his pike bent bravely, and to surgery bravely; to venture upon the charged chambers bravely,—

DOLL. Hang yourself, you muddy conger, hang yourself!

QUICKLY. By my troth, this is the old fashion; you two never meet but you fall to some discord: you are both, in good troth, as rheumatic as two dry toasts; you cannot one bear with another's confirmities. What the good-year! one must bear, and that must be you: you are the weaker vessel, as they say, the emptier vessel.

DOLL. Can a weak empty vessel bear such a huge full hogs-head? there's a whole merchant's venture of Bourdeaux stuff in him: you have not seen a hulk better stuffed in the hold. Come, I'll be friends with thee, Jack: thou art going to the wars; and whether I shall ever see thee again or no, there is nobody cares.

Re-enter First Drawer

FIRST DRAWER. Sir, Ancient Pistol's below, and would speak with you.

DOLL. Hang him, swaggering rascal! let him not come hither: it is the foul-mouthedest rogue in England.

QUICKLY. If he swagger, let him not come here: no, by my faith; I must live amongst my neighbours; I'll no swaggerers: I am in good name and fame with the very best. Shut the door; there comes no swaggerers here: I have not lived all this while to have swaggering now: shut the door, I pray you.

FALSTAFF. Dost thou hear, hostess?

QUICKLY. Pray you, pacify yourself, Sir John: there comes no swaggerers here.

FALSTAFF. Dost thou hear? it is mine ancient.

QUICKLY. Tilly-fally, Sir John, never tell me: your ancient swaggerer comes not in my doors. I was before Master Tisick, the deputy, t'other day; and, as he said to me,— 'twas no longer ago than Wednesday last,—'Neighbour Quickly,' says he;—Master Dumbe, our minister, was by then;—'Neighbour Quickly,' says he, 'receive those that are civil, for,' said he, 'you are in an ill name'; now, a' said so, I can tell whereupon; 'for,' says he, 'you are an honest woman, and well thought on; therefore take heed what guests you receive: receive,' says he, 'no swaggering companions.' There comes none here:—you would bless you to hear what he said. No, I 'll no swaggerers.

FALSTAFF. He 's no swaggerer, hostess; a tame cheater, i' faith; you may stroke him as gently as a puppy greyhound: he will not swagger with a Barbary hen if her feathers turn back in any show of resistance. Call him up, drawer.   *Exit First Drawer*

QUICKLY. Cheater, call you him? I will bar no honest man my house, nor no cheater; but I do not love swaggering, by my troth; I am the worse, when one says swagger. Feel, masters, how I shake; look you, I warrant you.

DOLL. So you do, hostess.

QUICKLY. Do I? yea, in very truth, do I, an 'twere an aspen leaf: I cannot abide swaggerers.

Enter Pistol, Bardolph, and Page

PISTOL. God save you, Sir John!

FALSTAFF. Welcome, Ancient Pistol. Here, Pistol, I charge you with a cup of sack: do you discharge upon mine hostess.

PISTOL. I will discharge upon her, Sir John, with two bullets.

FALSTAFF. She is pistol-proof, sir; you shall hardly offend her.

QUICKLY. Come, I 'll drink no proofs nor no bullets: I 'll drink no more than will do me good, for no man's pleasure, I.

PISTOL. Then to you, Mistress Dorothy; I will charge you.

DOLL. Charge me! I scorn you, scurvy companion. What! you poor, base, rascally, cheating, lack-linen mate! Away, you mouldy rogue, away! I am meat for your master.

PISTOL. I know you, Mistress Dorothy.

DOLL. Away, you cut-purse rascal! you filthy bung, away!

By this wine, I 'll thrust my knife in your mouldy chaps an
you play the saucy cuttle with me. Away, you bottle-ale
rascal! you basket-hilt stale juggler, you! Since when, I
pray you, sir? God's light! with two points on your shoul-
der? much!

PISTOL. God let me not live. I will murder your ruff for this!

FALSTAFF. No more, Pistol: I would not have you go off
here. Discharge yourself of our company, Pistol.

QUICKLY. No, good captain Pistol; not here, sweet captain.

DOLL. Captain! thou abominable damned cheater, art thou
not ashamed to be called captain? An captains were of
my mind, they would truncheon you out for taking their
names upon you before you have earned them. You a cap-
tain, you slave! for what? for tearing a poor whore's ruff
in a bawdy-house? He a captain! Hang him, rogue! He
lives upon mouldy stewed prunes and dried cakes. A cap-
tain! God's light, these villains will make the word captain
as odious as the word 'occupy,' which was an excellent
good word before it was ill sorted: therefore captains had
need look to it.

BARDOLPH. Pray thee, go down, good ancient.

FALSTAFF. Hark thee hither, Mistress Doll.

PISTOL. Not I; I tell thee what, Corporal Bardolph; I could
tear her. I 'll be revenged of her.

PAGE. Pray thee, go down.

PISTOL. I 'll see her damned first; to Pluto's damned lake, by
this hand, to the infernal deep, with Erebus and tortures
vile also. Hold hook and line, say I. Down, down, dogs!
down fates! Have we not Hiren here?

QUICKLY. Good Captain Peesel, be quiet; it is very late, i'
faith. I beseek you now, aggravate your choler.

PISTOL. These be good humours, indeed! Shall pack-horses,
And hollow pamper'd jades of Asia,
Which cannot go but thirty miles a day,
Compare with Cæsars, and with Cannibals,
And Trojan Greeks? nay, rather damn them with
King Cerberus; and let the welkin roar.
Shall we fall foul for toys?

QUICKLY. By my troth, captain, these are very bitter words.

BARDOLPH. Be gone, good ancient: this will grow to a brawl
anon.

PISTOL. Die men like dogs! give crowns like pins!
   Have we not Hiren here?

QUICKLY. O' my word, captain, there 's none such here.
   What the good-year! do you think I would deny her? for
   God's sake! be quiet.

PISTOL. Then feed, and be fat, my fair Calipolis.
   Come, give 's some sack.
   'Si fortuna me tormente, sperato me contento.'
   Fear we broadsides? no, let the fiend give fire:
   Give me some sack; and, sweetheart, lie thou there.
                                       Laying down his sword
   Come we to full points here, and are et ceteras nothing?

FALSTAFF. Pistol, I would be quiet.

PISTOL. Sweet knight, I kiss thy neif. What! we have seen
   the seven stars.

DOLL. For God's sake, thrust him down stairs! I cannot en-
   dure such a fustian rascal.

PISTOL. 'Thrust him down stairs!' know we not Galloway
   nags?

FALSTAFF. Quoit him down, Bardolph, like a shove-groat
   shilling: nay, an a' do nothing but speak nothing, a' shall
   be nothing here.

BARDOLPH. Come, get you down stairs.

PISTOL. What! shall we have incision? Shall we imbrue?
                                       Snatching up his sword
   Then death rock me asleep, abridge my doleful days!
   Why then, let grievous, ghastly, gaping wounds
   Untwine the Sisters Three! Come, Atropos, I say!

QUICKLY. Here 's goodly stuff toward!

FALSTAFF. Give me my rapier, boy.

DOLL. I pray thee, Jack, I pray thee, do not draw.

FALSTAFF. Get you down stairs.   *Drawing*

QUICKLY. Here 's a goodly tumult! I 'll forswear keeping
   house, afore I 'll be in these tirrits and frights. So; murder,
   I warrant now. Alas, alas! put up your naked weapons;
   put up your naked weapons.   *Exeunt Bardolph and Pistol*

DOLL. I pray thee, Jack, be quiet; the rascal 's gone. Ah! you
   whoreson little valiant villain, you!

QUICKLY. Are you not hurt i' the groin? methought a' made a
   shrewd thrust at your belly.
                          Re-enter Bardolph

FALSTAFF. Have you turned him out o' doors?

BARDOLPH. Yes, sir: the rascal 's drunk. You have hurt him, sir, i' the shoulder.

FALSTAFF. A rascal, to brave me!

DOLL. Ah, you sweet little rogue, you! Alas, poor ape, how thou sweatest! Come, let me wipe thy face; come on, you whoreson chops. Ah, rogue! i' faith, I love thee. Thou art as valorous as Hector of Troy, worth five of Agamemnon, and ten times better than the Nine Worthies. Ah, villain!

FALSTAFF. A rascally slave! I will toss the rogue in a blanket.

DOLL. Do, an thou darest for thy heart: an thou dost, I 'll canvass thee between a pair of sheets.

Enter Music

PAGE. The music is come, sir.

FALSTAFF. Let them play. Play, sirs. Sit on my knee, Doll. A rascal bragging slave! the rogue fled from me like quicksilver.

DOLL. I' faith, and thou followedst him like a church. Thou whoreson little tidy Bartholomew boar-pig, when wilt thou leave fighting o' days, and foining o' nights, and begin to patch up thine old body for heaven?

Enter, behind, the Prince and Poins, disguised like Drawers

FALSTAFF. Peace, good Doll! do not speak like a death's head: do not bid me remember mine end.

DOLL. Sirrah, what humour is the prince of?

FALSTAFF. A good shallow young fellow: a' would have made a good pantler, a' would have chipped bread well.

DOLL. They, say, Poins has a good wit.

FALSTAFF. He a good wit! hang him, baboon! his wit is as thick as Tewksbury mustard: there is no more conceit in him than is in a mallet.

DOLL. Why does the prince love him so, then?

FALSTAFF. Because their legs are both of a bigness, and he plays at quoits well, and eats conger and fennel, and drinks off candles' ends for flap-dragons, and rides the wild mare with the boys, and jumps upon joint-stools, and swears with a good grace, and wears his boots very smooth, like unto the sign of the leg, and breeds no bate with telling of discreet stories; and such other gambol faculties a' has, that show a weak mind and an able body, for the which the prince admits him: for the prince himself is such another; the weight of a hair will turn the scales between their avoirdupois.

PRINCE. Would not this nave of a wheel have his ears cut off?

POINS. Let 's beat him before his whore.

PRINCE. Look, whether the withered elder hath not his poll clawed like a parrot.

POINS. Is it not strange that desire should so many years out-live performance?

FALSTAFF. Kiss me, Doll.

PRINCE. Saturn and Venus this year in conjunction! what says the almanack to that?

POINS. And, look, whether the fiery Trigon, his man, be not lisping to his master's old tables, his note-book, his counsel-keeper.

FALSTAFF. Thou dost give me flattering busses.

DOLL. By my troth, I kiss thee with a most constant heart.

FALSTAFF. I am old, I am old.

DOLL. I love thee better than I love e'er a scurvy young boy of them all.

FALSTAFF. What stuff wilt have a kirtle of? I shall receive money o' Thursday; thou shalt have a cap to-morrow. A merry song! come: it grows late; we 'll to bed. Thou 'lt for-get me when I am gone.

DOLL. By my troth, thou 'lt set me a-weeping an thou sayst so: prove that ever I dress myself handsome till thy re-turn. Well, hearken at the end.

FALSTAFF. Some sack, Francis!

PRINCE. ⎫
POINS. ⎬ (*Coming forward*) Anon, anon, sir.

FALSTAFF. Ha! a bastard son of the king's? And art not thou Poins his brother?

PRINCE. Why, thou globe of sinful continents, what a life dost thou lead!

FALSTAFF. A better than thou: I am a gentleman; thou art a drawer.

PRINCE. Very true, sir; and I come to draw you out by the ears.

QUICKLY. O! the Lord preserve thy good Grace; by my troth, welcome to London. Now, the Lord bless that sweet face of thine! O Jesu! are you come from Wales?

FALSTAFF. Thou whoreson mad compound of majesty, by this light flesh and corrupt blood (*Pointing to Doll*), thou art welcome.

DOLL. How, you fat fool! I scorn you.

POINS. My lord, he will drive you out of your revenge and turn all to a merriment, if you take not the heat.

PRINCE. You whoreson candle-mine, you, how vilely did you speak of me even now before this honest, virtuous, civil gentlewoman!

QUICKLY. Blessing on your good heart! and so she is, by my troth.

FALSTAFF. Didst thou hear me?

PRINCE. Yea; and you knew me, as you did when you ran away by Gadshill: you knew I was at your back, and spoke it on purpose to try my patience.

FALSTAFF. No, no, no; not so; I did not think thou wast within hearing.

PRINCE. I shall drive you then to confess the wilful abuse; and then I know how to handle you.

FALSTAFF. No abuse, Hal, o' mine honour; no abuse.

PRINCE. Not to dispraise me, and call me pantler and bread-chipper and I know not what?

FALSTAFF. No abuse, Hal.

POINS. No abuse!

FALSTAFF. No abuse, Ned, in the world; honest Ned, none. I dispraised him before the wicked, that the wicked might not fall in love with him; in which doing I have done the part of a careful friend and a true subject, and thy father is to give me thanks for it. No abuse, Hal! none, Ned, none: no, faith, boys, none.

PRINCE. See now, whether pure fear and entire cowardice doth not make thee wrong this virtuous gentlewoman to close with us. Is she of the wicked? Is thine hostess here of the wicked? Or is thy boy of the wicked? Or honest Bardolph, whose zeal burns in his nose, of the wicked?

POINS. Answer, thou dead elm, answer.

FALSTAFF. The fiend hath pricked down Bardolph irrecoverable; and his face is Lucifer's privy-kitchen, where he doth nothing but roast malt-worms. For the boy, there is a good angel about him; but the devil outbids him too.

PRINCE. For the women?

FALSTAFF. For one of them, she is in hell already, and burns poor souls. For the other, I owe her money; and whether she be damned for that, I know not.

QUICKLY. No, I warrant you.

FALSTAFF. No, I think thou art not; I think thou art quit for
that. Marry, there is another indictment upon thee, for
suffering flesh to be eaten in thy house, contrary to the
law; for the which I think thou wilt howl.

QUICKLY. All victuallers do so: what 's a joint of mutton or
two in a whole Lent?

PRINCE. You, gentlewoman,—

DOLL. What says your Grace?

FALSTAFF. His grace says that which his flesh rebels against.
Knocking within

QUICKLY. Who knocks so loud at door? Look to the door
there, Francis.

Enter Peto

PRINCE. Peto, how now! what news?

PETO. The king your father is at Westminster;
And there are twenty weak and wearied posts
Come from the North: and as I came along,
I met and overtook a dozen captains,
Bare-headed, sweating, knocking at the taverns,
And asking every one for Sir John Falstaff.

PRINCE. By heaven, Poins, I feel me much to blame,
So idly to profane the precious time,
When tempest of commotion, like the South,
Borne with black vapour, doth begin to melt
And drop upon our bare unarmed heads.
Give me my sword and cloak. Falstaff, good-night.
Exeunt the Prince, Poins, Peto, and Bardolph

FALSTAFF. Now comes in the sweetest morsel of the night,
and we must hence and leave it unpicked. (*Knocking
within*) More knocking at the door!

Re-enter Bardolph

How now! what 's the matter?

BARDOLPH. You must away to court, sir, presently;
A dozen captains stay at door for you.

FALSTAFF. (*To the Page*) Pay the musicians, sirrah: Fare-
well, hostess; farewell, Doll. You see, my good wenches,
how men of merit are sought after: the undeserver may
sleep when the man of action is called on. Farewell, good
wenches. If I be not sent away post, I will see you again
ere I go.

DOLL. I cannot speak; if my heart be not ready to burst,—
well, sweet Jack, have a care of thyself.

FALSTAFF. Farewell, farewell.

Exeunt Falstaff and Bardolph

QUICKLY. Well, fare thee well: I have known thee these twenty-nine years, come peascod-time; but an honester, and truer-hearted man—well, fare thee well.

BARDOLPH. (*Within*) Mistress Tearsheet!

QUICKLY. What 's the matter?

BARDOLPH. (*Within*) Bid Mistress Tearsheet come to my master.

QUICKLY. O! run, Doll, run; run, good Doll.   *Exeunt*

ACT THREE

SCENE ONE

Westminster. A Room in the Palace.

Enter King Henry in his nightgown, with a Page

KING HENRY. Go, call the Earls of Surrey and of Warwick;
But, ere they come, bid them o'er-read these letters,
And well consider of them. Make good speed.   *Exit Page*
How many thousand of my poorest subjects
Are at this hour asleep! O sleep! O gentle sleep!
Nature's soft nurse, how have I frighted thee,
That thou no more wilt weigh my eyelids down
And steep my senses in forgetfulness?
Why rather, sleep, liest thou in smoky cribs,
Upon uneasy pallets stretching thee,
And hush'd with buzzing night-flies to thy slumber,
Than in the perfum'd chambers of the great,
Under the canopies of costly state,
And lull'd with sound of sweetest melody?
O thou dull god! why liest thou with the vile
In loathsome beds, and leav'st the kingly couch
A watch-case or a common 'larum bell?
Wilt thou upon the high and giddy mast
Seel up the ship-boy's eyes, and rock his brains
In cradle of the rude imperious surge,
And in the visitation of the winds,
Who take the ruffian billows by the top,
Curling their monstrous heads, and hanging them
With deaf'ning clamour in the slippery clouds,
That with the hurly death itself awakes?
Canst thou, O partial sleep! give thy repose
To the wet sea-boy in an hour so rude,
And in the calmest and most stillest night,
With all appliances and means to boot,

Deny it to a king? Then, happy low, lie down!
Uneasy lies the head that wears a crown.

Enter Warwick and Surrey

WARWICK. Many good-morrows to your Majesty!
KING HENRY. Is it good-morrow, lords?
WARWICK. 'Tis one o'clock, and past.
KING HENRY. Why then, good-morrow to you all, my lords.
Have you read o'er the letters that I sent you?
WARWICK. We have, my liege.
KING HENRY. Then you perceive the body of our kingdom,
How foul it is; what rank diseases grow,
And with what danger, near the heart of it.
WARWICK. It is but as a body, yet, distemper'd,
Which to his former strength may be restor'd
With good advice and little medicine:
My Lord Northumberland will soon be cool'd.
KING HENRY. O God! that one might read the book of fate,
And see the revolution of the times
Make mountains level, and the continent,—
Weary of solid firmness,—melt itself
Into the sea! and, other times, to see
The beachy girdle of the ocean
Too wide for Neptune's hips; how chances mock,
And changes fill the cup of alteration
With divers liquors! O! if this were seen,
The happiest youth, viewing his progress through,
What perils past, what crosses to ensue,
Would shut the book, and sit him down and die.
'Tis not ten years gone
Since Richard and Northumberland, great friends,
Did feast together, and in two years after
Were they at wars: it is but eight years since
This Percy was the man nearest my soul,
Who like a brother toil'd in my affairs
And laid his love and life under my foot;
Yea, for my sake, even to the eyes of Richard
Gave him defiance. But which of you was by,—
(*To Warwick*) You, cousin Nevil, as I may remember,—
When Richard, with his eye brimful of tears,
Then check'd and rated by Northumberland,
Did speak these words, now prov'd a prophecy?
'Northumberland, thou ladder, by the which

My cousin Bolingbroke ascends my throne';
Though then, God knows, I had no such intent,
But that necessity so bow'd the state
That I and greatness were compelled to kiss:
'The time shall come,' thus did he follow it,
'The time will come, that foul sin, gathering head,
Shall break into corruption':—so went on,
Foretelling this same time's condition
And the division of our amity.

WARWICK. There is a history in all men's lives,
Figuring the nature of the times deceas'd;
The which observ'd, a man may prophesy,
With a near aim, of the main chance of things
As yet not come to life, which in their seeds
And weak beginnings lie intreasured.
Such things become the hatch and brood of time;
And by the necessary form of this
King Richard might create a perfect guess
That great Northumberland, then false to him,
Would of that seed grow to a greater falseness,
Which should not find a ground to root upon,
Unless on you.

KING HENRY.   Are these things then necessities?
Then let us meet them like necessities;
And that same word even now cries out on us.
They say the bishop and Northumberland
Are fifty thousand strong.

WARWICK.   It cannot be, my lord!
Rumour doth double, like the voice and echo,
The numbers of the fear'd. Please it your Grace
To go to bed: upon my soul, my lord,
The powers that you already have sent forth
Shall bring this prize in very easily.
To comfort you the more, I have receiv'd
A certain instance that Glendower is dead.
Your Majesty hath been this fortnight ill,
And these unseason'd hours perforce must add
Unto your sickness.

KING HENRY.   I will take your counsel:
And were these inward wars once out of hand,
We would, dear lords, unto the Holy Land.   *Exeunt*

SCENE TWO

Court before Justice Shallow's House in Gloucestershire.

*Enter Shallow and Silence, meeting; Mouldy, Shadow,
Wart, Feeble, Bullcalf, and Servants, behind*

SHALLOW. Come on, come on, come on, sir; give me your
hand, sir, give me your hand, sir; an early stirrer, by the
rood! And how doth my good cousin Silence?

SILENCE. Good-morrow, good cousin Shallow.

SHALLOW. And how doth my cousin, your bedfellow? and
your fairest daughter and mine, my god-daughter Ellen?

SILENCE. Alas! a black ousel, cousin Shallow!

SHALLOW. By yea and nay, sir, I dare say my cousin William
is become a good scholar. He is at Oxford still, is he not?

SILENCE. Indeed, sir, to my cost.

SHALLOW. A' must, then, to the inns o' court shortly. I was
once of Clement's Inn; where I think they will talk of mad
Shallow yet.

SILENCE. You were called 'lusty Shallow' then, cousin.

SHALLOW. By the mass, I was called any thing; and I would
have done any thing indeed too, and roundly too. There
was I, and Little John Doit of Staffordshire, and black
George Barnes, and Francis Pickbone, and Will Squele, a
Cotswold man; you had not four such swinge-bucklers in
all the inns of court again: and, I may say to you, we knew
where the bona-robas were, and had the best of them all
at commandment. Then was Jack Falstaff, now Sir John,
a boy, and page to Thomas Mowbray, Duke of Norfolk.

SILENCE. This Sir John, cousin, that comes hither anon
about soldiers?

SHALLOW. The same Sir John, the very same. I saw him
break Skogan's head at the court-gate, when a' was a
crack not thus high: and the very same day did I fight
with one Sampson Stockfish, a fruiterer, behind Gray's
Inn. Jesu! Jesu! the mad days that I have spent; and to see
how many of mine old acquaintance are dead!

SILENCE. We shall all follow, cousin.

SHALLOW. Certain, 'tis certain; very sure, very sure: death, as the Psalmist saith, is certain to all; all shall die. How a good yoke of bullocks at Stamford fair?

SILENCE. Truly, cousin, I was not there.

SHALLOW. Death is certain. Is old Double of your town living yet?

SILENCE. Dead, sir.

SHALLOW. Jesu! Jesu! dead! a' drew a good bow; and dead! a' shot a fine shoot: John a Gaunt loved him well, and betted much money on his head. Dead! a' would have clapped i' the clout at twelve score; and carried you a forehand shaft a fourteen and fourteen and a half, that it would have done a man's heart good to see. How a score of ewes now?

SILENCE. Thereafter as they be: a score of good ewes may be worth ten pounds.

SHALLOW. And is old Double dead?

SILENCE. Here come two of Sir John Falstaff's men, as I think.

Enter Bardolph, and one with him

BARDOLPH. Good-morrow, honest gentlemen: I beseech you, which is Justice Shallow?

SHALLOW. I am Robert Shallow, sir; a poor esquire of this county, and one of the king's justices of the peace: what is your good pleasure with me?

BARDOLPH. My captain, sir, commends him to you; my captain, Sir John Falstaff: a tall gentleman, by heaven, and a most gallant leader.

SHALLOW. He greets me well, sir. I knew him a good backsword man. How doth the good knight? may I ask how my lady his wife doth?

BARDOLPH. Sir, pardon; a soldier is better accommodated than with a wife.

SHALLOW. It is well said, in faith, sir; and it is well said indeed too. 'Better accommodated!' it is good; yea indeed, is it: good phrases are surely and ever were, very commendable. Accommodated! it comes of 'accommodo': very good; a good phrase.

BARDOLPH. Pardon me, sir; I have heard the word. 'Phrase,' call you it? By this good day, I know not the phrase; but I will maintain the word with my sword to be a soldier-like word, and a word of exceeding good command, by heaven. Accommodated; that is, when a man is, as they

say, accommodated; or, when a man is, being, whereby a'
may be thought to be accommodated, which is an excel-
lent thing.

Enter Falstaff

SHALLOW. It is very just. Look, here comes good Sir John.
Give me your good hand, give me your worship's good
hand. By my troth, you look well and bear your years very
well: welcome, good Sir John.

FALSTAFF. I am glad to see you well, good Master Robert
Shallow. Master Surecard, as I think.

SHALLOW. No, Sir John; it is my cousin, Silence, in commis-
sion with me.

FALSTAFF. Good Master Silence, it well befits you should be
of the peace.

SILENCE. Your good worship is welcome.

FALSTAFF. Fie! this is hot weather, gentlemen. Have you
provided me here half a dozen sufficient men?

SHALLOW. Marry, have we, sir. Will you sit?

FALSTAFF. Let me see them, I beseech you.

SHALLOW. Where 's the roll? where 's the roll? where 's the
roll? Let me see, let me see, let me see. So, so, so, so, so,
so, so: yea, marry, sir: Ralph Mouldy! let them appear as
I call; let them do so, let them do so. Let me see; where is
Mouldy?

MOULDY. Here, an 't please you.

SHALLOW. What think you, Sir John? a good-limbed fellow;
young, strong, and of good friends.

FALSTAFF. Is thy name Mouldy?

MOULDY. Yea, an 't please you.

FALSTAFF. 'Tis the more time thou wert used.

SHALLOW. Ha, ha, ha! most excellent, i' faith! things that are
mouldy lack use: very singular good. In faith, well said,
Sir John; very well said.

FALSTAFF. Prick him.

MOULDY. I was pricked well enough before, an you could
have let me alone: my old dame will be undone now for
one to do her husbandry and her drudgery: you need not
to have pricked me; there are other men fitter to go out
than I.

FALSTAFF. Go to: peace, Mouldy! you shall go. Mouldy, it
is time you were spent.

MOULDY. Spent!

SHALLOW. Peace, fellow, peace! stand aside: know you where you are? For the other, Sir John: let me see. Simon Shadow!

FALSTAFF. Yea, marry, let me have him to sit under: he 's like to be a cold soldier.

SHALLOW. Where 's Shadow?

SHADOW. Here, sir.

FALSTAFF. Shadow, whose son art thou?

SHADOW. My mother's son, sir.

FALSTAFF. Thy mother's son! like enough, and thy father's shadow: so the son of the female is the shadow of the male: it is often so, indeed; but not of the father's substance.

SHALLOW. Do you like him, Sir John?

FALSTAFF. Shadow will serve for summer; prick him, for we have a number of shadows to fill up the muster-book.

SHALLOW. Thomas Wart!

FALSTAFF. Where 's he?

WART. Here, sir.

FALSTAFF. Is thy name Wart?

WART. Yea, sir.

FALSTAFF. Thou art a very ragged wart.

SHALLOW. Shall I prick him, Sir John?

FALSTAFF. It were superfluous; for his apparel is built upon his back, and the whole frame stands upon pins: prick him no more.

SHALLOW. Ha, ha, ha! you can do it, sir; you can do it: I commend you well. Francis Feeble!

FEEBLE. Here, sir.

FALSTAFF. What trade art thou, Feeble?

FEEBLE. A woman's tailor, sir.

SHALLOW. Shall I prick him, sir?

FALSTAFF. You may; but if he had been a man's tailor he'd have pricked you. Wilt thou make as many holes in an enemy's battle as thou hast done in a woman's petticoat?

FEEBLE. I will do my good will, sir: you can have no more.

FALSTAFF. Well said, good woman's tailor! well said, courageous Feeble! Thou wilt be as valiant as the wrathful dove or most magnanimous mouse. Prick the woman's tailor; well, Master Shallow; deep, Master Shallow.

FEEBLE. I would Wart might have gone, sir.

FALSTAFF. I would thou wert a man's tailor, that thou mightst mend him, and make him fit to go. I cannot put him to a private soldier that is the leader of so many thousands: let that suffice, most forcible Feeble.

FEEBLE. It shall suffice, sir.

FALSTAFF. I am bound to thee, reverend Feeble. Who is next?

SHALLOW. Peter Bullcalf o' the green!

FALSTAFF. Yea, marry, let's see Bullcalf.

BULLCALF. Here, sir.

FALSTAFF. 'Fore God, a likely fellow! Come, prick me Bullcalf till he roar again.

BULLCALF. O Lord! good my lord captain,—

FALSTAFF. What! dost thou roar before thou art pricked?

BULLCALF. O Lord, sir! I am a diseased man.

FALSTAFF. What disease hast thou?

BULLCALF. A whoreson cold, sir; a cough, sir, which I caught with ringing in the king's affairs upon his coronation day, sir.

FALSTAFF. Come, thou shalt go to the wars in a gown; we will have away thy cold; and I will take such order that thy friends shall ring for thee. Is here all?

SHALLOW. Here is two more called than your number; you must have but four here, sir: and so, I pray you, go in with me to dinner.

FALSTAFF. Come, I will go drink with you, but I cannot tarry dinner. I am glad to see you, by my troth, Master Shallow.

SHALLOW. O, Sir John, do you remember since we lay all night in the windmill in Saint George's fields?

FALSTAFF. No more of that, good Master Shallow, no more of that.

SHALLOW. Ha! it was a merry night. And is Jane Nightwork alive?

FALSTAFF. She lives, Master Shallow.

SHALLOW. She never could away with me.

FALSTAFF. Never, never; she would always say she could not abide Master Shallow.

SHALLOW. By the mass, I could anger her to the heart. She was then a bona-roba. Doth she hold her own well?

FALSTAFF. Old, old, Master Shallow.

SHALLOW. Nay, she must be old; she cannot choose but be old; certain she's old; and had Robin Nightwork by old Nightwork before I came to Clement's Inn.

SILENCE. That's fifty-five year ago.

SHALLOW. Ha! cousin Silence, that thou hadst seen that that this knight and I have seen. Ha! Sir John, said I well?

FALSTAFF. We have heard the chimes at midnight, Master Shallow.

SHALLOW. That we have, that we have, that we have; in faith, Sir John, we have. Our watchword was, 'Hem, boys!' Come, let's to dinner; come, let's to dinner. Jesus, the days that we have seen! Come, come.

Exeunt Falstaff, Shallow, and Silence

BULLCALF. Good Master Corporate Bardolph, stand my friend, and here's four Harry ten shillings in French crowns for you. In very truth, sir, I had as lief be hanged, sir, as go: and yet, for mine own part, sir, I do not care; but rather, because I am unwilling, and, for mine own part, have a desire to stay with my friends: else, sir, I did not care, for mine own part, so much.

BARDOLPH. Go to; stand aside.

MOULDY. And, good Master corporal captain, for my old dame's sake, stand my friend: she has nobody to do any thing about her, when I am gone; and she is old, and cannot help herself. You shall have forty, sir.

BARDOLPH. Go to; stand aside.

FEEBLE. By my troth, I care not; a man can die but once; we owe God a death. I'll ne'er bear a base mind: an't be my destiny, so; an't be not, so. No man's too good to serve's prince; and let it go which way it will, he that dies this year is quit for the next.

BARDOLPH. Well said; thou'rt a good fellow.

FEEBLE. Faith, I'll bear no base mind.

Re-enter Falstaff and the Justices

FALSTAFF. Come, sir, which men shall I have?

SHALLOW. Four, of which you please.

BARDOLPH. (*To Falstaff*) Sir, a word with you. I have three pound to free Mouldy and Bullcalf.

FALSTAFF. (*Aside to Bardolph*) Go to; well.

SHALLOW. Come, Sir John, which four will you have?

FALSTAFF. Do you choose for me.

SHALLOW. Marry, then, Mouldy, Bullcalf, Feeble, and Shadow.

FALSTAFF. Mouldy, and Bullcalf: for you, Mouldy, stay at

home till you are past service: and for your part, Bullcalf, grow till you come unto it: I will none of you.

SHALLOW. Sir John, Sir John, do not yourself wrong: they are your likeliest men, and I would have you served with the best.

FALSTAFF. Will you tell me, Master Shallow, how to choose a man? Care I for the limb, the thewes, the stature, bulk, and big assemblance of a man! Give me the spirit, Master Shallow. Here's Wart; you see what a ragged appearance it is: a' shall charge you and discharge you with the motion of a pewterer's hammer, come off and on swifter than he that gibbets on the brewer's bucket. And this same half-faced fellow, Shadow, give me this man: he presents no mark to the enemy; the foeman may with as great aim level at the edge of a penknife. And, for a retreat; how swiftly will this Feeble the woman's tailor run off! O! give me the spare men, and spare me the great ones. Put me a caliver into Wart's hand, Bardolph.

BARDOLPH. Hold, Wart, traverse; thus, thus, thus.

FALSTAFF. Come, manage me your caliver. So: very well: go to: very good: exceeding good. O, give me always a little, lean, old, chopp'd, bald shot. Well said, i' faith, Wart; thou 'rt a good scab: hold, there 's a tester for thee.

SHALLOW. He is not his craft's master, he doth not do it right. I remember at Mile-end Green, when I lay at Clement's Inn,—I was then Sir Dagonet in Arthur's show,— there was a little quiver fellow, and a' would manage you his piece thus: and a' would about and about, and come you in, and come you in; 'rah, tah, tah,' would a' say; 'bounce,' would a' say; and away again would a' go, and again would a' come: I shall never see such a fellow.

FALSTAFF. These fellows will do well, Master Shallow. God keep you, Master Silence: I will not use many words with you. Fare you well, gentlemen both: I thank you: I must a dozen mile to-night. Bardolph, give the soldiers coats.

SHALLOW. Sir John, the Lord bless you! and prosper your affairs! God send us peace! At your return visit our house; let our old acquaintance be renewed: peradventure I will with ye to the court.

FALSTAFF. 'Fore God, I would you would, Master Shallow.

SHALLOW. Go to; I have spoke at a word. God keep you.

FALSTAFF. Fare you well, gentle gentlemen. (*Exeunt Shal-*

low and Silence) On, Bardolph; lead the men away.
(*Exeunt Bardolph, Recruits, &c.*) As I return, I will fetch
off these justices: I do see the bottom of Justice Shallow.
Lord, Lord! how subject we old men are to this vice of ly-
ing. This same starved justice hath done nothing but prate
to me of the wildness of his youth and the feats he hath
done about Turnbull Street; and every third word a lie,
duer paid to the hearer than the Turk's tribute. I do re-
member him at Clement's Inn like a man made after sup-
per of a cheese-paring: when a' was naked he was for all
the world like a forked radish, with a head fantastically
carved upon it with a knife: a' was so forlorn that his di-
mensions to any thick sight were invincible: a' was the
very genius of famine; yet lecherous as a monkey, and the
whores called him mandrake: a' came ever in the rear-
ward of the fashion and sung those tunes to the over-
scutched huswives that he heard the carmen whistle, and
sware they were his fancies or his good-nights. And now is
this Vice's dagger become a squire, and talks as familiarly
of John a Gaunt as if he had been sworn brother to him;
and I 'll be sworn a' never saw him but once in the Tilt-
yard, and then he burst his head for crowding among the
marshal's men. I saw it and told John a Gaunt he beat his
own name; for you might have thrust him and all his ap-
parel into an eel-skin; the case of a treble hautboy was a
mansion for him, a court; and now has he land and beefs.
Well, I will be acquainted with him, if I return; and it
shall go hard but I will make him a philosopher's two
stones to me. If the young dace be a bait for the old pike,
I see no reason in the law of nature but I may snap at him.
Let time shape, and there an end.   *Exit*

ACT FOUR

SCENE ONE

A Forest in Yorkshire.

*Enter the Archbishop of York, Mowbray, Hastings,
and Others*

ARCHBISHOP. What is this forest call'd?

HASTINGS. 'Tis Gaultree Forest, an 't shall please your
    Grace.

ARCHBISHOP. Here stand, my lords, and send discoverers
    forth,
  To know the numbers of our enemies.

HASTINGS. We have sent forth already.

ARCHBISHOP.   'Tis well done.
  My friends and brethren in these great affairs,
  I must acquaint you that I have receiv'd
  New-dated letters from Northumberland;
  Their cold intent, tenour and substance, thus:
  Here doth he wish his person, with such powers
  As might hold sortance with his quality;
  The which he could not levy; whereupon
  He is retir'd, to ripe his growing fortunes,
  To Scotland; and concludes in hearty prayers
  That your attempts may overlive the hazard
  And fearful meeting of their opposite.

MOWBRAY. Thus do the hopes we have in him touch ground
  And dash themselves to pieces.

Enter a Messenger

HASTINGS.   Now, what news?

MESSENGER. West of this forest, scarcely off a mile,
  In goodly form comes on the enemy;
  And, by the ground they hide, I judge their number
  Upon or near the rate of thirty thousand.

MOWBRAY. The just proportion that we gave them out.
  Let us sway on and face them in the field.

Enter Westmoreland

ARCHBISHOP. What well-appointed leader fronts us here?

MOWBRAY. I think it is my Lord of Westmoreland.

WESTMORELAND. Health and fair greeting from our general,
    The prince, Lord John and Duke of Lancaster.

ARCHBISHOP. Say on, my Lord of Westmoreland, in peace,
    What doth concern your coming.

WESTMORELAND.   Then, my lord,
    Unto your Grace do I in chief address
    The substance of my speech. If that rebellion
    Came like itself, in base and abject routs,
    Led on by bloody youth, guarded with rags,
    And countenanc'd by boys and beggary;
    I say, if damn'd commotion so appear'd,
    In his true, native, and most proper shape,
    You, reverend father, and these noble lords
    Had not been here, to dress the ugly form
    Of base and bloody insurrection
    With your fair honours. You, Lord Archbishop,
    Whose see is by a civil peace maintain'd,
    Whose beard the silver hand of peace hath touch'd,
    Whose learning and good letters peace hath tutor'd,
    Whose white investments figure innocence,
    The dove and very blessed spirit of peace,
    Wherefore do you so ill translate yourself
    Out of the speech of peace that bears such grace
    Into the harsh and boisterous tongue of war;
    Turning your books to greaves, your ink to blood,
    Your pens to lances, and your tongue divine
    To a loud trumpet and a point of war?

ARCHBISHOP. Wherefore do I this? so the question stands.
    Briefly to this end: we are all diseas'd;
    And, with our surfeiting and wanton hours
    Have brought ourselves into a burning fever,
    And we must bleed for it: of which disease
    Our late king, Richard, being infected, died.
    But, my most noble Lord of Westmoreland,
    I take not on me here as a physician,
    Nor do I as an enemy to peace
    Troop in the throngs of military men;
    But rather show a while like fearful war,
    To diet rank minds sick of happiness

And purge the obstructions which begin to stop
Our very veins of life. Hear me more plainly:
I have in equal balance justly weigh'd
What wrongs our arms may do, what wrongs we suffer,
And find our griefs heavier than our offences.
We see which way the stream of time doth run
And are enforc'd from our most quiet sphere
By the rough torrent of occasion;
And have the summary of all our griefs,
When time shall serve, to show in articles,
Which long ere this we offer'd to the king,
And might by no suit gain our audience.
When we are wrong'd and would unfold our griefs,
We are denied access unto his person
Even by those men that most have done us wrong.
The dangers of the days but newly gone,—
Whose memory is written on the earth
With yet appearing blood,—and the examples
Of every minute's instance, present now,
Have put us in these ill-beseeming arms;
Not to break peace, or any branch of it,
But to establish here a peace indeed,
Concurring both in name and quality.

WESTMORELAND. When ever yet was your appeal denied?
Wherein have you been galled by the king?
What peer hath been suborn'd to grate on you,
That you should seal this lawless bloody book
Of forg'd rebellion with a seal divine,
And consecrate commotion's bitter edge?

ARCHBISHOP. My brother general, the commonwealth,
To brother born an household cruelty,
I make my quarrel in particular.

WESTMORELAND. There is no need of any such redress;
Or if there were, it not belongs to you.

MOWBRAY. Why not to him in part, and to us all
That feel the bruises of the days before,
And suffer the condition of these times
To lay a heavy and unequal hand
Upon our honours?

WESTMORELAND.   O! my good Lord Mowbray,
Construe the times to their necessities,
And you shall say indeed, it is the time,

And not the king, that doth you injuries.
Yet, for your part, it not appears to me
Either from the king or in the present time
That you should have an inch of any ground
To build a grief on: were you not restor'd
To all the Duke of Norfolk's signories,
Your noble and right well-remember'd father's?
MOWBRAY. What thing, in honour, had my father lost,
That need to be reviv'd and breath'd in me?
The king that lov'd him as the state stood then,
Was force perforce compell'd to banish him:
And then that Harry Bolingbroke and he,
Being mounted and both roused in their seats,
Their neighing coursers daring of the spur,
Their armed staves in charge, their beavers down,
Their eyes of fire sparkling through sights of steel,
And the loud trumpet blowing them together,
Then, then, when there was nothing could have stay'd
My father from the breast of Bolingbroke,
O! when the king did throw his warder down,
His own life hung upon the staff he threw;
Then threw he down himself and all their lives
That by indictment and by dint of sword
Have since miscarried under Bolingbroke.
WESTMORELAND. You speak, Lord Mowbray, now you
    know not what.
The Earl of Hereford was reputed then
In England the most valiant gentleman:
Who knows on whom Fortune would then have smil'd?
But if your father had been victor there,
He ne'er had borne it out of Coventry;
For all the country in a general voice
Cried hate upon him; and all their prayers and love
Were set on Hereford, whom they doted on
And bless'd and grac'd indeed, more than the king.
But this is mere digression from my purpose.
Here come I from our princely general
To know your griefs; to tell you from his Grace
That he will give you audience; and wherein
It shall appear that your demands are just,
You shall enjoy them; every thing set off
That might so much as think you enemies.

MOWBRAY. But he hath forc'd us to compel this offer,
    And it proceeds from policy, not love.
WESTMORELAND. Mowbray, you overween to take it so.
    This offer comes from mercy, not from fear:
    For, lo! within a ken our army lies
    Upon mine honour, all too confident
    To give admittance to a thought of fear.
    Our battle is more full of names than yours,
    Our men more perfect in the use of arms,
    Our armour all as strong, our cause the best;
    Then reason will our hearts should be as good:
    Say you not then our offer is compell'd.
MOWBRAY. Well, by my will we shall admit no parley.
WESTMORELAND. That argues but the shame of your
        offence:
    A rotten case abides no handling.
HASTINGS. Hath the Prince John a full commission,
    In very ample virtue of his father,
    To hear and absolutely to determine
    Of what conditions we shall stand upon?
WESTMORELAND. That is intended in the general's name.
    I muse you make so slight a question.
ARCHBISHOP. Then take, my Lord of Westmoreland, this
        schedule,
    For this contains our general grievances:
    Each several article herein redress'd;
    All members of our cause, both here and hence,
    That are insinew'd to this action,
    Acquitted by a true substantial form
    And present execution of our wills
    To us and to our purposes consign'd;
    We come within our awful banks again
    And knit our powers to the arm of peace.
WESTMORELAND. This will I show the general. Please you,
        lords,
    In sight of both our battles we may meet!
    And either end in peace, which God so frame!
    Or to the place of difference call the swords
    Which must decide it.
ARCHBISHOP.   My lord, we will do so.

                                    Exit Westmoreland
MOWBRAY. There is a thing within my bosom tells me

That no conditions of our peace can stand.

HASTINGS. Fear you not that: if we can make our peace
Upon such large terms, and so absolute
As our conditions shall consist upon,
Our peace shall stand as firm as rocky mountains.

MOWBRAY. Yea, but our valuation shall be such
That every slight and false-derived cause,
Yea, every idle, nice, and wanton reason
Shall to the king taste of this action;
That, were our royal faiths martyrs in love,
We shall be winnow'd with so rough a wind
That even our corn shall seem as light as chaff
And good from bad find no partition.

ARCHBISHOP. No, no, my lord. Note this; the king is weary
Of dainty and such picking grievances:
For he hath found to end one doubt by death
Revives two greater in the heirs of life;
And therefore will he wipe his tables clean,
And keep no tell-tale to his memory
That may repeat and history his loss
To new remembrance; for full well he knows
He cannot so precisely weed this land
As his misdoubts present occasion:
His foes are so enrooted with his friends
That, plucking to unfix an enemy,
He doth unfasten so and shake a friend.
So that this land, like an offensive wife,
That hath enrag'd him on to offer strokes,
As he is striking, holds his infant up
And hangs resolv'd correction in the arm
That was uprear'd to execution.

HASTINGS. Besides, the king hath wasted all his rods
On late offenders, that he now doth lack
The very instruments of chastisement;
So that his power, like to a fangless lion,
May offer, but not hold.

ARCHBISHOP.   'Tis very true:
And therefore be assur'd, my good Lord Marshal,
If we do now make our atonement well,
Our peace will, like a broken limb united,
Grow stronger for the breaking.

MOWBRAY.   Be it so.

Here is return'd my Lord of Westmoreland.

Re-enter Westmoreland

WESTMORELAND. The prince is here at hand: pleaseth your
lordship,
To meet his Grace just distance 'tween our armies?

MOWBRAY. Your Grace of York, in God's name then, set
forward.

ARCHBISHOP. Before, and greet his Grace: my lord, we
come.   *Exeunt*

SCENE   TWO

Another Part of the Forest.

*Enter, from one side, Mowbray, the Archbishop, Hastings,
and Others: from the other side, John of Lancaster,
Westmoreland, Officers, and Attendants*

LANCASTER. You are well encounter'd here, my cousin
Mowbray:
Good day to you, gentle Lord Archbishop;
And so to you, Lord Hastings, and to all.
My Lord of York, it better show'd with you,
When that your flock, assembled by the bell,
Encircled you to hear with reverence
Your exposition on the holy text
Than now to see you here an iron man,
Cheering a rout of rebels with your drum,
Turning the word to sword and life to death.
That man that sits within a monarch's heart
And ripens in the sunshine of his favour,
Would he abuse the countenance of the king,
Alack! what mischief might he set abroach
In shadow of such greatness. With you, Lord Bishop,
It is even so. Who hath not heard it spoken
How deep you were within the books of God?
To us, the speaker in his parliament;
To us the imagin'd voice of God himself;
The very opener and intelligencer
Between the grace, the sanctities of heaven,
And our dull workings. O! who shall believe
But you misuse the reverence of your place,

Employ the countenance and grace of heaven,
As a false favourite doth his prince's name,
In deeds dishonourable? You have taken up,
Under the counterfeited zeal of God,
The subjects of his substitute, my father;
And both against the peace of heaven and him
Have here upswarm'd them.
ARCHBISHOP.   Good my Lord of Lancaster,
I am not here against your father's peace;
But, as I told my Lord of Westmoreland,
The time misorder'd doth, in common sense,
Crowd us and crush us to this monstrous form,
To hold our safety up. I sent your Grace
The parcels and particulars of our grief,—
The which hath been with scorn shov'd from the court,—
Whereon this Hydra son of war is born;
Whose dangerous eyes may well be charm'd asleep
With grant of our most just and right desires,
And true obedience, of this madness cur'd,
Stoop tamely to the foot of majesty.
MOWBRAY. If not, we ready are to try our fortunes
To the last man.
HASTINGS.   And though we here fall down,
We have supplies to second our attempt:
If they miscarry, theirs shall second them:
And so success of mischief shall be born,
And heir from heir shall hold this quarrel up
Whiles England shall have generation.
LANCASTER. You are too shallow, Hastings, much to
    shallow,
To sound the bottom of the after-times.
WESTMORELAND. Pleaseth your Grace to answer them
    directly
How far forth you do like their articles.
LANCASTER. I like them all, and do allow them well;
And swear here, by the honour of my blood,
My father's purposes have been mistook,
And some about him have too lavishly
Wrested his meaning and authority.
My lord, these griefs shall be with speed redress'd;
Upon my soul, they shall. If this may please you,
Discharge your powers unto their several counties,

As we will ours: and here between the armies
Let's drink together friendly and embrace,
That all their eyes may bear those tokens home
Of our restored love and amity.

ARCHBISHOP. I take your princely word for these redresses.

LANCASTER. I give it you, and will maintain my word:
And thereupon I drink unto your Grace.

HASTINGS. (*To an Officer*) Go, captain, and deliver to the
army
This news of peace: let them have pay, and part:
I know it will well please them: hie thee, captain.

Exit Officer

ARCHBISHOP. To you, my noble Lord of Westmoreland.

WESTMORELAND. I pledge your Grace: and, if you knew
what pains
I have bestow'd to breed this present peace,
You would drink freely; but my love to you
Shall show itself more openly hereafter.

ARCHBISHOP. I do not doubt you.

WESTMORELAND.   I am glad of it.
Health to my lord and gentle cousin, Mowbray.

MOWBRAY. You wish me health in very happy season;
For I am, on the sudden, something ill.

ARCHBISHOP. Against ill chances men are ever merry,
But heaviness foreruns the good event.

WESTMORELAND. Therefore be merry, coz; since sudden
sorrow
Serves to say thus, Some good thing comes to-morrow.

ARCHBISHOP. Believe me, I am passing light in spirit.

MOWBRAY. So much the worse if your own rule be true.

Shouts within

LANCASTER. The word of peace is render'd: hark, how they
shout!

MOWBRAY. This had been cheerful, after victory.

ARCHBISHOP. A peace is of the nature of a conquest;
For then both parties nobly are subdu'd,
And neither party loser.

LANCASTER.   Go, my lord,
And let our army be discharged too.   *Exit Westmoreland*
And, good my lord, so please you, let our trains
March by us, that we may peruse the men
We should have cop'd withal.

ARCHBISHOP.   Go, good Lord Hastings,
   And, ere they be dismiss'd, let them march by.
                                        Exit Hastings
LANCASTER. I trust, lords, we shall lie to-night together.
                    Re-enter Westmoreland
   Now, cousin, wherefore stands our army still?
WESTMORELAND. The leaders, having charge from you to
      stand,
   Will not go off until they hear you speak.
LANCASTER. They know their duties.
                    Re-enter Hastings
HASTINGS. My lord, our army is dispers'd already:
   Like youthful steers unyok'd, they take their courses
   East, west, north, south; or, like a school broke up,
   Each hurries toward his home and sporting-place.
WESTMORELAND. Good tidings, my Lord Hastings; for the
      which
   I do arrest thee, traitor, of high treason:
   And you, Lord Archbishop, and you, Lord Mowbray,
   Of capital treason I attach you both.
MOWBRAY. Is this proceeding just and honourable?
WESTMORELAND. Is your assembly so?
ARCHBISHOP. Will you thus break your faith?
LANCASTER.   I pawn'd thee none.
   I promis'd you redress of these same grievances
   Whereof you did complain; which, by mine honour,
   I will perform with a most Christian care.
   But for you, rebels, look to taste the due
   Meet for rebellion and such acts as yours.
   Most shallowly did you these arms commence,
   Fondly brought here and foolishly sent hence.
   Strike up our drums! pursue the scatter'd stray:
   God, and not we, hath safely fought to-day.
   Some guard these traitors to the block of death;
   Treason's true bed, and yielder up of breath.   *Exeunt*

SCENE THREE

Another Part of the Forest.

Alarums. Excursions. Enter Falstaff and Colevile, meeting

FALSTAFF. What 's your name, sir? of what condition are
you, and of what place, I pray?

COLEVILE. I am a knight, sir; and my name is Colevile of the
dale.

FALSTAFF. Well then, Colevile is your name, a knight is your
degree, and your place the dale: Colevile shall still be
your name, a traitor your degree, and the dungeon your
place, a place deep enough; so shall you be still Colevile
of the dale.

COLEVILE. Are not you Sir John Falstaff?

FALSTAFF. As good a man as he, sir, whoe'er I am. Do ye
yield, sir, or shall I sweat for you? If I do sweat, they are
the drops of thy lovers, and they weep for thy death:
therefore rouse up fear and trembling, and do observance
to my mercy.

COLEVILE. I think you are Sir John Falstaff, and in that
thought yield me.

FALSTAFF. I have a whole school of tongues in this belly of
mine, and not a tongue of them all speaks any other word
but my name. An I had but a belly of any indifferency, I
were simply the most active fellow in Europe: my womb,
my womb, my womb undoes me. Here comes our general.

Enter John of Lancaster, Westmoreland, Blunt, and Others

LANCASTER. The heat is past, follow no further now.
Call in the powers, good cousin Westmoreland.

Exit Westmoreland

Now, Falstaff, where have you been all this while?
When every thing is ended, then you come:
These tardy tricks of yours will, on my life,
One time or other break some gallows' back.

FALSTAFF. I would be sorry, my lord, but it should be thus:
I never knew yet but rebuke and check was the reward of
valour. Do you think me a swallow, an arrow, or a bullet?
have I, in my poor and old motion, the expedition of
thought? I have speeded hither with the very extremest

inch of possibility; I have foundered nine score and odd
posts; and here, travel-tainted as I am, have, in my pure
and immaculate valour, taken Sir John Colevile of the
dale, a most furious knight and valorous enemy. But what
of that? he saw me, and yielded; that I may justly say with
the hook-nosed fellow of Rome, 'I came, saw, and over-
came.'

LANCASTER. It was more of his courtesy than your deserving.

FALSTAFF. I know not: here he is, and here I yield him; and
I beseech your Grace, let it be booked with the rest of this
day's deeds; or, by the Lord, I will have it in a particular
ballad else, with mine own picture on the top on't, Cole-
vile kissing my foot. To the which course if I be enforced,
if you do not all show like gilt twopences to me, and I in
the clear sky of fame o'ershine you as much as the full
moon doth the cinders of the element, which show like
pins' heads to her, believe not the word of the noble.
Therefore let me have right, and let desert mount.

LANCASTER. Thine 's too heavy to mount.

FALSTAFF. Let it shine then.

LANCASTER. Thine 's too thick to shine.

FALSTAFF. Let it do something, my good lord, that may do
me good, and call it what you will.

LANCASTER. Is thy name Colevile?

COLEVILE. It is, my lord.

LANCASTER. A famous rebel art thou, Colevile.

FALSTAFF. And a famous true subject took him.

COLEVILE. I am, my lord, but as my betters are
That led me hither: had they been rul'd by me
You should have won them dearer than you have.

FALSTAFF. I know not how they sold themselves: but thou,
like a kind fellow, gavest thyself away gratis, and I thank
thee for thee.

　　　　　　Re-enter Westmoreland

LANCASTER. Have you left pursuit?

WESTMORELAND. Retreat is made and execution stay'd.

LANCASTER. Send Colevile with his confederates
To York, to present execution.
Blunt, lead him hence, and see you guard him sure.

　　　　　Exit Blunt and Others with Colevile, guarded
And now dispatch we toward the court, my lords:
I hear, the king my father is sore sick:

Our news shall go before us to his Majesty,
Which, cousin (*addressing Westmoreland*), you shall
  bear, to comfort him;
And we with sober speed will follow you.

FALSTAFF. My lord, I beseech you, give me leave to go
Through Gloucestershire, and when you come to court
Stand my good lord, pray, in your good report.

LANCASTER. Fare you well, Falstaff: I, in my condition,
Shall better speak of you than you deserve.

Exeunt all but Falstaff

FALSTAFF. I would you had but the wit: 'twere better than
your dukedom. Good faith, this same young sober-blooded
boy doth not love me; nor a man cannot make him laugh;
but that 's no marvel, he drinks no wine. There 's never
none of these demure boys come to any proof; for thin
drink doth so overcool their blood, and making many fish-
meals, that they fall into a kind of male green-sickness;
and then, when they marry, they get wenches. They are
generally fools and cowards, which some of us should be
too but for inflammation. A good sherris-sack hath a two-
fold operation in it. It ascends me into the brain; dries me
there all the foolish and dull and crudy vapours which
environ it; makes it apprehensive, quick, forgetive, full of
nimble fiery and delectable shapes; which, deliver'd o'er
to the voice, the tongue, which is the birth, becomes ex-
cellent wit. The second property of your excellent sherris
is, the warming of the blood; which, before cold and
settled, left the liver white and pale, which is the badge
of pusillanimity and cowardice: but the sherris warms it
and makes it course from the inwards to the parts ex-
treme. It illumineth the face, which, as a beacon, gives
warning to all the rest of this little kingdom, man, to arm;
and then the vital commoners and inland petty spirits
muster me all to their captain, the heart, who, great and
puffed up with this retinue, doth any deed of courage;
and this valour comes of sherris. So that skill in the
weapon is nothing without sack, for that sets it a-work;
and learning, a mere hoard of gold kept by a devil till
sack commences it and sets it in act and use. Hereof
comes it that Prince Harry is valiant; for the cold blood
he did naturally inherit of his father, he hath, like lean,
sterile, and bare land, manured, husbanded, and tilled,

with excellent endeavour of drinking good and good store
of fertile sherris, that he is become very hot and valiant.
If I had a thousand sons, the first human principle I would
teach them should be, to forswear thin potations and to
addict themselves to sack.

Enter Bardolph

How now, Bardolph?

BARDOLPH. The army is discharged all and gone.

FALSTAFF. Let them go. I 'll through Gloucestershire; and
there will I visit Master Robert Shallow, esquire: I have
him already tempering between my finger and my thumb,
and shortly will I seal with him. Come away.   *Exeunt*

SCENE FOUR

Westminster. The Jerusalem Chamber.

Enter King Henry, Clarence, Gloucester,
Warwick, and Others

KING HENRY. Now, lords, if God doth give successful end
  To this debate that bleedeth at our doors,
  We will our youth lead on to higher fields
  And draw no swords but what are sanctified.
  Our navy is address'd, our power collected,
  Our substitutes in absence well invested,
  And every thing lies level to our wish:
  Only, we want a little personal strength;
  And pause us, till these rebels, now afoot,
  Come underneath the yoke of government.

WARWICK. Both which we doubt not but your Majesty
  Shall soon enjoy.

KING HENRY.   Humphrey, my son of Gloucester,
  Where is the prince your brother?

GLOUCESTER. I think he 's gone to hunt, my lord, at Windsor.

KING HENRY. And how accompanied?

GLOUCESTER.   I do not know, my lord.

KING HENRY. Is not his brother Thomas of Clarence with
  him?

GLOUCESTER. No, my good lord; he is in presence here.

CLARENCE. What would my lord and father?

KING HENRY. Nothing but well to thee, Thomas of Clarence.

How chance thou art not with the prince thy brother?
He loves thee, and thou dost neglect him, Thomas;
Thou hast a better place in his affection
Than all thy brothers: cherish it, my boy,
And noble offices thou mayst effect
Of mediation, after I am dead,
Between his greatness and thy other brethren:
Therefore omit him not; blunt not his love,
Nor lose the good advantage of his grace
By seeming cold or careless of his will;
For he is gracious, if he be observ'd:
He hath a tear for pity and a hand
Open as day for melting charity;
Yet, notwithstanding, being incens'd, he's flint;
As humorous as winter, and as sudden
As flaws congealed in the spring of day.
His temper therefore must be well observ'd:
Chide him for faults, and do it reverently,
When you perceive his blood inclin'd to mirth;
But, being moody, give him line and scope,
Till that his passions, like a whale on ground,
Confound themselves with working. Learn this, **Thomas,**
And thou shalt prove a shelter to thy friends,
A hoop of gold to bind thy brothers in,
That the united vessel of their blood,
Mingled with venom of suggestion—
As, force perforce, the age will pour it in—
Shall never leak, though it do work as strong
As aconitum or rash gunpowder.

CLARENCE. I shall observe him with all care and love.
KING HENRY. Why art thou not at Windsor with him,
    Thomas?
CLARENCE. He is not there to-day; he dines in London.
KING HENRY. And how accompanied? canst thou tell that?
CLARENCE. With Poins and other his continual followers.
KING HENRY. Most subject is the fattest soil to weeds;
    And he, the noble image of my youth,
    Is overspread with them: therefore my grief
    Stretches itself beyond the hour of death:
    The blood weeps from my heart when I do shape
    In forms imaginary the unguided days
    And rotten times that you shall look upon

When I am sleeping with my ancestors.
For when his headstrong riot hath no curb,
When rage and hot blood are his counsellors,
When means and lavish manners meet together,
O! with what wings shall his affections fly
Towards fronting peril and oppos'd decay.

WARWICK. My gracious lord, you look beyond him quite:
The prince but studies his companions
Like a strange tongue, wherein, to gain the language,
'Tis needful that the most immodest word
Be look'd upon, and learn'd; which once attain'd,
Your Highness knows, comes to no further use
But to be known and hated. So, like gross terms,
The prince will in the perfectness of time
Cast off his followers; and their memory
Shall as a pattern or a measure live,
By which his Grace must mete the lives of others,
Turning past evils to advantages.

KING HENRY. 'Tis seldom when the bee doth leave her comb
In the dead carrion.

Enter Westmoreland

Who 's here? Westmoreland!

WESTMORELAND. Health to my sovereign, and new happi-
ness
Added to that that I am to deliver!
Prince John your son doth kiss your Grace's hand:
Mowbray, the Bishop Scroop, Hastings and all
Are brought to the correction of your law.
There is not now a rebel's sword unsheath'd,
But Peace puts forth her olive every where.
The manner how this action hath been borne
Here at more leisure may your Highness read,
With every course in his particular.

KING HENRY. O Westmoreland! thou art a summer bird,
Which ever in the haunch of winter sings
The lifting up of day.

Enter Harcourt

Look! here 's more news.

HARCOURT. From enemies heaven keep your Majesty;
And, when they stand against you, may they fall
As those that I am come to tell you of!
The Earl Northumberland, and the Lord Bardolph,

With a great power of English and of Scots,
Are by the sheriff of Yorkshire overthrown.
The manner and true order of the fight
This packet, please it you, contains at large.

KING HENRY.   And wherefore should these good news make
me sick?
Will Fortune never come with both hands full
But write her fair words still in foulest letters?
She either gives a stomach and no food;
Such are the poor, in health; or else a feast
And takes away the stomach; such are the rich,
That have abundance and enjoy it not.
I should rejoice now at this happy news,
And now my sight fails, and my brain is giddy.
O me! come near me, now I am much ill.

GLOUCESTER.   Comfort, your Majesty!

CLARENCE.   O my royal father!

WESTMORELAND.   My sovereign lord, cheer up yourself: look
up!

WARWICK.   Be patient, princes: you do know these fits
Are with his Highness very ordinary:
Stand from him, give him air; he 'll straight be well.

CLARENCE.   No, no; he cannot long hold out these pangs:
The incessant care and labour of his mind
Hath wrought the mure that should confine it in
So thin, that life looks through and will break out.

GLOUCESTER.   The people fear me; for they do observe
Unfather'd heirs and loathly births of nature:
The seasons change their manners, as the year
Had found some months asleep and leap'd them over.

CLARENCE.   The river hath thrice flow'd, no ebb between;
And the old folk, time's doting chronicles,
Say it did so a little time before
That our great-grandsire, Edward, sick'd and died.

WARWICK.   Speak lower, princes, for the king recovers.

GLOUCESTER.   This apoplexy will certain be his end.

KING HENRY.   I pray you take me up, and bear me hence
Into some other chamber: softly, pray.

SCENE FIVE

Another Chamber.

King Henry lying on a bed: Clarence, Gloucester,
Warwick, and Others in attendance

KING HENRY. Let there be no noise made, my gentle friends;
  Unless some dull and favourable hand
  Will whisper music to my weary spirit.
WARWICK. Call for the music in the other room.
KING HENRY. Set me the crown upon my pillow here.
CLARENCE. His eye is hollow, and he changes much.
WARWICK. Less noise, less noise!
Enter the Prince

PRINCE.   Who saw the Duke of Clarence?
CLARENCE. I am here, brother, full of heaviness.
PRINCE. How now! rain within doors, and none abroad!
  How doth the king?
GLOUCESTER.   Exceeding ill.
PRINCE.   Heard he the good news yet?
  Tell it him.
GLOUCESTER. He alter'd much upon the hearing it.
PRINCE. If he be sick with joy, he will recover without
    physic.
WARWICK. Not so much noise, my lords. Sweet prince, speak
    low;
  The king your father is dispos'd to sleep.
CLARENCE. Let us withdraw into the other room.
WARWICK. Will 't please your Grace to go along with us?
PRINCE. No; I will sit and watch here by the king.
Exeunt all but the Prince

  Why doth the crown lie there upon his pillow,
  Being so troublesome a bedfellow?
  O polish'd perturbation! golden care!
  That keep'st the ports of slumber open wide
  To many a watchful night! Sleep with it now!
  Yet not so sound, and half so deeply sweet
  As he whose brow with homely biggin bound
  Snores out the watch of night. O majesty!
  When thou dost pinch thy bearer, thou dost sit

Like a rich armour worn in heat of day,
That scalds with safety. By his gates of breath
There lies a downy feather which stirs not:
Did he suspire, that light and weightless down
Perforce must move. My gracious lord! my father!
This sleep is sound indeed; this is a sleep
That from this golden rigol hath divorc'd
So many English kings. Thy due from me
Is tears and heavy sorrows of the blood,
Which nature, love, and filial tenderness
Shall, O dear father! pay thee plenteously:
My due from thee is this imperial crown,
Which, as immediate from thy place and blood,
Derives itself to me. Lo! here it sits, *Putting it on his head*
Which heaven shall guard; and put the world's whole
    strength
Into one giant arm, it shall not force
This lineal honour from me. This from thee
Will I to mine leave, as 'tis left to me.   *Exit*

KING HENRY. (*Waking*) Warwick! Gloucester! Clarence!
    Re-enter Warwick, Gloucester, Clarence, and the rest
CLARENCE.   Doth the king call?
WARWICK. What would your Majesty? How fares your
    Grace?
KING HENRY. Why did you leave me here alone, my lords?
CLARENCE. We left the prince my brother here, my liege,
    Who undertook to sit and watch by you.
KING HENRY. The Prince of Wales! Where is he? let me see
    him:
    He is not here.
WARWICK. This door is open; he is gone this way.
GLOUCESTER. He came not through the chamber where we
    stay'd.
KING HENRY. Where is the crown? who took it from my
    pillow?
WARWICK. When we withdrew, my liege, we left it here.
KING HENRY. The prince hath ta'en it hence: go, seek him
    out.
    Is he so hasty that he doth suppose
    My sleep my death?
    Find him, my Lord of Warwick; chide him hither.
                                        Exit Warwick

This part of his conjoins with my disease,
And helps to end me. See, sons, what things you are!
How quickly nature falls into revolt
When gold becomes her object!
For this the foolish over-careful fathers
Have broke their sleeps with thoughts,
Their brains with care, their bones with industry;
For this they have engrossed and pil'd up
The canker'd heaps of strange-achieved gold;
For this they have been thoughtful to invest
Their sons with arts and martial exercises:
When, like the bee, culling from every flower
The virtuous sweets,
Our thighs pack'd with wax, our mouths with honey,
We bring it to the hive, and like the bees,
Are murder'd for our pains. This bitter taste
Yield his engrossments to the ending father.

Re-enter Warwick

Now, where is he that will not stay so long
Till his friend sickness hath determin'd me?

WARWICK. My lord, I found the prince in the next room,
Washing with kindly tears his gentle cheeks,
With such a deep demeanour in great sorrow
That tyranny, which never quaff'd but blood,
Would, by beholding him, have wash'd his knife
With gentle eye-drops. He is coming hither.

KING HENRY. But wherefore did he take away the crown?

Re-enter the Prince

Lo, where he comes. Come hither to me, Harry.
Depart the chamber, leave us here alone.

Exeunt Warwick, and the rest

PRINCE. I never thought to hear you speak again.

KING HENRY. Thy wish was father, Harry, to that thought:
I stay too long by thee, I weary thee.
Dost thou so hunger for my empty chair
That thou wilt needs invest thee with mine honours
Before thy hour be ripe? O foolish youth!
Thou seek'st the greatness that will overwhelm thee.
Stay but a little; for my cloud of dignity
Is held from falling with so weak a wind
That it will quickly drop: my day is dim.
Thou hast stol'n that which after some few hours

Were thine without offence; and at my death
Thou hast seal'd up my expectation:
Thy life did manifest thou lov'dst me not,
And thou wilt have me die assur'd of it.
Thou hid'st a thousand daggers in thy thoughts,
Which thou hast whetted on thy stony heart,
To stab at half an hour of my life.
What! canst thou not forbear me half an hour?
Then get thee gone and dig my grave thyself,
And bid the merry bells ring to thine ear
That thou art crowned, not that I am dead.
Let all the tears that should bedew my hearse
Be drops of balm to sanctify thy head:
Only compound me with forgotten dust;
Give that which gave thee life unto the worms.
Pluck down my officers, break my decrees;
For now a time is come to mock at form.
Harry the Fifth is crown'd! Up, vanity!
Down, royal state! all you sage counsellors, hence!
And to the English court assemble now,
From every region, apes of idleness!
Now, neighbour confines, purge you of your scum:
Have you a ruffian that will swear, drink, dance,
Revel the night, rob, murder, and commit
The oldest sins the newest kind of ways?
Be happy, he will trouble you no more:
England shall double gild his treble guilt.
England shall give him office, honour, might;
For the fifth Harry from curb'd licence plucks
The muzzle of restraint, and the wild dog
Shall flesh his tooth in every innocent.
O my poor kingdom! sick with civil blows.
When that my care could not withhold thy riots,
What wilt thou do when riot is thy care?
O! thou wilt be a wilderness again,
Peopled with wolves, thy old inhabitants.
PRINCE. O! pardon me, my liege; but for my tears,
The moist impediments unto my speech,
I had forestall'd this dear and deep rebuke
Ere you with grief had spoke and I had heard
The course of it so far. There is your crown;
And he that wears the crown immortally

Long guard it yours! If I affect it more
Than as your honour and as your renown,
Let me no more from this obedience rise,—
Which my most true and inward duteous spirit
Teacheth,—this prostrate and exterior bending.
God witness with me, when I here came in,
And found no course of breath within your Majesty,
How cold it struck my heart! if I do feign,
O! let me in my present wildness die
And never live to show the incredulous world
The noble change that I have purposed.
Coming to look on you, thinking you dead,
And dead almost, my liege, to think you were,
I spake unto the crown as having sense,
And thus upbraided it: 'The care on thee depending
Hath fed upon the body of my father;
Therefore, thou best of gold art worst of gold:
Other, less fine in carat, is more precious,
Preserving life in medicine potable:
But thou most fine, most honour'd, most renown'd,
Hast eat thy bearer up.' Thus, my most royal liege,
Accusing it, I put it on my head,
To try with it, as with an enemy
That had before my face murder'd my father,
The quarrel of a true inheritor.
But if it did infect my blood with joy,
Or swell my thoughts to any strain of pride;
If any rebel or vain spirit of mine
Did with the least affection of a welcome
Give entertainment to the might of it,
Let God for ever keep it from my head,
And make me as the poorest vassal is
That doth with awe and terror kneel to it!
KING HENRY. O my son
God put it in thy mind to take it hence,
That thou mightst win the more thy father's love,
Pleading so wisely in excuse of it.
Come hither, Harry: sit thou by my bed;
And hear, I think, the very latest counsel
That ever I shall breathe. God knows, my son,
By what by-paths and indirect crook'd ways
I met this crown; and I myself know well

How troublesome it sat upon my head:
To thee it shall descend with better quiet,
Better opinion, better confirmation;
For all the soil of the achievement goes
With me into the earth. It seem'd in me
But as an honour snatch'd with boisterous hand,
And I had many living to upbraid
My gain of it by the'r assistances;
Which daily grew to quarrel and to bloodshed,
Wounding supposed peace. All these bold fears
Thou seest with peril I have answered;
For all my reign hath been but as a scene
Acting that argument; and now my death
Changes the mode: for what in me was purchas'd,
Falls upon thee in a more fairer sort;
So thou the garment wear'st successively.
Yet, though thou stand'st more sure than I could do,
Thou art not firm enough, since griefs are green;
And all my friends, which thou must make thy friends,
Have but their stings and teeth newly ta'en out;
By whose fell working I was first advanc'd,
And by whose power I well might lodge a fear
To be again displac'd: which to avoid,
I cut them off; and had a purpose now
To lead out many to the Holy Land,
Lest rest and lying still might make them look
Too near unto my state. Therefore, my Harry,
Be it thy course to busy giddy minds
With foreign quarrels; that action, hence borne out,
May waste the memory of the former days.
More would I, but my lungs are wasted so
That strength of speech is utterly denied me.
How I came by the crown, O God, forgive!
And grant it may with thee in true peace live.
PRINCE. My gracious liege,
You won it, wore it, kept it, gave it me;
Then plain and right must my possession be:
Which I with more than with a common pain
'Gainst all the world will rightfully maintain.
            Enter John of Lancaster
KING HENRY. Look, look, here comes my John of Lancaster.

LANCASTER. Health, peace, and happiness to my royal
     father!
KING HENRY. Thou bring'st me happiness and peace, son
     John;
  But health, alack, with youthful wings is flown
  From this bare wither'd trunk: upon thy sight
  My worldly business makes a period.
  Where is my Lord of Warwick?
PRINCE.   My Lord of Warwick!
          Re-enter Warwick and Others
KING HENRY. Doth any name particular belong
  Unto the lodging where I first did swound?
WARWICK. 'Tis call'd Jerusalem, my noble lord.
KING HENRY. Laud be to God! even there my life must end.
  It hath been prophesied to me many years
  I should not die but in Jerusalem,
  Which vainly I suppos'd the Holy Land.
  But bear me to that chamber; there I 'll lie:
  In that Jerusalem shall Harry die.   *Exeunt*

ACT FIVE

SCENE ONE

Gloucestershire. A Hall in Shallow's House.

Enter Shallow, Falstaff, Bardolph, and Page

SHALLOW. By cock and pie, sir, you shall not away to-night. What! Davy, I say.

FALSTAFF. You must excuse me, Master Robert Shallow.

SHALLOW. I will not excuse you; you shall not be excused; excuses shall not be admitted; there is no excuse shall serve; you shall not be excused. Why, Davy!

Enter Davy

DAVY. Here, sir.

SHALLOW. Davy, Davy, Davy, Davy, let me see, Davy; let me see: yea, marry, William cook, bid him come hither. Sir John, you shall not be excused.

DAVY. Marry, sir, thus; those precepts cannot be served: and again, sir, shall we sow the headland with wheat?

SHALLOW. With red wheat, Davy. But for William cook: are there no young pigeons?

DAVY. Yes, sir. Here is now the smith's note for shoeing and plough-irons.

SHALLOW. Let it be cast and paid. Sir John, you shall not be excused.

DAVY. Now, sir, a new link to the bucket must needs be had: and, sir, do you mean to stop any of William's wages, about the sack he lost the other day at Hinckley fair?

SHALLOW. A' shall answer it. Some pigeons, Davy, a couple of short-legged hens, a joint of mutton, and any pretty little tiny kickshaws, tell William cook.

DAVY. Doth the man of war stay all night, sir?

SHALLOW. Yea, Davy. I will use him well. A friend i' the court is better than a penny in purse. Use his men well, Davy, for they are arrant knaves, and will backbite.

DAVY. No worse than they are backbitten, sir; for they have marvellous foul linen.

SHALLOW. Well conceited, Davy: about thy business, Davy.

DAVY. I beseech you, sir, to countenance William Visor of Wincot against Clement Perkes of the hill.

SHALLOW. There are many complaints, Davy, against that Visor: that Visor is an arrant knave, on my knowledge.

DAVY. I grant your worship that he is a knave, sir; but yet, God forbid, sir, but a knave should have some countenance at his friend's request. An honest man, sir, is able to speak for himself, when a knave is not. I have served your worship truly, sir, this eight years; and if I cannot once or twice in a quarter bear out a knave against an honest man, I have but a very little credit with your worship. The knave is mine honest friend, sir; therefore, I beseech your worship, let him be countenanced.

SHALLOW. Go to; I say he shall have no wrong. Look about, Davy. (*Exit Davy*) Where are you, Sir John? Come, come, come; off with your boots. Give me your hand, Master Bardolph.

BARDOLPH. I am glad to see your worship.

SHALLOW. I thank thee with all my heart, kind Master Bardolph:—(*To the Page*) and welcome, my tall fellow. Come, Sir John.

FALSTAFF. I 'll follow you, good Master Robert Shallow. (*Exit Shallow*) Bardolph, look to our horses. (*Exeunt Bardolph and Page*) If I were sawed into quantities, I should make four dozen of such bearded hermit's staves as Master Shallow. It is a wonderful thing to see the semblable coherence of his men's spirits and his: they, by observing him, do bear themselves like foolish justices; he, by conversing with them, is turned into a justice-like serving-man. Their spirits are so married in conjunction with the participation of society that they flock together in consent, like so many wild geese. If I had a suit to Master Shallow, I would humour his men with the imputation of being near their master: if to his men, I would curry with Master Shallow that no man could better command his servants. It is certain that either wise bearing or ignorant carriage is caught, as men take diseases, one of another: therefore let men take heed of their company. I will devise matter enough out of this Shallow to keep

Prince Harry in continual laughter the wearing out of six fashions,—which is four terms, or two actions,—and a' shall laugh without intervallums. O! it is much that a lie with a slight oath and a jest with a sad brow will do with a fellow that never had the ache in his shoulders. O! you shall see him laugh till his face be like a wet cloak ill laid up!

SHALLOW. (*Within*) Sir John!

FALSTAFF. I come, Master Shallow: I come, Master Shallow.

Exit

SCENE TWO

Westminster. An Apartment in the Palace.

Enter Warwick and the Lord Chief Justice

WARWICK. How now, my Lord Chief Justice! whither away?

CHIEF JUSTICE. How doth the king?

WARWICK. Exceeding well: his cares are now all ended.

CHIEF JUSTICE. I hope not dead.

WARWICK.   He 's walk'd the way of nature;
And to our purposes he lives no more.

CHIEF JUSTICE. I would his Majesty had call'd me with him:
The service that I truly did his life
Hath left me open to all injuries.

WARWICK. Indeed I think the young king loves you not.

CHIEF JUSTICE. I know he doth not, and do arm myself,
To welcome the condition of the time;
Which cannot look more hideously upon me
Than I have drawn it in my fantasy.

Enter Lancaster, Clarence,
Gloucester, Westmoreland, and Others

WARWICK. Here come the heavy issue of dead Harry:
O! that the living Harry had the temper
Of him, the worst of these three gentlemen.
How many nobles then should hold their places,
That must strike sail to spirits of vile sort!

CHIEF JUSTICE. O God! I fear all will be overturn'd.

LANCASTER. Good-morrow, cousin Warwick, good-morrow.

GLOUCESTER.
CLARENCE. } Good-morrow, cousin.

LANCASTER. We meet like men that had forgot to speak.

WARWICK. We do remember; but our argument
Is all too heavy to admit much talk.

LANCASTER. Well, peace be with him that hath made us
heavy!

CHIEF JUSTICE. Peace be with us, lest we be heavier!

GLOUCESTER. O! good my lord, you have lost a friend indeed;
And I dare swear you borrow not that face
Of seeming sorrow; it is sure your own.

LANCASTER. Though no man be assur'd what grace to find,
You stand in coldest expectation.
I am the sorrier; would 'twere otherwise.

CLARENCE. Well, you must now speak Sir John Falstaff fair,
Which swims against your stream of quality.

CHIEF JUSTICE. Sweet princes, what I did, I did in honour,
Led by the impartial conduct of my soul;
And never shall you see that I will beg
A ragged and forestall'd remission.
If truth and upright innocency fail me,
I 'll to the king my master that is dead,
And tell him who hath sent me after him.

WARWICK. Here comes the prince.

Enter King Henry the Fifth, attended

CHIEF JUSTICE. Good-morrow, and God save your Majest·!

KING HENRY V. This new and gorgeous garment, majesty,
Sits not so easy on me as you think.
Brothers, you mix your sadness with some fear:
This is the English, not the Turkish court;
Not Amurath an Amurath succeeds,
But Harry Harry. Yet be sad, good brothers,
For, to speak truth, it very well becomes you:
Sorrow so royally in you appears
That I will deeply put the fashion on
And wear it in my heart. Why then, be sad;
But entertain no more of it, good brothers,
Than a joint burden laid upon us all.
For me, by heaven, I bid you be assur'd,
I 'll be your father and your brother too;
Let me but bear your love, I 'll bear your cares:
Yet weep that Harry's dead, and so will I;
But Harry lives that shall convert those tears
By number into hours of happiness.

LANCASTER, &C. We hope no other from your Majesty.

KING HENRY V. You all look strangely on me: (*To the Chief Justice*) and you most;
You are, I think, assur'd I love you not.

CHIEF JUSTICE. I am assur'd, if I be measur'd rightly.
Your Majesty hath no just cause to hate me.

KING HENRY V. No!
How might a prince of my great hopes forget
So great indignities you laid upon me?
What! rate, rebuke, and roughly send to prison
The immediate heir of England! Was this easy?
May this be wash'd in Lethe, and forgotten?

CHIEF JUSTICE. I then did use the person of your father;
The image of his power lay then in me:
And, in the administration of his law,
Whiles I was busy for the commonwealth,
Your Highness pleased to forget my place,
The majesty and power of law and justice,
The image of the king whom I presented,
And struck me in my very seat of judgment;
Whereon, as an offender to your father,
I gave bold way to my authority,
And did commit you. If the deed were ill,
Be you contented, wearing now the garland,
To have a son set your decrees at nought,
To pluck down justice from your awful bench,
To trip the course of law, and blunt the sword
That guards the peace and safety of your person:
Nay, more, to spurn at your most royal image
And mock your workings in a second body.
Question your royal thoughts, make the case yours;
Be now the father and propose a son,
Hear your own dignity so much profan'd,
See your most dreadful laws so loosely slighted,
Behold yourself so by a son disdain'd;
And then imagine me taking your part,
And in your power soft silencing your son:
After this cold considerance, sentence me;
And, as you are a king, speak in your state
What I have done that misbecame my place,
My person, or my liege's sovereignty.

KING HENRY V. You are right, justice; and you weigh this
        well;
Therefore still bear the balance and the sword:
And I do wish your honours may increase
Till you do live to see a son of mine
Offend you and obey you, as I did.
So shall I live to speak my father's words:
'Happy am I, that have a man so bold
That dares do justice on my proper son;
And not less happy, having such a son,
That would deliver up his greatness so
Into the hands of justice.' You did commit me:
For which, I do commit into your hand
The unstained sword that you have us'd to bear;
With this remembrance, that you use the same
With the like bold, just, and impartial spirit
As you have done 'gainst me. There is my hand:
You shall be as a father to my youth;
My voice shall sound as you do prompt mine ear,
And I will stoop and humble my intents
To your well-practis'd wise directions.
And, princes all, believe me, I beseech you;
My father is gone wild into his grave,
For in his tomb lie my affections;
And with his spirit sadly I survive,
To mock the expectation of the world,
To frustrate prophecies, and to raze out
Rotten opinion, who hath writ me down
After my seeming. The tide of blood in me
Hath proudly flow'd in vanity till now:
Now doth it turn and ebb back to the sea,
Where it shall mingle with the state of floods
And flow henceforth in formal majesty.
Now call we our high court of parliament;
And let us choose such limbs of noble counsel,
That the great body of our state may go
In equal rank with the best govern'd nation;
That war or peace, or both at once, may be
As things acquainted and familiar to us;
In which you, father, shall have foremost hand.
Our coronation done, we will accite,
As I before remember'd, all our state:

And, God consigning to my good intents,
No prince nor peer shall have just cause to say,
God shorten Harry's happy life one day.   *Exeunt*

SCENE THREE

Gloucestershire. The Garden of Shallow's House.

*Enter Falstaff, Shallow, Silence, Bardolph,
the Page, and Davy*

SHALLOW. Nay, you shall see mine orchard, where, in an ar-
bour, we will eat a last year's pippin of my own graffing,
with a dish of caraways, and so forth; come, cousin Si-
lence; and then to bed.

FALSTAFF. 'Fore God, you have here a goodly dwelling, and
a rich.

SHALLOW. Barren, barren, barren; beggars all, beggars all, Sir
John: marry, good air. Spread, Davy; spread, Davy: well
said, Davy.

FALSTAFF. This Davy serves you for good uses; he is your
serving-man and your husband.

SHALLOW. A good varlet, a good varlet, a very good varlet,
Sir John: by the mass, I have drunk too much sack at sup-
per: a good varlet. Now sit down, now sit down. Come,
cousin.

SILENCE.   Ah, sirrah! quoth a', we shall
              Do nothing but eat, and make good cheer,
              And praise God for the merry year;
              When flesh is cheap and females dear,
              And lusty lads roam here and there,
                      So merrily,
              And ever among so merrily.

FALSTAFF. There 's a merry heart! Good Master Silence, I 'll
give you a health for that anon.

SHALLOW. Give Master Bardolph some wine, Davy.

DAVY. Sweet sir, sit; I 'll be with you anon: most sweet sir,
sit. Master page, good master page, sit. Proface! What
you want in meat we 'll have in drink: but you must bear:
the heart 's all.   *Exit*

SHALLOW. Be merry, Master Bardolph; and my little sol-
dier there, be merry.

SILENCE.   Be merry, be merry, my wife has all;
                     For women are shrews, both short and tall:
                     'Tis merry in hall when beards wag all,
                         And welcome merry Shrove-tide.
                     Be merry, be merry.

FALSTAFF. I did not think Master Silence had been a man of
this mettle.

SILENCE. Who, I? I have been merry twice and once ere now.

Re-enter Davy

DAVY. There 's a dish of leather-coats for you.

Setting them before Bardolph

SHALLOW. Davy!

DAVY. Your worship! I 'll be with you straight.
A cup of wine, sir?

SILENCE.   A cup of wine that 's brisk and fine,
                     And drink unto the leman mine;
                         And a merry heart lives long-a.

FALSTAFF. Well said, Master Silence.

SILENCE. And we shall be merry, now comes in the sweet o'
the night.

FALSTAFF. Health and long life to you, Master Silence.

SILENCE.   Fill the cup, and let it come;
                     I 'll pledge you a mile to the bottom.

SHALLOW. Honest Bardolph, welcome: if thou wantest any-
thing and wilt not call, beshrew thy heart. (*To the Page*)
Welcome, my little tiny thief; and welcome indeed too.
I 'll drink to Master Bardolph and to all the cavaleiroes
about London.

DAVY. I hope to see London once ere I die.

BARDOLPH. An I might see you there, Davy,—

SHALLOW. By the mass, you 'll crack a quart together: ha!
will you not, Master Bardolph?

BARDOLPH. Yea, sir, in a pottle-pot.

SHALLOW. By God's liggens, I thank thee. The knave will
stick by thee, I can assure thee that: a' will not out; he is
true bred.

BARDOLPH. And I 'll stick by him, sir.

SHALLOW. Why, there spoke a king. Lack nothing: be
merry. (*Knocking within*) Look who 's at door there. Ho!
who knocks?   *Exit Davy*

FALSTAFF. (*To Silence, who drinks a bumper*) Why, now
you have done me right.

SILENCE.   Do me right,
                    And dub me knight:
                        Samingo.

Is 't not so?

FALSTAFF. 'Tis so.

SILENCE. Is 't so? Why, then, say an old man can do some-
what.

Re-enter Davy

DAVY. An 't please your worship, there 's one Pistol come
from the court with news.

FALSTAFF. From the court! let him come in.

Enter Pistol

How now, Pistol!

PISTOL. Sir John, God save you, sir!

FALSTAFF. What wind blew you hither, Pistol?

PISTOL. Not the ill wind which blows no man to good. Sweet
knight, thou art now one of the greatest men in this realm.

SILENCE. By 'r lady, I think a' be, but goodman Puff of Bar-
son.

PISTOL. Puff!
Puff in thy teeth, most recreant coward base!
Sir John, I am thy Pistol and thy friend,
And helter-skelter have I rode to thee,
And tidings do I bring and lucky joys
And golden times and happy news of price.

FALSTAFF. I prithee now, deliver them like a man of this
world.

PISTOL. A foutra for the world and worldlings base!
I speak of Africa and golden joys.

FALSTAFF. O base Assyrian knight, what is thy news?
Let King Cophetua know the truth thereof.

SILENCE. 'And Robin Hood, Scarlet, and John.'

PISTOL. Shall dunghill curs confront the Helicons?
And shall good news be baffled?
Then, Pistol, lay thy head in Furies' lap.

SHALLOW. Honest gentleman, I know not your breeding.

PISTOL. Why then, lament therefore.

SHALLOW. Give me pardon, sir: if, sir, you come with news
from the court, I take it there is but two ways: either to
utter them, or to conceal them. I am, sir, under the king,
in some authority.

PISTOL. Under which king, Bezonian? speak, or die.

SHALLOW. Under King Harry.

PISTOL.   Harry the Fourth? or Fifth?

SHALLOW. Harry the Fourth.

PISTOL.   A foutra for thine office!
   Sir John, thy tender lambkin now is king;
   Harry the Fifth 's the man. I speak the truth:
   When Pistol lies, do this; and fig me, like
   The bragging Spaniard.

FALSTAFF. What! is the old king dead?

PISTOL. As nail in door: the things I speak are just.

FALSTAFF. Away, Bardolph! saddle my horse. Master Rob-
   ert Shallow, choose what office thou wilt in the land, 'tis
   thine. Pistol, I will double-charge thee with dignities.

BARDOLPH. O joyful day!
   I would not take a knighthood for my fortune.

PISTOL. What! I do bring good news.

FALSTAFF. Carry Master Silence to bed. Master Shallow,
   my Lord Shallow, be what thou wilt, I am Fortune's stew-
   ard. Get on thy boots: we 'll ride all night. O sweet Pistol!
   Away, Bardolph! (*Exit Bardolph*) Come, Pistol, utter
   more to me; and withal devise something to do thyself
   good. Boot, boot, Master Shallow: I know the young king
   is sick for me. Let us take any man's horses; the laws of
   England are at my commandment. Happy are they which
   have been my friends, and woe unto my Lord Chief Jus-
   tice!

PISTOL. Let vultures vile seize on his lungs also!
   'Where is the life that late I led?' say they:
   Why, here it is: welcome these pleasant days!   *Exeunt*

SCENE FOUR

London. A Street.

*Enter Beadles, dragging in Mistress Quickly and
Doll Tearsheet*

QUICKLY. No, thou arrant knave: I would to God I might die
   that I might have thee hanged; thou hast drawn my
   shoulder out of joint.

FIRST BEADLE. The constables have delivered her over to
   me, and she shall have whipping-cheer enough, I warrant

her: there hath been a man or two lately killed about her.

DOLL. Nut-hook, nut-hook, you lie. Come on; I 'll tell thee what, thou damned tripe-visaged rascal, an the child I now go with do miscarry, thou hadst better thou hadst struck thy mother, thou paper-faced villain.

QUICKLY. O the Lord! that Sir John were come; he would make this a bloody day to somebody. But I pray God the fruit of her womb miscarry!

FIRST BEADLE. If it do, you shall have a dozen of cushions again; you have but eleven now. Come, I charge you both go with me; for the man is dead that you and Pistol beat among you.

DOLL. I 'll tell thee what, thou thin man in a censer, I will have you as soundly swinged for this, you blue-bottle rogue! you filthy famished correctioner! if you be not swinged, I 'll forswear half-kirtles.

FIRST BEADLE. Come, come, you she knight-errant, come.

QUICKLY. O, that right should thus overcome might! Well, of sufferance comes ease.

DOLL. Come, you rogue, come: bring me to a justice.

QUICKLY. Ay; come, you starved blood-hound.

DOLL. Goodman death! goodman bones!

QUICKLY. Thou atomy, thou!

DOLL. Come, you thin thing; come, you rascal!

FIRST BEADLE. Very well.   *Exeunt*

SCENE FIVE

A Public Place near Westminster Abbey.

Enter two Grooms, strewing rushes

FIRST GROOM. More rushes, more rushes.

SECOND GROOM. The trumpets have sounded twice.

FIRST GROOM. It will be two o'clock ere they come from the coronation. Dispatch, dispatch.   *Exeunt*

Enter Falstaff, Shallow, Pistol, Bardolph, and the Page

FALSTAFF. Stand here by me, Master Robert Shallow; I will make the king do you grace. I will leer upon him, as a' comes by; and do but mark the countenance that he will give me.

PISTOL. God bless thy lungs, good knight.

FALSTAFF. Come here, Pistol; stand behind me. O! if I had had time to have made new liveries, I would have bestowed the thousand pound I borrowed of you. But 'tis no matter; this poor show doth better: this doth infer the zeal I had to see him.

SHALLOW. It doth so.

FALSTAFF. It shows my earnestness of affection.

SHALLOW. It doth so.

FALSTAFF. My devotion.

SHALLOW. It doth, it doth, it doth.

FALSTAFF. As it were, to ride day and night; and not to deliberate, not to remember, not to have patience to shift me.

SHALLOW. It is most certain.

FALSTAFF. But to stand stained with travel, and sweating with desire to see him; thinking of nothing else; putting all affairs else in oblivion, as if there were nothing else to be done but to see him.

PISTOL. 'Tis 'semper idem,' for 'absque hoc nihil est': 'Tis all in every part.

SHALLOW. 'Tis so, indeed.

PISTOL. My knight, I will inflame thy noble liver,
And make thee rage.
Thy Doll, and Helen of thy noble thoughts,
Is in base durance and contagious prison;
Hal'd thither
By most mechanical and dirty hand:
Rouse up revenge from ebon den with fell Alecto's snake,
For Doll is in: Pistol speaks nought but truth.

FALSTAFF. I will deliver her.
                    Shouts within and trumpets sound

PISTOL. There roar'd the sea, and trumpet-clangor sounds.
            Enter King Henry the Fifth
   and his Train, the Lord Chief Justice among them

FALSTAFF. God save thy Grace, King Hal! my royal Hal!

PISTOL. The heavens thee guard and keep, most royal imp of fame!

FALSTAFF. God save thee, my sweet boy!

KING HENRY V. My Lord Chief Justice, speak to that vain man.

CHIEF JUSTICE. Have you your wits? know you what 'tis you speak?

FALSTAFF. My king! my Jove! I speak to thee, my heart!

KING HENRY V. I know thee not, old man: fall to thy prayers;

How ill white hairs become a fool and jester!
I have long dream'd of such a kind of man,
So surfeit-swell'd, so old, and so profane;
But, being awak'd, I do despise my dream.
Make less thy body hence, and more thy grace;
Leave gormandizing; know the grave doth gape
For thee thrice wider than for other men.
Reply not to me with a fool-born jest:
Presume not that I am the thing I was;
For God doth know, so shall the world perceive,
That I have turn'd away my former self;
So will I those that kept me company.
When thou dost hear I am as I have been,
Approach me, and thou shalt be as thou wast,
The tutor and the feeder of my riots:
Till then, I banish thee, on pain of death,
As I have done the rest of my misleaders,
Not to come near our person by ten mile.
For competence of life I will allow you,
That lack of means enforce you not to evil:
And, as we hear you do reform yourselves,
We will, according to your strength and qualities,
Give you advancement. Be it your charge, my lord,
To see perform'd the tenour of our word.
Set on.   *Exeunt King Henry V and his Train*

FALSTAFF. Master Shallow, I owe you a thousand pound.

SHALLOW. Ay, marry, Sir John; which I beseech you to let
me have home with me.

FALSTAFF. That can hardly be, Master Shallow. Do not you
grieve at this: I shall be sent for in private to him. Look
you, he must seem thus to the world. Fear not your ad-
vancements; I will be the man yet that shall make you
great.

SHALLOW. I cannot perceive how, unless you should give me
your doublet and stuff me out with straw. I beseech you,
good Sir John, let me have five hundred of my thousand.

FALSTAFF. Sir, I will be as good as my word: this that you
heard was but a colour.

SHALLOW. A colour that I fear you will die in, Sir John.

FALSTAFF. Fear no colours: go with me to dinner. Come,
Lieutenant Pistol; come, Bardolph: I shall be sent for
soon at night.

Re-enter John of Lancaster,
the Lord Chief Justice; Officers with them

CHIEF JUSTICE. Go, carry Sir John Falstaff to the Fleet;
   Take all his company along with him.

FALSTAFF. My lord, my lord!

CHIEF JUSTICE. I cannot now speak: I will hear you soon.
   Take them away.

PISTOL. 'Si fortuna me tormenta, spero contenta.'

> *Exeunt Falstaff, Shallow, Pistol,*
> *Bardolph, Page, and Officers*

LANCASTER. I like this fair proceeding of the king's.
   He hath intent his wonted followers
   Shall all be very well provided for;
   But all are banish'd till their conversations
   Appear more wise and modest to the world.

CHIEF JUSTICE. And so they are.

LANCASTER. The king hath call'd his parliament, my lord.

CHIEF JUSTICE. He hath.

LANCASTER. I will lay odds, that, ere this year expire,
   We bear our civil swords and native fire
   As far as France. I heard a bird so sing,
   Whose music, to my thinking, pleas'd the king.
   Come, will you hence?   *Exeunt*

EPILOGUE

Spoken by a Dancer

First, my fear; then, my curtsy; last my speech. My fear is, your displeasure, my curtsy, my duty, and my speech, to beg your pardon. If you look for a good speech now, you undo me; for what I have to say is of mine own making; and what indeed I should say will, I doubt, prove mine own marring. But to the purpose, and so to the venture. Be it known to you,—as it is very well,—I was lately here in the end of a displeasing play, to pray your patience for it and to promise you a better. I did mean indeed to pay you with this; which, if like an ill venture it come unluckily home, I break, and you, my gentle creditors, lose. Here I promised you I would be, and here I commit my body to your mercies; bate me some and I will pay you some; and, as most debtors do, promise you infinitely.

If my tongue cannot entreat you to acquit me, will you command me to use my legs? and yet that were but light payment, to dance out of your debt. But a good conscience will make any possible satisfaction, and so will I. All the gentlewomen here have forgiven me: if the gentlemen will not, then the gentlemen do not agree with the gentlewomen, which was never seen before in such an assembly.

One word more, I beseech you. If you be not too much cloyed with fat meat, our humble author will continue the story, with Sir John in it, and make you merry with fair Katharine of France: where, for any thing I know, Falstaff shall die of a sweat, unless already a' be killed with your hard opinions; for Oldcastle died a martyr, and this is not the man. My tongue is weary; when my legs are too, I will bid you good-night; and so kneel down before you—but, indeed, to pray for the queen.

THE LIFE OF KING
HENRY THE FIFTH

CAST OF CHARACTERS

KING HENRY THE FIFTH

DUKE OF GLOUCESTER } *Brothers to the King*
DUKE OF BEDFORD

DUKE OF EXETER, *Uncle to the King*

DUKE OF YORK, *Cousin to the King*

EARLS OF SALISBURY, WESTMORELAND, *and* WARWICK

ARCHBISHOP OF CANTERBURY

BISHOP OF ELY

EARL OF CAMBRIDGE

LORD SCROOP

SIR THOMAS GREY

SIR THOMAS ERPINGHAM, GOWER, FLUELLEN, MAC-
   MORRIS, JAMY, *Officers in King Henry's Army*

BATES, COURT, WILLIAMS, *Soldiers in the Same*

PISTOL, NYM, BARDOLPH

Boy

A Herald

CHARLES THE SIXTH, *King of France*

LEWIS, *the Dauphin*

DUKES OF BURGUNDY, ORLEANS, *and* BOURBON

THE CONSTABLE OF FRANCE

RAMBURES *and* GRANDPRÉ, *French Lords*

MONTJOY, *a French Herald*

Governor of Harfleur

Ambassadors to the King of England

ISABEL, *Queen of France*

KATHARINE, *Daughter to Charles and Isabel*

ALICE, *a Lady attending on the Princess Katharine*

Hostess of the Boar's Head Tavern, formerly Mis-
   tress Quickly, and now married to Pistol

Lords, Ladies, Officers, French and English Soldiers,
Citizens, Messengers, and Attendants

Chorus

SCENE

England; afterwards France

Enter Chorus

CHORUS. O! for a Muse of fire, that would ascend
      The brightest heaven of invention;
      A kingdom for a stage, princes to act
      And monarchs to behold the swelling scene.
      Then should the warlike Harry, like himself,
      Assume the port of Mars; and at his heels,
      Leash'd in like hounds, should famine, sword, and fire
      Crouch for employment. But pardon, gentles all,
      The flat unraised spirits that hath dar'd
      On this unworthy scaffold to bring forth
      So great an object: can this cockpit hold
      The vasty fields of France? or may we cram
      Within this wooden O the very casques
      That did affright the air at Agincourt?
      O, pardon! since a crooked figure may
      Attest in little place a million;
      And let us, ciphers to this great accompt,
      On your imaginary forces work.
      Suppose within the girdle of these walls
      Are now confin'd two mighty monarchies,
      Whose high upreared and abutting fronts
      The perilous narrow ocean parts asunder:
      Piece out our imperfections with your thoughts:
      Into a thousand parts divide one man,
      And make imaginary puissance;
      Think when we talk of horses that you see them
      Printing their proud hoofs i' the receiving earth;
      For 'tis your thoughts that now must deck our kings,
      Carry them here and there, jumping o'er times,
      Turning the accomplishment of many years
      Into an hour-glass: for the which supply,
      Admit me Chorus to this history;
      Who prologue-like your humble patience pray,
      Gently to hear, kindly to judge, our play.   *Exit*

THE LIFE OF KING HENRY
THE FIFTH

ACT ONE

SCENE ONE

London. An Antechamber in the King's Palace.

Enter the Archbishop of Canterbury and the Bishop of Ely

CANTERBURY. My lord, I 'll tell you; that self bill is urg'd,
    Which in the eleventh year of the last king's reign
    Was like, and had indeed against us pass'd,
    But that the scambling and unquiet time
    Did push it out of further question.
ELY. But how, my lord, shall we resist it now?
CANTERBURY. It must be thought on. If it pass against us,
    We lose the better half of our possession;
    For all the temporal lands which men devout
    By testament have given to the Church
    Would they strip from us; being valued thus:
    As much as would maintain, to the king's honour,
    Full fifteen earls and fifteen hundred knights,
    Six thousand and two hundred good esquires;
    And, to relief of lazars and weak age,
    Of indigent faint souls past corporal toil,
    A hundred almshouses right well supplied;
    And to the coffers of the king beside,
    A thousand pounds by the year. Thus runs the bill.
ELY. This would drink deep.
CANTERBURY.   'Twould drink the cup and all.
ELY. But what prevention?
CANTERBURY. The king is full of grace and fair regard.
ELY. And a true lover of the holy Church.
CANTERBURY. The courses of his youth promis'd it not.
    The breath no sooner left his father's body
    But that his wildness, mortified in him,
    Seem'd to die too; yea, at that very moment,

Consideration like an angel came,
And whipp'd the offending Adam out of him,
Leaving his body as a paradise,
To envelop and contain celestial spirits.
Never was such a sudden scholar made;
Never came reformation in a flood,
With such a heady currance, scouring faults;
Nor never Hydra-headed wilfulness
So soon did lose his seat and all at once
As in this king.

ELY.   We are blessed in the change.

CANTERBURY. Hear him but reason in divinity,
And, all-admiring, with an inward wish
You would desire the king were made a prelate:
Hear him debate of commonwealth affairs,
You would say it hath been all in all his study:
List his discourse of war, and you shall hear
A fearful battle render'd you in music:
Turn him to any cause of policy,
The Gordian knot of it he will unloose,
Familiar as his garter; that, when he speaks,
The air, a charter'd libertine, is still,
And the mute wonder lurketh in men's ears,
To steal his sweet and honey'd sentences;
So that the art and practic part of life
Must be the mistress to this theoric:
Which is a wonder how his Grace should glean it,
Since his addiction was to courses vain;
His companies unletter'd, rude, and shallow;
His hours fill'd up with riots, banquets, sports;
And never noted in him any study,
Any retirement, any sequestration
From open haunts and popularity.

ELY. The strawberry grows underneath the nettle,
And wholesome berries thrive and ripen best
Neighbour'd by fruit of baser quality:
And so the prince obscur'd his contemplation
Under the veil of wildness; which, no doubt,
Grew like the summer grass, fastest by night,
Unseen, yet crescive in his faculty.

CANTERBURY. It must be so; for miracles are ceas'd;
And therefore we must needs admit the means

How things are perfected.

ELY.   But, my good lord,
How now for mitigation of this bill
Urg'd by the commons? Doth his Majesty
Incline to it, or no?

CANTERBURY.   He seems indifferent,
Or rather swaying more upon our part
Than cherishing the exhibiters against us;
For I have made an offer to his Majesty,
Upon our spiritual convocation,
And in regard of causes now in hand,
Which I have open'd to his Grace at large,
As touching France, to give a greater sum
Than ever at one time the clergy yet
Did to his predecessors part withal.

ELY. How did this offer seem receiv'd, my lord?

CANTERBURY. With good acceptance of his Majesty;
Save that there was not time enough to hear,—
As I perceiv'd his Grace would fain have done,—
The severals and unhidden passages
Of his true titles to some certain dukedoms,
And generally to the crown and seat of France,
Deriv'd from Edward, his great-grandfather.

ELY. What was the impediment that broke this off?

CANTERBURY. The French ambassador upon that instant
Crav'd audience; and the hour I think is come
To give him hearing: is it four o'clock?

ELY. It is.

CANTERBURY. Then go we in to know his embassy;
Which I could with a ready guess declare
Before the Frenchman speak a word of it.

ELY. I 'll wait upon you, and I long to hear it.   *Exeunt*

SCENE TWO

The Same. The Presence Chamber.

*Enter King Henry, Gloucester, Bedford, Exeter,
Warwick, Westmoreland, and Attendants*

KING HENRY. Where is my gracious Lord of Canterbury?

EXETER. Not here in presence.

KING HENRY.   Send for him, good uncle.

WESTMORELAND. Shall we call in the ambassador, my liege?

KING HENRY. Not yet, my cousin: we would be resolv'd,
    Before we hear him, of some things of weight
    That task our thoughts, concerning us and France.

Enter the Archbishop of Canterbury and the Bishop of Ely

CANTERBURY. God and his angels guard your sacred throne,
    And make you long become it!

KING HENRY.   Sure, we thank you.
    My learned lord, we pray you to proceed,
    And justly and religiously unfold
    Why the law Salique that they have in France
    Or should, or should not, bar us in our claim.
    And God forbid, my dear and faithful lord,
    That you should fashion, wrest, or bow your reading,
    Or nicely charge your understanding soul
    With opening titles miscreate, whose right
    Suits not in native colours with the truth;
    For God doth know how many now in health
    Shall drop their blood in approbation
    Of what your reverence shall incite us to.
    Therefore take heed how you impawn our person,
    How you awake the sleeping sword of war:
    We charge you in the name of God, take heed;
    For never two such kingdoms did contend
    Without much fall of blood; whose guiltless drops
    Are every one a woe, a sore complaint,
    'Gainst him whose wrongs give edge unto the swords
    That make such waste in brief mortality.
    Under this conjuration speak, my lord,
    And we will hear, note, and believe in heart,
    That what you speak is in your conscience wash'd
    As pure as sin with baptism.

CANTERBURY. Then hear me, gracious sovereign, and you
    peers,
    That owe yourselves, your lives, and services
    To this imperial throne. There is no bar
    To make against your Highness' claim to France
    But this, which they produce from Pharamond,
    'In terram Salicam mulieres no succedant,'
    'No woman shall succeed in Salique land':
    Which Salique land the French unjustly gloze

To be the realm of France, and Pharamond
The founder of this law and female bar.
Yet their own authors faithfully affirm
That the land Salique is in Germany,
Between the floods of Sala and of Elbe;
Where Charles the Great, having subdu'd the Saxons,
There left behind and settled certain French;
Who, holding in disdain the German women
For some dishonest manners of their life,
Establish'd then this law; to wit, no female
Should be inheritrix in Salique land:
Which Salique, as I said, 'twixt Elbe and Sala,
Is at this day in Germany call'd Meisen.
Then doth it well appear the Salique law
Was not devised for the realm of France;
Nor did the French possess the Salique land
Until four hundred one-and-twenty years
After defunction of King Pharamond,
Idly suppos'd the founder of this law;
Who died within the year of our redemption
Four hundred twenty-six; and Charles the Great
Subdu'd the Saxons, and did seat the French
Beyond the river Sala, in the year
Eight hundred five. Besides, their writers say,
King Pepin, which deposed Childeric,
Did, as heir general, being descended
Of Blithild, which was daughter to King Clothair,
Make claim and title to the crown of France.
Hugh Capet also, who usurp'd the crown
Of Charles the Duke of Lorraine, sole heir male
Of the true line and stock of Charles the Great,
To find his title with some shows of truth,—
Though in pure truth, it was corrupt and nought,—
Convey'd himself as heir to the Lady Lingare,
Daughter to Charlemain, who was the son
To Lewis the emperor, and Lewis the son
Of Charles the Great. Also King Lewis the Tenth,
Who was sole heir to the usurper Capet,
Could not keep quiet in his conscience,
Wearing the crown of France, till satisfied
That fair Queen Isabel, his grandmother,
Was lineal of the Lady Ermengare,

Daughter to Charles the aforesaid Duke of Lorraine:
By the which marriage the line of Charles the Great
Was re-united to the crown of France.
So that, as clear as is the summer's sun,
King Pepin's title, and Hugh Capet's claim,
King Lewis his satisfaction, all appear
To hold in right and title of the female:
So do the kings of France unto this day;
Howbeit they would hold up this Salique law
To bar your Highness claiming from the female;
And rather choose to hide them in a net
Than amply to imbar their crooked titles
Usurp'd from you and your progenitors.

KING HENRY. May I with right and conscience make this
    claim?

CANTERBURY. The sin upon my head, dread sovereign!
For in the Book of Numbers is it writ:
'When the son dies, let the inheritance
Descend unto the daughter.' Gracious lord,
Stand for your own; unwind your bloody flag;
Look back into your mighty ancestors:
Go, my dread lord, to your great-grandsire's tomb,
From whom you claim; invoke his warlike spirit,
And your great-uncle's, Edward the Black Prince,
Who on the French ground play'd a tragedy,
Making defeat on the full power of France;
Whiles his most mighty father on a hill
Stood smiling to behold his lion's whelp
Forage in blood of French nobility.
O noble English! that could entertain
With half their forces the full pride of France,
And let another half stand laughing by,
All out of work, and cold for action.

ELY. Awake remembrance of these valiant dead,
And with your puissant arm renew their feats:
You are their heir, you sit upon their throne,
The blood and courage that renowned them
Runs in your veins; and my thrice-puissant liege
Is in the very May-morn of his youth,
Ripe for exploits and mighty enterprises.

EXETER. Your brother kings and monarchs of the earth
Do all expect that you should rouse yourself,

As did the former lions of your blood.

WESTMORELAND. They know your Grace hath cause and
   means and might;
   So hath your Highness; never King of England
   Had nobles richer, and more loyal subjects,
   Whose hearts have left their bodies here in England
   And lie pavilion'd in the fields of France.

CANTERBURY. O! let their bodies follow, my dear liege,
   With blood and sword and fire to win your right;
   In aid whereof we of the spiritualty
   Will raise your Highness such a mighty sum
   As never did the clergy at one time
   Bring in to any of your ancestors.

KING HENRY. We must not only arm to invade the French,
   But lay down our proportions to defend
   Against the Scot, who will make road upon us
   With all advantages.

CANTERBURY. They of those marches, gracious sovereign,
   Shall be a wall sufficient to defend
   Our inland from the pilfering borderers.

KING HENRY. We do not mean the coursing snatchers only,
   But fear the main intendment of the Scot,
   Who hath been still a giddy neighbour to us;
   For you shall read that my great-grandfather
   Never went with his forces into France
   But that the Scot on his unfurnish'd kingdom
   Came pouring, like the tide into a breach,
   With ample and brim fulness of his force,
   Galling the gleaned land with hot essays,
   Girding with grievous siege castles and towns;
   That England, being empty of defence,
   Hath shook and trembled at the ill neighbourhood.

CANTERBURY. She hath been then more fear'd than harm'd,
   my liege;
   For hear her but exampled by herself:
   When all her chivalry hath been in France
   And she a mourning widow of her nobles,
   She hath herself not only well defended,
   But taken and impounded as a stray
   The King of Scots; whom she did send to France,
   To fill King Edward's fame with prisoner kings,
   And make your chronicle as rich with praise

As is the ooze and bottom of the sea
With sunken wrack and sumless treasuries.

WESTMORELAND. But there 's a saying very old and true;
          If that you will France win,
               Then with Scotland first begin:
For once the eagle England being in prey,
To her unguarded nest the weasel Scot
Comes sneaking and so sucks her princely eggs,
Playing the mouse in absence of the cat,
To tear and havoc more than she can eat.

EXETER. It follows then the cat must stay at home:
Yet that is but a crush'd necessity;
Since we have locks to safeguard necessaries
And pretty traps to catch the petty thieves.
While that the armed hand doth fight abroad
The advised head defends itself at home:
For government, though high and low and lower,
Put into parts, doth keep in one consent,
Congreeing in a full and natural close,
Like music.

CANTERBURY. Therefore doth heaven divide
The state of man in divers functions,
Setting endeavour in continual motion;
To which is fixed, as an aim or butt,
Obedience: for so work the honey-bees,
Creatures that by a rule in nature teach
The act of order to a peopled kingdom.
They have a king and officers of sorts;
Where some, like magistrates, correct at home,
Others, like merchants, venture trade abroad,
Others, like soldiers, armed in their stings,
Make boot upon the summer's velvet buds;
Which pillage they with merry march bring home
To the tent-royal of their emperor:
Who, busied in his majesty, surveys
The singing masons building roofs of gold,
The civil citizens kneading up the honey,
The poor mechanic porters crowding in
Their heavy burdens at his narrow gate,
The sad-ey'd justice, with his surly hum,
Delivering o'er to executors pale
The lazy yawning drone. I this infer,

That many things, having full reference
To one consent, may work contrariously;
As many arrows, loosed several ways,
Fly to one mark; as many ways meet in one town;
As many fresh streams meet in one salt sea;
As many lines close in the dial's centre;
So may a thousand actions, once afoot,
End in one purpose, and be all well borne
Without defeat. Therefore to France, my liege.
Divide your happy England into four;
Whereof take you one quarter into France,
And you withal shall make all Gallia shake.
If we, with thrice such powers left at home,
Cannot defend our own doors from the dog,
Let us be worried and our nation lose
The name of hardiness and policy.

KING HENRY. Call in the messengers sent from the Dauphin.
                                    Exit an Attendant
Now are we well resolv'd; and by God's help,
And yours, the noble sinews of our power,
France being ours, we 'll bend it to our awe
Or break it all to pieces: or there we 'll sit,
Ruling in large and ample empery
O'er France and all her almost kingly dukedoms,
Or lay these bones in an unworthy urn,
Tombless, with no remembrance over them:
Either our history shall with full mouth
Speak freely of our acts, or else our grave,
Like Turkish mute, shall have a tongueless mouth,
Not worshipp'd with a waxen epitaph.
                Enter Ambassadors of France
Now are we well prepar'd to know the pleasure
Of our fair cousin Dauphin; for we hear
Your greeting is from him, not from the king.

FIRST AMBASSADOR. May 't please your Majesty to give us
    leave
Freely to render what we have in charge;
Or shall we sparingly show you far off
The Dauphin's meaning and our embassy?

KING HENRY. We are no tyrant, but a Christian king;
Unto whose grace our passion is as subject
As are our wretches fetter'd in our prisons:

Therefore with frank and with uncurbed plainness
Tell us the Dauphin's mind.

FIRST AMBASSADOR.   Thus then, in few.
Your Highness, lately sending into France,
Did claim some certain dukedoms, in the right
Of your great predecessor, King Edward the Third.
In answer of which claim, the prince our master
Says that you savour too much of your youth,
And bids you be advis'd there 's nought in France
That can be with a nimble galliard won;
You cannot revel into dukedoms there.
He therefore sends you, meeter for your spirit,
This tun of treasure; and, in lieu of this,
Desires you let the dukedoms that you claim
Hear no more of you. This the Dauphin speaks.

KING HENRY. What treasure, uncle?

EXETER.   Tennis-balls, my liege.

KING HENRY. We are glad the Dauphin is so pleasant with us:
His present and your pains we thank you for:
When we have match'd our rackets to these balls,
We will in France, by God's grace, play a set
Shall strike his father's crown into the hazard.
Tell him he hath made a match with such a wrangler
That all the courts of France will be disturb'd
With chaces. And we understand him well,
How he comes o'er us with our wilder days,
Not measuring what use we made of them.
We never valued this poor seat of England;
And therefore, living hence, did give ourself
To barbarous licence; as 'tis ever common
That men are merriest when they are from home.
But tell the Dauphin I will keep my state,
Be like a king and show my sail of greatness
When I do rouse me in my throne of France:
For that I have laid by my majesty
And plodded like a man for working-days,
But I will rise there with so full a glory
That I will dazzle all the eyes of France,
Yea, strike the Dauphin blind to look on us.
And tell the pleasant prince this mock of his
Hath turn'd his balls to gun-stones; and his soul
Shall stand sore-charged for the wasteful vengeance

That shall fly with them: for many a thousand widows
Shall this his mock mock out of their dear husbands;
Mock mothers from their sons, mock castles down;
And some are yet ungotten and unborn
That shall have cause to curse the Dauphin's scorn.
But this lies all within the will of God,
To whom I do appeal; and in whose name
Tell you the Dauphin I am coming on,
To venge me as I may and to put forth
My rightful hand in a well-hallow'd cause.
So get you hence in peace; and tell the Dauphin
His jest will savour but of shallow wit
When thousands weep more than did laugh at it.
Convey them with safe conduct. Fare you well.
                                        Exeunt Ambassadors
EXETER. This was a merry message.
KING HENRY. We hope to make the sender blush at it.
Therefore, my lords, omit no happy hour
That may give furtherance to our expedition;
For we have now no thought in us but France,
Save those to God, that run before our business.
Therefore let our proportions for these wars
Be soon collected, and all things thought upon
That may with reasonable swiftness add
More feathers to our wings; for, God before,
We 'll chide this Dauphin at his father's door.
Therefore let every man now task his thought,
That this fair action may on foot be brought.
                                        Exeunt. Flourish

ACT TWO

Enter Chorus

CHORUS. Now all the youth of England are on fire,
And silken dalliance in the wardrobe lies;
Now thrive the armourers, and honour's thought
Reigns solely in the breast of every man:
They sell the pasture now to buy the horse,
Following the mirror of all Christian kings
With winged heels, as English Mercuries.
For now sits Expectation in the air
And hides a sword from hilts unto the point
With crowns imperial, crowns and coronets,
Promis'd to Harry and his followers.
The French, advis'd by good intelligence
Of this most dreadful preparation,
Shake in their fear, and with pale policy
Seek to divert the English purposes.
O England! model to thy inward greatness,
Like little body with a mighty heart,
What mightst thou do, that honour would thee do,
Were all thy children kind and natural!
But see thy fault! France hath in thee found out
A nest of hollow bosoms, which he fills
With treacherous crowns; and three corrupted men,
One, Richard Earl of Cambridge, and the second,
Henry Lord Scroop of Masham, and the third,
Sir Thomas Grey, knight, of Northumberland,
Have, for the gilt of France,—O guilt, indeed!—
Confirm'd conspiracy with fearful France;
And by their hands this grace of kings must die,—
If hell and treason hold their promises,—
Ere he take ship for France, and in Southampton.
Linger your patience on; and well digest
The abuse of distance while we force a play.

The sum is paid; the traitors are agreed;
The king is set from London; and the scene
Is now transported, gentles, to Southampton:
There is the playhouse now, there must you sit:
And thence to France shall we convey you safe,
And bring you back, charming the narrow seas
To give you gentle pass; for, if we may,
We 'll not offend one stomach with our play.
But, till the king come forth and not till then,
Unto Southampton do we shift our scene.   *Exit*

SCENE ONE

London. Eastcheap.

Enter Nym and Bardolph

BARDOLPH. Well met, Corporal Nym.

NYM. Good-morrow, Lieutenant Bardolph.

BARDOLPH. What, are Ancient Pistol and you friends yet?

NYM. For my part, I care not: I say little; but when time shall serve, there shall be smiles; but that shall be as it may. I dare not fight; but I will wink and hold out mine iron. It is a simple one; but what though? it will toast cheese, and it will endure cold as another man's sword will: and there 's an end.

BARDOLPH. I will bestow a breakfast to make you friends, and we 'll be all three sworn brothers to France: let it be so, good Corporal Nym.

NYM. Faith, I will live so long as I may, that 's the certain of it; and when I cannot live any longer, I will do as I may: that is my rest, that is the rendezvous of it.

BARDOLPH. It is certain, corporal, that he is married to Nell Quickly; and, certainly she did you wrong, for you were troth-plight to her.

NYM. I cannot tell; things must be as they may: men may sleep, and they may have their throats about them at that time; and, some say, knives have edges. It must be as it may: though patience be a tired mare, yet she will plod. There must be conclusions. Well, I cannot tell.

Enter Pistol and Hostess

BARDOLPH. Here comes Ancient Pistol and his wife. Good
corporal, be patient here. How now, mine host Pistol!

PISTOL. Base tike, call'st thou me host?
Now, by this hand, I swear, I scorn the term;
Nor shall my Nell keep lodgers.

HOSTESS. No, by my troth, not long; for we cannot lodge and
board a dozen or fourteen gentlewomen that live honestly
by the prick of their needles, but it will be thought we
keep a bawdy-house straight. (*Nym and Pistol draw*) O
well-a-day, Lady! if he be not drawn now: we shall see
wilful adultery and murder committed.

BARDOLPH. Good lieutenant! good corporal! offer nothing
here.

NYM. Pish!

PISTOL. Pish for thee, Iceland dog! thou prick-eared cur of
Iceland!

HOSTESS. Good Corporal Nym, show thy valour and put up
your sword.

NYM. Will you shog off? I would have you solus.

Sheathing his sword

PISTOL. 'Solus,' egregious dog? O viper vile!
The 'solus' in thy most mervailous face;
The 'solus' in thy teeth, and in thy throat,
And in thy hateful lungs, yea, in thy maw, perdy;
And, which is worse, within thy nasty mouth!
I do retort the 'solus' in thy bowels:
For I can take, and Pistol's cock is up,
And flashing fire will follow.

NYM. I am not Barbason; you cannot conjure me. I have an
humour to knock you indifferently well. If you grow foul
with me, Pistol, I will scour you with my rapier, as I may,
in fair terms: if you would walk off, I would prick your
guts a little, in good terms, as I may; and that's the hu-
mour of it.

PISTOL. O braggart vile and damned furious wight!
The grave doth gape, and doting death is near;
Therefore exhale.

BARDOLPH. Hear me, hear me what I say: he that strikes the
first stroke, I'll run him up to the hilts, as I am a soldier.

Draws

PISTOL. An oath of mickle might, and fury shall abate.
Give me thy fist, thy fore-foot to me give;

Thy spirits are most tall.

NYM. I will cut thy throat, one time or other, in fair terms; that is the humour of it.

PISTOL. 'Coupe le gorge!'
That is the word. I thee defy again.
O hound of Crete, think'st thou my spouse to get?
No; to the spital go,
And from the powdering-tub of infamy
Fetch forth the lazar kite of Cressid's kind,
Doll Tearsheet she by name, and her espouse:
I have, and I will hold, the quondam Quickly
For the only she; and—pauca, there 's enough.
Go to.

Enter the Boy

BOY. Mine host Pistol, you must come to my master, and you, hostess: he is very sick, and would to bed. Good Bardolph, put thy face between his sheets and do the office of a warming-pan. Faith, he 's very ill.

BARDOLPH. Away, you rogue!

HOSTESS. By my troth, he 'll yield the crow a pudding one of these days. The king has killed his heart. Good husband, come home presently.   *Exeunt Hostess and Boy*

BARDOLPH. Come, shall I make you two friends? We must to France together. Why the devil should we keep knives to cut one another's throats?

PISTOL. Let floods o'erswell, and fiends for food howl on!

NYM. You 'll pay me the eight shillings I won of you at betting?

PISTOL. Base is the slave that pays.

NYM. That now I will have; that 's the humour of it.

PISTOL. As manhood shall compound: push home.

They draw

BARDOLPH. By this sword, he that makes the first thrust, I 'll kill him; by this sword, I will.

PISTOL. Sword is an oath, and oaths must have their course.

BARDOLPH. Corporal Nym, an thou wilt be friends, be friends: an thou wilt not, why then, be enemies with me too. Prithee, put up.

NYM. I shall have my eight shillings I won of you at betting?

PISTOL. A noble shalt thou have, and present pay;
And liquor likewise will I give to thee,
And friendship shall combine, and brotherhood:

I 'll live by Nym, and Nym shall live by me.
Is not this just? for I shall sutler be
Unto the camp, and profits will accrue.
Give me thy hand.

NYM. I shall have my noble?

PISTOL. In cash most justly paid.   *Paying him*

NYM. Well then, that 's the humour of it.

Re-enter Hostess

HOSTESS. As ever you came of women, come in quickly to
Sir John. Ah, poor heart! he is so shaked of a burning quo-
tidian tertian, that it is most lamentable to behold. Sweet
men, come to him.

NYM. The king hath run bad humours on the knight: that 's
the even of it.

PISTOL. Nym, thou hast spoke the right;
His heart is fracted and corroborate.

NYM. The king is a good king: but it must be as it may; he
passes some humours and careers.

PISTOL. Let us condole the knight; for, lambkins, we will
live.   *Exeunt*

SCENE TWO

Southampton. A Council-chamber.

Enter Exeter, Bedford, and Westmoreland

BEDFORD. 'Fore God, his Grace is bold to trust these traitors.

EXETER. They shall be apprehended by and by.

WESTMORELAND. How smooth and even they do bear
themselves!
As if allegiance in their bosoms sat,
Crowned with faith and constant loyalty.

BEDFORD. The king hath note of all that they intend,
By interception which they dream not of.

EXETER. Nay, but the man that was his bedfellow,
Whom he hath dull'd and cloy'd with gracious favours,
That he should, for a foreign purse, so sell
His sovereign's life to death and treachery!

*Trumpets sound. Enter King Henry,
Scroop, Cambridge, Grey, Lords, and Attendants*

KING HENRY. Now sits the wind fair, and we will aboard.

My Lord of Cambridge, and my kind Lord of Masham,
And you, my gentle knight, give me your thoughts:
Think you not that the powers we bear with us
Will cut their passage through the force of France,
Doing the execution and the act
For which we have in head assembled them?
SCROOP. No doubt, my liege, if each man do his best.
KING HENRY. I doubt not that; since we are well persuaded
We carry not a heart with us from hence
That grows not in a fair consent with ours;
Nor leave not one behind that doth not wish
Success and conquest to attend on us.
CAMBRIDGE. Never was monarch better fear'd and lov'd
Than is your Majesty: there's not, I think, a subject
That sits in heart-grief and uneasiness
Under the sweet shade of your government.
GREY. True: those that were your father's enemies
Have steep'd their galls in honey, and do serve you
With hearts create of duty and of zeal.
KING HENRY. We therefore have great cause of thankfulness,
And shall forget the office of our hand,
Sooner than quittance of desert and merit
According to the weight and worthiness.
SCROOP. So service shall with steeled sinews toil,
And labour shall refresh itself with hope,
To do your Grace incessant services.
KING HENRY. We judge no less. Uncle of Exeter,
Enlarge the man committed yesterday
That rail'd against our person: we consider
It was excess of wine that set him on;
And on his more advice we pardon him.
SCROOP. That's mercy, but too much security:
Let him be punish'd, sovereign, lest example
Breed, by his sufferance, more of such a kind.
KING HENRY. O! let us yet be merciful.
CAMBRIDGE. So may your Highness, and yet punish too.
GREY. Sir,
You show great mercy, if you give him life
After the taste of much correction.
KING HENRY. Alas! your too much love and care of me
Are heavy orisons 'gainst this poor wretch.
If little faults, proceeding on distemper,

Shall not be wink'd at, how shall we stretch our eye
When capital crimes, chew'd, swallow'd, and digested,
Appear before us? We 'll yet enlarge that man,
Though Cambridge, Scroop, and Grey, in their dear care,
And tender preservation of our person,
Would have him punish'd. And now to our French causes:
Who are the late commissioners?

CAMBRIDGE. I one, my lord:
Your Highness bade me ask for it to-day.

SCROOP. So did you me, my liege.

GREY. And I, my royal sovereign.

KING HENRY. Then, Richard, Earl of Cambridge, there is
    yours;
There yours, Lord Scroop of Masham; and, sir knight,
Grey of Northumberland, this same is yours:
Read them; and know, I know your worthiness.
My Lord of Westmoreland, and uncle Exeter,
We will aboard to-night. Why, how now, gentlemen!
What see you in those papers that you lose
So much complexion? Look ye, how they change!
Their cheeks are paper. Why, what read you there,
That hath so cowarded and chas'd your blood
Out of appearance?

CAMBRIDGE.   I do confess my fault,
And do submit me to your Highness' mercy.

GREY.
SCROOP. } To which we all appeal.

KING HENRY. The mercy that was quick in us but late
By your own counsel is suppress'd and kill'd:
You must not dare, for shame, to talk of mercy;
For your own reasons turn into your bosoms,
As dogs upon their masters, worrying you.
See you, my princes and my noble peers,
These English monsters! My Lord of Cambridge here,
You know how apt our love was to accord
To furnish him with all appertinents
Belonging to his honour; and this man
Hath, for a few light crowns, lightly conspir'd,
And sworn unto the practices of France,
To kill us here in Hampton: to the which
This knight, no less for bounty bound to us
Than Cambridge is, hath likewise sworn. But O!

What shall I say to thee, Lord Scroop? thou cruel,
Ingrateful, savage and inhuman creature!
Thou that didst bear the key of all my counsels,
That knew'st the very bottom of my soul,
That almost mightst have coin'd me into gold
Wouldst thou have practis'd on me for thy use!
May it be possible that foreign hire
Could out of thee extract one spark of evil
That might annoy my finger? 'tis so strange
That, though the truth of it stands off as gross
As black from white, my eye will scarcely see it.
Treason and murder ever kept together,
As two yoke-devils sworn to either's purpose,
Working so grossly in a natural cause
That admiration did not whoop at them:
But thou, 'gainst all proportion, didst bring in
Wonder to wait on treason and on murder:
And whatsoever cunning fiend it was
That wrought upon thee so preposterously
Hath got the voice in hell for excellence:
And other devils that suggest by treasons
Do botch and bungle up damnation
With patches, colours, and with forms, being fetch'd
From glistering semblances of piety;
But he that temper'd thee bade thee stand up,
Gave thee no instance why thou shouldst do treason,
Unless to dub thee with the name of traitor.
If that same demon that hath gull'd thee thus
Should with his lion gait walk the whole world,
He might return to vasty Tartar back,
And tell the legions, 'I can never win
A soul so easy as that Englishman's.'
O! how hast thou with jealousy infected
The sweetness of affiance. Show men dutiful?
Why, so didst thou: seem they grave and learned?
Why, so didst thou: come they of noble family?
Why, so didst thou: seem they religious?
Why, so didst thou: or are they spare in diet,
Free from gross passion or of mirth or anger,
Constant in spirit, not swerving with the blood,
Garnish'd and deck'd in modest complement,
Not working with the eye without the ear,

And but in purged judgment trusting neither?
Such and so finely bolted didst thou seem:
And thus thy fall hath left a kind of blot,
To mark the full-fraught man and best indued
With some suspicion. I will weep for thee;
For this revolt of thine, methinks, is like
Another fall of man. Their faults are open:
Arrest them to the answer of the law;
And God acquit them of their practices!

EXETER. I arrest thee of high treason, by the name of Rich-
ard Earl of Cambridge.

    I arrest thee of high treason, by the name of Henry
Lord Scroop of Masham.

    I arrest thee of high treason, by the name of Thomas
Grey, knight, of Northumberland.

SCROOP. Our purposes God justly hath discover'd,
And I repent my fault more than my death;
Which I beseech your Highness to forgive,
Although my body pay the price of it.

CAMBRIDGE. For me, the gold of France did not seduce,
Although I did admit it as a motive
The sooner to effect what I intended:
But God be thanked for prevention;
Which I in sufferance heartily will rejoice,
Beseeching God and you to pardon me.

GREY. Never did faithful subject more rejoice
At the discovery of most dangerous treason
Than I do at this hour joy o'er myself,
Prevented from a damned enterprise.
My fault, but not my body, pardon, sovereign.

KING HENRY. God quit you in his mercy! Hear your
    sentence.
You have conspir'd against our royal person,
Join'd with an enemy proclaim'd, and from his coffers
Receiv'd the golden earnest of our death;
Wherein you would have sold your king to slaughter,
His princes and his peers to servitude,
His subjects to oppression and contempt,
And his whole kingdom into desolation.
Touching our person seek we no revenge;
But we our kingdom's safety must so tender,
Whose ruin you have sought, that to her laws

We do deliver you. Get you therefore hence,
Poor miserable wretches, to your death;
The taste whereof, God of his mercy give you
Patience to endure, and true repentance
Of all your dear offences! Bear them hence.

Exeunt Cambridge, Scroop, and Grey, guarded

Now, lords, for France! the enterprise whereof
Shall be to you, as us, like glorious.
We doubt not of a fair and lucky war,
Since God so graciously hath brought to light
This dangerous treason lurking in our way
To hinder our beginnings. We doubt not now
But every rub is smoothed on our way.
Then forth, dear countrymen: let us deliver
Our puissance into the hand of God,
Putting it straight in expedition.
Cheerly to sea! the signs of war advance:
No king of England, if not King of France. *Exeunt*

SCENE THREE

London. Before a Tavern in Eastcheap.

Enter Pistol, Hostess, Nym, Bardolph, and Boy

HOSTESS. Prithee, honey-sweet husband, let me bring thee
to Staines.

PISTOL. No; for my manly heart doth yearn.
Bardolph, be blithe; Nym, rouse thy vaunting veins;
Boy, bristle thy courage up; for Falstaff he is dead,
And we must yearn therefore.

BARDOLPH. Would I were with him, wheresome'er he is,
either in heaven or in hell!

HOSTESS. Nay, sure, he 's not in hell: he 's in Arthur's bosom,
if ever man went to Arthur's bosom. A' made a finer end
and went away an it had been any christom child; a'
parted even just between twelve and one, even at the
turning o' the tide: for after I saw him fumble with the
sheets and play with flowers and smile upon his fingers'
ends, I knew there was but one way; for his nose was as
sharp as a pen, and a' babbled of green fields. 'How now,
Sir John!' quoth I: 'what man! be of good cheer.' So a'

cried out 'God, God, God!' three or four times: now I, to comfort him, bid him a' should not think of God, I hoped there was no need to trouble himself with any such thoughts yet. So a' bade me lay more clothes on his feet: I put my hand into the bed and felt them, and they were as cold as any stone; then I felt to his knees, and so upward, and upward, and all was as cold as any stone.

NYM. They say he cried out of sack.

HOSTESS. Ay, that a' did.

BARDOLPH. And of women.

HOSTESS. Nay, that a' did not.

BOY. Yes, that a' did; and said they were devils incarnate.

HOSTESS. A' could never abide carnation; 'twas a colour he never liked.

BOY. A' said once, the devil would have him about women.

HOSTESS. A' did in some sort, indeed, handle women; but then he was rheumatic, and talked of the whore of Babylon.

BOY. Do you not remember a' saw a flea stick upon Bardolph's nose, and a' said it was a black soul burning in hell-fire?

BARDOLPH. Well, the fuel is gone that maintained that fire: that's all the riches I got in his service.

NYM. Shall we shog? the king will be gone from Southampton.

PISTOL. Come, let's away. My love, give me thy lips.
Look to my chattels and my moveables:
Let senses rule, the word is 'Pitch and pay';
Trust none;
For oaths are straws, men's faiths are wafer-cakes,
And hold-fast is the only dog, my duck:
Therefore, caveto be thy counsellor.
Go, clear thy crystals. Yoke-fellows in arms,
Let us to France; like horse-leeches, my boys,
To suck, to suck, the very blood to suck!

BOY. And that's but unwholesome food, they say.

PISTOL. Touch her soft mouth, and march.

BARDOLPH. Farewell, hostess.   *Kissing her*

NYM. I cannot kiss, that is the humour of it; but, adieu.

PISTOL. Let housewifery appear: keep close, I thee command.

HOSTESS. Farewell; adieu.   *Exeunt*

SCENE FOUR

France. An Apartment in the French King's Palace.

*Flourish. Enter the French King, attended;
the Dauphin, the Dukes of Berri and Britaine,
the Constable, and Others*

FRENCH KING. Thus come the English with full power upon
  us;
  And more than carefully it us concerns
  To answer royally in our defences.
  Therefore the Dukes of Berri and Britaine,
  Of Brabant and of Orleans, shall make forth,
  And you, Prince Dauphin, with all swift dispatch,
  To line and new repair our towns of war
  With men of courage and with means defendant:
  For England his approaches makes as fierce
  As waters to the sucking of a gulf.
  It fits us then to be as provident
  As fear may teach us, out of late examples
  Left by the fatal and neglected English
  Upon our fields.
DAUPHIN.   My most redoubted father,
  It is most meet we arm us 'gainst the foe;
  For peace itself should not so dull a kingdom,—
  Though war nor no known quarrel were in question,—
  But that defences, musters, preparations,
  Should be maintain'd, assembled, and collected,
  As were a war in expectation.
  Therefore, I say 'tis meet we all go forth
  To view the sick and feeble parts of France:
  And let us do it with no show of fear;
  No, with no more than if we heard that England
  Were busied with a Whitsun morris-dance:
  For, my good liege, she is so idly king'd,
  Her sceptre so fantastically borne
  By a vain, giddy, shallow, humorous youth,
  That fear attends her not.
CONSTABLE.   O peace, Prince Dauphin!
  You are too much mistaken in this king.

Question your Grace the late ambassadors,
With what great state he heard their embassy,
How well supplied with noble counsellors,
How modest in exception, and, withal
How terrible in constant resolution,
And you shall find his vanities forespent
Were but the outside of the Roman Brutus,
Covering discretion with a coat of folly;
As gardeners do with ordure hide those roots
That shall first spring and be most delicate.

DAUPHIN. Well, 'tis not so, my Lord High Constable;
But though we think it so, it is no matter:
In cases of defence 'tis best to weigh
The enemy more mighty than he seems:
So the proportions of defence are fill'd;
Which of a weak and niggardly projection
Doth like a miser spoil his coat with scanting
A little cloth.

FRENCH KING.　　　Think we King Harry strong;
And, princes, look you strongly arm to meet him.
The kindred of him hath been flesh'd upon us,
And he is bred out of that bloody strain
That haunted us in our familiar paths:
Witness our too much memorable shame
When Cressy battle fatally was struck
And all our princes captiv'd by the hand
Of that black name, Edward, Black Prince of Wales;
Whiles that his mounting sire, on mountain standing,
Up in the air, crown'd with the golden sun,
Saw his heroical seed, and smil'd to see him
Mangle the work of nature, and deface
The patterns that by God and by French fathers
Had twenty years been made. This is a stem
Of that victorious stock; and let us fear
The native mightiness and fate of him.

Enter a Messenger

MESSENGER. Ambassadors from Harry King of England
Do crave admittance to your Majesty.

FRENCH KING. We 'll give them present audience. Go, and
　　　bring them.　　　*Exeunt Messenger and certain Lords*
You see this chase is hotly follow'd, friends.

DAUPHIN. Turn head, and stop pursuit; for coward dogs

Most spend their mouths when what they seem to
    threaten
Runs far before them. Good my sovereign,
Take up the English short, and let them know
Of what a monarchy you are the head:
Self-love, my liege, is not so vile a sin
As self-neglecting.

      Re-enter Lords, with Exeter and Train

FRENCH KING.   From our brother England?

EXETER. From him; and thus he greets your Majesty.
He wills you, in the name of God Almighty,
That you divest yourself, and lay apart
The borrow'd glories that by gift of heaven,
By law of nature and of nations, 'long
To him and to his heirs; namely, the crown
And all wide-stretched honours that pertain
By custom and the ordinance of times
Unto the crown of France. That you may know
'Tis no sinister nor no awkward claim,
Pick'd from the worm-holes of long-vanish'd days,
Nor from the dust of old oblivion rak'd,
He sends you this most memorable line, *Gives a pedigree*
In every branch truly demonstrative;
Willing you overlook this pedigree;
And when you find him evenly deriv'd
From his most fam'd of famous ancestors,
Edward the Third, he bids you then resign
Your crown and kingdom, indirectly held
From him the native and true challenger.

FRENCH KING. Or else what follows?

EXETER. Bloody constraint; for if you hid the crown
Even in your hearts, there will he rake for it:
Therefore in fierce tempest is he coming,
In thunder and in earthquake like a Jove,
That, if requiring fail, he will compel;
And bids you, in the bowels of the Lord,
Deliver up the crown, and to take mercy
On the poor souls for whom this hungry war
Opens his vasty jaws; and on your head
Turning the widows' tears, the orphans' cries,
The dead men's blood, the pining maidens' groans,
For husbands, fathers, and betrothed lovers,

That shall be swallow'd in this controversy.
This is his claim, his threatening, and my message;
Unless the Dauphin be in presence here,
To whom expressly I bring greeting too.

FRENCH KING. For us, we will consider of this further:
To-morrow shall you bear our full intent
Back to our brother England.

DAUPHIN.   For the Dauphin,
I stand here for him: what to him from England?

EXETER. Scorn and defiance, slight regard, contempt,
And anything that may not misbecome
The mighty sender, doth he prize you at.
Thus says my king: an if your father's Highness
Do not, in grant of all demands at large,
Sweeten the bitter mock you sent his Majesty,
He 'll call you to so hot an answer of it,
That caves and womby vaultages of France
Shall chide your trespass and return your mock
In second accent of his ordinance.

DAUPHIN. Say, if my father render fair return,
It is against my will; for I desire
Nothing but odds with England: to that end,
As matching to his youth and vanity,
I did present him with the Paris balls.

EXETER. He 'll make your Paris Louvre shake for it,
Were it the mistress-court of mighty Europe:
And, be assur'd, you 'll find a difference—
As we his subjects have in wonder found—
Between the promise of his greener days
And these he masters now. Now he weighs time
Even to the utmost grain; that you shall read
In your own losses, if he stay in France.

FRENCH KING. To-morrow shall you know our mind at full.

EXETER. Dispatch us with all speed, lest that our king
Come here himself to question our delay;
For he is footed in this land already.

FRENCH KING. You shall be soon dispatch'd with fair
    conditions:
A night is but small breath and little pause
To answer matters of this consequence. *Flourish. Exeunt*

ACT THREE

Enter Chorus

CHORUS. Thus with imagin'd wing our swift scene flies
      In motion of no less celerity
      Than that of thought. Suppose that you have seen
      The well-appointed king at Hampton pier
      Embark his royalty; and his brave fleet
      With silken streamers the young Phoebus fanning:
      Play with your fancies and in them behold
      Upon the hempen tackle ship-boys climbing;
      Hear the shrill whistle which doth order give
      To sounds confus'd; behold the threaden sails,
      Borne with the invisible and creeping wind,
      Draw the huge bottoms through the furrow'd sea,
      Breasting the lofty surge. O! do but think
      You stand upon the rivage and behold
      A city on the inconstant billows dancing;
      For so appears this fleet majestical,
      Holding due course to Harfleur. Follow, follow!
      Grapple your minds to sternage of this navy,
      And leave your England, as dead midnight still,
      Guarded with grandsires, babies, and old women,
      Either past or not arriv'd to pith and puissance:
      For who is he, whose chin is but enrich'd
      With one appearing hair, that will not follow
      Those cull'd and choice-drawn cavaliers to France?
      Work, work your thoughts, and therein see a siege;
      Behold the ordnance on their carriages,
      With fatal mouths gaping on girded Harfleur.
      Suppose the ambassador from the French comes back;
      Tells Harry that the king doth offer him
      Katharine his daughter; and with her, to dowry,
      Some petty and unprofitable dukedoms:
      The offer likes not: and the nimble gunner

With linstock now the devilish cannon touches,

Alarum, and chambers go off

And down goes all before them. Still be kind,
And eke out our performance with your mind.   *Exit*

SCENE ONE

France. Before Harfleur.

Alarums. Enter King Henry, Exeter, Bedford, Gloucester,
and Soldiers, with scaling ladders

KING HENRY. Once more unto the breach, dear friends, once
     more;
  Or close the wall up with our English dead!
  In peace there 's nothing so becomes a man
  As modest stillness and humility:
  But when the blast of war blows in our ears,
  Then imitate the action of the tiger;
  Stiffen the sinews, summon up the blood,
  Disguise fair nature with hard-favour'd rage;
  Then lend the eye a terrible aspect;
  Let it pry through the portage of the head
  Like the brass cannon; let the brow o'erwhelm it
  As fearfully as doth a galled rock
  O'erhang and jutty his confounded base,
  Swill'd with the wild and wasteful ocean.
  Now set the teeth and stretch the nostril wide,
  Hold hard the breath, and bend up every spirit
  To his full height! On, on, you noblest English!
  Whose blood is fet from fathers of war-proof;
  Fathers that, like so many Alexanders,
  Have in these parts from morn till even fought,
  And sheath'd their swords for lack of argument.
  Dishonour not your mothers; now attest
  That those whom you call'd fathers did beget you.
  Be copy now to men of grosser blood,
  And teach them how to war. And you, good yeomen,
  Whose limbs were made in England, show us here
  The mettle of your pasture; let us swear
  That you are worth your breeding; which I doubt not;
  For there is none of you so mean and base

That hath not noble lustre in your eyes.
I see you stand like greyhounds in the slips,
Straining upon the start. The game 's afoot:
Follow your spirit; and, upon this charge
Cry 'God for Harry! England and Saint George!'

Exeunt. Alarum, and chambers go off

SCENE TWO

The Same.

Enter Nym, Bardolph, Pistol, and Boy

BARDOLPH. On, on, on, on, on! to the breach, to the breach!

NYM. Pray thee, corporal, stay: the knocks are too hot; and
for mine own part, I have not a case of lives: the humour
of it is too hot, that is the very plain-song of it.

PISTOL. The plain-song is most just, for humours do abound:
Knocks go and come: God's vassals drop and die:

> And sword and shield
> In bloody field
> Doth win immortal fame.

BOY. Would I were in an alehouse in London! I would give
all my fame for a pot of ale, and safety.

PISTOL. And I:

> If wishes would prevail with me,
> My purpose should not fail with me,
> But thither would I hie.

BOY.

> As duly,
> But not as truly,
> As bird doth sing on bough.

Enter Fluellen

FLUELLEN. Up to the breach, you dogs! avaunt, you
cullions!   *Driving them forward*

PISTOL. Be merciful, great duke, to men of mould!
Abate thy rage, abate thy manly rage!
Abate thy rage, great duke!
Good bawcock, bate thy rage; use lenity, sweet chuck!

NYM. These be good humours! your honour wins bad hu-
mours.   *Exeunt Nym, Pistol,*
and Bardolph, followed by Fluellen

BOY. As young as I am, I have observed these three swash-

ers. I am boy to them all three, but all they three, though
they would serve me, could not be man to me; for, indeed
three such antiques do not amount to a man. For Bar-
dolph, he is white-livered and red-faced; by the means
whereof, a' faces it out, but fights not. For Pistol, he hath
a killing tongue and a quiet sword; by the means whereof
a' breaks words, and keeps whole weapons. For Nym, he
hath heard that men of few words are the best men; and
therefore he scorns to say his prayers, lest a' should be
thought a coward: but his few bad words are match'd
with as few good deeds; for a' never broke any man's head
but his own, and that was against a post when he was
drunk. They will steal any thing and call it purchase. Bar-
dolph stole a lute-case, bore it twelve leagues, and sold it
for three half-pence. Nym and Bardolph are sworn broth-
ers in filching, and in Calais they stole a fire-shovel;—I
knew by that piece of service the men would carry coals,
—they would have me as familiar with men's pockets as
their gloves or their handkerchers: which makes much
against my manhood if I should take from another's
pocket to put into mine; for it is plain pocketing up of
wrongs. I must leave them and seek some better service:
their villany goes against my weak stomach, and therefore
I must cast it up.　　　　　　　　　　　　　　　*Exit*

Re-enter Fluellen, Gower following

GOWER. Captain Fluellen, you must come presently to the
mines: the Duke of Gloucester would speak with you.

FLUELLEN. To the mines! tell you the duke is not so good
to come to the mines. For look you, the mines is not ac-
cording to the disciplines of the war; the concavities of it
is not sufficient; for, look you, th' athversary—you may dis-
cuss unto the duke, look you—is digt himself four yards
under the countermines; by Cheshu, I think, a' will plow
up all if there is not better directions.

GOWER. The Duke of Gloucester, to whom the order of the
siege is given, is altogether directed by an Irishman, a
very valiant gentleman, i' faith.

FLUELLEN. It is Captain Macmorris, is it not?

GOWER. I think it be.

FLUELLEN. By Cheshu, he is an ass, as in the world: I will
verify as much in his peard: he has no more directions in

the true disciplines of the wars, look you, of the Roman disciplines, than is a puppy-dog.

Enter Macmorris and Jamy, at a distance

GOWER. Here a' comes; and the Scots captain, Captain Jamy, with him.

FLUELLEN. Captain Jamy is a marvellous falorous gentleman, that is certain; and of great expedition and knowledge in th' aunchient wars, upon my particular knowledge of his directions: by Cheshu, he will maintain his argument as well as any military man in the world, in the disciplines of the pristine wars of the Romans.

JAMY. I say gud day, Captain Fluellen.

FLUELLEN. God-den to your worship, good Captain James.

GOWER. How now, Captain Macmorris! have you quit the mines? have the pioners given o'er?

MACMORRIS. By Chrish, la! tish ill done: the work ish give over, the trumpet sound the retreat. By my hand, I swear, and my father's soul, the work ish ill done; it ish give over: I would have blowed up the town, so Chrish save me, la! in an hour: O! tish ill done, tish ill done; by my hand, tish ill done!

FLUELLEN. Captain Macmorris, I beseech you now, will you voutsafe me, look you, a few disputations with you, as partly touching or concerning the disciplines of the war, the Roman wars, in the way of argument, look you, and friendly communication; partly to satisfy my opinion, and partly for the satisfaction, look you, of my mind, as touching the direction of the military discipline: that is the point.

JAMY. It sall be vary gud, gud feith, gud captains bath: (*Aside*) and I sall quit you with gud leve, as I may pick occasion; that sall I, marry.

MACMORRIS. It is no time to discourse, so Chrish save me: the day is hot, and the weather, and the wars, and the king, and the dukes: it is no time to discourse. The town is beseeched, and the trumpet calls us to the breach; and we talk, and be Chrish, do nothing: 'tis shame for us all; so God sa' me, 'tis shame to stand still; it is shame, by my hand; and there is throats to be cut, and works to be done; and there ish nothing done, so Chrish sa' me, la!

JAMY. By the mess, ere theise eyes of mine take themselves to slumber, aile do gud service, or aile lig i' the grund for

it; ay, or go to death; and aile pay it as valorously as I
may, that sal I suerly do, that is the breff and the long.
Marry, I wad full fain heard some question 'tween you
tway.

FLUELLEN. Captain Macmorris, I think, look you, under
your correction, there is not many of your nation—

MACMORRIS. Of my nation! What ish my nation? ish a vil-
lain, and a bastard, and a knave, and a rascal? What ish
my nation? Who talks of my nation?

FLUELLEN. Look you, if you take the matter otherwise than
is meant, Captain Macmorris, peradventure I shall think
you do not use me with that affability as in discretion you
ought to use me, look you; being as good a man as your-
self, both in the disciplines of wars, and in the derivation
of my birth, and in other particularities.

MACMORRIS. I do not know you so good a man as myself: so
Chrish save me, I will cut off your head.

GOWER. Gentlemen both, you will mistake each other.

JAMY. A! that's a foul fault.   *A parley sounded*

GOWER. The town sounds a parley.

FLUELLEN. Captain Macmorris, when there is more better
opportunity to be required, look you, I will be so bold as
to tell you I know the disciplines of wars; and there is an
end.   *Exeunt*

SCENE THREE

The Same. Before the Gates of Harfleur.

*The Governor and some Citizens on the walls; the English
forces below. Enter King Henry and his Train*

KING HENRY. How yet resolves the governor of the town?
This is the latest parle we will admit:
Therefore to our best mercy give yourselves;
Or like to men proud of destruction
Defy us to our worst: for, as I am a soldier,—
A name that in my thoughts, becomes me best,—
If I begin the battery once again,
I will not leave the half-achieved Harfleur
Till in her ashes she lie buried.
The gates of mercy shall be all shut up,

And the flesh'd soldier, rough and hard of heart,
In liberty of bloody hand shall range
With conscience wide as hell, mowing like grass
Your fresh-fair virgins and your flowering infants.
What is it then to me, if impious war,
Array'd in flames like to the prince of fiends,
Do, with his smirch'd complexion, all fell feats
Enlink'd to waste and desolation?
What is 't to me, when you yourselves are cause,
If your pure maidens fall into the hand
Of hot and forcing violation?
What rein can hold licentious wickedness
When down the hill he holds his fierce career?
We may as bootless spend our vain command
Upon the enraged soldiers in their spoil
As send precepts to the leviathan
To come ashore. Therefore, you men of Harfleur,
Take pity of your town and of your people,
Whiles yet my soldiers are in my command;
Whiles yet the cool and temperate wind of grace
O'erblows the filthy and contagious clouds
Of heady murder, spoil, and villany.
If not, why, in a moment, look to see
The blind and bloody soldier with foul hand
Defile the locks of your shrill-shrieking daughters;
Your fathers taken by the silver beards,
And their most reverend heads dash'd to the walls;
Your naked infants spitted upon pikes,
Whiles the mad mothers with their howls confus'd
Do break the clouds, as did the wives of Jewry
At Herod's bloody-hunting slaughtermen.
What say you? will you yield, and this avoid?
Or, guilty in defence, be thus destroy'd?

GOVERNOR. Our expectation hath this day an end.
The Dauphin, whom of succour we entreated,
Returns us that his powers are yet not ready
To raise so great a siege. Therefore, great king,
We yield our town and lives to thy soft mercy.
Enter our gates; dispose of us and ours;
For we no longer are defensible.

KING HENRY. Open your gates! Come, uncle Exeter,
Go you and enter Harfleur; there remain,

And fortify it strongly 'gainst the French:
Use mercy to them all. For us, dear uncle,
The winter coming on and sickness growing
Upon our soldiers, we will retire to Calais.
To-night in Harfleur will we be your guest;
To-morrow for the march are we addrest.

Flourish. King Henry and his Train enter the town

SCENE FOUR

Rouen. A Room in the Palace.

Enter Katharine and Alice

KATHARINE. Alice, tu as esté en Angleterre, et tu parles bien
le langage.

ALICE. Un peu, madame.

KATHARINE. Je te prie, m'enseignez; il faut que j'apprenne
à parler. Comment appellez vous la main en Anglois?

ALICE. La main? elle est appellée, de hand.

KATHARINE. De hand. Et les doigts?

ALICE. Les doigts? ma foy, j'oublie les doigts; mais je me
souviendray. Les doigts? je pense qu'ils sont appellés de
fingres; ouy, de fingres.

KATHARINE. La main, de hand; les doigts, de fingres. Je
pense que je suis le bon escolier. J'ai gagné deux mots
d'Anglois vistement. Comment appellez vous les ongles?

ALICE. Les ongles? nous les appellons, de nails.

KATHARINE. De nails. Escoutez; dites moy, si je parle bien:
de hands, de fingres, et de nails.

ALICE. C'est bien dict, madame; il est fort bon Anglois.

KATHARINE. Dites moy l'Anglois pour le bras.

ALICE. De arm, madame.

KATHARINE. Et le coude?

ALICE. De elbow.

KATHARINE. De elbow. Je m'en fais la répétition de tous les
mots que vous m'avez appris dès à présent.

ALICE. Il est trop difficile, madame, comme je pense.

KATHARINE. Excusez moy, Alice; escoutez: de hand, de fin-
gres, de nails, de arma, de bilbow.

ALICE. De elbow, madame.

KATHARINE. O Seigneur Dieu! je m'en oublie; de elbow.
Comment appellez vous le col?

ALICE. De nick, madame.

KATHARINE. De nick. Et le menton?

ALICE. De chin.

KATHARINE. De sin. Le col, de nick: le menton, de sin.

ALICE. Ouy. Sauf vostre honneur, en vérité vous prononcez
les mots aussi droict que les natifs d'Angleterre.

KATHARINE. Je ne doute point d'apprendre par la grace de
Dieu, et en peu de temps.

ALICE. N'avez vous déjà oublié ce que je vous ay enseignée?

KATHARINE. Non, je reciteray à vous promptement. De
hand, de fingre, de mails,—

ALICE. De nails, madame.

KATHARINE. De nails, de arme, de ilbow.

ALICE. Sauf vostre honneur, d'elbow.

KATHARINE. Ainsi dis je; d'elbow, de nick, et de sin. Com-
ment appellez vous le pied et la robe?

ALICE. De foot, madame; et le coun.

KATHARINE. De foot, et le coun? O Seigneur Dieu! ces sont
mots de son mauvais, corruptible, gros, et impudique, et
non pour les dames d'honneur d'user. Je ne voudrois pro-
noncer ces mots devant les seigneurs de France, pour tout
le monde. Foh! le foot, et le coun. Néantmoins je recitr ai
une autre fois ma leçon ensemble: de hand, de fingre ⸗
nails, d'arm, d'elbow, de nick, de sin, de foot, le coun.

ALICE. Excellent, madame!

KATHARINE. C'est assez pour une fois: allons nous à diner.

Exeunt

SCENE FIVE

The Same. Another Room in the Palace.

*Enter the French King, the Dauphin, Duke of Bourbon,
the Constable of France, and Others*

FRENCH KING. 'Tis certain, he hath pass'd the river Somme.

CONSTABLE. And if he be not fought withal, my lord,
Let us not live in France; let us quit all,
And give our vineyards to a barbarous people.

DAUPHIN. O Dieu vivant! shall a few sprays of us,

The emptying of our fathers' luxury,
Our scions, put in wild and savage stock,
Spirt up so suddenly into the clouds,
And overlook their grafters?

BOURBON. Normans, but bastard Normans, Norman
    bastards!
Mort de ma vie! if they march along
Unfought withal, but I will sell my dukedom,
To buy a slobbery and a dirty farm
In that nook-shotten isle of Albion.

CONSTABLE. Dieu de battailes! where have they this mettle?
Is not their climate foggy, raw, and dull,
On whom, as in despite, the sun looks pale,
Killing their fruit with frowns? Can sodden water,
A drench for sur-rein'd jades, their barley-broth,
Decoct their cold blood to such valiant heat?
And shall our quick blood, spirited with wine,
Seem frosty? O! for honour of our land,
Let us not hang like roping icicles
Upon our houses' thatch, whiles a more frosty people
Sweat drops of gallant youth in our rich fields;
Poor we may call them in their native lords.

DAUPHIN. By faith and honour,
Our madams mock at us, and plainly say
Our mettle is bred out; and they will give
Their bodies to the lust of English youth
To new-store France with bastard warriors.

BOURBON. They bid us to the English dancing-schools,
And teach lavoltas high and swift corantos;
Saying our grace is only in our heels,
And that we are most lofty runaways.

FRENCH KING. Where is Montjoy the herald? speed him
    hence:
Let him greet England with our sharp defiance.
Up, princes! and, with spirit of honour edg'd
More sharper than your swords, hie to the field:
Charles Delabreth, High Constable of France;
You Dukes of Orleans, Bourbon, and Berri,
Alençon, Brabant, Bar, and Burgundy;
Jaques Chatillon, Rambures, Vaudemont,
Beaumont, Grandpré, Roussi, and Fauconberg,
Foix, Lestrale, Bouciqualt, and Charolois;

High dukes, great princes, barons, lords, and knights,
For your great seats now quit you of great shames.
Bar Harry England, that sweeps through our land
With pennons painted in the blood of Harfleur:
Rush on his host, as doth the melted snow
Upon the valleys, whose low vassal seat
The Alps doth spit and void his rheum upon:
Go down upon him, you have power enough,
And in a captive chariot into Roan
Bring him our prisoner.

CONSTABLE.   This becomes the great.
Sorry am I his numbers are so few,
His soldiers sick and famish'd in their march,
For I am sure when he shall see our army
He 'll drop his heart into the sink of fear,
And for achievement offer us his ransom.

FRENCH KING. Therefore, Lord Constable, haste on Montjoy,
And let him say to England that we send
To know what willing ransom he will give.
Prince Dauphin, you shall stay with us in Roan.

DAUPHIN. Not so, I do beseech your Majesty.

FRENCH KING. Be patient, for you shall remain with us.
Now forth, Lord Constable and princes all,
And quickly bring us word of England's fall.   *Exeunt*

SCENE SIX

The English Camp in Picardy.

Enter Gower and Fluellen

GOWER. How now, Captain Fluellen! come you from the
bridge?

FLUELLEN. I assure you, there is very excellent services
committed at the pridge.

GOWER. Is the Duke of Exeter safe?

FLUELLEN. The Duke of Exeter is as magnanimous as Aga-
memnon; and a man that I love and honour with my soul,
and my heart, and my duty, and my life, and my living,
and my uttermost power: he is not—God be praised and
plessed!—any hurt in the world; but keeps the pridge most
valiantly, with excellent discipline. There is an aunchient

lieutenant there at the pridge, I think, in my very con-
science, he is as valiant a man as Mark Antony; and he is
a man of no estimation in the world; but I did see him do
as gallant service.

GOWER. What do you call him?

FLUELLEN. He is called Aunchient Pistol.

GOWER. I know him not.

Enter Pistol

FLUELLEN. Here is the man.

PISTOL. Captain, I thee beseech to do me favours:
      The Duke of Exeter doth love thee well.

FLUELLEN. Ay, I praise God; and I have merited some love
      at his hands.

PISTOL. Bardolph, a soldier firm and sound of heart,
      And of buxom valour, hath, by cruel fate
      And giddy Fortune's furious fickle wheel,
      That goddess blind,
      That stands upon the rolling restless stone,—

FLUELLEN. By your patience, Aunchient Pistol. Fortune is
      painted plind, with a muffler afore her eyes, to signify to
      you that Fortune is plind: and she is painted also with a
      wheel, to signify to you, which is the moral of it, that she
      is turning, and inconstant, and mutability, and variation:
      and her foot, look you, is fixed upon a spherical stone,
      which rolls, and rolls, and rolls: in good truth, the poet
      makes a most excellent description of it: Fortune is an ex-
      cellent moral.

PISTOL. Fortune is Bardolph's foe, and frowns on him;
      For he hath stol'n a pax, and hang'd must a' be,
      A damned death!
      Let gallows gape for dog, let man go free
      And let not hemp his wind-pipe suffocate.
      But Exeter hath given the doom of death
      For pax of little price.
      Therefore, go speak; the duke will hear thy voice;
      And let not Bardolph's vital thread be cut
      With edge of penny cord and vile reproach:
      Speak, captain, for his life, and I will thee requite.

FLUELLEN. Aunchient Pistol, I do partly understand your
      meaning.

PISTOL. Why then, rejoice therefore.

FLUELLEN. Certainly, aunchient, it is not a thing to rejoice

at; for, if, look you, he were my brother, I would desire
the duke to use his good pleasure and put him to execu-
tion; for discipline ought to be used.

PISTOL. Die and be damn'd; and figo for thy friendship!

FLUELLEN. It is well.

PISTOL. The fig of Spain!   *Exit*

FLUELLEN. Very good.

GOWER. Why, this is an arrant counterfeit rascal: I remem-
ber him now; a bawd, a cutpurse.

FLUELLEN. I'll assure you a' utter'd as prave words at the
pridge as you shall see in a summer's day. But it is very
well; what he has spoke to me, that is well, I warrant you,
when time is serve.

GOWER. Why, 'tis a gull, a fool, a rogue, that now and then
goes to the wars to grace himself at his return into London
under the form of a soldier. And such fellows are perfect
in the great commanders' names, and they will learn you
by rote where services were done; at such and such a
sconce, at such a breach, at such a convoy; who came off
bravely, who was shot, who disgraced, what terms the en-
emy stood on; and this they con perfectly in the phrase of
war, which they trick up with new-tuned oaths: and what
a beard of the general's cut and a horrid suit of the camp
will do among foaming bottles and ale-washed wits, is
wonderful to be thought on. But you must learn to know
such slanders of the age, or else you may be marvellously
mistook.

FLUELLEN. I tell you what, Captain Gower; I do perceive,
he is not the man that he would gladly make show to the
world he is: if I find a hole in his coat I will tell him my
mind. (*Drum heard*) Hark you, the king is coming; and
I must speak with him from the pridge.

    Enter King Henry, Gloucester, and Soldiers
God pless your Majesty!

KING HENRY. How now, Fluellen! cam'st thou from the
    bridge?

FLUELLEN. Ay, so please your Majesty. The Duke of Exeter
hath very gallantly maintained the pridge: the French is
gone off, look you, and there is gallant and most prave
passages. Marry, th' athversary was have possession of the
pridge, but he is enforced to retire, and the Duke of Exe-

ter is master of the pridge. I can tell your Majesty the duke is a prave man.

KING HENRY. What men have you lost, Fluellen?

FLUELLEN. The perdition of th' athversary hath been very great, reasonable great: marry, for my part, I think the duke hath lost never a man but one that is like to be executed for robbing a church; one Bardolph, if your Majesty know the man: his face is all bubukles, and whelks, and knobs, and flames o' fire; and his lips blows at his nose, and it is like a coal of fire, sometimes plue and sometimes red; but his nose is executed, and his fire 's out.

KING HENRY. We would have all such offenders so cut off: and we give express charge that in our marches through the country there be nothing compelled from the villages, nothing taken but paid for, none of the French upbraided or abused in disdainful language; for when lenity and cruelty play for a kingdom, the gentler gamester is the soonest winner.

Tucket. Enter Montjoy

MONTJOY. You know me by my habit.

KING HENRY. Well then I know thee; what shall I know of thee?

MONTJOY. My master's mind.

KING HENRY. Unfold it.

MONTJOY. Thus says my king: Say thou to Harry of England: Though we seemed dead, we did but sleep: advantage is a better soldier than rashness. Tell him, we could have rebuked him at Harfleur, but that we thought not good to bruise an injury till it were full ripe; now we speak upon our cue, and our voice is imperial: England shall repent his folly, see his weakness, and admire our sufferance. Bid him therefore consider of his ransom; which must proportion the losses we have borne, the subjects we have lost, the disgrace we have digested; which, in weight to re-answer, his pettiness would bow under. For our losses, his exchequer is too poor; for the effusion of our blood, the muster of his kingdom too faint a number; and for our disgrace, his own person, kneeling at our feet, but a weak and worthless satisfaction. To this add defiance: and tell him, for conclusion, he hath betrayed his followers, whose condemnation is pronounced. So far my king and master, so much my office.

KING HENRY. What is thy name? I know thy quality.

MONTJOY. Montjoy.

KING HENRY. Thou dost thy office fairly. Turn thee back,
And tell thy king I do not seek him now,
But could be willing to march on to Calais
Without impeachment; for, to say the sooth,—
Though 'tis no wisdom to confess so much
Unto an enemy of craft and vantage,—
My people are with sickness much enfeebled,
My numbers lessen'd, and those few I have
Almost no better than so many French:
Who, when they were in health, I tell thee, herald,
I thought upon one pair of English legs
Did march three Frenchmen. Yet, forgive me, God,
That I do brag thus! this your air of France
Hath blown that vice in me; I must repent.
Go therefore, tell thy master nere I am:
My ransom is this frail and worthless trunk,
My army but a weak and sickly guard;
Yet, God before, tell him we will come on,
Though France himself and such another neighbour
Stand in our way. There 's for thy labour, Montjoy.
Go, bid thy master well advise himself:
If we may pass, we will; if we be hinder'd,
We shall your tawny ground with your red blood
Discolour: and so, Montjoy, fare you well.
The sum of all our answer is but this:
We would not seek a battle as we are;
Nor, as we are, we say we will not shun it:
So tell your master.

MONTJOY. I shall deliver so. Thanks to your Highness. *Exit*

GLOUCESTER. I hope they will not come upon us now.

KING HENRY. We are in God's hand, brother, not in theirs.
March to the bridge; it now draws toward night:
Beyond the river we 'll encamp ourselves,
And on to-morrow bid them march away.   *Exeunt*

SCENE SEVEN

The French Camp, near Agincourt.

*Enter the Constable of France, the Lord Rambures, the
Duke of Orleans, the Dauphin, and Others*

CONSTABLE. Tut! I have the best armour of the world.
Would it were day!

ORLEANS. You have an excellent armour; but let my horse
have his due.

CONSTABLE. It is the best horse of Europe.

ORLEANS. Will it never be morning?

DAUPHIN. My Lord of Orleans, and my Lord High Con-
stable, you talk of horse and armour—

ORLEANS. You are as well provided of both as any prince in
the world.

DAUPHIN. What a long night is this! I will not change my
horse with any that treads but on four pasterns. Ça, ha!
He bounds from the earth as if his entrails were hairs: le
cheval volant, the Pegasus, qui a les narines de feu! When
I bestride him, I soar, I am a hawk: he trots the air; the
earth sings when he touches it; the basest horn of his hoof
is more musical than the pipe of Hermes.

ORLEANS. He 's of the colour of the nutmeg.

DAUPHIN. And of the heat of the ginger. It is a beast for
Perseus: he is pure air and fire; and the dull elements of
earth and water never appear in him but only in patient
stillness while his rider mounts him: he is indeed a horse;
and all other jades you may call beasts.

CONSTABLE. Indeed, my lord, it is a most absolute and excel-
lent horse.

DAUPHIN. It is the prince of palfreys; his neigh is like the
bidding of a monarch and his countenance enforces hom-
age.

ORLEANS. No more, cousin.

DAUPHIN. Nay, the man hath no wit that cannot, from the
rising of the lark to the lodging of the lamb, vary deserved
praise on my palfrey: it is a theme as fluent as the sea;
turn the sands into eloquent tongues, and my horse is ar-
gument for them all. 'Tis a subject for a sovereign to rea-

son on, and for a sovereign's sovereign to ride on; and for
the world—familiar to us, and unknown—to lay apart their
particular functions and wonder at him. I once writ a son-
net in his praise and began thus: 'Wonder of nature!'—

ORLEANS. I have heard a sonnet begin so to one's mistress.

DAUPHIN. Then did they imitate that which I composed to
my courser; for my horse is my mistress.

ORLEANS. Your mistress bears well.

DAUPHIN. Me well; which is the prescript praise and perfec-
tion of a good and particular mistress.

CONSTABLE. Ma foi, methought yesterday your mistress
shrewdly shook your back.

DAUPHIN. So perhaps did yours.

CONSTABLE. Mine was not bridled.

DAUPHIN. O! then belike she was old and gentle; and you
rode, like a kern of Ireland, your French hose off and in
your straight strossers.

CONSTABLE. You have good judgment in horsemanship.

DAUPHIN. Be warned by me, then: they that ride so, and
ride not warily, fall into foul bogs. I had rather have my
horse to my mistress.

CONSTABLE. I had as lief have my mistress a jade.

DAUPHIN. I tell thee, constable, my mistress wears his own
hair.

CONSTABLE. I could make as true a boast as that if I had a
sow to my mistress.

DAUPHIN. Le chien est retourné à son propre vomissement,
et la truie lavée au bourbier: thou makest use of any
thing.

CONSTABLE. Yet do I not use my horse for my mistress: or
any such proverb so little kin to the purpose.

RAMBURES. My Lord Constable, the armour that I saw in
your tent to-night, are those stars or suns upon it?

CONSTABLE. Stars, my lord.

DAUPHIN. Some of them will fall to-morrow, I hope.

CONSTABLE. And yet my sky shall not want.

DAUPHIN. That may be, for you bear a many superfluously,
and 'twere more honour some were away.

CONSTABLE. Even as your horse bears your praises; who
would trot as well were some of your brags dismounted.

DAUPHIN. Would I were able to load him with his desert!

Will it never be day? I will trot to-morrow a mile, and my way shall be paved with English faces.

CONSTABLE. I will not say so for fear I should be faced out of my way. But I would it were morning, for I would fain be about the ears of the English.

RAMBURES. Who will go to hazard with me for twenty prisoners?

CONSTABLE. You must first go yourself to hazard, ere you have them.

DAUPHIN. 'Tis midnight: I 'll go arm myself.   *Exit*

ORLEANS. The Dauphin longs for morning.

RAMBURES. He longs to eat the English.

CONSTABLE. I think he will eat all he kills.

ORLEANS. By the white hand of my lady, he 's a gallant prince.

CONSTABLE. Swear by her foot, that she may tread out the oath.

ORLEANS. He is simply the most active gentleman of France.

CONSTABLE. Doing is activity, and he will still be doing.

ORLEANS. He never did harm, that I heard of.

CONSTABLE. Nor will do none to-morrow: he will keep that good name still.

ORLEANS. I know him to be valiant.

CONSTABLE. I was told that by one that knows him better than you.

ORLEANS. What 's he?

CONSTABLE. Marry, he told me so himself; and he said he cared not who knew it.

ORLEANS. He needs not; it is no hidden virtue in him.

CONSTABLE. By my faith, sir, but it is; never any body saw it but his lackey: 'tis a hooded valour; and when it appears, it will bate.

ORLEANS. 'Ill will never said well.'

CONSTABLE. I will cap that proverb with 'There is flattery in friendship.'

ORLEANS. And I will take up that with 'Give the devil his due.'

CONSTABLE. Well placed: there stands your friend for the devil: have at the very eye of that proverb, with 'A pox of the devil.'

ORLEANS. You are the better at proverbs, by how much 'A fool's bolt is soon shot.'

CONSTABLE. You have shot over.

ORLEANS. 'Tis not the first time you were overshot.
Enter a Messenger

MESSENGER. My Lord High Constable, the English lie within fifteen hundred paces of your tents.

CONSTABLE. Who hath measured the ground?

MESSENGER. The Lord Grandpré.

CONSTABLE. A valiant and most expert gentleman. Would it were day! Alas! poor Harry of England, he longs not for the dawning as we do.

ORLEANS. What a wretched and peevish fellow is this King of England, to mope with his fat-brained followers so far out of his knowledge!

CONSTABLE. If the English had any apprehension they would run away.

ORLEANS. That they lack; for if their heads had any intellectual armour they could never wear such heavy headpieces.

RAMBURES. That island of England breeds very valiant creatures: their mastiffs are of unmatchable courage.

ORLEANS. Foolish curs! that run winking into the mouth of a Russian bear and have their heads crushed like rotten apples. You may as well say that 's a valiant flea that dare eat his breakfast on the lip of a lion.

CONSTABLE. Just, just; and the men do sympathize with the mastiffs in robustious and rough coming on, leaving their wits with their wives: and then give them great meals of beef and iron and steel, they will eat like wolves and fight like devils.

ORLEANS. Ay, but these English are shrewdly out of beef.

CONSTABLE. Then shall we find to-morrow they have only stomachs to eat and none to fight. Now is it time to arm; come, shall we about it?

ORLEANS. It is now two o'clock: but, let me see, by ten
We shall have each a hundred Englishmen.   *Exeunt*

ACT FOUR

Enter Chorus

Now entertain conjecture of a time
When creeping murmur and the poring dark
Fills the wide vessel of the universe.
From camp to camp, through the foul womb of night,
The hum of either army stilly sounds,
That the fix'd sentinels almost receive
The secret whispers of each other's watch:
Fire answers fire, and through their paly flames
Each battle sees the other's umber'd face:
Steed threatens steed, in high and boastful neighs
Piercing the night's dull ear; and from the tents
The armourers, accomplishing the knights,
With busy hammers closing rivets up,
Give dreadful note of preparation.
The country cocks do crow, the clocks do toll,
And the third hour of drowsy morning name.
Proud of their numbers, and secure in soul,
The confident and over-lusty French
Do the low-rated English play at dice;
And chide the cripple tardy-gaited night
Who, like a foul and ugly witch, doth limp
So tediously away. The poor condemned English,
Like sacrifices, by their watchful fires
Sit patiently, and inly ruminate
The morning's danger, and their gesture sad
Investing lank-lean cheeks and war-worn coats
Presenteth them unto the gazing moon
So many horrid ghosts. O! now, who will behold
The royal captain of this ruin'd band
Walking from watch to watch, from tent to tent,
Let him cry 'Praise and glory on his head!'
For forth he goes and visits all his host,
Bids them good-morrow with a modest smile,

And calls them brothers, friends, and countrymen.
Upon his royal face there is no note
How dread an army hath enrounded him;
Nor doth he dedicate one jot of colour
Unto the weary and all-watched night:
But freshly looks and overbears attaint
With cheerful semblance and sweet majesty;
That every wretch, pining and pale before,
Beholding him, plucks comfort from his looks.
A largess universal, like the sun
His liberal eye doth give to every one,
Thawing cold fear. Then mean and gentle all,
Behold, as may unworthiness define,
A little touch of Harry in the night.
And so our scene must to the battle fly;
Where,—O for pity,—we shall much disgrace,
With four or five most vile and ragged foils,
Right ill dispos'd in brawl ridiculous,
The name of Agincourt. Yet sit and see;
Minding true things by what their mockeries be.   *Exit*

SCENE ONE

The English Camp at Agincourt.

Enter King Henry, Bedford, and Gloucester

KING HENRY. Gloucester, 'tis true that we are in great
    danger;
  The greater therefore should our courage be.
  Good-morrow, brother Bedford. God Almighty!
  There is some soul of goodness in things evil,
  Would men observingly distil it out;
  For our bad neighbour makes us early stirrers,
  Which is both healthful, and good husbandry:
  Besides they are our outward consciences,
  And preachers to us all; admonishing
  That we should dress us fairly for our end.
  Thus may we gather honey from the weed,
  And make a moral of the devil himself.
          Enter Erpingham
  Good-morrow, old Sir Thomas Erpingham:

A good soft pillow for that good white head
Were better than a churlish turf of France.

ERPINGHAM. Not so, my liege: this lodging likes me better,
Since I may say, 'Now lie I like a king.'

KING HENRY. 'Tis good for men to love their present pains
Upon example; so the spirit is eas'd:
And when the mind is quicken'd, out of doubt,
The organs, though defunct and dead before,
Break up their drowsy grave, and newly move
With casted slough and fresh legerity.
Lend me thy cloak, Sir Thomas. Brothers both,
Commend me to the princes in our camp;
Do my good-morrow to them; and anon
Desire them all to my pavilion.

GLOUCESTER. We shall, my liege.

Exeunt Gloucester and Bedford

ERPINGHAM. Shall I attend your Grace?

KING HENRY.   No, my good knight;
Go with my brothers to my lords of England:
I and my bosom must debate awhile,
And then I would no other company.

ERPINGHAM. The Lord in heaven bless thee, noble Harry!

Exit

KING HENRY. God-a-mercy, old heart! thou speak'st cheer-
fully.

Enter Pistol

PISTOL. Qui va là?

KING HENRY. A friend.

PISTOL. Discuss unto me; art thou officer?
Or art thou base, common, and popular?

KING HENRY. I am a gentleman of a company.

PISTOL. Trail'st thou the puissant pike?

KING HENRY. Even so. What are you?

PISTOL. As good a gentleman as the emperor.

KING HENRY. Then you are a better than the king.

PISTOL. The king 's a bawcock, and a heart of gold,
A lad of life, an imp of fame:
Of parents good, of fist most valiant:
I kiss his dirty shoe, and from my heart-string
I love the lovely bully. What 's thy name?

KING HENRY. Harry le Roy.

PISTOL. Le Roy! a Cornish name: art thou of Cornish crew?

KING HENRY. No, I am a Welshman.

PISTOL. Know'st thou Fluellen?

KING HENRY. Yes.

PISTOL. Tell him, I 'll knock his leek about his pate
Upon Saint Davy's day.

KING HENRY. Do not you wear your dagger in your cap that
day, lest he knock that about yours.

PISTOL. Art thou his friend?

KING HENRY. And his kinsman too.

PISTOL. The figo for thee then!

KING HENRY. I thank you. God be with you!

PISTOL. My name is Pistol called.   *Exit*

KING HENRY. It sorts well with your fierceness.   *Retires*

    Enter Fluellen and Gower, severally

GOWER. Captain Fluellen!

FLUELLEN. So! in the name of Cheshu Christ, speak lower.
It is the greatest admiration in the universal world, when
the true and auncient prerogatifes and laws of the wars is
not kept. If you would take the pains but to examine the
wars of Pompey the Great, you shall find, I warrant you,
that there is no tiddle-taddle nor pibble-pabble in Pom-
pey's camp; I warrant you, you shall find the ceremonies
of the wars, and the cares of it, and the forms of it, and the
sobriety of it, and the modesty of it, to be otherwise.

GOWER. Why, the enemy is loud; you heard him all night.

FLUELLEN. If the enemy is an ass and a fool and a prating
coxcomb, is it meet, think you, that we should also, look
you, be an ass and a fool and a prating coxcomb, in your
own conscience now?

GOWER. I will speak lower.

FLUELLEN. I pray you and peseech you that you will.

    Exeunt Gower and Fluellen

KING HENRY. Though it appear a little out of fashion,
There is much care and valour in this Welshman.

  Enter John Bates, Alexander Court, and Michael Williams

COURT. Brother John Bates, is not that the morning which
breaks yonder?

BATES. I think it be; but we have no great cause to desire
the approach of day.

WILLIAMS. We see yonder the beginning of the day, but I
think we shall never see the end of it. Who goes there?

KING HENRY. A friend.

WILLIAMS. Under what captain serve you?

KING HENRY. Under Sir Thomas Erpingham.

WILLIAMS. A good old commander and a most kind gentle-
man: I pray you, what thinks he of our estate?

KING HENRY. Even as men wracked upon a sand, that look
to be washed off the next tide.

BATES. He hath not told his thought to the king?

KING HENRY. No; nor it is not meet he should. For, though I
speak it to you, I think the king is but a man, as I am: the
violet smells to him as it doth to me; the element shows to
him as it doth to me; all his senses have but human con-
ditions: his ceremonies laid by, in his nakedness he ap-
pears but a man; and though his affections are higher
mounted than ours, yet when they stoop, they stoop with
the like wing. Therefore when he sees reason of fears, as
we do, his fears, out of doubt, be of the same relish as ours
are: yet, in reason, no man should possess him with any
appearance of fear, lest he, by showing it, should dis-
hearten his army.

BATES. He may show what outward courage he will, but I
believe, as cold a night as 'tis, he could wish himself in
Thames up to the neck, and so I would he were, and I by
him, at all adventures, so we were quit here.

KING HENRY. By my troth, I will speak my conscience of the
king: I think he would not wish himself any where but
where he is.

BATES. Then I would he were here alone; so should he be
sure to be ransomed, and a many poor men's lives saved.

KING HENRY. I dare say you love him not so ill to wish him
here alone, howsoever you speak this to feel other men's
minds. Methinks I could not die any where so contented
as in the king's company, his cause being just and his
quarrel honourable.

WILLIAMS. That 's more than we know.

BATES. Ay, or more than we should seek after; for we know
enough if we know we are the king's subjects. If his cause
be wrong, our obedience to the king wipes the crime of it
out of us.

WILLIAMS. But if the cause be not good, the king himself
hath a heavy reckoning to make; when all those legs and
arms and heads, chopped off in a battle, shall join together
at the latter day, and cry all, 'We died at such a place';

some swearing, some crying for a surgeon, some upon their wives left poor behind them, some upon the debts they owe, some upon their children rawly left. I am afeard there are few die well that die in a battle; for how can they charitably dispose of any thing when blood is their argument? Now, if these men do not die well, it will be a black matter for the king that led them to it, whom to disobey were against all proportion of subjection.

KING HENRY. So, if a son that is by his father sent about merchandise do sinfully miscarry upon the sea, the imputation of his wickedness, by your rule, should be imposed upon his father that sent him: or if a servant, under his master's command transporting a sum of money, be assailed by robbers and die in many irreconciled iniquities, you may call the business of the master the author of the servant's damnation. But this is not so: the king is not bound to answer the particular endings of his soldiers, the father of his son, nor the master of his servant; for they purpose not their death when they purpose their services. Besides, there is no king, be his cause never so spotless, if it come to the arbitrement of swords, can try it out with all unspotted soldiers. Some, peradventure, have on them the guilt of premeditated and contrived murder; some, of beguiling virgins with the broken seals of perjury; some, making the wars their bulwark, that have before gored the gentle bosom of peace with pillage and robbery. Now, if these men have defeated the law and outrun native punishment, though they can outstrip men, they have no wings to fly from God: war is his beadle, war is his vengeance; so that here men are punished for before-breach of the king's laws in now the king's quarrel: where they feared the death they have borne life away, and where they would be safe they perish. Then, if they die unprovided, no more is the king guilty of their damnation than he was before guilty of those impieties for the which they are now visited. Every subject's duty is the king's; but every subject's soul is his own. Therefore should every soldier in the wars do as every sick man in his bed, wash every mote out of his conscience; and dying so, death is to him advantage; or not dying, the time was blessedly lost wherein such preparation was gained: and in him that escapes, it were not sin to think that, making God so free an offer, he let him outlive that day to see his greatness, and to teach others how they should prepare.

WILLIAMS. 'Tis certain, every man that dies ill, the ill upon his own head: the king is not to answer it.

BATES. I do not desire he should answer for me; and yet I determine to fight lustily for him.

KING HENRY. I myself heard the king say he would not be ransomed.

WILLIAMS. Ay, he said so, to make us fight cheerfully; but when our throats are cut he may be ransomed, and we ne'er the wiser.

KING HENRY. If I live to see it, I will never trust his word after.

WILLIAMS. You pay him then. That 's a perilous shot out of an elder-gun, that a poor and a private displeasure can do against a monarch. You may as well go about to turn the sun to ice with fanning in his face with a peacock's feather. You 'll never trust his word after! come, 'tis a foolish saying.

KING HENRY. Your reproof is something too round: I should be angry with you if the time were convenient.

WILLIAMS. Let it be a quarrel between us, if you live.

KING HENRY. I embrace it.

WILLIAMS. How shall I know thee again?

KING HENRY. Give me any gage of thine, and I will wear it in my bonnet: then, if ever thou darest acknowledge it, I will make it my quarrel.

WILLIAMS. Here 's my glove: give me another of thine.

KING HENRY. There.

WILLIAMS. This will I also wear in my cap: if ever thou come to me and say after to-morrow, 'This is my glove,' by this hand I will take thee a box on the ear.

KING HENRY. If ever I live to see it, I will challenge it.

WILLIAMS. Thou darest as well be hanged.

KING HENRY. Well, I will do it, though I take thee in the king's company.

WILLIAMS. Keep thy word: fare thee well.

BATES. Be friends, you English fools, be friends; we have French quarrels enow, if you could tell how to reckon.

KING HENRY. Indeed, the French may lay twenty French crowns to one, they will beat us; for they bear them on their shoulders: but it is no English treason to cut French crowns, and to-morrow the king himself will be a clipper.

Exeunt Soldiers

Upon the king! let us our lives, our souls,
Our debts, our careful wives,
Our children, and our sins lay on the king!
We must bear all. O hard condition!
Twin-born with greatness, subject to the breath
Of every fool, whose sense no more can feel
But his own wringing. What infinite heart's ease
Must kings neglect that private men enjoy!
And what have kings that privates have not too,
Save ceremony, save general ceremony?
And what art thou, thou idol ceremony?
What kind of god art thou, that suffer'st more
Of mortal griefs than do thy worshippers?
What are thy rents? what are thy comings in?
O ceremony! show me but thy worth:
What is thy soul of adoration?
Art thou aught else but place, degree, and form,
Creating awe and fear in other men?
Wherein thou art less happy, being fear'd,
Than they in fearing.
What drink'st thou oft, instead of homage sweet,
But poison'd flattery? O! be sick, great greatness,
And bid thy ceremony give thee cure.
Think'st thou the fiery fever will go out
With titles blown from adulation?
Will it give place to flexure and low-bending?
Canst thou, when thou command'st the beggar's knee,
Command the health of it? No, thou proud dream,
That play'st so subtly with a king's repose;
I am a king that find thee; and I know
'Tis not the balm, the sceptre and the ball,
The sword, the mace, the crown imperial,
The intertissued robe of gold and pearl,
The farced title running 'fore the king,
The throne he sits on, nor the tide of pomp
That beats upon the high shore of this world,
No, not all these, thrice-gorgeous ceremony,
Not all these, laid in bed majestical,
Can sleep so soundly as the wretched slave,
Who with a body fill'd and vacant mind

Gets him to rest, cramm'd with distressful bread;
Never sees horrid night, the child of hell,
But, like a lackey, from the rise to set
Sweats in the eye of Phœbus, and all night
Sleeps in Elysium; next day after dawn,
Doth rise and help Hyperion to his horse,
And follows so the ever-running year
With profitable labour to his grave:
And, but for ceremony, such a wretch,
Winding up days with toil and nights with sleep,
Had the fore-hand and vantage of a king.
The slave, a member of the country's peace,
Enjoys it; but in gross brain little wots
What watch the king keeps to maintain the peace,
Whose hours the peasant best advantages.

Re-enter Erpingham

ERPINGHAM. My lord, your nobles, jealous of your absence,
Seek through your camp to find you.

KING HENRY.   Good old knight,
Collect them all together at my tent:
I 'll be before thee.

ERPINGHAM.   I shall do 't, my lord.   *Exit*

KING HENRY. O God of battles! steel my soldiers' hearts;
Possess them not with fear; take from them now
The sense of reckoning, if the opposed numbers
Pluck their hearts from them. Not to-day, O Lord!
O! not to-day, think not upon the fault
My father made in compassing the crown.
I Richard's body have interr'd anew,
And on it have bestow'd more contrite tears
Than from it issu'd forced drops of blood.
Five hundred poor I have in yearly pay,
Who twice a day their wither'd hands hold up
Toward heaven, to pardon blood; and I have built
Two chantries, where the sad and solemn priests
Sing still for Richard's soul. More will I do;
Though all that I can do is nothing worth,
Since that my penitence comes after all,
Imploring pardon.

Re-enter Gloucester

GLOUCESTER. My liege!

KING HENRY. My brother Gloucester's voice! Ay;
  I know thy errand, I will go with thee:
  The day, my friends, and all things stay for me.   *Exeunt*

SCENE TWO

The French Camp.

Enter the Dauphin, Orleans, Rambures, and Others

ORLEANS. The sun doth gild our armour: up, my lords!
DAUPHIN. Montez à cheval! My horse! varlet! lacquais! ha!
ORLEANS. O brave spirit!
DAUPHIN. Via! les eaux et la terre!
ORLEANS. Rien puis? l'air et le feu.
DAUPHIN. Ciel! cousin Orleans.
                    Enter Constable
  Now, my Lord Constable!
CONSTABLE. Hark, how our steeds for present service neigh!
DAUPHIN. Mount them, and make incision in their hides,
  That their hot blood may spin in English eyes,
  And dout them with superfluous courage: ha!
RAMBURES. What! will you have them weep our horses'
    blood?
  How shall we then behold their natural tears?
                    Enter a Messenger
MESSENGER. The English are embattail'd, you French peers.
CONSTABLE. To horse, you gallant princes! straight to horse!
  Do but behold yon poor and starved band,
  And your fair show shall suck away their souls,
  Leaving them but the shales and husks of men.
  There is not work enough for all our hands;
  Scarce blood enough in all their sickly veins
  To give each naked curtal-axe a stain,
  That our French gallants shall to-day draw out,
  And sheathe for lack of sport: let us but blow on them,
  The vapour of our valour will o'erturn them.
  'Tis positive 'gainst all exceptions, lords,
  That our superfluous lackeys and our peasants,
  Who in unnecessary action swarm
  About our squares of battle, were enow

To purge this field of such a hilding foe,
Though we upon this mountain's basis by
Took stand for idle speculation:
But that our honours must not. What's to say?
A very little little let us do,
And all is done. Then let the trumpets sound
The tucket sonance and the note to mount:
For our approach shall so much dare the field,
That England shall couch down in fear and yield.

Enter Grandpré

GRANDPRÉ. Why do you stay so long, my lords of France?
Yon island carrions desperate of their bones,
Ill-favour'dly become the morning field:
Their ragged curtains poorly are let loose,
And our air shakes them passing scornfully:
Big Mars seems bankrupt in their beggar'd host,
And faintly through a rusty beaver peeps:
The horsemen sit like fixed candlesticks,
With torch-staves in their hand; and their poor jades
Lob down their heads, dropping the hides and hips,
The gum down-roping from their pale-dead eyes,
And in their pale dull mouths the gimmal bit
Lies foul with chew'd grass, still and motionless;
And their executors, the knavish crows,
Fly o'er them, all impatient for their hour.
Description cannot suit itself in words
To demonstrate the life of such a battle
In life so lifeless as it shows itself.

CONSTABLE. They have said their prayers, and they stay for
    death.
DAUPHIN. Shall we go send them dinners and fresh suits,
    And give their fasting horses provender,
    And after fight with them?
CONSTABLE. I stay but for my guard: on, to the field!
    I will the banner from a trumpet take,
    And use it for my haste. Come, come, away!
    The sun is high, and we outwear the day.   *Exeunt*

SCENE THREE

The English Camp.

Enter the English host; Gloucester, Bedford, Exeter, Salisbury, and Westmoreland

GLOUCESTER. Where is the king?

BEDFORD. The king himself is rode to view their battle.

WESTMORELAND. Of fighting men they have full three-
    score thousand.

EXETER. There 's five to one; besides, they all are fresh.

SALISBURY. God's arm strike with us! 'tis a fearful odds.
    God be wi' you, princes all; I 'll to my charge:
    If we no more meet till we meet in heaven,
    Then, joyfully, my noble Lord of Bedford,
    My dear Lord Gloucester, and my good Lord Exeter,
    And my kind kinsman, warriors all, adieu!

BEDFORD. Farewell, good Salisbury; and good luck go with
    thee!

EXETER. Farewell, kind lord. Fight valiantly to-day:
    And yet I do thee wrong to mind thee of it,
    For thou art fram'd of the firm truth of valour.

                                        Exit Salisbury

BEDFORD. He is as full of valour as of kindness;
    Princely in both.

                    Enter King Henry

WESTMORELAND.   O! that we now had here
    But one ten thousand of those men in England
    That do no work to-day.

KING HENRY.   What 's he that wishes so?
    My cousin Westmoreland? No, my fair cousin:
    If we are mark'd to die, we are enow
    To do our country loss; and if to live,
    The fewer men, the greater share of honour.
    God's will! I pray thee, wish not one man more.
    By Jove, I am not covetous for gold,
    Nor care I who doth feed upon my cost;
    It yearns me not if men my garments wear;
    Such outward things dwell not in my desires:
    But if it be a sin to covet honour,

I am the most offending soul alive.
No, faith, my coz, wish not a man from England:
God's peace! I would not lose so great an honour
As one man more, methinks, would share from me,
For the best hope I have. O! do not wish one more:
Rather proclaim it, Westmoreland, through my host,
That he which hath no stomach to this fight,
Let him depart; his passport shall be made,
And crowns for convoy put into his purse:
We would not die in that man's company
That fears his fellowship to die with us.
This day is call'd the feast of Crispian:
He that outlives this day, and comes safe home,
Will stand a tip-toe when this day is nam'd,
And rouse him at the name of Crispian.
He that shall live this day, and see old age,
Will yearly on the vigil feast his neighbours,
And say, 'To-morrow is Saint Crispian':
Then will he strip his sleeve and show his scars,
And say, 'These wounds I had on Crispin's day.'
Old men forget: yet all shall be forgot,
But he 'll remember with advantages
What feats he did that day. Then shall our names,
Familiar in his mouth as household words,
Harry the king, Bedford and Exeter,
Warwick and Talbot, Salisbury and Gloucester,
Be in their flowing cups freshly remember'd.
This story shall the good man teach his son;
And Crispin Crispian shall ne'er go by,
From this day to the ending of the world,
But we in it shall be remember'd;
We few, we happy few, we band of brothers;
For he to-day that sheds his blood with me
Shall be my brother; be he ne'er so vile
This day shall gentle his condition:
And gentlemen in England now a-bed
Shall think themselves accurs'd they were not here,
And hold their manhoods cheap whiles any speaks
That fought with us upon Saint Crispin's day.

Re-enter Salisbury

SALISBURY. My sovereign lord, bestow yourself with speed:
The French are bravely in their battles set,

And will with all expedience charge on us.

KING HENRY. All things are ready, if our minds be so.

WESTMORELAND. Perish the man whose mind is backward
    now!

KING HENRY. Thou dost not wish more help from England,
    coz?

WESTMORELAND. God's will! my liege, would you and I
    alone,

Without more help, could fight this royal battle!

KING HENRY. Why, now thou hast unwish'd five thousand
    men;

Which likes me better than to wish us one.

You know your places: God be with you all!

        Tucket. Enter Montjoy

MONTJOY. Once more I come to know of thee, King Harry,

If for thy ransom thou wilt now compound,

Before thy most assured overthrow:

For certainly thou art so near the gulf

Thou needs must be englutted. Besides, in mercy,

The constable desires thee thou wilt mind

Thy followers of repentance; that their souls

May make a peaceful and a sweet retire

From off these fields, where, wretches, their poor bodies

Must lie and fester.

KING HENRY.   Who hath sent thee now?

MONTJOY. The Constable of France.

KING HENRY. I pray thee, bear my former answer back:

Bid them achieve me and then sell my bones.

Good God! why should they mock poor fellows thus?

The man that once did sell the lion's skin

While the beast liv'd, was kill'd with hunting him.

A many of our bodies shall no doubt

Find native graves; upon the which, I trust,

Shall witness live in brass of this day's work;

And those that leave their valiant bones in France,

Dying like men, though buried in your dunghills,

They shall be fam'd; for there the sun shall greet them,

And draw their honours reeking up to heaven,

Leaving their earthly parts to choke your clime,

The smell whereof shall breed a plague in France.

Mark then abounding valour in our English,

That being dead, like to the bullet's grazing,

Break out into a second course of mischief,
Killing in relapse of mortality.
Let me speak proudly: tell the constable,
We are but warriors for the working-day;
Our gayness and our gilt are all besmirch'd
With rainy marching in the painful field;
There 's not a piece of feather in our host—
Good argument, I hope, we will not fly—
And time hath worn us into slovenry:
But, by the mass, our hearts are in the trim;
And my poor soldiers tell me, yet ere night
They 'll be in fresher robes, or they will pluck
The gay new coats o'er the French soldiers' heads,
And turn them out of service. If they do this,—
As, if God please, they shall,—my ransom then
Will soon be levied. Herald, save thou thy labour;
Come thou no more for ransom, gentle herald:
They shall have none, I swear, but these my joints;
Which if they have as I will leave 'em them,
Shall yield them little, tell the constable.

MONTJOY. I shall, King Harry. And so, fare thee well:
Thou never shalt hear herald any more.   *Exit*

KING HENRY. I fear thou 'lt once more come again for ransom.

Enter York

YORK. My lord, most humbly on my knee I beg
The leading of the vaward.

KING HENRY. Take it, brave York. Now, soldiers, march away:
And how thou pleasest, God, dispose the day!   *Exeunt*

SCENE FOUR

The Field of Battle.

Alarums. Excursions. Enter French Soldier, Pistol, and Boy

PISTOL. Yield, cur!

FRENCH SOLDIER. Je pense que vous estes le gentilhomme de
bonne qualité.

PISTOL. Quality? Calen O custure me! Art thou a gentle-
man?
What is thy name? Discuss.

FRENCH SOLDIER. O Seigneur Dieu!

PISTOL. O Signieur Dew should be a gentleman:—
Perpend my words, O Signieur Dew, and mark:
O Signieur Dew, thou diest on point of fox
Except, O signieur, thou do give to me
Egregious ransom.

FRENCH SOLDIER. O, prenez miséricorde! ayez pitié de moy!

PISTOL. Moy shall not serve; I will have forty moys;
Or I will fetch thy rim out at thy throat
In drops of crimson blood.

FRENCH SOLDIER. Est-il impossible d'eschapper la force de
ton bras?

PISTOL. Brass, cur!
Thou damned and luxurious mountain goat,
Offer'st me brass?

FRENCH SOLDIER. O pardonnez moy!

PISTOL. Sayst thou me so? is that a ton of moys?
Come hither, boy: ask me this slave in Franch
What is his name.

BOY. Escoutez: comment estes vous appellé?

FRENCH SOLDIER. Monsieur le Fer.

BOY. He says his name is Master Fer.

PISTOL. Master Fer! I 'll fer him, and firk him, and ferret
him. Discuss the same in French unto him.

BOY. I do not know the French for fer, and ferret, and firk.

PISTOL. Bid him prepare, for I will cut his throat.

FRENCH SOLDIER. Que dit-il, monsieur?

BOY. Il me commande à vous dire que vous faites vous prest;
car ce soldat icy est disposé tout à cette heure de couper
vostre gorge.

PISTOL. Ouy, cuppele gorge, permafoy,
Peasant, unless thou give me crowns, brave crowns;
Or mangled shalt thou be by this my sword.

FRENCH SOLDIER. O! je vous supplie pour l'amour de Dieu,
me pardonner! Je suis le gentilhomme de bonne maison:
gardez ma vie, et je vous donneray deux cents escus.

PISTOL. What are his words?

BOY. He prays you to save his life: he is a gentleman of a
good house; and, for his ransom he will give you two hun-
dred crowns.

PISTOL. Tell him, my fury shall abate, and I
The crowns will take.

FRENCH SOLDIER. Petit monsieur, que dit-il?

BOY. Encore qu'il est contre son jurement de pardonner aucun prisonnier; néantmoins, pour les escus que vous l'avez promis, il est content de vous donner la liberté, le franchisement.

FRENCH SOLDIER. Sur mes genoux, je vous donne mille remerciemens; et je m'estime heureux que je suis tombé entre les mains d'un chevalier, je pense, le plus brave, valiant, et très distingué seigneur d'Angleterre.

PISTOL. Expound unto me, boy.

BOY. He gives you, upon his knees, a thousand thanks; and he esteems himself happy that he hath fallen into the hands of one—as he thinks—the most brave, valorous, and thrice-worthy signieur of England.

PISTOL. As I suck blood, I will some mercy show.—Follow me!   *Exeunt Pistol and French Soldier*

BOY. Suivez vous le grand capitaine. I did never know so full a voice issue from so empty a heart: but the saying is true, 'The empty vessel makes the greatest sound.' Bardolph and Nym had ten times more valour than this roaring devil i' the old play, that every one may pare his nails with a wooden dagger; and they are both hanged; and so would this be if he durst steal anything adventurously. I must stay with the lackeys, with the luggage of our camp: the French might have a good prey of us, if he knew of it; for there is none to guard it but boys.   *Exit*

SCENE FIVE

Another Part of the Field.

Alarums. Enter Dauphin, Orleans, Bourbon, Constable, Rambures, and Others

CONSTABLE. O diable!

ORLEANS. O Seigneur! le jour est perdu! tout est perdu!

DAUPHIN. Mort de ma vie! all is confounded, all!
Reproach and everlasting shame
Sit mocking in our plumes. O meschante fortune!
Do not run away.   *A short alarum*

CONSTABLE.   Why, all our ranks are broke.

DAUPHIN. O perdurable shame! let 's stab ourselves.

Be these the wretches that we play'd at dice for?
ORLEANS. Is this the king we sent to for his ransom?
BOURBON. Shame, and eternal shame, nothing but shame!
    Let 's die in honour! once more back again;
    And he that will not follow Bourbon now,
    Let him go hence, and with his cap in hand,
    Like a base pander, hold the chamber-door
    Whilst by a slave, no gentler than my dog,
    His fairest daughter is contaminated.
CONSTABLE. Disorder, that hath spoil'd us, friend us now!
    Let us on heaps go offer up our lives.
ORLEANS. We are enough yet living in the field
    To smother up the English in our throngs,
    If any order might be thought upon.
BOURBON. The devil take order now! I 'll to the throng:
    Let life be short, else shame will be too long.   *Exeunt*

SCENE SIX

Another Part of the Field.

Alarums. Enter King Henry and Forces; Exeter, and Others

KING HENRY. Well have we done, thrice-valiant country-
    men:
    But all 's not done; yet keep the French the field.
EXETER. The Duke of York commends him to your Majesty.
KING HENRY. Lives he, good uncle? thrice within this hour
    I saw him down; thrice up again, and fighting;
    From helmet to the spur all blood he was.
EXETER. In which array, brave soldier, doth he lie,
    Larding the plain; and by his bloody side,—
    Yoke-fellow to his honour-owing wounds,—
    The noble Earl of Suffolk also lies.
    Suffolk first died: and York, all haggled over,
    Comes to him, where in gore he lay insteep'd,
    And takes him by the beard, kisses the gashes
    That bloodily did yawn upon his face;
    And cries aloud, 'Tarry, dear cousin Suffolk!
    My soul shall thine keep company to heaven;
    Tarry, sweet soul, for mine, then fly abreast,
    As in this glorious and well-foughten field,

We kept together in our chivalry!'
Upon these words I came and cheer'd him up:
He smil'd me in the face, raught me his hand,
And with a feeble gripe says, 'Dear my lord,
Commend my service to my sovereign.'
So did he turn, and over Suffolk's neck
He threw his wounded arm, and kiss'd his lips;
And so espous'd to death, with blood he seal'd
A testament of noble-ending love.
The pretty and sweet manner of it forc'd
Those waters from me which I would have stopp'd;
But I had not so much of man in me,
And all my mother came into mine eyes
And gave me up to tears.

KING HENRY.   I blame you not;
For, hearing this, I must perforce compound
With mistful eyes, or they will issue too.   *Alarum*
But hark! what new alarum is this same?
The French have reinforc'd their scatter'd men;
Then every soldier kill his prisoners!
Give the word through.   *Exeunt*

SCENE SEVEN

Another Part of the Field.

Alarums. Enter Fluellen and Gower

FLUELLEN. Kill the poys and the luggage! 'tis expressly
against the law of arms: 'tis as arrant a piece of knavery,
mark you now, as can be offer't: in your conscience now,
is it not?

GOWER. 'Tis certain, there 's not a boy left alive; and the
cowardly rascals that ran from the battle have done this
slaughter: besides, they have burned and carried away
all that was in the king's tent; wherefore the king most
worthily hath caused every soldier to cut his prisoner's
throat. O! 'tis a gallant king.

FLUELLEN. Ay, he was porn at Monmouth, Captain Gower.
What call you the town's name where Alexander the Pig
was born?

GOWER. Alexander the Great.

FLUELLEN. Why, I pray you, is not pig great? The pig, or the great, or the mighty, or the huge, or the magnanimous, are all one reckonings, save the phrase is a little variations.

GOWER. I think Alexander the Great was born in Macedon: his father was called Philip of Macedon, as I take it.

FLUELLEN. I think it is in Macedon where Alexander is porn. I tell you, captain, if you look in the maps of the 'orld, I warrant you sall find, in the comparisons between Macedon and Monmouth, that the situations, look you, is both alike. There is a river in Macedon, and there is also moreover a river at Monmouth: it is called Wye at Monmouth; but it is out of my prains what is the name of the other river; but 'tis all one, 'tis alike as my fingers is to my fingers, and there is salmon in both. If you mark Alexander's life well, Harry of Monmouth's life is come after it indifferent well; for there is figures in all things. Alexander,—God knows, and you know,—in his rages, and his furies, and his wraths, and his cholers, and his moods, and his displeasures, and his indignations, and also being a little intoxicates in his prains, did, in his ales and his angers, look you, kill his pest friend, Cleitus.

GOWER. Our king is not like him in that: he never killed any of his friends.

FLUELLEN. It is not well done, mark you now, to take the tales out of my mouth, ere it is made and finished. I speak but in the figures and comparisons of it: as Alexander killed his friend Cleitus, being in his ales and his cups, so also Harry Monmouth, being in his right wits and his good judgments, turned away the fat knight with the great belly-doublet: he was full of jests, and gipes, and knaveries, and mocks; I have forgot his name.

GOWER. Sir John Falstaff.

FLUELLEN. That is he. I 'll tell you, there is goot men porn at Monmouth.

GOWER. Here comes his Majesty.

Alarum. Enter King Henry, with a part of the English Forces; Warwick, Gloucester, Exeter, and Others

KING HENRY. I was not angry since I came to France
Until this instant. Take a trumpet, herald;
Ride thou unto the horsemen on yon hill:
If they will fight with us, bid them come down,

Or void the field; they do offend our sight.
If they 'll do neither, we will come to them,
And make them skirr away, as swift as stones
Enforced from the old Assyrian slings.
Besides, we 'll cut the throats of those we have,
And not a man of them that we shall take
Shall taste our mercy. Go and tell them so.

Enter Montjoy

EXETER. Here comes the herald of the French, my liege.

GLOUCESTER. His eyes are humbler than they us'd to be.

KING HENRY. How now! what means this, herald? know'st
    thou not
That I have fin'd these bones of mine for ransom?
Com'st thou again for ransom?

MONTJOY.   No, great king.
I come to thee for charitable licence,
That we may wander o'er this bloody field
To book our dead, and then to bury them;
To sort our nobles from our common men;
For many of our princes—woe the while!—
Lie drown'd and soak'd in mercenary blood;
So do our vulgar drench their peasant limbs
In blood of princes; and their wounded steeds
Fret fetlock-deep in gore, and with wild rage
Yerk out their armed heels at their dead masters,
Killing them twice. O! give us leave, great king,
To view the field in safety and dispose
Of their dead bodies.

KING HENRY.   I tell thee truly, herald,
I know not if the day be ours or no;
For yet a many of your horsemen peer
And gallop o'er the field.

MONTJOY.   The day is yours.

KING HENRY. Praised be God, and not our strength, for it!
What is this castle call'd that stands hard by?

MONTJOY. They call it Agincourt.

KING HENRY. Then call we this the field of Agincourt,
Fought on the day of Crispin Crispianus.

FLUELLEN. Your grandfather of famous memory, an 't please
your Majesty, and your great-uncle Edward the Plack
Prince of Wales, as I have read in the chronicles, fought a
most prave pattle here in France.

KING HENRY. They did, Fluellen.

FLUELLEN. Your Majesty says very true. If your Majesties is remembered of it, the Welshmen did good service in a garden where leeks did grow, wearing leeks in their Monmouth caps; which, your Majesty know, to this hour is an honourable badge of the service; and I do believe, your Majesty takes no scorn to wear the leek upon Saint Tavy's day.

KING HENRY. I wear it for a memorable honour; For I am Welsh, you know, good countryman.

FLUELLEN. All the water in Wye cannot wash your Majesty's Welsh plood out of your pody, I can tell you that: Got pless it and preserve it, as long as it pleases his Grace, and his Majesty too!

KING HENRY. Thanks, good my countryman.

FLUELLEN. By Jeshu, I am your Majesty's countryman, I care not who know it; I will confess it to all the 'orld: I need not be ashamed of your Majesty, praised be God, so long as your Majesty is an honest man.

KING HENRY. God keep me so! Our heralds go with him: Bring me just notice of the numbers dead On both our parts. Call yonder fellow hither.

Points to Williams. Exeunt Montjoy and others

EXETER. Soldier, you must come to the king.

KING HENRY. Soldier, why wear'st thou that glove in thy cap?

WILLIAMS. An 't please your Majesty, 'tis the gage of one that I should fight withal, if he be alive.

KING HENRY. An Englishman?

WILLIAMS. An 't please your Majesty, a rascal that swaggered with me last night; who, if a' live and ever dare to challenge this glove, I have sworn to take him a box o' the ear: or, if I can see my glove in his cap,—which he swore as he was a soldier he would wear if alive,—I will strike it out soundly.

KING HENRY. What think you, Captain Fluellen? is it fit this soldier keep his oath?

FLUELLEN. He is a craven and a villain else, an 't please your Majesty, in my conscience.

KING HENRY. It may be his enemy is a gentleman of great sort, quite from the answer of his degree.

FLUELLEN. Though he be as good a gentleman as the devil

is, as Lucifer and Belzebub himself, it is necessary, look your Grace, that he keep his vow and his oath. If he be perjured, see you now, his reputation is as arrant a villain and a Jack-sauce as ever his black shoe trod upon God's ground and his earth, in my conscience, la!

KING HENRY. Then keep thy vow, sirrah, when thou meetest the fellow.

WILLIAMS. So I will, my liege, as I live.

KING HENRY. Who servest thou under?

WILLIAMS. Under Captain Gower, my liege.

FLUELLEN. Gower is a goot captain, and is good knowledge and literatured in the wars.

KING HENRY. Call him hither to me, soldier.

WILLIAMS. I will, my liege.   *Exit*

KING HENRY. Here, Fluellen; wear thou this favour for me and stick it in thy cap. When Alençon and myself were down together I plucked this glove from his helm: if any man challenge this, he is a friend to Alençon, and an enemy to our person; if thou encounter any such, apprehend him, an thou dost me love.

FLUELLEN. Your Grace does me as great honours as can be desired in the hearts of his subjects: I would fain see the man that has but two legs that shall find himself aggriefed at this glove, that is all; but I would fain see it once, and please God of his grace that I might see.

KING HENRY. Knowest thou Gower?

FLUELLEN. He is my dear friend, an 't please you.

KING HENRY. Pray thee, go seek him, and bring him to my tent.

FLUELLEN. I will fetch him.   *Exit*

KING HENRY. My Lord of Warwick, and my brother
            Gloucester,
Follow Fluellen closely at the heels.
The glove which I have given him for a favour
May haply purchase him a box o' the ear;
It is the soldier's; I by bargain should
Wear it myself. Follow, good cousin Warwick:
If that the soldier strike him,—as, I judge
By his blunt bearing he will keep his word,—
Some sudden mischief may arise of it;
For I do know Fluellen valiant,
And touch'd with choler, hot as gunpowder,

And quickly will return an injury:
Follow and see there be no harm between them.
Go you with me, uncle of Exeter.   *Exeunt*

SCENE EIGHT

Before King Henry's Pavilion.

Enter Gower and Williams

WILLIAMS. I warrant it is to knight you, captain.
                    Enter Fluellen
FLUELLEN. God's will and his pleasure, captain, I peseech
you now come apace to the king: there is more good to-
ward you peradventure than is in your knowledge to
dream of.
WILLIAMS. Sir, know you this glove?
FLUELLEN. Know the glove! I know the glove is a glove.
WILLIAMS. I know this; and thus I challenge it.   *Strikes him*
FLUELLEN. 'Sblood! an arrant traitor as any 's in the univer-
sal 'orld, or in France, or in England.
GOWER. How now, sir! you villain!
WILLIAMS. Do you think I 'll be forsworn?
FLUELLEN. Stand away, Captain Gower; I will give treason
his payment into plows, I warrant you.
WILLIAMS. I am no traitor.
FLUELLEN. That 's a lie in thy throat. I charge you in his
Majesty's name, apprehend him: he is a friend of the
Duke Alençon's.
                    Enter Warwick and Gloucester
WARWICK. How now, how now! what 's the matter?
FLUELLEN. My Lord of Warwick, here is,—praised be God
for it!—a most contagious treason come to light, look you,
as you shall desire in a summer's day. Here is his Majesty.
                    Enter King Henry and Exeter
KING HENRY. How now! what 's the matter?
FLUELLEN. My liege, here is a villain and a traitor, that, look
your Grace, has struck the glove which your Majesty is
take out of the helmet of Alençon.
WILLIAMS. My liege, this was my glove; here is the fellow of
it; and he that I gave it to in change promised to wear it
in his cap; I promised to strike him, if he did: I met this

man with my glove in his cap, and I have been as good as
my word.

FLUELLEN. Your Majesty hear now,—saving your Majesty's
manhood,—what an arrant, rascally, beggarly, lousy knave
it is. I hope your Majesty is pear me testimony and wit-
ness, and avouchments, that this is the glove of Alençon
that your Majesty is give me; in your conscience now.

KING HENRY. Give me thy glove, soldier: look, here is the
fellow of it.

'Twas I, indeed, thou promisedst to strike;
And thou hast given me most bitter terms.

FLUELLEN. An 't please your Majesty, let his neck answer
for it, if there is any martial law in the 'orld.

KING HENRY. How canst thou make me satisfaction?

WILLIAMS. All offenses, my lord, come from the heart: never
came any from mine that might offend your Majesty.

KING HENRY. It was ourself thou didst abuse.

WILLIAMS. Your Majesty came not like yourself: you ap-
peared to me but as a common man; witness the night,
your garments, your lowliness; and what your Highness
suffered under that shape, I beseech you, take it for your
own fault and not mine: for had you been as I took you
for I made no offence; therefore, I beseech your Highness,
pardon me.

KING HENRY. Here, uncle Exeter, fill this glove with crowns,
And give it to this fellow. Keep it, fellow;
And wear it for an honour in thy cap
Till I do challenge it. Give him the crowns:
And, captain, you must needs be friends with him.

FLUELLEN. By this day and this light, the fellow has mettle
enough in his belly. Hold, there is twelve pence for you,
and I pray you to serve God, and keep you out of prawls,
and prabbles, and quarrels, and dissensions, and, I war-
rant you, it is the better for you.

WILLIAMS. I will none of your money.

FLUELLEN. It is with a good will; I can tell you it will serve
you to mend your shoes: come, wherefore should you be
so pashful? your shoes is not so good: 'tis a good shilling,
I warrant you, or I will change it.

Enter an English Herald

KING HENRY. Now, herald, are the dead number'd?

HERALD. Here is the number of the slaughter'd French.

Delivers a paper

KING HENRY. What prisoners of good sort are taken, uncle?
EXETER. Charles Duke of Orleans, nephew to the king;
   John Duke of Bourbon, and Lord Bouciqualt:
   Of other lords and barons, knights and squires,
   Full fifteen hundred, besides common men.
KING HENRY. This note doth tell me of ten thousand French
   That in the field lie slain: of princes, in this number,
   And nobles bearing banners, there lie dead
   One hundred twenty-six: added to these,
   Of knights, esquires, and gallant gentlemen,
   Eight thousand and four hundred; of the which
   Five hundred were but yesterday dubb'd knights:
   So that, in these ten thousand they have lost,
   There are but sixteen hundred mercenaries;
   The rest are princes, barons, lords, knights, squires,
   And gentlemen of blood and quality.
   The names of those their nobles that lie dead:
   Charles Delabreth, High Constable of France;
   Jaques of Chatillon, Admiral of France;
   The master of the cross-bows, Lord Rambures;
   Great-master of France, the brave Sir Guischard
      Dauphin;
   John Duke of Alençon; Anthony Duke of Brabant,
   The brother to the Duke of Burgundy,
   And Edward Duke of Bar: of lusty earls,
   Grandpré and Roussi, Fauconberg and Foix,
   Beaumont and Marle, Vaudemont and Lestrale.
   Here was a royal fellowship of death!
   Where is the number of our English dead?
                Herald presents another paper
   Edward the Duke of York, the Earl of Suffolk,
   Sir Richard Ketly, Davy Gam, esquire:
   None else of name: and of all other men
   But five and twenty. O God! thy arm was here;
   And not to us, but to thy arm alone,
   Ascribe we all. When, without stratagem,
   But in plain shock and even play of battle,
   Was ever known so great and little loss
   On one part and on the other? Take it, God,
   For it is none but thine!
EXETER.   'Tis wonderful!
KING HENRY. Come, go we in procession to the village:

And be it death proclaimed through our host
To boast of this or take the praise from God
Which is his only.

FLUELLEN. Is it not lawful, an please your Majesty, to tell
how many is killed?

KING HENRY. Yes, captain; but with this acknowledgment,
That God fought for us.

FLUELLEN. Yes, my conscience, he did us great good.

KING HENRY. Do we all holy rites:
Let there be sung Non nobis and Te Deum;
The dead with charity enclos'd in clay,
We 'll then to Calais; and to England then,
Where ne'er from France arriv'd more happy men.

Exeunt

ACT FIVE

Enter Chorus

CHORUS. Vouchsafe to those that have not read the story,
    That I may prompt them: and of such as have,
    I humbly pray them to admit the excuse
    Of time, of numbers, and due course of things,
    Which cannot, in their huge and proper life
    Be here presented. Now we bear the king
    Toward Calais: grant him there; there seen,
    Heave him away upon your winged thoughts
    Athwart the sea. Behold, the English beach
    Pales in the flood with men, with wives, and boys,
    Whose shouts and claps out-voice the deep-mouth'd sea,
    Which, like a mighty whiffler 'fore the king,
    Seems to prepare his way: so let him land
    And solemnly see him set on to London.
    So swift a pace hath thought that even now
    You may imagine him upon Blackheath;
    Where that his lords desire him to have borne
    His bruised helmet and his bended sword
    Before him through the city: he forbids it,
    Being free from vainness and self-glorious pride;
    Giving full trophy, signal and ostent,
    Quite from himself, to God. But now behold,
    In the quick forge and working-house of thought,
    How London doth pour out her citizens.
    The mayor and all his brethren in best sort,
    Like to the senators of the antique Rome,
    With the plebeians swarming at their heels,
    Go forth and fetch their conquering Cæsar in:
    As, by a lower but loving likelihood,
    Were now the general of our gracious empress,—
    As in good time he may,—from Ireland coming,
    Bringing rebellion broached on his sword,
    How many would the peaceful city quit

To welcome him! much more, and much more cause,
Did they this Harry. Now in London place him;
As yet the lamentation of the French
Invites the King of England's stay at home,—
The emperor's coming in behalf of France,
To order peace between them;—and omit
All the occurrences, whatever chanc'd,
Till Harry's back-return again to France:
There must we bring him; and myself have play'd
The interim, by remembering you 'tis past.
Then brook abridgment, and your eyes advance,
After your thoughts, straight back again to France.   *Exit*

SCENE ONE

France. An English Court of Guard.

Enter Fluellen and Gower

GOWER. Nay, that's right; but why wear you your leek to-day? Saint Davy's day is past.

FLUELLEN. There is occasions and causes why and where-fore in all things: I will tell you, asse my friend, Captain Gower. The rascally, scald, beggarly, lousy, pragging knave, Pistol,—which you and yourself and all the 'orld know to be no petter than a fellow,—look you now, of no merits, he is come to me and prings me pread and salt yesterday, look you, and pid me eat my leek. It was in a place where I could not preed no contention with him; but I will be so pold as to wear it in my cap till I see him once again, and then I will tell him a little piece of my desires.

GOWER. Why, here he comes, swelling like a turkey-cock.

Enter Pistol

FLUELLEN. 'Tis no matter for his swellings nor his turkey-cocks. God pless you, Aunchient Pistol! you scurvy, lousy knave, God pless you!

PISTOL. Ha! art thou bedlam? dost thou thirst, base Troyan, To have me fold up Parca's fatal web?
Hence! I am qualmish at the smell of leek.

FLUELLEN. I peseech you heartily, scurvy lousy knave, at my desires and my requests and my petitions to eat, look

you, this leek; pecause, look you, you do not love it, nor
your affections and your appetites and your digestions
does not agree with it, I would desire you to eat it.

PISTOL. Not for Cadwallader and all his goats.

FLUELLEN. (*Strikes him*) There is one goat for you. Will
you be so good, scald knave, as eat it?

PISTOL. Base Troyan, thou shalt die.

FLUELLEN. You say very true, scald knave, when God's will
is. I will desire you to live in the mean time and eat your
victuals; come, there is sauce for it. (*Strikes him again*)
You called me yesterday mountain-squire, but I will make
you to-day a squire of low degree. I pray you, fall to: if
you can mock a leek you can eat a leek.

GOWER. Enough, captain: you have astonished him.

FLUELLEN. I say, I will make him eat some part of my leek,
or I will peat his pate four days. Bite, I pray you; it is good
for your green wound and your ploody coxcomb.

PISTOL. Must I bite?

FLUELLEN. Yes, certainly, and out of doubt and out of ques-
tion too and ambiguities.

PISTOL. By this leek, I will most horribly revenge. I eat and
eat, I swear—

FLUELLEN. Eat, I pray you: will you have some more sauce
to your leek? there is not enough leek to swear by.

PISTOL. Quiet thy cudgel: thou dost see I eat.

FLUELLEN. Much good do you, scald knave, heartily. Nay,
pray you, throw none away; the skin is good for your
broken coxcomb. When you take occasions to see leeks
hereafter, I pray you, mock at 'em; that is all.

PISTOL. Good.

FLUELLEN. Ay, leeks is good. Hold you, there is a groat to
heal your pate.

PISTOL. Me a groat!

FLUELLEN. Yes, verily and in truth, you shall take it; or I
have another leek in my pocket, which you shall eat.

PISTOL. I take thy groat in earnest of revenge.

FLUELLEN. If I owe you anything I will pay you in cudgels:
you shall be a woodmonger, and buy nothing of me but
cudgels. God be wi' you, and keep you, and heal your
pate.   *Exit*

PISTOL. All hell shall stir for this.

GOWER. Go, go; you are a counterfeit cowardly knave. Will

you mock at an ancient tradition, begun upon an honour-
able respect, and worn as a memorable trophy of prede-
ceased valour, and dare not avouch in your deeds any of
your words? I have seen you gleeking and galling at this
gentleman twice or thrice. You thought, because he could
not speak English in the native garb, he could not there-
fore handle an English cudgel: you find it otherwise; and
henceforth let a Welsh correction teach you a good Eng-
lish condition. Fare ye well.   *Exit*

PISTOL. Doth Fortune play the huswife with me now?
News have I that my Nell is dead i' the spital
Of malady of France:
And there my rendezvous is quite cut off.
Old I do wax, and from my weary limbs
Honour is cudgelled. Well, bawd I 'll turn,
And something lean to cutpurse of quick hand.
To England will I steal, and there I 'll steal:
And patches will I get unto these cudgell'd scars,
And swear I got them in the Gallia wars.   *Exit*

SCENE TWO

*Troyes in Champagne. An Apartment in the French
King's Palace.*

*Enter, from one side, King Henry, Bedford, Gloucester, Ex-
eter, Warwick, Westmoreland, and other Lords; from the
other side, the French King, Queen Isabel, the Princess
Katharine, Alice and other Ladies; the Duke of
Burgundy, and his Train*

KING HENRY. Peace to this meeting, wherefore we are met!
Unto our brother France, and to our sister,
Health and fair time of day; joy and good wishes
To our most fair and princely cousin Katharine;
And, as a branch and member of this royalty,
By whom this great assembly is contriv'd,
We do salute you, Duke of Burgundy;
And, princes French, and peers, health to you all!
FRENCH KING. Right joyous are we to behold your face,
Most worthy brother England; fairly met:
So are you, princes English, every one.

QUEEN ISABEL. So happy be the issue, brother England,
　　Of this good day and of this gracious meeting,
　　As we are now glad to behold your eyes;
　　Your eyes, which hitherto have borne in them
　　Against the French, that met them in their bent,
　　The fatal balls of murdering basilisks:
　　The venom of such looks, we fairly hope,
　　Have lost their quality, and that this day
　　Shall change all griefs and quarrels into love.
KING HENRY. To cry amen to that, thus we appear.
QUEEN ISABEL. You English princes all, I do salute you.
BURGUNDY. My duty to you both, on equal love,
　　Great Kings of France and England! That I have labour'd
　　With all my wits, my pains, and strong endeavours,
　　To bring your most imperial Majesties
　　Unto this bar and royal interview,
　　Your mightiness on both parts best can witness.
　　Since then my office hath so far prevail'd
　　That face to face, and royal eye to eye,
　　You have congreeted, let it not disgrace me
　　If I demand before this royal view,
　　What rub or what impediment there is,
　　Why that the naked, poor, and mangled Peace,
　　Dear nurse of arts, plenties, and joyful births,
　　Should not in this best garden of the world,
　　Our fertile France, put up her lovely visage?
　　Alas! she hath from France too long been chas'd,
　　And all her husbandry doth lie on heaps,
　　Corrupting in its own fertility.
　　Her vine, the merry cheerer of the heart,
　　Unpruned dies; her hedges even-pleach'd,
　　Like prisoners wildly overgrown with hair,
　　Put forth disorder'd twigs; her fallow leas
　　The darnel, hemlock and rank fumitory
　　Doth root upon, while that the coulter rusts
　　That should deracinate such savagery;
　　The even mead, that erst brought sweetly forth
　　The freckled cowslip, burnet, and green clover,
　　Wanting the scythe, all uncorrected, rank,
　　Conceives by idleness, and nothing teems
　　But hateful docks, rough thistles, kecksies, burs,
　　Losing both beauty and utility;

And as our vineyards, fallows, meads, and hedges,
Defective in their natures, grow to wildness,
Even so our houses and ourselves and children
Have lost, or do not learn for want of time,
The sciences that should become our country,
But grow like savages,—as soldiers will,
That nothing do but meditate on blood,—
To swearing and stern looks, diffus'd attire,
And every thing that seems unnatural.
Which to reduce into our former favour
You are assembled; and my speech entreats
That I may know the let why gentle Peace
Should not expel these inconveniences,
And bless us with her former qualities.

KING HENRY. If, Duke of Burgundy, you would the peace,
Whose want gives growth to the imperfections
Which you have cited, you must buy that peace
With full accord to all our just demands;
Whose tenours and particular effects
You have, enschedul'd briefly, in your hands.

BURGUNDY. The king hath heard them; to the which as yet,
There is no answer made.

KING HENRY.   Well then the peace,
Which you before so urg'd, lies in his answer.

FRENCH KING. I have but with a cursorary eye
O'erglanc'd the articles: pleaseth your Grace
To appoint some of your council presently
To sit with us once more, with better heed
To re-survey them, we will suddenly
Pass our accept and peremptory answer.

KING HENRY. Brother, we shall. Go, uncle Exeter,
And brother Clarence, and you, brother Gloucester,
Warwick and Huntingdon, go with the king;
And take with you free power to ratify,
Augment, or alter, as your wisdoms best
Shall see advantageable for our dignity,
Anything in or out of our demands,
And we 'll consign thereto. Will you, fair sister,
Go with the princes, or stay here with us?

QUEEN ISABEL. Our gracious brother, I will go with them.
Haply a woman's voice may do some good
When articles too nicely urg'd be stood on.

KING HENRY. Yet leave our cousin Katharine here with us:
She is our capital demand, compris'd
Within the fore-rank of our articles.

QUEEN ISABEL. She hath good leave.

Exeunt all except King Henry, Katharine, and Alice

KING HENRY.   Fair Katharine, and most fair!
Will you vouchsafe to teach a soldier terms,
Such as will enter at a lady's ear,
And plead his love-suit to her gentle heart?

KATHARINE. Your Majesty sall mock at me; I cannot speak
your England.

KING HENRY. O fair Katharine! if you will love me soundly
with your French heart, I will be glad to hear you confess
it brokenly with your English tongue. Do you like me,
Kate?

KATHARINE. Pardonnez moy, I cannot tell vat is 'like me.'

KING HENRY. An angel is like you, Kate; and you are like an
angel.

KATHARINE. Que dit-il? que je suis semblable à les anges?

ALICE. Ouy, vrayment, sauf vostre grace, ainsi dit-il.

KING HENRY. I said so, dear Katharine; and I must not blush
to affirm it.

KATHARINE. O bon Dieu! les langues des hommes sont
pleines des tromperies.

KING HENRY. What says she, fair one? that the tongues of
men are full of deceits?

ALICE. Ouy, dat de tongues of de mans is be full of deceits:
dat is de princess.

KING HENRY. The princess is the better Englishwoman. I'
faith, Kate, my wooing is fit for thy understanding: I am
glad thou canst speak no better English; for, if thou
couldst, thou wouldst find me such a plain king that thou
wouldst think I had sold my farm to buy my crown. I
know no ways to mince it in love, but directly to say 'I
love you': then, if you urge me further than to say 'Do you
in faith?' I wear out my suit. Give me your answer; i'
faith, do: and so clap hands and a bargain. How say you,
lady?

KATHARINE. Sauf vostre honneur, me understand vell.

KING HENRY. Marry, if you would put me to verses, or to
dance for your sake, Kate, why you undid me: for the one,
I have neither words nor measure, and for the other, I

have no strength in measure, yet a reasonable measure in strength. If I could win a lady at leap-frog, or by vaulting into my saddle with my armour on my back, under the correction of bragging be it spoken, I should quickly leap into a wife. Or if I might buffet for my love, or bound my horse for her favours, I could lay on like a butcher and sit like a jack-an-apes, never off. But before God, Kate, I cannot look greenly nor gasp out my eloquence, nor I have no cunning in protestation; only downright oaths, which I never use till urged, nor never break for urging. If thou canst love a fellow of this temper, Kate, whose face is not worth sun-burning, that never looks in his glass for love of anything he sees there, let thine eye be thy cook. I speak to thee plain soldier: if thou canst love me for this, take me; if not, to say to thee that I shall die, is true; but for thy love, by the Lord, no; yet I love thee too. And while thou livest, dear Kate, take a fellow of plain and uncoined constancy, for he perforce must do thee right, because he hath not the gift to woo in other places; for these fellows of infinite tongue, that can rime themselves into ladies' favours, they do always reason themselves out again. What! a speaker is but a prater; a rime is but a ballad. A good leg will fall, a straight back will stoop, a black beard will turn white, a curled pate will grow bald, a fair face will wither, a full eye will wax hollow, but a good heart, Kate, is the sun and the moon; or, rather, the sun, and not the moon; for it shines bright and never changes, but keeps his course truly. If thou would have such a one, take me; and take me, take a soldier; take a soldier, take a king. And what sayest thou then to my love? speak, my fair, and fairly, I pray thee.

KATHARINE. Is it possible dat I sould love de enemy of France?

KING HENRY. No; it is not possible you should love the enemy of France, Kate; but, in loving me, you should love the friend of France; for I love France so well, that I will not part with a village of it; I will have it all mine: and, Kate, when France is mine and I am yours, then yours is France and you are mine.

KATHARINE. I cannot tell vat is dat.

KING HENRY. No, Kate? I will tell thee in French, which I am sure will hang upon my tongue like a new-married

wife about her husband's neck, hardly to be shook off. Je
quand sur le possession de France, et quand vous avez le
possession de moy,—let me see, what then? Saint Denis be
my speed!—donc vostre est France, et vous estes mienne.
It is as easy for me, Kate, to conquer the kingdom, as to
speak so much more French: I shall never move thee in
French, unless it be to laugh at me.

KATHARINE. Sauf vostre honneur, le François que vous par-
lez est meilleur que l'Anglois lequel je parle.

KING HENRY. No, faith, is 't not, Kate; but thy speaking of
my tongue, and I thine, most truly falsely, must needs be
granted to be much at one. But, Kate, dost thou under-
stand thus much English, Canst thou love me?

KATHARINE. I cannot tell.

KING HENRY. Can any of your neighbours tell, Kate? I 'll ask
them. Come, I know thou lovest me; and at night when
you come into your closet you 'll question this gentle-
woman about me; and I know, Kate, you will to her dis-
praise those parts in me that you love with your heart:
but, good Kate, mock me mercifully; the rather, gentle
princess, because I love thee cruelly. If ever thou be'st
mine, Kate,—as I have a saving faith within me tells me
thou shalt,—I get thee with scambling, and thou must
therefore needs prove a good soldier-breeder. Shall not
thou and I, between Saint Denis and Saint George, com-
pound a boy, half French, half English, that shall go to
Constantinople and take the Turk by the beard? shall we
not? what sayest thou, my fair flower-de-luce?

KATHARINE. I do not know dat.

KING HENRY. No; 'tis hereafter to know, but now to promise:
do but now promise, Kate, you will endeavour for your
French part of such a boy, and for my English moiety take
the word of a king and a bachelor. How answer you, la
plus belle Katharine du monde, mon très cher et divine
déesse?

KATHARINE. Your Majesté ave fausse French enough to de-
ceive de most sage demoiselle dat is en France.

KING HENRY. Now, fie upon my false French! By mine hon-
our, in true English I love thee, Kate: by which honour I
dare not swear thou lovest me; yet my blood begins to
flatter me that thou dost, notwithstanding the poor and
untempering effect of my visage. Now beshrew my fath-

er's ambition! he was thinking of civil wars when he got me: therefore was I created with a stubborn outside, with an aspect of iron, that, when I come to woo ladies I fright them. But, in faith, Kate, the elder I wax the better I shall appear: my comfort is, that old age, that ill layer-up of beauty, can do no more spoil upon my face: thou hast me, if thou hast me, at the worst; and thou shalt wear me, if thou wear me, better and better. And therefore tell me, most fair Katharine, will you have me? Put off your maiden blushes; avouch the thoughts of your heart with the looks of an empress; take me by the hand, and say 'Harry of England, I am thine': which word thou shalt no sooner bless mine ear withal, but I will tell thee aloud— 'England is thine, Ireland is thine, France is thine, and Henry Plantagenet is thine'; who, though I speak it before his face, if he be not fellow with the best king, thou shalt find the best king of good fellows. Come, your answer in broken music; for thy voice is music, and thy English broken; therefore, queen of all, Katharine, break thy mind to me in broken English: wilt thou have me?

KATHARINE. Dat is as it sall please de roy mon père.

KING HENRY. Nay, it will please him well, Kate; it shall please him, Kate.

KATHARINE. Den it sall also content me.

KING HENRY. Upon that I kiss your hand, and I call you my queen.

KATHARINE. Laissez, mon seigneur, laissez, laissez! Ma foy, je ne veux point que vous abaissez vostre grandeur, en baisant la main d'une vostre indigne serviteure: excusez moy, je vous supplie, mon très puissant seigneur.

KING HENRY. Then I will kiss your lips, Kate.

KATHARINE. Les dames, et demoiselles, pour estre baisées devant leur noces, il n'est pas la coutume de France.

KING HENRY. Madam my interpreter, what says she?

ALICE. Dat it is not be de fashion pour les ladies of France,— I cannot tell what is baiser in English.

KING HENRY. To kiss.

ALICE. Your Majesty entendre bettre que moy.

KING HENRY. It is not a fashion for the maids in France to kiss before they are married, would she say?

ALICE. Ouy, vrayment.

KING HENRY. O Kate! nice customs curtsy to great kings.

Dear Kate, you and I cannot be confined within the weak
list of a country's fashion: we are the makers of manners,
Kate; and the liberty that follows our places stops the
mouths of all find-faults, as I will do yours, for upholding
the nice fashion of your country in denying me a kiss:
therefore, patiently, and yielding. (*Kissing her*) You have
witchcraft in your lips, Kate: there is more eloquence in a
sugar touch of them, than in the tongues of the French
council; and they should sooner persuade Harry of Eng-
land than a general petition of monarchs. Here comes
your father.

> *Re-enter the King and Queen, Burgundy,*
> *Bedford, Gloucester, Exeter, Warwick, Westmoreland,*
> *and other French and English Lords*

BURGUNDY. God save your Majesty! My royal cousin, teach
you our princess English?

KING HENRY. I would have her learn, my fair cousin, how
perfectly I love her; and that is good English.

BURGUNDY. Is she not apt?

KING HENRY. Our tongue is rough, coz, and my condition is
not smooth; so that, having neither the voice nor the heart
of flattery about me, I cannot so conjure up the spirit of
love in her, that he will appear in his true likeness.

BURGUNDY. Pardon the frankness of my mirth if I answer
you for that. If you would conjure in her you must make a
circle; if conjure up love in her in his true likeness, he
must appear naked and blind. Can you blame her then,
being a maid yet rosed over with the virgin crimson of
modesty, if she deny the appearance of a naked blind boy
in her naked seeing self? It were, my lord, a hard condi-
tion for a maid to consign to.

KING HENRY. Yet they do wink and yield, as love is blind
and enforces.

BURGUNDY. They are then excused, my lord, when they see
not what they do.

KING HENRY. Then, good my lord, teach your cousin to con-
sent winking.

BURGUNDY. I will wink on her to consent, my lord, if you will
teach her to know my meaning: for maids, well summered
and warm kept, are like flies at Bartholomew-tide, blind,
though they have their eyes; and then they will endure
handling, which before would not abide looking on.

KING HENRY. This moral ties me over to time and a hot summer; and so I shall catch the fly, your cousin, in the latter end, and she must be blind too.

BURGUNDY. As love is, my lord, before it loves.

KING HENRY. It is so: and you may, some of you, thank love for my blindness, who cannot see many a fair French city for one fair French maid that stands in my way.

FRENCH KING. Yes, my lord, you see them perspectively, the cities turned into a maid; for they are all girdled with maiden walls that war hath never entered.

KING HENRY. Shall Kate be my wife?

FRENCH KING. So please you.

KING HENRY. I am content; so the maiden cities you talk of may wait on her: so the maid that stood in the way for my wish shall show me the way to my will.

FRENCH KING. We have consented to all terms of reason.

KING HENRY. Is 't so, my lords of England?

WESTMORELAND. The king hath granted every article:
His daughter first, and then in sequel all,
According to their firm proposed natures.

EXETER. Only he hath not yet subscribed this:
Where your Majesty demands, that the King of France,
having any occasion to write for matter of grant, shall
name your Highness in this form, and with this addition,
in French, Notre très cher fils Henry roy d'Angleterre,
Héretier de France; and thus in Latin, Præclarissimus
filius noster Henricus, Rex Angliæ, et Hæres Franciæ.

FRENCH KING. Nor this I have not, brother, so denied,
But your request shall make me let it pass.

KING HENRY. I pray you then, in love and dear alliance,
Let that one article rank with the rest;
And thereupon give me your daughter.

FRENCH KING. Take her, fair son; and from her blood raise
up
Issue to me; that the contending kingdoms
Of France and England, whose very shores look pale
With envy of each other's happiness,
May cease their hatred, and this dear conjunction
Plant neighbourhood and Christian-like accord
In their sweet bosoms, that never war advance
His bleeding sword 'twixt England and fair France.

ALL. Amen!

KING HENRY. Now, welcome, Kate: and bear me witness all,
  That here I kiss her as my sovereign queen.   *Flourish*
QUEEN ISABEL. God, the best maker of all marriages,
  Combine your hearts in one, your realms in one!
  As man and wife, being two, are one in love,
  So be there 'twixt your kingdoms such a spousal
  That never may ill office, or fell jealousy,
  Which troubles oft the bed of blessed marriage,
  Thrust in between the paction of these kingdoms,
  To make divorce of their incorporate league;
  That English may as French, French Englishmen,
  Receive each other! God speak this Amen!
ALL. Amen!
KING HENRY. Prepare we for our marriage: on which day,
  My Lord of Burgundy, we 'll take your oath,
  And all the peers', for surety of our leagues.
  Then shall I swear to Kate, and you to me;
  And may our oaths well kept and prosperous be!
                                    Sennet. Exeunt

Enter Chorus
Thus far, with rough and all-unable pen,
  Our bending author hath pursu'd the story;
In little room confining mighty men,
  Mangling by starts the full course of their glory.
Small time, but in that small most greatly liv'd
  This star of England: Fortune made his sword,
By which the world's best garden he achiev'd,
  And of it left his son imperial lord.
Henry the Sixth, in infant bands crown'd King
  Of France and England, did this king succeed;
Whose state so many had the managing,
  That they lost France and made his England bleed:
Which oft our stage hath shown; and, for their sake,
In your fair minds let this acceptance take.   *Exit*

THE FIRST PART OF
KING HENRY THE SIXTH

CAST OF CHARACTERS

KING HENRY THE SIXTH

DUKE OF GLOUCESTER, *Uncle to the King, and Protector*

DUKE OF BEDFORD, *Uncle to the King, Regent of France*

THOMAS BEAUFORT, *Duke of Exeter, Great-uncle to the King*

HENRY BEAUFORT, *Great-uncle to the King; Bishop of Winchester, and afterwards Cardinal*

JOHN BEAUFORT, *Earl, afterwards Duke, of Somerset*

RICHARD PLANTAGENET, *Son of Richard, late Earl of Cambridge; afterwards Duke of York*

EARL OF WARWICK

EARL OF SALISBURY

EARL OF SUFFOLK

LORD TALBOT, *afterwards Earl of Shrewsbury*

JOHN TALBOT, *his Son*

EDMUND MORTIMER, *Earl of March*

SIR JOHN FASTOLFE

SIR WILLIAM LUCY

SIR WILLIAM GLANSDALE

SIR THOMAS GARGRAVE

WOODVILLE, *Lieutenant of the Tower*

Mayor of London, Mortimer's Keepers, A Lawyer

VERNON, *of the White-Rose, or York Faction*

BASSET, *of the Red-Rose, or Lancaster Faction*

CHARLES, *Dauphin, and afterwards King of France*

REIGNIER, *Duke of Anjou, and titular King of Naples*

DUKE OF BURGUNDY

DUKE OF ALENCON

(*continued on next page*)

Bastard of Orleans
Governor of Paris
Master-Gunner of Orleans, and his Son
General of the French Forces in Bourdeaux
A French Sergeant
A Porter
An old Shepherd, Father to Joan la Pucelle

Margaret, *Daughter to Reignier; afterwards married to King Henry*
Countess of Auvergne
Joan la Pucelle, *commonly called Joan of Arc*

Fiends appearing to La Pucelle

Lords, Warders of the Tower, Heralds, Officers, Soldiers, Messengers, and Attendants

SCENE

Partly in England, and partly in France

THE FIRST PART OF KING
HENRY THE SIXTH

ACT ONE

SCENE ONE

Westminster Abbey.

Dead March. Enter the Funeral of King Henry the Fifth attended on by the Dukes of Bedford, Gloucester, and Exeter; the Earl of Warwick, the Bishop of Winchester, Heralds, &c.

BEDFORD. Hung be the heavens with black, yield day to
 night!
 Comets, importing change of times and states,
 Brandish your crystal tresses in the sky,
 And with them scourge the bad revolting stars,
 That have consented unto Henry's death!
 King Henry the Fifth, too famous to live long!
 England ne'er lost a king of so much worth.
GLOUCESTER. England ne'er had a king until his time.
 Virtue he had, deserving to command:
 His brandish'd sword did blind men with his beams;
 His arms spread wider than a dragon's wings;
 His sparkling eyes, replete with wrathful fire,
 More dazzled and drove back his enemies
 Than mid-day sun fierce bent against their faces.
 What should I say? his deeds exceed all speech:
 He ne'er lift up his hand but conquered.
EXETER. We mourn in black: why mourn we not in blood?
 Henry is dead and never shall revive.
 Upon a wooden coffin we attend,
 And death's dishonourable victory
 We with our stately presence glorify,
 Like captives bound to a triumphant car.

What! shall we curse the planets of mishap
That plotted thus our glory's overthrow?
Or shall we think the subtle-witted French
Conjurers and sorcerers, that, afraid of him,
By magic verses have contriv'd his end?

WINCHESTER. He was a king bless'd of the King of Kings.
Unto the French the dreadful judgment-day
So dreadful will not be as was his sight.
The battles of the Lord of Hosts he fought:
The Church's prayers made him so prosperous.

GLOUCESTER. The Church! where is it? Had not churchmen
    pray'd,
His thread of life had not so soon decay'd:
None do you like but an effeminate prince,
Whom like a school-boy you may over-awe.

WINCHESTER. Gloucester, whate'er we like thou art
    Protector,
And lookest to command the prince and realm.
Thy wife is proud; she holdeth thee in awe,
More than God or religious churchmen may.

GLOUCESTER. Name not religion, for thou lov'st the flesh,
And ne'er throughout the year to church thou go'st,
Except it be to pray against thy foes.

BEDFORD. Cease, cease these jars and rest your minds in
    peace!
Let 's to the altar: heralds, wait on us:
Instead of gold we 'll offer up our arms,
Since arms avail not, now that Henry 's dead.
Posterity, await for wretched years,
When at their mothers' moist eyes babes shall suck,
Our isle be made a marish of salt tears,
And none but women left to wail the dead.
Henry the Fifth! thy ghost I invocate:
Prosper this realm, keep it from civil broils!
Combat with adverse planets in the heavens!
A far more glorious star thy soul will make,
Than Julius Cæsar, or bright—

Enter a Messenger

MESSENGER. My honourable lords, health to you all!
Sad tidings bring I to you out of France,
Of loss, of slaughter, and discomfiture:
Guienne, Champaigne, Rheims, Orleans,

Paris, Guysors, Poictiers, are all quite lost.

BEDFORD. What sayst thou, man, before dead Henry's
  corse?
Speak softly; or the loss of those great towns
Will make him burst his lead and rise from death.

GLOUCESTER. Is Paris lost? is Roan yielded up?
If Henry were recall'd to life again
These news would cause him once more yield the ghost.

EXETER. How were they lost? what treachery was us'd?

MESSENGER. No treachery; but want of men and money.
Among the soldiers this is muttered,
That here you maintain several factions;
And, whilst a field should be dispatch'd and fought,
You are disputing of your generals.
One would have lingering wars with little cost;
Another would fly swift, but wanteth wings;
A third thinks, without expense at all,
By guileful fair words peace may be obtain'd.
Awake, awake, English nobility!
Let not sloth dim your honours new-begot:
Cropp'd are the flower-de-luces in your arms;
Of England's coat one half is cut away.

EXETER. Were our tears wanting to this funeral
These tidings would call forth their flowing tides.

BEDFORD. Me they concern; Regent I am of France.
Give me my steeled coat: I 'll fight for France.
Away with these disgraceful wailing robes!
Wounds will I lend the French instead of eyes,
To weep their intermissive miseries.

                 Enter another Messenger

SECOND MESSENGER. Lords, view these letters, full of bad
  mischance.
France is revolted from the English quite,
Except some petty towns of no import:
The Dauphin Charles is crowned king in Rheims;
The Bastard of Orleans with him is join'd;
Reignier, Duke of Anjou, doth take his part;
The Duke of Alençon flieth to his side.

EXETER. The Dauphin crowned king! all fly to him!
O! whither shall we fly from this reproach?

GLOUCESTER. We will not fly, but to our enemies' throats.
Bedford, if thou be slack, I 'll fight it out.

BEDFORD. Gloucester, why doubt'st thou of my forward-
ness?
An army have I muster'd in my thoughts,
Wherewith already France is overrun.

Enter a third Messenger

THIRD MESSENGER. My gracious lords, to add to your
laments,
Wherewith you now bedew King Henry's hearse,
I must inform you of a dismal fight
Betwixt the stout Lord Talbot and the French.

WINCHESTER. What! wherein Talbot overcame? is't so?

THIRD MESSENGER. O, no! wherein Lord Talbot was o'er-
thrown:
The circumstance I 'll tell you more at large.
The tenth of August last this dreadful lord,
Retiring from the siege of Orleans,
Having full scarce six thousand in his troop,
By three-and-twenty thousand of the French
Was round encompassed and set upon.
No leisure had he to enrank his men;
He wanted pikes to set before his archers;
Instead whereof sharp stakes pluck'd out of hedges
They pitched in the ground confusedly,
To keep the horsemen off from breaking in.
More than three hours the fight continued;
Where valiant Talbot above human thought
Enacted wonders with his sword and lance.
Hundreds he sent to hell, and none durst stand him;
Here, there, and every where, enrag'd he flew:
The French exclaim'd the devil was in arms;
All the whole army stood agaz'd on him.
His soldiers, spying his undaunted spirit,
A Talbot! A Talbot! cried out amain,
And rush'd into the bowels of the battle.
Here had the conquest fully been seal'd up,
If Sir John Fastolfe had not play'd the coward.
He, being in the vaward,—plac'd behind,
With purpose to relieve and follow them,—
Cowardly fled, not having struck one stroke.
Hence grew the general wrack and massacre;
Enclosed were they with their enemies.
A base Walloon, to win the Dauphin's grace,

Thrust Talbot with a spear into the back;
Whom all France, with their chief assembled strength,
Durst not presume to look once in the face.

BEDFORD. Is Talbot slain? then I will slay myself,
For living idly here in pomp and ease
Whilst such a worthy leader, wanting aid,
Unto his dastard foemen is betray'd.

THIRD MESSENGER. O no! he lives; but is took prisoner,
And Lord Scales with him, and Lord Hungerford:
Most of the rest slaughter'd or took likewise.

BEDFORD. His ransom there is none but I shall pay:
I 'll hale the Dauphin headlong from his throne;
His crown shall be the ransom of my friend;
Four of their lords I 'll change for one of ours.
Farewell, my masters; to my task will I;
Bonfires in France forthwith I am to make,
To keep our great Saint George's feast withal:
Ten thousand soldiers with me I will take,
Whose bloody deeds shall make all Europe quake.

THIRD MESSENGER. So you had need; for Orleans is besieg'd;
The English army is grown weak and faint;
The Earl of Salisbury craveth supply,
And hardly keeps his men from mutiny,
Since they, so few, watch such a multitude.

EXETER. Remember, lords, your oaths to Henry sworn,
Either to quell the Dauphin utterly,
Or bring him in obedience to your yoke.

BEDFORD. I do remember it; and here take my leave,
To go about my preparation.   *Exit*

GLOUCESTER. I 'll to the Tower with all the haste I can,
To view the artillery and munition;
And then I will proclaim young Henry king.   *Exit*

EXETER. To Eltham will I, where the young king is,
Being ordain'd his special governor;
And for his safety there I 'll best devise.   *Exit*

WINCHESTER. Each hath his place and function to attend:
I am left out; for me nothing remains.
But long I will not be Jack-out-of-office.
The king from Eltham I intend to steal,
And sit at chiefest stern of public weal.   *Exit*

SCENE TWO

France. Before Orleans.

*Flourish. Enter Charles, with his Forces: Alençon,
Reignier, and Others*

CHARLES. Mars his true moving, even as in the heavens
So in the earth, to this day is not known.
Late did he shine upon the English side;
Now we are victors; upon us he smiles.
What towns of any moment but we have?
At pleasure here we lie near Orleans;
Otherwhiles the famish'd English, like pale ghosts,
Faintly besiege us one hour in a month.
ALENÇON. They want their porridge and their fat bull-
beeves:
Either they must be dieted like mules
And have their provender tied to their mouths,
Or piteous they will look, like drowned mice.
REIGNIER. Let's raise the siege: why live we idly here?
Talbot is taken, whom we wont to fear:
Remaineth none but mad-brain'd Salisbury,
And he may well in fretting spend his gall;
Nor men nor money hath he to make war.
CHARLES. Sound, sound alarum! we will rush on them.
Now for the honour of the forlorn French!
Him I forgive my death that killeth me
When he sees me go back one foot or fly.   *Exeunt*
*Alarums; Excursions; afterwards a retreat. Re-enter
Charles, Alençon, Reignier, and Others*
CHARLES. Who ever saw the like? what men have I!
Dogs! cowards! dastards! I would ne'er have fled
But that they left me 'midst my enemies.
REIGNIER. Salisbury is a desperate homicide;
He fighteth as one weary of his life:
The other lords, like lions wanting food,
Do rush upon us as their hungry prey.
ALENÇON. Froissart, a countryman of ours, records
England all Olivers and Rowlands bred
During the time Edward the Third did reign.

More truly now may this be verified;
For none but Samsons and Goliases,
It sendeth forth to skirmish. One to ten!
Lean raw-bon'd rascals! who would e'er suppose
They had such courage and audacity?

CHARLES. Let 's leave this town; for they are hare-brain'd slaves,
And hunger will enforce them to be more eager:
Of old I know them; rather with their teeth
The walls they 'll tear down than forsake the siege.

REIGNIER. I think, by some odd gimmals or device,
Their arms are set like clocks, still to strike on;
Else ne'er could they hold out so as they do.
By my consent, we 'll e'en let them alone.

ALENÇON. Be it so.

Enter the Bastard of Orleans

THE BASTARD. Where 's the Prince Dauphin? I have news for him.

CHARLES. Bastard of Orleans, thrice welcome to us.

THE BASTARD. Methinks your looks are sad, your cheer appall'd:
Hath the late overthrow wrought this offence?
Be not dismay'd, for succour is at hand:
A holy maid hither with me I bring,
Which by a vision sent to her from heaven
Ordained is to raise this tedious siege,
And drive the English forth the bounds of France.
The spirit of deep prophecy she hath,
Exceeding the nine sibyls of old Rome;
What 's past and what 's to come she can descry.
Speak, shall I call her in? Believe my words,
For they are certain and unfallible.

CHARLES. Go, call her in. (*Exit Bastard*) But first, to try her skill,
Reignier, stand thou as Dauphin in my place:
Question her proudly; let thy looks be stern:
By this means shall we sound what skill she hath.   *Retires*

Re-enter the Bastard of
Orleans, with Joan la Pucelle and Others

REIGNIER. Fair maid, is 't thou wilt do these wondrous feats?

JOAN. Reignier, is 't thou that thinkest to beguile me?
Where is the Dauphin? Come, come from behind;

I know thee well, though never seen before.
Be not amaz'd, there 's nothing hid from me:
In private will I talk with thee apart.
Stand back, you lords, and give us leave a while.
REIGNIER. She takes upon her bravely at first dash.
JOAN. Dauphin, I am by birth a shepherd's daughter,
My wit untrain'd in any kind of art.
Heaven and our Lady gracious hath it pleas'd
To shine on my contemptible estate:
Lo! whilst I waited on my tender lambs,
And to sun's parching heat display'd my cheeks,
God's mother deigned to appear to me,
And in a vision full of majesty
Will'd me to leave my base vocation
And free my country from calamity:
Her aid she promis'd and assur'd success;
In complete glory she reveal'd herself;
And, whereas I was black and swart before,
With those clear rays which she infus'd on me,
That beauty am I bless'd with which you see.
Ask me what question thou canst possible
And I will answer unpremeditated:
My courage try by combat, if thou dar'st,
And thou shalt find that I exceed my sex.
Resolve on this, thou shalt be fortunate
If thou receive me for thy warlike mate.
CHARLES. Thou hast astonish'd me with thy high terms.
Only this proof I 'll of thy valour make,
In single combat thou shalt buckle with me,
And if thou vanquishest, thy words are true;
Otherwise I renounce all confidence.
JOAN. I am prepar'd: here is my keen-edg'd sword,
Deck'd with five flower-de-luces on each side;
The which at Touraine, in Saint Katharine's churchyard,
Out of a great deal of old iron I chose forth.
CHARLES. Then come, o' God's name; I fear no woman.
JOAN. And, while I live, I 'll ne'er fly from a man.
                    They fight, and Joan la Pucelle overcomes
CHARLES. Stay, stay thy hands! thou art an Amazon,
And fightest with the sword of Deborah.
JOAN. Christ's mother helps me, else I were too weak.
CHARLES. Whoe'er helps thee, 'tis thou that must help me:

Impatiently I burn with thy desire;
My heart and hands thou hast at once subdu'd.
Excellent Pucelle, if thy name be so,
Let me thy servant and not sovereign be;
'Tis the French Dauphin sueth to thee thus.

JOAN. I must not yield to any rites of love
For my profession 's sacred from above:
When I have chased all thy foes from hence,
Then will I think upon a recompense.

CHARLES. Meantime look gracious on thy prostrate thrall.

REIGNIER. My lord, methinks, is very long in talk.

ALENÇON. Doubtless he shrives this woman to her smock;
Else ne'er could he so long protract his speech.

REIGNIER. Shall we disturb him, since he keeps no mean?

ALENÇON. He may mean more than we poor men do know:
These women are shrewd tempters with their tongues.

REIGNIER. My lord, where are you? what devise you on?
Shall we give over Orleans, or no?

JOAN. Why, no, I say, distrustful recreants!
Fight till the last gasp; I will be your guard.

CHARLES. What she says, I 'll confirm: we 'll fight it out.

JOAN. Assign'd am I to be the English scourge.
This night the siege assuredly I 'll raise:
Expect Saint Martin's summer, halcyon days,
Since I have entered into these wars.
Glory is like a circle in the water,
Which never ceaseth to enlarge itself,
Till by broad spreading it disperse to nought.
With Henry's death the English circle ends;
Dispersed are the glories it included.
Now am I like that proud insulting ship
Which Cæsar and his fortune bare at once.

CHARLES. Was Mahomet inspired with a dove?
Thou with an eagle art inspired then.
Helen, the mother of great Constantine,
Nor yet Saint Philip's daughters were like thee.
Bright star of Venus, fall'n down on the earth,
How may I reverently worship thee enough?

ALENÇON. Leave off delays and let us raise the siege.

REIGNIER. Woman, do what thou canst to save our honours;
Drive them from Orleans and be immortaliz'd.

CHARLES. Presently we 'll try. Come, let 's away about it:
No prophet will I trust if she prove false.   *Exeunt*

SCENE THREE

London. Before the Tower.

Enter at the Gates the Duke of Gloucester, with his
Serving-men, in blue coats

GLOUCESTER. I am come to survey the Tower this day;
Since Henry's death, I fear, there is conveyance.
Where be these warders that they wait not here?
Open the gates! 'Tis Gloucester that calls. *Servants knock*
FIRST WARDER. (*Within*) Who's there that knocks so
imperiously?
FIRST SERVING-MAN. It is the noble Duke of Gloucester.
SECOND WARDER. (*Within*) Whoe'er he be, you may not be
let in.
FIRST SERVING-MAN. Villains, answer you so the Lord
Protector?
FIRST WARDER. (*Within*) The Lord protect him! so we
answer him:
We do not otherwise than we are will'd.
GLOUCESTER. Who willed you? or whose will stands but
mine?
There's none protector of the realm but I.
Break up the gates, I'll be your warrantize:
Shall I be flouted thus by dunghill grooms?
                    Gloucester's men rush at the Tower
                    gates, and Woodvile the lieutenant speaks within
WOODVILE. What noise is this? what traitors have we here?
GLOUCESTER. Lieutenant, is it you whose voice I hear?
Open the gates! here's Gloucester that would enter.
WOODVILE. (*Within*) Have patience, noble Duke; I may not
open;
The Cardinal of Winchester forbids:
From him I have express commandment
That thou nor none of thine shall be let in.
GLOUCESTER. Faint-hearted Woodvile, prizest him 'fore me?
Arrogant Winchester, that haughty prelate,
Whom Henry, our late sovereign, ne'er could brook?
Thou art no friend to God or to the king:

Open the gates, or I 'll shut thee out shortly.

FIRST SERVING-MAN. Open the gates unto the Lord
    Protector;
Or we 'll burst them open, if that you come not quickly.

Enter Winchester, attended by Serving-men in tawny coats

WINCHESTER. How now, ambitious Humphrey! what means
    this?

GLOUCESTER. Peel'd priest, dost thou command me to be
    shut out?

WINCHESTER. I do, thou most usurping proditor,
And not protector, of the king or realm.

GLOUCESTER. Stand back, thou manifest conspirator,
Thou that contriv'dst to murder our dead lord;
Thou that giv'st whores indulgences to sin:
I 'll canvass thee in thy broad cardinal's hat,
If thou proceed in this thy insolence.

WINCHESTER. Nay, stand thou back; I will not budge a foot:
This be Damascus, be thou cursed Cain,
To slay thy brother Abel, if thou wilt.

GLOUCESTER. I will not slay thee, but I 'll drive thee back:
Thy scarlet robes as a child's bearing-cloth
I 'll use to carry thee out of this place.

WINCHESTER. Do what thou dar'st; I 'll beard thee to thy
    face.

GLOUCESTER. What! am I dar'd and bearded to my face?—
Draw, men, for all this privileged place;
Blue-coats to tawny-coats. Priest, beware your beard;
          Gloucester and his men attack the Cardinal
I mean to tug it and to cuff you soundly.
Under my feet I stamp thy cardinal's hat,
In spite of pope or dignities of church,
Here by the cheeks I 'll drag thee up and down.

WINCHESTER. Gloucester, thou 'lt answer this before the
    pope.

GLOUCESTER. Winchester goose! I cry a rope! a rope!
Now beat them hence; why do you let them stay?
Thee I 'll chase hence, thou wolf in sheep's array.
Out, tawny-coats! out, scarlet hypocrite!

*Here Gloucester's Men beat out the Cardinal's Men, and en-
ter in the hurly-burly the Mayor of London and his Officers*

MAYOR. Fie, lords! that you, being supreme magistrates,

Thus contumeliously should break the peace!

GLOUCESTER. Peace, mayor! thou know'st little of my
 wrongs:
Here 's Beaufort, that regards nor God nor King,
Hath here distrain'd the Tower to his use.

WINCHESTER. Here 's Gloucester, a foe to citizens;
One that still motions war and never peace,
O'ercharging your free purses with large fines,
That seeks to overthrow religion
Because he is protector of the realm,
And would have armour here out of the Tower,
To crown himself king and suppress the prince.

GLOUCESTER. I will not answer thee with words, but blows.

        Here they skirmish again

MAYOR. Nought rests for me, in this tumultuous strife
But to make open proclamation.
Come, officer: as loud as e'er thou canst;
Cry.

OFFICER. All manner of men, assembled here in arms this
day, against God's peace and the king's, we charge and
command you, in his Highness' name, to repair to your
several dwelling-places; and not to wear, handle, or use,
any sword, weapon, or dagger, henceforward, upon pain
of death.

GLOUCESTER. Cardinal, I 'll be no breaker of the law;
But we shall meet and break our minds at large.

WINCHESTER. Gloucester, we will meet; to thy cost, be sure:
Thy heart-blood I will have for this day's work.

MAYOR. I 'll call for clubs if you will not away.
This cardinal 's more haughty than the devil.

GLOUCESTER. Mayor, farewell: thou dost but what thou
 mayst.

WINCHESTER. Abominable Gloucester! guard thy head;
For I intend to have it ere long.

      Exeunt, severally, Gloucester
     and Winchester, with their Serving-men

MAYOR. See the coast clear'd, and then we will depart.
Good God! these nobles should such stomachs bear;
I myself fight not once in forty year.   *Exeunt*

SCENE FOUR

France. Before Orleans.

Enter, on the walls, the Master-Gunner and his Boy

MASTER-GUNNER. Sirrah, thou know'st how Orleans is
    besieg'd,
And how the English have the suburbs won.
SON. Father, I know; and oft have shot at them,
    Howe'er unfortunate I miss'd my aim.
MASTER-GUNNER. But now thou shalt not. Be thou rul'd by
    me:
Chief master-gunner am I of this town;
Something I must do to procure me grace.
The prince's espials have informed me
How the English, in the suburbs close entrench'd,
Wont through a secrèt gate of iron bars
In yonder tower to overpeer the city,
And thence discover how with most advantage
They may vex us with shot or with assault.
To intercept this inconvenience,
A piece of ordnance 'gainst it I have plac'd;
And fully even these three days have I watch'd
If I could see them. Now, boy, do thou watch,
For I can stay no longer.
If thou spy'st any, run and bring me word;
And thou shalt find me at the governor's.   *Exit*
SON. Father, I warrant you; take you no care;
    I 'll never trouble you if I may spy them.   *Exit*

Enter, on the turrets, the Lords Salisbury and Talbot;
Sir William Glansdale, Sir Thomas Gargrave, and Others

SALISBURY. Talbot, my life, my joy! again return'd!
    How wert thou handled being prisoner?
Or by what means got'st thou to be releas'd,
Discourse, I prithee, on this turret's top.
TALBOT. The Duke of Bedford had a prisoner
    Called the brave Lord Ponton de Santrailles;
For him I was exchang'd and ransomed.
But with a baser man at arms by far
Once in contempt they would have barter'd me:

Which I disdaining scorn'd, and craved death
Rather than I would be so vile-esteem'd.
In fine, redeem'd I was as I desir'd.
But, O! the treacherous Fastolfe wounds my heart:
Whom with my bare fists I would execute
If I now had him brought into my power.

SALISBURY. Yet tell'st thou not how thou wert entertain'd.

TALBOT. With scoffs and scorns and contumelious taunts.
In open market-place produc'd they me,
To be a public spectacle to all:
Here, said they, is the terror of the French,
The scarecrow that affrights our children so.
Then broke I from the officers that led me,
And with my nails digg'd stones out of the ground
To hurl at the beholders of my shame.
My grisly countenance made others fly.
None durst come near for fear of sudden death.
In iron walls they deem'd me not secure;
So great fear of my name 'mongst them was spread
That they suppos'd I could rend bars of steel
And spurn in pieces posts of adamant:
Wherefore a guard of chosen shot I had,
That walk'd about me every minute-while;
And if I did but stir out of my bed
Ready they were to shoot me to the heart.

Enter the Boy with a linstock

SALISBURY. I grieve to hear what torments you endur'd;
But we will be reveng'd sufficiently.
Now it is supper-time in Orleans:
Here, through this grate, I count each one,
And view the Frenchmen how they fortify:
Let us look in; the sight will much delight thee.
Sir Thomas Gargrave, and Sir William Glansdale,
Let me have your express opinions
Where is best place to make our battery next.

GARGRAVE. I think at the North gate; for there stand lords.

GLANSDALE. And I, here, at the bulwark of the bridge.

TALBOT. For aught I see, this city must be famish'd,
Or with light skirmishes enfeebled.

Here they shoot.
Salisbury and Sir Thomas Gargrave fall

SALISBURY. O Lord! have mercy on us, wretched sinners.

GARGRAVE. O Lord! have mercy on me, woeful man.
TALBOT. What chance is this that suddenly hath cross'd us?
Speak, Salisbury; at least, if thou canst speak:
How far'st thou, mirror of all martial men?
One of thy eyes and thy cheek's side struck off!
Accursed tower! accursed fatal hand
That hath contriv'd this woeful tragedy!
In thirteen battles Salisbury o'ercame;
Henry the Fifth he first train'd to the wars;
Whilst any trump did sound or drum struck up,
His sword did ne'er leave striking in the field.
Yet liv'st thou, Salisbury? though thy speech doth fail,
One eye thou hast to look to heaven for grace:
The sun with one eye vieweth all the world.
Heaven, be thou gracious to none alive,
If Salisbury wants mercy at thy hands!
Bear hence his body; I will help to bury it.
Sir Thomas Gargrave, hast thou any life?
Speak unto Talbot; nay, look up to him.
Salisbury, cheer thy spirit with this comfort;
Thou shalt not die, whiles—
He beckons with his hand and smiles on me,
As who should say, 'When I am dead and gone,
Remember to avenge me on the French.'
Plantagenet, I will; and like thee, Nero,
Play on the lute, beholding the towns burn:
Wretched shall France be only in my name.
                    It thunders and lightens. An alarum
What stir is this? What tumult 's in the heavens?
Whence cometh this alarum and the noise?
                    Enter a Messenger
MESSENGER. My lord, my lord! the French have gather'd
    head:
The Dauphin, with one Joan la Pucelle join'd,
A holy prophetess new risen up
Is come with a great power to raise the siege.
                    Here Salisbury lifteth himself up and groans
TALBOT. Hear, hear how dying Salisbury doth groan!
It irks his heart he cannot be reveng'd.
Frenchmen, I 'll be a Salisbury to you:
Pucelle or puzzel, dolphin or dogfish,
Your hearts I 'll stamp out with my horse's heels

And make a quagmire of your mingled brains.   1-23]
Convey me Salisbury into his tent,
And then we 'll try what these dastard Frenchmen dare.
Exeunt, bearing out the bodies

SCENE FIVE

The Same. Before one of the Gates.

*Alarum. Skirmishings. Enter Talbot, pursuing the Dauphin;
drives him in, and exit: then enter Joan la Pucelle, driving
Englishmen before her, and exit after them.
Then re-enter Talbot*

TALBOT. Where is my strength, my valour, and my force?
Our English troops retire, I cannot stay them;
A woman clad in armour chaseth them.
Re-enter Joan la Pucelle
Here, here she comes. I 'll have a bout with thee:
Devil, or devil's dam, I 'll conjure thee:
Blood will I draw on thee, thou art a witch,
And straightway give thy soul to him thou serv'st.
JOAN. Come, come; 'tis only I that must disgrace thee.
They fight
TALBOT. Heavens, can you suffer hell so to prevail?
My breast I 'll burst with straining of my courage,
And from my shoulders crack my arms asunder,
But I will chastise this high-minded strumpet.
They fight again
JOAN. Talbot, farewell; thy hour is not yet come:
I must go victual Orleans forthwith.
*A short alarum; then
La Pucelle enters the town with Soldiers*
O'ertake me if thou canst; I scorn thy strength.
Go, go, cheer up thy hunger-starved men;
Help Salisbury to make his testament:
This day is ours, as many more shall be.   *Exit*
TALBOT. My thoughts are whirled like a potter's wheel;
I know not where I am, nor what I do:
A witch, my fear, not force, like Hannibal,
Drives back our troops and conquers as she lists:
So bees with smoke, and doves with noisome stench,

Are from their hives and houses driven away.
They call'd us for our fierceness English dogs;
Now, like to whelps, we crying run away. *A short alarum*
Hark, countrymen! either renew the fight,
Or tear the lions out of England's coat;
Renounce your soil, give sheep in lions' stead:
Sheep run not half so treacherous from the wolf,
Or horse or oxen from the leopard,
As you fly from your oft-subdued slaves.
                              Alarum. Another skirmish
It will not be: retire into your trenches:
You all consented unto Salisbury's death,
For none would strike a stroke in his revenge.
Pucelle is entered into Orleans
In spite of us or aught that we could do.
O! would I were to die with Salisbury.
The shame hereof will make me hide my head.
        Alarum. Retreat. Exeunt Talbot and his Forces, &c.

SCENE SIX

The Same.

*Flourish. Enter, on the walls, Joan la Pucelle, Charles,
Reignier, Alençon, and Soldiers*

JOAN. Advance our waving colours on the walls;
    Rescu'd is Orleans from the English:
    Thus Joan la Pucelle hath perform'd her word.
CHARLES. Divinest creature, Astræa's daughter,
    How shall I honour thee for this success?
    Thy promises are like Adonis' gardens,
    That one day bloom'd and fruitful were the next.
    France, triumph in thy glorious prophetess!
    Recover'd is the town of Orleans:
    More blessed hap did ne'er befall our state.
REIGNIER. Why ring not out the bells throughout the town?
    Dauphin, command the citizens make bonfires
    And feast and banquet in the open streets,
    To celebrate the joy that God hath given us.
ALENÇON. All France will be replete with mirth and joy,
    When they shall hear how we have play'd the men.

CHARLES. 'Tis Joan, not we, by whom the day is won;
   For which I will divide my crown with her;
   And all the priests and friars in my realm
   Shall in procession sing her endless praise.
   A statelier pyramis to her I 'll rear
   Than Rhodope's of Memphis ever was:
   In memory of her when she is dead,
   Her ashes, in an urn more precious
   Than the rich-jewell'd coffer of Darius,
   Transported shall be at high festivals
   Before the kings and queens of France.
   No longer on Saint Denis will we cry,
   But Joan la Pucelle shall be France's saint.
   Come in, and let us banquet royally,
   After this golden day of victory.   *Flourish. Exeunt*

ACT TWO

SCENE ONE

Before Orleans.

Enter to the Gates, a French Sergeant, and two Sentinels

SERGEANT. Sirs, take your places and be vigilant.
  If any noise or soldier you perceive
  Near to the walls, by some apparent sign
  Let us have knowledge at the court of guard.
FIRST SENTINEL. Sergeant, you shall.   *Exit Sergeant*
                       Thus are poor servitors—
  When others sleep upon their quiet beds—
  Constrain'd to watch in darkness, rain, and cold.
            *Enter Talbot, Bedford, Burgundy, and Forces
  with scaling-ladders; their drums beating a dead march*
TALBOT. Lord Regent, and redoubted Burgundy,
  By whose approach the regions of Artois,
  Walloon, and Picardy, are friends to us,
  This happy night the Frenchmen are secure,
  Having all day carous'd and banqueted:
  Embrace we then this opportunity,
  As fitting best to quittance their deceit
  Contriv'd by art and baleful sorcery.
BEDFORD. Coward of France! how much he wrongs his
        fame,
  Despairing of his own arm's fortitude,
  To join with witches and the help of hell!
BURGUNDY. Traitors have never other company.
  But what's that Pucelle whom they term so pure?
TALBOT. A maid, they say.
BEDFORD.   A maid, and be so martial!
BURGUNDY. Pray God she prove not masculine ere long;
  If underneath the standard of the French
  She carry armour, as she hath begun.
TALBOT. Well, let them practise and converse with spirits;

God is our fortress, in whose conquering name
Let us resolve to scale their flinty bulwarks.
BEDFORD. Ascend, brave Talbot; we will follow thee.
TALBOT. Not all together: better far, I guess,
That we do make our entrance several ways,
That if it chance the one of us do fail,
The other yet may rise against their force.
BEDFORD. Agreed: I 'll to yond corner.
BURGUNDY.   And I to this.
TALBOT. And here will Talbot mount, or make his grave.
Now, Salisbury, for thee, and for the right
Of English Henry, shall this night appear
How much in duty I am bound to both.

> *The English scale the walls, crying,*
> *'Saint George!' 'A Talbot!' and all enter the town*

FIRST SENTINEL. Arm, arm! the enemy doth make assault!

> *The French leap over the Walls in their shirts.*
> *Enter, several ways, the Bastard of Orleans, Alençon, and*
> *Reignier, half ready, and half unready*

ALENÇON. How now, my lords! what! all unready so?
THE BASTARD. Unready! ay, and glad we 'scap'd so well.
REIGNIER. 'Twas time, I trow, to wake and leave our beds,
Hearing alarums at our chamber-doors.
ALENÇON. Of all exploits since first I follow'd arms,
Ne'er heard I of a warlike enterprise
More venturous or desperate than this.
THE BASTARD. I think this Talbot be a fiend of hell.
REIGNIER. If not of hell, the heavens, sure, favour him.
ALENÇON. Here cometh Charles: I marvel how he sped.
THE BASTARD. Tut! holy Joan was his defensive guard.

> *Enter Charles and Joan la Pucelle*

CHARLES. Is this thy cunning, thou deceitful dame?
Didst thou at first, to flatter us withal,
Make us partakers of a little gain,
That now our loss might be ten times so much?
JOAN. Wherefore is Charles impatient with his friend?
At all times will you have my power alike?
Sleeping or waking must I still prevail,
Or will you blame and lay the fault on me?
Improvident soldiers! had your watch been good,
This sudden mischief never could have fall'n.
CHARLES. Duke of Alençon, this was your default,

That, being captain of the watch to-night,
Did look no better to that weighty charge.
ALENÇON. Had all your quarters been so safely kept
As that whereof I had the government,
We had not been thus shamefully surpris'd.
THE BASTARD. Mine was secure.
REIGNIER.   And so was mine, my lord.
CHARLES. And for myself, most part of all this night,
Within her quarter and mine own precinct
I was employ'd in passing to and fro,
About relieving of the sentinels:
Then how or which way should they first break in?
JOAN. Question, my lords, no further of the case,
How or which way: 'tis sure they found some place
But weakly guarded, where the breach was made.
And now there rests no other shift but this;
To gather our soldiers, scatter'd and dispers'd,
And lay new platforms to endamage them.
                    Alarum. Enter an English Soldier, crying,
        'A Talbot! a Talbot!' They fly, leaving their clothes behind
SOLDIER. I'll be so bold to take what they have left.
The cry of Talbot serves me for a sword;
For I have loaden me with many spoils,
Using no other weapon but his name.   *Exit*

SCENE TWO

Orleans. Within the Town.

Enter Talbot, Bedford, Burgundy, a Captain, and Others

BEDFORD. The day begins to break, and night is fled,
Whose pitchy mantle over-veil'd the earth.
Here sound retreat, and cease our hot pursuit.
                                    Retreat sounded
TALBOT. Bring forth the body of old Salisbury,
And here advance it in the market-place,
The middle centre of this cursed town.
Now have I paid my vow unto his soul;
For every drop of blood was drawn from him
There hath at least five Frenchmen died to-night.
And that hereafter ages may behold

What ruin happen'd in revenge of him,
Within their chiefest temple I 'll erect
A tomb wherein his corse shall be interr'd:
Upon the which, that every one may read,
Shall be engrav'd the sack of Orleans,
The treacherous manner of his mournful death,
And what a terror he had been to France.
But, lords, in all our bloody massacre,
I muse we met not with the Dauphin's Grace,
His new-come champion, virtuous Joan of Arc,
Nor any of his false confederates.

BEDFORD. 'Tis thought, Lord Talbot, when the fight began,
Rous'd on the sudden from their drowsy beds,
They did amongst the troops of armed men
Leap o'er the walls for refuge in the field.

BURGUNDY. Myself—as far as I could well discern
For smoke and dusky vapours of the night—
Am sure I scar'd the Dauphin and his trull,
When arm in arm they both came swiftly running,
Like to a pair of loving turtle-doves
That could not live asunder day or night.
After that things are set in order here,
We 'll follow them with all the power we have.

Enter a Messenger

MESSENGER. All hail, my lords! Which of this princely train
Call ye the warlike Talbot, for his acts
So much applauded through the realm of France?

TALBOT. Here is the Talbot: who would speak with him?

MESSENGER. The virtuous lady, Countess of Auvergne,
With modesty admiring thy renown,
By me entreats, great lord, thou wouldst vouchsafe
To visit her poor castle where she lies,
That she may boast she hath beheld the man
Whose glory fills the world with loud report.

BURGUNDY. Is it even so? Nay, then, I see our wars
Will turn into a peaceful comic sport,
When ladies crave to be encounter'd with.
You may not, my lord, despise her gentle suit.

TALBOT. Ne'er trust me then; for when a world of men
Could not prevail with all their oratory, ·
Yet hath a woman's kindness over-rul'd:
And therefore tell her I return great thanks,

And in submission will attend on her.
Will not your honours bear me company?
BEDFORD. No, truly; it is more than manners will;
And I have heard it said, unbidden guests
Are often welcomest when they are gone.
TALBOT. Well then, alone,—since there 's no remedy,—
I mean to prove this lady's courtesy.
Come hither, captain. (*Whispers*) You perceive my mind.
CAPTAIN. I do, my lord, and mean accordingly.   *Exeunt*

SCENE THREE

Auvergne. Court of the Castle.

Enter the Countess and her Porter

COUNTESS. Porter, remember what I gave in charge;
And when you have done so, bring the keys to me.
PORTER. Madam, I will.   *Exit*
COUNTESS. The plot is laid: if all things fall out right,
I shall as famous be by this exploit
As Scythian Tomyris by Cyrus' death.
Great is the humour of this dreadful knight,
And his achievements of no less account:
Fain would mine eyes be witness with mine ears,
To give their censure of these rare reports.
                    Enter Messenger and Talbot
MESSENGER. Madam,
According as your ladyship desir'd,
By message crav'd, so is Lord Talbot come.
COUNTESS. And he is welcome. What! is this the man?
MESSENGER. Madam, it is.
COUNTESS.   Is this the scourge of France?
Is this the Talbot, so much fear'd abroad,
That with his name the mothers still their babes?
I see report is fabulous and false:
I thought I should have seen some Hercules,
A second Hector, for his grim aspect,
And large proportion of his strong-knit limbs.
Alas! this is a child, a silly dwarf:
It cannot be this weak and writhled shrimp

Should strike such terror to his enemies.

TALBOT. Madam, I have been bold to trouble you;
But since your ladyship is not at leisure,
I 'll sort some other time to visit you.

COUNTESS. What means he now? Go ask him whither he
goes.

MESSENGER. Stay, my Lord Talbot, for my lady craves
To know the cause of your abrupt departure.

TALBOT. Marry, for that she 's in a wrong belief,
I go to certify her Talbot 's here.

Re-enter Porter, with keys

COUNTESS. If thou be he, then art thou prisoner.

TALBOT. Prisoner! to whom?

COUNTESS.   To me, blood-thirsty lord;
And for that cause I train'd thee to my house.
Long time thy shadow hath been thrall to me,
For in my gallery thy picture hangs:
But now the substance shall endure the like,
And I will chain these legs and arms of thine,
That hast by tyranny, these many years
Wasted our country, slain our citizens,
And sent our sons and husbands captivate.

TALBOT. Ha, ha, ha!

COUNTESS. Laughest thou, wretch? thy mirth shall turn to
moan.

TALBOT. I laugh to see your ladyship so fond
To think that you have aught but Talbot's shadow,
Whereon to practise your severity.

COUNTESS. Why, art not thou the man?

TALBOT.   I am, indeed.

COUNTESS. Then have I substance too.

TALBOT. No, no, I am but shadow of myself:
You are deceiv'd, my substance is not here;
For what you see is but the smallest part
And least proportion of humanity.
I tell you, madam, were the whole frame here,
It is of such a spacious lofty pitch,
Your roof were not sufficient to contain it.

COUNTESS. This is a riddling merchant for the nonce;
He will be here, and yet he is not here:
How can these contrarieties agree?

TALBOT. That will I show you presently.

He winds a horn. Drums strike up;
a peal of ordnance. The Gates being forced, enter Soldiers

    How say you, madam? are you now persuaded
    That Talbot is but shadow of himself?
    These are his substance, sinews, arms, and strength,
    With which he yoketh your rebellious necks,
    Razeth your cities, and subverts your towns,
    And in a moment makes them desolate.
COUNTESS. Victorious Talbot! pardon my abuse:
    I find thou art no less than fame hath bruited,
    And more than may be gather'd by thy shape.
    Let my presumption not provoke thy wrath;
    For I am sorry that with reverence
    I did not entertain thee as thou art.
TALBOT. Be not dismay'd, fair lady; nor misconster
    The mind of Talbot as you did mistake
    The outward composition of his body.
    What you have done hath not offended me;
    Nor other satisfaction do I crave,
    But only, with your patience, that we may
    Taste of your wine and see what cates you have;
    For soldiers' stomachs always serve them well.
COUNTESS. With all my heart, and think me honoured
    To feast so great a warrior in my house.   *Exeunt*

SCENE FOUR

London. The Temple Garden.

Enter the Earls of Somerset, Suffolk, and Warwick; Richard
Plantagenet, Vernon, and a Lawyer

PLANTAGENET. Great lords, and gentlemen, what means
    this silence?
    Dare no man answer in a case of truth?
SUFFOLK. Within the Temple hall we were too loud;
    The garden here is more convenient.
PLANTAGENET. Then say at once if I maintained the truth,
    Or else was wrangling Somerset in the error?
SUFFOLK. Faith, I have been a truant in the law,
    And never yet could frame my will to it;
    And therefore frame the law unto my will.

SOMERSET. Judge you, my Lord of Warwick, then, between
us.

WARWICK. Between two hawks, which flies the higher pitch;
Between two dogs, which hath the deeper mouth;
Between two blades, which bears the better temper;
Between two horses, which doth bear him best;
Between two girls, which hath the merriest eye;
I have, perhaps, some shallow spirit of judgment;
But in these nice sharp quillets of the law,
Good faith, I am no wiser than a daw.

PLANTAGENET. Tut, tut! here is a mannerly forbearance:
The truth appears so naked on my side,
That any purblind eye may find it out.

SOMERSET. And on my side it is so well apparell'd,
So clear, so shining, and so evident,
That it will glimmer through a blind man's eye.

PLANTAGENET. Since you are tongue-tied, and so loath to
speak,
In dumb significants proclaim your thoughts:
Let him that is a true-born gentleman,
And stands upon the honour of his birth,
If he suppose that I have pleaded truth,
From off this brier pluck a white rose with me.

SOMERSET. Let him that is no coward nor no flatterer,
But dare maintain the party of the truth,
Pluck a red rose from off this thorn with me.

WARWICK. I love no colours, and without all colour
Of base insinuating flattery
I pluck this white rose with Plantagenet.

SUFFOLK. I pluck this red rose with young Somerset:
And say withal I think he held the right.

VERNON. Stay, lords and gentlemen, and pluck no more,
Till you conclude that he, upon whose side
The fewest roses are cropp'd from the tree,
Shall yield the other in the right opinion.

SOMERSET. Good Master Vernon, it is well objected:
If I have fewest I subscribe in silence.

PLANTAGENET. And I.

VERNON. Then for the truth and plainness of the case,
I pluck this pale and maiden blossom here,
Giving my verdict on the white rose side.

SOMERSET. Prick not your finger as you pluck it off,

Lest bleeding you do paint the white rose red,
And fall on my side so, against your will.
VERNON. If I, my lord, for my opinion bleed,
Opinion shall be surgeon to my hurt,
And keep me on the side where still I am.
SOMERSET. Well, well, come on: who else?
LAWYER. (*To Somerset*) Unless my study and my books be
false,
The argument you held was wrong in you,
In sign whereof I pluck a white rose too.
PLANTAGENET. Now, Somerset, where is your argument?
SOMERSET. Here, in my scabbard; meditating that
Shall dye your white rose in a bloody red.
PLANTAGENET. Meantime, your cheeks do counterfeit our
roses;
For pale they look with fear, as witnessing
The truth on our side.
SOMERSET.   No, Plantagenet,
'Tis not for fear but anger that thy cheeks
Blush for pure shame to counterfeit our roses,
And yet thy tongue will not confess thy error.
PLANTAGENET. Hath not thy rose a canker, Somerset?
SOMERSET. Hath not thy rose a thorn, Plantagenet?
PLANTAGENET. Ay, sharp and piercing, to maintain his
truth;
Whiles thy consuming canker eats his falsehood.
SOMERSET. Well, I'll find friends to wear my bleeding roses,
That shall maintain what I have said is true,
Where false Plantagenet dare not be seen.
PLANTAGENET. Now, by this maiden blossom in my hand,
I scorn thee and thy faction, peevish boy.
SUFFOLK. Turn not thy scorns this way, Plantagenet.
PLANTAGENET. Proud Pole, I will, and scorn both him and
thee.
SUFFOLK. I'll turn my part thereof into thy throat.
SOMERSET. Away, away! good William de la Pole:
We grace the yeoman by conversing with him.
WARWICK. Now, by God's will, thou wrong'st him,
Somerset:
His grandfather was Lionel, Duke of Clarence,
Third son to the third Edward, King of England.
Spring crestless yeomen from so deep a root?

PLANTAGENET. He bears him on the place's privilege,
  Or durst not, for his craven heart, say thus.
SOMERSET. By him that made me, I 'll maintain my words
  On any plot of ground in Christendom.
  Was not thy father, Richard Earl of Cambridge,
  For treason executed in our late king's days?
  And, by his treason stand'st not thou attainted,
  Corrupted, and exempt from ancient gentry?
  His trespass yet lives guilty in thy blood;
  And, till thou be restor'd, thou art a yeoman.
PLANTAGENET. My father was attached, not attainted;
  Condemn'd to die for treason, but no traitor;
  And that I 'll prove on better men than Somerset,
  Were growing time once ripen'd to my will.
  For your partaker Pole and you yourself,
  I 'll note you in my book of memory,
  To scourge you for this apprehension:
  Look to it well and say you are well warn'd.
SOMERSET. Ah, thou shalt find us ready for thee still,
  And know us by these colours for thy foes;
  For these my friends in spite of thee shall wear.
PLANTAGENET. And, by my soul, this pale and angry rose,
  As cognizance of my blood-drinking hate,
  Will I for ever and my faction wear,
  Until it wither with me to my grave
  Or flourish to the height of my degree.
SUFFOLK. Go forward, and be chok'd with thy ambition:
  And so farewell until I meet thee next.   *Exit*
SOMERSET. Have with thee, Pole. Farewell, ambitious
      Richard.   *Exit*
PLANTAGENET. How I am brav'd and must perforce endure
      it!
WARWICK. This blot that they object against your house
  Shall be wip'd out in the next parliament,
  Call'd for the truce of Winchester and Gloucester;
  And if thou be not then created York,
  I will not live to be accounted Warwick.
  Meantime in signal of my love to thee,
  Against proud Somerset and William Pole,
  Will I upon thy party wear this rose.
  And here I prophesy: this brawl to-day,
  Grown to this faction in the Temple garden,

Shall send between the red rose and the white
A thousand souls to death and deadly night.
PLANTAGENET. Good Master Vernon, I am bound to you,
That you on my behalf would pluck a flower.
VERNON. In your behalf still would I wear the same.
LAWYER. And so will I.
PLANTAGENET. Thanks, gentle sir.
Come, let us four to dinner: I dare say
This quarrel will drink blood another day.   *Exeunt*

SCENE FIVE

London. A Room in the Tower.

Enter Mortimer, brought in a chair by two Gaolers

MORTIMER. Kind keepers of my weak decaying age,
Let dying Mortimer here rest himself.
Even like a man new haled from the rack,
So fare my limbs with long imprisonment;
And these grey locks, the pursuivants of death,
Nestor-like aged, in an age of care,
Argue the end of Edmund Mortimer.
These eyes, like lamps whose wasting oil is spent,
Wax dim, as drawing to their exigent;
Weak shoulders, overborne with burdening grief,
And pithless arms, like to a wither'd vine
That droops his sapless branches to the ground:
Yet are these feet, whose strengthless stay is numb,
Unable to support this lump of clay,
Swift-winged with desire to get a grave,
As witting I no other comfort have.
But tell me, keeper, will my nephew come?
FIRST KEEPER. Richard Plantagenet, my lord, will come:
We sent unto the Temple, unto his chamber,
And answer was return'd that he will come.
MORTIMER. Enough: my soul shall then be satisfied.
Poor gentleman! his wrong doth equal mine.
Since Henry Monmouth first began to reign,
Before whose glory I was great in arms,
This loathsome sequestration have I had;
And even since then hath Richard been obscur'd,

Depriv'd of honour and inheritance.
But now the arbitrator of despairs,
Just death, kind umpire of men's miseries,
With sweet enlargement doth dismiss me hence:
I would his troubles likewise were expir'd,
That so he might recover what was lost.

Enter Richard Plantagenet

FIRST KEEPER. My lord, your loving nephew now is come.

MORTIMER. Richard Plantagenet, my friend, is he come?

PLANTAGENET. Ay, noble uncle, thus ignobly us'd,
Your nephew, late despised Richard, comes.

MORTIMER. Direct mine arms I may embrace his neck,
And in his bosom spend my latter gasp:
O! tell me when my lips do touch his cheeks,
That I may kindly give one fainting kiss.
And now declare, sweet stem from York's great stock,
Why didst thou say of late thou wert despis'd?

PLANTAGENET. First, lean thine aged back against mine
     arm;
And in that ease, I 'll tell thee my disease.
This day, in argument upon a case,
Some words there grew 'twixt Somerset and me;
Among which terms he us'd a lavish tongue
And did upbraid me with my father's death:
Which obloquy set bars before my tongue,
Else with the like I had requited him.
Therefore, good uncle, for my father's sake,
In honour of a true Plantagenet,
And for alliance sake, declare the cause
My father, Earl of Cambridge, lost his head.

MORTIMER. That cause, fair nephew, that imprison'd me,
And hath detain'd me all my flowering youth
Within a loathsome dungeon, there to pine,
Was cursed instrument of his decease.

PLANTAGENET. Discover more at large what cause that was,
For I am ignorant and cannot guess.

MORTIMER. I will, if that my fading breath permit,
And death approach not ere my tale be done.
Henry the Fourth, grandfather to this king,
Depos'd his nephew Richard, Edward's son,
The first-begotten, and the lawful heir
Of Edward king, the third of that descent:

During whose reign the Percies of the North,
Finding his usurpation most unjust,
Endeavour'd my advancement to the throne.
The reason mov'd these warlike lords to this
Was, for that—young King Richard thus remov'd,
Leaving no heir begotten of his body—
I was the next by birth and parentage;
For by my mother I derived am
From Lionel Duke of Clarence, the third son
To King Edward the Third; whereas he
From John of Gaunt doth bring his pedigree,
Being but fourth of that heroic line.
But mark: as, in this haughty great attempt
They laboured to plant the rightful heir,
I lost my liberty, and they their lives.
Long after this, when Henry the Fifth
Succeeding his father Bolingbroke, did reign,
Thy father, Earl of Cambridge, then deriv'd
From famous Edmund Langley, Duke of York,
Marrying my sister that thy mother was,
Again in pity of my hard distress
Levied an army, weening to redeem
And have install'd me in the diadem;
But, as the rest, so fell that noble earl,
And was beheaded. Thus the Mortimers,
In whom the title rested, were suppress'd.

PLANTAGENET. Of which, my lord, your honour is the last.

MORTIMER. True; and thou seest that I no issue have,
And that my fainting words do warrant death:
Thou art my heir; the rest I wish thee gather:
But yet be wary in thy studious care.

PLANTAGENET. Thy grave admonishments prevail with me.
But yet methinks my father's execution
Was nothing less than bloody tyranny.

MORTIMER. With silence, nephew, be thou politic:
Strong-fixed is the house of Lancaster,
And like a mountain, not to be remov'd.
But now thy uncle is removing hence,
As princes do their courts, when they are cloy'd
With long continuance in a settled place.

PLANTAGENET. O uncle! would some part of my young years
Might but redeem the passage of your age.

MORTIMER. Thou dost then wrong me,—as the slaughterer
    doth,
  Which giveth many wounds when one will kill.—
  Mourn not, except thou sorrow for my good;
  Only give order for my funeral:
  And so farewell; and fair be all thy hopes,
  And prosperous be thy life in peace and war!   *Dies*
PLANTAGENET. And peace, no war, befall thy parting soul!
  In prison hast thou spent a pilgrimage,
  And like a hermit overpass'd thy days.
  Well, I will lock his counsel in my breast;
  And what I do imagine let that rest.
  Keepers, convey him hence; and I myself
  Will see his burial better than his life.
      Exeunt Keepers, bearing out the body of Mortimer
  Here dies the dusky torch of Mortimer,
  Chok'd with ambition of the meaner sort:
  And, for those wrongs, those bitter injuries,
  Which Somerset hath offer'd to my house,
  I doubt not but with honour to redress;
  And therefore haste I to the parliament,
  Either to be restored to my blood,
  Or make my ill the advantage of my good.   *Exit*

ACT THREE

SCENE ONE

London. The Parliament House.

Flourish. Enter King Henry, Exeter, Gloucester, Warwick, Somerset, and Suffolk; the Bishop of Winchester, Richard Plantagenet, and Others. Gloucester offers to put up a bill; Winchester snatches it, and tears it

WINCHESTER. Com'st thou with deep premeditated lines,
With written pamphlets studiously devis'd,
Humphrey of Gloucester? If thou canst accuse,
Or aught intend'st to lay unto my charge,
Do it without invention, suddenly;
As I, with sudden and extemporal speech
Purpose to answer what thou canst object.
GLOUCESTER. Presumptuous priest! this place commands
    my patience
Or thou shouldst find thou hast dishonour'd me.
Think not, although in writing I preferr'd
The manner of thy vile outrageous crimes,
That therefore I have forg'd, or am not able
Verbatim to rehearse the method of my pen:
No, prelate; such is thy audacious wickedness,
Thy lewd, pestiferous, and dissentious pranks,
As very infants prattle of thy pride.
Thou art a most pernicious usurer,
Froward by nature, enemy to peace;
Lascivious, wanton, more than well beseems
A man of thy profession and degree;
And for thy treachery, what's more manifest?
In that thou laid'st a trap to take my life
As well at London Bridge as at the Tower.
Beside, I fear me, if thy thoughts were sifted,
The king, thy sovereign, is not quite exempt

From envious malice of thy swelling heart.

WINCHESTER. Gloucester, I do defy thee. Lords, vouchsafe
To give me hearing what I shall reply.
If I were covetous, ambitious, or perverse,
As he will have me, how am I so poor?
Or how haps it I seek not to advance
Or raise myself, but keep my wonted calling?
And for dissension, who preferreth peace
More than I do, except I be provok'd?
No, my good lords, it is not that offends;
It is not that that hath incens'd the duke:
It is, because no one should sway but he;
No one but he should be about the king;
And that engenders thunder in his breast,
And makes him roar these accusations forth.
But he shall know I am as good—

GLOUCESTER.   As good!
Thou bastard of my grandfather!

WINCHESTER. Ay, lordly sir; for what are you, I pray,
But one imperious in another's throne?

GLOUCESTER. Am I not protector, saucy priest?

WINCHESTER. And am not I a prelate of the church?

GLOUCESTER. Yes, as an outlaw in a castle keeps,
And useth it to patronage his theft.

WINCHESTER. Unreverent Gloucester!

GLOUCESTER.   Thou art reverent,
Touching thy spiritual function, not thy life.

WINCHESTER. Rome shall remedy this.

WARWICK.   Roam thither then.

SOMERSET. My lord, it were your duty to forbear.

WARWICK. Ay, see the bishop be not overborne.

SOMERSET. Methinks my lord should be religious,
And know the office that belongs to such.

WARWICK. Methinks his lordship should be humbler;
It fitteth not a prelate so to plead.

SOMERSET. Yes, when his holy state is touch'd so near.

WARWICK. State holy, or unhallow'd, what of that?
Is not his Grace protector to the king?

PLANTAGENET. (*Aside*) Plantagenet, I see, must hold his
tongue,
Lest it be said, 'Speak, sirrah, when you should;
Must your bold verdict enter talk with lords?'

Else would I have a fling at Winchester.

KING HENRY. Uncles of Gloucester and of Winchester,
　　The special watchmen of our English weal,
　　I would prevail, if prayers might prevail,
　　To join your hearts in love and amity.
　　O! what a scandal is it to our crown,
　　That two such noble peers as ye should jar.
　　Believe me, lords, my tender years can tell
　　Civil dissension is a viperous worm,
　　That gnaws the bowels of the commonwealth.
　　　　　　　(*A noise within*) 'Down with the tawny-coats!'
　　What tumult 's this?

WARWICK.　　　　　　　An uproar, I dare warrant,
　　Begun through malice of the bishop's men.
　　　　　　　　　(*A noise again within*) 'Stones! Stones!'
　　　　　　Enter the Mayor of London, attended

MAYOR. O, my good lords, and virtuous Henry,
　　Pity the city of London, pity us!
　　The bishop and the Duke of Gloucester's men,
　　Forbidden late to carry any weapon,
　　Have fill'd their pockets full of pebble stones,
　　And banding themselves in contrary parts
　　Do pelt so fast at one another's pate,
　　That many have their giddy brains knock'd out:
　　Our windows are broke down in every street,
　　And we for fear compell'd to shut our shops.
　　　　　　*Enter, skirmishing, the Serving-men
　　　　　　of Gloucester and Winchester, with bloody pates*

KING HENRY. We charge you, on allegiance to ourself,
　　To hold your slaught'ring hands, and keep the peace.—
　　Pray, uncle Gloucester, mitigate this strife.

FIRST SERVING-MAN. Nay, if we be forbidden stones, we 'll
　　fall to it with our teeth.

SECOND SERVING-MAN. Do what ye dare, we are as resolute.
　　　　　　　　　　　　　　　　　　Skirmish again

GLOUCESTER. You of my household, leave this peevish broil,
　　And set this unaccustom'd fight aside.

THIRD SERVING-MAN. My lord, we know your Grace to be a
　　man
　　Just and upright, and, for your royal birth,
　　Inferior to none but to his Majesty;
　　And ere that we will suffer such a prince,

So kind a father of the commonweal,
To be disgraced by an inkhorn mate,
We and our wives and children all will fight,
And have our bodies slaughter'd by thy foes.

FIRST SERVING-MAN. Ay, and the very parings of our nails
Shall pitch a field when we are dead.   *Skirmish again*

GLOUCESTER.   Stay, stay, I say!
And, if you love me, as you say you do,
Let me persuade you to forbear a while.

KING HENRY. O! how this discord doth afflict my soul!
Can you, my Lord of Winchester, behold
My sighs and tears and will not once relent?
Who should be pitiful if you be not?
Or who should study to prefer a peace
If holy churchmen take delight in broils?

WARWICK. Yield, my Lord Protector; yield, Winchester;
Except you mean with obstinate repulse
To slay your sovereign and destroy the realm.
You see what mischief and what murder too
Hath been enacted through your enmity:
Then be at peace, except ye thirst for blood.

WINCHESTER. He shall submit, or I will never yield.

GLOUCESTER. Compassion on the king commands me stoop;
Or I would see his heart out ere the priest
Should ever get that privilege of me.

WARWICK. Behold, my Lord of Winchester, the duke
Hath banish'd moody discontented fury,
As by his smoothed brows it doth appear:
Why look you still so stern and tragical?

GLOUCESTER. Here, Winchester, I offer thee my hand.

KING HENRY. Fie, uncle Beaufort! I have heard you preach,
That malice was a great and grievous sin;
And will not you maintain the thing you teach,
But prove a chief offender in the same?

WARWICK. Sweet king! the bishop hath a kindly gird.
For shame, my Lord of Winchester, relent!
What! shall a child instruct you what to do?

WINCHESTER. Well, Duke of Gloucester, I will yield to thee;
Love for thy love and hand for hand I give.

GLOUCESTER. (*Aside*) Ay; but I fear me, with a hollow heart.
See here, my friends and loving countrymen,
This token serveth for a flag of truce,

Betwixt ourselves and all our followers.
So help me God, as I dissemble not!

WINCHESTER. (*Aside*) So help me God, as I intend it not!

KING HENRY. O loving uncle, kind Duke of Gloucester,
How joyful am I made by this contract!
Away, my masters! trouble us no more;
But join in friendship, as your lords have done.

FIRST SERVING-MAN. Content: I 'll to the surgeon's.

SECOND SERVING-MAN.   And so will I.

THIRD SERVING-MAN. And I will see what physic the tavern
affords.   *Exeunt Mayor, Serving-men, &c.*

WARWICK. Accept this scroll, most gracious sovereign,
Which in the right of Richard Plantagenet
We do exhibit to your Majesty.

GLOUCESTER. Well urg'd, my Lord of Warwick: for, sweet
prince,
An if your Grace mark every circumstance,
You have great reason to do Richard right;
Especially for those occasions
At Eltham-place I told your Majesty.

KING HENRY. And those occasions, uncle, were of force:
Therefore, my loving lords, our pleasure is
That Richard be restored to his blood.

WARWICK. Let Richard be restored to his blood;
So shall his father's wrongs be recompens'd.

WINCHESTER. As will the rest, so willeth Winchester.

KING HENRY. If Richard will be true, not that alone,
But all the whole inheritance I give
That doth belong unto the house of York,
From whence you spring by lineal descent.

PLANTAGENET. Thy humble servant vows obedience,
And humble service till the point of death.

KING HENRY. Stoop then and set your knee against my foot;
And, in reguerdon of that duty done,
I girt thee with the valiant sword of York:
Rise, Richard, like a true Plantagenet,
And rise created princely Duke of York.

PLANTAGENET. And so thrive Richard as thy foes may fall!
And as my duty springs, so perish they
That grudge one thought against your Majesty!

ALL. Welcome, high prince, the mighty Duke of York!

SOMERSET. (*Aside*) Perish, base prince, ignoble Duke of York!

GLOUCESTER. Now, will it best avail your Majesty
    To cross the seas and to be crown'd in France.
    The presence of a king engenders love
    Amongst his subjects and his loyal friends,
    As it disanimates his enemies.

KING HENRY. When Gloucester says the word, King Henry
    goes;
    For friendly counsel cuts off many foes.

GLOUCESTER. Your ships already are in readiness.

                Flourish. Exeunt all except Exeter

EXETER. Ay, we may march in England or in France,
    Not seeing what is likely to ensue.
    This late dissension grown betwixt the peers
    Burns under feigned ashes of forg'd love,
    And will at last break out into a flame:
    As fester'd members rot but by degree,
    Till bones and flesh and sinews fall away,
    So will this base and envious discord breed.
    And now I fear that fatal prophecy
    Which in the time of Henry, nam'd the Fifth,
    Was in the mouth of every sucking babe;
    That Henry born at Monmouth should win all;
    And Henry born at Windsor should lose all:
    Which is so plain that Exeter doth wish
    His days may finish ere that hapless time.   *Exit*

SCENE TWO

France. Before Roan.

*Enter Joan la Pucelle, disguised, and Soldiers dressed like
countrymen, with sacks upon their backs*

JOAN. These are the city gates, the gates of Roan,
    Through which our policy must make a breach:
    Take heed, be wary how you place your words;
    Talk like the vulgar sort of market-men
    That come to gather money for their corn.
    If we have entrance,—as I hope we shall,—
    And that we find the slothful watch but weak,
    I 'll by a sign give notice to our friends,

That Charles the Dauphin may encounter them.

FIRST SOLDIER. Our sacks shall be a mean to sack the city,
And we be lords and rulers over Roan;
Therefore we 'll knock.   *Knocks*

GUARD. (*Within*) Qui est là?

JOAN. Paysans, pauvres gens de France:
Poor market-folks that come to sell their corn.

GUARD. (*Opening the gates*) Enter, go in; the market-bell is
rung.

JOAN. Now, Roan, I 'll shake thy bulwarks to the ground.
Joan la Pucelle, &c., enter the city
Enter Charles, the Bastard of Orleans, Alençon, and Forces

CHARLES. Saint Denis bless this happy stratagem!
And once again we 'll sleep secure in Roan.

THE BASTARD. Here enter'd Pucelle and her practisants;
Now she is there how will she specify
Where is the best and safest passage in?

ALENÇON. By thrusting out a torch from yonder tower;
Which, once discern'd, shows that her meaning is,
No way to that, for weakness, which she enter'd.
Enter Joan la Pucelle
on a battlement, holding out a torch burning

JOAN. Behold! this is the happy wedding torch
That joineth Roan unto her countrymen,
But burning fatal to the Talbotites!   *Exit*

THE BASTARD. See, noble Charles, the beacon of our friend,
The burning torch in yonder turret stands.

CHARLES. Now shine it like a comet of revenge,
A prophet to the fall of all our foes!

ALENÇON. Defer no time, delays have dangerous ends;
Enter and cry 'The Dauphin!' presently,
And then do execution on the watch. *They enter the town*
Alarum. Enter Talbot in an Excursion

TALBOT. France, thou shalt rue this treason with thy tears,
If Talbot but survive thy treachery.
Pucelle, that witch, that damned sorceress,
Hath wrought this hellish mischief unawares,
That hardly we escap'd the pride of France.   *Exit*
Alarum: Excursions. Enter from the town, Bedford,
brought in sick in a chair. Enter Talbot and Burgundy, and
the English Forces. Then, enter on the walls, Joan la Pucelle,
Charles, the Bastard of Orleans, Alençon, and Others

JOAN. Good-morrow, gallants! Want ye corn for bread?
I think the Duke of Burgundy will fast
Before he 'll buy again at such a rate.
'Twas full of darnel; do you like the taste?

BURGUNDY. Scoff on, vile fiend and shameless courtezan!
I trust ere long to choke thee with thine own,
And make thee curse the harvest of that corn.

CHARLES. Your Grace may starve perhaps before that time.

BEDFORD. O! let no words, but deeds, revenge this treason!

JOAN. What will you do, good grey-beard? break a lance,
And run a tilt at death within a chair?

TALBOT. Foul fiend of France, and hag of all despite,
Encompass'd with thy lustful paramours!
Becomes it thee to taunt his valiant age
And twit with cowardice a man half dead?
Damsel, I 'll have a bout with you again,
Or else let Talbot perish with this shame.

JOAN. Are you so hot, sir? Yet, Pucelle, hold thy peace;
If Talbot do but thunder, rain will follow.

      Talbot and the rest consult together
God speed the parliament! who shall be the speaker?

TALBOT. Dare ye come forth and meet us in the field?

JOAN. Belike your lordship takes us then for fools,
To try if that our own be ours or no.

TALBOT. I speak not to that railing Hecate,
But unto thee, Alençon, and the rest;
Will ye, like soldiers, come and fight it out?

ALENÇON. Signior, no.

TALBOT. Signior, hang! base muleters of France!
Like peasant foot-boys do they keep the walls,
And dare not take up arms like gentlemen.

JOAN. Away, captains! let 's get us from the walls;
For Talbot means no goodness, by his looks.
God be wi' you, my lord! we came but to tell you
That we are here.

    Exeunt Joan La Pucelle, &c., from the Walls

TALBOT. And there will we be too, ere it be long,
Or else reproach be Talbot's greatest fame!
Vow, Burgundy, by honour of thy house,—
Prick'd on by public wrongs sustain'd in France,—
Either to get the town again, or die;
And I, as sure as English Henry lives,

And as his father here was conqueror,
As sure as in this late-betrayed town
Great Cœur-de-Lion's heart was buried,
So sure I swear to get the town or die.

BURGUNDY. My vows are equal partners with thy vows.

TALBOT. But, ere we go, regard this dying prince,
The valiant Duke of Bedford. Come, my lord,
We will bestow you in some better place,
Fitter for sickness and for crazy age.

BEDFORD. Lord Talbot, do not so dishonour me:
Here will I sit before the walls of Roan,
And will be partner of your weal or woe.

BURGUNDY. Courageous Bedford, let us now persuade you.

BEDFORD. Not to be gone from hence; for once I read
That stout Pendragon in his litter, sick,
Came to the field and vanquished his foes:
Methinks I should revive the soldiers' hearts,
Because I ever found them as myself.

TALBOT. Undaunted spirit in a dying breast!
Then be it so: heavens keep old Bedford safe!
And now no more ado, brave Burgundy,
But gather we our forces out of hand,
And set upon our boasting enemy.

Exeunt all but Bedford and Attendants
Alarum: Excursions; in one
of which, enter Sir John Fastolfe and a Captain

CAPTAIN. Whither away, Sir John Fastolfe, in such haste?

FASTOLFE. Whither away! to save myself by flight:
We are like to have the overthrow again.

CAPTAIN. What! will you fly, and leave Lord Talbot?

FASTOLFE.   Ay,
All the Talbots in the world, to save my life.   *Exit*

CAPTAIN. Cowardly knight! ill fortune follow thee!   *Exit*
Retreat: Excursions. Re-enter, from the town,
Joan la Pucelle, Alençon, Charles, &c., and exeunt, flying

BEDFORD. Now, quiet soul, depart when Heaven please,
For I have seen our enemies' overthrow.
What is the trust or strength of foolish man?
They, that of late were daring with their scoffs
Are glad and fain by flight to save themselves.

Dies, and is carried off in his chair
Alarum. Re-enter Talbot, Burgundy, and Others

TALBOT. Lost, and recover'd in a day again!
   This is a double honour, Burgundy:
   Yet heavens have glory for this victory!
BURGUNDY. Warlike and martial Talbot, Burgundy
   Enshrines thee in his heart, and there erects
   Thy noble deeds as valour's monument.
TALBOT. Thanks, gentle duke. But where is Pucelle now?
   I think her old familiar is asleep.
   Now where 's the Bastard's braves, and Charles his gleeks?
   What! all amort? Roan hangs her head for grief,
   That such a valiant company are fled.
   Now will we take some order in the town,
   Placing therein some expert officers,
   And then depart to Paris to the king;
   For there young Henry with his nobles lie.
BURGUNDY. What wills Lord Talbot pleaseth Burgundy.
TALBOT. But yet, before we go, let 's not forget
   The noble Duke of Bedford late deceas'd,
   But see his exequies fulfill'd in Roan:
   A braver soldier never couched lance,
   A gentler heart did never sway in court;
   But kings and mightiest potentates must die,
   For that 's the end of human misery.   *Exeunt*

SCENE THREE

The Plains near Roan.

*Enter Charles, the Bastard of Orleans, Alençon, Joan
la Pucelle, and Forces*

JOAN. Dismay not, princes, at this accident,
   Nor grieve that Roan is so recovered:
   Care is no cure, but rather corrosive,
   For things that are not to be remedied.
   Let frantic Talbot triumph for a while,
   And like a peacock sweep along his tail;
   We 'll pull his plumes and take away his train,
   If Dauphin and the rest will be but rul'd.
CHARLES. We have been guided by thee hitherto,
   And of thy cunning had no diffidence:
   One sudden foil shall never breed distrust.

THE BASTARD. Search out thy wit for secret policies,
  And we will make thee famous through the world.
ALENÇON. We 'll set thy statue in some holy place
  And have thee reverenc'd like a blessed saint:
  Employ thee, then, sweet virgin, for our good.
JOAN. Then thus it must be; this doth Joan devise:
  By fair persuasions, mix'd with sugar'd words,
  We will entice the Duke of Burgundy
  To leave the Talbot and to follow us.
CHARLES. Ay, marry, sweeting, if we could do that,
  France were no place for Henry's warriors;
  Nor should that nation boast it so with us,
  But be extirped from our provinces.
ALENÇON. For ever should they be expuls'd from France,
  And not have title of an earldom here.
JOAN. Your honours shall perceive how I will work
  To bring this matter to the wished end.
                              Drums heard afar off
  Hark! by the sound of drum you may perceive
  Their powers are marching unto Paris-ward.
                    *Here sound an English
     march. Enter, and pass over, Talbot and his Forces*
  There goes the Talbot, with his colours spread,
  And all the troops of English after him.
                              *A French march.
     Enter the Duke of Burgundy and his Forces*
  Now in the rearward comes the duke and his:
  Fortune in favour makes him lag behind.
  Summon a parley; we will talk with him.   *A parley*
CHARLES. A parley with the Duke of Burgundy!
BURGUNDY. Who craves a parley with the Burgundy?
JOAN. The princely Charles of France, thy countryman.
BURGUNDY. What sayst thou, Charles? for I am marching
    hence.
CHARLES. Speak, Pucelle, and enchant him with thy words.
JOAN. Brave Burgundy, undoubted hope of France!
  Stay, let thy humble handmaid speak to thee.
BURGUNDY. Speak on; but be not over-tedious.
JOAN. Look on thy country, look on fertile France,
  And see the cities and the towns defac'd
  By wasting ruin of the cruel foe.
  As looks the mother on her lowly babe

When death doth close his tender dying eyes,
See, see the pining malady of France;
Behold the wounds, the most unnatural wounds,
Which thou thyself hast given her woeful breast.
O! turn thy edged sword another way;
Strike those that hurt, and hurt not those that help.
One drop of blood drawn from thy country's bosom,
Should grieve thee more than streams of foreign gore:
Return thee therefore, with a flood of tears,
And wash away thy country's stained spots.

BURGUNDY. Either she hath bewitch'd me with her words,
Or nature makes me suddenly relent.

JOAN. Besides, all French and France exclaims on thee,
Doubting thy birth and lawful progeny.
Who join'st thou with but with a lordly nation
That will not trust thee but for profit's sake?
When Talbot hath set footing once in France,
And fashion'd thee that instrument of ill,
Who then but English Henry will be lord,
And thou be thrust out like a fugitive?
Call we to mind, and mark but this for proof,
Was not the Duke of Orleans thy foe,
And was he not in England prisoner?
But when they heard he was thine enemy,
They set him free, without his ransom paid,
In spite of Burgundy and all his friends.
See then, thou fight'st against thy countrymen!
And join'st with them will be thy slaughtermen.
Come, come, return; return, thou wand'ring lord;
Charles and the rest will take thee in their arms.

BURGUNDY. I am vanquished; these haughty words of hers
Have batter'd me like roaring cannon-shot,
And made me almost yield upon my knees.
Forgive me, country, and sweet countrymen!
And, lords, accept this hearty kind embrace:
My forces and my power of men are yours.
So, farewell, Talbot; I'll no longer trust thee.

JOAN. Done like a Frenchman: turn, and turn again!

CHARLES. Welcome, brave duke! thy friendship makes us
fresh.

THE BASTARD. And doth beget new courage in our breasts.

ALENÇON. Pucelle hath bravely play'd her part in this,

And doth deserve a coronet of gold.
CHARLES. Now let us on, my lords, and join our powers:
    And seek how we may prejudice the foe.   *Exeunt*

SCENE FOUR

Paris. A Room in the Palace.

Enter King Henry, Gloucester, Bishop of Winchester, York,
Suffolk, Somerset, Warwick, Exeter; Vernon, Basset, and
Others. To them with his Soldiers, Talbot

TALBOT. My gracious prince, and honourable peers,
    Hearing of your arrival in this realm,
    I have a while given truce unto my wars,
    To do my duty to my sovereign:
    In sign whereof, this arm,—that hath reclaim'd
    To your obedience fifty fortresses,
    Twelve cities, and seven walled towers of strength,
    Beside five hundred prisoners of esteem,—
    Lets fall his sword before your Highness' feet,   *Kneels*
    And with submissive loyalty of heart,
    Ascribes the glory of his conquest got,
    First to my God, and next unto your Grace.
KING HENRY. Is this the Lord Talbot, uncle Gloucester,
    That hath so long been resident in France?
GLOUCESTER. Yes, if it please your Majesty, my liege.
KING HENRY. Welcome, brave captain and victorious lord!
    When I was young,—as yet I am not old,—
    I do remember how my father said,
    A stouter champion never handled sword.
    Long since we were resolved of your truth,
    Your faithful service and your toil in war;
    Yet never have you tasted our reward,
    Or been reguerdon'd with so much as thanks,
    Because till now we never saw your face:
    Therefore, stand up; and for these good deserts,
    We here create you Earl of Shrewsbury;
    And in our coronation take your place.
                    Flourish. Exeunt all but Vernon and Basset
VERNON. Now, sir, to you, that were so hot at sea,
    Disgracing of these colours that I wear

In honour of my noble Lord of York,
Dar'st thou maintain the former words thou spak'st?

BASSET. Yes, sir: as well as you dare patronage
The envious barking of your saucy tongue
Against my lord the Duke of Somerset.

VERNON. Sirrah, thy lord I honour as he is.

BASSET. Why, what is he? as good a man as York.

VERNON. Hark ye; not so: in witness, take ye that.

Strikes him

BASSET. Villain, thou know'st the law of arms is such
That whoso draws a sword, 'tis present death,
Or else this blow should broach thy dearest blood.
But I 'll unto his Majesty, and crave
I may have liberty to venge this wrong;
When thou shalt see I 'll meet thee to thy cost.

VERNON. Well, miscreant, I 'll be there as soon as you;
And, after, meet you sooner than you would.   *Exeunt*

ACT FOUR

SCENE ONE

Paris. A Room of State.

Enter King Henry, Gloucester, Exeter, York, Suffolk, Somer-
set, the Bishop of Winchester, Warwick, Talbot,
the Governor of Paris, and Others

GLOUCESTER. Lord Bishop, set the crown upon his head.
WINCHESTER. God save King Henry, of that name the sixth.
GLOUCESTER. Now, Governor of Paris, take your oath,—
                                                Governor kneels
 That you elect no other king but him,
 Esteem none friends but such as are his friends,
 And none your foes but such as shall pretend
 Malicious practices against his state:
 This shall ye do, so help you righteous God!
                              Exeunt Governor and his Train
                              Enter Sir John Fastolfe.
FASTOLFE. My gracious sovereign, as I rode from Calais,
 To haste unto your coronation,
 A letter was deliver'd to my hands,
 Writ to your Grace from the Duke of Burgundy.
TALBOT. Shame to the Duke of Burgundy and thee!
 I vow'd, base knight, when I did meet thee next,
 To tear the garter from thy craven's lage;   *Plucking it off*
 Which I have done, because unworthily
 Thou wast installed in that high degree.
 Pardon me, princely Henry, and the rest:
 This dastard, at the battle of Patay,
 When but in all I was six thousand strong,
 And that the French were almost ten to one,
 Before we met or that a stroke was given,
 Like to a trusty squire did run away:
 In which assault we lost twelve hundred men;
 Myself, and divers gentlemen beside,

Were there surpris'd and taken prisoners.
Then judge, great lords, if I have done amiss;
Or whether that such cowards ought to wear
This ornament of knighthood, yea, or no?

GLOUCESTER. To say the truth, this fact was infamous
And ill beseeming any common man,
Much more a knight, a captain and a leader.

TALBOT. When first this order was ordain'd, my lords,
Knights of the garter were of noble birth,
Valiant and virtuous, full of haughty courage,
Such as were grown to credit by the wars;
Not fearing death, nor shrinking for distress,
But always resolute in most extremes.
He then that is not furnish'd in this sort
Doth but usurp the sacred name of knight,
Profaning this most honourable order;
And should—if I were worthy to be judge—
Be quite degraded, like a hedge-born swain
That doth presume to boast of gentle blood.

KING HENRY. Stain to thy countrymen! thou hear'st thy
    doom.
Be packing therefore, thou that wast a knight;
Henceforth we banish thee on pain of death. *Exit Fastolfe*
And now, my Lord Protector, view the letter
Sent from our uncle Duke of Burgundy.

GLOUCESTER (*Viewing superscription*) What means his
    Grace, that he hath chang'd his style?
No more but, plain and bluntly, 'To the King!'
Hath he forgot he is his sovereign?
Or doth this churlish superscription
Pretend some alteration in good will?
What's here? 'I have, upon especial cause,
Mov'd with compassion of my country's wrack,
Together with the pitiful complaints
Of such as your oppression feeds upon,
Forsaken your pernicious faction,
And join'd with Charles, the rightful King of France.'
O monstrous treachery! Can this be so,
That in alliance, amity, and oaths,
There should be found such false dissembling guile?

KING HENRY. What! doth my uncle Burgundy revolt?

GLOUCESTER. He doth, my lord, and is become your foe.

KING HENRY. Is that the worst this letter doth contain?

GLOUCESTER. It is the worst, and all, my lord, he writes.

KING HENRY. Why then, Lord Talbot there shall talk with
    him,
  And give him chastisement for this abuse.
  How say you, my lord? are you not content?

TALBOT. Content, my liege! Yes: but that I am prevented,
  I should have begg'd I might have been employ'd.

KING HENRY. Then gather strength, and march unto him
    straight:
  Let him perceive how ill we brook his treason,
  And what offence it is to flout his friends.

TALBOT. I go, my lord; in heart desiring still
  You may behold confusion of your foes.   *Exit*

       Enter Vernon and Basset

VERNON. Grant me the combat, gracious sovereign!

BASSET. And me, my lord; grant me the combat too!

YORK. This is my servant: hear him, noble prince!

SOMERSET. And this is mine: sweet Henry, favour him!

KING HENRY. Be patient, lords; and give them leave to
    speak.
  Say, gentlemen, what makes you thus exclaim?
  And wherefore crave you combat? or with whom?

VERNON. With him, my lord; for he hath done me wrong.

BASSET. And I with him; for he hath done me wrong.

KING HENRY. What is that wrong whereof you both com-
    plain?
  First let me know, and then I 'll answer you.

BASSET. Crossing the sea from England into France,
  This fellow here, with envious carping tongue,
  Upbraided me about the rose I wear;
  Saying, the sanguine colour of the leaves
  Did represent my master's blushing cheeks,
  When stubbornly he did repugn the truth
  About a certain question in the law
  Argu'd betwixt the Duke of York and him;
  With other vile and ignominious terms:
  In confutation of which rude reproach,
  And in defence of my lord's worthiness,
  I crave the benefit of law of arms.

VERNON. And that is my petition, noble lord:
  For though he seem with forged quaint conceit,

To set a gloss upon his bold intent,
Yet know, my lord, I was provok'd by him;
And he first took exceptions at this badge,
Pronouncing that the paleness of this flower
Bewray'd the faintness of my master's heart.

YORK. Will not this malice, Somerset, be left?

SOMERSET. Your private grudge, my Lord of York, will out,
Though ne'er so cunningly you smother it.

KING HENRY. Good Lord! what madness rules in brainsick
    men,
When, for so slight and frivolous a cause,
Such factious emulations shall arise!
Good cousins both, of York and Somerset,
Quiet yourselves, I pray, and be at peace.

YORK. Let this dissension first be tried by fight,
And then your Highness shall command a peace.

SOMERSET. The quarrel toucheth none but us alone;
Betwixt ourselves let us decide it, then.

YORK. There is my pledge; accept it, Somerset.

VERNON. Nay, let it rest where it began at first.

BASSET. Confirm it so, mine honourable lord.

GLOUCESTER. Confirm it so! Confounded be your strife!
And perish ye, with your audacious prate!
Presumptuous vassals! are you not asham'd,
With this immodest clamorous outrage
To trouble and disturb the king and us?—
And you, my lords, methinks you do not well
To bear with their perverse objections;
Much less to take occasion from their mouths
To raise a mutiny betwixt yourselves:
Let me persuade you take a better course.

EXETER. It grieves his Highness: good my lords, be friends.

KING HENRY. Come hither, you that would be combatants.
Henceforth I charge you, as you love our favour,
Quite to forget this quarrel and the cause.
And you, my lords, remember where we are;
In France, amongst a fickle wavering nation.
If they perceive dissension in our looks,
And that within ourselves we disagree,
How will their grudging stomachs be provok'd
To wilful disobedience, and rebel!
Beside, what infamy will there arise,

When foreign princes shall be certified
That for a toy, a thing of no regard,
King Henry's peers and chief nobility
Destroy'd themselves, and lost the realm of France!
O! think upon the conquest of my father,
My tender years, and let us not forego
That for a trifle that was bought with blood!
Let me be umpire in this doubtful strife.
I see no reason, if I wear this rose.   *Putting on a red rose*
That any one should therefore be suspicious
I more incline to Somerset than York:
Both are my kinsmen, and I love them both.
As well they may upbraid me with my crown,
Because, forsooth, the King of Scots is crown'd.
But your discretions better can persuade
Than I am able to instruct or teach:
And therefore, as we hither came in peace,
So let us still continue peace and love.
Cousin of York, we institute your Grace
To be our regent in these parts of France:
And, good my Lord of Somerset, unite
Your troops of horsemen with his bands of foot;
And like true subjects, sons of your progenitors,
Go cheerfully together and digest
Your angry choler on your enemies.
Ourself, my Lord Protector, and the rest,
After some respite will return to Calais;
From thence to England; where I hope ere long
To be presented, by your victories,
With Charles, Alençon, and that traitorous rout.

Flourish. Exeunt all
but York, Warwick, Exeter, and Vernon

WARWICK. My Lord of York, I promise you, the king
Prettily, methought, did play the orator.
YORK. And so he did; but yet I like it not,
In that he wears the badge of Somerset.
WARWICK. Tush! that was but his fancy, blame him not;
I dare presume, sweet prince, he thought no harm.
YORK. An if I wist he did,—But let it rest;
Other affairs must now be managed.

Exeunt York, Warwick, and Vernon

EXETER. Well didst thou, Richard, to suppress thy voice;

For had the passions of thy heart burst out,
I fear we should have seen decipher'd there
More rancorous spite, more furious raging broils,
Than yet can be imagin'd or suppos'd.
But howsoe'er, no simple man that sees
This jarring discord of nobility,
This shouldering of each other in the court,
This factious bandying of their favourites,
But that it doth presage some ill event.
'Tis much when sceptres are in children's hands;
But more, when envy breeds unkind division:
There comes the ruin, there begins confusion.   *Exit*

SCENE TWO

Before Bourdeaux.

Enter Talbot, with his Forces

TALBOT. Go to the gates of Bourdeaux, trumpeter;
Summon their general unto the wall.
          *Trumpet sounds a parley. Enter, on
the Walls, the General of the French Forces, and Others*
English John Talbot, captains, calls you forth,
Servant in arms to Harry King of England;
And thus he would: Open your city gates,
Be humble to us, call my sovereign yours,
And do him homage as obedient subjects,
And I 'll withdraw me and my bloody power;
But, if you frown upon this proffer'd peace,
You tempt the fury of my three attendants,
Lean famine, quartering steel, and climbing fire;
Who in a moment even with the earth
Shall lay your stately and air-braving towers,
If you forsake the offer of their love.
GENERAL. Thou ominous and fearful owl of death,
Our nation's terror and their bloody scourge!
The period of thy tyranny approacheth.
On us thou canst not enter but by death;
For, I protest, we are well fortified,
And strong enough to issue out and fight:
If thou retire, the Dauphin, well appointed,

Stands with the snares of war to tangle thee:
On either hand thee there are squadrons pitch'd,
To wall thee from the liberty of flight;
And no way canst thou turn thee for redress
But death doth front thee with apparent spoil,
And pale destruction meets thee in the face.
Ten thousand French have ta'en the sacrament,
To rive their dangerous artillery
Upon no Christian soul but English Talbot.
Lo! there thou stand'st, a breathing valiant man,
Of an invincible unconquer'd spirit:
This is the latest glory of thy praise,
That I, thy enemy, 'due thee withal;
For ere the glass, that now begins to run,
Finish the process of his sandy hour,
These eyes, that see thee now well coloured,
Shall see thee wither'd, bloody, pale, and dead.

Drum afar off

Hark! hark! the Dauphin's drum, a warning bell,
Sings heavy music to thy timorous soul;
And mine shall ring thy dire departure out.

Exeunt General, &c., from the Walls

TALBOT. He fables not; I hear the enemy:
Out, some light horsemen, and peruse their wings.
O! negligent and heedless discipline;
How are we park'd and bounded in a pale,
A little herd of England's timorous deer,
Maz'd with a yelping kennel of French curs!
If we be English deer, be then in blood;
Not rascal-like, to fall down with a pinch,
But rather moody-mad and desperate stags,
Turn on the bloody hounds with heads of steel,
And make the cowards stand aloof at bay:
Sell every man his life as dear as mine,
And they shall find dear deer of us, my friends.
God and Saint George, Talbot and England's right,
Prosper our colours in this dangerous fight!   *Exeunt*

SCENE THREE

Plains in Gascony.

Enter York, with Forces; to him a Messenger

YORK. Are not the speedy scouts return'd again,
    That dogg'd the mighty army of the Dauphin?
MESSENGER. They are return'd, my lord; and give it out
    That he is march'd to Bourdeaux with his power,
    To fight with Talbot. As he march'd along,
    By your espials were discovered
    Two mightier troops than that the Dauphin led,
    Which join'd with him and made their march for Bour-
        deaux.
YORK. A plague upon that villain Somerset,
    That thus delays my promised supply
    Of horsemen that were levied for this siege!
    Renowned Talbot doth expect my aid,
    And I am louted by a traitor villain,
    And cannot help the noble chevalier.
    God comfort him in this necessity!
    If he miscarry, farewell wars in France.
                Enter Sir William Lucy
LUCY. Thou princely leader of our English strength,
    Never so needful on the earth of France,
    Spur to the rescue of the noble Talbot,
    Who now is girdled with a waist of iron
    And hemm'd about with grim destruction.
    To Bourdeaux, warlike duke! To Bourdeaux, York!
    Else, farewell Talbot, France, and England's honour.
YORK. O God! that Somerset, who in proud heart
    Doth stop my cornets, were in Talbot's place;
    So should we save a valiant gentleman
    By forfeiting a traitor and a coward.
    Mad ire and wrathful fury, make me weep
    That thus we die, while remiss traitors sleep.
LUCY. O! send some succour to the distress'd lord.
YORK. He dies, we lose; I break my warlike word;
    We mourn, France smiles; we lose, they daily get;
    All 'long of this vile traitor Somerset.

LUCY. Then God take mercy on brave Talbot's soul;
    And on his son young John, whom two hours since
    I met in travel toward his warlike father.
    This seven years did not Talbot see his son;
    And now they meet where both their lives are done.
YORK. Alas! what joy shall noble Talbot have
    To bid his young son welcome to his grave?
    Away! vexation almost stops my breath
    That sunder'd friends greet in the hour of death.
    Lucy, farewell: no more my fortune can,
    But curse the cause I cannot aid the man.
    Maine, Blois, Poictiers, and Tours, are won away,
    'Long all of Somerset and his delay.

                              Exit, with his Soldiers

LUCY. Thus, while the vulture of sedition
    Feeds in the bosom of such great commanders,
    Sleeping neglection doth betray to loss
    The conquest of our scarce cold conqueror,
    That ever living man of memory,
    Henry the Fifth: Whiles they each other cross,
    Lives, honours, lands, and all hurry to loss.   *Exit*

SCENE FOUR

Other Plains in Gascony.

*Enter Somerset, with his Army; a Captain of Talbot's
with him*

SOMERSET. It is too late; I cannot send them now:
    This expedition was by York and Talbot
    Too rashly plotted: all our general force
    Might with a sally of the very town
    Be buckled with: the over-daring Talbot
    Hath sullied all his gloss of former honour
    By this unheedful, desperate, wild adventure:
    York set him on to fight and die in shame,
    That, Talbot dead, great York might bear the name.
CAPTAIN. Here is Sir William Lucy, who with me
    Set from our o'ermatch'd forces forth for aid.
                    Enter Sir William Lucy
SOMERSET. How now, Sir William! whither were you sent?

LUCY. Whither, my lord? from bought and sold Lord
    Talbot;
  Who, ring'd about with bold adversity,
  Cries out for noble York and Somerset,
  To beat assailing death from his weak legions:
  And whiles the honourable captain there
  Drops bloody sweat from his war-wearied limbs,
  And, in advantage lingering, looks for rescue,
  You, his false hopes, the trust of England's honour,
  Keep off aloof with worthless emulation.
  Let not your private discord keep away
  The levied succours that should lend him aid,
  While he, renowned noble gentleman,
  Yields up his life unto a world of odds:
  Orleans the Bastard, Charles, Burgundy,
  Alençon, Reignier, compass him about,
  And Talbot perisheth by your default.
SOMERSET. York set him on; York should have sent him aid.
LUCY. And York as fast upon your Grace exclaims;
  Swearing that you withhold his levied host
  Collected for this expedition.
SOMERSET. York lies; he might have sent and had the horse:
  I owe him little duty, and less love;
  And take foul scorn to fawn on him by sending.
LUCY. The fraud of England, not the force of France,
  Hath now entrapp'd the noble-minded Talbot.
  Never to England shall he bear his life,
  But dies, betray'd to fortune by your strife.
SOMERSET. Come, go; I will dispatch the horsemen straight:
  Within six hours they will be at his aid.
LUCY. Too late comes rescue: he is ta'en or slain,
  For fly he could not if he would have fled;
  And fly would Talbot never, though he might.
SOMERSET. If he be dead, brave Talbot, then adieu!
LUCY. His fame lives in the world, his shame in you.
                                        Exeunt

SCENE FIVE

The English Camp near Bourdeaux.

Enter Talbot and John his Son

TALBOT. O young John Talbot! I did send for thee
　　To tutor thee in stratagems of war,
　　That Talbot's name might be in thee reviv'd
　　When sapless age, and weak unable limbs
　　Should bring thy father to his drooping chair.
　　But,—O malignant and ill-boding stars!
　　Now thou art come unto a feast of death,
　　A terrible and unavoided danger:
　　Therefore, dear boy, mount on my swiftest horse,
　　And I 'll direct thee how thou shalt escape
　　By sudden flight: come, dally not, be gone.
JOHN. Is my name Talbot? and am I your son?
　　And shall I fly? O! if you love my mother,
　　Dishonour not her honourable name,
　　To make a bastard and a slave of me:
　　The world will say he is not Talbot's blood
　　That basely fled when noble Talbot stood.
TALBOT. Fly, to revenge my death, if I be slain.
JOHN. He that flies so will ne'er return again.
TALBOT. If we both stay, we both are sure to die.
JOHN. Then let me stay; and, father, do you fly:
　　Your loss is great, so your regard should be;
　　My worth unknown, no loss is known in me.
　　Upon my death the French can little boast;
　　In yours they will, in you all hopes are lost.
　　Flight cannot stain the honour you have won;
　　But mine it will that no exploit have done:
　　You fled for vantage everyone will swear;
　　But if I bow, they 'll say it was for fear.
　　There is no hope that ever I will stay
　　If the first hour I shrink and run away.
　　Here, on my knee, I beg mortality,
　　Rather than life preserv'd with infamy.
TALBOT. Shall all thy mother's hopes lie in one tomb?
JOHN. Ay, rather than I 'll shame my mother's womb.

TALBOT. Upon my blessing I command thee go.

JOHN. To fight I will, but not to fly the foe.

TALBOT. Part of thy father may be sav'd in thee.

JOHN. No part of him but will be shame in me.

TALBOT. Thou never hadst renown, nor canst not lose it.

JOHN. Yes, your renowned name: shall flight abuse it?

TALBOT. Thy father's charge shall clear thee from that stain.

JOHN. You cannot witness for me, being slain.
    If death be so apparent, then both fly.

TALBOT. And leave my followers here to fight and die?
    My age was never tainted with such shame.

JOHN. And shall my youth be guilty of such blame?
    No more can I be sever'd from your side
    Than can yourself yourself in twain divide.
    Stay, go, do what you will, the like do I;
    For live I will not if my father die.

TALBOT. Then here I take my leave of thee, fair son,
    Born to eclipse thy life this afternoon.
    Come, side by side together live and die,
    And soul with soul from France to heaven fly.   *Exeunt*

SCENE SIX

A Field of Battle.

*Alarum: Excursions, wherein Talbot's Son is hemmed
about, and Talbot rescues him*

TALBOT. Saint George and victory! fight, soldiers, fight!
    The regent hath with Talbot broke his word,
    And left us to the rage of France his sword.
    Where is John Talbot? Pause, and take thy breath:
    I gave thee life and rescued thee from death.

JOHN. O! twice my father, twice am I thy son:
    The life thou gav'st me first was lost and done,
    Till with thy warlike sword, despite of fate,
    To my determin'd time thou gavest new date.

TALBOT. When from the Dauphin's crest thy sword struck
        fire,
    It warm'd thy father's heart with proud desire

Of bold-fac'd victory. Then leaden age,
Quicken'd with youthful spleen and warlike rage,
Beat down Alençon, Orleans, Burgundy,
And from the pride of Gallia rescued thee.
The ireful bastard Orleans,—that drew blood
From thee, my boy, and had the maidenhood
Of thy first fight,—I soon encountered
And, interchanging blows, I quickly shed
Some of his bastard blood; and, in disgrace,
Bespoke him thus, 'Contaminated, base,
And misbegotten blood I spill of thine,
Mean and right poor, for that pure blood of mine
Which thou didst force from Talbot, my brave boy':
Here, purposing the Bastard to destroy,
Came in strong rescue. Speak, thy father's care,
Art thou not weary, John? How dost thou fare?
Wilt thou yet leave the battle, boy, and fly,
Now thou art seal'd the son of chivalry?
Fly, to revenge my death when I am dead;
The help of one stands me in little stead.
O! too much folly is it, well I wot,
To hazard all our lives in one small boat.
If I to-day die not with Frenchmen's rage,
To-morrow I shall die with mickle age:
By me they nothing gain an if I stay;
'Tis but the shortening of my life one day.
In thee thy mother dies, our household's name,
My death's revenge, thy youth, and England's fame.
All these and more we hazard by thy stay;
All these are sav'd if thou wilt fly away.
JOHN. The sword of Orleans hath not made me smart;
These words of yours draw life-blood from my heart.
On that advantage, bought with such a shame,
To save a paltry life and slay bright fame,
Before young Talbot from old Talbot fly,
The coward horse that bears me fall and die
And like me to the peasant boys of France,
To be shame's scorn and subject of mischance!
Surely, by all the glory you have won,
An if I fly, I am not Talbot's son:
Then talk no more of flight, it is no boot;
If son to Talbot, die at Talbot's foot.

TALBOT. Then follow thou thy desperate sire of Crete,
Thou Icarus. Thy life to me is sweet:
If thou wilt fight, fight by thy father's side,
And, commendable prov'd, let 's die in pride.   *Exeunt*

SCENE SEVEN

Another Part of the Field.

Alarum: Excursions. Enter Old Talbot, wounded,
led by a Servant

TALBOT. Where is my other life?—mine own is gone;—
O! where 's young Talbot? where is valiant John?
Triumphant death, smear'd with captivity,
Young Talbot's valour makes me smile at thee.
When he perceiv'd me shrink and on my knee,
His bloody sword he brandish'd over me,
And like a hungry lion did commence
Rough deeds of rage and stern impatience;
But when my angry guardant stood alone,
Tendering my ruin and assail'd of none,
Dizzy-ey'd fury and great rage of heart
Suddenly made him from my side to start
Into the clustering battle of the French;
And in that sea of blood my boy did drench
His overmounting spirit; and there died
My Icarus, my blossom, in his pride.
    Enter Soldiers, bearing the body of Young Talbot
SERVANT. O, my dear lord! lo, where your son is borne!
TALBOT. Thou antick, death, which laugh'st us here to
    scorn,
Anon, from thy insulting tyranny,
Coupled in bonds of perpetuity,
Two Talbots, winged through the lither sky,
In thy despite shall 'scape mortality.
O! thou, whose wounds become hard-favour'd death,
Speak to thy father ere thou yield thy breath;
Brave death by speaking whether he will or no;
Imagine him a Frenchman and thy foe.
Poor boy! he smiles, methinks, as who should say,
Had death been French, then death had died to-day.
Come, come, and lay him in his father's arms:
My spirit can no longer bear these harms.

Soldiers, adieu! I have what I would have,
Now my old arms are young John Talbot's grave.   *Dies*
                Alarums. Exeunt Soldiers and Servant,
leaving the two bodies. Enter Charles, Alençon, Burgundy,
    the Bastard of Orleans, Joan la Pucelle, and Forces

CHARLES. Had York and Somerset brought rescue in
We should have found a bloody day of this.

THE BASTARD. How the young whelp of Talbot's, raging-
    wood,
Did flesh his puny sword in Frenchmen's blood!

JOAN. Once I encounter'd him, and thus I said:
'Thou maiden youth, be vanquish'd by a maid':
But with a proud majestical high scorn,
He answer'd thus: 'Young Talbot was not born
To be the pillage of a giglot wench.'
So, rushing in the bowels of the French,
He left me proudly, as unworthy fight.

BURGUNDY. Doubtless he would have made a noble knight;
See, where he lies inhearsed in the arms
Of the most bloody nurser of his harms.

THE BASTARD. Hew them to pieces, hack their bones
    asunder,
Whose life was England's glory, Gallia's wonder.

CHARLES. O, no! forbear; for that which we have fled
During the life, let us not wrong it dead.
            Enter Sir William Lucy,
        attended: a French Herald preceding

LUCY. Herald, conduct me to the Dauphin's tent,
To know who hath obtain'd the glory of the day.

CHARLES On what submissive message art thou sent?

LUCY. Submission, Dauphin! 'tis a mere French word;
We English warriors wot not what it means.
I come to know what prisoners thou hast ta'en,
And to survey the bodies of the dead.

CHARLES. For prisoners ask'st thou? hell our prison is.
But tell me whom thou seek'st.

LUCY. Where is the great Alcides of the field,
Valiant Lord Talbot, Earl of Shrewsbury?
Created, for his rare success in arms,
Great Earl of Washford, Waterford, and Valence;
Lord Talbot of Goodrig and Urchinfield,
Lord Strange of Blackmere, Lord Verdun of Alton,

Lord Cromwell of Wingfield, Lord Furnival of Sheffield,
The thrice-victorious Lord of Falconbridge;
Knight of the noble order of Saint George,
Worthy Saint Michael and the Golden Fleece;
Great Mareschal to Henry the Sixth
Of all his wars within the realm of France?

JOAN. Here is a silly stately style indeed!
The Turk, that two-and-fifty kingdoms hath,
Writes not so tedious a style as this.
Him that thou magnifiest with all these titles,
Stinking and fly-blown lies here at our feet.

LUCY. Is Talbot slain, the Frenchmen's only scourge,
Your kingdom's terror and black Nemesis?
O! were mine eye-balls into bullets turn'd,
That I in rage might shoot them at your faces!
O! that I could but call these dead to life!
It were enough to fright the realm of France.
Were but his picture left among you here
It would amaze the proudest of you all.
Give me their bodies, that I may bear them hence,
And give them burial as beseems their worth.

JOAN. I think this upstart is old Talbot's ghost,
He speaks with such a proud commanding spirit.
For God's sake, let him have 'em; to keep them here
They would but stink and putrefy the air.

CHARLES. Go, take their bodies hence.

LUCY.   I 'll bear them hence:
But from their ashes shall be rear'd
A phœnix that shall make all France afeard.

CHARLES. So we be rid of them, do with 'em what thou wilt.
And now to Paris, in this conquering vein:
All will be ours now bloody Talbot's slain.   *Exeunt*

ACT FIVE

SCENE ONE

London. A Room in the Palace.

Enter King Henry, Gloucester, and Exeter

KING HENRY. Have you perus'd the letters from the pope,
   The emperor, and the Earl of Armagnac?
GLOUCESTER. I have, my lord; and their intent is this:
   They humbly sue unto your excellence
   To have a godly peace concluded of
   Between the realms of England and of France.
KING HENRY. How doth your Grace affect their motion?
GLOUCESTER. Well, my good lord; and as the only means
   To stop effusion of our Christian blood,
   And stablish quietness on every side.
KING HENRY. Ay, marry, uncle; for I always thought
   It was both impious and unnatural
   That such immanity and bloody strife
   Should reign among professors of one faith.
GLOUCESTER. Beside, my lord, the sooner to effect
   And surer bind this knot of amity,
   The Earl of Armagnac, near knit to Charles,
   A man of great authority in France,
   Proffers his only daughter to your Grace
   In marriage, with a large and sumptuous dowry.
KING HENRY. Marriage, uncle! alas! my years are young,
   And fitter is my study and my books
   Than wanton dalliance with a paramour.
   Yet call the ambassadors; and, as you please,
   So let them have their answers every one:
   I shall be well content with any choice
   Tends to God's glory and my country's weal.
      Enter a Legate, and two Ambassadors, with
   Winchester, now Cardinal Beaufort, and habited accordingly

EXETER. (*Aside*) What! is my Lord of Winchester install'd,
And call'd unto a cardinal's degree?
Then, I perceive that will be verified
Henry the Fifth did sometime prophesy,—
'If once he come to be a cardinal,
He 'll make his cap co-equal with the crown.'

KING HENRY. My Lords Ambassadors, your several suits
Have been consider'd, and debated on.
Your purpose is both good and reasonable;
And therefore are we certainly resolv'd
To draw conditions of a friendly peace;
Which by my Lord of Winchester we mean
Shall be transported presently to France.

GLOUCESTER. And for the proffer of my lord your master,
I have inform'd his Highness so at large,
As,—liking of the lady's virtuous gifts
Her beauty, and the value of her dower,—
He doth intend she shall be England's queen.

KING HENRY. (*To the Ambassador*) In argument and proof
of which contract,
Bear her this jewel, pledge of my affection.
And so, my Lord Protector, see them guarded,
And safely brought to Dover; where inshipp'd
Commit them to the fortune of the sea.

> *Exeunt King Henry and Train;*
> *Gloucester, Exeter, and Ambassadors*

CARDINAL. Stay, my Lord Legate: you shall first receive
The sum of money which I promised
Should be deliver'd to his Holiness
For clothing me in these grave ornaments.

LEGATE. I will attend upon your lordship's leisure.

CARDINAL. (*Aside*) Now Winchester will not submit, I trow,
Or be inferior to the proudest peer.
Humphrey of Gloucester, thou shalt well perceive
That neither in birth or for authority
The bishop will be overborne by thee:
I 'll either make thee stoop and bend thy knee,
Or sack this country with a mutiny.   *Exeunt*

SCENE TWO

France. Plains in Anjou.

*Enter Charles, Burgundy, Alençon, Joan la Pucelle,
and Forces, marching*

CHARLES. These news, my lord, may cheer our drooping
        spirits;
    'Tis said the stout Parisians do revolt,
    And turn again unto the warlike French.
ALENÇON. Then, march to Paris, royal Charles of France,
    And keep not back your powers in dalliance.
JOAN. Peace be amongst them if they turn to us;
    Else, ruin combat with their palaces!
                Enter a Scout
SCOUT. Success unto our valiant general,
    And happiness to his accomplices!
CHARLES. What tidings send our scouts? I prithee speak.
SCOUT. The English army, that divided was
    Into two parties, is now conjoin'd in one,
    And means to give you battle presently.
CHARLES. Somewhat too sudden, sirs, the warning is:
    But we will presently provide for them.
BURGUNDY. I trust the ghost of Talbot is not there:
    Now he is gone, my lord, you need not fear.
JOAN. Of all base passions, fear is most accurs'd.
    Command the conquest, Charles, it shall be thine;
    Let Henry fret and all the world repine.
CHARLES. Then on, my lords; and France be fortunate!
                                            Exeunt

SCENE THREE

France. Before Angiers.

Alarum: Excursions. Enter Joan la Pucelle

JOAN. The regent conquers and the Frenchmen fly.
    Now help, ye charming spells and periapts;
    And ye choice spirits that admonish me
    And give me signs of future accidents: *Thunder*

You speedy helpers, that are substitutes
Under the lordly monarch of the north,
Appear, and aid me in this enterprise!
Enter Fiends
This speedy and quick appearance argues proof
Of your accustom'd diligence to me.
Now, ye familiar spirits, that are cull'd
Out of the powerful regions under earth,
Help me this once, that France may get the field.
They walk, and speak not
O! hold me not with silence over-long.
Where I was wont to feed you with my blood,
I 'll lop a member off and give it you,
In earnest of a further benefit,
So you do condescend to help me now.
They hang their heads
No hope to have redress? My body shall
Pay recompense, if you will grant my suit.
They shake their heads
Cannot my body nor blood-sacrifice
Entreat you to your wonted furtherance?
Then take my soul; my body, soul, and all,
Before that England give the French the foil. *They depart*
See! they forsake me. Now the time is come,
That France must vail her lofty-plumed crest,
And let her head fall into England's lap.
My ancient incantations are too weak,
And hell too strong for me to buckle with:
Now, France, thy glory droopeth to the dust.   *Exit*
Alarum. Enter French and English fighting:
Joan la Pucelle and York fight hand to hand: Joan la
Pucelle is taken. The French fly
YORK. Damsel of France, I think I have you fast:
Unchain your spirits now with spelling charms,
And try if they can gain your liberty.
A goodly prize, fit for the devil's grace!
See how the ugly witch doth bend her brows,
As if with Circe she would change my shape.
JOAN. Chang'd to a worser shape thou canst not be.
YORK. O! Charles the Dauphin is a proper man;
No shape but his can please your dainty eye.

JOAN. A plaguing mischief light on Charles and thee!
  And may ye both be suddenly surpris'd
  By bloody hands, in sleeping on your beds!
YORK. Fell banning hag, enchantress, hold thy tongue!
JOAN. I prithee, give me leave to curse a while.
YORK. Curse, miscreant, when thou comest to the stake.

Exeunt

Alarum. Enter Suffolk, with Margaret in his hand
SUFFOLK. Be what thou wilt, thou art my prisoner.

Gazes on her

  O fairest beauty! do not fear nor fly,
  For I will touch thee but with reverent hands.
  I kiss these fingers for eternal peace,
  And lay them gently on thy tender side.
  What art thou? say, that I may honour thee.
MARGARET. Margaret my name, and daughter to a king,
  The King of Naples, whosoe'er thou art.
SUFFOLK. An earl I am, and Suffolk am I call'd.
  Be not offended, nature's miracle,
  Thou art allotted to be ta'en by me:
  So doth the swan her downy cygnets save,
  Keeping them prisoners underneath her wings.
  Yet if this servile usage once offend,
  Go and be free again, as Suffolk's friend.

She turns away as going

  O stay! I have no power to let her pass;
  My hand would free her, but my heart says no.
  As plays the sun upon the glassy streams,
  Twinkling another counterfeited beam,
  So seems this gorgeous beauty to mine eyes.
  Fain would I woo her, yet I dare not speak:
  I'll call for pen and ink and write my mind.
  Fie, De la Pole! disable not thyself;
  Hast not a tongue? is she not here thy prisoner?
  Wilt thou be daunted at a woman's sight?
  Ay; beauty's princely majesty is such
  Confounds the tongue and makes the senses rough.
MARGARET. Say, Earl of Suffolk,—if thy name be so,—
  What ransom must I pay before I pass?
  For I perceive I am thy prisoner.
SUFFOLK. (*Aside*) How canst thou tell she will deny thy suit,
  Before thou make a trial of her love?

MARGARET. Why speak'st thou not? what ransom must I
     pay?
SUFFOLK. (*Aside*) She 's beautiful and therefore to be woo'd,
     She is a woman, therefore to be won.
MARGARET. Wilt thou accept of ransom, yea or no?
SUFFOLK. (*Aside*) Fond man! remember that thou hast a
     wife;
     Then how can Margaret be thy paramour?
MARGARET. I were best to leave him, for he will not hear.
SUFFOLK. (*Aside*) There all is marr'd; there lies a cooling
     card.
MARGARET. He talks at random; sure, the man is mad.
SUFFOLK. (*Aside*) And yet a dispensation may be had.
MARGARET. And yet I would that you would answer me.
SUFFOLK. (*Aside*) I 'll win this Lady Margaret. For whom?
     Why, for my king: tush! that 's a wooden thing.
MARGARET. (*Overhearing him*) He talks of wood: it is some
     carpenter.
SUFFOLK. (*Aside*) Yet so my fancy may be satisfied,
     And peace established between these realms.
     But there remains a scruple in that too;
     For though her father be the King of Naples,
     Duke of Anjou and Maine, yet is he poor,
     And our nobility will scorn the match.
MARGARET. Hear ye, captain? Are you not at leisure?
SUFFOLK. (*Aside*) It shall be so, disdain they ne'er so much:
     Henry is youthful and will quickly yield.
     Madam, I have a secret to reveal.
MARGARET. (*Aside*) What though I be enthrall'd? he seems
     a knight,
     And will not any way dishonour me.
SUFFOLK. Lady, vouchsafe to listen what I say.
MARGARET. (*Aside*) Perhaps I shall be rescu'd by the
     French;
     And then I need not crave his courtesy.
SUFFOLK. Sweet madam, give me hearing in a cause—
MARGARET. Tush, women have been captivate ere now.
SUFFOLK. Lady, wherefore talk you so?
MARGARET. I cry you mercy, 'tis but quid for quo.
SUFFOLK. Say, gentle princess, would you not suppose
     Your bondage happy to be made a queen?
MARGARET. To be a queen in bondage is more vile

Than is a slave in base servility;
For princes should be free.
SUFFOLK.   And so shall you,
If happy England's royal king be free.
MARGARET. Why, what concerns his freedom unto me?
SUFFOLK. I 'll undertake to make thee Henry's queen,
To put a golden sceptre in thy hand
And set a precious crown upon thy head,
If thou wilt condescend to be my—
MARGARET.   What?
SUFFOLK.   His love.
MARGARET. I am unworthy to be Henry's wife.
SUFFOLK. No, gentle madam; I unworthy am
To woo so fair a dame to be his wife
And have no portion in the choice myself.
How say you, madam, are you so content?
MARGARET. An if my father please, I am content.
SUFFOLK. Then call our captains and our colours forth!
And, madam, at your father's castle walls
We 'll crave a parley, to confer with him.

Troops come forward

A Parley sounded. Enter Reignier on the Walls

SUFFOLK. See, Reignier, see thy daughter prisoner!
REIGNIER. To whom?
SUFFOLK.   To me.
REIGNIER.   Suffolk, what remedy?
I am a soldier, and unapt to weep,
Or to exclaim on Fortune's fickleness.
SUFFOLK. Yes, there is remedy enough, my lord:
Consent, and for thy honour, give consent,
Thy daughter shall be wedded to my king,
Whom I with pain have woo'd and won thereto;
And this her easy-held imprisonment
Hath gain'd thy daughter princely liberty.
REIGNIER. Speaks Suffolk as he thinks?
SUFFOLK.   Fair Margaret knows
That Suffolk doth not flatter, face, or feign.
REIGNIER. Upon thy princely warrant, I descend
To give thee answer of thy just demand.

Exit from the walls

SUFFOLK. And here I will expect thy coming.

Trumpets sound. Enter Reignier, below

REIGNIER. Welcome, brave earl, into our territories:
　Command in Anjou what your honour pleases.
SUFFOLK. Thanks, Reignier, happy for so sweet a child,
　Fit to be made companion with a king.
　What answer makes your Grace unto my suit?
REIGNIER. Since thou dost deign to woo her little worth
　To be the princely bride of such a lord,
　Upon condition I may quietly
　Enjoy mine own, the county Maine and Anjou,
　Free from oppression or the stroke of war,
　My daughter shall be Henry's if he please.
SUFFOLK. That is her ransom; I deliver her;
　And those two counties I will undertake
　Your Grace shall well and quietly enjoy.
REIGNIER. And I again, in Henry's royal name,
　As deputy unto that gracious king,
　Give thee her hand for sign of plighted faith.
SUFFOLK. Reignier of France, I give thee kingly thanks,
　Because this is in traffic of a king:
　(*Aside*) And yet, methinks, I could be well content
　To be mine own attorney in this case.
　I 'll over then, to England with this news,
　And make this marriage to be solemniz'd.
　So farewell, Reignier: set this diamond safe,
　In golden palaces, as it becomes.
REIGNIER. I do embrace thee, as I would embrace
　The Christian prince, King Henry, were he here.
MARGARET. Farewell, my lord. Good wishes, praise, and
　　prayers
　Shall Suffolk ever have of Margaret.　　　　　　*Going*
SUFFOLK. Farewell, sweet madam! but hark you, Margaret;
　No princely commendations to my king?
MARGARET. Such commendations as become a maid,
　A virgin, and his servant, say to him.
SUFFOLK. Words sweetly plac'd and modestly directed.
　But madam, I must trouble you again,
　No loving token to his Majesty?
MARGARET. Yes, my good lord; a pure unspotted heart,
　Never yet taint with love, I send the king.
SUFFOLK. And this withal.　　　　　　　　　*Kisses her*
MARGARET. That for thyself: I will not so presume,
　To send such peevish tokens to a king.

Exeunt Reignier and Margaret

SUFFOLK. O! wert thou for myself! But Suffolk, stay;
Thou mayst not wander in that labyrinth;
There Minotaurs and ugly treasons lurk.
Solicit Henry with her wondrous praise:
Bethink thee on her virtues that surmount
And natural graces that extinguish art;
Repeat their semblance often on the seas,
That, when thou com'st to kneel at Henry's feet,
Thou mayst bereave him of his wits with wonder.   *Exit*

SCENE FOUR

Camp of the Duke of York, in Anjou.

Enter York, Warwick, and Others

YORK. Bring forth that sorceress, condemn'd to burn.
Enter Joan la Pucelle, guarded; and a Shepherd
SHEPHERD. Ah, Joan; this kills thy father's heart outright.
Have I sought every country far and near,
And, now it is my chance to find thee out,
Must I behold thy timeless cruel death?
Ah, Joan! sweet daughter Joan, I 'll die with thee.
JOAN. Decrepit miser! base ignoble wretch!
I am descended of a gentler blood:
Thou art no father nor no friend of mine.
SHEPHERD. Out, out! My lords, an please you, 'tis not so;
I did beget her, all the parish knows:
Her mother liveth yet, can testify
She was the first fruit of my bachelorship.
WARWICK. Graceless! wilt thou deny thy parentage?
YORK. This argues what her kind of life hath been:
Wicked and vile; and so her death concludes.
SHEPHERD. Fie, Joan, that thou wilt be so obstacle!
God knows, thou art a collop of my flesh;
And for thy sake have I shed many a tear:
Deny me not, I prithee, gentle Joan.
JOAN. Peasant, avaunt! You have suborn'd this man,
Of purpose to obscure my noble birth.
SHEPHERD. 'Tis true, I gave a noble to the priest,
The morn that I was wedded to her mother.

Kneel down and take my blessing, good my girl.
Wilt thou not stoop? Now cursed be the time
Of thy nativity! I would the milk
Thy mother gave thee, when thou suck'dst her breast,
Had been a little ratsbane for thy sake!
Or else, when thou didst keep my lambs a-field
I wish some ravenous wolf had eaten thee!
Dost thou deny thy father, cursed drab?
O! burn her, burn her! hanging is too good.   *Exit*

YORK. Take her away; for she hath liv'd too long,
To fill the world with vicious qualities.

JOAN. First, let me tell you whom you have condemn'd:
Not me begotten of a shepherd swain,
But issu'd from the progeny of kings;
Virtuous and holy; chosen from above,
By inspiration of celestial grace,
To work exceeding miracles on earth.
I never had to do with wicked spirits:
But you,—that are polluted with your lusts,
Stain'd with the guiltless blood of innocents,
Corrupt and tainted with a thousand vices,—
Because you want the grace that others have,
You judge it straight a thing impossible
To compass wonders but by help of devils.
No, misconceived! Joan of Arc hath been
A virgin from her tender infancy,
Chaste and immaculate in very thought;
Whose maiden blood, thus rigorously effus'd,
Will cry for vengeance at the gates of heaven.

YORK. Ay, ay: away with her to execution!

WARWICK. And hark ye, sirs; because she is a maid,
Spare for no faggots, let there be enow:
Place barrels of pitch upon the fatal stake,
That so her torture may be shortened.

JOAN. Will nothing turn your unrelenting hearts?
Then, Joan, discover thine infirmity;
That warranteth by law to be thy privilege.
I am with child, ye bloody homicides:
Murder not then the fruit within my womb,
Although ye hale me to a violent death.

YORK. Now, heaven forefend! the holy maid with child!

WARWICK. The greatest miracle that e'er ye wrought!

Is all your strict preciseness come to this?

YORK. She and the Dauphin have been juggling:
I did imagine what would be her refuge.

WARWICK. Well, go to; we will have no bastards live;
Especially since Charles must father it.

JOAN. You are deceiv'd; my child is none of his:
It was Alencon that enjoy'd my love.

YORK. Alençon! that notorious Machiavel!
It dies an if it had a thousand lives.

JOAN. O! give me leave, I have deluded you:
'Twas neither Charles, nor yet the duke I nam'd,
But Reignier, King of Naples, that prevail'd.

WARWICK. A married man: that's most intolerable.

YORK. Why, here's a girl! I think she knows not well,
There were so many, whom she may accuse.

WARWICK. It's sign she hath been liberal and free.

YORK. And yet, forsooth, she is a virgin pure.
Strumpet, thy words condemn thy brat and thee:
Use no entreaty, for it is in vain.

JOAN. Then lead me hence; with whom I leave my curse:
May never glorious sun reflex his beams
Upon the country where you make abode;
But darkness and the gloomy shade of death
Environ you, till mischief and despair
Drive you to break your necks or hang yourselves!

Exit, guarded

YORK. Break thou in pieces and consume to ashes,
Thou foul accursed minister of hell!

Enter Cardinal Beaufort, attended

CARDINAL. Lord Regent, I do greet your Excellence
With letters of commission from the king.
For know, my lords, the states of Christendom,
Mov'd with remorse of these outrageous broils,
Have earnestly implor'd a general peace
Betwixt our nation and the aspiring French;
And here at hand the Dauphin, and his train,
Approacheth to confer about some matter.

YORK. Is all our travail turn'd to this effect?
After the slaughter of so many peers,
So many captains, gentlemen, and soldiers,
That in this quarrel have been overthrown,
And sold their bodies for their country's benefit,

Shall we at last conclude effeminate peace?
Have we not lost most part of all the towns,
By treason, falsehood, and by treachery,
Our great progenitors had conquered?
O! Warwick, Warwick! I foresee with grief
The utter loss of all the realm of France.

WARWICK. Be patient, York: if we conclude a peace,
It shall be with such strict and severe covenants
As little shall the Frenchmen gain thereby.

Enter Charles, attended;
Alençon, the Bastard of Orleans, Reignier, and Others

CHARLES. Since, lords of England, it is thus agreed,
That peaceful truce shall be proclaim'd in France,
We come to be informed by yourselves
What the conditions of that league must be.

YORK. Speak, Winchester; for boiling choler chokes
The hollow passage of my poison'd voice,
By sight of these our baleful enemies.

CARDINAL. Charles, and the rest, it is enacted thus:
That, in regard King Henry gives consent,
Of mere compassion and of lenity,
To ease your country of distressful war,
And suffer you to breathe in fruitful peace,
You shall become true liegemen to his crown:
And, Charles, upon condition thou wilt swear
To pay him tribute, and submit thyself,
Thou shalt be plac'd as viceroy under him,
And still enjoy the regal dignity.

ALENÇON. Must he be then as shadow of himself?
Adorn his temples with a coronet,
And yet, in substance and authority,
Retain but privilege of a private man?
This proffer is absurd and reasonless.

CHARLES. 'Tis known already that I am possess'd
With more than half the Gallian territories,
And therein reverenc'd for their lawful king:
Shall I, for lucre of the rest unvanquish'd,
Detract so much from that prerogative
As to be call'd but viceroy of the whole?
No, Lord Ambassador; I'll rather keep
That which I have than, coveting for more,
Be cast from possibility of all.

YORK. Insulting Charles! hast thou by secret means
  Us'd intercession to obtain a league,
  And now the matter grows to compromise,
  Stand'st thou aloof upon comparison?
  Either accept the title thou usurp'st,
  Of benefit proceeding from our king
  And not of any challenge of desert,
  Or we will plague thee with incessant wars.
REIGNIER. My lord, you do not well in obstinacy
  To cavil in the course of this contract:
  If once it be neglected, ten to one,
  We shall not find like opportunity.
ALENÇON. (*Aside to Charles*) To say the truth, it is your
    policy
  To save your subjects from such massacre
  And ruthless slaughters as are daily seen
  By our proceeding in hostility;
  And therefore take this compact of a truce,
  Although you break it when your pleasure serves.
WARWICK. How sayst thou, Charles? shall our condition
    stand?
CHARLES. It shall;
  Only reserv'd, you claim no interest
  In any of our towns of garrison.
YORK. Then swear allegiance to his Majesty;
  As thou art knight, never to disobey
  Nor be rebellious to the crown of England,
  Thou, nor thy nobles, to the crown of England.
                    Charles, &c., give tokens of fealty
  So, now dismiss your army when ye please;
  Hang up your ensigns, let your drums be still,
  For here we entertain a solemn peace.   *Exeunt*

SCENE FIVE

London. A Room in the Palace

*Enter King Henry, in conference with Suffolk; Gloucester
and Exeter following*

KING HENRY. Your wondrous rare description, noble earl,
  Of beauteous Margaret hath astonish'd me:

Her virtues, graced with external gifts
Do breed love's settled passions in my heart:
And like as rigour of tempestuous gusts
Provokes the mightiest hulk against the tide,
So am I driven by breath of her renown
Either to suffer shipwrack, or arrive
Where I may have fruition of her love.

SUFFOLK. Tush! my good lord, this superficial tale
Is but a preface of her worthy praise:
The chief perfections of that lovely dame—
Had I sufficient skill to utter them—
Would make a volume of enticing lines,
Able to ravish any dull conceit:
And, which is more, she is not so divine,
So full replete with choice of all delights,
But with as humble lowliness of mind
She is content to be at your command;
Command, I mean, of virtuous chaste intents,
To love and honour Henry as her lord.

KING HENRY. And otherwise will Henry ne'er presume.
Therefore, my Lord Protector, give consent
That Margaret may be England's royal queen.

GLOUCESTER. So should I give consent to flatter sin.
You know, my lord, your Highness is betroth'd
Unto another lady of esteem;
How shall we then dispense with that contract,
And not deface your honour with reproach?

SUFFOLK. As doth a ruler with unlawful oaths;
Or one that, at a triumph having vow'd
To try his strength, forsaketh yet the lists
By reason of his adversary's odds.
A poor earl's daughter is unequal odds,
And therefore may be broke without offence.

GLOUCESTER. Why, what, I pray, is Margaret more than
        that?
Her father is no better than an earl,
Although in glorious titles he excel.

SUFFOLK. Yes, my good lord, her father is a king,
The King of Naples and Jerusalem;
And of such great authority in France
As his alliance will confirm our peace,
And keep the Frenchmen in allegiance.

GLOUCESTER. And so the Earl of Armagnac may do,
    Because he is near kinsman unto Charles.
EXETER. Beside, his wealth doth warrant liberal dower,
    Where Reignier sooner will receive than give.
SUFFOLK. A dower, my lords! disgrace not so your king,
    That he should be so abject, base, and poor,
    To choose for wealth and not for perfect love.
    Henry is able to enrich his queen,
    And not to seek a queen to make him rich:
    So worthless peasants bargain for their wives,
    As market-men for oxen, sheep, or horse.
    Marriage is a matter of more worth
    Than to be dealt in by attorneyship:
    Not whom we will, but whom his Grace affects,
    Must be companion of his nuptial bed;
    And therefore, lords, since he affects her most,
    It most of all these reasons bindeth us,
    In our opinions she should be preferr'd.
    For what is wedlock forced, but a hell,
    An age of discord and continual strife?
    Whereas the contrary bringeth bliss,
    And is a pattern of celestial peace.
    Whom should we match with Henry, being a king,
    But Margaret, that is daughter to a king?
    Her peerless feature, joined with her birth,
    Approves her fit for none but for a king:
    Her valiant courage and undaunted spirit—
    More than in women commonly is seen—
    Will answer our hope in issue of a king;
    For Henry, son unto a conqueror,
    Is likely to beget more conquerors,
    If with a lady of so high resolve
    As is fair Margaret he be link'd in love.
    Then yield, my lords; and here conclude with me
    That Margaret shall be queen, and none but she.
KING HENRY. Whether it be through force of your report,
    My noble lord of Suffolk, or for that
    My tender youth was never yet attaint
    With any passion of inflaming love,
    I cannot tell; but this I am assur'd,
    I feel such sharp dissension in my breast,
    Such fierce alarums both of hope and fear,

As I am sick with working of my thoughts.
Take, therefore, shipping; post, my lord, to France;
Agree to any covenants, and procure
That Lady Margaret do vouchsafe to come
To cross the seas to England and be crown'd
King Henry's faithful and anointed queen:
For your expenses and sufficient charge,
Among the people gather up a tenth.
Be gone, I say; for till you do return
I rest perplexed with a thousand cares.
And you, good uncle, banish all offence:
If you do censure me by what you were,
Not what you are, I know it will excuse
This sudden execution of my will.
And so, conduct me, where, from company
I may revolve and ruminate my grief.   *Exit*
GLOUCESTER. Ay, grief, I fear me, both at first and last.
                    Exeunt Gloucester and Exeter
SUFFOLK. Thus Suffolk hath prevail'd; and thus he goes,
As did the youthful Paris once to Greece;
With hope to find the like event in love,
But prosper better than the Trojan did.
Margaret shall now be queen, and rule the king;
But I will rule both her, the king, and realm.   *Exit*

THE SECOND PART OF KING HENRY THE SIXTH

CAST OF CHARACTERS

KING HENRY THE SIXTH
HUMPHREY, *Duke of Gloucester, his Uncle*
CARDINAL BEAUFORT, *Bishop of Winchester, Great-Uncle to the King*
RICHARD PLANTAGENET, *Duke of York*
EDWARD *and* RICHARD, *his Sons*

DUKE OF SOMERSET
DUKE OF SUFFOLK
DUKE OF BUCKINGHAM } *Of the King's Party*
LORD CLIFFORD
YOUNG CLIFFORD, *his Son*

EARL OF SALISBURY } *of the York Faction*
EARL OF WARWICK

LORD SCALES, *Governor of the Tower*
SIR HUMPHREY STAFFORD, *and* WILLIAM STAFFORD, *his Brother*
LORD SAY
A Sea-Captain, Master, and Master's Mate
WALTER WHITMORE
SIR JOHN STANLEY
Two Gentlemen, prisoners with Suffolk
VAUX
MATTHEW GOFFE
JOHN HUME *and* JOHN SOUTHWELL, *Priests*
BOLINGBROKE, *a Conjurer*
A Spirit raised by him
THOMAS HORNER, *an Armourer*
PETER, *his Man*
Clerk of Chatham
Mayor of St. Alban's
SIMPCOX, *an Impostor*

(*continued on next page*)

Two Murderers
JACK CADE, *a Rebel*
GEORGE BEVIS, JOHN HOLLAND, DICK *the Butcher,*
SMITH *the Weaver,* MICHAEL, *&c., Followers of
Cade*
ALEXANDER IDEN, *a Kentish Gentleman*

MARGARET, *Queen to King Henry*
ELEANOR, *Duchess of Gloucester*
MARGERY JOURDAIN, *a Witch*
Wife to Simpcox

Lords, Ladies, and Attendants; Herald, Petitioners,
Aldermen, a Beadle, Sheriff, and Officers; Citizens,
Prentices, Falconers, Guards, Soldiers, Messengers,
&c.

SCENE

In various parts of England

THE SECOND PART OF KING HENRY THE SIXTH

ACT ONE

SCENE ONE

London. A Room of State in the Palace.

Flourish of Trumpets: then hautboys. Enter, on one side, King Henry, Duke of Gloucester, Salisbury, Warwick, and Cardinal Beaufort; on the other, Queen Margaret, led in by Suffolk; York, Somerset, Buckingham, and Others, following

SUFFOLK. As by your high imperial Majesty
   I had in charge at my depart for France,
   As procurator to your Excellence,
   To marry Princess Margaret for your Grace;
   So, in the famous ancient city, Tours,
   In presence of the Kings of France and Sicil,
   The Dukes of Orleans, Calaber, Britaine, and Alençon,
   Seven earls, twelve barons, and twenty reverend bishops,
   I have perform'd my task, and was espous'd:
   And humbly now upon my bended knee,
   In sight of England and her lordly peers,
   Deliver up my title in the queen
   To your most gracious hands, that are the substance
   Of that great shadow I did represent;
   The happiest gift that ever marquess gave,
   The fairest queen that ever king receiv'd.
KING HENRY. Suffolk, arise. Welcome, Queen Margaret:
   I can express no kinder sign of love
   Than this kind kiss. O Lord! that lends me life,
   Lend me a heart replete with thankfulness;
   For thou hast given me in this beauteous face
   A world of earthly blessings to my soul,
   If sympathy of love unite our thoughts.

QUEEN MARGARET. Great King of England and my gracious
lord,
  The mutual conference that my mind hath had
  By day, by night, waking, and in my dreams,
  In courtly company, or at my beads,
  With you, mine alderliefest sovereign,
  Makes me the bolder to salute my king
  With ruder terms, such as my wit affords,
  And over-joy of heart doth minister.

KING HENRY. Her sight did ravish, but her grace in speech,
  Her words y-clad with wisdom's majesty,
  Makes me from wondering fall to weeping joys;
  Such is the fulness of my heart's content.
  Lords, with one cheerful voice welcome my love.

ALL. Long live Queen Margaret, England's happiness!

QUEEN MARGARET. We thank you all. *Flourish*

SUFFOLK. My Lord Protector, so it please your Grace,
  Here are the articles of contracted peace
  Between our sovereign and the French King Charles,
  For eighteen months concluded by consent.

GLOUCESTER. 'Imprimis, It is agreed between the French
king, Charles, and William De la Pole, Marquess of Suf-
folk, ambassador for Henry King of England, that the said
Henry shall espouse the Lady Margaret, daughter unto
Reignier King of Naples, Sicilia, and Jerusalem, and
crown her Queen of England ere the thirtieth of May
next ensuing. Item, That the duchy of Anjou and the
county of Maine shall be released and delivered to the
king her father.'— *Lets the paper fall*

KING HENRY. Uncle, how now!

GLOUCESTER.   Pardon me, gracious lord;
  Some sudden qualm hath struck me at the heart
  And dimm'd mine eyes, that I can read no further.

KING HENRY. Uncle of Winchester, I pray, read on.

CARDINAL. 'Item, It is further agreed between them, that
the duchies of Anjou and Maine shall be released and de-
livered over to the king her father; and she sent over of
the King of England's own proper cost and charges, with-
out having any dowry.'

KING HENRY. They please us well. Lord Marquess, kneel
down:
  We here create thee the first Duke of Suffolk,

And girt thee with the sword. Cousin of York,
We here discharge your Grace from being regent
I' the parts of France, till term of eighteen months
Be full expir'd. Thanks, uncle Winchester,
Gloucester, York, Buckingham, Somerset,
Salisbury, and Warwick;
We thank you all for this great favour done,
In entertainment to my princely queen.
Come, let us in, and with all speed provide
To see her coronation be perform'd.

Exeunt King, Queen, and Suffolk

GLOUCESTER. Brave peers of England, pillars of the state,
To you Duke Humphrey must unload his grief,
Your grief, the common grief of all the land.
What! did my brother Henry spend his youth,
His valour, coin, and people, in the wars?
Did he so often lodge in open field,
In winter's cold, and summer's parching heat,
To conquer France, his true inheritance?
And did my brother Bedford toil his wits,
To keep by policy what Henry got?
Have you yourselves, Somerset, Buckingham,
Brave York, Salisbury, and victorious Warwick,
Receiv'd deep scars in France and Normandy?
Or hath mine uncle Beaufort and myself,
With all the learned council of the realm,
Studied so long, sat in the council-house
Early and late, debating to and fro
How France and Frenchmen might be kept in awe?
And hath his Highness in his infancy
Been crown'd in Paris, in despite of foes?
And shall these labours and these honours die?
Shall Henry's conquest, Bedford's vigilance,
Your deeds of war and all our counsel die?
O peers of England! shameful is this league,
Fatal this marriage, cancelling your fame,
Blotting your names from books of memory,
Razing the characters of your renown,
Defacing monuments of conquer'd France,
Undoing all, as all had never been.

CARDINAL. Nephew, what means this passionate discourse,
This peroration with such circumstance?

For France, 'tis ours; and we will keep it still.
GLOUCESTER. Ay, uncle; we will keep it, if we can;
But now it is impossible we should.
Suffolk, the new-made duke that rules the roast,
Hath given the duchies of Anjou and Maine
Unto the poor King Reignier, whose large style
Agrees not with the leanness of his purse.
SALISBURY. Now, by the death of him who died for all,
These counties were the keys of Normandy.
But wherefore weeps Warwick, my valiant son?
WARWICK. For grief that they are past recovery:
For, were there hope to conquer them again,
My sword should shed hot blood, mine eyes no tears.
Anjou and Maine! myself did win them both;
Those provinces these arms of mine did conquer:
And are the cities, that I got with wounds,
Deliver'd up again with peaceful words?
Mort Dieu!
YORK. For Suffolk's duke, may he be suffocate,
That dims the honour of this warlike isle!
France should have torn and rent my very heart
Before I would have yielded to this league.
I never read but England's kings have had
Large sums of gold and dowries with their wives;
And our King Henry gives away his own,
To match with her that brings no vantages.
GLOUCESTER. A proper jest, and never heard before,
That Suffolk should demand a whole fifteenth
For costs and charges in transporting her!
She should have stay'd in France, and starv'd in France,
Before—
CARDINAL. My Lord of Gloucester, now you grow too hot:
It was the pleasure of my lord the king.
GLOUCESTER. My Lord of Winchester, I know your mind:
'Tis not my speeches that you do mislike,
But 'tis my presence that doth trouble ye.
Rancour will out: proud prelate, in thy face
I see thy fury. If I longer stay
We shall begin our ancient bickerings.
Lordings, farewell; and say, when I am gone,
I prophesied France will be lost ere long.   *Exit*
CARDINAL. So, there goes our protector in a rage.

'Tis known to you he is mine enemy,
Nay, more, an enemy unto you all,
And no great friend, I fear me, to the king.
Consider, lords, he is the next of blood,
And heir apparent to the English crown:
Had Henry got an empire by his marriage,
And all the wealthy kingdoms of the west,
There 's reason he should be displeas'd at it.
Look to it, lords; let not his smoothing words
Bewitch your hearts; be wise and circumspect.
What though the common people favour him,
Calling him, 'Humphrey, the good Duke of Gloucester';
Clapping their hands, and crying with loud voice,
'Jesu maintain your royal excellence!'
With 'God preserve the good Duke Humphrey!'
I fear me, lords, for all this flattering gloss,
He will be found a dangerous protector.

BUCKINGHAM. Why should he then protect our sovereign,
He being of age to govern of himself?
Cousin of Somerset, join you with me,
And all together, with the Duke of Suffolk,
We 'll quickly hoise Duke Humphrey from his seat.

CARDINAL. This weighty business will not brook delay;
I 'll to the Duke of Suffolk presently.   *Exit*

SOMERSET. Cousin of Buckingham, though Humphrey's
        pride
And greatness of his place be grief to us,
Yet let us watch the haughty cardinal:
His insolence is more intolerable
Than all the princes in the land beside:
If Gloucester be displac'd, he 'll be protector.

BUCKINGHAM. Or thou, or I, Somerset, will be protector,
Despite Duke Humphrey or the cardinal.
                Exeunt Buckingham and Somerset

SALISBURY. Pride went before, ambition follows him.
While these do labour for their own preferment,
Behoves it us to labour for the realm.
I never saw but Humphrey, Duke of Gloucester,
Did bear him like a noble gentleman.
Oft have I seen the haughty cardinal
More like a soldier than a man o' the church,
As stout and proud as he were lord of all,

Swear like a ruffian and demean himself
Unlike the ruler of a commonweal.
Warwick, my son, the comfort of my age,
Thy deeds, thy plainness, and thy house-keeping,
Have won the greatest favour of the commons,
Excepting none but good Duke Humphrey:
And, brother York, thy acts in Ireland,
In bringing them to civil discipline,
Thy late exploits done in the heart of France,
When thou wert regent for our sovereign,
Have made thee fear'd and honour'd of the people.
Join we together for the public good,
In what we can to bridle and suppress
The pride of Suffolk and the cardinal,
With Somerset's and Buckingham's ambition;
And, as we may, cherish Duke Humphrey's deeds,
While they do tend the profit of the land.

WARWICK. So God help Warwick, as he loves the land,
And common profit of his country!

YORK. (*Aside*) And so says York, for he hath greatest cause.

SALISBURY. Then let 's make haste away, and look unto the
    main.

WARWICK. Unto the main! O father, Maine is lost!
That Maine which by main force Warwick did win,
And would have kept so long as breath did last:
Main chance, father, you meant; but I meant Maine,
Which I will win from France, or else be slain.

                    Exeunt Warwick and Salisbury

YORK. Anjou and Maine are given to the French;
Paris is lost; the state of Normandy
Stands on a tickle point now they are gone.
Suffolk concluded on the articles,
The peers agreed, and Henry was well pleas'd
To change two dukedoms for a duke's fair daughter.
I cannot blame them all: what is 't to them?
'Tis thine they give away, and not their own.
Pirates may make cheap pennyworths of their pillage,
And purchase friends, and give to courtezans,
Still revelling like lords till all be gone;
While as the silly owner of the goods
Weeps over them, and wrings his hapless hands,
And shakes his head, and trembling stands aloof,

While all is shar'd and all is borne away,
Ready to starve and dare not touch his own:
So York must sit and fret and bite his tongue
While his own lands are bargain'd for and sold.
Methinks the realms of England, France, and Ireland
Bear that proportion to my flesh and blood
As did the fatal brand Althæa burn'd
Unto the prince's heart of Calydon.
Anjou and Maine both given unto the French!
Cold news for me, for I had hope of France,
Even as I have of fertile England's soil.
A day will come when York shall claim his own;
And therefore I will take the Nevils' parts
And make a show of love to proud Duke Humphrey,
And, when I spy advantage, claim the crown,
For that 's the golden mark I seek to hit.
Nor shall proud Lancaster usurp my right,
Nor hold the sceptre in his childish fist,
Nor wear the diadem upon his head,
Whose church-like humours fit not for a crown.
Then, York, be still awhile, till time do serve:
Watch thou and wake when others be asleep,
To pry into the secrets of the state;
Till Henry, surfeiting in joys of love,
With his new bride and England's dear-bought queen,
And Humphrey with the peers be fall'n at jars:
Then will I raise aloft the milk-white rose,
With whose sweet smell the air shall be perfum'd,
And in my standard bear the arms of York,
To grapple with the house of Lancaster;
And, force perforce, I 'll make him yield the crown,
Whose bookish rule hath pull'd fair England down.   *Exit*

SCENE TWO

The Same. A Room in the Duke of Gloucester's House.

Enter Gloucester and his Duchess

DUCHESS. Why droops my lord, like over-ripen'd corn
    Hanging the head at Ceres' plenteous load?
    Why doth the great Duke Humphrey knit his brows,

As frowning at the favours of the world?
Why are thine eyes fix'd to the sullen earth,
Gazing on that which seems to dim thy sight?
What seest thou there? King Henry's diadem
Enchas'd with all the honours of the world?
If so, gaze on, and grovel on thy face,
Until thy head be circled with the same.
Put forth thy hand, reach at the glorious gold:
What! is 't too short? I 'll lengthen it with mine;
And having both together heav'd it up,
We 'll both together lift our heads to heaven,
And never more abase our sight so low
As to vouchsafe one glance unto the ground.

GLOUCESTER. O Nell, sweet Nell, if thou dost love thy lord,
Banish the canker of ambitious thoughts:
And may that thought, when I imagine ill
Against my king and nephew, virtuous Henry,
Be my last breathing in this mortal world!
My troublous dream this night doth make me sad.

DUCHESS. What dream'd my lord? tell me, and I 'll requite it
With sweet rehearsal of my morning's dream.

GLOUCESTER. Methought this staff, mine office-badge in court,
Was broke in twain; by whom I have forgot,
But, as I think, it was by the cardinal;
And on the pieces of the broken wand
Were plac'd the heads of Edmund Duke of Somerset,
And William De la Pole, first Duke of Suffolk.
This was my dream: what it doth bode, God knows.

DUCHESS. Tut! this was nothing but an argument
That he that breaks a stick of Gloucester's grove
Shall lose his head for his presumption.
But list to me, my Humphrey, my sweet duke:
Methought I sat in seat of majesty
In the cathedral church of Westminster,
And in that chair where kings and queens are crown'd;
Where Henry and Dame Margaret kneel'd to me,
And on my head did set the diadem.

GLOUCESTER. Nay, Eleanor, then must I chide outright:
Presumptuous dame! ill-natur'd Eleanor!
Art thou not second woman in the realm,
And the protector's wife, belov'd of him?

Hast thou not worldly pleasure at command,
Above the reach or compass of thy thought?
And wilt thou still be hammering treachery,
To tumble down thy husband and thyself
From top of honour to disgrace's feet?
Away from me, and let me hear no more.

DUCHESS. What, what, my lord! are you so choleric
With Eleanor, for telling but her dream?
Next time I 'll keep my dreams unto myself,
And not be check'd.

GLOUCESTER. Nay, be not angry; I am pleas'd again.

Enter a Messenger

MESSENGER. My Lord Protector, 'tis his Highness' pleasure
You do prepare to ride unto Saint Alban's,
Whereas the king and queen do mean to hawk.

GLOUCESTER. I go. Come, Nell, thou wilt ride with us?

DUCHESS. Yes, my good lord, I 'll follow presently.

Exeunt Gloucester and Messenger

Follow I must; I cannot go before,
While Gloucester bears this base and humble mind.
Were I a man, a duke, and next of blood,
I would remove these tedious stumbling-blocks
And smooth my way upon their headless necks;
And, being a woman, I will not be slack
To play my part in Fortune's pageant.
Where are you there? Sir John! nay, fear not, man,
We are alone; here 's none but thee and I.

Enter Hume

HUME. Jesus preserve your royal Majesty!

DUCHESS. What sayst thou? Majesty! I am but Grace.

HUME. But, by the grace of God, and Hume's advice,
Your Grace's title shall be multiplied.

DUCHESS. What sayst thou, man? hast thou as yet conferr'd
With Margery Jourdain, the cunning witch,
With Roger Bolingbroke, the conjurer?
And will they undertake to do me good?

HUME. This they have promised, to show your highness
A spirit rais'd from depth of under-ground,
That shall make answer to such questions
As by your Grace shall be propounded him.

DUCHESS. It is enough: I 'll think upon the questions.
When from Saint Alban's we do make return

We 'll see these things effected to the full.

Here, Hume, take this reward; make merry, man,

With thy confederates in this weighty cause.   *Exit*

HUME. Hume must make merry with the duchess' gold;

Marry and shall. But how now, Sir John Hume!

Seal up your lips, and give no words but mum:

The business asketh silent secrecy.

Dame Eleanor gives gold to bring the witch:

Gold cannot come amiss, were she a devil.

Yet have I gold flies from another coast:

I dare not say from the rich cardinal

And from the great and new-made Duke of Suffolk;

Yet I do find it so: for, to be plain,

They, knowing Dame Eleanor's aspiring humour,

Have hired me to undermine the duchess

And buzz these conjurations in her brain.

They say, 'A crafty knave does need no broker';

Yet am I Suffolk and the cardinal's broker.

Hume, if you take not heed, you shall go near

To call them both a pair of crafty knaves.

Well, so it stands; and thus, I fear, at last

Hume's knavery will be the duchess' wrack,

And her attainture will be Humphrey's fall.

Sort how it will I shall have gold for all.   *Exit*

SCENE THREE

The Same. A Room in the Palace.

Enter three or four Petitioners, Peter, the Armourer's man, being one

FIRST PETITIONER. My masters, let 's stand close: my Lord Protector will come this way by and by, and then we may deliver our supplications in the quill.

SECOND PETITIONER. Marry, the Lord protect him, for he 's a good man! Jesu bless him!

Enter Suffolk and Queen Margaret

FIRST PETITIONER. Here a' comes, methinks, and the queen with him. I 'll be the first, sure.

SECOND PETITIONER. Come back, fool! this is the Duke of Suffolk and not my Lord Protector.

SUFFOLK. How now, fellow! wouldst any thing with me?

FIRST PETITIONER. I pray, my lord, pardon me: I took ye for my Lord Protector.

QUEEN MARGARET. (*Glancing at the superscriptions*) 'To my Lord Protector!' are your supplications to his lordship? Let me see them: what is thine?

FIRST PETITIONER. Mine is, an 't please your Grace, against John Goodman, my Lord Cardinal's man, for keeping my house, and lands, my wife and all, from me.

SUFFOLK. Thy wife too! that is some wrong indeed. What 's yours? What 's here? 'Against the Duke of Suffolk, for enclosing the commons of Melford!' How now, sir knave!

SECOND PETITIONER. Alas! sir, I am but a poor petitioner of our whole township.

PETER. (*Presenting his petition*) Against my master, Thomas Horner, for saying that the Duke of York was rightful heir to the crown.

QUEEN MARGARET. What sayst thou? Did the Duke of York say he was rightful heir to the crown?

PETER. That my master was? No, forsooth: my master said that he was; and that the king was an usurper.

SUFFOLK. Who is there?

Enter Servants

Take this fellow in, and send for his master with a pursuivant presently. We 'll hear more of your matter before the king.   *Exeunt Servants with Peter*

QUEEN MARGARET. And as for you, that love to be protected
Under the wings of our protector's grace,
Begin your suits anew and sue to him. *Tears the petitions*
Away, base cullions! Suffolk, let them go.

ALL. Come, let 's be gone.   *Exeunt Petitioners*

QUEEN MARGARET. My Lord of Suffolk, say, is this the guise,
Is this the fashion of the court of England?
Is this the government of Britain's isle,
And this the royalty of Albion's king?
What! shall King Henry be a pupil still
Under the surly Gloucester's governance?
Am I a queen in title and in style,
And must be made a subject to a duke?
I tell thee, Pole, when in the city Tours
Thou ran'st a tilt in honour of my love,
And stol'st away the ladies' hearts of France,

I thought King Henry had resembled thee
In courage, courtship, and proportion:
But all his mind is bent to holiness,
To number Ave-Maries on his beads;
His champions are the prophets and apostles;
His weapons holy saws of sacred writ;
His study is his tilt-yard, and his loves
Are brazen images of canoniz'd saints.
I would the college of the cardinals
Would choose him pope, and carry him to Rome,
And set the triple crown upon his head:
That were a state fit for his holiness.

SUFFOLK. Madam, be patient; as I was cause
Your Highness came to England, so will I
In England work your Grace's full content.

QUEEN MARGARET. Beside the haught protector, have we Beaufort
The imperious churchman, Somerset, Buckingham,
And grumbling York; and not the least of these
But can do more in England than the king.

SUFFOLK. And he of these that can do most of all
Cannot do more in England than the Nevils:
Salisbury and Warwick are no simple peers.

QUEEN MARGARET. Not all these lords do vex me half so much
As that proud dame, the Lord Protector's wife:
She sweeps it through the court with troops of ladies,
More like an empress than Duke Humphrey's wife.
Strangers in court do take her for the queen:
She bears a duke's revenues on her back,
And in her heart she scorns our poverty.
Shall I not live to be aveng'd on her?
Contemptuous base-born callot as she is,
She vaunted 'mongst her minions t' other day
The very train of her worst wearing gown
Was better worth than all my father's lands,
Till Suffolk gave two dukedoms for his daughter.

SUFFOLK. Madam, myself have lim'd a bush for her,
And plac'd a quire of such enticing birds
That she will light to listen to the lays,
And never mount to trouble you again.
So, let her rest: and, madam, list to me;

For I am bold to counsel you in this.
Although we fancy not the cardinal,
Yet must we join with him and with the lords
Till we have brought Duke Humphrey in disgrace.
As for the Duke of York, this late complaint
Will make but little for his benefit:
So, one by one, we 'll weed them all at last,
And you yourself shall steer the happy helm.

Sound a sennet. Enter King Henry,
York, and Somerset, Duke and Duchess of Gloucester, Car-
dinal Beaufort, Buckingham, Salisbury, and Warwick

KING HENRY. For my part, noble lords, I care not which;
  Or Somerset or York, all 's one to me.

YORK. If York have ill demean'd himself in France,
  Then let him be denay'd the regentship.

SOMERSET. If Somerset be unworthy of the place,
  Let York be regent; I will yield to him.

WARWICK. Whether your Grace be worthy, yea or no,
  Dispute not that: York is the worthier.

CARDINAL. Ambitious Warwick, let thy betters speak.

WARWICK. The cardinal 's not my better in the field.

BUCKINGHAM. All in this presence are thy betters, Warwick.

WARWICK. Warwick may live to be the best of all.

SALISBURY. Peace, son! and show some reason, Buckingham,
  Why Somerset should be preferr'd in this.

QUEEN MARGARET. Because the king, forsooth, will have it so.

GLOUCESTER. Madam, the king is old enough himself
  To give his censure: these are no women's matters.

QUEEN MARGARET. If he be old enough, what needs your
    Grace
  To be protector of his Excellence?

GLOUCESTER. Madam, I am protector of the realm;
  And at his pleasure will resign my place.

SUFFOLK. Resign it then and leave thine insolence.
  Since thou wert king,—as who is king but thou?—
  The commonwealth hath daily run to wrack;
  The Dauphin hath prevail'd beyond the seas;
  And all the peers and nobles of the realm
  Have been as bondmen to thy sovereignty.

CARDINAL. The commons hast thou rack'd; the clergy's bags
  Are lank and lean with thy extortions.

SOMERSET. Thy sumptuous buildings and thy wife's attire

Have cost a mass of public treasury.

BUCKINGHAM. Thy cruelty in execution
Upon offenders hath exceeded law,
And left thee to the mercy of the law.

QUEEN MARGARET. Thy sale of offices and towns in France,
If they were known, as the suspect is great,
Would make thee quickly hop without thy head.

Exit Gloucester. The Queen drops her fan

Give me my fan: what, minion! can ye not?

Giving the Duchess a box on the ear

I cry you mercy, madam, was it you?

DUCHESS. Was 't I? yea, I it was, proud Frenchwoman:
Could I come near your beauty with my nails
I 'd set my ten commandments in your face.

KING HENRY. Sweet aunt, be quiet; 'twas against her will.

DUCHESS. Against her will! Good king, look to 't in time;
She 'll hamper thee and dandle thee like a baby:
Though in this place most master wear no breeches,
She shall not strike Dame Eleanor unreveng'd.   *Exit*

BUCKINGHAM. Lord Cardinal, I will follow Eleanor,
And listen after Humphrey, how he proceeds:
She 's tickled now; her fume can need no spurs,
She'll gallop far enough to her destruction.

Exit Buckingham

Re-enter Gloucester

GLOUCESTER. Now, lords, my choler being over-blown
With walking once about the quadrangle,
I come to talk of commonwealth affairs.
As for your spiteful false objections,
Prove them, and I lie open to the law:
But God in mercy so deal with my soul
As I in duty love my king and country!
But to the matter that we have in hand.
I say, my sovereign, York is meetest man
To be your regent in the realm of France.

SUFFOLK. Before we make election, give me leave
To show some reason, of no little force,
That York is most unmeet of any man.

YORK. I 'll tell thee, Suffolk, why I am unmeet:
First, for I cannot flatter thee in pride;
Next, if I be appointed for the place,
My Lord of Somerset will keep me here,

Without discharge, money, or furniture,
Till France be won into the Dauphin's hands.
Last time I danc'd attendance on his will
Till Paris was besieg'd, famish'd, and lost.

WARWICK. That can I witness; and a fouler fact
Did never traitor in the land commit.

SUFFOLK. Peace, headstrong Warwick!

WARWICK. Image of pride, why should I hold my peace?
Enter Servants of Suffolk, bringing in Horner and Peter

SUFFOLK. Because here is a man accus'd of treason:
Pray God the Duke of York excuse himself!

YORK. Doth any one accuse York for a traitor?

KING HENRY. What mean'st thou, Suffolk? tell me, what are
these?

SUFFOLK. Please it your Majesty, this is the man
That doth accuse his master of high treason.
His words were these: that Richard, Duke of York,
Was rightful heir unto the English crown,
And that your Majesty was an usurper.

KING HENRY. Say, man, were these thy words?

HORNER. An 't shall please your Majesty, I never said nor
thought any such matter: God is my witness, I am falsely
accused by the villain.

PETER. By these ten bones, my lords, he did speak them to
me in the garret one night, as we were scouring my Lord
of York's armour.

YORK. Base dunghill villain, and mechanical,
I 'll have thy head for this thy traitor's speech.
I do beseech your royal Majesty
Let him have all the rigour of the law.

HORNER. Alas! my lord, hang me if ever I spake the words.
My accuser is my prentice; and when I did correct him
for his fault the other day, he did vow upon his knees he
would be even with me: I have good witness of this:
therefore I beseech your Majesty, do not cast away an
honest man for a villain's accusation.

KING HENRY. Uncle, what shall we say to this in law?

GLOUCESTER. This doom, my lord, if I may judge.
Let Somerset be regent o'er the French,
Because in York this breeds suspicion;
And let these have a day appointed them
For single combat in convenient place;

For he hath witness of his servant's malice.

This is the law, and this Duke Humphrey's doom.

KING HENRY. Then be it so. My Lord of Somerset,
We make your Grace Lord Regent o'er the French.

SOMERSET. I humbly thank your royal Majesty.

HORNER. And I accept the combat willingly.

PETER. Alas! my lord, I cannot fight: for God's sake, pity
my case! the spite of man prevaileth against me. O Lord,
have mercy upon me! I shall never be able to fight a blow.
O Lord, my heart!

GLOUCESTER. Sirrah, or you must fight, or else be hang'd.

KING HENRY. Away with them to prison; and the day
Of combat shall be the last of the next month.
Come, Somerset, we 'll see thee sent away.   *Exeunt*

SCENE FOUR

The Same. The Duke of Gloucester's Garden.

Enter Margery Jourdain, Hume, Southwell, and Bolingbroke

HUME. Come, my masters; the duchess, I tell you, expects
performance of your promises.

BOLINGBROKE. Master Hume, we are therefore provided.
Will her ladyship behold and hear our exorcisms?

HUME. Ay; what else? fear you not her courage.

BOLINGBROKE. I have heard her reported to be a woman of
invincible spirit: but it shall be convenient, Master Hume,
that you be by her aloft while we be busy below; and so,
I pray you, go in God's name, and leave us. (*Exit Hume*)
Mother Jourdain, be you prostrate, and grovel on the
earth; John Southwell, read you; and let us to our work.
              Enter Duchess aloft, Hume following

DUCHESS. Well said, my masters, and welcome all.
To this gear the sooner the better.

BOLINGBROKE. Patience, good lady; wizards know their
times:

Deep night, dark night, the silent of the night,
The time of night when Troy was set on fire;
The time when screech-owls cry, and ban-dogs howl,
And spirits walk, and ghosts break up their graves,
That time best fits the work we have in hand.

Madam, sit you, and fear not: whom we raise
We will make fast within a hallow'd verge.
Here they perform the ceremonies belonging, and make the
circle; Bolingbroke or Southwell reads, 'Conjuro te,' &c. It
    thunders and lightens terribly; then the Spirit riseth
SPIRIT. Adsum.
MARGERY JOURDAIN. Asmath!
By the eternal God, whose name and power
Thou tremblest at, answer that I shall ask;
For till thou speak, thou shalt not pass from hence.
SPIRIT. Ask what thou wilt. That I had said and done!
BOLINGBROKE. First, of the king: what shall of him become?
SPIRIT. The duke yet lives that Henry shall depose;
But him outlive, and die a violent death.
            As the Spirit speaks, Southwell writes the answers
BOLINGBROKE. What fate awaits the Duke of Suffolk?
SPIRIT. By water shall he die and take his end.
BOLINGBROKE. What shall befall the Duke of Somerset?
SPIRIT. Let him shun castles:
Safer shall he be upon the sandy plains
Than where castles mounted stand.
Have done, for more I hardly can endure.
BOLINGBROKE. Descend to darkness and the burning lake!
False fiend, avoid. *Thunder and lightning. Spirit descends*
                Enter York and Buck-
    ingham, hastily, with their Guards, and Others
YORK. Lay hands upon these traitors and their trash.
Beldam, I think we watch'd you at an inch.
What! madam, are you there? the king and commonweal
Are deeply indebted for this piece of pains:
My Lord Protector will, I doubt it not,
See you well guerdon'd for these good deserts.
DUCHESS. Not half so bad as thine to England's king,
Injurious duke, that threat'st where is no cause.
BUCKINGHAM. True, madam, none at all. What call you this?
                        Showing her the papers
Away with them! let them be clapp'd up close
And kept asunder. You, madam, shall with us:
Stafford, take her to thee.—
                Exeunt above, Duchess and Hume guarded
We 'll see your trinkets here all forthcoming.
All, away!

Exeunt Southwell, Bolingbroke, &c., guarded

YORK. Lord Buckingham, methinks you watch'd her well:
A pretty plot, well chosen to build upon!
Now, pray, my lord, let 's see the devil's writ.
What have we here?
'The duke yet lives that Henry shall depose;
But him outlive, and die a violent death.'
Why, this is just
'Aio te, Æacida, Romanos vincere posse.'
Well, to the rest:
'Tell me what fate awaits the Duke of Suffolk?
By water shall he die and take his end.
What shall betide the Duke of Somerset?
Let him shun castles:
Safer shall he be upon the sandy plains
Than where castles mounted stand.'
Come, come, my lords; these oracles
Are hardly attain'd, and hardly understood.
The king is now in progress towards Saint Alban's;
With him, the husband of this lovely lady:
Thither go these news as fast as horse can carry them,
A sorry breakfast for my Lord Protector.

BUCKINGHAM. Your Grace shall give me leave, my Lord of
York.
To be the post, in hope of his reward.

YORK. At your pleasure, my good lord. Who 's within there,
ho!

Enter a Serving-man

Invite my Lords of Salisbury and Warwick
To sup with me to-morrow night. Away!

Flourish. Exeunt

ACT TWO

SCENE ONE

St. Alban's.

*Enter King Henry, Queen Margaret, Gloucester, Cardinal
Beaufort, and Suffolk, with Falconers, hollaing*

QUEEN MARGARET. Believe me, lords, for flying at the brook,
  I saw not better sport these seven years' day:
  Yet, by your leave, the wind was very high,
  And, ten to one, old Joan had not gone out.
KING HENRY. But what a point, my lord, your falcon made,
  And what a pitch she flew above the rest!
  To see how God in all his creatures works!
  Yea, man and birds are fain of climbing high.
SUFFOLK. No marvel, an it like your Majesty,
  My Lord Protector's hawks do tower so well;
  They know their master loves to be aloft,
  And bears his thoughts above his falcon's pitch.
GLOUCESTER. My lord, 'tis but a base ignoble mind
  That mounts no higher than a bird can soar.
CARDINAL. I thought as much; he 'd be above the clouds.
GLOUCESTER. Ay, my Lord Cardinal; how think you by that?
  Were it not good your Grace could fly to heaven?
KING HENRY. The treasury of everlasting joy.
CARDINAL. Thy heaven is on earth; thine eyes and thoughts
  Beat on a crown, the treasure of thy heart;
  Pernicious protector, dangerous peer,
  That smooth'st it so with king and commonweal!
GLOUCESTER. What! cardinal, is your priesthood grown
      peremptory?
  Tantæne animis cœlestibus iræ?
  Churchmen so hot? good uncle, hide such malice;
  With such holiness can you do it?
SUFFOLK. No malice, sir; no more than well becomes
  So good a quarrel and so bad a peer.

GLOUCESTER. As who, my lord?

SUFFOLK.   Why, as you, my lord,
An 't like your lordly lord-protectorship.

GLOUCESTER. Why, Suffolk, England knows thine insolence.

QUEEN MARGARET. And thy ambition, Gloucester.

KING HENRY.   I prithee, peace,
Good queen, and whet not on these furious peers;
For blessed are the peacemakers on earth.

CARDINAL. Let me be blessed for the peace I make
Against this proud protector with my sword!

GLOUCESTER. (*Aside to the Cardinal*) Faith, holy uncle,
would 'twere come to that!

CARDINAL. (*Aside to Gloucester*) Marry, when thou darest.

GLOUCESTER. (*Aside to the Cardinal*) Make up no factious
numbers for the matter;
In thine own person answer thy abuse.

CARDINAL. (*Aside to Gloucester*) Ay, where thou darest not
peep: an if thou darest,
This evening on the east side of the grove.

KING HENRY. How now, my lords!

CARDINAL.   Believe me, cousin Gloucester,
Had not your man put up the fowl so suddenly,
We had had more sport. (*Aside to Gloucester*) Come with
thy two-hand sword.

GLOUCESTER. True, uncle.

CARDINAL. Are you advis'd? (*Aside to Gloucester*) the east
side of the grove.

GLOUCESTER. (*Aside to the Cardinal*) Cardinal, I am with
you.

KING HENRY. Why, how now, uncle Gloucester!

GLOUCESTER. Talking of hawking; nothing else, my lord.—
(*Aside to the Cardinal*) Now, by God's mother, priest, I 'll
shave your crown
For this, or all my fence shall fail.

CARDINAL. (*Aside to Gloucester*) Medice teipsum;
Protector, see to 't well, protect yourself.

KING HENRY. The winds grow high; so do your stomachs,
lords.
How irksome is this music to my heart!
When such strings jar, what hope of harmony?
I pray, my lords, let me compound this strife.
                    Enter One crying 'A Miracle'

GLOUCESTER. What means this noise?
  Fellow, what miracle dost thou proclaim?
ONE. A miracle! a miracle!
SUFFOLK. Come to the king, and tell him what miracle.
ONE. Forsooth, a blind man at Saint Alban's shrine,
  Within this half hour hath receiv'd his sight;
  A man that ne'er saw in his life before.
KING HENRY. Now, God be prais'd, that to believing souls
  Gives light in darkness, comfort in despair!

Enter the Mayor of Saint Alban's, and his
Brethren, and Simpcox, bore between two persons in a chair;
his Wife and a great multitude following

CARDINAL. Here comes the townsmen on procession,
  To present your Highness with the man.
KING HENRY. Great is his comfort in this earthly vale,
  Although by his sight his sin be multiplied.
GLOUCESTER. Stand by, my masters; bring him near the
    king:
  His Highness' pleasure is to talk with him.
KING HENRY. Good fellow, tell us here the circumstance,
  That we for thee may glorify the Lord.
  What! hast thou been long blind, and now restor'd?
SIMPCOX. Born blind, an 't please your Grace.
WIFE. Ay, indeed, was he.
SUFFOLK. What woman is this?
WIFE. His wife an 't like your worship.
GLOUCESTER. Hadst thou been his mother, thou couldst
    have better told.
KING HENRY. Where wert thou born?
SIMPCOX. At Berwick in the north, an 't like your Grace.
KING HENRY. Poor soul! God's goodness hath been great to
    thee:
  Let never day nor night unhallow'd pass,
  But still remember what the Lord hath done.
QUEEN MARGARET. Tell me, good fellow, cam'st thou here
    by chance,
  Or of devotion, to this holy shrine?
SIMPCOX. God knows, of pure devotion; being call'd
  A hundred times and oftener in my sleep,
  By good Saint Alban; who said, 'Simpcox, come;
  Come, offer at my shrine, and I will help thee.'
WIFE. Most true, forsooth; and many time and oft

Myself have heard a voice to call him so.

CARDINAL. What! art thou lame?

SIMPCOX.   Ay, God Almighty help me!

SUFFOLK. How cam'st thou so?

SIMPCOX.   A fall off of a tree.

WIFE. A plum-tree, master.

GLOUCESTER.   How long hast thou been blind?

SIMPCOX. O! born so, master.

GLOUCESTER.   What! and wouldst climb a tree?

SIMPCOX. But that in all my life, when I was a youth.

WIFE. Too true; and bought his climbing very dear.

GLOUCESTER. Mass, thou lov'dst plums well, that wouldst
    venture so.

SIMPCOX. Alas! master, my wife desir'd some damsons,
    And made me climb with danger of my life.

GLOUCESTER. A subtle knave! but yet it shall not serve.
    Let me see thine eyes: wink now: now open them:
    In my opinion yet thou seest not well.

SIMPCOX. Yes, master, clear as day; I thank God and Saint
    Alban.

GLOUCESTER. Sayst thou me so? What colour is this cloak of?

SIMPCOX. Red, master; red as blood.

GLOUCESTER. Why, that's well said. What colour is my
    gown of?

SIMPCOX. Black, forsooth; coal-black as jet.

KING HENRY. Why then, thou know'st what colour jet is of?

SUFFOLK. And yet, I think, jet did he never see.

GLOUCESTER. But cloaks and gowns before this day a many.

WIFE. Never, before this day, in all his life.

GLOUCESTER. Tell me, sirrah, what's my name?

SIMPCOX. Alas! master, I know not.

GLOUCESTER. What's his name?

SIMPCOX. I know not.

GLOUCESTER. Nor his?

SIMPCOX. No, indeed, master.

GLOUCESTER. What's thine own name?

SIMPCOX. Saunder Simpcox, an if it please you, master.

GLOUCESTER. Then, Saunder, sit there, the lyingest knave in
    Christendom. If thou hadst been born blind, thou mightst
    as well have known all our names as thus to name the
    several colours we do wear. Sight may distinguish of col-
    ours, but suddenly to nominate them all, it is impossible.

My lords, Saint Alban here hath done a miracle; and
would ye not think that cunning to be great, that could
restore this cripple to his legs again?

SIMPCOX. O, master, that you could!

GLOUCESTER. My masters of Saint Alban's, have you not
beadles in your town, and things called whips?

MAYOR. Yes, my lord, if it please your Grace.

GLOUCESTER. Then send for one presently.

MAYOR. Sirrah, go fetch the beadle hither straight.

Exit an Attendant

GLOUCESTER. Now fetch me a stool hither by and by. (*A
stool brought out*) Now, sirrah, if you mean to save your-
self from whipping, leap me over this stool and run away.

SIMPCOX. Alas! master, I am not able to stand alone:
You go about to torture me in vain.

Re-enter Attendant, and a Beadle with a whip

GLOUCESTER. Well, sir, we must have you find your legs.
Sirrah beadle, whip him till he leap over that same stool.

BEADLE. I will, my lord. Come on, sirrah; off with your
doublet quickly.

SIMPCOX. Alas! master, what shall I do? I am not able to
stand.

*After the Beadle hath hit him once, he leaps over the stool,
and runs away: and the people follow and cry, 'A miracle!'*

KING HENRY. O God! seest thou this, and bearest so long?

QUEEN MARGARET. It made me laugh to see the villain run.

GLOUCESTER. Follow the knave; and take this drab away.

WIFE. Alas! sir, we did it for pure need.

GLOUCESTER. Let them be whipp'd through every market
town

Till they come to Berwick, from whence they came.

Exeunt Mayor, Beadle, Wife, &c.

CARDINAL. Duke Humphrey has done a miracle to-day.

SUFFOLK. True; made the lame to leap and fly away.

GLOUCESTER. But you have done more miracles than I;
You made in a day, my lord, whole towns to fly.

Enter Buckingham

KING HENRY. What tidings with our cousin Buckingham?

BUCKINGHAM. Such as my heart doth tremble to unfold.
A sort of naughty persons, lewdly bent,
Under the countenance and confederacy
Of Lady Eleanor, the protector's wife,

The ringleader and head of all this rout,
Have practis'd dangerously against your state,
Dealing with witches and with conjurers:
Whom we have apprehended in the fact;
Raising up wicked spirits from under-ground,
Demanding of King Henry's life and death,
And other of your Highness' privy council,
As more at large your Grace shall understand.

CARDINAL. And so, my Lord Protector, by this means
Your lady is forthcoming yet at London.
This news, I think, hath turn'd your weapon's edge;
'Tis like, my lord, you will not keep your hour.

GLOUCESTER. Ambitious churchman, leave to afflict my
      heart:
Sorrow and grief have vanquish'd all my powers;
And, vanquish'd as I am, I yield to thee,
Or to the meanest groom.

KING HENRY. O God! what mischiefs work the wicked ones,
Heaping confusion on their own heads thereby.

QUEEN MARGARET. Gloucester, see here the tainture of thy
      nest;
And look thyself be faultless, thou were best.

GLOUCESTER. Madam, for myself, to heaven I do appeal,
How I have lov'd my king and commonweal;
And, for my wife, I know not how it stands.
Sorry I am to hear what I have heard:
Noble she is, but if she have forgot
Honour and virtue, and convers'd with such
As, like to pitch, defile nobility,
I banish her my bed and company,
And give her, as a prey, to law and shame,
That hath dishonour'd Gloucester's honest name.

KING HENRY. Well, for this night we will repose us here:
To-morrow toward London back again,
To look into this business thoroughly,
And call these foul offenders to their answers;
And poise the cause in justice' equal scales,
Whose beam stands sure, whose rightful cause prevails.
                              Flourish. Exeunt

SCENE TWO

London. The Duke of York's Garden.

Enter York, Salisbury, and Warwick

YORK. Now, my good Lords of Salisbury and Warwick,
  Our simple supper ended, give me leave
  In this close walk to satisfy myself,
  In craving your opinion of my title,
  Which is infallible to England's crown.
SALISBURY. My lord, I long to hear it at full.
WARWICK. Sweet York, begin; and if thy claim be good,
  The Nevils are thy subjects to command.
YORK. Then thus:
  Edward the Third, my lords, had seven sons:
  The first, Edward the Black Prince, Prince of Wales;
  The second, William of Hatfield; and the third,
  Lionel, Duke of Clarence; next to whom
  Was John of Gaunt, the Duke of Lancaster;
  The fifth was Edmund Langley, Duke of York;
  The sixth was Thomas of Woodstock, Duke of Gloucester;
  William of Windsor was the seventh and last.
  Edward the Black Prince died before his father,
  And left behind him Richard, his only son,
  Who after Edward the Third's death, reign'd as king;
  Till Henry Bolingbroke, Duke of Lancaster,
  The eldest son and heir of John of Gaunt,
  Crown'd by the name of Henry the Fourth,
  Seiz'd on the realm, depos'd the rightful king,
  Sent his poor queen to France, from whence she came,
  And him to Pomfret; where as all you know,
  Harmless Richard was murder'd traitorously.
WARWICK. Father, the duke hath told the truth;
  Thus got the house of Lancaster the crown.
YORK. Which now they hold by force and not by right;
  For Richard, the first son's heir, being dead,
  The issue of the next son should have reign'd.
SALISBURY. But William of Hatfield died without an heir.
YORK. The third son, Duke of Clarence, from whose line
  I claim the crown, had issue, Philippe a daughter,

Who married Edmund Mortimer, Earl of March:
Edmund had issue Roger, Earl of March:
Roger had issue Edmund, Anne, and Eleanor.
SALISBURY. This Edmund, in the reign of Bolingbroke,
    As I have read, laid claim unto the crown;
    And but for Owen Glendower, had been king,
    Who kept him in captivity till he died.
    But to the rest.
YORK.   His eldest sister, Anne,
    My mother, being heir unto the crown,
    Married Richard, Earl of Cambridge, who was son
    To Edmund Langley, Edward the Third's fifth son.
    By her I claim the kingdom: she was heir
    To Roger, Earl of March; who was the son
    Of Edmund Mortimer; who married Philippe,
    Sole daughter unto Lionel, Duke of Clarence:
    So, if the issue of the eldest son
    Succeed before the younger, I am king.
WARWICK. What plain proceeding is more plain than this?
    Henry doth claim the crown from John of Gaunt,
    The fourth son; York claims it from the third.
    Till Lionel's issue fails, his should not reign:
    It fails not yet, but flourishes in thee,
    And in thy sons, fair slips of such a stock.
    Then, father Salisbury, kneel we together,
    And in this private plot be we the first
    That shall salute our rightful sovereign
    With honour of his birthright to the crown.
BOTH. Long live our sovereign Richard, England's king!
YORK. We thank you, lords! But I am not your king
    Till I be crown'd and that my sword be stain'd
    With heart-blood of the house of Lancaster;
    And that 's not suddenly to be perform'd,
    But with advice and silent secrecy.
    Do you as I do in these dangerous days,
    Wink at the Duke of Suffolk's insolence,
    At Beaufort's pride, at Somerset's ambition,
    At Buckingham and all the crew of them,
    Till they have snar'd the shepherd of the flock,
    That virtuous prince, the good Duke Humphrey:
    'Tis that they seek; and they, in seeking that
    Shall find their deaths, if York can prophesy.

SALISBURY. My lord, break we off; we know your mind at
   full.
WARWICK. My heart assures me that the Earl of Warwick
   Shall one day make the Duke of York a king.
YORK. And, Nevil, this I do assure myself,
   Richard shall live to make the Earl of Warwick
   The greatest man in England but the king.   *Exeunt*

SCENE THREE

The Same. A Hall of Justice.

*Trumpets sounded. Enter King Henry, Queen Margaret,
Gloucester, York, Suffolk, and Salisbury; the Duchess of
Gloucester, Margery Jourdain, Southwell, Hume,
and Bolingbroke, under guard*

KING HENRY. Stand forth, Dame Eleanor Cobham, Glou-
   cester's wife.
   In sight of God and us, your guilt is great:
   Receive the sentence of the law for sins
   Such as by God's book are adjudg'd to death.
   You four, from hence to prison back again;
   From thence, unto the place of execution:
   The witch in Smithfield shall be burn'd to ashes,
   And you three shall be strangled on the gallows.
   You, madam, for you are more nobly born,
   Despoiled of your honour in your life,
   Shall, after three days' open penance done,
   Live in your country here, in banishment,
   With Sir John Stanley, in the Isle of Man.
DUCHESS. Welcome is banishment; welcome were my death.
GLOUCESTER. Eleanor, the law, thou seest, hath judged thee:
   I cannot justify whom the law condemns.—
      Exeunt the Duchess, and the other Prisoners, guarded
   Mine eyes are full of tears, my heart of grief.
   Ah, Humphrey! this dishonour in thine age
   Will bring thy head with sorrow to the ground.
   I beseech your Majesty, give me leave to go;
   Sorrow would solace and mine age would ease.
KING HENRY. Stay, Humphrey, Duke of Gloucester: ere thou
   go,

Give up thy staff: Henry will to himself
Protector be; and God shall be my hope,
My stay, my guide, and lantern to my feet.
And go in peace, Humphrey; no less belov'd
Than when thou wert protector to thy king.

QUEEN MARGARET. I see no reason why a king of years
  Should be to be protected like a child.
  God and King Henry govern England's helm!
  Give up your staff, sir, and the king his realm.

GLOUCESTER. My staff! here, noble Henry, is my staff:
  As willingly do I the same resign
  As e'er thy father Henry made it mine;
  And even as willingly at thy feet I leave it
  As others would ambitiously receive it.
  Farewell, good king! when I am dead and gone,
  May honourable peace attend thy throne.   *Exit*

QUEEN MARGARET. Why, now is Henry king, and Margaret
    queen;
  And Humphrey, Duke of Gloucester, scarce himself,
  That bears so shrewd a maim: two pulls at once;
  His lady banish'd, and a limb lopp'd off;
  This staff of honour raught: there let it stand,
  Where it best fits to be, in Henry's hand.

SUFFOLK. Thus droops this lofty pine and hangs his sprays;
  Thus Eleanor's pride dies in her youngest days.

YORK. Lords, let him go. Please it your Majesty,
  This is the day appointed for the combat;
  And ready are the appellant and defendant,
  The armourer and his man, to enter the lists,
  So please your Highness to behold the fight.

QUEEN MARGARET. Ay, good my lord; for purposely there-
    fore
  Left I the court, to see this quarrel tried.

KING HENRY. O' God's name, see the lists and all things fit:
  Here let them end it; and God defend the right!

YORK. I never saw a fellow worse bested,
  Or more afraid to fight, than is the appellant,
  The servant of this armourer, my lords.

       Enter, on one side, Horner, and his
Neighbours drinking to him so much that he is drunk; and
he enters bearing his staff with a sand-bag fastened to it; a

drum before him: on the other side, Peter, with a drum and
a sand-bag; and Prentices drinking to him

FIRST NEIGHBOUR. Here, neighbour Horner, I drink to you
in a cup of sack: and fear not, neighbour, you shall do well
enough.

SECOND NEIGHBOUR. And here, neighbour, here 's a cup of
charneco.

THIRD NEIGHBOUR. And here 's a pot of good double beer,
neighbour: drink, and fear not your man.

HORNER. Let it come, i' faith, and I 'll pledge you all; and a
fig for Peter!

FIRST PRENTICE. Here, Peter, I drink to thee; and be not
afraid.

SECOND PRENTICE. Be merry, Peter, and fear not thy master:
fight for credit of the prentices.

PETER. I thank you all: drink, and pray for me, I pray you;
for, I think, I have taken my last draught in this world.
Here, Robin, an if I die, I give thee my apron: and, Will,
thou shalt have my hammer: and here, Tom, take all the
money that I have. O Lord bless me! I pray God, for I am
never able to deal with my master, he hath learnt so much
fence already.

SALISBURY. Come, leave your drinking and fall to blows.
Sirrah, what 's thy name?

PETER. Peter, forsooth.

SALISBURY. Peter! what more?

PETER. Thump.

SALISBURY. Thump! then see thou thump thy master well.

HORNER. Masters, I am come hither, as it were, upon my
man's instigation, to prove him a knave, and myself an
honest man: and touching the Duke of York, I will take
my death I never meant him any ill, nor the king, nor the
queen; and therefore, Peter, have at thee with a down-
right blow!

YORK. Dispatch: this knave's tongue begins to double.
Sound, trumpets, alarum to the combatants.

    Alarum. They fight, and Peter strikes down his Master

HORNER. Hold, Peter, hold! I confess, I confess treason. *Dies*

YORK. Take away his weapon. Fellow, thank God, and the
good wine in thy master's way.

PETER. O God! have I overcome mine enemies in this pres-
ence? O Peter, thou hast prevailed in right!

KING HENRY. Go, take hence that traitor from our sight;
  For by his death we do perceive his guilt:
  And God in justice hath reveal'd to us
  The truth and innocence of this poor fellow,
  Which he had thought to have murder'd wrongfully.
  Come, fellow, follow us for thy reward.

                    Sound a flourish. Exeunt

SCENE FOUR

The Same. A Street.

Enter Gloucester and Serving-men, in mourning cloaks

GLOUCESTER. Thus sometimes hath the brightest day a
      cloud;
  And after summer evermore succeeds
  Barren winter, with his wrathful nipping cold:
  So cares and joys abound, as seasons fleet.
  Sirs, what 's o'clock?
SERVING-MAN.   Ten, my lord.
GLOUCESTER. Ten is the hour that was appointed me
  To watch the coming of my punish'd duchess:
  Uneath may she endure the flinty streets,
  To tread them with her tender-feeling feet.
  Sweet Nell, ill can thy noble mind abrook
  The abject people, gazing on thy face
  With envious looks still laughing at thy shame,
  That erst did follow thy proud chariot wheels
  When thou didst ride in triumph through the streets.
  But, soft! I think she comes; and I 'll prepare
  My tear-stain'd eyes to see her miseries.
            Enter the Duchess of Gloucester,
*with papers pinned upon her back, in a white sheet, her feet
bare, and a taper burning in her hand; Sir John Stanley, a
                Sheriff, and Officers*
SERVING-MAN. So please your Grace, we 'll take her from the
      sheriff.
GLOUCESTER. No, stir not, for your lives; let her pass by.
DUCHESS. Come you, my lord, to see my open shame?
  Now thou dost penance too. Look! how they gaze.
  See! how the giddy multitude do point.

And nod their heads, and throw their eyes on thee.
Ah, Gloucester, hide thee from their hateful looks,
And, in thy closet pent up, rue my shame,
And ban thine enemies, both mine and thine!
GLOUCESTER. Be patient, gentle Nell; forget this grief.
DUCHESS. Ay, Gloucester, teach me to forget myself;
  For whilst I think I am thy wedded wife,
  And thou a prince, protector of this land,
  Methinks I should not thus be led along,
  Mail'd up in shame, with papers on my back,
  And follow'd with a rabble that rejoice
  To see my tears and hear my deep-fet groans.
  The ruthless flint doth cut my tender feet,
  And when I start, the envious people laugh,
  And bid me be advised how I tread.
  Ah, Humphrey! can I bear this shameful yoke?
  Trow'st thou that e'er I 'll look upon the world,
  Or count them happy that enjoy the sun?
  No; dark shall be my light, and night my day;
  To think upon my pomp shall be my hell.
  Sometime I 'll say, I am Duke Humphrey's wife;
  And he a prince and ruler of the land:
  Yet so he rul'd and such a prince he was
  As he stood by whilst I, his forlorn duchess,
  Was made a wonder and a pointing-stock
  To every idle rascal follower.
  But be thou mild and blush not at my shame;
  Nor stir at nothing till the axe of death
  Hang over thee, as, sure, it shortly will;
  For Suffolk, he that can do all in all
  With her that hateth thee, and hates us all,
  And York, and impious Beaufort, that false priest,
  Have all lim'd bushes to betray thy wings;
  And, fly thou how thou canst, they 'll tangle thee:
  But fear not thou, until thy foot be snar'd,
  Nor never seek prevention of thy foes.
GLOUCESTER. Ah, Nell! forbear: thou aimest all awry;
  I must offend before I be attainted;
  And had I twenty times so many foes,
  And each of them had twenty times their power,
  All these could not procure me any scath,
  So long as I am loyal, true, and crimeless.

Wouldst have me rescue thee from this reproach?
Why, yet thy scandal were not wip'd away,
But I in danger for the breach of law.
Thy greatest help is quiet, gentle Nell:
I pray thee, sort thy heart to patience;
These few days' wonder will be quickly worn.

Enter a Herald

HERALD. I summon your Grace to his Majesty's parliament,
  holden at Bury the first of this next month.
GLOUCESTER. And my consent ne'er ask'd herein before!
  This is close dealing. Well, I will be there.   *Exit Herald*
  My Nell, I take my leave: and, master sheriff,
  Let not her penance exceed the king's commission.
SHERIFF. An 't please your Grace, here my commission
      stays;
  And Sir John Stanley is appointed now
  To take her with him to the Isle of Man.
GLOUCESTER. Must you, Sir John, protect my lady here?
STANLEY. So am I given in charge, may 't please your Grace.
GLOUCESTER. Entreat her not the worse in that I pray
  You use her well. The world may laugh again;
  And I may live to do you kindness if
  You do it her: and so, Sir John, farewell.
DUCHESS. What! gone, my lord, and bid me not farewell!
GLOUCESTER. Witness my tears, I cannot stay to speak.

Exeunt Gloucester and Serving-men

DUCHESS. Art thou gone too? All comfort go with thee!
  For none abides with me: my joy is death;
  Death, at whose name I oft have been afear'd,
  Because I wish'd this world's eternity.
  Stanley, I prithee, go, and take me hence;
  I care not whither, for I beg no favour,
  Only convey me where thou art commanded.
STANLEY. Why, madam, that is to the Isle of Man;
  There to be us'd according to your state.
DUCHESS. That 's bad enough, for I am but reproach:
  And shall I then be us'd reproachfully?
STANLEY. Like to a duchess, and Duke Humphrey's lady:
  According to that state you shall be us'd.
DUCHESS. Sheriff, farewell, and better than I fare,
  Although thou hast been conduct of my shame.
SHERIFF. It is my office; and, madam, pardon me.

DUCHESS. Ay, ay, farewell; thy office is discharg'd.
Come, Stanley, shall we go?
STANLEY. Madam, your penance done, throw off this sheet,
And go we to attire you for our journey.
DUCHESS. My shame will not be shifted with my sheet:
No; it will hang upon my richest robes,
And show itself, attire me how I can.
Go, lead the way; I long to see my prison.   *Exeunt*

ACT THREE

SCENE ONE

The Abbey at Bury St. Edmund's.

Sound a sennet. Enter to the Parliament, King Henry, Queen Margaret, Cardinal Beaufort, Suffolk, York, Buckingham, and Others

KING HENRY. I muse my Lord of Gloucester is not come:
  'Tis not his wont to be the hindmost man,
  Whate'er occasion keeps him from us now.
QUEEN MARGARET. Can you not see? or will ye not observe
  The strangeness of his alter'd countenance?
  With what a majesty he bears himself,
  How insolent of late he is become,
  How proud, how peremptory, and unlike himself?
  We know the time since he was mild and affable,
  An if we did but glance a far-off look,
  Immediately he was upon his knee,
  That all the court admir'd him for submission:
  But meet him now, and, be it in the morn,
  When everyone will give the time of day,
  He knits his brow and shows an angry eye,
  And passeth by with stiff unbowed knee,
  Disdaining duty that to us belongs.
  Small curs are not regarded when they grin,
  But great men tremble when the lion roars;
  And Humphrey is no little man in England.
  First note that he is near you in descent,
  And should you fall, he is the next will mount.
  Me seemeth then it is no policy,
  Respecting what a rancorous mind he bears,
  And his advantage following your decease,
  That he should come about your royal person
  Or be admitted to your Highness' council.
  By flattery hath he won the commons' hearts,

And when he please to make commotion,
'Tis to be fear'd they all will follow him.
Now 'tis the spring, and weeds are shallow-rooted;
Suffer them now and they 'll o'ergrow the garden,
And choke the herbs for want of husbandry.
The reverent care I bear unto my lord
Made me collect these dangers in the duke.
If it be fond, call it a woman's fear;
Which fear if better reasons can supplant,
I will subscribe and say I wrong'd the duke.
My Lord of Suffolk, Buckingham, and York,
Reprove my allegation if you can
Or else conclude my words effectual.

SUFFOLK. Well hath your Highness seen into this duke;
And had I first been put to speak my mind,
I think I should have told your Grace's tale.
The duchess, by his subornation,
Upon my life, began her devilish practices:
Or if he were not privy to those faults,
Yet, by reputing of his high descent,
As, next the king he was successive heir,
And such high vaunts of his nobility,
Did instigate the bedlam brain-sick duchess,
By wicked means to frame our sovereign's fall.
Smooth runs the water where the brook is deep,
And in his simple show he harbours treason.
The fox barks not when he would steal the lamb:
No, no, my sovereign; Gloucester is a man
Unsounded yet, and full of deep deceit.

CARDINAL. Did he not, contrary to form of law,
Devise strange deaths for small offences done?

YORK. And did he not, in his protectorship,
Levy great sums of money through the realm
For soldiers' pay in France, and never sent it?
By means whereof the towns each day revolted.

BUCKINGHAM. Tut! these are petty faults to faults unknown,
Which time will bring to light in smooth Duke Humphrey.

KING HENRY. My lords, at once: the care you have of us,
To mow down thorns that would annoy our foot,
Is worthy praise; but shall I speak my conscience,
Our kinsman Gloucester is as innocent
From meaning treason to our royal person,

As is the sucking lamb or harmless dove.
The duke is virtuous, mild, and too well given
To dream on evil, or to work my downfall.

QUEEN MARGARET. Ah! what 's more dangerous than this
    fond affiance!
Seems he a dove? his feathers are but borrow'd,
For he 's disposed as the hateful raven:
Is he a lamb? his skin is surely lent him,
For he 's inclin'd as is the ravenous wolf.
Who cannot steal a shape that means deceit?
Take heed, my lord; the welfare of us all
Hangs on the cutting short that fraudful man.

Enter Somerset

SOMERSET. All health unto my gracious sovereign!

KING HENRY. Welcome, Lord Somerset. What news from
    France?

SOMERSET. That all your interest in those territories
Is utterly bereft you; all is lost.

KING HENRY. Cold news, Lord Somerset: but God's will be
    done!

YORK. (*Aside*) Cold news for me; for I had hope of France,
As firmly as I hope for fertile England.
Thus are my blossoms blasted in the bud,
And caterpillars eat my leaves away;
But I will remedy this gear ere long,
Or sell my title for a glorious grave.

Enter Gloucester

GLOUCESTER. All happiness unto my lord the king!
Pardon, my liege, that I have stay'd so long.

SUFFOLK. Nay, Gloucester, know that thou art come too
    soon,
Unless thou wert more loyal than thou art:
I do arrest thee of high treason here.

GLOUCESTER. Well, Suffolk's duke, thou shalt not see me
    blush,
Nor change my countenance for this arrest:
A heart unspotted is not easily daunted.
The purest spring is not so free from mud
As I am clear from treason to my sovereign.
Who can accuse me? wherein am I guilty?

YORK. 'Tis thought, my lord, that you took bribes of France,
And, being protector, stay'd the soldiers' pay;

By means whereof his Highness hath lost France.

GLOUCESTER. Is it but thought so? What are they that think
    it?
  I never robb'd the soldiers of their pay,
  Nor ever had one penny bribe from France.
  So help me God, as I have watch'd the night,
  Ay, night by night, in studying good for England,
  That doit that e'er I wrested from the king,
  Or any groat I hoarded to my use,
  Be brought against me at my trial-day!
  No; many a pound of mine own proper store,
  Because I would not tax the needy commons,
  Have I disbursed to the garrisons,
  And never ask'd for restitution.

CARDINAL. It serves you well, my lord, to say so much.

GLOUCESTER. I say no more than truth, so help me God!

YORK. In your protectorship you did devise
  Strange tortures for offenders, never heard of,
  That England was defam d by tyranny.

GLOUCESTER. Why, 'tis well known that, whiles I was pro-
    tector,
  Pity was all the fault that was in me;
  For I should melt at an offender's tears,
  And lowly words were ransom for their fault.
  Unless it were a bloody murderer,
  Or foul felonious thief that fleec'd poor passengers,
  I never gave them condign punishment:
  Murder, indeed, that bloody sin, I tortur'd
  Above the felon or what trespass else.

SUFFOLK. My lord, these faults are easy, quickly answer'd:
  But mightier crimes are laid unto your charge,
  Whereof you cannot easily purge yourself.
  I do arrest you in his Highness' name;
  And here commit you to my Lord Cardinal
  To keep until your further time of trial.

KING HENRY. My Lord of Gloucester, 'tis my special hope
  That you will clear yourself from all suspect:
  My conscience tells me you are innocent.

GLOUCESTER. Ah! gracious lord, these days are dangerous.
  Virtue is chok'd with foul ambition,
  And charity chas'd hence by rancour's hand;
  Foul subornation is predominant,

And equity exil'd your Highness' land.
I know their complot is to have my life;
And if my death might make this island happy,
And prove the period of their tyranny,
I would expend it with all willingness;
But mine is made the prologue to their play;
For thousands more, that yet suspect no peril,
Will not conclude their plotted tragedy.
Beaufort's red sparkling eyes blab his heart's malice,
And Suffolk's cloudy brow his stormy hate;
Sharp Buckingham unburdens with his tongue
The envious load that lies upon his heart;
And dogged York, that reaches at the moon,
Whose overweening arm I have pluck'd back,
By false accuse doth level at my life:
And you, my sovereign lady, with the rest,
Causeless have laid disgraces on my head,
And with your best endeavour have stirr'd up
My liefest liege to be mine enemy.
Ay, all of you have laid your heads together;
Myself had notice of your conventicles;
And all to make away my guiltless life.
I shall not want false witness to condemn me,
Nor store of treasons to augment my guilt;
The ancient proverb will be well effected:
'A staff is quickly found to beat a dog.'
CARDINAL. My liege, his railing is intolerable.
If those that care to keep your royal person
From treason's secret knife and traitor's rage
Be thus upbraided, chid, and rated at,
And the offender granted scope of speech,
'Twill make them cool in zeal unto your Grace.
SUFFOLK. Hath he not twit our sovereign lady here
With ignominious words, though clerkly couch'd,
As if she had suborned some to swear
False allegations to o'erthrow his state?
QUEEN MARGARET. But I can give the loser leave to chide.
GLOUCESTER. Far truer spoke than meant: I lose, indeed;
Beshrew the winners, for they play'd me false!
And well such losers may have leave to speak.
BUCKINGHAM. He 'll wrest the sense and hold us here all day.
Lord Cardinal, he is your prisoner.

CARDINAL. Sirs, take away the duke, and guard him sure.
GLOUCESTER. Ah! thus King Henry throws away his crutch
    Before his legs be firm to bear his body:
    Thus is the shepherd beaten from thy side,
    And wolves are gnarling who shall gnaw thee first.
    Ah! that my fear were false, ah! that it were;
    For, good King Henry, thy decay I fear.
                    Exeunt Attendants with Gloucester
KING HENRY. My lords, what to your wisdoms seemeth best
    Do or undo, as if ourself were here.
QUEEN MARGARET. What! will your Highness leave the par-
        liament?
KING HENRY. Ay, Margaret; my heart is drown'd with grief,
    Whose flood begins to flow within mine eyes,
    My body round engirt with misery,
    For what 's more miserable than discontent?
    Ah! uncle Humphrey, in thy face I see
    The map of honour, truth, and loyalty;
    And yet, good Humphrey, is the hour to come
    That e'er I prov'd thee false, or fear'd thy faith.
    What lowering star now envies thy estate,
    That these great lords, and Margaret our queen,
    Do seek subversion of thy harmless life?
    Thou never didst them wrong, nor no man wrong;
    And as the butcher takes away the calf,
    And binds the wretch, and beats it when it strays,
    Bearing it to the bloody slaughter-house,
    Even so, remorseless, have they borne him hence;
    And as the dam runs lowing up and down,
    Looking the way her harmless young one went,
    And can do nought but wail her darling's loss;
    Even so myself bewails good Gloucester's case,
    With sad unhelpful tears, and with dimm'd eyes
    Look after him, and cannot do him good;
    So mighty are his vowed enemies.
    His fortunes I will weep; and, 'twixt each groan,
    Say 'Who 's a traitor, Gloucester he is none.'   *Exit*
QUEEN MARGARET. Fair lords, cold snow melts with the sun's
        hot beams.
    Henry my lord is cold in great affairs,
    Too full of foolish pity; and Gloucester's show
    Beguiles him as the mournful crocodile

With sorrow snares relenting passengers;
Or as the snake, roll'd in a flowering bank,
With shining checker's slough, doth sting a child
That for the beauty thinks it excellent.
Believe me, lords, were none more wise than I,—
And yet herein I judge mine own wit good,—
This Gloucester should be quickly rid the world,
To rid us from the fear we have of him.

CARDINAL. That he should die is worthy policy;
And yet we want a colour for his death.
'Tis meet he be condemn'd by course of law.

SUFFOLK. But in my mind that were no policy:
The king will labour still to save his life;
The commons haply rise to save his life;
And yet we have but trivial argument,
More than mistrust, that shows him worthy death.

YORK. So that, by this, you would not have him die.

SUFFOLK. Ah! York, no man alive so fain as I.

YORK. 'Tis York that hath more reason for his death.
But my Lord Cardinal, and you, my Lord of Suffolk,
Say as you think, and speak it from your souls,
Were 't not all one an empty eagle were set
To guard the chicken from a hungry kite,
As place Duke Humphrey for the king's protector?

QUEEN MARGARET. So the poor chicken should be sure of
death.

SUFFOLK. Madam, 'tis true: and were 't not madness, then,
To make the fox surveyor of the fold?
Who, being accus'd a crafty murderer,
His guilt should be but idly posted over
Because his purpose is not executed.
No; let him die, in that he is a fox,
By nature prov'd an enemy to the flock,
Before his chaps be stain'd with crimson blood,
As Humphrey, prov'd by reasons, to my liege.
And do not stand on quillets how to slay him:
Be it by gins, by snares, by subtilty,
Sleeping or waking, 'tis no matter how,
So he be dead; for that is good deceit
Which mates him first that first intends deceit.

QUEEN MARGARET. Thrice noble Suffolk, 'tis resolutely
spoke.

SUFFOLK. Not resolute, except so much were done,
  For things are often spoke and seldom meant;
  But, that my heart accordeth with my tongue,
  Seeing the deed is meritorious,
  And to preserve my sovereign from his foe,
  Say but the word and I will be his priest.
CARDINAL. But I would have him dead, my Lord of Suffolk,
  Ere you can take due orders for a priest:
  Say you consent and censure well the deed,
  And I 'll provide his executioner;
  I tender so the safety of my liege.
SUFFOLK. Here is my hand, the deed is worthy doing.
QUEEN MARGARET. And so say I.
YORK. And I: and now we three have spoke it,
  It skills not greatly who impugns our doom.

Enter a Messenger

MESSENGER. Great lords, from Ireland am I come amain,
  To signify that rebels there are up,
  And put the Englishmen unto the sword.
  Send succours, lords, and stop the rage betime,
  Before the wound do grow uncurable;
  For, being green, there is great hope of help.
CARDINAL. A breach that craves a quick expedient stop!
  What counsel give you in this weighty cause?
YORK. That Somerset be sent as regent thither.
  'Tis meet that lucky ruler be employ'd;
  Witness the fortune he hath had in France.
SOMERSET. If York, with all his far-fet policy,
  Had been the regent there instead of me,
  He never would have stay'd in France so long.
YORK. No, not to lose it all, as thou hast done:
  I rather would have lost my life betimes
  Than bring a burden of dishonour home,
  By staying there so long till all were lost.
  Show me one scar character'd on thy skin:
  Men's flesh preserv'd so whole do seldom win.
QUEEN MARGARET. Nay then, this spark will prove a raging
    fire,
  If wind and fuel be brought to feed it with.
  No more, good York; sweet Somerset, be still:
  Thy fortune, York, hadst thou been regent there,
  Might happily have prov'd far worse than his.

YORK. What! worse than nought? nay, then a shame take all.
SOMERSET. And in the number three, that wishest shame.
CARDINAL. My Lord of York, try what your fortune is.
　The uncivil kerns of Ireland are in arms
　And temper clay with blood of Englishmen:
　To Ireland will you lead a band of men,
　Collected choicely, from each county some,
　And try your hap against the Irishmen?
YORK. I will, my lord, so please his Majesty.
SUFFOLK. Why, our authority is his consent,
　And what we do establish he confirms:
　Then, noble York, take thou this task in hand.
YORK. I am content: provide me soldiers, lords,
　Whiles I take order for mine own affairs.
SUFFOLK. A charge, Lord York, that I will see perform'd.
　But now return we to the false Duke Humphrey.
CARDINAL. No more of him: for I will deal with him
　That henceforth he shall trouble us no more.
　And so break off; the day is almost spent.
　Lord Suffolk, you and I must talk of that event.
YORK. My Lord of Suffolk, within fourteen days
　At Bristol I expect my soldiers;
　For there I 'll ship them all for Ireland.
SUFFOLK. I 'll see it truly done, my Lord of York.
　　　　　　　　　　　　　Exeunt all except York
YORK. Now, York, or never, steel thy fearful thoughts,
　And change misdoubt to resolution:
　Be that thou hopest to be, or what thou art
　Resign to death; it is not worth the enjoying.
　Let pale-fac'd fear keep with the mean-born man,
　And find no harbour in a royal heart.
　Faster than spring-time showers comes thought on
　　　thought,
　And not a thought but thinks on dignity.
　My brain, more busy than the labouring spider,
　Weaves tedious snares to trap mine enemies.
　Well, nobles, well; 'tis politicly done,
　To send me packing with a host of men:
　I fear me you but warm the starved snake,
　Who, cherish'd in your breasts, will sting your hearts.
　'Twas men I lack'd, and you will give them me:
　I take it kindly; yet be well assur'd

You put sharp weapons in a madman's hands.
Whiles I in Ireland nourish a mighty band,
I will stir up in England some black storm
Shall blow ten thousand souls to heaven or hell;
And this fell tempest shall not cease to rage
Until the golden circuit on my head,
Like to the glorious sun's transparent beams,
Do calm the fury of this mad-bred flaw.
And, for a minister of my intent,
I have seduc'd a headstrong Kentishman,
John Cade of Ashford,
To make commotion, as full well he can,
Under the title of John Mortimer.
In Ireland have I seen this stubborn Cade
Oppose himself against a troop of kerns,
And fought so long, till that his thighs with darts
Were almost like a sharp-quill'd porpentine:
And, in the end being rescu'd, I have seen
Him caper upright like a wild Morisco,
Shaking the bloody darts as he his bells.
Full often, like a shag-hair'd crafty kern,
Hath he conversed with the enemy,
And undiscover'd come to me again,
And given me notice of their villanies.
This devil here shall be my substitute;
For that John Mortimer, which now is dead,
In face, in gait, in speech, he doth resemble;
By this I shall perceive the commons' mind,
How they affect the house and claim of York.
Say he be taken, rack'd, and tortured,
I know no pain they can inflict upon him
Will make him say I mov'd him to those arms.
Say that he thrive,—as 'tis great like he will,—
Why, then from Ireland come I with my strength,
And reap the harvest which that rascal sow'd;
For, Humphrey being dead, as he shall be,
And Henry put apart, the next for me.   *Exit*

SCENE TWO

Bury St. Edmund's. A Room in the Palace.

Enter certain Murderers, hastily

FIRST MURDERER. Run to my Lord of Suffolk; let him know
We have dispatch'd the duke, as he commanded.

SECOND MURDERER. O! that it were to do. What have we
done?
Didst ever hear a man so penitent?

Enter Suffolk

FIRST MURDERER. Here comes my lord.

SUFFOLK. Now, sirs, have you dispatch'd this thing?

FIRST MURDERER. Ay, my good lord, he 's dead.

SUFFOLK. Why, that 's well said. Go, get you to my house;
I will reward you for this venturous deed.
The king and all the peers are here at hand.
Have you laid fair the bed? is all things well,
According as I gave directions?

FIRST MURDERER. 'Tis, my good lord.

SUFFOLK. Away! be gone.   *Exeunt Murderers*

*Sound trumpets. Enter King Henry, Queen
Margaret, Cardinal Beaufort, Somerset, Lords, and Others*

KING HENRY. Go, call our uncle to our presence straight;
Say, we intend to try his Grace to-day,
If he be guilty, as 'tis published.

SUFFOLK. I 'll call him presently, my noble lord.   *Exit*

KING HENRY. Lords, take your places; and, I pray you all,
Proceed no straiter 'gainst our uncle Gloucester
Than from true evidence, of good esteem,
He be approv'd in practice culpable.

QUEEN MARGARET. God forbid any malice should prevail
That faultless may condemn a nobleman!
Pray God, he may acquit him of suspicion!

KING HENRY. I thank thee, Meg; these words content me
much.

Re-enter Suffolk

How now! why look'st thou pale? why tremblest thou?
Where is our uncle? what 's the matter, Suffolk?

SUFFOLK. Dead in his bed, my lord; Gloucester is dead.

QUEEN MARGARET. Marry, God forfend!

CARDINAL. God's secret judgment: I did dream to-night
  The duke was dumb, and could not speak a word.

The King swoons

QUEEN MARGARET. How fares my lord! Help, lords! the
  king is dead.

SOMERSET. Rear up his body; wring him by the nose.

QUEEN MARGARET. Run, go, help, help! O Henry, ope thine
  eyes!

SUFFOLK. He doth revive again. Madam, be patient.

KING HENRY. O heavenly God!

QUEEN MARGARET.   How fares my gracious lord?

SUFFOLK. Comfort, my sovereign! gracious Henry, comfort!

KING HENRY. What! doth my Lord of Suffolk comfort me?
  Came he right now to sing a raven's note,
  Whose dismal tune bereft my vital powers,
  And thinks he that the chirping of a wren,
  By crying comfort from a hollow breast,
  Can chase away the first-conceived sound?
  Hide not thy poison with such sugar'd words:
  Lay not thy hands on me; forbear, I say:
  Their touch affrights me as a serpent's sting.
  Thou baleful messenger, out of my sight!
  Upon thy eyeballs murderous tyranny
  Sits in grim majesty to fright the world.
  Look not upon me, for thine eyes are wounding:
  Yet do not go away; come, basilisk,
  And kill the innocent gazer with thy sight;
  For in the shade of death I shall find joy,
  In life but double death, now Gloucester's dead.

QUEEN MARGARET. Why do you rate my Lord of Suffolk
  thus?
  Although the duke was enemy to him,
  Yet he, most Christian-like, laments his death:
  And for myself, foe as he was to me,
  Might liquid tears or heart-offending groans
  Or blood-consuming sighs recall his life,
  I would be blind with weeping, sick with groans,
  Look pale as primrose with blood-drinking sighs,
  And all to have the noble duke alive.
  What know I how the world may deem of me?
  For it is known we were but hollow friends:

It may be judg'd I made the duke away:
So shall my name with slander's tongue be wounded,
And princes' courts be fill'd with my reproach.
This get I by his death. Ay me, unhappy!
To be a queen, and crown'd with infamy!
KING HENRY. Ah! woe is me for Gloucester, wretched man.
QUEEN MARGARET. Be woe for me, more wretched than he
    is.
What! dost thou turn away and hide thy face?
I am no loathsome leper; look on me.
What! art thou, like the adder, waxen deaf?
Be poisonous too and kill thy forlorn queen.
Is all thy comfort shut in Gloucester's tomb?
Why, then, Dame Margaret was ne'er thy joy:
Erect his statua and worship it,
And make my image but an alehouse sign.
Was I for this nigh wrack'd upon the sea,
And twice by awkward wind from England's bank
Drove back again unto my native clime?
What boded this, but well forewarning wind
Did seem to say, 'Seek not a scorpion's nest,
Nor set no footing on this unkind shore'?
What did I then, but curs'd the gentle gusts
And he that loos'd them forth their brazen caves;
And bid them blow towards England's blessed shore,
Or turn our stern upon a dreadful rock?
Yet Æolus would not be a murderer,
But left that hateful office unto thee:
The pretty vaulting sea refus'd to drown me,
Knowing that thou wouldst have me drown'd on shore
With tears as salt as sea through thy unkindness:
The splitting rocks cower'd in the sinking sands,
And would not dash me with their ragged sides,
Because thy flinty heart, more hard than they,
Might in thy palace perish Margaret.
As far as I could ken thy chalky cliffs,
When from thy shore the tempest beat us back,
I stood upon the hatches in the storm,
And when the dusky sky began to rob
My earnest-gaping sight of thy land's view,
I took a costly jewel from my neck,
A heart it was, bound in with diamonds,

And threw it towards thy land: the sea receiv'd it,
And so I wish'd thy body might my heart:
And even with this I lost fair England's view,
And bid mine eyes be packing with my heart,
And call'd them blind and dusky spectacles
For losing ken of Albion's wished coast.
How often have I tempted Suffolk's tongue—
The agent of thy foul inconstancy—
To sit and witch me, as Ascanius did
When he to madding Dido would unfold
His father's acts, commenc'd in burning Troy!
Am I not witch'd like her? or thou not false like him?
Ay me! I can no more. Die, Margaret!
For Henry weeps that thou dost live so long.

   Noise within. Enter Warwick
  and Salisbury. The Commons press to the door

WARWICK. It is reported, mighty sovereign,
 That good Duke Humphrey traitorously is murder'd
 By Suffolk and the Cardinal Beaufort's means.
 The commons, like an angry hive of bees
 That want their leader, scatter up and down,
 And care not who they sting in his revenge.
 Myself have calm'd their spleenful mutiny,
 Until they hear the order of his death.
KING HENRY. That he is dead, good Warwick, 'tis too true;
 But how he died God knows, not Henry.
 Enter his chamber, view his breathless corpse,
 And comment then upon his sudden death.
WARWICK. That shall I do, my liege. Stay, Salisbury,
 With the rude multitude till I return.

  Warwick goes into an inner chamber. Salisbury retires

KING HENRY. O! Thou that judgest all things, stay my
  thoughts,
 My thoughts that labour to persuade my soul
 Some violent hands were laid on Humphrey's life.
 If my suspect be false, forgive me, God,
 For judgment only doth belong to thee.
 Fain would I go to chafe his paly lips
 With twenty thousand kisses, and to drain
 Upon his face an ocean of salt tears,
 To tell my love unto his deaf dumb trunk,
 And with my fingers feel his hand unfeeling:

But all in vain are these mean obsequies,
And to survey his dead and earthly image
What were it but to make my sorrow greater?
Re-enter Warwick
and Others, bearing Gloucester's body on a bed

WARWICK. Come hither, gracious sovereign, view this body.

KING HENRY. That is to see how deep my grave is made;
For with his soul fled all my wordly solace,
For seeing him I see my life in death.

WARWICK. As surely as my soul intends to live
With that dread King that took our state upon him
To free us from his Father's wrathful curse,
I do believe that violent hands were laid
Upon the life of this thrice-famed duke.

SUFFOLK. A dreadful oath, sworn with a solemn tongue!
What instance gives Lord Warwick for his vow?

WARWICK. See how the blood is settled in his face.
Oft have I seen a timely-parted ghost,
Of ashy semblance, meagre, pale, and bloodless,
Being all descended to the labouring heart;
Who, in the conflict that it holds with death,
Attracts the same for aidance 'gainst the enemy;
Which with the heart there cools, and ne'er returneth
To blush and beautify the cheek again.
But see, his face is black and full of blood,
His eyeballs further out than when he liv'd,
Staring full ghastly like a strangled man;
His hair uprear'd, his nostrils stretch'd with struggling:
His hands abroad display'd, as one that grasp'd
And tugg'd for life, and was by strength subdu'd.
Look on the sheets, his hair, you see, is sticking;
His well-proportion'd beard made rough and rugged,
Like to the summer's corn by tempest lodg'd.
It cannot be but he was murder'd here;
The least of all these signs were probable.

SUFFOLK. Why, Warwick, who should do the duke to death?
Myself and Beaufort had him in protection;
And we, I hope, sir, are no murderers.

WARWICK. But both of you were vow'd Duke Humphrey's
    foes,
And you, forsooth, had the good duke to keep:
'Tis like you would not feast him like a friend,

And 'tis well seen he found an enemy.

QUEEN MARGARET. Then you, belike, suspect these noble-
men
As guilty of Duke Humphrey's timeless death.

WARWICK. Who finds the heifer dead, and bleeding fresh,
And sees fast by a butcher with an axe,
But will suspect 'twas he that made the slaughter?
Who finds the partridge in the puttock's nest,
But may imagine how the bird was dead,
Although the kite soar with unbloodied beak?
Even so suspicious is this tragedy.

QUEEN MARGARET. Are you the butcher, Suffolk? where 's
your knife?
Is Beaufort term'd a kite? where are his talons?

SUFFOLK. I wear no knife to slaughter sleeping men;
But here 's a vengeful sword, rusted with ease,
That shall be scoured in his rancorous heart
That slanders me with murder's crimson badge.
Say, if thou dar'st, proud Lord of Warwickshire,
That I am faulty in Duke Humphrey's death.
                Exeunt Cardinal Beaufort, Somerset, and Others

WARWICK. What dares not Warwick, if false Suffolk dare
him?

QUEEN MARGARET. He dares not calm his contumelious
spirit,
Nor cease to be an arrogant controller,
Though Suffolk dare him twenty thousand times.

WARWICK. Madam, be still, with reverence may I say;
For every word you speak in his behalf
Is slander to your royal dignity.

SUFFOLK. Blunt-witted lord, ignoble in demeanour!
If ever lady wrong'd her lord so much,
Thy mother took into her blameful bed
Some stern untutor'd churl, and noble stock
Was graft with crab-tree slip; whose fruit thou art,
And never of the Nevils' noble race.

WARWICK. But that the guilt of murder bucklers thee,
And I should rob the deathsman of his fee,
Quitting thee thereby of ten thousand shames,
And that my sovereign's presence makes me mild,
I would, false murderous coward, on thy knee
Make thee beg pardon for thy passed speech,

And say it was thy mother that thou meant'st;
That thou thyself wast born in bastardy:
And after all this fearful homage done,
Give thee thy hire, and send thy soul to hell,
Pernicious blood-sucker of sleeping men.

SUFFOLK. Thou shalt be waking while I shed thy blood,
If from this presence thou dar'st go with me.

WARWICK. Away even now, or I will drag thee hence:
Unworthy though thou art, I 'll cope with thee,
And do some service to Duke Humphrey's ghost.

Exeunt Suffolk and Warwick

KING HENRY. What stronger breastplate than a heart
untainted!
Thrice is he arm'd that hath his quarrel just,
And he but naked, though lock'd up in steel,
Whose conscience with injustice is corrupted.

A noise within

QUEEN MARGARET. What noise is this?

Re-enter Suffolk and Warwick, with their weapons drawn

KING HENRY. Why, how now, lords! your wrathful weapons
drawn
Here in our presence! dare you be so bold?
Why, what tumultuous clamour have we here?

SUFFOLK. The traitorous Warwick, with the men of Bury,
Set all upon me, mighty sovereign.

Noise of a crowd within. Re-enter Salisbury

SALISBURY. (*Speaking to those within*) Sirs, stand apart; the
king shall know your mind.
Dread lord, the commons send you word by me,
Unless false Suffolk straight be done to death,
Or banished fair England's territories,
They will by violence tear him from your palace
And torture him with grievous lingering death.
They say, by him the good Duke Humphrey died;
They say, in him they fear your Highness' death;
And mere instinct of love and loyalty,
Free from a stubborn opposite intent,
As being thought to contradict your liking,
Makes them thus forward in his banishment.
They say, in care of your most royal person,
That if your Highness should intend to sleep,
And charge that no man should disturb your rest

In pain of your dislike or pain of death,
Yet, notwithstanding such a strait edict,
Were there a serpent seen, with forked tongue,
That slily glided towards your Majesty,
It were but necessary you were wak'd,
Lest, being suffer'd in that harmful slumber,
The mortal worm might make the sleep eternal:
And therefore do they cry, though you forbid,
That they will guard you, whe'r you will or no,
From such fell serpents as false Suffolk is;
With whose envenomed and fatal sting,
Your loving uncle, twenty times his worth,
They say, is shamefully bereft of life.

COMMONS. (*Within*) An answer from the king, my Lord of
    Salisbury!
SUFFOLK. 'Tis like the commons, rude unpolish'd hinds,
    Could send such message to their sovereign;
    But you, my lord, were glad to be employ'd,
    To show how quaint an orator you are:
    But all the honour Salisbury hath won
    Is that he was the lord ambassador
    Sent from a sort of tinkers to the king.
COMMONS (*Within*) An answer from the king, or we will all
        break in!
KING HENRY. Go, Salisbury, and tell them all from me,
    I thank them for their tender loving care;
    And had I not been cited so by them,
    Yet did I purpose as they do entreat;
    For, sure, my thoughts do hourly prophesy
    Mischance unto my state by Suffolk's means:
    And therefore, by his majesty I swear,
    Whose far unworthy deputy I am,
    He shall not breathe infection in this air
    But three days longer, on the pain of death.
                                    Exit Salisbury
QUEEN MARGARET. O Henry! let me plead for gentle Suffolk.
KING HENRY. Ungentle queen, to call him gentle Suffolk!
    No more, I say; if thou dost plead for him
    Thou wilt but add increase unto my wrath.
    Had I but said, I would have kept my word,
    But when I swear, it is irrevocable.

(*To Suffolk*) If after three days' space thou here be'st
    found
On any ground that I am ruler of,
The world shall not be ransom for thy life.
Come, Warwick, come, good Warwick, go with me;
I have great matters to impart to thee.

Exeunt King Henry, Warwick, Lords, &c.

QUEEN MARGARET. Mischance and sorrow go along with
    you!
Heart's discontent and sour affliction
Be playfellows to keep you company!
There 's two of you; the devil make a third,
And threefold vengeance tend upon your steps!

SUFFOLK. Cease, gentle queen, these execrations,
And let thy Suffolk take his heavy leave.

QUEEN MARGARET. Fie, coward woman and soft-hearted
    wretch!
Hast thou not spirit to curse thine enemy?

SUFFOLK. A plague upon them! Wherefore should I curse
    them?
Would curses kill, as doth the mandrake's groan,
I would invent as bitter-searching terms,
As curst, as harsh and horrible to hear,
Deliver'd strongly through my fixed teeth,
With full as many signs of deadly hate,
As lean-fac'd Envy in her loathsome cave.
My tongue should stumble in mine earnest words;
Mine eyes should sparkle like the beaten flint;
My hair be fix'd on end, as one distract;
Ay, every joint should seem to curse and ban:
And even now my burden'd heart would break,
Should I not curse them. Poison be their drink!
Gall, worse than gall, the daintiest that they taste!
Their sweetest shade a grove of cypress trees!
Their chiefest prospect murdering basilisks!
Their softest touch as smart as lizard's stings!
Their music frightful as the serpent's hiss,
And boding screech-owls make the concert full!
All the foul terrors in dark-seated hell—

QUEEN MARGARET. Enough, sweet Suffolk; thou torment'st
    thyself;
And these dread curses, like the sun 'gainst glass,

    Or like an over-charged gun, recoil,
    And turn the force of them upon thyself.
SUFFOLK. You bade me ban, and will you bid me leave?
    Now, by the ground that I am banish'd from,
    Well could I curse away a winter's night,
    Though standing naked on a mountain top,
    Where biting cold would never let grass grow,
    And think it but a minute spent in sport.
QUEEN MARGARET. O! let me entreat thee, cease! Give me
      thy hand,
    That I may dew it with my mournful tears;
    Nor let the rain of heaven wet this place,
    To wash away my woeful monuments.
    O! could this kiss be printed in thy hand,   *Kisses his hand*
    That thou mightst think upon these by the seal,
    Through whom a thousand sighs are breath'd for thee.
    So, get thee gone, that I may know my grief;
    'Tis but surmis'd whiles thou art standing by,
    As one that surfeits thinking on a want.
    I will repeal thee, or, be well assur'd,
    Adventure to be banished myself;
    And banished I am, if but from thee.
    Go; speak not to me; even now be gone.
    O! go not yet. Even thus two friends condemn'd
    Embrace and kiss, and take ten thousand leaves,
    Loather a hundred times to part than die.
    Yet now farewell; and farewell life with thee!
SUFFOLK. Thus is poor Suffolk ten times banished,
    Once by the king, and three times thrice by thee.
    'Tis not the land I care for, wert thou thence;
    A wilderness is populous enough,
    So Suffolk had thy heavenly company:
    For where thou art, there is the world itself,
    With every several pleasure in the world,
    And where thou art not, desolation.
    I can no more: live thou to joy thy life;
    Myself to joy in nought but that thou livest.
                Enter Vaux
QUEEN MARGARET. Whither goes Vaux so fast? what news, I
      prithee?
VAUX. To signify unto his Majesty
    That Cardinal Beaufort is at point of death;

For suddenly a grievous sickness took him,
That makes him gasp and stare, and catch the air,
Blaspheming God, and cursing men on earth.
Sometime he talks as if Duke Humphrey's ghost
Were by his side; sometime he calls the king,
And whispers to his pillow, as to him,
The secrets of his overcharged soul:
And I am sent to tell his Majesty
That even now he cries aloud for him.

QUEEN MARGARET. Go tell this heavy message to the king.

Exit Vaux

Ay me! what is this world! what news are these!
But wherefore grieve I at an hour's poor loss,
Omitting Suffolk's exile, my soul's treasure?
Why only, Suffolk, mourn I not for thee,
And with the southern clouds contend in tears,
Theirs for the earth's increase, mine for my sorrows?
Now get thee hence: the king, thou know'st, is coming;
If thou be found by me thou art but dead.

SUFFOLK. If I depart from thee I cannot live;
And in thy sight to die, what were it else
But like a pleasant slumber in thy lap?
Here could I breathe my soul into the air,
As mild and gentle as the cradle-babe,
Dying with mother's dug between its lips;
Where, from thy sight, I should be raging mad,
And cry out for thee to close up mine eyes,
To have thee with thy lips to stop my mouth:
So shouldst thou either turn my flying soul,
Or I should breathe it so into thy body,
And then it liv'd in sweet Elysium.
To die by thee, were but to die in jest;
From thee to die were torture more than death.
O! let me stay, befall what may befall!

QUEEN MARGARET. Away! though parting be a fretful
    corsive,
It is applied to a deathful wound.
To France, sweet Suffolk: let me hear from thee;
For wheresoe'er thou art in this world's globe,
I 'll have an Iris that shall find thee out.

SUFFOLK. I go.

QUEEN MARGARET. And take my heart with thee.

SUFFOLK. A jewel, lock'd into the woefull'st cask
  That ever did contain a thing of worth.
  Even as a splitted bark, so sunder we:
  This way fall I to death.
QUEEN MARGARET.   This way for me.
                              Exeunt severally.

SCENE THREE

London. Cardinal Beaufort's Bedchamber.

*Enter King Henry, Salisbury, Warwick, and Others. The
Cardinal in bed; Attendants with him*

KING HENRY. How fares my lord? speak, Beaufort, to thy
    sovereign.
CARDINAL. If thou be'st death, I 'll give thee England's
    treasure,
  Enough to purchase such another island,
  So thou wilt let me live, and feel no pain.
KING HENRY. Ah! what a sign it is of evil life
  Where death's approach is seen so terrible.
WARWICK. Beaufort, it is thy sovereign speaks to thee.
CARDINAL. Bring me unto my trial when you will.
  Died he not in his bed? where should he die?
  Can I make men live whe'r they will or no?
  O! torture me no more, I will confess.
  Alive again? then show me where he is:
  I 'll give a thousand pounds to look upon him.
  He hath no eyes, the dust hath blinded them.
  Comb down his hair; look! look! it stands upright,
  Like lime-twigs set to catch my winged soul.
  Give me some drink; and bid the apothecary
  Bring the strong poison that I bought of him.
KING HENRY. O thou eternal Mover of the heavens!
  Look with a gentle eye upon this wretch;
  O! beat away the busy meddling fiend
  That lays strong siege unto this wretch's soul,
  And from his bosom purge this black despair.
WARWICK. See how the pangs of death do make him grin!
SALISBURY. Disturb him not! let him pass peaceably.
KING HENRY. Peace to his soul, if God's good pleasure be!

Lord Cardinal, if thou think'st on heaven's bliss,
Hold up thy hand, make signal of thy hope.
He dies, and makes no sign. O God, forgive him!
WARWICK. So bad a death argues a monstrous life.
KING HENRY. Forbear to judge, for we are sinners all.
Close up his eyes, and draw the curtain close;
And let us all to meditation.   *Exeunt*

ACT FOUR

SCENE ONE

Kent. The Seashore near Dover.

Firing heard at Sea. Then enter from a boat, a Captain, a Master, a Master's-Mate, Walter Whitmore, and Others; with them Suffolk disguised, and other Gentlemen, prisoners

CAPTAIN. The gaudy, blabbing, and remorseful day
  Is crept into the bosom of the sea,
  And now loud-howling wolves arouse the jades
  That drag the tragic melancholy night;
  Who with their drowsy, slow, and flagging wings
  Clip dead men's graves, and from their misty jaws
  Breathe foul contagious darkness in the air.
  Therefore bring forth the soldiers of our prize,
  For, whilst our pinnace anchors in the Downs
  Here shall they make their ransom on the sand,
  Or with their blood stain this discolour'd shore.
  Master, this prisoner freely give I thee:
  And thou that art his mate make boot of this;
  The other (*Pointing to Suffolk*), Walter Whitmore, is thy
    share.
FIRST GENTLEMAN. What is my ransom, master? let me
  know.
MASTER. A thousand crowns, or else lay down your head.
MATE. And so much shall you give, or off goes yours.
CAPTAIN. What! think you much to pay two thousand
  crowns,
  And bear the name and port of gentlemen?
  Cut both the villains' throats! for die you shall:
  The lives of those which we have lost in fight
  Cannot be counterpois'd with such a petty sum!
FIRST GENTLEMAN. I'll give it, sir; and therefore spare my
  life.

SECOND GENTLEMAN. And so will I, and write home for it
    straight.
WHITMORE. I lost mine eye in laying the prize aboard,
    (*To Suffolk*) And therefore to revenge it shalt thou die;
    And so should these if I might have my will.
CAPTAIN. Be not so rash: take ransom; let him live.
SUFFOLK. Look on my George; I am a gentleman:
    Rate me at what thou wilt, thou shalt be paid.
WHITMORE. And so am I; my name is Walter Whitmore.
    How now! why start'st thou? what! doth death affright?
SUFFOLK. Thy name affrights me, in whose sound is death.
    A cunning man did calculate my birth,
    And told me that by Water I should die:
    Yet let not this make thee be bloody-minded;
    Thy name is—Gaultier, being rightly sounded.
WHITMORE. Gaultier, or Walter, which it is I care not;
    Never yet did base dishonour blur our name
    But with our sword we wip'd away the blot:
    Therefore, when merchant-like I sell revenge,
    Broke be my sword, my arms torn and defac'd,
    And I proclaim'd a coward through the world!
                            Lays hold on Suffolk
SUFFOLK. Stay, Whitmore; for thy prisoner is a prince,
    The Duke of Suffolk, William de la Pole.
WHITMORE. The Duke of Suffolk muffled up in rags!
SUFFOLK. Ay, but these rags are no part of the duke:
    Jove sometimes went disguis'd, and why not I?
CAPTAIN. But Jove was never slain, as thou shalt be.
SUFFOLK. Obscure and lowly swain, King Henry's blood,
    The honourable blood of Lancaster,
    Must not be shed by such a jaded groom.
    Hast thou not kiss'd thy hand and held my stirrup?
    Bare-headed plodded by my foot-cloth mule,
    And thought thee happy when I shook my head?
    How often hast thou waited at my cup,
    Fed from my trencher, kneel'd down at the board,
    When I have feasted with Queen Margaret?
    Remember it and let it make thee crest-fall'n;
    Ay, and allay this thy abortive pride.
    How in our voiding lobby hast thou stood
    And duly waited for my coming forth?
    This hand of mine hath writ in thy behalf,

And therefore shall it charm thy riotous tongue.

WHITMORE. Speak, captain, shall I stab the forlorn swain?

CAPTAIN. First let my words stab him, as he hath me.

SUFFOLK. Base slave, thy words are blunt, and so art thou.

CAPTAIN. Convey him hence, and on our longboat's side
　　Strike off his head.

SUFFOLK.　　　　　Thou dar'st not for thy own.

CAPTAIN. Yes, Pole.

SUFFOLK.　　　　Pole!

CAPTAIN.　　　　　　　Pool! Sir Pool! lord!
Ay, kennel, puddle, sink; whose filth and dirt
Troubles the silver spring where England drinks.
Now will I dam up this thy yawning mouth
For swallowing the treasure of the realm:
Thy lips, that kiss'd the queen, shall sweep the ground;
And thou, that smil'dst at good Duke Humphrey's death,
Against the senseless winds shall grin in vain,
Who in contempt shall hiss at thee again:
And wedded be thou to the hags of hell,
For daring to affy a mighty lord
Unto the daughter of a worthless king,
Having neither subject, wealth, nor diadem.
By devilish policy art thou grown great,
And, like ambitious Sylla, overgorg'd
With gobbets of thy mother's bleeding heart.
By thee Anjou and Maine were sold to France,
The false revolting Normans thorough thee
Disdain to call us lord, and Picardy
Hath slain their governors, surpris'd our forts,
And sent the ragged soldiers wounded home.
The princely Warwick, and the Nevils all,
Whose dreadful swords were never drawn in vain,
As hating thee, are rising up in arms:
And now the house of York, thrust from the crown
By shameful murder of a guiltless king,
And lofty proud encroaching tyranny,
Burns with revenging fire; whose hopeful colours
Advance our half-fac'd sun, striving to shine,
Under the which is writ 'Invitis nubibus.'
The commons here in Kent are up in arms;
And to conclude, reproach and beggary
Is crept into the palace of our king,

And all by thee. Away! convey him hence.

SUFFOLK. O! that I were a god, to shoot forth thunder
Upon these paltry, servile, abject drudges.
Small things make base men proud: this villain here,
Being captain of a pinnace, threatens more
Than Bargulus the strong Illyrian pirate.
Drones suck not eagles' blood, but rob beehives.
It is impossible that I should die
By such a lowly vassal as thyself.
Thy words move rage, and not remorse in me:
I go of message from the queen to France;
I charge thee, waft me safely cross the Channel.

CAPTAIN. Walter!

WHITMORE. Come, Suffolk, I must waft thee to thy death.

SUFFOLK. Gelidus timor occupat artus: 'tis thee I fear.

WHITMORE. Thou shalt have cause to fear before I leave
thee.
What! are ye daunted now? now will ye stoop?

FIRST GENTLEMAN. My gracious lord, entreat him, speak
him fair.

SUFFOLK. Suffolk's imperial tongue is stern and rough,
Us'd to command, untaught to plead for favour.
Far be it we should honour such as these
With humble suit: no, rather let my head
Stoop to the block than these knees bow to any
Save to the God of heaven, and to my king;
And sooner dance upon a bloody pole
Than stand uncover'd to the vulgar groom.
True nobility is exempt from fear:
More can I bear than you dare execute.

CAPTAIN. Hale him away, and let him talk no more.

SUFFOLK. Come, soldiers, show what cruelty ye can,
That this my death may never be forgot.
Great men oft die by vile bezonians.
A Roman sworder and banditto slave
Murder'd sweet Tully; Brutus' bastard hand
Stabb'd Julius Cæsar; savage islanders
Pompey the Great; and Suffolk dies by pirates.

Exit with Suffolk, Whitmore and Others

CAPTAIN. And as for these whose ransom we have set,
It is our pleasure one of them depart:
Therefore come you with us and let him go.

Exeunt all but First Gentleman
Re-enter Whitmore, with Suffolk's body

WHITMORE. There let his head and lifeless body lie,
Until the queen his mistress bury it. *Exit*
FIRST GENTLEMAN. O barbarous and bloody spectacle!
His body will I bear unto the king:
If he revenge it not, yet will his friends;
So will the queen, that living held him dear.

Exit with the body

SCENE TWO

Blackheath.

Enter George Bevis and John Holland

GEORGE. Come, and get thee a sword, though made of a
lath: they have been up these two days.
JOHN. They have the more need to sleep now then.
GEORGE. I tell thee, Jack Cade the clothier means to dress
the commonwealth, and turn it, and set a new nap upon it.
JOHN. So he had need, for 'tis threadbare. Well, I say it was
never merry world in England since gentlemen came up.
GEORGE. O miserable age! Virtue is not regarded in handi-
crafts-men.
JOHN. The nobility think scorn to go in leather aprons.
GEORGE. Nay, more; the king's council are no good work-
men.
JOHN. True; and yet it is said, 'Labour in thy vocation':
which is as much to say as, let the magistrates be labour-
ing men; and therefore should we be magistrates.
GEORGE. Thou hast hit it; for there 's no better sign of a
brave mind than a hard hand.
JOHN. I see them! I see them! There 's Best's son, the tanner
of Wingham,—
GEORGE. He shall have the skins of our enemies to make
dog's-leather of.
JOHN. And Dick the butcher,—
GEORGE. Then is sin struck down like an ox, and iniquity's
throat cut like a calf.
JOHN. And Smith the weaver,—
GEORGE. Argo,.their thread of life is spun.

JOHN. Come, come, let's fall in with them.

Drum. Enter Cade, Dick the Butcher,
Smith the Weaver, and a Sawyer, with infinite numbers

CADE. We John Cade, so termed of our supposed father,—

DICK. (*Aside*) Or rather, of stealing a cade of herrings.

CADE. For our enemies shall fall before us, inspired with the
spirit of putting down kings and princes,—Command si-
lence.

DICK. Silence!

CADE. My father was a Mortimer.—

DICK. (*Aside*) He was an honest man, and a good bricklayer.

CADE. My mother a Plantagenet,—

DICK. (*Aside*) I knew her well; she was a midwife.

CADE. My wife descended of the Lacies,—

DICK. (*Aside*) She was, indeed, a pedlar's daughter, and sold
many laces.

SMITH. (*Aside*) But now of late, not able to travel with her
furred pack, she washes bucks here at home.

CADE. Therefore am I of an honourable house.

DICK. (*Aside*) Ay, by my faith, the field is honourable; and
there was he born, under a hedge; for his father had never
a house but the cage.

CADE. Valiant I am.

SMITH. (*Aside*) A' must needs, for beggary is valiant.

CADE. I am able to endure much.

DICK. (*Aside*) No question of that, for I have seen him
whipped three market-days together.

CADE. I fear neither sword nor fire.

SMITH. (*Aside*) He need not fear the sword, for his coat is of
proof.

DICK. (*Aside*) But methinks he should stand in fear of fire,
being burnt i' the hand for stealing of sheep.

CADE. Be brave, then; for your captain is brave, and vows
reformation. There shall be in England seven halfpenny
loaves sold for a penny; the three-hooped pot shall have
ten hoops; and I will make it felony to drink small beer.
All the realm shall be in common, and in Cheapside shall
my palfrey go to grass. And when I am king,—as king I
will be,—

ALL. God save your Majesty!

CADE. I thank you, good people: there shall be no money;
all shall eat and drink on my score; and I will apparel

them all in one livery, that they may agree like brothers, and worship me their lord.

DICK. The first thing we do, let's kill all the lawyers.

CADE. Nay, that I mean to do. Is not this a lamentable thing, that of the skin of an innocent lamb should be made parchment? that parchment, being scribbled o'er, should undo a man? Some say the bee stings; but I say, 'tis the bee's wax, for I did but seal once to a thing, and I was never mine own man since. How now! who's there?

Enter some, bringing in the Clerk of Chatham

SMITH. The Clerk of Chatham: he can write and read and cast accompt.

CADE. O monstrous!

SMITH. We took him setting of boys' copies.

CADE. Here's a villain!

SMITH. Has a book in his pocket with red letters in 't.

CADE. Nay, then he is a conjurer.

DICK. Nay, he can make obligations, and write court-hand.

CADE. I am sorry for 't: the man is a proper man, of mine honour; unless I find him guilty, he shall not die. Come hither, sirrah, I must examine thee. What is thy name?

CLERK. Emmanuel.

DICK. They use to write it on the top of letters. 'Twill go hard with you.

CADE. Let me alone. Dost thou use to write thy name, or hast thou a mark to thyself, like an honest plain-dealing man?

CLERK. Sir, I thank God, I have been so well brought up, that I can write my name.

ALL. He hath confessed: away with him! he's a villain and a traitor.

CADE. Away with him! I say: hang him with his pen and ink-horn about his neck.   *Exeunt some with the Clerk*

Enter Michael

MICHAEL. Where's our general?

CADE. Here I am, thou particular fellow.

MICHAEL. Fly, fly, fly! Sir Humphrey Stafford and his brother are hard by, with the king's forces.

CADE. Stand, villain, stand, or I'll fell thee down. He shall be encountered with a man as good as himself: he is but a knight, is a'?

MICHAEL. No.

CADE. To equal him, I will make myself a knight presently.
(*Kneels*) Rise up Sir John Mortimer. (*Rises*) Now have
at him.

Enter Sir Humphrey Stafford
and William his Brother, with drum and Forces

STAFFORD. Rebellious hinds, the filth and scum of Kent,
Mark'd for the gallows, lay your weapons down;
Home to your cottages, forsake this groom:
The king is merciful, if you revolt.

WILLIAM STAFFORD. But angry, wrathful, and inclin'd to
blood,
If you go forward: therefore yield, or die.

CADE. As for these silken-coated slaves, I pass not:
It is to you, good people, that I speak,
O'er whom, in time to come I hope to reign;
For I am rightful heir unto the crown.

STAFFORD. Villain! thy father was a plasterer;
And thou thyself a shearman, art thou not?

CADE. And Adam was a gardener.

WILLIAM STAFFORD. And what of that?

CADE. Marry, this: Edmund Mortimer, Earl of March,
Married the Duke of Clarence' daughter, did he not?

STAFFORD. Ay, sir.

CADE. By her he had two children at one birth.

WILLIAM STAFFORD. That 's false.

CADE. Ay, there 's the question; but I say, 'tis true:
The elder of them, being put to nurse,
Was by a beggar-woman stolen away;
And, ignorant of his birth and parentage,
Became a bricklayer when he came to age:
His son am I; deny it if you can.

DICK. Nay, 'tis too true; therefore he shall be king.

SMITH. Sir, he made a chimney in my father's house, and the
bricks are alive at this day to testify it; therefore deny it
not.

STAFFORD. And will you credit this base drudge's words,
That speaks he knows not what?

ALL. Ay, marry, will we; therefore get ye gone.

WILLIAM STAFFORD. Jack Cade, the Duke of York hath
taught you this.

CADE (*Aside*) He lies, for I invented it myself. Go to, sirrah;
tell the king from me, that, for his father's sake, Henry the

Fifth, in whose time boys went to span-counter for French crowns, I am content he shall reign; but I 'll be protector over him.

DICK. And furthermore, we 'll have the Lord Say's head for selling the dukedom of Maine.

CADE. And good reason; for thereby is England mained, and fain to go with a staff, but that my puissance holds it up. Fellow kings, I tell you that that Lord Say hath gelded the commonwealth, and made it a eunuch; and more than that, he can speak French; and therefore he is a traitor.

STAFFORD. O gross and miserable ignorance!

CADE. Nay, answer, if you can: the Frenchmen are our enemies; go to then, I ask but this, can he that speaks with the tongue of an enemy be a good counsellor, or no?

ALL. No, no; and therefore we 'll have his head.

WILLIAM STAFFORD. Well, seeing gentle words will not prevail,
Assail them with the army of the king.

STAFFORD. Herald, away; and throughout every town
Proclaim them traitors that are up with Cade;
That those which fly before the battle ends
May, even in their wives' and children's sight,
Be hang'd up for example at their doors:
And you, that be the king's friends, follow me.

Exeunt the two Staffords and Forces

CADE. And you, that love the commons, follow me.
Now show yourselves men; 'tis for liberty.
We will not leave one lord, one gentleman:
Spare none but such as go in clouted shoon,
For they are thrifty honest men, and such
As would, but that they dare not, take our parts.

DICK. They are all in order, and march toward us.

CADE. But then are we in order when we are most out of order. Come, march! forward! *Exeunt*

SCENE THREE

Another Part of Blackheath.

Alarums. The two parties enter and fight, and both the Staffords are slain

CADE. Where 's Dick, the butcher of Ashford?

DICK. Here, sir.

CADE. They fell before thee like sheep and oxen, and thou behavedst thyself as if thou hadst been in thine own slaughter-house: therefore thus will I reward thee, the Lent shall be as long again as it is; and thou shalt have a licence to kill for a hundred lacking one.

DICK. I desire no more.

CADE. And, to speak truth, thou deservest no less. This monument of the victory will I bear; (*Puts on Sir Humphrey Stafford's armour*) and the bodies shall be dragged at my horse' heels, till I do come to London, where we will have the Mayor's sword borne·before us.

DICK. If we mean to thrive and do good, break open the gaols and let out the prisoners.

CADE. Fear not that, I warrant thee. Come; let 's march towards London.   *Exeunt*

SCENE FOUR

London. A Room in the Palace.

Enter King Henry, reading a supplication; the Duke of Buckingham and Lord Say with him: at a distance, Queen Margaret, mourning over Suffolk's head

QUEEN MARGARET. Oft have I heard that grief softens the mind,
And makes it fearful and degenerate;
Think therefore on revenge, and cease to weep.
But who can cease to weep and look on this?
Here may his head lie on my throbbing breast;
But where 's the body that I should embrace?

BUCKINGHAM. What answer makes your Grace to the rebels'
　　supplication?

KING HENRY. I 'll send some holy bishop to entreat;
　　For God forbid so many simple souls
　　Should perish by the sword! And I myself,
　　Rather than bloody war shall cut them short,
　　Will parley with Jack Cade their general.
　　But stay, I 'll read it over once again.

QUEEN MARGARET. Ah, barbarous villains! hath this lovely
　　face
　　Rul'd like a wandering planet over me,
　　And could it not enforce them to relent,
　　That were unworthy to behold the same?

KING HENRY. Lord Say, Jack Cade hath sworn to have thy
　　head.

SAY. Ay, but I hope your Highness shall have his.

KING HENRY. How now, madam!
　　Still lamenting and mourning for Suffolk's death?
　　I fear me, love, if that I had been dead,
　　Thou wouldest not have mourn'd so much for me.

QUEEN MARGARET. No, my love; I should not mourn, but die
　　for thee.

Enter a Messenger

KING HENRY. How now! what news? why com'st thou in
　　such haste?

MESSENGER. The rebels are in Southwark; fly, my lord!
　　Jack Cade proclaims himself Lord Mortimer,
　　Descended from the Duke of Clarence' house,
　　And calls your Grace usurper openly,
　　And vows to crown himself in Westminster.
　　His army is a ragged multitude
　　Of hinds and peasants, rude and merciless:
　　Sir Humphrey Stafford and his brother's death
　　Hath given them heart and courage to proceed.
　　All scholars, lawyers, courtiers, gentlemen,
　　They call false caterpillars, and intend their death.

KING HENRY. O graceless men! they know not what they do.

BUCKINGHAM. My gracious lord, retire to Killingworth,
　　Until a power be rais'd to put them down.

QUEEN MARGARET. Ah! were the Duke of Suffolk now alive,
　　These Kentish rebels would be soon appeas'd.

KING HENRY. Lord Say, the traitors hate thee,

Therefore away with us to Killingworth.

SAY. So might your Grace's person be in danger.
The sight of me is odious in their eyes;
And therefore in this city will I stay,
And live alone as secret as I may.

Enter a second Messenger

SECOND MESSENGER. Jack Cade hath gotten London bridge;
The citizens fly and forsake their houses;
The rascal people, thirsting after prey,
Join with the traitor; and they jointly swear
To spoil the city and your royal court.

BUCKINGHAM. Then linger not, my lord; away! take horse.

KING HENRY. Come, Margaret; God, our hope, will succour
us.

QUEEN MARGARET. My hope is gone, now Suffolk is deceas'd.

KING HENRY. (*To Lord Say*) Farewell, my lord: trust not the
Kentish rebels.

BUCKINGHAM. Trust nobody, for fear you be betray'd.

SAY. The trust I have is in mine innocence,
And therefore am I bold and resolute.   *Exeunt*

SCENE FIVE

The Same. The Tower.

*Enter Lord Scales and Others, on the Walls. Then enter
certain Citizens, below*

SCALES. How now! is Jack Cade slain?

FIRST CITIZEN. No, my lord, nor likely to be slain; for they
have won the bridge, killing all those that withstand them.
The Lord Mayor craves aid of your honour from the
Tower, to defend the city from the rebels.

SCALES. Such aid as I can spare you shall command;
But I am troubled here with them myself;
The rebels have assay'd to win the Tower.
But get you to Smithfield and gather head,
And thither I will send you Matthew Goffe:
Fight for your king, your country, and your lives;
And so, farewell, for I must hence again.   *Exeunt*

SCENE SIX

London. Cannon Street.

*Enter Jack Cade and his Followers. He strikes his staff
on London-stone*

CADE. Now is Mortimer lord of this city. And here, sitting
upon London-stone, I charge and command that, of the
city's cost, the pissing-conduit run nothing but claret wine
this first year of our reign. And now, henceforward, it shall
be treason for any that calls me other than Lord Mortimer.
Enter a Soldier, running
SOLDIER. Jack Cade! Jack Cade!
CADE. Knock him down there.   *They kill him*
SMITH. If this fellow be wise, he 'll never call you Jack Cade
more; I think he hath a very fair warning.
DICK. My lord, there 's an army gathered together in Smith-
field.
CADE. Come then, let 's go fight with them. But first, go and
set London bridge on fire, and, if you can, burn down the
Tower too. Come, let 's away.   *Exeunt*

SCENE SEVEN

The Same. Smithfield.

*Alarums. Enter, on one side, Cade and his company; on the
other, Citizens, and the King's Forces, headed by Matthew
Goffe. They fight; the Citizens are routed, and
Matthew Goffe is slain*

CADE. So, sirs:—Now go some and pull down the Savoy;
others to the inns of court: down with them all.
DICK. I have a suit unto your lordship.
CADE. Be it a lordship, thou shalt have it for that word.
DICK. Only that the laws of England may come out of your
mouth.
JOHN. (*Aside*) Mass, 'twill be sore law then; for he was
thrust in the mouth with a spear, and 'tis not whole yet.

SMITH. (*Aside*) Nay, John, it will be stinking law; for his breath stinks with eating toasted cheese.

CADE. I have thought upon it; it shall be so. Away! burn all the records of the realm: my mouth shall be the parliament of England.

JOHN. (*Aside*) Then we are like to have biting statutes, unless his teeth be pulled out.

CADE. And henceforward all things shall be in common.

Enter a Messenger

MESSENGER. My lord, a prize, a prize! here 's the Lord Say, which sold the towns in France; he that made us pay one-and-twenty fifteens, and one shilling to the pound, the last subsidy.

Enter George Bevis, with the Lord Say

CADE. Well, he shall be beheaded for it ten times. Ah! thou say, thou serge, nay, thou buckram lord; now art thou within point-blank of our jurisdiction regal. What canst thou answer to my Majesty for giving up of Normandy unto Monsieur Basimecu, the Dauphin of France? Be it known unto thee by these presence, even the presence of Lord Mortimer, that I am the besom that must sweep the court clean of such filth as thou art. Thou hast most traitorously corrupted the youth of the realm in erecting a grammar-school; and whereas, before, our forefathers had no other books but the score and the tally, thou hast caused printing to be used; and, contrary to the king, his crown, and dignity, thou hast built a paper-mill. It will be proved to thy face that thou hast men about thee that usually talk of a noun and a verb, and such abominable words as no Christian ear can endure to hear. Thou hast appointed justices of peace, to call poor men before them about matters they were not able to answer. Moreover, thou hast put them in prison; and because they could not read, thou hast hanged them; when indeed only for that cause they have been most worthy to live. Thou dost ride on a foot-cloth, dost thou not?

SAY. What of that?

CADE. Marry, thou oughtest not to let thy horse wear a cloak, when honester men than thou go in their hose and doublets.

DICK. And work in their shirt too; as myself, for example, that am a butcher.

SAY. You men of Kent,—

DICK. What say you of Kent?

SAY. Nothing but this: 'tis bona terra, mala gens.

CADE. Away with him! away with him! he speaks Latin.

SAY. Hear me but speak, and bear me where you will.
  Kent, in the Commentaries Cæsar writ,
  Is term'd the civil'st place of all this isle:
  Sweet is the country, because full of riches;
  The people liberal, valiant, active, wealthy;
  Which makes me hope you are not void of pity.
  I sold not Maine, I lost not Normandy;
  Yet, to recover them, would lose my life.
  Justice with favour have I always done;
  Prayers and tears have moved me, gifts could never.
  When have I aught exacted at your hands,
  But to maintain the king, the realm, and you?
  Large gifts have I bestow'd on learned clerks,
  Because my book preferr'd me to the king,
  And seeing ignorance is the curse of God,
  Knowledge the wing wherewith we fly to heaven,
  Unless you be possess'd with devilish spirits,
  You cannot but forbear to murder me:
  This tongue hath parley'd unto foreign kings
  For your behoof,—

CADE. Tut! when struck'st thou one blow in the field?

SAY. Great men have reaching hands: oft have I struck
  Those that I never saw, and struck them dead.

GEORGE. O monstrous coward! what, to come behind folks!

SAY. These cheeks are pale for watching for your good.

CADE. Give him a box o' the ear, and that will make 'em red
  again.

SAY. Long sitting, to determine poor men's causes,
  Hath made me full of sickness and diseases.

CADE. Ye shall have a hempen caudle then, and the help of
  hatchet.

DICK. Why dost thou quiver, man?

SAY. The palsy, and not fear, provokes me.

CADE. Nay, he nods at us; as who should say, I 'll be even
  with you: I 'll see if his head will stand steadier on a pole,
  or no. Take him away and behead him.

SAY. Tell me wherein have I offended most?
  Have I affected wealth, or honour? speak.

Are my chests fill'd up with extorted gold?
Is my apparel sumptuous to behold?
Whom have I injur'd, that ye seek my death?
These hands are free from guiltless blood-shedding,
This breast from harbouring foul deceitful thoughts.
O! let me live.

CADE. (*Aside*) I feel remorse in myself with his words; but
I 'll bridle it: he shall die, an it be but for pleading so well
for his life. Away with him! he has a familiar under his
tongue; he speaks not o' God's name. Go, take him away,
I say, and strike off his head presently; and then break
into his son-in-law's house, Sir James Cromer, and strike
off his head, and bring them both upon two poles hither.

ALL. It shall be done.

SAY. Ah, countrymen! if when you make your prayers,
God should be so obdurate as yourselves,
How would it fare with your departed souls?
And therefore yet relent, and save my life.

CADE. Away with him! and do as I command ye. (*Exeunt
some, with Lord Say*) The proudest peer in the realm
shall not wear a head on his shoulders, unless he pay me
tribute; there shall not a maid be married, but she shall
pay to me her maidenhead, ere they have it; men shall
hold of me in capite; and we charge and command that
their wives be as free as heart can wish or tongue can tell.

DICK. My lord, when shall we go to Cheapside, and take up
commodities upon our bills?

CADE. Marry, presently.

ALL. O! brave!

*Re-enter Rebels, with
the heads of Lord Say and his Son-in-Law*

CADE. But is not this braver? Let them kiss one another, for
they loved well when they were alive. Now part them
again, lest they consult about the giving up of some more
towns in France. Soldiers, defer the spoil of the city until
night: for with these borne before us, instead of maces,
will we ride through the streets; and at every corner have
them kiss. Away!   *Exeunt*

SCENE EIGHT

The Same. Southwark.

Alarum. Enter Cade and all his Rabblement

CADE. Up Fish Street! down St. Magnus' Corner! kill and
knock down! throw them into Thames! (*A parley sounded,
then a retreat*) What noise is this I hear? Dare any be so
bold to sound retreat or parley, when I command them kill?
Enter Buckingham, and Old Clifford, with Forces

BUCKINGHAM. Ay, here they be that dare and will disturb
thee.
Know, Cade, we come ambassadors from the king
Unto the commons whom thou hast misled;
And here pronounce free pardon to them all
That will forsake thee and go home in peace.

CLIFFORD. What say ye, countrymen? will ye relent,
And yield to mercy, whilst 'tis offer'd you,
Or let a rebel lead you to your deaths?
Who loves the king, and will embrace his pardon,
Fling up his cap, and say 'God save his Majesty!'
Who hateth him, and honours not his father,
Henry the Fifth, that made all France to quake,
Shake he his weapon at us, and pass by.

ALL. God save the king! God save the king!

CADE. What! Buckingham and Clifford, are ye so brave?
And you, base peasants, do ye believe him? will you needs
be hanged with your pardons about your necks? Hath my
sword therefore broke through London Gates, that you
should leave me at the White Hart in Southwark? I
thought ye would never have given out these arms till you
had recovered your ancient freedom; but you are all rec-
reants and dastards, and delight to live in slavery to the
nobility. Let them break your backs with burdens, take
your houses over your heads, ravish your wives and
daughters before your faces: for me, I will make shift for
one, and so, God's curse light upon you all!

ALL. We 'll follow Cade, we 'll follow Cade!

CLIFFORD. Is Cade the son of Henry the Fifth,

That thus you do exclaim you 'll go with him?
Will he conduct you through the heart of France,
And make the meanest of you earls and dukes?
Alas! he hath no home, no place to fly to;
Nor knows he how to live but by the spoil,
Unless by robbing of your friends and us.
Were 't not a shame, that whilst you live at jar,
The fearful French, whom you late vanquished,
Should make a start o'er seas and vanquish you?
Methinks already in this civil broil
I see them lording it in London streets,
Crying Villiago! unto all they meet.
Better ten thousand base-born Cades miscarry,
Than you should stoop unto a Frenchman's mercy.
To France, to France! and get what you have lost;
Spare England, for it is your native coast.
Henry hath money, you are strong and manly;
God on our side, doubt not of victory.

ALL. A Clifford! a Clifford! we 'll follow the king and Clifford.

CADE. (*Aside*) Was ever feather so lightly blown to and fro as this multitude? The name of Henry the Fifth hales them to a hundred mischiefs, and makes them leave me desolate. I see them lay their heads together to surprise me. My sword make way for me, for here is no staying. In despite of the devils and hell, have through the very middest of you! and heavens and honour be witness, that no want of resolution in me, but only my followers' base and ignominious treasons, makes me betake me to my heels.

Exit

BUCKINGHAM. What, is he fled? go some, and follow him;
And he that brings his head unto the king
Shall have a thousand crowns for his reward.

Exeunt some of them

Follow me, soldiers; we 'll devise a mean
To reconcile you all unto the king.   *Exeunt*

SCENE NINE

Kenilworth Castle

Trumpets sounded. Enter King Henry, Queen Margaret,
and Somerset, on the terrace

KING HENRY. Was ever king that joy'd an earthly throne,
And could command no more content than I?
No sooner was I crept out of my cradle
But I was made a king at nine months old:
Was never subject long'd to be a king
As I do long and wish to be a subject.
          Enter Buckingham and Old Clifford
BUCKINGHAM. Health, and glad tidings, to your Majesty!
KING HENRY. Why, Buckingham, is the traitor Cade
     surpris'd?
Or is he but retir'd to make him strong?
          Enter, below, a number of
     Cade's followers, with halters about their necks
CLIFFORD. He 's fled, my lord, and all his powers do yield;
And humbly thus, with halters on their necks,
Expect your Highness' doom, of life, or death.
KING HENRY. Then, heaven, set ope thy everlasting gates,
To entertain my vows of thanks and praise!
Soldiers, this day have you redeem'd your lives,
And show'd how well you love your prince and country:
Continue still in this so good a mind,
And Henry, though he be infortunate,
Assure yourselves, will never be unkind:
And so, with thanks and pardon to you all,
I do dismiss you to your several countries.
ALL. God save the king! God save the king!
          Enter a Messenger
MESSENGER. Please it your Grace to be advertised,
The Duke of York is newly come from Ireland;
And with a puissant and a mighty power
Of gallowglasses, and stout kerns,
Is marching hitherward in proud array;
And still proclaimeth, as he comes along,
His arms are only to remove from thee

The Duke of Somerset, whom he terms a traitor.

KING HENRY. Thus stands my state, 'twixt Cade and York
    distress'd;
Like to a ship that, having scap'd a tempest,
Is straightway calm'd, and boarded with a pirate.
But now is Cade driven back, his men dispers'd;
And now is York in arms to second him.
I pray thee, Buckingham, go and meet him,
And ask him what 's the reason of these arms.
Tell him I 'll send Duke Edmund to the Tower;
And, Somerset, we will commit thee thither,
Until his army be dismissed from him.

SOMERSET. My lord,
I 'll yield myself to prison willingly,
Or unto death, to do my country good.

KING HENRY. In any case, be not too rough in terms;
For he is fierce and cannot brook hard language.

BUCKINGHAM. I will, my lord; and doubt not so to deal
As all things shall redound unto your good.

KING HENRY. Come, wife, let 's in, and learn to govern
    better;
For yet may England curse my wretched reign.   *Exeunt*

SCENE TEN

Kent. Iden's Garden.

Enter Cade

CADE. Fie on ambition! fie on myself, that have a sword, and
yet am ready to famish! These five days have I hid me in
these woods and durst not peep out, for all the country is
laid for me; but now I am so hungry, that if I might have
a lease of my life for a thousand years I could stay no
longer. Wherefore, on a brick wall have I climbed into
this garden, to see if I can eat grass, or pick a sallet an-
other while, which is not amiss to cool a man's stomach
this hot weather. And I think this word 'sallet' was born to
do me good: for many a time, but for a sallet, my brain-
pan had been cleft with a brown bill; and many a time,
when I have been dry, and bravely marching, it hath

served me instead of a quart-pot to drink in; and now the
word 'sallet' must serve me to feed on.

Enter Iden with Servants behind

IDEN. Lord! who would live turmoiled in the court,
And may enjoy such quiet walks as these?
This small inheritance my father left me
Contenteth me, and worth a monarchy.
I seek not to wax great by others' waning,
Or gather wealth I care not with what envy:
Sufficeth that I have maintains my state,
And sends the poor well pleased from my gate.

CADE. (*Aside*) Here 's the lord of the soil come to seize me
for a stray, for entering his fee-simple without leave. Ah,
villain! thou wilt betray me, and get a thousand crowns of
the king by carrying my head to him; but I 'll make thee
eat iron like an ostrich, and swallow my sword like a great
pin, ere thou and I part.

IDEN. Why, rude companion, whatsoe'er thou be,
I know thee not; why then should I betray thee?
Is 't not enough to break into my garden,
And like a thief to come to rob my grounds,
Climbing my walls in spite of me the owner,
But thou wilt brave me with these saucy terms?

CADE. Brave thee! ay, by the best blood that ever was
broached, and beard thee too. Look on me well: I have
eat no meat these five days; yet, come thou and thy five
men, and if I do not leave you all as dead as a door-nail, I
pray God I may never eat grass more.

IDEN. Nay, it shall ne'er be said, while England stands,
That Alexander Iden, an esquire of Kent,
Took odds to combat a poor famish'd man.
Oppose thy steadfast-gazing eyes to mine,
See if thou canst outface me with thy looks:
Set limb to limb, and thou art far the lesser;
Thy hand is but a finger to my fist;
Thy leg a stick compared with this truncheon;
My foot shall fight with all the strength thou hast;
And if mine arm be heaved in the air
Thy grave is digg'd already in the earth.
As for more words, whose greatness answers words,
Let this my sword report what speech forbears.

CADE. By my valour, the most complete champion that ever

I heard! Steel, if thou turn the edge, or cut not out the
burly-boned clown in chines of beef ere thou sleep in thy
sheath, I beseech Jove on my knees, thou mayst be turned
to hobnails. (*They fight; Cade falls*) O, I am slain! Fam-
ine and no other hath slain me: let ten thousand devils
come against me, and give me but the ten meals I have
lost, and I 'll defy them all. Wither, garden; and be hence-
forth a burying-place to all that do dwell in this house,
because the unconquered soul of Cade is fled.

IDEN. Is 't Cade that I have slain, that monstrous traitor?
Sword, I will hallow thee for this thy deed,
And hang thee o'er my tomb when I am dead:
Ne'er shall this blood be wiped from thy point,
But thou shalt wear it as a herald's coat,
To emblaze the honour that thy master got.

CADE. Iden, farewell; and be proud of thy victory. Tell Kent
from me, she hath lost her best man, and exhort all the
world to be cowards; for I, that never feared any, am van-
quished by famine, not by valour.   *Dies*

IDEN. How much thou wrong'st me, heaven be my judge.
Die, damned wretch, the curse of her that bare thee!
And as I thrust thy body in with my sword,
So wish I, I might thrust thy soul to hell.
Hence will I drag thee headlong by the heels
Unto a dunghill which shall be thy grave,
And there cut off thy most ungracious head;
Which I will bear in triumph to the king,
Leaving thy trunk for crows to feed upon.
                    Exit, with Servants, dragging out the body

ACT FIVE

SCENE ONE

Kent. Fields between Dartford and Blackheath.

The King's camp on one side. On the other, enter York, and his army of Irish, with drum and colours

YORK. From Ireland thus comes York to claim his right,
    And pluck the crown from feeble Henry's head:
    Ring, bells, aloud; burn, bonfires, clear and bright,
    To entertain great England's lawful king.
    Ah, sancta majestas, who would not buy thee dear?
    Let them obey that know not how to rule;
    This hand was made to handle nought but gold:
    I cannot give due action to my words,
    Except a sword or sceptre balance it.
    A sceptre shall it have, have I a soul,
    On which I'll toss the flower-de-luce of France.
             Enter Buckingham
    Whom have we here? Buckingham, to disturb me?
    The king hath sent him, sure: I must dissemble.
BUCKINGHAM. York, if thou meanest well, I greet thee well.
YORK. Humphrey of Buckingham, I accept thy greeting.
    Art thou a messenger, or come of pleasure?
BUCKINGHAM. A messenger from Henry, our dread liege,
    To know the reason of these arms in peace;
    Or why thou,—being a subject as I am,—
    Against thy oath and true allegiance sworn,
    Shouldst raise so great a power without his leave,
    Or dare to bring thy force so near the court.
YORK. (*Aside*) Scarce can I speak, my choler is so great:
    O! I could hew up rocks and fight with flint,
    I am so angry at these abject terms;
    And now, like Ajax Telamonius,
    On sheep or oxen could I spend my fury.

I am far better born than is the king,
More like a king, more kingly in my thoughts;
But I must make fair weather yet awhile,
Till Henry be more weak, and I more strong.
(*Aloud*) Buckingham, I prithee, pardon me,
That I have given no answer all this while;
My mind was troubled with deep melancholy.
The cause why I have brought this army hither
Is to remove proud Somerset from the king,
Seditious to his Grace and to the state.

BUCKINGHAM. That is too much presumption on thy part:
But if thy arms be to no other end,
The king hath yielded unto thy demand:
The Duke of Somerset is in the Tower.

YORK. Upon thine honour, is he a prisoner?

BUCKINGHAM. Upon mine honour, he is a prisoner.

YORK. Then, Buckingham, I do dismiss my powers.
Soldiers, I thank you all; disperse yourselves;
Meet me to-morrow in Saint George's field,
You shall have pay, and everything you wish,
And let my sovereign, virtuous Henry,
Command my eldest son, nay, all my sons,
As pledges of my fealty and love;
I 'll send them all as willing as I live:
Lands, goods, horse, armour, anything I have
Is his to use, so Somerset may die.

BUCKINGHAM. York, I commend this kind submission:
We twain will go into his Highness' tent.

Enter King Henry, attended

KING HENRY. Buckingham, doth York intend no harm to us,
That thus he marcheth with thee arm in arm?

YORK. In all submission and humility
York doth present himself unto your Highness.

KING HENRY. Then what intend these forces thou dost bring?

YORK. To heave the traitor Somerset from hence,
And fight against that monstrous rebel, Cade,
Who since I heard to be discomfited.

Enter Iden, with Cade's head

IDEN. If one so rude and of so mean condition
May pass into the presence of a king,
Lo! I present your Grace a traitor's head,
The head of Cade, whom I in combat slew.

KING HENRY. The head of Cade! Great God, how just art
     thou!
     O! let me view his visage, being dead,
     That living wrought me such exceeding trouble.
     Tell me, my friend, art thou the man that slew him?
IDEN. I was, an 't like your Majesty.
KING HENRY. How art thou call'd, and what is thy degree?
IDEN. Alexander Iden, that 's my name;
     A poor esquire of Kent, that loves his king.
BUCKINGHAM. So please it you, my lord, 'twere not amiss
     He were created knight for his good service.
KING HENRY. Iden, kneel down. (*He kneels*) Rise up a
     knight.
     We give thee for reward a thousand marks;
     And will that thou henceforth attend on us.
IDEN. May Iden live to merit such a bounty,
     And never live but true unto his liege!
KING HENRY. See! Buckingham! Somerset comes with the
     queen:
     Go, bid her hide him quickly from the duke.
               Enter Queen Margaret and Somerset
QUEEN MARGARET. For thousand Yorks he shall not hide his
     head,
     But boldly stand and front him to his face.
YORK. How now! is Somerset at liberty?
     Then, York, unloose thy long-imprison'd thoughts
     And let thy tongue be equal with thy heart.
     Shall I endure the sight of Somerset?
     False king! why hast thou broken faith with me,
     Knowing how hardly I can brook abuse?
     King did I call thee? no, thou art not king;
     Not fit to govern and rule multitudes,
     Which darest not, no, nor canst not rule a traitor.
     That head of thine doth not become a crown;
     Thy hand is made to grasp a palmer's staff,
     And not to grace an awful princely sceptre.
     That gold must round engirt these brows of mine,
     Whose smile and frown, like to Achilles' spear,
     Is able with the change to kill and cure.
     Here is a hand to hold a sceptre up,
     And with the same to act controlling laws.
     Give place: by heaven, thou shalt rule no more

O'er him whom heaven created for thy ruler.

SOMERSET. O monstrous traitor:—I arrest thee, York,
Of capital treason 'gainst the king and crown.
Obey, audacious traitor; kneel for grace.

YORK. Wouldst have me kneel? first let me ask of these
If they can brook I bow a knee to man.
Sirrah, call in my sons to be my bail: *Exit an Attendant*
I know ere they will have me go to ward,
They 'll pawn their swords for my enfranchisement.

QUEEN MARGARET. Call hither Clifford; bid him come
amain,
To say if that the bastard boys of York
Shall be the surety for their traitor father.

Exit Buckingham

YORK. O blood-bespotted Neapolitan,
Outcast of Naples, England's bloody scourge!
The sons of York, thy betters in their birth,
Shall be their father's bail; and bane to those
That for my surety will refuse the boys!

*Enter Edward and Richard Plantagenet, with Forces at one
side; at the other, with Forces also, Old Clifford and his Son*
See where they come: I 'll warrant they 'll make it good.

QUEEN MARGARET. And here comes Clifford, to deny their
bail.

CLIFFORD. (*Kneeling*) Health and all happiness to my lord
the king!

YORK. I thank thee, Clifford: say, what news with thee?
Nay, do not fright us with an angry look:
We are thy sovereign, Clifford, kneel again;
For thy mistaking so, we pardon thee.

CLIFFORD. This is my king, York, I do not mistake;
But thou mistakest me much to think I do.
To Bedlam with him! is the man grown mad?

KING HENRY. Ay, Clifford; a bedlam and ambitious humour
Makes him oppose himself against his king.

CLIFFORD. He is a traitor; let him to the Tower,
And chop away that factious pate of his.

QUEEN MARGARET. He is arrested, but will not obey:
His sons, he says, shall give their words for him.

YORK. Will you not, sons?

EDWARD. Ay, noble father, if our words will serve.

RICHARD. And if words will not, then our weapons shall.

CLIFFORD. Why, what a brood of traitors have we here!
YORK. Look in a glass, and call thy image so:
  I am thy king, and thou a false-heart traitor.
  Call hither to the stake my two brave bears.
  That with the very shaking of their chains
  They may astonish these fell-lurking curs:
  Bid Salisbury and Warwick come to me.
    Drums. Enter Warwick and Salisbury, with Forces
CLIFFORD. Are these thy bears? we 'll bait thy bears to death,
  And manacle the bear-ward in their chains,
  If thou darest bring them to the baiting-place.
RICHARD. Oft have I seen a hot o'erweening cur
  Run back and bite, because he was withheld;
  Who, being suffer'd with the bear's fell paw,
  Hath clapp'd his tail between his legs, and cried:
  And such a piece of service will you do,
  If you oppose yourselves to match Lord Warwick.
CLIFFORD. Hence, heap of wrath, foul indigested lump,
  As crooked in thy manners as thy shape!
YORK. Nay, we shall heat you thoroughly anon.
CLIFFORD. Take heed, lest by your heat you burn your-
  selves.
KING HENRY. Why, Warwick, hath thy knee forgot to bow?
  Old Salisbury, shame to thy silver hair,
  Thou mad misleader of thy brain-sick son!
  What! wilt thou on thy death-bed play the ruffian,
  And seek for sorrow with thy spectacles?
  O, where is faith? O, where is loyalty?
  If it be banish'd from the frosty head,
  Where shall it find a harbour in the earth?
  Wilt thou go dig a grave to find out war,
  And shame thine honourable age with blood?
  Why art thou old, and want'st experience?
  Or wherefore dost abuse it, if thou hast it?
  For shame! in duty bend thy knee to me,
  That bows unto the grave with mickle age.
SALISBURY. My lord, I have consider'd with myself
  The title of this most renowned duke;
  And in my conscience do repute his Grace
  The rightful heir to England's royal seat.
KING HENRY. Hast thou not sworn allegiance unto me?
SALISBURY. I have.

KING HENRY. Canst thou dispense with heaven for such an
　　oath?

SALISBURY. It is great sin to swear unto a sin,
　　But greater sin to keep a sinful oath.
　　Who can be bound by any solemn vow
　　To do a murderous deed, to rob a man,
　　To force a spotless virgin's chastity,
　　To reave the orphan of his patrimony,
　　To wring the widow from her custom'd right,
　　And have no other reason for this wrong
　　But that he was bound by a solemn oath?

QUEEN MARGARET. A subtle traitor needs no sophister.

KING HENRY. Call Buckingham, and bid him arm himself.

YORK. Call Buckingham, and all the friends thou hast,
　　I am resolv'd for death, or dignity.

CLIFFORD. The first I warrant thee, if dreams prove true.

WARWICK. You were best to go to bed and dream again,
　　To keep thee from the tempest of the field.

CLIFFORD. I am resolv'd to bear a greater storm
　　Than any thou canst conjure up to-day;
　　And that I'll write upon thy burgonet,
　　Might I but know thee by thy household badge.

WARWICK. Now, by my father's badge, old Nevil's crest,
　　The rampant bear chain'd to the ragged staff,
　　This day I'll wear aloft my burgonet,—
　　As on a mountain-top the cedar shows,
　　That keeps his leaves in spite of any storm,—
　　Even to affright thee with the view thereof.

CLIFFORD. And from thy burgonet I'll rend thy bear,
　　And tread it underfoot with all contempt,
　　Despite the bear-ward that protects the bear.

YOUNG CLIFFORD. And so to arms, victorious father,
　　To quell the rebels and their complices.

RICHARD. Fie! charity! for shame! speak not in spite,
　　For you shall sup with Jesu Christ to-night.

YOUNG CLIFFORD. Foul stigmatic, that's more than thou
　　canst tell.

RICHARD. If not in heaven, you'll surely sup in hell.

Exeunt severally

SCENE TWO

Saint Alban's.

Alarums: Excursions. Enter Warwick

WARWICK. Clifford of Cumberland, 'tis Warwick calls:
  And if thou dost not hide thee from the bear,
  Now, when the angry trumpet sounds alarm,
  And dead men's cries do fill the empty air,
  Clifford, I say, come forth, and fight with me!
  Proud northern lord, Clifford of Cumberland,
  Warwick is hoarse with calling thee to arms.
                Enter York
  How now, my noble lord! what! all afoot?
YORK. The deadly-handed Clifford slew my steed;
  But match to match I have encounter'd him,
  And made a prey for carrion kites and crows
  Even of the bonny beast he lov'd so well.
                Enter Old Clifford
WARWICK. Of one or both of us the time is come.
YORK. Hold, Warwick! seek thee out some other chase,
  For I myself must hunt this deer to death.
WARWICK. Then, nobly, York; 'tis for a crown thou fight'st.
  As I intend, Clifford, to thrive to-day,
  It grieves my soul to leave thee unassail'd.   *Exit*
CLIFFORD. What seest thou in me, York? why dost thou
    pause?
YORK. With thy brave bearing should I be in love,
  But that thou art so fast mine enemy.
CLIFFORD. Nor should thy prowess want praise and esteem,
  But that 'tis shown ignobly and in treason.
YORK. So let it help me now against thy sword
  As I in justice and true right express it.
CLIFFORD. My soul and body on the action both!
YORK. A dreadful lay! address thee instantly.
CLIFFORD. La fin couronne les œuvres.
                They fight, and Clifford falls and dies
YORK. Thus war hath given thee peace, for thou art still.
  Peace with his soul, heaven, if it be thy will!   *Exit*
                Enter Young Clifford

YOUNG CLIFFORD. Shame and confusion! all is on the rout:
  Fear frames disorder, and disorder wounds
  Where it should guard. O war! thou son of hell,
  Whom angry heavens do make their minister,
  Throw in the frozen bosoms of our part
  Hot coals of vengeance! Let no soldier fly:
  He that is truly dedicate to war
  Hath no self-love; nor he that loves himself
  Hath not essentially, but by circumstance,
  The name of valour.   *Seeing his father's body*
              O! let the vile world end,
  And the premised flames of the last day
  Knit heaven and earth together;
  Now let the general trumpet blow his blast,
  Particularities and petty sounds
  To cease!—Wast thou ordain'd, dear father,
  To lose thy youth in peace, and to achieve
  The silver livery of advised age,
  And, in thy reverence and thy chair-days thus
  To die in ruffian battle? Even at this sight
  My heart is turn'd to stone: and while 'tis mine
  It shall be stony. York not our old men spares;
  No more will I their babes: tears virginal
  Shall be to me even as the dew to fire;
  And beauty, that the tyrant oft reclaims,
  Shall to my flaming wrath be oil and flax.
  Henceforth I will not have to do with pity:
  Meet I an infant of the house of York,
  Into as many gobbets will I cut it
  As mild Medea young Absyrtus did:
  In cruelty will I seek out my fame.
  Come, thou new ruin of old Clifford's house:
                          Taking up the body
  As did Æneas old Anchises bear,
  So bear I thee upon my manly shoulders;
  But then Æneas bare a living load,
  Nothing so heavy as these woes of mine.   *Exit*
  Enter Richard and Somerset, fighting; Somerset is killed
RICHARD. So, lie thou there;
  For underneath an alehouse' paltry sign,
  The Castle in Saint Alban's, Somerset
  Hath made the wizard famous in his death.

Sword, hold thy temper; heart, be wrathful still:

Priests pray for enemies, but princes kill.   *Exit*

Alarums: Excursions. Enter
King Henry, Queen Margaret, and Others, retreating

QUEEN MARGARET. Away, my lord! you are slow: for shame, away!

KING HENRY. Can we outrun the heavens? good Margaret, stay.

QUEEN MARGARET. What are you made of? you 'll nor fight nor fly:

Now is it manhood, wisdom, and defence,

To give the enemy way, and to secure us

By what we can, which can no more but fly.

Alarum afar off

If you be ta'en, we then should see the bottom

Of all our fortunes: but if we haply scape,

As well we may, if not through your neglect,

We shall to London get, where you are lov'd,

And where this breach now in our fortunes made

May readily be stopp'd.

Re-enter Young Clifford

YOUNG CLIFFORD. But that my heart 's on future mischief set,

I would speak blasphemy ere bid you fly;

But fly you must: uncurable discomfit

Reigns in the hearts of all our present parts.

Away, for your relief! and we will live

To see their day and them our fortune give.

Away, my lord, away!   *Exeunt*

SCENE THREE

Field near Saint Alban's.

Alarum. Retreat. Flourish; then enter York, Richard,
Warwick, and Soldiers, with drum and colours

YORK. Of Salisbury, who can report of him;

That winter lion, who in rage forgets

Aged contusions and all brush of time,

And, like a gallant in the brow of youth,

Repairs him with occasion? this happy day

Is not itself, nor have we won one foot,

If Salisbury be lost.

RICHARD.   My noble father,
Three times to-day I holp him to his horse,
Three times bestrid him; thrice I led him off,
Persuaded him from any further act:
But still, where danger was, still there I met him;
And like rich hangings in a homely house,
So was his will in his old feeble body.
But, noble as he is, look where he comes.

Enter Salisbury

SALISBURY. Now, by my sword, well hast thou fought
    to-day;
By the mass, so did we all. I thank you, Richard:
God knows how long it is I have to live;
And it hath pleas'd him that three times to-day
You have defended me from imminent death.
Well, lords, we have not got that which we have:
'Tis not enough our foes are this time fled,
Being opposites of such repairing nature.

YORK. I know our safety is to follow them;
For, as I hear, the king is fled to London,
To call a present court of parliament:
Let us pursue him ere the writs go forth:—
What says Lord Warwick? shall we after them?

WARWICK. After them! nay, before them, if we can.
Now, by my hand, lords, 'twas a glorious day:
Saint Alban's battle, won by famous York,
Shall be eterniz'd in all age to come.
Sound, drums and trumpets, and to London all:
And more such days as these to us befall!   *Exeunt*

THE THIRD PART OF
KING HENRY THE SIXTH

CAST OF CHARACTERS

KING HENRY THE SIXTH
EDWARD, *Prince of Wales, his Son*
LEWIS THE ELEVENTH, *King of France*

DUKE OF SOMERSET
DUKE OF EXETER
EARL OF OXFORD   } *on King Henry's*
EARL OF NORTHUMBERLAND   *side*
EARL OF WESTMORELAND
LORD CLIFFORD

RICHARD PLANTAGENET, *Duke of York*

EDWARD, *Earl of March, afterwards*
  King Edward the Fourth   } *his*
EDMUND, *Earl of Rutland*   *Sons*
GEORGE, *afterwards Duke of Clarence*
RICHARD, *afterwards Duke of Gloucester*

DUKE OF NORFOLK
MARQUESS OF MONTAGUE
EARL OF WARWICK   } *of the Duke*
EARL OF PEMBROKE   *of York's Party*
LORD HASTINGS
LORD STAFFORD

SIR JOHN MORTIMER } *Uncles to the Duke of York*
SIR HUGH MORTIMER

HENRY, EARL OF RICHMOND, *a Youth*
LORD RIVERS, *Brother to Lady Grey*
SIR WILLIAM STANLEY
SIR JOHN MONTGOMERY
SIR JOHN SOMERVILLE

(*continued on next page*)

Tutor to Rutland
Mayor of York
Lieutenant of the Tower
A Nobleman
Two Keepers
A Huntsman
A Son that has killed his Father
A Father that has killed his Son

QUEEN MARGARET
LADY GREY, *afterwards Queen to Edward the Fourth*
BONA, *Sister to the French Queen*

Soldiers, and other Attendants on King Henry and King Edward, Messengers, Watchmen, &c.

SCENE

During part of the Third Act, in France; during the rest of the Play, in England

THE THIRD PART OF KING
HENRY THE SIXTH

ACT ONE

SCENE ONE

London. The Parliament-House.

*Drums. Some soldiers of York's party break in. Then, enter
the Duke of York, Edward, Richard, Norfolk, Montague,
Warwick, and Others, with white roses in their hats*

WARWICK. I wonder how the king escap'd our hands.
YORK. While we pursu'd the horsemen of the north,
  He slily stole away and left his men:
  Whereat the great Lord of Northumberland,
  Whose warlike ears could never brook retreat,
  Cheer'd up the drooping army; and himself,
  Lord Clifford, and Lord Stafford, all abreast,
  Charg'd our main battle's front, and breaking in
  Were by the swords of common soldiers slain.
EDWARD. Lord Stafford's father, Duke of Buckingham,
  Is either slain or wounded dangerously;
  I cleft his beaver with a downright blow:
  That this is true, father, behold his blood.
                        Showing his bloody sword
MONTAGUE. And, brother, here 's the Earl of Wiltshire's
    blood,   *To York, showing his*
  Whom I encounter'd as the battles join'd.
RICHARD. Speak thou for me, and tell them what I did.
          Throwing down the Duke of Somerset's head
YORK. Richard hath best deserv'd of all my sons.
  But, is your Grace dead, my Lord of Somerset?
NORFOLK. Such hope have all the line of John of Gaunt!
RICHARD. Thus do I hope to shake King Henry's head.
WARWICK. And so do I. Victorious Prince of York,
  Before I see thee seated in that throne

Which now the house of Lancaster usurps,
I vow by heaven these eyes shall never close.
This is the palace of the fearful king,
And this the regal seat: possess it, York;
For this is thine, and not King Henry's heirs'.

YORK. Assist me, then, sweet Warwick, and I will;
For hither we have broken in by force.

NORFOLK. We 'll all assist you; he that flies shall die.

YORK. Thanks, gentle Norfolk. Stay by me, my lords;
And, soldiers, stay and lodge by me this night.

WARWICK. And when the king comes, offer him no violence,
Unless he seeks to thrust you out perforce.

The Soldiers retire

YORK. The queen this day here holds her parliament,
But little thinks we shall be of her council:
By words or blows here let us win our right.

RICHARD. Arm'd as we are, let 's stay within this house.

WARWICK. The bloody parliament shall this be call'd,
Unless Plantagenet, Duke of York, be king,
And bashful Henry depos'd, whose cowardice
Hath made us by-words to our enemies.

YORK. Then leave me not, my lords; be resolute;
I mean to take possession of my right.

WARWICK. Neither the king, nor he that loves him best,
The proudest he that holds up Lancaster,
Dares stir a wing if Warwick shake his bells.
I 'll plant Pantagenet, root him up who dares.
Resolve thee, Richard; claim the English crown.

Warwick leads York to the throne, who seats himself
Flourish. Enter King Henry, Clifford, Northumberland,
Westmoreland, Exeter, and Others, with red roses in
their hats

KING HENRY. My lords, look where the sturdy rebel sits,
Even in the chair of state! belike he means—
Back'd by the power of Warwick, that false peer—
To aspire unto the crown and reign as king.
Earl of Northumberland, he slew thy father,
And thine, Lord Clifford; and you both have vow'd
    revenge
On him, his sons, his favourites, and his friends.

NORTHUMBERLAND. If I be not, heavens be reveng'd on me!

CLIFFORD. The hope thereof makes Clifford mourn in steel.

WESTMORELAND. What! shall we suffer this? let's pluck him
    down:
  My heart for anger burns; I cannot brook it.
KING HENRY. Be patient, gentle Earl of Westmoreland.
CLIFFORD. Patience is for poltroons, such as he:
  He durst not sit there had your father liv'd.
  My gracious lord, here in the parliament
  Let us assail the family of York.
NORTHUMBERLAND. Well hast thou spoken, cousin: be it so.
KING HENRY. Ah! know you not the city favours them,
  And they have troops of soldiers at their beck?
EXETER. But when the duke is slain they'll quickly fly.
KING HENRY. Far be the thought of this from Henry's heart,
  To make a shambles of the parliament-house!
  Cousin of Exeter, frowns, words, and threats,
  Shall be the war that Henry means to use.
                        They advance to the Duke
  Thou factious Duke of York, descend my throne,
  And kneel for grace and mercy at my feet;
  I am thy sovereign.
YORK.   I am thine.
EXETER. For shame! come down: he made thee Duke of
    York.
YORK. 'Twas my inheritance, as the earldom was.
EXETER. Thy father was a traitor to the crown.
WARWICK. Exeter, thou art a traitor to the crown
  In following this usurping Henry.
CLIFFORD. Whom should he follow but his natural king?
WARWICK. True, Clifford; and that's Richard, Duke of York.
KING HENRY. And shall I stand, and thou sit in my throne?
YORK. It must and shall be so: content thyself.
WARWICK. Be Duke of Lancaster: let him be king.
WESTMORELAND. He is both king and Duke of Lancaster;
  And that the Lord of Westmoreland shall maintain.
WARWICK. And Warwick shall disprove it. You forget
  That we are those which chas'd you from the field
  And slew your fathers, and with colours spread
  March'd through the city to the palace gates.
NORTHUMBERLAND. Yes, Warwick, I remember it to my
    grief;
  And, by his soul, thou and thy house shall rue it.
WESTMORELAND. Plantagenet, of thee, and these thy sons,

Thy kinsmen and thy friends, I 'll have more lives
Than drops of blood were in my father's veins.

CLIFFORD. Urge it no more; lest that instead of words,
I send thee, Warwick, such a messenger
As shall revenge his death before I stir.

WARWICK. Poor Clifford! how I scorn his worthless threats.

YORK. Will you we show our title to the crown?
If not, our swords shall plead it in the field.

KING HENRY. What title hast thou, traitor, to the crown?
Thy father was, as thou art, Duke of York;
Thy grandfather, Roger Mortimer, Earl of March;
I am the son of Henry the Fifth,
Who made the Dauphin and the French to stoop,
And seiz'd upon their towns and provinces.

WARWICK. Talk not of France, sith thou hast lost it all.

KING HENRY. The Lord Protector lost it, and not I:
When I was crown'd I was but nine months old.

RICHARD. You are old enough now, and yet, methinks, you
lose.
Father, tear the crown from the usurper's head.

EDWARD. Sweet father, do so; set it on your head.

MONTAGUE. (To York) Good brother, as thou lov'st and
honour'st arms,
Let 's fight it out and not stand cavilling thus.

RICHARD. Sound drums and trumpets, and the king will fly.

YORK. Sons, peace!

KING HENRY. Peace thou! and give King Henry leave to
speak.

WARWICK. Plantagenet shall speak first: hear him, lords;
And be you silent and attentive too,
For he that interrupts him shall not live.

KING HENRY. Think'st thou that I will leave my kingly
throne,
Wherein my grandsire and my father sat?
No: first shall war unpeople this my realm;
Ay, and their colours, often borne in France,
And now in England to our heart's great sorrow,
Shall be my winding-sheet. Why faint you, lords?
My title 's good, and better far than his.

WARWICK. Prove it, Henry, and thou shalt be king.

KING HENRY. Henry the Fourth by conquest got the crown.

YORK. 'Twas by rebellion against his king.

KING HENRY. (*Aside*) I know not what to say: my title 's
  weak.
  (*Aloud*) Tell me, may not a king adopt an heir?
YORK. What then?
KING HENRY. An if he may, then am I lawful king;
  For Richard, in the view of many lords,
  Resign'd the crown to Henry the Fourth,
  Whose heir my father was, and I am his.
YORK. He rose against him, being his sovereign,
  And made him to resign his crown perforce.
WARWICK. Suppose, my lords, he did it unconstrain'd,
  Think you 'twere prejudicial to his crown?
EXETER. No; for he could not so resign his crown
  But that the next heir should succeed and reign.
KING HENRY. Art thou against us, Duke of Exeter?
EXETER. His is the right, and therefore pardon me.
YORK. Why whisper you, my lords, and answer not?
EXETER. My conscience tells me he is lawful king.
KING HENRY. (*Aside*) All will revolt from me, and turn to
  him.
NORTHUMBERLAND. Plantagenet, for all the claim thou
    lay'st,
  Think not that Henry shall be so depos'd.
WARWICK. Depos'd he shall be in despite of all.
NORTHUMBERLAND. Thou art deceiv'd: 'tis not thy southern
    power,
  Of Essex, Norfolk, Suffolk, nor of Kent,
  Which makes thee thus presumptuous and proud,
  Can set the duke up in despite of me.
CLIFFORD. King Henry, be thy title right or wrong,
  Lord Clifford vows to fight in thy defence:
  May that ground gape and swallow me alive,
  Where I shall kneel to him that slew my father!
KING HENRY. O Clifford, how thy words revive my heart!
YORK. Henry of Lancaster, resign thy crown.
  What mutter you, or what conspire you, lords?
WARWICK. Do right unto this princely Duke of York,
  Or I will fill the house with armed men,
  And o'er the chair of state, where now he sits,
  Write up his title with usurping blood.
He stamps with his foot, and the Soldiers show themselves
KING HENRY. My Lord of Warwick, hear me but one word:—

Let me for this my life-time reign as king.

YORK. Confirm the crown to me and to mine heirs,
And thou shalt reign in quiet while thou livest.

KING HENRY. I am content: Richard Plantagenet,
Enjoy the kingdom after my decease.

CLIFFORD. What wrong is this unto the prince your son!

WARWICK. What good is this to England and himself!

WESTMORELAND. Base, fearful, and despairing Henry!

CLIFFORD. How hast thou injur'd both thyself and us!

WESTMORELAND. I cannot stay to hear these articles.

NORTHUMBERLAND. Nor I.

CLIFFORD. Come, cousin, let us tell the queen these news.

WESTMORELAND. Farewell, faint-hearted and degenerate
    king,
In whose cold blood no spark of honour bides.

NORTHUMBERLAND. Be thou a prey unto the house of York,
And die in bands for this unmanly deed!

CLIFFORD. In dreadful war mayst thou be overcome,
Or live in peace abandon'd and despis'd!

Exeunt Northumberland, Clifford, and Westmoreland

WARWICK. Turn this way, Henry, and regard them not.

EXETER. They seek revenge and therefore will not yield.

KING HENRY. Ah! Exeter.

WARWICK.   Why should you sigh, my lord?

KING HENRY. Not for myself, Lord Warwick, but my son,
Whom I unnaturally shall disinherit.
But be it as it may; I here entail
The crown to thee and to thine heirs for ever;
Conditionally, that here thou take an oath
To cease this civil war, and, whilst I live,
To honour me as thy king and sovereign;
And neither by treason nor hostility
To seek to put me down and reign thyself.

YORK. This oath I willingly take and will perform.

Coming from the throne

WARWICK. Long live King Henry! Plantagenet, embrace
    him.

KING HENRY. And long live thou and these thy forward sons!

YORK. Now York and Lancaster are reconcil'd.

EXETER. Accurs'd be he that seeks to make them foes!

Sennet. The Lords come forward

YORK. Farewell, my gracious lord; I 'll to my castle.

WARWICK. And I'll keep London with my soldiers.
NORFOLK. And I to Norfolk with my followers.
MONTAGUE. And I unto the sea from whence I came.

Exeunt York and his Sons, Warwick,
Norfolk, Montague, Soldiers, and Attendants

KING HENRY. And I, with grief and sorrow, to the court.

Enter Queen Margaret and the Prince of Wales

EXETER. Here comes the queen, whose looks bewray her
    anger:
    I'll steal away.   *Going*
KING HENRY.   Exeter, so will I.   *Going*
QUEEN MARGARET. Nay, go not from me; I will follow thee.
KING HENRY. Be patient, gentle queen, and I will stay.
QUEEN MARGARET. Who can be patient in such extremes?
    Ah! wretched man; would I had died a maid,
    And never seen thee, never borne thee son,
    Seeing thou hast prov'd so unnatural a father.
    Hath he deserv'd to lose his birthright thus?
    Hadst thou but lov'd him half so well as I,
    Or felt that pain which I did for him once,
    Or nourish'd him as I did with my blood,
    Thou wouldst have left thy dearest heart-blood there,
    Rather than have made that savage duke thine heir,
    And disinherited thine only son.
PRINCE. Father, you cannot disinherit me:
    If you be king, why should not I succeed?
KING HENRY. Pardon me, Margaret; pardon me, sweet son;
    The Earl of Warwick, and the duke, enforc'd me.
QUEEN MARGARET. Enforc'd thee! art thou king, and wilt be
    forc'd?
    I shame to hear thee speak. Ah! timorous wretch;
    Thou hast undone thyself, thy son, and me;
    And given unto the house of York such head
    As thou shalt reign but by their sufferance.
    To entail him and his heirs unto the crown,
    What is it but to make thy sepulchre,
    And creep into it far before thy time?
    Warwick is chancellor and the Lord of Calais;
    Stern Faulconbridge commands the narrow seas;
    The duke is made protector of the realm;
    And yet shalt thou be safe? such safety finds
    The trembling lamb environed with wolves.

Had I been there, which am a silly woman,
The soldiers should have toss'd me on their pikes
Before I would have granted to that act;
But thou preferr'st thy life before thine honour:
And seeing thou dost, I here divorce myself
Both from thy table, Henry, and thy bed,
Until that act of parliament be repeal'd
Whereby my son is disinherited.
The northern lords that have forsworn thy colours
Will follow mine, if once they see them spread;
And spread they shall be, to thy foul disgrace,
And utter ruin of the house of York.
Thus do I leave thee. Come, son, let's away;
Our army is ready; come, we 'll after them.

KING HENRY. Stay, gentle Margaret, and hear me speak.

QUEEN MARGARET. Thou hast spoke too much already: get
thee gone.

KING HENRY. Gentle son Edward, thou wilt stay with me?

QUEEN MARGARET. Ay, to be murder'd by his enemies.

PRINCE. When I return with victory from the field
I 'll see your Grace: till then, I 'll follow her.

QUEEN MARGARET. Come, son, away; we may not linger
thus.   *Exeunt Queen Margaret and the Prince of Wales*

KING HENRY. Poor queen! how love to me and to her son
Hath made her break out into terms of rage.
Reveng'd may she be on that hateful duke,
Whose haughty spirit, winged with desire,
Will cost my crown, and like an empty eagle
Tire on the flesh of me and of my son!
The loss of those three lords torments my heart:
I 'll write unto them, and entreat them fair.
Come, cousin; you shall be the messenger.

EXETER. And I, I hope, shall reconcile them all.   *Exeunt*

SCENE TWO

A Room in Sandal Castle, near Wakefield, in Yorkshire.

Enter Edward, Richard, and Montague

RICHARD. Brother, though I be youngest, give me leave.

EDWARD. No, I can better play the orator.

MONTAGUE. But I have reasons strong and forcible.
Enter York
YORK. Why, how now, sons and brother! at a strife?
  What is your quarrel? how began it first?
EDWARD. No quarrel, but a slight contention.
YORK. About what?
RICHARD. About that which concerns your Grace and us;
  The crown of England, father, which is yours.
YORK. Mine, boy? not till King Henry be dead.
RICHARD. Your right depends not on his life or death.
EDWARD. Now you are heir, therefore enjoy it now:
  By giving the house of Lancaster leave to breathe,
  It will outrun you, father, in the end.
YORK. I took an oath that he should quietly reign.
EDWARD. But for a kingdom any oath may be broken;
  I would break a thousand oaths to reign one year.
RICHARD. No; God forbid your Grace should be forsworn.
YORK. I shall be, if I claim by open war.
RICHARD. I'll prove the contrary, if you'll hear me speak.
YORK. Thou canst not, son; it is impossible.
RICHARD. An oath is of no moment, being not took
  Before a true and lawful magistrate
  That hath authority over him that swears:
  Henry had none, but did usurp the place;
  Then, seeing 'twas he that made you to depose,
  Your oath, my lord, is vain and frivolous,
  Therefore, to arms! And, father, do but think
  How sweet a thing it is to wear a crown,
  Within whose circuit is Elysium,
  And all that poets feign of bliss and joy.
  Why do we linger thus? I cannot rest
  Until the white rose that I wear be dy'd
  Even in the lukewarm blood of Henry's heart.
YORK. Richard, enough, I will be king, or die.
  Brother, thou shalt to London presently,
  And whet on Warwick to this enterprise.
  Thou, Richard, shalt unto the Duke of Norfolk,
  And tell him privily of our intent.
  You, Edward, shall unto my Lord Cobham,
  With whom the Kentishmen will willingly rise:
  In them I trust; for they are soldiers,
  Witty, courteous, liberal, full of spirit.

While you are thus employ'd, what resteth more,
But that I seek occasion how to rise,
And yet the king not privy to my drift,
Nor any of the house of Lancaster?

Enter a Messenger

But, stay: what news? Why comest thou in such post?
MESSENGER. The queen with all the northern earls and lords
Intend here to besiege you in your castle.
She is hard by with twenty thousand men,
And therefore fortify your hold, my lord.
YORK. Ay, with my sword. What! think'st thou that we fear
them?
Edward and Richard, you shall stay with me;
My brother Montague shall post to London:
Let noble Warwick, Cobham, and the rest,
Whom we have left protectors of the king,
With powerful policy strengthen themselves,
And trust not simple Henry nor his oaths.
MONTAGUE. Brother, I go; I 'll win them, fear it not:
And thus most humbly I do take my leave.   *Exit*

Enter Sir John and Sir Hugh Mortimer

YORK. Sir John, and Sir Hugh Mortimer, mine uncles,
You are come to Sandal in a happy hour;
The army of the queen mean to besiege us.
SIR JOHN. She shall not need, we 'll meet her in the field.
YORK. What! with five thousand men?
RICHARD. Ay, with five hundred, father, for a need:
A woman's general; what should we fear? *A march afar off*
EDWARD. I hear their drums; let 's set our men in order,
And issue forth and bid them battle straight.
YORK. Five men to twenty! though the odds be great,
I doubt not, uncle, of our victory.
Many a battle have I won in France,
When as the enemy hath been ten to one:
Why should I not now have the like success?

Alarum. Exeunt

SCENE THREE

Field of Battle between Sandal Castle and Wakefield.

Alarums: Excursions. Enter Rutland and his Tutor

RUTLAND. Ah, whither shall I fly to 'scape their hands?
Ah! tutor, look, where bloody Clifford comes!
    Enter Clifford and Soldiers
CLIFFORD. Chaplain, away! thy priesthood saves thy life.
As for the brat of this accursed duke,
Whose father slew my father, he shall die.
TUTOR. And I, my lord, will bear him company.
CLIFFORD. Soldiers, away with him.
TUTOR. Ah! Clifford, murder not this innocent child,
Lest thou be hated both of God and man!
     Exit, forced off by Soldiers
CLIFFORD. How now! is he dead already? Or is it fear
That makes him close his eyes? I 'll open them.
RUTLAND. So looks the pent-up lion o'er the wretch
That trembles under his devouring paws;
And so he walks, insulting o'er his prey,
And so he comes to rend his limbs asunder.
Ah! gentle Clifford, kill me with thy sword,
And not with such a cruel threatening look.
Sweet Clifford! hear me speak before I die:
I am too mean a subject for thy wrath;
Be thou reveng'd on men, and let me live.
CLIFFORD. In vain thou speak'st, poor boy; my father's blood
Hath stopp'd the passage where thy words should enter.
RUTLAND. Then let my father's blood open it again:
He is a man, and, Clifford, cope with him.
CLIFFORD. Had I thy brethren here, their lives and thine
Were not revenge sufficient for me:
No, if I digg'd up thy forefathers' graves,
And hung their rotten coffins up in chains,
It could not slake mine ire, nor ease my heart.
The sight of any of the house of York
Is as a fury to torment my soul;
And till I root out their accursed line,
And leave not one alive, I live in hell.

Therefore—   *Lifting his hand*

RUTLAND. O! let me pray before I take my death.

  To thee I pray; sweet Clifford, pity me!

CLIFFORD. Such pity as my rapier's point affords.

RUTLAND. I never did thee harm: why wilt thou slay me?

CLIFFORD. Thy father hath.

RUTLAND.   But 'twas ere I was born.

  Thou hast one son; for his sake pity me,

  Lest in revenge thereof, sith God is just,

  He be as miserably slain as I.

  Ah! let me live in prison all my days;

  And when I give occasion of offence,

  Then let me die, for now thou hast no cause.

CLIFFORD. No cause!

  Thy father slew my father; therefore, die.   *Stabs him*

RUTLAND. Di faciant laudis summa sit ista tuæ!   *Dies*

CLIFFORD. Plantagenet! I come, Plantagenet!

  And this thy son's blood cleaving to my blade

  Shall rust upon my weapon, till thy blood,

  Congeal'd with this, do make me wipe off both.   *Exit*

SCENE FOUR

Another Part of the Plains.

Alarum. Enter York

YORK. The army of the queen hath got the field:

  My uncles both are slain in rescuing me;

  And all my followers to the eager foe

  Turn back and fly, like ships before the wind,

  Or lambs pursu'd by hunger-starved wolves.

  My sons, God knows what hath bechanced them:

  But this I know, they have demean'd themselves

  Like men born to renown by life or death.

  Three times did Richard make a lane to me,

  And thrice cried, 'Courage, father! fight it out!'

  And full as oft came Edward to my side,

  With purple falchion, painted to the hilt

  In blood of those that had encounter'd him:

  And when the hardiest warriors did retire,

  Richard cried, 'Charge! and give no foot of ground!'

And cried, 'A crown, or else a glorious tomb!
A sceptre, or an earthly sepulchre!'
With this, we charg'd again; but out, alas!
We bodg'd again: as I have seen a swan
With bootless labour swim against the tide,
And spend her strength with over-matching waves.

A short alarum within

Ah, hark! the fatal followers do pursue;
And I am faint and cannot fly their fury;
And were I strong I would not shun their fury:
The sands are number'd that make up my life;
Here must I stay, and here my life must end.

*Enter Queen Margaret, Clifford,
Northumberland, the young Prince, and Soldiers*

Come, bloody Clifford, rough Northumberland,
I dare your quenchless fury to more rage:
I am your butt, and I abide your shot.

NORTHUMBERLAND. Yield to our mercy, proud Plantagenet.

CLIFFORD. Ay, to such mercy as his ruthless arm
With downright payment show'd unto my father.
Now Phæthon hath tumbled from his car,
And made an evening at the noontide prick.

YORK. My ashes, as the phœnix, may bring forth
A bird that will revenge upon you all;
And in that hope I throw mine eyes to heaven,
Scorning whate'er you can afflict me with.
Why come you not? what! multitudes, and fear?

CLIFFORD. So cowards fight when they can fly no further;
So doves do peck the falcon's piercing talons;
So desperate thieves, all hopeless of their lives,
Breathe out invectives 'gainst the officers.

YORK. O Clifford! but bethink thee once again,
And in thy thought o'er-run my former time
And, if thou canst for blushing, view this face,
And bite thy tongue, that slanders him with cowardice
Whose frown hath made thee faint and fly ere this.

CLIFFORD. I will not bandy with thee word for word.
But buckle with thee blows, twice two for one.   *Draws*

QUEEN MARGARET. Hold, valiant Clifford! for a thousand causes
I would prolong awhile the traitor's life.
Wrath makes him deaf: speak thou, Northumberland.

NORTHUMBERLAND. Hold, Clifford! do not honour him so
   much
   To prick thy finger, though to wound his heart.
   What valour were it, when a cur doth grin,
   For one to thrust his hand between his teeth,
   When he might spurn him with his foot away?
   It is war's prize to take all vantages,
   And ten to one is no impeach of valour.
                       They lay hands on York, who struggles
CLIFFORD. Ay, ay; so strives the woodcock with the gin.
NORTHUMBERLAND. So doth the cony struggle in the net.
                       York is taken prisoner
YORK. So triumph thieves upon their conquer'd booty;
   So true men yield, with robbers so o'er-matched.
NORTHUMBERLAND. What would your Grace have done
   unto him now?
QUEEN MARGARET. Brave warriors, Clifford and Northum-
   berland,
   Come, make him stand upon this molehill here,
   That raught at mountains with outstretched arms,
   Yet parted but the shadow with his hand.
   What! was it you that would be England's king?
   Was 't you that revell'd in our parliament,
   And made a preachment of your high descent?
   Where are your mess of sons to back you now?
   The wanton Edward, and the lusty George?
   And where 's that valiant crook-back prodigy,
   Dicky your boy, that with his grumbling voice
   Was wont to cheer his dad in mutinies?
   Or, with the rest, where is your darling Rutland?
   Look, York: I stain'd this napkin with the blood
   That valiant Clifford with his rapier's point
   Made issue from the bosom of the boy;
   And if thine eyes can water for his death,
   I give thee this to dry thy cheeks withal.
   Alas, poor York! but that I hate thee deadly,
   I should lament thy miserable state.
   I prithee grieve, to make me merry, York.
   What! hath thy fiery heart so parch'd thine entrails
   That not a tear can fall for Rutland's death?
   Why art thou patient, man? thou shouldst be mad;
   And I, to make thee mad, do mock thee thus.

Stamp, rave, and fret, that I may sing and dance.
Thou wouldst be fee'd, I see, to make me sport:
York cannot speak unless he wear a crown.
A crown for York! and, lords, bow low to him:
Hold you his hands whilst I do set it on.
Putting a paper crown on his head
Ay, marry, sir, now looks he like a king!
Ay, this is he that took King Henry's chair;
And this is he was his adopted heir.
But how is it that great Plantagenet
Is crown'd so soon, and broke his solemn oath?
As I bethink me, you should not be king
Till our King Henry had shook hands with death.
And will you pale your head in Henry's glory,
And rob his temples of the diadem,
Now in his life, against your holy oath?
O! 'tis a fault too-too unpardonable.
Off with the crown; and, with the crown, his head;
And, whilst we breathe, take time to do him dead.

CLIFFORD. That is my office, for my father's sake.

QUEEN MARGARET. Nay, stay; let 's hear the orisons he
makes.

YORK. She-wolf of France, but worse than wolves of France,
Whose tongue more poisons than the adder's tooth!
How ill-beseeming is it in thy sex
To triumph, like an Amazonian trull,
Upon their woes whom fortune captivates!
But that thy face is, visor-like, unchanging,
Made impudent with use of evil deeds,
I would assay, proud queen, to make thee blush:
To tell thee whence thou cam'st, of whom deriv'd,
Were shame enough to shame thee, were thou not shame-
less.
Thy father bears the type of King of Naples,
Of both the Sicils and Jerusalem;
Yet not so wealthy as an English yeoman.
Hath that poor monarch taught thee to insult?
It needs not, nor it boots thee not, proud queen,
Unless the adage must be verified,
That beggars mounted run their horse to death.
'Tis beauty that doth oft make women proud;
But, God he knows, thy share thereof is small:

'Tis virtue that doth make them most admir'd;
The contrary doth make thee wonder'd at:
'Tis government that makes them seem divine;
The want thereof makes thee abominable.
Thou art as opposite to every good
As the Antipodes are unto us,
Or as the south to the septentrion.
O tiger's heart wrapp'd in a woman's hide!
How couldst thou drain the life-blood of the child,
To bid the father wipe his eyes withal,
And yet be seen to bear a woman's face?
Women are soft, mild, pitiful, and flexible;
Thou stern, obdurate, flinty, rough, remorseless.
Bidd'st thou me rage? why, now thou hast thy wish:
Wouldst have me weep? why, now thou hast thy will;
For raging wind blows up incessant showers,
And when the rage allays, the rain begins.
These tears are my sweet Rutland's obsequies,
And every drop cries vengeance for his death,
'Gainst thee, fell Clifford, and thee, false Frenchwoman.

NORTHUMBERLAND.   Beshrew me, but his passion moves me
    so
That hardly can I check my eyes from tears.

YORK.   That face of his the hungry cannibals
    Would not have touch'd, would not have stain'd with
        blood;
    But you are more inhuman, more inexorable,—
    O! ten times more, than tigers of Hyrcania.
    See, ruthless queen, a hapless father's tears:
    This cloth thou dipp'dst in blood of my sweet boy,
    And I with tears do wash the blood away.
    Keep thou the napkin, and go boast of this;
                        Giving back the handkerchief
    And if thou tell'st the heavy story right,
    Upon my soul, the hearers will shed tears;
    Yea, even my foes will shed fast-falling tears,
    And say, 'Alas! it was a piteous deed!'
    There, take the crown, and, with the crown my curse,
    And in thy need such comfort come to thee
    As now I reap at thy too cruel hand!
    Hard-hearted Clifford, take me from the world;
    My soul to heaven, my blood upon your heads!

NORTHUMBERLAND. Had he been slaughter-man to all my
    kin,
  I should not for my life but weep with him,
  To see how inly sorrow gripes his soul.
QUEEN MARGARET. What! weeping-ripe, my Lord Northum-
    berland?
  Think but upon the wrong he did us all,
  And that will quickly dry thy melting tears.
CLIFFORD. Here 's for my oath; here 's for my father's death.
                                Stabbing him
QUEEN MARGARET. And here 's to right our gentle-hearted
    king.   *Stabbing him*
YORK. Open thy gate of mercy, gracious God!
  My soul flies through these wounds to seek out thee. *Dies*
QUEEN MARGARET. Off with his head, and set it on York
    gates;
  So York may overlook the town of York. *Flourish. Exeunt*

ACT TWO

SCENE ONE

A Plain near Mortimer's Cross in Herefordshire.

Drums. Enter Edward and Richard, with their Forces,
marching

EDWARD. I wonder how our princely father 'scap'd,
  Or whether he be 'scap'd away or no
  From Clifford's and Northumberland's pursuit.
  Had he been ta'en we should have heard the news;
  Had he been slain we should have heard the news;
  Or had he 'scap'd, methinks we should have heard
  The happy tidings of his good escape.
  How fares my brother? why is he so sad?
RICHARD. I cannot joy until I be resolv'd
  Where our right valiant father is become.
  I saw him in the battle range about,
  And watch'd him how he singled Clifford forth.
  Methought he bore him in the thickest troop
  As doth a lion in a herd of neat;
  Or as a bear, encompass'd round with dogs,
  Who having pinch'd a few and made them cry,
  The rest stand all aloof and bark at him.
  So far'd our father with his enemies;
  So fled his enemies my warlike father:
  Methinks, 'tis prize enough to be his son.
  See how the morning opes her golden gates,
  And takes her farewell of the glorious sun;
  How well resembles it the prime of youth,
  Trimm'd like a younker prancing to his love.
EDWARD. Dazzle mine eyes, or do I see three suns?
RICHARD. Three glorious suns, each one a perfect sun;
  Not separated with the racking clouds,
  But sever'd in a pale clear-shining sky.
  See, see! they join, embrace, and seem to kiss,

As if they vow'd some league inviolable:
Now are they but one lamp, one light, one sun.
In this the heaven figures some event.

EDWARD. 'Tis wondrous strange, the like yet never heard of.
I think it cites us, brother, to the field;
That we, the sons of brave Plantagenet,
Each one already blazing by our meeds,
Should notwithstanding join our lights together.
And over-shine the earth, as this the world.
Whate'er it bodes, henceforward will I bear
Upon my target three fair-shining suns.

RICHARD. Nay, bear three daughters: by your leave I speak it,
You love the breeder better than the male.

Enter a Messenger

But what art thou, whose heavy looks foretell
Some dreadful story hanging on thy tongue?

MESSENGER. Ah! one that was a woeful looker-on,
When as the noble Duke of York was slain,
Your princely father, and my loving lord.

EDWARD. O! speak no more, for I have heard too much.

RICHARD. Say how he died, for I will hear it all.

MESSENGER. Environed he was with many foes,
And stood against them, as the hope of Troy
Against the Greeks that would have enter'd Troy.
But Hercules himself must yield to odds;
And many strokes, though with a little axe,
Hew down and fell the hardest-timber'd oak.
By many hands your father was subdu'd;
But only slaughter'd by the ireful arm
Of unrelenting Clifford and the queen,
Who crown'd the gracious duke in high despite;
Laugh'd in his face; and when with grief he wept,
The ruthless queen gave him to dry his cheeks
A napkin steeped in the harmless blood
O sweet young Rutland, by rough Clifford slain:
And after many scorns, many foul taunts,
They took his head, and on the gates of York
They set the same; and there it doth remain,
The saddest spectacle that e'er I view'd.

EDWARD. Sweet Duke of York! our prop to lean upon,
Now thou art gone, we have no staff, no stay!
O Clifford! boisterous Clifford! thou hast slain

The flower of Europe for his chivalry;
And treacherously hast thou vanquish'd him,
For hand to hand he would have vanquish'd thee.
Now my soul's palace is become a prison:
Ah! would she break from hence, that this my body
Might in the ground be closed up in rest,
For never henceforth shall I joy again,
Never, O! never, shall I see more joy.

RICHARD. I cannot weep, for all my body's moisture
Scarce serves to quench my furnace-burning heart:
Nor can my tongue unload my heart's great burden;
For selfsame wind, that I should speak withal
Is kindling coals that fire all my breast,
And burn me up with flames, that tears would quench.
To weep is to make less the depth of grief:
Tears then, for babes; blows and revenge for me!
Richard, I bear thy name; I 'll venge thy death,
Or die renowned by attempting it.

EDWARD. His name that valiant duke hath left with thee;
His dukedom and his chair with me is left.

RICHARD. Nay, if thou be that princely eagle's bird,
Show thy descent by gazing 'gainst the sun:
For chair and dukedom, throne and kingdom say;
Either that is thine, or else thou wert not his.

March. Enter Warwick
and the Marquess of Montague, with Forces

WARWICK. How now, fair lords! What fare? what news
abroad?

RICHARD. Great Lord of Warwick, if we should recount
Our baleful news, and at each word's deliverance
Stab poinards in our flesh till all were told,
The words would add more anguish than the wounds.
O valiant lord! the Duke of York is slain.

EDWARD. O Warwick! Warwick! that Plantagenet
Which held thee dearly as his soul's redemption,
Is by the stern Lord Clifford done to death.

WARWICK. Ten days ago I drown'd these news in tears,
And now, to add more measure to your woes,
I come to tell you things sith then befallen.
After the bloody fray at Wakefield fought,
Where your brave father breath'd his latest gasp,
Tidings, as swiftly as the posts could run,

Were brought me of your loss and his depart.
I, then in London, keeper of the king,
Muster'd my soldiers, gather'd flocks of friends,
And very well appointed, as I thought,
March'd towards Saint Alban's to intercept the queen,
Bearing the king in my behalf along;
For by my scouts I was advertised
That she was coming with a full intent
To dash our late decree in parliament,
Touching King Henry's oath and your succession.
Short tale to make, we at Saint Alban's met,
Our battles join'd, and both sides fiercely fought:
But whether 'twas the coldness of the king,
Who look'd full gently on his warlike queen,
That robb'd my soldiers of their heated spleen;
Or whether 'twas report of her success;
Or more than common fear of Clifford's rigour,
Who thunders to his captives blood and death,
I cannot judge: but, to conclude with truth,
Their weapons like to lightning came and went;
Our soldiers'—like the night-owl's lazy flight,
Or like a lazy thresher with a flail—
Fell gently down, as if they struck their friends.
I cheer'd them up with justice of our cause,
With promise of high pay, and great rewards:
But all in vain; they had no heart to fight,
And we in them no hope to win the day;
So that we fled: the king unto the queen;
Lord George your brother, Norfolk, and myself,
In haste, post-haste, are come to join with you;
For in the marches here we heard you were,
Making another head to fight again.
EDWARD. Where is the Duke of Norfolk, gentle Warwick?
And when came George from Burgundy to England?
WARWICK. Some six miles off the duke is with the soldiers;
And for your brother, he was lately sent
From your kind aunt, Duchess of Burgundy,
With aid of soldiers to this needful war.
RICHARD. 'Twas odds, belike, when valiant Warwick fled:
Oft have I heard his praises in pursuit,
But ne'er till now his scandal of retire.
WARWICK. Nor now my scandal, Richard, dost thou hear;

For thou shalt know, this strong right hand of mine
Can pluck the diadem from faint Henry's head,
And wring the awful sceptre from his fist,
Were he as famous and as bold in war
As he is fam'd for mildness, peace, and prayer.

RICHARD. I know it well, Lord Warwick; blame me not:
'Tis love I bear thy glories makes me speak.
But in this troublous time what's to be done?
Shall we go throw away our coats of steel,
And wrap our bodies in black mourning gowns,
Numbering our Ave-Maries with our beads?
Or shall we on the helmets of our foes
Tell our devotion with revengeful arms?
If for the last, say 'Ay,' and to it, lords.

WARWICK. Why, therefore Warwick came to seek you out;
And therefore comes my brother Montague.
Attend me, lords. The proud insulting queen,
With Clifford and the haught Northumberland,
And of their feather many more proud birds,
Have wrought the easy-melting king like wax.
He swore consent to your succession,
His oath enrolled in the parliament;
And now to London all the crew are gone,
To frustrate both his oath and what beside
May make against the house of Lancaster.
Their power, I think, is thirty thousand strong:
Now, if the help of Norfolk and myself,
With all the friends that thou, brave Earl of March,
Amongst the loving Welshmen canst procure,
Will but amount to five and twenty thousand,
Why, Via! to London will we march amain,
And once again bestride our foaming steeds,
And once again cry 'Charge upon our foes!'
But never once again turn back and fly.

RICHARD. Ay, now methinks I hear great Warwick speak:
Ne'er may he live to see a sunshine day,
That cries 'Retire,' if Warwick bid him stay.

EDWARD. Lord Warwick, on thy shoulder will I lean;
And when thou fail'st—as God forbid the hour!—
Must Edward fall, which peril heaven forfend!

WARWICK. No longer Earl of March, but Duke of York:
The next degree is England's royal throne;

For King of England shalt thou be proclaim'd
In every borough as we pass along;
And he that throws not up his cap for joy
Shall for the fault make forfeit of his head.
King Edward, valiant Richard, Montague,
Stay we no longer dreaming of renown,
But sound the trumpets, and about our task.

RICHARD. Then Clifford, were thy heart as hard as steel,—
As thou hast shown it flinty by thy deeds,—
I come to pierce it, or to give thee mine.

EDWARD. Then strike up, drums! God, and Saint George for
us!

Enter a Messenger.

WARWICK. How now! what news?

MESSENGER. The Duke of Norfolk sends you word by me,
The queen is coming with a puissant host;
And craves your company for speedy counsel.

WARWICK. Why then it sorts; brave warriors, let 's away.

Exeunt

SCENE TWO

Before York.

*Flourish. Enter King Henry, Queen Margaret, the Prince
of Wales, Clifford, and Northumberland, with
drums and trumpets*

QUEEN MARGARET. Welcome, my lord, to this brave town of
York.
Yonder 's the head of that arch-enemy,
That sought to be encompass'd with your crown:
Doth not the object cheer your heart, my lord?

KING HENRY. Ay, as the rocks cheer them that fear their
wrack:
To see this sight, it irks my very soul.
Withhold revenge, dear God! 'tis not my fault,
Nor wittingly have I infring'd my vow.

CLIFFORD. My gracious liege, this too much lenity
And harmful pity must be laid aside.
To whom do lions cast their gentle looks?
Not to the beast that would usurp their den.

Whose hand is that the forest bear doth lick?
Not his that spoils her young before her face.
Who 'scapes the lurking serpent's mortal sting?
Not he that sets his foot upon her back.
The smallest worm will turn being trodden on,
And doves will peck in safeguard of their brood.
Ambitious York did level at thy crown;
Thou smiling while he knit his angry brows:
He, but a duke, would have his son a king,
And raise his issue like a loving sire;
Thou, being a king, bless'd with a goodly son,
Didst yield consent to disinherit him,
Which argu'd thee a most unloving father.
Unreasonable creatures feed their young;
And though man's face be fearful to their eyes,
Yet, in protection of their tender ones,
Who hath not seen them, even with those wings
Which sometime they have us'd with fearful flight,
Make war with him that climb'd unto their nest,
Offering their own lives in their young's defence?
For shame, my liege! make them your precedent.
Were it not pity that this goodly boy
Should lose his birthright by his father's fault,
And long hereafter say unto his child,
'What my great-grandfather and grandsire got,
My careless father fondly gave away'?
Ah! what a shame were this. Look on the boy:
And let his manly face, which promiseth
Successful fortune, steel thy melting heart
To hold thine own and leave thine own with him.
KING HENRY. Full well hath Clifford play'd the orator,
Inferring arguments of mighty force.
But, Clifford, tell me, didst thou never hear
That things ill-got had ever bad success?
And happy always was it for that son
Whose father for his hoarding went to hell?
I 'll leave my son my virtuous deeds behind;
And would my father had left me no more!
For all the rest is held at such a rate
As brings a thousand-fold more care to keep
Than in possession any jot of pleasure.
Ah! cousin York, would thy best friends did know

How it doth grieve me that thy head is here!

QUEEN MARGARET. My lord, cheer up your spirits: our foes
　　are nigh,
And this soft courage makes your followers faint.
You promis'd knighthood to our forward son:
Unsheathe your sword, and dub him presently.
Edward, kneel down.

KING HENRY. Edward Plantagenet, arise a knight;
And learn this lesson, draw thy sword in right.

PRINCE. My gracious father, by your kingly leave,
I'll draw it as apparent to the crown,
And in that quarrel use it to the death.

CLIFFORD. Why, that is spoken like a toward prince.

Enter a Messenger.

MESSENGER. Royal commanders, be in readiness:
For with a band of thirty thousand men
Comes Warwick, backing of the Duke of York;
And in the towns, as they do march along,
Proclaims him king, and many fly to him:
Darraïgn your battle, for they are at hand.

CLIFFORD. I would your Highness would depart the field:
The queen hath best success when you are absent.

QUEEN MARGARET. Ay, good my lord, and leave us to our
　　fortune.

KING HENRY. Why, that's my fortune too; therefore I'll stay.

NORTHUMBERLAND. Be it with resolution then to fight.

PRINCE. My royal father, cheer these noble lords,
And hearten those that fight in your defence:
Unsheathe your sword, good father: cry, 'Saint George!'

March. Enter Edward, George,
Richard, Warwick, Norfolk, Montague, and Soldiers

EDWARD. Now, perjud'd Henry, wilt thou kneel for grace,
And set thy diadem upon my head;
Or bide the mortal fortune of the field?

QUEEN MARGARET. Go, rate thy minions, proud insulting
　　boy!
Becomes it thee to be thus bold in terms
Before thy sovereign and thy lawful king?

EDWARD. I am his king, and he should bow his knee;
I was adopted heir by his consent:
Since when, his oath is broke; for, as I hear,
You, that are king, though he do wear the crown,

Have caus'd him, by new act of parliament,
To blot out me, and put his own son in.

CLIFFORD. And reason too:
Who should succeed the father but the son?

RICHARD. Are you there, butcher? O! I cannot speak.

CLIFFORD. Ay, crook-back; here I stand to answer thee,
Or any he the proudest of thy sort.

RICHARD. 'Twas you that kill'd young Rutland, was it not?

CLIFFORD. Ay, and old York, and yet not satisfied.

RICHARD. For God's sake, lords, give signal to the fight.

WARWICK. What sayst thou, Henry, wilt thou yield the
crown?

QUEEN MARGARET. Why, how now, long-tongu'd Warwick!
dare you speak?
When you and I met at Saint Alban's last,
Your legs did better service than your hands.

WARWICK. Then 'twas my turn to fly, and now 'tis thine.

CLIFFORD. You said so much before, and yet you fled.

WARWICK. 'Twas not your valour, Clifford, drove me thence.

NORTHUMBERLAND. No, nor your manhood that durst make
you stay.

RICHARD. Northumberland, I hold thee reverently.
Break off the parley; for scarce I can refrain
The execution of my big-swoln heart
Upon that Clifford, that cruel child-killer.

CLIFFORD. I slew thy father: call'st thou him a child?

RICHARD. Ay, like a dastard and a treacherous coward,
As thou didst kill our tender brother Rutland;
But ere sunset I 'll make thee curse the deed.

KING HENRY. Have done with words, my lords, and hear me
speak.

QUEEN MARGARET. Defy them, then, or else hold close thy
lips.

KING HENRY. I prithee, give no limits to my tongue:
I am a king, and privileg'd to speak.

CLIFFORD. My liege, the wound that bred this meeting here
Cannot be cur'd by words; therefore be still.

RICHARD. Then, executioner, unsheathe thy sword.
By him that made us all, I am resolv'd
That Clifford's manhood lies upon his tongue.

EDWARD. Say, Henry, shall I have my right or no?
A thousand men have broke their fasts to-day,

That ne'er shall dine unless thou yield the crown.
WARWICK. If thou deny, their blood upon thy head;
  For York in justice puts his armour on.
PRINCE. If that be right which Warwick says is right,
  There is no wrong, but everything is right.
RICHARD. Whoever got thee, there thy mother stands;
  For well I wot thou hast thy mother's tongue.
QUEEN MARGARET. But thou art neither like thy sire nor dam,
  But like a foul mis-shapen stigmatic,
  Mark'd by the destinies to be avoided,
  As venom toads, or lizards' dreadful stings.
RICHARD. Iron of Naples hid with English gilt,
  Whose father bears the title of a king,—
  As if a channel should be call'd the sea,—
  Sham'st thou not, knowing whence thou art extraught,
  To let thy tongue detect thy base-born heart?
EDWARD. A wisp of straw were worth a thousand crowns,
  To make this shameless callet know herself.
  Helen of Greece was fairer far than thou,
  Although thy husband may be Menelaus;
  And ne'er was Agamemnon's brother wrong'd
  By that false woman as this king by thee.
  His father revell'd in the heart of France,
  And tam'd the king, and made the Dauphin stoop;
  And had he match'd according to his state,
  He might have kept that glory to this day;
  But when he took a beggar to his bed,
  And grac'd thy poor sire with his bridal day,
  Even then that sunshine brew'd a shower for him,
  That wash'd his father's fortunes forth of France,
  And heap'd sedition on his crown at home.
  For what hath broach'd this tumult but thy pride?
  Hadst thou been meek, our title still had slept,
  And we, in pity of the gentle king,
  Had slipp'd our claim until another age.
GEORGE. But when we saw our sunshine made thy spring,
  And that thy summer bred us no increase,
  We set the axe to thy usurping root;
  And though the edge hath something hit ourselves,
  Yet know thou, since we have begun to strike,
  We 'll never leave, till we have hewn thee down,
  Or bath'd thy growing with our heated bloods.

EDWARD. And in this resolution I defy thee;
    Not willing any longer conference,
    Since thou deniest the gentle king to speak.
    Sound trumpets!—let our bloody colours wave!
    And either victory, or else a grave.
QUEEN MARGARET. Stay, Edward.
EDWARD. No, wrangling woman, we 'll no longer stay:
    These words will cost ten thousand lives this day. *Exeunt*

SCENE THREE

*A Field of Battle between Towton and
Saxton, in Yorkshire*

Alarums: Excursions. Enter Warwick

WARWICK. Forspent with toil, as runners with a race,
    I lay me down a little while to breathe;
    For strokes receiv'd, and many blows repaid,
    Have robb'd my strong-knit sinews of their strength,
    And spite of spite needs must I rest a while.
        Enter Edward, running
EDWARD. Smile, gentle heaven! or strike, ungentle death!
    For this world frowns, and Edward's sun is clouded.
WARWICK. How now, my lord! what hap? what hope of
    good?
        Enter George
GEORGE. Our hap is loss, our hope but sad despair,
    Our ranks are broke, and ruin follows us.
    What counsel give you? whither shall we fly?
EDWARD. Bootless is flight, they follow us with wings;
    And weak we are and cannot shun pursuit.
        Enter Richard
RICHARD. Ah! Warwick, why hast thou withdrawn thyself?
    Thy brother's blood the thirsty earth hath drunk,
    Broach'd with the steely point of Clifford's lance;
    And in the very pangs of death he cried,
    Like to a dismal clangor heard from far,
    'Warwick, revenge! brother, revenge my death!'
    So, underneath the belly of their steeds,
    That stain'd their fetlocks in his smoking blood,
    The noble gentleman gave up the ghost.

WARWICK. Then let the earth be drunken with our blood:
    I 'll kill my horse because I will not fly.
    Why stand we like soft-hearted women here,
    Wailing our losses, whiles the foe doth rage;
    And look upon, as if the tragedy
    Were play'd in jest by counterfeiting actors?
    Here on my knee I vow to God above,
    I 'll never pause again, never stand still
    Till either death hath clos'd these eyes of mine,
    Or fortune given me measure of revenge.
EDWARD. O Warwick! I do bend my knee with thine;
    And in this vow do chain by soul to thine.
    And, ere my knee rise from the earth's cold face,
    I throw my hands, mine eyes, my heart to thee,
    Thou setter up and plucker down of kings,
    Beseeching thee, if with thy will it stands
    That to my foes this body must be prey,
    Yet that thy brazen gates of heaven may ope,
    And give sweet passage to my sinful soul!
    Now, lords, take leave until we meet again,
    Where'er it be, in heaven or in earth.
RICHARD. Brother, give me thy hand; and, gentle Warwick,
    Let me embrace thee in my weary arms:
    I, that did never weep, now melt with woe
    That winter should cut off our spring-time so.
WARWICK. Away, away! Once more, sweet lords, farewell.
GEORGE. Yet let us all together to our troops,
    And give them leave to fly that will not stay,
    And call them pillars that will stand to us;
    And if we thrive, promise them such rewards
    As victors wear at the Olympian games.
    This may plant courage in their quailing breasts;
    For yet is hope of life and victory.
    Forslow no longer; make we hence amain.   *Exeunt*

SCENE FOUR

Another Part of the Field.

Excursions. Enter Richard and Clifford

RICHARD. Now, Clifford, I have singled thee alone.
Suppose this arm is for the Duke of York,
And this for Rutland; both bound to revenge,
Wert thou environ'd with a brazen wall.
CLIFFORD. Now, Richard, I am with thee here alone.
This is the hand that stabb'd thy father York,
And this the hand that slew thy brother Rutland;
And here 's the heart that triumphs in their death
And cheers these hands that slew thy sire and brother,
To execute the like upon thy self;
And so, have at thee.
                    They fight. Warwick enters; Clifford flies
RICHARD. Nay, Warwick, single out some other chase;
For I myself will hunt this wolf to death.   *Exeunt*

SCENE FIVE

Another Part of the Field.

Alarum. Enter King Henry

KING HENRY. This battle fares like to the morning's war,
When dying clouds contend with growing light,
What time the shepherd, blowing of his nails,
Can neither call it perfect day nor night.
Now sways it this way, like a mighty sea
Forc'd by the tide to combat with the wind;
Now sways it that way, like the selfsame sea
Forc'd to retire by fury of the wind:
Sometime the flood prevails, and then the wind;
Now one the better, then another best;
Both tugging to be victors, breast to breast,
Yet neither conqueror nor conquered:
So is the equal poise of this fell war.
Here on this molehill will I sit me down.

To whom God will, there be the victory!
For Margaret my queen, and Clifford too,
Have chid me from the battle; swearing both
They prosper best of all when I am thence.
Would I were dead! if God's good will were so;
For what is in this world but grief and woe?
O God! methinks it were a happy life,
To be no better than a homely swain;
To sit upon a hill, as I do now,
To carve out dials quaintly, point by point,
Thereby to see the minutes how they run,
How many make the hour full complete;
How many hours bring about the day;
How many days will finish up the year;
How many years a mortal man may live.
When this is known, then to divide the times:
So many hours must I tend my flock;
So many hours must I take my rest;
So many hours must I contemplate;
So many hours must I sport myself;
So many days my ewes have been with young;
So many weeks ere the poor fools will ean;
So many years ere I shall shear the fleece:
So minutes, hours, days, months, and years,
Pass'd over to the end they were created,
Would bring white hairs unto a quiet grave.
Ah! what a life were this! how sweet! how lovely!
Gives not the hawthorn bush a sweeter shade
To shepherds, looking on their silly sheep,
Than doth a rich embroider'd canopy
To kings, that fear their subjects' treachery?
O, yes! it doth; a thousand-fold it doth.
And to conclude, the shepherd's homely curds,
His cold thin drink out of his leather bottle,
His wonted sleep under a fresh tree's shade,
All which secure and sweetly he enjoys,
Is far beyond a prince's delicates,
His viands sparkling in a golden cup,
His body couched in a curious bed,
When care, mistrust, and treason wait on him.
                Alarum. Enter a Son
      that hath killed his Father, with the dead body

SON. Ill blows the wind that profits nobody.
This man whom hand to hand I slew in fight,
May be possessed with some store of crowns;
And I, that haply take them from him now,
May yet ere night yield both my life and them
To some man else, as this dead man doth me.
Who 's this? O God! it is my father's face,
Whom in this conflict I unwares have kill'd.
O heavy times, begetting such events!
From London by the king was I press'd forth;
My father, being the Earl of Warwick's man,
Came on the part of York, press'd by his master;
And I, who at his hands receiv'd my life,
Have by my hands of life bereaved him.
Pardon me, God, I knew not what I did!
And pardon, father, for I knew not thee!
My tears shall wipe away these bloody marks;
And no more words till they have flow'd their fill.

KING HENRY. O piteous spectacle! O bloody times!
Whiles lions war and battle for their dens,
Poor harmless lambs abide their enmity.
Weep, wretched man, I 'll aid thee tear for tear;
And let our hearts and eyes, like civil war,
Be blind with tears, and break o'ercharg'd with grief.

Enter a Father
that hath killed his Son, with the body in his arms

FATHER. Thou that so stoutly hast resisted me,
Give me thy gold, if thou hast any gold,
For I have bought it with a hundred blows.
But let me see: is this our foeman's face?
Ah! no, no, no, it is mine only son.
Ah! boy, if any life be left in thee,
Throw up thine eye: see, see! what showers arise,
Blown with the windy tempest of my heart,
Upon thy wounds, that kill mine eye and heart.
O! pity, God, this miserable age.
What stratagems, how fell, how butcherly,
Erroneous, mutinous, and unnatural,
This deadly quarrel daily both beget!
O boy! thy father gave thee life too soon,
And hath bereft thee of thy life too late.

KING HENRY. Woe above woe! grief more than common
   grief!
  O! that my death would stay these ruthful deeds.
  O! pity, pity; gentle heaven, pity.
  The red rose and the white are on his face,
  The fatal colours of our striving houses:
  The one his purple blood right well resembles;
  The other his pale cheeks, methinks, presenteth:
  Wither one rose, and let the other flourish!
  If you contend, a thousand lives must wither.

SON. How will my mother for a father's death
  Take on with me and ne'er be satisfied!

FATHER. How will my wife for slaughter of my son
  Shed seas of tears and ne'er be satisfied!

KING HENRY. How will the country for these woeful chances
  Misthink the king and not be satisfied!

SON. Was ever son so ru'd a father's death?

FATHER. Was ever father so bemoan'd a son?

KING HENRY. Was ever king so griev'd for subjects' woe?
  Much is your sorrow; mine, ten times so much.

SON. I 'll bear thee hence, where I may weep my fill.

                          Exit with the body

FATHER. These arms of mine shall be thy windingsheet;
  My heart, sweet boy, shall be thy sepulchre,
  For from my heart thine image ne'er shall go:
  My sighing breast shall be thy funeral bell;
  And so obsequious will thy father be,
  E'en for the loss of thee, having no more,
  As Priam was for all his valiant sons.
  I 'll bear thee hence; and let them fight that will,
  For I have murder'd where I should not kill.

                          Exit with the body

KING HENRY. Sad-hearted men, much overgone with care,
  Here sits a king more woeful than you are.

        Alarum. Excursions. Enter Queen
      Margaret, Prince of Wales, and Exeter

PRINCE. Fly, father, fly! for all your friends are fled,
  And Warwick rages like a chafed bull.
  Away! for death doth hold us in pursuit.

QUEEN MARGARET. Mount you, my lord; towards Berwick
   post amain.
  Edward and Richard, like a brace of greyhounds

Having the fearful flying hare in sight,
With fiery eyes sparkling for very wrath,
And bloody steel grasp'd in their ireful hands,
Are at our backs; and therefore hence amain.

EXETER. Away! for vengeance comes along with them.
Nay, stay not to expostulate; make speed,
Or else come after: I 'll away before.

KING HENRY. Nay, take me with thee, good sweet Exeter:
Not that I fear to stay, but love to go
Whither the queen intends. Forward! away!   *Exeunt*

SCENE SIX

The Same.

A loud alarum. Enter Clifford, wounded

CLIFFORD. Here burns my candle out; ay, here it dies,
Which, while it lasted, gave King Henry light.
O Lancaster! I fear thy overthrow
More than my body's parting with my soul.
My love and fear glu'd many friends to thee;
And, now I fall, thy tough commixtures melt,
Impairing Henry, strengthening misproud York:
The common people swarm like summer flies;
And whither fly the gnats but to the sun?
And who shines now but Henry's enemies?
O Phœbus! hadst thou never given consent
That Phæthon should check thy fiery steeds,
Thy burning car never had scorch'd the earth;
And, Henry, hadst thou sway'd as kings should do,
Or as thy father and his father did,
Giving no ground unto the house of York,
They never then had sprung like summer flies;
I and ten thousand in this luckless realm
Had left no mourning widows for our death,
And thou this day hadst kept thy chair in peace.
For what doth cherish weeds but gentle air?
And what makes robbers bold but too much lenity?
Bootless are plaints, and cureless are my wounds;
No way to fly, nor strength to hold out flight;
The foe is merciless, and will not pity;

For at their hands I have deserv'd no pity.
The air hath got into my deadly wounds,
And much effuse of blood doth make me faint.
Come, York and Richard, Warwick and the rest;
I stabb'd your fathers' bosoms, split my breast.   *He faints*
   Alarum and Retreat. Enter Edward,
  George, Richard, Montague, Warwick, and Soldiers

EDWARD. Now breathe we, lords: good fortune bids us
  pause,
 And smooth the frowns of war with peaceful looks.
 Some troops pursue the bloody-minded queen,
 That led calm Henry, though he were a king,
 As doth a sail, fill'd with a fretting gust,
 Command an argosy to stem the waves.
 But think you, lords, that Clifford fled with them?
WARWICK. No, 'tis impossible he should escape;
 For, though before his face I speak the words,
 Your brother Richard mark'd him for the grave;
 And wheresoe'er he is, he 's surely dead.
     Clifford groans and dies
EDWARD. Whose soul is that which takes her heavy leave?
RICHARD. A deadly groan, like life and death's departing.
EDWARD. See who it is: and, now the battle 's ended,
 If friend or foe, let him be gently us'd.
RICHARD. Revoke that doom of mercy, for 'tis Clifford;
 Who not contented that he lopp'd the branch
 In hewing Rutland when his leaves put forth,
 But set his murdering knife unto the root
 From whence that tender spray did sweetly spring,
 I mean our princely father, Duke of York.
WARWICK. From off the gates of York fetch down the head,
 Your father's head, which Clifford placed there;
 Instead whereof let this supply the room:
 Measure for measure must be answered.
EDWARD. Bring forth that fatal screech-owl to our house,
 That nothing sung but death to us and ours:
 Now death shall stop his dismal threatening sound,
 And his ill-boding tongue no more shall speak.
   Attendants bring the body forward
WARWICK. I think his understanding is bereft.
 Speak, Clifford; dost thou know who speaks to thee?
 Dark cloudy death o'ershades his beams of life,

And he nor sees, nor hears us what we say.

RICHARD. O! would he did; and so perhaps he doth:
'Tis but his policy to counterfeit,
Because he would avoid such bitter taunts
Which in the time of death he gave our father.

GEORGE. If so thou think'st, vex him with eager words.

RICHARD. Clifford! ask mercy and obtain no grace.

EDWARD. Clifford! repent in bootless penitence.

WARWICK. Clifford! devise excuses for thy faults.

GEORGE. While we devise fell tortures for thy faults.

RICHARD. Thou didst love York, and I am son to York.

EDWARD. Thou pitiedst Rutland, I will pity thee.

GEORGE. Where 's Captain Margaret, to fence you now?

WARWICK. They mock thee, Clifford: swear as thou wast
wont.

RICHARD. What! not an oath? nay, then the world goes hard
When Clifford cannot spare his friends an oath.
I know by that he 's dead; and, by my soul,
If this right hand would buy two hours' life,
That I in all despite might rail at him,
This hand should chop it off, and with the issuing blood
Stifle the villain whose unstanched thirst
York and young Rutland could not satisfy.

WARWICK. Ay, but he 's dead: off with the traitor's head,
And rear it in the place your father's stands.
And now to London with triumphant march,
There to be crowned England's royal king:
From whence shall Warwick cut the sea to France,
And ask the Lady Bona for thy queen.
So shalt thou sinew both these lands together;
And, having France thy friend, thou shalt not dread
The scatter'd foe that hopes to rise again;
For though they cannot greatly sting to hurt,
Yet look to have them buzz to offend thine ears.
First will I see the coronation;
And then to Brittany I 'll cross the sea,
To effect this marriage, so it please my lord.

EDWARD. Even as thou wilt, sweet Warwick, let it be;
For on thy shoulder do I build my seat,
And never will I undertake the thing
Wherein thy counsel and consent is wanting.
Richard, I will create thee Duke of Gloucester;

    And George, of Clarence; Warwick, as ourself,
    Shall do and undo as him pleaseth best.
RICHARD. Let me be Duke of Clarence, George of
      Gloucester,
    For Gloucester's dukedom is too ominous.
WARWICK. Tut! that 's a foolish observation:
    Richard, be Duke of Gloucester. Now to London,
    To see these honours in possession.   *Exeunt*

ACT THREE

SCENE ONE

A Chase in the North of England.

Enter two Keepers, with cross-bows in their hands

FIRST KEEPER. Under this thick-grown brake we 'll shroud
    ourselves;
  For through this laund anon the deer will come;
  And in this covert will we make our stand,
  Culling the principal of all the deer.
SECOND KEEPER. I 'll stay above the hill, so both may shoot.
FIRST KEEPER. That cannot be; the noise of thy cross-bow
  Will scare the herd, and so my shoot is lost.
  Here stand we both, and aim we at the best:
  And, for the time shall not seem tedious,
  I 'll tell thee what befell me on a day
  In this self place where now we mean to stand.
SECOND KEEPER. Here comes a man; let 's stay till he be past.
    Enter King Henry, disguised, with a prayer-book
KING HENRY. From Scotland am I stol'n, even of pure love,
  To greet mine own land with my wishful sight.
  No, Harry, Harry, 'tis no land of thine;
  Thy place is fill'd, thy sceptre wrung from thee,
  Thy balm wash'd off wherewith thou wast anointed:
  No bending knee will call thee Cæsar now,
  No humble suitors press to speak for right,
  No, not a man comes for redress of thee;
  For how can I help them, and not myself?
FIRST KEEPER. Ay, here 's a deer whose skin 's a keeper's fee:
  This is the quondam king; let 's seize upon him.
KING HENRY. Let me embrace thee, sour adversity,
  For wise men say it is the wisest course.
SECOND KEEPER. Why linger we? let us lay hands upon him.
FIRST KEEPER. Forbear awhile; we 'll hear a little more.
KING HENRY. My queen and son are gone to France for aid;

And, as I hear, the great commanding Warwick
Is thither gone, to crave the French king's sister
To wife for Edward. If this news be true,
Poor queen and son, your labour is but lost;
For Warwick is a subtle orator,
And Lewis a prince soon won with moving words.
By this account then Margaret may win him.
For she 's a woman to be pitied much:
Her sighs will make a battery in his breast;
Her tears will pierce into a marble heart;
The tiger will be mild whiles she doth mourn;
And Nero will be tainted with remorse,
To hear and see her plaints, her brinish tears.
Ay, but she 's come to beg; Warwick, to give:
She on his left side craving aid for Henry;
He on his right asking a wife for Edward.
She weeps, and says her Henry is depos'd;
He smiles, and says his Edward is install'd;
That she, poor wretch, for grief can speak no more:
Whiles Warwick tells his title, smooths the wrong,
Inferreth arguments of mighty strength,
And in conclusion wins the king from her,
With promise of his sister, and what else,
To strengthen and support King Edward's place.
O Margaret! thus 'twill be; and thou, poor soul,
Art then forsaken, as thou went'st forlorn.

SECOND KEEPER. Say, what art thou, that talk'st of kings and
    queens?
KING HENRY. More than I seem, and less than I was born to:
    A man at least, for less I should not be;
    And men may talk of kings, and why not I?
SECOND KEEPER. Ay, but thou talk'st as if thou wert a king.
KING HENRY. Why, so I am, in mind; and that 's enough.
SECOND KEEPER. But, if thou be a king, where is thy crown?
KING HENRY. My crown is in my heart, not on my head;
    Not deck'd with diamonds and Indian stones,
    Nor to be seen: my crown is call'd content;
    A crown it is that seldom kings enjoy.
SECOND KEEPER. Well, if you be a king crown'd with
    content,
    Your crown content and you must be contented
    To go along with us; for, as we think,

You are the king King Edward hath depos'd;
And we his subjects, sworn in all allegiance,
Will apprehend you as his enemy.

KING HENRY. But did you never swear, and break an oath?

SECOND KEEPER. No, never such an oath; nor will not now.

KING HENRY. Where did you dwell when I was King of
  England?

SECOND KEEPER. Here in this country, where we now
  remain.

KING HENRY. I was anointed king at nine months old;
  My father and my grandfather were kings,
  And you were sworn true subjects unto me:
  And tell me, then, have you not broke your oaths?

FIRST KEEPER. No;
  For we were subjects but while you were king.

KING HENRY. Why, am I dead? do I not breathe a man?
  Ah! simple men, you know not what you swear.
  Look, as I blow this feather from my face,
  And as the air blows it to me again;
  Obeying with my wind when I do blow,
  And yielding to another when it blows,
  Commanded always by the greater gust;
  Such is the lightness of you common men.
  But do not break your oaths; for of that sin
  My mild entreaty shall not make you guilty.
  Go where you will, the king shall be commanded;
  And be you kings: command, and I 'll obey.

FIRST KEEPER. We are true subjects to the king, King
  Edward.

KING HENRY. So would you be again to Henry,
  If he were seated as King Edward is.

FIRST KEEPER. We charge you, in God's name, and in the
  king's,
  To go with us unto the officers.

KING HENRY. In God's name, lead; your king's name be
  obey'd:
  And what God will, that let your king perform;
  And what he will, I humbly yield unto.   *Exeunt*

SCENE TWO

London. A Room in the Palace.

Enter King Edward, Gloucester, Clarence, and Lady Grey

KING EDWARD. Brother of Gloucester, at Saint Alban's field
  This lady's husband, Sir John Grey, was slain,
  His lands then seiz'd on by the conqueror:
  Her suit is now, to repossess those lands;
  Which we in justice cannot well deny,
  Because in quarrel of the house of York
  The worthy gentleman did lose his life.
GLOUCESTER. Your Highness shall do well to grant her suit;
  It were dishonour to deny it her.
KING EDWARD. It were no less: but yet I 'll make a pause.
GLOUCESTER. (*Aside to Clarence*) Yea; is it so?
  I see the lady hath a thing to grant
  Before the king will grant her humble suit.
CLARENCE. (*Aside to Gloucester*) He knows the game: how
  true he keeps the wind!
GLOUCESTER. (*Aside to Clarence*) Silence!
KING EDWARD. Widow, we will consider of your suit,
  And come some other time to know our mind.
LADY GREY. Right gracious lord, I cannot brook delay:
  May it please your Highness to resolve me now,
  And what your pleasure is shall satisfy me.
GLOUCESTER. (*Aside to Clarence*) Ay, widow? then I 'll
  warrant you all your lands,
  An if what pleases him shall pleasure you.
  Fight closer, or, good faith, you 'll catch a blow.
CLARENCE. (*Aside to Gloucester*) I fear her not, unless she
  chance to fall.
GLOUCESTER. (*Aside to Clarence*) God forbid that! for he 'll
  take vantages.
KING EDWARD. How many children hast thou, widow? tell
  me.
CLARENCE. (*Aside to Gloucester*) I think he means to beg a
  child of her.
GLOUCESTER. (*Aside to Clarence*) Nay, whip me, then; he 'll
  rather give her two.

LADY GREY. Three, my most gracious lord.

GLOUCESTER. (*Aside to Clarence*) You shall have four, if
    you 'll be rul'd by him.

KING EDWARD. 'Twere pity they should lose their father's
    lands.

LADY GREY. Be pitiful, dread lord, and grant it then.

KING EDWARD. Lords, give us leave: I 'll try this widow's wit.

GLOUCESTER. (*Aside to Clarence*) Ay, good leave have you;
    for you will have leave,

  Till youth take leave and leave you to the crutch.

                               Retiring with Clarence

KING EDWARD. Now, tell me, madam, do you love your
    children?

LADY GREY. Ay, full as dearly as I love myself.

KING EDWARD. And would you not do much to do them
    good?

LADY GREY. To do them good I would sustain some harm.

KING EDWARD. Then get your husband's lands, to do them
    good.

LADY GREY. Therefore I came unto your Majesty.

KING EDWARD. I 'll tell you how these lands are to be got.

LADY GREY. So shall you bind me to your Highness' service.

KING EDWARD. What service wilt thou do me, if I give them?

LADY GREY. What you command, that rests in me to do.

KING EDWARD. But you will take exceptions to my boon.

LADY GREY. No, gracious lord, except I cannot do it.

KING EDWARD. Ay, but thou canst do what I mean to ask.

LADY GREY. Why, then I will do what your Grace
    commands.

GLOUCESTER. (*Aside to Clarence*) He plies her hard; and
    much rain wears the marble.

CLARENCE. (*Aside to Gloucester*) As red as fire! nay, then
    her wax must melt.

LADY GREY. Why stops my lord? shall I not hear my task?

KING EDWARD. An easy task: 'tis but to love a king.

LADY GREY. That 's soon perform'd, because I am a subject.

KING EDWARD. Why then, thy husband's lands I freely give
    thee.

LADY GREY. I take my leave with many thousand thanks.

GLOUCESTER. (*Aside to Clarence*) The match is made; she
    seals it with a curtsy.

KING EDWARD. But stay thee; 'tis the fruits of love I mean.

LADY GREY. The fruits of love I mean, my loving liege.
KING EDWARD. Ay, but, I fear me, in another sense.
  What love think'st thou I sue so much to get?
LADY GREY. My love till death, my humble thanks, my
    prayers:
  That love which virtue begs and virtue grants.
KING EDWARD. No, by my troth, I did not mean such love.
LADY GREY. Why, then you mean not as I thought you did.
KING EDWARD. But now you partly may perceive my mind.
LADY GREY. My mind will never grant what I perceive
  Your Highness aims at, if I aim right.
KING EDWARD. To tell thee plain, I aim to lie with thee.
LADY GREY. To tell you plain, I had rather lie in prison.
KING EDWARD. Why, then thou shalt not have thy husband's
    lands.
LADY GREY. Why, then mine honesty shall be my dower;
  For by that loss I will not purchase them.
KING EDWARD. Therein thou wrong'st thy children mightily.
LADY GREY. Herein your Highness wrongs both them and
    me.
  But, mighty lord, this merry inclination
  Accords not with the sadness of my suit:
  Please you dismiss me, either with 'ay' or 'no.'
KING EDWARD. Ay, if thou wilt say 'ay' to my request;
  No, if thou dost say 'no' to my demand.
LADY GREY. Then, no, my lord. My suit is at an end.
GLOUCESTER. (*Aside to Clarence*) The widow likes him not,
    she knits her brows.
CLARENCE. (*Aside to Gloucester*) He is the bluntest wooer
    in Christendom.
KING EDWARD. (*Aside*) Her looks do argue her replete with
    modesty;·
  Her words do show her wit incomparable;
  All her perfections challenge sovereignty:
  One way or other, she is for a king;
  And she shall be my love, or else my queen.
  Say that King Edward take thee for his queen?
LADY GREY. 'Tis better said than done, my gracious lord:
  I am a subject fit to jest withal,
  But far unfit to be a sovereign.
KING EDWARD. Sweet widow, by my state I swear to thee
  I speak no more than what my soul intends;

And that is, to enjoy thee for my love.

LADY GREY. And that is more than I will yield unto.
I know I am too mean to be your queen,
And yet too good to be your concubine.

KING EDWARD. You cavil, widow: I did mean, my queen.

LADY GREY. 'Twill grieve your Grace my sons should call
you father.

KING EDWARD. No more than when my daughters call thee
mother.
Thou art a widow, and thou hast some children;
And, by God's mother, I, being but a bachelor,
Have other some: why, 'tis a happy thing
To be the father unto many sons.
Answer no more, for thou shalt be my queen.

GLOUCESTER. (*Aside to Clarence*) The ghostly father now
hath done his shrift.

CLARENCE. (*Aside to Gloucester*) When he was made a
shriver, 'twas for shift.

KING EDWARD. Brothers, you muse what chat we two have
had.

GLOUCESTER. The widow likes it not, for she looks very sad.

KING EDWARD. You 'd think it strange if I should marry her.

CLARENCE. To whom, my lord?

KING EDWARD.   Why, Clarence, to myself.

GLOUCESTER. That would be ten days' wonder at the least.

CLARENCE. That 's a day longer than a wonder lasts.

GLOUCESTER. By so much is the wonder in extremes.

KING EDWARD. Well, jest on, brothers: I can tell you both
Her suit is granted for her husband's lands.

Enter a Nobleman

NOBLEMAN. My gracious lord, Henry your foe is taken,
And brought as prisoner to your palace gate.

KING EDWARD. See that he be convey'd unto the Tower:
And go we, brothers, to the man that took him,
To question of his apprehension.
Widow, go you along. Lords, use her honourably.

Exeunt all but Gloucester

GLOUCESTER. Ay, Edward will use women honourably.
Would he were wasted, marrow, bones, and all,
That from his loins no hopeful branch may spring,
To cross me from the golden time I look for!
And yet, between my soul's desire and me—

The lustful Edward's title buried,—
Is Clarence, Henry, and his son young Edward,
And all the unlook'd for issue of their bodies,
To take their rooms, ere I can place myself:
A cold premeditation for my purpose!
Why then, I do but dream on sovereignty;
Like one that stands upon a promontory,
And spies a far-off shore where he would tread,
Wishing his foot were equal with his eye;
And chides the sea that sunders him from thence,
Saying, he 'll lade it dry to have his way:
So do I wish the crown, being so far off,
And so I chide the means that keep me from it,
And so I say I 'll cut the causes off,
Flattering me with impossibilities.
My eye 's too quick, my heart o'erweens too much,
Unless my hand and strength could equal them.
Well, say there is no kingdom then for Richard;
What other pleasure can the world afford?
I 'll make my heaven in a lady's lap,
And deck my body in gay ornaments,
And witch sweet ladies with my words and looks.
O miserable thought! and more unlikely
Than to accomplish twenty golden crowns.
Why, love forswore me in my mother's womb:
And, for I should not deal in her soft laws,
She did corrupt frail nature with some bribe,
To shrink mine arm up like a wither'd shrub;
To make an envious mountain on my back,
Where sits deformity to mock my body;
To shape my legs of an unequal size;
To disproportion me in every part,
Like to a chaos, or an unlick'd bear-whelp
That carries no impression like the dam.
And am I then a man to be belov'd?
O monstrous fault! to harbour such a thought.
Then, since this earth affords no joy to me
But to command, to check, to o'erbear such
As are of better person than myself,
I 'll make my heaven to dream upon the crown;
And, whiles I live, to account this world but hell,
Until my mis-shap'd trunk that bears this head

Be round impaled with a glorious crown.
And yet I know not how to get the crown,
For many lives stand between me and home:
And I, like one lost in a thorny wood,
That rents the thorns and is rent with the thorns,
Seeking a way and straying from the way;
Not knowing how to find the open air,
But toiling desperately to find it out,
Torment myself to catch the English crown:
And from that torment I will free myself,
Or hew my way out with a bloody axe.
Why, I can smile, and murder while I smile,
And cry, 'Content,' to that which grieves my heart,
And wet my cheeks with artificial tears,
And frame my face to all occasions.
I 'll drown more sailors than the mermaid shall;
I 'll slay more gazers than the basilisk;
I 'll play the orator as well as Nestor,
Deceive more slily than Ulysses could,
And, like a Sinon, take another Troy.
I can add colours to the chameleon,
Change shapes with Proteus for advantages,
And set the murderous Machiavel to school.
Can I do this, and cannot get a crown?
Tut! were it farther off, I 'll pluck it down.   *Exit*

SCENE THREE

France. A Room in the Palace.

Flourish. Enter Lewis the French King, his sister Lady Bona, attended: his Admiral called Bourbon; the King takes his state. Then enter Queen Margaret, Prince Edward, and the Earl of Oxford. Lewis sits, and riseth up again

KING LEWIS. Fair Queen of England, worthy Margaret,
    Sit down with us: it ill befits thy state
    And birth, that thou shouldst stand while Lewis doth sit.
QUEEN MARGARET. No, mighty King of France: now Margaret
    Must strike her sail, and learn a while to serve
    Where kings command. I was, I must confess,

Great Albion's queen in former golden days;
But now mischance hath trod my title down,
And with dishonour laid me on the ground,
Where I must take like seat unto my fortune,
And to my humble seat conform myself.

KING LEWIS. Why, say, fair queen, whence springs this deep despair?

QUEEN MARGARET. From such a cause as fills mine eyes with tears
And stops my tongue, while heart is drown'd in cares.

KING LEWIS. Whate'er it be, be thou still like thyself,
And sit thee by our side. (*Seats her by him*) Yield not thy neck
To fortune's yoke, but let thy dauntless mind
Still ride in triumph over all mischance.
Be plain, Queen Margaret, and tell thy grief:
It shall be eas'd, if France can yield relief.

QUEEN MARGARET. Those gracious words revive my drooping thoughts,
And give my tongue-tied sorrows leave to speak.
Now, therefore, be it known to noble Lewis,
That Henry, sole possessor of my love,
Is of a king become a banish'd man,
And forc'd to live in Scotland a forlorn;
While proud ambitious Edward Duke of York
Usurps the regal title and the seat
Of England's true-anointed lawful king.
This is the cause that I, poor Margaret,
With this my son, Prince Edward, Henry's heir,
Am come to crave thy just and lawful aid;
And if thou fail us, all our hope is done.
Scotland hath will to help, but cannot help;
Our people and our peers are both misled,
Our treasure seiz'd, our soldiers put to flight,
And, as thou seest, ourselves in heavy plight.

KING LEWIS. Renowned queen, with patience calm the storm,
While we bethink a means to break it off.

QUEEN MARGARET. The more we stay, the stronger grows our foe.

KING LEWIS. The more I stay, the more I 'll succour thee.

QUEEN MARGARET. O! but impatience waiteth on true
    sorrow:
  And see where comes the breeder of my sorrow.
             Enter Warwick, attended
KING LEWIS. What 's he approacheth boldly to our presence?
QUEEN MARGARET. Our Earl of Warwick, Edward's greatest
    friend.
KING LEWIS. Welcome, brave Warwick! What brings thee to
    France?
      Descending from his state. Queen Margaret rises
QUEEN MARGARET. Ay, now begins a second storm to rise;
  For this is he that moves both wind and tide.
WARWICK. From worthy Edward, King of Albion,
  My lord and sovereign, and thy vowed friend,
  I come, in kindness and unfeigned love,
  First, to do greetings to thy royal person;
  And then to crave a league of amity;
  And lastly to confirm that amity
  With nuptial knot, if thou vouchsafe to grant
  That virtuous Lady Bona, thy fair sister,
  To England's king in lawful marriage.
QUEEN MARGARET. If that go forward, Henry's hope is done.
WARWICK. (*To Bona*) And, gracious madam, in our king's
    behalf,
  I am commanded, with your leave and favour,
  Humbly to kiss your hand, and with my tongue
  To tell the passion of my sovereign's heart;
  Where fame, late entering at his heedful ears,
  Hath plac'd thy beauty's image and thy virtue.
QUEEN MARGARET. King Lewis and Lady Bona, hear me
    speak,
  Before you answer Warwick. His demand
  Springs not from Edward's well-meant honest love,
  But from deceit bred by necessity;
  For how can tyrants safely govern home,
  Unless abroad they purchase great alliance?
  To prove him tyrant this reason may suffice,
  That Henry liveth still; but were he dead,
  Yet here Prince Edward stands, King Henry's son.
  Look, therefore, Lewis, that by this league and marriage
  Thou draw not on thy danger and dishonour;
  For though usurpers sway the rule awhile,

Yet heavens are just, and time suppresseth wrongs.

WARWICK. Injurious Margaret!

PRINCE.   And why not queen?

WARWICK. Because thy father Henry did usurp,
And thou no more are prince than she is queen.

OXFORD. Then Warwick disannuls great John of Gaunt,
Which did subdue the greatest part of Spain;
And, after John of Gaunt, Henry the Fourth,
Whose wisdom was a mirror to the wisest;
And, after that wise prince, Henry the Fifth,
Who by his prowess conquered all France:
From these our Henry lineally descends.

WARWICK. Oxford, how haps it, in this smooth discourse,
You told not how Henry the Sixth hath lost
All that which Henry the Fifth had gotten?
Methinks these peers of France should smile at that.
But for the rest, you tell a pedigree
Of threescore and two years; a silly time
To make prescription for a kingdom's worth.

OXFORD. Why, Warwick, canst thou speak against thy liege,
Whom thou obeyedst thirty and six years,
And not bewray thy treason with a blush?

WARWICK. Can Oxford, that did ever fence the right,
Now buckler falsehood with a pedigree?
For shame! leave Henry, and call Edward king.

OXFORD. Call him my king, by whose injurious doom
My elder brother, the Lord Aubrey Vere,
Was done to death? and more than so, my father,
Even in the downfall of his mellow'd years,
When nature brought him to the door of death?
No, Warwick, no; while life upholds this arm,
This arm upholds the house of Lancaster.

WARWICK. And I the house of York.

KING LEWIS. Queen Margaret, Prince Edward, and Oxford,
Vouchsafe at our request to stand aside,
While I use further conference with Warwick.

                                        They stand aloof

QUEEN MARGARET. Heaven grant that Warwick's words
bewitch him not!

KING LEWIS. Now, Warwick, tell me, even upon thy
conscience,
Is Edward your true king? for I were loath

To link with him that were not lawful chosen.

WARWICK.   Thereon I pawn my credit and mine honour.

KING LEWIS.   But is he gracious in the people's eye?

WARWICK.   The more that Henry was unfortunate.

KING LEWIS.   Then further, all dissembling set aside,
Tell me for truth the measure of his love
Unto our sister Bona.

WARWICK.   Such it seems
As may beseem a monarch like himself.
Myself have often hear him say and swear
That this his love was an eternal plant,
Whereof the root was fix'd in virtue's ground,
The leaves and fruit maintain'd with beauty's sun,
Exempt from envy, but not from disdain,
Unless the Lady Bona quit his pain.

KING LEWIS.   Now, sister, let us hear your firm resolve.

BONA.   Your grant, or your denial, shall be mine:
(*To Warwick*) Yet I confess that often ere this day,
When I have heard your king's desert recounted,
Mine ear hath tempted judgment to desire.

KING LEWIS.   Then, Warwick, thus: our sister shall be
Edward's;
And now forthwith shall articles be drawn
Touching the jointure that your king must make,
Which with her dowry shall be counterpois'd.
Draw near, Queen Margaret, and be a witness
That Bona shall be wife to the English king.

PRINCE.   To Edward, but not to the English king.

QUEEN MARGARET.   Deceitful Warwick! it was thy device
By this alliance to make void my suit:
Before thy coming Lewis was Henry's friend.

KING LEWIS.   And still is friend to him and Margaret:
But if your title to the crown be weak,
As may appear by Edward's good success,
Then 'tis but reason that I be releas'd
From giving aid which late I promised.
Yet shall you have all kindness at my hand
That your estate requires and mine can yield.

WARWICK.   Henry now lives in Scotland at his ease,
Where having nothing, nothing can he lose.
And as for you yourself, our quondam queen,
You have a father able to maintain you,

And better 'twere you troubled him than France.

QUEEN MARGARET. Peace! impudent and shameless
    Warwick, peace;
Proud setter up and puller down of kings;
I will not hence, till, with my talk and tears,
Both full of truth, I make King Lewis behold
Thy sly conveyance and thy lord's false love;
For both of you are birds of selfsame feather.

                 A horn winded within

KING LEWIS. Warwick, this is some post to us or thee.

                 Enter a Post

MESSENGER. My Lord Ambassador, these letters are for you,
Sent from your brother, Marquess Montague:
These from our king unto your Majesty;
  (*To Margaret*) And, madam, these for you; from whom I
  know not.   *They all read their letters*

OXFORD. I like it well that our fair queen and mistress
Smiles at her news, while Warwick frowns at his.

PRINCE. Nay, mark how Lewis stamps as he were nettled:
I hope all 's for the best.

KING LEWIS. Warwick, what are thy news? and yours, fair
  queen?

QUEEN MARGARET. Mine, such as fill my heart with unhop'd
  joys.

WARWICK. Mine, full of sorrow and heart's discontent.

KING LEWIS. What! has your king married the Lady Grey?
And now, to soothe your forgery and his,
Sends me a paper to persuade me patience?
Is this the alliance that he seeks with France?
Dare he presume to scorn us in this manner?

QUEEN MARGARET. I told your Majesty as much before:
This proveth Edward's love and Warwick's honesty.

WARWICK. King Lewis, I here protest, in sight of heaven,
And by the hope I have of heavenly bliss,
That I am clear from this misdeed of Edward's;
No more my king, for he dishonours me;
But most himself, if he could see his shame.
Did I forget that by the house of York
My father came untimely to his death?
Did I let pass the abuse done to my niece?
Did I impale him with the regal crown?
Did I put Henry from his native right?

And am I guerdon'd at the last with shame?
Shame on himself! for my desert is honour:
And, to repair my honour, lost for him,
I here renounce him and return to Henry.
My noble queen, let former grudges pass,
And henceforth I am thy true servitor.
I will revenge his wrong to Lady Bona,
And replant Henry in his former state.

QUEEN MARGARET. Warwick, these words have turn'd my
　　hate to love;
And I forgive and quite forget old faults,
And joy that thou becomest King Henry's friend.

WARWICK. So much his friend, ay, his unfeigned friend,
That, if King Lewis vouchsafe to furnish us
With some few bands of chosen soldiers,
I 'll undertake to land them on our coast,
And force the tyrant from his seat by war.
'Tis not his new-made bride shall succour him:
And as for Clarence, as my letters tell me,
He 's very likely now to fall from him,
For matching more for wanton lust than honour,
Or than for strength and safety of our country.

BONA. Dear brother, how shall Bona be reveng'd,
But by thy help to this distressed queen?

QUEEN MARGARET. Renowned prince, how shall poor Henry
　　live,
Unless thou rescue him from foul despair?

BONA. My quarrel and this English queen's are one.

WARWICK. And mine, fair Lady Bona, joins with yours.

KING LEWIS. And mine with hers, and thine and Margaret's.
Therefore, at last, I firmly am resolv'd
You shall have aid.

QUEEN MARGARET. Let me give humble thanks for all at
　　once.

KING LEWIS. Then, England's messenger, return in post,
And tell false Edward, thy supposed king,
That Lewis of France is sending over masquers
To revel it with him and his new bride.
Thou seest what 's past; go fear thy king withal.

BONA. Tell him, in hope he 'll prove a widower shortly,
I 'll wear the willow garland for his sake.

QUEEN MARGARET. Tell him, my mourning weeds are laid
      aside,
   And I am ready to put armour on.
WARWICK. Tell him from me that he hath done me wrong,
   And therefore I 'll uncrown him ere 't be long.
   There 's thy reward: be gone.   *Exit Messenger*
KING LEWIS.   But, Warwick,
   Thou and Oxford, with five thousand men,
   Shall cross the seas, and bid false Edward battle;
   And, as occasion serves, this noble queen
   And prince shall follow with a fresh supply.
   Yet ere thou go, but answer me one doubt:
   What pledge have we of thy firm loyalty?
WARWICK. This shall assure my constant loyalty:
   That if our queen and this young prince agree,
   I 'll join mine eldest daughter and my joy
   To him forthwith in holy wedlock bands.
QUEEN MARGARET. Yes, I agree, and thank you for your
      motion.
   Son Edward, she is fair and virtuous,
   Therefore delay not, give thy hand to Warwick;
   And, with thy hand, thy faith irrevocable,
   That only Warwick's daughter shall be thine.
PRINCE. Yes, I accept her, for she well deserves it;
   And here, to pledge my vow, I give my hand.
                    He gives his hand to Warwick
KING LEWIS. Why stay we now? These soldiers shall be
      levied,
   And thou, Lord Bourbon, our high admiral,
   Shall waft them over with our royal fleet.
   I long till Edward fall by war's mischance,
   For mocking marriage with a dame of France.
                    Exeunt all except Warwick
WARWICK. I came from Edward as ambassador,
   But I return his sworn and mortal foe:
   Matter of marriage was the charge he gave me,
   But dreadful war shall answer his demand.
   Had he none else to make a stale but me?
   Then none but I shall turn his jest to sorrow.
   I was the chief that rais'd him to the crown,
   And I 'll be chief to bring him down again:
   Not that I pity Henry's misery,
   But seek revenge on Edward's mockery.   *Exit*

ACT FOUR

SCENE ONE

London. A Room in the Palace.

Enter Gloucester, Clarence, Somerset, Montague, and Others

GLOUCESTER. Now tell me, brother Clarence, what think
 you
 Of this new marriage with the Lady Grey?
 Hath not our brother made a worthy choice?
CLARENCE. Alas! you know, 'tis far from hence to France;
 How could he stay till Warwick made return?
SOMERSET. My lords, forbear this talk; here comes the king.
GLOUCESTER. And his well-chosen bride.
CLARENCE. I mind to tell him plainly what I think.
  Flourish. Enter King Edward, attended; Lady
 Grey, as Queen; Pembroke, Stafford, Hastings, and Others
KING EDWARD. Now, brother Clarence, how like you our
  choice,
 That you stand pensive, as half malcontent?
CLARENCE. As well as Lewis of France, or the Earl of War-
  wick;
 Which are so weak of courage and in judgment
 That they 'll take no offence at our abuse.
KING EDWARD. Suppose they take offence without a cause,
 They are but Lewis and Warwick: I am Edward,
 Your king and Warwick's, and must have my will.
GLOUCESTER. And you shall have your will, because our
  king:
 Yet hasty marriage seldom proveth well.
KING EDWARD. Yea, brother Richard, are you offended too?
GLOUCESTER. Not I:
 No, God forbid, that I should wish them sever'd
 Whom God hath join'd together; ay, and 'twere pity
 To sunder them that yoke so well together.

KING EDWARD. Setting your scorns and your mislike aside,
Tell me some reason why the Lady Grey
Should not become my wife and England's queen:
And you too, Somerset and Montague,
Speak freely what you think.

CLARENCE. Then this is mine opinion: that King Lewis
Becomes your enemy for mocking him
About the marriage of the Lady Bona.

GLOUCESTER. And Warwick, doing what you gave in charge,
Is now dishonoured by this new marriage.

KING EDWARD. What if both Lewis and Warwick be
appeas'd
By such invention as I can devise?

MONTAGUE. Yet to have join'd with France in such alliance
Would more have strengthen'd this our commonwealth
'Gainst foreign storms, than any home-bred marriage.

HASTINGS. Why, knows not Montague, that of itself
England is safe, if true within itself?

MONTAGUE. Yes; but the safer when 'tis back'd with France.

HASTINGS. 'Tis better using France than trusting France:
Let us be back'd with God and with the seas
Which he hath given for fence impregnable,
And with their helps only defend ourselves:
In them and in ourselves our safety lies.

CLARENCE. For this one speech Lord Hastings well deserves
To have the heir of the Lord Hungerford.

KING EDWARD. Ay, what of that? it was my will and grant;
And for this once my will shall stand for law.

GLOUCESTER. And yet methinks your Grace hath not done
well,
To give the heir and daughter of Lord Scales
Unto the brother of your loving bride:
She better would have fitted me or Clarence:
But in your bride you bury brotherhood.

CLARENCE. Or else you would not have bestow'd the heir
Of the Lord Bonville on your new wife's son,
And leave your brothers to go speed elsewhere.

KING EDWARD. Alas, poor Clarence, is it for a wife
That thou art malcontent? I will provide thee.

CLARENCE. In choosing for yourself you show'd your
judgment,
Which being shallow, you shall give me leave

To play the broker on mine own behalf;
And to that end I shortly mind to leave you.

KING EDWARD. Leave me, or tarry, Edward will be king,
And not be tied unto his brother's will.

QUEEN ELIZABETH. My lords, before it pleas'd his Majesty
To raise my state to title of a queen,
Do me but right, and you must all confess
That I was not ignoble of descent;
And meaner than myself have had like fortune.
But as this title honours me and mine,
So your dislikes, to whom I would be pleasing,
Do cloud my joys with danger and with sorrow.

KING EDWARD. My love, forbear to fawn upon their frowns:
What danger or what sorrow can befall thee,
So long as Edward is thy constant friend,
And their true sovereign, whom they must obey?
Nay, whom they shall obey, and love thee too,
Unless they seek for hatred at my hands;
Which if they do, yet will I keep thee safe,
And they shall feel the vengeance of my wrath.

GLOUCESTER. (*Aside*) I hear, yet say not much, but think the
more.

Enter a Messenger

KING EDWARD. Now, messenger, what letters or what news
From France?

MESSENGER. My sovereign liege, no letters; and few words;
But such as I, without your special pardon,
Dare not relate.

KING EDWARD. Go to, we pardon thee: therefore, in brief,
Tell me their words as near as thou canst guess them.
What answer makes King Lewis unto our letters?

MESSENGER. At my depart these were his very words:
'Go tell false Edward, thy supposed king,
That Lewis of France is sending over masquers,
To revel it with him and his new bride.'

KING EDWARD. Is Lewis so brave? belike he thinks me
Henry.
But what said Lady Bona to my marriage?

MESSENGER. These were her words, utter'd with mild
disdain:
'Tell him, in hope he 'll prove a widower shortly,
I 'll wear the willow garland for his sake.'

KING EDWARD. I blame not her, she could say little less;
  She had the wrong. But what said Henry's queen?
  For I have heard that she was there in place.
MESSENGER. 'Tell him,' quoth she, 'my mourning weeds are
    done,
  And I am ready to put armour on.'
KING EDWARD. Belike she minds to play the Amazon.
  But what said Warwick to these injuries?
MESSENGER. He, more incens'd against your Majesty
  Than all the rest, discharg'd me with these words:
  'Tell him from me that he hath done me wrong,
  And therefore I 'll uncrown him ere 't be long.'
KING EDWARD. Ha! durst the traitor breathe out so proud
    words?
  Well, I will arm me, being thus forewarn'd:
  They shall have wars, and pay for their presumption.
  But say, is Warwick friends with Margaret?
MESSENGER. Ay, gracious sovereign; they are so link'd in
    friendship,
  That young Prince Edward marries Warwick's daughter.
CLARENCE. Belike the elder; Clarence will have the
    younger.
  Now, brother king, farewell, and sit you fast,
  For I will hence to Warwick's other daughter;
  That, though I want a kingdom, yet in marriage
  I may not prove inferior to yourself.
  You that love me and Warwick, follow me.
                    Exit Clarence, and Somerset follows
GLOUCESTER. (*Aside*) Not I.
  My thoughts aim at a further matter; I
  Stay not for love of Edward, but the crown.
KING EDWARD. Clarence and Somerset both gone to
    Warwick!
  Yet am I arm'd against the worst can happen,
  And haste is needful in this desperate case.
  Pembroke and Stafford, you in our behalf
  Go levy men, and make prepare for war:
  They are already, or quickly will be landed:
  Myself in person will straight follow you,
                    Exeunt Pembroke and Stafford
  But ere I go, Hastings and Montague,
  Resolve my doubt. You twain, of all the rest,

Are near to Warwick by blood, and by alliance:
Tell me if you love Warwick more than me?
If it be so, then both depart to him;
I rather wish you foes than hollow friends:
But if you mind to hold your true obedience,
Give me assurance with some friendly vow
That I may never have you in suspect.

MONTAGUE. So God help Montague as he proves true!

HASTINGS. And Hastings as he favours Edward's cause!

KING EDWARD. Now, brother Richard, will you stand by us?

GLOUCESTER. Ay, in despite of all that shall withstand you.

KING EDWARD. Why, so! then am I sure of victory.
Now therefore let us hence; and lose no hour
Till we meet Warwick with his foreign power.   *Exeunt*

SCENE TWO

A Plain in Warwickshire.

Enter Warwick and Oxford, with French and other Forces

WARWICK. Trust me, my lord, all hitherto goes well;
The common people by numbers swarm to us.
            Enter Clarence and Somerset
But see where Somerset and Clarence come!
Speak suddenly, my lords, are we all friends?

CLARENCE. Fear not that, my lord.

WARWICK. Then, gentle Clarence, welcome unto Warwick;
And welcome, Somerset; I hold it cowardice,
To rest mistrustful where a noble heart
Hath pawn'd an open hand in sign of love;
Else might I think that Clarence, Edward's brother,
Were but a feigned friend to our proceedings:
But welcome, sweet Clarence; my daughter shall be thine.
And now what rests but, in night's coverture,
Thy brother being carelessly encamp'd,
His soldiers lurking in the towns about,
And but attended by a simple guard,
We may surprise and take him at our pleasure?
Our scouts have found the adventure very easy:
That as Ulysses, and stout Diomede,
With sleight and manhood stole to Rhesus' tents,

And brought from thence the Thracian fatal steeds;
So we, well cover'd with the night's black mantle,
At unawares may beat down Edward's guard,
And seize himself; I say not, slaughter him,
For I intend but only to surprise him.
You, that will follow me to this attempt,
Applaud the name of Henry with your leader.

They all cry 'Henry!'

Why, then, let 's on our way in silent sort.
For Warwick and his friends, God and Saint George!

Exeunt

SCENE THREE

Edward's Camp near Warwick.

Enter certain Watchmen to guard the King's tent

FIRST WATCHMAN. Come on, my masters, each man take his
stand;
The king, by this, is set him down to sleep.
SECOND WATCHMAN. What, will he not to bed?
FIRST WATCHMAN. Why, no: for he hath made a solemn vow
Never to lie and take his natural rest
Till Warwick or himself be quite suppress'd.
SECOND WATCHMAN. To-morrow then belike shall be the
day,
If Warwick be so near as men report.
THIRD WATCHMAN. But say, I pray, what nobleman is that
That with the king here resteth in his tent?
FIRST WATCHMAN. 'Tis the Lord Hastings, the king's
chiefest friend.
THIRD WATCHMAN. O! is it so? But why commands the king
That his chief followers lodge in towns about him,
While he himself keeps in the cold field?
SECOND WATCHMAN. 'Tis the more honour, because the
more dangerous.
THIRD WATCHMAN. Ay, but give me worship and quietness;
I like it better than a dangerous honour.
If Warwick knew in what estate he stands,
'Tis to be doubted he would waken him.

FIRST WATCHMAN. Unless our halberds did shut up his
   passage.
SECOND WATCHMAN. Ay; wherefore else guard we his royal
   tent,
  But to defend his person from night-foes?
Enter Warwick, Clarence, Oxford, Somerset, and Forces
WARWICK. This is his tent; and see where stand his guard.
  Courage, my masters! honour now or never!
  But follow me, and Edward shall be ours.
FIRST WATCHMAN. Who goes there?
SECOND WATCHMAN. Stay, or thou diest.
Warwick and the rest cry all,
   'Warwick! Warwick!' and set upon the Guard; who fly,
   crying 'Arm! Arm!' Warwick and the rest following them.
   Drums beating, and Trumpets sounding, re-enter Warwick
   and the rest, bringing the King out in his gown, sitting in a
   chair. Gloucester and Hastings fly over the stage
SOMERSET.   What are they that fly there?
WARWICK. Richard and Hastings: let them go; here 's the
   duke.
KING EDWARD. The duke! Why, Warwick, when we parted
   last,
  Thou call'dst me king!
WARWICK.   Ay, but the case is alter'd:
  When you disgrac'd me in my embassade,
  Then I degraded you from being king,
  And come now to create you Duke of York.
  Alas! how should you govern any kingdom,
  That know not how to use ambassadors,
  Nor how to be contented with one wife,
  Nor how to use your brothers brotherly,
  Nor how to study for the people's welfare,
  Nor how to shroud yourself from enemies?
KING EDWARD. Yea, brother of Clarence, art thou here too?
  Nay, then, I see that Edward needs must down.
  Yet, Warwick, in despite of all mischance,
  Of thee thyself, and all thy complices,
  Edward will always bear himself as king:
  Though Fortune's malice overthrow my state,
  My mind exceeds the compass of her wheel.
WARWICK. Then, for his mind, be Edward England's king:
                              Takes off his crown

But Henry now shall wear the English crown,
And be true king indeed, thou but the shadow.
My Lord of Somerset, at my request,
See that forthwith Duke Edward be convey'd
Unto my brother, Archbishop of York.
When I have fought with Pembroke and his fellows,
I 'll follow you, and tell what answer
Lewis and the Lady Bona send to him:
Now, for a while farewell, good Duke of York.
KING EDWARD. What fates impose, that men must needs
    abide;
It boots not to resist both wind and tide.

Exit, led out; Somerset with him

OXFORD. What now remains, my lords, for us to do,
But march to London with our soldiers?
WARWICK. Ay, that 's the first thing that we have to do;
To free King Henry from imprisonment,
And see him seated in the regal throne.   *Exeunt*

SCENE FOUR

London. A Room in the Palace.

Enter Queen Elizabeth and Rivers

RIVERS. Madam, what makes you in this sudden change?
QUEEN ELIZABETH. Why, brother Rivers, are you yet to
    learn
What late misfortune is befall'n King Edward?
RIVERS. What! loss of some pitch'd battle against Warwick?
QUEEN ELIZABETH. No, but the loss of his own royal person.
RIVERS. Then is my sovereign slain?
QUEEN ELIZABETH. Ay, almost slain, for he is taken prisoner;
Either betray'd by falsehood of his guard
Or by his foe surpris'd at unawares:
And, as I further have to understand,
Is new committed to the Bishop of York,
Fell Warwick's brother, and by that our foe.
RIVERS. These news, I must confess, are full of grief;
Yet, gracious madam, bear it as you may:
Warwick may lose, that now hath won the day.

QUEEN ELIZABETH. Till then fair hope must hinder
  life's decay.
And I the rather wean me from despair
For love of Edward's offspring in my womb:
This is it that makes me bridle passion,
And bear with mildness my misfortune's cross;
Ay, ay, for this I draw in many a tear,
And stop the rising of blood-sucking sighs,
Lest with my sighs or tears I blast or drown
King Edward's fruit, true heir to the English crown.
RIVERS. But, madam, where is Warwick then become?
QUEEN ELIZABETH. I am inform'd that he comes towards
  London,
To set the crown once more on Henry's head:
Guess thou the rest; King Edward's friends must down.
But, to prevent the tyrant's violence,—
For trust not him that hath once broken faith,—
I 'll hence forthwith unto the sanctuary,
To save at least the heir of Edward's right:
There shall I rest secure from force and fraud.
Come, therefore; let us fly while we may fly:
If Warwick take us we are sure to die.   *Exeunt*

SCENE FIVE

A Park near Middleham Castle in Yorkshire.

Enter Gloucester, Hastings, Sir William Stanley, and Others

GLOUCESTER. Now, my Lord Hastings and Sir William
  Stanley,
Leave off to wonder why I drew you hither,
Into this chiefest thicket of the park.
Thus stands the case. You know, our king, my brother,
Is prisoner to the bishop here, at whose hands
He hath good usage and great liberty,
And often but attended with weak guard,
Comes hunting this way to disport himself.
I have advertis'd him by secret means,
That if about this hour he make this way,
Under the colour of his usual game,
He shall here find his friends, with horse and men

To set him free from his captivity.

Enter King Edward and a Huntsman

HUNTSMAN. This way, my lord, for this way lies the game.

KING EDWARD. Nay, this way, man: see where the huntsmen
  stand.

  Now, brother of Gloucester, Lord Hastings, and the rest,
  Stand you thus close to steal the bishop's deer?

GLOUCESTER. Brother, the time and case requireth haste.
  Your horse stands ready at the park-corner.

KING EDWARD. But whither shall we then?

HASTINGS. To Lynn, my lord; and ship from thence to
  Flanders.

GLOUCESTER. Well guess'd, believe me; for that was my
  meaning.

KING EDWARD. Stanley, I will requite thy forwardness.

GLOUCESTER. But wherefore stay we? 'tis no time to talk.

KING EDWARD. Huntsman, what sayst thou? wilt thou go
  along?

HUNTSMAN. Better do so than tarry and be hang'd.

GLOUCESTER. Come then, away; let 's ha' no more ado.

KING EDWARD. Bishop, farewell: shield thee from Warwick's
  frown,

  And pray that I may repossess the crown.   *Exeunt*

SCENE SIX

A Room in the Tower.

*Enter King Henry, Clarence, Warwick, Somerset, young
Richmond, Oxford, Montague, Lieutenant of the
Tower, and Attendants*

KING HENRY. Master lieutenant, now that God and friends
  Have shaken Edward from the regal seat,
  And turn'd my captive state to liberty,
  My fear to hope, my sorrows unto joys,
  At our enlargement what are thy due fees?

LIEUTENANT. Subjects may challenge nothing of their sov-
  ereigns;
  But if a humble prayer may prevail,
  I then crave pardon of your Majesty.

KING HENRY. For what, lieutenant? for well using me?

Nay, be thou sure, I 'll well requite thy kindness,
For that it made my imprisonment a pleasure;
Ay, such a pleasure as encaged birds
Conceive, when, after many moody thoughts
At last by notes of household harmony
They quite forget their loss of liberty.
But, Warwick, after God, thou set'st me free,
And chiefly therefore I thank God and thee;
He was the author, thou the instrument.
Therefore, that I may conquer Fortune's spite
By living low, where Fortune cannot hurt me,
And that the people of this blessed land
May not be punish'd with my thwarting stars,
Warwick, although my head still wear the crown,
I here resign my government to thee,
For thou art fortunate in all thy deeds.

WARWICK.   Your Grace hath still been fam'd for virtuous;
And now may seem as wise as virtuous,
By spying and avoiding Fortune's malice;
For few men rightly temper with the stars:
Yet in this one thing let me blame your Grace,
For choosing me when Clarence is in place.

CLARENCE.   No, Warwick, thou art worthy of the sway,
To whom the heavens, in thy nativity
Adjudg'd an olive branch and laurel crown,
As likely to be blest in peace, and war;
And therefore I yield thee my free consent.

WARWICK. And I choose Clarence only for protector.

KING HENRY.   Warwick and Clarence, give me both your
    hands:
Now join your hands, and with your hands your hearts,
That no dissension hinder government:
I make you both protectors of this land,
While I myself will lead a private life,
And in devotion spend my latter days,
To sin's rebuke and my Creator's praise.

WARWICK. What answers Clarence to his sovereign's will?

CLARENCE. That he consents, if Warwick yield consent;
For on thy fortune I repose myself.

WARWICK. Why then, though loath, yet must I be content:
We 'll yoke together, like a double shadow
To Henry's body, and supply his place;

I mean, in bearing weight of government,
While he enjoys the honour and his ease.
And, Clarence, now then it is more than needful
Forthwith that Edward be pronounc'd a traitor,
And all his lands and goods be confiscate.

CLARENCE. What else? and that succession be determin'd.

WARWICK. Ay, therein Clarence shall not want his part.

KING HENRY. But, with the first of all your chief affairs,
Let me entreat, for I command no more,
That Margaret your queen, and my son Edward,
Be sent for, to return from France with speed:
For, till I see them here, by doubtful fear
My joy of liberty is half eclips'd.

CLARENCE. It shall be done, my sovereign, with all speed.

KING HENRY. My Lord of Somerset, what youth is that
Of whom you seem to have so tender care?

SOMERSET. My liege, it is young Henry, Earl of Richmond.

KING HENRY. Come hither, England's hope: (*Lays his hand
on his head*) If secret powers
Suggest but truth to my divining thoughts,
This pretty lad will prove our country's bliss.
His looks are full of peaceful majesty,
His head by nature fram'd to wear a crown,
His hand to wield a sceptre, and himself
Likely in time to bless a regal throne.
Make much of him, my lords; for this is he
Must help you more than you are hurt by me.

Enter a Post

WARWICK. What news, my friend?

MESSENGER. That Edward is escaped from your brother,
And fled, as he hears since, to Burgundy.

WARWICK. Unsavoury news! but how made he escape?

MESSENGER. He was convey'd by Richard Duke of
Gloucester,
And the Lord Hastings, who attended him
In secret ambush on the forest side,
And from the bishop's huntsmen rescu'd him:
For hunting was his daily exercise.

WARWICK. My brother was too careless of his charge.
But let us hence, my sovereign, to provide
A salve for any sore that may betide.

Exeunt King Henry, Warwick,
Clarence, Lieutenant, and Attendant

SOMERSET. My lord, I like not of this flight of Edward's;
For doubtless Burgundy will yield him help,
And we shall have more wars before 't be long.
As Henry's late presaging prophecy
Did glad my heart with hope of this young Richmond,
So doth my heart misgive me, in these conflicts
What may befall him to his harm and ours:
Therefore, Lord Oxford, to prevent the worst,
Forthwith we 'll send him hence to Brittany,
Till storms be past of civil enmity.

OXFORD. Ay, for if Edward repossess the crown,
'Tis like that Richmond with the rest shall down.

SOMERSET. It shall be so; he shall to Brittany.
Come, therefore, let 's about it speedily.   *Exeunt*

SCENE SEVEN

Before York.

Enter King Edward, Gloucester, Hastings, and Forces

KING EDWARD. Now, brother Richard, Lord Hastings, and
        the rest,
Yet thus far Fortune maketh us amends,
And says, that once more I shall interchange
My waned state for Henry's regal crown.
Well have we pass'd, and now repass'd the seas,
And brought desired help from Burgundy:
What then remains, we being thus arriv'd
From Ravenspurgh haven before the gates of York,
But that we enter, as into our dukedom?

GLOUCESTER. The gates made fast! Brother, I like not this;
For many men that stumble at the threshold
Are well foretold that danger lurks within.

KING EDWARD. Tush, man! abodements must not now
        affright us.
By fair or foul means we must enter in,
For hither will our friends repair to us.

HASTINGS. My liege, I 'll knock once more to summon them
Enter, on the Walls, the Mayor of York and his Brethren

MAYOR. My lords, we were forewarned of your coming,
    And shut the gates for safety of ourselves;
    For now we owe allegiance unto Henry.
KING EDWARD. But, Master Mayor, if Henry be your king,
    Yet Edward, at the least, is Duke of York.
MAYOR. True, my good lord, I know you for no less.
KING EDWARD. Why, and I challenge nothing but my duke-
    dom,
    As being well content with that alone.
GLOUCESTER. (*Aside*) But when the fox hath once got in his
    nose,
    He 'll soon find means to make the body follow.
HASTINGS. Why, Master Mayor, why stand you in a doubt?
    Open the gates; we are King Henry's friends.
MAYOR. Ay, say you so? the gates shall then be open'd.
                        Exit, with Aldermen, above
GLOUCESTER. A wise stout captain, and soon persuaded.
HASTINGS. The good old man would fain that all were well,
    So 'twere not 'long of him; but being enter'd,
    I doubt not, I, but we shall soon persuade
    Both him and all his brothers unto reason.
            Re-enter the Mayor and two Aldermen
KING EDWARD. So, Master Mayor: these gates must not be
    shut
    But in the night, or in the time of war.
    What! fear not, man, but yield me up the keys;
                        Takes his keys
    For Edward will defend the town and thee,
    And all those friends that deign to follow me.
            Enter Montgomery and Forces
GLOUCESTER. Brother, this is Sir John Montgomery,
    Our trusty friend, unless I be deceiv'd.
KING EDWARD. Welcome, Sir John! but why come you in
    arms?
MONTGOMERY. To help King Edward in his time of storm,
    As every loyal subject ought to do.
KING EDWARD. Thanks, good Montgomery; bu. we now
    forget
    Our title to the crown, and only claim
    Our dukedom till God please to send the rest.
MONTGOMERY. Then fare you well, for I will hence again.
    I came to serve a king and not a duke.

Drummer, strike up, and let us march away.

A march begun

KING EDWARD. Nay, stay, Sir John, awhile; and we 'll debate
By what safe means the crown may be recover'd.

MONTGOMERY. What talk you of debating? in few words,
If you 'll not here proclaim yourself our king,
I 'll leave you to your fortune, and be gone
To keep them back that come to succour you.
Why shall we fight, if you pretend no title?

GLOUCESTER. Why, brother, wherefore stand you on nice
points?

KING HENRY. When we grow stronger then we 'll make our
claim;
Till then, 'tis wisdom to conceal our meaning.

HASTINGS. Away with scrupulous wit! now arms must rule.

GLOUCESTER. And fearless minds climb soonest unto crowns.
Brother, we will proclaim you out of hand;
The bruit thereof will bring you many friends.

KING EDWARD. Then be it as you will; for 'tis my right,
And Henry but usurps the diadem.

MONTGOMERY. Ay, now my sovereign speaketh like himself;
And now will I be Edward's champion.

HASTINGS. Sound, trumpet! Edward shall be here pro-
claim'd;
Come, fellow soldier, make thou proclamation.

Gives him a paper. Flourish

SOLDIER. Edward the Fourth, by the grace of God, King of
England and France, and Lord of Ireland, &c.'

MONTGOMERY. And whosoe'er gainsays King Edward's
right,
By this I challenge him to single fight.

Throws down his gauntlet

ALL. Long live Edward the Fourth!

KING EDWARD. Thanks, brave Montgomery;—and thanks
unto you all:
If Fortune serve me, I 'll requite this kindness.
Now, for this night, let 's harbour here in York;
And when the morning sun shall raise his car
Above the border of this horizon,
We 'll forward towards Warwick and his mates;
For well I wot that Henry is no soldier.
Ah, froward Clarence, how evil it beseems thee

To flatter Henry, and forsake thy brother!
Yet, as we may, we 'll meet both thee and Warwick.
Come on, brave soldiers: doubt not of the day;
And, that once gotten, doubt not of large pay.   *Exeunt*

SCENE EIGHT

London. A Room in the Palace.

*Flourish. Enter King Henry, Warwick, Clarence,
Montague, Exeter, and Oxford*

WARWICK. What counsel, lords? Edward from Belgia,
With hasty Germans and blunt Hollanders,
Hath pass'd in safety through the narrow seas,
And with his troops doth march amain to London;
And many giddy people flock to him.
OXFORD. Let 's levy men, and beat him back again.
CLARENCE. A little fire is quickly trodden out,
Which, being suffer'd, rivers cannot quench.
WARWICK. In Warwickshire I have true-hearted friends,
Not mutinous in peace, yet bold in war;
Those will I muster up: and thou, son Clarence,
Shalt stir up in Suffolk, Norfolk, and in Kent,
The knights and gentlemen to come with thee:
Thou, brother Montague, in Buckingham,
Northampton, and in Leicestershire, shalt find
Men well inclin'd to hear what thou command'st:
And thou, brave Oxford, wondrous well belov'd
In Oxfordshire, shalt muster up thy friends.
My sovereign, with the loving citizens,
Like to his island girt in with the ocean,
Or modest Dian circled with her nymphs,
Shall rest in London till we come to him.
Fair lords, take leave, and stand not to reply.
Farewell, my sovereign.
KING HENRY. Farewell, my Hector, and my Troy's true hope.
CLARENCE. In sign of truth, I kiss your Highness' hand.
KING HENRY. Well-minded Clarence, be thou fortunate!
MONTAGUE. Comfort, my lord; and so I take my leave.
OXFORD. (*Kissing Henry's hand*) And thus I seal my truth,
and bid adieu.

KING HENRY. Sweet Oxford, and my loving Montague,
And all at once, once more a happy farewell.
WARWICK. Farewell, sweet lords: let 's meet at Coventry.
                    Exeunt all but King Henry and Exeter
KING HENRY. Here at the palace will I rest awhile.
Cousin of Exeter, what thinks your lordship?
Methinks the power that Edward hath in field
Should not be able to encounter mine.
EXETER. The doubt is that he will seduce the rest.
KING HENRY. That 's not my fear; my meed hath got me
    fame:
I have not stopp'd mine ears to their demands,
Nor posted off their suits with slow delays;
My pity hath been balm to heal their wounds,
My mildness hath allay'd their swelling griefs,
My mercy dried their water-flowing tears;
I have not been desirous of their wealth;
Nor much oppress'd them with great subsidies,
Nor forward of revenge, though they much err'd.
Then why should they love Edward more than me?
No, Exeter, these graces challenge grace:
And, when the lion fawns upon the lamb,
The lamb will never cease to follow him.
                    Shout within, 'A Lancaster! A Lancaster!'
EXETER. Hark, hark, my lord! what shouts are these?
                    Enter King Edward, Gloucester, and Soldiers
KING EDWARD. Seize on the shame-fac'd Henry! bear him
    hence:
And once again proclaim us King of England.
You are the fount that makes small brooks to flow:
Now stops thy spring; my sea shall suck them dry,
And swell so much the higher by their ebb.
Hence with him to the Tower! let him not speak.
                    Exeunt some with King Henry
And, lords, towards Coventry bend we our course,
Where peremptory Warwick now remains:
The sun shines hot; and, if we use delay,
Cold biting winter mars our hop'd-for hay.
GLOUCESTER. Away betimes, before his forces join,
And take the great-grown traitor unawares:
Brave warriors, march amain towards Coventry. *Exeunt*

ACT FIVE

SCENE ONE

Coventry.

Enter, upon the Walls, Warwick, the Mayor of Coventry,
two Messengers, and Others

WARWICK. Where is the post that came from valiant Oxford?
  How far hence is thy lord, mine honest fellow?
FIRST MESSENGER. By this at Dunsmore, marching hither-
  ward.
WARWICK. How far off is our brother Montague?
  Where is the post that came from Montague?
SECOND MESSENGER. By this at Daintry, with a puissant
  troop.

Enter Sir John Somerville

WARWICK. Say, Somerville, what says my loving son?
  And, by thy guess, how nigh is Clarence now?
SOMERVILLE. At Southam I did leave him with his forces,
  And do expect him here some two hours hence.

                                        Drum heard

WARWICK. Then Clarence is at hand, I hear his drum.
SOMERVILLE. It is not his, my lord; here Southam lies:
  The drum your honour hears marcheth from Warwick.
WARWICK. Who should that be? belike, unlook'd for friends.
SOMERVILLE. They are at hand, and you shall quickly know.

Enter King Edward, Gloucester, and Forces

KING EDWARD. Go, trumpet, to the walls, and sound a parle.
GLOUCESTER. See how the surly Warwick mans the wall.
WARWICK. O, unbid spite! is sportful Edward come?
  Where slept our scouts, or how are they seduc'd,
  That we could hear no news of his repair?
KING EDWARD. Now, Warwick, wilt thou ope the city gates,
  Speak gentle words, and humbly bend thy knee?—
  Call Edward king, and at his hands beg mercy?

And he shall pardon thee these outrages.

WARWICK. Nay, rather, wilt thou draw thy forces hence,—
Confess who set thee up and pluck'd thee down?—
Call Warwick patron, and be penitent;
And thou shalt still remain the Duke of York.

GLOUCESTER. I thought, at least, he would have said the
    king;
Or did he make the jest against his will?

WARWICK. Is not a dukedom, sir, a goodly gift?

GLOUCESTER. Ay, by my faith, for a poor earl to give:
I 'll do thee service for so good a gift.

WARWICK. 'Twas I that gave the kingdom to thy brother.

KING EDWARD. Why then 'tis mine, if but by Warwick's gift.

WARWICK. Thou art no Atlas for so great a weight:
And, weakling, Warwick takes his gift again;
And Henry is my king, Warwick his subject.

KING EDWARD. But Warwick's king is Edward's prisoner;
And, gallant Warwick, do but answer this,
What is the body, when the head is off?

GLOUCESTER. Alas! that Warwick had no more forecast,
But, whiles he thought to steal the single ten,
The king was slily finger'd from the deck.
You left poor Henry at the bishop's palace,
And, ten to one, you 'll meet him in the Tower.

KING EDWARD. 'Tis even so: yet you are Warwick still.

GLOUCESTER. Come, Warwick, take the time; kneel down,
    kneel down:
Nay, when? strike now, or else the iron cools.

WARWICK. I had rather chop this hand off at a blow,
And with the other fling it at thy face,
Than bear so low a sail to strike to thee.

KING EDWARD. Sail how thou canst, have wind and tide thy
    friend;
This hand, fast wound about thy coal-black hair,
Shall, whiles thy head is warm and new cut off,
Write in the dust this sentence with thy blood:
'Wind-changing Warwick now can change no more.'
        Enter Oxford, with Soldiers, drum, and colours

WARWICK. O cheerful colours! see where Oxford comes!

OXFORD. Oxford, Oxford, for Lancaster!
                He and his Forces enter the city

GLOUCESTER. The gates are open, let us enter too.

KING EDWARD. So other foes may set upon our backs.
　Stand we in good array; for they no doubt
　Will issue out again and bid us battle:
　If not, the city being but of small defence,
　We 'll quickly rouse the traitors in the same.
WARWICK. O! welcome, Oxford! for we want thy help.
　　　　Enter Montague, with Soldiers, drum, and colours
MONTAGUE. Montague, Montague, for Lancaster!
　　　　　　　He and his Forces enter the city
GLOUCESTER. Thou and thy brother both shall buy this
　treason
　Even with the dearest blood your bodies bear.
KING EDWARD. The harder match'd, the greater victory:
　My mind presageth happy gain, and conquest.
　　　　Enter Somerset, with Soldiers, drum, and colours
SOMERSET. Somerset, Somerset, for Lancaster!
　　　　　　　He and his Forces enter the city
GLOUCESTER. Two of thy name, both Dukes of Somerset,
　Have sold their lives unto the house of York;
　And thou shalt be the third, if this sword hold.
　　　　Enter Clarence, with Forces, drum, and colours
WARWICK. And lo! where George of Clarence sweeps along,
　Of force enough to bid his brother battle;
　With whom an upright zeal to right prevails
　More than the nature of a brother's love.
　Come, Clarence, come; thou wilt, if Warwick call.
CLARENCE. Father of Warwick, know you what this means?
　　　　　　Taking the red rose out of his hat
　Look here, I throw my infamy at thee:
　I will not ruinate my father's house,
　Who gave his blood to lime the stones together,
　And set up Lancaster. Why, trow'st thou, Warwick,
　That Clarence is so harsh, so blunt, unnatural,
　To bend the fatal instruments of war
　Against his brother and his lawful king?
　Perhaps thou wilt object my holy oath:
　To keep that oath were more impiety
　Than Jephthah's, when he sacrific'd his daughter.
　I am so sorry for my trespass made
　That, to deserve well at my brother's hands,
　I here proclaim myself thy mortal foe;
　With resolution, wheresoe'er I meet thee—

As I will meet thee if thou stir abroad—
To plague thee for thy foul misleading me.
And so, proud-hearted Warwick, I defy thee,
And to my brother turn my blushing cheeks.
Pardon me, Edward, I will make amends;
And, Richard, do not frown upon my faults,
For I will henceforth be no more unconstant.

KING EDWARD. Now welcome more, and ten times more
    belov'd,
Than if thou never hadst deserv'd our hate.

GLOUCESTER. Welcome, good Clarence; this is brother-like.

WARWICK. O passing traitor, perjur'd, and unjust!

KING EDWARD. What, Warwick, wilt thou leave the town,
    and fight?
Or shall we beat the stones about thine ears?

WARWICK. Alas! I am not coop'd here for defence:
I will away towards Barnet presently,
And bid thee battle, Edward, if thou darest.

KING EDWARD. Yes, Warwick, Edward dares, and leads the
    way.
Lords, to the field; Saint George and victory!

                                         March. Exeunt

SCENE TWO

A Field of Battle near Barnet.

*Alarums and Excursions. Enter King Edward, bringing
in Warwick, wounded*

KING EDWARD. So, lie thou there: die thou, and die our fear;
For Warwick was a bug that fear'd us all.
Now Montague, sit fast; I seek for thee,
That Warwick's bones may keep thine company.   *Exit*

WARWICK. Ah! who is nigh? come to me, friend or foe,
And tell me who is victor, York or Warwick?
Why ask I that? my mangled body shows,
My blood, my want of strength, my sick heart shows,
That I must yield my body to the earth,
And, by my fall, the conquest to my foe.
Thus yields the cedar to the axe's edge,
Whose arms gave shelter to the princely eagle,

Under whose shade the ramping lion slept,
Whose top branch overpeer'd Jove's spreading tree,
And kept low shrubs from winter's powerful wind.
These eyes, that now are dimm'd with death's black veil,
Have been as piercing as the mid-day sun,
To search the secret treasons of the world:
The wrinkles in my brows, now fill'd with blood,
Were liken'd oft to kingly sepulchres;
For who liv'd king, but I could dig his grave?
And who durst smile when Warwick bent his brow?
Lo! now my glory smear'd in dust and blood;
My parks, my walks, my manors that I had,
Even now forsake me; and of all my lands
Is nothing left me but my body's length.
Why, what is pomp, rule, reign, but earth and dust?
And, live we how we can, yet die we must.
                 Enter Oxford and Somerset
SOMERSET. Ah! Warwick, Warwick, wert thou as we are,
    We might recover all our loss again.
    The queen from France hath brought a puissant power;
    Even now we heard the news. Ah! couldst thou fly.
WARWICK. Why, then, I would not fly. Ah! Montague,
    If thou be there, sweet brother, take my hand,
    And with thy lips keep in my soul awhile.
    Thou lov'st me not; for, brother, if thou didst,
    Thy tears would wash this cold congealed blood
    That glues my lips and will not let me speak.
    Come quickly, Montague, or I am dead.
SOMERSET. Ah! Warwick, Montague hath breath'd his last;
    And to the latest gasp, cried out for Warwick,
    And said, 'Commend me to my valiant brother.'
    And more he would have said; and more he spoke,
    Which sounded like a clamour in a vault,
    That mought not be distinguish'd: but at last
    I well might hear, deliver'd with a groan,
    'O! farewell, Warwick!'
WARWICK. Sweet rest his soul! Fly, lords, and save your-
        selves;
    For Warwick bids you all farewell, to meet in heaven.
                                                    Dies
OXFORD. Away, away, to meet the queen's great power.
                 Exeunt, bearing off Warwick's body

SCENE THREE

Another Part of the Field.

Flourish. Enter King Edward, in triumph: with Clarence,
Gloucester, and the rest

KING EDWARD. Thus far our fortune keeps an upward course,
  And we are grac'd with wreaths of victory.
  But in the midst of this bright-shining day,
  I spy a black, suspicious, threatening cloud,
  That will encounter with our glorious sun,
  Ere he attain his easeful western bed:
  I mean, my lords, those powers that the queen
  Hath rais'd in Gallia, have arriv'd our coast,
  And, as we hear, march on to fight with us.
CLARENCE. A little gale will soon disperse that cloud,
  And blow it to the source from whence it came:
  Thy very beams will dry those vapours up,
  For every cloud engenders not a storm.
GLOUCESTER. The queen is valu'd thirty thousand strong,
  And Somerset, with Oxford, fled to her:
  If she have time to breathe, be well assur'd
  Her faction will be full as strong as ours.
KING EDWARD. We are advertis'd by our loving friends
  That they do hold their course toward Tewksbury.
  We, having now the best at Barnet field,
  Will thither straight, for willingness rids way;
  And, as we march, our strength will be augmented
  In every county as we go along.
  Strike up the drum! cry 'Courage!' and away.

                                        Flourish. Exeunt

SCENE FOUR

Plains near Tewksbury.

March. Enter Queen Margaret, Prince Edward,
Somerset, Oxford, and Soldiers

QUEEN MARGARET. Great lords, wise men ne'er sit and wail
their loss,
But cheerly seek how to redress their harms.
What though the mast be now blown overboard,
The cable broke, the holding anchor lost,
And half our sailors swallow'd in the flood?
Yet lives our pilot still: is 't meet that he
Should leave the helm and like a fearful lad
With tearful eyes add water to the sea,
And give more strength to that which hath too much;
Whiles in his moan the ship splits on the rock,
Which industry and courage might have sav'd?
Ah! what a shame! ah, what a fault were this.
Say, Warwick was our anchor; what of that?
And Montague our top-mast; what of him?
Our slaughter'd friends the tackles; what of these?
Why, is not Oxford here another anchor?
And Somerset, another goodly mast?
The friends of France our shrouds and tacklings?
And, though unskilful, why not Ned and I
For once allow'd the skilful pilot's charge?
We will not from the helm, to sit and weep,
But keep our course, though the rough wind say no,
From shelves and rocks that threaten us with wrack.
As good to chide the waves as speak them fair.
And what is Edward but a ruthless sea?
What Clarence but a quicksand of deceit?
And Richard but a ragged fatal rock?
All those the enemies to our poor bark.
Say you can swim; alas! 'tis but a while:
Tread on the sand; why, there you quickly sink:
Bestride the rock; the tide will wash you off,
Or else you famish; that 's a threefold death.
This speak I, lords, to let you understand,

In case some one of you would fly from us,
That there 's no hop'd-for mercy with the brothers
More than with ruthless waves, with sands and rocks.
Why, courage, then! what cannot be avoided
'Twere childish weakness to lament or fear.

PRINCE. Methinks a woman of this valiant spirit
Should, if a coward heard her speak these words,
Infuse his breast with magnanimity,
And make him, naked, foil a man at arms.
I speak not this, as doubting any here;
For did I but suspect a fearful man,
He should have leave to go away betimes,
Lest in our need he might infect another,
And make him of like spirit to himself.
If any such be here, as God forbid!
Let him depart before we need his help.

OXFORD. Women and children of so high a courage,
And warriors faint! why, 'twere perpetual shame.
O brave young prince! thy famous grandfather
Doth live again in thee: long mayst thou live
To bear his image and renew his glories!

SOMERSET. And he that will not fight for such a hope,
Go home to bed, and, like the owl by day,
If he arise, be mock'd and wonder'd at.

QUEEN MARGARET. Thanks, gentle Somerset: sweet Oxford,
   thanks.

PRINCE. And take his thanks that yet hath nothing else.

Enter a Messenger

MESSENGER. Prepare you, lords, for Edward is at hand,
Ready to fight; therefore be resolute.

OXFORD. I thought no less: it is his policy
To haste thus fast, to find us unprovided.

SOMERSET. But he 's deceiv'd; we are in readiness.

QUEEN MARGARET. This cheers my heart to see your forward-
   ness.

OXFORD. Here pitch our battle; hence we will not budge.

March. Enter, at a distance, King Edward, Clarence,
Gloucester, and Forces

KING EDWARD. Brave followers, yonder stands the thorny
   wood,
Which, by the heavens' assistance, and your strength,
Must by the roots be hewn up yet ere night.

I need not add more fuel to your fire,
For well I wot ye blaze to burn them out:
Give signal to the fight, and to it, lords.
QUEEN MARGARET. Lords, knights, and gentlemen, what I
　should say
My tears gainsay; for every word I speak,
Ye see, I drink the water of mine eyes.
Therefore, no more but this: Henry, your sovereign,
Is prisoner to the foe; his state usurp'd,
His realm a slaughter-house, his subjects slain,
His statutes cancell'd, and his treasure spent;
And yonder is the wolf that makes this spoil.
You fight in justice: then, in God's name, lords,
Be valiant, and give signal to the fight. *Exeunt both armies*

SCENE FIVE

Another Part of the Same.

*Alarums: Excursions: and afterwards a retreat. Then enter
King Edward, Clarence, Gloucester, and Forces; with Queen
Margaret, Oxford, and Somerset, prisoners*

KING EDWARD. Now, here a period of tumultuous broils.
Away with Oxford to Hames Castle straight:
For Somerset, off with his guilty head.
Go, bear them hence; I will not hear them speak.
OXFORD. For my part, I 'll not trouble thee with words.
SOMERSET. Nor I, but stoop with patience to my fortune.
　　　　　　　Exeunt Oxford and Somerset, guarded
QUEEN MARGARET. So part we sadly in this troublous world,
To meet with joy in sweet Jerusalem.
KING EDWARD. Is proclamation made, that who finds Edward
Shall have a high reward, and he his life?
GLOUCESTER. It is: and lo, where youthful Edward comes.
　　　　　　　Enter Soldiers, with Prince Edward
KING EDWARD. Bring forth the gallant: let us hear him speak.
What! can so young a thorn begin to prick?
Edward, what satisfaction canst thou make
For bearing arms, for stirring up my subjects,
And all the trouble thou hast turn'd me to?

PRINCE. Speak like a subject, proud ambitious York!
  Suppose that I am now my father's mouth:
  Resign thy chair, and where I stand kneel thou,
  Whilst I propose the selfsame words to thee,
  Which, traitor, thou wouldst have me answer to.

QUEEN MARGARET. Ah! that thy father had been so resolv'd.

GLOUCESTER. That you might still have worn the petticoat,
  And ne'er have stol'n the breech from Lancaster.

PRINCE. Let Æsop fable in a winter's night;
  His currish riddles sort not with this place.

GLOUCESTER. By heaven, brat, I 'll plague you for that word.

QUEEN MARGARET. Ay, thou wast born to be a plague to
  men.

GLOUCESTER. For God's sake, take away this captive scold.

PRINCE. Nay, take away this scolding crook-back rather.

KING EDWARD. Peace, wilful boy, or I will charm your
  tongue.

CLARENCE. Untutor'd lad, thou art too malapert.

PRINCE. I know my duty; you are all undutiful:
  Lascivious Edward, and thou perjur'd George,
  And thou mis-shapen Dick, I tell ye all,
  I am your better, traitors as ye are;
  And thou usurp'st my father's right and mine.

KING EDWARD. Take that, the likeness of this railer here.
                                        Stabs him

GLOUCESTER. Sprawl'st thou? take that, to end thy agony.
                                        Stabs him

CLARENCE. And there 's for twitting me with perjury.
                                        Stabs him

QUEEN MARGARET. O, kill me too!

GLOUCESTER. Marry, and shall.   *Offers to kill her*

KING EDWARD. Hold, Richard, hold! for we have done too
  much.

GLOUCESTER. Why should she live, to fill the world with
  words?

KING EDWARD. What! doth she swoon? use means for her
  recovery.

GLOUCESTER. Clarence, excuse me to the king, my brother;
  I 'll hence to London on a serious matter:
  Ere ye come there, be sure to hear some news.

CLARENCE. What? what?

GLOUCESTER. The Tower! the Tower!   *Exit*

QUEEN MARGARET. O Ned, sweet Ned! speak to thy mother,
    boy!
  Canst thou not speak? O traitors! murderers!
  They that stabb'd Cæsar shed no blood at all,
  Did not offend, nor were not worthy blame,
  If this foul deed were by, to equal it:
  He was a man; this, in respect, a child;
  And men ne'er spend their fury on a child.
  What's worse than murderer, that I may name it?
  No, no, my heart will burst, an if I speak:
  And I will speak, that so my heart may burst.
  Butchers and villains! bloody cannibals!
  How sweet a plant have you untimely cropp'd!
  You have no children, butchers! if you had,
  The thought of them would have stirr'd up remorse;
  But if you ever chance to have a child,
  Look in his youth to have him so cut off
  As, deathsmen, you have rid this sweet young prince!
KING EDWARD. Away with her! go, bear her hence perforce.
QUEEN MARGARET. Nay, never bear me hence, dispatch me
    here:
  Here sheathe thy sword, I'll pardon thee my death.
  What! wilt thou not? then, Clarence, do it thou.
CLARENCE. By heaven, I will not do thee so much ease.
QUEEN MARGARET. Good Clarence, do; sweet Clarence, do
    thou do it.
CLARENCE. Didst thou not hear me swear I would not do it?
QUEEN MARGARET. Ay, but thou usest to forswear thyself:
  'Twas sin before, but now 'tis charity.
  What! wilt thou not? Where is that devil's butcher,
  Hard-favour'd Richard? Richard, where art thou?
  Thou art not here; murder is thy alms-deed;
  Petitioners for blood thou ne'er put'st back.
KING EDWARD. Away, I say! I charge ye, bear her hence.
QUEEN MARGARET. So come to you and yours, as to this
    prince!   *Exit, led out forcibly*
KING EDWARD. Where's Richard gone?
CLARENCE. To London, all in post; and, as I guess,
  To make a bloody supper in the Tower.
KING EDWARD. He's sudden if a thing comes in his head.
  Now march we hence: discharge the common sort
  With pay and thanks, and let's away to London

And see our gentle queen how well she fares;
By this, I hope, she hath a son for me.   *Exeunt*

SCENE SIX

London. A Room in the Tower.

*King Henry is discovered sitting with a book in his hand,
the Lieutenant attending. Enter Gloucester.*

GLOUCESTER. Good day, my lord. What! at your book so
  hard?
KING HENRY. Ay, my good lord:—my lord, I should say
  rather;
  'Tis sin to flatter; 'good' was little better:
  'Good Gloucester' and 'good devil' were alike,
  And both preposterous; therefore, not 'good lord.'
GLOUCESTER. Sirrah, leave us to ourselves: we must confer.
                                        Exit Lieutenant
KING HENRY. So flies the reckless shepherd from the wolf;
  So first the harmless sheep doth yield his fleece,
  And next his throat unto the butcher's knife.
  What scene of death hath Roscius now to act?
GLOUCESTER. Suspicion always haunts the guilty mind;
  The thief doth fear each bush an officer.
KING HENRY. The bird that hath been limed in a bush,
  With trembling wings misdoubteth every bush;
  And I, the hapless male to one sweet bird,
  Have now the fatal object in my eye
  Where my poor young was lim'd, was caught, and kill'd.
GLOUCESTER. Why, what a peevish fool was that of Crete,
  That taught his son the office of a fowl!
  And yet, for all his wings, the fool was drown'd.
KING HENRY. I, Dædalus; my poor boy, Icarus;
  Thy father, Minos, that denied our course;
  The sun, that sear'd the wings of my sweet boy,
  Thy brother Edward, and thyself the sea,
  Whose envious gulf did swallow up his life.
  Ah! kill me with thy weapon, not with words.
  My breast can better brook thy dagger's point
  Than can my ears that tragic history.
  But wherefore dost thou come? is 't for my life?

GLOUCESTER. Think'st thou I am an executioner?

KING HENRY. A persecutor, I am sure, thou art:
  If murdering innocents be executing,
  Why, then thou art an executioner.

GLOUCESTER. Thy son I kill'd for his presumption.

KING HENRY. Hadst thou been kill'd, when first thou didst presume,
  Thou hadst not liv'd to kill a son of mine.
  And thus I prophesy: that many a thousand,
  Which now mistrust no parcel of my fear,
  And many an old man's sigh, and many a widow's,
  And many an orphan's water-standing eye,
  Men for their sons', wives for their husbands',
  And orphans for their parents' timeless death,
  Shall rue the hour that ever thou wast born.
  The owl shriek'd at thy birth, an evil sign;
  The night-crow cried, aboding luckless time;
  Dogs howl'd, and hideous tempest shook down trees!
  The raven rook'd her on the chimney's top,
  And chattering pies in dismal discords sung.
  Thy mother felt more than a mother's pain,
  And yet brought forth less than a mother's hope;
  To wit, an indigest deformed lump,
  Not like the fruit of such a goodly tree.
  Teeth hadst thou in thy head when thou wast born,
  To signify thou camest to bite the world:
  And, if the rest be true which I have heard,
  Thou camest—

GLOUCESTER. I 'll hear no more: die, prophet, in thy speech:
                                        Stabs him
  For this, amongst the rest, was I ordain'd.

KING HENRY. Ay, and for much more slaughter after this.
  O, God forgive my sins, and pardon thee!   *Dies*

GLOUCESTER. What! will the aspiring blood of Lancaster
  Sink in the ground? I thought it would have mounted.
  See how my sword weeps for the poor king's death!
  O! may such purple tears be always shed
  From those that wish the downfall of our house.
  If any spark of life be yet remaining,
  Down, down to hell; and say I sent thee thither,
                                        Stabs him again
  I, that have neither pity, love, nor fear.

Indeed, 'tis true, that Henry told me of;
For I have often heard my mother say
I came into the world with my legs forward.
Had I not reason, think ye, to make haste,
And seek their ruin that usurp'd our right?
The midwife wonder'd, and the women cried
'O! Jesus bless us, he is born with teeth.'
And so I was; which plainly signified
That I should snarl and bite and play the dog.
Then, since the heavens have shap'd my body so,
Let hell make crook'd my mind to answer it.
I have no brother, I am like no brother;
And this word 'love,' which greybeards call divine,
Be resident in men like one another
And not in me: I am myself alone.
Clarence, beware; thou keep'st me from the light:
But I will sort a pitchy day for thee;
For I will buzz abroad such prophecies
That Edward shall be fearful of his life;
And then, to purge his fear, I 'll be thy death.
King Henry and the prince his son are gone:
Clarence, thy turn is next, and then the rest,
Counting myself but bad till I be best.
I 'll throw thy body in another room,
And triumph, Henry, in thy day of doom.

Exit, with the body

SCENE SEVEN

The Same. A Room in the Palace.

*King Edward is discovered sitting on his throne: Queen Eliz-
abeth with the infant Prince, Clarence, Gloucester,
Hastings, and Others, near him.*

KING EDWARD. Once more we sit in England's royal throne,
Re-purchas'd with the blood of enemies.
What valiant foemen like to autumn's corn,
Have we mow'd down, in tops of all their pride!
Three Dukes of Somerset, threefold renown'd
For hardy and undoubted champions;
Two Cliffords, as the father and the son;
And two Northumberlands: two braver men

Ne'er spurr'd their coursers at the trumpet's sound;
With them, the two brave bears, Warwick and Montague,
That in their chains fetter'd the kingly lion,
And made the forest tremble when they roar'd.
Thus have we swept suspicion from our seat,
And made our footstool of security.
Come hither, Bess, and let me kiss my boy.
Young Ned, for thee thine uncles and myself
Have in our armours watch'd the winter's night;
Went all a-foot in summer's scalding heat,
That thou might'st repossess the crown in peace;
And of our labours thou shalt reap the gain.

GLOUCESTER. (*Aside*) I 'll blast his harvest, if your head were
   laid;
For yet I am not look'd on in the world.
This shoulder was ordain'd so thick to heave;
And heave it shall some weight, or break my back:
Work thou the way, and thou shalt execute.

KING EDWARD. Clarence and Gloucester, love my lovely
   queen;
And kiss your princely nephew, brothers both.

CLARENCE. The duty, that I owe unto your Majesty,
I seal upon the lips of this sweet babe.

KING EDWARD. Thanks, noble Clarence; worthy brother,
   thanks.

GLOUCESTER. And, that I love the tree from whence thou
   sprang'st,
Witness the loving kiss I give the fruit.
(*Aside*) To say the truth, so Judas kiss'd his master,
And cried 'all hail' when as he meant all harm.

KING EDWARD. Now am I seated as my soul delights,
Having my country's peace and brothers' loves.

CLARENCE. What will your Grace have done with Margaret?
Reignier, her father, to the King of France
Hath pawn'd the Sicils and Jerusalem,
And hither have they sent it for her ransom.

KING EDWARD. Away with her, and waft her hence to
   France.
And now what rests but that we spend the time
With stately triumphs, mirthful comic shows,
Such as befit the pleasure of the court?
Sound, drums and trumpets! farewell, sour annoy!
For here, I hope, begins our lasting joy.   *Exeunt*

THE TRAGEDY OF KING
RICHARD THE THIRD

CAST OF CHARACTERS

KING EDWARD THE FOURTH

EDWARD, *Prince of Wales; after-*
 wards King Edward the Fifth } *Sons to the*
RICHARD, *Duke of York*   *King*

GEORGE, *Duke of Clarence*
RICHARD, *Duke of Gloucester;* } *Brothers to*
 afterwards King Richard   *the King*
 the Third

A young Son of Clarence
HENRY, *Earl of Richmond; afterwards King Henry*
 the Seventh
CARDINAL BOURCHIER, *Archbishop of Canterbury*
THOMAS ROTHERHAM, *Archbishop of York*
JOHN MORTON, *Bishop of Ely*
DUKE OF BUCKINGHAM
DUKE OF NORFOLK
EARL OF SURREY, *his Son*
EARL RIVERS, *Brother to King Edward's Queen*
MARQUESS OF DORSET, *and* LORD GREY, *her Sons*
EARL OF OXFORD
LORD HASTINGS
LORD STANLEY, *called also* EARL OF DERBY
LORD LOVEL
SIR THOMAS VAUGHAN
SIR RICHARD RATCLIFF
SIR WILLIAM CATESBY
SIR JAMES TYRRELL
SIR JAMES BLOUNT
SIR WALTER HERBERT
SIR ROBERT BRAKENBURY, *Lieutenant of the Tower*
SIR WILLIAM BRANDON

(*continued on next page*)

CHRISTOPHER URSWICK, *a Priest*
Another Priest
Lord Mayor of London
Sheriff of Wiltshire
TRESSEL *and* BERKELEY, *Gentlemen attending on
Lady Anne*

ELIZABETH, *Queen of King Edward the Fourth*
MARGARET, *Widow of King Henry the Sixth*
DUCHESS OF YORK, *Mother to King Edward the
Fourth, Clarence, and Gloucester*
LADY ANNE, *Widow of Edward, Prince of Wales,
Son to King Henry the Sixth; afterwards married
to the Duke of Gloucester*
LADY MARGARET PLANTAGENET, *a young Daughter
of Clarence*

Lords, and other Attendants; two Gentlemen, a Pur-
suivant, Scrivener, Citizens, Murderers, Messengers,
Ghosts of those murdered by Richard the Third,
Soldiers, &c.

SCENE

England

THE TRAGEDY OF KING
RICHARD THE THIRD

ACT ONE

SCENE ONE

London. A Street.

Enter Gloucester

GLOUCESTER. Now is the winter of our discontent
Made glorious summer by this sun of York;
And all the clouds that lowr'd upon our house
In the deep bosom of the ocean buried.
Now all our brows bound with victorious wreaths;
Our bruised arms hung up for monuments;
Our stern alarums chang'd to merry meetings;
Our dreadful marches to delightful measures.
Grim-visag'd war hath smooth'd his wrinkled front;
And now,—instead of mounting barbed steeds,
To fright the souls of fearful adversaries,—
He capers nimbly in a lady's chamber
To the lascivious pleasing of a lute.
But I, that am not shap'd for sportive tricks,
Nor made to court an amorous looking-glass;
I, that am rudely stamp'd, and want love's majesty
To strut before a wanton ambling nymph;
I, that am curtail'd of this fair proportion,
Cheated of feature by dissembling nature,
Deform'd, unfinish'd, sent before my time
Into this breathing world, scarce half made up,
And that so lamely and unfashionable
That dogs bark at me, as I halt by them;
Why, I, in this weak piping time of peace,
Have no delight to pass away the time,
Unless to see my shadow in the sun
And descant on mine own deformity:
And therefore, since I cannot prove a lover,

To entertain these fair well-spoken days,
I am determined to prove a villain,
And hate the idle pleasures of these days.
Plots have I laid, inductions dangerous,
By drunken prophecies, libels, and dreams,
To set my brother Clarence and the king
In deadly hate the one against the other:
And if King Edward be as true and just
As I am subtle, false, and treacherous,
This day should Clarence closely be mew'd up,
About a prophecy, which says, that G
Of Edward's heirs the murderer shall be.
Dive, thoughts, down to my soul: here Clarence comes.
            Enter Clarence, guarded, and Brakenbury
Brother, good day: what means this armed guard
That waits upon your Grace?

CLARENCE.   His Majesty,
Tendering my person's safety, hath appointed
This conduct to convey me to the Tower.

GLOUCESTER. Upon what cause?

CLARENCE.   Because my name is George.

GLOUCESTER. Alack! my lord, that fault is none of yours;
He should, for that, commit your godfathers.
O! belike his Majesty hath some intent
That you should be new-christen'd in the Tower.
But what 's the matter, Clarence? may I know?

CLARENCE. Yea, Richard, when I know; for I protest
As yet I do not: but, as I can learn,
He hearkens after prophecies and dreams;
And from the cross-row plucks the letter G,
And says a wizard told him that by G
His issue disinherited should be;
And, for my name of George begins with G,
It follows in his thoughts that I am he.
These, as I learn, and such like toys as these,
Have mov'd his Highness to commit me now.

GLOUCESTER. Why, this it is, when men are rul'd by women:
'Tis not the king that sends you to the Tower;
My Lady Grey, his wife, Clarence, 'tis she
That tempers him to this extremity.
Was it not she and that good man of worship,
Anthony Woodville, her brother there,

That made him send Lord Hastings to the Tower,
From whence this present day he is deliver'd?
We are not safe, Clarence; we are not safe.

CLARENCE. By heaven, I think there is no man secure
But the queen's kindred and night-walking heralds
That trudge betwixt the king and Mistress Shore.
Heard you not what a humble suppliant
Lord Hastings was to her for his delivery?

GLOUCESTER. Humbly complaining to her deity
Got my Lord Chamberlain his liberty.
I 'll tell you what; I think it is our way,
If we will keep in favour with the king,
To be her men and wear her livery:
The jealous o'er-worn widow and herself,
Since that our brother dubb'd them gentlewomen,
Are mighty gossips in our monarchy.

BRAKENBURY. I beseech your Graces both to pardon me;
His Majesty hath straitly given in charge
That no man shall have private conference,
Of what degree soever, with your brother.

GLOUCESTER. Even so; an please your worship, Brakenbury,
You may partake of any thing we say:
We speak no treason, man: we say the king
Is wise and virtuous, and his noble queen
Well struck in years, fair, and not jealous;
We say that Shore's wife hath a pretty foot,
A cherry lip, a bonny eye, a passing pleasing tongue;
And that the queen's kindred are made gentlefolks.
How say you, sir? can you deny all this?

BRAKENBURY. With this, my lord, myself have nought to do.

GLOUCESTER. Naught to do with Mistress Shore! I tell thee,
   fellow,
He that doth naught with her, excepting one,
Were best to do it secretly, alone.

BRAKENBURY. What one, my lord?

GLOUCESTER. Her husband, knave. Wouldst thou betray me?

BRAKENBURY. I beseech your Grace to pardon me; and
   withal
Forbear your conference with the noble duke.

CLARENCE. We know thy charge, Brakenbury, and will
   obey.

GLOUCESTER. We are the queen's abjects, and must obey.

Brother, farewell: I will unto the king;
And whatsoe'er you will employ me in,
Were it to call King Edward's widow sister,
I will perform it to enfranchise you.
Meantime, this deep disgrace in brotherhood
Touches me deeper than you can imagine.

CLARENCE. I know it pleaseth neither of us well.

GLOUCESTER. Well, your imprisonment shall not be long;
I will deliver you, or else lie for you:
Meantime, have patience.

CLARENCE.   I must perforce: farewell.

Exeunt Clarence, Brakenbury, and Guard

GLOUCESTER. Go, tread the path that thou shalt ne'er return,
Simple, plain Clarence! I do love thee so
That I will shortly send thy soul to heaven,
If heaven will take the present at our hands.
But who comes here? the new-deliver'd Hastings!

Enter Hastings

HASTINGS. Good time of day unto my gracious lord!

GLOUCESTER. As much unto my good Lord Chamberlain!
Well are you welcome to this open air.
How hath your lordship brook'd imprisonment?

HASTINGS. With patience, noble lord, as prisoners must:
But I shall live, my lord, to give them thanks
That were the cause of my imprisonment.

GLOUCESTER. No doubt, no doubt; and so shall Clarence too;
For they that were your emenies are his,
And have prevail'd as much on him as you.

HASTINGS. More pity that the eagles should be mew'd,
While kites and buzzards prey at liberty.

GLOUCESTER. What news abroad?

HASTINGS. No news so bad abroad as this at home;
The king is sickly, weak, and melancholy,
And his physicians fear him mightily.

GLOUCESTER. Now by Saint Paul, this news is bad indeed.
O! he hath kept an evil diet long,
And over-much consum'd his royal person:
'Tis very grievous to be thought upon.
What, is he in his bed?

HASTINGS.   He is.

GLOUCESTER. Go you before, and I will follow you.

Exit Hastings

He cannot live, I hope; and must not die
Till George be pack'd with post-horse up to heaven.
I 'll in, to urge his hatred more to Clarence,
With lies well steel'd with weighty arguments;
And, if I fail not in my deep intent,
Clarence hath not another day to live:
Which done, God take King Edward to his mercy,
And leave the world for me to bustle in!
For then I 'll marry Warwick's youngest daughter.
What though I kill'd her husband and her father,
The readiest way to make the wench amends
Is to become her husband and her father:
The which will I; not all so much for love
As for another secret close intent,
By marrying her, which I must reach unto.
But yet I run before my horse to market:
Clarence still breathes; Edward still lives and reigns:
When they are gone, then must I count my gains.   *Exit*

SCENE TWO

London. Another Street.

*Enter the corpse of King Henry the Sixth, borne in an open
coffin; Gentlemen bearing halberds to guard it; and
Lady Anne, as mourner*

ANNE. Set down, set down your honourable load,
If honour may be shrouded in a hearse,
Whilst I awhile obsequiously lament
The untimely fall of virtuous Lancaster.
Poor key-cold figure of a holy king!
Pale ashes of the house of Lancaster!
Thou bloodless remnant of that royal blood!
Be it lawful that I invocate thy ghost,
To hear the lamentations of poor Anne,
Wife to thy Edward, to thy slaughter'd son,
Stabb'd by the selfsame hand that made these wounds!
Lo, in these windows that let forth thy life,
I pour the helpless balm of my poor eyes.
O! cursed be the hand that made these holes;
Cursed the heart that had the heart to do it!

Cursed the blood that let this blood from hence!
More direful hap betide that hated wretch,
That makes us wretched by the death of thee,
Than I can wish to adders, spiders, toads,
Or any creeping venom'd thing that lives!
If ever he have child, abortive be it,
Prodigious, and untimely brought to light,
Whose ugly and unnatural aspect
May fright the hopeful mother at the view;
And that be heir to his unhappiness!
If ever he have wife, let her be made
More miserable by the death of him
Than I am made by my young lord and thee!
Come, now towards Chertsey with your holy load,
Taken from Paul's to be interred there;
And still, as you are weary of the weight,
Rest you, whiles I lament King Henry's corse.

The Bearers take up the corpse and advance
Enter Gloucester

GLOUCESTER. Stay, you that bear the corse, and set it down.
ANNE. What black magician conjures up this fiend,
  To stop devoted charitable deeds?
GLOUCESTER. Villains! set down the corse; or, by Saint Paul,
  I 'll make a corse of him that disobeys.
FIRST GENTLEMAN. My lord, stand back, and let the coffin
  pass.
GLOUCESTER. Unmanner'd dog! stand thou when I com-
  mand:
  Advance thy halberd higher than my breast,
  Or, by Saint Paul, I 'll strike thee to my foot,
  And spurn upon thee, beggar, for thy boldness.

The Bearers set down the coffin

ANNE. What! do you tremble? are you all afraid?
  Alas! I blame you not; for you are mortal,
  And mortal eyes cannot endure the devil.
  Avaunt! thou dreadful minister of hell,
  Thou hadst but power over his mortal body,
  His soul thou canst not have: therefore, be gone.
GLOUCESTER. Sweet saint, for charity, be not so curst.
ANNE. Foul devil, for God's sake hence, and trouble us not;
  For thou hast made the happy earth thy hell,
  Fill'd it with cursing cries and deep exclaims.

If thou delight to view thy heinous deeds,
Behold this pattern of thy butcheries.
O! gentlemen; see, see! dead Henry's wounds
Open their congeal'd mouths and bleed afresh.
Blush, blush, thou lump of foul deformity,
For 'tis thy presence that exhales this blood
From cold and empty veins, where no blood dwells:
Thy deed, inhuman and unnatural,
Provokes this deluge most unnatural.
O God! which this blood mad'st, revenge his death;
O earth! which this blood drink'st, revenge his death;
Either heaven with lightning strike the murderer dead,
Or earth, gape open wide, and eat him quick,
As thou dost swallow up this good king's blood,
Which his hell-govern'd arm hath butchered!

GLOUCESTER. Lady, you know no rules of charity,
Which renders good for bad, blessings for curses.

ANNE. Villain, thou know'st no law of God nor man:
No beast so fierce but knows some touch of pity.

GLOUCESTER. But I know none, and therefore am no beast.

ANNE. O! wonderful, when devils tell the truth.

GLOUCESTER. More wonderful when angels are so angry.
Vouchsafe, divine perfection of a woman,
Of these supposed evils, to give me leave,
By circumstance, but to acquit myself.

ANNE. Vouchsafe, diffus'd infection of a man,
For these known evils, but to give me leave,
By circumstance, to curse thy cursed self.

GLOUCESTER. Fairer than tongue can name thee, let me have
Some patient leisure to excuse myself.

ANNE. Fouler than heart can think thee, thou canst make
No excuse current, but to hang thyself.

GLOUCESTER. By such despair I should accuse myself.

ANNE. And by despairing shouldst thou stand excus'd
For doing worthy vengeance on thyself,
Which didst unworthy slaughter upon others.

GLOUCESTER. Say that I slew them not.

ANNE.   Then say they were not slain:
But dead they are, and, devilish slave, by thee.

GLOUCESTER. I did not kill your husband.

ANNE.   Why, then he is alive.

GLOUCESTER. Nay, he is dead; and slain by Edward's hand.

ANNE. In thy foul throat thou liest: Queen Margaret saw
Thy murderous falchion smoking in his blood;
The which thou once didst bend against her breast,
But that thy brothers beat aside the point.

GLOUCESTER. I was provoked by her slanderous tongue,
That laid their guilt upon my guiltless shoulders.

ANNE. Thou was provoked by thy bloody mind,
That never dreamt on aught but butcheries.
Didst thou not kill this king?

GLOUCESTER. I grant ye.

ANNE. Dost grant me, hedgehog? Then, God grant me too
Thou mayst be damned for that wicked deed!
O! he was gentle, mild, and virtuous.

GLOUCESTER. The fitter for the King of Heaven, that hath
him.

ANNE. He is in heaven, where thou shalt never come.

GLOUCESTER. Let him thank me, that help'd to send him
thither;
For he was fitter for that place than earth.

ANNE. And thou unfit for any place but hell.

GLOUCESTER. Yes, one place else, if you will hear me name it.

ANNE. Some dungeon.

GLOUCESTER.   Your bed-chamber.

ANNE. Ill rest betide the chamber where thou liest!

GLOUCESTER. So will it, madam, till I lie with you.

ANNE. I hope so.

GLOUCESTER.   I know so. But, gentle Lady Anne,
To leave this keen encounter of our wits,
And fall somewhat into a slower method,
Is not the causer of the timeless deaths
Of these Plantagenets, Henry and Edward,
As blameful as the executioner?

ANNE. Thou wast the cause, and most accurs'd effect.

GLOUCESTER. Your beauty was the cause of that effect;
Your beauty, that did haunt me in my sleep
To undertake the death of all the world,
So might I live one hour in your sweet bosom.

ANNE. If I thought that, I tell thee, homicide,
These nails should rend that beauty from my cheeks.

GLOUCESTER. These eyes could not endure that beauty's
wrack;

You should not blemish it if I stood by:
As all the world is cheered by the sun,
So I by that; it is my day, my life.

ANNE. Black night o'ershade thy day, and death thy life!

GLOUCESTER. Curse not thyself, fair creature; thou art both.

ANNE. I would I were, to be reveng'd on thee.

GLOUCESTER. It is a quarrel most unnatural,
To be reveng'd on him that loveth thee.

ANNE. It is a quarrel just and reasonable,
To be reveng'd on him that kill'd my husband.

GLOUCESTER. He that bereft thee, lady, of thy husband,
Did it to help thee to a better husband.

ANNE. His better doth not breathe upon the earth.

GLOUCESTER. He lives that loves thee better than he could.

ANNE. Name him.

GLOUCESTER.   Plantagenet.

ANNE.   Why, that was he.

GLOUCESTER. The selfsame name, but one of better nature.

ANNE. Where is he?

GLOUCESTER.   Here. (*She spitteth at him*) Why dost
thou spit at me?

ANNE. Would it were mortal poison, for thy sake!

GLOUCESTER. Never came poison from so sweet a place.

ANNE. Never hung poison on a fouler toad.
Out of my sight! thou dost infect mine eyes.

GLOUCESTER. Thine eyes, sweet lady, have infected mine.

ANNE. Would they were basilisks, to strike thee dead!

GLOUCESTER. I would they were, that I might die at once;
For now they kill me with a living death.
Those eyes of thine from mine have drawn salt tears,
Sham'd their aspects with store of childish drops;
These eyes, which never shed remorseful tear;
No, when my father York and Edward wept
To hear the piteous moan that Rutland made
When black-fac'd Clifford shook his sword at him;
Nor when thy warlike father like a child,
Told the sad story of my father's death,
And twenty times made pause to sob and weep,
That all the standers-by had wet their cheeks,
Like trees bedash'd with rain: in that sad time
My manly eyes did scorn an humble tear;
And what these sorrows could not thence exhale,

Thy beauty hath, and made them blind with weeping.
I never su'd to friend nor enemy;
My tongue could never learn sweet smoothing words;
But, now thy beauty is propos'd my fee,
My proud heart sues, and prompts my tongue to speak.

She looks scornfully at him

Teach not thy lip such scorn, for it was made
For kissing, lady, not for such contempt.
If thy revengeful heart cannot forgive,
Lo! here I lend thee this sharp-pointed sword;
Which if thou please to hide in this true breast,
And let the soul forth that adoreth thee,
I lay it open to the deadly stroke,
And humbly beg the death upon my knee.

He lays his breast open: she offers at it with his sword

Nay, do not pause; for I did kill King Henry;
But 'twas thy beauty that provoked me.
Nay, now dispatch; 'twas I that stabb'd young Edward;

She again offers at his breast

But 'twas thy heavenly face that set me on.

She lets fall the sword

Take up the sword again, or take up me.

ANNE. Arise, dissembler: though I wish thy death,
I will not be thy executioner.

GLOUCESTER. Then bid me kill myself, and I will do it.

ANNE. I have already.

GLOUCESTER.   That was in thy rage:
Speak it again, and, even with the word,
This hand, which for thy love did kill thy love,
Shall, for thy love, kill a far truer love:
To both their deaths shalt thou be accessary.

ANNE. I would I knew thy heart.

GLOUCESTER. 'Tis figur'd in my tongue.

ANNE. I fear me both are false.

GLOUCESTER. Then never man was true.

ANNE. Well, well, put up your sword.

GLOUCESTER. Say, then, my peace is made.

ANNE. That shalt thou know hereafter.

GLOUCESTER. But shall I live in hope?

ANNE. All men, I hope, live so.

GLOUCESTER. Vouchsafe to wear this ring.

ANNE. To take is not to give.   *She puts on the ring*

GLOUCESTER. Look, how my ring encompasseth thy finger,
   Even so thy breast encloseth my poor heart;
   Wear both of them, for both of them are thine.
   And if thy poor devoted servant may
   But beg one favour at thy gracious hand,
   Thou dost confirm his happiness for ever.
ANNE. What is it?
GLOUCESTER. That it may please you leave these sad
      designs
   To him that hath most cause to be a mourner,
   And presently repair to Crosby-place;
   Where, after I have solemnly interr'd
   At Chertsey monastery this noble king,
   And wet his grave with my repentant tears,
   I will with all expedient duty see you:
   For divers unknown reasons, I beseech you,
   Grant me this boon.
ANNE. With all my heart; and much it joys me too
   To see you are become so penitent.
   Tressel and Berkeley, go along with me.
GLOUCESTER. Bid me farewell.
ANNE.   'Tis more than you deserve;
   But since you teach me how to flatter you,
   Imagine I have said farewell already.
             Exeunt Lady Anne, Tressel, and Berkeley
GLOUCESTER. Sirs, take up the corse.
GENTLEMAN. Towards Chertsey, noble lord?
GLOUCESTER. No, to White-Friars; there attend my coming.
                    Exeunt all but Gloucester
   Was ever woman in this humour woo'd?
   Was ever woman in this humour won?
   I 'll have her; but I will not keep her long.
   What! I, that kill'd her husband, and his father,
   To take her in her heart's extremest hate;
   With curses in her mouth, tears in her eyes,
   The bleeding witness of her hatred by;
   Having God, her conscience, and these bars against me,
   And nothing I to back my suit withal
   But the plain devil and dissembling looks,
   And yet to win her, all the world to nothing!
   Ha!
   Hath she forgot already that brave prince,

Edward, her lord, whom I, some three months since,
Stabb'd in my angry mood at Tewksbury?
A sweeter and a lovelier gentleman,
Fram'd in the prodigality of nature,
Young, valiant, wise, and, no doubt, right royal,
The spacious world cannot again afford:
And will she yet abase her eyes on me,
That cropp'd the golden prime of this sweet prince,
And made her widow to a woeful bed?
On me, whose all not equals Edward's moiety?
On me, that halt and am mis-shapen thus?
My dukedom to a beggarly denier
I do mistake my person all this while:
Upon my life, she finds, although I cannot,
Myself to be a marvellous proper man.
I 'll be at charges for a looking-glass,
And entertain a score or two of tailors,
To study fashions to adorn my body:
Since I am crept in favour with myself,
I will maintain it with some little cost.
But first I 'll turn yon fellow in his grave,
And then return lamenting to my love.
Shine out, fair sun, till I have bought a glass,
That I may see my shadow as I pass.   *Exit*

SCENE THREE

London. A Room in the Palace.

Enter Queen Elizabeth, Lord Rivers, and Lord Grey

RIVERS. Have patience, madam: there 's no doubt his Majesty
    Will soon recover his accustom'd health.
GREY. In that you brook it ill, it makes him worse:
    Therefore, for God's sake, entertain good comfort,
    And cheer his Grace with quick and merry words.
QUEEN ELIZABETH. If he were dead, what would betide on me?
GREY. No other harm but loss of such a lord.
QUEEN ELIZABETH. The loss of such a lord includes all harms.

GREY. The heavens have bless'd you with a goodly son,
  To be your comforter when he is gone.
QUEEN ELIZABETH. Ah! he is young; and his minority
  Is put into the trust of Richard Gloucester,
  A man that loves not me, nor none of you.
RIVERS. Is it concluded he shall be protector?
QUEEN ELIZABETH. It is determin'd, not concluded yet:
  But so it must be if the king miscarry.
          Enter Buckingham and Stanley
GREY. Here come the Lords of Buckingham and Stanley.
BUCKINGHAM. Good time of day unto your royal Grace!
STANLEY. God make your Majesty joyful as you have been!
QUEEN ELIZABETH. The Countess Richmond, good my Lord
      of Stanley,
  To your good prayer will scarcely say amen.
  Yet, Stanley, notwithstanding she 's your wife,
  And loves not me, be you, good lord, assur'd
  I hate not you for her proud arrogance.
STANLEY. I do beseech you, either not believe
  The envious slanders of her false accusers;
  Or, if she be accus'd on true report,
  Bear with her weakness, which, I think, proceeds
  From wayward sickness, and no grounded malice.
QUEEN ELIZABETH. Saw you the king to-day, my Lord of
      Stanley?
STANLEY. But now the Duke of Buckingham and I
  Are come from visiting his Majesty.
QUEEN ELIZABETH. What likelihood of his amendment,
      lords?
BUCKINGHAM. Madam, good hope; his Grace speaks cheer-
      fully.
QUEEN ELIZABETH. God grant him health! did you confer
  with him?
BUCKINGHAM. Ay, madam: he desires to make atonement
  Between the Duke of Gloucester and your brothers,
  And between them and my Lord Chamberlain;
  And sent to warn them to his royal presence.
QUEEN ELIZABETH. Would all were well! But that will never
  be.
  I fear our happiness is at the highest.
          Enter Gloucester, Hastings, and Dorset
GLOUCESTER. They do me wrong, and I will not endure it:

Who are they that complain unto the king,
That I, forsooth, am stern and love them not?
By holy Paul, they love his Grace but lightly
That fill his ears with such dissentious rumours.
Because I cannot flatter and speak fair,
Smile in men's faces, smooth, deceive, and cog,
Duck with French nods and apish courtesy,
I must be held a rancorous enemy.
Cannot a plain man live and think no harm,
But thus his simple truth must be abus'd
By silken, sly, insinuating Jacks?

GREY. To whom in all this presence speaks your Grace?
GLOUCESTER. To thee, that hast nor honesty nor grace.
When have I injur'd thee? when done thee wrong?
Or thee? or thee? or any of your faction?
A plague upon you all! His royal person,—
Whom God preserve better than you would wish!—
Cannot be quiet scarce a breathing-while,
But you must trouble him with lewd complaints.

QUEEN ELIZABETH. Brother of Gloucester, you mistake the
      matter.
The king, on his own royal disposition,
And not provok'd by any suitor else,
Aiming, belike, at your interior hatred,
That in your outward action shows itself
Against my children, brothers, and myself,
Makes him to send; that thereby he may gather
The ground of your ill-will, and so remove it.

GLOUCESTER. I cannot tell; the world is grown so bad
That wrens make prey where eagles dare not perch:
Since every Jack became a gentleman
There 's many a gentle person made a Jack.

QUEEN ELIZABETH. Come, come, we know your meaning,
      brother Gloucester;
You envy my advancement and my friends'.
God grant we never may have need of you!

GLOUCESTER. Meantime, God grants that we have need of
      you:
Our brother is imprison'd by your means,
Myself disgrac'd, and the nobility
Held in contempt; while great promotions
Are daily given to ennoble those

That scarce, some two days since, were worth a noble.

QUEEN ELIZABETH. By him that rais'd me to this careful
 height
From that contented hap which I enjoy'd,
I never did incense his Majesty
Against the Duke of Clarence, but have been
An earnest advocate to plead for him.
My lord, you do me shameful injury,
Falsely to draw me in these vile suspects.

GLOUCESTER. You may deny that you were not the mean
Of my Lord Hastings' late imprisonment.

RIVERS. She may, my lord; for—

GLOUCESTER. She may, Lord Rivers! why, who knows not
 so?
She may do more, sir, than denying that:
She may help you to many fair preferments,
And then deny her aiding hand therein,
And lay those honours on your high desert.
What may she not? She may,—ay, marry, may she,—

RIVERS. What, marry, may she?

GLOUCESTER. What, marry, may she! marry with a king,
A bachelor, a handsome stripling too.
I wis your grandam had a worser match.

QUEEN ELIZABETH. My Lord of Gloucester, I have too long
 borne
Your blunt upbraiding and your bitter scoffs;
By heaven, I will acquaint his Majesty
Of those gross taunts that oft I have endur'd.
I had rather be a country servantmaid
Than a great queen, with this condition,
To be so baited, scorn'd, and stormed at:
Small joy have I in being England's queen.

    Enter Queen Margaret, behind

QUEEN MARGARET. (*Apart*) And lessen'd be that small, God,
I beseech him!
Thy honour, state, and seat is due to me.

GLOUCESTER. What! threat you me with telling of the king?
Tell him, and spare not: look, what I have said
I will avouch in presence of the king:
I dare adventure to be sent to the Tower.
'Tis time to speak; my pains are quite forgot.

QUEEN MARGARET. (*Apart*) Out, devil! I remember them too
    well:
  Thou kill'dst my husband Henry in the Tower,
  And Edward, my poor son, at Tewksbury.
GLOUCESTER. Ere you were queen, ay, or your husband king,
  I was a pack-horse in his great affairs,
  A weeder-out of his proud adversaries,
  A liberal rewarder of his friends;
  To royalize his blood I spilt mine own.
QUEEN MARGARET. Ay, and much better blood than his, or
    thine.
GLOUCESTER. In all which time you and your husband Grey
  Were factious for the house of Lancaster;
  And, Rivers, so were you. Was not your husband
  In Margaret's battle at Saint Alban's slain?
  Let me put in your minds, if you forget,
  What you have been ere now, and what you are;
  Withal, what I have been, and what I am.
QUEEN MARGARET. A murderous villain, and so still thou art.
GLOUCESTER. Poor Clarence did forsake his father,
    Warwick,
  Ay, and forswore himself,—which Jesu pardon!—
QUEEN MARGARET. Which God revenge!
GLOUCESTER. To fight on Edward's party for the crown;
  And for his meed, poor lord, he is mew'd up.
  I would to God my heart were flint, like Edward's;
  Or Edward's soft and pitiful, like mine:
  I am too childish-foolish for this world.
QUEEN MARGARET. Hie thee to hell for shame, and leave this
    world,
  Thou cacodemon! there thy kingdom is.
RIVERS. My Lord of Gloucester, in those busy days
  Which here you urge to prove us enemies,
  We follow'd then our lord, our lawful king;
  So should we you, if you should be our king.
GLOUCESTER. If I should be! I had rather be a pedlar.
  Far be it from my heart the thought thereof!
QUEEN ELIZABETH. As little joy, my lord, as you suppose
  You should enjoy, were you this country's king,
  As little joy you may suppose in me
  That I enjoy, being the queen thereof.
QUEEN MARGARET. As little joy enjoys the queen thereof;

For I am she, and altogether joyless.
I can no longer hold me patient.   *Advancing*
Hear me, you wrangling pirates, that fall out
In sharing that which you have pill'd from me!
Which of you trembles not that looks on me?
If not, that, I being queen, you bow like subjects,
Yet that, by you depos'd, you quake like rebels?
Ah! gentle villain, do not turn away.

GLOUCESTER. Foul wrinkled witch, what makest thou in my
        sight?

QUEEN MARGARET. But repetition of what thou hast marr'd;
    That will I make before I let thee go.

GLOUCESTER. Wert thou not banished on pain of death?

QUEEN MARGARET. I was; but I do find more pain in
        banishment
    Than death can yield me here by my abode.
    A husband and a son thou owest to me;
    And thou, a kingdom; all of you, allegiance:
    This sorrow that I have, by right is yours,
    And all the pleasures you usurp are mine.

GLOUCESTER. The curse my noble father laid on thee,
    When thou didst crown his warlike brows with paper,
    And with thy scorns drew'st rivers from his eyes;
    And then, to dry them, gavest the duke a clout
    Steep'd in the faultless blood of pretty Rutland;
    His curses, then from bitterness of soul
    Denounc'd against thee, are all fall'n upon thee;
    And God, not we, hath plagu'd thy bloody deed.

QUEEN ELIZABETH. So just is God, to right the innocent.

HASTINGS. O! 'twas the foulest deed to slay that babe,
    And the most merciless, that e'er was heard of.

RIVERS. Tyrants themselves wept when it was reported.

DORSET. No man but prophesied revenge for it.

BUCKINGHAM. Northumberland, then present, wept to see it.

QUEEN MARGARET. What! were you snarling all before I
        came,
    Ready to catch each other by the throat,
    And turn you all your hatred now on me?
    Did York's dread curse prevail so much with heaven
    That Henry's death, my lovely Edward's death,
    Their kingdom's loss, my woeful banishment,
    Should all but answer for that peevish brat?

Can curses pierce the clouds and enter heaven?
Why then, give way, dull clouds, to my quick curses!
Though not by war, by surfeit die your king,
As ours by murder, to make him a king!
Edward, thy son, that now is Prince of Wales,
For Edward, my son, which was Prince of Wales,
Die in his youth by like untimely violence!
Thyself a queen, for me that was a queen,
Outlive thy glory, like my wretched self!
Long mayst thou live to wail thy children's loss,
And see another, as I see thee now,
Deck'd in thy rights, as thou art stall'd in mine!
Long die thy happy days before thy death;
And, after many lengthen'd hours of grief,
Die neither mother, wife, nor England's queen!
Rivers, and Dorset, you were standers-by,—
And so wast thou, Lord Hastings,—when my son
Was stabb'd with bloody daggers: God, I pray him,
That none of you may live your natural age,
But by some unlook'd accident cut off.

GLOUCESTER. Have done thy charm, thou hateful wither'd
hag!

QUEEN MARGARET. And leave out thee? stay, dog, for thou
shalt hear me.
If heaven have any grievous plague in store
Exceeding those that I can wish upon thee,
O! let them keep it till thy sins be ripe,
And then hurl down their indignation
On thee, the troubler of the poor world's peace.
The worm of conscience still begnaw thy soul!
Thy friends suspect for traitors while thou livest
And take deep traitors for thy dearest friends!
No sleep close up that deadly eye of thine,
Unless it be while some tormenting dream
Affrights thee with a hell of ugly devils!
Thou elvish-mark'd, abortive, rooting hog!
Thou that wast seal'd in thy nativity
The slave of nature and the son of hell!
Thou slander of thy mother's heavy womb!
Thou loathed issue of thy father's loins!
Thou rag of honour! thou detested—

GLOUCESTER. Margaret!

QUEEN MARGARET.   Richard!

GLOUCESTER.   Ha!

QUEEN MARGARET.   I call thee not.

GLOUCESTER. I cry thee mercy then, for I did think
  That thou hadst call'd me all these bitter names.

QUEEN MARGARET. Why, so I did; but look'd for no reply.
  O! let me make the period to my curse.

GLOUCESTER. 'Tis done by me, and ends in 'Margaret.'

QUEEN ELIZABETH. Thus have you breath'd your curse
    against yourself.

QUEEN MARGARET. Poor painted queen, vain flourish of my
    fortune!
  Why strew'st thou sugar on that bottled spider,
  Whose deadly web ensnareth thee about?
  Fool, fool! thou whet'st a knife to kill thyself.
  The day will come that thou shalt wish for me
  To help thee curse this poisonous bunch-back'd toad.

HASTINGS. False-boding woman, end thy frantic curse,
  Lest to thy harm thou move our patience.

QUEEN MARGARET. Foul shame upon you! you have all
    mov'd mine.

RIVERS. Were you well serv'd, you would be taught your
    duty.

QUEEN MARGARET. To serve me well, you all should do me
    duty,
  Teach me to be your queen, and you my subjects:
  O! serve me well, and teach yourselves that duty.

DORSET. Dispute not with her, she is lunatic.

QUEEN MARGARET. Peace! Master marquess, you are
    malapert:
  Your fire-new stamp of honour is scarce current.
  O! that your young nobility could judge
  What 'twere to lose it, and be miserable!
  They that stand high have many blasts to shake them,
  And if they fall, they dash themselves to pieces.

GLOUCESTER. Good counsel, marry: learn it, learn it,
    marquess.

DORSET. It touches you, my lord, as much as me.

GLOUCESTER. Ay, and much more; but I was born so high,
  Our aery buildeth in the cedar's top,
  And dallies with the wind, and scorns the sun.

QUEEN MARGARET. And turns the sun to shade; alas! alas!

Witness my son, now in the shade of death;
Whose bright out-shining beams thy cloudy wrath
Hath in eternal darkness folded up.
Your aery buildeth in our aery's nest:
O God! that seest it, do not suffer it;
As it was won with blood, lost be it so!

BUCKINGHAM. Peace, peace! for shame, if not for charity.

QUEEN MARGARET. Urge neither charity nor shame to me:
Uncharitably with me have you dealt,
And shamefully my hopes by you are butcher'd.
My charity is outrage, life my shame;
And in that shame still live my sorrow's rage!

BUCKINGHAM. Have done, have done.

QUEEN MARGARET. O princely Buckingham! I 'll kiss thy
hand,
In sign of league and amity with thee:
Now fair befall thee and thy noble house!
Thy garments are not spotted with our blood,
Nor thou within the compass of my curse.

BUCKINGHAM. Nor no one here; for curses never pass
The lips of those that breathe them in the air.

QUEEN MARGARET. I will not think but they ascend the sky,
And there awake God's gentle-sleeping peace.
O Buckingham! take heed of yonder dog:
Look, when he fawns, he bites; and when he bites
His venom tooth will rankle to the death:
Have not to do with him, beware of him;
Sin, death and hell have set their marks on him,
And all their ministers attend on him.

GLOUCESTER. What doth she say, my Lord of Buckingham?

BUCKINGHAM. Nothing that I respect, my gracious lord.

QUEEN MARGARET. What! dost thou scorn me for my gentle
counsel,
And soothe the devil that I warn thee from?
O! but remember this another day,
When he shall split thy very heart with sorrow,
And say poor Margaret was a prophetess.
Live each of you the subject to his hate,
And he to yours, and all of you to God's!   *Exit*

HASTINGS. My hair doth stand on end to hear her curses.

RIVERS. And so doth mine. I muse why she 's at liberty.

GLOUCESTER. I cannot blame her: by God's holy mother,

She hath had too much wrong, and I repent
My part thereof that I have done to her.

QUEEN ELIZABETH. I never did her any, to my knowledge.

GLOUCESTER. Yet you have all the vantage of her wrong.
I was too hot to do somebody good,
That is too cold in thinking of it now.
Marry, as for Clarence, he is well repaid;
He is frank'd up to fatting for his pains:
God pardon them that are the cause thereof!

RIVERS. A virtuous and a Christian-like conclusion,
To pray for them that have done scath to us.

GLOUCESTER. So do I ever, (*Aside*) being well-advis'd;
For had I curs'd now, I had curs'd myself.

Enter Catesby

CATESBY. Madam, his Majesty doth call for you;
And for your Grace; and you, my noble lords.

QUEEN ELIZABETH. Catesby, I come. Lords, will you go with
me?

RIVERS. We wait upon your Grace.

Exeunt all but Gloucester

GLOUCESTER. I do the wrong, and first begin to brawl.
The secret mischiefs that I set abroach
I lay unto the grievous charge of others.
Clarence, whom I, indeed, have cast in darkness,
I do beweep to many simple gulls;
Namely, to Stanley, Hastings, Buckingham;
And tell them 'tis the queen and her allies
That stir the king against the duke my brother.
Now they believe it; and withal whet me
To be reveng'd on Rivers, Vaughan, Grey;
But then I sigh, and, with a piece of scripture,
Tell them that God bids us do good for evil:
And thus I clothe my naked villany
With odd old ends stolen forth of holy writ,
And seem a saint when most I play the devil.

Enter two Murderers

But soft! here come my executioners.
How now, my hardy, stout, resolved mates!
Are you now going to dispatch this thing?

FIRST MURDERER. We are, my lord; and come to have the
warrant,
That we may be admitted where he is.

GLOUCESTER. Well thought upon; I have it here about me:

Gives the warrant

When you have done, repair to Crosby-place.
But, sirs, be sudden in the execution,
Withal obdurate, do not hear him plead;
For Clarence is well-spoken, and perhaps
May move your hearts to pity, if you mark him.

FIRST MURDERER. Tut, tut, my lord, we will not stand to
    prate;
Talkers are no good doers: be assur'd
We go to use our hands and not our tongues.

GLOUCESTER. Your eyes drop millstones, when fools' eyes
    fall tears:
I like you, lads; about your business straight;
Go, go, dispatch.

FIRST MURDERER.   We will, my noble lord.   *Exeunt*

SCENE FOUR

The Same. The Tower.

Enter Clarence and Brakenbury

BRAKENBURY. Why looks your Grace so heavily to-day?

CLARENCE. O, I have pass'd a miserable night,
So full of ugly sights, of ghastly dreams,
That, as I am a Christian faithful man,
I would not spend another such a night,
Though 'twere to buy a world of happy days,
So full of dismal terror was the time.

BRAKENBURY. What was your dream, my lord? I pray you,
    tell me.

CLARENCE. Methought that I had broken from the Tower,
And was embark'd to cross to Burgundy;
And in my company my brother Gloucester,
Who from my cabin tempted me to walk
Upon the hatches: thence we look'd toward England,
And cited up a thousand heavy times,
During the wars of York and Lancaster,
That had befall'n us. As we pac'd along
Upon the giddy footing of the hatches,
Methought that Gloucester stumbled; and, in falling,

Struck me, that thought to stay him, overboard,
Into the tumbling billows of the main.
Lord, Lord! methought what pain it was to drown:
What dreadful noise of water in mine ears!
What sights of ugly death within mine eyes!
Methought I saw a thousand fearful wracks;
A thousand men that fishes gnaw'd upon;
Wedges of gold, great anchors, heaps of pearl,
Inestimable stones, unvalu'd jewels,
All scatter'd in the bottom of the sea.
Some lay in dead men's skulls; and in those holes
Where eyes did once inhabit, there were crept,
As 'twere in scorn of eyes, reflecting gems,
That woo'd the slimy bottom of the deep,
And mock'd the dead bones that lay scatter'd by.
BRAKENBURY. Had you such leisure in the time of death
To gaze upon these secrets of the deep?
CLARENCE. Methought I had; and often did I strive
To yield the ghost; but still the envious flood
Stopt in my soul, and would not let it forth
To find the empty, vast, and wandering air;
But smother'd it within my panting bulk,
Which almost burst to belch it in the sea.
BRAKENBURY. Awak'd you not with this sore agony?
CLARENCE. No, no, my dream was lengthen'd after life;
O! then began the tempest to my soul.
I pass'd, methought, the melancholy flood,
With that grim ferryman which poets write of,
Unto the kingdom of perpetual night.
The first that there did greet my stranger soul,
Was my great father-in-law, renowned Warwick;
Who cried aloud, 'What scourge for perjury
Can this dark monarchy afford false Clarence?'
And so he vanish'd: then came wandering by
A shadow like an angel, with bright hair
Dabbled in blood; and he shriek'd out aloud,
'Clarence is come,—false, fleeting, perjur'd Clarence,
That stabb'd me in the field by Tewksbury;—
Seize on him! Furies, take him unto torment.'
With that, methought, a legion of foul fiends
Environ'd me, and howled in mine ears
Such hideous cries, that with the very noise

I trembling wak'd, and, for a season after,
Could not believe but that I was in hell,
Such terrible impression made my dream.

BRAKENBURY. No marvel, lord, though it affrighted you;
I am afraid, methinks, to hear you tell it.

CLARENCE. O Brakenbury! I have done these things
That now give evidence against my soul,
For Edward's sake; and see how he requites me.
O God! if my deep prayers cannot appease thee,
But thou wilt be aveng'd on my misdeeds,
Yet execute thy wrath on me alone:
O! spare my guiltless wife and my poor children.
I pray thee, gentle keeper, stay by me;
My soul is heavy, and I fain would sleep.

BRAKENBURY. I will, my lord. God give your Grace good
rest!   *Clarence sleeps*

Sorrow breaks seasons and reposing hours,
Makes the night morning, and the noon-tide night.
Princes have but their titles for their glories,
An outward honour for an inward toil;
And, for unfelt imaginations,
They often feel a world of restless cares:
So that, between their titles and low names,
There's nothing differs but the outward fame.

Enter the two Murderers

FIRST MURDERER. Ho! who's here?

BRAKENBURY. What wouldst thou, fellow? and how cam'st
thou hither?

FIRST MURDERER. I would speak with Clarence, and
I came hither on my legs.

BRAKENBURY. What! so brief?

SECOND MURDERER. 'Tis better, sir, than to be tedious.—
Let him see our commission, and talk no more.

A paper is delivered to Brakenbury, who reads it

BRAKENBURY. I am, in this, commanded to deliver
The noble Duke of Clarence to your hands:
I will not reason what is meant hereby,
Because I will be guiltless of the meaning.
There lies the duke asleep, and there the keys.
I'll to the king; and signify to him
That thus I have resign'd to you my charge.

FIRST MURDERER. You may, sir; 'tis a point of wisdom: fare
   you well.   *Exit Brakenbury*
SECOND MURDERER. What! shall we stab him as he sleeps?
FIRST MURDERER. No; he 'll say 'twas done cowardly, when
   he wakes.
SECOND MURDERER. When he wakes! why, fool, he shall
   never wake till the judgment-day.
FIRST MURDERER. Why, then he 'll say we stabbed him sleep-
   ing.
SECOND MURDERER. The urging of that word 'judgment'
   hath bred a kind of remorse in me.
FIRST MURDERER. What! art thou afraid?
SECOND MURDERER. Not to kill him, having a warrant for it;
   but to be damn'd for killing him, from the which no war-
   rant can defend me.
FIRST MURDERER. I thought thou hadst been resolute.
SECOND MURDERER. So I am, to let him live.
FIRST MURDERER. I 'll back to the Duke of Gloucester, and
   tell him so.
SECOND MURDERER. Nay, I prithee, stay a little: I hope my
   holy humour will change; it was wont to hold me but
   while one tells twenty.
FIRST MURDERER. How dost thou feel thyself now?
SECOND MURDERER. Some certain dregs of conscience a·e
   yet within me.
FIRST MURDERER. Remember our reward when the deed's
   done.
SECOND MURDERER. 'Zounds! he dies: I had forgot the re-
   ward.
FIRST MURDERER. Where 's thy conscience now?
SECOND MURDERER. In the Duke of Gloucester's purse.
FIRST MURDERER. So when he opens his purse to give us our
   reward, thy conscience flies out.
SECOND MURDERER. 'Tis no matter; let it go: there 's few or
   none will entertain it.
FIRST MURDERER. What if it comes to thee again?
SECOND MURDERER. I 'll not meddle with it; it makes a man a
   coward; a man cannot steal, but it accuseth him; a man
   cannot swear, but it checks him; a man cannot lie with his
   neighbour's wife, but it detects him: 'tis a blushing shame-
   fast spirit, that mutinies in a man's bosom; it fills one full

of obstacles; it made me once restore a purse of gold that
I found; it beggars any man that keeps it; it is turned out
of all towns and cities for a dangerous thing; and every
man that means to live well, endeavours to trust to himself
and live without it.

FIRST MURDERER. 'Zounds! it is even now at my elbow, per-
suading me not to kill the duke.

SECOND MURDERER. Take the devil in thy mind, and believe
him not: he would insinuate with thee but to make thee
sigh.

FIRST MURDERER. Tut, I am strong-framed; he cannot pre-
vail with me.

SECOND MURDERER. Spoke like a tall fellow that respects his
reputation. Come, shall we to this gear?

FIRST MURDERER. Take him over the costard with the hilts
of thy sword, and then throw him into the malmsey-butt
in the next room.

SECOND MURDERER. O, excellent device! make a sop of him.

FIRST MURDERER. Soft! he wakes.

SECOND MURDERER. Strike!

FIRST MURDERER. No, we 'll reason with him.

CLARENCE. Where art thou, keeper? give me a cup of wine.

FIRST MURDERER. You shall have wine enough, my lord,
anon.

CLARENCE. In God's name, what art thou?

FIRST MURDERER. A man, as you are.

CLARENCE. But not, as I am, royal.

FIRST MURDERER. Nor you, as we are, loyal.

CLARENCE. Thy voice is thunder, but thy looks are humble.

FIRST MURDERER. My voice is now the king's, my looks mine
own.

CLARENCE. How darkly, and how deadly dost thou speak!
Your eyes do menace me: why look you pale?
Who sent you hither? Wherefore do you come?

BOTH MURDERERS. To, to, to—

CLARENCE. To murder me?

BOTH MURDERERS. Ay, ay.

CLARENCE. You scarcely have the hearts to tell me so,
And therefore cannot have the hearts to do it.
Wherein, my friends, have I offended you?

FIRST MURDERER. Offended us you have not, but the king.

CLARENCE. I shall be reconcil'd to him again.

SECOND MURDERER. Never, my lord; therefore prepare to
 die.

CLARENCE. Are you call'd forth from out a world of men
 To slay the innocent? What is my offence?
 Where is the evidence that doth accuse me?
 What lawful quest have given their verdict up
 Unto the frowning judge? or who pronounc'd
 The bitter sentence of poor Clarence' death?
 Before I be convict by course of law,
 To threaten me with death is most unlawful.
 I charge you, as you hope to have redemption
 By Christ's dear blood shed for our grievous sins,
 That you depart and lay no hands on me;
 The deed you undertake is damnable.

FIRST MURDERER. What we will do, we do upon command.

SECOND MURDERER. And he that hath commanded is our
 king.

CLARENCE. Erroneous vassal! the great King of Kings
 Hath in the table of his law commanded
 That thou shalt do no murder: will you, then,
 Spurn at his edict and fulfil a man's?
 Take heed; for he holds vengeance in his hand,
 To hurl upon their heads that break his law.

SECOND MURDERER. And that same vengeance doth he hurl
 on thee,
 For false forswearing and for murder too:
 Thou didst receive the sacrament to fight
 In quarrel of the house of Lancaster.

FIRST MURDERER. And, like a traitor to the name of God,
 Didst break that vow, and, with thy treacherous blade
 Unripp'dst the bowels of thy sovereign's son.

SECOND MURDERER. Whom thou wast sworn to cherish and
 defend.

FIRST MURDERER. How canst thou urge God's dreadful law
 to us,
 When thou hast broke it in such dear degree?

CLARENCE. Alas! for whose sake did I that ill deed?
 For Edward, for my brother, for his sake:
 He sends you not to murder me for this;
 For in that sin he is as deep as I.
 If God will be avenged for the deed,
 O! know you yet, he doth it publicly:

Take not the quarrel from his powerful arm;
He needs no indirect or lawless course
To cut off those that have offended him.

FIRST MURDERER. Who made thee then a bloody minister,
When gallant-springing, brave Plantagenet,
That princely novice, was struck dead by thee?

CLARENCE. My brother's love, the devil, and my rage.

FIRST MURDERER. Thy brother's love, our duty, and thy
fault,
Provoke us hither now to slaughter thee.

CLARENCE. If you do love my brother, hate not me;
I am his brother, and I love him well.
If you are hir'd for meed, go back again,
And I will send you to my brother Gloucester,
Who shall reward you better for my life
Than Edward will for tidings of my death.

SECOND MURDERER. You are deceiv'd, your brother
Gloucester hates you.

CLARENCE. O, no! he loves me, and he holds me dear:
Go you to him from me.

BOTH MURDERERS.   Ay, so we will.

CLARENCE. Tell him, when that our princely father York
Bless'd his three sons with his victorious arm,
And charg'd us from his soul to love each other,
He little thought of this divided friendship:
Bid Gloucester think on this, and he will weep.

FIRST MURDERER. Ay, millstones; as he lesson'd us to weep.

CLARENCE. O! do not slander him, for he is kind.

FIRST MURDERER. Right;
As snow in harvest. Thou deceiv'st thyself:
'Tis he that sends us to destroy you here.

CLARENCE. It cannot be; for he bewept my fortune,
And hugg'd me in his arms, and swore, with sobs,
That he would labour my delivery.

FIRST MURDERER. Why, so he doth, when he delivers you
From this earth's thraldom to the joys of heaven.

SECOND MURDERER. Make peace with God, for you must die,
my lord.

CLARENCE. Hast thou that holy feeling in thy soul,
To counsel me to make my peace with God,
And art thou yet to thy own soul so blind,
That thou wilt war with God by murdering me?

O! sirs, consider, he that set you on
To do this deed, will hate you for the deed.
SECOND MURDERER. What shall we do?
CLARENCE.   Relent, and save your souls.
FIRST MURDERER. Relent! 'tis cowardly, and womanish.
CLARENCE. Not to relent is beastly, savage, devilish.
    Which of you, if you were a prince's son,
    Being pent from liberty, as I am now,
    If two such murderers as yourselves came to you,
    Would not entreat for life?
    My friend, I spy some pity in thy looks;
    O! if thine eye be not a flatterer,
    Come thou on my side, and entreat for me,
    As you would beg, were you in my distress:
    A begging prince what beggar pities not?
SECOND MURDERER. Look behind you, my lord.
FIRST MURDERER. (*Stabs him*) Take that, and that: if all this
        will not do,
    I 'll drown you in the malmsey-butt within.
                                                Exit with the body
SECOND MURDERER. A bloody deed, and desperately
        dispatch'd!
    How fain, like Pilate, would I wash my hands
    Of this most grievous murder.
                    Re-enter first Murderer
FIRST MURDERER. How now! what mean'st thou, that thou
        help'st me not?
    By heaven, the duke shall know how slack you have been.
SECOND MURDERER. I would he knew that I had sav'd his
        brother!
    Take thou the fee, and tell him what I say;
    For I repent me that the duke is slain.   *Exit*
FIRST MURDERER. So do not I: go, coward as thou art.
    Well, I 'll go hide the body in some hole,
    Till that the duke give order for his burial:
    And when I have my meed, I will away;
    For this will out, and here I must not stay.   *Exit*

ACT TWO

SCENE ONE

London. A Room in the Palace.

Enter King Edward sick, Queen Elizabeth, Dorset, Rivers, Hastings, Buckingham, Grey, and Others

KING EDWARD. Why, so: now have I done a good day's work.
  You peers, continue this united league:
  I every day expect an embassage
  From my Redeemer to redeem me hence;
  And more in peace my soul shall part to heaven,
  Since I have made my friends at peace on earth.
  Rivers and Hastings, take each other's hand;
  Dissemble not your hatred, swear your love.
RIVERS. By heaven, my soul is purg'd from grudging hate;
  And with my hand I seal my true heart's love.
HASTINGS. So thrive I, as I truly swear the like!
KING EDWARD. Take heed, you dally not before your king;
  Lest he that is the supreme King of Kings
  Confound your hidden falsehood, and award
  Either of you to be the other's end.
HASTINGS. So prosper I, as I swear perfect love!
RIVERS. And I, as I love Hastings with my heart!
KING EDWARD. Madam, yourself are not exempt in this,
  Nor you, son Dorset, Buckingham, nor you;
  You have been factious one against the other.
  Wife, love Lord Hastings, let him kiss your hand;
  And what you do, do it unfeignedly.
QUEEN ELIZABETH. There, Hastings; I will never more remember
  Our former hatred, so thrive I and mine!
KING EDWARD. Dorset, embrace him; Hastings, love Lord Marquess.
DORSET. This interchange of love, I here protest,
  Upon my part shall be inviolable.

HASTINGS. And so swear I. *They embrace*
KING EDWARD. Now, princely Buckingham, seal thou this league
　With thy embracements to my wife's allies,
　And make me happy in your unity.
BUCKINGHAM. (*To the Queen*) Whenever Buckingham doth turn his hate
　Upon your Grace, but with all duteous love
　Doth cherish you and yours, God punish me
　With hate in those where I expect most love!
　When I have most need to employ a friend,
　And most assured that he is a friend,
　Deep, hollow, treacherous, and full of guile,
　Be he unto me! This do I beg of God,
　When I am cold in love to you or yours. *They embrace*
KING EDWARD. A pleasing cordial, princely Buckingham,
　Is this thy vow unto my sickly heart.
　There wanteth now our brother Gloucester here
　To make the blessed period of this peace.
BUCKINGHAM. And, in good time, here comes the noble duke.

　　　　　Enter Gloucester

GLOUCESTER. Good-morrow to my sovereign king and queen;
　And princely peers, a happy time of day!
KING EDWARD. Happy, indeed, as we have spent the day.
　Gloucester, we have done deeds of charity;
　Made peace of enmity, fair love of hate,
　Between these swelling wrong-incensed peers.
GLOUCESTER. A blessed labour, my most sovereign lord.
　Among this princely heap, if any here,
　By false intelligence, or wrong surmise,
　Hold me a foe;
　If I unwittingly, or in my rage,
　Have aught committed that is hardly borne
　By any in this presence, I desire
　To reconcile me to his friendly peace:
　'Tis death to me to be at enmity;
　I hate it, and desire all good men's love.
　First, madam, I entreat true peace of you,
　Which I will purchase with my duteous service;
　Of you, my noble cousin Buckingham,

If ever any grudge were lodg'd between us;
Of you, Lord Rivers, and Lord Grey, of you,
That all without desert have frown'd on me;
Of you, Lord Woodvile, and Lord Scales, of you;
Dukes, earls, lords, gentlemen; indeed, of all.
I do not know that Englishman alive
With whom my soul is any jot at odds
More than the infant that is born to-night:
I thank my God for my humility.

QUEEN ELIZABETH. A holy day shall this be kept hereafter:
I would to God all strifes were well compounded.
My sovereign lord, I do beseech your Highness
To take our brother Clarence to your grace.

GLOUCESTER. Why, madam, have I offer'd love for this,
To be so flouted in this royal presence?
Who knows not that the gentle duke is dead?

They all start

You do him injury to scorn his corse.

KING EDWARD. Who knows not he is dead! who knows he is?

QUEEN ELIZABETH. All-seeing heaven, what a world is this!

BUCKINGHAM. Look I so pale, Lord Dorset, as the rest?

DORSET. Ay, my good lord; and no man in the presence
But his red colour hath forsook his cheeks.

KING EDWARD. Is Clarence dead? the order was revers'd.

GLOUCESTER. But he, poor man, by your first order died,
And that a winged Mercury did bear;
Some tardy cripple bore the countermand,
That came too lag to see him buried.
God grant that some, less noble and less loyal,
Nearer in bloody thoughts, and not in blood,
Deserve not worse than wretched Clarence did,
And yet go current from suspicion.

Enter Stanley

STANLEY. A boon, my sovereign, for my service done!

KING EDWARD. I prithee, peace: my soul is full of sorrow.

STANLEY. I will not rise, unless your Highness hear me.

KING EDWARD. Then say at once, what is it thou request'st.

STANLEY. The forfeit, sovereign, of my servant's life;
Who slew to-day a riotous gentleman
Lately attendant on the Duke of Norfolk.

KING EDWARD. Have I a tongue to doom my brother's death,
And shall that tongue give pardon to a slave?

My brother kill'd no man, his fault was thought;
And yet his punishment was bitter death.
Who su'd to me for him? who, in my wrath,
Kneel'd at my feet, and bade me be advis'd?
Who spoke of brotherhood? who spoke of love?
Who told me how the poor soul did forsake
The mighty Warwick, and did fight for me?
Who told me, in the field at Tewksbury,
When Oxford had me down, he rescu'd me,
And said, 'Dear brother, live, and be a king'?
Who told me, when we both lay in the field
Frozen almost to death, how he did lap me
Even in his garments; and did give himself,
All thin and naked, to the numb cold night?
All this from my remembrance brutish wrath
Sinfully pluck'd, and not a man of you
Had so much grace to put it in my mind.
But when your carters or your waiting-vassals
Have done a drunken slaughter, and defac'd
The precious image of our dear Redeemer,
You straight are on your knees for pardon, pardon;
And I, unjustly too, must grant it you;
But for my brother not a man would speak,
Nor I, ungracious, speak unto myself
For him, poor soul. The proudest of you all
Have been beholding to him in his life,
Yet none of you would once beg for his life.
O God! I fear, thy justice will take hold
On me and you and mine and yours for this.
Come, Hastings, help me to my closet. O! poor Clarence!
                    Exeunt King Edward,
          Queen, Hastings, Rivers, Dorset, and Grey
GLOUCESTER. This is the fruit of rashness. Mark'd you not
    How that the guilty kindred of the queen
    Look'd pale when they did hear of Clarence' death?
    O! they did urge it still unto the king:
    God will revenge it. Come, lords; will you go
    To comfort Edward with our company?
BUCKINGHAM. We wait upon your Grace.   *Exeunt*

SCENE TWO

The Same. A Room in the Palace.

Enter the Duchess of York, with a Son and Daughter of Clarence

BOY. Good grandam, tell us, is our father dead?
DUCHESS. No, boy.
DAUGHTER. Why do you wring your hands, and beat your
    breast,
    And cry—'O Clarence, my unhappy son'?
BOY. Why do you look on us, and shake your head,
    And call us orphans, wretches, castaways,
    If that our noble father be alive?
DUCHESS. My pretty cousins, you mistake me much;
    I do lament the sickness of the king,
    As loath to lose him, not your father's death;
    It were lost sorrow to wail one that's lost.
BOY. Then, grandam, you conclude that he is dead.
    The king mine uncle is to blame for it:
    God will revenge it; whom I will importune
    With earnest prayers all to that effect.
DAUGHTER. And so will I.
DUCHESS. Peace, children, peace! the king doth love you
    well:
    Incapable and shallow innocents,
    You cannot guess who caus'd your father's death.
BOY. Grandam, we can; for my good uncle Gloucester
    Told me, the king, provok'd to 't by the queen,
    Devis'd impeachments to imprison him:
    And when my uncle told me so, he wept,
    And pitied me, and kindly kiss'd my cheek;
    Bade me rely on him, as on my father,
    And he would love me dearly as his child.
DUCHESS. Ah! that deceit should steal such gentle shape,
    And with a virtuous vizard hide deep vice.
    He is my son, ay, and therein my shame,
    Yet from my dugs he drew not this deceit.
BOY. Think you my uncle did dissemble, grandam?
DUCHESS. Ay, boy.

BOY. I cannot think it. Hark! what noise is this?

Enter Queen Elizabeth,
distractedly; Rivers and Dorset following her

QUEEN ELIZABETH. Oh! who shall hinder me to wail and
weep,
To chide my fortune, and torment myself?
I 'll join with black despair against my soul,
And to myself become an enemy.

DUCHESS. What means this scene of rude impatience?

QUEEN ELIZABETH. To make an act of tragic violence:
Edward, my lord, thy son, our king, is dead!
Why grow the branches now the root is wither'd?
Why wither not the leaves that want their sap?
If you will live, lament: if die, be brief,
That our swift-winged souls may catch the king's;
Or, like obedient subjects, follow him
To his new kingdom of perpetual rest.

DUCHESS. Ah! so much interest have I in thy sorrow
As I had title in thy noble husband.
I have bewept a worthy husband's death,
And liv'd with looking on his images;
But now two mirrors of his princely semblance
Are crack'd in pieces by malignant death,
And I for comfort have but one false glass,
That grieves me when I see my shame in him.
Thou art a widow; yet thou art a mother,
And hast the comfort of thy children left thee:
But death hath snatch'd my husband from mine arms,
And pluck'd two crutches from my feeble limbs,
Clarence and Edward. O! what cause have I—
Thine being but a moiety of my grief—
To overgo thy plaints, and drown thy cries!

BOY. Ah, aunt, you wept not for our father's death;
How can we aid you with our kindred tears?

DAUGHTER. Our fatherless distress was left unmoan'd;
Your widow-dolour likewise be unwept.

QUEEN ELIZABETH. Give me no help in lamentation;
I am not barren to bring forth complaints:
All springs reduce their currents to mine eyes,
That I, being govern'd by the watery moon,
May send forth plenteous tears to drown the world!
Ah! for my husband, for my dear Lord Edward!

CHILDREN. Ah! for our father, for our dear Lord Clarence!

DUCHESS. Alas! for both, both mine, Edward and Clarence!

QUEEN ELIZABETH. What stay had I but Edward? and he 's gone.

CHILDREN. What stay had we but Clarence? and he 's gone.

DUCHESS. What stays had I but they? and they are gone.

QUEEN ELIZABETH. Was never widow had so dear a loss.

CHILDREN. Were never orphans had so dear a loss.

DUCHESS. Was never mother had so dear a loss.
 Alas! I am the mother of these griefs:
 Their woes are parcell'd, mine are general.
 She for an Edward weeps, and so do I;
 I for a Clarence weep, so doth not she:
 These babes for Clarence weep, and so do I;
 I for an Edward weep, so do not they:
 Alas! you three, on me, threefold distress'd,
 Pour all your tears; I am your sorrow's nurse,
 And I will pamper it with lamentation.

DORSET. Comfort, dear mother: God is much displeas'd
 That you take with unthankfulness his doing.
 In common worldly things 'tis call'd ungrateful
 With dull unwillingness to repay a debt
 Which with a bounteous hand was kindly lent;
 Much more to be thus opposite with heaven,
 For it requires the royal debt it lent you.

RIVERS. Madam, bethink you, like a careful mother,
 Of the young prince your son: send straight for him;
 Let him be crown'd; in him your comfort lives.
 Drown desperate sorrow in dead Edward's grave,
 And plant your joys in living Edward's throne.
 Enter Gloucester, Buckingham,
 Stanley, Hastings, Ratcliff, and Others

GLOUCESTER. Sister, have comfort: all of us have cause
 To wail the dimming of our shining star;
 But none can cure their harms by wailing them.
 Madam, my mother, I do cry you mercy;
 I did not see your Grace: humbly on my knee
 I crave your blessing.

DUCHESS. God bless thee! and put meekness in thy mind,
 Love, charity, obedience, and true duty.

GLOUCESTER. Amen; (*Aside*) and make me die a good old man!

That is the butt-end of a mother's blessing;
I marvel that her Grace did leave it out.

BUCKINGHAM. You cloudy princes and heart-sorrowing
    peers,
That bear this heavy mutual load of moan,
Now cheer each other in each other's love:
Though we have spent our harvest of this king,
We are to reap the harvest of his son.
The broken rancour of your high-swoln hearts,
But lately splinter'd, knit, and join'd together,
Must gently be preserv'd, cherish'd, and kept:
Me seemeth good, that, with some little train,
Forthwith from Ludlow the young prince be fetch'd
Hither to London, to be crown'd our king.

RIVERS. Why with some little train, my Lord of Buck-
    ingham?

BUCKINGHAM. Marry, my lord, lest, by a multitude,
The new-heal'd wound of malice should break out;
Which would be so much the more dangerous.
By how much the estate is green and yet ungovern'd:
Where every horse bears his commanding rein,
And may direct his course as please himself,
As well the fear of harm, as harm apparent,
In my opinion, ought to be prevented.

GLOUCESTER. I hope the king made peace with all of us;
And the compact is firm and true in me.

RIVERS. And so in me; and so, I think, in all:
Yet, since it is but green, it should be put
To no apparent likelihood of breach,
Which haply by much company might be urg'd:
Therefore I say with noble Buckingham,
That it is meet so few should fetch the prince.

HASTINGS. And so say I.

GLOUCESTER. Then be it so; and go we to determine
Who they shall be that straight shall post to Ludlow.
Madam, and you my mother, will you go
To give your censures in this business?

       Exeunt all except Buckingham and Gloucester

BUCKINGHAM. My lord, whoever journeys to the prince,
For God's sake, let not us two stay at home:
For by the way I'll sort occasion,
As index to the story we late talk'd of,

To part the queen's proud kindred from the prince.   1-21]

GLOUCESTER. My other self, my counsel's consistory,
  My oracle, my prophet! My dear cousin,
  I, as a child, will go by thy direction.
  Towards Ludlow then, for we 'll not stay behind. *Exeunt*

SCENE THREE

The Same. A Street.

Enter two Citizens, meeting

FIRST CITIZEN. Good-morrow, neighbour: whither away so
  fast?

SECOND CITIZEN. I promise you, I scarcely know myself:
  Hear you the news abroad?

FIRST CITIZEN.   Ay; that the king is dead.

SECOND CITIZEN. Ill news, by 'r lady; seldom comes the
  better:
  I fear, I fear, 'twill prove a giddy world.

Enter a third Citizen

THIRD CITIZEN. Neighbours, God speed!

FIRST CITIZEN.   Give you good-morrow, sir.

THIRD CITIZEN. Doth the news hold of good King Edward's
  death?

SECOND CITIZEN. Ay, sir, it is too true; God help the while!

THIRD CITIZEN. Then, masters, look to see a troublous world.

FIRST CITIZEN. No, no; by God's good grace, his son shall
  reign.

THIRD CITIZEN. Woe to that land that 's govern'd by a child!

SECOND CITIZEN. In him there is a hope of government,
  That in his nonage council under him,
  And in his full and ripen'd years himself,
  No doubt, shall then and till then govern well.

FIRST CITIZEN. So stood the state when Henry the Sixth
  Was crown'd at Paris but at nine months old.

THIRD CITIZEN. Stood the state so? no, no, good friends, God
  wot;
  For then this land was famously enrich'd
  With politic grave counsel; then the king
  Had virtuous uncles to protect his Grace.

FIRST CITIZEN. Why, so hath this, both by his father and
    mother.
THIRD CITIZEN. Better it were they all came by his father,
    Or by his father there were none at all;
    For emulation, who shall now be nearest,
    Will touch us all too near, if God prevent not.
    O! full of danger is the Duke of Gloucester!
    And the queen's sons and brothers haught and proud;
    And were they to be rul'd, and not to rule,
    This sickly land might solace as before.
FIRST CITIZEN. Come, come, we fear the worst; all will be
    well.
THIRD CITIZEN. When clouds are seen, wise men put on their
    cloaks;
    When great leaves fall, then winter is at hand;
    When the sun sets, who doth not look for night?
    Untimely storms make men expect a dearth.
    All may be well; but, if God sort it so,
    'Tis more than we deserve, or I expect.
SECOND CITIZEN. Truly, the hearts of men are full of fear:
    You cannot reason almost with a man
    That looks not heavily and full of dread.
THIRD CITIZEN. Before the days of change, still is it so:
    By a divine instinct men's minds mistrust
    Ensuing danger; as, by proof, we see
    The waters swell before a boisterous storm.
    But leave it all to God. Whither away?
SECOND CITIZEN. Marry, we were sent for to the justices.
THIRD CITIZEN. And so was I: I'll bear you company. *Exeunt*

SCENE FOUR

The Same. A Room in the Palace.

*Enter the Archbishop of York, the young Duke of York,
Queen Elizabeth, and the Duchess of York*

ARCHBISHOP. Last night, I hear, they lay at Northampton;
    At Stony-Stratford they do rest to-night:
    To-morrow, or next day, they will be here.
DUCHESS. I long with all my heart to see the prince.
    I hope he is much grown since last I saw him.

QUEEN ELIZABETH. But I hear, no; they say my son of York
  Hath almost overta'en him in his growth.
YORK. Ay, mother, but I would not have it so.
DUCHESS. Why, my young cousin, it is good to grow.
YORK. Grandam, one night, as we did sit at supper,
  My uncle Rivers talk'd how I did grow
  More than my brother: 'Ay,' quoth my uncle Gloucester,
  'Small herbs have grace, great weeds do grow apace':
  And since, methinks, I would not grow so fast,
  Because sweet flowers are slow and weeds make haste.
DUCHESS. Good faith, good faith, the saying did not hold
  In him that did object the same to thee:
  He was the wretched'st thing when he was young,
  So long a-growing, and so leisurely,
  That, if his rule were true, he should be gracious.
ARCHBISHOP. And so, no doubt, he is, my gracious madam.
DUCHESS. I hope he is; but yet let mothers doubt.
YORK. Now, by my troth, if I had been remember'd,
  I could have given my uncle's grace a flout,
  To touch his growth nearer than he touch'd mine.
DUCHESS. How, my young York? I prithee, let me hear it.
YORK. Marry, they say my uncle grew so fast,
  That he could gnaw a crust at two hours old:
  'Twas full two years ere I could get a tooth.
  Grandam, this would have been a biting jest.
DUCHESS. I prithee, pretty York, who told thee this?
YORK. Grandam, his nurse.
DUCHESS. His nurse! why, she was dead ere thou wast born.
YORK. If 'twere not she, I cannot tell who told me.
QUEEN ELIZABETH. A parlous boy: go to, you are too
  shrewd.
ARCHBISHOP. Good madam, be not angry with the child.
QUEEN ELIZABETH. Pitchers have ears.
                    Enter a Messenger
ARCHBISHOP. Here comes a messenger. What news?
MESSENGER. Such news, my lord, as grieves me to report.
QUEEN ELIZABETH. How doth the prince?
MESSENGER.   Well, madam, and in health.
DUCHESS. What is thy news?
MESSENGER. Lord Rivers and Lord Grey are sent to
    Pomfret,
  With them Sir Thomas Vaughan, prisoners.

DUCHESS. Who hath committed them?

MESSENGER. The mighty dukes,
    Gloucester and Buckingham.

ARCHBISHOP. For what offence?

MESSENGER. The sum of all I can I have disclos'd:
    Why or for what the nobles were committed
    Is all unknown to me, my gracious lord.

QUEEN ELIZABETH. Ah me! I see the ruin of my house!
    The tiger now hath seiz'd the gentle hind;
    Insulting tyranny begins to jet
    Upon the innocent and aweless throne:
    Welcome, destruction, death, and massacre!
    I see, as in a map, the end of all.

DUCHESS. Accursed and unquiet wrangling days,
    How many of you have mine eyes beheld!
    My husband lost his life to get the crown,
    And often up and down my sons were toss'd,
    For me to joy and weep their gain and loss:
    And being seated, and domestic broils
    Clean over-blown, themselves, the conquerors,
    Make war upon themselves; brother to brother,
    Blood to blood, self against self: O! preposterous
    And frantic outrage, end thy damned spleen;
    Or let me die, to look on death no more.

QUEEN ELIZABETH. Come, come, my boy; we will to
    sanctuary.
    Madam, farewell.

DUCHESS. Stay, I will go with you.

QUEEN ELIZABETH. You have no cause.

ARCHBISHOP. (*To the Queen*) My gracious lady, go;
    And thither bear your treasure and your goods.
    For my part, I 'll resign unto your Grace
    The seal I keep: and so betide to me
    As well I tender you and all of yours!
    Come; I 'll conduct you to the sanctuary. *Exeunt*

ACT THREE

SCENE ONE

The Same. A Street.

The Trumpets sound. Enter the Prince of Wales, Gloucester, Buckingham, Catesby, Cardinal Bourchier, and Others

BUCKINGHAM. Welcome, sweet prince, to London, to your
    chamber.
GLOUCESTER. Welcome, dear cousin, my thoughts'
    sovereign;
  The weary way hath made you melancholy.
PRINCE. No, uncle; but our crosses on the way
  Have made it tedious, wearisome, and heavy:
  I want more uncles here to welcome me.
GLOUCESTER. Sweet prince, the untainted virtue of your
    years
  Hath not yet div'd into the world's deceit:
  No more can you distinguish of a man
  Than of his outward show; which, God he knows,
  Seldom or never jumpeth with the heart.
  Those uncles which you want were dangerous;
  Your Grace attended to their sugar'd words,
  But look'd not on the poison of their hearts:
  God keep you from them, and from such false friends!
PRINCE. God keep me from false friends! but they were
    none.
GLOUCESTER. My lord, the Mayor of London comes to greet
    you.
      Enter the Lord Mayor and his Train
MAYOR. God bless your Grace with health and happy days!
PRINCE. I thank you, good my lord; and thank you all.
  I thought my mother and my brother York
  Would long ere this have met us on the way:
  Fie! what a slug is Hastings, that he comes not

To tell us whether they will come or no.

Enter Hastings

BUCKINGHAM. And in good time here comes the sweating
  lord.

PRINCE. Welcome, my lord. What, will our mother come?

HASTINGS. On what occasion, God he knows, not I,
  The queen your mother, and your brother York,
  Have taken sanctuary: the tender prince
  Would fain have come with me to meet your Grace,
  But by his mother was perforce withheld.

BUCKINGHAM. Fie! what an indirect and peevish course
  Is this of hers! Lord Cardinal, will your Grace
  Persuade the queen to send the Duke of York
  Unto his princely brother presently?
  If she deny, Lord Hastings, go with him,
  And from her jealous arms pluck him perforce.

CARDINAL. My Lord of Buckingham, if my weak oratory
  Can from his mother win the Duke of York,
  Anon expect him here; but if she be obdurate
  To mild entreaties, God in heaven forbid
  We should infringe the holy privilege
  Of blessed sanctuary! not for all this land
  Would I be guilty of so great a sin.

BUCKINGHAM. You are too senseless-obstinate, my lord,
  Too ceremonious and traditional:
  Weigh it but with the grossness of this age,
  You break not sanctuary in seizing him.
  The benefit thereof is always granted
  To those whose dealings have deserved the place
  And those who have the wit to claim the place:
  This prince hath neither claim'd it, nor deserv'd it;
  And therefore, in mine opinion, cannot have it:
  Then, taking him from thence that is not there,
  You break no privilege nor charter there.
  Oft have I heard of sanctuary men,
  But sanctuary children ne'er till now.

CARDINAL. My lord, you shall o'er-rule my mind for once.
  Come on, Lord Hastings, will you go with me?

HASTINGS. I go, my lord.

PRINCE. Good lords, make all the speedy haste you may.

> *Exeunt Cardinal Bourchier and Hastings*

Say, uncle Gloucester, if our brother come,

Where shall we sojourn till our coronation?

GLOUCESTER. Where it seems best unto your royal self.
If I may counsel you, some day or two
Your Highness shall repose you at the Tower:
Then where you please, and shall be thought most fit
For your best health and recreation.

PRINCE. I do not like the Tower, of any place:
Did Julius Cæsar build that place, my lord?

BUCKINGHAM. He did, my gracious lord, begin that place,
Which, since, succeeding ages have re-edified.

PRINCE. Is it upon record, or else reported
Successively from age to age, he built it?

BUCKINGHAM. Upon record, my gracious lord.

PRINCE. But say, my lord, it were not register'd,
Methinks the truth should live from age to age,
As 'twere retail'd to all posterity,
Even to the general all-ending day.

GLOUCESTER. (Aside) So wise so young, they say, do never
live long.

PRINCE. What say you, uncle?

GLOUCESTER. I say, without characters, fame lives long.
(Aside) Thus, like the formal Vice, Iniquity,
I moralize two meanings in one word.

PRINCE. That Julius Cæsar was a famous man;
With what his valour did enrich his wit,
His wit set down to make his valour live:
Death makes no conquest of this conqueror,
For now he lives in fame, though not in life.
I 'll tell you what, my cousin Buckingham,—

BUCKINGHAM. What, my gracious lord?

PRINCE. An if I live until I be a man,
I 'll win our ancient right in France again,
Or die a soldier, as I liv'd a king.

GLOUCESTER. (Aside) Short summers lightly have a forward
spring.

Enter York, Hastings, and Cardinal Bourchier

BUCKINGHAM. Now, in good time, here comes the Duke of
York.

PRINCE. Richard of York! how fares our loving brother?

YORK. Well, my dread lord; so must I call you now.

PRINCE. Ay, brother, to our grief, as it is yours:
Too late he died that might have kept that title,

Which by his death hath lost much majesty.

GLOUCESTER. How fares our cousin, noble Lord of York?

YORK. I thank you, gentle uncle. O, my lord,
You said that idle weeds are fast in growth:
The prince my brother hath outgrown me far.

GLOUCESTER. He hath, my lord.

YORK.   And therefore is he idle?

GLOUCESTER. O, my fair cousin, I must not say so.

YORK. Then he is more beholding to you than I.

GLOUCESTER. He may command me as my sovereign;
But you have power in me as in a kinsman.

YORK. I pray you, uncle, give me this dagger.

GLOUCESTER. My dagger, little cousin? with all my heart.

PRINCE. A beggar, brother?

YORK. Of my kind uncle, that I know will give;
And, being but a toy, which is no grief to give.

GLOUCESTER. A greater gift than that I 'll give my cousin.

YORK. A greater gift! O, that 's the sword to it.

GLOUCESTER. Ay, gentle cousin, were it light enough.

YORK. O, then, I see, you 'll part but with light gifts;
In weightier things you 'll say a beggar nay.

GLOUCESTER. It is too weighty for your Grace to wear.

YORK. I weigh it lightly, were it heavier.

GLOUCESTER. What! would you have my weapon, little lord?

YORK. I would, that I might thank you as you call me.

GLOUCESTER. How?

YORK. Little.

PRINCE. My Lord of York will still be cross in talk.
Uncle, your Grace knows how to bear with him.

YORK. You mean, to bear me, not to bear with me:
Uncle, my brother mocks both you and me.
Because that I am little, like an ape,
He thinks that you should bear me on your shoulders.

BUCKINGHAM. With what a sharp provided wit he reasons!
To mitigate the scorn he gives his uncle,
He prettily and aptly taunts himself:
So cunning and so young is wonderful.

GLOUCESTER. My lord, will 't please you pass along?
Myself and my good cousin Buckingham
Will to your mother, to entreat of her
To meet you at the Tower and welcome you.

YORK. What! will you go unto the Tower, my lord?

PRINCE. My Lord Protector needs will have it so.

YORK. I shall not sleep in quiet at the Tower.

GLOUCESTER. Why, what would you fear?

YORK. Marry, my uncle Clarence' angry ghost:
My grandam told me he was murder'd there.

PRINCE. I fear no uncles dead.

GLOUCESTER. Nor none that live, I hope.

PRINCE. An if they live, I hope, I need not fear.
But come, my lord; and, with a heavy heart,
Thinking on them, go I unto the Tower.

Sennet. Exeunt all
but Gloucester, Buckingham, and Catesby

BUCKINGHAM. Think you, my lord, this little prating York
Was not incensed by his subtle mother
To taunt and scorn you thus opprobriously?

GLOUCESTER. No doubt, no doubt: O! 'tis a parlous boy;
Bold, quick, ingenious, forward, capable:
He 's all the mother's, from the top to toe.

BUCKINGHAM. Well, let them rest. Come hither, Catesby;
thou art sworn
As deeply to effect what we intend
As closely to conceal what we impart.
Thou know'st our reasons urg'd upon the way:
What think'st thou? is it not an easy matter
To make William Lord Hastings of our mind,
For the instalment of this noble duke
In the seat royal of this famous isle?

CATESBY. He for his father's sake so loves the prince
That he will not be won to aught against him.

BUCKINGHAM. What think'st thou then of Stanley? what will
he?

CATESBY. He will do all in all as Hastings doth.

BUCKINGHAM. Well then, no more but this: go, gentle
Catesby,
And, as it were far off, sound thou Lord Hastings,
How he doth stand affected to our purpose;
And summon him to-morrow to the Tower,
To sit about the coronation.
If thou dost find him tractable to us,
Encourage him, and tell him all our reasons:
If he be leaden, icy-cold, unwilling,
Be thou so too, and so break off the talk,

And give us notice of his inclination;
For we to-morrow hold divided councils,
Wherein thyself shalt highly be employ'd.
GLOUCESTER. Commend me to Lord William: tell him,
    Catesby,
His ancient knot of dangerous adversaries
To-morrow are let blood at Pomfret Castle;
And bid my lord, for joy of this good news,
Give Mistress Shore one gentle kiss the more.
BUCKINGHAM. Good Catesby, go, effect this business
    soundly.
CATESBY. My good lords both, with all the heed I can.
GLOUCESTER. Shall we hear from you, Catesby, ere we
    sleep?
CATESBY. You shall, my lord.
GLOUCESTER. At Crosby-place, there shall you find us both.
                                            Exit Catesby
BUCKINGHAM. Now, my lord, what shall we do if we
    perceive
Lord Hastings will not yield to our complots?
GLOUCESTER. Chop off his head; something we will deter-
    mine:
And, look, when I am king, claim thou of me
The earldom of Hereford, and all the moveables
Whereof the king my brother stood possess'd.
BUCKINGHAM. I 'll claim that promise at your Grace's hand.
GLOUCESTER. And look to have it yielded with all kindness.
Come, let us sup betimes, that afterwards
We may digest our complots in some form.   *Exeunt*

SCENE TWO

The Same. Before Lord Hastings' House.

Enter a Messenger

MESSENGER. (*Knocking*) My lord! my lord!
HASTINGS. (*Within*) Who knocks?
MESSENGER. One from the Lord Stanley.
HASTINGS. (*Within*) What is 't o'clock?
MESSENGER. Upon the stroke of four.

Enter Hastings

HASTINGS. Cannot my Lord Stanley sleep these tedious
  nights?

MESSENGER. So it appears by that I have to say.
  First, he commends him to your noble self.

HASTINGS. What then?

MESSENGER. Then certifies your lordship, that this night
  He dreamt the boar had razed off his helm:
  Besides, he says there are two councils held;
  And that may be determin'd at the one
  Which may make you and him to rue at the other.
  Therefore he sends to know your lordship's pleasure,
  If you will presently take horse with him,
  And with all speed post with him toward the north,
  To shun the danger that his soul divines.

HASTINGS. Go, fellow, go, return unto thy lord;
  Bid him not fear the separated councils:
  His honour and myself are at the one,
  And at the other is my good friend Catesby;
  Where nothing can proceed that toucheth us
  Whereof I shall not have intelligence.
  Tell him his fears are shallow, wanting instance:
  And for his dreams, I wonder he's so fond
  To trust the mockery of unquiet slumbers.
  To fly the boar before the boar pursues,
  Were to incense the boar to follow us
  And make pursuit where he did mean no chase.
  Go, bid thy master rise and come to me;
  And we will both together to the Tower,
  Where, he shall see, the boar will use us kindly.

MESSENGER. I'll go, my lord, and tell him what you say. *Exit*

Enter Catesby

CATESBY. Many good-morrows to my noble lord.

HASTINGS. Good-morning, Catesby; you are early stirring.
  What news, what news, in this our tottering state?

CATESBY. It is a reeling world, indeed, my lord;
  And I believe will never stand upright
  Till Richard wear the garland of the realm.

HASTINGS. How! wear the garland! dost thou mean the
  crown?

CATESBY. Ay, my good lord.

HASTINGS. I 'll have this crown of mine cut from my
    shoulders
    Before I 'll see the crown so foul misplac'd.
    But canst thou guess that he doth aim at it?
CATESBY. Ay, on my life; and hopes to find you forward
    Upon his party for the gain thereof:
    And thereupon he sends you this good news,
    That this same very day your enemies,
    The kindred of the queen, must die at Pomfret.
HASTINGS. Indeed, I am no mourner for that news,
    Because they have been still my adversaries;
    But that I 'll give my voice on Richard's side,
    To bar my master's heirs in true descent,
    God knows I will not do it, to the death.
CATESBY. God keep your lordship in that gracious mind!
HASTINGS. But I shall laugh at this a twelvemonth hence,
    That they which brought me in my master's hate,
    I live to look upon their tragedy.
    Well, Catesby, ere a fortnight make me older,
    I 'll send some packing that yet think not on 't.
CATESBY. 'Tis a vile thing to die, my gracious lord,
    When men are unprepar'd and look not for it.
HASTINGS. O monstrous, monstrous! and so falls it out
    With Rivers, Vaughan, Grey; and so 'twill do
    With some men else, who think themselves as safe
    As thou and I; who, as thou know'st, are dear
    To princely Richard and to Buckingham.
CATESBY. The princes both make high account of you;
    (*Aside*) For they account his head upon the bridge.
HASTINGS. I know they do, and I have well deserv'd it.
               Enter Stanley
    Come on, come on; where is your boar-spear, man?
    Fear you the boar, and go so unprovided?
STANLEY. My lord, good-morrow; good-morrow, Catesby:
    You may jest on, but by the holy rood,
    I do not like these several councils, I.
HASTINGS. My Lord, I hold my life as dear as you do yours;
    And never, in my days, I do protest,
    Was it so precious to me as 'tis now.
    Think you, but that I know our state secure,
    I would be so triumphant as I am?

STANLEY. The lords at Pomfret, when they rode from
    London,
Were jocund and suppos'd their state was sure,
And they indeed had no cause to mistrust;
But yet you see how soon the day o'ercast.
This sudden stab of rancour I misdoubt;
Pray God, I say, I prove a needless coward!
What, shall we toward the Tower? the day is spent.

HASTINGS. Come, come, have with you. Wot you what, my
    lord?
To-day the lords you talk of are beheaded.

STANLEY. They, for their truth, might better wear their
    heads,
Than some that have accus'd them wear their hats.
But come, my lord, let's away.

Enter a Pursuivant

HASTINGS. Go on before; I'll talk with this good fellow.

Exeunt Stanley and Catesby

How now, sirrah! how goes the world with thee?

PURSUIVANT. The better that your lordship please to ask.

HASTINGS. I tell thee, man, 'tis better with me now
Than when I met thee last where now we meet:
Then was I going prisoner to the Tower,
By the suggestion of the queen's allies;
But now, I tell thee,—keep it to thyself,—
This day those enemies are put to death,
And I in better state than e'er I was.

PURSUIVANT. God hold it to your honour's good content!

HASTINGS. Gramercy, fellow: there, drink that for me.

Throws him his purse

PURSUIVANT. God save your lordship.   *Exit*

Enter a Priest

PRIEST. Well met, my lord; I am glad to see your honour.

HASTINGS. I thank thee, good Sir John, with all my heart.
I am in your debt for your last exercise;
Come the next Sabbath, and I will content you.

Enter Buckingham

BUCKINGHAM. What, talking with a priest, Lord Cham-
    berlain?
Your friends of Pomfret, they do need the priest:
Your honour hath no shriving work in hand.

HASTINGS. Good faith, and when I met this holy man,

The men you talk of came into my mind.
What, go you toward the Tower?
BUCKINGHAM. I do, my lord; but long I shall not stay:
I shall return before your lordship thence.
HASTINGS. Nay, like enough, for I stay dinner there.
BUCKINGHAM. (*Aside*) And supper too, although thou
know'st it not.
Come, will you go?
HASTINGS.   I 'll wait upon your lordship.   *Exeunt*

SCENE THREE

Pomfret. Before the Castle.

*Enter Ratcliff, with halberds, carrying Rivers, Grey,
and Vaughan to death*

RIVERS. Sir Richard Ratcliff, let me tell thee this:
To-day shalt thou behold a subject die
For truth, for duty, and for loyalty.
GREY. God bless the prince from all the pack of you!
A knot you are of damned blood-suckers.
VAUGHAN. You live that shall cry woe for this hereafter.
RATCLIFF. Dispatch; the limit of your lives is out.
RIVERS. O Pomfret, Pomfret! O thou bloody prison!
Fatal and ominous to noble peers!
Within the guilty closure of thy walls
Richard the Second here was hack'd to death;
And, for more slander to thy dismal seat,
We give thee up our guiltless blood to drink.
GREY. Now Margaret's curse is fall'n upon our heads,
When she exclaim'd on Hastings, you, and I,
For standing by when Richard stabb'd her son.
RIVERS. Then curs'd she Richard, then curs'd she Buck-
ingham,
Then curs'd she Hastings: O! remember, God,
To hear her prayer for them, as now for us;
And for my sister and her princely sons,
Be satisfied, dear God, with our true blood,
Which, as thou know'st, unjustly must be spilt.
RATCLIFF. Make haste; the hour of death is expiate.
RIVERS. Come, Grey, come, Vaughan; let us here embrace:
And take our leave until we meet in heaven.   *Exeunt*

SCENE FOUR

London. The Tower.

Buckingham, Stanley, Hastings, the Bishop of Ely, Ratcliff,
Lovel, and Others, sitting at a table. Officers
of the Council attending

HASTINGS. My lords, at once: the cause why we are met
Is to determine of the coronation:
In God's name, speak, when is the royal day?
BUCKINGHAM. Are all things ready for that royal time?
STANLEY. It is; and wants but nomination.
ELY. To-morrow then I judge a happy day.
BUCKINGHAM. Who knows the Lord Protector's mind
herein?
Who is most inward with the noble duke?
ELY. Your Grace, we think, should soonest know his mind.
BUCKINGHAM. We know each other's faces; for our hearts,
He knows no more of mine than I of yours;
Nor I of his, my lord, than you of mine.
Lord Hastings, you and he are near in love.
HASTINGS. I thank his Grace, I know he loves me well;
But, for his purpose in the coronation,
I have not sounded him, nor he deliver'd
His gracious pleasure any way therein:
But you, my noble lords, may name the time;
And in the duke's behalf I 'll give my voice,
Which, I presume, he 'll take in gentle part.
Enter Gloucester
ELY. In happy time, here comes the duke himself.
GLOUCESTER. My noble lords and cousins all, good-morrow.
I have been long a sleeper; but, I trust,
My absence doth neglect no great design,
Which by my presence might have been concluded.
BUCKINGHAM. Had you not come upon your cue, my lord,
William Lord Hastings had pronounc'd your part,
I mean, your voice, for crowning of the king.
GLOUCESTER. Than my Lord Hastings no man might be
bolder:
His lordship knows me well, and loves me well.
My Lord of Ely, when I was last in Holborn,

I saw good strawberries in your garden there;
I do beseech you send for some of them.
ELY. Marry, and will, my lord, with all my heart.   *Exit*
GLOUCESTER. Cousin of Buckingham, a word with you.
Takes him aside
Catesby hath sounded Hastings in our business,
And finds the testy gentleman so hot,
That he will lose his head ere give consent
His master's child, as worshipfully he terms it,
Shall lose the royalty of England's throne.
BUCKINGHAM. Withdraw yourself a while; I 'll go with you.
Exeunt Gloucester and Buckingham
STANLEY. We have not yet set down this day of triumph.
To-morrow, in my judgment, is too sudden;
For I myself am not so well provided
As else I would be, were the day prolong'd.
Re-enter Bishop of Ely
ELY. Where is my lord, the Duke of Gloucester?
I have sent for these strawberries.
HASTINGS. His Grace looks cheerfully and smooth this
morning:
There 's some conceit or other likes him well,
When that he bids good-morrow with such spirit.
I think there 's never a man in Christendom
Can lesser hide his hate or love than he;
For by his face straight shall you know his heart.
STANLEY. What of his heart perceiv'd you in his face
By any livelihood he show'd to-day?
HASTINGS. Marry, that with no man here he is offended;
For, were he, he had shown it in his looks.
Re-enter Gloucester and Buckingham
GLOUCESTER. I pray you all, tell me what they deserve
That do conspire my death with devilish plots
Of damned witchcraft, and that have prevail'd
Upon my body with their hellish charms?
HASTINGS. The tender love I bear your Grace, my lord,
Makes me most forward in this princely presence
To doom th' offenders, whosoe'er they be:
I say, my lord, they have deserved death.
GLOUCESTER. Then be your eyes the witness of their evil.
Look how I am bewitch'd; behold mine arm
Is like a blasted sapling, wither'd up:

And this is Edward's wife, that monstrous witch
Consorted with that harlot strumpet Shore,
That by their witchcraft thus have marked me.
HASTINGS. If they have done this thing, my noble lord,—
GLOUCESTER. If! thou protector of this damned strumpet,
Talk'st thou to me of ifs? Thou art a traitor:
Off with his head! now, by Saint Paul, I swear,
I will not dine until I see the same.
Lovel and Ratcliff, look that it be done:
The rest, that love me, rise, and follow me.

Exeunt all but Hastings, Ratcliff, and Lovel

HASTINGS. Woe, woe, for England! not a whit for me;
For I, too fond, might have prevented this.
Stanley did dream the boar did raze his helm;
And I did scorn it, and disdain'd to fly.
Three times to-day my foot-cloth horse did stumble,
And startled when he looked upon the Tower,
As loath to bear me to the slaughter-house.
O! now I need the priest that spake to me:
I now repent I told the pursuivant,
As too triumphing, how mine enemies
To-day at Pomfret bloodily were butcher'd
And I myself secure in grace and favour.
O Margaret, Margaret! now thy heavy curse
Is lighted on poor Hastings' wretched head.
RATCLIFF. Come, come, dispatch; the duke would be at
      dinner:
Make a short shrift, he longs to see your head.
HASTINGS. O momentary grace of mortal man,
Which we more hunt for than the grace of God!
Who builds his hope in air of your good looks,
Lives like a drunken sailor on a mast;
Ready with every nod to tumble down
Into the fatal bowels of the deep.
LOVEL. Come, come, dispatch; 'tis bootless to exclaim.
HASTINGS. O bloody Richard! miserable England!
I prophesy the fearfull'st time to thee
That ever wretched age hath look'd upon.
Come, lead me to the block; bear him my head:
They smile at me who shortly shall be dead.   *Exeunt*

SCENE FIVE

London. The Tower Walls.

*Enter Gloucester and Buckingham, in rotten armour,
marvellous ill-favoured*

GLOUCESTER. Come, cousin, canst thou quake, and change
      thy colour,
   Murder. thy breath in middle of a word,
   And then again begin, and stop again,
   As if thou wert distraught and mad with terror?
BUCKINGHAM. Tut! I can counterfeit the deep tragedian,
   Speak and look back, and pry on every side,
   Tremble and start at wagging of a straw,
   Intending deep suspicion: ghastly looks
   Are at my service, like enforced smiles;
   And both are ready in their offices,
   At any time, to grace my stratagems.
   But what! is Catesby gone?
GLOUCESTER. He is; and, see, he brings the mayor along.
         Enter the Lord Mayor and Catesby
BUCKINGHAM. Lord Mayor,—
GLOUCESTER. Look to the drawbridge there!
BUCKINGHAM.   Hark! a drum.
GLOUCESTER. Catesby, o'erlook the walls.
BUCKINGHAM. Lord Mayor, the reason we have sent,—
GLOUCESTER. Look back, defend thee; here are enemies.
BUCKINGHAM. God and our innocency defend and guard us!
      Enter Lovel and Ratcliff, with Hastings' head
GLOUCESTER. Be patient, they are friends, Ratcliff and
      Lovel.
LOVEL. Here is the head of that ignoble traitor,
   The dangerous and unsuspected Hastings.
GLOUCESTER. So dear I lov'd the man, that I must weep.
   I took him for the plainest harmless creature
   That breath'd upon the earth a Christian;
   Made him my book, wherein my soul recorded
   The history of all her secret thoughts:
   So smooth he daub'd his vice with show of virtue,
   That, his apparent open guilt omitted,
   I mean his conversation with Shore's wife,

He liv'd from all attainder of suspect.

BUCKINGHAM. Well, well, he was the covert'st shelter'd
     traitor
That ever liv'd.
Would you imagine, or almost believe,—
Were 't not that by great preservation
We live to tell it, that the subtle traitor
This day had plotted, in the council-house,
To murder me and my good Lord of Gloucester?

MAYOR. Had he done so?

GLOUCESTER. What! think you we are Turks or infidels?
Or that we would, against the form of law,
Proceed thus rashly in the villain's death,
But that the extreme peril of the case,
The peace of England and our person's safety,
Enforc'd us to this execution?

MAYOR. Now, fair befall you! he deserv'd his death;
And your good Graces both have well proceeded,
To warn false traitors from the like attempts.
I never look'd for better at his hands,
After he once fell in with Mistress Shore.

BUCKINGHAM. Yet had we not determin'd he should die,
Until your lordship came to see his end;
Which now the loving haste of these our friends,
Something against our meaning, hath prevented:
Because, my lord, we would have had you heard
The traitor speak, and timorously confess
The manner and the purpose of his treason;
That you might well have signified the same
Unto the citizens, who haply may
Misconster us in him, and wail his death.

MAYOR. But, my good lord, your Grace's word shall serve,
As well as I had seen and heard him speak:
And do not doubt, right noble princes both,
But I 'll acquaint our duteous citizens
With all your just proceedings in this cause.

GLOUCESTER. And to that end we wish'd your lordship here,
To avoid the censures of the carping world.

BUCKINGHAM. But since you come too late of our intent,
Yet witness what you hear we did intend:
And so, my good Lord Mayor, we bid farewell.

                              Exit Lord Mayor

GLOUCESTER. Go, after, after, cousin Buckingham.
  The mayor towards Guildhall hies him in all post:
  There, at your meetest vantage of the time,
  Infer the bastardy of Edward's children:
  Tell them how Edward put to death a citizen,
  Only for saying he would make his son
  Heir to the crown; meaning indeed his house,
  Which by the sign thereof was termed so.
  Moreover, urge his hateful luxury
  And bestial appetite in change of lust;
  Which stretch'd unto their servants, daughters, wives,
  Even where his raging eye or savage heart
  Without control lusted to make a prey.
  Nay, for a need, thus far come near my person:
  Tell them, when that my mother went with child
  Of that insatiate Edward, noble York
  My princely father then had wars in France;
  And, by true computation of the time,
  Found that the issue was not his begot;
  Which well appeared in his lineaments,
  Being nothing like the noble duke my father.
  Yet touch this sparingly, as 'twere far off;
  Because, my lord, you know my mother lives.
BUCKINGHAM. Doubt not, my lord, I 'll play the orator
  As if the golden fee for which I plead
  Were for myself: and so, my lord, adieu.
GLOUCESTER. If you thrive well, bring them to Baynard's
    Castle;
  Where you shall find me well accompanied
  With reverend fathers and well-learned bishops.
BUCKINGHAM. I go; and towards three or four o'clock
  Look for the news that the Guildhall affords.   *Exit*
GLOUCESTER. Go, Lovel, with all speed to Doctor Shaw;
  (*To Catesby*) Go thou to Friar Penker; bid them both
  Meet me within this hour at Baynard's Castle.
                          Exeunt Lovel and Catesby
  Now will I in, to take some privy order,
  To draw the brats of Clarence out of sight;
  And to give notice that no manner person
  Have any time recourse unto the princes.   *Exit*

SCENE SIX

The Same. A Street.

Enter a Scrivener

SCRIVENER. Here is the indictment of the good Lord
      Hastings;
   Which in a set hand fairly is engross'd,
   That it may be to-day read o'er in Paul's:
   And mark how well the sequel hangs together.
   Eleven hours I have spent to write it over,
   For yesternight by Catesby was it sent me.
   The precedent was full as long a-doing;
   And yet within these five hours Hastings liv'd,
   Untainted, unexamin'd, free, at liberty.
   Here's a good world the while! Who is so gross
   That cannot see this palpable device?
   Yet who so bold but says he sees it not?
   Bad is the world; and all will come to naught,
   When such ill dealing must be seen in thought.   *Exit*

SCENE SEVEN

The Same. The Court of Baynard's Castle.

Enter Gloucester and Buckingham, meeting

GLOUCESTER. How now, how now! what say the citizens?
BUCKINGHAM. Now, by the holy mother of our Lord,
   The citizens are mum, say not a word.
GLOUCESTER. Touch'd you the bastardy of Edward's
      children?
BUCKINGHAM. I did; with his contract with Lady Lucy,
   And his contract by deputy in France;
   The insatiate greediness of his desires,
   And his enforcement of the city wives;
   His tyranny for trifles; his own bastardy,
   As being got, your father then in France,
   And his resemblance, being not like the duke:
   Withal I did infer your lineaments,

Being the right idea of your father,
Both in your form and nobleness of mind;
Laid open all your victories in Scotland,
Your discipline in war, wisdom in peace,
Your bounty, virtue, fair humility;
Indeed, left nothing fitting for your purpose
Untouch'd or slightly handled in discourse;
And when my oratory drew toward end,
I bade them that did love their country's good
Cry 'God save Richard, England's royal king!'

GLOUCESTER. And did they so?

BUCKINGHAM. No, so God help me, they spake not a word;
But, like dumb statuas or breathing stones,
Star'd each on other, and look'd deadly pale.
Which when I saw, I reprehended them;
And ask'd the mayor what meant this wilful silence:
His answer was, the people were not wont
To be spoke to but by the recorder.
Then he was urg'd to tell my tale again:
'Thus saith the duke, thus hath the duke inferr'd';
But nothing spoke in warrant from himself.
When he had done, some followers of mine own,
At lower end of the hall, hurl'd up their caps,
And some ten voices cried, 'God save King Richard!'
And thus I took the vantage of those few,
'Thanks, gentle citizens and friends,' quoth I;
'This general applause and cheerful shout
Argues your wisdom and your love to Richard':
And even here brake off, and came away.

GLOUCESTER. What tongueless blocks were they! would they
not speak?
Will not the mayor then and his brethren come?

BUCKINGHAM. The mayor is here at hand. Intend some fear;
Be not you spoke with but by mighty suit:
And look you get a prayer-book in your hand,
And stand between two churchmen, good my lord:
For on that ground I 'll make a holy descant:
And be not easily won to our requests;
Play the maid's part, still answer nay, and take it.

GLOUCESTER. I go; and if you plead as well for them
As I can say nay to thee for myself,
No doubt we bring it to a happy issue.

BUCKINGHAM. Go, go, up to the leads! the Lord Mayor
    knocks.   *Exit Gloucester*
       Enter the Lord Mayor, Aldermen, and Citizens
    Welcome, my lord: I dance attendance here;
    I think the duke will not be spoke withal.
           Enter, from the Castle, Catesby
    Now, Catesby! what says your lord to my request?
CATESBY. He doth entreat your Grace, my noble lord,
    To visit him to-morrow or next day.
    He is within, with two right reverend fathers,
    Divinely bent to meditation;
    And in no worldly suit would he be mov'd,
    To draw him from his holy exercise.
BUCKINGHAM. Return, good Catesby, to the gracious duke:
    Tell him, myself, the mayor and aldermen,
    In deep designs in matter of great moment,
    No less importing than our general good,
    Are come to have some conference with his Grace.
CATESBY. I 'll signify so much unto him straight.   *Exit*
BUCKINGHAM. Ah, ha, my lord, this prince is not an Edward!
    He is not lolling on a lewd day-bed,
    But on his knees at meditation;
    Not dallying with a brace of courtezans,
    But meditating with two deep divines;
    Not sleeping, to engross his idle body,
    But praying, to enrich his watchful soul.
    Happy were England, would this virtuous prince
    Take on his Grace the sovereignty thereof:
    But sure, I fear, we shall not win him to it.
MAYOR. Marry, God defend his Grace should say us nay!
BUCKINGHAM. I fear he will. Here Catesby comes again.
             Re-enter Catesby
    Now, Catesby, what says his Grace?
CATESBY. He wonders to what end you have assembled
    Such troops of citizens to come to him,
    His Grace not being warn'd thereof before:
    My lord, he fears you mean no good to him.
BUCKINGHAM. Sorry I am my noble cousin should
    Suspect me that I mean no good to him.
    By heaven, we come to him in perfect love;
    And so once more return, and tell his Grace. *Exit Catesby*
    When holy and devout religious men

Are at their beads, 'tis much to draw them thence;
So sweet is zealous contemplation.

Enter Gloucester, in a
gallery above, between two Bishops. Catesby returns

MAYOR. See, where his Grace stands 'tween two clergymen!
BUCKINGHAM. Two props of virtue for a Christian prince,
　To stay him from the fall of vanity;
　And, see, a book of prayer in his hand;
　True ornament to know a holy man.
　Famous Plantagenet, most gracious prince,
　Lend favourable ear to our requests,
　And pardon us the interruption
　Of thy devotion and right Christian zeal.
GLOUCESTER. My lord, there needs no such apology;
　I do beseech your Grace to pardon me,
　Who, earnest in the service of my God,
　Deferr'd the visitation of my friends.
　But, leaving this, what is your Grace's pleasure?
BUCKINGHAM. Even that, I hope, which pleaseth God above,
　And all good men of this ungovern'd isle.
GLOUCESTER. I do suspect I have done some offence
　That seems disgracious in the city's eye;
　And that you come to reprehend my ignorance.
BUCKINGHAM. You have, my lord: would it might please
　　your Grace,
　On our entreaties to amend your fault!
GLOUCESTER. Else wherefore breathe I in a Christian land?
BUCKINGHAM. Know then, it is your fault that you resign
　The supreme seat, the throne majestical,
　The sceptred office of your ancestors,
　Your state of fortune and your due of birth,
　The lineal glory of your royal house,
　To the corruption of a blemish'd stock;
　Whiles, in the mildness of your sleepy thoughts,—
　Which here we waken to our country's good,—
　This noble isle doth want her proper limbs;
　Her face defac'd with scars of infamy,
　Her royal stock graft with ignoble plants,
　And almost shoulder'd in the swallowing gulf
　Of dark forgetfulness and deep oblivion.
　Which to recure we heartily solicit
　Your gracious self to take on you the charge

And kingly government of this your land;
Not as protector, steward, substitute,
Or lowly factor for another's gain;
But as successively from blood to blood,
Your right of birth, your empery, your own.
For this, consorted with the citizens,
Your very worshipful and loving friends,
And by their vehement instigation,
In this just cause come I to move your Grace.

GLOUCESTER. I cannot tell if to depart in silence,
Or bitterly to speak in your reproof,
Best fitteth my degree or your condition:
If not to answer, you might haply think
Tongue-tied ambition, not replying, yielded
To bear the golden yoke of sovereignty,
Which fondly you would here impose on me;
If to reprove you for this suit of yours,
So season'd with your faithful love to me,
Then, on the other side, I check'd my friends.
Therefore, to speak, and to avoid the first,
And then, in speaking, not to incur the last,
Definitively thus I answer you.
Your love deserves my thanks; but my desert
Unmeritable shuns your high request.
First, if all obstacles were cut away,
And that my path were even to the crown,
As the ripe revenue and due of birth,
Yet so much is my poverty of spirit,
So mighty and so many my defects,
That I would rather hide me from my greatness,
Being a bark to brook no mighty sea,
Than in my greatness covet to be hid,
And in the vapour of my glory smother'd.
But, God be thank'd, there is no need of me;
And much I need to help you, were there need;
The royal tree hath left us royal fruit,
Which, mellow'd by the stealing hours of time,
Will well become the seat of majesty,
And make, no doubt, us happy by his reign.
On him I lay that you would lay on me,
The right and fortune of his happy stars;
Which God defend that I should wring from him!

BUCKINGHAM. My lord, this argues conscience in your
    Grace;
    But the respects thereof are nice and trivial,
    All circumstances well considered.
    You say that Edward is your brother's son:
    So say we too, but not by Edward's wife;
    For first was he contract to Lady Lucy,
    Your mother lives a witness to his vow,
    And afterward by substitute betroth'd
    To Bona, sister to the King of France.
    These both put by, a poor petitioner,
    A care-craz'd mother to a many sons,
    A beauty-waning and distressed widow,
    Even in the afternoon of her best days,
    Made prize and purchase of his wanton eye,
    Seduc'd the pitch and height of his degree
    To base declension and loath'd bigamy:
    By her, in his unlawful bed, he got
    This Edward, whom our manners call the prince.
    More bitterly could I expostulate,
    Save that, for reverence to some alive,
    I give a sparing limit to my tongue.
    Then, good my lord, take to your royal self
    This proffer'd benefit of dignity;
    If not to bless us and the land withal,
    Yet to draw forth your noble ancestry
    From the corruption of abusing times,
    Unto a lineal true-derived course.
MAYOR. Do, good my lord; your citizens entreat you.
BUCKINGHAM. Refuse not, mighty lord, this proffer'd love.
CATESBY. O! make them joyful: grant their lawful suit:
GLOUCESTER. Alas! why would you heap those cares on me?
    I am unfit for state and majesty:
    I do beseech you, take it not amiss,
    I cannot nor I will not yield to you.
BUCKINGHAM. If you refuse it, as, in love and zeal,
    Loath to depose the child, your brother's son;
    As well we know your tenderness of heart
    And gentle, kind, effeminate remorse,
    Which we have noted in you to your kindred,
    And egally, indeed, to all estates,
    Yet whether you accept our suit or no,

Your brother's son shall never reign our king;
But we will plant some other in the throne,
To the disgrace and downfall of your house:
And in this resolution here we leave you.
Come, citizens, we will entreat no more.

Exit Buckingham and Citizens

CATESBY. Call them again, sweet prince; accept their suit:
If you deny them, all the land will rue it.

GLOUCESTER. Will you enforce me to a world of cares?
Call them again: I am not made of stone,
But penetrable to your kind entreats   *Exit Catesby*
Albeit against my conscience and my soul.

Re-enter Buckingham and the rest

Cousin of Buckingham, and sage, grave men,
Since you will buckle fortune on my back,
To bear her burden, whe'r I will or no,
I must have patience to endure the load:
But if black scandal or foul-fac'd reproach
Attend the sequel of your imposition,
Your mere enforcement shall acquittance me
From all the impure blots and stains thereof;
For God doth know, and you may partly see,
How far I am from the desire of this.

MAYOR. God bless your Grace! we see it, and will say it.

GLOUCESTER. In saying so, you shall but say the truth.

BUCKINGHAM. Then I salute you with this royal title:
Long live King Richard, England's worthy king!

ALL. Amen.

BUCKINGHAM. To-morrow may it please you to be crown'd?

GLOUCESTER. Even when you please, for you will have it so.

BUCKINGHAM. To-morrow then we will attend your Grace:
And so most joyfully we take our leave.

GLOUCESTER. (*To the Bishops*) Come, let us to our holy
work again.
Farewell, my cousin;—farewell, gentle friends.   *Exeunt*

ACT FOUR

SCENE ONE

London. Before the Tower.

Enter on one side, Queen Elizabeth, Duchess of York, and Marquess of Dorset; on the other, Anne, Duchess of Glouces- ter, leading Lady Margaret Plantagenet, Clarence's young daughter

DUCHESS. Who meets us here? my niece Plantagenet,
Led in the hand of her kind aunt of Gloucester?
Now, for my life, she 's wandering to the Tower,
On pure heart's love, to greet the tender princes.
Daughter, well met.

ANNE.   God give your Graces both
A happy and a joyful time of day!

QUEEN ELIZABETH. As much to you, good sister! whither
away?

ANNE. No farther than the Tower; and, as I guess,
Upon the like devotion as yourselves,
To gratulate the gentle princes there.

QUEEN ELIZABETH. Kind sister, thanks: we 'll enter all to-
gether:—

Enter Brakenbury

And, in good time, here the lieutenant comes.
Master lieutenant, pray you, by your leave,
How doth the prince, and my young son of York?

BRAKENBURY. Right well, dear madam. By your patience,
I may not suffer you to visit them:
The king hath strictly charg'd the contrary.

QUEEN ELIZABETH. The king! who 's that?

BRAKENBURY.   I mean the Lord Protector.

QUEEN ELIZABETH. The Lord protect him from that kingly
title!
Hath he set bounds between their love and me?

I am their mother; who shall bar me from them?

DUCHESS. I am their father's mother; I will see them.

ANNE. Their aunt I am in law, in love their mother:
Then bring me to their sights; I 'll bear thy blame,
And take thy office from thee, on my peril.

BRAKENBURY. No, madam, no, I may not leave it so:
I am bound by oath, and therefore pardon me.   *Exit*

Enter Stanley

STANLEY. Let me but meet you, ladies, one hour hence,
And I 'll salute your Grace of York as mother,
And reverend looker-on, of two fair queens.
(*To the Duchess of Gloucester*) Come, madam, you must
straight to Westminster,
There to be crowned Richard's royal queen.

QUEEN ELIZABETH. Ah! cut my lace asunder,
That my pent heart may have some scope to beat,
Or else I swoon with this dead-killing news.

ANNE. Despiteful tidings! O! unpleasing news!

DORSET. Be of good cheer: mother, how fares your Grace?

QUEEN ELIZABETH. O, Dorset! speak not to me, get thee
gone;
Death and destruction dog thee at the heels:
Thy mother's name is ominous to children.
If thou wilt outstrip death, go cross the seas,
And live with Richmond, from the reach of hell:
Go, hie thee, hie thee, from this slaughter-house,
Lest thou increase the number of the dead,
And make me die the thrall of Margaret's curse,
Nor mother, wife, nor England's counted queen.

STANLEY. Full of wise care is this your counsel, madam.
(*To Dorset*) Take all the swift advantage of the hours;
You shall have letters from me to my son
In your behalf, to meet you on the way:
Be not ta'en tardy by unwise delay.

DUCHESS. O ill-dispersing wind of misery!
O! my accursed womb, the bed of death,
A cockatrice hast thou hatch'd to the world,
Whose unavoided eye is murderous!

STANLEY. Come, madam, come; I in all haste was sent.

ANNE. And I with all unwillingness will go.
O! would to God that the inclusive verge
Of golden metal that must round my brow

Were red-hot steel to sear me to the brain.
Anointed let me be with deadly venom;
And die, ere men can say 'God save the queen!'
QUEEN ELIZABETH. Go, go, poor soul, I envy not thy glory;
To feed my humour, wish thyself no harm.
ANNE. No! why? When he, that is my husband now
Came to me, as I follow'd Henry's corse;
When scarce the blood was well wash'd from his hands,
Which issu'd from my other angel husband,
And that dead saint which then I weeping follow'd;
O! when I say, I look'd on Richard's face,
This was my wish, 'Be thou,' quoth I, 'accurs'd,
For making me so young, so old a widow!
And, when thou wedd'st, let sorrow haunt thy bed;
And be thy wife—if any be so mad—
More miserable by the life of thee
Than thou hast made me by my dear lord's death!'
Lo! ere I can repeat this curse again,
Within so small a time, my woman's heart
Grossly grew captive to his honey words,
And prov'd the subject of mine own soul's curse:
Which hitherto hath held mine eyes from rest;
For never yet one hour in his bed
Did I enjoy the golden dew of sleep,
But with his timorous dreams was still awak'd.
Besides, he hates me for my father Warwick,
And will, no doubt, shortly be rid of me.
QUEEN ELIZABETH. Poor heart, adieu! I pity thy com-
    plaining.
ANNE. No more than with my soul I mourn for yours.
QUEEN ELIZABETH. Farewell! thou woeful welcomer of
    glory!
ANNE. Adieu, poor soul, that takest thy leave of it!
DUCHESS. (*To Dorset*) Go thou to Richmond, and good for-
    tune guide thee!
    (*To Anne*) Go thou to Richard, and good angels tend
    thee!
    (*To Queen Elizabeth*) Go thou to sanctuary, and good
    thoughts possess thee!
I to my grave, where peace and rest lie with me!
Eighty odd years of sorrow have I seen,
And each hour's joy wrack'd with a week of teen.

QUEEN ELIZABETH. Stay yet, look back with me unto the
    Tower.
  Pity, you ancient stones, those tender babes
  Whom envy hath immur'd within your walls,
  Rough cradle for such little pretty ones!
  Rude ragged nurse, old sullen playfellow
  For tender princes, use my babies well.
  So foolish sorrow bids your stones farewell.   *Exeunt*

SCENE TWO

The Same. A Room of State in the Palace.

*Sennet. Richard, in pomp, crowned: Buckingham,
    Catesby, a Page, and Others*

KING RICHARD. Stand all apart. Cousin of Buckingham.
BUCKINGHAM. My gracious sovereign!
KING RICHARD. Give me thy hand.   *He ascends the throne*
    Thus high, by thy advice,
  And thy assistance, is King Richard seated:
  But shall we wear these glories for a day?
  Or shall they last, and we rejoice in them?
BUCKINGHAM. Still live they, and for ever let them last!
KING RICHARD. Ah! Buckingham, now do I play the touch,
  To try if thou be current gold indeed:
  Young Edward lives: think now what I would speak.
BUCKINGHAM. Say on, my loving lord.
KING RICHARD. Why, Buckingham, I say, I would be king.
BUCKINGHAM. Why, so you are, my thrice-renowned liege.
KING RICHARD. Ha! am I king? 'Tis so: but Edward lives.
BUCKINGHAM. True, noble prince.
KING RICHARD.   O bitter consequence,
  That Edward still should live! 'True, noble prince!'
  Cousin, thou wast not wont to be so dull:
  Shall I be plain? I wish the bastards dead;
  And I would have it suddenly perform'd.
  What sayest thou now? speak suddenly, be brief.
BUCKINGHAM. Your Grace may do your pleasure.
KING RICHARD. Tut, tut! thou art all ice, thy kindness freezes:
  Say, have I thy consent that they shall die?
BUCKINGHAM. Give me some little breath, some pause, dear
    lord,

Before I positively speak in this:
I will resolve you herein presently. *Exit*

CATESBY. (*Aside to another*) The king is angry: see, he
   gnaws his lip.

KING RICHARD. (*Descends from his throne*) I will converse
   with iron-witted fools
And unrespective boys: none are for me
That look into me with considerate eyes.
High-reaching Buckingham grows circumspect.
Boy!

PAGE. My lord!

KING RICHARD. Know'st thou not any whom corrupting gold
   Will tempt unto a close exploit of death?

PAGE. I know a discontented gentleman,
   Whose humble means match not his haughty spirit:
   Gold were as good as twenty orators,
   And will, no doubt, tempt him to any thing.

KING RICHARD. What is his name?

PAGE.   His name, my lord, is Tyrrell.

KING RICHARD. I partly know the man: go, call him hither.
Exit Page

The deep-revolving witty Buckingham
No more shall be the neighbour to my counsel.
Hath he so long held out with me untir'd,
And stops he now for breath? well, be it so.
Enter Stanley
How now, Lord Stanley! what's the news?

STANLEY. Know, my loving lord,
   The Marquess Dorset, as I hear, is fled
   To Richmond, in the parts where he abides.

KING RICHARD. Come hither, Catesby: rumour it abroad,
   That Anne my wife is very grievous sick;
   I will take order for her keeping close.
   Inquire me out some mean poor gentleman,
   Whom I will marry straight to Clarence' daughter:
   The boy is foolish, and I fear not him.
   Look, how thou dream'st! I say again, give out
   That Anne my queen is sick, and like to die:
   About it; for it stands me much upon,
   To stop all hopes whose growth may damage me.
Exit Catesby

I must be married to my brother's daughter,

Or else my kingdom stands on brittle glass.
Murder her brothers, and then marry her!
Uncertain way of gain! But I am in
So far in blood, that sin will pluck on sin:
Tear-falling pity dwells not in this eye.

Re-enter Page, with Tyrrell

Is thy name Tyrrell?

TYRRELL. James Tyrrell, and your most obedient subject.

KING RICHARD. Art thou, indeed?

TYRRELL.   Prove me, my gracious lord.

KING RICHARD. Darest thou resolve to kill a friend of mine?

TYRRELL. Please you; but I had rather kill two enemies.

KING RICHARD. Why, then thou hast it: two deep enemies,
    Foes to my rest and my sweet sleep's disturbers,
    Are they that I would have thee deal upon.
    Tyrrell, I mean those bastards in the Tower.

TYRRELL. Let me have open means to come to them,
    And soon I'll rid you from the fear of them.

KING RICHARD. Thou sing'st sweet music. Hark, come hither,
        Tyrrell:
    Go, by this token: rise, and lend thine ear.   *Whispers*
    There is no more but so: say it is done,
    And I will love thee, and prefer thee for it.

TYRRELL. I will dispatch it straight.   *Exit*

Re-enter Buckingham

BUCKINGHAM. My lord, I have consider'd in my mind
    The late demand that you did sound me in.

KING RICHARD. Well, let that rest. Dorset is fled to Richmond.

BUCKINGHAM. I hear the news, my lord.

KING RICHARD. Stanley, he is your wife's son: well, look to it.

BUCKINGHAM. My lord, I claim the gift, my due by promise,
    For which your honour and your faith is pawn'd;
    The earldom of Hereford and the moveables
    Which you have promised I shall possess.

KING RICHARD. Stanley, look to your wife: if she convey
    Letters to Richmond, you shall answer it.

BUCKINGHAM. What says your Highness to my just request?

KING RICHARD. I do remember me, Henry the Sixth
    Did prophesy that Richmond should be king,
    When Richmond was a little peevish boy.
    A king! perhaps—

BUCKINGHAM. My lord!

KING RICHARD. How chance the prophet could not at that
    time
    Have told me, I being by, that I should kill him?
BUCKINGHAM. My lord, your promise for the earldom,—
KING RICHARD. Richmond! When last I was at Exeter,
    The mayor in courtesy show'd me the castle,
    And call'd it Rougemont: at which name I started,
    Because a bard of Ireland told me once
    I should not live long after I saw Richmond.
BUCKINGHAM. My lord!
KING RICHARD. Ay, what's o'clock?
BUCKINGHAM. I am thus bold to put your Grace in mind
    Of what you promis'd me.
KING RICHARD. Well, but what is 't o'clock?
BUCKINGHAM.   Upon the stroke of ten.
KING RICHARD. Well, let it strike.
BUCKINGHAM.   Why let it strike?
KING RICHARD. Because that, like a Jack, thou keep'st the
    stroke
    Betwixt thy begging and my meditation.
    I am not in the giving vein to-day.
BUCKINGHAM. Why, then resolve me whether you will or no.
KING RICHARD. Thou troublest me: I am not in the vein.
                Exeunt King Richard and train
BUCKINGHAM. And is it thus? repays he my deep service
    With such contempt? made I him king for this?
    O, let me think on Hastings, and be gone
    To Brecknock, while my fearful head is on.   *Exit*

SCENE THREE

The Same.

Enter Tyrrell

TYRRELL. The tyrannous and bloody act is done;
    The most arch deed of piteous massacre
    That ever yet this land was guilty of.
    Dighton and Forrest, whom I did suborn
    To do this piece of ruthless butchery,
    Albeit they were flesh'd villains, bloody dogs,
    Melting with tenderness and mild compassion,

Wept like to children in their death's sad story.
'Oh! thus,' quoth Dighton, 'lay the gentle babes':
'Thus, thus,' quoth Forrest, 'girdling one another
Within their alabaster innocent arms:
Their lips were four red roses on a stalk,
Which in their summer beauty kiss'd each other.
A book of prayers on their pillow lay;
Which once,' quoth Forrest, 'almost chang'd my mind;
But, O, the devil'—there the villain stopp'd;
When Dighton thus told on: 'We smothered
The most replenished sweet work of nature,
That from the prime creation e'er she fram'd.'
Hence both are gone with conscience and remorse;
They could not speak; and so I left them both,
To bear this tidings to the bloody king:
And here he comes.

Enter King Richard

All health, my sovereign lord!
KING RICHARD. Kind Tyrrell, am I happy in thy news?
TYRRELL. If to have done the thing you gave in charge
Beget your happiness, be happy then,
For it is done.
KING RICHARD.   But didst thou see them dead?
TYRRELL. I did, my lord.
KING RICHARD.   And buried, gentle Tyrrell?
TYRRELL. The chaplain of the Tower hath buried them;
But how or in what place I do not know.
KING RICHARD. Come to me, Tyrrell, soon at after supper,
When thou shalt tell the process of their death.
Meantime, but think how I may do thee good,
And be inheritor of thy desire.
Farewell till then.
TYRRELL.   I humbly take my leave.   *Exit*
KING RICHARD. The son of Clarence have I pent up close;
His daughter meanly have I match'd in marriage;
The sons of Edward sleep in Abraham's bosom,
And Anne my wife hath bid the world good night.
Now, for I know the Breton Richmond aims
At young Elizabeth, my brother's daughter,
And, by that knot, looks proudly on the crown,
To her go I, a jolly thriving wooer.

Enter Catesby

CATESBY. My lord!

KING RICHARD. Good or bad news, that thou comest in so
    bluntly?

CATESBY. Bad news, my lord: Morton is fled to Richmond;
    And Buckingham, back'd with the hardy Welshmen,
    Is in the field, and still his power increaseth.

KING RICHARD. Ely with Richmond troubles me more near
    Than Buckingham and his rash-levied strength.
    Come; I have learn'd that fearful commenting
    Is leaden servitor to dull delay:
    Delay leads impotent and snail-pac'd beggary:
    Then fiery expedition be my wing,
    Jove's Mercury, and herald for a king!
    Go, muster men: my counsel is my shield;
    We must be brief when traitors brave the field.   *Exeunt*

SCENE FOUR

The Same. Before the Palace.

Enter Queen Margaret

QUEEN MARGARET. So, now prosperity begins to mellow
    And drop into the rotten mouth of death.
    Here in these confines slily have I lurk'd
    To watch the waning of mine enemies.
    A dire induction am I witness to,
    And will to France, hoping the consequence
    Will prove as bitter, black, and tragical.
    Withdraw thee, wretched Margaret: who comes here?
    Enter Queen Elizabeth and the Duchess of York.

QUEEN ELIZABETH. Ah! my poor princes! ah, my tender
    babes,
    My unknown flowers, new-appearing sweets,
    If yet your gentle souls fly in the air
    And be not fix'd in doom perpetual,
    Hover about me with your airy wings,
    And hear your mother's lamentation.

QUEEN MARGARET. Hover about her; say, that right for right
    Hath dimm'd your infant morn to aged night.

DUCHESS. So many miseries have craz'd my voice,
That my woe-wearied tongue is still and mute.
Edward Plantagenet, why art thou dead?

QUEEN MARGARET. Plantagenet doth quit Plantagenet;
Edward for Edward pays a dying debt.

QUEEN ELIZABETH. Wilt thou, O God! fly from such gentle
lambs,
And throw them in the entrails of the wolf?
When didst thou sleep when such a deed was done?

QUEEN MARGARET. When holy Harry died, and my sweet
son.

DUCHESS. Dead life, blind sight, poor mortal living ghost,
Woe's scene, world's shame, grave's due by life usurp'd,
Brief abstract and record of tedious days,
Rest thy unrest on England's lawful earth, *Sitting down*
Unlawfully made drunk with innocent blood!

QUEEN ELIZABETH. Ah! that thou wouldst as soon afford a
grave
As thou canst yield a melancholy seat;
Then would I hide my bones, not rest them here.
Ah! who hath any cause to mourn but I?
                              Sitting down by her

QUEEN MARGARET. If ancient sorrow be most reverend,
Give mine the benefit of seniory,
And let my griefs frown on the upper hand,
If sorrow can admit society.   *Sitting down with them*
Tell o'er your woes again by viewing mine:
I had an Edward, till a Richard kill'd him;
I had a Harry, till a Richard kill'd him;
Thou hadst an Edward, till a Richard kill'd him;
Thou hadst a Richard, till a Richard kill'd him.

DUCHESS. I had a Richard too, and thou didst kill him;
I had a Rutland too, thou holp'st to kill him.

QUEEN MARGARET. Thou hadst a Clarence too, and Richard
kill'd him.
From forth the kennel of thy womb hath crept
A hell-hound that doth hunt us all to death:
That dog, that had his teeth before his eyes,
To worry lambs, and lap their gentle blood,
That foul defacer of God's handiwork,
That excellent grand tyrant of the earth,
That reigns in galled eyes of weeping souls,

Thy womb let loose, to chase us to our graves.
O! upright, just, and true-disposing God,
How do I thank thee that this carnal cur
Preys on the issue of his mother's body,
And makes her pew-fellow with others' moan.

DUCHESS. O! Harry's wife, triumph not in my woes:
God witness with me, I have wept for thine.

QUEEN MARGARET. Bear with me; I am hungry for revenge,
And now I cloy me with beholding it.
Thy Edward he is dead, that kill'd my Edward;
Thy other Edward dead, to quit my Edward;
Young York he is but boot, because both they
Match not the high perfection of my loss:
Thy Clarence he is dead that stabb'd my Edward;
And the beholders of this tragic play,
The adulterate Hastings, Rivers, Vaughan, Grey,
Untimely smother'd in their dusky graves.
Richard yet lives, hell's black intelligencer,
Only reserv'd their factor, to buy souls
And send them thither; but at hand, at hand,
Ensues his piteous and unpitied end:
Earth gapes, hell burns, fiends roar, saints pray,
To have him suddenly convey'd from hence.
Cancel his bond of life, dear God! I pray,
That I may live to say, The dog is dead.

QUEEN ELIZABETH. O! thou didst prophesy the time would
come
That I should wish for thee to help me curse
That bottled spider, that foul bunch-back'd toad.

QUEEN MARGARET. I call'd thee then vain flourish of my
fortune;
I call'd thee then poor shadow, painted queen;
The presentation of but what I was;
The flattering index of a direful pageant;
One heav'd a-high to be hurl'd down below;
A mother only mock'd with two fair babes;
A dream of what thou wert, a breath, a bubble,
A sign of dignity, a garish flag,
To be the aim of every dangerous shot;
A queen in jest, only to fill the scene.
Where is thy husband now? where be thy brothers?
Where are thy children? wherein dost thou joy?

Who sues and kneels and cries God save the queen?
Where be the bending peers that flatter'd thee?
Where be the thronging troops that follow'd thee?
Decline all this, and see what now thou art:
For happy wife, a most distressed widow;
For joyful mother, one that wails the name;
For one being su'd to, one that humbly sues;
For queen, a very caitiff crown'd with care;
For one that scorn'd at me, now scorn'd of me;
For one being fear'd of all, now fearing one;
For one commanding all, obey'd of none.
Thus hath the course of justice whirl'd about,
And left thee but a very prey to time;
Having no more but thought of what thou wert,
To torture thee the more, being what thou art.
Thou didst usurp my place, and dost thou not
Usurp the just proportion of my sorrow?
Now thy proud neck bears half my burden'd yoke;
From which even here, I slip my wearied head,
And leave the burden of it all on thee.
Farewell, York's wife, and queen of sad mischance:
These English woes shall make me smile in France.

QUEEN ELIZABETH. O thou, well skill'd in curses, stay awhile,
And teach me how to curse mine enemies.

QUEEN MARGARET. Forbear to sleep the night, and fast the
    day;
Compare dead happiness with living woe;
Think that thy babes were fairer than they were,
And he that slew them fouler than he is:
Bettering thy loss makes the bad causer worse:
Revolving this will teach thee how to curse.

QUEEN ELIZABETH. My words are dull; O! quicken them
    with thine!

QUEEN MARGARET. Thy woes will make them sharp, and
    pierce like mine.   *Exit*

DUCHESS. Why should calamity be full of words?

QUEEN ELIZABETH. Windy attorneys to their client woes,
Airy succeeders of intestate joys,
Poor breathing orators of miseries!
Let them have scope: though what they do impart
Help nothing else, yet do they ease the heart.

DUCHESS. If so, then be not tongue-tied: go with me,

And in the breath of bitter words let 's smother
My damned son, that thy two sweet sons smother'd.
                                   A trumpet heard
The trumpet sounds: be copious in exclaims.
     Enter King Richard, and his Train, marching
KING RICHARD. Who intercepts me in my expedition?
DUCHESS. O! she that might have intercepted thee,
     By strangling thee in her accursed womb,
     From all the slaughters, wretch, that thou hast done!
QUEEN ELIZABETH. Hid'st thou that forehead with a golden
          crown,
     Where should be branded, if that right were right,
     The slaughter of the prince that ow'd that crown,
     And the dire death of my poor sons and brothers?
     Tell me, thou villain slave, where are my children?
DUCHESS. Thou toad, thou toad, where is thy brother
          Clarence
     And little Ned Plantagenet, his son?
QUEEN ELIZABETH. Where is the gentle Rivers, Vaughan,
          Grey?
DUCHESS. Where is kind Hastings?
KING RICHARD. A flourish, trumpets! strike alarum, drums!
     Let not the heavens hear these tell-tale women
     Rail on the Lord's anointed. Strike, I say!
                                   Flourish. Alarums
     Either be patient, and entreat me fair,
     Or with the clamorous report of war
     Thus will I drown your exclamations.
DUCHESS. Art thou my son?
KING RICHARD. Ay; I thank God, my father, and yourself.
DUCHESS. Then patiently hear my impatience.
KING RICHARD. Madam, I have a touch of your condition,
     That cannot brook the accent of reproof.
DUCHESS. O, let me speak!
KING RICHARD.   Do, then; but I 'll not hear.
DUCHESS. I will be mild and gentle in my words.
KING RICHARD. And brief, good mother; for I am in haste.
DUCHESS. Art thou so hasty? I have stay'd for thee,
     God knows, in torment and in agony.
KING RICHARD. And came I not at last to comfort you?
DUCHESS. No, by the holy rood, thou know'st it well,
     Thou cam'st on earth to make the earth my hell.

A grievous burden was thy birth to me;
Tetchy and wayward was thy infancy;
Thy school-days frightful, desperate, wild and furious;
Thy prime of manhood daring, bold, and venturous;
Thy age confirm'd, proud, subtle, sly, and bloody,
More mild, but yet more harmful, kind in hatred:
What comfortable hour canst thou name
That ever grac'd me in thy company?

KING RICHARD. Faith, none, but Humphrey Hour, that
      call'd your Grace
To breakfast once forth of my company.
If I be so disgracious in your eye,
Let me march on, and not offend you, madam.
Strike up the drum!

DUCHESS.   I prithee, hear me speak.

KING RICHARD. You speak too bitterly.

DUCHESS.   Hear me a word;
For I shall never speak to thee again.

KING RICHARD. So!

DUCHESS. Either thou wilt die by God's just ordinance,
Ere from this war thou turn a conqueror;
Or I with grief and extreme age shall perish
And never look upon thy face again.
Therefore take with thee my most grievous curse,
Which, in the day of battle, tire thee more
Than all the complete armour that thou wear'st!
My prayers on the adverse party fight;
And there the little souls of Edward's children
Whisper the spirits of thine enemies
And promise them success and victory.
Bloody thou art, bloody will be thy end;
Shame serves thy life and doth thy death attend.   *Exit*

QUEEN ELIZABETH. Though far more cause, yet much less
      spirit to curse
Abides in me: I say amen to her.   *Going*

KING RICHARD. Stay, madam; I must talk a word with you.

QUEEN ELIZABETH. I have no moe sons of the royal blood
For thee to slaughter: for my daughters, Richard,
They shall be praying nuns, not weeping queens;
And therefore level not to hit their lives.

KING RICHARD. You have a daughter call'd Elizabeth,
Virtuous and fair, royal and gracious.

QUEEN ELIZABETH. And must she die for this? O! let her live,
  And I 'll corrupt her manners, stain her beauty;
  Slander myself as false to Edward's bed;
  Throw over her the veil of infamy:
  So she may live unscarr'd of bleeding slaughter,
  I will confess she was not Edward's daughter.
KING RICHARD. Wrong not her birth; she is of royal blood.
QUEEN ELIZABETH. To save her life, I 'll say she is not so.
KING RICHARD. Her life is safest only in her birth.
QUEEN ELIZABETH. And only in that safety died her brothers.
KING RICHARD. Lo! at their births good stars were opposite!
QUEEN ELIZABETH. No, to their lives ill friends were
      contrary.
KING RICHARD. All unavoided is the doom of destiny.
QUEEN ELIZABETH. True, when avoided grace makes
      destiny.
  My babes were destin'd to a fairer death,
  If grace had bless'd thee with a fairer life.
KING RICHARD. You speak as if that I had slain my cousins.
QUEEN ELIZABETH. Cousins, indeed; and by their uncle
      cozen'd
  Of comfort, kingdom, kindred, freedom, life.
  Whose hand soever lanc'd their tender hearts,
  Thy head, all indirectly, gave direction:
  No doubt the murderous knife was dull and blunt
  Till it was whetted on thy stone-hard heart,
  To revel in the entrails of my lambs.
  But that still use of grief makes wild grief tame,
  My tongue should to thy ears not name my boys
  Till that my nails were anchor'd in thine eyes;
  And I, in such a desperate bay of death,
  Like a poor bark, of sails and tackling reft,
  Rush all to pieces on thy rocky bosom.
KING RICHARD. Madam, so thrive I in my enterprise
  And dangerous success of bloody wars,
  As I intend more good to you and yours
  Than ever you or yours by me were harm'd.
QUEEN ELIZABETH. What good is cover'd with the face of
      heaven,
  To be discover'd, that can do me good?
KING RICHARD. The advancement of your children, gentle
      lady.

QUEEN ELIZABETH. Up to some scaffold, there to lose their
    heads?
KING RICHARD. No, to the dignity and height of fortune,
    The high imperial type of this earth's glory.
QUEEN ELIZABETH. Flatter my sorrow with report of it:
    Tell me what state, what dignity, what honour,
    Canst thou demise to any child of mine?
KING RICHARD. Even all I have; ay, and myself and all,
    Will I withal endow a child of thine;
    So in the Lethe of thy angry soul
    Thou drown the sad remembrance of those wrongs
    Which thou supposest I have done to thee.
QUEEN ELIZABETH. Be brief, lest that the process of thy
        kindness
    Last longer telling than thy kindness' date.
KING RICHARD. Then know, that from my soul I love thy
        daughter.
QUEEN ELIZABETH. My daughter's mother thinks it with her
    soul.
KING RICHARD. What do you think?
QUEEN ELIZABETH. That thou dost love my daughter from
        thy soul:
    So from thy soul's love didst thou love her brothers;
    And from my heart's love I do thank thee for it.
KING RICHARD. Be not too hasty to confound my meaning:
    I mean, that with my soul I love thy daughter,
    And do intend to make her Queen of England.
QUEEN ELIZABETH. Well then, who dost thou mean shall be
    her king?
KING RICHARD. Even he that makes her queen: who else
    should be?
QUEEN ELIZABETH. What! thou?
KING RICHARD. Even so: what think you of it?
QUEEN ELIZABETH. How canst thou woo her?
KING RICHARD.   That I would learn of you,
    As one being best acquainted with her humour.
QUEEN ELIZABETH. And wilt thou learn of me?
KING RICHARD.   Madam, with all my heart.
QUEEN ELIZABETH. Send to her, by the man that slew her
        brothers,
    A pair of bleeding hearts; thereon engrave
    Edward and York; then haply will she weep:

Therefore present to her, as sometime Margaret
Did to thy father, steep'd in Rutland's blood,
A handkerchief, which, say to her, did drain
The purple sap from her sweet brother's body,
And bid her wipe her weeping eyes withal.
If this inducement move her not to love,
Send her a letter of thy noble deeds;
Tell her thou madest away her uncle Clarence,
Her uncle Rivers; ay, and for her sake,
Madest quick conveyance with her good aunt Anne.
KING RICHARD. You mock me, madam; this is not the way
  To win your daughter.
QUEEN ELIZABETH.   There is no other way
  Unless thou couldst put on some other shape,
  And not be Richard that hath done all this.
KING RICHARD. Say, that I did all this for love of her.
QUEEN ELIZABETH. Nay, then indeed she cannot choose **but**
    hate thee,
  Having bought love with such a bloody spoil.
KING RICHARD. Look, what is done cannot be now amended:
  Men shall deal unadvisedly sometimes,
  Which after-hours give leisure to repent.
  If I did take the kingdom from your sons,
  To make amends I 'll give it to your daughter.
  If I have kill'd the issue of your womb,
  To quicken your increase, I will beget
  Mine issue of your blood upon your daughter:
  A grandam's name is little less in love
  Than is the doting title of a mother;
  They are as children but one step below,
  Even of your mettle, of your very blood;
  Of all one pain, save for a night of groans
  Endur'd of her for whom you bid like sorrow.
  Your children were vexation to your youth,
  But mine shall be a comfort to your age.
  The loss you have is but a son being king,
  And by that loss your daughter is made queen.
  I cannot make you what amends I would,
  Therefore accept such kindness as I can.
  Dorset your son, that with a fearful soul
  Leads discontented steps in foreign soil,
  This fair alliance quickly shall call home

To high promotions and great dignity:
The king that calls your beauteous daughter wife,
Familiarly shall call thy Dorset brother;
Again shall you be mother to a king,
And all the ruins of distressful times
Repair'd with double riches of content.
What! we have many goodly days to see:
The liquid drops of tears that you have shed
Shall come again, transform'd to orient pearl,
Advantaging their loan with interest
Of ten times double gain of happiness.
Go then, my mother; to thy daughter go:
Make bold her bashful years with your experience;
Prepare her ears to hear a wooer's tale;
Put in her tender heart the aspiring flame
Of golden sovereignty; acquaint the princess
With the sweet silent hours of marriage joys:
And when this arm of mine hath chastised
The petty rebel, dull-brain'd Buckingham,
Bound with triumphant garlands will I come,
And lead thy daughter to a conqueror's bed;
To whom I will retail my conquest won,
And she shall be sole victress, Cæsar's Cæsar.

QUEEN ELIZABETH. What were I best to say? her father's
   brother
Would be her lord? Or shall I say, her uncle?
Or, he that slew her brothers and her uncles?
Under what title shall I woo for thee,
That God, the law, my honour, and her love
Can make seem pleasing to her tender years?

KING RICHARD. Infer fair England's peace by this alliance.

QUEEN ELIZABETH. Which she shall purchase with still
   lasting war.

KING RICHARD. Tell her, the king, that may command,
   entreats.

QUEEN ELIZABETH. That at her hands which the king's King
   forbids.

KING RICHARD. Say, she shall be a high and mighty queen.

QUEEN ELIZABETH. To wail the title, as her mother doth.

KING RICHARD. Say, I will love her everlastingly.

QUEEN ELIZABETH. But how long shall that title 'ever' last?

KING RICHARD. Sweetly in force unto her fair life's end.

QUEEN ELIZABETH. But how long fairly shall her sweet life
    last?

KING RICHARD. As long as heaven and nature lengthens it.

QUEEN ELIZABETH. As long as hell and Richard likes of it.

KING RICHARD. Say, I, her sovereign, am her subject low.

QUEEN ELIZABETH. But she, your subject, loathes such
    sovereignty.

KING RICHARD. Be eloquent in my behalf to her.

QUEEN ELIZABETH. An honest tale speeds best being plainly
    told.

KING RICHARD. Then plainly to her tell my loving tale.

QUEEN ELIZABETH. Plain and not honest is too harsh a style.

KING RICHARD. Your reasons are too shallow and too quick.

QUEEN ELIZABETH. O, no! my reasons are too deep and
    dead;
  Too deep and dead, poor infants, in their graves.

KING RICHARD. Harp not on that string, madam; that is past.

QUEEN ELIZABETH. Harp on it still shall I till heart-strings
    break.

KING RICHARD. Now, by my George, my garter, and my
    crown,—

QUEEN ELIZABETH. Profan'd, dishonour'd, and the third
    usurp'd.

KING RICHARD. I swear,—

QUEEN ELIZABETH. By nothing; for this is no oath.
  Thy George, profan'd, hath lost his holy honour;
  Thy garter, blemish'd, pawn'd his knightly virtue;
  Thy crown, usurp'd, disgrac'd his kingly glory.
  If something thou wouldst swear to be believ'd,
  Swear, then, by something that thou hast not wrong'd.

KING RICHARD. Now, by the world,—

QUEEN ELIZABETH.   'Tis full of thy foul wrongs.

KING RICHARD. My father's death,—

QUEEN ELIZABETH.   Thy life hath that dishonour'd.

KING RICHARD. Then, by myself,—

QUEEN ELIZABETH.   Thyself is self-misus'd.

KING RICHARD. Why, then, by God,—

QUEEN ELIZABETH.   God's wrong is most of all.
  If thou hadst fear'd to break an oath by him,
  The unity the king my husband made
  Had not been broken, nor my brothers died:
  If thou hadst fear'd to break an oath by him,

The imperial metal, circling now thy head,
Had grac'd the tender temples of my child,
And both the princes had been breathing here,
Which now, too tender bedfellows for dust,
Thy broken faith hath made a prey for worms.
What canst thou swear by now?

KING RICHARD.   The time to come.

QUEEN ELIZABETH. That thou hast wronged in the time
     o'erpast;
For I myself have many tears to wash
Hereafter time for time past wrong'd by thee.
The children live, whose parents thou hast slaughter'd,
Ungovern'd youth, to wail it in their age:
The parents live, whose children thou hast butcher'd,
Old barren plants, to wail it with their age.
Swear not by time to come; for that thou hast
Misus'd ere us'd, by times ill-us'd o'erpast.

KING RICHARD. As I intend to prosper, and repent,
So thrive I in my dangerous affairs
Of hostile arms! myself myself confound!
Heaven and fortune bar me happy hours!
Day, yield me not thy light; nor, night, thy rest!
Be opposite all planets of good luck
To my proceeding, if, with pure heart's love,
Immaculate devotion, holy thoughts,
I tender not thy beauteous princely daughter!
In her consists my happiness and thine;
Without her, follows to myself, and thee,
Herself, the land, and many a Christian soul,
Death, desolation, ruin, and decay:
It cannot be avoided but by this;
It will not be avoided but by this.
Therefore, dear mother,—I must call you so,—
Be the attorney of my love to her:
Plead what I will be, not what I have been;
Not my deserts, but what I will deserve:
Urge the necessity and state of times,
And be not peevish-fond in great designs.

QUEEN ELIZABETH. Shall I be tempted of the devil thus?

KING RICHARD. Ay, if the devil tempt thee to do good.

QUEEN ELIZABETH. Shall I forget myself to be myself?

KING RICHARD. Ay, if your self's remembrance wrong
     yourself.

QUEEN ELIZABETH. Yet thou didst kill my children.

KING RICHARD. But in your daughter's womb I bury them:
Where, in that nest of spicery, they shall breed
Selves of themselves, to your recomforture.

QUEEN ELIZABETH. Shall I go win my daughter to thy will?

KING RICHARD. And be a happy mother by the deed.

QUEEN ELIZABETH. I go. Write to me very shortly,
And you shall understand from me her mind.

KING RICHARD. Bear her my true love's kiss; and so, farewell.
                    Kissing her. Exit Queen Elizabeth
Relenting fool, and shallow changing woman!
            Enter Ratcliff; Catesby following
How now! what news?

RATCLIFF. Most mighty sovereign, on the western coast
Rideth a puissant navy; to the shores
Throng many doubtful hollow-hearted friends,
Unarm'd, and unresolv'd to beat them back.
'Tis thought that Richmond is their admiral;
And there they hull, expecting but the aid
Of Buckingham to welcome them ashore.

KING RICHARD. Some light-foot friend post to the Duke of
      Norfolk:
Ratcliff, thyself, or Catesby; where is he?

CATESBY. Here, my good lord.

KING RICHARD.   Catesby, fly to the duke.

CATESBY. I will, my lord, with all convenient haste.

KING RICHARD. Ratcliff, come hither. Post to Salisbury:
When thou com'st thither,—(*To Catesby*) Dull, unmind-
      ful villain,
Why stay'st thou here, and go'st not to the duke?

CATESBY. First, mighty liege, tell me your Highness'
      pleasure,
What from your Grace I shall deliver to him.

KING RICHARD. O! true, good Catesby: bid him levy straight
The greatest strength and power he can make,
And meet me suddenly at Salisbury.

CATESBY. I go.   *Exit*

RATCLIFF. What, may it please you, shall I do at Salisbury?

KING RICHARD. Why, what wouldst thou do there before I
      go?

RATCLIFF. Your Highness told me I should post before.
                    Enter Stanley

KING RICHARD. My mind is chang'd. Stanley, what news
   with you?

STANLEY. None good, my liege, to please you with the
   hearing;

   Nor none so bad but well may be reported.

KING RICHARD. Hoyday, a riddle! neither good nor bad!

   What need'st thou run so many miles about,

   When thou mayst tell thy tale the nearest way?

   Once more, what news?

STANLEY.   Richmond is on the seas.

KING RICHARD. There let him sink, and be the seas on him!

   White-liver'd runagate! what doth he there?

STANLEY. I know not, mighty sovereign, but by guess.

KING RICHARD. Well, as you guess?

STANLEY. Stirr'd up by Dorset, Buckingham, and Morton,

   He makes for England, here to claim the crown.

KING RICHARD. Is the chair empty? is the sword unsway'd?

   Is the king dead? the empire unpossess'd?

   What heir of York is there alive but we?

   And who is England's king but great York's heir?

   Then, tell me, what makes he upon the seas?

STANLEY. Unless for that, my liege, I cannot guess.

KING RICHARD. Unless for that he comes to be your liege,

   You cannot guess wherefore the Welshman comes.

   Thou wilt revolt and fly to him, I fear.

STANLEY. No, my good lord; therefore mistrust me not.

KING RICHARD. Where is thy power then to beat him back?

   Where be thy tenants and thy followers?

   Are they not now upon the western shore,

   Safe-conducting the rebels from their ships?

STANLEY. No, my good lord, my friends are in the North.

KING RICHARD. Cold friends to me: what do they in the
   North,

   When they should serve their sovereign in the West?

STANLEY. They have not been commanded, mighty king:

   Pleaseth your Majesty to give me leave,

   I 'll muster up my friends, and meet your Grace,

   Where and what time your Majesty shall please.

KING RICHARD. Ay, ay, thou wouldst be gone to join with
   Richmond:

   But I 'll not trust thee.

STANLEY.   Most mighty sovereign,

   You have no cause to hold my friendship doubtful.

I never was nor never will be false.

KING RICHARD. Go then and muster men: but leave behind
Your son, George Stanley: look your heart be firm,
Or else his head's assurance is but frail.

STANLEY. So deal with him as I prove true to you.   *Exit*

Enter a Messenger

MESSENGER. My gracious sovereign, now in Devonshire,
As I by friends am well advertised,
Sir Edward Courtney, and the haughty prelate,
Bishop of Exeter, his brother there,
With many moe confederates are in arms.

Enter a second Messenger

SECOND MESSENGER. In Kent, my liege, the Guildfords are in
arms;
And every hour more competitors
Flock to the rebels, and their power grows strong.

Enter a third Messenger

THIRD MESSENGER. My lord, the army of great Bucking-
ham—

KING RICHARD. Out on ye, owls! nothing but songs of death?
He strikes him
There, take thou that, till thou bring better news.

THIRD MESSENGER. The news I have to tell your Majesty
Is, that by sudden floods and fall of waters,
Buckingham's army is dispers'd and scatter'd;
And he himself wander'd away alone,
No man knows whither.

KING RICHARD.   I cry thee mercy:
There is my purse, to cure that blow of thine.
Hath any well-advised friend proclaim'd
Reward to him that brings the traitor in?

THIRD MESSENGER. Such proclamation hath been made, my
liege.

Enter a fourth Messenger

FOURTH MESSENGER. Sir Thomas Lovel, and Lord Marquess
Dorset,
'Tis said, my liege, in Yorkshire are in arms:
But this good comfort bring I to your Highness,
The Breton navy is dispers'd by tempest.
Richmond, in Dorsetshire, sent out a boat
Unto the shore to ask those on the banks
If they were his assistants, yea or no;
Who answer'd him, they came from Buckingham

Upon his party: he, mistrusting them,
Hois'd sail, and made away for Brittany.

KING RICHARD. March on, march on, since we are up in arms;
If not to fight with foreign enemies,
Yet to beat down these rebels here at home.

Re-enter Catesby

CATESBY. My liege, the Duke of Buckingham is taken,
That is the best news: that the Earl of Richmond
Is with a mighty power landed at Milford
Is colder news, but yet they must be told.

KING RICHARD. Away towards Salisbury! while we reason here,
A royal battle might be won and lost.
Some one take order Buckingham be brought
To Salisbury; the rest march on with me.   *Exeunt*

SCENE FIVE

The Same. A Room in Lord Stanley's House.

Enter Stanley and Sir Christopher Urswick

STANLEY. Sir Christopher, tell Richmond this from me:
That in the sty of this most bloody boar
My son George Stanley is frank'd up in hold:
If I revolt, off goes young George's head;
The fear of that holds off my present aid.
So, get thee gone: commend me to thy lord.
Withal, say that the queen hath heartily consented
He should espouse Elizabeth her daughter.
But, tell me, where is princely Richmond now?

CHRISTOPHER. At Pembroke, or at Ha'rford-west, in Wales.

STANLEY. What men of name resort to him?

CHRISTOPHER. Sir Walter Herbert, a renowned soldier,
Sir Gilbert Talbot, Sir William Stanley,
Oxford, redoubted Pembroke, Sir James Blunt,
And Rice ap Thomas, with a valiant crew;
And many other of great name and worth:
And towards London do they bend their power,
If by the way they be not fought withal.

STANLEY. Well, hie thee to thy lord; I kiss his hand:
My letter will resolve him of my mind.
Farewell.   *Exeunt*

ACT FIVE

SCENE ONE

Salisbury. An open Place.

Enter the Sheriff and Guard, with Buckingham,
led to execution

BUCKINGHAM. Will not King Richard let me speak with him?
SHERIFF. No, my good lord; therefore be patient.
BUCKINGHAM. Hastings, and Edward's children, Grey and
 Rivers,
 Holy King Henry, and thy fair son Edward,
 Vaughan, and all that have miscarried
 By underhand corrupted foul injustice,
 If that your moody discontented souls
 Do through the clouds behold this present hour,
 Even for revenge mock my destruction!
 This is All-Souls' day, fellows, is it not?
SHERIFF. It is, my lord.
BUCKINGHAM. Why, then All-Souls' day is my body's
 doomsday.
 This is the day that, in King Edward's time,
 I wish'd might fall on me, when I was found
 False to his children or his wife's allies;
 This is the day wherein I wish'd to fall
 By the false faith of him whom most I trusted;
 This, this All-Souls' day to my fearful soul
 Is the determin'd respite of my wrongs.
 That high All-Seer which I dallied with
 Hath turn'd my feigned prayer on my head,
 And given in earnest what I begg'd in jest.
 Thus doth he force the swords of wicked men
 To turn their own points on their masters' bosoms:
 Thus Margaret's curse falls heavy on my neck:

'When he,' quoth she, 'shall split thy heart with sorrow,
Remember Margaret was a prophetess.'
Come, lead me, officers, to the block of shame:
Wrong hath but wrong, and blame the due of blame.

Exeunt

SCENE TWO

A Plain near Tamworth.

*Enter with drum and colours, Richmond, Oxford, Sir James
Blunt, Sir Walter Herbert, and Others, with Forces,
marching*

RICHMOND. Fellows in arms, and my most loving friends,
Bruis'd underneath the yoke of tyranny,
Thus far into the bowels of the land
Have we march'd on without impediment:
And here receive we from our father Stanley
Lines of fair comfort and encouragement.
The wretched, bloody, and usurping boar,
That spoil'd your summer fields and fruitful vines,
Swills your warm blood like wash, and makes his trough
In your embowell'd bosoms, this foul swine
Is now even in the centre of this isle,
Near to the town of Leicester, as we learn:
From Tamworth thither is but one day's march.
In God's name, cheerly on, courageous friends,
To reap the harvest of perpetual peace
By this one bloody trial of sharp war.
OXFORD. Every man's conscience is a thousand men,
To fight against this guilty homicide.
HERBERT. I doubt not but his friends will turn to us.
BLUNT. He hath no friends but what are friends for fear,
Which in his dearest need will fly from him.
RICHMOND. All for our vantage: then, in God's name,
march:
True hope is swift, and flies with swallow's wings;
Kings it makes gods, and meaner creatures kings. *Exeunt*

SCENE THREE

Bosworth Field.

Enter King Richard and Forces; the Duke of Norfolk, Earl of Surrey, and Others

KING RICHARD. Here pitch our tent, even here in Bosworth field.
My Lord of Surrey, why look you so sad?
SURREY. My heart is ten times lighter than my looks.
KING RICHARD. My Lord of Norfolk,—
NORFOLK.   Here, most gracious liege.
KING RICHARD. Norfolk, we must have knocks; ha! must we not?
NORFOLK. We must both give and take, my loving lord.
KING RICHARD. Up with my tent! here will I lie to-night;
        Soldiers begin to set up the King's tent
But where to-morrow? Well, all 's one for that.
Who hath descried the number of the traitors?
NORFOLK. Six or seven thousand is their utmost power.
KING RICHARD. Why, our battalia trebles that account;
Besides, the king's name is a tower of strength,
Which they upon the adverse faction want.
Up with the tent! Come, noble gentlemen,
Let us survey the vantage of the ground;
Call for some men of sound direction:
Let 's lack no discipline, make no delay;
For, lords, to-morrow is a busy day.   *Exeunt*
*Enter on the other side of
the field, Richmond, Sir William Brandon, Oxford, and other
Officers. Some of the Soldiers pitch Richmond's tent*
RICHMOND. The weary sun hath made a golden set,
And, by the bright track of his fiery car,
Gives token of a goodly day to-morrow.
Sir William Brandon, you shall bear my standard.
Give me some ink and paper in my tent:
I 'll draw the form and model of our battle.
Limit each leader to his several charge,
And part in just proportion our small power.
My Lord of Oxford, you, Sir William Brandon,
And you, Sir Walter Herbert, stay with me.

The Earl of Pembroke keeps his regiment:
Good Captain Blunt, bear my good-night to him,
And by the second hour in the morning
Desire the earl to see me in my tent.
Yet one thing more, good captain, do for me;
Where is Lord Stanley quarter'd, do you know?
BLUNT. Unless I have mista'en his colours much,—
Which, well I am assur'd, I have not done,—
His regiment lies half a mile at least
So th'rom the mighty power of the king.
RICHMOND. If without peril it be possible,
Good Captain Blunt, bear my good-night to him.
And give him from me this most needful note.
BLUNT. Upon my life, my lord, I 'll undertake it;
And so, God give you quiet rest to-night!
RICHMOND. Good-night, good Captain Blunt. Come,
    gentlemen,
Let us consult upon to-morrow's business;
Into my tent, the air is raw and cold.

                They withdraw into the tent
           Enter, to his tent,
    King Richard, Norfolk, Ratcliff, and Catesby

KING RICHARD. What is 't o'clock?
CATESBY.   It 's supper-time, my lord;
It 's nine o'clock.
KING RICHARD.   I will not sup to-night.
Give me some ink and paper.
What, is my beaver easier than it was,
And all my armour laid into my tent?
CATESBY. It is, my liege; and all things are in readiness.
KING RICHARD. Good Norfolk, hie thee to thy charge;
Use careful watch; choose trusty sentinels.
NORFOLK. I go, my lord.
KING RICHARD. Stir with the lark to-morrow, gentle Norfolk.
NORFOLK. I warrant you, my lord.   *Exit*
KING RICHARD. Ratcliff!
RATCLIFF. My lord?
KING RICHARD.   Send out a pursuivant at arms
To Stanley's regiment; bid him bring his power
Before sunrising, lest his son George fall
Into the blind cave of eternal night.
Fill me a bowl of wine. Give me a watch.

Saddle white Surrey for the field to-morrow.
Look that my staves be sound, and not too heavy.
Ratcliff!

RATCLIFF. My lord?

KING RICHARD. Saw'st thou the melancholy Lord
    Northumberland?

RATCLIFF. Thomas the Earl of Surrey, and himself,
    Much about cock-shut time, from troop to troop
    Went through the army, cheering up the soldiers.

KING RICHARD. So, I am satisfied. Give me a bowl of wine:
    I have not that alacrity of spirit,
    Nor cheer of mind, that I was wont to have.
    Set it down. Is ink and paper ready?

RATCLIFF. It is, my lord.

KING RICHARD. Bid my guard watch; leave me.
    Ratcliff, about the mid of night come to my tent
    And help to arm me. Leave me, I say.

> *King Richard retires into
> his tent. Exeunt Ratcliff and Catesby
> Richmond's tent opens,
> and discovers him and his Officers, &c. Enter Stanley*

STANLEY. Fortune and victory sit on thy helm!

RICHMOND. All comfort that the dark night can afford
    Be to thy person, noble father-in-law!
    Tell me, how fares our loving mother?

STANLEY. I, by attorney, bless thee from thy mother,
    Who prays continually for Richmond's good:
    So much for that. The silent hours steal on,
    And flaky darkness breaks within the east.
    In brief, for so the season bids us be,
    Prepare thy battle early in the morning,
    And put thy fortune to the arbitrement
    Of bloody strokes and mortal-staring war.
    I, as I may,—that which I would I cannot,—
    With best advantage will deceive the time,
    And aid thee in this doubtful shock of arms.
    But on thy side I may not be too forward,
    Lest, being seen, thy brother, tender George,
    Be executed in his father's sight.
    Farewell: the leisure and the fearful time
    Cuts of the ceremonious vows of love
    And ample interchange of sweet discourse,

Which so long sunder'd friends should dwell upon:
God give us leisure for these rites of love!
Once more, adieu: be valiant, and speed well!
RICHMOND. Good lords, conduct him to his regiment.
I 'll strive, with troubled thoughts, to take a nap,
Lest leaden slumber peise me down to-morrow,
When I should mount with wings of victory.
Once more, good-night, kind lords and gentlemen.

Exeunt all but Richmond

O! thou, whose captain I account myself,
Look on my forces with a gracious eye;
Put in their hands thy bruising irons of wrath,
That they may crush down with a heavy fall
The usurping helmets of our adversaries!
Make us thy ministers of chastisement,
That we may praise thee in thy victory!
To thee I do commend my watchful soul,
Ere I let fall the windows of mine eyes:
Sleeping and waking, O! defend me still!   *Sleeps*

The Ghost of Prince Edward,
Son to Henry the Sixth, rises between the two tents

GHOST. (*To King Richard*) Let me sit heavy on thy soul
    to-morrow!
Think how thou stab'dst me in my prime of youth
At Tewksbury: despair, therefore, and die!
    (*To Richmond*) Be cheerful, Richmond; for the wronged
    souls
Of butcher'd princes fight in thy behalf:
King Henry's issue, Richmond, comforts thee.

The Ghost of King Henry the Sixth rises

GHOST. (*To King Richard*) When I was mortal, my anointed
    body
By thee was punched full of deadly holes:
Think on the Tower and me; despair and die!
Henry the Sixth bids thee despair and die.
    (*To Richmond*) Virtuous and holy, be thou conqueror!
Harry, that prophesied thou shouldst be king,
Doth comfort thee in thy sleep: live thou and flourish!

The Ghost of Clarence rises

GHOST. (*To King Richard*) Let me sit heavy on thy soul
    to-morrow!
I, that was wash'd to death with fulsome wine,

Poor Clarence, by thy guile betray'd to death!
To-morrow in the battle think on me,
And fall thy edgeless sword: despair, and die!
(*To Richmond*) Thou offspring of the house of Lancaster,
The wronged heirs of York do pray for thee:
Good angels guard thy battle! live, and flourish!
    The Ghosts of Rivers, Grey, and Vaughan rise
GHOST OF RIVERS. (*To King Richard*) Let me sit heavy on
    thy soul to-morrow!
Rivers, that died at Pomfret! despair, and die!
GHOST OF GREY. (*To King Richard*) Think upon Grey, and
    let thy soul despair.
GHOST OF VAUGHAN. (*To King Richard*) Think upon
        Vaughan, and with guilty fear
Let fall thy pointless lance: despair, and die!—
ALL THREE. (*To Richmond*) Awake! and think our wrongs
    in Richard's bosom
Will conquer him: awake, and win the day!
            The Ghost of Hastings rises
GHOST. (*To King Richard*) Bloody and guilty, guiltily awake;
And in a bloody battle end thy days!
Think on Lord Hastings, so despair, and die!—
(*To Richmond*) Quiet, untroubled soul, awake, awake!
Arm, fight, and conquer, for fair England's sake!
        The Ghosts of the two young Princes rise
GHOSTS. (*To King Richard*) Dream on thy cousins
    smother'd in the Tower:
Let us be lead within thy bosom, Richard,
And weigh thee down to ruin, shame, and death!
Thy nephews' souls bid thee despair and die!
(*To Richmond*) Sleep, Richmond, sleep in peace, and
    wake in joy;
Good angels guard thee from the boar's annoy!
Live, and beget a happy race of kings!
Edward's unhappy sons do bid thee flourish.
            The Ghost of Lady Anne rises
GHOST. (*To King Richard*) Richard, thy wife, that wretched
        Anne thy wife,
That never slept a quiet hour with thee,
Now fills thy sleep with perturbations:
To-morrow in the battle think on me,
And fall thy edgeless sword: despair, and die!

(*To Richmond*) Thou quiet soul, sleep thou a quiet sleep,
Dream of success and happy victory!
Thy adversary's wife doth pray for thee.

The Ghost of Buckingham rises

GHOST. (*To King Richard*) The first was I that help'd thee to
     the crown;
The last was I that felt thy tyranny.
O! in the battle think on Buckingham,
And die in terror of thy guiltiness!
Dream on, dream on, of bloody deeds and death:
Fainting, despair; despairing, yield thy breath!
(*To Richmond*) I died for hope ere ˙ ⸀ould lend thee aid:
But cheer thy heart, and be thou not dismay'd:
God and good angels fight on Richmond's side;
And Richard fall in height of all his pride.

The Ghosts vanish. King Richard starts out of his dream

KING RICHARD. Give me another horse! bind up my wounds!
Have mercy, Jesu! Soft! I did but dream.
O coward conscience, how dost thou afflict me!
The lights burn blue. It is now dead midnight.
Cold fearful drops stand on my trembling flesh.
What! do I fear myself? there 's none else by:
Richard loves Richard; that is, I am I.
Is there a murderer here? No. Yes, I am:
Then fly: what! from myself? Great reason why:
Lest I revenge. What! myself upon myself?
Alack! I love myself. Wherefore? for any good
That I myself have done unto myself?
O! no: alas! I rather hate myself
For hateful deeds committed by myself.
I am a villain. Yet I lie; I am not.
Fool, of thyself speak well: fool, do not flatter.
My conscience hath a thousand several tongues,
And every tongue brings in a several tale,
And every tale condemns me for a villain.
Perjury, perjury, in the high'st degree:
Murder, stern murder, in the direst degree;
All several sins, all us'd in each degree,
Throng to the bar, crying all, 'Guilty! guilty!'
I shall despair. There is no creature loves me;
And if I die, no soul will pity me:
Nay, wherefore should they, since that I myself

Find in myself no pity to myself?
Methought the souls of all that I had murder'd
Came to my tent; and every one did threat
To-morrow's vengeance on the head of Richard.

Enter Ratcliff

RATCLIFF. My lord!

KING RICHARD. 'Zounds! who 's there?

RATCLIFF. Ratcliff, my lord; 'tis I. The early village cock
Hath twice done salutation to the morn;
Your friends are up, and buckle on their armour.

KING RICHARD. O Ratcliff! I have dream'd a fearful dream.
What thinkest thou, will our friends prove all true?

RATCLIFF. No doubt, my lord.

KING RICHARD.   O Ratcliff! I fear, I fear,—

RATCLIFF. Nay, good my lord, be not afraid of shadows.

KING RICHARD. By the apostle Paul, shadows to-night
Have struck more terror to the soul of Richard
Than can the substance of ten thousand soldiers
Armed in proof, and led by shallow Richmond.
It is not yet near day. Come, go with me;
Under our tents I 'll play the eaves-dropper,
To hear if any mean to shrink from me.   *Exeunt*

Richmond wakes. Enter Oxford and others.

LORDS. Good-morrow, Richmond!

RICHMOND. Cry mercy, lords, and watchful gentlemen,
That you have ta'en a tardy sluggard here.

LORDS. How have you slept, my lord?

RICHMOND. The sweetest sleep, the fairest-boding dreams
That ever enter'd in a drowsy head,
Have I since your departure had, my lords.
Methought their souls, whose bodies Richard murder'd,
Came to my tent and cried on victory:
I promise you, my heart is very jocund
In the remembrance of so fair a dream.
How far into the morning is it, lords?

LORDS. Upon the stroke of four.

RICHMOND. Why, then 'tis time to arm and give direction.

Richmond's oration to his Soldiers

More than I have said, loving countrymen,
The leisure and enforcement of the time
Forbids to dwell on: yet remember this,
God and our good cause fight upon our side;

The prayers of holy saints and wronged souls,
Like high-rear'd bulwarks, stand before our faces;
Richard except, those whom we fight against
Had rather have us win than him they follow.
For what is he they follow? truly, gentlemen,
A bloody tyrant and a homicide;
One rais'd in blood, and one in blood establish'd;
One that made means to come by what he hath,
And slaughter'd those that were the means to help him;
A base foul stone, made precious by the foil
Of England's chair, where he is falsely set;
One that hath ever been God's enemy.
Then, if you fight against God's enemy,
God will in justice ward you as his soldiers;
If you do sweat to put a tyrant down,
You sleep in peace, the tyrant being slain;
If you do fight against your country's foes,
Your country's fat shall pay your pains the hire;
If you do fight in safeguard of your wives,
Your wives shall welcome home the conquerors;
If you do free your children from the sword,
Your children's children quit it in your age.
Then, in the name of God and all these rights,
Advance your standards, draw your willing swords.
For me, the ransom of my bold attempt
Shall be this cold corse on the earth's cold face;
But if I thrive, the gain of my attempt
The least of you shall share his part thereof.
Sound drums and trumpets, boldly and cheerfully;
God and Saint George! Richmond and victory!   *Exeunt*
Re-enter King Richard, Ratcliff, Attendants, and Forces

KING RICHARD. What said Northumberland as touching
    Richmond?
RATCLIFF. That he was never trained up in arms.
KING RICHARD. He said the truth: and what said Surrey
    then?
RATCLIFF. He smil'd, and said, 'The better for our purpose.'
KING RICHARD. He was i' the right; and so, indeed, it is.
                                           Clock strikes
  Tell the clock there. Give me a calendar.
  Who saw the sun to-day?
RATCLIFF.   Not I, my lord.

KING RICHARD. Then he disdains to shine; for by the book
    He should have brav'd the East an hour ago:
    A black day will it be to somebody.
    Ratcliff!
RATCLIFF. My lord?
KING RICHARD.   The sun will not be seen to-day;
    The sky doth frown and lower upon our army.
    I would these dewy tears were from the ground.
    Not shine to-day! Why, what is that to me
    More than to Richmond? for the selfsame heaven
    That frowns on me looks sadly upon him.
Enter Norfolk

NORFOLK. Arm, arm, my lord! the foe vaunts in the field.
KING RICHARD. Come, bustle, bustle; caparison my horse.
    Call up Lord Stanley, bid him bring his power:
    I will lead forth my soldiers to the plain,
    And thus my battle shall be ordered:
    My foreward shall be drawn out all in length
    Consisting equally of horse and foot;
    Our archers shall be placed in the midst:
    John Duke of Norfolk, Thomas Earl of Surrey,
    Shall have the leading of this foot and horse.
    They thus directed, we will follow
    In the main battle, whose puissance on either side
    Shall be well winged with our chiefest horse.
    This, and Saint George to boot! What think'st thou,
      Norfolk?
NORFOLK. A good direction, warlike sovereign.
    This found I on my tent this morning.   *Giving a scroll*
KING RICHARD. 'Jockey of Norfolk, be not too bold,
    For Dickon thy master is bought and sold.'
    A thing devised by the enemy.
    Go, gentlemen; every man to his charge:
    Let not our babbling dreams affright our souls;
    Conscience is but a word that cowards use,
    Devis'd at first to keep the strong in awe:
    Our strong arms be our conscience, swords our law.
    March on, join bravely, let us to 't pell-mell;
    If not to heaven, then hand in hand to hell.
His oration to his Army

    What shall I say more than I have inferr'd?
    Remember whom you are to cope withal:

A sort of vagabonds, rascals, and runaways,
A scum of Bretons and base lackey peasants,
Whom their o'er-cloyed country vomits forth
To desperate adventures and assur'd destruction.
You sleeping safe, they bring you to unrest;
You having lands, and bless'd with beauteous wives,
They would restrain the one, distain the other.
And who doth lead them but a paltry fellow,
Long kept in Britaine at our mother's cost?
A milksop, one that never in his life
Felt so much cold as over shoes in snow?
Let 's whip these stragglers o'er the sea again;
Lash hence these overweening rags of France,
These famish'd beggars, weary of their lives;
Who, but for dreaming on this fond exploit,
For want of means, poor rats, had hang'd themselves:
If we be conquer'd, let men conquer us,
And not these bastard Bretons, whom our fathers
Have in their own land beaten, bobb'd, and thump'd,
And, on record, left them the heirs of shame.
Shall these enjoy our lands? lie with our wives?
Ravish our daughters?   *Drum afar off*
                 Hark! I hear their drum.
Fight, gentlemen of England! fight, bold yeomen!
Draw, archers, draw your arrows to the head!
Spur your proud horses hard, and ride in blood;
Amaze the welkin with your broken staves!
                   Enter a Messenger
What says Lord Stanley? will he bring his power?
MESSENGER. My lord, he doth deny to come.
KING RICHARD. Off with his son George's head!
NORFOLK. My lord, the enemy is pass'd the marsh:
  After the battle let George Stanley die.
KING RICHARD. A thousand hearts are great within my
    bosom:
  Advance our standards! set upon our foes!
  Our ancient word of courage, fair Saint George,
  Inspire us with the spleen of fiery dragons!
  Upon them! Victory sits upon our helms.   *Exeunt*

SCENE FOUR

Another Part of the Field.

Alarum: Excursions. Enter Norfolk and Forces; to him
Catesby

CATESBY. Rescue, my Lord of Norfolk! rescue, rescue!
   The king enacts more wonders than a man,
   Daring an opposite to every danger:
   His horse is slain, and all on foot he fights,
   Seeking for Richmond in the throat of death.
   Rescue, fair lord, or else the day is lost!
            Alarum. Enter King Richard
KING RICHARD. A horse! a horse! my kingdom for a horse!
CATESBY. Withdraw, my lord; I 'll help you to a horse.
KING RICHARD. Slave! I have set my life upon a cast,
   And I will stand the hazard of the die.
   I think there be six Richmonds in the field;
   Five have I slain to-day, instead of him.—
   A horse! a horse! my kingdom for a horse!   *Exeunt*
   Alarums. Enter from opposite sides King Richard
and Richmond, and exeunt fighting. Retreat and flourish.
Then re-enter Richmond, Stanley, bearing the crown, with
        divers other Lords, and Forces
RICHMOND. God and your arms be prais'd, victorious
   friends;
   The day is ours, the bloody dog is dead.
STANLEY. Courageous Richmond, well hast thou acquit
   thee!
   Lo! here, this long-usurped royalty
   From the dead temples of this bloody wretch
   Have I pluck'd off, to grace thy brows withal:
   Wear it, enjoy it, and make much of it.
RICHMOND. Great God of heaven, say amen to all!
   But, tell me, is young George Stanley living?
STANLEY. He is, my lord, and safe in Leicester town;
   Whither, if you please, we may withdraw us.
RICHMOND. What men of name are slain on either side?
STANLEY. John Duke of Norfolk, Walter Lord Ferrers,
   Sir Robert Brakenbury, and Sir William Brandon.
RICHMOND. Inter their bodies as becomes their births:

Proclaim a pardon to the soldiers fled
That in submission will return to us;
And then, as we have ta'en the sacrament,
We will unite the white rose and the red:
Smile, heaven, upon this fair conjunction,
That long hath frown'd upon their enmity!
What traitor hears me, and says not amen?
England hath long been mad, and scarr'd herself;
The brother blindly shed the brother's blood,
The father rashly slaughter'd his own son,
The son, compell'd, been butcher to the sire:
All this divided York and Lancaster,
Divided in their dire division,
O! now, let Richmond and Elizabeth,
The true succeeders of each royal house,
By God's fair ordinance conjoin together;
And let their heirs—God, if thy will be so,—
Enrich the time to come with smooth-fac'd peace,
With smiling plenty, and fair prosperous days!
Abate the edge of traitors, gracious Lord,
That would reduce these bloody days again,
And make poor England weep in streams of blood!
Let them not live to taste this land's increase,
That would with treason wound this fair land's peace!
Now civil wounds are stopp'd, peace lives again:
That she may long live here, God say amen!   *Exeunt*

THE FAMOUS HISTORY OF THE LIFE OF KING HENRY THE EIGHTH

CAST OF CHARACTERS

KING HENRY THE EIGHTH
CARDINAL WOLSEY
CARDINAL CAMPEIUS
CAPUCIUS, *Ambassador from the Emperor Charles the Fifth*
CRANMER, *Archbishop of Canterbury*
DUKE OF NORFOLK
DUKE OF SUFFOLK
DUKE OF BUCKINGHAM
EARL OF SURREY
Lord Chancellor
Lord Chamberlain
GARDINER, *Bishop of Winchester*
BISHOP OF LINCOLN
LORD ABERGAVENNY
LORD SANDS
SIR THOMAS LOVELL
SIR HENRY GUILDFORD
SIR ANTHONY DENNY
SIR NICHOLAS VAUX
Secretaries to Wolsey
CROMWELL, *Servant to Wolsey*
GRIFFITH, *Gentleman-Usher to Queen Katharine*
Three Gentlemen
Garter King-at-Arms
DOCTOR BUTTS, *Physician to the King*
Surveyor to the Duke of Buckingham
BRANDON, *and a Sergeant-at-Arms*
Door-keeper of the Council Chamber

(*continued on next page*)

Porter, and his Man
Page to Gardiner
A Crier

QUEEN KATHARINE, *Wife to King Henry; afterwards divorced*
ANNE BULLEN, *her Maid of Honour; afterwards Queen*
An Old Lady, Friend to Anne Bullen
PATIENCE, *Woman to Queen Katharine*

Several Lords and Ladies in the Dumb Shows; Women attending upon the Queen; Spirits which appear to her; Scribes, Officers, Guards, and other Attendants

SCENE

Chiefly in London and Westminster; once, at Kimbolton

PROLOGUE

I come no more to make you laugh: things now,
That bear a weighty and a serious brow,
Sad, high, and working, full of state and woe,
Such noble scenes as draw the eye to flow,
We now present. Those that can pity, here
May, if they think it well, let fall a tear;
The subject will deserve it. Such as give
Their money out of hope they may believe,
May here find truth too. Those that come to see
Only a show or two, and so agree
The play may pass, if they be still and willing,
I 'll undertake may see away their shilling
Richly in two short hours. Only they
That come to hear a merry, bawdy play,
A noise of targets, or to see a fellow
In a long motley coat guarded with yellow,
Will be deceiv'd; for, gentle hearers, know,
To rank our chosen truth with such a show
As fool and fight is, besides forfeiting
Our own brains, and the opinion that we bring,
To make that only true we now intend,
Will leave us never an understanding friend.
Therefore, for goodness' sake, and as you are known
The first and happiest hearers of the town,
Be sad, as we would make ye: think ye see
The very persons of our noble story
As they were living; think you see them great,
And follow'd with the general throng and sweat
Of thousand friends; then, in a moment see
How soon this mightiness meets misery:
And if you can be merry then, I 'll say
A man may weep upon his wedding-day.

THE FAMOUS HISTORY OF THE LIFE OF KING HENRY THE EIGHTH

ACT ONE

SCENE ONE

London. An Ante-chamber in the Palace.

Enter at one door the Duke of Norfolk; at the other, the Duke of Buckingham and the Lord Abergavenny

BUCKINGHAM. Good-morrow, and well met. How have you done,
 Since last we saw in France?
NORFOLK.   I thank your Grace,
 Healthful; and ever since a fresh admirer
 Of what I saw there.
BUCKINGHAM.   An untimely ague
 Stay'd me a prisoner in my chamber, when
 Those suns of glory, those two lights of men,
 Met in the vale of Andren.
NORFOLK.   Twixt Guynes and Arde:
 I was then present, saw them salute on horseback;
 Beheld them, when they lighted, how they clung
 In their embracement, as they grew together;
 Which had they, what four thron'd ones could have
  weigh'd
 Such a compounded one?
BUCKINGHAM.   All the whole time
 I was my chamber's prisoner.
NORFOLK.   Then you lost
 The view of earthly glory: men might say,
 Till this time, pomp was single, but now married
 To one above itself. Each following day
 Became the next day's master, till the last
 Made former wonders its. To-day the French
 All clinquant, all in gold, like heathen gods,

Shone down the English; and to-morrow they
Made Britain India: every man that stood
Show'd like a mine. Their dwarfish pages were
As cherubins, all gilt: the madams, too,
Not us'd to toil, did almost sweat to bear
The pride upon them, that their very labour
Was to them as a painting. Now this masque
Was cried incomparable; and the ensuing night
Made it a fool, and beggar. The two kings,
Equal in lustre, were now best, now worst,
As presence did present them; him in eye,
Still him in praise; and, being present both,
'Twas said they saw but one; and no discerner
Durst wag his tongue in censure. When these suns—
For so they phrase 'em—by their heralds challeng'd
The noble spirits to arms, they did perform
Beyond thought's compass; that former fabulous story,
Being now seen possible enough, got credit,
That Bevis was believ'd.

BUCKINGHAM.   O! you go far.

NORFOLK. As I belong to worship, and affect
In honour honesty, the tract of every thing
Would by a good discourser lose some life,
Which action's self was tongue to. All was royal;
To the disposing of it nought rebell'd,
Order gave each thing view; the office did
Distinctly his full function.

BUCKINGHAM.   Who did guide,
I mean, who set the body and the limbs
Of this great sport together, as you guess?

NORFOLK. One certes, that promises no element
In such a business.

BUCKINGHAM.   I pray you, who, my lord?

NORFOLK. All this was order'd by the good discretion
Of the right reverend Cardinal of York.

BUCKINGHAM. The devil speed him! no man's pie is freed
From his ambitious finger. What had he
To do in these fierce vanities? I wonder
That such a keech can with his very bulk
Take up the rays o' the beneficial sun,
And keep it from the earth.

NORFOLK.   Surely, sir,
There 's in him stuff that puts him to these ends;

For, being not propp'd by ancestry, whose grace
Chalks successors their way, nor call'd upon
For high feats done to the crown; neither allied
To eminent assistants; but, spider-like,
Out of his self-drawing web, he gives us note,
The force of his own merit makes his way;
A gift that heaven gives for him, which buys
A place next to the king.

ABERGAVENNY.   I cannot tell
What heaven hath given him: let some graver eye
Pierce into that; but I can see his pride
Peep through each part of him: whence has he that?
If not from hell, the devil is a niggard,
Or has given all before, and he begins
A new hell in himself.

BUCKINGHAM.   Why the devil,
Upon this French going-out took he upon him,
Without the privity o' the king, to appoint
Who should attend on him? He makes up the file
Of all the gentry; for the most part such
To whom as great a charge as little honour
He meant to lay upon: and his own letter,—
The honourable board of council out,—
Must fetch him in he papers.

ABERGAVENNY.   I do know
Kinsmen of mine, three at the least, that have
By this so sicken'd their estates that never
They shall abound as formerly.

BUCKINGHAM.   O! many
Have broke their backs with laying manors on 'em
For this great journey. What did this vanity
But minister communication of
A most poor issue?

NORFOLK.   Grievingly I think,
The peace between the French and us not values
The cost that did conclude it.

BUCKINGHAM.   Every man,
After the hideous storm that follow'd, was
A thing inspir'd; and, not consulting, broke
Into a general prophecy: That this tempest,
Dashing the garment of this peace, aboded
The sudden breach on 't.

NORFOLK.   Which is budded out;

For France hath flaw'd the league, and hath attach'd
Our merchants' goods at Bourdeaux.

ABERGAVENNY.   Is it therefore
The ambassador is silenc'd?

NORFOLK.   Marry, is 't.

ABERGAVENNY. A proper title of a peace; and purchas'd
At a superfluous rate!

BUCKINGHAM.   Why, all this business
Our reverend cardinal carried.

NORFOLK.   Like it your Grace,
The state takes notice of the private difference
Betwixt you and the cardinal. I advise you,—
And take it from a heart that wishes towards you
Honour and plenteous safety,—that you read
The cardinal's malice and his potency
Together; to consider further that
What his high hatred would effect wants not
A minister in his power. You know his nature,
That he 's revengeful; and I know his sword
Hath a sharp edge: it 's long, and 't may be said,
It reaches far; and where 'twill not extend,
Thither he darts it. Bosom up my counsel,
You 'll find it wholesome. Lo, where comes that rock
That I advise your shunning.

  Enter Cardinal Wolsey,—the Purse borne before
him,—certain of the Guard, and two Secretaries with papers.
The Cardinal in his passage fixeth his eye on Buckingham,
  and Buckingham on him, both full of disdain

WOLSEY. The Duke of Buckingham's surveyor, ha?
Where 's his examination?

FIRST SECRETARY.   Here, so please you.

WOLSEY. Is he in person ready?

FIRST SECRETARY.   Ay, please your Grace.

WOLSEY. Well, we shall then know more; and Buckingham
Shall lessen this big look.   *Exeunt Wolsey and Train*

BUCKINGHAM. This butcher's cur is venom-mouth'd, and I
Have not the power to muzzle him; therefore best
Not wake him in his slumber. A beggar's book
Outworths a noble's blood.

NORFOLK.   What! are you chaf'd?
Ask God for temperance; that 's the appliance only
Which your disease requires.

BUCKINGHAM.   I read in 's looks
    Matter against me; and his eye revil'd
    Me, as his abject object: at this instant
    He bores me with some trick: he 's gone to the king;
    I 'll follow, and outstare him.
NORFOLK.   Stay, my lord,
    And let your reason with your choler question
    What 'tis you go about. To climb steep hills
    Requires slow pace at first: anger is like
    A full-hot horse, who being allow'd his way,
    Self-mettle tires him. Not a man in England
    Can advise me like you: be to yourself
    As you would to your friend.
BUCKINGHAM.   I 'll to the king;
    And from a mouth of honour quite cry down
    This Ipswich fellow's insolence, or proclaim
    There 's difference in no persons.
NORFOLK.   Be advis'd;
    Heat not a furnace for your foe so hot
    That it do singe yourself. We may outrun
    By violent swiftness that which we run at,
    And lose by over-running. Know you not,
    The fire that mounts the liquor till it run o'er,
    In seeming to augment it wastes it? Be advis'd:
    I say again, there is no English soul
    More stronger to direct you than yourself,
    If with the sap of reason you would quench,
    Or but allay, the fire of passion.
BUCKINGHAM.   Sir,
    I am thankful to you, and I 'll go along
    By your prescription: but this top-proud fellow,
    Whom from the flow of gall I name not, but
    From sincere motions,—by intelligence,
    And proofs as clear as founts in July, when
    We see each grain of gravel,—I do know
    To be corrupt and treasonous.
NORFOLK.   Say not 'treasonous.'
BUCKINGHAM. To the king I 'll say 't; and make my vouch as
    strong
    As shore of rock. Attend. This holy fox,
    Or wolf, or both,—for he is equal ravenous
    As he is subtle, and as prone to mischief

As able to perform 't, his mind and place
Infecting one another, yea, reciprocally,
Only to show his pomp as well in France
As here at home, suggests the king our master
To this last costly treaty, the interview,
That swallow'd so much treasure, and like a glass
Did break i' the rinsing.
NORFOLK.   Faith, and so it did.
BUCKINGHAM. Pray give me favour, sir. This cunning
     cardinal
The articles o' the combination drew
As himself pleas'd; and they were ratified
As he cried 'Thus let be,' to as much end
As give a crutch to the dead. But our count-cardinal
Has done this, and 'tis well; for worthy Wolsey,
Who cannot err, he did it. Now this follows,—
Which, as I take it, is a kind of puppy
To the old dam, treason,—Charles the emperor,
Under pretence to see the queen his aunt,—
For 'twas indeed his colour, but he came
To whisper Wolsey,—here makes visitation:
His fears were, that the interview betwixt
England and France might, through their amity,
Breed him some prejudice; for from this league
Peep'd harms that menac'd him. He privily
Deals with our cardinal, and, as I trow,
Which I do well; for, I am sure the emperor
Paid ere he promis'd; whereby his suit was granted
Ere it was ask'd; but when the way was made,
And pav'd with gold, the emperor thus desir'd:
That he would please to alter the king's course,
And break the foresaid peace. Let the king know—
As soon he shall by me—that thus the cardinal
Does buy and sell his honour as he pleases,
And for his own advantage.
NORFOLK.   I am sorry
To hear this of him; and could wish he were
Something mistaken in 't.
BUCKINGHAM.   No, not a syllable:
I do pronounce him in that very shape
He shall appear in proof.
     Enter Brandon; a Sergeant-at-Arms before him

BRANDON. Your office, sergeant; execute it.

SERGEANT.   Sir,
My Lord the Duke of Buckingham, and Earl
Of Hereford, Stafford, and Northampton, I
Arrest thee of high treason, in the name
Of our most sovereign king.

BUCKINGHAM.   Lo you, my lord,
The net has fall'n upon me! I shall perish
Under device and practice.

BRANDON.   I am sorry
To see you ta'en from liberty, to look on
The business present. 'Tis his Highness' pleasure
You shall to the Tower.

BUCKINGHAM.   It will help me nothing
To plead mine innocence, for that dye is on me
Which makes my whitest part black. The will of heaven
Be done in this and all things! I obey.
O! my Lord Abergavenny, fare you well!

BRANDON. Nay, he must bear you company. (*To Aber-
   gavenny*) The king
Is pleas'd you shall to the Tower, till you know
How he determines further.

ABERGAVENNY.   As the duke said,
The will of heaven be done, and the king's pleasure
By me obey'd!

BRANDON.   Here is a warrant from
The king to attach Lord Montacute; and the bodies
Of the duke's confessor, John de la Car,
One Gilbert Peck, his chancellor,—

BUCKINGHAM.   So, so;
These are the limbs o' the plot: no more, I hope.

BRANDON. A monk o' the Chartreux.

BUCKINGHAM.   O! Nicholas Hopkins?

BRANDON.   He.

BUCKINGHAM. My surveyor is false; the o'er-great cardinal
Hath show'd him gold. My life is spann'd already:
I am the shadow of poor Buckingham,
Whose figure even this instant cloud puts on,
By darkening my clear sun. My lord, farewell.   *Exeunt*

SCENE TWO

The Council-Chamber.

*Enter the King, leaning on the Cardinal's shoulder, the Lords
of the Council, Sir Thomas Lovell, Officers, and Attendants.
The Cardinal places himself under the
King's feet on the right side*

KING HENRY. My life itself, and the best heart of it,
  Thanks you for this great care: I stood i' the level
  Of a full-charg'd confederacy, and give thanks
  To you that chok'd it. Let be call'd before us
  That gentleman of Buckingham's; in person
  I 'll hear him his confessions justify;
  And point by point the treasons of his master
  He shall again relate.
      A noise within, crying, 'Room for the Queen!'
*Enter Queen Katharine, ushered by the Dukes of Norfolk
and Suffolk: she kneels. The King riseth from his state, takes
her up, kisses, and placeth her by him*

QUEEN KATHARINE. Nay, we must longer kneel: I am a
  suitor.

KING HENRY. Arise, and take place by us: half your suit
  Never name to us; you have half our power:
  The other moiety, ere you ask, is given;
  Repeat your will, and take it.

QUEEN KATHARINE.   Thank your Majesty.
  That you would love yourself, and in that love
  Not unconsider'd leave your honour, nor
  The dignity of your office, is the point
  Of my petition.

KING HENRY.   Lady mine, proceed.

QUEEN KATHARINE. I am solicited, not by a few,
  And those of true condition, that your subjects
  Are in great grievance: there have been commissions
  Sent down among 'em, which hath flaw'd the heart
  Of all their loyalties: wherein although,
  My good Lord Cardinal, they vent reproaches
  Most bitterly on you, as putter-on
  Of these exactions, yet the king our master,—

Whose honour heaven shield from soil!—even he escapes
    not
Language unmannerly; yea, such which breaks
The sides of loyalty, and almost appears
In loud rebellion.

NORFOLK.   Not almost appears,
It doth appear; for, upon these taxations,
The clothiers all, not able to maintain
The many to them 'longing, have put off
The spinsters, carders, fullers, weavers, who,
Unfit for other life, compell'd by hunger
And lack of other means, in desperate manner
Daring the event to the teeth, are all in uproar,
And danger serves among them.

KING HENRY.   Taxation!
Wherein? and what taxation? My Lord Cardinal,
You that are blam'd for it alike with us,
Know you of this taxation?

WOLSEY.   Please you, sir,
I know but of a single part in aught
Pertains to the state; and front but in that file
Where others tell steps with me.

QUEEN KATHARINE.   No, my lord,
You know no more than others; but you frame
Things that are known alike; which are not wholesome
To those which would not know them, and yet must
Perforce be their acquaintance. These exactions,
Whereof my sovereign would have note, they are
Most pestilent to the hearing; and to bear 'em,
The back is sacrifice to the load. They say
They are devis'd by you, or else you suffer
Too hard an exclamation.

KING HENRY.   Still exaction!
The nature of it? In what kind, let 's know,
Is this exaction?

QUEEN KATHARINE. I am much too venturous
In tempting of your patience; but am bolden'd
Under your promis'd pardon. The subjects' grief
Comes through commissions, which compel from each
The sixth part of his substance, to be levied
Without delay; and the pretence for this
Is nam'd your wars in France. This makes bold mouths:

Tongues spit their duties out, and cold hearts freeze
Allegiance in them; their curses now
Live where their prayers did; and it 's come to pass,
This tractable obedience is a slave
To each incensed will. I would your Highness
Would give it quick consideration, for
There is no primer business.

KING HENRY.   By my life,
This is against our pleasure.

WOLSEY.   And for me,
I have no further gone in this than by
A single voice, and that not pass'd me but
By learned approbation of the judges. If I am
Traduc'd by ignorant tongues, which neither know
My faculties nor person, yet will be
The chronicles of my doing, let me say
'Tis but the fate of place, and the rough brake
That virtue must go through. We must not stint
Our necessary actions, in the fear
To cope malicious censurers; which ever,
As ravenous fishes, do a vessel follow
That is new-trimm'd, but benefit no further
Than vainly longing. What we oft do best,
By sick interpreters, once weak ones, is
Not ours, or not allow'd; what worst, as oft,
Hitting a grosser quality, is cried up
For our best act. If we shall stand still,
In fear our motion will be mock'd or carp'd at,
We should take root here where we sit, or sit
State-statues only.

KING HENRY.   Things done well,
And with a care, exempt themselves from fear;
Things done without example, in their issue
Are to be fear'd. Have you a precedent
Of this commission? I believe, not any.
We must not rend our subjects from our laws,
And stick them in our will. Sixth part of each?
A trembling contribution! Why, we take
From every tree, lop, bark, and part o' the timber;
And, though we leave it with a root, thus hack'd,
The air will drink the sap. To every county
Where this is question'd, send our letters, with

Free pardon to each man that has denied
The force of this commission. Pray, look to 't;
I put it to your care.

WOLSEY. *(To the Secretary)* A word with you.
Let there be letters writ to every shire,
Of the king's grace and pardon. The griev'd commons
Hardly conceive of me; let it be nois'd
That through our intercession this revokement
And pardon comes: I shall anon advise you
Further in the proceeding.   *Exit Secretary*

Enter Surveyor

QUEEN KATHARINE. I am sorry that the Duke of Buckingham
Is run in your displeasure.

KING HENRY.   It grieves many:
The gentleman is learn'd, and a most rare speaker,
To nature none more bound; his training such
That he may furnish and instruct great teachers,
And never seek for aid out of himself. Yet see,
When these so noble benefits shall prove
Not well dispos'd, the mind growing once corrupt,
They turn to vicious forms, ten times more ugly
Than ever they were fair. This man so complete,
Who was enroll'd 'mongst wonders, and when we,
Almost with ravish'd listening, could not find
His hour of speech a minute; he, my lady,
Hath into monstrous habits put the graces
That once were his, and is become as black
As if beswear'd in hell. Sit by us; you shall hear—
This was his gentleman in trust—of him
Things to strike honour sad. Bid him recount
The fore-recited practices; whereof
We cannot feel too little, hear too much.

WOLSEY. Stand forth; and with bold spirit relate what you,
Most like a careful subject, have collected
Out of the Duke of Buckingham.

KING HENRY.   Speak freely.

SURVEYOR. First, it was usual with him, every day
It would infect his speech, that if the king
Should without issue die, he'd carry it so
To make the sceptre his. These very words
I 've heard him utter to his son-in-law,
Lord Abergavenny, to whom by oath he menac'd

Revenge upon the cardinal.

WOLSEY.　　　　　　　　　Please your Highness, note
This dangerous conception in this point.
Not friended by his wish, to your high person
His will is most malignant; and it stretches
Beyond you, to your friends.

QUEEN KATHARINE.　　　　　My learn'd Lord Cardinal,
Deliver all with charity.

KING HENRY.　　　　　　Speak on:
How grounded he his title to the crown
Upon our fail? to this point hast thou heard him
At any time speak aught?

SURVEYOR.　　　　　　　He was brought to this
By a vain prophecy of Nicholas Hopkins.

KING HENRY. What was that Hopkins?

SURVEYOR.　　　　　　　Sir, a Chartreux friar,
His confessor, who fed him every minute
With words of sovereignty.

KING HENRY.　　　　　How know'st thou this?

SURVEYOR. Not long before your Highness sped to France,
The duke being at the Rose, within the parish
Saint Lawrence Poultney, did of me demand
What was the speech among the Londoners
Concerning the French journey: I replied,
Men fear'd the French would prove perfidious,
To the king's danger. Presently the duke
Said, 'twas the fear, indeed; and that he doubted
'Twould prove the verity of certain words
Spoke by a holy monk; 'that oft,' says he,
'Hath sent to me, wishing me to permit
John de la Car, my chaplain, a choice hour
To hear from him a matter of some moment:
Whom after under the confession's seal
He solemnly had sworn that what he spoke
My chaplain to no creature living but
To me should utter, with demure confidence
This pausingly ensu'd: neither the king nor 's heirs—
Tell you the duke—shall prosper: bid him strive
To gain the love o' the commonalty; the duke
Shall govern England.'

QUEEN KATHARINE.　　　If I know you well,
You were the duke's surveyor, and lost your office

On the complaint o' the tenants: take good heed
You charge not in your spleen a noble person,
And spoil your nobler soul. I say, take heed;
Yes, heartily beseech you.

KING HENRY.   Let him on.
Go forward.

SURVEYOR.   On my soul, I 'll speak but truth.
I told my lord the duke, by the devil's illusions
The monk might be deceiv'd; and that 'twas dangerous for
    him
To ruminate on this so far, until
It forg'd him some design, which, being believ'd,
It was much like to do. He answer'd, 'Tush!
It can do me no damage'; adding further,
That had the king in his last sickness fail'd,
The cardinal's and Sir Thomas Lovell's heads
Should have gone off.

KING HENRY.   Ha! what, so rank? Ah, ha!
There 's mischief in this man. Canst thou say further?

SURVEYOR. I can, my liege.

KING HENRY.   Proceed.

SURVEYOR.   Being at Greenwich,
After your highness had reprov'd the duke
About Sir William Blomer,—

KING HENRY.   I remember
Of such a time: being my sworn servant,
The duke retain'd him his. But on; what hence?

SURVEYOR. 'If,' quoth he, 'I for this had been committed,
As, to the Tower, I thought, I would have play'd
The part my father meant to act upon
The usurper Richard; who, being at Salisbury,
Made suit to come in 's presence; which if granted,
As he made semblance of his duty, would
Have put his knife into him.'

KING HENRY.   A giant traitor!

WOLSEY. Now, madam, may his Highness live in freedom,
And this man out of prison?

QUEEN KATHARINE.   God mend all!

KING HENRY. There 's something more would out of thee?
    what sayst?

SURVEYOR. After 'the duke his father,' with 'the knife,'
He stretch'd him, and, with one hand on his dagger,

Another spread on 's breast, mounting his eyes,
He did discharge a horrible oath; whose tenour
Was, were he evil us'd, he would outgo
His father by as much as a performance
Does an irresolute purpose.

KING HENRY.   There 's his period;
To sheathe his knife in us. He is attach'd;
Call him to present trial: if he may
Find mercy in the law, 'tis his; if none,
Let him not seek 't of us: by day and night!
He 's traitor to the height.   *Exeunt*

SCENE THREE

A Room in the Palace.

Enter the Lord Chamberlain and Lord Sands

CHAMBERLAIN. Is 't possible the spells of France should
      juggle
Men into such strange mysteries?

SANDS.   New customs,
Though they be never so ridiculous,
Nay, let 'em be unmanly, yet are follow'd.

CHAMBERLAIN. As far as I see, all the good our English
Have got by the late voyage is but merely
A fit or two o' the face; but they are shrewd ones;
For when they hold 'em, you would swear directly
Their very noses had been counsellors
To Pepin or Clotharius, they keep state so.

SANDS. They have all new legs, and lame ones: one would
      take it,
That never saw 'em pace before, the spavin
Or springhalt reign'd among 'em.

CHAMBERLAIN.   Death! my lord,
Their clothes are after such a pagan cut too,
That, sure, they 've worn out Christendom.

                    Enter Sir Thomas Lovell

                                          How now!
What news, Sir Thomas Lovell?

LOVELL.   Faith, my lord,
I hear of none, but the new proclamation

That 's clapp'd upon the court-gate.

CHAMBERLAIN.   What is 't for?

LOVELL. The reformation of our travell'd gallants,
That fill the court with quarrels, talk, and tailors.

CHAMBERLAIN. I am glad 'tis there: now I would pray our
    monsieurs
To think an English courtier may be wise,
And never see the Louvre.

LOVELL.   They must either—
For so run the conditions—leave those remnants
Of fool and feather that they got in France,
With all their honourable points of ignorance
Pertaining thereunto, as fights and fireworks;
Abusing better men than they can be,
Out of a foreign wisdom;—renouncing clean
The faith they have in tennis and tall stockings,
Short blister'd breeches, and those types of travel,
And understand again like honest men;
Or pack to their old playfellows: there, I take it,
They may, cum privilegio, wear away
The lag end of their lewdness, and be laugh'd at.

SANDS. 'Tis time to give 'em physic, their diseases
Are grown so catching.

CHAMBERLAIN.   What a loss our ladies
Will have of these trim vanities!

LOVELL.   Ay, marry,
There will be woe indeed, lords: the sly whoresons
Have got a speeding trick to lay down ladies;
A French song and a fiddle has no fellow.

SANDS. The devil fiddle 'em! I am glad they 're going:
For, sure, there 's no converting of 'em: now
An honest country lord, as I am, beaten
A long time out of play, may bring his plain-song
And have an hour of hearing; and, by 'r lady,
Held current music too.

CHAMBERLAIN.   Well said, Lord Sands;
Your colt's tooth is not cast yet.

SANDS.   No, my lord;
Nor shall not, while I have a stump.

CHAMBERLAIN.   Sir Thomas,
Whither were you a-going?

LOVELL.   To the cardinal's:

Your lordship is a guest too.

CHAMBERLAIN.   O! 'tis true:
This night he makes a supper, and a great one,
To many lords and ladies; there will be
The beauty of this kingdom, I 'll assure you.

LOVELL. That churchman bears a bounteous mind indeed,
A hand as fruitful as the land that feeds us:
His dews fall every where.

CHAMBERLAIN.   No doubt he 's noble.
He had a black mouth that said other of him.

SANDS. He may, my lord; he has wherewithal: in him
Sparing would show a worse sin than ill doctrine:
Men of his way should be most liberal;
They are set here for examples.

CHAMBERLAIN.   True, they are so;
But few now give so great ones. My barge stays;
Your lordship shall along. Come, good Sir Thomas,
We shall be late else; which I would not be,
For I was spoke to, with Sir Henry Guildford,
This night to be comptrollers.

SANDS.   I am your lordship's.   *Exeunt*

SCENE FOUR

The Presence-Chamber in York Place.

*Hautboys. A small table under a state for Cardinal Wolsey, a
longer table for the guests. Enter, at one door, Anne Bullen,
and divers Lords, Ladies, and Gentlewomen, as guests; at
another door, enter Sir Henry Guildford*

GUILDFORD. Ladies, a general welcome from his Grace
Salutes ye all; this night he dedicates
To fair content and you. None here, he hopes,
In all this noble bevy, has brought with her
One care abroad; he would have all as merry
As, first, good company, good wine, good welcome,
Can make good people.

Enter Lord Chamberlain, Lord Sands, and Sir Thomas Lovell
                         O, my lord! you 're tardy:
The very thought of this fair company
Clapp'd wings to me.

CHAMBERLAIN. You are young, Sir Harry Guildford.

SANDS. Sir Thomas Lovell, had the cardinal
But half my lay-thoughts in him, some of these
Should find a running banquet ere they rested,
I think would better please 'em: by my life,
They are a sweet society of fair ones.

LOVELL. O! that your lordship were but now confessor
To one or two of these!

SANDS.   I would I were;
They should find easy penance.

LOVELL.   Faith, how easy?

SANDS. As easy as a down-bed would afford it.

CHAMBERLAIN. Sweet ladies, will it please you sit? Sir
    Harry,
Place you that side, I 'll take the charge of this;
His Grace is entering. Nay, you must not freeze!
Two women plac'd together makes cold weather:
My Lord Sands, you are one will keep 'em waking;
Pray, sit between these ladies.

SANDS.   By my faith,
And thank your lordship. By your leave, sweet ladies:
        Seats himself between Anne Bullen and another Lady
If I chance to talk a little wild, forgive me;
I had it from my father.

ANNE.   Was he mad, sir?

SANDS. O! very mad, exceeding mad; in love too:
But he would bite none; just as I do now,
He would kiss you twenty with a breath.   *Kisses her*

CHAMBERLAIN.   Well said, my lord.
So, now you 're fairly seated. Gentlemen,
The penance lies on you, if these fair ladies
Pass away frowning.

SANDS.   For my little cure,
Let me alone.

        Hautboys. Enter Cardinal
        Wolsey, attended, and takes his state

WOLSEY. You 're welcome, my fair guests: that noble lady,
Or gentleman, that is not freely merry,
Is not my friend: this, to confirm my welcome;
And to you all, good health.   *Drinks*

SANDS.   Your Grace is noble:
Let me have such a bowl may hold my thanks,

And save me so much talking.

WOLSEY.   My Lord Sands,
I am beholding to you: cheer your neighbours.
Ladies, you are not merry: gentlemen,
Whose fault is this?

SANDS.   The red wine first must rise
In their fair cheeks, my lord; then, we shall have 'em
Talk us to silence.

ANNE.   You are a merry gamester,
My Lord Sands.

SANDS.   Yes, if I make my play.
Here 's to your ladyship; and pledge it, madam,
For 'tis to such a thing,—

ANNE.   You cannot show me.

SANDS. I told your Grace they would talk anon.

Drum and trumpets within; chambers discharged

WOLSEY.   What 's that?

CHAMBERLAIN. Look out there, some of ye.

Exit a Servant

WOLSEY.   What warlike voice,
And to what end, is this? Nay, ladies, fear not;
By all the laws of war you 're privileg'd.

Re-enter Servant

CHAMBERLAIN. How now, what is 't?

SERVANT.   A noble troop of strangers;
For so they seem: they 've left their barge and landed;
And hither make, as great ambassadors
From foreign princes.

WOLSEY.   Good Lord Chamberlain,
Go, give 'em welcome; you can speak the French tongue;
And, pray, receive 'em nobly, and conduct 'em
Into our presence, where this heaven of beauty
Shall shine at full upon them. Some attend him.

Exit the Lord Chamberlain,
attended. All arise, and tables removed

You have now a broken banquet; but we 'll mend it.
A good digestion to you all; and once more
I shower a welcome on ye; welcome all.

Hautboys. Enter the King, and Others, as masquers, habit-
ed like shepherds, ushered by the Lord Chamberlain. They
pass directly before the Cardinal, and gracefully salute him

A noble company! what are their pleasures?

CHAMBERLAIN. Because they speak no English, thus they
    pray'd
    To tell your Grace: that, having heard by fame
    Of this so noble and so fair assembly
    This night to meet here, they could do no less,
    Out of the great respect they bear to beauty,
    But leave their flocks; and, under your fair conduct,
    Crave leave to view these ladies, and entreat
    An hour of revels with 'em.

WOLSEY.   Say, Lord Chamberlain,
    They have done my poor house grace; for which I pay 'em
    A thousand thanks, and pray 'em take their pleasures.

                          They choose Ladies for
            the dance. The King chooses Anne Bullen

KING HENRY. The fairest hand I ever touch'd! O beauty,
    Till now I never knew thee!   *Music. Dance*

WOLSEY. My lord.

CHAMBERLAIN.   Your Grace?

WOLSEY.   Pray tell them thus much from me:
    There should be one amongst 'em, by his person,
    More worthy this place than myself; to whom,
    If I but knew him, with my love and duty
    I would surrender it.

CHAMBERLAIN. I will, my lord.   *Whispers the Masquers*

WOLSEY. What say they?

CHAMBERLAIN.   Such a one, they all confess,
    There is indeed; which they would have your Grace
    Find out, and he will take it.

WOLSEY.   Let me see then.

                       Comes from his state
    By all your good leaves, gentlemen, here I 'll make
    My royal choice.

KING HENRY. (*Unmasking*) You have found him, cardinal.
    You hold a fair assembly; you do well, lord:
    You are a churchman, or, I 'll tell you, cardinal,
    I should judge now unhappily.

WOLSEY.   I am glad
    Your Grace is grown so pleasant.

KING HENRY.   My Lord Chamberlain,
    Prithee, come hither. What fair lady 's that?

CHAMBERLAIN. An 't please your Grace, Sir Thomas Bullen's
    daughter,

The Viscount Rochford, one of her highness' women.

KING HENRY. By heaven, she is a dainty one. Sweetheart,
I were unmannerly to take you out,
And not to kiss you. A health, gentlemen!
Let it go round.

WOLSEY. Sir Thomas Lovell, is the banquet ready
I' the privy chamber?

LOVELL.   Yes, my lord.

WOLSEY.   Your Grace,
I fear, with dancing is a little heated.

KING HENRY. I fear, too much.

WOLSEY.   There 's fresher air, my lord,
In the next chamber.

KING HENRY. Lead in your ladies, every one. Sweet partner,
I must not yet forsake you. Let 's be merry:
Good my Lord Cardinal, I have half a dozen healths
To drink to these fair ladies, and a measure
To lead 'em once again; and then let 's dream
Who 's best in favour. Let the music knock it.

Exeunt with trumpets

ACT TWO

SCENE ONE

Westminster. A Street.

Enter two Gentlemen, meeting

FIRST GENTLEMAN. Whither away so fast?

SECOND GENTLEMAN.   O! God save ye.
  E'en to the hall, to hear what shall become
  Of the great Duke of Buckingham.

FIRST GENTLEMAN.   I 'll save you
  That labour, sir. All 's now done but the ceremony
  Of bringing back the prisoner.

SECOND GENTLEMAN.   Were you there?

FIRST GENTLEMAN. Yes, indeed, was I.

SECOND GENTLEMAN.   Pray speak what has happen'd.

FIRST GENTLEMAN. You may guess quickly what.

SECOND GENTLEMAN.   Is he found guilty?

FIRST GENTLEMAN. Yes, truly is he, and condemn'd upon 't.

SECOND GENTLEMAN. I am sorry for 't.

FIRST GENTLEMAN.   So are a number more.

SECOND GENTLEMAN. But, pray, how pass'd it?

FIRST GENTLEMAN. I 'll tell you in a little. The great duke
  Came to the bar; where, to his accusations
  He pleaded still not guilty, and alleg'd
  Many sharp reasons to defeat the law.
  The king's attorney on the contrary
  Urg'd on the examinations, proofs, confessions
  Of divers witnesses, which the duke desir'd
  To have brought, viva voce, to his face:
  At which appear'd against him his surveyor;
  Sir Gilbert Peck his chancellor; and John Car,
  Confessor to him; with that devil-monk,
  Hopkins, that made this mischief.

SECOND GENTLEMAN.   That was he

That fed him with his prophecies?

FIRST GENTLEMAN.   The same.
All these accus'd him strongly; which he fain
Would have flung from him, but, indeed, he could not:
And so his peers, upon this evidence,
Have found him guilty of high treason. Much
He spoke, and learnedly, for life; but all
Was either pitied in him or forgotten.

SECOND GENTLEMAN.   After all this how did he bear himself?

FIRST GENTLEMAN.   When he was brought again to the bar,
    to hear
His knell rung out, his judgment, he was stirr'd
With such an agony, he sweat extremely,
And something spoke in choler, ill and hasty:
But he fell to himself again, and sweetly
In all the rest show'd a most noble patience.

SECOND GENTLEMAN.   I do not think he fears death.

FIRST GENTLEMAN.   Sure, he does not;
He never was so womanish; the cause
He may a little grieve at.

SECOND GENTLEMAN.   Certainly
The cardinal is the end of this.

FIRST GENTLEMAN.   'Tis likely
By all conjectures: first, Kildare's attainder,
Then deputy of Ireland; who remov'd,
Earl Surrey was sent thither, and in haste too,
Lest he should help his father.

SECOND GENTLEMAN.   That trick of state
Was a deep envious one.

FIRST GENTLEMAN.   At his return,
No doubt he will requite it. This is noted,
And generally, whoever the king favours,
The cardinal instantly will find employment,
And far enough from court too.

SECOND GENTLEMAN.   All the commons
Hate him perniciously, and o' my conscience,
Wish him ten fathom deep: this duke as much
They love and dote on; call him bounteous **Buckingham,**
The mirror of all courtesy;—

FIRST GENTLEMAN.   Stay there, sir,
And see the noble ruin'd man you speak of.

Enter Buckingham from his arraignment;
tipstaves before him; the axe with the edge towards him;
halberds on each side: with him Sir Thomas Lovell, Sir
Nicholas Vaux, Sir William Sands, and common people

SECOND GENTLEMAN. Let's stand close, and behold him.

BUCKINGHAM.   All good people,
        You that thus far have come to pity me,
        Hear what I say, and then go home and lose me.
        I have this day receiv'd a traitor's judgment,
        And by that name must die: yet, heaven bear witness,
        And if I have a conscience, let it sink me,
        Even as the axe falls, if I be not faithful!
        The law I bear no malice for my death,
        'T has done upon the premisses but justice;
        But those that sought it I could wish more Christians:
        Be what they will, I heartily forgive 'em.
        Yet let 'em look they glory not in mischief,
        Nor build their evils on the graves of great men;
        For then my guiltless blood must cry against 'em.
        For further life in this world I ne'er hope,
        Nor will I sue, although the king have mercies
        More than I dare make faults. You few that lov'd me,
        And dare be bold to weep for Buckingham,
        His noble friends and fellows, whom to leave
        Is only bitter to him, only dying,
        Go with me, like good angels, to my end;
        And, as the long divorce of steel falls on me,
        Make of your prayers one sweet sacrifice,
        And lift my soul to heaven. Lead on, o' God's name.

LOVELL. I do beseech your Grace, for charity,
        If ever any malice in your heart
        Were hid against me, now to forgive me frankly.

BUCKINGHAM. Sir Thomas Lovell, I as free forgive you
        As I would be forgiven: I forgive all.
        There cannot be those numberless offences
        'Gainst me that I cannot take peace with: no black envy
        Shall mark my grave. Commend me to his Grace;
        And, if he speak of Buckingham, pray, tell him
        You met him half in heaven. My vows and prayers
        Yet are the king's; and, till my soul forsake,
        Shall cry for blessings on him: may he live

Longer than I have time to tell his years!
Ever belov'd and loving may his rule be!
And when old time shall lead him to his end,
Goodness and he fill up one monument!

LOVELL. To the water side I must conduct your Grace;
Then give my charge up to Sir Nicholas Vaux,
Who undertakes you to your end.

VAUX.   Prepare there!
The duke is coming: see the barge be ready;
And fit it with such furniture as suits
The greatness of his person.

BUCKINGHAM.   Nay, Sir Nicholas,
Let it alone; my state now will but mock me.
When I came hither, I was Lord High Constable
And Duke of Buckingham; now, poor Edward Bohun:
Yet I am richer than my base accusers,
That never knew what truth meant: I now seal it;
And with that blood will make them one day groan for 't.
My noble father, Henry of Buckingham,
Who first rais'd head against usurping Richard,
Flying for succour to his servant Banister,
Being distress'd, was by that wretch betray'd,
And without trial fell: God's peace be with him!
Henry the Seventh succeeding, truly pitying
My father's loss, like a most royal prince
Restor'd me to my honours, and, out of ruins,
Made my name once more noble. Now his son,
Henry the Eighth, life, honour, name, and all
That made me happy, at one stroke has taken
For ever from the world. I had my trial,
And, must needs say, a noble one; which makes me
A little happier than my wretched father:
Yet thus far we are one in fortunes; both
Fell by our servants, by those men we lov'd most:
A most unnatural and faithless service!
Heaven has an end in all; yet, you that hear me,
This from a dying man receive as certain:
Where you are liberal of your loves and counsels
Be sure you be not loose; for those you make friends
And give your hearts to, when they once perceive
The least rub in your fortunes, fall away
Like water from ye, never found again

But where they mean to sink ye. All good people,
Pray for me! I must now forsake ye: the last hour
Of my long weary life is come upon me.
Farewell:
And when you would say something that is sad,
Speak how I fell. I have done; and God forgive me!

Exeunt Buckingham and Train

FIRST GENTLEMAN. O! this is full of pity! Sir, it calls,
I fear, too many curses on their heads
That were the authors.

SECOND GENTLEMAN.   If the duke be guiltless,
'Tis full of woe; yet I can give you inkling
Of an ensuing evil, if it fall,
Greater than this.

FIRST GENTLEMAN.   Good angels keep it from us!
What may it be? You do not doubt my faith, sir?

SECOND GENTLEMAN. This secret is so weighty, 'twill require
A strong faith to conceal it.

FIRST GENTLEMAN.   Let me have it;
I do not talk much.

SECOND GENTLEMAN. I am confident:
You shall, sir. Did you not of late days hear
A buzzing of a separation
Between the king and Katharine?

FIRST GENTLEMAN.   Yes, but it held not;
For when the king once heard it, out of anger
He sent command to the Lord Mayor straight
To stop the rumour, and allay those tongues
That durst disperse it.

SECOND GENTLEMAN.   But that slander, sir,
Is found a truth now; for it grows again
Fresher than e'er it was; and held for certain
The king will venture at it. Either the cardinal,
Or some about him near, have, out of malice
To the good queen, possess'd him with a scruple
That will undo her: to confirm this too,
Cardinal Campeius is arriv'd, and lately;
As all think, for this business.

FIRST GENTLEMAN.   'Tis the cardinal;
And merely to revenge him on the emperor
For not bestowing on him, at his asking,
The archbishopric of Toledo, this is purpos'd.

SECOND GENTLEMAN. I think you have hit the mark: but is 't
    not cruel
    That she should feel the smart of this? The cardinal
    Will have his will, and she must fall.
FIRST GENTLEMAN.   'Tis woeful.
    We are too open here to argue this;
    Let 's think in private more.   *Exeunt*

SCENE TWO

An Ante-chamber in the Palace.

Enter the Lord Chamberlain, reading a letter

CHAMBERLAIN. 'My lord, The horses your lordship sent for,
    with all the care I had, I saw well chosen, ridden, and fur-
    nished. They were young and handsome, and of the best
    breed in the north. When they were ready to set out for
    London, a man of my Lord Cardinal's, by commission and
    main power, took them from me; with this reason: His
    master would be served before a subject, if not before the
    king; which stopped our mouths, sir.'

    I fear he will indeed. Well, let him have them:
    He will have all, I think.
          Enter the Dukes of Norfolk and Suffolk
NORFOLK. Well met, my Lord Chamberlain.
CHAMBERLAIN. Good day to both your Graces.
SUFFOLK. How is the king employ'd?
CHAMBERLAIN.   I left him private,
    Full of sad thoughts and troubles.
NORFOLK.   What 's the cause?
CHAMBERLAIN. It seems the marriage with his brother's wife
    Has crept too near his conscience.
SUFFOLK.   No; his conscience
    Has crept too near another lady.
NORFOLK.   'Tis so:
    This is the cardinal's doing, the king-cardinal:
    That blind priest, like the eldest son of Fortune,
    Turns what he list. The king will know him one day.
SUFFOLK. Pray God he do! he 'll never know himself else.
NORFOLK. How holily he works in all his business,

And with what zeal! for, now he has crack'd the league
Between us and the emperor, the queen's great nephew,
He dives into the king's soul, and there scatters
Dangers, doubts, wringing of the conscience,
Fears, and despairs; and all these for his marriage:
And out of all these, to restore the king,
He counsels a divorce; a loss of her
That like a jewel has hung twenty years
About his neck, yet never lost her lustre;
Of her, that loves him with that excellence
That angels love good men with; even of her,
That, when the greatest stroke of fortune falls,
Will bless the king: and is not this course pious?

CHAMBERLAIN. Heaven keep me from such counsel! 'Tis
    most true
These news are every where; every tongue speaks 'em,
And every true heart weeps for 't. All that dare
Look into these affairs, see this main end,
The French king's sister. Heaven will one day open
The king's eyes, that so long have slept upon
This bold bad man.

SUFFOLK.   And free us from his slavery.

NORFOLK. We had need pray,
And heartily, for our deliverance;
Or this imperious man will work us all
From princes into pages. All men's honours
Lie like one lump before him, to be fashion'd
Into what pitch he please.

SUFFOLK.   For me, my lords,
I love him not, nor fear him; there 's my creed.
As I am made without him, so I 'll stand,
If the king please; his curses and his blessings
Touch me alike, they 're breath I not believe in.
I knew him, and I know him; so I leave him
To him that made him proud, the pope.

NORFOLK.   Let 's in;
And with some other business put the king
From these sad thoughts, that work too much upon him.
My lord, you 'll bear us company?

CHAMBERLAIN.   Excuse me;
The king hath sent me otherwhere: besides,
You 'll find a most unfit time to disturb him:

Health to your lordships.

NORFOLK.   Thanks, my good Lord Chamberlain.

Exit Lord Chamberlain

Norfolk opens a folding-door.

The King is discovered sitting and reading pensively

SUFFOLK. How sad he looks! sure, he is much afflicted.

KING HENRY. Who is there, ha?

NORFOLK.   Pray God he be not angry.

KING HENRY. Who 's there, I say? How dare you thrust
    yourselves
  Into my private meditations?
  Who am I, ha?

NORFOLK. A gracious king that pardons all offences
  Malice ne'er meant: our breach of duty this way
  Is business of estate; in which we come
  To know your royal pleasure.

KING HENRY.   Ye are too bold.
  Go to; I 'll make ye know your times of business:
  Is this an hour for temporal affairs, ha?

Enter Wolsey and Campeius

  Who 's there? my good Lord Cardinal? O! my Wolsey,
  The quiet of my wounded conscience;
  Thou art a cure fit for a king. (*To Campeius*) You 're
    welcome,
  Most learned reverend sir, into our kingdom:
  Use us, and it. (*To Wolsey*) My good lord, have great
    care
  I be not found a talker.

WOLSEY.   Sir, you cannot.
  I would your Grace would give us but an hour
  Of private conference.

KING HENRY. (*To Norfolk and Suffolk*) We are busy: go.

NORFOLK. (*Aside to Suffolk*) This priest has no pride in him!

SUFFOLK. (*Aside to Norfolk*)   Not to speak of;
  I would not be so sick though for his place:
  But this cannot continue.

NORFOLK. (*Aside to Suffolk*) If it do,
  I 'll venture one have-at-him.

SUFFOLK. (*Aside to Norfolk*)   I another.

Exeunt Norfolk and Suffolk

WOLSEY. Your Grace has given a precedent of wisdom
  Above all princes, in committing freely

Your scruple to the voice of Christendom.
Who can be angry now? what envy reach you?
The Spaniard, tied by blood and favour to her,
Must now confess, if they have any goodness,
The trial just and noble. All the clerks,
I mean the learned ones, in Christian kingdoms
Have their free voices: Rome, the nurse of judgment,
Invited by your noble self, hath sent
One general tongue unto us, this good man,
This just and learned priest, Cardinal Campeius;
Whom once more I present unto your Highness.

KING HENRY. And once more in my arms I bid him welcome,
And thank the holy conclave for their loves:
They have sent me such a man I would have wish'd for.

CAMPEIUS. Your Grace must needs deserve all strangers'
    loves,
You are so noble. To your Highness' hand
I tender my commission, by whose virtue,—
The court of Rome commanding,—you, my Lord
Cardinal of York, are join'd with me, their servant,
In the impartial judging of this business.

KING HENRY. Two equal men. The queen shall be
    acquainted
Forthwith for what you come. Where 's Gardiner?

WOLSEY. I know your Majesty has always lov'd her
So dear in heart, not to deny her that
A woman of less place might ask by law,
Scholars, allow'd freely to argue for her.

KING HENRY. Ay, and the best, she shall have; and my
    favour
To him that does best: God forbid else. Cardinal,
Prithee, call Gardiner to me, my new secretary:
I find him a fit fellow.   *Exit Wolsey*
            Re-enter Wolsey, with Gardiner

WOLSEY. (*Aside to Gardiner*) Give me your hand; much joy
    and favour to you;
You are the king's now.

GARDINER. (*Aside to Wolsey*) But to be commanded
For ever by your Grace, whose hand has rais'd me.

KING HENRY. Come hither, Gardiner.   *They converse apart*

CAMPEIUS. My Lord of York, was not one Doctor Pace
    In this man's place before him?

WOLSEY.   Yes, he was.
CAMPEIUS. Was he not held a learned man?
WOLSEY.   Yes, surely.
CAMPEIUS. Believe me, there 's an ill opinion spread then
  Even of yourself, Lord Cardinal.
WOLSEY.   How! of me?
CAMPEIUS. They will not stick to say, you envied him,
  And fearing he would rise, he was so virtuous,
  Kept him a foreign man still; which so griev'd him
  That he ran mad and died.
WOLSEY.   Heaven's peace be with him!
  That 's Christian care enough: for living murmurers
  There 's places of rebuke. He was a fool,
  For he would needs be virtuous: that good fellow,
  If I command him, follows my appointment:
  I will have none so near else. Learn this, brother,
  We live not to be grip'd by meaner persons.
KING HENRY. Deliver this with modesty to the queen.
                                           Exit Gardiner

  The most convenient place that I can think of
  For such receipt of learning, is Black-Friars;
  There ye shall meet about this weighty business.
  My Wolsey, see it furnish'd. O my lord!
  Would it not grieve an able man to leave
  So sweet a bedfellow? But, conscience, conscience!
  O! 'tis a tender place, and I must leave her.   *Exeunt*

                    SCENE THREE

        An Ante-chamber in the Queen's Apartments.

        Enter Anne Bullen and an Old Lady

ANNE. Not for that neither: here 's the pang that pinches:
  His Highness having liv'd so long with her, and she
  So good a lady that no tongue could ever
  Pronounce dishonour of her; by my life,
  She never knew harm-doing; O! now, after
  So many courses of the sun enthron'd,
  Still growing in a majesty and pomp, the which
  To leave a thousand-fold more bitter than
  'Tis sweet at first to acquire, after this process

To give her the avaunt! it is a pity
Would move a monster.

OLD LADY.   Hearts of most hard temper
Melt and lament for her.

ANNE.   O! God's will; much better
She ne'er had known pomp: though 't be temporal,
Yet, if that quarrel, Fortune, do divorce
It from the bearer, 'tis a sufferance panging
As soul and body's severing.

OLD LADY.   Alas! poor lady,
She 's a stranger now again.

ANNE.   So much the more
Must pity drop upon her. Verily,
I swear, 'tis better to be lowly born,
And range with humble livers in content,
Than to be perk'd up in a glistering grief
And wear a golden sorrow.

OLD LADY.   Our content
Is our best having.

ANNE.   By my troth and maidenhead
I would not be a queen.

OLD LADY.   Beshrew me, I would,
And venture maidenhead for 't; and so would you,
For all this spice of your hypocrisy.
You, that have so fair parts of woman on you,
Have too a woman's heart; which ever yet
Affected eminence, wealth, sovereignty:
Which, to say sooth, are blessings, and which gifts—
Saving your mincing—the capacity
Of your soft cheveril conscience would receive,
If you might please to stretch it.

ANNE.   Nay, good troth.

OLD LADY. Yes, troth, and troth; you would not be a queen?

ANNE. No, not for all the riches under heaven.

OLD LADY. 'Tis strange; a three-pence bow'd would hire me,
Old as I am, to queen it. But, I pray you,
What think you of a duchess? have you limbs
To bear that load of title?

ANNE.   No, in truth.

OLD LADY. Then you are weakly made. Pluck off a little:
I would not be a young count in your way,
For more than blushing comes to: if your back

Cannot vouchsafe this burden, 'tis too weak
Ever to get a boy.

ANNE.   How you do talk!
I swear again, I would not be a queen
For all the world.

OLD LADY.   In faith, for little England
You 'd venture an emballing: I myself
Would for Carnarvonshire, although there 'long'd
No more to the crown but that. Lo! who comes here?

Enter the Lord Chamberlain

CHAMBERLAIN. Good-morrow, ladies. What were 't worth to
     know
The secret of your conference?

ANNE.   My good lord,
Not your demand; it values not your asking:
Our mistress' sorrows we were pitying.

CHAMBERLAIN. It was a gentle business, and becoming
The action of good women: there is hope
All will be well.

ANNE.   Now, I pray God, amen!

CHAMBERLAIN. You bear a gentle mind, and heavenly
     blessings
Follow such creatures. That you may, fair lady,
Perceive I speak sincerely, and high note 's
Ta'en of your many virtues, the king's Majesty
Commends his good opinion of you, and
Does purpose honour to you no less flowing
Than Marchioness of Pembroke; to which title
A thousand pound a year, annual support,
Out of his grace he adds.

ANNE.   I do not know
What kind of my obedience I should tender;
More than my all is nothing, nor my prayers
Are not words duly hallow'd, nor my wishes
More worth than empty vanities; yet prayers and wishes
Are all I can return. Beseech your lordship,
Vouchsafe to speak my thanks and my obedience
As from a blushing handmaid, to his Highness,
Whose health and royalty I pray for.

CHAMBERLAIN.   Lady,
I shall not fail to approve the fair conceit
The king hath of you. (*Aside*) I have perus'd her well;

Beauty and honour in her are so mingled
That they have caught the king; and who knows yet
But from this lady may proceed a gem
To lighten all this isle? (*To her*) I 'll to the king,
And say, I spoke with you.

ANNE. My honour'd lord.   *Exit Lord Chamberlain*

OLD LADY. Why, this it is; see, see!
I have been begging sixteen years in court,
Am yet a courtier beggarly, nor could
Come pat betwixt too early and too late
For any suit of pounds; and you, O fate!
A very fresh-fish here,—fie, fie, upon
This compell'd fortune!—have your mouth fill'd up
Before you open it.

ANNE.   This is strange to me.

OLD LADY. How tastes it? is it bitter? forty pence, no.
There was a lady once,—'tis an old story,—
That would not be a queen, that would she not,
For all the mud in Egypt: have you heard it?

ANNE. Come, you are pleasant.

OLD LADY.   With your theme I could
O'ermount the lark. The Marchioness of Pembroke!
A thousand pounds a year, for pure respect!
No other obligation! By my life
That promises more thousands: honour's train
Is longer than his foreskirt. By this time
I know your back will bear a duchess: say,
Are you not stronger than you were?

ANNE.   Good lady,
Make yourself mirth with your particular fancy,
And leave me out on 't. Would I had no being,
If this salute my blood a jot: it faints me,
To think what follows.
The queen is comfortless, and we forgetful
In our long absence. Pray, do not deliver
What here you 've heard to her.

OLD LADY.   What do you think me?
                              Exeunt

SCENE FOUR

A Hall in Black-Friars.

*Trumpets, sennet, and cornets. Enter two Vergers, with
short silver wands; next them, two Scribes, in the habit of
doctors; after them, the Archbishop of Canterbury, alone;
after him, the Bishops of Lincoln, Ely, Rochester, and Saint
Asaph; next them, at some small distance, follows a Gentle-
man bearing the purse, with the great seal, and a cardinal's
hat; then two Priests, bearing each a silver cross; then a
Gentleman-Usher bare-headed, accompanied with a Ser-
geant-at-Arms, bearing a silver mace; then two Gentlemen,
bearing two great silver pillars; after them, side by side, the
two Cardinals; two Noblemen with the sword and mace.
Then enter the King and Queen, and their Trains. The King
takes place under the cloth of state; the two Cardinals sit
under him as judges. The Queen takes place at some dis-
tance from the King. The Bishops place themselves on each
side the court, in manner of a consistory; below them, the
Scribes. The Lords sit next the Bishops. The Crier
and the rest of the Attendants stand in convenient
order about the Stage*

WOLSEY. Whilst our commission from Rome is read,
  Let silence be commanded.
KING HENRY.   What 's the need?
  It hath already publicly been read,
  And on all sides the authority allow'd;
  You may then spare that time.
WOLSEY.   Be 't so. Proceed.
SCRIBE. Say, Henry King of England, come into the court.
CRIER. Henry King of England, come into the court.
KING HENRY. Here.
SCRIBE. Say, Katharine Queen of England, come into the
  court.
CRIER. Katharine Queen of England, come into the court.
          The Queen makes no answer,
*rises out of her chair, goes about the court, comes to the
      King, and kneels at his feet; then speaks*
QUEEN KATHARINE. Sir, I desire you do me right and justice;
  And to bestow your pity on me; for

I am a most poor woman, and a stranger,
Born out of your dominions; having here
No judge indifferent, nor no more assurance
Of equal friendship and proceeding. Alas! sir,
In what have I offended you? what cause
Hath my behaviour given to your displeasure,
That thus you should proceed to put me off
And take your good grace from me? Heaven witness,
I have been to you a true and humble wife,
At all times to your will conformable;
Ever in fear to kindle your dislike,
Yea, subject to your countenance, glad or sorry
As I saw it inclin'd. When was the hour
I ever contradicted your desire,
Or made it not mine too? Or which of your friends
Have I not strove to love, although I knew
He were mine enemy? what friend of mine
That had to him deriv'd your anger, did I
Continue in my liking? nay, gave notice
He was from thence discharg'd. Sir, call to mind
That I have been your wife, in this obedience,
Upward of twenty years, and have been blest
With many children by you: if, in the course
And process of this time, you can report,
And prove it too, against mine honour aught,
My bond to wedlock, or my love and duty,
Against your sacred person, in God's name
Turn me away; and let the foul'st contempt
Shut door upon me, and so give me up
To the sharp'st kind of justice. Please you, sir,
The king, your father, was reputed for
A prince most prudent, of an excellent
And unmatch'd wit and judgment: Ferdinand,
My father, King of Spain, was reckon'd one
The wisest prince that there had reign'd by many
A year before: it is not to be question'd
That they had gather'd a wise council to them
Of every realm, that did debate this business,
Who deem'd our marriage lawful. Wherefore I humbly
Beseech you, sir, to spare me, till I may
Be by my friends in Spain advis'd, whose counsel
I will implore: if not, i' the name of God,

Your pleasure be fulfill'd!

WOLSEY.   You have here, lady,—
And of your choice,—these reverend fathers; men
Of singular integrity and learning,
Yea, the elect o' the land, who are assembled
To plead your cause. It shall be therefore bootless
That longer you desire the court, as well
For your own quiet, as to rectify
What is unsettled in the king.

CAMPEIUS.   His Grace
Hath spoken well and justly: therefore, madam,
It 's fit this royal session do proceed,
And that, without delay, their arguments
Be now produc'd and heard.

QUEEN KATHARINE.   Lord Cardinal,
To you I speak.

WOLSEY.   Your pleasure, madam?

QUEEN KATHARINE.   Sir,
I am about to weep; but, thinking that
We are a queen,—or long have dream'd so,—certain
The daughter of a king, my drops of tears
I 'll turn to sparks of fire.

WOLSEY.   Be patient yet.

QUEEN KATHARINE. I will, when you are humble; nay,
    before,
Or God will punish me. I do believe,
Induc'd by potent circumstances, that
You are mine enemy; and make my challenge
You shall not be my judge; for it is you
Have blown this coal betwixt my lord and me,
Which God's dew quench! Therefore I say again,
I utterly abhor, yea, from my soul
Refuse you for my judge, whom, yet once more,
I hold my most malicious foe, and think not
At all a friend to truth.

WOLSEY.   I do profess
You speak not like yourself; who ever yet
Have stood to charity, and display'd the effects
Of disposition gentle, and of wisdom
O'ertopping woman's power. Madam, you do me wrong:
I have no spleen against you; nor injustice
For you or any: how far I have proceeded,

Or how far further shall, is warranted
By a commission from the consistory,
Yea, the whole consistory of Rome. You charge me
That I have blown this coal: I do deny it.
The king is present: if it be known to him
That I gainsay my deed, how may he wound,
And worthily, my falsehood; yea, as much
As you have done my truth. If he know
That I am free of your report, he knows
I am not of your wrong. Therefore in him
It lies to cure me; and the cure is, to
Remove these thoughts from you: the which before
His Highness shall speak in, I do beseech
You, gracious madam, to unthink your speaking,
And to say so no more.

QUEEN KATHARINE.   My lord, my lord,
I am a simple woman, much too weak
To oppose your cunning. You 're meek and humble-
     mouth'd;
You sign your place and calling, in full seeming,
With meekness and humility; but your heart
Is cramm'd with arrogancy, spleen, and pride.
You have, by fortune and his Highness' favours,
Gone slightly o'er low steps, and now are mounted
Where powers are your retainers, and your words,
Domestics to you, serve your will as 't please
Yourself pronounce their office. I must tell you,
You tender more your person's honour than
Your high profession spiritual; that again
I do refuse you for my judge; and here,
Before you all, appeal unto the pope,
To bring my whole cause 'fore his holiness,
And to be judg'd by him.

                    She curtsies to the King, and offers to depart
CAMPEIUS.   The queen is obstinate,
Stubborn to justice, apt to accuse it, and
Disdainful to be tried by 't: 'tis not well.
She 's going away.

KING HENRY. Call her again.

CRIER. Katharine Queen of England, come into the court.

GRIFFITH. Madam, you are call'd back.

QUEEN KATHARINE. What need you note it? pray you, keep
 your way:
 When you are call'd, return. Now, the Lord help!
 They vex me past my patience. Pray you, pass on:
 I will not tarry; no, nor ever more
 Upon this business my appearance make
 In any of their courts. *Exeunt Queen, and her Attendants*
KING HENRY.   Go thy ways, Kate:
 That man i' the world who shall report he has
 A better wife, let him in nought be trusted,
 For speaking false in that: thou art, alone,—
 If thy rare qualities, sweet gentleness,
 Thy meekness saint-like, wife-like government,
 Obeying in commanding, and thy parts
 Sovereign and pious else, could speak thee out,—
 The queen of earthly queens. She 's noble born;
 And, like her true nobility, she has
 Carried herself towards me.
WOLSEY.   Most gracious sir,
 In humblest manner I require your Highness,
 That it shall please you to declare, in hearing
 Of all these ears,—for where I am robb'd and bound
 There must I be unloos'd, although not there
 At once and fully satisfied,—whether ever I
 Did broach this business to your Highness, or
 Laid any scruple in your way, which might
 Induce you to the question on 't? or ever
 Have to you, but with thanks to God for such
 A royal lady, spake one the least word that might
 Be to the prejudice of her present state,
 Or touch of her good person?
KING HENRY.   My Lord Cardinal,
 I do excuse you; yea, upon mine honour
 I free you from 't. You are not to be taught
 That you have many enemies, that know not
 Why they are so, but, like to village curs,
 Bark when their fellows do: by some of these
 The queen is put in anger. You 're excus'd:
 But will you be more justified? you ever
 Have wish'd the sleeping of this business; never
 Desir'd it to be stirr'd; but oft have hinder'd, oft,
 The passages made toward it. On my honour,

I speak my good Lord Cardinal to this point,
And thus far clear him. Now, what mov'd me to 't,
I will be bold with time and your attention:
Then mark the inducement. Thus it came; give heed to 't:
My conscience first receiv'd a tenderness,
Scruple, and prick, on certain speeches utter'd
By the Bishop of Bayonne, then French ambassador,
Who had been hither sent on the debating
A marriage 'twixt the Duke of Orleans and
Our daughter Mary. I' the progress of this business,
Ere a determinate resolution, he—
I mean, the bishop—did require a respite;
Wherein he might the king his lord advertise
Whether our daughter were legitimate,
Respecting this our marriage with the dowager,
Sometimes our brother's wife. This respite shook
The bosom of my conscience, enter'd me,
Yea, with a splitting power, and made to tremble
The region of my breast; which forc'd such way
That many maz'd considerings did throng,
And press'd in with this caution. First, methought
I stood not in the smile of heaven, who had
Commanded nature, that my lady's womb,
If it conceiv'd a male child by me, should
Do no more offices of life to 't than
The grave does to the dead; for her male issue
Or died where they were made, or shortly after
This world had air'd them. Hence I took a thought
This was a judgment on me; that my kingdom,
Well worthy the best heir o' the world, should not
Be gladded in 't by me. Then follows that
I weigh'd the danger which my realms stood in
By this my issue's fail; and that gave to me
Many a groaning throe. Thus hulling in
The wild sea of my conscience, I did steer
Toward this remedy, whereupon we are
Now present here together; that 's to say,
I meant to rectify my conscience, which
I then did feel full sick, and yet not well,
By all the reverend fathers of the land
And doctors learn'd. First, I began in private
With you, my Lord of Lincoln; you remember

How under my oppression I did reek,
When I first mov'd you.

LINCOLN.   Very well, my liege.

KING HENRY. I have spoke long: be pleas'd yourself to say
How far you satisfied me.

LINCOLN.   So please your Highness,
The question did at first so stagger me,
Bearing a state of mighty moment in 't,
And consequence of dread, that I committed
The daring'st counsel that I had to doubt;
And did entreat your Highness to this course
Which you are running here.

KING HENRY.   Then I mov'd you,
My Lord of Canterbury, and got your leave
To make this present summons. Unsolicited
I left no reverend person in this court;
But my particular consent proceeded
Under your hands and seals: therefore, go on;
For no dislike i' the world against the person
Of the good queen, but the sharp thorny points
Of my alleged reasons drive this forward.
Prove but our marriage lawful, by my life
And kingly dignity, we are contented
To wear our mortal state to come with her,
Katharine our queen, before the primest creature
That 's paragon'd o' the world.

CAMPEIUS.   So please your Highness,
The queen being absent, 'tis a needful fitness
That we adjourn this court till further day:
Meanwhile must be an earnest motion
Made to the queen, to call back her appeal
She intends unto his Holiness.   *They rise to depart*

KING HENRY.   (*Aside*) I may perceive
These cardinals trifle with me: I abhor
This dilatory sloth and tricks of Rome.
My learn'd and well-beloved servant Cranmer,
Prithee, return: with thy approach, I know,
My comfort comes along. Break up the court:
I say, set on.   *Exeunt, in manner as they entered*

ACT THREE

SCENE ONE

The Palace at Bridewell. A Room in the Queen's Apartment.

The Queen and her Women at work.

QUEEN KATHARINE. Take thy lute, wench: my soul grows
    sad with troubles;
    Sing and disperse 'em, if thou canst. Leave working.

SONG

    Orpheus with his lute made trees,
    And the mountain tops that freeze,
      Bow themselves, when he did sing:

    To his music plants and flowers
    Ever sprung; as sun and showers
      There had made a lasting spring.

    Every thing that heard him play,
    Even the billows of the sea,
      Hung their heads, and then lay by.
    In sweet music is such art,
    Killing care and grief of heart
      Fall asleep, or hearing, die.

Enter a Gentleman

QUEEN KATHARINE. How now!

GENTLEMAN. An 't please your Grace, the two great cardinals
    Wait in the presence.

QUEEN KATHARINE.   Would they speak with me?

GENTLEMAN. They will'd me say so, madam.

QUEEN KATHARINE.   Pray their Graces
    To come near. (*Exit Gentleman*) What can be their busi-
    ness
    With me, a poor weak woman, fall'n from favour?

I do not like their coming, now I think on 't.
They should be good men, their affairs as righteous;
But all hoods make not monks.

Enter Wolsey and Campeius

WOLSEY.   Peace to your Highness!

QUEEN KATHARINE. Your Graces find me here part of a
     housewife,
I would be all, against the worst may happen.
What are your pleasures with me, reverend lords?

WOLSEY. May it please you, noble madam, to withdraw
Into your private chamber, we shall give you
The full cause of our coming.

QUEEN KATHARINE.   Speak it here;
There 's nothing I have done yet, o' my conscience,
Deserves a corner: would all other women
Could speak this with as free a soul as I do!
My lords, I care not—so much I am happy
Above a number—if my actions
Were tried by every tongue, every eye saw 'em,
Envy and base opinion set against 'em,
I know my life so even. If your business
Seek me out, and that way I am wife in,
Out with it boldly: truth loves open dealing.

WOLSEY. Tanta est erga te mentis integritas, regina
     serenissima,—

QUEEN KATHARINE. O, good my lord, no Latin;
I am not such a truant since my coming
As not to know the language I have liv'd in:
A strange tongue makes my cause more strange, suspi-
     cious;
Pray, speak in English: here are some will thank you,
If you speak truth, for their poor mistress' sake:
Believe me, she has had much wrong. Lord Cardinal,
The willing'st sin I ever yet committed
May be absolv'd in English.

WOLSEY.   Noble Lady,
I am sorry my integrity should breed,—
And service to his Majesty and you,—
So deep suspicion, where all faith was meant.
We come not by the way of accusation,
To taint that honour every good tongue blesses,
Nor to betray you any way to sorrow—

You have too much, good lady; but to know
How you stand minded in the weighty difference
Between the king and you; and to deliver,
Like free and honest men, our just opinions
And comforts to your cause.

CAMPEIUS.   Most honour'd madam,
My Lord of York, out of his noble nature,
Zeal and obedience he still bore your Grace,
Forgetting, like a good man, your late censure
Both of his truth and him,—which was too far,—
Offers, as I do, in sign of peace,
His service and his counsel.

QUEEN KATHARINE. (*Aside*)   To betray me.
My lords, I thank you both for your good wills;
Ye speak like honest men,—pray God, ye prove so!—
But how to make ye suddenly an answer,
In such a point of weight, so near mine honour,—
More near my life, I fear,—with my weak wit,
And to such men of gravity and learning,
In truth, I know not. I was set at work
Among my maids; full little, God knows, looking
Either for such men or such business.
For her sake that I have been,—for I feel
The last fit of my greatness,—good your Graces,
Let me have time and counsel for my cause:
Alas! I am a woman, friendless, hopeless.

WOLSEY. Madam, you wrong the king's love with these
     fears:
Your hopes and friends are infinite.

QUEEN KATHARINE.   In England
But little for my profit. Can you think, lords,
That any Englishman dare give me counsel?
Or be a known friend, 'gainst his Highness' pleasure,—
Though he be grown so desperate to be honest,—
And live a subject? Nay, forsooth, my friends,
They that must weigh out my afflictions,
They that my trust must grow to, live not here:
They are, as all my other comforts, far hence
In mine own country, lords.

CAMPEIUS.   I would your Grace
Would leave your griefs, and take my counsel.

QUEEN KATHARINE.   How, sir?

CAMPEIUS. Put your main cause into the king's protection;
 He 's loving and most gracious: 'twill be much
 Both for your honour better and your cause;
 For if the trial of the law o'ertake ye,
 You 'll part away disgrac'd.
WOLSEY.   He tells you rightly.
QUEEN KATHARINE. Ye tell me what ye wish for both; my
  ruin.
 Is this your Christian counsel? out upon ye!
 Heaven is above all yet; there sits a judge
 That no king can corrupt.
CAMPEIUS.   Your rage mistakes us.
QUEEN KATHARINE. The more shame for ye! holy men I
  thought ye,
 Upon my soul, two reverend cardinal virtues;
 But cardinal sins and hollow hearts I fear ye.
 Mend 'em, for shame, my lords. Is this your comfort?
 The cordial that ye bring a wretched lady,
 A woman lost among ye, laugh'd at, scorn'd?
 I will not wish ye half my miseries,
 I have more charity; but say, I warn'd ye:
 Take heed, for heaven's sake, take heed, lest at once
 The burden of my sorrows fall upon ye.
WOLSEY. Madam, this is a mere distraction;
 You turn the good we offer into envy.
QUEEN KATHARINE. Ye turn me into nothing: woe upon ye,
 And all such false professors! Would ye have me,—
 If ye have any justice, any pity;
 If ye be anything but churchmen's habits,—
 Put my sick cause into his hands that hates me?
 Alas! he has banish'd me his bed already,
 His love, too long ago! I am old, my lords,
 And all the fellowship I hold now with him
 Is only my obedience. What can happen
 To me above this wretchedness? all your studies
 Make me a curse like this.
CAMPEIUS.   Your fears are worse.
QUEEN KATHARINE. Have I liv'd thus long—let me speak
  myself,
 Since virtue finds no friends—a wife, a true one?
 A woman, I dare say without vain-glory,
 Never yet branded with suspicion?

Have I with all my full affections
Still met the king? lov'd him next heaven? obey'd him?
Been, out of fondness, superstitious to him?
Almost forgot my prayers to content him?
And am I thus rewarded? 'tis not well, lords.
Bring me a constant woman to her husband,
One that ne'er dream'd a joy beyond his pleasure,
And to that woman, when she has done most,
Yet will I add an honour, a great patience.

WOLSEY. Madam, you wander from the good we aim at.

QUEEN KATHARINE. My lord, I dare not make myself so
        guilty,
To give up willingly that noble title
Your master wed me to: nothing but death
Shall e'er divorce my dignities.

WOLSEY.   Pray hear me.

QUEEN KATHARINE. Would I had never trod this English
        earth,
Or felt the flatteries that grow upon it!
Ye have angels' faces, but heaven knows your hearts.
What will become of me now, wretched lady?
I am the most unhappy woman living.
(*To her women*) Alas! poor wenches, where are now your
        fortunes?
Shipwrack'd upon a kingdom, where no pity,
No friends, no hope; no kindred weep for me;
Almost no grave allow'd me. Like the lily,
That once was mistress of the field and flourish'd,
I 'll hang my head and perish.

WOLSEY.   If your Grace
Could but be brought to know our ends are honest,
You 'd feel more comfort. Why should we, good lady,
Upon what cause, wrong you? alas! our places,
The way of our profession is against it:
We are to cure such sorrows, not to sow them.
For goodness' sake, consider what you do;
How you may hurt yourself, ay, utterly
Grown from the king's acquaintance, by this carriage.
The hearts of princes kiss obedience,
So much they love it; but to stubborn spirits
They swell, and grow as terrible as storms.
I know you have a gentle, noble temper,

A soul as even as a calm: pray think us
Those we profess, peace-makers, friends, and servants.
CAMPEIUS. Madam, you 'll find it so. You wrong your virtues
With these weak women's fears: a noble spirit,
As yours was put into you, ever casts
Such doubts, as false coin, from it. The king loves you;
Beware you lose it not: for us, if you please
To trust us in your business, we are ready
To use our utmost studies in your service.
QUEEN KATHARINE. Do what ye will, my lords: and, pray, forgive me
If I have us'd myself unmannerly.
You know I am a woman, lacking wit
To make a seemly answer to such persons.
Pray do my service to his Majesty:
He has my heart yet; and shall have my prayers
While I shall have my life. Come, reverend fathers,
Bestow your counsels on me: she now begs
That little thought, when she set footing here,
She should have bought her dignities so dear.   *Exeunt*

SCENE TWO

Ante-chamber to the King's Apartment.

*Enter the Duke of Norfolk, the Duke of Suffolk, the Earl
of Surrey, and the Lord Chamberlain*

NORFOLK. If you will now unite in your complaints,
And force them with a constancy, the cardinal
Cannot stand under them: if you omit
The offer of this time, I cannot promise
But that you shall sustain moe new disgraces
With these you bear already.
SURREY.   I am joyful
To meet the least occasion that may give me
Remembrance of my father-in-law, the duke,
To be reveng'd on him.
SUFFOLK.   Which of the peers
Have uncontemn'd gone by him, or at least
Strangely neglected? when did he regard
The stamp of nobleness in any person,

Out of himself?

CHAMBERLAIN.   My lords, you speak your pleasures:
What he deserves of you and me, I know;
What we can do to him,—though now the time
Gives way to us,—I much fear. If you cannot
Bar his access to the king, never attempt
Any thing on him, for he hath a witchcraft
Over the king in 's tongue.

NORFOLK.   O! fear him not;
His spell in that is out: the king hath found
Matter against him that for ever mars
The honey of his language. No, he 's settled,
Not to come off, in his displeasure.

SURREY.   Sir,
I should be glad to hear such news as this
Once every hour.

NORFOLK.   Believe it, this is true:
In the divorce his contrary proceedings
Are all unfolded; wherein he appears
As I would wish mine enemy.

SURREY.   How came
His practices to light?

SUFFOLK.   Most strangely.

SURREY.   O! how? how?

SUFFOLK. The cardinal's letter to the pope miscarried,
And came to the eye o' the king; wherein was read
That the cardinal did entreat his Holiness
To stay the judgment o' the divorce; for if
It did take place, 'I do,' quoth he, 'perceive
My king is tangled in affection to
A creature of the queen's, Lady Anne Bullen.'

SURREY. Has the king this?

SUFFOLK.   Believe it.

SURREY.   Will this work?

CHAMBERLAIN. The king in this perceives him, how he
          coasts
And hedges his own way. But in this point
All his tricks founder, and he brings his physic
After his patient's death: the king already
Hath married the fair lady.

SURREY.   Would he had!

SUFFOLK. May you be happy in your wish, my lord!

For I profess, you have it.

SURREY.   Now all my joy
Trace the conjunction!

SUFFOLK.   My amen to 't!

NORFOLK.   All men's.

SUFFOLK. There 's order given for her coronation:
Marry, this is yet but young, and may be left
To some ears unrecounted. But, my lords,
She is a gallant creature, and complete
In mind and feature: I persuade me, from her
Will fall some blessing to this land, which shall
In it be memoriz'd.

SURREY.   But will the king
Digest this letter of the cardinal's?
The Lord forbid!

NORFOLK.   Marry, amen!

SUFFOLK.   No, no;
There be moe wasps that buzz about his nose
Will make this sting the sooner. Cardinal Campeius
Is stol'n away to Rome; hath ta'en no leave;
Has left the cause o' the king unhandled; and
Is posted, as the agent of our cardinal,
To second all his plot. I do assure you
The king cried Ha! at this.

CHAMBERLAIN.   Now, God incense him,
And let him cry Ha! louder.

NORFOLK.   But, my lord,
When returns Cranmer?

SUFFOLK. He is return'd in his opinions, which
Have satisfied the king for his divorce,
Together with all famous colleges
Almost in Christendom. Shortly, I believe,
His second marriage shall be publish'd, and
Her coronation. Katharine no more
Shall be call'd queen, but princess dowager,
And widow to Prince Arthur.

NORFOLK.   This same Cranmer 's
A worthy fellow, and hath ta'en much pain
In the king's business.

SUFFOLK.   He has; and we shall see him
For it an archbishop.

NORFOLK.   So I hear.

SUFFOLK.   'Tis so.
   The cardinal!

Enter Wolsey and Cromwell

NORFOLK.   Observe, observe; he 's moody.
WOLSEY. The packet, Cromwell,
   Gave 't you the king?
CROMWELL.   To his own hand, in his bedchamber.
WOLSEY. Look'd he o' the inside of the paper?
CROMWELL.   Presently
   He did unseal them; and the first he view'd,
   He did it with a serious mind; a heed
   Was in his countenance. You he bade
   Attend him here this morning.
WOLSEY.   Is he ready
   To come abroad?
CROMWELL.   I think, by this he is.
WOLSEY. Leave me awhile.   *Exit Cromwell*
   (*Aside*) It shall be to the Duchess of Alençon,
   The French King's sister; he shall marry her.
   Anne Bullen! No; I 'll no Anne Bullens for him:
   There 's more in 't than fair visage. Bullen!
   No, we 'll no Bullens. Speedily I wish
   To hear from Rome. The Marchioness of Pembroke!
NORFOLK. He 's discontented.
SUFFOLK.   May be he hears the king
   Does whet his anger to him.
SURREY.   Sharp enough,
   Lord, for thy justice!
WOLSEY. The late queen's gentlewoman, a knight's
     daughter,
   To be her mistress' mistress! the queen's queen!
   This candle burns not clear: 'tis I must snuff it;
   Then, out it goes. What though I know her virtuous
   And well deserving? yet I know her for
   A spleeny Lutheran; and not wholesome to
   Our cause, that she should lie i' the bosom of
   Our hard-rul'd king. Again, there is sprung up
   A heretic, an arch one, Cranmer; one
   Hath crawl'd into the favour of the king,
   And is his oracle.
NORFOLK.   He is vex'd at something.

SURREY. I would 'twere something that would fret the
 string,
 The master-cord on 's heart!
  Enter the King, reading a schedule; and Lovell
SUFFOLK.   The king, the king!
KING HENRY. What piles of wealth hath he accumulated
 To his own portion! and what expense by the hour
 Seems to flow from him! How, i' the name of thrift,
 Does he rake this together? Now, my lords,
 Saw you the cardinal?
NORFOLK.   My lord, we have
 Stood here observing him; some strange commotion
 Is in his brain: he bites his lip, and starts;
 Stops on a sudden, looks upon the ground,
 Then lays his finger on his temple; straight
 Springs out into fast gait; then stops again,
 Strikes his breast hard; and anon he casts
 His eye against the moon: in most strange postures
 We have seen him set himself.
KING HENRY.   It may well be:
 There is a mutiny in 's mind. This morning
 Papers of state he sent me to peruse,
 As I requir'd; and wot you what I found
 There, on my conscience, put unwittingly?
 Forsooth, an inventory, thus importing;
 The several parcels of his plate, his treasure,
 Rich stuffs and ornaments of household, which
 I find at such a proud rate that it out-speaks
 Possession of a subject.
NORFOLK.   It 's heaven's will:
 Some spirit put this paper in the packet
 To bless your eye withal.
KING HENRY.   If we did think
 His contemplation were above the earth,
 And fix'd on spiritual object, he should still
 Dwell in his musings: but I am afraid
 His thinkings are below the moon, not worth
 His serious considering.
       *He takes his seat, and
    whispers Lovell, who goes to Wolsey*
WOLSEY.   Heaven forgive me!
 Ever God bless your Highness!

KING HENRY. Good my lord,
You are full of heavenly stuff, and bear the inventory
Of your best graces in your mind, the which
You were now running o'er: you have scarce time
To steal from spiritual leisure a brief span
To keep your earthly audit: sure, in that
I deem you an ill husband, and am glad
To have you therein my companion.

WOLSEY. Sir,
For holy offices I have a time; a time
To think upon the part of business which
I bear i' the state; and nature does require
Her times of preservation, which perforce
I, her frail son, amongst my brethren mortal,
Must give my tendance to.

KING HENRY. You have said well.

WOLSEY. And ever may your Highness yoke together,
As I will lend you cause, my doing well
With my well saying!

KING HENRY. 'Tis well said again;
And 'tis a kind of good deed to say well:
And yet words are no deeds. My father lov'd you:
He said he did; and with his deed did crown
His word upon you. Since I had my office,
I have kept you next my heart; have not alone
Employ'd you where high profits might come home,
But par'd my present havings, to bestow
My bounties upon you.

WOLSEY. (Aside) What should this mean?

SURREY. (Aside) The Lord increase this business!

KING HENRY. Have I not made you
The prime man of the state? I pray you, tell me
If what I now pronounce you have found true;
And if you may confess it, say withal,
If you are bound to us or no. What say you?

WOLSEY. My sovereign, I confess your royal graces,
Shower'd on me daily, have been more than could
My studied purposes requite; which went
Beyond all man's endeavours: my endeavours
Have ever come too short of my desires,
Yet fil'd with my abilities. Mine own ends
Have been mine so, that evermore they pointed

To the good of your most sacred person and
The profit of the state. For your great graces
Heap'd upon me, poor undeserver, I
Can nothing render but allegiant thanks,
My prayers to heaven for you, my loyalty,
Which ever has and ever shall be growing,
Till death, that winter, kill it.

KING HENRY.   Fairly answer'd;
A loyal and obedient subject is
Therein illustrated; the honour of it
Does pay the act of it, as, i' the contrary,
The foulness is the punishment. I presume
That as my hand has open'd bounty to you,
My heart dropp'd love, my power rain'd honour, more
On you than any; so your hand and heart,
Your brain, and every function of your power,
Should, notwithstanding that your bond of duty,
As 'twere in love's particular, be more
To me, your friend, than any.

WOLSEY.   I do profess,
That for your Highness' good I ever labour'd
More than mine own; that am, have, and will be—
Though all the world should crack their duty to you,
And throw it from their soul; though perils did
Abound as thick as thought could make 'em, and
Appear in forms more horrid, yet my duty,
As doth a rock against the chiding flood,
Should the approach of this wild river break,
And stand unshaken yours.

KING HENRY.   'Tis nobly spoken.
Take notice, lords, he has a loyal breast,
For you have seen him open 't. Read o'er this;
                              Giving him papers
And after, this: and then to breakfast with
What appetite you have.
              Exit King, frowning upon Cardinal Wolsey;
      the Nobles throng after him, smiling, and whispering

WOLSEY.   What should this mean?
What sudden anger 's this? how have I reap'd it?
He parted frowning from me, as if ruin
Leap'd from his eyes: so looks the chafed lion
Upon the daring huntsman that has gall'd him;

Then makes him nothing. I must read this paper;
I fear, the story of his anger. 'Tis so;
This paper has undone me! 'Tis the account
Of all that world of wealth I have drawn together
For mine own ends; indeed, to gain the popedom,
And fee my friends in Rome. O negligence!
Fit for a fool to fall by: what cross devil
Made me put this main secret in the packet
I sent the king? Is there no way to cure this?
No new device to beat this from his brains?
I know 'twill stir him strongly; yet I know
A way, if it take right, in spite of fortune
Will bring me off again. What 's this?—'To the Pope!'
The letter, as I live, with all the business
I writ to 's Holiness. Nay then, farewell!
I have touch'd the highest point of all my greatness;
And from that full meridian of my glory,
I haste now to my setting: I shall fall
Like a bright exhalation in the evening,
And no man see me more.

Re-enter the Dukes of Norfolk
and Suffolk, the Earl of Surrey, and the Lord Chamberlain

NORFOLK. Hear the king's pleasure, cardinal: who com-
    mands you
To render up the great seal presently
Into our hands; and to confine yourself
To Asher-house, my Lord of Winchester's,
Till you hear further from his Highness.

WOLSEY.   Stay,
Where 's your commission, lord? words cannot carry
Authority so weighty.

SUFFOLK.   Who dares cross 'em,
Bearing the king's will from his mouth expressly?

WOLSEY. Till I find more than will or words to do it,
I mean your malice, know, officious lords,
I dare and must deny it. Now I feel
Of what coarse metal ye are moulded, envy:
How eagerly ye follow my disgraces,
As if it fed ye! and how sleek and wanton
Ye appear in every thing may bring my ruin!
Follow your envious courses, men of malice;
You have Christian warrant for 'em, and, no doubt,

In time will find their fit rewards. That seal
You ask with such a violence, the king—
Mine and your master—with his own hand gave me;
Bade me enjoy it with the place and honours
During my life; and to confirm his goodness,
Tied it by letters-patents: now who 'll take it?
SURREY. The king, that gave it.
WOLSEY.   It must be himself then.
SURREY. Thou art a proud traitor, priest.
WOLSEY.   Proud lord, thou liest:
Within these forty hours Surrey durst better
Have burnt that tongue than said so.
SURREY.   Thy ambition,
Thou scarlet sin, robb'd this bewailing land
Of noble Buckingham, my father-in-law:
The heads of all thy brother cardinals—
With thee and all thy best parts bound together—
Weigh'd not a hair of his. Plague of your policy!
You sent me deputy for Ireland,
Far from his succour, from the king, from all
That might have mercy on the fault thou gavest him;
Whilst your great goodness, out of holy pity,
Absolv'd him with an axe.
WOLSEY.   This, and all else
This talking lord can lay upon my credit,
I answer, is most false. The duke by law
Found his deserts: how innocent I was
From any private malice in his end,
His noble jury and foul cause can witness.
If I lov'd many words, lord, I should tell you,
You have as little honesty as honour,
That in the way of loyalty and truth
Toward the king, my ever royal master,
Dare mate a sounder man than Surrey can be,
And all that love his follies.
SURREY.   By my soul,
Your long coat, priest, protects you; thou shouldst feel
My sword i' the life-blood of thee else. My lords,
Can ye endure to hear this arrogance?
And from this fellow? If we live thus tamely,
To be thus jaded by a piece of scarlet,
Farewell nobility; let his Grace go forward,

And dare us with his cap like larks.

WOLSEY.   All goodness
Is poison to thy stomach.

SURREY.   Yes, that goodness
Of gleaning all the land's wealth into one,
Into your own hands, cardinal, by extortion;
The goodness of your intercepted packets,
You writ to the pope against the king; your goodness,
Since you provoke me, shall be most notorious.
My Lord of Norfolk, as you are truly noble,
As you respect the common good, the state
Of our despis'd nobility, our issues,
Who, if he live, will scarce be gentlemen,
Produce the grand sum of his sins, the articles
Collected from his life; I 'll startle you
Worse than the sacring bell, when the brown wench
Lay kissing in your arms, Lord Cardinal.

WOLSEY. How much, methinks, I could despise this man,
But that I am bound in charity against it!

NORFOLK. Those articles, my lord, are in the king's hand;
But, thus much, they are foul ones.

WOLSEY.   So much fairer
And spotless shall mine innocence arise
When the king knows my truth.

SURREY.   This cannot save you:
I thank my memory, I yet remember
Some of these articles; and out they shall.
Now, if you can blush, and cry 'guilty,' cardinal,
You 'll show a little honesty.

WOLSEY.   Speak on, sir;
I dare your worst objection; if I blush,
It is to see a nobleman want manners.

SURREY. I had rather want those than my heart. Have at
  you!
First, that, without the king's assent or knowledge,
You wrought to be a legate; by which power
You maim'd the jurisdiction of all bishops.

NORFOLK. Then, that in all you writ to Rome, or else
To foreign princes, 'Ego et Rex meus'
Was still inscrib'd; in which you brought the king
To be your servant.

SUFFOLK.   Then, that without the knowledge

Either of king or council, when you went
Ambassador to the emperor, you made bold
To carry into Flanders the great seal.
SURREY. Item, you sent a large commission
To Gregory de Cassado, to conclude,
Without the king's will or the state's allowance,
A league between his Highness and Ferrara.
SUFFOLK. That, out of mere ambition, you have caus'd
Your holy hat to be stamp'd on the king's coin.
SURREY. Then, that you have sent innumerable substance,—
By what means got I leave to your own conscience,—
To furnish Rome, and to prepare the ways
You have for dignities; to the mere undoing
Of all the kingdom. Many more there are;
Which, since they are of you, and odious,
I will not taint my mouth with.
CHAMBERLAIN.   O my lord!
Press not a falling man too far; 'tis virtue:
His faults lie open to the laws; let them,
Not you, correct him. My heart weeps to see him
So little of his great self.
SURREY.   I forgive him.
SUFFOLK. Lord Cardinal, the king's further pleasure is,
Because all those things you have done of late,
By your power legatine, within this kingdom,
Fall into the compass of a præmunire,
That therefore such a writ be su'd against you;
To forfeit all your goods, lands, tenements,
Chattels, and whatsoever, and to be
Out of the king's protection. This is my charge.
NORFOLK. And so we 'll leave you to your meditations
How to live better. For your stubborn answer
About the giving back the great seal to us,
The king shall know it, and, no doubt, shall thank you.
So fare you well, my little good Lord Cardinal.
                              Exeunt all except Wolsey
WOLSEY. So farewell to the little good you bear me.
Farewell! a long farewell, to all my greatness!
This is the state of man: to-day he puts forth
The tender leaves of hopes; to-morrow blossoms,
And bears his blushing honours thick upon him;
The third day comes a frost, a killing frost;

And, when he thinks, good easy man, full surely
His greatness is a-ripening, nips his root,
And then he falls, as I do. I have ventur'd,
Like little wanton boys that swim on bladders,
This many summers in a sea of glory,
But far beyond my depth: my high-blown pride
At length broke under me, and now has left me,
Weary and old with service, to the mercy
Of a rude stream, that must for ever hide me.
Vain pomp and glory of this world, I hate ye:
I feel my heart new open'd. O! how wretched
Is that poor man that hangs on princes' favours!
There is, betwixt that smile we would aspire to,
That sweet aspect of princes, and their ruin,
More pangs and fears than wars or women have;
And when he falls, he falls like Lucifer,
Never to hope again.
              Enter Cromwell, and stands amazed
                        Why, how now, Cromwell!
CROMWELL. I have no power to speak, sir.
WOLSEY.   What! amaz'd
    At my misfortunes? can thy spirit wonder
    A great man should decline? Nay, an you weep,
    I am fall'n indeed.
CROMWELL.   How does your Grace?
WOLSEY.   Why, well;
    Never so truly happy, my good Cromwell.
    I know myself now; and I feel within me
    A peace above all earthly dignities,
    A still and quiet conscience. The king has cur'd me,
    I humbly thank his Grace; and from these shoulders,
    These ruin'd pillars, out of pity taken
    A load would sink a navy, too much honour:
    O! 'tis a burden, Cromwell, 'tis a burden
    Too heavy for a man that hopes for heaven.
CROMWELL. I am glad your Grace has made that right use
    of it.
WOLSEY. I hope I have: I am able now, methinks,—
    Out of a fortitude of soul I feel,—
    To endure more miseries and greater far
    Than my weak-hearted enemies dare offer.
    What news abroad?

CROMWELL.   The heaviest and the worst,
  Is your displeasure with the king.
WOLSEY.   God bless him!
CROMWELL. The next is, that Sir Thomas More is chosen
  Lord Chancellor in your place.
WOLSEY.   That 's somewhat sudden:
  But he 's a learned man. May he continue
  Long in his Highness' favour, and do justice
  For truth's sake and his conscience; that his bones,
  When he has run his course and sleeps in blessings,
  May have a tomb of orphans' tears wept on 'em!
  What more?
CROMWELL.   That Cranmer is return'd with welcome,
  Install'd Lord Archbishop of Canterbury.
WOLSEY. That 's news indeed.
CROMWELL.   Last, that the Lady Anne,
  Whom the king hath in secrecy long married,
  This day was view'd in open as his queen,
  Going to chapel; and the voice is now
  Only about her coronation.
WOLSEY. There was the weight that pull'd me down.
    O Cromwell!
  The king has gone beyond me: all my glories
  In that one woman I have lost for ever.
  No sun shall ever usher forth mine honours,
  Or gild again the noble troops that waited
  Upon my smiles. Go, get thee from me, Cromwell;
  I am a poor fall'n man, unworthy now
  To be thy lord and master: seek the king;—
  That sun, I pray, may never set!—I have told him
  What, and how true thou art: he will advance thee;
  Some little memory of me will stir him—
  I know his noble nature—not to let
  Thy hopeful service perish too. Good Cromwell,
  Neglect him not; make use now, and provide
  For thine own future safety.
CROMWELL.   O my lord!
  Must I then leave you? must I needs forego
  So good, so noble, and so true a master?
  Bear witness all that have not hearts of iron,
  With what a sorrow Cromwell leaves his lord.
  The king shall have my service; but my prayers

For ever and for ever shall be yours.

WOLSEY. Cromwell, I did not think to shed a tear
In all my miseries; but thou hast forc'd me,
Out of thy honest truth, to play the woman.
Let 's dry our eyes: and thus far hear me, Cromwell;
And, when I am forgotten, as I shall be,
And sleep in dull cold marble, where no mention
Of me more must be heard of, say, I taught thee,
Say, Wolsey, that once trod the ways of glory,
And sounded all the depths and shoals of honour,
Found thee a way, out of his wrack, to rise in;
A sure and safe one, though thy master miss'd it.
Mark but my fall, and that that ruin'd me.
Cromwell, I charge thee, fling away ambition:
By that sin fell the angels; how can man then,
The image of his Maker, hope to win by it?
Love thyself last: cherish those hearts that hate thee;
Corruption wins not more than honesty.
Still in thy right hand carry gentle peace,
To silence envious tongues: be just, and fear not.
Let all the ends thou aim'st at be thy country's,
Thy God's, and truth's; then if thou fall'st, O Cromwell!
Thou fall'st a blessed martyr. Serve the king;
And,—prithee, lead me in:
There take an inventory of all I have,
To the last penny; 'tis the king's: my robe,
And my integrity to heaven is all
I dare now call mine own. O Cromwell, Cromwell!
Had I but served my God with half the zeal
I serv'd my king, he would not in mine age
Have left me naked to mine enemies.

CROMWELL. Good sir, have patience.

WOLSEY.   So I have. Farewell
The hopes of court! my hopes in heaven do dwell. *Exeunt*

ACT FOUR

SCENE ONE

A Street in Westminster.

Enter two Gentlemen, meeting

FIRST GENTLEMAN. You 're well met once again.

SECOND GENTLEMAN.   So are you.

FIRST GENTLEMAN. You come to take your stand here, and
  behold

The Lady Anne pass from her coronation?

SECOND GENTLEMAN. 'Tis all my business. At our last
  encounter

The Duke of Buckingham came from his trial.

FIRST GENTLEMAN. 'Tis very true: but that time offer'd
  sorrow;

This, general joy.

SECOND GENTLEMAN. 'Tis well: the citizens,

I am sure, have shown at full their royal minds,

As, let 'em have their rights, they are ever forward,

In celebration of this day with shows,

Pageants, and sights of honour.

FIRST GENTLEMAN.   Never greater;

Nor, I 'll assure you, better taken, sir.

SECOND GENTLEMAN. May I be bold to ask what that
  contains,

That paper in your hand?

FIRST GENTLEMAN.   Yes; 'tis the list

Of those that claim their offices this day

By custom of the coronation.

The Duke of Suffolk is the first, and claims

To be high-steward; next, the Duke of Norfolk,

He to be earl marshal: you may read the rest.

SECOND GENTLEMAN. I thank you, sir: had I not known
  those customs,

I should have been beholding to your paper.
But, I beseech you, what 's become of Katharine,
The princess dowager? how goes her business?

FIRST GENTLEMAN. That I can tell you too. The Archbishop
Of Canterbury, accompanied with other
Learned and reverend fathers of his order,
Held a late court at Dunstable, six miles off
From Ampthill, where the princess lay; to which
She was often cited by them, but appear'd not:
And, to be short, for not appearance and
The king's late scruple, by the main assent
Of all these learned men she was divorc'd,
And the late marriage made of none effect:
Since which she was remov'd to Kimbolton,
Where she remains now sick.

SECOND GENTLEMAN.   Alas! good lady! *Trumpets*
The trumpets sound: stand close, the queen is coming.
                                    Hautboys

THE ORDER OF THE CORONATION

A lively flourish of trumpets.

1. *Two Judges.*
2. *Lord Chancellor, with the purse and mace before him.*
3. *Choristers, singing.*   **Music**
4. *Mayor of London, bearing the mace. Then Garter, in his coat of arms, and on his head a gilt copper crown.*
5. *Marquess Dorset, bearing a sceptre of gold, on his head a demi-coronal of gold. With him, the Earl of Surrey, bearing the rod of silver with the dove, crowned with an earl's coronet. Collars of SS.*
6. *Duke of Suffolk, in his robe of estate, his coronet on his head, bearing a long white wand, as high-steward. With him, the Duke of Norfolk, with the rod of marshalship, a coronet on his head. Collars of SS.*
7. *A canopy borne by four of the Cinque-ports; under it, the Queen in her robe; in her hair richly adorned with pearl, crowned. On each side of her, the Bishops of London and Winchester.*
8. *The old Duchess of Norfolk, in a coronal of gold, wrought with flowers, bearing the Queen's train.*
9. *Certain Ladies or Countesses, with plain circlets of gold without flowers.*

          They pass over the stage in order and state

SECOND GENTLEMAN. A royal train, believe me. These I
    know;
Who 's that that bears the sceptre?
FIRST GENTLEMAN.   Marquess Dorset:
    And that the Earl of Surrey with the rod.
SECOND GENTLEMAN. A bold brave gentleman. That should
    be
The Duke of Suffolk?
FIRST GENTLEMAN.   'Tis the same; high-steward.
SECOND GENTLEMAN. And that my Lord of Norfolk?
                                            Yes.
SECOND GENTLEMAN. (*Looking on the Queen*) Heaven bless
    thee!
Thou hast the sweetest face I ever look'd on.
Sir, as I have a soul, she is an angel;
Our king has all the Indies in his arms,
And more and richer, when he strains that lady:
I cannot blame his conscience.
FIRST GENTLEMAN.   They that bear
    The cloth of honour over her, are four barons
Of the Cinque-ports.
SECOND GENTLEMAN. Those men are happy; and so are all
    are near her.
I take it, she that carries up the train
Is that old noble lady, Duchess of Norfolk.
FIRST GENTLEMAN. It is; and all the rest are countesses.
SECOND GENTLEMAN. Their coronets say so. These are stars
    indeed;
And sometimes falling ones.
FIRST GENTLEMAN.   No more of that.
    Exit Procession, with a great flourish of trumpets
          Enter a third Gentleman
God save you, sir! Where have you been broiling?
THIRD GENTLEMAN. Among the crowd i' the Abbey; where a
    finger
Could not be wedg'd in more: I am stifled
With the mere rankness of their joy.
SECOND GENTLEMAN.   You saw
    The ceremony?
THIRD GENTLEMAN. That I did.
FIRST GENTLEMAN.   How was it?

THIRD GENTLEMAN. Well worth the seeing.

SECOND GENTLEMAN.   Good sir, speak it to us.

THIRD GENTLEMAN. As well as I am able. The rich stream
Of lords and ladies, having brought the queen
To a prepar'd place in the choir, fell off
A distance from her; while her Grace sat down
To rest awhile, some half an hour or so,
In a rich chair of state, opposing freely
The beauty of her person to the people.
Believe me, sir, she is the goodliest woman
That ever lay by man: which when the people
Had the full view of, such a noise arose
As the shrouds make at sea in a stiff tempest,
As loud, and to as many tunes: hats, cloaks,—
Doublets, I think,—flew up; and had their faces
Been loose, this day they had been lost. Such joy
I never saw before. Great-bellied women,
That had not half a week to go, like rams
In the old time of war, would shake the press,
And make 'em reel before 'em. No man living
Could say, 'This is my wife,' there; all were woven
So strangely in one piece.

SECOND GENTLEMAN.   But what follow'd?

THIRD GENTLEMAN. At length her Grace rose, and with
        modest paces
Came to the altar; where she kneel'd, and, saint-like,
Cast her fair eyes to heaven and pray'd devoutly.
Then rose again and bow'd her to the people:
When by the Archbishop of Canterbury
She had all the royal makings of a queen;
As holy oil, Edward Confessor's crown,
The rod, and bird of peace, and all such emblems
Laid nobly on her: which perform'd, the choir,
With all the choicest music of the kingdom,
Together sung Te Deum. So she parted,
And with the same full state pac'd back again
To York-place, where the feast is held.

FIRST GENTLEMAN.   Sir,
You must no more call it York-place, that 's past;
For, since the cardinal fell, that title 's lost:
'Tis now the king's, and call'd Whitehall.

THIRD GENTLEMAN. I know it;
But 'tis so lately alter'd that the old name
Is fresh about me.
SECOND GENTLEMAN. What two reverend bishops
Were those that went on each side of the queen?
THIRD GENTLEMAN. Stokesly and Gardiner; the one of
    Winchester,—
Newly preferr'd from the king's secretary,—
The other, London.
SECOND GENTLEMAN. He of Winchester
Is held no great good lover of the archbishop's,
The virtuous Cranmer.
THIRD GENTLEMAN. All the land knows that:
However, yet there 's no great breach; when it comes,
Cranmer will find a friend will not shrink from him.
SECOND GENTLEMAN. Who may that be, I pray you?
THIRD GENTLEMAN. Thomas Cromwell:
A man in much esteem with the king, and truly
A worthy friend. The king
Has made him master o' the jewel house,
And one, already, of the privy council.
SECOND GENTLEMAN. He will deserve more.
THIRD GENTLEMAN. Yes, without all doubt.
Come, gentlemen, ye shall go my way, which
Is to the court, and there ye shall be my guests:
Something I can command. As I walk thither,
I 'll tell ye more.
BOTH. You may command us, sir. *Exeunt*

SCENE TWO

Kimbolton.

*Enter Katharine, Dowager, sick: led between Griffith
and Patience*

GRIFFITH. How does your Grace?
KATHARINE. O Griffith! sick to death!
My legs, like loaden branches, bow to the earth,
Willing to leave their burden. Reach a chair:
So; now, methinks, I feel a little ease.

Didst thou not tell me, Griffith, as thou ledd'st me,
That the great child of honour, Cardinal Wolsey,
Was dead?

GRIFFITH.   Yes, madam; but I think your Grace,
Out of the pain you suffer'd, gave no ear to 't.

KATHARINE. Prithee, good Griffith, tell me how he died:
If well, he stepp'd before me, happily,
For my example.

GRIFFITH.   Well, the voice goes, madam:
For after the stout Earl Northumberland
Arrested him at York, and brought him forward,
As a man sorely tainted, to his answer,
He fell sick suddenly, and grew so ill
He could not sit his mule.

KATHARINE.   Alas! poor man.

GRIFFITH. At last, with easy roads, he came to Leicester;
Lodg'd in the abbey, where the reverend abbot,
With all his covent, honourably receiv'd him:
To whom he gave these words: 'O! father abbot,
An old man, broken with the storms of state,
Is come to lay his weary bones among ye;
Give him a little earth for charity.'
So went to bed, where eagerly his sickness
Pursu'd him still; and three nights after this,
About the hour of eight,—which he himself
Foretold should be his last,—full of repentance,
Continual meditations, tears, and sorrows,
He gave his honours to the world again,
His blessed part to heaven, and slept in peace.

KATHARINE. So may he rest; his faults lie gently on him!
Yet thus far, Griffith, give me leave to speak him,
And yet with charity. He was a man
Of an unbounded stomach, ever ranking
Himself with princes; one, that by suggestion
Tied all the kingdom; simony was fair-play;
His own opinion was his law; i' the presence
He would say untruths, and be ever double
Both in his words and meaning. He was never,
But where he meant to ruin, pitiful;
His promises were, as he then was, mighty;
But his performance, as he is now, nothing:
Of his own body he was ill, and gave

The clergy ill example.

GRIFFITH. Noble madam,
Men's evil manners live in brass; their virtues
We write in water. May it please your Highness
To hear me speak his good now?

KATHARINE. Yes, good Griffith,
I were malicious else.

GRIFFITH. This cardinal,
Though from a humble stock, undoubtedly
Was fashion'd to much honour from his cradle.
He was a scholar, and a ripe and good one;
Exceeding wise, fair-spoken, and persuading;
Lofty and sour to them that lov'd him not;
But, to those men that sought him sweet as summer.
And though he were unsatisfied in getting,—
Which was a sin,—yet in bestowing, madam,
He was most princely. Ever witness for him
Those twins of learning that he rais'd in you,
Ipswich, and Oxford! one of which fell with him,
Unwilling to outlive the good that did it;
The other, though unfinish'd, yet so famous,
So excellent in art, and still so rising,
That Christendom shall ever speak his virtue.
His overthrow heap'd happiness upon him;
For then, and not till then, he felt himself,
And found the blessedness of being little:
And, to add greater honours to his age
Than man could give him, he died fearing God.

KATHARINE. After my death I wish no other herald,
No other speaker of my living actions,
To keep mine honour from corruption,
But such an honest chronicler as Griffith.
Whom I most hated living, thou hast made me,
With thy religious truth and modesty,
Now in his ashes honour. Peace be with him!
Patience, be near me still; and set me lower:
I have not long to trouble thee. Good Griffith,
Cause the musicians play me that sad note
I nam'd my knell, whilst I sit meditating
On that celestial harmony I go to. *Sad and solemn music*

GRIFFITH. She is asleep: good wench, let's sit down quiet,
For fear we wake her: softly, gentle Patience.

THE VISION

Enter, solemnly tripping one after another, six Personages,
clad in white robes, wearing on their heads garlands of bays,
and golden vizards on their faces; branches of bays or palm
in their hands. They first congee unto her, then dance; and,
at certain changes, the first two hold a spare garland over her
head; at which, the other four make reverend curtsies: then,
the two that held the garland deliver the same to the other
next two, who observe the same order in their changes, and
holding the garland over her head: which done, they deliver
the same garland to the last two, who likewise observe the
same order, at which,—as it were by inspiration,—she makes
in her sleep signs of rejoicing, and holdeth up her hands to
heaven: and so in their dancing they vanish, carrying the
garland with them. The music continues

KATHARINE. Spirits of peace, where are ye? Are ye all gone,
  And leave me here in wretchedness behind ye?
GRIFFITH. Madam, we are here.
KATHARINE.   It is not you I call for:
  Saw ye none enter since I slept?
GRIFFITH.   None, madam.
KATHARINE. No? Saw you not, even now, a blessed troop
  Invite me to a banquet; whose bright faces
  Cast thousand beams upon me, like the sun?
  They promis'd me eternal happiness,
  And brought me garlands, Griffith, which I feel
  I am not worthy yet to wear: I shall, assuredly.
GRIFFITH. I am most joyful, madam, such good dreams
  Possess your fancy.
KATHARINE.   Bid the music leave,
  They are harsh and heavy to me.   *Music ceases*
PATIENCE.   Do you note
  How much her Grace is alter'd on the sudden?
  How long her face is drawn? How pale she looks,
  And of an earthy cold? Mark her eyes!
GRIFFITH. She is going, wench. Pray, pray.
PATIENCE. Heaven comfort her!
                    Enter a Messenger
MESSENGER. An 't like your Grace,—
KATHARINE.   You are a saucy fellow:
  Deserve we no more reverence?

GRIFFITH.   You are to blame,
  Knowing she will not lose her wonted greatness,
  To use so rude behaviour; go to, kneel
MESSENGER. I humbly do entreat your Highness' pardon;
  My haste made me unmannerly. There is staying
  A gentleman, sent from the king, to see you.
KATHARINE. Admit him entrance, Griffith: but this fellow
  Let me ne'er see again.   *Exeunt Griffith and Messenger*
               Re-enter Griffith, with Capucius
                     If my sight fail not,
  You should be Lord Ambassador from the emperor,
  My royal nephew, and your name Capucius.
CAPUCIUS. Madam, the same; your servant.
KATHARINE.   O my lord!
  The times and titles now are alter'd strangely
  With me since first you knew me. But, I pray you,
  What is your pleasure with me?
CAPUCIUS.   Noble lady,
  First, mine own service to your Grace; the next,
  The king's request that I would visit you;
  Who grieves much for your weakness, and by me
  Sends you his princely commendations,
  And heartily entreats you take good comfort.
KATHARINE. O! my good lord, that comfort comes too late;
  'Tis like a pardon after execution:
  That gentle physic, given in time, had cur'd me;
  But now I am past all comforts here but prayers.
  How does his Highness?
CAPUCIUS.   Madam, in good health.
KATHARINE. So may he ever do; and ever flourish,
  When I shall dwell with worms, and my poor name
  Banish'd the kingdom. Patience, is that letter
  I caus'd you write, yet sent away?
PATIENCE.   No, madam.
                     Giving it to Katharine
KATHARINE. Sir, I most humbly pray you to deliver
  This to my lord the king.
CAPUCIUS.   Most willing, madam.
KATHARINE. In which I have commended to his goodness
  The model of our chaste loves, his young daughter,—
  The dews of heaven fall thick in blessings on her!
  Beseeching him to give her virtuous breeding,—

She is young, and of a noble modest nature,
I hope she will deserve well,—and a little
To love her for her mother's sake, that lov'd him,
Heaven knows how dearly. My next poor petition
Is, that his noble Grace would have some pity
Upon my wretched women, that so long
Have follow'd both my fortunes faithfully:
Of which there is not one, I dare avow,—
And now I should not lie,—but will deserve,
For virtue, and true beauty of the soul,
For honesty and decent carriage,
A right good husband, let him be a noble;
And, sure, those men are happy that shall have 'em.
The last is, for my men: they are the poorest,
But poverty could never draw 'em from me;
That they may have their wages duly paid 'em,
And something over to remember me by:
If heaven had pleas'd to have given me longer life
And able means, we had not parted thus.
These are the whole contents: and, good my lord,
By that you love the dearest in this world,
As you wish Christian peace to souls departed,
Stand these poor people's friend, and urge the king
To do me this last right.
CAPUCIUS.   By heaven, I will,
Or let me lose the fashion of a man!
KATHARINE. I thank you, honest lord. Remember me
In all humility unto his Highness:
Say his long trouble now is passing
Out of this world; tell him, in death I bless'd him,
For so I will. Mine eyes grow dim. Farewell,
My lord. Griffith, farewell. Nay, Patience,
You must not leave me yet: I must to bed;
Call in more women. When I am dead, good wench,
Let me be us'd with honour: strew me over
With maiden flowers, that all the world may know
I was a chaste wife to my grave: embalm me,
Then lay me forth: although unqueen'd, yet like
A queen, and daughter to a king, inter me.
I can no more.   *Exeunt, leading Katharine*

ACT FIVE

SCENE ONE

London. A Gallery in the Palace.

Enter Gardiner, Bishop of Winchester, a Page with a torch before him, met by Sir Thomas Lovell

GARDINER. It 's one o'clock, boy, is 't not?
BOY.   It hath struck.
GARDINER. These should be hours for necessities,
  Not for delights; times to repair our nature
  With comforting repose, and not for us
  To waste these times. Good hour of night, Sir Thomas!
  Whither so late?
LOVELL.   Came you from the king, my lord?
GARDINER. I did, Sir Thomas; and left him at primero
  With the Duke of Suffolk.
LOVELL.   I must to him too,
  Before he go to bed. I 'll take my leave.
GARDINER. Not yet, Sir Thomas Lovell. What 's the matter?
  It seems you are in haste: an if there be
  No great offence belongs to 't, give your friend
  Some touch of your late business: affairs that walk—
  As they say spirits do—at midnight, have
  In them a wilder nature than the business
  That seeks dispatch by day.
LOVELL.   My lord, I love you,
  And durst commend a secret to your ear
  Much weightier than this work. The queen 's in labour,
  They say, in great extremity; and fear'd
  She 'll with the labour end.
GARDINER.   The fruit she goes with
  I pray for heartily, that it may find
  Good time, and live: but for the stock, Sir Thomas,
  I wish it grubb'd up now.

LOVELL.   Methinks I could
Cry the amen; and yet my conscience says
She's a good creature, and, sweet lady, does
Deserve our better wishes.
GARDINER.   But, sir, sir,
Hear me, Sir Thomas: you're a gentleman
Of mine own way; I know you wise, religious;
And, let me tell you, it will ne'er be well,
'Twill not, Sir Thomas Lovell, take 't of me,
Till Cranmer, Cromwell, her two hands, and she,
Sleep in their graves.
LOVELL.   Now, sir, you speak of two
The most remark'd i' the kingdom. As for Cromwell,
Beside that of the jewel-house, is made master
O' the rolls, and the king's secretary; further, sir,
Stands in the gap and trade of moe preferments,
With which the time will load him. The archbishop
Is the king's hand and tongue; and who dare speak
One syllable against him?
GARDINER.   Yes, yes, Sir Thomas,
There are that dare; and I myself have ventur'd
To speak my mind of him: and indeed this day,
Sir,—I may tell it you,—I think I have
Incens'd the lords o' the council that he is—
For so I know he is, they know he is—
A most arch-heretic, a pestilence
That does infect the land: with which they mov'd
Have broken with the king; who hath so far
Given ear to our complaint,—of his great grace
And princely care, foreseeing those fell mischiefs
Our reasons laid before him,—hath commanded
To-morrow morning to the council-board
He be convented. He's a rank weed, Sir Thomas,
And we must root him out. From your affairs
I hinder you too long: good-night, Sir Thomas!
LOVELL. Many good-nights, my lord. I rest your servant.
                              Exeunt Gardiner and Page
                    Enter the King and Suffolk
KING HENRY. Charles, I will play no more to-night;
My mind's not on 't; you are too hard for me.
SUFFOLK. Sir, I did never win of you before.
KING HENRY. But little, Charles;

Nor shall not when my fancy's on my play.
Now, Lovell, from the queen what is the news?
LOVELL. I could not personally deliver to her
What you commanded me, but by her woman
I sent your message; who return'd her thanks
In the great'st humbleness, and desir'd your Highness
Most heartily to pray for her.
KING HENRY.   What sayst thou, ha?
To pray for her? what! is she crying out?
LOVELL. So said her woman; and that her sufferance made
Almost each pang a death.
KING HENRY.   Alas! good lady.
SUFFOLK. God safely quit her of her burden, and
With gentle travail, to the gladding of
Your Highness with an heir!
KING HENRY.   'Tis midnight, Charles;
Prithee, to bed; and in thy prayers remember
The estate of my poor queen. Leave me alone;
For I must think of that which company
Would not be friendly to.
SUFFOLK.   I wish your Highness
A quiet night; and my good mistress will
Remember in my prayers.
KING HENRY.   Charles, good night.
                              Exit Suffolk
            Enter Sir Anthony Denny
Well, sir, what follows?
DENNY. Sir, I have brought my lord the archbishop,
As you commanded me.
KING HENRY.   Ha! Canterbury?
DENNY. Ay, my good lord.
KING HENRY.   'Tis true: where is he, Denny?
DENNY. He attends your Highness' pleasure.
KING HENRY.   Bring him to us.
                              Exit Denny
LOVELL. (*Aside*) This is about that which the bishop spake:
I am happily come hither.
            Re-enter Denny, with Cranmer
KING HENRY.   Avoid the gallery.
                         Lovell seems to stay

Ha! I have said. Begone.
What!—   *Exeunt Lovell and Denny*

CRANMER. I am fearful. Wherefore frowns he thus?
   'Tis his aspect of terror: all 's not well.
KING HENRY. How now, my lord! You do desire to know
   Wherefore I sent for you.
CRANMER.   (*Kneeling*) It is my duty
   To attend your Highness' pleasure.
KING HENRY.   Pray you, arise,
   My good and gracious Lord of Canterbury.
   Come, you and I must walk a turn together;
   I have news to tell you: come, come, give me your hand.
   Ah! my good lord, I grieve at what I speak,
   And am right sorry to repeat what follows.
   I have, and most unwillingly, of late
   Heard many grievous, I do say, my lord,
   Grievous complaints of you; which, being consider'd,
   Have mov'd us and our council, that you shall
   This morning come before us; where, I know,
   You cannot with such freedom purge yourself,
   But that, till further trial in those charges
   Which will require your answer, you must take
   Your patience to you, and be well contented
   To make your house our Tower: you a brother of us,
   It fits we thus proceed, or else no witness
   Would come against you.
CRANMER. (*Kneeling*) I humbly thank your Highness;
   And am right glad to catch this good occasion
   Most throughly to be winnow'd, where my chaff
   And corn shall fly asunder; for I know
   There 's none stands under more calumnious tongues
   Than I myself, poor man.
KING HENRY.   Stand up, good Canterbury:
   Thy truth and thy integrity is rooted
   In us, thy friend: give me thy hand, stand up:
   Prithee, let 's walk. Now, by my holidame,
   What manner of man are you? My lord, I look'd
   You would have given me your petition, that
   I should have ta'en some pains to bring together
   Yourself and your accusers; and to have heard you,
   Without indurance, further.
CRANMER.   Most dread liege,
   The good I stand on is my truth and honesty:
   If they shall fail, I, with mine enemies,

Will triumph o'er my person; which I weigh not,
Being of those virtues vacant. I fear nothing
What can be said against me.

KING HENRY.   Know you not
How your state stands i' the world, with the whole world?
Your enemies are many, and not small; their practices
Must bear the same proportion; and not ever
The justice and the truth o' the question carries
The due o' the verdict with it. At what ease
Might corrupt minds procure knaves as corrupt
To swear against you? such things have been done.
You are potently oppos'd, and with a malice
Of as great size. Ween you of better luck,
I mean in perjur'd witness, than your master,
Whose minister you are, whiles here he liv'd
Upon this naughty earth? Go to, go to;
You take a precipice for no leap of danger,
And woo your own destruction.

CRANMER.   God and your Majesty
Protect mine innocence! or I fall into
The trap is laid for me!

KING HENRY.   Be of good cheer;
They shall no more prevail than we give way to.
Keep comfort to you; and this morning see
You do appear before them. If they shall chance,
In charging you with matters, to commit you,
The best persuasions to the contrary
Fail not to use, and with what vehemency
The occasion shall instruct you: if entreaties
Will render you no remedy, this ring
Deliver them, and your appeal to us
There make before them. Look! the good man weeps;
He's honest, on mine honour. God's blest mother!
I swear he is true-hearted; and a soul
None better in my kingdom. Get you gone,
And do as I have bid you. (*Exit Cranmer*) He has
    strangled
His language in his tears.
                Enter an Old Lady
GENTLEMAN. (*Within*) Come back: what mean you?
OLD LADY. I'll not come back; the tidings that I bring
Will make my boldness manners. Now, good angels

Fly o'er thy royal head, and shade thy person
Under their blessed wings!

KING HENRY.   Now, by thy looks
I guess thy message. Is the queen deliver'd?
Say, ay; and of a boy.

OLD LADY.   Ay, ay, my liege;
And of a lovely boy: the God of heaven
Both now and ever bless her! 'tis a girl,
Promises boys hereafter. Sir, your queen
Desires your visitation, and to be
Acquainted with this stranger: 'tis as like you
As cherry is to cherry.

KING HENRY.   Lovell!

Re-enter Lovell

LOVELL.   Sir!

KING HENRY. Give her a hundred marks. I 'll to the queen.

             Exit

OLD LADY. A hundred marks! By this light, I 'll ha' more.
An ordinary groom is for such payment:
I will have more, or scold it out of him.
Said I for this the girl was like to him?
I will have more, or else unsay 't; and now,
While it is hot, I 'll put it to the issue.   *Exeunt*

SCENE TWO

The Lobby before the Council-Chamber

Enter Cranmer; Pursuivants, Pages, &c., attending

CRANMER. I hope I am not too late; and yet the gentleman,
That was sent to me from the council, pray'd me
To make great haste. All fast? what means this? Ho!
Who waits there?

     Enter Keeper
    Sure, you know me?

KEEPER.   Yes, my lord;
But yet I cannot help you.

CRANMER.   Why?

KEEPER. Your Grace must wait till you be call'd for.

     Enter Doctor Butts

CRANMER.   So.

BUTTS. (*Aside*) This is a piece of malice. I am glad
　I came this way so happily: the king
　Shall understand it presently.
CRANMER.　　　　　　　　　(*Aside*) 'Tis Butts,
　The king's physician. As he pass'd along,
　How earnestly he cast his eyes upon me.
　Pray heaven he sound not my disgrace! For certain,
　This is of purpose laid by some that hate me,—
　God turn their hearts! I never sought their malice,—
　To quench mine honour; they would shame to make me
　Wait else at door, a fellow-counsellor,
　'Mong boys, grooms, and lackeys. But their pleasures
　Must be fulfill'd, and I attend with patience.
　　　Enter, at a window above, the King and Butts
BUTTS. I'll show your Grace the strangest sight—
KING HENRY.　　　　　　　　　　What's that, Butts?
BUTTS. I think your Highness saw this many a day.
KING HENRY. Body o' me, where is it?
BUTTS.　　　　　　　　　There, my lord,
　The high promotion of his Grace of Canterbury;
　Who holds his state at door, 'mongst pursuivants,
　Pages, and footboys.
KING HENRY.　　　　Ha! 'Tis he, indeed:
　Is this the honour they do one another?
　'Tis well there's one above 'em yet. I had thought
　They had parted so much honesty among 'em,—
　At least, good manners,—as not thus to suffer
　A man of his place, and so near our favour,
　To dance attendance on their lordship's pleasures,
　And at the door too, like a post with packets.
　By holy Mary, Butts, there's knavery:
　Let 'em alone, and draw the curtain close;
　We shall hear more anon.　　　　　*Exeunt above*

SCENE THREE

The Council-Chamber.

Enter the Lord Chancellor, the Duke of Suffolk, the Duke of Norfolk, Earl of Surrey, Lord Chamberlain, Gardiner, and Cromwell. The Chancellor places himself at the upper end of the table on the left hand; a seat being left void above him, as for the Archbishop of Canterbury. The rest seat themselves in order on each side. Cromwell at the lower end as secretary. Keeper at the door

CHANCELLOR. Speak to the business, Master Secretary:
  Why are we met in council?
CROMWELL.   Please, your honours,
  The chief cause concerns his Grace of Canterbury.
GARDINER. Has he had knowledge of it?
CROMWELL.   Yes.
NORFOLK.   Who waits there?
KEEPER. Without, my noble lords?
GARDINER.   Yes.
KEEPER.   My Lord Archbishop:
  And has done half an hour, to know your pleasures.
CHANCELLOR. Let him come in.
KEEPER.   Your Grace may enter now.
    Cranmer enters and approaches the council-table
CHANCELLOR. My good Lord Archbishop, I 'm very sorry
  To sit here at this present and behold
  That chair stand empty: but we all are men,
  In our own natures frail, and capable
  Of our flesh; few are angels: out of which frailty
  And want of wisdom, you, that best should teach us,
  Have misdemean'd yourself, and not a little,
  Toward the king first, then his laws, in filling
  The whole realm, by your teaching and your chaplains,—
  For so we are inform'd,—with new opinions,
  Divers and dangerous; which are heresies,
  And, not reform'd, may prove pernicious.
GARDINER. Which reformation must be sudden too,
  My noble lords; for those that tame wild horses
  Pace 'em not in their hands to make 'em gentle,
  But stop their mouths with stubborn bits, and spur 'em,

Till they obey the manage. If we suffer—
Out of our easiness and childish pity
To one man's honour—this contagious sickness,
Farewell all physic: and what follows then?
Commotions, uproars, with a general taint
Of the whole state: as, of late days, our neighbours,
The upper Germany, can dearly witness,
Yet freshly pitied in our memories.

CRANMER. My good lords, hitherto in all the progress
Both of my life and office, I have labour'd,
And with no little study, that my teaching
And the strong course of my authority
Might go one way, and safely; and the end
Was ever to do well: nor is there living,—
I speak it with a single heart, my lords,—
A man that more detests, more stirs against,
Both in his private conscience and his place,
Defacers of a public peace, than I do.
Pray heaven the king may never find a heart
With less allegiance in it! Men, that make
Envy and crooked malice nourishment
Dare bite the best. I do beseech your lordships
That, in this case of justice, my accusers,
Be what they will, may stand forth face to face,
And freely urge against me.

SUFFOLK.   Nay, my lord,
That cannot be: you are a counsellor,
And by that virtue no man dare accuse you.

GARDINER. My lord, because we have business of more
    moment,
We will be short with you. 'Tis his Highness' pleasure,
And our consent, for better trial of you,
From hence you be committed to the Tower;
Where, being but a private man again,
You shall know many dare accuse you boldly,
More than, I fear, you are provided for.

CRANMER. Ah! my good Lord of Winchester, I thank you;
You are always my good friend: if your will pass,
I shall both find your lordship judge and juror,
You are so merciful. I see your end;
'Tis my undoing: love and meekness, lord,
Become a churchman better than ambition:

Win straying souls with modesty again,
Cast none away. That I shall clear myself,
Lay all the weight ye can upon my patience,
I make as little doubt, as you do conscience
In doing daily wrongs. I could say more,
But reverence to your calling makes me modest.

GARDINER. My lord, my lord, you are a sectary;
That 's the plain truth: your painted gloss discovers,
To men that understand you, words and weakness.

CROMWELL. My Lord of Winchester, you are a little,
By your good favour, too sharp; men so noble,
However faulty, yet should find respect
For what they have been: 'tis a cruelty
To load a falling man.

GARDINER. Good Master Secretary,
I cry your honour mercy; you may, worst
Of all this table, say so.

CROMWELL. Why, my lord?

GARDINER. Do not I know you for a favourer
Of this new sect? ye are not sound.

CROMWELL. Not sound?

GARDINER. Not sound, I say.

CROMWELL. Would you were half so honest!
Men's prayers then would seek you, not their fears.

GARDINER. I shall remember this bold language.

CROMWELL. Do.
Remember your bold life too.

CHANCELLOR. This is too much;
Forbear, for shame, my lords.

GARDINER. I have done.

CROMWELL. And I.

CHANCELLOR. Then thus for you, my lord: it stands agreed,
I take it, by all voices, that forthwith
You be convey'd to the Tower a prisoner;
There to remain till the king's further pleasure
Be known unto us. Are you all agreed, lords?

ALL. We are.

CRANMER. Is there no other way of mercy,
But I must needs to the Tower, my lords?

GARDINER. What other
Would you expect? You are strangely troublesome.
Let some o' the guard be ready there.

Enter Guard

CRANMER.   For me?
 Must I go like a traitor thither?
GARDINER.   Receive him,
 And see him safe i' the Tower.
CRANMER.   Stay, good my lords;
 I have a little yet to say. Look there, my lords;
 By virtue of that ring I take my cause
 Out of the gripes of cruel men, and give it
 To a most noble judge, the king my master.
CHANCELLOR. This is the king's ring.
SURREY.   'Tis no counterfeit.
SUFFOLK. 'Tis the right ring, by heaven! I told ye all,
 When we first put this dangerous stone a-rolling,
 'Twould fall upon ourselves.
NORFOLK.   Do you think, my lords,
 The king will suffer but the little finger
 Of this man to be vex'd?
CHAMBERLAIN.   'Tis now too certain:
 How much more is his life in value with him?
 Would I were fairly out on 't.
CROMWELL.   My mind gave me,
 In seeking tales and informations
 Against this man—whose honesty the devil
 And his disciples only envy at—
 Ye blew the fire that burns ye: now have at ye!
 Enter the King, frowning on them: he takes his seat
GARDINER. Dread sovereign, how much are we bound to
  heaven
 In daily thanks, that gave us such a prince;
 Not only good and wise, but most religious:
 One that in all obedience makes the Church
 The chief aim of his honour; and, to strengthen
 That holy duty, out of dear respect,
 His royal self in judgment comes to hear
 The cause betwixt her and this great offender.
KING HENRY. You were ever good at sudden commendations,
 Bishop of Winchester; but know, I come not
 To hear such flattery now, and in my presence;
 They are too thin and bare to hide offences.
 To me you cannot reach; you play the spaniel,
 And think with wagging of your tongue to win me;

But, whatsoe'er thou takest me for, I 'm sure
Thou hast a cruel nature and a bloody.
(*To Cranmer*) Good man, sit down. Now let me see the
    proudest
He, that dares most, but wag his finger at thee:
By all that 's holy, he had better starve
Than but once think this place becomes thee not.

SURREY. May it please your Grace.—

KING HENRY.   No, sir, it does not please me.
I had thought I had had men of some understanding
And wisdom of my council; but I find none.
Was it discretion, lords, to let this man,
This good man,—few of you deserve that title,—
This honest man, wait like a lousy footboy
At chamber-door? and one as great as you are?
Why, what a shame was this! Did my commission
Bid ye so far forget yourselves? I gave ye
Power as he was a counsellor to try him,
Not as a groom. There 's some of ye, I see,
More out of malice than integrity,
Would try him to the utmost, had ye mean;
Which ye shall never have while I live.

CHANCELLOR.   Thus far,
My most dread sovereign, may it like your Grace
To let my tongue excuse all. What was purpos'd
Concerning his imprisonment, was rather—
If there be faith in men—meant for his trial
And fair purgation to the world, than malice,
I 'm sure, in me.

KING HENRY.   Well, well, my lords, respect him;
Take him, and use him well; he 's worthy of it.
I will say thus much for him, if a prince
May be beholding to a subject, I
Am, for his love and service, so to him.
Make me no more ado, but all embrace him:
Be friends, for shame, my lords! My Lord of Canterbury,
I have a suit which you must not deny me;
That is, a fair young maid that yet wants baptism,
You must be godfather, and answer for her.

CRANMER. The greatest monarch now alive may glory
In such an honour: how may I deserve it,
That am a poor and humble subject to you?

KING HENRY. Come, come, my lord, you 'd spare your spoons;
you shall have two noble partners with you; the old
Duchess of Norfolk, and Lady Marquess Dorset: will
these please you?
Once more, my Lord of Winchester, I charge you,
Embrace and love this man.

GARDINER.   With a true heart
And brother-love I do it.

CRANMER.   And let heaven
Witness, how dear I hold this confirmation.

KING HENRY. Good man! those joyful tears show thy true
heart:
The common voice, I see, is verified
Of thee, which says thus, 'Do my Lord of Canterbury
A shrewd turn, and he is your friend for ever.'
Come, lords, we trifle time away; I long
To have this young one made a Christian.
As I have made ye one, lords, one remain;
So I grow stronger, you more honour gain.   *Exeunt*

SCENE FOUR

The Palace Yard.

Noise and tumult within. Enter Porter and his Man

PORTER. You 'll leave your noise anon, ye rascals. Do you
take the court for Paris-garden? ye rude slaves leave your
gaping.
(*Within*) Good Master porter, I belong to the larder.

PORTER. Belong to the gallows, and be hang'd, you rogue!
Is this a place to roar in? Fetch me a dozen crab-tree
staves, and strong ones: there are but switches to 'em. I 'll
scratch your heads: you must be seeing christenings! Do
you look for ale and cakes here, you rude rascals?

MAN. Pray, sir, be patient: 'tis as much impossible—
Unless we sweep 'em from the door with cannons—
To scatter 'em, as 'tis to make 'em sleep
On May-day morning; which will never be.
We may as well push against Paul's as stir 'em.

PORTER. How got they in, and be hang'd?

MAN. Alas, I know not; how gets the tide in?

As much as one sound cudgel of four foot—
You see the poor remainder—could distribute,
I made no spare, sir.

PORTER.   You did nothing, sir.

MAN. I am not Samson, nor Sir Guy, nor Colbrand,
To mow 'em down before me; but if I spar'd any
That had a head to hit, either young or old,
He or she, cuckold or cuckold-maker,
Let me ne'er hope to see a chine again;
And that I would not for a cow, God save her!
(*Within*) Do you hear, Master porter?

PORTER. I shall be with you presently, good Master puppy.
Keep the door close, sirrah.

MAN. What would you have me do?

PORTER. What should you do, but knock 'em down by the
dozens? Is this Moorfields to muster in? or have we some
strange Indian with the great tool come to court, the
women so besiege us? Bless me, what a fry of fornication is
at door! On my Christian conscience, this one christening
will beget a thousand: here will be father, godfather, and
all together.

MAN. The spoons will be the bigger, sir. There is a fellow
somewhat near the door, he should be a brazier by his
face, for, o' my conscience, twenty of the dog-days now
reign in 's nose: all that stand about him are under the
line, they need no other penance. That fire-drake did I hit
three times on the head, and three times was his nose dis-
charged against me: he stands there, like a mortar-piece,
to blow us. There was a haberdasher's wife of small wit
near him, that railed upon me till her pinked porringer fell
off her head, for kindling such a combustion in the state.
I missed the meteor once, and hit that woman, who cried
out, 'Clubs!' when I might see from far some forty trun-
cheoners draw to her succour, which were the hope o' the
Strand, where she was quartered. They fell on; I made
good my place; at length they came to the broomstaff to
me; I defied 'em still; when suddenly a file of boys behind
'em, loose shot, delivered such a shower of pebbles, that
I was fain to draw mine honour in, and let 'em win the
work. The devil was amongst 'em, I think, surely.

PORTER. These are the youths that thunder at a playhouse,
and fight for bitten apples; that no audience, but the

Tribulation of Tower-hill, or the Limbs of Limehouse,
their dear brothers, are able to endure. I have some of 'em
in Limbo Patrum, and there they are like to dance these
three days; besides the running banquet of two beadles,
that is to come.

Enter the Lord Chamberlain

CHAMBERLAIN. Mercy o' me, what a multitude are here!
They grow still too, from all parts they are coming,
As if we kept a fair here! Where are these porters,
These lazy knaves? Ye have made a fine hand, fellows:
There 's a trim rabble let in. Are all these
Your faithful friends o' the suburbs? We shall have
Great store of room, no doubt, left for the ladies,
When they pass back from the christening.

PORTER.   An 't please your honour,
We are but men; and what so many may do,
Not being torn a-pieces, we have done:
An army cannot rule 'em.

CHAMBERLAIN.   As I live,
If the king blame me for 't, I 'll lay ye all
By the heels, and suddenly; and on your heads
Clap round fines for neglect: ye 're lazy knaves;
And here ye lie baiting of bombards, when
Ye should do service. Hark! the trumpets sound;
They 're come already from the christening.
Go, break among the press, and find a way out
To let the troop pass fairly, or I 'll find
A Marshalsea shall hold ye play these two months.

PORTER. Make way there for the princess.

MAN.   You great fellow,
Stand close up, or I 'll make your head ache.

PORTER. You i' the camlet, get up o' the rail:
I 'll pick you o'er the pales else.   *Exeunt*

SCENE FIVE

The Palace.

Enter trumpets, sounding; then two Aldermen, Lord Mayor,
Garter, Cranmer, Duke of Norfolk, with his marshal's staff,
Duke of Suffolk, two Noblemen bearing great standing-
bowls for the christening gifts; then, four Noblemen bearing
a canopy, under which the Duchess of Norfolk, godmother,
bearing the child, richly habited in a mantle, &c., train borne
by a Lady; then follows the Marchioness Dorset, the other
godmother, and Ladies. The troop pass once
about the stage, and Garter speaks

GARTER. Heaven, from thy endless goodness, send pros-
  perous life, long, and ever happy, to the high and mighty
  Princess of England, Elizabeth!
            Flourish. Enter King and Train
CRANMER. (*Kneeling*) And to your royal Grace, and the
      good queen,
  My noble partners, and myself, thus pray:
  All comfort, joy, in this most gracious lady,
  Heaven ever laid up to make parents happy,
  May hourly fall upon ye!
KING HENRY.   Thank you, good Lord Archbishop:
  What is her name?
CRANMER.   Elizabeth.
KING HENRY.   Stand up, lord.
                          The King kisses the Child
  With this kiss take my blessing; God protect thee!
  Into whose hand I give thy life.
CRANMER.   Amen.
KING HENRY. My noble gossips, ye have been too prodigal:
  I thank ye heartily: so shall this lady
  When she has so much English.
CRANMER.   Let me speak, sir,
  For heaven now bids me; and the words I utter
  Let none think flattery, for they 'll find 'em truth.
  This royal infant,—heaven still move about her!—
  Though in her cradle, yet now promises
  Upon this land a thousand thousand blessings,
  Which time shall bring to ripeness: she shall be—

But few now living can behold that goodness—
A pattern to all princes living with her,
And all that shall succeed: Saba was never
More covetous of wisdom and fair virtue
Than this pure soul shall be: all princely graces,
That mould up such a mighty piece as this is,
With all the virtues that attend the good,
Shall still be doubled on her; truth shall nurse her;
Holy and heavenly thoughts still counsel her;
She shall be lov'd and fear'd; her own shall bless her;
Her foes shake like a field of beaten corn,
And hang their heads with sorrow; good grows with her.
In her days every man shall eat in safety
Under his own vine what he plants; and sing
The merry songs of peace to all his neighbours.
God shall be truly known; and those about her
From her shall read the perfect ways of honour,
And by those claim their greatness, not by blood.
Nor shall this peace sleep with her; but as when
The bird of wonder dies, the maiden phoenix,
Her ashes new-create another heir
As great in admiration as herself,
So shall she leave her blessedness to one,—
When heaven shall call her from this cloud of darkness,
Who, from the sacred ashes of her honour,
Shall star-like rise, as great in fame as she was,
And so stand fix'd. Peace, plenty, love, truth, terror,
That were the servants to this chosen infant,
Shall then be his, and like a vine grow to him:
Wherever the bright sun of heaven shall shine,
His honour and the greatness of his name
Shall be, and make new nations; he shall flourish,
And, like a mountain cedar, reach his branches
To all the plains about him; our children's children
Shall see this, and bless heaven.
KING HENRY.   Thou speakest wonders.
CRANMER. She shall be, to the happiness of England,
An aged princess; many days shall see her,
And yet no day without a deed to crown it.
Would I had known no more! but she must die,
She must, the saints must have her, yet a virgin;
A most unspotted lily shall she pass

To the ground, and all the world shall mourn her.
KING HENRY. O Lord Archbishop!
Thou hast made me now a man: never, before
This happy child, did I get any thing.
This oracle of comfort has so pleas'd me,
That when I am in heaven, I shall desire
To see what this child does, and praise my Maker.
I thank ye all. To you, my good Lord Mayor,
And your good brethren, I am much beholding;
I have receiv'd much honour by your presence,
And ye shall find me thankful. Lead the way, lords:
Ye must all see the queen, and she must thank ye;
She will be sick else. This day, no man think
He has business at his house; for all shall stay:
This little one shall make it holiday.   *Exeunt*

EPILOGUE

'Tis ten to one, this play can never please
All that are here: some come to take their ease
And sleep an act or two; but those, we fear,
We 've frighted with our trumpets; so, 'tis clear
They 'll say 'tis naught: others, to hear the city
Abus'd extremely, and to cry, 'That 's witty!'
Which we have not done neither: that, I fear,
All the expected good we 're like to hear
For this play at this time, is only in
The merciful construction of good women;
For such a one we show'd 'em: if they smile,
And say 'twill do, I know, within a while
All the best men are ours; for 'tis ill hap
If they hold when their ladies bid 'em clap.

POEMS

VENUS AND ADONIS

'Vilia miretur vulgus; mihi flavus Apollo
Pocula Castalia plena ministret aqua.'

TO THE RIGHT HONOURABLE
HENRY WRIOTHESLEY,
EARL OF SOUTHAMPTON, AND
BARON OF TICHFIELD

Right Honourable,

I know not how I shall offend in dedicating my unpolished lines to your lordship, nor how the world will censure me for choosing so strong a prop to support so weak a burthen: only, if your honour seem but pleased, I account myself highly praised, and vow to take advantage of all idle hours, till I have honoured you with some graver labour. But if the first heir of my invention prove deformed, I shall be sorry it had so noble a godfather, and never after ear so barren a land, for fear it yield me still so bad a harvest. I leave it to your honourable survey, and your honour to your heart's content; which I wish may always answer your own wish and the world's hopeful expectation.

Your honour's in all duty,

William Shakespeare

VENUS AND ADONIS

Even as the sun with purple-colour'd face
Had ta'en his last leave of the weeping morn,
Rose-cheek'd Adonis hied him to the chase;
Hunting he lov'd, but love he laugh'd to scorn;
   Sick-thoughted Venus makes amain unto him,
   And like a bold-fac'd suitor 'gins to woo him.

'Thrice fairer than myself,' thus she began,
'The field's chief flower, sweet above compare,
Stain to all nymphs, more lovely than a man,
More white and red than doves or roses are;
   Nature that made thee, with herself at strife,
   Saith that the world hath ending with thy life.

Vouchsafe, thou wonder, to alight thy steed,
And rein his proud head to the saddle-bow;
If thou wilt deign this favour, for thy meed
A thousand honey secrets shalt thou know:
   Here come and sit, where never serpent hisses;
   And being set, I'll smother thee with kisses:

And yet not cloy thy lips with loath'd satiety,
But rather famish them amid their plenty,
Making them red and pale with fresh variety;
Ten kisses short as one, one long as twenty:
   A summer's day will seem an hour but short,
   Being wasted in such time-beguiling sport.'

With this she seizeth on his sweating palm,
The precedent of pith and livelihood,
And, trembling in her passion, calls it balm,
Earth's sovereign salve to do a goddess good:
   Being so enrag'd, desire doth lend her force
   Courageously to pluck him from his horse.

Over one arm the lusty courser's rein,
Under her other was the tender boy,
Who blush'd and pouted in a dull disdain,
With leaden appetite, unapt to toy;
    She red and hot as coals of glowing fire,
    He red for shame, but frosty in desire.

The studded bridle on a ragged bough
Nimbly she fastens;—O! how quick is love:—
The steed is stalled up, and even now
To tie the rider she begins to prove:
    Backward she push'd him, as she would be thrust,
    And govern'd him in strength, though not in lust.

So soon was she along, as he was down,
Each leaning on their elbows and their hips:
Now doth she stroke his cheek, now doth he frown,
And 'gins to chide, but soon she stops his lips;
    And kissing speaks, with lustful language broken,
    'If thou wilt chide, thy lips shall never open.'

He burns with bashful shame; she with her tears
Doth quench the maiden burning of his cheeks;
Then with her windy sighs and golden hairs
To fan and blow them dry again she seeks:
    He saith she is immodest, blames her miss;
    What follows more she murders with a kiss.

Even as an empty eagle, sharp by fast,
Tires with her beak on feathers, flesh and bone,
Shaking her wings, devouring all in haste,
Till either gorge be stuff'd or prey be gone;
    Even so she kiss'd his brow, his cheek, his chin,
    And where she ends she doth anew begin.

Forc'd to content, but never to obey,
Panting he lies, and breatheth in her face;
She feedeth on the steam, as on a prey,
And calls it heavenly moisture, air of grace;
    Wishing her cheeks were gardens full of flowers,
    So they were dew'd with such distilling showers.

Look! how a bird lies tangled in a net,
So fasten'd in her arms Adonis lies;
Pure shame and aw'd resistance made him fret,
Which bred more beauty in his angry eyes:
    Rain added to a river that is rank
    Perforce will force it overflow the bank.

Still she entreats, and prettily entreats,
For to a pretty ear she tunes her tale;
Still is he sullen, still he lours and frets,
'Twixt crimson shame and anger ashy-pale;
    Being red, she loves him best; and being white,
    Her best is better'd with a more delight.

Look how he can, she cannot choose but love;
And by her fair immortal hand she swears,
From his soft bosom never to remove,
Till he take truce with her contending tears,
    Which long have rain'd, making her cheeks all wet;
    And one sweet kiss shall pay this countless debt.

Upon this promise did he raise his chin
Like a dive-dapper peering through a wave,
Who, being look'd on, ducks as quickly in;
So offers he to give what she did crave;
    But when her lips were ready for his pay,
    He winks, and turns his lips another way.

Never did passenger in summer's heat
More thirst for drink than she for this good turn.
Her help she sees, but help she cannot get;
She bathes in water, yet her fire must burn:
    'O! pity,' 'gan she cry, 'flint-hearted boy:
    'Tis but a kiss I beg; why art thou coy?

'I have been woo'd, as I entreat thee now,
Even by the stern and direful god of war,
Whose sinewy neck in battle ne'er did bow,
Who conquers where he comes in every jar;
    Yet hath he been my captive and my slave,
    And begg'd for that which thou unask'd shalt have.

'Over my altars hath he hung his lance,
His batter'd shield, his uncontrolled crest,
And for my sake hath learn'd to sport and dance,
To toy, to wanton, dally, smile, and jest;
 Scorning his churlish drum and ensign red,
 Making my arms his field, his tent my bed.

'Thus he that overrul'd I oversway'd,
Leading him prisoner in a red-rose chain:
Strong-temper'd steel his stronger strength obey'd,
Yet was he servile to my coy disdain.
 O! be not proud, nor brag not of thy might,
 For mastering her that foil'd the god of fight.

'Touch but my lips with those fair lips of thine,—
Though mine be not so fair, yet are they red,—
The kiss shall be thine own as well as mine:
What seest thou in the ground? hold up thy head:
 Look in mine eyeballs, there thy beauty lies;
 Then why not lips on lips, since eyes in eyes?

'Art thou asham'd to kiss? then wink again,
And I will wink; so shall the day seem night;
Love keeps his revels where there are but twain;
Be bold to play, our sport is not in sight:
 These blue-vein'd violets whereon we lean
 Never can blab, nor know not what we mean.

'The tender spring upon thy tempting lip
Shows thee unripe, yet mayst thou well be tasted:
Make use of time, let not advantage slip;
Beauty within itself should not be wasted:
 Fair flowers that are not gather'd in their prime
 Rot and consume themselves in little time.

'Were I hard-favour'd, foul, or wrinkled-old,
Ill-nurtur'd, crooked, churlish, harsh in voice,
O'erworn, despised, rheumatic, and cold,
Thick-sighted, barren, lean, and lacking juice,
 Then mightst thou pause, for then I were not for thee;
 But having no defects, why dost abhor me?

'Thou canst not see one wrinkle in my brow;
Mine eyes are grey and bright, and quick in turning;
My beauty as the spring doth yearly grow;
My flesh is soft and plump, my marrow burning;
　My smooth moist hand, were it with thy hand felt,
　Would in thy palm dissolve, or seem to melt.

'Bid me discourse, I will enchant thine ear,
Or, like a fairy, trip upon the green,
Or, like a nymph, with long dishevell'd hair,
Dance on the sands, and yet no footing seen:
　Love is a spirit all compact of fire,
　Not gross to sink, but light, and will aspire.

'Witness this primrose bank whereon I lie;
These forceless flowers like sturdy trees support me;
Two strengthless doves will draw me through the sky,
From morn till night, even where I list to sport me:
　Is love so light, sweet boy, and may it be
　That thou shouldst think it heavy unto thee?

'Is thine own heart to thine own face affected?
Can thy right hand seize love upon thy left?
Then woo thyself, be of thyself rejected,
Steal thine own freedom, and complain on theft.
　Narcissus so himself himself forsook,
　And died to kiss his shadow in the brook.

'Torches are made to light, jewels to wear,
Dainties to taste, fresh beauty for the use,
Herbs for their smell, and sappy plants to bear;
Things growing to themselves are growth's abuse:
　Seeds spring from seeds, and beauty breedeth beauty;
　Thou wast begot; to get it is thy duty.

'Upon the earth's increase why shouldst thou feed,
Unless the earth with thy increase be fed?
By law of nature thou art bound to breed,
That thine may live when thou thyself art dead;
　And so in spite of death thou dost survive,
　In that thy likeness still is left alive.'

By this the love-sick queen began to sweat,
For where they lay the shadow had forsook them,
And Titan, tired in the mid-day heat,
With burning eye did hotly overlook them,
    Wishing Adonis had his team to guide,
    So he were like him and by Venus' side.

And now Adonis with a lazy spright,
And with a heavy, dark, disliking eye,
His louring brows o'erwhelming his fair sight,
Like misty vapours when they blot the sky,
    Souring his cheeks, cries, 'Fie! no more of love:
    The sun doth burn my face; I must remove.'

'Ay me,' quoth Venus 'young, and so unkind!
What bare excuses mak'st thou to be gone!
I 'll sigh celestial breath, whose gentle wind
Shall cool the heat of this descending sun:
    I 'll make a shadow for thee of my hairs;
    If they burn too, I 'll quench them with my tears.

'The sun that shines from heaven shines but warm,
And lo! I lie between that sun and thee:
The heat I have from thence doth little harm,
Thine eye darts forth the fire that burneth me;
    And were I not immortal, life were done
    Between this heavenly and earthly sun.

'Art thou obdurate, flinty, hard as steel?
Nay, more than flint, for stone at rain relenteth:
Art thou a woman's son, and canst not feel
What 'tis to love? how want of love tormenteth?
    O! had thy mother borne so hard a mind,
    She had not brought forth thee, but died unkind.

'What am I that thou shouldst contemn me this?
Or what great danger dwells upon my suit?
What were thy lips the worse for one poor kiss?
Speak, fair; but speak fair words, or else be mute:
    Give me one kiss, I 'll give it thee again,
    And one for interest, if thou wilt have twain.

'Fie! lifeless picture, cold and senseless stone,
Well-painted idol, image dull and dead,
Statue contenting but the eye alone,
Thing like a man, but of no woman bred:
   Thou art no man, though of a man's complexion,
   For men will kiss even by their own direction.'

This said, impatience chokes her pleading tongue,
And swelling passion doth provoke a pause;
Red cheeks and fiery eyes blaze forth her wrong;
Being judge in love, she cannot right her cause:
   And now she weeps, and now she fain would speak,
   And now her sobs do her intendments break.

Sometimes she shakes her head, and then his hand;
Now gazeth she on him, now on the ground;
Sometimes her arms infold him like a band:
She would, he will not in her arms be bound;
   And when from thence he struggles to be gone,
   She locks her lily fingers one in one.

'Fondling,' she saith, 'since I have hemm'd thee here
Within the circuit of this ivory pale,
I 'll be a park, and thou shalt be my deer;
Feed where thou wilt, on mountain or in dale:
   Graze on my lips, and if those hills be dry,
   Stray lower, where the pleasant fountains lie.

'Within this limit is relief enough,
Sweet bottom-grass and high delightful plain,
Round rising hillocks, brakes obscure and rough,
To shelter thee from tempest and from rain:
   Then be my deer, since I am such a park;
   No dog shall rouse thee, though a thousand bark.'

At this Adonis smiles as in disdain,
That in each cheek appears a pretty dimple:
Love made those hollows, if himself were slain,
He might be buried in a tomb so simple;
   Foreknowing well, if there he came to lie,
   Why, there Love liv'd, and there he could not die.

These lovely caves, these round enchanting pits,
Open'd their mouths to swallow Venus' liking.
Being mad before, how doth she now for wits?
Struck dead at first, what needs a second striking?
      Poor queen of love, in thine own law forlorn,
      To love a cheek that smiles at thee in scorn!

Now which way shall she turn? what shall she say?
Her words are done, her woes the more increasing;
The time is spent, her object will away,
And from her twining arms doth urge releasing:
      'Pity,' she cries; 'some favour, some remorse!'
      Away he springs, and hasteth to his horse.

But, lo! from forth a copse that neighbours by,
A breeding jennet, lusty, young, and proud,
Adonis' trampling courser doth espy,
And forth she rushes, snorts and neighs aloud:
      The strong-neck'd steed, being tied unto a tree,
      Breaketh his rein, and to her straight goes he.

Imperiously he leaps, he neighs, he bounds,
And now his woven girths he breaks asunder;
The bearing earth with his hard hoof he wounds,
Whose hollow womb resounds like heaven's thunder;
      The iron bit he crusheth 'tween his teeth,
      Controlling what he was controlled with.

His ears up-prick'd; his braided hanging mane
Upon his compass'd crest now stand on end;
His nostrils drink the air, and forth again,
As from a furnace, vapours doth he send:
      His eye, which scornfully glisters like fire,
      Shows his hot courage and his high desire.

Sometime he trots, as if he told the steps,
With gentle majesty and modest pride;
Anon he rears upright, curvets and leaps,
As who should say, 'Lo! thus my strength is tried;
      And this I do to captivate the eye
      Of the fair breeder that is standing by.'

What recketh he his rider's angry stir,
His flattering 'Holla,' or his 'Stand, I say'?
What cares he now for curb or pricking spur?
For rich caparisons or trapping gay?
    He sees his love, and nothing else he sees,
    Nor nothing else with his proud sight agrees.

Look, when a painter would surpass the life,
In limning out a well-proportion'd steed,
His art with nature's workmanship at strife,
As if the dead the living should exceed;
    So did this horse excel a common one.
    In shape, in courage, colour, pace and bone.

Round-hoof'd, short-jointed, fetlocks shag and long
Broad breast, full eye, small head, and nostril wide,
High crest, short ears, straight legs and passing strong,
Thin mane, thick tail, broad buttock, tender hide:
    Look, what a horse should have he did not lack,
    Save a proud rider on so proud a back.

Sometimes he scuds far off, and there he stares;
Anon he starts at stirring of a feather;
To bid the wind a base he now prepares,
And whe'r he run or fly they know not whether;
    For through his mane and tail the high wind sings,
    Fanning the hairs, who wave like feather'd wings.

He looks upon his love, and neighs unto her;
She answers him as if she knew his mind;
Being proud, as females are, to see him woo her,
She puts on outward strangeness, seems unkind,
    Spurns at his love and scorns the heat he feels,
    Beating his kind embracements with her heels.

Then, like a melancholy malcontent,
He vails his tail, that, like a falling plume,
Cool shadow to his melting buttock lent:
He stamps, and bites the poor flies in his fume.
    His love, perceiving how he is enrag'd,
    Grew kinder, and his fury was assuag'd.

His testy master goeth about to take him;
When lo! the unback'd breeder, full of fear,
Jealous of catching, swiftly doth forsake him,
With her the horse, and left Adonis there:
    As they were mad, unto the wood they hie them,
    Outstripping crows that strive to overfly them.

All swoln with chafing, down Adonis sits,
Banning his boisterous and unruly beast:
And now the happy season once more fits,
That love-sick Love by pleading may be blest;
    For lovers say, the heart hath treble wrong
    When it is barr'd the aidance of the tongue.

An oven that is stopp'd, or river stay'd,
Burneth more hotly, swelleth with more rage:
So of concealed sorrow may be said;
Free vent of words love's fire doth assuage;
    But when the heart's attorney once is mute,
    The client breaks, as desperate in his suit.

He sees her coming, and begins to glow,—
Even as a dying coal revives with wind,—
And with his bonnet hides his angry brow;
Looks on the dull earth with disturbed mind,
    Taking no notice that she is so nigh,
    For all askance he holds her in his eye.

O! what a sight it was, wistly to view
How she came stealing to the wayward boy;
To note the fighting conflict of her hue,
How white and red each other did destroy:
    But now her cheek was pale, and by and by
    It flash'd forth fire, as lightning from the sky.

Now was she just before him as he sat,
And like a lowly lover down she kneels;
With one fair hand she heaveth up his hat,
Her other tender hand his fair cheek feels:
    His tenderer cheek receives her soft hand's print,
    As apt as new-fall'n snow takes any dint.

O! what a war of looks was then between them;
Her eyes petitioners to his eyes suing;
His eyes saw her eyes as they had not seen them;
Her eyes woo'd still, his eyes disdain'd the wooing:
    And all this dumb play had his acts made plain
    With tears, which, chorus-like, her eyes did rain.

Full gently now she takes him by the hand,
A lily prison'd in a gaol of snow,
Or ivory in an alabaster band;
So white a friend engirts so white a foe:
    This beauteous combat, wilful and unwilling,
    Show'd like two silver doves that sit a-billing.

Once more the engine of her thoughts began:
'O fairest mover on this mortal round,
Would thou wert as I am, and I a man,
My heart all whole as thine, thy heart my wound;
    For one sweet look thy help I would assure thee,
    Though nothing but my body's bane would cure thee.'

'Give me my hand,' saith he, 'why dost thou feel it?'
'Give me my heart,' saith she, 'and thou shalt have it;
O! give it me, lest thy hard heart do steel it,
And being steel'd, soft sighs can never grave it:
    Then love's deep groans I never shall regard,
    Because Adonis' heart hath made mine hard.'

'For shame,' he cries, 'let go, and let me go;
My day's delight is past, my horse is gone,
And 'tis your fault I am bereft him so:
I pray you hence, and leave me here alone:
    For all my mind, my thought, my busy care,
    Is how to get my palfrey from the mare.'

Thus she replies: 'Thy palfrey, as he should,
Welcomes the warm approach of sweet desire:
Affection is a coal that must be cool'd;
Else, suffer'd, it will set the heart on fire:
    The sea hath bounds, but deep desire hath none;
    Therefore no marvel though thy horse be gone.

'How like a jade he stood, tied to the tree,
Servilely master'd with a leathern rein!
But when he saw his love, his youth's fair fee,
He held such petty bondage in disdain;
    Throwing the base thong from his bending crest,
    Enfranchising his mouth, his back, his breast.

'Who sees his true-love in her naked bed,
Teaching the sheets a whiter hue than white,
But, when his glutton eye so full hath fed,
His other agents aim at like delight?
    Who is so faint, that dare not be so bold
    To touch the fire, the weather being cold?

'Let me excuse thy courser, gentle boy;
And learn of him, I heartily beseech thee,
To take advantage on presented joy;
Though I were dumb, yet his proceedings teach thee.
    O learn to love; the lesson is but plain,
    And once made perfect, never lost again.'

'I know not love,' quoth he, 'nor will not know it,
Unless it be a boar, and then I chase it;
'Tis much to borrow, and I will not owe it;
My love to love is love but to disgrace it;
    For I have heard it is a life in death,
    That laughs and weeps, and all but with a breath.

'Who wears a garment shapeless and unfinish'd?
Who plucks the bud before one leaf put forth?
If springing things be any jot diminish'd,
They wither in their prime, prove nothing worth:
    The colt that 's back'd and burden'd being young
    Loseth his pride, and never waxeth strong.

'You hurt my hand with wringing; let us part,
And leave this idle theme, this bootless chat:
Remove your siege from my unyielding heart;
To love's alarms it will not ope the gate:
    Dismiss your vows, your feigned tears, your flattery;
    For where a heart is hard they make no battery.'

'What! canst thou talk?' quoth she, 'hast thou a tongue?
O! would thou hadst not, or I had no hearing;
Thy mermaid's voice hath done me double wrong;
I had my load before, now press'd with bearing:
  Melodious discord, heavenly tune, harsh-sounding,
  Ear's deep-sweet music, and heart's deep-sore wound-
    ing.

'Had I no eyes but ears, my ears would love
That inward beauty and invisible;
Or were I deaf, thy outward parts would move
Each part in me that were but sensible:
  Though neither eyes nor ears, to hear nor see,
  Yet should I be in love by touching thee.

'Say, that the sense of feeling were bereft me,
And that I could not see, nor hear, nor touch,
And nothing but the very smell were left me,
Yet would my love to thee be still as much;
  For from the stillitory of thy face excelling
  Comes breath perfum'd that breedeth love by smelling.

'But O! what banquet wert thou to the taste,
Being nurse and feeder of the other four;
Would they not wish the feast might ever last,
And bid Suspicion double-lock the door,
  Lest Jealousy, that sour unwelcome guest,
  Should, by his stealing in, disturb the feast?'

Once more the ruby-colour'd portal open'd,
Which to his speech did honey passage yield,
Like a red morn, that ever yet betoken'd
Wrack to the seaman, tempest to the field,
  Sorrow to shepherds, woe unto the birds,
  Gusts and foul flaws to herdmen and to herds.

This ill presage advisedly she marketh:
Even as the wind is hush'd before it raineth,
Or as the wolf doth grin before he barketh,
Or as the berry breaks before it staineth,
  Or like the deadly bullet of a gun,
  His meaning struck her ere his words begun.

And at his look she flatly falleth down,
For looks kill love, and love by looks reviveth;
A smile recures the wounding of a frown;
But blessed bankrupt, that by love so thriveth!
    The silly boy, believing she is dead,
    Claps her pale cheek, till clapping makes it red;

And all amaz'd brake off his late intent,
For sharply he did think to reprehend her,
Which cunning love did wittily prevent:
Fair fall the wit that can so well defend her!
    For on the grass she lies as she were slain,
    Till his breath breatheth life in her again.

He wrings her nose, he strikes her on the cheeks,
He bends her fingers, holds her pulses hard,
He chafes her lips; a thousand ways he seeks
To mend the hurt that his unkindness marr'd:
    He kisses her; and she, by her good will,
    Will never rise, so he will kiss her still.

The night of sorrow now is turn'd to day:
Her two blue windows faintly she up-heaveth,
Like the fair sun, when in his fresh array
He cheers the morn, and all the world relieveth:
    And as the bright sun glorifies the sky,
    So is her face illumin'd with her eye;

Whose beams upon his hairless face are fix'd,
As if from thence they borrow'd all their shine.
Were never four such lamps together mix'd,
Had not his clouded with his brow's repine;
    But hers, which through the crystal tears gave light,
    Shone like the moon in water seen by night.

'O! where am I?' quoth she, 'in earth or heaven,
Or in the ocean drench'd, or in the fire?
What hour is this? or morn or weary even?
Do I delight to die, or life desire?
    But now I liv'd, and life was death's annoy;
    But now I died, and death was lively joy.

'O! thou didst kill me; kill me once again:
Thy eyes' shrewd tutor, that hard heart of thine,
Hath taught them scornful tricks, and such disdain,
That they have murder'd this poor heart of mine;
  And these mine eyes, true leaders to their queen,
  But for thy piteous lips no more had seen.

'Long may they kiss each other for this cure!
O! never let their crimson liveries wear;
And as they last, their verdure still endure,
To drive infection from the dangerous year:
  That the star-gazers, having writ on death,
  May say, the plague is banish'd by thy breath.

'Pure lips, sweet seals in my soft lips imprinted,
What bargains may I make, still to be sealing?
To sell myself I can be well contented,
So thou wilt buy and pay and use good dealing;
  Which purchase if thou make, for fear of slips
  Set thy seal-manual on my wax-red lips.

'A thousand kisses buys my heart from me;
And pay them at thy leisure, one by one.
What is ten hundred touches unto thee?
Are they not quickly told and quickly gone?
  Say, for non-payment that the debt should double,
  Is twenty hundred kisses such a trouble?'

'Fair queen,' quoth he, 'if any love you owe me,
Measure my strangeness with my unripe years:
Before I know myself, seek not to know me;
No fisher but the ungrown fry forbears:
  The mellow plum doth fall, the green sticks fast,
  Or being early pluck'd is sour to taste.

'Look! the world's comforter, with weary gait
His day's hot task hath ended in the west;
The owl, night's herald, shrieks, 'tis very late;
The sheep are gone to fold, birds to their nest,
  And coal-black clouds that shadow heaven's light
  Do summon us to part, and bid good-night.

'Now let me say good-night, and so say you;
If you will say so, you shall have a kiss.'
'Good-night,' quoth she; and ere he says adieu,
The honey fee of parting tender'd is:
    Her arms do lend his neck a sweet embrace;
    Incorporate then they seem, face grows to face.

Till, breathless, he disjoin'd, and backward drew
The heavenly moisture, that sweet coral mouth,
Whose precious taste her thirsty lips well knew,
Whereon they surfeit, yet complain on drouth:
    He with her plenty press'd, she faint with dearth,
    Their lips together glu'd, fall to the earth.

Now quick desire hath caught the yielding prey,
And glutton-like she feeds, yet never filleth;
Her lips are conquerors, his lips obey,
Paying what ransom the insulter willeth;
    Whose vulture thought doth pitch the price so high,
    That she will draw his lips' rich treasure dry.

And having felt the sweetness of the spoil,
With blindfold fury she begins to forage;
Her face doth reek and smoke, her blood doth boil,
And careless lust stirs up a desperate courage;
    Planting oblivion, beating reason back,
    Forgetting shame's pure blush and honour's wrack.

Hot, faint, and weary, with her hard embracing,
Like a wild bird being tam'd with too much handling,
Or as the fleet-foot roe that 's tir'd with chasing,
Or like the froward infant still'd with dandling,
    He now obeys, and now no more resisteth,
    While she takes all she can, not all she listeth.

What wax so frozen but dissolves with tempering,
And yields at last to every light impression?
Things out of hope are compass'd oft with venturing,
Chiefly in love, whose leave exceeds commission:
    Affection faints not like a pale-fac'd coward,
    But then woos best when most his choice is froward.

When he did frown, O! had she then gave over,
Such nectar from his lips she had not suck'd.
Foul words and frowns must not repel a lover;
What though the rose have prickles, yet 'tis pluck'd:
    Were beauty under twenty locks kept fast,
    Yet love breaks through and picks them all at last.

For pity now she can no more detain him;
The poor fool prays her that he may depart:
She is resolv'd no longer to restrain him,
Bids him farewell, and look well to her heart,
    The which, by Cupid's bow she doth protest,
    He carries thence incaged in his breast.

'Sweet boy,' she says, 'this night I 'll waste in sorrow,
For my sick heart commands mine eyes to watch.
Tell me, Love's master, shall we meet to-morrow?
Say, shall we? shall we? wilt thou make the match?'
    He tells her, no; to-morrow he intends
    To hunt the boar with certain of his friends.

'The boar!' quoth she; whereat a sudden pale,
Like lawn being spread upon the blushing rose,
Usurps her cheeks, she trembles at his tale,
And on his neck her yoking arms she throws:
    She sinketh down, still hanging by his neck,
    He on her belly falls, she on her back.

Now is she in the very lists of love,
Her champion mounted for the hot encounter:
All is imaginary she doth prove,
He will not manage her, although he mount her;
    That worse than Tantalus' is her annoy,
    To clip Elysium and to lack her joy.

Even as poor birds, deceiv'd with painted grapes,
Do surfeit by the eye and pine the maw,
Even so she languisheth in her mishaps,
As those poor birds that helpless berries saw.
    The warm effects which she in him finds missing,
    She seeks to kindle with continual kissing.

But all in vain; good queen, it will not be:
She hath assay'd as much as may be prov'd;
Her pleading hath deserv'd a greater fee;
She 's Love, she loves, and yet she is not lov'd.
　　'Fie, fie!' he says, 'you crush me; let me go;
　　You have no reason to withhold me so.'

'Thou hadst been gone,' quoth she, 'sweet boy, ere this,
But that thou told'st me thou wouldst hunt the boar.
O! be advis'd; thou know'st not what it is
With javelin's point a churlish swine to gore,
　　Whose tushes never sheath'd he whetteth still,
　　Like to a mortal butcher, bent to kill.

'On his bow-back he hath a battle set
Of bristly pikes, that ever threat his foes;
His eyes like glow-worms shine when he doth fret;
His snout digs sepulchres where'er he goes;
　　Being mov'd, he strikes whate'er is in his way,
　　And whom he strikes his crooked tushes slay.

'His brawny sides, with hairy bristles arm'd,
Are better proof than thy spear's point can enter;
His short thick neck cannot be easily harm'd;
Being ireful, on the lion he will venture:
　　The thorny brambles and embracing bushes,
　　As fearful of him, part, through whom he rushes.

'Alas! he nought esteems that face of thine,
To which Love's eyes pay tributary gazes;
Nor thy soft hands, sweet lips, and crystal eyne,
Whose full perfection all the world amazes;
　　But having thee at vantage, wondrous dread!
　　Would root these beauties as he roots the mead.

'O! let him keep his loathsome cabin still;
Beauty hath nought to do with such foul fiends:
Come not within his danger by thy will;
They that thrive well take counsel of their friends.
　　When thou didst name the boar, not to dissemble,
　　I fear'd thy fortune, and my joints did tremble.

'Didst thou not mark my face? was it not white?
Saw'st thou not signs of fear lurk in mine eye?
Grew I not faint? And fell I not downright?
Within my bosom, whereon thou dost lie,
    My boding heart pants, beats, and takes no rest,
    But, like an earthquake, shakes thee on my breast.

'For where Love reigns, disturbing Jealousy
Doth call himself Affection's sentinel;
Gives false alarms, suggesteth mutiny,
And in a peaceful hour doth cry "Kill, kill!"
    Distempering gentle Love in his desire,
    As air and water do abate the fire.

'This sour informer, this bate-breeding spy,
This canker that eats up Love's tender spring,
This carry-tale, dissentious Jealousy,
That sometime true news, sometime false doth bring,
    Knocks at my heart, and whispers in mine ear
    That if I love thee, I thy death should fear:

'And more than so, presenteth to mine eye
The picture of an angry-chafing boar,
Under whose sharp fangs on his back doth lie
An image like thyself, all stain'd with gore;
    Whose blood upon the fresh flowers being shed
    Doth make them droop with grief and hang the head.

'What should I do, seeing thee so indeed,
That tremble at the imagination?
The thought of it doth make my faint heart bleed,
And fear doth teach it divination:
    I prophesy thy death, my living sorrow,
    If thou encounter with the boar to-morrow.

'But if thou needs wilt hunt, be rul'd by me;
Uncouple at the timorous flying hare,
Or at the fox which lives by subtilty,
Or at the roe which no encounter dare:
    Pursue these fearful creatures o'er the downs,
    And on thy well-breath'd horse keep with thy hounds.

'And when thou hast on foot the purblind hare,
Mark the poor wretch, to overshoot his troubles
How he outruns the winds, and with what care
He cranks and crosses with a thousand doubles:
    The many musits through the which he goes
    Are like a labyrinth to amaze his foes.

'Sometimes he runs among a flock of sheep,
To make the cunning hounds mistake their smell,
And sometime where earth-delving conies keep,
To stop the loud pursuers in their yell,
    And sometimes sorteth with a herd of deer;
    Danger deviseth shifts, wit waits on fear:

'For there his smell with others being mingled,
The hot scent-snuffing hounds are driven to doubt,
Ceasing their clamorous cry till they have singled
With much ado the cold fault cleanly out;
    Then do they spend their mouths: Echo replies,
    As if another chase were in the skies.

'By this, poor Wat, far off upon a hill,
Stands on his hinder legs with listening ear,
To hearken if his foes pursue him still:
Anon their loud alarums he doth hear;
    And now his grief may be compared well
    To one sore sick that hears the passing bell.

'Then shalt thou see the dew-bedabbled wretch
Turn, and return, indenting with the way;
Each envious briar his weary legs doth scratch,
Each shadow makes him stop, each murmur stay:
    For misery is trodden on by many,
    And being low never reliev'd by any.

'Lie quietly, and hear a little more;
Nay, do not struggle, for thou shalt not rise:
To make thee hate the hunting of the boar,
Unlike myself thou hear'st me moralize,
    Applying this to that, and so to so;
    For love can comment upon every woe.

'Where did I leave?' 'No matter where,' quoth he;
'Leave me, and then the story aptly ends:
The night is spent.' 'Why, what of that?' quoth she.
'I am,' quoth he, 'expected of my friends;
    And now 'tis dark, and going I shall fall.'
    'In night,' quoth she, 'desire sees best of all.'

'But if thou fall, O! then imagine this,
The earth, in love with thee, thy footing trips,
And all is but to rob thee of a kiss.
Rich preys make true men thieves; so do thy lips
    Make modest Dian cloudy and forlorn,
    Lest she should steal a kiss and die forsworn.

'Now of this dark night I perceive the reason:
Cynthia for shame obscures her silver shine,
Till forging Nature be condemn'd of treason,
For stealing moulds from heaven that were divine;
    Wherein she fram'd thee in high heaven's despite,
    To shame the sun by day and her by night.

'And therefore hath she brib'd the Destinies,
To cross the curious workmanship of nature,
To mingle beauty with infirmities,
And pure perfection with impure defeature;
    Making it subject to the tyranny
    Of mad mischances and much misery;

'As burning fevers, agues pale and faint,
Life-poisoning pestilence and frenzies wood,
The marrow-eating sickness, whose attaint
Disorder breeds by heating of the blood;
    Surfeits, imposthumes, grief, and damn'd despair,
    Swear nature's death for framing thee so fair.

'And not the least of all these maladies
But in one minute's fight brings beauty under:
Both favour, savour, hue, and qualities,
Whereat the impartial gazer late did wonder,
    Are on the sudden wasted, thaw'd and done,
    As mountain-snow melts with the mid-day sun.

'Therefore, despite of fruitless chastity,
Love-lacking vestals and self-loving nuns,
That on the earth would breed a scarcity
And barren dearth of daughters and of sons,
　　Be prodigal: the lamp that burns by night
　　Dries up his oil to lend the world his light.

'What is thy body but a swallowing grave,
Seeming to bury that posterity
Which by the rights of time thou needs must have,
If thou destroy them not in dark obscurity?
　　If so, the world will hold thee in disdain,
　　Sith in thy pride so fair a hope is slain.

'So in thyself thyself art made away;
A mischief worse than civil home-bred strife,
Or theirs whose desperate hands themselves do slay,
Or butcher-sire that reaves his son of life.
　　Foul-cankering rust the hidden treasure frets,
　　But gold that 's put to use more gold begets.'

'Nay then,' quoth Adon, 'you will fall again
Into your idle over-handled theme;
The kiss I gave you is bestow'd in vain,
And all in vain you strive against the stream;
　　For by this black-fac'd night, desire's foul nurse,
　　Your treatise makes me like you worse and worse.

'If love have lent you twenty thousand tongues,
And every tongue more moving than your own,
Bewitching like the wanton mermaid's songs,
Yet from mine ear the tempting tune is blown;
　　For know, my heart stands armed in mine ear,
　　And will not let a false sound enter there;

'Lest the deceiving harmony should run
Into the quiet closure of my breast;
And then my little heart were quite undone,
In his bedchamber to be barr'd of rest.
　　No, lady, no; my heart longs not to groan,
　　But soundly sleeps, while now it sleeps alone.

'What have you urg'd that I cannot reprove?
The path is smooth that leadeth on to danger;
I hate not love, but your device in love,
That lends embracements unto every stranger.
    You do it for increase: O strange excuse!
    When reason is the bawd to lust's abuse.

'Call it not love, for Love to heaven is fled,
Since sweating Lust on earth usurp'd his name;
Under whose simple semblance he hath fed
Upon fresh beauty, blotting it with blame;
    Which the hot tyrant stains and soon bereaves,
    As caterpillars do the tender leaves.

'Love comforteth like sunshine after rain,
But Lust's effect is tempest after sun;
Love's gentle spring doth always fresh remain,
Lust's winter comes ere summer half be done.
    Love surfeits not, Lust like a glutton dies;
    Love is all truth, Lust full of forged lies.

'More I could tell, but more I dare not say;
The text is old, the orator too green.
Therefore, in sadness, now I will away;
My face is full of shame, my heart of teen:
    Mine ears, that to your wanton talk attended,
    Do burn themselves for having so offended.'

With this he breaketh from the sweet embrace
Of those fair arms which bound him to her breast,
And homeward through the dark laund runs apace;
Leaves Love upon her back deeply distress'd.
    Look, how a bright star shooteth from the sky
    So glides he in the night from Venus' eye;

Which after him she darts, as one on shore
Gazing upon a late-embarked friend,
Till the wild waves will have him seen no more,
Whose ridges with the meeting clouds contend:
    So did the merciless and pitchy night
    Fold in the object that did feed her sight.

Whereat amaz'd, as one that unaware
Hath dropp'd a precious jewel in the flood,
Or 'stonish'd as night-wanderers often are,
Their light blown out in some mistrustful wood;
    Even so confounded in the dark she lay,
    Having lost the fair discovery of her way.

And now she beats her heart, whereat it groans,
That all the neighbour caves, as seeming troubled,
Make verbal repetition of her moans;
Passion on passion deeply is redoubled:
    'Ay me!' she cries, and twenty times, 'Woe, woe!'
    And twenty echoes twenty times cry so.

She marking them, begins a wailing note,
And sings extemporally a woeful ditty;
How love makes young men thrall and old men dote;
How love is wise in folly, foolish-witty:
    Her heavy anthem still concludes in woe,
    And still the choir of echoes answer so.

Her song was tedious, and outwore the night,
For lovers' hours are long, though seeming short:
If pleas'd themselves, others, they think, delight
In such like circumstance, with such like sport:
    Their copious stories, oftentimes begun,
    End without audience, and are never done.

For who hath she to spend the night withal,
But idle sounds resembling parasites;
Like shrill-tongu'd tapsters answering every call,
Soothing the humour of fantastic wits?
    She says, ' 'Tis so': they answer all, ' 'Tis so';
    And would say after her, if she said 'No.'

Lo! here the gentle lark, weary of rest,
From his moist cabinet mounts up on high,
And wakes the morning, from whose silver breast
The sun ariseth in his majesty;
    Who doth the world so gloriously behold,
    That cedar-tops and hills seem burnish'd gold.

Venus salutes him with this fair good-morrow:
'O thou clear god, and patron of all light,
From whom each lamp and shining star doth borrow
The beauteous influence that makes him bright,
    There lives a son that suck'd an earthly mother,
    May lend thee light, as thou dost lend to other.'

This said, she hasteth to a myrtle grove,
Musing the morning is so much o'erworn,
And yet she hears no tidings of her love;
She hearkens for his hounds and for his horn:
    Anon she hears them chant it lustily,
    And all in haste she coasteth to the cry.

And as she runs, the bushes in the way
Some catch her by the neck, some kiss her face,
Some twine about her thigh to make her stay:
She wildly breaketh from their strict embrace,
    Like a milch doe, whose swelling dugs do ache,
    Hasting to feed her fawn hid in some brake.

By this she hears the hounds are at a bay;
Whereat she starts, like one that spies an adder
Wreath'd up in fatal folds just in his way,
The fear whereof doth make him shake and shudder;
    Even so the timorous yelping of the hounds
    Appals her senses, and her spirit confounds.

For now she knows it is no gentle chase,
But the blunt boar, rough bear, or lion proud,
Because the cry remaineth in one place,
Where fearfully the dogs exclaim aloud:
    Finding their enemy to be so curst,
    They all strain courtesy who shall cope him first.

This dismal cry rings sadly in her ear,
Through which it enters to surprise her heart;
Who, overcome by doubt and bloodless fear,
With cold-pale weakness numbs each feeling part;
    Like soldiers, when their captain once doth yield,
    They basely fly and dare not stay the field.

Thus stands she in a trembling ecstasy,
Till, cheering up her senses sore dismay'd,
She tells them 'tis a causeless fantasy,
And childish error, that they are afraid;
    Bids them leave quaking, bids them fear no more:
    And with that word she spied the hunted boar;

Whose frothy mouth bepainted all with red,
Like milk and blood being mingled both together,
A second fear through all her sinews spread,
Which madly hurries her she knows not whither:
    This way she runs, and now she will no further,
    But back retires to rate the boar for murther.

A thousand spleens bear her a thousand ways,
She treads the path that she untreads again;
Her more than haste is mated with delays,
Like the proceedings of a drunken brain,
    Full of respects, yet nought at all respecting,
    In hand with all things, nought at all effecting.

Here kennel'd in a brake she finds a hound,
And asks the weary caitiff for his master,
And there another licking of his wound,
'Gainst venom'd sores the only sovereign plaster;
    And here she meets another sadly scowling,
    To whom she speaks, and he replies with howling.

When he hath ceas'd his ill-resounding noise,
Another flap-mouth'd mourner, black and grim,
Against the welkin volleys out his voice;
Another and another answer him,
    Clapping their proud tails to the ground below,
    Shaking their scratch'd ears, bleeding as they go.

Look, how the world's poor people are amaz'd
At apparitions, signs, and prodigies,
Whereon with fearful eyes they long have gaz'd,
Infusing them with dreadful prophecies;
    So she at these sad sighs draws up her breath,
    And, sighing it again, exclaims on Death.

'Hard-favour'd tyrant, ugly, meagre, lean,
Hateful divorce of love,'—thus chides she Death,—
'Grim-grinning ghost, earth's worm, what dost thou mean
To stifle beauty and to steal his breath,
    Who when he liv'd, his breath and beauty set
    Gloss on the rose, smell to the violet?

'If he be dead—O no! it cannot be,
Seeing his beauty, thou shouldst strike at it;
O yes! it may; thou hast no eyes to see,
But hatefully at random dost thou hit.
    Thy mark is feeble age, but thy false dart
    Mistakes that aim and cleaves an infant's heart.

'Hadst thou but bid beware, then he had spoke,
And, hearing him, thy power had lost his power.
The Destinies will curse thee for this stroke;
They bid thee crop a weed, thou pluck'st a flower.
    Love's golden arrow at him should have fled,
    And not Death's ebon dart, to strike him dead.

'Dost thou drink tears, that thou provok'st such weeping?
What may a heavy groan advantage thee?
Why hast thou cast into eternal sleeping
Those eyes that taught all other eyes to see?
    Now Nature cares not for thy mortal vigour,
    Since her best work is ruin'd with thy rigour.'

Here overcome, as one full of despair,
She vail'd her eyelids, who, like sluices, stopp'd
The crystal tide that from her two cheeks fair
In the sweet channel of her bosom dropp'd;
    But through the flood-gates breaks the silver rain,
    And with his strong course opens them again.

O! how her eyes and tears did lend and borrow;
Her eyes seen in the tears, tears in her eye;
Both crystals, where they view'd each other's sorrow,
Sorrow that friendly sighs sought still to dry;
    But like a stormy day, now wind, now rain,
    Sighs dry her cheeks, tears make them wet again.

Variable passions throng her constant woe,
As striving who should best become her grief;
All entertain'd, each passion labours so,
That every present sorrow seemeth chief,
     But none is best; then join they all together,
     Like many clouds consulting for foul weather.

By this, far off she hears some huntsman holloa;
A nurse's song ne'er pleas'd her babe so well:
The dire imagination she did follow
This sound of hope doth labour to expel;
     For now reviving joy bids her rejoice,
     And flatters her it is Adonis' voice.

Whereat her tears began to turn their tide,
Being prison'd in her eye, like pearls in glass;
Yet sometimes falls an orient drop beside,
Which her cheek melts, as scorning it should pass
     To wash the foul face of the sluttish ground,
     Who is but drunken when she seemeth drown'd.

O hard-believing love! how strange it seems
Not to believe, and yet too credulous;
Thy weal and woe are both of them extremes;
Despair and hope make thee ridiculous:
     The one doth flatter thee in thoughts unlikely,
     In likely thoughts the other kills thee quickly.

Now she unweaves the web that she hath wrought,
Adonis lives, and Death is not to blame;
It was not she that call'd him all to naught.
Now she adds honours to his hateful name;
     She clepes him king of graves, and grave for kings,
     Imperious supreme of all mortal things.

'No, no,' quoth she, 'sweet Death, I did but jest;
Yet pardon me, I felt a kind of fear
Whenas I met the boar, that bloody beast,
Which knows no pity, but is still severe;
     Then, gentle shadow,—truth I must confess—
     I rail'd on thee, fearing my love's decease.

' 'Tis not my fault: the boar provok'd my tongue;
Be wreak'd on him, invisible commander;
'Tis he, foul creature, that hath done thee wrong;
I did but act, he 's author of my slander:
  Grief hath two tongues: and never woman yet,
  Could rule them both without ten women's wit.'

Thus hoping that Adonis is alive,
Her rash suspect she doth extenuate;
And that his beauty may the better thrive,
With Death she humbly doth insinuate;
  Tells him of trophies, statues, tombs; and stories
  His victories, his triumphs, and his glories.

'O Jove!' quoth she, 'how much a fool was I,
To be of such a weak and silly mind
To wail his death who lives and must not die
Till mutual overthrow of mortal kind;
  For he being dead, with him is beauty slain,
  And, beauty dead, black chaos comes again.

'Fie, fie, fond love! thou art so full of fear
As one with treasure laden, hemm'd with thieves
Trifles, unwitnessed with eye or ear,
Thy coward heart with false bethinking grieves.'
  Even at this word she hears a merry horn,
  Whereat she leaps that was but late forlorn.

As falcon to the lure, away she flies;
The grass stoops not, she treads on it so light;
And in her haste unfortunately spies
The foul boar's conquest on her fair delight;
  Which seen, her eyes, as murder'd with the view,
  Like stars asham'd of day, themselves withdrew:

Or, as the snail, whose tender horns being hit,
Shrinks backwards in his shelly cave with pain,
And there, all smother'd up, in shade doth sit,
Long after fearing to creep forth again;
  So, at his bloody view, her eyes are fled
  Into the deep dark cabins of her head;

Where they resign their office and their light
To the disposing of her troubled brain;
Who bids them still consort with ugly night,
And never wound the heart with looks again;
   Who, like a king perplexed in his throne,
   By their suggestion gives a deadly groan,

Whereat each tributary subject quakes;
As when the wind, imprison'd in the ground,
Struggling for passage, earth's foundation shakes,
Which with cold terror doth men's minds confound.
   This mutiny each part doth so surprise
   That from their dark beds once more leap her eyes;

And, being open'd, threw unwilling light
Upon the wide wound that the boar had trench'd
In his soft flank; whose wonted lily white
With purple tears, that his wound wept, was drench'd:
   No flower was nigh, no grass, herb, leaf, or weed,
   But stole his blood and seem'd with him to bleed.

This solemn sympathy poor Venus noteth,
Over one shoulder doth she hang her head,
Dumbly she passions, franticly she doteth;
She thinks he could not die, he is not dead:
   Her voice is stopp'd, her joints forget to bow,
   Her eyes are mad that they have wept till now.

Upon his hurt she looks so steadfastly,
That her sight dazzling makes the wound seem three;
And then she reprehends her mangling eye,
That makes more gashes where no breach should be:
   His face seems twain, each several limb is doubled;
   For oft the eye mistakes, the brain being troubled.

'My tongue cannot express my grief for one,
And yet,' quoth she, 'behold two Adons dead!
My sighs are blown away, my salt tears gone,
Mine eyes are turn'd to fire, my heart to lead:
   Heavy heart's lead, melt at mine eyes' red fire!
   So shall I die by drops of hot desire.

'Alas! poor world, what treasure hast thou lost!
What face remains alive that 's worth the viewing?
Whose tongue is music now? what canst thou boast
Of things long since, or anything ensuing?
    The flowers are sweet, their colours fresh and trim;
    But true-sweet beauty liv'd and died with him.

'Bonnet nor veil henceforth no creature wear!
Nor sun nor wind will ever strive to kiss you:
Having no fair to lose, you need not fear;
The sun doth scorn you, and the wind doth hiss you:
    But when Adonis liv'd, sun and sharp air
    Lurk'd like two thieves, to rob him of his fair:

'And therefore would he put his bonnet on,
Under whose brim the gaudy sun would peep;
The wind would blow it off, and, being gone,
Play with his locks: then would Adonis weep;
    And straight, in pity of his tender years,
    They both would strive who first should dry his tears.

'To see his face the lion walk'd along
Behind some hedge, because he would not fear him;
To recreate himself when he hath sung,
The tiger would be tame and gently hear him;
    If he had spoke, the wolf would leave his prey,
    And never fright the silly lamb that day.

'When he beheld his shadow in the brook,
The fishes spread on it their golden gills;
When he was by, the birds such pleasure took,
That some would sing, some other in their bills
    Would bring him mulberries and ripe-red cherries.
    He fed them with his sight, they him with berries.

'But this foul, grim, and urchin-snouted boar,
Whose downward eye still looketh for a grave,
Ne'er saw the beauteous livery that he wore;
Witness the entertainment that he gave:
    If he did see his face, why then I know
    He thought to kiss him, and hath kill'd him so.

' 'Tis true, 'tis true; thus was Adonis slain:
He ran upon the boar with his sharp spear,
Who did not whet his teeth at him again,
But by a kiss thought to persuade him there;
   And nuzzling in his flank, the loving swine
   Sheath'd unaware the tusk in his soft groin.

'Had I been tooth'd like him, I must confess,
With kissing him I should have kill'd him first;
But he is dead, and never did he bless
My youth with his; the more am I accurst.'
   With this she falleth in the place she stood,
   And stains her face with his congealed blood.

She looks upon his lips, and they are pale;
She takes him by the hand, and that is cold;
She whispers in his ears a heavy tale,
As if they heard the woeful words she told;
   She lifts the coffer-lids that close his eyes,
   Where, lo! two lamps, burnt out, in darkness lies;

Two glasses where herself herself beheld
A thousand times, and now no more reflect;
Their virtue lost, wherein they late excell'd,
And every beauty robb'd of his effect:
   'Wonder of time,' quoth she, 'this is my spite,
   That, you being dead, the day should yet be light.

'Since thou art dead, lo! here I prophesy,
Sorrow on love hereafter shall attend:
It shall be waited on with jealousy,
Find sweet beginning, but unsavoury end;
   Ne'er settled equally, but high or low;
   That all love's pleasure shall not match his woe.

'It shall be fickle, false, and full of fraud,
Bud and be blasted in a breathing-while;
The bottom poison, and the top o'erstraw'd
With sweets that shall the truest sight beguile:
   The strongest body shall it make most weak,
   Strike the wise dumb and teach the fool to speak.

'It shall be sparing and too full of riot,
Teaching decrepit age to tread the measures;
The staring ruffian shall it keep in quiet,
Pluck down the rich, enrich the poor with treasures;
    It shall be raging mad, and silly mild,
    Make the young old, the old become a child.

'It shall suspect where is no cause of fear;
It shall not fear where it should most mistrust;
It shall be merciful, and too severe,
And most deceiving when it seems most just;
    Perverse it shall be, where it shows most toward,
    Put fear to valour, courage to the coward.

'It shall be cause of war and dire events,
And set dissension 'twixt the son and sire;
Subject and servile to all discontents,
As dry combustious matter is to fire:
    Sith in his prime Death doth my love destroy,
    They that love best their love shall not enjoy.'

By this, the boy that by her side lay kill'd
Was melted like a vapour from her sight,
And in his blood that on the ground lay spill'd,
A purple flower sprung up, chequer'd with white;
    Resembling well his pale cheeks, and the blood
    Which in round drops upon their whiteness stood.

She bows her head, the new-sprung flower to smell,
Comparing it to her Adonis' breath;
And says within her bosom it shall dwell,
Since he himself is reft from her by death:
    She crops the stalk, and in the breach appears
    Green dropping sap, which she compares to tears.

'Poor flower,' quoth she, 'this was thy father's guise,
Sweet issue of a more sweet-smelling sire,
For every little grief to wet his eyes:
To grow unto himself was his desire,
    And so 'tis thine; but know, it is as good
    To wither in my breast as in his blood.

'Here was thy father's bed, here in my breast;
Thou art the next of blood, and 'tis thy right:
Lo! in this hollow cradle take thy rest,
My throbbing heart shall rock thee day and night:
    There shall not be one minute in an hour
    Wherein I will not kiss my sweet love's flower.'

Thus weary of the world, away she hies,
And yokes her silver doves; by whose swift aid
Their mistress, mounted, through the empty skies
In her light chariot quickly is convey'd;
    Holding their course to Paphos, where their queen
    Means to immure herself and not be seen.

THE RAPE OF LUCRECE

TO THE RIGHT HONOURABLE
HENRY WRIOTHESLEY
EARL OF SOUTHAMPTON AND
BARON OF TICHFIELD

The love I dedicate to your lordship is without end; whereof this pamphlet, without beginning, is but a superfluous moiety. The warrant I have of your honourable disposition, not the worth of my untutored lines, makes it assured of acceptance. What I have done is yours; what I have to do is yours; being part in all I have, devoted yours. Were my worth greater, my duty would show greater; meantime, as it is, it is bound to your lordship, to whom I wish long life, still lengthened with happiness.

Your lordship's in all duty,

William Shakespeare

THE ARGUMENT

Lucius Tarquinius,—for his excessive pride surnamed Superbus,—after he had caused his own father-in-law, Servius Tullius, to be cruelly murdered, and, contrary to the Roman laws and customs, not requiring or staying for the people's suffrages, had possessed himself of the kingdom, went, accompanied with his sons and other noblemen of Rome, to besiege Ardea. During which siege the principal men of the army meeting one evening at the tent of Sextus Tarquinius, the king's son, in their discourses after supper every one commended the virtues of his own wife: among whom Collatinus extolled the incomparable chastity of his wife Lucretia. In that pleasant humour they all posted to Rome; and intending, by their secret and sudden arrival, to make trial of that which every one had before avouched, only Collatinus finds his wife—though it were late in the night—spinning amongst her maids: the other ladies were all found dancing and revelling, or in several disports. Whereupon the noblemen yielded Collatinus the victory, and his wife the fame. At that time Sextus Tarquinius, being inflamed with Lucrece' beauty, yet smothering his passions for the present, departed with the rest back to the camp; from whence he shortly after privily withdrew himself, and was, according to his estate, royally entertained and lodged by Lucrece at Collatium. The same night he treacherously stealeth into her chamber, violently ravished her, and early in the morning speedeth away. Lucrece, in this lamentable plight, hastily dispatcheth messengers, one to Rome for her father, and another to the camp for Collatine. They came, the one accompanied with Junius Brutus, the other with Publius Valerius; and finding Lucrece attired in mourning habit, demanded the cause of her sorrow. She, first taking an oath of them for her revenge, revealed the actor, and the whole manner of his dealing, and withal suddenly stabbed herself. Which done, with one consent they all vowed to root out the whole hated family of the Tarquins; and, bearing the dead body to Rome, Brutus acquainted the people with the doer and manner of the vile deed, with a bitter invective against the tyranny of the king: wherewith the people were so moved, that with one consent and a general acclamation the Tarquins were all exiled, and the state government changed from kings to consuls.

THE RAPE OF LUCRECE

From the besieged Ardea all in post,
Borne by the trustless wings of false desire,
Lust-breathed Tarquin leaves the Roman host,
And to Collatium bears the lightless fire
Which, in pale embers hid, lurks to aspire,
    And girdle with embracing flames the waist
    Of Collatine's fair love, Lucrece the chaste.

Haply that name of chaste unhappily set
This bateless edge on his keen appetite;
When Collatine unwisely did not let
To praise the clear unmatched red and white
Which triumph'd in that sky of his delight,
    Where mortal stars, as bright as heaven's beauties,
    With pure aspects did him peculiar duties.

For he the night before, in Tarquin's tent,
Unlock'd the treasure of his happy state;
What priceless wealth the heavens had him lent
In the possession of his beauteous mate;
Reckoning his fortune at such high-proud rate,
    That kings might be espoused to more fame,
    But king nor peer to such a peerless dame.

O happiness enjoy'd but of a few!
And, if possess'd, as soon decay'd and done
As is the morning's silver-melting dew
Against the golden splendour of the sun;
An expir'd date, cancell'd ere well begun:
    Honour and beauty, in the owner's arms,
    Are weakly fortress'd from a world of harms.

Beauty itself doth of itself persuade
The eyes of men without an orator;
What needeth then apology be made
To set forth that which is so singular?
Or why is Collatine the publisher
    Of that rich jewel he should keep unknown
    From thievish ears, because it is his own?

Perchance his boast of Lucrece' sovereignty
Suggested this proud issue of a king;
For by our ears our hearts oft tainted be:
Perchance that envy of so rich a thing,
Braving compare, disdainfully did sting
      His high-pitch'd thoughts, that meaner men should
          vaunt
      That golden hap which their superiors want.

But some untimely thought did instigate
His all-too-timeless speed, if none of those:
His honour, his affairs, his friends, his state,
Neglected all, with swift intent he goes
To quench the coal which in his liver glows.
      O! rash false heat, wrapp'd in repentant cold,
      Thy hasty spring still blasts, and ne'er grows old.

When at Collatium this false lord arriv'd,
Well was he welcom'd by the Roman dame,
Within whose face beauty and virtue striv'd
Which of them both should underprop her fame:
When virtue bragg'd, beauty would blush for shame;
      When beauty boasted blushes, in despite
      Virtue would stain that o'er with silver white.

But beauty, in that white intituled,
From Venus' doves doth challenge that fair field;
Then virtue claims from beauty beauty's red,
Which virtue gave the golden age to gild
Their silver cheeks, and call'd it then their shield;
      Teaching them thus to use it in the fight,
      When shame assail'd, the red should fence the white.

This heraldry in Lucrece' face was seen,
Argu'd by beauty's red and virtue's white:
Of either's colour was the other queen,
Proving from world's minority their right:
Yet their ambition makes them still to fight;
      The sovereignty of either being so great,
      That oft they interchange each other's seat.

This silent war of lilies and of roses,
Which Tarquin view'd in her fair face's field,
In their pure ranks his traitor eye encloses;
Where, lest between them both it should be kill'd,
The coward captive vanquished doth yield
  To those two armies that would let him go,
  Rather than triumph in so false a foe.

Now thinks he that her husband's shallow tongue—
The niggard prodigal that prais'd her so—
In that high task hath done her beauty wrong,
Which far exceeds his barren skill to show:
Therefore that praise which Collatine doth owe
  Enchanted Tarquin answers with surmise,
  In silent wonder of still-gazing eyes.

This earthly saint, adored by this devil,
Little suspecteth the false worshipper;
For unstain'd thoughts do seldom dream on evil,
Birds never lim'd no secret bushes fear:
So guiltless she securely gives good cheer
  And reverend welcome to her princely guest,
  Whose inward ill no outward harm express'd:

For that he colour'd with his high estate,
Hiding base sin in plaits of majesty;
That nothing in him seem'd inordinate,
Save sometime too much wonder of his eye,
Which, having all, all could not satisfy;
  But, poorly rich, so wanteth in his store,
  That, cloy'd with much, he pineth still for more.

But she, that never cop'd with stranger eyes,
Could pick no meaning from their parling looks,
Nor read the subtle-shining secrecies
Writ in the glassy margents of such books:
She touch'd no unknown baits, nor fear'd no hooks;
  Nor could she moralize his wanton sight,
  More than his eyes were open'd to the light.

He stories to her ears her husband's fame,
Won in the fields of fruitful Italy;
And decks with praises Collatine's high name,
Made glorious by his manly chivalry
With bruised arms and wreaths of victory:
    Her joy with heav'd-up hand she doth express,
    And wordless so greets heaven for his success.

Far from the purpose of his coming thither,
He makes excuses for his being there:
No cloudy show of stormy blustering weather
Doth yet in his fair welkin once appear;
Till sable Night, mother of Dread and Fear,
    Upon the world dim darkness doth display,
    And in her vaulty prison stows the Day.

For then is Tarquin brought unto his bed,
Intending weariness with heavy spright;
For after supper long he questioned
With modest Lucrece, and wore out the night:
Now leaden slumber with life's strength doth fight,
    And every one to rest themselves betake,
    Save thieves, and cares, and troubled minds, that wake.

As one of which doth Tarquin lie revolving
The sundry dangers of his will's obtaining;
Yet ever to obtain his will resolving,
Though weak-built hopes persuade him to abstaining:
Despair to gain doth traffic oft for gaining;
    And when great treasure is the meed propos'd,
    Though death be adjunct, there 's no death suppos'd.

Those that much covet are with gain so fond,
For what they have not, that which they possess
They scatter and unloose it from their bond,
And so, by hoping more, they have but less;
Or, gaining more, the profit of excess
    Is but to surfeit, and such griefs sustain,
    That they prove bankrupt in this poor-rich gain.

The aim of all is but to nurse the life
With honour, wealth, and ease, in waning age;
And in this aim there is such thwarting strife,
That one for all, or all for one we gage;
As life for honour in fell battles' rage;
    Honour for wealth; and oft that wealth doth cost
    The death of all, and all together lost.

So that in venturing ill we leave to be
The things we are for that which we expect;
And this ambitious foul infirmity,
In having much, torments us with defect
Of that we have: so then we do neglect
    The thing we have, and, all for want of wit,
    Make something nothing by augmenting it.

Such hazard now must doting Tarquin make,
Pawning his honour to obtain his lust,
And for himself himself he must forsake:
Then where is truth, if there be no self-trust?
When shall he think to find a stranger just,
    When he himself himself confounds, betrays
    To slanderous tongues and wretched hateful days?

Now stole upon the time the dead of night,
When heavy sleep had closed up mortal eyes;
No comfortable star did lend his light,
No noise but owls' and wolves' death-boding cries;
Now serves the season that they may surprise
    The silly lambs; pure thoughts are dead and still,
    While lust and murder wake to stain and kill.

And now this lustful lord leap'd from his bed,
Throwing his mantle rudely o'er his arm;
Is madly toss'd between desire and dread;
Th' one sweetly flatters, th' other feareth harm;
But honest fear, bewitch'd with lust's foul charm,
    Doth too too oft betake him to retire,
    Beaten away by brain-sick rude desire.

His falchion on a flint he softly smiteth,
That from the cold stone sparks of fire do fly;
Whereat a waxen torch forthwith he lighteth,
Which must be lode-star to his lustful eye;
And to the flame thus speaks advisedly:
   'As from this cold flint I enforc'd this fire,
   So Lucrece must I force to my desire.'

Here pale with fear he doth premeditate
The dangers of his loathsome enterprise,
And in his inward mind he doth debate
What following sorrow may on this arise:
Then looking scornfully, he doth despise
   His naked armour of still-slaughter'd lust,
   And justly thus controls his thoughts unjust:

'Fair torch, burn out thy light, and lend it not
To darken her whose light excelleth thine;
And die, unhallow'd thoughts, before you blot
With your uncleanness that which is divine;
Offer pure incense to so pure a shrine:
   Let fair humanity abhor the deed
   That spots and stains love's modest snow-white weed.

'O shame to knighthood and to shining arms,
O foul dishonour to my household's grave!
O impious act, including all foul harms!
A martial man to be soft fancy's slave!
True valour still a true respect should have;
   Then my digression is so vile, so base,
   That it will live engraven in my face.

'Yea, though I die, the scandal will survive,
And be an eye-sore in my golden coat;
Some loathsome dash the herald will contrive,
To cipher me how fondly I did dote;
That my posterity sham'd with the note,
   Shall curse my bones, and hold it for no sin
   To wish that I their father had not been.

'What win I if I gain the thing I seek?
A dream, a breath, a froth of fleeting joy.
Who buys a minute's mirth to wail a week?
Or sells eternity to get a toy?
For one sweet grape who will the vine destroy?
    Or what fond beggar, but to touch the crown,
    Would with the sceptre straight be strucken down?

'If Collatinus dream of my intent,
Will he not wake, and in a desperate rage
Post hither, this vile purpose to prevent?
This siege that hath engirt his marriage,
This blur to youth, this sorrow to the sage,
    This dying virtue, this surviving shame,
    Whose crime will bear an ever-during blame?

'O! what excuse can my invention make,
When thou shalt charge me with so black a deed?
Will not my tongue be mute, my frail joints shake,
Mine eyes forego their light, my false heart bleed?
The guilt being great, the fear doth still exceed;
    And extreme fear can neither fight nor fly,
    But coward-like with trembling terror die.

'Had Collatinus kill'd my son or sire,
Or lain in ambush to betray my life,
Or were he not my dear friend, this desire
Might have excuse to work upon his wife,
As in revenge or quittal of such strife:
    But as he is my kinsman, my dear friend,
    The shame and fault finds no excuse nor end.

'Shameful it is; ay, if the fact be known:
Hateful it is; there is no hate in loving:
I 'll beg her love; but she is not her own:
The worst is but denial and reproving:
My will is strong, past reason's weak removing.
    Who fears a sentence or an old man's saw,
    Shall by a painted cloth be kept in awe.'

Thus, graceless, holds he disputation
'Tween frozen conscience and hot burning will,
And with good thoughts makes dispensation,
Urging the worser sense for vantage still;
Which in a moment doth confound and kill
    All pure effects, and doth so far proceed,
    That what is vile shows like a virtuous deed.

Quoth he, 'She took me kindly by the hand,
And gaz'd for tidings in my eager eyes,
Fearing some hard news from the warlike band
Where her beloved Collatinus lies.
O! how her fear did make her colour rise:
    First red as roses that on lawn we lay,
    Then white as lawn, the roses took away.

'And how her hand, in my hand being lock'd,
Forc'd it to tremble with her loyal fear!
Which struck her sad, and then it faster rock'd,
Until her husband's welfare she did hear;
Whereat she smiled with so sweet a cheer,
    That had Narcissus seen her as she stood,
    Self-love had never drown'd him in the flood.

'Why hunt I then for colour or excuses?
All orators are dumb when beauty pleadeth;
Poor wretches have remorse in poor abuses;
Love thrives not in the heart that shadows dreadeth:
Affection is my captain, and he leadeth;
    And when his gaudy banner is display'd,
    The coward fights, and will not be dismay'd.

'Then, childish fear, avaunt! debating, die!
Respect and reason, wait on wrinkled age!
My heart shall never countermand mine eye:
Sad pause and deep regard beseems the sage;
My part is youth, and beats these from the stage.
    Desire my pilot is, beauty my prize;
    Then who fears sinking where such treasure lies?'

As corn o'ergrown by weeds, so heedful fear
Is almost chok'd by unresisted lust.
Away he steals with open listening ear,
Full of foul hope, and full of fond mistrust;
Both which, as servitors to the unjust,
    So cross him with their opposite persuasion,
    That now he vows a league, and now invasion.

Within his thought her heavenly image sits,
And in the self-same seat sits Collatine:
That eye which looks on her confounds his wits;
That eye which him beholds, as more divine,
Unto a view so false will not incline;
    But with a pure appeal seeks to the heart,
    Which once corrupted, takes the worser part;

And therein heartens up his servile powers,
Who, flatter'd by their leader's jocund show,
Stuff up his lust, as minutes fill up hours;
And as their captain, so their pride doth grow,
Paying more slavish tribute than they owe.
    By reprobate desire thus madly led,
    The Roman lord marcheth to Lucrece' bed.

The locks between her chamber and his will,
Each one by him enforc'd, retires his ward;
But as they open they all rate his ill,
Which drives the creeping thief to some regard:
The threshold grates the door to have him heard;
    Night-wandering weasels shriek to see him there;
    They fright him, yet he still pursues his fear.

As each unwilling portal yields him way,
Through little vents and crannies of the place
The wind wars with his torch to make him stay,
And blows the smoke of it into his face,
Extinguishing his conduct in this case;
    But his hot heart, which fond desire doth scorch,
    Puffs forth another wind that fires the torch:

And being lighted, by the light he spies
Lucretia's glove, wherein her needle sticks:
He takes it from the rushes where it lies,
And griping it, the needle his finger pricks;
As who should say, 'This glove to wanton tricks
    Is not inur'd; return again in haste;
    Thou seest our mistress' ornaments are chaste.'

But all these poor forbiddings could not stay him;
He in the worst sense construes their denial:
The door, the wind, the glove, that did delay him,
He takes for accidental things of trial;
Or as those bars which stop the hourly dial,
    Who with a lingering stay his course doth let,
    Till every minute pays the hour his debt.

'So, so,' quoth he, 'these lets attend the time,
Like little frosts that sometime threat the spring,
To add a more rejoicing to the prime,
And give the sneaped birds more cause to sing.
Pain pays the income of each precious thing;
    Huge rocks, high winds, strong pirates, shelves and
        sands,
    The merchant fears, ere rich at home he lands.'

Now is he come unto the chamber door,
That shuts him from the heaven of his thought,
Which with a yielding latch, and with no more,
Hath barr'd him from the blessed thing he sought.
So from himself impiety hath wrought,
    That for his prey to pray he doth begin,
    As if the heavens should countenance his sin.

But in the midst of his unfruitful prayer,
Having solicited the eternal power
That his foul thoughts might compass his fair fair,
And they would stand auspicious to the hour,
Even there he starts: quoth he, 'I must deflower;
    The powers to whom I pray abhor this fact,
    How can they then assist me in the act?

'Then Love and Fortune be my gods, my guide!
My will is back'd with resolution:
Thoughts are but dreams till their effects be tried;
The blackest sin is clear'd with absolution;
Against love's fire fear's frost hath dissolution.
   The eye of heaven is out, and misty night
   Covers the shame that follows sweet delight.'

This said, his guilty hand pluck'd up the latch,
And with his knee the door he opens wide.
The dove sleeps fast that this night-owl will catch:
Thus treason works ere traitors be espied.
Who sees the lurking serpent steps aside;
   But she, sound sleeping, fearing no such thing,
   Lies at the mercy of his mortal sting.

Into the chamber wickedly he stalks,
And gazeth on her yet unstained bed.
The curtains being close, about he walks,
Rolling his greedy eyeballs in his head:
By their high treason is his heart misled;
   Which gives the watchword to his hand full soon,
   To draw the cloud that hides the silver moon.

Look, as the fair and fiery-pointed sun,
Rushing from forth a cloud, bereaves our sight;
Even so, the curtain drawn, his eyes begun
To wink, being blinded with a greater light:
Whether it is that she reflects so bright,
   That dazzleth them, or else some shame supposed,
   But blind they are, and keep themselves enclosed.

O! had they in that darksome prison died,
Then had they seen the period of their ill;
Then Collatine again, by Lucrece' side,
In his clear bed might have reposed still:
But they must ope, this blessed league to kill,
   And holy-thoughted Lucrece to their sight
   Must sell her joy, her life, her world's delight.

Her lily hand her rosy cheek lies under,
Cozening the pillow of a lawful kiss;
Who, therefore angry, seems to part in sunder,
Swelling on either side to want his bliss;
Between whose hills her head entombed is:
   Where, like a virtuous monument she lies,
   To be admir'd of lewd unhallow'd eyes.

Without the bed her other fair hand was,
On the green coverlet; whose perfect white
Show'd like an April daisy on the grass,
With pearly sweat, resembling dew of night.
Her eyes, like marigolds, had sheath'd their light,
   And canopied in darkness sweetly lay,
   Till they might open to adorn the day.

Her hair, like golden threads, play'd with her breath;
O modest wantons! wantons modesty!
Showing life's triumph in the map of death,
And death's dim look in life's mortality:
Each in her sleep themselves so beautify,
   As if between them twain there were no strife,
   But that life liv'd in death, and death in life.

Her breasts, like ivory globes circled with blue,
A pair of maiden worlds unconquered,
Save of their lord no bearing yoke they knew,
And him by oath they truly honoured.
These worlds in Tarquin new ambition bred;
   Who, like a foul usurper, went about
   From this fair throne to heave the owner out.

What could he see but mightily he noted?
What did he note but strongly he desir'd?
What he beheld, on that he firmly doted,
And in his will his wilful eye he tir'd.
With more than admiration he admir'd
   Her azure veins, her alabaster skin,
   Her coral lips, her snow-white dimpled chin.

As the grim lion fawneth o'er his prey,
Sharp hunger by the conquest satisfied,
So o'er this sleeping soul doth Tarquin stay,
His rage of lust by gazing qualified;
Slack'd, not suppress'd; for standing by her side,
    His eye, which late this mutiny restrains,
    Unto a greater uproar tempts his veins:

And they, like straggling slaves for pillage fighting,
Obdurate vassals fell exploits effecting,
In bloody death and ravishment delighting,
Nor children's tears nor mother's groans respecting,
Swell in their pride, the onset still expecting:
    Anon his beating heart, alarum striking,
    Gives the hot charge and bids them do their liking.

His drumming heart cheers up his burning eye,
His eye commends the leading to his hand;
His hand, as proud of such a dignity,
Smoking with pride, march'd on to make his stand
On her bare breast, the heart of all her land;
    Whose ranks of blue veins, as his hand did scale,
    Left their round turrets destitute and pale.

They, mustering to the quiet cabinet
Where their dear governess and lady lies,
Do tell her she is dreadfully beset,
And fright her with confusion of their cries:
She, much amaz'd, breaks ope her lock'd-up eyes,
    Who, peeping forth this tumult to behold,
    Are by his flaming torch dimm'd and controll'd.

Imagine her as one in dead of night
From forth dull sleep by dreadful fancy waking,
That thinks she hath beheld some ghastly sprite,
Whose grim aspect sets every joint a-shaking;
What terror 'tis! but she, in worser taking,
    From sleep disturbed, heedfully doth view
    The sight which makes supposed terror true.

Wrapp'd and confounded in a thousand fears,
Like to a new-kill'd bird she trembling lies;
She dares not look; yet, winking, there appears
Quick-shifting antics, ugly in her eyes:
Such shadows are the weak brain's forgeries;
   Who, angry that the eyes fly from their lights,
   In darkness daunts them with more dreadful sights.

His hand, that yet remains upon her breast,—
Rude ram to batter such an ivory wall!—
May feel her heart,—poor citizen,—distress'd,
Wounding itself to death, rise up and fall,
Beating her bulk, that his hand shakes withal.
   This moves in him more rage and lesser pity,
   To make the breach and enter this sweet city.

First, like a trumpet, doth his tongue begin
To sound a parley to his heartless foe;
Who o'er the white sheet peers her whiter chin,
The reason of this rash alarm to know,
Which he by dumb demeanour seeks to show;
   But she with vehement prayers urgeth still
   Under what colour he commits this ill.

Thus he replies: 'The colour in thy face,
That even for anger makes the lily pale,
And the red rose blush at her own disgrace,
Shall plead for me and tell my loving tale;
Under that colour am I come to scale
   Thy never-conquer'd fort: the fault is thine,
   For those thine eyes betray thee unto mine.

'Thus I forestall thee, if thou mean to chide:
Thy beauty hath ensnar'd thee to this night,
Where thou with patience must my will abide,
My will that marks thee for my earth's delight,
Which I to conquer sought with all my might;
   But as reproof and reason beat it dead,
   By thy bright beauty was it newly bred.

'I see what crosses my attempt will bring;
I know what thorns the growing rose defends;
I think the honey guarded with a sting;
All this, beforehand, counsel comprehends:
But will is deaf and hears no heedful friends;
 Only he hath an eye to gaze on beauty,
 And dotes on what he looks, 'gainst law or duty.

'I have debated, even in my soul,
What wrong, what shame, what sorrow I shall breed;
But nothing can affection's course control,
Or stop the headlong fury of his speed.
I know repentant tears ensue the deed,
 Reproach, disdain, and deadly enmity;
 Yet strive I to embrace mine infamy.

This said, he shakes aloft his Roman blade,
Which like a falcon towering in the skies,
Coucheth the fowl below with his wings' shade,
Whose crooked beak threats if he mount he dies:
So under his insulting falchion lies
 Harmless Lucretia, marking what he tells
 With trembling fear, as fowl hear falcon's bells.

'Lucrece,' quoth he, 'this night I must enjoy thee:
If thou deny, then force must work my way,
For in thy bed I purpose to destroy thee:
That done, some worthless slave of thine I 'll slay,
To kill thine honour with thy life's decay;
 And in thy dead arms do I mean to place him,
 Swearing I slew him, seeing thee embrace him.

'So thy surviving husband shall remain
The scornful mark of every open eye;
Thy kinsmen hang their heads at this disdain,
Thy issue blurr'd with nameless bastardy:
And thou, the author of their obloquy,
 Shalt have thy trespass cited up in rimes,
 And sung by children in succeeding times.

'But if thou yield, I rest thy secret friend:
The fault unknown is as a thought unacted;
A little harm done to a great good end,
For lawful policy remains enacted.
The poisonous simple sometime is compacted
   In a pure compound; being so applied,
   His venom in effect is purified.

'Then for thy husband and thy children's sake,
Tender my suit: bequeath not to their lot
The shame that from them no device can take,
The blemish that will never be forgot;
Worse than a slavish wipe or birth-hour's blot:
   For marks descried in men's nativity
   Are nature's faults, not their own infamy.'

Here with a cockatrice' dead-killing eye
He rouseth up himself, and makes a pause;
While she, the picture of pure piety,
Like a white hind under the gripe's sharp claws,
Pleads in a wilderness where are no laws,
   To the rough beast that knows no gentle right,
   Nor aught obeys but his foul appetite.

But when a black-fac'd cloud the world doth threat,
In his dim mist the aspiring mountains hiding,
From earth's dark womb some gentle gust doth get,
Which blows these pitchy vapours from their biding,
Hindering their present fall by this dividing;
   So his unhallow'd haste her words delays,
   And moody Pluto winks while Orpheus plays.

Yet, foul night-waking cat, he doth but dally,
While in his hold-fast foot the weak mouse panteth:
Her sad behaviour feeds his vulture folly,
A swallowing gulf that even in plenty wanteth:
His ear her prayers admits, but his heart granteth
   No penetrable entrance to her plaining:
   Tears harden lust though marble wear with raining.

Her pity-pleading eyes are sadly fix'd
In the remorseless wrinkles of his face;
Her modest eloquence with sighs is mix'd,
Which to her oratory adds more grace.
She puts the period often from his place,
    And midst the sentence so her accent breaks,
    That twice she doth begin ere once she speaks.

She conjures him by high almighty Jove,
By knighthood, gentry, and sweet friendship's oath,
By her untimely tears, her husband's love,
By holy human law, and common troth,
By heaven and earth, and all the power of both,
    That to his borrow'd bed he make retire,
    And stoop to honour, not to foul desire.

Quoth she, 'Reward not hospitality
With such black payment as thou hast pretended;
Mud not the fountain that gave drink to thee;
Mar not the thing that cannot be amended;
End thy ill aim before thy shoot be ended;
    He is no woodman that doth bend his bow
    To strike a poor unseasonable doe.

'My husband is thy friend, for his sake spare me;
Thyself art mighty, for thine own sake leave me;
Myself a weakling, do not, then, ensnare me;
Thou look'dst not like deceit, do not deceive me.
My sighs, like whirlwinds, labour hence to heave thee;
    If ever man were mov'd with woman's moans,
    Be moved with my tears, my sighs, my groans.

'All which together, like a troubled ocean,
Beat at thy rocky and wrack-threatening heart,
To soften it with their continual motion;
For stones dissolv'd to water do convert.
O! if no harder than a stone thou art,
    Melt at my tears, and be compassionate;
    Soft pity enters at an iron gate.

'In Tarquin's likeness I did entertain thee;
Hast thou put on his shape to do him shame?
To all the host of heaven I complain me,
Thou wrong'st his honour, wound'st his princely name.
Thou art not what thou seem'st; and if the same,
   Thou seem'st not what thou art, a god, a king;
   For kings like gods should govern every thing.

'How will thy shame be seeded in thine age,
When thus thy vices bud before thy spring!
If in thy hope thou dar'st do such outrage,
What dar'st thou not when once thou art a king?
O! be remembered, no outrageous thing
   From vassal actors can be wip'd away;
   Then kings' misdeeds cannot be hid in clay.

'This deed will make thee only lov'd for fear;
But happy monarchs still are fear'd for love:
With foul offenders thou perforce must bear,
When they in thee the like offences prove:
If but for fear of this, thy will remove;
   For princes are the glass, the school, the book,
   Where subjects' eyes do learn, do read, do look.

'And wilt thou be the school where Lust shall learn?
Must he in thee read lectures of such shame?
Wilt thou be glass wherein it shall discern
Authority for sin, warrant for blame,
To privilege dishonour in thy name?
   Thou back'st reproach against long-living laud,
   And mak'st fair reputation but a bawd.

'Hast thou command? by him that gave it thee,
From a pure heart command thy rebel will:
Draw not thy sword to guard iniquity,
For it was lent thee all that brood to kill.
Thy princely office how canst thou fulfil,
   When, pattern'd by thy fault, foul Sin may say,
   He learn'd to sin, and thou didst teach the way?

'Think but how vile a spectacle it were,
To view thy present trespass in another.
Men's faults do seldom to themselves appear;
Their own transgressions partially they smother:
This guilt would seem death-worthy in thy brother.
    O! how are they wrapp'd in with infamies
    That from their own misdeeds askance their eyes.

'To thee, to thee, my heav'd-up hands appeal,
Not to seducing lust, thy rash relier:
I sue for exil'd majesty's repeal;
Let him return, and flattering thoughts retire:
His true respect will prison false desire,
    And wipe the dim mist from thy doting eyne,
    That thou shalt see thy state and pity mine.'

'Have done,' quoth he; 'my uncontrolled tide
Turns not, but swells the higher by this let.
Small lights are soon blown out, huge fires abide,
And with the wind in greater fury fret:
The petty streams that pay a daily debt
    To their salt sovereign, with their fresh falls' haste
    Add to his flow, but alter not his taste.'

'Thou art,' quoth she, 'a sea, a sovereign king;
And lo! there falls into thy boundless flood
Black lust, dishonour, shame, misgoverning,
Who seek to stain the ocean of thy blood.
If all these petty ills shall change thy good,
    Thy sea within a puddle's womb is hears'd,
    And not the puddle in thy sea dispers'd.

'So shall these slaves be king, and thou their slave;
Thou nobly base, they basely dignified;
Thou their fair life, and they thy fouler grave;
Thou loathed in their shame, they in thy pride:
The lesser thing should not the greater hide;
    The cedar stoops not to the base shrub's foot,
    But low shrubs wither at the cedar's root.

'So let thy thoughts, low vassals to thy state'—
'No more,' quoth he; 'by heaven, I will not hear thee:
Yield to my love; if not, enforced hate,
Instead of love's coy touch, shall rudely tear thee;
That done, despitefully I mean to bear thee
    Unto the base bed of some rascal groom,
    To be thy partner in this shameful doom.'

This said, he sets his foot upon the light,
For light and lust are deadly enemies:
Shame folded up in blind concealing night,
When most unseen, then most doth tyrannize.
The wolf hath seiz'd his prey, the poor lamb cries;
    Till with her own white fleece her voice controll'd
    Entombs her outcry in her lips' sweet fold:

For with the nightly linen that she wears
He pens her piteous clamours in her head,
Cooling his hot face in the chastest tears
That ever modest eyes with sorrow shed.
O! that prone lust should stain so pure a bed,
    The spots whereof could weeping purify,
    Her tears should drop on them perpetually.

But she hath lost a dearer thing than life,
And he hath won what he would lose again;
This forced league doth force a further strife;
This momentary joy breeds months of pain;
This hot desire converts to cold disdain:
    Pure Chastity is rifled of her store,
    And Lust, the thief, far poorer than before.

Look! as the full-fed hound or gorged hawk,
Unapt for tender smell or speedy flight,
Make slow pursuit, or altogether balk
The prey wherein by nature they delight;
So surfeit-taking Tarquin fares this night:
    His taste delicious, in digestion souring,
    Devours his will, that liv'd by foul devouring.

O! deeper sin than bottomless conceit
Can comprehend in still imagination;
Drunken Desire must vomit his receipt,
Ere he can see his own abomination.
While Lust is in his pride, no exclamation
   Can curb his heat, or rein his rash desire,
   Till, like a jade, Self-will himself doth tire.

And then with lank and lean discolour'd cheek,
With heavy eye, knit brow, and strengthless pace,
Feeble Desire, all recreant, poor, and meek,
Like to a bankrupt beggar wails his case:
The flesh being proud, Desire doth fight with Grace,
   For there it revels; and when that decays,
   The guilty rebel for remission prays.

So fares it with this faultful lord of Rome,
Who this accomplishment so hotly chas'd;
For now against himself he sounds this doom,
That through the length of times he stands disgrac'd;
Besides, his soul's fair temple is defac'd;
   To whose weak ruins muster troops of cares,
   To ask the spotted princess how she fares.

She says, her subjects with foul insurrection
Have batter'd down her consecrated wall,
And by their mortal fault brought in subjection
Her immortality, and made her thrall
To living death and pain perpetual:
   Which in her prescience she controlled still,
   But her foresight could not forestall their will.

Even in this thought through the dark night he stealeth,
A captive victor that hath lost in gain;
Bearing away the wound that nothing healeth,
The scar that will despite of cure remain;
Leaving his spoil perplex'd in greater pain.
   She bears the load of lust he left behind,
   And he the burden of a guilty mind.

He like a thievish dog creeps sadly thence,
She like a wearied lamb lies panting there;
He scowls and hates himself for his offence,
She desperate with her nails her flesh doth tear;
He faintly flies, sweating with guilty fear,
    She stays, exclaiming on the direful night;
    He runs, and chides his vanish'd, loath'd delight.

He thence departs a heavy convertite,
She there remains a hopeless castaway;
He in his speed looks for the morning light;
She prays she never may behold the day;
'For day,' quoth she, 'night's 'scapes doth open lay,
    And my true eyes have never practis'd how
    To cloak offences with a cunning brow.

'They think not but that every eye can see
The same disgrace which they themselves behold;
And therefore would they still in darkness be,
To have their unseen sin remain untold;
For they their guilt with weeping will unfold,
    And grave, like water that doth eat in steel,
    Upon my cheeks what helpless shame I feel.'

Here she exclaims against repose and rest,
And bids her eyes hereafter still be blind.
She wakes her heart by beating on her breast,
And bids it leap from thence, where it may find
Some purer chest to close so pure a mind.
    Frantic with grief thus breathes she forth her spite
    Against the unseen secrecy of night:

'O comfort-killing Night, image of hell!
Dim register and notary of shame!
Black stage for tragedies and murders fell!
Vast sin-concealing chaos! nurse of blame!
Blind muffled bawd! dark harbour for defame!
    Grim cave of death! whispering conspirator
    With close-tongu'd treason and the ravisher!

'O hateful, vaporous, and foggy Night!
Since thou art guilty of my cureless crime,
Muster thy mists to meet the eastern light,
Make war against proportion'd course of time;
Or if thou wilt permit the sun to climb
　　His wonted height, yet ere he go to bed,
　　Knit poisonous clouds about his golden head.

'With rotten damps ravish the morning air;
Let their exhal'd unwholesome breaths make sick
The life of purity, the supreme fair,
Ere he arrive his weary noontide prick;
And let thy misty vapours march so thick,
　　That in their smoky ranks his smother'd light
　　May set at noon and make perpetual night.

'Were Tarquin Night, as he is but Night's child,
The silver-shining queen he would disdain;
Her twinkling handmaids too, by him defil'd,
Through Night's black bosom should not peep again:
So should I have co-partners in my pain;
　　And fellowship in woe doth woe assuage,
　　As palmers' chat makes short their pilgrimage.

'Where now I have no one to blush with me,
To cross their arms and hang their heads with mine,
To mask their brows and hide their infamy;
But I alone alone must sit and pine,
Seasoning the earth with showers of silver brine,
　　Mingling my talk with tears, my grief with groans,
　　Poor wasting monuments of lasting moans.

'O Night! thou furnace of foul-reeking smoke,
Let not the jealous Day behold that face
Which underneath thy black all-hiding cloak
Immodestly lies martyr'd with disgrace:
Keep still possession of thy gloomy place,
　　That all the faults which in thy reign are made
　　May likewise be sepulchred in thy shade.

'Make me not object to the tell-tale Day!
The light will show, character'd in my brow,
The story of sweet chastity's decay,
The impious breach of holy wedlock vow:
Yea, the illiterate, that know not how
    To 'cipher what is writ in learned books,
    Will quote my loathsome trespass in my looks.

'The nurse, to still her child, will tell my story,
And fright her crying babe with Tarquin's name;
The orator, to deck his oratory,
Will couple my reproach to Tarquin's shame;
Feast-finding minstrels, tuning my defame,
    Will tie the hearers to attend each line,
    How Tarquin wronged me, I Collatine.

'Let my good name, that senseless reputation,
For Collatine's dear love be kept unspotted:
If that be made a theme for disputation,
The branches of another root are rotted,
And undeserv'd reproach to him allotted
    That is as clear from this attaint of mine,
    As I ere this was pure to Collatine.

'O unseen shame! invisible disgrace!
O unfelt sore! crest-wounding, private scar!
Reproach is stamp'd in Collatinus' face,
And Tarquin's eye may read the mot afar,
How he in peace is wounded, not in war.
    Alas! how many bear such shameful blows,
    Which not themselves, but he that gives them knows.

'If, Collatine, thine honour lay in me,
From me by strong assault it is bereft.
My honey lost, and I, a drone-like bee,
Have no perfection of my summer left,
But robb'd and ransack'd by injurious theft:
    In thy weak hive a wandering wasp hath crept,
    And suck'd the honey which thy chaste bee kept.

'Yet am I guilty of thy honour's wrack;
Yet for thy honour did I entertain him;
Coming from thee, I could not put him back,
For it had been dishonour to disdain him:
Besides, of weariness he did complain him,
    And talk'd of virtue: O! unlook'd-for evil,
    When virtue is profan'd in such a devil.

'Why should the worm intrude the maiden bud?
Or hateful cuckoos hatch in sparrows' nests?
Or toads infect fair founts with venom mud?
Or tyrant folly lurk in gentle breasts?
Or kings be breakers of their own behests?
    But no perfection is so absolute,
    That some impurity doth not pollute.

'The aged man that coffers up his gold
Is plagu'd with cramps and gouts and painful fits;
And scarce hath eyes his treasure to behold,
But like still-pining Tantalus he sits,
And useless barns the harvest of his wits;
    Having no other pleasure of his gain
    But torment that it cannot cure his pain.

'So then he hath it when he cannot use it,
And leaves it to be master'd by his young;
Who in their pride do presently abuse it:
Their father was too weak, and they too strong,
To hold their cursed-blessed fortune long.
    The sweets we wish for turn to loathed sours
    Even in the moment that we call them ours.

'Unruly blasts wait on the tender spring;
Unwholesome weeds take root with precious flowers;
The adder hisses where the sweet birds sing;
What virtue breeds iniquity devours:
We have no good that we can say is ours,
    But ill-annexed Opportunity
    Or kills his life, or else his quality.

'O Opportunity! thy guilt is great,
'Tis thou that execut'st the traitor's treason;
Thou sett'st the wolf where he the lamb may get;
Whoever plots the sin, thou point'st the season;
'Tis thou that spurn'st at right, at law, at reason;
   And in thy shady cell, where none may spy him,
   Sits Sin to seize the souls that wander by him.

'Thou makest the vestal violate her oath;
Thou blow'st the fire when temperance is thaw'd;
Thou smother'st honesty, thou murder'st troth;
Thou foul abettor! thou notorious bawd!
Thou plantest scandal and displacest laud:
   Thou ravisher, thou traitor, thou false thief,
   Thy honey turns to gall, thy joy to grief!

'Thy secret pleasure turns to open shame,
Thy private feasting to a public fast,
Thy smoothing titles to a ragged name,
Thy sugar'd tongue to bitter wormwood taste:
Thy violent vanities can never last.
   How comes it then, vile Opportunity,
   Being so bad, such numbers seek for thee?

'When wilt thou be the humble suppliant's friend,
And bring him where his suit may be obtain'd?
When wilt thou sort an hour great strifes to end?
Or free that soul which wretchedness hath chain'd?
Give physic to the sick, ease to the pain'd?
   The poor, lame, blind, halt, creep, cry out for thee;
   But they ne'er meet with Opportunity.

'The patient dies while the physician sleeps;
The orphan pines while the oppressor feeds;
Justice is feasting while the widow weeps;
Advice is sporting while infection breeds:
Thou grant'st no time for charitable deeds:
   Wrath, envy, treason, rape, and murder's rages,
   Thy heinous hours wait on them as their pages.

'When Truth and Virtue have to do with thee,
A thousand crosses keep them from thy aid:
They buy thy help; but Sin ne'er gives a fee,
He gratis comes; and thou art well appaid
As well to hear as grant what he hath said.
   My Collatine would else have come to me
   When Tarquin did, but he was stay'd by thee.

'Guilty thou art of murder and of theft,
Guilty of perjury and subornation,
Guilty of treason, forgery, and shift,
Guilty of incest, that abomination;
An accessary by thine inclination
   To all sins past and all that are to come,
   From the creation to the general doom.

'Mis-shapen Time, copesmate of ugly Night,
Swift subtle post, carrier of grisly care,
Eater of youth, false slave to false delight,
Base watch of woes, sin's pack-horse, virtue's snare;
Thou nursest all, and murderest all that are:
   O! hear me then, injurious, shifting Time,
   Be guilty of my death, since of my crime.

'Why hath thy servant Opportunity
Betray'd the hours thou gav'st me to repose?
Cancell'd my fortunes, and enchained me
To endless date of never-ending woes?
Time's office is to fine the hate of foes,
   To eat up errors by opinion bred,
   Not spend the dowry of a lawful bed.

'Time's glory is to calm contending kings,
To unmask falsehood and bring truth to light,
To stamp the seal of time in aged things,
To wake the morn and sentinel the night,
To wrong the wronger till he render right,
   To ruinate proud buildings with thy hours,
   And smear with dust their glittering golden towers;

'To fill with worm-holes stately monuments,
To feed oblivion with decay of things,
To blot old books and alter their contents,
To pluck the quills from ancient ravens' wings,
To dry the old oak's sap and cherish springs,
　　To spoil antiquities of hammer'd steel,
　　And turn the giddy round of Fortune's wheel;

'To show the beldam daughters of her daughter,
To make the child a man, the man a child,
To slay the tiger that doth live by slaughter,
To tame the unicorn and lion wild,
To mock the subtle, in themselves beguil'd,
　　To cheer the ploughman with increaseful crops,
　　And waste huge stones with little water-drops.

'Why work'st thou mischief in thy pilgrimage,
Unless thou couldst return to make amends?
One poor retiring minute in an age
Would purchase thee a thousand thousand friends,
Lending him wit that to bad debtors lends:
　　O! this dread night, wouldst thou one hour come back,
　　I could prevent this storm and shun thy wrack.

'Thou ceaseless lackey to eternity,
With some mischance cross Tarquin in his flight:
Devise extremes beyond extremity,
To make him curse this cursed crimeful night:
Let ghastly shadows his lewd eyes affright,
　　And the dire thought of his committed evil
　　Shape every bush a hideous shapeless devil.

'Disturb his hours of rest with restless trances,
Afflict him in his bed with bedrid groans;
Let there bechance him pitiful mischances,
To make him moan, but pity not his moans:
Stone him with harden'd hearts, harder than stones;
　　And let mild women to him lose their mildness,
　　Wilder to him than tigers in their wildness.

'Let him have time to tear his curled hair,
Let him have time against himself to rave,
Let him have time of Time's help to despair,
Let him have time to live a loathed slave,
Let him have time a beggar's orts to crave,
    And time to see one that by alms doth live
    Disdain to him disdained scraps to give.

'Let him have time to see his friends his foes,
And merry fools to mock at him resort;
Let him have time to mark how slow time goes
In time of sorrow, and how swift and short
His time of folly and his time of sport;
    And ever let his unrecalling crime
    Have time to wail the abusing of his time.

'O Time! thou tutor both to good and bad,
Teach me to curse him that thou taught'st this ill;
At his own shadow let the thief run mad,
Himself himself seek every hour to kill:
Such wretched hands such wretched blood should spill;
    For who so base would such an office have
    As slanderous deathsman to so base a slave?

'The baser is he, coming from a king,
To shame his hope with deeds degenerate:
The mightier man, the mightier is the thing
That makes him honour'd, or begets him hate;
For greatest scandal waits on greatest state,
    The moon being clouded presently is miss'd,
    But little stars may hide them when they list.

'The crow may bathe his coal-black wings in mire,
And unperceiv'd fly with the filth away;
But if the like the snow-white swan desire,
The stain upon his silver down will stay.
Poor grooms are sightless night, kings glorious day:
    Gnats are unnoted wheresoe'er they fly,
    But eagles gaz'd upon with every eye.

'Out, idle words! servants to shallow fools,
Unprofitable sounds, weak arbitrators!
Busy yourselves in skill-contending schools;
Debate where leisure serves with dull debaters;
To trembling clients be you mediators;
    For me, I force not argument a straw,
    Since that my case is past the help of law.

'In vain I rail at Opportunity,
At Time, at Tarquin, and uncheerful Night;
In vain I cavil with mine infamy,
In vain I spurn at my confirm'd despite;
This helpless smoke of words doth me no right.
    The remedy indeed to do me good,
    Is to let forth my foul-defiled blood.

'Poor hand, why quiver'st thou at this decree?
Honour thyself to rid me of this shame;
For if I die, my honour lives in thee,
But if I live, thou liv'st in my defame;
Since thou couldst not defend thy loyal dame,
    And wast afeard to scratch her wicked foe,
    Kill both thyself and her for yielding so.'

This said, from her be-tumbled couch she starteth,
To find some desperate instrument of death;
But this no slaughter-house no tool imparteth
To make more vent for passage of her breath;
Which, thronging through her lips, so vanisheth
    As smoke from Ætna, that in air consumes,
    Or that which from discharged cannon fumes.

'In vain,' quoth she, 'I live, and seek in vain
Some happy mean to end a hapless life.
I fear'd by Tarquin's falchion to be slain,
Yet for the self-same purpose seek a knife:
But when I fear'd I was a loyal wife:
    So am I now: O no! that cannot be;
    Of that true type hath Tarquin rifled me.

'O! that is gone for which I sought to live,
And therefore now I need not fear to die.
To clear this spot by death, at least I give
A badge of fame to slander's livery,
A dying life to living infamy:
 Poor helpless help, the treasure stol'n away,
 To burn the guiltless casket where it lay!

'Well, well, dear Collatine, thou shalt not know
The stained taste of violated troth;
I will not wrong thy true affection so,
To flatter thee with an infringed oath;
This bastard graff shall never come to growth;
 He shall not boast who did thy stock pollute
 That thou art doting father of his fruit.

'Nor shall he smile at thee in secret thought,
Nor laugh with his companions at thy state;
But thou shalt know thy interest was not bought
Basely with gold, but stol'n from forth thy gate.
For me, I am the mistress of my fate,
 And with my trespass never will dispense,
 Till life to death acquit my forc'd offence.

'I will not poison thee with my attaint,
Nor fold my fault in cleanly-coin'd excuses;
My sable ground of sin I will not paint,
To hide the truth of this false night's abuses:
My tongue shall utter all; mine eyes, like sluices,
 As from a mountain-spring that feeds a dale,
 Shall gush pure streams to purge my impure tale.'

By this, lamenting Philomel had ended
The well-tun'd warble of her nightly sorrow,
And solemn night with slow sad gait descended
To ugly hell; when, lo! the blushing morrow
Lends light to all fair eyes that light will borrow:
 But cloudy Lucrece shames herself to see,
 And therefore still in night would cloister'd be.

Revealing day through every cranny spies,
And seems to point her out where she sits weeping;
To whom she sobbing speaks: 'O eye of eyes,
Why pry'st thou through my window? leave thy peeping;
Mock with thy tickling beams eyes that are sleeping:
　　Brand not my forehead with thy piercing light,
　　For day hath nought to do what 's done by night.'

Thus cavils she with everything she sees.
True grief is fond and testy as a child,
Who wayward once, his mood with nought agrees:
Old woes, not infant sorrows, bear them mild;
Continuance tames the one; the other wild,
　　Like an unpractis'd swimmer plunging still,
　　With too much labour drowns for want of skill.

So she, deep-drenched in a sea of care,
Holds disputation with each thing she views,
And to herself all sorrow doth compare;
No object but her passion's strength renews,
And as one shifts, another straight ensues:
　　Sometime her grief is dumb and hath no words;
　　Sometime 'tis mad and too much talk affords.

The little birds that tune their morning's joy
Make her moans mad with their sweet melody:
For mirth doth search the bottom of annoy;
Sad souls are slain in merry company;
Grief best is pleas'd with grief's society:
　　True sorrow then is feelingly suffic'd
　　When with like semblance it is sympathiz'd.

'Tis double death to drown in ken of shore;
He ten times pines that pines beholding food;
To see the salve doth make the wound ache more;
Great grief grieves most at that would do it good;
Deep woes roll forward like a gentle flood,
　　Who, being stopp'd, the bounding banks o'erflows;
　　Grief dallied with nor law nor limit knows.

'You mocking birds,' quoth she, 'your tunes entomb
Within your hollow-swelling feather'd breasts,
And in my hearing be you mute and dumb:
My restless discord loves no stops nor rests;
A woeful hostess brooks not merry guests:
    Relish your nimble notes to pleasing ears;
    Distress likes dumps when time is kept with tears.

'Come, Philomel, that sing'st of ravishment,
Make thy sad grove in my dishevell'd hair:
As the dank earth weeps at thy languishment,
So I at each sad strain will strain a tear,
And with deep groans the diapason bear;
    For burthen-wise I 'll hum on Tarquin still,
    While thou on Tereus descant'st better skill.

'And whiles against a thorn thou bear'st thy part,
To keep thy sharp woes waking, wretched I,
To imitate thee well, against my heart
Will fix a sharp knife to affright mine eye,
Who, if it wink, shall thereon fall and die.
    These means, as frets upon an instrument,
    Shall tune our heart-strings to true languishment.

'And for, poor bird, thou sing'st not in the day,
As shaming any eye should thee behold,
Some dark deep desert, seated from the way,
That knows not parching heat nor freezing cold,
Will we find out; and there we will unfold
    To creatures stern sad tunes, to change their kinds:
    Since men prove beasts, let beasts bear gentle minds.

As the poor frighted deer, that stands at gaze,
Wildly determining which way to fly,
Or one encompass'd with a winding maze,
That cannot tread the way out readily;
So with herself is she in mutiny,
    To live or die which of the twain were better,
    When life is sham'd, and death reproach's debtor.

'To kill myself,' quoth she, 'alack! what were it
But with my body my poor soul's pollution?
They that lose half with greater patience bear it
Than they whose whole is swallow'd in confusion.
That mother tries a merciless conclusion,
    Who, having two sweet babes, when death takes one,
    Will slay the other and be nurse to none.

'My body or my soul, which was the dearer,
When the one pure, the other made divine?
Whose love of either to myself was nearer,
When both were kept for heaven and Collatine?
Ay me! the bark peel'd from the lofty pine,
    His leaves will wither and his sap decay;
    So must my soul, her bark being peel'd away.

'Her house is sack'd, her quiet interrupted,
Her mansion batter'd by the enemy;
Her sacred temple spotted, spoil'd, corrupted,
Grossly engirt with daring infamy:
Then let it not be call'd impiety,
    If in this blemish'd fort I make some hole
    Through which I may convey this troubled soul.

'Yet die I will not till my Collatine
Have heard the cause of my untimely death;
That he may vow, in that sad hour of mine,
Revenge on him that made me stop my breath.
My stained blood to Tarquin I 'll bequeath,
    Which by him tainted, shall for him be spent,
    And as his due writ in my testament.

'My honour I 'll bequeath unto the knife
That wounds my body so dishonoured.
'Tis honour to deprive dishonour'd life;
The one will live, the other being dead:
So of shame's ashes shall my fame be bred;
    For in my death I murder shameful scorn:
    My shame so dead, mine honour is new-born.

'Dear lord of that dear jewel I have lost,
What legacy shall I bequeath to thee?
My resolution, love, shall be thy boast,
By whose example thou reveng'd mayst be.
How Tarquin must be us'd, read it in me:
    Myself, thy friend, will kill myself, thy foe,
    And for my sake serve thou false Tarquin so.

'This brief abridgment of my will I make:
My soul and body to the skies and ground;
My resolution, husband, do thou take;
Mine honour be the knife's that makes my wound;
My shame be his that did my fame confound;
    And all my fame that lives disbursed be
    To those that live, and think no shame of me.

'Thou, Collatine, shalt oversee this will;
How was I overseen that thou shalt see it!
My blood shall wash the slander of mine ill;
My life's foul deed, my life's fair end shall free it.
Faint not, faint heart, but stoutly say "So be it":
    Yield to my hand; my hand shall conquer thee:
    Thou dead, both die, and both shall victors be.'

This plot of death when sadly she had laid,
And wip'd the brinish pearl from her bright eyes,
With untun'd tongue she hoarsely calls her maid,
Whose swift obedience to her mistress hies;
For fleet-wing'd duty with thought's feathers flies.
    Poor Lucrece' cheeks unto her maid seem so
    As winter meads when sun doth melt their snow.

Her mistress she doth give demure good-morrow,
With soft slow tongue, true mark of modesty,
And sorts a sad look to her lady's sorrow,
For why her face wore sorrow's livery;
But durst not ask of her audaciously
    Why her two suns were cloud-eclipsed so,
    Nor why her fair cheeks over-wash'd with woe.

But as the earth doth weep, the sun being set,
Each flower moisten'd like a melting eye;
Even so the maid with swelling drops 'gan wet
Her circled eyne, enforc'd by sympathy
Of those fair suns set in her mistress' sky,
    Who in a salt-wav'd ocean quench their light,
    Which makes the maid weep like the dewy night.

A pretty while these pretty creatures stand,
Like ivory conduits coral cisterns filling:
One justly weeps, the other takes in hand
No cause, but company, of her drops spilling:
Their gentle sex to weep are often willing,
    Grieving themselves to guess at others' smarts,
    And then they drown their eyes or break their hearts.

For men have marble, women waxen, minds,
And therefore are they form'd as marble will;
The weak oppress'd, the impression of strange kinds
Is form'd in them by force, by fraud, or skill:
Then call them not the authors of their ill,
    No more than wax shall be accounted evil
    Wherein is stamp'd the semblance of a devil.

Their smoothness, like a goodly champaign plain,
Lays open all the little worms that creep;
In men, as in a rough-grown grove, remain
Cave-keeping evils that obscurely sleep:
Through crystal walls each little mote will peep:
    Though men can cover crimes with bold stern looks,
    Poor women's faces are their own faults' books.

No man inveigh against the wither'd flower,
But chide rough winter that the flower hath kill'd:
Not that devour'd, but that which doth devour,
Is worthy blame. O! let it not be hild
Poor women's faults, that they are so fulfill'd
    With men's abuses: those proud lords, to blame,
    Make weak-made women tenants to their shame.

The precedent whereof in Lucrece view,
Assail'd by night with circumstances strong
Of present death, and shame that might ensue
By that her death, to do her husband wrong:
Such danger to resistance did belong,
    That dying fear through all her body spread;
    And who cannot abuse a body dead?

By this, mild patience bid fair Lucrece speak
To the poor counterfeit of her complaining:
'My girl,' quoth she, 'on what occasion break
Those tears from thee, that down thy cheeks are raining?
If thou dost weep for grief of my sustaining,
    Know, gentle wench, it small avails my mood:
    If tears could help, mine own would do me good.

'But tell me, girl, when went'—and there she stay'd
Till after a deep groan—'Tarquin from hence?'—
'Madam, ere I was up,' replied the maid,
'The more to blame my sluggard negligence:
Yet with the fault I thus far can dispense;
    Myself was stirring ere the break of day,
    And, ere I rose, was Tarquin gone away.

'But, lady, if your maid may be so bold,
She would request to know your heaviness.'
'O! peace,' quoth Lucrece; 'if it should be told,
The repetition cannot make it less;
For more it is than I can well express:
    And that deep torture may be call'd a hell,
    When more is felt than one hath power to tell.

'Go, get me hither paper, ink, and pen:
Yet save that labour, for I have them here.
What should I say? One of my husband's men
Bid thou be ready, by and by, to bear
A letter to my lord, my love, my dear:
    Bid him with speed prepare to carry it;
    The cause craves haste, and it will soon be writ.'

Her maid is gone, and she prepares to write,
First hovering o'er the paper with her quill:
Conceit and grief an eager combat fight;
What wit sets down is blotted straight with will;
This is too curious-good, this blunt and ill:
 Much like a press of people at a door,
 Throng her inventions, which shall go before.

At last she thus begins: 'Thou worthy lord
Of that unworthy wife that greeteth thee,
Health to thy person! next vouchsafe t' afford—
If ever, love, thy Lucrece thou wilt see—
Some present speed to come and visit me.
 So I commend me from our house in grief:
 My woes are tedious, though my words are brief.'

Here folds she up the tenour of her woe,
Her certain sorrow writ uncertainly.
By this short schedule Collatine may know
Her grief, but not her grief's true quality:
She dares not thereof make discovery,
 Lest he should hold it her own gross abuse,
 Ere she with blood had stain'd her stain'd excuse.

Besides, the life and feeling of her passion
She hoards, to spend when he is by to hear her;
When sighs, and groans, and tears may grace the fashion
Of her disgrace, the better so to clear her
From that suspicion which the world might bear her.
 To shun this blot, she would not blot the letter
 With words, till action might become them better.

To see sad sights moves more than hear them told;
For then the eye interprets to the ear
The heavy motion that it doth behold,
When every part a part of woe doth bear.
'Tis but a part of sorrow that we hear;
 Deep sounds make lesser noise than shallow fords,
 And sorrow ebbs, being blown with wind of words.

Her letter now is seal'd, and on it writ
'At Ardea to my lord with more than haste.'
The post attends, and she delivers it,
Charging the sour-fac'd groom to hie as fast
As lagging fowls before the northern blast:
    Speed more than speed but dull and slow she deems:
    Extremity still urgeth such extremes.

The homely villain curtsies to her low;
And, blushing on her, with a steadfast eye
Receives the scroll without or yea or no,
And forth with bashful innocence doth hie.
But they whose guilt within their bosoms lie
    Imagine every eye beholds their blame;
    For Lucrece thought he blush'd to see her shame:

When, silly groom! God wot, it was defect
Of spirit, life, and bold audacity.
Such harmless creatures have a true respect
To talk in deeds, while others saucily
Promise more speed, but do it leisurely:
    Even so this pattern of the worn-out age
    Pawn'd honest looks, but laid no words to gage.

His kindled duty kindled her mistrust,
That two red fires in both their faces blaz'd;
She thought he blush'd, as knowing Tarquin's lust,
And, blushing with him, wistly on him gaz'd;
Her earnest eye did make him more amaz'd:
    The more she saw the blood his cheeks replenish,
    The more she thought he spied in her some blemish.

But long she thinks till he return again,
And yet the duteous vassal scarce is gone.
The weary time she cannot entertain,
For now 'tis stale to sigh, to weep, and groan:
So woe hath wearied woe, moan tired moan,
    That she her plaints a little while doth stay,
    Pausing for means to mourn some newer way.

At last she calls to mind where hangs a piece
Of skilful painting, made for Priam's Troy;
Before the which is drawn the power of Greece,
For Helen's rape the city to destroy,
Threat'ning cloud-kissing Ilion with annoy;
    Which the conceited painter drew so proud,
    As heaven, it seem'd, to kiss the turrets bow'd.

A thousand lamentable objects there,
In scorn of nature, art gave lifeless life;
Many a dry drop seem'd a weeping tear,
Shed for the slaughter'd husband by the wife:
The red blood reek'd, to show the painter's strife;
    And dying eyes gleam'd forth their ashy lights,
    Like dying coals burnt out in tedious nights.

There might you see the labouring pioner
Begrim'd with sweat, and smeared all with dust;
And from the towers of Troy there would appear
The very eyes of men through loop-holes thrust,
Gazing upon the Greeks with little lust:
    Such sweet observance in this work was had,
    That one might see those far-off eyes look sad.

In great commanders grace and majesty
You might behold, triumphing in their faces;
In youth quick bearing and dexterity;
And here and there the painter interlaces
Pale cowards, marching on with trembling paces;
    Which heartless peasants did so well resemble,
    That one would swear he saw them quake and tremble.

In Ajax and Ulysses, O! what art
Of physiognomy might one behold;
The face of either cipher'd either's heart;
Their face their manners most expressly told:
In Ajax' eyes blunt rage and rigour roll'd;
    But the mild glance that sly Ulysses lent
    Show'd deep regard and smiling government.

There pleading might you see grave Nestor stand,
As 'twere encouraging the Greeks to fight;
Making such sober action with his hand,
That it beguil'd attention, charm'd the sight:
In speech, it seem'd, his beard, all silver white,
    Wagg'd up and down, and from his lips did fly
    Thin winding breath, which purl'd up to the sky.

About him were a press of gaping faces,
Which seem'd to swallow up his sound advice;
All jointly listening, but with several graces,
As if some mermaid did their ears entice,
Some high, some low, the painter was so nice;
    The scalps of many, almost hid behind,
    To jump up higher seem'd, to mock the mind.

Here one man's hand lean'd on another's head,
His nose being shadow'd by his neighbour's ear;
Here one being throng'd bears back, all boll'n and red;
Another smother'd, seems to pelt and swear;
And in their rage such signs of rage they bear,
    As, but for loss of Nestor's golden words,
    It seem'd they would debate with angry swords.

For much imaginary work was there;
Conceit deceitful, so compact, so kind,
That for Achilles' image stood his spear,
Grip'd in an armed hand; himself behind
Was left unseen, save to the eye of mind:
    A hand, a foot, a face, a leg, a head,
    Stood for the whole to be imagined.

And from the walls of strong-besieged Troy,
When their brave hope, bold Hector, march'd to field,
Stood many Trojan mothers, sharing joy
To see their youthful sons bright weapons wield;
And to their hope they such odd action yield,
    That through their light joy seemed to appear,—
    Like bright things stain'd—a kind of heavy fear.

And from the strand of Dardan, where they fought,
To Simois' reedy banks the red blood ran,
Whose waves to imitate the battle sought
With swelling ridges; and their ranks began
To break upon the galled shore, and then
　　Retire again, till meeting greater ranks
　　They join, and shoot their foam at Simois' banks.

To this well-painted piece is Lucrece come,
To find a face where all distress is stell'd.
Many she sees where cares have carved some,
But none where all distress and dolour dwell'd,
Till she despairing Hecuba beheld,
　　Staring on Priam's wounds with her old eyes,
　　Which bleeding under Pyrrhus' proud foot lies.

In her the painter had anatomiz'd
Time's ruin, beauty's wrack, and grim care's reign:
Her cheeks with chaps and wrinkles were disguis'd;
Of what she was no semblance did remain:
Her blue blood chang'd to black in every vein,
　　Wanting the spring that those shrunk pipes had fed,
　　Show'd life imprison'd in a body dead.

On this sad shadow Lucrece spends her eyes,
And shapes her sorrow to the beldam's woes,
Who nothing wants to answer her but cries,
And bitter words to ban her cruel foes:
The painter was no god to lend her those;
　　And therefore Lucrece swears he did her wrong,
　　To give her so much grief and not a tongue.

'Poor instrument,' quoth she, 'without a sound,
I 'll tune thy woes with my lamenting tongue;
And drop sweet balm in Priam's painted wound,
And rail on Pyrrhus that hath done him wrong;
And with my tears quench Troy that burns so long;
　　And with my knife scratch out the angry eyes
　　Of all the Greeks that are thine enemies.

'Show me the strumpet that began this stir,
That with my nails her beauty I may tear.
Thy heat of lust, fond Paris, did incur
This load of wrath that burning Troy doth bear:
Thy eye kindled the fire that burneth here;
   And here in Troy, for trespass of thine eye,
   The sire, the son, the dame, and daughter die.

'Why should the private pleasure of some one
Become the public plague of many moe?
Let sin, alone committed, light alone
Upon his head that hath transgressed so;
Let guiltless souls be freed from guilty woe;
   For one's offence why should so many fall,
   To plague a private sin in general?

'Lo! here weeps Hecuba, here Priam dies,
Here manly Hector faints, here Troilus swounds,
Here friend by friend in bloody channel lies,
And friend to friend gives unadvised wounds,
And one man's lust these many lives confounds:
   Had doting Priam check'd his son's desire,
   Troy had been bright with fame and not with fire.'

Here feelingly she weeps Troy's painted woes;
For sorrow, like a heavy-hanging bell,
Once set on ringing, with his own weight goes;
Then little strength rings out the doleful knell:
So Lucrece, set a-work, sad tales doth tell
   To pencil'd pensiveness and colour'd sorrow;
   She lends them words, and she their looks doth borrow.

She throws her eyes about the painting round,
And whom she finds forlorn she doth lament:
At last she sees a wretched image bound,
That piteous looks to Phrygian shepherds lent;
His face, though full of cares, yet show'd content;
   Onward to Troy with the blunt swains he goes,
   So mild, that Patience seem'd to scorn his woes.

In him the painter labour'd with his skill
To hide deceit, and give the harmless show
An humble gait, calm looks, eyes wailing still,
A brow unbent that seem'd to welcome woe;
Cheeks neither red nor pale, but mingled so
   That blushing red no guilty instance gave,
   Nor ashy pale the fear that false hearts have.

But, like a constant and confirmed devil,
He entertain'd a show so seeming-just,
And therein so ensconc'd his secret evil,
That jealousy itself could not mistrust
False-creeping craft and perjury should thrust
   Into so bright a day such black-fac'd storms,
   Or blot with hell-born sin such saint-like forms.

The well-skill'd workman this mild image drew
For perjur'd Sinon, whose enchanting story
The credulous old Priam after slew;
Whose words like wildfire burnt the shining glory
Of rich-built Ilion, that the skies were sorry,
   And little stars shot from their fixed places,
   When their glass fell wherein they view'd their faces.

This picture she advisedly perus'd,
And chid the painter for his wondrous skill,
Saying, some shape in Sinon's was abus'd;
So fair a form lodg'd not a mind so ill:
And still on him she gaz'd, and gazing still,
   Such signs of truth in his plain face she spied,
   That she concludes the picture was belied.

'It cannot be,' quoth she, 'that so much guile'—
She would have said—'can lurk in such a look';
But Tarquin's shape came in her mind the while,
And from her tongue 'can lurk' from 'cannot' took:
'It cannot be,' she in that sense forsook,
   And turn'd it thus, 'It cannot be, I find,
   But such a face should bear a wicked mind:

'For even as subtle Sinon here is painted,
So sober-sad, so weary, and so mild,
As if with grief or travail he had fainted,
To me came Tarquin armed; so beguil'd
With outward honesty, but yet defil'd
    With inward vice; as Priam him did cherish,
    So did I Tarquin; so my Troy did perish.

'Look, look, how listening Priam wets his eyes,
To see those borrow'd tears that Sinon sheds!
Priam, why art thou old and yet not wise?
For every tear he falls a Trojan bleeds:
His eye drops fire, no water thence proceeds;
    Those round clear pearls of his, that move thy pity,
    Are balls of quenchless fire to burn thy city.

'Such devils steal effects from lightless hell;
For Sinon in his fire doth quake with cold,
And in that cold hot-burning fire doth dwell;
These contraries such unity do hold,
Only to flatter fools and make them bold:
    So Priam's trust false Sinon's tears doth flatter,
    That he finds means to burn his Troy with water.'

Here, all enrag'd, such passion her assails,
That patience is quite beaten from her breast.
She tears the senseless Sinon with her nails,
Comparing him to that unhappy guest
Whose deed hath made herself herself detest:
    At last she smilingly with this gives o'er;
    'Fool, fool!' quoth she, 'his wounds will not be sore.'

Thus ebbs and flows the current of her sorrow,
And time doth weary time with her complaining.
She looks for night, and then she longs for morrow,
And both she thinks too long with her remaining:
Short time seems long in sorrow's sharp sustaining:
    Though woe be heavy, yet it seldom sleeps;
    And they that watch see time how slow it creeps.

While all this time hath overslipp'd her thought,
That she with painted images hath spent;
Being from the feeling of her own grief brought
By deep surmise of others' detriment;
Losing her woes in shows of discontent.
    It easeth some, though none it ever cur'd,
    To think their dolour others have endur'd.

But now the mindful messenger, come back,
Brings home his lord and other company;
Who finds his Lucrece clad in mourning black;
And round about her tear-distained eye
Blue circles stream'd, like rainbows in the sky:
    These water-galls in her dim element
    Foretell new storms to those already spent.

Which when her sad-beholding husband saw,
Amazedly in her sad face he stares:
Her eyes, though sod in tears, look'd red and raw,
Her lively colour kill'd with deadly cares.
He hath no power to ask her how she fares:
    Both stood like old acquaintance in a trance,
    Met far from home, wondering each other's chance.

At last he takes her by the bloodless hand,
And thus begins: 'What uncouth ill event
Hath thee befall'n, that thou dost trembling stand?
Sweet love, what spite hath thy fair colour spent?
Why art thou thus attir'd in discontent?
    Unmask, dear dear, this moody heaviness,
    And tell thy grief, that we may give redress.'

Three times with sighs she gives her sorrow fire,
Ere once she can discharge one word of woe:
At length address'd to answer his desire,
She modestly prepares to let them know
Her honour is ta'en prisoner by the foe;
    While Collatine and his consorted lords
    With sad attention long to hear her words.

And now this pale swan in her watery nest
Begins the sad dirge of her certain ending.
'Few words,' quoth she, 'shall fit the trespass best,
Where no excuse can give the fault amending;
In me moe woe than words are now depending;
    And my laments would be drawn out too long,
    To tell them all with one poor tired tongue.

'Then be this all the task it hath to say:
Dear husband, in the interest of thy bed
A stranger came, and on that pillow lay
Where thou wast wont to rest thy weary head;
And what wrong else may be imagined
    By foul enforcement might be done to me,
    From that, alas! thy Lucrece is not free.

'For in the dreadful dead of dark midnight,
With shining falchion in my chamber came
A creeping creature with a flaming light,
And softly cried, "Awake, thou Roman dame,
And entertain my love; else lasting shame
    On thee and thine this night I will inflict,
    If thou my love's desire do contradict.

' "For some hard-favour'd groom of thine," quoth he,
"Unless thou yoke thy liking to my will,
I 'll murder straight, and then I 'll slaughter thee,
And swear I found you where you did fulfil
The loathsome act of lust, and so did kill
    The lechers in their deed; this act will be
    My fame, and thy perpetual infamy."

'With this I did begin to start and cry,
And then against my heart he set his sword,
Swearing, unless I took all patiently,
I should not live to speak another word;
So should my shame still rest upon record,
    And never be forgot in mighty Rome
    Th' adulterate death of Lucrece and her groom.

'Mine enemy was strong, my poor self weak,
And far the weaker with so strong a fear:
My bloody judge forbade my tongue to speak;
No rightful plea might plead for justice there:
His scarlet lust came evidence to swear
    That my poor beauty had purloin'd his eyes;
    And when the judge is robb'd the prisoner dies.

'O! teach me how to make mine own excuse,
Or, at the least, this refuge let me find;
Though my gross blood be stain'd with this abuse,
Immaculate and spotless is my mind;
That was not forc'd; that never was inclin'd
    To accessary yieldings, but still pure
    Doth in her poison'd closet yet endure.'

Lo! here the helpless merchant of this loss,
With head declin'd, and voice damm'd up with woe,
With sad set eyes, and wretched arms across,
From lips new-waxen pale begins to blow
The grief away that stops his answer so:
    But, wretched as he is, he strives in vain;
    What he breathes out his breath drinks up again.

As through an arch the violent roaring tide
Outruns the eye that doth behold his haste,
Yet in the eddy boundeth in his pride
Back to the strait that forc'd him on so fast;
In rage sent out, recall'd in rage, being past:
    Even so his sighs, his sorrows, make a saw,
    To push grief on, and back the same grief draw.

Which speechless woe of his poor she attendeth,
And his untimely frenzy thus awaketh:
'Dear lord, thy sorrow to my sorrow lendeth
Another power; no flood by raining slaketh.
My woe too sensible thy passion maketh
    More feeling-painful: let it then suffice
    To drown one woe, one pair of weeping eyes.

'And for my sake, when I might charm thee so,
For she that was thy Lucrece, now attend me:
Be suddenly revenged on my foe,
Thine, mine, his own: suppose thou dost defend me
From what is past: the help that thou shalt lend me
   Comes all too late, yet let the traitor die;
   For sparing justice feeds iniquity.

'But ere I name him, you fair lords,' quoth she,—
Speaking to those that came with Collatine,—
'Shall plight your honourable faiths to me,
With swift pursuit to venge this wrong of mine;
For 'tis a meritorious fair design
   To chase injustice with revengeful arms:
   Knights, by their oaths, should right poor ladies' harms.'

At this request, with noble disposition
Each present lord began to promise aid,
As bound in knighthood to her imposition,
Longing to hear the hateful foe bewray'd.
But she, that yet her sad task hath not said,
   The protestation stops. 'O! speak,' quoth she,
   'How may this forced stain be wip'd from me?

'What is the quality of mine offence,
Being constrain'd with dreadful circumstance?
May my pure mind with the foul act dispense,
My low-declined honour to advance?
May any terms acquit me from this chance?
   The poison'd fountain clears itself again;
   And why not I from this compelled stain?'

With this, they all at once began to say,
Her body's stain her mind untainted clears;
While with a joyless smile she turns away
The face, that map which deep impression bears
Of hard misfortune, carv'd in it with tears.
   'No, no,' quoth she, 'no dame, hereafter living,
   By my excuse shall claim excuse's giving.'

Here with a sigh, as if her heart would break,
She throws forth Tarquin's name: 'He, he,' she says,
But more than 'he' her poor tongue could not speak;
Till after many accents and delays,
Untimely breathings, sick and short assays,
　　She utters this, 'He, he, fair lords, 'tis he,
　　That guides this hand to give this wound to me.'

Even here she sheathed in her harmless breast
A harmful knife, that thence her soul unsheath'd:
That blow did bail it from the deep unrest
Of that polluted prison where it breath'd;
Her contrite sighs unto the clouds bequeath'd
　　Her winged sprite, and through her wounds doth fly
　　Life's lasting date from cancell'd destiny.

Stone-still, astonish'd with this deadly deed,
Stood Collatine and all his lordly crew;
Till Lucrece' father, that beholds her bleed,
Himself on her self-slaughter'd body threw;
And from the purple fountain Brutus drew
　　The murderous knife, and as it left the place,
　　Her blood, in poor revenge, held it in chase;

And bubbling from her breast, it doth divide
In two slow rivers, that the crimson blood
Circles her body in on every side,
Who, like a late-sack'd island, vastly stood,
Bare and unpeopled in this fearful flood.
　　Some of her blood still pure and red remain'd,
　　And some look'd black, and that false Tarquin stain'd.

About the mourning and congealed face
Of that black blood a watery rigol goes,
Which seems to weep upon the tainted place:
And ever since, as pitying Lucrece' woes,
Corrupted blood some watery token shows;
　　And blood untainted still doth red abide,
　　Blushing at that which is so putrified.

'Daughter, dear daughter!' old Lucretius cries,
'That life was mine which thou hast here depriv'd.
If in the child the father's image lies,
Where shall I live now Lucrece is unliv'd?
Thou wast not to this end from me deriv'd.
   If children pre-decease progenitors,
   We are their offspring, and they none of ours.

'Poor broken glass, I often did behold
In thy sweet semblance my old age new born;
But now that fair fresh mirror, dim and old,
Shows me a bare-bon'd death by time outworn:
O! from thy cheeks my image thou hast torn,
   And shiver'd all the beauty of my glass,
   That I no more can see what once I was.

'O Time! cease thou thy course and last no longer,
If they surcease to be that should survive.
Shall rotten death make conquest of the stronger,
And leave the faltering feeble souls alive?
The old bees die, the young possess their hive:
   Then live, sweet Lucrece, live again and see
   Thy father die, and not thy father thee!'

By this, starts Collatine as from a dream,
And bids Lucretius give his sorrow place;
And then in key-cold Lucrece' bleeding stream
He falls, and bathes the pale fear in his face,
And counterfeits to die with her a space;
   Till manly shame bids him possess his breath
   And live to be revenged on her death.

The deep vexation of his inward soul
Hath serv'd a dumb arrest upon his tongue;
Who, mad that sorrow should his use control,
Or keep him from heart-easing words so long,
Begins to talk; but through his lips do throng
   Weak words, so thick come in his poor heart's aid,
   That no man could distinguish what he said.

Yet sometime 'Tarquin' was pronounced plain,
But through his teeth, as if the name he tore.
This windy tempest, till it blow up rain,
Held back his sorrow's tide, to make it more;
At last it rains, and busy winds give o'er:
    Then son and father weep with equal strife
    Who should weep most, for daughter or for wife.

The one doth call her his, the other his,
Yet neither may possess the claim they lay.
The father says, 'She 's mine.' 'O! mine she is,'
Replies her husband; 'do not take away
My sorrow's interest; let no mourner say
    He weeps for her, for she was only mine,
    And only must be wail'd by Collatine.'

'O!' quoth Lucretius, 'I did give that life
Which she too early and too late hath spill'd.'
'Woe, woe,' quoth Collatine, 'she was my wife,
I ow'd her, and 'tis mine that she hath kill'd.'
'My daughter' and 'my wife' with clamours fill'd
    The dispers'd air, who, holding Lucrece' life,
    Answer'd their cries, 'my daughter' and 'my wife.'

Brutus, who pluck'd the knife from Lucrece' side,
Seeing such emulation in their woe,
Began to clothe his wit in state and pride,
Burying in Lucrece' wound his folly's show.
He with the Romans was esteemed so
    As silly-jeering idiots are with kings,
    For sportive words and uttering foolish things:

But now he throws that shallow habit by,
Wherein deep policy did him disguise;
And arm'd his long-hid wits advisedly,
To check the tears in Collatinus' eyes.
'Thou wronged lord of Rome,' quoth he, 'arise:
    Let my unsounded self, suppos'd a fool,
    Now set thy long-experienc'd wit to school.

'Why, Collatine, is woe the cure for woe?
Do wounds help wounds, or grief help grievous deeds?
Is it revenge to give thyself a blow
For his foul act by whom thy fair wife bleeds?
Such childish humour from weak minds proceeds:
    Thy wretched wife mistook the matter so,
    To slay herself, that should have slain her foe.

'Courageous Roman, do not steep thy heart
In such relenting dew of lamentations;
But kneel with me and help to bear thy part,
To rouse our Roman gods with invocations,
That they will suffer these abominations,
    Since Rome herself in them doth stand disgrac'd,
    By our strong arms from forth her fair streets chas'd.

'Now, by the Capitol that we adore,
And by this chaste blood so unjustly stain'd,
By heaven's fair sun that breeds the fat earth's store,
By all our country rights in Rome maintain'd,
And by chaste Lucrece' soul that late complain'd
    Her wrongs to us, and by this bloody knife,
    We will revenge the death of this true wife.'

This said, he struck his hand upon his breast,
And kiss'd the fatal knife to end his vow;
And to his protestation urg'd the rest,
Who, wondering at him, did his words allow:
Then jointly to the ground their knees they bow;
    And that deep vow, which Brutus made before,
    He doth again repeat, and that they swore.

When they had sworn to this advised doom,
They did conclude to bear dead Lucrece thence;
To show her bleeding body thorough Rome,
And so to publish Tarquin's foul offence:
Which being done with speedy diligence,
    The Romans plausibly did give consent
    To Tarquin's everlasting banishment.

SONNETS

I

FROM fairest creatures we desire increase,
That thereby beauty's rose might never die,
But as the riper should by time decease,
His tender heir might bear his memory:
But thou, contracted to thine own bright eyes,
Feed'st thy light's flame with self-substantial fuel,
Making a famine where abundance lies,
Thyself thy foe, to thy sweet self too cruel.
Thou that art now the world's fresh ornament
And only herald to the gaudy spring,
Within thine own bud buriest thy content
And, tender churl, mak'st waste in niggarding.
  Pity the world, or else this glutton be,
    To eat the world's due, by the grave and thee.

II

When forty winters shall besiege thy brow,
And dig deep trenches in thy beauty's field,
Thy youth's proud livery, so gaz'd on now,
Will be a tatter'd weed, of small worth held:
Then being ask'd where all thy beauty lies,
Where all the treasure of thy lusty days,
To say, within thine own deep-sunken eyes,
Were an all-eating shame and thriftless praise.

How much more praise deserv'd thy beauty's use,
If thou couldst answer 'This fair child of mine
Shall sum my count, and make my old excuse,'
Proving his beauty by succession thine!
  This were to be new made when thou art old,
  And see thy blood warm when thou feel'st it cold.

III

Look in thy glass, and tell the face thou viewest
Now is the time that face should form another;
Whose fresh repair if now thou not renewest,
Thou dost beguile the world, unbless some mother.
For where is she so fair whose unear'd womb
Disdains the tillage of thy husbandry?
Or who is he so fond will be the tomb
Of his self-love, to stop posterity?
Thou art thy mother's glass, and she in thee
Calls back the lovely April of her prime;
So thou through windows of thine age shalt see,
Despite of wrinkles, this thy golden time.
  But if thou live, remember'd not to be,
  Die single, and thine image dies with thee.

IV

Unthrifty loveliness, why dost thou spend
Upon thyself thy beauty's legacy?
Nature's bequest gives nothing, but doth lend,
And being frank, she lends to those are free:
Then, beauteous niggard, why dost thou abuse
The bounteous largess given thee to give?
Profitless usurer, why dost thou use
So great a sum of sums, yet canst not live?
For having traffic with thyself alone,
Thou of thyself thy sweet self dost deceive:
Then how, when Nature calls thee to be gone,
What acceptable audit canst thou leave?
  Thy unus'd beauty must be tomb'd with thee,
  Which, used, lives th' executor to be.

V

Those hours, that with gentle work did frame
The lovely gaze where every eye doth dwell,
Will play the tyrants to the very same
And that unfair which fairly doth excel;
For never-resting time leads summer on
To hideous winter, and confounds him there;
Sap check'd with frost, and lusty leaves quite gone,
Beauty o'ersnow'd and bareness every where:
Then, were not summer's distillation left,
A liquid prisoner pent in walls of glass,
Beauty's effect with beauty were bereft,
Nor it, nor no remembrance what it was:
　　But flowers distill'd, though they with winter meet,
　　Leese but their show; their substance still lives sweet.

VI

Then let not winter's ragged hand deface
In thee thy summer, ere thou be distill'd:
Make sweet some vial; treasure thou some place
With beauty's treasure, ere it be self-kill'd.
That use is not forbidden usury,
Which happies those that pay the willing loan;
That 's for thyself to breed another thee,
Or ten times happier, be it ten for one;
Ten times thyself were happier than thou art,
If ten of thine ten times refigur'd thee;
Then what could death do, if thou shouldst depart,
Leaving thee living in posterity?
　　Be not self-will'd, for thou art much too fair
　　To be death's conquest and make worms thine heir.

VII

Lo! in the Orient when the gracious light
Lifts up his burning head, each under eye
Doth homage to his new-appearing sight,
Serving with looks his sacred majesty;
And having climb'd the steep-up heavenly hill,
Resembling strong youth in his middle age,
Yet mortal looks adore his beauty still,
Attending on his golden pilgrimage;

But when from highmost pitch, with weary car,
Like feeble age, he reeleth from the day,
The eyes, 'fore duteous, now converted are
From his low tract, and look another way:
  So thou, thyself outgoing in thy noon,
  Unlook'd on diest, unless thou get a son.

VIII

Music to hear, why hear'st thou music sadly?
Sweets with sweets war not, joy delights in joy:
Why lov'st thou that which thou receiv'st not gladly,
Or else receiv'st with pleasure thine annoy?
If the true concord of well-tuned sounds,
By unions married, do offend thine ear,
They do but sweetly chide thee, who confounds
In singleness the parts that thou shouldst bear.
Mark how one string, sweet husband to another,
Strikes each in each by mutual ordering;
Resembling sire and child and happy mother,
Who, all in one, one pleasing note do sing:
  Whose speechless song, being many, seeming one,
  Sings this to thee: 'Thou single wilt prove none.'

IX

Is it for fear to wet a widow's eye
That thou consum'st thyself in single life?
Ah! if thou issueless shalt hap to die,
The world will wail thee, like a makeless wife;
The world will be thy widow, and still weep
That thou no form of thee hast left behind,
When every private widow well may keep
By children's eyes her husband's shape in mind.
Look! what an unthrift in the world doth spend
Shifts but his place, for still the world enjoys it;
But beauty's waste hath in the world an end,
And kept unus'd, the user so destroys it.
  No love toward others in that bosom sits
  That on himself such murderous shame commits.

X

For shame! deny that thou bear'st love to any,
Who for thyself art so unprovident.
Grant, if thou wilt, thou art belov'd of many,
But that thou none lov'st is most evident;
For thou art so possess'd with murderous hate
That 'gainst thyself thou stick'st not to conspire,
Seeking that beauteous roof to ruinate
Which to repair should be thy chief desire.
O! change thy thought, that I may change my mind:
Shall hate be fairer lodg'd than gentle love?
Be, as thy presence is, gracious and kind,
Or to thyself at least kind-hearted prove:
    Make thee another self, for love of me,
    That beauty still may live in thine or thee.

XI

As fast as thou shalt wane, so fast thou grow'st
In one of thine, from that which thou departest;
And that fresh blood which youngly thou bestow'st
Thou mayst call thine when thou from youth convertest.
Herein lives wisdom, beauty and increase;
Without this, folly, age and cold decay:
If all were minded so, the times should cease
And threescore year would make the world away.
Let those whom Nature hath not made for store,
Harsh, featureless, and rude, barrenly perish:
Look, whom she best endow'd she gave the more;
Which bounteous gift thou shouldst in bounty cherish:
    She carv'd thee for her seal, and meant thereby
    Thou shouldst print more, not let that copy die.

XII

When I do count the clock that tells the time,
And see the brave day sunk in hideous night;
When I behold the violet past prime,
And sable curls, all silver'd o'er with white;
When lofty trees I see barren of leaves,
Which erst from heat did canopy the herd,
And summer's green all girded up in sheaves,
Borne on the bier with white and bristly beard,

Then of thy beauty do I question make,
That thou among the wastes of time must go,
Since sweets and beauties do themselves forsake
And die as fast as they see others grow;
    And nothing 'gainst Time's scythe can make defence
    Save breed, to brave him when he takes thee hence.

XIII

O! that you were yourself; but, love, you are
No longer yours than you yourself here live:
Against this coming end you should prepare,
And your sweet semblance to some other give:
So should that beauty which you hold in lease
Find no determination; then you were
Yourself again, after yourself's decease,
When your sweet issue your sweet form should bear.
Who lets so fair a house fall to decay,
Which husbandry in honour might uphold
Against the stormy gusts of winter's day
And barren rage of death's eternal cold?
    O! none but unthrifts. Dear my love, you know
    You had a father: let your son say so.

XIV

Not from the stars do I my judgment pluck;
And yet methinks I have astronomy,
But not to tell of good or evil luck,
Of plagues, of dearths, or seasons' quality;
Nor can I fortune to brief minutes tell,
Pointing to each his thunder, rain, and wind,
Or say with princes if it shall go well,
By oft predict that I in heaven find:
But from thine eyes my knowledge I derive,
And, constant stars, in them I read such art
As 'Truth and beauty shall together thrive,
If from thyself to store thou wouldst convert';
    Or else of thee this I prognosticate:
    'Thy end is truth's and beauty's doom and date.

XV

When I consider every thing that grows
Holds in perfection but a little moment,
That this huge stage presenteth nought but shows
Whereon the stars in secret influence comment;
When I perceive that men as plants increase,
Cheered and check'd even by the self-same sky,
Vaunt in their youthful sap, at height decrease,
And wear their brave state out of memory;
Then the conceit of this inconstant stay
Sets you most rich in youth before my sight,
Where wasteful Time debateth with Decay,
To change your day of youth to sullied night;
 And, all in war with Time for love of you,
 As he takes from you, I engraft you new.

XVI

But wherefore do not you a mightier way
Make war upon this bloody tyrant, Time?
And fortify yourself in your decay
With means more blessed than my barren rime?
Now stand you on the top of happy hours,
And many maiden gardens, yet unset,
With virtuous wish would bear you living flowers,
Much liker than your painted counterfeit:
So should the lines of life that life repair,
Which this, Time's pencil, or my pupil pen,
Neither in inward worth nor outward fair,
Can make you live yourself in eyes of men.
 To give away yourself keeps yourself still;
 And you must live, drawn by your own sweet skill.

XVII

Who will believe my verse in time to come,
If it were fill'd with your most high deserts?
Though yet, heaven knows, it is but as a tomb
Which hides your life and shows not half your parts.
If I could write the beauty of your eyes
And in fresh numbers number all your graces,
The age to come would say 'This poet lies;
Such heavenly touches ne'er touch'd earthly faces.'

So should my papers, yellow'd with their age,
Be scorn'd, like old men of less truth than tongue,
And your true rights be term'd a poet's rage
And stretched metre of an antique song:
    But were some child of yours alive that time,
    You should live twice,—in it and in my rime.

XVIII

Shall I compare thee to a summer's day?
Thou art more lovely and more temperate:
Rough winds do shake the darling buds of May,
And summer's lease hath all too short a date:
Sometime too hot the eye of heaven shines,
And often is his gold complexion dimm'd;
And every fair from fair sometimes declines,
By chance, or nature's changing course untrimm'd;
But thy eternal summer shall not fade,
Nor lose possession of that fair thou ow'st,
Nor shall death brag thou wander'st in his shade,
When in eternal lines to time thou grow'st;
    So long as men can breathe, or eyes can see,
    So long lives this, and this gives life to thee.

XIX

Devouring Time, blunt thou the lion's paws,
And make the earth devour her own sweet brood;
Pluck the keen teeth from the fierce tiger's jaws,
And burn the long-liv'd phœnix in her blood;
Make glad and sorry seasons as thou fleets,
And do whate'er thou wilt, swift-footed Time,
To the wide world and all her fading sweets;
But I forbid thee one most heinous crime:
O! carve not with thy hours my love's fair brow,
Nor draw no lines there with thine antique pen;
Him in thy course untainted do allow
For beauty's pattern to succeeding men.
    Yet, do thy worst, old Time: despite thy wrong,
    My love shall in my verse ever live young.

XX

A woman's face with Nature's own hand painted
Hast thou, the master-mistress of my passion;
A woman's gentle heart, but not acquainted
With shifting change, as is false women's fashion;
An eye more bright than theirs, less false in rolling,
Gilding the object whereupon it gazeth;
A man in hue all 'hues' in his controlling,
Which steals men's eyes and women's souls amazeth.
And for a woman wert thou first created;
Till Nature, as she wrought thee, fell a-doting,
And by addition me of thee defeated,
By adding one thing to my purpose nothing.
    But since she prick'd thee out for women's pleasure,
    Mine be thy love, and thy love's use their treasure.

XXI

So is it not with me as with that Muse
Stirr'd by a painted beauty to his verse,
Who heaven itself for ornament doth use
And every fair with his fair doth rehearse,
Making a couplement of proud compare,
With sun and moon, with earth and sea's rich gems,
With April's first-born flowers, and all things rare
That heaven's air in this huge rondure hems.
O! let me, true in love, but truly write,
And then believe me, my love is as fair
As any mother's child, though not so bright
As those gold candles fix'd in heaven's air:
    Let them say more that like of hear-say well;
    I will not praise that purpose not to sell.

XXII

My glass shall not persuade me I am old,
So long as youth and thou are of one date;
But when in thee time's furrows I behold,
Then look I death my days should expiate.
For all that beauty that doth cover thee
Is but the seemly raiment of my heart,
Which in thy breast doth live, as thine in me:
How can I then be elder than thou art?

O! therefore, love, be of thyself so wary
As I, not for myself, but for thee will;
Bearing thy heart, which I will keep so chary
As tender nurse her babe from faring ill.
   Presume not on thy heart when mine is slain;
   Thou gav'st me thine, not to give back again.

XXIII

As an unperfect actor on the stage,
Who with his fear is put besides his part,
Or some fierce thing replete with too much rage,
Whose strength's abundance weakens his own heart;
So I, for fear of trust, forget to say
The perfect ceremony of love's rite,
And in mine own love's strength seem to decay,
O'ercharg'd with burthen of mine own love's might.
O! let my books be then the eloquence
And dumb presagers of my speaking breast,
Who plead for love, and look for recompense,
More than that tongue that more hath more express'd.
   O! learn to read what silent love hath writ:
   To hear with eyes belongs to love's fine wit.

XXIV

Mine eye hath play'd the painter and hath stell'd
Thy beauty's form in table of my heart;
My body is the frame wherein 'tis held,
And perspective it is best painter's art.
For through the painter must you see his skill,
To find where your true image pictur'd lies,
Which in my bosom's shop is hanging still,
That hath his windows glazed with thine eyes.
Now see what good turns eyes for eyes have done:
Mine eyes have drawn thy shape, and thine for me
Are windows to my breast, where-through the sun
Delights to peep, to gaze therein on thee;
   Yet eyes this cunning want to grace their art,
   They draw but what they see, know not the heart.

XXV

Let those who are in favour with their stars
Of public honour and proud titles boast,
Whilst I, whom fortune of such triumph bars
Unlook'd for joy in that I honour most.
Great princes' favourites their fair leaves spread
But as the marigold at the sun's eye,
And in themselves their pride lies buried,
For at a frown they in their glory die.
The painful warrior famoused for fight,
After a thousand victories once foil'd,
Is from the book of honour razed quite,
And all the rest forgot for which he toil'd:
    Then happy I, that love and am belov'd,
    Where I may not remove nor be remov'd.

XXVI

Lord of my love, to whom in vassalage
Thy merit hath my duty strongly knit,
To thee I send this written ambassage,
To witness duty, not to show my wit:
Duty so great, which wit so poor as mine
May make seem bare, in wanting words to show it,
But that I hope some good conceit of thine
In thy soul's thought, all naked, will bestow it;
Till whatsoever star that guides my moving,
Points on me graciously with fair aspect,
And puts apparel on my tatter'd loving,
To show me worthy of thy sweet respect:
    Then may I dare to boast how I do love thee;
    Till then not show my head where thou mayst prove
    me.

XXVII

Weary with toil, I haste me to my bed,
The dear repose for limbs with travel tir'd;
But then begins a journey in my head
To work my mind, when body's work 's expir'd:
For then my thoughts—from far where I abide—
Intend a zealous pilgrimage to thee,
And keep my drooping eyelids open wide,
Looking on darkness which the blind do see:

Save that my soul's imaginary sight
Presents thy shadow to my sightless view,
Which, like a jewel hung in ghastly night,
Makes black night beauteous and her old face new.
    Lo! thus, by day my limbs, by night my mind,
    For thee, and for myself no quiet find.

XXVIII

How can I then return in happy plight,
That am debarr'd the benefit of rest?
When day's oppression is not eas'd by night,
But day by night and night by day oppress'd,
And each, though enemies to either's reign,
Do in consent shake hands to torture me,
The one by toil, the other to complain
How far I toil, still farther off from thee.
I tell the day, to please him thou art bright,
And dost him grace when clouds do blot the heaven:
So flatter I the swart-complexion'd night;
When sparkling stars twire not thou gild'st the even.
    But day doth daily draw my sorrows longer,
    And night doth nightly make grief's strength seem
       stronger.

XXIX

When in disgrace with fortune and men's eyes
I all alone beweep my outcast state,
And trouble deaf heaven with my bootless cries,
And look upon myself, and curse my fate,
Wishing me like to one more rich in hope,
Featur'd like him, like him with friends possess'd,
Desiring this man's art, and that man's scope,
With what I most enjoy contented least;
Yet in these thoughts myself almost despising,
Haply I think on thee,—and then my state,
Like to the lark at break of day arising
From sullen earth, sings hymns at heaven's gate;
    For thy sweet love remember'd such wealth brings
    That then I scorn to change my state with kings.

XXX

When to the sessions of sweet silent thought
I summon up remembrance of things past,
I sigh the lack of many a thing I sought,
And with old woes new wail my dear times' waste:
Then can I drown an eye, unus'd to flow,
For precious friends hid in death's dateless night,
And weep afresh love's long since cancell'd woe,
And moan the expense of many a vanish'd sight:
Then can I grieve at grievances foregone,
And heavily from woe to woe tell o'er
The sad account of fore-bemoaned moan,
Which I new pay as if not paid before.
   But if the while I think on thee, dear friend,
   All losses are restor'd and sorrows end.

XXXI

Thy bosom is endeared with all hearts,
Which I by lacking have supposed dead;
And there reigns Love, and all Love's loving parts,
And all those friends which I thought buried.
How many a holy and obsequious tear
Hath dear religious love stol'n from mine eye,
As interest of the dead, which now appear
But things remov'd that hidden in thee lie!
Thou art the grave where buried love doth live,
Hung with the trophies of my lovers gone,
Who all their parts of me to thee did give,
That due of many now is thine alone:
   Their images I lov'd I view in thee,
   And thou—all they—hast all the all of me.

XXXII

If thou survive my well-contented day,
When that churl Death my bones with dust shall cover,
And shalt by fortune once more re-survey
These poor rude lines of thy deceased lover,
Compare them with the bettering of the time,
And though they be outstripp'd by every pen,
Reserve them for my love, not for their rime,
Exceeded by the height of happier men.

O! then vouchsafe me but this loving thought:
'Had my friend's Muse grown with this growing age,
A dearer birth than this his love had brought,
To march in ranks of better equipage:
   But since he died, and poets better prove,
   Theirs for their style I 'll read, his for his love.'

XXXIII

Full many a glorious morning have I seen
Flatter the mountain-tops with sovereign eye,
Kissing with golden face the meadows green,
Gilding pale streams with heavenly alchemy;
Anon permit the basest clouds to ride
With ugly rack on his celestial face,
And from the forlorn world his visage hide,
Stealing unseen to west with this disgrace:
Even so my sun one early morn did shine,
With all-triumphant splendour on my brow;
But out! alack! he was but one hour mine,
The region cloud hath mask'd him from me now.
   Yet him for this my love no whit disdaineth;
   Suns of the world may stain when heaven's sun stain-
    eth.

XXXIV

Why didst thou promise such a beauteous day,
And make me travel forth without my cloak,
To let base clouds o'ertake me in my way,
Hiding thy bravery in their rotten smoke?
'Tis not enough that through the cloud thou break,
To dry the rain on my storm-beaten face,
For no man well of such a salve can speak
That heals the wound and cures not the disgrace:
Nor can thy shame give physic to my grief;
Though thou repent, yet I have still the loss:
The offender's sorrow lends but weak relief
To him that bears the strong offence's cross.
   Ah! but those tears are pearl which thy love sheds,
   And they are rich and ransom all ill deeds.

XXXV

No more be griev'd at that which thou hast done:
Roses have thorns, and silver fountains mud;
Clouds and eclipses stain both moon and sun,
And loathsome canker lives in sweetest bud.
All men make faults, and even I in this,
Authorizing thy trespass with compare,
Myself corrupting, salving thy amiss,
Excusing thy sins more than thy sins are;
For to thy sensual fault I bring in sense,—
Thy adverse party is thy advocate,—
And 'gainst myself a lawful plea commence:
Such civil war is in my love and hate,
 That I an accessary needs must be
 To that sweet thief which sourly robs from me.

XXXVI

Let me confess that we two must be twain,
Although our undivided loves are one:
So shall those blots that do with me remain,
Without thy help, by me be borne alone.
In our two loves there is but one respect,
Though in our lives a separable spite,
Which, though it alter not love's sole effect,
Yet doth it steal sweet hours from love's delight.
I may not evermore acknowledge thee,
Lest my bewailed guilt should do thee shame,
Nor thou with public kindness honour me,
Unless thou take that honour from thy name:
 But do not so; I love thee in such sort
 As thou being mine, mine is thy good report.

XXXVII

As a decrepit father takes delight
To see his active child do deeds of youth,
So I, made lame by fortune's dearest spite,
Take all my comfort of thy worth and truth;
For whether beauty, birth, or wealth, or wit,
Or any of these all, or all, or more,
Entitled in thy parts do crowned sit,
I make my love engrafted to this store:

So then I am not lame, poor, nor despis'd,
Whilst that this shadow doth such substance give
That I in thy abundance am suffic'd
And by a part of all thy glory live.
  Look what is best, that best I wish in thee:
  This wish I have; then ten times happy me!

XXXVIII

How can my Muse want subject to invent,
While thou dost breathe, that pour'st into my verse
Thine own sweet argument, too excellent
For every vulgar paper to rehearse?
O! give thyself the thanks, if aught in me
Worthy perusal stand against thy sight;
For who's so dumb that cannot write to thee,
When thou thyself dost give invention light?
Be thou the tenth Muse, ten times more in worth
Than those old nine which rimers invocate;
And he that calls on thee, let him bring forth
Eternal numbers to outlive long date.
  If my slight Muse do please these curious days,
  The pain be mine, but thine shall be the praise.

XXXIX

O! how thy worth with manners may I sing,
When thou art all the better part of me?
What can mine own praise to mine own self bring?
And what is 't but mine own when I praise thee?
Even for this let us divided live,
And our dear love lose name of single one,
That by this separation I may give
That due to thee, which thou deserv'st alone.
O absence! what a torment wouldst thou prove,
Were it not thy sour leisure gave sweet leave
To entertain the time with thoughts of love,
Which time and thoughts so sweetly doth deceive,
  And that thou teachest how to make one twain,
  By praising him here who doth hence remain.

XL

Take all my loves, my love, yea, take them all;
What hast thou then more than thou hadst before?
No love, my love, that thou mayst true love call;
All mine was thine before thou hadst this more.
Then, if for my love thou my love receivest,
I cannot blame thee for my love thou usest;
But yet be blam'd, if thou thyself deceivest
By wilful taste of what thyself refusest.
I do forgive thy robbery, gentle thief,
Although thou steal thee all my poverty:
And yet, love knows it is a greater grief
To bear love's wrong than hate's known injury.
   Lascivious grace, in whom all ill well shows,
   Kill me with spites; yet we must not be foes.

XLI

Those pretty wrongs that liberty commits,
When I am sometime absent from thy heart,
Thy beauty and thy years full well befits,
For still temptation follows where thou art.
Gentle thou art, and therefore to be won,
Beauteous thou art, therefore to be assail'd;
And when a woman woos, what woman's son
Will sourly leave her till she have prevail'd?
Ay me! but yet thou mightst my seat forbear,
And chide thy beauty and thy straying youth,
Who lead thee in their riot even there
Where thou art forc'd to break a twofold truth;—
   Hers, by thy beauty tempting her to thee,
   Thine, by thy beauty being false to me.

XLII

That thou hast her, it is not all my grief,
And yet it may be said I lov'd her dearly;
That she hath thee, is of my wailing chief,
A loss in love that touches me more nearly.
Loving offenders, thus I will excuse ye:
Thou dost love her, because thou know'st I love her;
And for my sake even so doth she abuse me,
Suffering my friend for my sake to approve her.

If I lose thee, my loss is my love's gain,
And losing her, my friend hath found that loss;
Both find each other, and I lose both twain,
And both for my sake lay on me this cross:
    But here 's the joy; my friend and I are one;
    Sweet flattery! then she loves but me alone.

XLIII

When most I wink, then do mine eyes best see,
For all the day they view things unrespected;
But when I sleep, in dreams they look on thee,
And darkly bright, are bright in dark directed.
Then thou, whose shadow shadows doth make bright,
How would thy shadow's form form happy show
To the clear day with thy much clearer light,
When to unseeing eyes thy shade shines so!
How would, I say, mine eyes be blessed made
By looking on thee in the living day,
When in dead night thy fair imperfect shade
Through heavy sleep on sightless eyes doth stay!
    All days are nights to see till I see thee,
    And nights bright days when dreams do show thee me.

XLIV

If the dull substance of my flesh were thought,
Injurious distance should not stop my way;
For then, despite of space, I would be brought,
From limits far remote, where thou dost stay.
No matter then although my foot did stand
Upon the farthest earth remov'd from thee;
For nimble thought can jump both sea and land,
As soon as think the place where he would be.
But, ah! thought kills me that I am not thought,
To leap large lengths of miles when thou art gone,
But that, so much of earth and water wrought,
I must attend time's leisure with my moan;
    Receiving nought by elements so slow
    But heavy tears, badges of either's woe.

XLV

The other two, slight air and purging fire
Are both with thee, wherever I abide;
The first my thought, the other my desire
These present-absent with swift motion slide.
For when these quicker elements are gone
In tender embassy of love to thee,
My life, being made of four, with two alone
Sinks down to death, oppress'd with melancholy;
Until life's composition be recur'd
By those swift messengers return'd from thee,
Who even but now come back again, assur'd
Of thy fair health, recounting it to me:
    This told, I joy; but then no longer glad,
    I send them back again, and straight grow sad.

XLVI

Mine eye and heart are at a mortal war,
How to divide the conquest of thy sight;
Mine eye my heart thy picture's sight would bar,
My heart mine eye the freedom of that right.
My heart doth plead that thou in him dost lie,—
A closet never pierc'd with crystal eyes,—
But the defendant doth that plea deny,
And says in him thy fair appearance lies.
To 'cide this title is impannelled
A quest of thoughts, all tenants to the heart;
And by their verdict is determined
The clear eye's moiety and the dear heart's part:
    As thus; mine eye's due is thine outward part,
    And my heart's right thine inward love of heart.

XLVII

Betwixt mine eye and heart a league is took,
And each doth good turns now unto the other:
When that mine eye is famish'd for a look,
Or heart in love with sighs himself doth smother,
With my love's picture then my eye doth feast,
And to the painted banquet bids my heart;
Another time mine eye is my heart's guest,
And in his thoughts of love doth share a part:

So, either by thy picture or my love,
Thyself away art present still with me;
For thou not farther than my thoughts canst move,
And I am still with them and they with thee;
    Or, if they sleep, thy picture in my sight
    Awakes my heart to heart's and eye's delight.

XLVIII

How careful was I when I took my way,
Each trifle under truest bars to thrust,
That to my use it might unused stay
From hands of falsehood, in sure wards of trust!
But thou, to whom my jewels trifles are,
Most worthy comfort, now my greatest grief,
Thou, best of dearest and mine only care,
Art left the prey of every vulgar thief.
Thee have I not lock'd up in any chest,
Save where thou art not, though I feel thou art,
Within the gentle closure of my breast,
From whence at pleasure thou mayst come and part;
    And even thence thou wilt be stol'n, I fear,
    For truth proves thievish for a prize so dear.

XLIX

Against that time, if ever that time come,
When I shall see thee frown on my defects,
When as thy love hath cast his utmost sum,
Call'd to that audit by advis'd respects;
Against that time when thou shalt strangely pass,
And scarcely greet me with that sun, thine eye,
When love, converted from the thing it was,
Shall reasons find of settled gravity;
Against that time do I ensconce me here
Within the knowledge of mine own desert,
And this my hand against myself uprear,
To guard the lawful reasons on thy part:
    To leave poor me thou hast the strength of laws,
    Since why to love I can allege no cause.

L

How heavy do I journey on the way,
When what I seek, my weary travel's end,
Doth teach that ease and that repose to say,
'Thus far the miles are measur'd from thy friend!'
The beast that bears me, tired with my woe,
Plods dully on, to bear that weight in me,
As if by some instinct the wretch did know
His rider lov'd not speed, being made from thee:
The bloody spur cannot provoke him on
That sometimes anger thrusts into his hide,
Which heavily he answers with a groan,
More sharp to me than spurring to his side;
 For that same groan doth put this in my mind:
 My grief lies onward, and my joy behind.

LI

Thus can my love excuse the slow offence
Of my dull bearer when from thee I speed:
From where thou art why should I haste me thence?
Till I return, of posting is no need.
O! what excuse will my poor beast then find,
When swift extremity can seem but slow?
Then should I spur, though mounted on the wind,
In winged speed no motion shall I know:
Then can no horse with my desire keep pace;
Therefore desire, of perfect'st love being made,
Shall neigh—no dull flesh—in his fiery race;
But love, for love, thus shall excuse my jade,—
 'Since from thee going he went wilful-slow,
 Towards thee I 'll run and give him leave to go.'

LII

So am I as the rich, whose blessed key
Can bring him to his sweet up-locked treasure,
The which he will not every hour survey,
For blunting the fine point of seldom pleasure.
Therefore are feasts so solemn and so rare,
Since, seldom coming, in the long year set,
Like stones of worth they thinly placed are,
Or captain jewels in the carconet.

So is the time that keeps you as my chest,
Or as the wardrobe which the robe doth hide,
To make some special instant special blest,
By new unfolding his imprison'd pride.
   Blessed are you, whose worthiness gives scope,
   Being had, to triumph; being lack'd, to hope.

LIII

What is your substance, whereof are you made,
That millions of strange shadows on you tend?
Since every one hath, every one, one shade,
And you, but one, can every shadow lend.
Describe Adonis, and the counterfeit
Is poorly imitated after you;
On Helen's cheek all art of beauty set,
And you in Grecian tires are painted new:
Speak of the spring and foison of the year,
The one doth shadow of your beauty show,
The other as your bounty doth appear;
And you in every blessed shape we know.
   In all external grace you have some part,
   But you like none, none you, for constant heart.

LIV

O! how much more doth beauty beauteous seem
By that sweet ornament which truth doth give.
The rose looks fair, but fairer we it deem
For that sweet odour which doth in it live.
The canker-blooms have full as deep a dye
As the perfumed tincture of the roses.
Hang on such thorns, and play as wantonly
When summer's breath their masked buds discloses:
But, for their virtue only is their show,
They live unwoo'd, and unrespected fade,
Die to themselves. Sweet roses do not so;
Of their sweet deaths are sweetest odours made:
   And so of you, beauteous and lovely youth,
   When that shall vade, my verse distils your truth.

LV

Not marble, nor the gilded monuments
Of princes, shall outlive this powerful rime;
But you shall shine more bright in these contents
Than unswept stone, besmear'd with sluttish time.
When wasteful war shall statues overturn,
And broils root out the work of masonry,
Nor Mars his sword nor war's quick fire shall burn
The living record of your memory.
'Gainst death and all-oblivious enmity
Shall you pace forth; your praise shall still find room
Even in the eyes of all posterity
That wear this world out to the ending doom.
 So, till the judgment that yourself arise,
 You live in this, and dwell in lovers' eyes.

LVI

Sweet love, renew thy force; be it not said
Thy edge should blunter be than appetite,
Which but to-day by feeding is allay'd,
To-morrow sharpen'd in his former might:
So, love, be thou; although to-day thou fill
Thy hungry eyes, even till they wink with fulness,
To-morrow see again, and do not kill
The spirit of love with a perpetual dulness.
Let this sad interim like the ocean be
Which parts the shore, where two contracted new
Come daily to the banks, that, when they see
Return of love, more blest may be the view;
 Or call it winter, which, being full of care,
 Makes summer's welcome thrice more wish'd, more
  rare.

LVII

Being your slave, what should I do but tend
Upon the hours and times of your desire?
I have no precious time at all to spend,
Nor services to do, till you require.
Nor dare I chide the world-without-end hour
Whilst I, my sovereign, watch the clock for you,
Nor think the bitterness of absence sour
When you have bid your servant once adieu;

Nor dare I question with my jealous thought
Where you may be, or your affairs suppose,
But, like a sad slave, stay and think of nought
Save, where you are how happy you make those.
　　So true a fool is love that in your will,
　　Though you do any thing, he thinks no ill.

LVIII

That god forbid that made me first your slave,
I should in thought control your times of pleasure,
Or at your hand the account of hours to crave,
Being your vassal, bound to stay your leisure!
O! let me suffer, being at your beck,
The imprison'd absence of your liberty;
And patience, tame to sufferance, bide each check,
Without accusing you of injury.
Be where you list, your charter is so strong
That you yourself may privilege your time
To what you will; to you it doth belong
Yourself to pardon of self-doing crime.
　　I am to wait, though waiting so be hell,
　　Not blame your pleasure, be it ill or well.

LIX

If there be nothing new, but that which is
Hath been before, how are our brains beguil'd,
Which, labouring for invention, bear amiss
The second burthen of a former child!
O! that record could with a backward look,
Even of five hundred courses of the sun,
Show me your image in some antique book,
Since mind at first in character was done!
That I might see what the old world could say
To this composed wonder of your frame;
Whe'r we are mended, or whe'r better they,
Or whether revolution be the same.
　　O! sure I am, the wits of former days
　　To subjects worse have given admiring praise.

LX

Like as the waves make towards the pebbled shore,
So do our minutes hasten to their end;
Each changing place with that which goes before,
In sequent toil all forwards do contend.
Nativity, once in the main of light,
Crawls to maturity, wherewith being crown'd,
Crooked eclipses 'gainst his glory fight,
And Time that gave doth now his gift confound.
Time doth transfix the flourish set on youth
And delves the parallels in beauty's brow,
Feeds on the rarities of nature's truth,
And nothing stands but for his scythe to mow:
   .And yet to times in hope my verse shall stand,
    Praising thy worth, despite his cruel hand.

LXI

Is it thy will thy image should keep open
My heavy eyelids to the weary night?
Dost thou desire my slumbers should be broken,
While shadows, like to thee, do mock my sight?
Is it thy spirit that thou send'st from thee
So far from home, into my deeds to pry,
To find out shames and idle hours in me,
The scope and tenour of thy jealousy?
O, no! thy love, though much, is not so great:
It is my love that keeps mine eye awake;
Mine own true love that doth my rest defeat,
To play the watchman ever for thy sake:
    For thee watch I whilst thou dost wake elsewhere,
    From me far off, with others all too near.

LXII

Sin of self-love possesseth all mine eye
And all my soul and all my every part;
And for this sin there is no remedy,
It is so grounded inward in my heart.
Methinks no face so gracious is as mine,
No shape so true, no truth of such account;
And for myself mine own worth do define,
As I all other in all worths surmount.

But when my glass shows me myself indeed,
Beated and chopp'd with tann'd antiquity,
Mine own self-love quite contrary I read;
Self so self-loving were iniquity.
 'Tis thee,—myself,—that for myself I praise,
 Painting my age with beauty of thy days.

LXIII

Against my love shall be, as I am now,
With Time's injurious hand crush'd and o'erworn;
When hours have drain'd his blood and fill'd his brow
With lines and wrinkles; when his youthful morn
Hath travell'd on to age's steepy night;
And all those beauties whereof now he 's king
Are vanishing or vanish'd out of sight,
Stealing away the treasure of his spring;
For such a time do I now fortify
Against confounding age's cruel knife,
That he shall never cut from memory
My sweet love's beauty, though my lover's life:
 His beauty shall in these black lines be seen,
 And they shall live, and he in them still green.

LXIV

When I have seen by Time's fell hand defac'd
The rich-proud cost of outworn buried age;
When sometime lofty towers I see down-raz'd,
And brass eternal slave to mortal rage;
When I have seen the hungry ocean gain
Advantage on the kingdom of the shore,
And the firm soil win of the watery main,
Increasing store with loss, and loss with store;
When I have seen such interchange of state,
Or state itself confounded to decay;
Ruin hath taught me thus to ruminate—
That time will come and take my love away.
 This thought is as a death, which cannot choose
 But weep to have that which it fears to lose.

LXV

Since brass, nor stone, nor earth, nor boundless sea,
But sad mortality o'ersways their power,
How with this rage shall beauty hold a plea,
Whose action is no stronger than a flower?
O! how shall summer's honey breath hold out
Against the wrackful siege of battering days,
When rocks impregnable are not so stout,
Nor gates of steel so strong, but Time decays?
O fearful meditation! where, alack,
Shall time's best jewel from Time's chest lie hid?
Or what strong hand can hold his swift foot back?
Or who his spoil of beauty can forbid?
    O! none, unless this miracle have might,
    That in black ink my love may still shine bright.

LXVI

Tir'd with all these, for restful death I cry,
As to behold desert a beggar born,
And needy nothing trimm'd in jollity,
And purest faith unhappily forsworn,
And gilded honour shamefully misplac'd,
And maiden virtue rudely strumpeted,
And right perfection wrongfully disgrac'd,
And strength by limping sway disabled,
And art made tongue-tied by authority,
And folly—doctor-like—controlling skill,
And simple truth miscall'd simplicity,
And captive good attending captain ill:
    Tir'd with all these, from these would I be gone,
    Save that, to die, I leave my love alone.

LXVII

Ah! wherefore with infection should he live,
And with his presence grace impiety,
That sin by him advantage should achieve,
And lace itself with his society?
Why should false painting imitate his cheek,
And steel dead seeing of his living hue?
Why should poor beauty indirectly seek
Roses of shadow, since his rose is true?

Why should he live, now Nature bankrupt is,
Beggar'd of blood to blush through lively veins?
For she hath no exchequer now but his,
And, proud of many, lives upon his gains.
    O! him she stores, to show what wealth she had
    In days long since, before these last so bad.

LXVIII

Thus is his cheek the map of days outworn,
When beauty liv'd and died as flowers do now,
Before these bastard signs of fair were born,
Or durst inhabit on a living brow;
Before the golden tresses of the dead,
The right of sepulchres, were shorn away,
To live a second life on second head;
Ere beauty's dead fleece made another gay:
In him those holy antique hours are seen,
Without all ornament, itself and true,
Making no summer of another's green,
Robbing no old to dress his beauty new;
    And him as for a map doth Nature store,
    To show false Art what beauty was of yore.

LXIX

Those parts of thee that the world's eye doth view
Want nothing that the thought of hearts can mend;
All tongues—the voice of souls—give thee that due,
Uttering bare truth, even so as foes commend.
Thy outward thus with outward praise is crown'd;
But those same tongues, that give thee so thine own,
In other accents do this praise confound
By seeing farther than the eye hath shown.
They look into the beauty of thy mind,
And that, in guess, they measure by thy deeds;
Then,—churls,—their thoughts, although their eyes were
        kind,
To thy fair flower add the rank smell of weeds:
    But why thy odour matcheth not thy show,
    The soil is this, that thou dost common grow.

LXX

That thou art blam'd shall not be thy defect,
For slander's mark was ever yet the fair;
The ornament of beauty is suspect,
A crow that flies in heaven's sweetest air.
So thou be good, slander doth but approve
Thy worth the greater, being woo'd of time;
For canker vice the sweetest buds doth love,
And thou present'st a pure unstained prime.
Thou hast pass'd by the ambush of young days
Either not assail'd, or victor being charg'd;
Yet this thy praise cannot be so thy praise,
To tie up envy evermore enlarg'd:
   If some suspect of ill mask'd not thy show,
   Then thou alone kingdoms of hearts shouldst owe.

LXXI

No longer mourn for me when I am dead
Than you shall hear the surly sullen bell
Give warning to the world that I am fled
From this vile world, with vilest worms to dwell:
Nay, if you read this line, remember not
The hand that writ it; for I love you so,
That I in your sweet thoughts would be forgot,
If thinking on me then should make you woe.
O! if,—I say, you look upon this verse,
When I perhaps compounded am with clay,
Do not so much as my poor name rehearse,
But let your love even with my life decay;
   Lest the wise world should look into your moan,
   And mock you with me after I am gone.

LXXII

O! lest the world should task you to recite
What merit lived in me, that you should love
After my death,—dear love, forget me quite,
For you in me can nothing worthy prove;
Unless you would devise some virtuous lie,
To do more for me than mine own desert,
And hang more praise upon deceased I
Than niggard truth would willingly impart:

O! lest your true love may seem false in this
That you for love speak well of me untrue,
My name be buried where my body is,
And live no more to shame nor me nor you.
    For I am sham'd by that which I bring forth,
    And so should you, to love things nothing worth.

LXXIII

That time of year thou mayst in me behold
When yellow leaves, or none, or few, do hang
Upon those boughs which shake against the cold,
Bare ruin'd choirs, where late the sweet birds sang.
In me thou see'st the twilight of such day
As after sunset fadeth in the West;
Which by and by black night doth take away,
Death's second self, that seals up all in rest.
In me thou see'st the glowing of such fire,
That on the ashes of his youth doth lie,
As the death-bed whereon it must expire,
Consum'd with that which it was nourish'd by.
    This thou perceiv'st, which makes thy love more strong,
    To love that well which thou must leave ere long.

LXXIV

But be contented: when that fell arrest
Without all bail shall carry me away,
My life hath in this line some interest,
Which for memorial still with thee shall stay.
When thou reviewest this, thou dost review
The very part was consecrate to thee:
The earth can have but earth, which is his due;
My spirit is thine, the better part of me:
So then thou hast but lost the dregs of life,
The prey of worms, my body being dead;
The coward conquest of a wretch's knife,
Too base of thee to be remembered.
    The worth of that is that which it contains,
    And that is this, and this with thee remains.

LXXV

So are you to my thoughts as food to life,
Or as sweet-season'd showers are to the ground;
And for the peace of you I hold such strife
As 'twixt a miser and his wealth is found;
Now proud as an enjoyer, and anon
Doubting the filching age will steal his treasure;
Now counting best to be with you alone,
Then better'd that the world may see my pleasure:
Sometime at full with feasting on your sight,
And by and by clean starved for a look;
Possessing or pursuing no delight,
Save what is had or must from you be took.
    Thus do I pine and surfeit day by day,
     Or gluttoning on all, or all away.

LXXVI

Why is my verse so barren of new pride,
So far from variation or quick change?
Why with the time do I not glance aside
To new-found methods and to compounds strange?
Why write I still all one, ever the same,
And keep invention in a noted weed,
That every word doth almost tell my name,
Showing their birth, and where they did proceed?
O! know, sweet love, I always write of you,
And you and love are still my argument;
So all my best is dressing old words new,
Spending again what is already spent:
    For as the sun is daily new and old,
     So is my love still telling what is told.

LXXVII

Thy glass will show thee how thy beauties wear,
Thy dial how thy precious minutes waste;
The vacant leaves thy mind's imprint will bear,
And of this book this learning mayst thou taste.
The wrinkles which thy glass will truly show
Of mouthed graves will give thee memory;
Thou by thy dial's shady stealth mayst know
Time's thievish progress to eternity.

Look! what thy memory cannot contain,
Commit to these waste blanks, and thou shalt find
Those children nursed, deliver'd from thy brain,
To take a new acquaintance of thy mind.
   These offices, so oft as thou wilt look,
    Shall profit thee and much enrich thy book.

LXXVIII

So oft have I invok'd thee for my Muse
And found such fair assistance in my verse
As every alien pen hath got my use
And under thee their poesy disperse.
Thine eyes, that taught the dumb on high to sing
And heavy ignorance aloft to fly,
Have added feathers to the learned's wing
And given grace a double majesty.
Yet be most proud of that which I compile,
Whose influence is thine, and born of thee:
In others' works thou dost but mend the style,
And arts with thy sweet graces graced be;
   But thou art all my art, and dost advance
    As high as learning my rude ignorance.

LXXIX

Whilst I alone did call upon thy aid,
My verse alone had all thy gentle grace;
But now my gracious numbers are decay'd,
And my sick Muse doth give another place.
I grant, sweet love, thy lovely argument
Deserves the travail of a worthier pen;
Yet what of thee thy poet doth invent
He robs thee of, and pays it thee again.
He lends thee virtue, and he stole that word
From thy behaviour; beauty doth he give,
And found it in thy cheek: he can afford
No praise to thee but what in thee doth live.
   Then thank him not for that which he doth say,
    Since what he owes thee thou thyself dost pay.

LXXX

O! how I faint when I of you do write,
Knowing a better spirit doth use your name,
And in the praise thereof spends all his might,
To make me tongue-tied, speaking of your fame!
But since your worth—wide as the ocean is,—
The humble as the proudest sail doth bear,
My saucy bark, inferior far to his,
On your broad main doth wilfully appear.
Your shallowest help will hold me up afloat,
Whilst he upon your soundless deep doth ride;
Or, being wrack'd, I am a worthless boat,
He of tall building and of goodly pride:
    Then if he thrive and I be cast away,
    The worst was this,—my love was my decay.

LXXXI

Or I shall live your epitaph to make,
Or you survive when I in earth am rotten;
From hence your memory death cannot take,
Although in me each part will be forgotten.
Your name from hence immortal life shall have,
Though I, once gone, to all the world must die:
The earth can yield me but a common grave,
When you entombed in men's eyes shall lie.
Your monument shall be my gentle verse,
Which eyes not yet created shall o'er-read;
And tongues to be your being shall rehearse,
When all the breathers of this world are dead;
    You still shall live,—such virtue hath my pen,—
    Where breath most breathes, even in the mouths of
      men.

LXXXII

I grant thou wert not married to my Muse,
And therefore mayst without attaint o'erlook
The dedicated words which writers use
Of their fair subject, blessing every book.
Thou art as fair in knowledge as in hue,
Finding thy worth a limit past my praise;
And therefore art enforc'd to seek anew
Some fresher stamp of the time-bettering days.

And do so, love; yet when they have devis'd
What strained touches rhetoric can lend,
Thou truly fair wert truly sympathiz'd
In true plain words by thy true-telling friend;
   And their gross painting might be better us'd
   Where cheeks need blood; in thee it is abus'd.

LXXXIII

I never saw that you did painting need,
And therefore to your fair no painting set;
I found, or thought I found, you did exceed
The barren tender of a poet's debt:
And therefore have I slept in your report,
That you yourself, being extant, well might show
How far a modern quill doth come too short,
Speaking of worth, what worth in you doth grow.
This silence for my sin you did impute,
Which shall be most my glory, being dumb;
For I impair not beauty being mute,
When others would give life, and bring a tomb.
   There lives more life in one of your fair eyes
   Than both your poets can in praise devise.

LXXXIV

Who is it that says most? which can say more
Than this rich praise,—that you alone are you?
In whose confine immured is the store
Which should example where your equal grew.
Lean penury within that pen doth dwell
That to his subject lends not some small glory;
But he that writes of you, if he can tell
That you are you, so dignifies his story,
Let him but copy what in you is writ,
Not making worse what nature made so clear,
And such a counterpart shall fame his wit,
Making his style admired every where.
   You to your beauteous blessings add a curse,
   Being fond on praise, which makes your praises worse.

LXXXV

My tongue-tied Muse in manners holds her still,
While comments of your praise, richly compil'd,
Reserve their character with golden quill,
And precious phrase by all the Muses fil'd.
I think good thoughts, whilst others write good words,
And, like unletter'd clerk, still cry 'Amen'
To every hymn that able spirit affords,
In polish'd form of well-refinéd pen.
Hearing you prais'd, I say, ' 'Tis so, 'tis true,'
And to the most of praise add something more;
But that is in my thought, whose love to you,
Though words come hindmost, holds his rank before.
　　Then others for the breath of words respect,
　　Me for my dumb thoughts, speaking in effect.

LXXXVI

Was it the proud full sail of his great verse,
Bound for the prize of all too precious you,
That did my ripe thoughts in my brain inhearse,
Making their tomb the womb wherein they grew?
Was it his spirit, by spirits taught to write
Above a mortal pitch, that struck me dead?
No, neither he, nor his compeers by night
Giving him aid, my verse astonished.
He, nor that affable familiar ghost
Which nightly gulls him with intelligence,
As victors of my silence cannot boast;
I was not sick of any fear from thence:
　　But when your countenance fill'd up his line,
　　Then lack'd I matter; that enfeebled mine.

LXXXVII

Farewell! thou art too dear for my possessing,
And like enough thou know'st thy estimate:
The charter of thy worth gives thee releasing;
My bonds in thee are all determinate.
For how do I hold thee but by thy granting?
And for that riches where is my deserving?
The cause of this fair gift in me is wanting,
And so my patent back again is swerving.

Thyself thou gav'st, thy own worth then not knowing,
Or me, to whom thou gav'st it, else mistaking;
So thy great gift, upon misprision growing,
Comes home again, on better judgment making.
   Thus have I had thee, as a dream doth flatter,
   In sleep a king, but, waking, no such matter.

LXXXVIII

When thou shalt be dispos'd to set me light,
And place my merit in the eye of scorn,
Upon thy side against myself I'll fight,
And prove thee virtuous, though thou art forsworn.
With mine own weakness, being best acquainted,
Upon thy part I can set down a story
Of faults conceal'd, wherein I am attainted;
That thou in losing me shalt win much glory:
And I by this will be a gainer too;
For bending all my loving thoughts on thee,
The injuries that to myself I do,
Doing thee vantage, double-vantage me.
   Such is my love, to thee I so belong,
   That for thy right myself will bear all wrong.

LXXXIX

Say that thou didst forsake me for some fault,
And I will comment upon that offence:
Speak of my lameness, and I straight will halt,
Against thy reasons making no defence.
Thou canst not, love, disgrace me half so ill,
To set a form upon desired change,
As I'll myself disgrace; knowing thy will,
I will acquaintance strangle, and look strange;
Be absent from thy walks; and in my tongue
Thy sweet beloved name no more shall dwell,
Lest I, too much profane, should do it wrong,
And haply of our old acquaintance tell.
   For thee, against myself I'll vow debate,
   For I must ne'er love him whom thou dost hate.

XC

Then hate me when thou wilt; if ever, now;
Now, while the world is bent my deeds to cross,
Join with the spite of fortune, make me bow,
And do not drop in for an after-loss:
Ah! do not, when my heart hath 'scap'd this sorrow,
Come in the rearward of a conquer'd woe;
Give not a windy night a rainy morrow,
To linger out a purpos'd overthrow.
If thou wilt leave me, do not leave me last,
When other petty griefs have done their spite,
But in the onset come: so shall I taste
At first the very worst of fortune's might;
    And other strains of woe, which now seem woe,
    Compar'd with loss of thee will not seem so.

XCI

Some glory in their birth, some in their skill,
Some in their wealth, some in their body's force,
Some in their garments, though new-fangled ill;
Some in their hawks and hounds, some in their horse;
And every humour hath his adjunct pleasure,
Wherein it finds a joy above the rest:
But these particulars are not my measure:
All these I better in one general best.
Thy love is better than high birth to me,
Richer than wealth, prouder than garments' cost,
Of more delight than hawks or horses be;
And having thee, of all men's pride I boast:
    Wretched in this alone, that thou mayst take
    All this away, and me most wretched make.

XCII

But do thy worst to steal thyself away,
For term of life thou art assured mine;
And life no longer than thy love will stay,
For it depends upon that love of thine.
Then need I not to fear the worst of wrongs,
When in the least of them my life hath end.
I see a better state to me belongs
Than that which on thy humour doth depend:

Thou canst not vex me with inconstant mind,
Since that my life on thy revolt doth lie.
O! what a happy title do I find,
Happy to have thy love, happy to die!
    But what 's so blessed-fair that fears no blot?
    Thou mayst be false, and yet I know it not.

XCIII

So shall I live, supposing thou art true,
Like a deceived husband; so love's face
May still seem love to me, though alter'd new;
Thy looks with me, thy heart in other place:
For there can live no hatred in thine eye,
Therefore in that I cannot know thy change.
In many's looks the false heart's history
Is writ in moods, and frowns, and wrinkles strange,
But heaven in thy creation did decree
That in thy face sweet love should ever dwell;
Whate'er thy thoughts or thy heart's workings be,
Thy looks should nothing thence but sweetness tell.
    How like Eve's apple doth thy beauty grow,
    If thy sweet virtue answer not thy show!

XCIV

They that have power to hurt and will do none,
That do not do the thing they most do show,
Who, moving others, are themselves as stone,
Unmoved, cold, and to temptation slow;
They rightly do inherit heaven's graces,
And husband nature's riches from expense;
They are the lords and owners of their faces,
Others but stewards of their excellence.
The summer's flower is to the summer sweet,
Though to itself it only live and die,
But if that flower with base infection meet,
The basest weed outbraves his dignity:
    For sweetest things turn sourest by their deeds;
    Lilies that fester smell far worse than weeds.

XCV

How sweet and lovely dost thou make the shame
Which, like a canker in the fragrant rose,
Doth spot the beauty of thy budding name!
O! in what sweets dost thou thy sins enclose.
That tongue that tells the story of thy days,
Making lascivious comments on thy sport,
Cannot dispraise but in a kind of praise;
Naming thy name blesses an ill report.
O! what a mansion have those vices got
Which for their habitation chose out thee,
Where beauty's veil doth cover every blot
And all things turn to fair that eyes can see!
    Take heed, dear heart, of this large privilege;
    The hardest knife ill-us'd doth lose his edge.

XCVI

Some say thy fault is youth, some wantonness;
Some say thy grace is youth and gentle sport;
Both grace and faults are lov'd of more and less:
Thou makest faults graces that to thee resort.
As on the finger of a throned queen
The basest jewel will be well esteem'd,
So are those errors that in thee are seen
To truths translated and for true things deem'd.
How many lambs might the stern wolf betray,
If like a lamb he could his looks translate!
How many gazers mightst thou lead away,
If thou wouldst use the strength of all thy state!
    But do not so; I love thee in such sort,
    As, thou being mine, mine is thy good report.

XCVII

How like a winter hath my absence been
From thee, the pleasure of the fleeting year!
What freezings have I felt, what dark days seen!
What old December's bareness every where!
And yet this time remov'd was summer's time;
The teeming autumn, big with rich increase,
Bearing the wanton burthen of the prime,
Like widow'd wombs after their lords' decease:

Yet this abundant issue seem'd to me
But hope of orphans and unfather'd fruit;
For summer and his pleasures wait on thee,
And, thou away, the very birds are mute:
　Or, if they sing, 'tis with so dull a cheer,
　That leaves look pale, dreading the winter 's near.

XCVIII

From you have I been absent in the spring,
When proud-pied April, dress'd in all his trim,
Hath put a spirit of youth in every thing,
That heavy Saturn laugh'd and leap'd with him.
Yet nor the lays of birds, nor the sweet smell
Of different flowers in odour and in hue,
Could make me any summer's story tell,
Or from their proud lap pluck them where they grew:
Nor did I wonder at the lily's white,
Nor praise the deep vermilion in the rose;
They were but sweet, but figures of delight,
Drawn after you, you pattern of all those.
　Yet seem'd it winter still, and, you away,
　As with your shadow I with these did play.

XCIX

The forward violet thus did I chide:
Sweet thief, whence didst thou steal thy sweet that smells,
If not from my love's breath? The purple pride
Which on thy soft cheek for complexion dwells
In my love's veins thou hast too grossly dy'd.
The lily I condemned for thy hand,
And buds of marjoram had stol'n thy hair;
The roses fearfully on thorns did stand,
One blushing shame, another white despair;
A third, nor red nor white, had stol'n of both,
And to his robbery had annex'd thy breath;
But, for his theft, in pride of all his growth
A vengeful canker eat him up to death.
　More flowers I noted, yet I none could see
　But sweet or colour it had stol'n from thee.

C

Where art thou, Muse, that thou forget'st so long
To speak of that which gives thee all thy might?
Spend'st thou thy fury on some worthless song,
Darkening thy power to lend base subjects light?
Return, forgetful Muse, and straight redeem
In gentle numbers time so idly spent;
Sing to the ear that doth thy lays esteem
And gives thy pen both skill and argument.
Rise, resty Muse, my love's sweet face survey,
If Time have any wrinkle graven there;
If any, be a satire to decay,
And make Time's spoils despised every where.
     Give my love fame faster than Time wastes life;
     So thou prevent'st his scythe and crooked knife.

CI

O truant Muse, what shall be thy amends
For thy neglect of truth in beauty dy'd?
Both truth and beauty on my love depends;
So dost thou too, and therein dignified.
Make answer, Muse: wilt thou not haply say,
'Truth needs no colour, with his colour fix'd;
Beauty no pencil, beauty's truth to lay;
But best is best, if never intermix'd'?
Because he needs no praise, wilt thou be dumb?
Excuse not silence so, for 't lies in thee
To make him much outlive a gilded tomb
And to be prais'd of ages yet to be.
     Then do thy office, Muse; I teach thee how
     To make him seem long hence as he shows now.

CII

My love is strengthen'd, though more weak in seeming;
I love not less, though less the show appear:
That love is merchandiz'd whose rich esteeming
The owner's tongue doth publish every where.
Our love was new, and then but in the spring,
When I was wont to greet it with my lays;
As Philomel in summer's front doth sing,
And stops her pipe in growth of riper days:

Not that the summer is less pleasant now
Than when her mournful hymns did hush the night,
But that wild music burthens every bough,
And sweets grown common lose their dear delight.
   Therefore, like her, I sometime hold my tongue,
   Because I would not dull you with my song.

CIII

Alack! what poverty my Muse brings forth,
That having such a scope to show her pride,
The argument, all bare, is of more worth
Than when it hath my added praise beside!
O! blame me not, if I no more can write!
Look in your glass, and there appears a face
That over-goes my blunt invention quite,
Dulling my lines and doing me disgrace.
Were it not sinful then, striving to mend,
To mar the subject that before was well?
For to no other pass my verses tend
Than of your graces and your gifts to tell;
   And more, much more, than in my verse can sit,
   Your own glass shows you when you look in it.

CIV

To me, fair friend, you never can be old,
For as you were when first your eye I ey'd,
Such seems your beauty still. Three winters cold
Have from the forests shook three summers' pride,
Three beauteous springs to yellow autumn turn'd
In process of the seasons have I seen,
Three April perfumes in three hot Junes burn'd,
Since first I saw you fresh, which yet are green.
Ah! yet doth beauty, like a dial-hand,
Steal from his figure, and no pace perceiv'd;
So your sweet hue, which methinks still doth stand,
Hath motion, and mine eye may be deceiv'd:
   For fear of which, hear this, thou age unbred:
   Ere you were born was beauty's summer dead.

CV

Let not my love be call'd idolatry,
Nor my beloved as an idol show,
Since all alike my songs and praises be
To one, of one, still such, and ever so.
Kind is my love to-day, to-morrow kind,
Still constant in a wondrous excellence;
Therefore my verse, to constancy confin'd,
One thing expressing, leaves out difference.
'Fair, kind, and true,' is all my argument,
'Fair, kind, and true,' varying to other words;
And in this change is my invention spent,
Three themes in one, which wondrous scope affords.
   'Fair, kind, and true,' have often liv'd alone,
   Which three till now never kept seat in one.

CVI

When in the chronicle of wasted time
I see descriptions of the fairest wights,
And beauty making beautiful old rime,
In praise of ladies dead and lovely knights,
Then, in the blazon of sweet beauty's best,
Of hand, of foot, of lip, of eye, of brow,
I see their antique pen would have express'd
Even such a beauty as you master now.
So all their praises are but prophecies
Of this our time, all you prefiguring;
And, for they look'd but with divining eyes,
They had not skill enough your worth to sing:
   For we, which now behold these present days,
   Have eyes to wonder, but lack tongues to praise.

CVII

Not mine own fears, nor the prophetic soul
Of the wide world dreaming on things to come,
Can yet the lease of my true love control,
Suppos'd as forfeit to a confin'd doom.
The mortal moon hath her eclipse endur'd,
And the sad augurs mock their own presage;
Incertainties now crown themselves assur'd,
And peace proclaims olives of endless age.

Now with the drops of this most balmy time
My love looks fresh, and Death to me subscribes,
Since, spite of him, I 'll live in this poor rime,
While he insults o'er dull and speechless tribes:
 And thou in this shalt find thy monument,
 When tyrants' crests and tombs of brass are spent.

CVIII

What 's in the brain, that ink may character,
Which hath not figur'd to thee my true spirit?
What 's new to speak, what new to register,
That may express my love, or thy dear merit?
Nothing, sweet boy; but yet, like prayers divine,
I must each day say o'er the very same;
Counting no old thing old, thou mine, I thine,
Even as when first I hallow'd thy fair name.
So that eternal love in love's fresh case
Weighs not the dust and injury of age,
Nor gives to necessary wrinkles place,
But makes antiquity for aye his page;
 Finding the first conceit of love there bred,
 Where time and outward form would show it dead.

CIX

O! never say that I was false of heart,
Though absence seem'd my flame to qualify.
As easy might I from myself depart
As from my soul, which in thy breast doth lie:
That is my home of love: if I have rang'd,
Like him that travels, I return again;
Just to the time, not with the time exchang'd,
So that myself bring water for my stain.
Never believe, though in my nature reign'd
All frailties that besiege all kinds of blood,
That it could so preposterously be stain'd,
To leave for nothing all thy sum of good;
 For nothing this wide universe I call,
 Save thou, my rose; in it thou art my all.

CX

Alas! 'tis true I have gone here and there,
And made myself a motley to the view,
Gor'd mine own thoughts, sold cheap what is most dear,
Made old offences of affections new;
Most true it is that I have look'd on truth
Askance and strangely; but, by all above,
These blenches gave my heart another youth,
And worse essays prov'd thee my best of love.
Now all is done, save what shall have no end:
Mine appetite I never more will grind
On newer proof, to try an older friend,
A god in love, to whom I am confin'd.
　　Then give me welcome, next my heaven the best,
　　Even to thy pure and most loving breast.

CXI

O! for my sake do you with Fortune chide,
The guilty goddess of my harmful deeds,
That did not better for my life provide
Than public means which public manners breeds.
Thence comes it that my name receives a brand,
And almost thence my nature is subdu'd
To what it works in, like the dyer's hand:
Pity me, then, and wish I were renew'd;
Whilst, like a willing patient, I will drink
Potions of eisel 'gainst my strong infection;
No bitterness that I will bitter think,
Nor double penance, to correct correction.
　　Pity me, then, dear friend, and I assure ye
　　Even that your pity is enough to cure me.

CXII

Your love and pity doth the impression fill
Which vulgar scandal stamp'd upon my brow;
For what care I who calls me well or ill,
So you o'er-green my bad, my good allow?
You are my all-the-world, and I must strive
To know my shames and praises from your tongue;
None else to me, nor I to none alive,
That my steel'd sense or changes right or wrong.

In so profound abysm I throw all care
Of others' voices, that my adder's sense
To critic and to flatterer stopped are.
Mark how with my neglect I do dispense:
    You are so strongly in my purpose bred,
    That all the world besides methinks are dead.

CXIII

Since I left you, mine eye is in my mind;
And that which governs me to go about
Doth part his function and is partly blind,
Seems seeing, but effectually is out;
For it no form delivers to the heart
Of bird, of flower, or shape, which it doth latch:
Of his quick objects hath the mind no part,
Nor his own vision holds what it doth catch;
For if it see the rud'st or gentlest sight,
The most sweet favour or deformed'st creature,
The mountain or the sea, the day or night,
The crow or dove, it shapes them to your feature.
    Incapable of more, replete with you,
    My most true mind thus maketh mine untrue.

CXIV

Or whether doth my mind, being crown'd with you,
Drink up the monarch's plague, this flattery?
Or whether shall I say, mine eye saith true,
And that your love taught it this alchemy,
To make of monsters and things indigest
Such cherubins as your sweet self resemble,
Creating every bad a perfect best,
As fast as objects to his beams assemble?
O! 'tis the first, 'tis flattery in my seeing,
And my great mind most kingly drinks it up:
Mine eye well knows what with his gust is 'greeing,
And to his palate doth prepare the cup:
    If it be poison'd, 'tis the lesser sin
    That mine eye loves it and doth first begin.

CXV

Those lines that I before have writ do lie,
Even those that said I could not love you dearer:
Yet then my judgment knew no reason why
My most full flame should afterwards burn clearer.
But reckoning Time, whose million'd accidents
Creep in 'twixt vows, and change decrees of kings,
Tan sacred beauty, blunt the sharp'st intents,
Divert strong minds to the course of altering things;
Alas! why, fearing of Time's tyranny,
Might I not then say, 'Now I love you best,'
When I was certain o'er incertainty,
Crowning the present, doubting of the rest?
    Love is a babe; then might I not say so,
      To give full growth to that which still doth grow?

CXVI

Let me not to the marriage of true minds
Admit impediments. Love is not love
Which alters when it alteration finds,
Or bends with the remover to remove:
O, no! it is an ever-fixed mark,
That looks on tempests and is never shaken;
It is the star to every wandering bark,
Whose worth 's unknown, although his height be taken.
Love 's not Time's fool, though rosy lips and cheeks
Within his bending sickle's compass come;
Love alters not with his brief hours and weeks,
But bears it out even to the edge of doom.
    If this be error, and upon me prov'd,
      I never writ, nor no man ever lov'd.

CXVII

Accuse me thus: that I have scanted all
Wherein I should your great deserts repay,
Forgot upon your dearest love to call,
Whereto all bonds do tie me day by day;
That I have frequent been with unknown minds,
And given to time your own dear-purchas'd right;
That I have hoisted sail to all the winds
Which should transport me farthest from your sight.

Book both my wilfulness and errors down,
And on just proof surmise accumulate;
Bring me within the level of your frown,
But shoot not at me in your waken'd hate;
    Since my appeal says I did strive to prove
    The constancy and virtue of your love.

CXVIII

Like as, to make our appetites more keen,
With eager compounds we our palate urge;
As, to prevent our maladies unseen,
We sicken to shun sickness when we purge;
Even so, being full of your ne'er-cloying sweetness,
To bitter sauces did I frame my feeding;
And, sick of welfare, found a kind of meetness
To be diseas'd, ere that there was true needing.
Thus policy in love, to anticipate
The ills that were not, grew to faults assur'd,
And brought to medicine a healthful state,
Which, rank of goodness, would by ill be cur'd;
    But thence I learn, and find the lesson true,
    Drugs poison him that so fell sick of you.

CXIX

What potions have I drunk of Siren tears,
Distill'd from limbecks foul as hell within,
Applying fears to hopes, and hopes to fears,
Still losing when I saw myself to win!
What wretched errors hath my heart committed,
Whilst it hath thought itself so blessed never!
How have mine eyes out of their spheres been fitted,
In the distraction of this madding fever!
O benefit of ill! now I find true
That better is by evil still made better;
And ruin'd love, when it is built anew,
Grows fairer than at first, more strong, far greater.
    So I return rebuk'd to my content,
    And gain by ill thrice more than I have spent.

CXX

That you were once unkind befriends me now,
And for that sorrow, which I then did feel,
Needs must I under my transgression bow,
Unless my nerves were brass or hammer'd steel.
For if you were by my unkindness shaken,
As I by yours, you 've pass'd a hell of time;
And I, a tyrant, have no leisure taken
To weigh how once I suffer'd in your crime.
O! that our night of woe might have remember'd
My deepest sense, how hard true sorrow hits,
And soon to you, as you to me, then tender'd
The humble salve which wounded bosoms fits!
    But that your trespass now becomes a fee;
    Mine ransoms yours, and yours must ransom me.

CXXI

'Tis better to be vile than vile esteem'd,
When not to be receives reproach of being;
And the just pleasure lost, which is so deem'd
Not by our feeling, but by others' seeing:
For why should others' false adulterate eyes
Give salutation to my sportive blood?
Or on my frailties why are frailer spies,
Which in their wills count bad what I think good?
No, I am that I am, and they that level
At my abuses reckon up their own:
I may be straight though they themselves be bevel;
By their rank thoughts my deeds must not be shown;
    Unless this general evil they maintain,
    All men are bad and in their badness reign.

CXXII

Thy gift, thy tables, are within my brain
Full character'd with lasting memory,
Which shall above that idle rank remain,
Beyond all date, even to eternity:
Or, at the least, so long as brain and heart
Have faculty by nature to subsist;
Till each to raz'd oblivion yield his part
Of thee, thy record never can be miss'd.

That poor retention could not so much hold,
Nor need I tallies thy dear love to score;
Therefore to give them from me was I bold,
To trust those tables that receive thee more:
　　To keep an adjunct to remember thee
　　Were to import forgetfulness in me.

CXXIII

No, Time, thou shalt not boast that I do change:
Thy pyramids built up with newer might
To me are nothing novel, nothing strange;
They are but dressings of a former sight.
Our dates are brief, and therefore we admire
What thou dost foist upon us that is old;
And rather make them born to our desire
Than think that we before have heard them told.
Thy registers and thee I both defy,
Not wondering at the present nor the past,
For thy records and what we see doth lie,
Made more or less by thy continual haste.
　　This I do vow, and this shall ever be;
　　I will be true, despite thy scythe and thee.

CXXIV

If my dear love were but the child of state,
It might for Fortune's bastard be unfather'd,
As subject to Time's love or to Time's hate,
Weeds among weeds, or flowers with flowers gather'd.
No, it was builded far from accident;
It suffers not in smiling pomp, nor falls
Under the blow of thralled discontent,
Whereto th' inviting time our fashion calls:
It fears not Policy, that heretic,
Which works on leases of short number'd hours,
But all alone stands hugely politic,
That it nor grows with heat, nor drowns with showers.
　　To this I witness call the fools of time,
　　Which die for goodness, who have liv'd for crime.

CXXV

Were 't aught to me I bore the canopy,
With my extern the outward honouring,
Or laid great bases for eternity,
Which proves more short than waste or ruining?
Have I not seen dwellers on form and favour
Lose all and more by paying too much rent,
For compound sweet foregoing simple savour,
Pitiful thrivers, in their gazing spent?
No; let me be obsequious in thy heart,
And take thou my oblation, poor but free,
Which is not mix'd with seconds, knows no art,
But mutual render, only me for thee.
　　Hence, thou suborn'd informer! a true soul
　　When most impeach'd stands least in thy control.

CXXVI

O thou, my lovely boy, who in thy power
Dost hold Time's fickle glass, his sickle hour;
Who hast by waning grown, and therein show'st
Thy lovers withering as thy sweet self grow'st;
If Nature, sovereign mistress over wrack,
As thou goest onwards, still will pluck thee back,
She keeps thee to this purpose, that her skill
May time disgrace and wretched minutes kill.
Yet fear her, O thou minion of her pleasure!
She may detain, but not still keep, her treasure:
　　Her audit, though delay'd, answer'd must be,
　　And her quietus is to render thee.

CXXVII

In the old age black was not counted fair,
Or if it were, it bore not beauty's name;
But now is black beauty's successive heir,
And beauty slander'd with a bastard's shame:
For since each hand hath put on Nature's power,
Fairing the foul with Art's false borrow'd face,
Sweet beauty hath no name, no holy bower,
But is profan'd, if not lives in disgrace.

Therefore my mistress' brows are raven black,
Her eyes so suited, and they mourners seem
At such who, not born fair, no beauty lack,
Sland'ring creation with a false esteem:
    Yet so they mourn, becoming of their woe,
    That every tongue says beauty should look so.

CXXVIII

How oft, when thou, my music, music play'st,
Upon that blessed wood whose motion sounds
With thy sweet fingers, when thou gently sway'st
The wiry concord that mine ear confounds,
Do I envy those jacks that nimble leap
To kiss the tender inward of thy hand,
Whilst my poor lips, which should that harvest reap,
At the wood's boldness by thee blushing stand!
To be so tickled, they would change their state
And situation with those dancing chips,
O'er whom thy fingers walk with gentle gait,
Making dead wood more bless'd than living lips.
    Since saucy jacks so happy are in this,
    Give them thy fingers, me thy lips to kiss.

CXXIX

The expense of spirit in a waste of shame
Is lust in action; and till action, lust
Is perjur'd, murderous, bloody, full of blame,
Savage, extreme, rude, cruel, not to trust;
Enjoy'd no sooner but despised straight;
Past reason hunted; and no sooner had,
Past reason hated, as a swallow'd bait,
On purpose laid to make the taker mad:
Mad in pursuit, and in possession so;
Had, having, and in quest to have, extreme;
A bliss in proof,—and prov'd, a very woe;
Before, a joy propos'd; behind, a dream.
    All this the world well knows; yet none knows well
    To shun the heaven that leads men to this hell.

CXXX

My mistress' eyes are nothing like the sun;
Coral is far more red than her lips' red:
If snow be white, why then her breasts are dun;
If hairs be wires, black wires grow on her head.
I have seen roses damask'd, red and white,
But no such roses see I in her cheeks;
And in some perfumes is there more delight
Than in the breath that from my mistress reeks.
I love to hear her speak, yet well I know
That music hath a far more pleasing sound:
I grant I never saw a goddess go,—
My mistress, when she walks, treads on the ground:
　　And yet, by heaven, I think my love as rare
　　As any she belied with false compare.

CXXXI

Thou art as tyrannous, so as thou art,
As those whose beauties proudly make them cruel;
For well thou know'st to my dear doting heart
Thou art the fairest and most precious jewel.
Yet, in good faith, some say that thee behold,
Thy face hath not the power to make love groan:
To say they err I dare not be so bold,
Although I swear it to myself alone.
And to be sure that is not false I swear,
A thousand groans, but thinking on thy face,
One on another's neck, do witness bear
Thy black is fairest in my judgment's place.
　　In nothing art thou black save in thy deeds,
　　And thence this slander, as I think, proceeds.

CXXXII

Thine eyes I love, and they, as pitying me,
Knowing thy heart torments me with disdain,
Have put on black and loving mourners be,
Looking with pretty ruth upon my pain.
And truly not the morning sun of heaven
Better becomes the grey cheeks of the East,
Nor that full star that ushers in the even,
Doth half that glory to the sober West,

As those two mourning eyes become thy face:
O! let it then as well beseem thy heart
To mourn for me, since mourning doth thee grace,
And suit thy pity like in every part.
  Then will I swear beauty herself is black,
  And all they foul that thy complexion lack.

CXXXIII

Beshrew that heart that makes my heart to groan
For that deep wound it gives my friend and me!
Is 't not enough to torture me alone,
But slave to slavery my sweet'st friend must be?
Me from myself thy cruel eye hath taken,
And my next self thou harder hast engross'd:
Of him, myself, and thee, I am forsaken;
A torment thrice threefold thus to be cross'd.
Prison my heart in thy steel bosom's ward,
But then my friend's heart let my poor heart bail;
Whoe'er keeps me, let my heart be his guard;
Thou canst not then use rigour in my jail:
  And yet thou wilt; for I, being pent in thee,
  Perforce am thine, and all that is in me.

CXXXIV

So, now I have confess'd that he is thine,
And I myself am mortgag'd to thy will,
Myself I 'll forfeit, so that other mine
Thou wilt restore, to be my comfort still:
But thou wilt not, nor he will not be free,
For thou art covetous and he is kind;
He learn'd but surety-like to write for me,
Under that bond that him as fast doth bind.
The statute of thy beauty thou wilt take,
Thou usurer, that putt'st forth all to use,
And sue a friend came debtor for my sake;
So him I lose through my unkind abuse.
  Him have I lost; thou hast both him and me:
  He pays the whole, and yet am I not free.

CXXXV

Whoever hath her wish, thou hast thy 'Will,'
And 'Will!' to boot, and 'Will' in over-plus;
More than enough am I that vex'd thee still,
To thy sweet will making addition thus.
Wilt thou, whose will is large and spacious,
Not once vouchsafe to hide my will in thine?
Shall will in others seem right gracious,
And in my will no fair acceptance shine?
The sea, all water, yet receives rain still,
And in abundance addeth to his store;
So thou, being rich in 'Will,' add to thy 'Will'
One will of mine, to make thy large 'Will' more.
    Let no unkind 'No' fair beseechers kill;
    Think all but one, and me in that one 'Will.'

CXXXVI

If thy soul check thee that I come so near,
Swear to thy blind soul that I was thy 'Will,'
And will, thy soul knows, is admitted there;
Thus far for love, my love-suit, sweet, fulfil.
'Will' will fulfil the treasure of thy love,
Ay, fill it full with wills, and my will one.
In things of great receipt with ease we prove
Among a number one is reckon'd none:
Then in the number let me pass untold,
Though in thy stores' account I one must be;
For nothing hold me, so it please thee hold
That nothing me, a something sweet to thee:
    Make but my name thy love, and love that still,
    And then thou lovest me, for my name is 'Will.'

CXXXVII

Thou blind fool, Love, what dost thou to mine eyes,
That they behold, and see not what they see?
They know what beauty is, see where it lies,
Yet what the best is take the worst to be.
If eyes, corrupt by over-partial looks,
Be anchor'd in the bay where all men ride,
Why of eyes' falsehood hast thou forged hooks,
Whereto the judgment of my heart is tied?

Why should my heart think that a several plot
Which my heart knows the wide world's common place?
Or mine eyes, seeing this, say this is not,
To put fair truth upon so foul a face?
   In things right true my heart and eyes have err'd,
   And to this false plague are they now transferr'd.

CXXXVIII

When my love swears that she is made of truth,
I do believe her, though I know she lies,
That she might think me some untutor'd youth,
Unlearned in the world's false subtleties.
Thus vainly thinking that she thinks me young,
Although she knows my days are past the best,
Simply I credit her false-speaking tongue:
On both sides thus is simple truth supprest.
But wherefore says she not she is unjust?
And wherefore say not I that I am old?
O! love's best habit is in seeming trust,
And age in love loves not to have years told:
   Therefore I lie with her, and she with me,
   And in our faults by lies we flatter'd be.

CXXXIX

O! call not me to justify the wrong
That thy unkindness lays upon my heart;
Wound me not with thine eye, but with thy tongue:
Use power with power, and slay me not by art.
Tell me thou lovest elsewhere; but in my sight,
Dear heart, forbear to glance thine eye aside:
What need'st thou wound with cunning, when thy might
Is more than my o'erpress'd defence can bide?
Let me excuse thee: ah! my love well knows
Her pretty looks have been mine enemies;
And therefore from my face she turns my foes,
That they elsewhere might dart their injuries:
   Yet do not so; but since I am near slain,
   Kill me outright with looks, and rid my pain.

CXL

Be wise as thou art cruel; do not press
My tongue-tied patience with too much disdain;
Lest sorrow lend me words, and words express
The manner of my pity-wanting pain.
If I might teach thee wit, better it were,
Though not to love, yet, love, to tell me so;—
As testy sick men, when their deaths be near,
No news but health from their physicians know;—
For, if I should despair, I should grow mad,
And in my madness might speak ill of thee:
Now this ill-wresting world is grown so bad,
Mad slanderers by mad ears believed be.
    That I may not be so, nor thou belied,
    Bear thine eyes straight, though thy proud heart go
        wide.

CXLI

In faith, I do not love thee with mine eyes,
For they in thee a thousand errors note;
But 'tis my heart that loves what they despise,
Who, in despite of view, is pleas'd to dote.
Nor are mine ears with thy tongue's tune delighted;
Nor tender feeling, to base touches prone,
Nor taste, nor smell, desire to be invited
To any sensual feast with thee alone:
But my five wits nor my five senses can
Dissuade one foolish heart from serving thee,
Who leaves unsway'd the likeness of a man,
Thy proud heart's slave and vassal wretch to be:
    Only my plague thus far I count my gain,
    That she that makes me sin awards me pain.

CXLII

Love is my sin, and thy dear virtue hate,
Hate of my sin, grounded on sinful loving:
O! but with mine compare thou thine own state,
And thou shalt find it merits not reproving;
Or, if it do, not from those lips of thine,
That have profan'd their scarlet ornaments
And seal'd false bonds of love as oft as mine,
Robb'd others' beds' revenues of their rents.

Be it lawful I love thee, as thou lov'st those
Whom thine eyes woo as mine importune thee:
Root pity in thy heart, that, when it grows,
Thy pity may deserve to pitied be.
  If thou dost seek to have what thou dost hide,
  By self-example mayst thou be denied!

CXLIII

Lo, as a careful housewife runs to catch
One of her feather'd creatures broke away,
Sets down her babe, and makes all swift dispatch
In pursuit of the thing she would have stay;
Whilst her neglected child holds her in chase,
Cries to catch her whose busy care is bent
To follow that which flies before her face,
Not prizing her poor infant's discontent:
So runn'st thou after that which flies from thee,
Whilst I thy babe chase thee afar behind;
But if thou catch thy hope, turn back to me,
And play the mother's part, kiss me, be kind;
  So will I pray that thou mayst have thy 'Will,'
  If thou turn back and my loud crying still.

CXLIV

Two loves I have of comfort and despair,
Which like two spirits do suggest me still:
The better angel is a man right fair,
The worser spirit a woman colour'd ill.
To win me soon to hell, my female evil
Tempteth my better angel from my side,
And would corrupt my saint to be a devil,
Wooing his purity with her foul pride.
And whether that my angel be turn'd fiend
Suspect I may, yet not directly tell;
But being both from me, both to each friend,
I guess one angel in another's hell:
  Yet this shall I ne'er know, but live in doubt,
  Till my bad angel fire my good one out.

CXLV

Those lips that Love's own hand did make,
Breath'd forth the sound that said 'I hate,'
To me that languish'd for her sake:
But when she saw my woeful state,
Straight in her heart did mercy come,
Chiding that tongue that ever sweet
Was us'd in giving gentle doom;
And taught it thus anew to greet;
'I hate,' she alter'd with an end,
That follow'd it as gentle day
Doth follow night, who like a fiend
From heaven to hell is flown away.
 'I hate' from hate away she threw,
  And sav'd my life, saying 'Not you.'

CXLVI

Poor soul, the centre of my sinful earth,
Fool'd by these rebel powers that thee array,
Why dost thou pine within and suffer dearth,
Painting thy outward walls so costly gay?
Why so large cost, having so short a lease,
Dost thou upon thy fading mansion spend?
Shall worms, inheritors of this excess,
Eat up thy charge? Is this thy body's end?
Then, soul, live thou upon thy servant's loss,
And let that pine to aggravate thy store;
Buy terms divine in selling hours of dross;
Within be fed, without be rich no more:
 So shalt thou feed on Death, that feeds on men,
  And Death once dead, there's no more dying then.

CXLVII

My love is as a fever, longing still
For that which longer nurseth the disease;
Feeding on that which doth preserve the ill,
The uncertain sickly appetite to please.
My reason, the physician to my love,
Angry that his prescriptions are not kept,
Hath left me, and I desperate now approve
Desire is death, which physic did except.

Past cure I am, now Reason is past care,
And frantic-mad with evermore unrest;
My thoughts and my discourse as madmen's are,
As random from the truth vainly express'd;
 For I have sworn thee fair, and thought thee bright,
 Who art as black as hell, as dark as night.

CXLVIII

O me! what eyes hath Love put in my head,
Which have no correspondence with true sight;
Or, if they have, where is my judgment fled,
That censures falsely what they see aright?
If that be fair whereon my false eyes dote,
What means the world to say it is not so?
If it be not, then love doth well denote
Love's eye is not so true as all men's: no,
How can it? O! how can Love's eye be true,
That is so vex'd with watching and with tears?
No marvel then, though I mistake my view;
The sun itself sees not till heaven clears.
 O cunning Love! with tears thou keep'st me blind,
 Lest eyes well-seeing thy foul faults should find.

CXLIX

Canst thou, O cruel! say I love thee not,
When I against myself with thee partake?
Do I not think on thee, when I forgot
Am of myself, all tyrant, for thy sake?
Who hateth thee that I do call my friend?
On whom frown'st thou that I do fawn upon?
Nay, if thou low'r'st on me, do I not spend
Revenge upon myself with present moan?
What merit do I in myself respect,
That is so proud thy service to despise,
When all my best doth worship thy defect,
Commanded by the motion of thine eyes?
 But, love, hate on, for now I know thy mind;
 Those that can see thou lov'st, and I am blind.

CL

O! from what power hast thou this powerful might,
With insufficiency my heart to sway?
To make me give the lie to my true sight,
And swear that brightness doth not grace the day?
Whence hast thou this becoming of things ill,
That in the very refuse of thy deeds
There is such strength and warrantise of skill.
That, in my mind, thy worst all best exceeds?
Who taught thee how to make me love thee more,
The more I hear and see just cause of hate?
O! though I love what others do abhor,
With others thou shouldst not abhor my state:
    If thy unworthiness rais'd love in me,
    More worthy I to be belov'd of thee.

CLI

Love is too young to know what conscience is;
Yet who knows not conscience is born of love?
Then, gentle cheater, urge not my amiss,
Lest guilty of my faults thy sweet self prove:
For, thou betraying me, I do betray
My nobler part to my gross body's treason;
My soul doth tell my body that he may
Triumph in love; flesh stays no farther reason,
But rising at thy name doth point out thee
As his triumphant prize. Proud of this pride,
He is contented thy poor drudge to be,
To stand in thy affairs, fall by thy side.
    No want of conscience hold it that I call
    Her 'love' for whose dear love I rise and fall.

CLII

In loving thee thou know'st I am forsworn,
But thou art twice forsworn, to me love swearing;
In act thy bed-vow broke, and new faith torn,
In vowing new hate after new love bearing.
But why of two oaths' breach do I accuse thee,
When I break twenty? I am perjur'd most;
For all my vows are oaths but to misuse thee,
And all my honest faith in thee is lost:

For I have sworn deep oaths of thy deep kindness,
Oaths of thy love, thy truth, thy constancy;
And, to enlighten thee, gave eyes to blindness,
Or made them swear against the thing they see;
 For I have sworn thee fair; more perjur'd I,
 To swear against the truth so foul a lie!

CLIII

Cupid laid by his brand and fell asleep:
A maid of Dian's this advantage found,
And his love-kindling fire did quickly steep
In a cold valley-fountain of that ground;
Which borrow'd from this holy fire of Love
A dateless lively heat, still to endure,
And grew a seething bath, which yet men prove
Against strange maladies a sovereign cure.
But at my mistress' eye Love's brand new-fired,
The boy for trial needs would touch my breast;
I, sick withal, the help of bath desired,
And thither hied, a sad distemper'd guest,
 But found no cure: the bath for my help lies
 Where Cupid got new fire, my mistress' eyes.

CLIV

The little Love-god lying once asleep
Laid by his side his heart-inflaming brand,
Whilst many nymphs that vow'd chaste life to keep
Came tripping by; but in her maiden hand
The fairest votary took up that fire
Which many legions of true hearts had warm'd;
And so the general of hot desire
Was, sleeping, by a virgin hand disarm'd.
This brand she quenched in a cool well by,
Which from Love's fire took heat perpetual,
Growing a bath and healthful remedy
For men diseas'd; but I, my mistress' thrall,
 Came there for cure, and this by that I prove,
 Love's fire heats water, water cools not love.

A LOVER'S COMPLAINT

From off a hill whose concave womb re-worded
A plaintful story from a sistering vale,
My spirits to attend this double voice accorded,
And down I laid to list the sad-tun'd tale;
Ere long espied a fickle maid full pale,
Tearing of papers, breaking rings a-twain,
Storming her world with sorrow's wind and rain.

Upon her head a platted hive of straw,
Which fortified her visage from the sun,
Whereon the thought might think sometime it saw
The carcass of a beauty spent and done:
Time had not scythed all that youth begun,
Nor youth all quit; but, spite of heaven's fell rage,
Some beauty peep'd through lattice of sear'd age.

Oft did she heave her napkin to her eyne,
Which on it had conceited characters,
Laundering the silken figures in the brine
That season'd woe had pelleted in tears,
And often reading what content it bears;
As often shrieking undistinguish'd woe,
In clamours of all size, both high and low.

Sometimes her levell'd eyes their carriage ride,
As they did battery to the spheres intend;
Sometime diverted, their poor balls are tied
To the orbed earth; sometimes they do extend
Their view right on; anon their gazes lend
To every place at once, and nowhere fix'd,
The mind and sight distractedly commix'd.

Her hair, nor loose nor tied in formal plat,
Proclaim'd in her a careless hand of pride;
For some, untuck'd, descended her sheav'd hat,
Hanging her pale and pined cheek beside;
Some in her threaden fillet still did bide,
And true to bondage would not break from thence,
Though slackly braided in loose negligence.

A thousand favours from a maund she drew
Of amber, crystal, and of beaded jet,
Which one by one she in a river threw,
Upon whose weeping margent she was set;
Like usury, applying wet to wet,
Or monarch's hands that let not bounty fall
Where want cries some, but where excess begs all.

Of folded schedules had she many a one,
Which she perus'd, sigh'd, tore, and gave the flood;
Crack'd many a ring of posied gold and bone,
Bidding them find their sepulchres in mud;
Found yet more letters sadly penn'd in blood,
With sleided silk feat and affectedly
Enswath'd, and seal'd to curious secrecy.

These often bath'd she in her fluxive eyes,
And often kiss'd, and often 'gan to tear;
Cried 'O false blood, thou register of lies,
What unapproved witness dost thou bear!
Ink would have seem'd more black and damned here!
This said, in top of rage the lines she rents,
Big discontent so breaking their contents.

A reverend man that graz'd his cattle nigh—
Sometime a blusterer, that the ruffle knew
Of court, of city, and had let go by
The swiftest hours, observed as they flew—
Towards this afflicted fancy fastly drew;
And, privileg'd by age, desires to know
In brief the grounds and motives of her woe.

So slides he down upon his grained bat,
And comely-distant sits he by her side;
When he again desires her, being sat,
Her grievance with his hearing to divide:
If that from him there may be aught applied
Which may her suffering ecstasy assuage,
'Tis promis'd in the charity of age.

'Father,' she says, 'though in me you behold
The injury of many a blasting hour,
Let it not tell your judgment I am old;
Not age, but sorrow, over me hath power:
I might as yet have been a spreading flower,
Fresh to myself, if I had self-applied
Love to myself, and to no love beside.

'But woe is me! too early I attended
A youthful suit, it was to gain my grace,
Of one by nature's outwards so commended,
That maidens' eyes stuck over all his face.
Love lack'd a dwelling and made him her place;
And when in his fair parts she did abide,
She was new lodg'd and newly deified.

'His browny locks did hang in crooked curls,
And every light occasion of the wind
Upon his lips their silken parcels hurls.
What 's sweet to do, to do will aptly find:
Each eye that saw him did enchant the mind,
For on his visage was in little drawn
What largeness thinks in Paradise was sawn.

'Small show of man was yet upon his chin;
His phœnix down began but to appear
Like unshorn velvet on that termless skin
Whose bare out-bragg'd the web it seem'd to wear;
Yet show'd his visage by that cost more dear,
And nice affections wavering stood in doubt
If best were as it was, or best without.

'His qualities were beauteous as his form,
For maiden-tongu'd he was, and thereof free;
Yet, if men mov'd him, was he such a storm
As oft 'twixt May and April is to see,
When winds breathe sweet, unruly though they be.
His rudeness so with his authoriz'd youth
Did livery falseness in a pride of truth.

'Well could he ride, and often men would say
"That horse his mettle from his rider takes:
Proud of subjection, noble by the sway,
What rounds, what bounds, what course, what stop he
    makes!"
And controversy hence a question takes,
Whether the horse by him became his deed,
Or he his manage by the well-doing steed.

'But quickly on this side the verdict went:
His real habitude gave life and grace
To appertainings and to ornament,
Accomplish'd in himself, not in his case:
All aids, themselves made fairer by their place,
Came for additions; yet their purpos'd trim
Piec'd not his grace, but were all grac'd by him.

'So on the tip of his subduing tongue
All kind of arguments and question deep,
All replication prompt, and reason strong,
For his advantage still did wake and sleep:
To make the weeper laugh, the laugher weep,
He had the dialect and different skill,
Catching all passions in his craft of will:

'That he did in the general bosom reign
Of young, of old, and sexes both enchanted,
To dwell with him in thoughts, or to remain
In personal duty, following where he haunted:
Consents bewitch'd, ere he desire, have granted,
And dialogu'd for him what he would say,
Ask'd their own wills and made their wills obey.

'Many there were that did his picture get,
To serve their eyes, and in it put their mind;
Like fools that in the imagination set
The goodly objects which abroad they find
Of lands and mansions, theirs in thought assign'd;
And labouring in more pleasures to bestow them
Than the true gouty landlord which doth owe them.

'So many have, that never touch'd his hand,
Sweetly suppos'd them mistress of his heart.
My woeful self, that did in freedom stand,
And was my own fee-simple, not in part,
What with his art in youth and youth in art
Threw my affections in his charmed power,
Reserv'd the stalk and gave him all my flower.

'Yet did I not, as some my equals did,
Demand of him, nor being desired yielded;
Finding myself in honour so forbid,
With safest distance I mine honour shielded.
Experience for me many bulwarks builded
Of proofs new-bleeding, which remain'd the foil
Of this false jewel, and his amorous spoil.

'But, ah! who ever shunn'd by precedent
The destin'd ill she must herself assay?
Or forc'd examples, 'gainst her own content,
To put the by-past perils in her way?
Counsel may stop awhile what will not stay;
For when we rage, advice is often seen
By blunting us to make our wits more keen.

'Nor gives it satisfaction to our blood,
That we must curb it upon others' proof;
To be forbid the sweets that seem so good,
For fear of harms that preach in our behoof.
O appetite! from judgment stand aloof!
The one a palate hath that needs will taste,
Though Reason weep, and cry "It is thy last."

'For further I could say "This man 's untrue,"
And knew the patterns of his foul beguiling;
Heard where his plants in others' orchards grew;
Saw how deceits were gilded in his smiling;
Knew vows were ever brokers to defiling;
Thought characters and words merely but art,
And bastards of his foul adulterate heart.

'And long upon these terms I held my city,
Till thus he 'gan besiege me: "Gentle maid,
Have of my suffering youth some feeling pity,
And be not of my holy vows afraid:
That 's to ye sworn to none was ever said;
For feasts of love I have been call'd unto,
Till now did ne'er invite, nor never woo.

' "All my offences that abroad you see
Are errors of the blood, none of the mind;
Love made them not: with acture they may be,
Where neither party is nor true nor kind:
They sought their shame that so their shame did find,
And so much less of shame in me remains,
By how much of me their reproach contains.

' "Among the many that mine eyes have seen,
Not one whose flame my heart so much as warm'd,
Or my affection put to the smallest teen,
Or any of my leisures ever charm'd:
Harm have I done to them, but ne'er was harm'd;
Kept hearts in liveries, but mine own was free,
And reign'd, commanding in his monarchy.

' "Look here, what tributes wounded fancies sent me,
Of paled pearls and rubies red as blood;
Figuring that they their passions likewise lent me
Of grief and blushes, aptly understood
In bloodless white and the encrimson'd mood;
Effects of terror and dear modesty,
Encamp'd in hearts, but fighting outwardly.

' "And, lo! behold these talents of their hair,
With twisted metal amorously impleach'd,
I have receiv'd from many a several fair,
Their kind acceptance weepingly beseech'd,
With the annexions of fair gems enrich'd,
And deep-brain'd sonnets, that did amplify
Each stone's dear nature, worth, and quality.

' "The diamond; why, 'twas beautiful and hard,
Whereto his invis'd properties did tend;
The deep-green emerald, in whose fresh regard
Weak sights their sickly radiance do amend;
The heaven-hu'd sapphire and the opal blend
With objects manifold: each several stone,
With wit well blazon'd, smil'd or made some moan.

' "Lo! all these trophies of affections hot,
Of pensiv'd and subdu'd desires the tender,
Nature hath charg'd me that I hoard them not,
But yield them up where I myself must render,
That is, to you, my origin and ender;
For these, of force, must your oblations be,
Since I their altar, you enpatron me.

' "O! then, advance of yours that phraseless hand,
Whose white weighs down the airy scale of praise;
Take all these similes to your own command,
Hallow'd with sighs that burning lungs did raise;
What me your minister, for you obeys,
Works under you; and to your audit comes
Their distract parcels in combined sums.

' "Lo! this device was sent me from a nun,
Or sister sanctified, of holiest note;
Which late her noble suit in court did shun,
Whose rarest havings made the blossoms dote;
For she was sought by spirits of richest coat,
But kept cold distance, and did thence remove,
To spend her living in eternal love.

' "But, O my sweet! what labour is 't to leave
The thing we have not, mastering what not strives,
Paling the place which did no form receive,
Playing patient sports in unconstrained gyves?
She that her fame so to herself contrives,
The scars of battle 'scapeth by the flight,
And makes her absence valiant, not her might.

' "O! pardon me, in that my boast is true;
The accident which brought me to her eye
Upon the moment did her force subdue,
And now she would the caged cloister fly:
Religious love put out Religion's eye:
Not to be tempted, would she be immur'd,
And now, to tempt, all liberty procur'd.

' "How mighty then you are, O! hear me tell:
The broken bosoms that to me belong
Have emptied all their fountains in my well,
And mine I pour your ocean all among:
I strong o'er them, and you o'er me being strong,
Must for your victory us all congest,
As compound love to physic your cold breast.

' "My parts had power to charm a sacred nun,
Who, disciplin'd, ay, dieted in grace,
Believ'd her eyes when they to assail begun,
All vows and consecrations giving place:
O most potential love! vow, bond, nor space,
In thee hath neither sting, knot, nor confine,
For thou art all, and all things else are thine.

' "When thou impressest, what are precepts worth
Of stale example? When thou wilt inflame,
How coldly those impediments stand forth
Of wealth, of filial fear, law, kindred, fame!
Love's arms are peace, 'gainst rule, 'gainst sense, 'gainst
    shame,
And sweetens, in the suffering pangs it bears,
The aloes of all forces, shocks, and fears.

' "Now all these hearts that do on mine depend,
Feeling it break, with bleeding groans they pine;
And supplicant their sighs to you extend,
To leave the battery that you make 'gainst mine
Lending soft audience to my sweet design,
And credent soul to that strong-bonded oath
That shall prefer and undertake my troth."

'This said, his watery eyes he did dismount,
Whose sights till then were levell'd on my face;
Each cheek a river running from a fount
With brinish current downward flow'd apace:
O, how the channel to the stream gave grace!
Who glaz'd with crystal gate the glowing roses
That flame through water which their hue encloses.

'O father, what a hell of witchcraft lies
In the small orb of one particular tear!
But with the inundation of the eyes
What rocky heart to water will not wear?
What breast so cold that is not warmed here?
O cleft effect! cold modesty, hot wrath,
Both fire from hence and chill extincture hath.

'For, lo! his passion, but an art of craft,
Even there resolv'd my reason into tears;
There my white stole of chastity I daff'd,
Shook off my sober guards and civil fears;
Appear to him, as he to me appears,
All melting; though our drops this difference bore,
His poison'd me, and mine did him restore.

'In him a plenitude of subtle matter,
Applied to cautels, all strange forms receives,
Of burning blushes, or of weeping water,
Or swounding paleness; and he takes and leaves,
In either's aptness, as it best deceives,
To blush at speechless rank, to weep at woes,
Or to turn white and swound at tragic shows:

'That not a heart which in his level came
Could 'scape the hail of his all-hurting aim,
Showing fair nature is both kind and tame;
And, veil'd in them, did win whom he would maim:
Against the thing he sought he would exclaim;
When he most burn'd in heart-wish'd luxury,
He preach'd pure maid, and prais'd cold chastity.

'Thus merely with the garment of a Grace
The naked and concealed fiend he cover'd;
That the unexperient gave the tempter place,
Which like a cherubin above them hover'd.
Who, young and simple, would not be so lover'd?
Ay me! I fell; and yet do question make
What I should do again for such a sake.

'O! that infected moisture of his eye,
O! that false fire which in his cheek so glow'd,
O! that forc'd thunder from his heart did fly,
O! that sad breath his spongy lungs bestow'd,
O! all that borrow'd motion seeming ow'd,
Would yet again betray the fore-betray'd,
And new pervert a reconciled maid.'

THE PASSIONATE PILGRIM

I

WHEN my love swears that she is made of truth,
I do believe her, though I know she lies,
That she might think me some untutor'd youth,
Unskilful in the world's false forgeries.
Thus vainly thinking that she thinks me young,
Although I know my years be past the best,
I smiling credit her false-speaking tongue,
Outfacing faults in love with love's ill rest.
But wherefore says my love that she is young?
And wherefore say not I that I am old?
O! love's best habit is a soothing tongue,
And age, in love, loves not to have years told.
    Therefore I 'll lie with love, and love with me,
    Since that our faults in love thus smother'd be.

II

Two loves I have, of comfort and despair,
Which like two spirits do suggest me still;
The better angel is a man, right fair,
The worser spirit a woman, colour'd ill.
To win me soon to hell, my female evil
Tempteth my better angel from my side,
And would corrupt my saint to be a devil,
Wooing his purity with her fair pride:
And whether that my angel be turn'd fiend
Suspect I may, but not directly tell;
For being both to me, both to each friend,
I guess one angel in another's hell.
    The truth I shall not know, but live in doubt,
    Till my bad angel fire my good one out.

III

Did not the heavenly rhetoric of thine eye,
'Gainst whom the world could not hold argument,
Persuade my heart to this false perjury?
Vows for thee broke deserve not punishment.
A woman I forswore; but I will prove,

Thou being a goddess, I forswore not thee:
My vow was earthly, thou a heavenly love;
Thy grace being gain'd cures all disgrace in me.
My vow was breath, and breath a vapour is;
Then thou, fair sun, that on this earth doth shine,
Exhale this vapour vow; in thee it is:
If broken, then it is no fault of mine.
    If by me broke, what fool is not so wise
    To break an oath, to win a paradise?

IV

Sweet Cytherea, sitting by a brook
With young Adonis, lovely, fresh, and green,
Did court the lad with many a lovely look,
Such looks as none could look but beauty's queen.
She told him stories to delight his ear;
She show'd him favours to allure his eye;
To win his heart, she touch'd him here and there,—
Touches so soft still conquer chastity.
But whether unripe years did want conceit,
Or he refus'd to take her figur'd proffer,
The tender nibbler would not touch the bait,
But smile and jest at every gentle offer:
    Then fell she on her back, fair queen, and toward:
    He rose and ran away; ah! fool too froward.

V

If love make me forsworn, how shall I swear to love?
O! never faith could hold, if not to beauty vow'd:
Though to myself forsworn, to thee I 'll constant prove;
Those thoughts, to me like oaks, to thee like osiers bow'd.
Study his bias leaves, and makes his book thine eyes,
Where all those pleasures live that art can comprehend.
If knowledge be the mark, to know thee shall suffice;
Well learned is that tongue that well can thee commend;
All ignorant that soul that sees thee without wonder;
Which is to me some praise, that I thy parts admire:
Thine eye Jove's lightning seems, thy voice his dreadful
    thunder,
Which, not to anger bent, is music and sweet fire.
    Celestial as thou art, O! do not love that wrong,
    To sing heaven's praise with such an earthly tongue.

VI

Scarce had the sun dried up the dewy morn,
And scarce the herd gone to the hedge for shade,
When Cytherea, all in love forlorn,
A longing tarriance for Adonis made
Under an osier growing by a brook,
A brook where Adon us'd to cool his spleen:
Hot was the day; she hotter that did look
For his approach, that often there had been.
Anon he comes, and throws his mantle by,
And stood stark naked on the brook's green brim:
The sun look'd on the world with glorious eye,
Yet not so wistly as this queen on him:
   He, spying her, bounc'd in, whereas he stood:
   'O Jove,' quoth she, 'why was not I a flood!'

VII

Fair is my love, but not so fair as fickle;
Mild as a dove, but neither true nor trusty;
Brighter than glass, and yet, as glass is, brittle;
Softer than wax, and yet, as iron, rusty:
   A lily pale, with damask dye to grace her,
   None fairer, nor none falser to deface her.

Her lips to mine how often hath she join'd,
Between each kiss her oaths of true love swearing!
How many tales to please me hath she coin'd,
Dreading my love, the loss thereof still fearing!
   Yet in the midst of all her pure protestings,
   Her faith, her oaths, her tears, and all were jestings.

She burn'd with love, as straw with fire flameth;
She burn'd out love, as soon as straw outburneth;
She fram'd the love, and yet she foil'd the framing;
She bade love last, and yet she fell a-turning.
   Was this a lover, or a lecher whether?
   Bad in the best, though excellent in neither.

VIII

If music and sweet poetry agree,
As they must needs, the sister and the brother,
Then must the love be great 'twixt thee and me,
Because thou lov'st the one, and I the other.
Dowland to thee is dear, whose heavenly touch
Upon the lute doth ravish human sense;
Spenser to me, whose deep conceit is such
As, passing all conceit, needs no defence.
Thou lov'st to hear the sweet melodious sound
That Phœbus' lute, the queen of music, makes;
And I in deep delight am chiefly drown'd
When as himself to singing he betakes.
  One god is god of both, as poets feign;
  One knight loves both, and both in thee remain.

IX

Fair was the morn when the fair queen of love,

. . . .

Paler for sorrow than her milk-white dove,
For Adon's sake, a youngster proud and wild;
Her stand she takes upon a steep-up hill:
Anon Adonis comes with horn and hounds;
She, silly queen, with more than love's good will,
Forbade the boy he should not pass those grounds:
'Once,' quoth she, 'did I see a fair sweet youth
Here in these brakes deep-wounded with a boar,
Deep in the thigh, a spectacle of ruth!
See, in my thigh,' quoth she, 'here was the sore.'
She showed hers: he saw more wounds than one,
  And blushing fled, and left her all alone.

X

Sweet rose, fair flower, untimely pluck'd, soon vaded,
Pluck'd in the bud, and vaded in the spring!
Bright orient pearl, alack! too timely shaded;
Fair creature, kill'd too soon by death's sharp sting!
  Like a green plum that hangs upon a tree,
  And falls, through wind, before the fall should be.

I weep for thee, and yet no cause I have;
For why thou left'st me nothing in thy will:
And yet thou left'st me more than I did crave;
For why I craved nothing of thee still:
  O yes, dear friend, I pardon crave of thee,
  Thy discontent thou didst bequeath to me.

XI

Venus, with young Adonis sitting by her
Under a myrtle shade, began to woo him:
She told the youngling how god Mars did try her,
And as he fell to her, so fell she to him.
'Even thus,' quoth she, 'the warlike god embrac'd me,'
And then she clipp'd Adonis in her arms;
'Even thus,' quoth she, 'the warlike god unlac'd me,'
As if the boy should use like loving charms.
'Even thus,' quoth she, 'he seized on my lips,'
And with her lips on his did act the seizure;
And as she fetched breath, away he skips,
And would not take her meaning nor her pleasure.
  Ah! that I had my lady at this bay,
  To kiss and clip me till I ran away.

XII

Crabbed age and youth cannot live together:
Youth is full of pleasance, age is full of care;
Youth like summer morn, age like winter weather;
Youth like summer brave, age like winter bare.
Youth is full of sport, age's breath is short;
  Youth is nimble, age is lame;
Youth is hot and bold, age is weak and cold;
Youth is wild, and age is tame.
Age, I do abhor thee; youth, I do adore thee;
  O! my love, my love is young:
Age, I do defy thee: O! sweet shepherd, hie thee,
  For methinks thou stay'st too long.

XIII

Beauty is but a vain and doubtful good;
A shining gloss that vadeth suddenly;
A flower that dies when first it 'gins to bud;
A brittle glass that 's broken presently:
    A doubtful good, a gloss, a glass, a flower,
    Lost, vaded, broken, dead within an hour.

And as goods lost are seld or never found,
As vaded gloss no rubbing will refresh,
As flowers dead lie wither'd on the ground,
As broken glass no cement can redress,
    So beauty blemish'd once 's for ever lost,
    In spite of physic, painting, pain, and cost.

XIV

Good-night, good rest. Ah! neither be my share:
She bade good-night that kept my rest away;
And daff'd me to a cabin hang'd with care,
To descant on the doubts of my decay.
    'Farewell,' quoth she, 'and come again to-morrow':
    Fare well I could not, for I supp'd with sorrow.

Yet at my parting sweetly did she smile,
In scorn or friendship, nill I construe whether:
'T may be, she joy'd to jest at my exile,
'T may be, again to make me wander thither:
    'Wander,' a word for shadows like myself,
    As take the pain, but cannot pluck the pelf.

Lord! how mine eyes throw gazes to the East;
My heart doth charge the watch; the morning rise
Doth cite each moving sense from idle rest.
Not daring trust the office of mine eyes,
    While Philomela sits and sings, I sit and mark,
    And wish her lays were tuned like the lark;

For she doth welcome daylight with her ditty,
And drives away dark dismal-dreaming night:
The night so pack'd, I post unto my pretty;
Heart hath his hope, and eyes their wished sight.
  Sorrow chang'd to solace, solace mix'd with sorrow;
  For why, she sigh'd, and bade me come to-morrow.

Were I with her, the night would post too soon;
But now are minutes added to the hours;
To spite me now, each minute seems a moon;
Yet not for me, shine sun to succour flowers!
  Pack night, peep day; good day, of night now borrow:
  Short, night, to-night, and length thyself to-morrow.

SONNETS TO SUNDRY NOTES
OF MUSIC

I

It was a lording's daughter, the fairest one of three,
That liked of her master as well as well might be,
Till looking on an Englishman, the fair'st that eye could see,
  Her fancy fell a-turning.
Long was the combat doubtful that love with love did fight,
To leave the master loveless, or kill the gallant knight:
To put in practice either, alas! it was a spite
  Unto the silly damsel.
But one must be refused; more mickle was the pain
That nothing could be used to turn them both to gain,
For of the two the trusty knight was wounded with disdain:
  Alas! she could not help it.
Thus art with arms contending was victor of the day,
Which by a gift of learning did bear the maid away;
Then lullaby, the learned man hath got the lady gay;
  For now my song is ended.

II

On a day, alack the day!
Love, whose month was ever May,
Spied a blossom passing fair,
Playing in the wanton air:
Through the velvet leaves the wind
All unseen 'gan passage find;
That the lover, sick to death,
Wish'd himself the heaven's breath.
'Air,' quoth he, 'thy cheeks may blow;
Air, would I might triumph so!
But, alas! my hand hath sworn
Ne'er to pluck thee from thy thorn:
Vow, alack! for youth unmeet:
Youth, so apt to pluck a sweet.
Thou for whom Jove would swear
Juno but an Ethiope were;
And deny himself for Jove,
Turning mortal for thy love.'

III

My flocks feed not,
My ewes breed not,
My rams speed not,
   All is amiss:
Love 's denying,
Faith 's defying,
Heart 's renying,
   Causer of this.
All my merry jigs are quite forgot,
All my lady's love is lost, God wot:
Where her faith was firmly fix'd in love,
There a nay is plac'd without remove.
One silly cross
Wrought all my loss;
   O frowning Fortune, cursed, fickle dame;
For now I see
Inconstancy
   More in women than in men remain.

In black mourn I,
All fears scorn I,
Love hath forlorn me,
   Living in thrall:
Heart is bleeding,
All help needing,
O cruel speeding,
   Fraughted with gall.
My shepherd's pipe can sound no deal,
My wether's bell rings doleful knell;
My curtal dog, that wont to have play'd,
Plays not at all, but seems afraid;
My sighs so deep
Procure to weep,
   In howling wise, to see my doleful plight.
How sighs resound
Through heartless ground,
   Like a thousand vanquish'd men in bloody fight!

Clear wells spring not,
Sweet birds sing not,
Green plants bring not
  Forth their dye;
Herds stand weeping,
Flocks all sleeping,
Nymphs back peeping
  Fearfully:
All our pleasure known to us poor swains,
All our merry meetings on the plains,
All our evening sport from us is fled,
All our love is lost, for Love is dead.
Farewell, sweet lass,
Thy like ne'er was
  For a sweet content, the cause of all my moan
Poor Corydon
Must live alone;
  Other help for him I see that there is none.

IV

When as thine eye hath chose the dame,
And stall'd the deer that thou shouldst strike,
Let reason rule things worthy blame,
As well as fancy, partial wight:
  Take counsel of some wiser head,
  Neither too young nor yet unwed.

And when thou com'st thy tale to tell,
Smooth not thy tongue with filed talk,
Lest she some subtle practice smell;
A cripple soon can find a halt:
  But plainly say thou lov'st her well,
  And set thy person forth to sell.

What though her frowning brows be bent,
Her cloudy looks will clear ere night;
And then too late she will repent
That thus dissembled her delight:
  And twice desire, ere it be day,
  That which with scorn she put away.

What though she strive to try her strength,
And ban and brawl, and say thee nay,
Her feeble force will yield at length,
When craft hath taught her thus to say,
'Had women been so strong as men,
In faith, you had not had it then.'

And to her will frame all thy ways;
Spare not to spend, and chiefly there
Where thy desert may merit praise,
By ringing in thy lady's ear:
The strongest castle, tower, and town,
The golden bullet beats it down.

Serve always with assured trust,
And in thy suit be humble true;
Unless thy lady prove unjust,
Seek never thou to choose anew.
When time shall serve, be thou not slack
To proffer, though she put thee back.

The wiles and guiles that women work,
Dissembled with an outward show,
The tricks and toys that in them lurk,
The cock that treads them shall not know.
Have you not heard it said full oft,
A woman's nay doth stand for nought?

Think, women love to match with men,
And not to live so like a saint:
Here is no heaven; they holy then
Begin, when age doth them attaint.
Were kisses all the joys in bed,
One woman would another wed.

But, soft! enough! too much, I fear;
For if my mistress hear my song,
She will not stick to ring my ear,
To teach my tongue to be so long:
Yet will she blush, here be it said,
To hear her secrets so bewray'd.

V

Live with me, and be my love,
And we will all the pleasures prove
That hills and valleys, dales and fields,
And all the craggy mountains yields.

There will we sit upon the rocks,
And see the shepherds feed their flocks,
By shallow rivers, by whose falls
Melodious birds sing madrigals.

There will I make thee a bed of roses,
With a thousand fragrant posies,
A cap of flowers, and a kirtle
Embroider'd all with leaves of myrtle.

A belt of straw and ivy buds,
With coral clasps and amber studs;
And if these pleasures may thee move,
Then live with me and be my love.

LOVE'S ANSWER

If that the world and love were young,
And truth in every shepherd's tongue,
These pretty pleasures might me move,
To live with thee and be thy love.

VI

As it fell upon a day
In the merry month of May,
Sitting in a pleasant shade
Which a grove of myrtles made,
Beasts did leap, and birds did sing,
Trees did grow, and plants did spring;
Every thing did banish moan,
Save the nightingale alone:
She, poor bird, as all forlorn,
Lean'd her breast up-till a thorn,
And there sung the dolefull'st ditty,
That to hear it was great pity:
'Fie, fie, fie,' now would she cry;
'Tereu, Tereu!' by and by;
That to hear her so complain,

Scarce I could from tears refrain;
For her griefs, so lively shown,
Made me think upon mine own.
Ah! thought I, thou mourn'st in vain,
None takes pity on thy pain:
Senseless trees they cannot hear thee,
Ruthless beasts they will not cheer thee:
King Pandion he is dead,
All thy friends are lapp'd in lead,
All thy fellow birds do sing,
Careless of thy sorrowing.
Even so, poor bird, like thee,
None alive will pity me.
Whilst as fickle Fortune smil'd,
Thou and I were both beguil'd.

  Every one that flatters thee
Is no friend in misery.
Words are easy, like the wind;
Faithful friends are hard to find:
Every man will be thy friend
Whilst thou hast wherewith to spend;
But if store of crowns be scant,
No man will supply thy want.
If that one be prodigal,
Bountiful they will him call,
And with such-like flattering,
'Pity but he were a king.'
If he be addict to vice,
Quickly him they will entice;
If to women he be bent,
They have him at commandement:
But if Fortune once do frown,
Then farewell his great renown;
They that fawn'd on him before
Use his company no more.
He that is thy friend indeed,
He will help thee in thy need:
If thou sorrow, he will weep;
If thou wake, he cannot sleep:
Thus of every grief in heart
He with thee does bear a part.
These are certain signs to know
Faithful friend from flattering foe.

THE PHŒNIX AND THE
TURTLE

LET the bird of loudest lay,
On the sole Arabian tree,
Herald sad and trumpet be,
To whose sound chaste wings obey.

But thou shrieking harbinger,
Foul precurrer of the fiend,
Augur of the fever's end,
To this troop come thou not near.

From this session interdict
Every fowl of tyrant wing,
Save the eagle, feather'd king:
Keep the obsequy so strict.

Let the priest in surplice white,
That defunctive music can,
Be the death-divining swan,
Lest the requiem lack his right.

And thou treble-dated crow,
That thy sable gender mak'st
With the breath thou giv'st and tak'st,
'Mongst our mourners shalt thou go.

Here the anthem doth commence:
Love and constancy is dead;
Phœnix and the turtle fled
In a mutual flame from hence.

So they lov'd, as love in twain
Had the essence but in one;
Two distincts, division none:
Number there in love was slain.

Hearts remote, yet not asunder;
Distance, and no space was seen
'Twixt the turtle and his queen:
But in them it were a wonder.

So between them love did shine,
That the turtle saw his right
Flaming in the phœnix' sight;
Either was the other's mine.

Property was thus appall'd,
That the self was not the same;
Single nature's double name
Neither two nor one was call'd.

Reason, in itself confounded,
Saw division grow together;
To themselves yet either neither,
Simple were so well compounded,

That it cried, 'How true a twain
Seemeth this concordant one!
Love hath reason, reason none,
If what parts can so remain.'

Whereupon it made this threne
To the phœnix and the dove,
Co-supremes and stars of love,
As chorus to their tragic scene.

THRENOS

Beauty, truth, and rarity,
Grace in all simplicity,
Here enclos'd in cinders lie.

Death is now the phœnix' nest;
And the turtle's loyal breast
To eternity doth rest,

Leaving no posterity:
'Twas not their infirmity,
It was married chastity.

Truth may seem, but cannot be;
Beauty brag, but 'tis not she;
Truth and beauty buried be.

To this urn let those repair
That are either true or fair;
For these dead birds sigh a prayer.

NOTES

THE LIFE AND DEATH OF KING JOHN

I. i. 20. According to the Cambridge editors the line must probably be scanned as an Alexandrine, reading the first *'control-ment'* in the time of a trisyllable and the second as a quadrisyllable. This seems very doubtful; the irregularity of the line is not remarkable; there is merely an extra syllable before the pause:—

Contról|ment fór| contrólment ‖ so áns|wer Fránce.|

I. i. 28. *'sullen presage of your own decay'*; there is perhaps an allusion here to the dismal passing-bell, as Steevens suggested; according to Delius, the trumpet of doom is alluded to. There is, however, no difficulty in the thought as it stands, without these references to a secondary idea.

I. i. 49. *'expedition's'*; first Folio *'expeditious'*; an obvious misprint.

I. i. 54. *'Cœur-de-lion'*; *'Cordelion'* in the Folios and old play; perhaps the spelling should be kept as the popular form of the name.

'knighted in the field'; in *'The Troublesome Reign'* he is knighted at the siege of Acon or Acre, by the title of Sir Robert Fauconbridge of Montbery.

I. i. 85. *'trick'*; it has been suggested that *'trick'* is used here in the heraldic sense of 'copy'; it would seem, however, to be used in a less definite sense.

I. i. 139. *'sir Robert's his,'* so the Folios; Theobald proposed *'sir Robert his,'* regarding *'his'* as the old genitive form; Vaughan *'just sir Robert's shape'*; Schmidt takes the *"s his"* as a reduplicative possessive. Surely *'his'* is used substantively with that rollicking effect which is so characteristic of Faulconbridge. There is no need to explain the phrase as equivalent to 'his shape, which is also his father Sir Robert's'; *'sir Robert's his'* = 'sir Robert's shape,' *'his'* emphasizing substantively the previous pronominal use of the word.

I. i. 143. *'Look, where three-farthings goes'*; three-farthing pieces of silver were coined in 1561 (discontinued in 1582); they were very thin, and were distinguished from the silver pence by an impression of the queen's profile, with a rose behind her ear.

I. i. 147. *'I would not'*; Folio 1 reads *'It would not,'* probably a misprint, though Delius makes *'it'* refer to *'His face.'*

I. i. 234-5. *'eat his part in me upon Good-Friday'*; evidently a popular proverb, *cp.* Heywood's *Dialogue upon Proverbs:*

"He may his part on Good Friday eat,
    And fast never the wurs for ought he shall geat" (*i.e. get*).

I. i. 244. '*Knight, knight, good mother, Basilisco-like*'; an allusion to the old play called '*Soliman and Perseda*' (printed 1599, written probably some ten years before); Piston the buffoon, representing the old Vice of the Morality Plays, jumps on the back of Basilisco, the bragging coward, and makes him take oath on his dagger:—

BAS. '*I, the aforesaid Basilisco,—knight, good fellow, knight, knight,—*

PIST. *Knave, good fellow, knave, knave.*'

(*cp*. Dodsley's *Old Plays*, ed. Hazlitt, *Vol. v.* 271-2.)

II. i. 2. '*that great forerunner of thy blood*'; Shakespeare, by some oversight, here makes Arthur directly descended from Richard.

II. i. 5. '*by this brave duke*,' so the old play. Richard was, however, slain by an arrow at the siege of Chaluz, some years after the Duke's death.

II. i. 64. '*her niece, the Lady Blanch of Spain*,' *i.e.* her granddaughter; Blanch was the daughter of John's sister Eleanor and Alphonso VIII, King of Castile.

II. i. 65. '*of the king's deceased*,' *i.e.* 'of the deceased king'; Folios 2, 3, 4, '*king*'; but Folio 1, '*kings*' = 'king's' is idiomatically correct.

II. i. 103. '*huge*'; Rowe read '*large*,' doubtless a misprint for '*huge*' restored by Capell.

II. i. 113. '*breast*'; Folio 1, '*beast*.'

II. i. 119. '*Excuse; it is*,' &c.; Malone's correction of the Folios, '*Excuse it is*'; Rowe (ed. 2) '*Excuse it, 'tis*.'

II. i. 137. '*of whom the proverb goes*,' *i.e.* '*Mortuo leoni et lepores insultant*'; *cp*. Kyd's *Spanish Tragedy*, '*Hares may pull dead lions by the beard.*'

II. i. 144. '*Great Alcides' shows upon an ass*'; alluding to the skin of the Nemean lion won by Hercules. The Folios read '*shooes*'; the reading of the text was first proposed by Theobald.

II. i. 149. '*King Philip*,' &c.; the line is printed in the Folios as part of Austria's speech, with '*King Lewis*' instead of '*King Philip*'; the error was first corrected by Theobald.

II. i. 152. '*Anjou*,' Theobald's correction of '*Angiers*' of the Folios.

II. i. 156. '*Bretagne*'; Folios 1, 2, '*Britaine*'; Folio 3, '*Britain*'; Folio 4, '*Brittain.*'

II. i. 159. ll. 159 to 197 considered as spurious by Pope.

II. i. 160, 161. '*it*,' old form of possessive, so Folios 2, 3, 4; Folio 1, '*yt . . . it*'; Johnson, '*it' . . . it' *'; Capell, '*it's . . . it's.*' In the Lancashire dialect '*hit*' is still the common form of the possessive, an archaism used here in imitation of the language of the nursery.

II. i. 167. '*whether*,' monosyllabic; Folios 1, 2, 3, '*where*'; Folio 4, '*whe're*.'

II. i. 177. '*this is thy eld'st*'; Capell's emendation of the Folios, '*this is thy eldest*'; Fleay proposed '*this*' *thy eld'st*'; Ritson, '*thy eld'st*,' omitting '*this is*.'

II. i. 180. '*the canon of the law*,' *cp.* Exodus xx. 5.

II. i. 187. '*And with her plague; her sin his injury*,' &c.; the Folios, '*And with her plague her sin: his injury*,' &c. The punctuation adopted was first proposed by Mr. Roby, who explains the passage thus:—"God hath made her sin and herself to be a plague to this distant child, who is punished for her and with the punishment belonging to her: God has made her sin to be an injury to Arthur, and her injurious deeds to be the executioner to punish her sin: all which (viz., her first sin and her now injurious deeds) are punished in the person of this child."

II. i. 196. '*aim*'; Folio 1, '*ayme*'; Folios 2, 3, 4, '*ay me*'; Rowe conjectured '*amen*'; Moberly, '*hem*'; Jackson, '*shame*'; Johnson, '*j'aime*.'

II. i. 215. '*Confronts your*,' Capell's emendation; Folios 1, 2, '*Comfort yours*'; Folios 3, 4, '*Comfort your*'; Rowe suggested, '*Confront your*'; Collier, *Come 'fore your*.'

II. i. 217. '*waist*'; Folios 1, 2, 3, '*waste*'; Folio 4, '*waiste*'; '*doth*'; the singular by attraction to the preceding word; Rowe, '*do*.'

II. i. 234. '*Crave*,' so Pope; Folios read '*Craues*.'

II. i. 259. '*roundure*,' so Capell; Folios read '*rounder*'; Singer, '*rondure*.'

II. i. 262. '*rude*'; Williams conjectured '*wide*.'

II. i. 323. '*Dyed*'; Folios 1, 2, 3, '*Dide*'; Folio 4, '*dy'd*.' Pope suggested '*Stain'd*'; Vaughan, '*Dipp'd*.'

II. i. 325. In the Folios 'the first citizen' is throughout named 'Hubert,' in all probability owing to the fact that the actor of the part of Hubert also took this minor character of the play.

II. i. 335. '*run*,' so Folios 2, 3, 4; Folio 1, '*rome*'; Malone reads, '*roam*'; Nicholson conjectured, '*foam*.'

II. i. 353. '*fangs*,' Steevens' spelling for '*phangs*' of the Folios.

II. i. 358. '*equal potents*'; Collier reads '*equal potent*'; Delius, '*equal-potents*'; Dyce, '*equal-potent*.'

'*fiery kindled*,' so Folios 2, 3, 4; Folio 1, '*fierie kindled*'; Pope, '*fiery-kindled*'; Collier (ed. 2), '*fire-ykindled*'; Lettsom conjectures '*fire-enkindled*.'

II. i. 371. '*King'd of our fears*'; the Folios, '*Kings of our fear*'; the excellent emendation adopted in the text was first proposed by Tyrwhitt.

II. i. 378. '*the mutines of Jerusalem*,' *i.e.* the mutineers of Jerusalem, evidently alluding to John of Giscala and Simon bar Gioras, the leaders of the opposing factions, who combined in order to resist the Roman attack. Shakespeare probably derived his knowledge from Peter Morwyng's translation (1558) of the spurious Josephus, the 'joseppon,' as it is called: Josephus was first Englished in 1602.

II. i. 425. *'Dauphin,'* so Rowe; Folios, *'Dolphin'* (*passim*).

II. i. 584. *'aid'*; Collier (ed. 2, Mason's conjecture) *'aim.'*

III. i. 16-17. *'thou didst but jest, With my vex'd spirits,'* &c.; Rowe's emendation of the punctuation of the Folios, *'jest . . . spirits.'*

III. i. 148. *'task,'* Theobald's correction of the Folios; Folios 1, 2, *'tast'*; Folios 3, 4, *'taste'*; Rowe conjectured *'tax.'*

III. i. 210. *'new untrimmed bride'*; so the Folios; Theobald, *'new and trimmed,'* or *'new untamed,'* *'new betrimmed'*; Dyce *'new-uptrimmed.'* Staunton was probably right when he suggested that *'untrimmed'* is descriptive of the bride with her hair hanging loose.

III. i. 260. *'chafed lion'*; Theobald's correction of the Folios, *'cased.'*

III. i. 281-285. In the first Folio the reading is:—

'But thou hast sworn against religion;
  By what thou swear'st against the thing thou swear'st,
  And mak'st an oath the surety for thy truth,
  Against an oath the truth, thou art unsure
  To swear, sweares only not to be foresworn.'

In line 281 a plausible emendation is *'swar'st'* (= 'swor'st) for the second *'swear'st.'* *'By what'* = 'in so far as'; lines 281, 282 are evidently parallel in sense; a slight obscurity may perhaps be cleared away by taking the first *'truth'* as used with a suggestion of the secondary meaning 'troth'; lines 283, 284 are considered the crux of the passage, but possibly all difficulty is removed by placing a semicolon after *'unsure,'* and rendering *'to swear'* with the force of 'if a man swear.'

III. ii. 4. *'Philip'*; Theobald, *'Richard'*; the error was probably Shakespeare's; *'Philip'* was *'Sir Richard.'*

III. iii. 26. *'time,'* Pope's emendation for *'tune'* of the Folios.

III. iii. 39. *'Sound on into the drowsy ear of night'*; the Folios, *'race'*; Dyce and Staunton, *'ear'*; Bulloch, *'face,'* &c. Theobald suggested *'sound one unto,'* as plausible an emendation as so many of his excellent readings.

III. iii. 52. *'brooded watchful day'*; Pope's *'broad-ey'd,'* Mitford's *'broad and,'* and various emendations have been proposed, but *'brooded'* = 'having a brood to watch over,' hence *'brooding'* = 'sitting on brood.'

III. iii. 72. *'attend on you,'* so Folios 1, 2; Folios 3, 4, *'to attend'*; Pope reads *'t' attend.'*

III. iv. 2. *'convicted,'* i.e. 'overcome'; there is perhaps a reference here to the Spanish Armada. Pope proposed *'collected'*;

other suggestions have been *'convented,' 'connected,' 'combined,' 'convexed,'* &c.

III. iv. 6. *'Is not Angiers lost?'* &c. Arthur was made prisoner at the capture of Mirabeau in 1202. Angiers was captured by John four years later.

III. iv. 44. *'not holy,'* so Folio 4; Folios 1, 2, 3, *'holy'*; Delius and Staunton (Steevens' conjecture) *'unholy.'*

III. iv. 64. *'friends,'* Rowe's emendation of *'fiends'* of the Folios.

III. iv. 98. *'Then have I reason to be fond of grief,'* Rowe's reading; Folios 1, 2, 3 read *'Then, have I reason to be fond of grief?'*; Folio 4, *'Then . . . grief?'*

III. iv. 110. *'world's taste,'* Pope's emendation of the Folios, *'words taste'*; Jackson's conjecture, *'word, state.'*

III. iv. 182. *'strong actions,'* so Folios 2, 3, 4. Folio 1 misprints *'strange actions.'*

IV. i. 92. *'mote,'* Steevens' emendation for *'moth'* of the Folios, a frequent spelling of the word.

IV. ii. 42. *'then lesser is my fear,'* so Folio 1; *'then'* a common spelling of *'than'* in Elizabethan English; Folios 2, 3, 4, *'then less is my fear'*; Pope, *'the lesser is my fear.'*

IV. ii. 50. *'myself and them'* = (perhaps) 'myself and themselves'; hence the ungrammatical *'them.'*

IV. ii. 65. *'than whereupon our weal,'* &c. The meaning of the passage seems to be, 'we ask for his liberty only in so far as the commonwealth (*i.e.* *'our weal, on you depending'*) counts it your welfare,' &c.

IV. ii. 117. *'care'*; it is impossible to determine whether th first Folio reads *'eare'* or *'care'*; the other Folios *'care.'* There is considerable doubt as to whether the first letter is Roman or Italic, and taking all the evidence into account it seems possible that *'care'* was corrected to *'eare'* in some copies of the first Folio.

IV. ii. 120. *'first of April'*; according to history, Eleanor died in 1204 in the month of July.

IV. ii. 123. *'Three days before'*; Constance died in reality three years, and not three days before, in August, 1201.

IV. ii. 147. *'a prophet,' i.e.* Peter of Pomfret (Pontefract).

IV. iii. 11. *'him'* = the Dauphin.

V. i. 8. *'counties'*; it is difficult to determine whether *'counties'* = (i.) 'counts,' *i.e.* 'the nobility,' or (ii.) 'the divisions of the country': probably the former.

V. ii. 1. *'this,' i.e.* 'this compact with the English lords.'

V. ii. 27. *'step after a stranger, march,'* so the Folios; Theobald *'stranger march,'* but the original reading seems preferable.

V. ii. 36. *'grapple,'* Pope's emendation of *'cripple'* of the Folios; Steevens conjectured *'gripple,'* Gould *'souple.'*

V. ii. 59. *'Full of warm blood,'* Heath's conjecture of *'Full warm of blood'* of the Folios.

V. ii. 64. *'an angel spake'*; *'angel'* used probably equivocally with a play upon 'angel' the gold coin, the quibble being suggested by the previous *'purse,' 'nobles.'*

V. ii. 133. *'unhair'd,'* Theobald's correction of Folios; Folio 1, *'vnheard'*; Folios 2, 3, 4, *'unheard'*; Keightley proposed *'unbeard.'*

V. iii. 8. *'Swinstead,'* so in *'The Troublesome Reign'*; *'Swinstead'* = Swineshead, near Spalding, in Lincolnshire.

V. iv. 15. *'He,' i.e.* the Dauphin; perhaps *'lords'* in the previous line is an error for *'lord.'*

V. iv. 24-5. *'even as a form of wax Resolveth from his figure 'gainst the fire,'* alluding to the images of wax used in witchcraft; as the figure melted before the fire, so the person it represented dwindled away.

V. iv. 60. *'Right in thine eye'*; it has been suggested that *'right'* is a misprint for *'riot'*; *'pight,' 'fight,' 'fright,'* &c., have been proposed: there is no reason at all for emending the word.

V. vi. 12. *'eyeless night,'* Theobald's emendation of the Folios, *'endles.'*

V. vii. 16. *'Leaves them invisible, and his siege'*; so Folio 1; the other Folios, *'and her siege'*; Pope, *'leaves them; invisible his siege'*; Hanmer, *'leaves them insensible; his siege'*; Steevens, *'invisible'*; &c.

V. vii. 21. *'cygnet'*; Rowe's correction of *'Symet'* of the Folios.

THE TRAGEDY OF KING
RICHARD II

I. i. 1. *'Old John of Gaunt'*; Gaunt was only fifty-eight years old at the time when the play opens, but Shakespeare refers to him throughout as an old man.

I. i. 20. *'Many years of happy days befal'*; Pope suggested *'May many'*; Tate, *'Now many'*; Collier, *'Full many'*; others suggest that *'years'* is to be read as a dissyllable. No change is necessary; the emphatic monosyllabic foot at the beginning of the speech is not very remarkable, and may easily be paralleled.

I. i. 65. *'inhabitable'*; Theobald suggested *'unhabitable.'*

I. i. 77. *'What I have spoke, or thou canst worse deuise'*; this is the reading of Quarto 1; Quarto 2, *'spoke, or thou canst deuise'*; Quartos 3, 4, *'spoke, or what thou canst deuise'*; Folios and Quarto 5, *'spoken, or thou canst deuise'*; Hanmer conjectured, *'spoke, as what thou hast devised.'*

I. i. 95. *'for these eighteen years'*; since the insurrection of Wat Tyler, in 1381.

I. i. 189. *'beggar-fear'*; so Quartos 1, 5, and Folios 1, 2; Quartos 2, 3, 4, *'beggar-face'*; Folios 3, 4, *'beggar'd fear'*; Hanmer proposed *'haggard fear'*; others have suggested, *'bugbear fear'*; *'bug-bear-face'*; *'stagger'd fear.'*

I. i. 199. *'Saint Lambert's day'*; thus Quartos 1, 5, and Folios; Quartos 2, 3, 4, *'St Lambards Day.'* This was September 17th.

I. i. 204. *'Lord marshal'*; Norfolk was himself Earl Marshal of England; this made therefore a deputy appointed for the occasion: Holinshed tells us that he was Thomas Holland, Duke of Surrey. Capell suggested *'Marshal'* for *'Lord Marshal'* in order to normalise the scansion of the line: otherwise *'marshal'* must be taken as equivalent to a monosyllable, or a monosyllable with an unessential extra syllable before a pause.

I. ii. 1. *'Woodstock's blood'*; thus Quartos 1, 2, 3, 4; Folios 1, 2, 3, read *'Glousters'*; Folio 4 and Quarto 5, *'Glosters.'* The Duke of Gloucester was also called Thomas of Woodstock.

I. ii. 47. *'sit'*; so the Folios and Quarto 5; Quartos 1, 2, 3, 4, *'set.'*

I. ii. 66. *'Plashy'*; the seat of Thomas of Woodstock, as Lord High Constable, near Dunmow, in Essex.

I. ii. 70. *'hear there'*; so Quarto 2; Quarto 1 reads *'cheere there.'*

I. iii. 20. *'and my succeeding issue'*; so Quartos 1, 2, 3, 4; the Folios and Quarto 5, *'and his succeeding issue.'*

I. iii. 43. *'daring-hardy'*; Theobald's emendation of the Quartos and Folios; Quarto 1, *'daring, hardy'*; Quartos 2, 3, 4, *'daring hardie'*; Folios 1, 2, *'daring hardie'*; Quarto 5 and Folios 3, 4, *'daring hardy.'*

I. iii. 58. *'thee dead'*; Quartos 1, 2, *'the dead.'*

I. iii. 67, 68. *'at English feasts, . . . The daintiest last'*; referring to the English custom of having sweets as the last course at a dinner.

I. iii. 84. *'innocency'*; the Quartos and Folios, *'innocence,'* changed by Capell to *'innocency.'*

I. iii. 128. *'Of civil wounds plough'd up with neighbours' sword'*; Quarto 1, *'cruell'* for *'civil'*; Quartos 1, 2, 3, 4, *'sword'*; the Folios and Quarto 5, *'swords'*; Theobald conjectured *'neighbour'* for *'neighbours'.'*

I. iii. 136. *'wrathful iron arms'*; Quarto 1 reads *'harsh resounding arms.'*

I. iii. 138. *'kindred's'*; Quartos 1, 2, read *'kinreds.'*

I. iii. 140. *'upon pain of life'*; the reading of Quartos 1, 2, 3, 4; the Folios and Quarto 5, *'upon pain of death.'*

I. iii. 193. *'so far'*; the Quartos and Folio 1, *'so fare'*; Folios 2, 3, and Quarto 5, *'so farre'*; Folio 4, *'so far.'*

I. iii. 276. *'wise man'*; written as one word in the first two Quartos, and evidently pronounced with the accent on the first syllable.

I. iv. 23. *'Bagot here and Green'*; omitted in Quartos 1, 2, 3, 4; inserted in the Folios and Quarto 5.

I. iv. 58. *'Ely House'*; the Bishop of Ely's palace in Holborn. 'Ely-Place' marks its site.

II. i. 18. *'of whose taste the wise are fond'*; Quarto 1 reads *'of whose taste the wise are fond'*; Quarto 2, *'of whose state the wise are found'*; Quartos 3, 4, 5 and Folios read *'of his state: then there are found'*; Folio 1, *'sound'*; the reading in the text was first suggested by Collier.

II. i. 40-55. *'This royal throne . . . Jewry'*; with the exception of line 50, this passage is quoted more or less correctly in *England's Parnassus* (1600), but is attributed by mistake to Michael Drayton.

II. i. 73-83. These famous lines suggest comparison with the word play of Ajax upon his name in Sophocles' drama.

II. i. 102. *'incaged'*; the reading of Folios 1, 2; Quartos 1, 2, 3, 4 read *'inraged'*; Quarto 5 reads *'encaged'*; Folios 3, 4 read *'ingaged.'*

II. i. 113. *'thou now, not king'*; Theobald's emendation of the Quartos and Folios; Quartos 1, 2, 3 read *'thou now not, not king'*; Quarto 4 reads *'thou now not, nor king'*; the Folios and Quartos 5 read *'thou and not king.'*

II. i. 115. *'And thou'*—King Richard. 'A lunatic,' &c. Quarto 1, 'And thou.' King. 'A lunatike'; Quarto 2, 'And thou.' King. 'A lunatick'; Quartos 3, 4 read 'And thou.' King 'Ah lunaticke'; the Folios and Quarto 5, 'And—' Rich. 'And thou, a lunaticke'; Warburton, 'And thou—' K. Rich. 'And thou, a lunatick.'

II. i. 246. *' 'Gainst us, our lives'*; Vaughan conjectured *'Against ourselves'*; Collier MS., *' 'Gainst us, our wives.'*

II. i. 248. Pope proposed the omission of *'quite'* in order to improve the scansion of the line. It has been suggested that Shakespeare may have written *'The gentlemen and nobles hath he fined.'* Sidney Walker rearranged the passage thus:—

> *'The commons hath he pill'd*
> *With grievous taxes, and quite lost their hearts;*
> *The nobles hath he fined for ancient quarrels.'*

The text as it stands is better than the readings which result from these emendations.

II. i. 253. *'Wars have,'* &c.; Rowe's emendation; Quartos 1, 2, and the Folios read *'Wars hath,'* &c.; Capell conjectured *'War hath,'* &c.

II. i. 254. "The allusion here is to the treaty which Richard made with Charles VI. of France in the year 1393."

II. i. 255. The Folios omit *'noble'* but there are many similar quasi-Alexandrines in the play.

II. i. 278. *'Then thus: I have from le Port Blanc.'* The first Quarto reads:—

> *'Then thus, I have from le Port Blan*
> *A Bay in Brittaine,'* &c.

Dr. Wright notes that as the Quartos have *'le Port Blan,'* and Holinshed *'le Porte Blanc,'* he adopts the reading *'le Port Blanc,'* which is the name of a small port in the department of Côtes du Nord, near Tréguier.

II. i. 280. Malone, having Holinshed before him, assumed that a line has been lost, and introduced the following words after *'Cobham'*:—

> *'The son of Richard Earl of Arundel.'*

II. i. 283. *'Sir John Ramston'*; according to Holinshed *'Sir Thomas,'* not *'Sir John.'*

II. i. 284. *'Quoint'*; Quartos 1, 2, 3, 4 read *'Coines.'*

II. ii. 18. *'perspectives'*; "at the right Honourable the Lord Gerards at Gerards Bromley, there are the pictures of Henry the Great of France and his Queen, both upon the same indented board, which if beheld directly, you only perceive a confused piece of work; but, if obliquely, of one side you see the King's, and on the other the Queen's picture"; Plot's *Natural History of Staffordshire* (quoted by Staunton).

II. ii. 31. *'though'*; Quarto 1 reads *'thought'*; *'on thinking on'*; Folios 3, 4 read *'one thinking, on'*; Collier MS., *'unthinking on'*; *'no thought'*; Lettsom conjectured *'no thing.'*

II. ii. 57. *'all the rest'*; the reading of Quarto 1; Quartos 2, 3, 4, 5 and Folios 1, 2 read *'the rest of the'*; Folios 3, 4, *'the rest of that'*; Pope, *'all of that,' 'revolt'*; Quartos 3, 4 read *'revolting'*; *'faction'*; Daniel conjectured *'factious.'*

II. ii. 58. *'The Earl of Worcester'*; Thomas Percy, Steward of the King's household: he was brother to the Earl of Northumberland.

II. iii. 9. *'Cotswold'*; Quartos 1, 2, 3, 4 read *'Cotshall'*; the Folios and Quarto 5 read *'Coltshold.'*

II. iii. 100. The Clarendon Press editors suggest that this passage bears considerable resemblance to the speech of Nestor (*Iliad,* vii. 157). (Hall's translation of Homer was published in 1581.)

II. iii. 164. *'Bristol'*; the reading of Quarto 5; all the rest Quartos and Folios *'Bristow.'*

III. ii. 1. *'Barkloughly'*; the name was derived from Holinshed, where it was undoubtedly a copyist's or printer's error for *'Hertlowli,' i.e. 'Harlech.'*

III. ii. 14. Alluding to the old idea that spiders were venomous.

III. ii. 40. *'boldly'*; Collier's conjecture; Quarto 1, *'bouldly'*; Quarto 2, *'bloudy'*; Quartos 3, 4, 5, and Folios, *'bloody.'*

III. ii. 157. *'sad stories of the death of kings'*; Shakespeare was probably thinking of the *Mirror for Magistrates* with its 'tragedies' of English princes, Richard among the earliest of them.

III. ii. 161-164. Douce plausibly suggested that this image was suggested to Shakespeare by the seventh print in the

Imagines Mortis, where *"a King is represented sitting on his throne, sword in hand, with courtiers round him, while from his crown rises a grinning skeleton."*

III. iii. 105. *'the honourable tomb';* the tomb of Edward III. in Westminster Abbey.

III. iv. 11. *'joy';* Rowe's emendation; Quarto and Folios, *'griefe.'*

III. iv. 22. *'And I could sing';* Pope's emendation; *'weep,'* has been generally adopted, but the Cambridge editors adhere to the reading of the Quartos and Folios. They explain that "the Queen speaks with an emphasis on *'sing.'* 'And I could even sing for joy if thy troubles were only such as weeping could alleviate, and then I could not ask you weep for me.' "

IV. i. 55. *'sun to sun';* Capell's emendation of *'sinne to sinne'* of the Quartos.

IV. i. 148. *'Prevent it, resist it';* Pope proposed *'prevent, resist it';* others scan *'resist'* by apocope (*'sist*); the natural movement of the line suggests:—

'prevént it, | resíst it, | —lét | it nót | be so.'

IV. i. 155-319. This part of the 'deposition scene' appeared for the first time in the Quarto of 1608. In the earlier editions line 320 reads: *'Let it be so, and lo on Wednesday next We solemnly proclaim.'*

IV. i. 215. *'that swear';* i.e. 'of those that swear'; Folios and Quarto 5, *'are made.'*

IV. i. 271. *'torment'st';* Rowe's emendation of Quartos 3, 4, 5 and Folios, *'torments.'*

IV. i. 282-289. A reminiscence of Marlowe's famous lines in Faustus: *'Was this the face that launch'd a thousand ships,'* &c.

V. i. 88. *'Better far off than near, be ne'er the near,'* i.e. 'better to be far apart than to be near, and yet never the nearer.'

V. iii. 42. *'secure, foolhardy king';* Quartos, *'secure foole hardy king';* Folio 4, *'secure foul-hardy king.'*

V. iii. 87. *'Love loving not itself,'* &c.; i.e. 'love which is indifferent to the claims of kindred can be loving to none.'

V. iii. 143. The reading of Quarto 5; the other editions omit *'too.'*

V. v. 9 *'this little world';* alluding to the conception of man as a 'microcosm,' i.e. 'an abstract or model of the world.'

V. v. 31. *'person';* so Quarto 1; the rest *'prison.'*

THE FIRST PART OF
KING HENRY IV

I. i. 5. *'No more the thirsty entrance of this soil,'* &c.; Folio 4, *'entrails'* for *'entrance';* Steevens, *'entrants;* Mason *'Erinnys';* Malone compares Genesis iv. 11: "And now art thou cursed from the earth, which hath opened *her mouth* to receive thy brother's blood from thy hand"; *'entrance'* probably = *'the mouth* of the earth or *soil.'*

I. i. 28. *'now is twelve month old,'* so Quartos 1, 2; Folios, *'is a twelvemonth old'*; Quartos 7, 8, *'is but twelve months old.'*

I. i. 71. *'Mordake the Earl of Fife'*; this was "Murdach Stewart, *not* the son of Douglas, but the eldest son of Robert, Duke of Albany, Regent of Scotland, third son of King Robert II." (*'the'* first supplied by Pope).

I. ii. 14. *'that wandering knight so fair,'* an allusion to 'El Donzel del Febo,' the 'Knight of the Sun,' whose adventures were translated from the Spanish:—*"The First Part of the Mirrour of Princely deeds and Knighthood: Wherein is shewed the Worthiness of the Knight of the Sunne and his brother Rosicleer. . . .* Now newly translated out of Spanish into our vulgar English tongue, by M(argaret) T(iler)"; eight parts of the book were published between 1579 and 1601. Shirley alludes to the Knight in the *Gamester* (iii. 1):—

"*He has knocked the flower of chivalry, the very Donzel del Phebo of the time.*"

I. ii. 40. *'Of Hybla,'* reading of Quartos; omitted in Folios; *'my old lad of the castle'*; probably a pun on the original name of Falstaff (*cp.* Preface).

I. ii. 84-85. *'For wisdom cries out in the streets, and no man regards it'*; an adaptation of Proverbs i. 20, omitted in Folios.

I. iii. 128. *'Albeit I make a hazard of my head'*; the reading of Quartos; Folios, *'Although it be with hazard of my head.'*

I. iii. 202, &c. This rant of Hotspur has been compared with the similar sentiment put into the mouth of Eteocles by Euripides—"I will not disguise my thoughts; I would scale heaven; I would descend to the very entrails of the earth, if so be that by that price I could obtain a kingdom."

In *The Knight of the Burning Pestle* (Induction), Beaumont and Fletcher put these lines into the mouth of Ralph, the apprentice, "apparently with the design of raising a good-natured laugh at Shakespeare's expense" (Johnson).

I. iii. 254. *'when his . . . age,'* cp. *Richard II.* Act II. iii. 48, 49, *'as my fortune ripens with thy love, It shall be still thy true love's recompense.'*

II. i. 72-73. *'great oneyers,'* probably a jocose term for 'great ones,' with perhaps a pun on *'owners'*; various emendations have been proposed, *e.g. 'oneraires,' 'moneyers,' 'seignors,' 'owners,' 'mynheers,' 'overseers,'* &c.

II. iii. 87. *'I'll break thy little finger,'* an ancient token of amorous dalliance, as Steevens has shown by quotations.

II. iv. *'Boar's-Head Tavern,'* the original tavern in Eastcheap was burnt down in the great fire, but was subsequently rebuilt, and stood until 1757, when it was demolished. Goldsmith visited the tavern, and wrote of it enthusiastically in his *Essays*.

II. iv. 114. *'pitiful-hearted Titan,'* so the early eds.: Theobald suggested *'butter'* for *'Titan,'* and the emendation has been generally adopted.

II. iv. 116. *'here's lime in this sack,'* cp. Sir Richard Hawkins' statement in his *Voyages*, that the Spanish sacks "for conservation are mingled with the lime in the making," and hence give rise to "the stone, the dropsy, and infinite other distempers, not heard of before this wine came into frequent use."

II. iv. 124. *'I would I were a weaver'*; weavers were good singers, especially of psalms, most of them being Calvinists who had fled from Flanders to escape persecution.

II. iv. 128. *'dagger of lath,'* like that carried by the Vice in the old Morality plays.

II. iv. 229. *'you elf-skin'*; so the Quartos and Folios; Hanmer, *'eel-skin'* (*cp.* 2 *Henry IV*. III. ii. 322); Johnson, *'elfkin.'*

II. iv. 363-364. *'King Cambyses' vein'*; an allusion to a ranting play called *'A Lamentable Tragedie, mixed full of pleasant mirth, containing the Life of Cambises, King of Persia'* (1570).

II. iv. 377. *'The camomile,'* &c., *cp.* Lyly's *Euphues* (quoted by Farmer): *"Though the camomile the more it is trodden and pressed down, the more it spreadeth; yet the violet the oftener it is handled and touched, the sooner it withereth and decayeth."*

II. iv. 425-426. *'that reverend vice,'* &c., alluding to the Vice of the Morality plays; 'Iniquity' and 'Vanity' were among the names given to the character, according to the particular 'Vice' held up to ridicule.

II. iv. 463. *'mad,'* Folios 3, 4; the rest *'made.'*

II. iv. 473. *'Peto'*; probably 'Poins,' according to Johnson; perhaps, the prefix in the MS. was simply 'P.' The Cambridge editors, however, remark that the formal address is appropriate to Peto rather than to Poins.

III. i. 148, &c. *'telling me of the mold-warp.'* cp. *Legend of Glendour* (stanza 23) in *The Mirror for Magistrates*, 1559:—

> *'And for it to sit us hereon more agog,*
> *A prophet came (a vengeance take them all!)*
> *Affirming Henry to be Gogmagog,*
> *Whom Merlin doth a mouldwarp ever call,*
> *Accurst of God, that must be brought in thrall*
> *By a wolf, a dragon, and a lion strong,*
> *Which should divide his kingdom them among.'*

III. i. 159-160. Compare Chaucer, *Canterbury Tales*, 5860:—

> *'Thou saist, that dropping houses, and eek smoke,*
> *And chiding wives maken men to flee*
> *Out of her owen hous';*

Vaughan adds the following:—"It is singular that Shakespeare should have combined two annoyances commemorated together by an old Welsh proverb, which I would translate:

'Three things will drive a man from home:
A roof that leaks,
A house that reeks,
A wife who scolds whene'er she speaks.' "

III. ii. 32. *'Thy place in council thou hast rudely lost,'* i.e. 'by thy rude or violent conduct'; there is an anachronism here, as the Prince was removed from the council for striking the Chief-Justice in 1403, some years after the battle of Shrewsbury.

III. ii. 38. *'doth'*; Quartos and Folios, *'do,'* which may be explained as due to the plural implied in *'every man'*; Rowe, *'does'*; Collier MS., *'doth.'*

III. ii. 62. *'carded his state'*; *'to card'* is often used in Elizabethan English in the sense of 'to mix, or debase by mixing' (*e.g.* *"You card your beer if you see your guests begin to get drunk, half small, half strong."* Green's *Quip for an Upstart Courtier*); Warburton suggested *'carded,' ' 'scarded,'* i.e. 'discarded'; but the former explanation is undoubtedly correct. 'To stir and mix with cards, to stir together, to mix,' the meaning is brought out by 1607 quotation from Topsell, *Four-foot Beasts,* "As for his diet, let it be warm mashes, sodden wheat and hay, thoroughly carded with wool-cards."

III. ii. 154. *'If He be pleased I shall perform'*; the reading of Quartos; Folio 1, *'if I performe, and doe survive'*; Folios 2, 3, 4, *'if I promise, and doe survive,'* &c.

III. ii. 164. *'Lord Mortimer of Scotland,'* a mistake for Lord March of Scotland, George Dunbar, who took sides with the English.

III. iii. 32-33. *'By this fire, that's God's angel'*; the latter words omitted in Folios and Quartos after Quarto 2; evidently a familiar expression. Vaughan thinks the allusion is to Hebrews i. 7; but it is more probably to Exodus iii. 2.

III. iii. 120. *'neither fish nor flesh,'* alluding to the old proverb, "Neither fish nor flesh, nor good red herring."

III. iii. 144. *'I pray God my girdle break'*; an allusion to the old adage, *"ungirt, unblessed"*; the breaking of the girdle was formerly a serious matter, as the purse generally hung on to the girdle, and would, in the event of the girdle breaking, probably be lost.

IV. i. 31. *'that inward sickness—'*; Rowe first suggested the dash in place of the comma of the early editions; the sentence is suddenly broken off.

IV. i. 85. *'term of fear'*; the Folios and later Quartos (7 and 8), *'dream'* for *'term.'*

IV. i. 98.

> *'All plumed like estridges that with the wind*
> *Baited like eagles having lately bathed':*

This, the reading of the early editions, has been variously
emended; Steevens and Malone suggested that a line has dropped
out after *wind*, and the former (too boldly) proposed as the miss-
ing line:—

> *'Run on, in gallant trim they now advance';*

on the other hand, Rowe's proposal to read *'wing the wind'* for
'with' has had many supporters, though it is said that *'wing the
wind'* applies to ostriches less than to any other birds; Dyce, how-
ever, quotes a passage from Claudian (*In Eutropium II.,* 310-
313) to justify it:—

> *'Vasta velut Libyæ venantum vocibus ales*
> *Cum premitur, calidas cursu transmittet arenas,*
> *Inque modum veli sinuatis flamina pennis*
> *Pulverulenta volat';*

the Cambridge editors maintain that this means that the bird
spreads its wings like a sail bellying with the wind—a different
thing from *'winging the wind.'* "But the Cambridge editors,"
Dyce replies, "take no notice of the important word *volat,* by
which Claudian means, of course, that the ostrich, *when once her
wings are filled with the wind, flies* along the ground (though
she does not mount into the air)"; he adds the following apt quo-
tation from Rogers:—

> *'Such to their grateful ear the gush of springs*
> *Who course the ostrich, as away she wings.'*
>
> COLUMBUS, Canto VIII.

baited = baiting; *to bait* or *bate* = 'to flap wings, as the
hawk did when unhooded and ready to fly.'

'having lately bathed'; "writers on falconry," says Steevens,
"often mention the bathing of hawks and eagles as highly neces-
sary for their health and spirits. All birds, after bathing, spread
out their wings to catch the wind, and flutter violently with them
in order to dry themselves. This, in the falconer's language, is
called *bating.*"

IV. ii. 26-27. *'younger sons to younger brothers,' i.e.* 'men of
desperate fortune and wild adventure'; the phrase, as Johnson
pointed out, occurs in Raleigh's *Discourse on War.*

V. i. *Stage direction.* The Quartos and Folios make the Earl of
Westmoreland one of the characters; but, as Malone pointed out,
he was in the rebel camp as a pledge for Worcester's safe con-
duct.

V. i. 13. *'old limbs';* Henry was, in reality, only thirty years old
at this time.

V. ii. 8. *'suspicion';* Rowe's emendation for *'supposition'* of the
early editions. Johnson points out that the same image of *'suspi-*

cion' is exhibited in a Latin tragedy, called *Roxana,* written about the same time by Dr. William Alabaster.

V. ii. 18. *'adopted name of privilege,' i.e.* the name of *Hotspur* will suggest that his temperament must be his excuse.

V. ii. 32. *'Douglas'* must here be read as a trisyllable.

V. ii. 59. *'By still dispraising praise valued with you'*; omitted by Pope and others as 'foolish,' but defended by Johnson:—"to vilify praise, compared or valued with merit, superior to praise, is no harsh expression."

V. ii. 71. *'so wild a libertine'*; Capell's emendation for the reading of the Folios, *'at libertie,'* and Quartos 1-4, *'a libertie'*; Theobald punctuated the line thus: *'of any prince, so wild, at liberty'*; others proposed *'wild o' liberty,'* which Collier erroneously declared to be the reading of the three oldest Quartos.

V. iii. 44. *'Turk Gregory never did such deeds in arms'*; Warburton observes:—"Fox, in his *History,* hath made Gregory (*i.e.* Pope Gregory VII., called Hildebrand) so odious that I don't doubt but the good Protestants of that time were well pleased to hear him thus characterized, as uniting the attributes of their two great enemies, the Turk and Pope, in one."

V. iv. 81. *'But thought's the slave of life,'* &c.; Dyce and others prefer the reading of Quarto 1:—

> *'But thoughts the slaves of life, and life time's fool,*
> *And time that takes survey of all the world,*
> *Must have a stop.'*

i.e. "Thoughts, which are the slaves of life, aye, and life itself, which is but the fool of Time, aye, and Time itself, which measures the existence of the whole world, must come to an end" (Vaughan).

V. iv. 161. *'Grow great,'* so Quartos; Folios, *'grow great again.'*

V. v. 41. *'sway'*; Folios and later Quartos, *'way.'*

THE SECOND PART OF
KING HENRY IV

INDUCTION. *'Enter Rumour, painted full of tongues,'* so Quarto; Folios, *'Enter Rumour.'* In ancient pageants Rumour was often represented as apparelled in a robe *'full of toongs'*; Stephen Hawes, in his *Pastimes of Pleasure,* describes Rumour as

> *'A goodly lady, environed about*
> *With tongues of fire.'*

Similarly Chaucer, *House of Fame,* 298-300. Probably the idea was ultimately derived from Virgil, *Æneid,* IV. 173-188.

Induct. 6. *'tongues,'* so Quarto; Folios, *'tongue.'*

Induct. 8. *'men,'* so Quarto; Folios, *'them.'*

I. i. 62. '*whereon,*' so Quarto; Folios, '*when.*'

I. i. 164. '*Lean*'; Quarto, '*leaue*'; '*your*'; Quarto, '*you.*'

I. i. 166-179; 189-190; omitted in Quarto.

I. ii. 7. '*foolish-compounded clay, man*'; Quarto and Folios, '*foolish compounded clay-man.*'

I. ii. 32-33. '*his tongue be hotter,*' alluding to the rich man in the Parable, Luke xvi. 24.

I. ii. 33-34. '*a rascally yea-forsooth knave*'; Quarto, '*rascall.*'

I. ii. 51-52. '*here comes the nobleman who committed the Prince*', &c.; this was Sir William Gascoigne, Chief-Justice of the King's Bench.

I. ii. 157. '*I cannot go; I cannot tell*'; Johnson was probably right in seeing here a play on *go* and *tell* in the sense of 'pass current' and 'count as good money.'

I. ii. 197. '*Spit white*'; cp. *Batman uppon Bartholome*, ed. 1582 (quoted by Dr. Furnivall):—"*If the spittle be white viscus, the sickness cometh of fleam; if black, of melancholy; the white spittle not knottie signifieth health.*" Other passages indicate that it was also regarded as a sign of thirst.

I. ii. 199-205. Omitted in Folios.

I. iii. 36-55. Omitted in Quarto.

I. iii. 36, &c.

> '*If this present quality of war*
> *Indeed the instant action: a cause on foot,*' &c.

Various attempts have been made to restore the meaning of the lines. Malone's reading has been generally accepted:—

> '*Yes, in this present quality of war:*
> *Indeed the instant action—a cause on foot—*
> *Lives so in hope as in an early spring.*'

which Grant White paraphrases, "Yes, in this present quality, function, or business of war, it is harmful to lay down likelihoods, etc. Indeed this very action or affair—a cause on foot—is no more hopeful for fruition than the buds of an unseasonably early spring." Pope proposed '*Impede the instant act*'; Johnson, '*in this present. . . . Indeed of instant action*'; Mason, '*if this prescient quality of war Induc'd the instant action,*' &c.

I. iii. 71. '*against the French.*' A French army of 12,000 men landed at Mitford Haven in Wales, for the aid of Glendower, during this rebellion.

I. iii. 85-108. Omitted in Quarto.

II. i. 145. '*so God save me, la!*'; Quarto, '*so God save me law*'; Folios, '*in good earnest la.*'

II. ii. 23-25. Omitted in Folios.

II. ii. 68. '*virtuous*'; Folios, '*pernicious*'; Capell conjectured '*precious.*'

II. ii. 78. '*Althæa*'; the boy here confounds Althæa's firebrand with Hecuba's; perhaps the blunder was the poet's.

iI. ii. 103. *'borrower's cap'*; Theobald's emendation; Folios and Quartos, *'borrowed cap.'*

II. ii. 154. *'leathern jerkins,'* commonly worn by vintners and tapsters.

II. iii. 12. *'heart's dear Harry'*; Folios, *'heart-deere-Harry.'*

II. iii. 19. *'the grey vault of heaven'*; cp. the use of *'grey'* applied to the eyes, where we generally use 'blue'; *'grey-eyed morn'* (*Romeo and Juliet*, II. iii. 1) may perhaps illustrate the same fact.

II. iv. 31. *'When Arthur's first in court'*; from the ballad of *Sir Lancelot du Lake*, printed in Percy's *Reliques*.

II. iv. 45. *'your brooches, pearls, and ouches'*; a scrap of an old ballad, first marked as a quotation by Capell.

II. iv. 49. Omitted in Folios.

II. iv. 100. PISTOL has been likened to the character of 'the swaggering ruffian,' CENTURIO, in the famous Spanish play by Rojas, called *Celestina*, which was translated into English by James Mabbe; and though entered on the Stationers' Registers in 1598, the translation was not issued till 1630. It is more than probable that Mabbe was one of Shakespeare's friends; at all events, the dramatist may easily have read the English *Tragicke-Comedye of Celestina* in MS. (Mabbe's fascinating book has recently been reprinted as a volume of Mr. Nutt's *Tudor Translations*.)

II. iv. 116-117. *'Since when, I pray you, sir?'* a scoffing form of enquiry.

II. iv. 119. Omitted in Folios.

II. iv. 142. *'Have we not Hiren here?'* probably a quotation from a lost play by George Peele called *The Turkish Mahomet and Hyren the Fair Greek*; *'Hiren,'* a corruption of 'Irene.'

II. iv. 146. *'And hollow pamper'd jades of Asia'*; cp. 2 *Tamburlaine*, IV. iv:—

> *'Holla, ye pamper'd jades of Asia!*
> *What! can ye draw but twenty miles a day?'*

II. iv. 150. *'Let the welkin roar'*; a commonplace tag in old ballads of the time.

II. iv. 160. *'Then feed, and be fat, my fair Calipolis'*; a burlesque of passages in Peele's *Battle of Alcazar* (1594); Muley Mahomet enters to his wife with lion's flesh on his sword, and says, *'Feed then, and faint not, my fair Calipolis.'*

II. iv. 162. *'Si fortune me tormente, sperato me contento'*; the line probably purposely corrupted, was restored by Hanmer:— *'Si fortuna me tormenta, il sperare me contenta'* (*i.e.* 'If fortune torments me, hope contents me'). "Pistol is only a copy of Hannibal Gonsaga," remarked Farmer, "who vaunted on yielding himself a prisoner, as you may read in an old collection of tales, called *Wits, Fits, Fancies*:—

> *'Si Fortuna me tormenta,*
> *Il speranza me contenta.'* "

II. iv. 178. *'Then death rock me asleep,'* &c.; said to be a fragment of an old song written by Anne Boleyn.

II. iv. 180. *'Untwine the Sisters Three'; cp. A Midsummer-Night's Dream*, V. i. 325-330, where there is a reference to the *'shears'* of Atropos, the Fate that cut the thread of human destiny.

II. iv. 253. *'Fiery Trigon'*; alluding to the astrological division of the zodiacal signs into four *trigons* or *triplicities;* one consisting of the three *fiery* signs (Aries, Leo, and Sagittarius); the others, respectively, of three airy, three watery, and three earthly signs. When the three superior planets were in the three fiery signs they formed a *fiery trigon*; when in Cancer, Scorpio, and Pisces, a *watery* one, &c.

III. i. The whole scene omitted in Quarto 1 (*i.e.* the earlier copies of the edition).

III. i. 30. *'Then happy low, lie down!'*; Quarto reads *'Then (happy) low lie downe'*; Coleridge suggested *'Then, happy low-lie-down'*; Warburton, *'happy lowly clown.'* The Folio seems to make the meaning quite clear:—*'Then happy Lowe, lye downe'*; *'low'* is used substantively, 'You who are happy in your humble situations, lay down your heads to rest,' &c.

III. i. 43. *'little,' i.e.* 'a little.'

III. i. 53-56. Omitted in Folios.

III. i. 66. *'cousin Nevil'*; the earldom of Warwick did not come into the family of the Nevilles till the latter part of the reign of Henry IV.; at this time it was in the family of Beauchamp.

III. ii. *'Justice Shallow'*; the character has, with much reason, been identified with Sir Thomas Lucy of Charlecote (*cp. The Merry Wives of Windsor*); perhaps there is a reference to his arms in the words, *'If the young dace be a bait for the old pike, I see no reason in the law of nature but I may snap at line'* (*cp. infra*, ll. 356, 357; *'luce'* = 'pike,' *cp.* Note, line 1, *Merry Wives of Windsor*).

III. ii. 22-23. *'Then was Jack Falstaff, now Sir John, a boy, and page to Thomas Mowbray, Duke of Norfolk.'* This is generally given as one of the points of evidence that Falstaff was originally called Oldcastle, Sir John Oldcastle having actually been in his youth page to the Duke of Norfolk: but it would seem that the same is true of Sir John Fastolf.

III. ii. 26-27. *'I see* (Folios *'saw'*) *him break Skogan's heal'* = (Quarto *Skoggins*; Folio 1, *'Scoggans'*); two Scogans must be carefully differentiated, though probably both are confused by Shakespeare in this passage:—(i.) Henry Scogan, the poet, Chaucer's Scogan, described by Ben Jonson in *The Fortunate Isles*, as

> *'a fine gentleman, and master of arts*
> *Of Henry the Fourth's times, that made disguises*
> *For the King's sons, and writ in ballad royal*
> *Daintily well';*

(ii.) John Scogan, "an excellent mimick, and of great pleasantry in conversation, the favourite buffoon of the court of Edward IV." A book of *'Scogins Jests'* was published in 1565 by Andrew Borde, and probably suggested the name to Shakespeare.

III. ii. 126-127. *'but much of the father's substance'*; so Quarto; Folios, *'not'*; the Variorum of 1821 proposed *'not much'*; the Quarto reading must be understood as ironical.

III. ii. 262. *'Dagonet in Arthur's show'*; Sir Dagonet is Arthur's fool in the story of Tristram de Lyonesse; *'Arthur's show'* was an exhibition of archery by a society of 58 members which styled itself *"The Ancient Order, Society, and Unitie laudable of Prince Arthur and his Knightly Armory of the Round Table,"* and took the names of the knights of the old romance. Mulcaster referred to it in his *Positions, concerning the training up of children* (1581). The meeting-place of the society was Mile-end Green.

III. ii. 291. *'invisible'*; Rowe's emendation; Quarto and Folios, *'invincible,' i.e.* (?) "not to be evinced, not to be made out, indeterminable" (Schmidt).

III. ii. 292-293. *'yet . . . mandrake'*; 310-314, *'a' came . . . good-nights'*; omitted in Folios.

III. ii. 306-307. *'philosopher's two stones'*; "one of which was an universal medicine, the other a transmuter of base metals into gold"; so Warburton; Malone explains:—"I will make him of *twice* the value of the philosopher's stone."

IV. i. 55-79. Omitted in Quarto.

IV. i. 71. *'there'*; the reading of the Folios; Hanmer conjectured *'sphere'*; Collier *'chair.'*

IV. i. 93. Neither this line nor 95 is to be found in the Folios, and they are omitted in some copies of the Quarto. To some corruption of the text is due the obscurity of ll. 94-96, which Clarke paraphrases:—"The grievances of my brother general, the commonwealth, and the home cruelty to my born brother, cause me to make this quarrel my own." The archbishop's brother had been beheaded by the King's order.

IV. i. 103-139. Omitted in Quarto.

IV. i. 173. *'true substantial form,' i.e.* 'in due form and legal validity.'

IV. iii. 39. *'hook-nosed fellow of Rome'*; Quarto adds *'there cosin'* before *'I came,'* which Johnson took to be a corruption of *'there, Cæsar.'*

IV. iii. 109. *'commences it and sets it in act and use'*; Tyrwhitt saw in these words an allusion "to the Cambridge *Commencement* and the Oxford *Act*; for by those different names the two Universities have long distinguished the season at which each gives to her respective students a complete authority to use *those hoards of learning* which have entitled them to their several degrees."

IV. iv. 35. '*as flaws congealed in the spring of day*'; according to Warburton the allusion is "to the opinion of some philosophers that the vapours being congealed in the air by the cold (which is most intense in the morning), and being afterwards rarefied and let loose by the warmth of the sun, occasion those sudden and impetuous gusts of wind which are called flaws"; Malone explained '*flaws*' to mean "small blades of ice which are stuck on the edges of the water in winter mornings."

IV. iv. 122. '*loathly births of nature*,' *i.e.* 'unnatural births.'

IV. v. 202. '*And all my friends*'; Tyrwhitt's conjecture for '*thy friends*' of the Folios and Quarto. Dyce, '*my foes.*' Clarke explains the original reading thus:—"By the first *thy friends* the King means those who are friendly inclined to the prince, and who, he goes on to say, must be made securely friends."

IV. v. 232. ' '*Tis called Jerusalem*'; probably from the tapestries of the history of Jerusalem with which it was hung; now used for the meetings of Convocation.

V. i. 26-27. '*A friend i' court is better than a penny in purse*'; *cp. The Romaunt of the Rose*, 5540:—

> '*For frende in court aie better is*
> *Than peny is in purse, certis*';

Camden gives the same proverbial expression.

V. ii. 38. '*A ragged and forestall'd remission*'; '*forestall'd*' has been variously interpreted; the simplest interpretation seems to be 'anticipated, asked for before being granted,' not necessarily by the Chief-Justice himself, but by his friends; the explanation fits in well with the dignified utterance of the speaker. Others explain, 'a pardon that is sure not to be granted, the case having been prejudged'; 'a pardon which is precluded from being absolute, by the refusal of the offender to accuse or alter his conduct,' &c.

V. iii. 72. '*Do me right*'; 'to do a man right' was formerly, according to Steevens, the usual expression in pledging healths.

'*And dub me knight*'; it was a custom in Shakespeare's day to drink a bumper kneeling to the health of one's mistress. He who performed this exploit was *dubbed a knight* for the evening, *cp. A Yorkshire Tragedy*. "They call it knighting in London when they drink upon their knees" (Malone).

V. iii. 116, 117. '*Dead?· As nail in door*'; an ancient proverbial expression; the door-nail was probably the nail on which the knocker struck. "It is therefore used as a comparison to any one irrevocably dead, one who has fallen (as Virgil says)*multa morte*, that is, with abundant death, such as iteration of strokes on the head would naturally produce."

V. iii. 134. '*Where is the life that late I led*'; a scrap of an old song; *cp. Taming of the Shrew*, IV. i.

V. v. 27. '*obsque hoc nihil est*,' ' 'tis all in every part'; the second and later Folios correct '*obsque*' to '*absque*,' but the error may have been intentional on the author's part. Pistol uses a Latin expression 'ever the same, for without this there is nothing,' and then goes on to allude to an English proverbial expression, '*All in all, and all in every part*,' which he seems to give as its free rendering.

V. v. 106. '*I heard a bird so sing*'; a proverbial expression still extant.

EPILOGUE. Shakespeare's authorship of this epilogue has been doubted, and it has been described as 'a manifest and poor imitation of the epilogue to *As You Like It*.' It is noteworthy that it occurs already in the Quarto (1600), though with one important difference; the words '*and so kneel down . . . queen*' (ll. 33, 34) are printed there at the end of the first paragraph, after '*infinitely*.' It seems probable, therefore, that the epilogue originally ended there, and that the remaining lines were added somewhat later. One is strongly tempted to infer that the additions to the epilogue were called forth by the success of the first and second parts of the play of *Sir John Oldcastle*, written evidently to vindicate the character of Falstaff's original, and put on the stage as a counter-attraction to *Henry IV*., hence the words, added in a spirit of playful defiance, '*for Oldcastle died a martyr, and this is not the man*' (l. 31). The first part of *Sir John Oldcastle* was performed for the first time about the 1st of November, 1599, the second part, dealing with the Lollard's death, was evidently written by the end of the year. *The First Part of the true and honourable history of the Life of Sir John Oldcastle, the good Lord Cobham*, appeared in two editions in 1600; Shakespeare's name had been impudently printed on the title-page of the former and less correct edition; the authors were Munday, Drayton, Wilson, and Chettle. The 'Second Part' is not known to exist.

l. 23-25. '*our humble author will continue the story, with Sir John in it, and make you merry with fair Katherine in France*'; Shakespeare changed his mind. "The public was not to be indulged in laughter for laughter's sake at the expense of his play. The tone of the entire play of *Henry V.* would have been altered if Falstaff had been allowed to appear in it. . . . Agincourt is not the field for splendid mendacity. . . . There is no place for Falstaff any longer on earth; he must find refuge 'in Arthur's bosom.' " But the public would not absolve "our humble author of his promise, and they were to make merry again with their favourite

'*round about the oak
Of Herne the hunter*.' "

THE LIFE OF KING HENRY V

PROLOGUE. 9. *'spirits that have dared'*; so Staunton; Folios 1, 2, 3, *'hath'*; Folio 4, *'spirit, that hath.'*

I. ii. 45, 52. *'Elbe,'* restored by Capell; Folios, *'Elue'*; (Holinshed, *'Elbe'*; Hall, *'Elve'*).

I. ii. 61-64. Theobald (Warburton); *cp.* Montaigne's *Essays*, III. 9 (*vide* Florio's translation).

I. ii. 77. *'Lewis the tenth'*; the reading of Folios, following Holinshed; Pope, from Hall, reads *'ninth.'*

I. ii. 94. *'amply to imbar'*; so Folios (Folios 1, 2, *'imbarre'*); Quartos, 1, 2 *'imbace,'* Quarto 3, *'imbrace'*; Rowe, *'make bare'*; Theobald (Warburton), *'imbare'*; Pope, *'openly imbrace,'* &c. Schmidt explains the lines:—"They strive to exclude you, instead of excluding amply, *i.e.* without restriction or subterfuge, their own false titles." Perhaps Mr. W. A. Wright's explanation is the truer, taking *'imbar'* in the sense of 'to bar in,' 'secure':—"The Kings of France, says the Archbishop, whose own right is derived only through the female line, prefer to shelter themselves under the flimsy protection of an appeal to the Salic law, which would exclude Henry's claim, instead of fully securing and defending their own titles by maintaining that though, like Henry's, derived through the female line, their claim was stronger than his."

I. ii. 98. *'in the Book of Numbers'*; *cp.* Numbers xxvii. 1-11.

I. ii. 99. *'man'*; the reading of Folios; Quartos, *'sonne.'*

I. ii. 110. *'Forage in,'* Folios, *'Forrage in'*; Quarto 1, *'Foraging'*; Quarto 3, *'Forraging the.'*

I. ii. 125. *'Your grace hath cause and means.'* Hanmer reads *'Your race hath had cause, means.'* Various readings have been suggested, but there seems to be no difficulty whatever in understanding the text as it stands.

I. ii. 131. *'blood'*; so Folios 3, 4; Folio 1, *'Bloods'*; Folio 2, *'Blouds.'*

I. ii. 150. *'with ample and brim fulness'*; probably *'brim'* is here adjectival; Pope reads *'brimfulness'*; but the accent favours the present reading.

I. ii. 154. *'the ill neighbourhood'*; Boswell, from Quartos, reads *'the bruit thereof.'*

I. ii. 163. *'her chronicle'*; Capell, Johnson conjectured; Folios read, *'their C.'*; Quartos, *'your Chronicles'*; Rowe, *'his Chronicle.'*

I. ii. 173. *'tear'*; so Rowe, ed. 2; Folios, *'tame'*; Quartos, *'spoil'*; Theobald, *'taint.'*

I. ii. 180-183. Theobald first compared these lines with Cicero, *De Republica*, ii. 42, and thought that Shakespeare had perhaps borrowed from Cicero.

I. ii. 187-203. Lyly, in his *Euphues* (Arber's Reprint, pp. 262-

4), has a similar description of the common-wealth of the bees: its *ultimate* source is probably Pliny's *Natural History*, Book xi. (*n.b.*, Holland's translation did not appear till 1601).

I. ii. 197. *'majesty'*; so Rowe from Quartos; Folios, *'Maiesties.'*

I. ii. 208. *'Come,'* so Folios; Capell, from Quartos, *'fly'*; *'as many ways meet in one town'*; Capell, from Quartos, reads *'As many seuerall wayes meete in one towne'*; Dyce, Lettsom conjectured *'As many several streets,'* &c.

I. ii. 209. *'meet in one salt sea'*; Capell, from Quartos, reads *'run in one self sea'*; Vaughan conjectured *'run in one salt sea.'*

I. ii. 212. *'End'*; Pope's emendation from Quartos; Folios, *'And.'*

I. ii. 255. *'This tun of treasure'*; probably suggested by the corresponding words in *The Famous Victories*.

I. ii. 263. *'shall strike his father's crown into the hazard'*; *'hazard'* used technically, "the hazard in a tennis-court"; glosses, *'grille de tripot'* in old French dictionaries.

Prol. II. Pope transferred the Prologue to the end of the first scene.

Prol. II. 32. *'The abuse of distance; force a play'*: so Folios; Pope, *'while we force a play'*; Warburton conjectured *'while we farce a play,'* &c.; *'to force a play'* is interpreted by Steevens to mean 'to produce a play by compressing many circumstances into a narrow compass.' Various emendations have been proposed, but in spite of the imperfection of the line as it stands, no suggestions seem to improve upon it. Perhaps, after all, the line is correct as it stands, with a pause for a syllable at the cæsura, and with a vocalic *r* in *'force,'* making the word dissyllabic; *cp.* *'fierce,'* II. iv. 100.

Prol. II. 41. *'But, till the king come forth,'* &c., *i.e.* 'until the King come forth we shall not shift our scene unto Southampton.'

II. i. 5. *'there shall be smiles'*; Hanmer conjectures, Warburton, *'there shall be—*(smiles)'; Farmer, Collier, 2 ed., *'smites'* (*i.e.* 'blows').

II. i. 22. *'mare'*; restored by Theobald from Quartos; Folios read *'name'*; Hanmer, *'dame'*; Collier MS., *'jade.'*

II. i. 25. *'How now, mine host Pistol!'* Quartos, *'How do you my Hoste?'* giving the words to Nym.

II. i. 32-33. *'O well a day, Lady, if he be not drawn now'*; *'drawn,'* Theobald's emendation; Folios, *'hewne'*; Malone from Quarto 1, *'O Lord! here's corporal Nym's——.'*

II. i. 38. *'Iceland dog!'* Steevens, Johnson conjectured; Folios read *'Island dog'*; Quartos, *'Iseland.'* There are several allusions to "these shaggy, sharp-eared, white dogs, much imported formerly as favourites for ladies."

II. i. 71. *'lazar kite of Cressid's kind'*; probably a scrap from some old play. In certain parallel passages the readings vary between 'Kite,' 'Kit,' 'Catte'; 'Kit,' too, is the spelling of Folio 4.

II. i. 76-77. 'and you, hostess'; Folios, 'and your Hostesse'; Folio 4, 'Hostes you must come straight to my master, and you Hoste Pistole.'

II. i. 89. 'Base is the slave that pays,' a quotation from an old play, Steevens quotes "My motto shall be, Base is the man that pays" (Heywood's Fair Maid of the West).

II. i. 98. Omitted in Folios.

II. ii. 9. 'Whom he hath dull'd and cloy'd with gracious favours'; Folios 3, 4, 'lull'd.' Quartos, followed by Steevens, 'whom he hath cloy'd and grac'd with princely favours.'

II. ii. 61. 'Who are the late commissioners?'; Vaughan conjectured 'Who ask the late commissions?'; Collier MS. 'the state c.'; but no change is necessary; 'late commissioners' = 'lately appointed commissioners.'

II. ii. 63. 'for it,' i.e. 'for my commission.'

II. ii. 114. 'by treasons'; Mason conjectured 'to treasons'; Moberly conjectured 'by reasons.'

II. ii. 118. 'But he that temper'd thee bade thee stand up'; Moberly conjectured 'But he that tempter-fiend that stirr'd thee up'; Dyce, Johnson conjectured 'tempted'; Folios, 'bad'; Vaughan conjectured 'sin thus.' No emendation is necessary, though it is uncertain what the exact force of 'bade thee stand up' may be, whether (1) 'like an honest-man,' or (2) 'rise in rebellion.'

II. ii. 139-140. 'To mark the full-fraught man and best indued With some suspicion'; Malone's emendation; Theobald, 'The best,' &c.; Folios, 'To make thee full fraught man, and best indued,' &c.; Pope, 'To make the full-fraught man, the best, endu'd With,' &c.

II. ii. 147. 'Henry'; Theobald's correction from Quartos; Folios, 'Thomas.'

II. iii. 10. 'A' made a finer end'; Folios 1, 2, 'a finer'; Folios 3, 4, 'finer'; Capell, 'a fine'; Johnson conjectured 'a final'; Vaughan conjectured 'a fair.' Probably Mistress Quickly's words are correctly reported, and should not be edited.

II. iii. 13-14. 'fumble with the sheets'; popularly supposed to be a sign of approaching death.

II. iii. 16. 'and a' babbled of green fields'; Theobald's famous correction of Folios, 'and a Table of greene fields'; Theobald's reading was suggested to him by a MS. note written in a copy of Shakespeare by 'a gentleman sometime deceased,' who proposed 'And a' talked of green fields.' The Quartos omit the line, giving the passage thus:—

> 'His nose was as sharp as a pen,
> For when I saw him fumble with the sheetes,
> And talk of floures, and smile vpo his fingers ends,
> I knew there was no way but one'

(*n.b. 'talk of floures'*). Many suggestions have been put forward since Pope explained that the words were part of a stage direction, and that 'Greenfield was the name of the propertyman in that time who furnished implements, &c., for the actors.' The marginal stage-direction was, according to him, '*A table of greenfields.*' Malone, '*in a table of green fields,*' Collin MSS., '*on a table of green freese.*' Recently M. Henry Bradley has pointed out that 'green field' was occasionally used for the exchequer table, a table of green baize. A combination of this suggestion with the reading of the Collier MS. would require merely the change of '*and*' to '*on,*' but one cannot easily give up one's perfect faith in Theobald's most brilliant conjecture.

II. iii. 43. '*Let senses rule*'; *i.e.* 'let prudence govern you' (Steevens).

II. iii. 46. '*And hold-fast is the only dog*'; *cp.* 'Brag is a good dog, but holdfast is a better.'

II. iii. 47. '*Caveto,*' Quartos, '*cophetua.*'

II. iv. 57. '*mountain sire*'; Theobald, '*mounting sire*'; Collier, Mitford conjectured '*mighty sire*'; '*mountain*' evidently means 'huge as a mountain.'

Prol. III. 4. '*Hampton,*' Theobald's correction of Folios, '*Dover.*'

Prol. III. 6. '*fanning*'; Rowe's emendation of Folios 1, 2, '*fayning,*' Folios 3, 4, '*faining*'; Gould conjectured '*playing.*'

Prol. III. 35. '*Eke*'; the first Folio, '*eech*'; the others, '*ech*'; probably representing the pronunciation of the word.

III. i. 7. '*summon up,*' Rowe's emendation of Folios, '*commune up.*'

III. i. 15. '*nostril*'; Rowe's emendation of Folios, '*nosthrill.*'

III. i. 32. '*straining*'; Rowe's emendation of Folios, '*Straying.*'

III. ii. 19. '*Up to the breach, you dogs! avaunt, you cullions!*'; so Folios; Capell reads, from Quartos, '*God's plud!—Up to the preaches you rascals! will you not up to the preaches?*'

III. v. 46. '*Knights*'; Theobald's emendation of Folios, '*Kings.*'

III. v. 54. '*Rouen*'; Malone's emendation of '*Rone,*' Quartos; '*Roan,*' Folios.

III. vi. 26. '*And giddy Fortune's furious fickle wheel,*' &c.; *cp.* '*Fortune is blind . . . whose foot is standing on a rolling stone,*' Kyd's *Spanish Tragedy.*

III. vi. 29-30. '*Fortune is painted blind*'; Warburton proposed the omission of '*blind,*' which may have been caught up from the next line.

III. vi. 38. '*Fortune is Bardolph's foe*'; a reference to the old ballad, '*Fortune, my foe!*'

III. vi. 74. '*new-tuned*'; Pope reads '*new-turned*'; Collier MS., '*new-coined*'; Grant White, '*new-found.*'

III. vi. 98-102. Fluellen's description of Bardolph forcibly recalls Chaucer's Sompnour in the *Prologue to the Canterbury Tales* (Quartos, '*whelkes, and knubs, and pumples*' for '*bubukles, and whelks, and knobs*').

III. vi. 107. '*lenity*,' Rowe's emendation from Quartos; Folios, '*Levity*.'

III. vi. 110. '*habit*'; *i.e.* 'sleeveless coat, the herald's tabard.'

III. vii. 14. '*chez les narines*'; Capell, '*qui a*'; Folios, '*ches*'; Heath conjectured '*voyez*,' &c.

III. vii. 37. '*Wonder of Nature*,' probably the first words of a sonnet or lyric of the time.

III. vii. 60-61. '*Le chien . . . au bourbier*'; 'the dog is returned to his own vomit, and the washed out sow to the mire,' *cp.* 2 Peter ii. 22.

Prol. IV. 16. '*name*'; Tyrwhitt's conjecture; Folios, '*nam'd*.'

Prol. IV. 20. '*cripple tardy-gaited*'; Folios, '*creeple-tardy-gated*.'

Prol. IV. 26. '*Investing lank-lean cheeks and war-worn coats*'; Capell, '*And war-worn coats, investing lank-lean cheeks*'; Hanmer, '*In wasted*'; Warburton, '*Invest in*'; Becket conjectured '*Infesting*,' &c.

IV. i. 35. '*Qui va là*'; Rowe's emendation of Folios, '*Che vous la?*'

IV. i. 65. '*speak lower*'; so Quarto 3, adopted by Malone; Quartos 1, 2, '*lewer*'; Folios, '*fewer*'; *cp.* 'to speak few,' a provincialism for 'to speak low,' (according to Steevens, who prefers the Folio reading).

IV. i. 91. '*Sir Thomas*'; Theobald's correction of Folios, '*John*.'

IV. i. 141. '*sinfully miscarry upon the sea*'; Pope reads from Quartos, '*fall into some lewd action and miscarry*.'

IV. i. 170. '*mote*'; Malone's emendation of Folios, '*Moth*'; Quartos, '*moath*.'

IV. i. 231. '*What is thy soul of adoration?*'; Knight's reading; Folio I reads, '*What? is thy Soule of Odoration?*'; Folios 2, 3, 4, '*Adoration*'; Warburton, '*What is thy toll, O adoration?*'; Hanmer, '*What is thy shew of adoration?*'; Johnson, '*What is thy soul, O adoration?*'; &c., &c. (*v.* Glossary).

IV. i. 276-277. '*take from them now the sense of reckoning, if the opposed numbers*'; Tyrwhitt's reading; Folios, '*take . . . reck'ning of the opposed numbers:*'; Theobald, '*take . . . reck'ning; lest th' opposed numbers,*' &c. &c.

IV. iii. 40. '*the feast of Crispian*' falls upon the 25th October.

IV. iii. 44. '*He that shall live this day, and see*'; Pope's reading; Folios, '*He that shall see this day and live*'; Quartos, '*He that outlives this day and sees*.'

IV. iii. 48. Omitted in Folios.

IV. iii. 52. '*his mouth*'; so Folios; Quartos, '*their mouths*'; Pope, '*their mouth*.'

IV. iv. 4. *'Qualtitie calmie custure me'*; probably Pistol catches the last word of the French soldier's speech, repeats it, and adds the refrain of a popular Irish song, *'Galen, O custure me'* = 'colleen oge astore,' *i.e.* 'young girl, my treasure.' The popularity of the song is evidenced by the following heading of one of the songs in Robinson's *Handful of Pleasant Delights* (*cp.* Arber's Reprint, p. 33): *'A Sonet of a Lover in the praise of his lady. To Galen o custure me; sung at eurie lines end'*; first pointed out by Malone.

IV. iv. 66-67. *'this roaring devil? the old play'*; alluding to the standing character of the Devil in the Morality plays.

IV. v. 11. *'Let us die in honour; once'*; Knight's emendation; Folio 1, *'Let us dye in once'*; Folios 2, 3, 4, *'Let us flye in once'*; &c. Omitted by Pope.

IV. v. 18. *'our lives'*; Steevens adds from Quartos, *'Unto these English, or else die with fame'*; Vaughan conjectured *'Unto these English, or else die with shame.'*

IV. vii. 24. *'alike'*; so Folios; Rowe reads *'as like.'*

IV. vii. 39. *'made'*; Capell, following Quartos, reads *'made an end.'*

IV. vii. 57. *'Assyrian slings'*; Theobald compared Judith ix. 7, and defended the reading against Warburton's proposed *'Balearian'* (afterwards withdrawn).

IV. vii. 63. *'what means this, herald?'* Steevens' reading; Folio 1, *'what meanes this herald?'*; Folios 2, 3, 4, *'what means their herald'*; Hanmer conjectured *'what mean'st thou, herald?'*

IV. vii. 73. *'their wounded steeds'*; Folios, *'with,'* corrected by Malone. The Quartos omit the line.

Prol. V. 30-35. The allusion is to Robert Devereux, Earl of Essex, who was sent to Ireland in 1599 to suppress Tyrone's rebellion; he left London on March 27, and returned on September 28 (*v.* Preface).

Prol. V. 38. *'The emperor's coming'*; *i.e.* 'the emperor is coming,' or (better) 'the emperor's coming,' parallel to *'the King of England's stay at home.'* The line refers to the visit of Sigismund, Emperor of Germany, 1st May 1416. Malone supposed that a line had dropped out before *'The Emperor,'* &c.; Capell re-wrote the passage. It seems, however, that if instead of a semi-colon, a comma is placed after *'at home,'* the lines are perfectly intelligible as they stand.

V. i. 74. *'Doll'*; Capell, *'Nell'*; which is probably the correct reading, though Shakespeare may himself have made the mistake.

V. ii. 7. *'Burgundy'*; Rowe's emendation, from Quartos, of Folio 1, *'Burgogne'*; Folios 2, 4, *'Burgoigne'*; Folio 3, *'Bargoigne.'*

V. ii. 11. *'So are you, princes English, every one'*; Folios 1, 2, 3, *'So are you princes (English) every one'*; Folio 4, *'So are you princes (English every one).'*

V. ii. 12. *'England'*; so Folios 2, 3, 4; Folio 1 reads *'Ireland.'*

V. ii. 50. *'all'*; Rowe's reading; Folios, *'withall.'*

V. ii. 82. *'Pass our accept'*; Warburton reads, *'Pass, or accept'*; Malone conjectured *'Pass, or except,'* &c.

V. ii. 237. *'queen of all, Katharine'*; Capell conjectured, adopted by Dyce, *'queen of all Katharines.'*

V. ii. 325. *'Héritier'*; Folios read *'Heretere'*; *'Præclarissimus'*; so Folios; Rann reads *'Percarissimus'*; the error is, however, copied from Holinshed.

V. ii. 358. *'Sennet'*; Folio 1, *'Senet'*; Folio 2, *'Sonet,'* as though referring to the fourteen lines of the Epilogue.

Epil. 13. *'Which oft our stage hath shown'*; *vide* Preface to 1, 2, 3 *Henry VI.*

THE FIRST PART OF
KING HENRY VI

I. i. 3. *'crystal,'* unnecessarily changed by Hanmer to *'crisped'*; Warburton, *'cristed'* or *'crested'*; Roderick, *'tristful tresses in the sky,'* or *'tresses in the crystal sky.'*

I. i. 6. *'King Henry the Fifth'*; Pope, *'Henry the Fifth'*; Walker, *'King Henry Fifth'*; Pope's reading has been generally followed by modern editors.

I. i. 12. *'wrathful'*; Rowe, *'awful.'*

I. i. 24. *'glory's'*; Folios, *'Glories.'*

I. i. 27. *'By magic verses have contrived his end'*; alluding to the old notion "that life might be taken away by metrical charms" (Johnson). Folios 2, 3, 4, *'Verse'*; Pope, *'verse have thus.'*

I. i. 33. *'had not'*; Vaughan proposed *'had but'* (but *cp.* ll. 41-43).

I. i. 49. *'moist'*; so Folios 2, 3, 4; Folio 1, *'moistned.'*

I. i. 56. *'or bright——'*; various attempts have been made to fill up the blank, which some editors explain as due to the inability of the compositor to read the name in the MS.; Francis Drake, Berenice, Cassiopeia, Alexander, &c., have been suggested. Probably the speech is interrupted by the entrance of the messenger.

I. i. 60. *'Rheims'*; Folios, *'Rheimes'*; evidently intended as a dissyllable; but Capell's *'Rheims. Roan,'* derives some support from the fact that *'Roan,'* i.e. *'Rouen,'* is mentioned by Gloucester in line 65 (Cambridge ed.).

I. i. 65. *'Rouen'*; Folio 1, *'Roan.'*

I. i. 76. *'A third'*; Folios 2, 3, 4, *'A third man'*; Walker, *'A third one'*; Delius, *'A third thinketh'*; Keightley, *'A third thinks that'*; Dyce, *'And a third thinks,'* &c. Surely a simpler solution of the difficulty is to read *'third'* as a dissyllable with a trilled *r*.

I. i. 78. *'Awake, awake'*; Folio 2, *'Awake, away.'*

I. i. 83. '*their*'; Theobald's emendation; Folios, '*her*'; Anon. conjectured '*our.*'

I. i. 94. '*Reignier*'; Rowe's emendation of '*Reynold*' of the Folios.

I. i. 95. '*The Duke of Alençon*'; Walker omits '*of,*' to improve the rhythm of the line.

I. i. 96. '*crowned*'; Rowe's emendation; '*crown'd,*' the reading of the Folios.

I. i. 124. '*flew,*' Rowe's correction; Folios, '*slew.*'

I. i. 128. '*A Talbot! a Talbot! cried out amain.*' The line has been variously emended as being defective, metrically. Pope, '*A Talbot! Talbot! cried*'; Seymour, '*A Talbot! cried, a Talbot!*'; Vaughan, '*Talbot! a Talbot! cried.*' If, however, '*cried*' is read as a dissyllable, the movement of the line is parallel to that of '*prevent it, resist it, let it not be so,*' in *Richard II.* IV. i. 148, and no correction seems necessary—

A Tálbot! | A Tálbot! crí|ed óut | amáin |

I. i. 131. '*Sir John Fastolfe*'; Theobald's emendation here and elsewhere of Folios, '*Sir John Falstaffe*'; but in all probability Falstaff was the popular form of the name and it is questionable whether the text should be altered here. "He was a lieutenant-general, deputy regent to the Duke of Bedford in Normandy, and a Knight of the Garter."

I. i. 176. '*steal,*' Mason's conjecture; Folios, '*send*'; Keightley '*fetch.*'

I. ii. 1. '*Mars his true moving*'; cp. "You are as ignorant in the true *movings* of my muse as the astronomers are in the *true movings of Mars,* which to this day they could not attain to," quoted by Steevens from one of Nash's prefaces to '*Gabriel Harvey's Hunt's Up,*' 1596. Kepler's work on Mars (*Comment. de Motibus Stellæ Martis*) was published in 1609.

I. ii. 13. '*live*'; Capell, '*sit*'; Walker, '*lie.*'

I. ii. 30. '*bred*'; Folios, '*bread.*'

I. ii. 56. '*nine sibyls of old Rome.*' The number of the Sibyls is variously given as three, four, seven, ten; possibly the '*nine*' is here due to confusion with the nine Sibylline books.

I. ii. 86. '*which you see,*' reading of Folios 2, 3, 4; Folio 1, '*which you may see.*'

I. ii. 99. '*five*'; Folios, '*fine.*'

I. ii. 101. '*Out of a great deal of old iron*'; Dyce's conjecture, '*out of a deal old iron,*' seems the best of the emendations proposed.

I. ii. 103. '*ne'er fly from a man*'; so Folio 1; Folios 2, 3, 4, '*ne're flye no man*'; Collier MS., '*ne'er fly from no man*'; there was probably some jingle intended:—

CHAR. *Then come, o' God's name; I fear no woman.*
PUC. *And while I live, I'll ne'er fly from no man.*

I. ii. 108. *'thy desire,'* = 'desire for thee.'

I. ii. 131. *'Except Saint Martin's summer'*; "except prosperity after misfortune, like fair weather at Martlemas, after winter has begun" (Johnson). St. Martin's Day is November 11th.

I. ii. 138. *'That proud insulting ship, Which Cæsar and his fortune bare at once,'* evidently suggested by the following passage in North's translation of Plutarch's "Life of Cæsar":— "Cæsar hearing that, straight discovered himself unto the faster of the pynnace, who at first was amazed when he saw him; but Cæsar, then taking him by the hand, said unto him, good fellow, be of good cheer, . . . and fear not, for *thou hast Cæsar and his fortune with thee.*"

I. ii. 140. *'Mohamet inspired with a dove'*; cp. "he (Mahomet) used to feed (a dove) with wheat out of his ear; which dove, when it was hungry, lighted on Mahomet's shoulder, and thrust its bill in to find its breakfast; Mahomet persuading the rude and simple Arabians that it was the Holy Ghost that gave him advice" (Raleigh's *History of the World,* I. i. vi.).

I. ii. 143. *'Saint Philip's daughters'*; "the four daughters of Philip mentioned in the Acts" (Hanmer).

I. ii. 145. *'reverently worship'*; Capell, *'ever worship'*; Steevens, *'reverence, worship'*; Dyce (Collier MS.), *'reverent worship'*; the last seems the only plausible reading.

I. ii. 148. *'Orleans'*; Folios, *'Orleance'*; Capell, *'hence.'*

I. iii. 4. *' 'tis Gloucester'*; Pope's emendation; Folios, *' 'tis Gloster'*; Steevens, *'it is Gloster,'* &c.; cp. l. 62 below, where Folios similarly read *'Gloster.'*

I. iii. 29. *'ambitious Humphry'*; Folio 4, *'ambition'*; *'Humphrey,'* Theobald's emendation; Folio 1, *'Vmpheir'*; Folios 2, 3, 4, *'Umpire.'*

I. iii. 35. *'indulgences to sin'*; "the public stews were formerly under the jurisdiction of the bishop of Winchester" (Pope).

I. iii. 72. *'as e'er thou canst; Cry'*; Folios, *'as e're thou canst, cry'*; Collier MS., *'as thou canst cry.'*

I. iii. 82. *'cost,'* Folios 2, 3, 4, *'deare cost.'*

I. iii. 88. *'it ere long'*; so Folios 1, 2; Folios 3, 4, *'it e're be long'*; Capell, *'it ere 't be long'*; Collier MS., *'it off, ere long'*; Orson, *'at it.'*

I. iv. 22. *'on the turrets,'* Folios, *'in an upper chamber of a tower'* (Malone).

I. iv. 27. *'Duke'*; Theobald's emendation of *'Earle'* of the Folios.

I. iv. 33. *'so vile-esteem'd'*; Pope, *'so vilde esteem'd'*; Folios, *'so pil'd esteem'd'*; Capell, *'so pill'd esteem'd'*; Mason, *'so ill-esteemed,'* &c.

I. iv. 95. *'like thee, Nero,'* Malone; Folio 1, *'like thee'*; Folio 2, *'Nero like will'*; Folios 3, 4, *'Nero like, will'*; Pope, *'Nero-like,'* &c.

I. iv. 101. '*Joan la Pucelle*'; Folios, '*Joan de Puzel*' (and elsewhere).

I. v. 6. '*Blood will I draw on thee, thou art a witch*'; "the superstition of those times taught that he that could draw the witch's blood was free from her power" (Johnson).

I. v. 21. '*like Hannibal,*' who, in order to escape, devised the stratagem of fixing lighted twigs to the horns of oxen. (*Cp.* Livy, xxii. 16.)

I. v. 30. '*treacherous from*'; so Folios 3, 4; Folios 1, 2, '*trecherous from*'; Pope, '*tim'rous from.*'

I. vi. 2. '*English*' (trisyllabic), so Folio 1; Folios 2, 3, 4, '*English wolves*'; Staunton, '*English dogs.*'

I. vi. 6. '*Adonis' gardens.*' "The proverb alluded to seems always to have been used in a bad sense, for things which make a fair show for a few days, and then wither away; but the author of this play, desirous of making a show of his learning, without considering its propriety, has made the Dauphin apply it as an encomium" (Blakeway). *Cp. Faerie Queene,* III. vi. 29; Folio 1, '*Garden.*'

I. vi. 22. '*Than Rhodope's or Memphis*' ' Hanmer's emendation; Folios '*or Memphis*'; Capell's '*of Memphis*' has been generally adopted. Pliny, writing of the pyramids near Memphis, records that "the fairest and most commended for workmanship was built at the cost and charges of *one Rhodope,* a verie strumpet."

I. vi. 25. '*the rich-jewel'd coffer of Darius*'; referred to by Plutarch in his "Life of Alexander," as the "*preciousest thing, and the richest that was gotten of all spoyls and riches, taken at the overthrow of Darius . . . he said he would put the Iliads of Homer into it, as the worthiest thing.*"

II. i. 8. '*redoubted Burgundy*'; Duke of Burgundy, surnamed Philip the Good.

II. i. 29. '*all together*'; Rowe's emendation of '*altogether*' of Folios.

II. i. 40. '*ay, and glad*'; Folios, '*I and glad*'; Pope, '*I am glad.*'

II. i. 63. '*your quarters*'; '*your,*' so Folio 1; Folios 2, 3, 4, '*our*'; '*quarters*'; so Folios 1, 2, 3; Folio 4, '*Quarter.*'

II. ii. 20. '*Arc,*' Rowe's emendation of '*acre*' of Folios.

II. ii. 38. '*Auvergne*'; Rowe's emendation of Folio 1, '*Ouergne*'; Folios 2, 3, '*Auergne*'; Folio 4, '*Avergne.*'

II. iii. 49. '*I substance*'; Vaughan proposed to read, '*I shadow, aye and substance.*'

II. iv. 6. '*in the error*'; Johnson (adopted by Capell), '*i' the right*'; Hudson, '*in error.*'

II. iv. 83. '*His grandfather was Lionel Duke of Clarence*'; this is erroneous; Duke Lionel was his maternal great-great-grandfather.

II. iv. 91. 'executed'; Pope, 'headed'; Steevens, 'execute' (probably to be read as a dissyllable).

II. iv. 117. 'wiped'; Folios 2, 3, 4, 'wip't'; Folio 1, 'whipt.'

II. iv. 127. 'a thousand'; Collier MS., 'Ten thousand.'

II. iv. 132. 'gentle sir'; so Folios 2, 3, 4; Folio 1, 'gentle.' Anon. conjectured 'gentlemen.'

II. v. 'enter Mortimer'; Edmund Mortimer served under Henry V. in 1422, and died in his castle in Ireland in 1424.

II. v. 6. 'an age of care'; Collier MS., 'a cage of care.'

II. v. 74. 'For by my mother I derived am'; 'mother' should strictly be 'grandmother,' i.e. his father's mother.

II. v. 113. 'fair be all'; Theobald, 'fair befal.'

II. v. 123. 'choked with ambition of the meaner sort,' i.e. "shifted by the ambition of those whose right to the crown was inferior to his own" (Clarke).

II. v. 129. 'ill the advantage'; 'ill,' Theobald's emendation of 'will' of the Folios. Collier MS., 'will the advancer.'

III. i. 53. 'Ay, see'; Rowe's emendation of 'I, see' of the Folios; Hanmer, 'I'll see.'

III. i. 143. 'kind'; Pope, 'gentle'; Capell, 'kind, kind'; Collier MS., 'and kind'; probably the line should be read:

> O loving úncle. || Kind Dûke | of Glóucéster.

III. i. 199. 'lose,' 'should lose'; Folio 1, 'loose'; Folios 2, 3, 4, 'should lose.'

III. ii. 14. 'Paysans, pauvres gens de France'; Rowe's emendation of Folios, 'Peasauns la pouure,' &c.

III. ii. 40. 'the pride'; Theobald, 'the prize'; Hanmer, 'being prize'; Jackson, 'the bride'; Vaughan, 'the gripe.'

III. ii. 52. 'all despite'; Collier MS., 'hell's despite.'

III. ii. 73. 'God be wi' you'; Rowe's emendation of Folios, 'God b' uy.'

III. ii. 118. 'and martial'; Collier MS., 'and matchless'; Vaughan, 'unmatchable.'

III. iii. 85. 'Done like a Frenchman: turn, and turn again'; "the inconstancy of the French was always a subject of satire. I have read a dissertation to prove that the index of the wind upon our steeples was made in form of a cock to ridicule the French for their frequent changes" (Johnson).

III. iv. 18. 'I do remember'; "Henry was but nine months old when his father died, and never even saw him" (Malone).

III. iv. 38. 'the law of arms is such'; "By the ancient law before the Conquest, fighting in the king's palace, or before the king's judges, was punished with death. And by Statute 33, Henry VIII., malicious striking in the king's palace, whereby blood is drawn, is punishable by perpetual imprisonment and fine at the king's pleasure and also with loss of the offender's right hand" (Blackstone).

IV. i. 19. '*at the battle of Patay*'; Capell's emendation (adopted by Malone) of '*Poictiers*' of the Folios. The battle of Poictiers was fought 1357; the date of the present scene is 1428.

IV. i. 180. '*An if I wist he did*,' Capell; Folios, '*And if I wish he did*'; Rowe, '*And if I wish he did.—*'; Theobald (in text), '*An if I wis he did.—*'; (in note), '*And if I wis, he did.—*'; Johnson, '*And if—I wish—he did—*' or '*And if he did,—I wish—*'; Steevens, '*And, if I wist, he did,—.*'

IV. ii. 14. '*their love*'; Hanmer, '*our love.*'

IV. ii. 22. '*war*'; Capell, '*death.*'

IV. ii. 26. '*spoil*'; Vaughan, '*steel.*'

IV. iii. 51. '*That ever living man of memory*,' *i.e.* 'that ever man of living memory.' Lettsom, '*man of ever-living.*'

IV. iv. 16. '*legions*,' Rowe's emendation of Folios, '*Regions.*'

IV. iv. 19. '*in advantage lingering*'; Staunton, '*in disadvantage ling'ring*'; Lettsom, '*in disvantage lingering*'; Vaughan, '*disadvantage ling'ring.*' Johnson explains the phrase, "Protracting his resistance by the advantage of a strong post"; Malone, "Endeavouring by every means, with advantage to himself, to linger out the action."

IV. iv. 31. '*host*'; so Folios 3, 4; Folios 1, 2, '*hoast*'; Theobald's conjecture (adopted by Hanmer), '*horse.*'

IV. iv. 42. '*rescue: he is*'; Folios 1, 2, '*rescue, he is*'; Folios 3, 4, '*rescue, if he is*'; Rowe (ed. 1), '*rescue, if he's*'; (ed. 2) '*rescue, he's*'; Pope, '*rescue now, he's.*'

IV. v. 39. '*shame*'; Walker, '*sham'd.*'

IV. vi. 44. '*On that advantage*,' so the Folios; Theobald conjectured '*On that bad vantage*,' but subsequently read, '*Out on that vantage*'; Hanmer, '*Oh! what advantage*'; Vaughan, '*Oh, hated vantage!*' &c.

IV. vii. 3.

> *Triumphant Death, smear'd with captivity,*
> *Young Talbot's valour makes me smile at thee*;

the phrase '*smear'd with captivity*,' has not been clearly explained; at first sight it is difficult to determine its exact force, and whether the words refer to Death or to the speaker (Talbot). Leo explains that 'Death is supposed to go triumphantly over the battlefield, *smeared* with the *terrible* aspect of captivity'; but possibly the reference is to the Christian belief that Christ took Death captive. Death the Victor is, from this point of view, Death the Victim; it is, as it were, unconsciously *smeared* (*i.e.* smirched) with the wretched (not the *terrible*) aspect of captivity.

IV. vii. 60. '*But where's*'; so Folios; Rowe, '*Where is*'; Lettsom proposed, '*First, where's.*'

IV. vii. 70. '*Henry*'; so Folio 1; Folios 2, 3, 4, '*our King Henry.*' The line is probably to be read:—

'Great mareshal to Henry the Sixth.'

V. i. 17. *'Knit,'* the reading of the Folios; Pope first suggested *'kin,'* which was also adopted by Theobald, Hanmer, Warburton, and Johnson; Capell restored *'knit,'* which was adopted by Steevens and Malone. The Cambridge editions see in *'knit,'* "a conceit suggested by the *'Knot of amity'* in the preceding line."

V. i. 21. *'Marriage, uncle! alas, my years are young!'* Pope reads, *'Marriage, alas! my years are yet too young';* Capell, *'Marriage, good uncle! alas, my years are young';* Walker, *'Marriage, uncle, 'las my years are young.'*

V. i. 21. *'My years are young';* "His Majesty was, however, twenty-four years old" (Malone).

V. i. 49. *'where inshipp'd';* the reading of Folio 4; Folios 1, 2, *'wherein ship'd';* Folio 3, *'wherein shipp'd.'*

V. iii. 8. *'speedy and quick';* Pope, *'speedy quick';* Walker, *'speed and quick.' 'argues';* Vaughan, *'urges.'*

V. iii. 10. *'cull'd';* Collier MS., *'call'd.'*

V. iii. 11. *'regions';* Folios, *'Regions';* Warburton, *'legions.'*

V. iii. 48, 49. *'I kiss . . . side';* Capell and other editors transpose these lines:—*'And lay . . . side. I kiss . . .* [kissing her hand] *. . . peace.'*

V. iii. 57. *'Keeping them prisoner underneath her wings';* Folios 1, 2, *'prisoner';* Folios 3, 4, *'prisoners';* Vaughan, *'prisoned'; 'her wings,'* Folios 3, 4; Folio 1, *'his wings';* Folio 2, *'hir wings';* Vaughan, *'its wings.'*

V. iii. 63. *'Twinkling another counterfeited beam';* Vaughan, *'Kindling another counterfeited beam';* or *'Twinkling in other counterfeited beams.'*

V. iii. 68. *'Hast not a tongue? is she not here?'* Anon. conjectured *'tongue to speak?' 'here?';* Folio 1, *'heere?';* Folios 2, 3, 4, *'heere thy prisoner';* Keightley, *'here alone';* Lettsom, *'here in place,'* cr *'here beside thee';* Vaughan, *'present here.'*

V. iii. 71. *'makes the senses rough';* so the Folios; Hanmer, *'makes the senses crouch';* Capell, *'make . . . crouch';* Jackson, *'makes the senses touch';* Collier MS., *'mocks the sense of touch.'*

V. iii. 78, 79. *'She's beautiful, and therefore to be woo'd,'* &c. These lines were evidently proverbial; *cp. Richard III.,* I. ii. 227, 228, and *Titus Andronicus,* II. i. 82, 83.

V. iii. 108. *'Lady';* Capell, *'Nay, hear me, Lady';* Collier MS., *'Lady, pray tell me';* Lettsom, *'Lady, sweet lady';* Dyce, *'I prithee, lady.'*

V. iii. 144. *'And here I will expect thy coming';* Dyce, *'here, my lord';* Folio 4, *'coming';* Folios 1, 2, 3, *'comming';* Capell, *'coming, Reignier';* Collier MS., *'coming down';* Anon. conjectured *'coming, king';* Anon. conjectured *'communing.'*

V. iii. 153. *'country';* so the Folios; Theobald, *'counties';* Capell, *'countries';* Malone, *'county.'*

V. iii. 178. *'modestly'*; Folio 1, *'modestie.'*

V. iii. 191. *'And natural'*; Perring, *'Maid-natural'*; Capell, *'And'*; Folio 1, *'Mad'*; Folios 2, 3, 4, *'Made'*; Pope, *'Her'*; Collier, *' 'Mid'*; Jackson conjectured *'Man'*; Barry, *'Made'*; Vaughan, *'Mild.'*

V. iv. 37. *'Not me begotten'*; Anon. conjectured *'Me, not begotten'*; Malone, *'Not one begotten'*; Anon. conjectured *'Not mean-begotten.'*

V. iv. 49. *'No, misconceived!'*; so Steevens; Folios 1, 2, 3, *'No misconceived,'* Folio 4, *'no, misconceived Joan'*; Capell, *'No, misconceivers'*; Vaughan, *'No, misconceited!'*

V. iv. 121. *'Poison'd'*; Theobald, *'prison'd.'*

V. iv. 150. *'Stand'st thou aloof upon comparison?'* 'Do you stand to compare your present state, a state which you have neither right nor power to maintain, with the terms which we offer?' (Johnson).

V. v. 39. *'Yes, my lord'*; so Folio 1; Folios 2, 3, 4, *'Yes, my good lord'*; Anon. conjectured, *'Yes, yes, my lord,'* or *'Why, yes, my lord'*; Dyce, *'O, yes, my lord'*; Vaughan, *'Yes, my lord—more.'*

V. v. 55. *'Marriage'*; so Folio 1; Folios 2, 3, 4, read *'But marriage'*; perhaps we should read *'marriage.'*

V. v. 64. *'bringeth,'* the reading of Folio 1; Folios 2, 3, 4, *'bringeth forth'*; perhaps the difficulty of the line is due to the quadrisyllabic nature of the word *'contrary'* *'cónteráry.'*

V. v. 90. *'To cross'*; Walker, *'Across.'*

THE SECOND PART OF KING HENRY VI

I. i. 1. *'As by your high,'* &c.; *'The Contention'* reads:—*'As by your high imperial majesty's command.'*

I. i. 7. *'and'*; the reading of Folio 1; Folios 2, 3, 4, omit it.

I. i. 19. *'lends'*; Rowe, *'lend'st.'*

I. i. 49-50. *'duchy of Anjou and the county of Maine'*; changed by Capell from Quartos to *'dutchies of Anjou and Maine.'*

I. i. 61. *'kneel down'*; Pope reads *'kneel you down'*; Keightley, Collier MS., *'kneel thee down.'* Perhaps *'kneel'* is to be read as a dissyllable.

I. i. 86. *'Beaufort'*; Folios read *'Beauford'*; Rowe, *'Bedford.'*

I. i. 91. *'And had his highness in his infancy Crowned'*; Grant White's emendation of Folios, *'And hath . . . Crowned'*; Rowe reads *'And was . . . Crowned'*; Capell, *'O hath . . . Been crown'd'*; Malone, *'And hath . . . Been crown'd.'*

I. i. 100. *'Defacing'*; Capell reads, *'Reversing,'* following, *'The Contention.'*

I. i. 245. *'humours fits'*; so Folios, Quartos; Rowe reads *'humour fits'*; Malone, *'humours fit.'*

I. ii. 22. *'My troublous dream this night doth make me sad'*; Capell's emendation of Folios, *'My troublous dreames . . . doth,'* &c.

I. ii. 38. *'And in that chair where kings and queens are crown'd'; 'are,'* Hanmer's correction from Quartos; Folios 1, 2, read, *'wer'*; Folios 3, 4, *'were.'*

I. ii. 59. *'thou wilt ride with us'*; Dyce, from Quartos, *'thou 'lt ride with us, I'm sure'*; Hanmer, *'thou too wilt ride with us'*; Vaughan, *'thou; thou wilt ride with us.'*

I. ii. 71. *'What say'st thou? majesty!'*; Capell reads from Quartos, *'My majesty! why, man'*; Vaughan, *'What say'st thou, "Majesty"?'* &c.

I. ii. 100. *'A crafty knave does need no broker'*; an old proverb given in Ray's collection.

I. iii. 3. *'In the quill'*; Hanmer, *'in quill'*; Jackson, *'in quiet'*; Singer, *'in the coil'*; Collier MS., *'in sequel,'* &c. In Ainsworth's Latin Dictionary, 1761, the phrase is rendered, *'ex compacto agunt.'* Halliwell and others explain it also as 'all together in a body.' This interpretation is borne out by a passage in *'The Devonshire Damsel's Frolic,'* one of the 'Songs and Sonnets' in the collection called 'Choyce Drollery,' &c. (1656):—

> *'Thus those females were all in a quill*
> *And following on their pastimes still.'*

No satisfactory explanation has yet been given of the origin of the phrase. The following solution is suggested:—*'the quill'* I take to be a popular elaboration of the more correct phrase *'a quill,'* which occurs in the ballad quoted; the latter seems to be a corruption of French *accueil,* O. F. *acueil, acoil, akel, achoil,* &c., 'a gathering together.' It is noteworthy that a verb *'aquyle'* occurs in one passage in Middle English, where in all probability it is the English form of the verb *'accueillir.'* (*Cp. Pearl,* ed. Gollancz, p. 122.)

I. iii. 29. *'master was'*; Warburton's emendation of Folios, *'mistress was.'*

I. iii. 66. *'haughty'*; probably an error for *'haught,'* the reading of Folios 2, 3, 4; Pope, *'proud.'*

I. iii. 88. *'to the lays'*; Rowe, *'their lays.'*

I. iii. 144. *'most master wear'; 'master,'* Halliwell; *'master'; 'wear,'* so Folio 1; Folios 2, 3, 4, *'wears'; 'most master'* $=$ 'the one who is most master,' *i.e.* 'the queen.'

I. iii. 148. *'fume needs'*; Grant White (Dyce and Walker conjectured) *'fury,'* which seems a most plausible emendation; *'needs,'* the reading of Folio 1; Folios 2, 3, 4, *'can need'*; Keightley, *'needs now.'*

I. iii. 149. *'far'*; Pope reads *'fast,'* adopted by many editors.

I. iii. 202. 'This doom, my lord, if I may judge'; Capell reads, 'This do, my lord, if I may be the judge'; Dyce from Quartos, 'This is my doom, my lord, if I may judge'; Vaughan conjectured, 'This doom, my lord, if I may judge, is law'; Collier MS., 'This doom, my gracious lord, if I may judge.'

I. iii. 214. 'the spite of man'; Capell reads 'the sight of my master'; Folios 2, 3, read 'the spite of my man'; Folio 4, 'the spite of my master'; Collier MS., 'the spite of this man'; Steevens, 'the spite of a man'; Vaughan conjectured 'the spite of many.'

I. iv. 31. 'What fates await'; so Folios; Pope reads 'Tell me what fates await'; Capell, 'What fate awaits'; Vaughan, 'What fate awaiteth then'; Wordsworth, 'Tell me what fate awaits.'

I. iv. 40. 'we watch'd you at an inch'; Daniel, 'we've catch'd in the nick,' or 'at the nick.'

I. iv. 61. 'Aio te Æacida, Romanos vincere posse'; the ambiguous answer which Pyrrhus received from the oracle at Delphi before his war against the Romans; meaning either 'I say that thou the descendant of Æacus, mayest conquer the Romans,' or 'I say that the Romans may conquer thee, descendant of Æacus'; 'te' inserted by Warburton; Folios 1, 2, read, 'Æacida'; Folios 3, 4 'Æacide'; Rowe, 'te Æacidem.'

II. i. 24. 'Tantæne animis cœlestibus iræ?' 'Is such resentment found in heavenly minds?' (Æneid, i. 15). Omitted by Pope.

II. i. 26. 'With such holiness can you do it'; omitted by Pope. Warburton, 'With such holiness can you not do it?'; Johnson, 'A churchman, with such,' &c.; Collier MS., 'And with such holiness you well can do it'; the old play 'dote' for 'do it.' Many emendations have been proposed. If the original reading is retained, it must be considered ironical.

II. i. 29. 'you'; Pope, 'yourself.'

II. i. 33. 'furious'; Folio 2, 'too-too furious.'

II. i. 47. given in Folios to Gloucester; corrected by Theobald.

II. i. 53. 'Medice, teipsum—'; 'Physician, heal thyself'; from the Vulgate (Luke iv. 23). Folios read 'Medice teipsum'; Rowe, 'Medice cura teipsum'; &c. omitted by Pope.

II. i. 69. 'To present your highness with the man'; Pope reads, 'Before your highness to present the man'; Capell, 'Come to present your highness with the man,' &c.

II. i. 91. 'Simpcox'; Pope's emendation (Theobald conjecture) of Folios 'Symon'; Capell, 'Saunder.'

II. i. 134. 'things called whips'; Halliwell and others quote from Armin's Nest of Ninnies (1608); "There are, as Hamlet saies, things cold whips in store"; this cannot refer, as has been supposed, to Hamlet's 'whips and scorns of time,' but may well have occurred in the pre-Shakespearian Hamlet. The actual words are to be found in Kyd's Spanish Tragedy:—

'Well heaven is heaven still!

> *And there is Nemesis, and furies,*
> *And things call'd whips.'*

Perhaps Armin wrote '*Hamlet*' when he meant '*Jeronimy.*'

II. i. 177. '*vanquished*'; Walker, '*languish'd*'; Vaughan, '*banish'd.*'

II. ii. 6. '*at full*'; Folios 3, 4, '*thus at full*'; Capell, '*at the full*'; Keightley, '*at full length*'; Marshall, '*told at full.*'

II. ii. 15. '*Edmund*'; Folio 1 reads '*Edmond*'; Folios 2, 3, 4, '*Edward.*'

II. ii. 27. '*Richard was murder'd traitorously*'; Folio 1 reads '*Richard . . . traiterously*'; Folios 2, 3, 4, '*King Richard . . . traiterously*'; Pope, '*King Richard trait'rously was murther'd*'; Dyce, '*was harmless Richard murder'd traitorously.*'

II. ii. 28. '*told the truth*'; Hanmer reads '*told the very truth*'; Capell, '*surely told the truth*'; Keightley, '*told the truth in this*'; Marshall, '*the Duke of York hath told the truth.*'

II. ii. 35. '*Philippe,*' Hanmer's correction; Folio 1, '*Phillip*'; Folios 2, 3, 4, '*Philip*'; Collier MS., '*Philippa.*'

II. ii. 42. '*Who kept him in captivity till he died*'; 'it was really his son-in-law, Lord Grey of Ruthvyn, and not Edmund Mortimer, whom, according to Hall, Owen Glendower kept in captivity till he died' (Malone).

II. ii. 55. '*York claims*'; Pope, '*York here claims*'; Capell, '*but York claims*'; Dyce, '*while York claims*'; Hudson, '*York doth claim.*'

II. iii. 3. '*sins*'; Theobald's emendation of '*sinne,*' Folios 1, 2; '*sin*' Folio 3.

II. iii. 14. '*Welcome is banishment; welcome were my death*'; Pope reads '*Welcome is exile,*' &c.; Anon. conjecture '*Welcome is banishment; welcomer my death*'; Wordsworth, '*Welcome is banishment; welcome were death*'; '*banishment*' is probably to be considered a dissyllable.

II. iii. 20. '*I beseech*'; Hanmer, '*Beseech.*'

II. iii. 21. '*ease,*' the reading of Folios 1, 4; Folios 2, 3, '*cease.*

II. iii. 29. '*Should be to be protected like a child*'; Collier MS. reads '*Should be protected like a child by peers.*' '*Should be to be*' = '*should need to be.*'

II. iii. 30. '*God and King Henry govern England's realm*'; omitted by Capell; '*Realm,*' the reading of Folios; Steevens (Johnson conjectured), '*helm*'; Dyce and Staunton, '*helm!*' In the next line Keightley proposed '*helm*' for '*realm.*'

II. iii. 32. Collier MS. inserts after l. 32, '*To think I fain would keep it makes me laugh.*'

II. iii. 35. '*willingly*'; Pope, '*willing*' (from Quartos).

II. iii. 46. '*youngest*'; so Folios 1, 2; Folios 3, 4, '*younger*'; Singer (Anon. conjectured MS.), '*strongest*'; Collier MS., '*proud-*

est'; Staunton, *'haughtiest'*; Kinnear, *'highest.'* Perhaps *'her'* may be taken to refer to *'pride.'*

II. iii. 55. *'defend'*; Pope, *'guard'*; Vaughan, *'feed.'*

II. iii. 90. *'blow'*; Warburton adds, from Quartos, *'as Bevis of Southampton fell upon Ascapart.'*

II. iii. 98. *'Go, take hence that traitor from our sight'*; Hanmer, *'Go, and take hence,'* &c.; perhaps *'traitor'* should be read as a trisyllable.

II. iv. 3. *'Barren winter, with his wrathful nipping cold'*; Pope, *'The barren winter, with his nipping cold'*; Capell, *'Bare winter with his wrathful nipping cold'*; Mitford, *'The barren winter with his wrathful cold.'*

II. iv. 5. *'ten'*; Steevens, *''Tis ten o'clock'*; Lettsom, from Quartos, *''Tis almost ten.'*

II. iv. 12. *'laughing'*; so Folio 1; Folios 2, 3, 4, *'still laughing'*; Hudson (Lettsom conj.), *'and laughing.'*

II. iv. 25. *'thine enemies'*; Folios 4, *'their enemies'*; Rowe, *'our enemies.'*

II. iv. 31. *'with papers on my back'*; 'criminals undergoing punishment usually wore papers on their backs containing their offence.'

II. iv. 87. *'gone too?'*; so Folios 2, 3, 4; Folio 1, *'gone to?'*; Collier MS., *'gone so?'*

III. i. 78. *'as is the ravenous wolf'*; Rowe's correction of Folios, *'as is . . . Wolues'*; Malone, *'as are . . . wolves'*; Vaughan, *'as the ravenous wolves.'*

III. i. 98. *'Well, Suffolk, thou shalt not see me blush'*; the reading of Folio 1; Folios 2, 3, 4, *'Well, Suffolk, yet thou,'* &c.; Malone, from Quartos, *'Well, Suffolk's duke, thou,'* &c.; Dyce (Walker conj.), *'Well, Suffolk, well, thou,'* &c.

III. i. 133. *'easy'*; Collier MS., *'easily'*; Walker, *'very'*; omitted by Wordsworth.

III. i. 151. *'But mine is,'* &c.; Hudson (Lettsom conj.), from Quartos, reads, *'But I am,'* &c.; *'mine'* = 'my death.'

III. i. 211. *'strays'*; Theobald (adopting the conj. Thirlby), *'strives'*; Vaughan, *'strains.'*

III. i. 223. *'Free lords'*; Hanmer, *'See, lords'*; Dyce (Collier MS.), *'Fair lords'*; Cambridge editors suggest *'My lords.'*

III. i. 280. *'spoke'*; so Folios; Hanmer, *'spoken.'*

III. i. 348. *'nourish'* (monosyllabic), = 'nurse' (verb); (Collier MS. reads *'march'*).

III. i. 357. *'John Cade of Ashford'*; Seymour adds, *'with a headlong crew.'*

III. ii. 26. *'Nell'*; Theobald, *'Well'*; Capell, *'Meg'*; Malone, *'Margaret'*; Clark MS., *'well.'* The playwright here, as in other places (*cp.* below, ll. 79, 100, 120), seems, by some strange error, to have thought of Eleanor instead of Margaret.

III. ii. 70. *'ay me'*; Pope reads *'ah me.'*

III. ii. 78. ll. 78 to 121 struck out in Collier MS.

III. ii. 79. *'Eleanor'*; cp. *supra*, Note, III. ii. 26.

III. ii. 80. *'Statuë and worship it'*; Keightley correction of Folios, *'Statue, and worship it'*; Rowe reads *'statue, and do worship to it'*; Capell, *'statue then, and worship it'*; Dyce, *'statua and worship it.'*

III. ii. 88. *'gentle'*; Singer (Anon. MS. conj. and Collier MS.) reads *'ungentle'*; destroying the whole point of the passage.

III. ii. 89. *'he,'* i.e. Æolus, the God of the winds.

III. ii. 100, 120. *'Eleanor,'* cp. *supra*, Note, III. ii. 26.

III. ii. 152. *'For seeing him I see my life in death'*; Folio 4 reads *'For . . . life is Death'*; Johnson *'For . . . death in life'*; Capell, *'And . . . death in life'*; Rann, *'And . . . life in death'*; Vaughan, *'So . . . my self in death.'*

III. ii. 163. *'being all descended,'* i.e. 'the blood being.'

III. ii. 182. *'And both of you were vow'd Duke Humphrey's foes,'* the reading of Folio 1; Folio 2, *'were . . . death'*; Folios 3, 4, *'have . . . death'*; Capell first suggested true reading.

III. ii. 192. *'was dead'*; Vaughan, *'is dead,'* or *'was deaded,'* or *'was ended.'*

III. ii. 244. *'Lord Suffolk'*; the reading of Folios; Malone reads from Quartos, *'false Suffolk.'*

III. ii. 262. *'harmful'*; Folios 2, 3, 4 read *'harmless.'*

III. ii. 308. *'enemy'*; Capell (from Quartos), *'enemies.'*

III. ii. 322. *'daintiest that'*; Theobald, *'daintiest meat'*; Hanmer (from Quarto), *'daintiest thing'*; Vaughan, *'daintiest cate.'*

III. ii. 344-5. *'That thou mightst think,'* &c. "That by the impression of my kiss forever remaining on thy hand, thou mightest think on those lips through which a thousand sighs will be breathed for thee" (Johnson).

III. ii. 359. *'thence,'* away from the land; Folios 2, 3, 4, *'hence.'*

III. ii. 366. *'no joy'*; Singer (Collier MS.), *'to joy'*; *'nought,'* Folios 3, 4, *'ought.'*

III. iii. 4. *'and feel no pain'*; Theobald reads, from Quartos, *'but one whole year.'*

IV. i. 21, 22. *'The lives of those,'* &c., so Folios, with the exception of the note of exclamation, added by Grant White; Knight prints a note of interrogation; Nicholson, *'Shall the lives . . . sum?'*; Marshall, *'The lives . . . shall they Be counterpoised,'* &c.

IV. i. 48. Omitted in Folios; restored by Pope (from Quartos).

IV. i. 50. In Folios this line is made part of preceding speech, with *'lowsie'* for *'lowly,'* restored by Pope (from Quartos).

IV. i. 70. *'Cap. Yes, Pole. Suf. Pole!'* added by Capell from Quartos.

IV. i. 85. *'mother's bleeding,'* Rowe's correction of Folios, *'Mother-bleeding.'*

IV. i. 117. *'Gelidus timor occupat artus,' i.e.* 'chill fear seizes my limbs'; the reading of Folios 2, 3, 4; Folio 1 reads, *'Pine gelidus'*; Theobald, *'Pœne gelidus,'* &c. (*cp. Æneid,* vii. 446).

IV. i. 129. Lloyd, *'Exempt from fear is true nobility.'*

IV. i. 136. *'Brutus' bastard hand'*; Theobald proposed *'dastard,'* but afterwards withdrew his suggestion; Servilia, the mother of Brutus, became, it is true, the mistress of Julius Cæsar, but not until after the birth of Brutus.

IV. i. 137, 138. *'savage islanders Pompey the Great'*; the story of Pompey's death is given in Plutarch; the murderers were Achillas, an Egyptian, and Septimius, who had served under him; perhaps they are described as 'islanders,' because the murder was committed at Pelusium, an island-like spot in the midst of morasses, easternmost mouth of the Nile.

IV. ii. 73. *'Chatham'*; Rowe's emendation; Folio 1, *'Chartam'*; Folios 2, 3, 4, *'Chattam,'* &c.

IV. iii. 7. *'a hundred lacking one'*; Malone, *'a hundred lacking one, a week,'* from Quartos. In the reign of Elizabeth butchers were not allowed to sell flesh-meat in Lent; by special licenses, however, a limited number of beasts might be killed each week.

IV. iv. 22. Pope, *'Lamenting still and mourning Suffolk's death?'*

IV. iv. 43. *'Lord Say, the traitors hate thee'*; Folio 1, *'hateth'*; Capell, *'traitor rebel hateth'*; Marshall, *'the traitor Jack Cade hateth thee.'*

IV. vii. 31-32. *'thou hast caused printing to be used'*; printing was not really introduced into England until twenty years later.

IV. vii. 54-55. Cæsar says in Book V. of the "Commentaries," *'Ex his omnibus sunt humanissimi qui Cantium incolunt,'* which Golding rendered (1590), *'Of all the inhabitants of this isle, the civilest are the Kentish folke.'*

IV. vii. 56. *'because full'*; Hanmer reads *'beauteous, full'*; Vaughan, *'bounteous, full,'* &c.

IV. vii. 64. *'But to maintain'* (Johnson; Rann); *'Kent to m.,'* the reading of Folios; Steevens, *'Bent to m.'*; Malone, *'Kent to m.,'* &c.

IV. vii. 82-83. *'The help of hatchet'*; so Folio 1; Folios 2, 3, 4, *'the help of a hatchet'*; Farmer, *'pap with a hatchet,'* a singularly happy emendation, &c.

IV. vii. 102. *'Sir James Cromer'*; it was Sir William Cromer whom Cade beheaded.

IV. viii. 12. *'rebel'*; Singer's emendation (Collier MS. and Anon. MS.) of Folios, *'rabble'*; Vaughan, *'ribald.'*

IV. ix. 26. *'Of gallowglasses and stout kernes'*; Hanmer reads, *'Of desp'rate gallowglasses,'* &c.; Capell, *'Of nimble g.,'* &c.;

Dyce, '*Of savage g.*,' &c.; '*stout*'; Mitford, '*stout Irish*'; '*kernes*'; Keightley, '*kernes, he*'; Vaughan, '*kernes supplied.*'

IV. ix. 29. '*arms*'; Folio 1, '*Armes*'; Folios 2, 3, 4, '*Armies.*'

IV. ix. 33. '*calm'd*'; the reading of Folio 4; Folio 1, '*calme*'; Folio 2, '*claimd*'; Folio 3, '*claim'd*'; Becket, '*cramp'd*'; Walker, '*chased.*'

IV. ix. 36. '*I pray thee, Buckingham, go and meet him*'; Staunton, '*Go, I pray thee, B.,*' &c.; Rowe reads, '*go and meet with him*'; Malone, '*to go and meet him*'; Steevens (1793), '*go forth and meet him*'; Collier (Collier MS.), '*then go and meet him*'; Dyce, '*go thou and meet him.*'

IV. x. 1. '*Fie on ambition*'; so the later Folios; Folio 1, '*Ambitions.*'

IV. x. 41. '*That Alexander Iden, an esquire of Kent*'; Capell, '*'squir*'; Marshall omits '*an,*' following Hall.

IV. x. 51. '*As for words, whose greatness answers words*'; Rowe reads, '*As for more words,*' &c.; Mason, '*As for mere words,*' &c.; Dyce (Anon. conj.), '*But as for words,*' &c., &c.

IV. x. 56. '*God*'; Malone's correction (from Quartos) of '*Ioue*' of the Folios.

IV. x. 75. '*And as I thrust thy body in with my sword*'; Dyce (Lloyd conj.) omits '*in.*'

V. i. 74. '*Alexander Iden, that's my name*'; Capell, '*My name is Alexander Iden, sir*'; Hanmer, '*Ev'n Alexander,*' &c.; Edd, '*Iden, Alexander Iden,*' &c.; Keightley, '*Alexander Iden, that's my name, my liege,*' &c.

V. i. 78. '*Iden, kneel down. Rise up a knight*'; Hanmer reads, '*Iden kneel down; and rise thou up a knight*'; Dyce (Lettsom conj.), '*Iden, kneel down. Iden, rise up a knight*'; Vaughan, '*Iden, kneel down; and now rise up Sir Alexander.*'

V. i. 95. '*darest*'; monosyllabic; Folio 1, '*dar'st*'; Folios 2, 3, 4, '*durst.*'

V. i. 109. '*these*'; Theobald's correction of '*thee*' of the Folios.

V. i. 130. '*mistakest*'; so Folios 2, 3, 4; Folio 1, '*mistakes.*'

V. i. 146. '*fell-lurking*'; Roderick, '*fell-barking*'; Hudson (Heath conj.), '*fell-lurching*'; Collier (Collier MS.), '*fell-looking*'; Capell, '*fell lurking.*'

V. i. 170. '*shame*'; Dyce (Walker conj.), '*stain.*'

V. i. 211. '*victorious*'; so Folio 1; Folios 2, 3, 4, read '*victorious noble.*'

V. ii. 28. '*La fin couronne les œuvres*'; *i.e.* 'the end crowns the work'; Folio 1 reads, '*Corrone les eumenes*'; Folios 2, 3, 4, '*Corronne les oevres.*'

V. ii. 42. '*Knit earth and heaven together*'; Vaughan adds '*in one blase.*'

V. ii. 66. '*So, lie thou there*'; Malone supposes that a line has been omitted here, equivalent to '*Behold the prophecy is come to pass*'; Vaughan's conjecture adds '*fulfilling prophecy.*'

V. ii. 87. '*parts*'; Hanmer reads '*powers*'; Warburton, '*party*'; Collier MS., '*frends*'; Dyce (Walker conj.), '*part.*'

V. iii. 1. '*of*'; Collier MS. (from Quartos), '*Old,*' adopted by Dyce.

V. iii. 29. '*faith*'; Malone's correction (from Quartos): Folios, '*hand.*'

THE THIRD PART OF
KING HENRY VI

I. i. 11. '*dangerously,*' Theobald's correction (from Quartos); Folios, '*dangerous.*'

I. i. 18. '*But is your grace*'; Pope, '*Is his grace*'; Capell, '*Is your grace*'; Malone (from Quartos), '*What, is your grace*'; Steevens, '*What, 's your grace*'; Lettsom, '*What, Is your grace.*'

I. i. 19. '*hope*'; Capell, '*end*'; Dyce (Anon. conj.), '*hap.*'

I. i. 34. '*thrust you out perforce*'; Rowe, '*thrust you out by force*'; Capell (from Quartos), '*put us out by force.*'

I. i. 36. '*council*'; Pope's emendation of Folios 1, 2, '*counsaile*'; Folio 3, '*counsell*'; Folio 4, '*counsel.*'

I. i. 41. '*And bashful Henry deposed, whose cowardice*'; Quartos, '*be deposde*'; as the line stands in the Folios '*Henry*' must be either dissyllabic or monosyllabic.

I. i. 55. '*You both have vow'd*'; Folio 4, '*you have both vow'd*'; Pope, '*you vow'd*'; Collier MS., '*you have vow'd*'; Collier conjectured '*both have vow'd*'; Vaughan conjectured '*you both vow'd.*'

I. i. 56. '*favourites*'; Capell, '*favourers.*'

I. i. 62. '*poltroons, such as he*'; Folio 1, '*Poultroones, such as he*'; Folios 2, 3, '*Poultroones, and such is he*'; Folio 4, '*Poltroons, and such is he*'; Capell, '*poltroons, and such as he.*'

I. i. 70. '*Far be the thought of this from Henry's heart*'; Capell (from Quartos), '*Far be it from the thoughts of Henry's heart.*'

I. i. 76. '*I am thine*'; Rowe, '*Henry, I am thine*'; Theobald (from Quartos), '*Thou 'rt deceiv'd, I'm thine.*'

I. i. 78. '*The earldom was,*' *i.e.* the earldom of March, by which he claimed the throne; Theobald (from Quartos), '*The kingdom is.*'

I. i. 83. '*and that's,*' the reading of Folios 2, 3, 4; Folio 1, '*that's*'; Quartos, '*and that is*'; Collier, '*that is.*'

I. i. 105. '*Thy father*'; '*Thy,*' Rowe's correction (from Quartos) of Folios, '*My*'; '*father*'; Capell conjectured '*uncle.*'

I. i. 144. '*his crown*'; Johnson, '*his son*'; Dr. Percy pointed out that Richard II. had no son; Capell (from Quartos), *'the crown'*; Vaughan, *'his line'*; Wordsworth, *'the throne.'*

I. i. 171. *'for this my life-time reign as king,'* the reading of Folio 1; Folios 2, 3, 4, *'for this time,'* &c.; Theobald (from Quartos), *'but reign in quiet, while I live.'*

I. i. 261. *'from,'* the reading of Folios 2, 3, 4, and Quartos; Folio 1, *'to.'*

I. i. 268. *'cost,'* so Folios; Hanmer, *'truss'*; Warburton, *'coast,' i.e.* 'watch and follow, or hover round'; Steevens, *'cote'*; Jackson, *'court'*; Dyce, *'souse.'* Warburton's emendation is generally adopted by modern editors.

I. ii. 16. *'any'*; Dyce, *'an.'* (?) *'But for a kingdom may an oath be broken.'*

I. ii. 38. *'shalt to the Duke of Norfolk'*; the reading of Folios 1, 2, 3; Folio 4, *'shalt be D. of N.'*; Rowe, *'shall go to the D. of N.'*; Pope, *'shalt to th' D. of N. go'*; Steevens, *'shalt unto the D. of N.'*; Vaughan, *'shalt straight to the D. of N.'*

I. ii. 40. *'Lord Cobham'*; Hanmer, *'Lord of Cobham.'*

I. iii. 48. *'Di faciant laudis summa sit ista tuæ'*; *i.e.* 'The gods grant that this be the sum of thy glory'; (Ovid, *Epistle from Phillis to Demophoon*).

I. iv. 109. *'sake'*; Capell (from Quartos), *'death.'*

I. iv. 150. *'passion moves'*; Folios 2, 3, 4, *'passions move'*; Folio 1, *'passions moues.'*

I. iv. 152, 153. *'That face of his the hungry cannibals Would not have touch'd, would not have stain'd with blood'*; Warburton's arrangement (from Quartos); printed as three lines in Folios, ending *'his . . . toucht . . . blood.'* For *'with blood'* Folios 2, 3, 4 read *'the roses just with blood'*; Theobald, *'the roses juic'd with blood'*; Hanmer, *'the roses just i' th' bud'*; Collier MS., *'the rose's hues with blood.'*

I. iv. 169. *'to all'*; Capell (from Quartos), *'of all.'*

II. i. 20. *'Methinks, 'tis prize enough to be his son'*; so Folios; Warburton (from Quartos), *'pride.'*

II. i. 113. Omitted in Folios, added by Steevens (from Quartos).

II. i. 131. *'idle,'* Capell's emendation (from Quartos) of Folios, *'lazy.'*

II. i. 146. *'Your kind aunt, Duchess of Burgundy,'* *i.e.* Isabel, daughter of John I., King of Portugal, by Philippa of Lancaster, eldest daughter of John of Gaunt; she was, therefore, really third cousin to Edward, and not aunt.

II. i. 182. *'to London will we march amain'*; Theobald's emendation (from Quartos); Folios read *'to London will we march'*; Hanmer, *'straight to London will we march.'*

II. i. 190. *'fail'st'*; Steevens, *'fall'st'*; Quartos, *'faints.'*

II. ii. 47-48. cp. Greene's *Royal Exchange:*—"It hath been an *old proverb, that happy is that son whose father goes to the devil,"* &c.

II. ii. 147. *'Although thy husband may be Menelaus,'* cp. *Troilus and Cressida,* V. i. 53, where Thersites calls Menelaus *"the primitive statue and oblique memorial of cuckolds."*

II. ii. 172. *'deniest,'* Wharburton's correction (from Quartos); Folios 1, 2, *'denied'st'*; Folios 3, 4, *'deni'dst.'*

II. ii. 177. *'these'*; Capell (from Quartos), *'thy.'*

II. iii. 37. *'Thou setter up and plucker down of kings'*; cp. Daniel ii. 21, *"He removeth kings and setteth up kings."*

II. iii. 43. *'in earth'*; the reading of Folios 1, 2; Folios 3, 4, *'in the earth'*; Pope, *'on earth.'*

II. iii. 49. *'all together,'* Rowe's emendation of Folios, *'altogether.'*

II. iii. 53. *'wear'*; Collier MS., *'wore'*; Collier (ed. 2), *'ware.'*

II. v. 26. *'make'*; Folios, *'makes.'*

II. v. 38. *'months'*; Rowe, *'weeks, months.'*

II. v. 60. *'as this dead man doth me'*; Hanmer, *'as this dead man to me'*; Wordsworth, *'as this dead doth to me.'*

II. v. 80. *'hast,'* the reading of Folios 3, 4; Folios 1, 2, *'hath.'*

II. v. 87. *'kill,'* Rowe's correction of Folios, *'kills.'*

II. v. 92, 93. *'O boy, thy father gave thee life too soon, And hath bereft thee of thy life too late'*; much has been written on these lines, the difficulty being in the words *'too late'*; the simplest meaning of the phrase seems to be 'when too late'; others explain *'too late'* = 'too recently.' The Quartos read *'too late'* in the first line, and *'too soon'* in the second.

The force of the crude couplet seems to be:—O boy, too soon thy father gave thee life (better thou had'st never been born!), too late he discovers that the fatal blow was aimed at *thee.*

II. v. 119. *'Even,'* Capell's emendation; Folios 1, 2, 3, *'Men'*; Folio 4, *'Man'*; Rowe, *'Sad'*; Mitford, *'Mere'*; Delius (Mitford conj.), *'Son'*; Collier MS., *'E'en'*; Keightley conjectured, *''Fore men'* or *'To men'*; Anonymous conjecture, *'Main,'* &c.

II. vi. 6. *'And, now I fall, thy tough commixture melts,'* Rowe's reading; Folios, *'fall. Thy'*; Rann, *'fall, that'*; Johnson conjectured *'fall, the'*; *'commixture melts,'* Steevens' correction (from Quartos); Folio 1, *'Commixtures melt'*; Folios 2, 3, 4, *'Commixtures melt.'*

II. vi. 8. Omitted in Folios. Restored by Theobald (from Quartos).

II. vi. 17. Omitted by Capell, following Quartos.

II. vi. 42, 45. The assignment to the speakers is due to Capell, following Quartos, which here are more correct than Folios.

II. vi. 80. *'If this right hand would buy two hours' life'*; Capell (from Quartos), *'would this right hand buy but an hour's life,'* Folio 1, *'two hours''*; Folios 2, 3, 4, *'but two hours.''*

II. vi. 82. *'This hand should'*; Capell (from Quartos), *'I'd.'*

II. vi. 100. *'in thy shoulder'*; so Folio 1; Folios 2, 3, 4, *'on thy s.'*

III. i. *'Enter two keepers'*; Folios, *'Enter Sinklo and Humfrey'*; "as Sinklo is certainly the name of an Actor who is mentioned in the stage directions in the *Taming of the Shrew* (Ind. i. 81), and in *Henry IV.*, Part II. (Act v. Sc. 4), there is a great probability that Humphrey is the name of another Actor; perhaps, as Malone suggests, Humfrey Jeaffes. Neither of these is mentioned in the list of 'Principall Actors' prefixed to the first Folio" (Camb. Editors).

III. i. 13. *'Enter King Henry, disguised, with a Prayer-book,'* Malone's emendation; Folios, *'Enter the King with a Prayer booke'*; Collier MS. adds, *'disguised as a Churchman'*; Capell (from Quartos), *'Enter King Henrie disguisde.'*

III. i. 14. *'To greet mine own land with my wishful sight'*; Rann (from Quartos), *'and thus disguis'd to greet my native land.'*

III. i. 17. *'wast,'* the reading of Folios 3, 4; Folios, 1, 2, *'was.'*

III. i. 24. *'thee, sour adversity'*; Dyce's emendation; Folios, *'the sower Adversaries'*; Pope, *'these sour adversities'*; Clarke's Concordance, *'these sour adversaries'*; Delius, *'the sour adversities.'*

III. i. 55. *'thou that talk'st,'* &c.; Rowe's emendation; Quartos, *'thou that talkes,'* &c.; Folios, *'thou talk'st,'* &c.; Collier, *'thou talkest,'* &c.

III. i. 60. *'and that's enough'*; Rann (from Quartos), *'though not in shew.'*

III. i. 97. *'We charge you, in God's name, and the king's'*; *'You'*; Anonymous conjecture, *'you now'* or *'you then'*; *'and the king's'*; Rowe, *'and in the king's.'*

III. ii. 2. *'Richard'*; the reading of Folios and Quartos; Pope (from Hall), *'John.'*

III. ii. 3. *'lands'*; Capell's correction (from Quartos); Folios, *'land.'*

III. ii. 6-7. *'In quarrel of the house of York,'* &c.; but in reality Sir John Grey fell in the second battle of St. Albans, fighting on the side of King Henry.

III. ii. 32. *'then'*; Quartos, *'them.'*

III. ii. 108. *''twas for shift'*; so Folios 1, 2; Folio 3 reads, *''twas for a shift'*; Folio 4, *'it was for a shift.'*

III. ii. 110. *'very sad'*; so Folio 1; Folios 2, 3, 4, *'sad.'*

III. ii. 119. *'your prisoner'*; the reading of Folios, Capell (from Quartos), *'as prisoner'*; Id. conj. *'a prisoner.'*

III. ii. 143. *'Flattering me with impossibilities'*; Pope, *'Flatt'ring my mind with things impossible'* (*'me'* = 'myself').

III. ii. 156. *'shrub'*; Quartos, *'shrimpe.'*

III. ii. 170. '*Until my mis-shaped trunk that bears this head*'; the reading of Folios 1, 2; Folios 3, 4, '*Until this . . . head*'; Pope, '*Until the . . . head*'; Thirlby, '*Until the head of this mis-shapen trunk*'; Hanmer, '*Until the head this mis-shap'd trunk doth bear*,' &c.

III. ii. 193. '*the murderous Machiavel*'; Warburton (from Quartos), '*th' aspiring Catiline*'; Folios 1, 2, '*Macheuill*'; Folio 4, '*Matchevil*.'

III. iii. 3. '*while Lewis doth sit*'; Rowe, '*whiles Lewis sits*'; Pope, '*while Lewis sits*.'

III. iii. 11. '*seat*'; Walker conjectured '*state*.'

III. iii. 42. '*waiteth on true sorrow*'; Warburton, '*waiting rues to-morrow*.'

III. iii. 45. '*Our*'; Collier MS., '*The*'; Vaughan conjectured '*Proud*.'

III. iii. 75. '*thy*'; Johnson, '*thee*.'

III. iii. 96. '*thirty and six years*'; Quartos, '*thirtie and eight*'; the correct number according to Malone.

III. iii. 124. '*an eternal plant*'; Warburton's emendation (from Quartos); Folios read '*an externall p*.'; Hanmer, '*a perennial p*.'

III. iii. 127. '*Exempt from envy, but not from disdain*'; *i.e.* 'not liable to malice or hatred, although not secured from female disdain.'

III. iii. 133. '*tempted*'; Vaughan, '*temper'd*.'

III. iii. 156. '*Warwick, peace*'; the reading of Folios 2, 3, 4; Folio 1, '*Warwick*.'

III. iii. 228. '*I'll*,' Capell (from Quartos); Folios read '*I*.'

III. iii. 233, 234. '*But, Warwick, Thou and Oxford, with five thousand men*'; Theobald, '*But, Warwick, Thyself and . . . men*'; Hanmer, '*But Warwick, thou Thyself and . . . men*'; Steevens, '*But, Warwick, thou And . . . men*'; Collier MS., '*But, Warwick, thou And . . . warlike men*'; Keightley, '*But, Warwick, Thou and Lord . . . men*'; 'Anon. conjectured '*But, Warwick, thou And . . . men of mine*.' Perhaps, as an anonymous scholar has suggested, the line should be read as an Alexandrine.

III. iii. 242. '*Mine eldest daughter*'; the reading of Folios (following Quartos); Theobald (from Holinshed), '*my younger d*.' It was, however, Anne, Warwick's second daughter, whom Edward married.

III. iii. 253. '*Shalt*,' the reading of Folios 2, 3, 4; Folio 1, '*Shall*.'

IV. i. 13. '*our*'; Capell, '*your*.'

IV. i. 17. '*And shall*'; Rowe, '*And you shall*'; Walker, '*Ay, and shall*,' or '*Marry, and shall*.'

IV. i. 41. '*But the safer*'; Folios 2, 3, 4, '*Yes, but the safer*'; S. Walker conjectured '*But then the safer*'; Keightley, '*Ay, but the safer*'; Anon. conjectured '*But yet the safer*'; Vaughan, '*But all the safer*'; Folio 2, '*safter.*'

IV. i. 42. '*using*'; Vaughan, '*losing.*'

IV. i. 66. '*brother's*'; Rowe's emendation of Folios, '*Brothers*'; Anon. conjectured '*brothers*'.'

IV. i. 73, 74. '*dislike . . . Doth*'; Folios, '*dislikes . . . Doth*'; Rowe, '*dislikes . . . Do.*'

IV. i. 89, 90. '*therefore, in brief, Tell me*'; Folio 1, '*Therefore, in briefe, tell me*'; Folios 2, 3, 4, '*Therefore, in briefe, tell*'; Pope, '*So tell.*'

IV. i. 93. '*thy*'; Rowe (from Quartos); Folios, '*the.*'

IV. i. 118. '*elder . . . younger*'; Folios (from Quartos); Theobald, '*younger . . . elder.*'

IV. i. 126. '*the love*'; Pope, '*love.*'

IV. i. 128. '*Yet am I arm'd*'; Vaughan, '*Yet am I warn'd.*'

IV. ii. 12. '*Sweet Clarence*'; Pope, '*friend*'; Capell, '*Clarence.*' Many modern editions omit '*but.*'

IV. ii. 15. '*towns*'; Theobald (Thirlby conj.); Folios, '*town.*'

IV. ii. 21. It had been prophesied that if the horses of the Thracian Rhesus drank of the Xanthus and grazed on the Trojan plains, the Greeks would never take Troy. Wherefore Diomede and Ulysses killed him at night, and carried off his horses. *v. Iliad*, x.; Ovid, *Metamorphoses*, xiii. 98-108, 249-252; Virgil, *Æneid*, i. 469-473.

IV. iii. 14. '*keeps*'; so Folios 3, 4; Folios 1, 2, '*keepes*'; Theobald, '*keepeth*'; Hanmer, '*keeps here*'; Vaughan, '*keeps out*'; Keightley, '*field here.*'

IV. iii. 15. '*more dangerous*'; so Folios 1, 2; Folios 3, 4, '*the more d.*'; Hanmer, '*dangerous.*'

IV. iii. 40. '*Yea, brother of Clarence, art thou here too?*'; Pope, '*Brother of C., and art thou here too?*'; Capell, '*Yea, brother of C., and art thou here too?*'

IV. iii. 54. '*tell what answer*'; Pope, '*tell you what reply*'; Capell, '*tell his grace what answer*'; Keightley, '*tell him what answer*'; Anon. conjectured '*tell the duke what answer*'; Dyce, '*tell him there what answer.*'

IV. iv. 11. '*new committed*'; Rowe, '*now committed.*'

IV. iv. 19. '*is it that makes me bridle passion*'; the reading of Folio 1; Folios 2, 3, '*is it . . . my passion*'; Folio 4, '*is . . . my passion*'; Rowe, '*is it . . . in my passion*'; Pope, '*is 't . . . in my passion*'; Vaughan, '*is it, makes . . . passion.*'

IV. v. 16. '*brother of Gloucester, Lord Hastings*'; Pope, '*brother Glo'ster, Hastings*'; Collier MS., '*brother of Gloster, Hastings.*'

IV. v. 21. '*Flanders*'; Vaughan suggests the addition of the words, '*as I guess.*'

IV. vi. 55. '*be confiscate*'; Malone's emendation, Folio 1, '*confiscate*'; Folios 2, 3, 4, '*confiscated.*'

IV. vii. 8. *Ravenspurgh*, the name of a seaport in Yorkshire; the reading of Folios 2, 3, 4; Folio 1, *'Rauenspurre'*; Quarto 1, 3, *'Raunspur'*; *'Ravenspurgh haven before'*; Pope omits *'haven'*; Steevens conjectured *'fore.'*

IV. vii. 30. *'A wise stout captain, and soon persuaded'*; *'captain'* probably trisyllabic; Keightley, *'I' faith, a wise'*; Collier MS., *'captain he'*; Delius (Lettsom conj.), *'capitain'*; Cartwright, *'captain, faith'*; Pope, *'persuaded soon.'*

IV. vii. 57. *'shall'*; Capell (from Quartos), *'should.'*

IV. viii. In the Folios, Somerset is named in the stage direction, though he had gone with young Richmond into Brittany. The mistake arose, as the Cambridge Eds. point out, from the Quartos, in which Scenes vi. and viii. form but one.

IV. viii. 2. *'hasty Germans'*; S. Walker, *'lusty'*; Cartwright, *'hardy.'*

IV. viii. 43. *'water-flowing tears'*; Capell, *'water-flowing eyes'*; Collier MS., *'bitter-flowing tears'*; Vaughan, *'wet o'erflowing tears.'*

IV. viii. 61. *'hoped-for hay'*; Quartos, *'hope for haie'*; Malone proposed, altogether unnecessarily, to change the words to *'hope for aye.'*

V. i. 6. *'Daintry,'* popular pronunciation of Daventry.

V. i. 50. *'I had'*; Pope, *'I'd.'*

V. i. 73. *'Two of thy name, both Dukes of Somerset'*; "Edmund slain at battle of St. Alban's, 1455; and Henry, his son, beheaded after the battle of Hexham, 1463" (Ritson).

V. i. 78. *'whom an'*; Rowe's emendation; Folios 2, 3, 4, *'whom, an'*; Folio 1, *'whom, in.'*

V. i. 86. *'That Clarence is'*; Steevens conjectured *'Clarence, so harsh, so blunt'*; Quartos, *'so harsh'* (*so blunt* omitted); Collier conjectured *'so harsh, so blind'*; Mitford, *'so harsh'* or *'so blunt'*; S. Walker, *'blunt-unnatural'*; Anon. conjectured *'brute-unnatural.'*

V. i. 91. *'Jephthah's'*; Rowe, *'Jepthah's'*; Folios 1, 2, *'Iephah'*; Folios 3, 4, *'Jepthah.'*

V. ii. 44. *'clamour,'* Warburton's reading from Quartos; Folios, *'cannon.'*

V. ii. 47-49. The arrangement of the lines in the Quartos; they form three lines in Folios, and have been variously arranged by editors.

V. iii. 5. *'our glorious sun,'* alluding to the cognizance of Edward.

V. iv. 18. *'The friends of France our shrouds and tacklings'*; S. Walker, *'Our . . . our,'* or *'These . . . our,'* &c.; Cartwright, *'Our . . . the,'* &c.; Pope, *'tacklings still'*; Johnson, *'tackling still'*; *'tacklings'* is evidently trisyllabic in this passage.

V. iv. 75. *'mine eyes'*; Capell (from Quartos); Folios, *'my eye.'*

V. v. 1. 'Now here'; the reading of Folio 1; Folios 2, 3, 4, 'Now here's'; Capell (from Quartos), 'Lo, here.'

V. v. 2. 'Hames'; the reading of Quartos and Folios; 'Ham' in Picardy; Rowe reads 'Hammes'; Hanmer, 'Holmes'; Capell, 'Hammes''; Delius, 'Ham's.'

V. v. 38. 'thou'; Rowe (from Quarto 3); Folios (Quartos 1, 2), 'the.'

V. v. 50. 'The Tower, the Tower'; Capell's reading; Folios, 'Tower, the Tower'; Theobald (from Quartos), 'The Tower, man, the Tower!—I'll root 'em out'; Steevens, 'The Tower, man, Tower!'

V. v. 77, 78. Steevens' reading, which is nearest to Quartos; Folio 1, 'Where is that devil's butcher, Richard? Hard favor'd Richard,' &c.

V. vi. 20. 'fool'; Seymour conjectured (from Quartos), 'fowl.'

V. vi. 41. 'Men for their sons, wives for their husbands'; Anon. conjectured (from Quartos), 'Wives for their husbands, fathers for their sons'; Folio 1, 'sonnes, . . . husbands'; Folio 2, 'sonnes, . . . husbands fate'; Folios 3, 4, 'sons . . . husbands fate'; Warburton, 'sons . . . husbands fate'; Knight, 'sons' . . . husbands,' &c.

V. vi. 45. 'boding luckless time'; Quartos, 'aboding . . . tune'; Theobald, 'a boding . . . tune.'

V. vi. 48. 'discords'; Grant White (from Quartos), 'discord.'

V. vi. 51. 'To wit, an indigested and deformed lump'; Capell (from Quartos), 'to wit an indigest deformed lump'; Dyce (Capell conj.) omits 'to wit.'

V. vi. 79. After this line, Theobald inserts from Quartos, 'I had no father, I am like no father.'

V. vii. 30. The Camb. editor quotes from Steevens:—"In my copy of the second Folio, which had belonged to King Charles the First, his Majesty has erased Cla. and written King in its stead. Shakespeare, therefore, in the catalogue of his restorers, may boast a Royal name."

THE TRAGEDY OF KING RICHARD III

I. i. 2. 'Sun of York'; probably an allusion to the device of a sun, the cognizance of Edward IV.. Quartos, 'sonne'; Folios, 'Son'; Rowe, 'sun.'

I. i. 15. 'to court an amorous looking-glass'; Vaughan thought the line might be improved by a slight emendation:—'an amorous looking lass.' (!).

I. i. 26. 'spy'; so Quartos; Folios, 'see.'

I. i. 61. 'have'; so Quartos and Folio 4; Folios 1, 2, 3, 'hath.'

I. i. 65. 'That tempers him to this extremity'; so Quarto 1; Quartos 2-8 read, 'That tempts him,' &c. (Quarto 3, 'tempts'); Folios read, 'That tempts him to this harsh extremity'; Anon. conjectured, 'That tempts him now to this extremity.'

I. i. 75. 'was to her for his'; so Quartos; Folio 1, 'was, for her'; Folios 2, 3, 'was, for his.'

I. i. 132. 'eagle'; so Quartos; Folios, 'Eagles.'

I. i. 133. 'prey'; so Quartos; Folios, 'play.'

I. i. 138. 'by Saint Paul'; the reading of Quartos; Folios, 'by S. Iohn,' a favourite oath of Richard's.

I. ii. 8. 'be it,' monosyllabic.

I. ii. 14. 'Cursed be the hand that made these fatal holes'; Quartos, 'Curst'; Folios, 'O cursed'; Quartos 1, 2, 'these fatal'; Quartos 3-8, 'the fatall'; Folios, 'these.'

I. ii. ll. 16, 25. Omitted in Quartos.

I. ii. 19. 'to adders, spiders'; the reading of Quartos; Folios read, 'to wolves, to spiders.'

I. ii. 60, 61. 'Thy deed . . . Provokes'; so Quartos; Folios 1, 2, 3, 'Deeds . . . Prouokes'; Folio 4, 'deeds . . . Provoke.'

I. ii. 76. 'evils'; so Quartos; Folios, 'crimes.'

I. ii. 89. 'Why, then they are not dead'; the reading of Quartos; Folios read, 'Then say they were not slaine.'

I. ii. 128. 'These eyes could never endure sweet beauty's wreck'; Quartos, 'never'; Folios read, 'not'; Quartos, 'sweet'; Folios 1, 2, 'yt'; Folios 3, 4, 'that'; 'wreck,' Theobald's emendation of 'wrack' of Quartos and Folios.

I. ii. 136. 'you'; Folios, 'thee.'

I. ii. 148. 'Never hung poison on a fouler toad'; alluding to the old belief that toads were venomous.

I. ii. 157, 168. Omitted in Quartos.

I. ii. 180. 'for I did kill King Henry'; Quartos read, 'twas I that kild your husband.'

I. ii. 182. ' 'twas I that stabb'd young Edward'; Quartos read, 'twas I that kild King Henry.'

I. ii. 186. 'the'; Folios, 'thy.'

I. ii. 203. Omitted in Folios.

I. ii. 207. 'devoted suppliant'; so Quarto 1; Folios read, 'devoted servant'; the rest, 'suppliant.'

I. ii. 211. 'would,' the reading of Quartos; Folios, 'may'; 'thee,' so Quartos; Folios, 'you.'

I. ii. 212. 'more'; so Quartos; Folios, 'most.'

I. ii. 226. 'Sirs, take up the corse'; omitted in Folios.

I. ii. 229-230:—

'Was ever woman in this humour woo'd?
Was ever woman in this humour won?'

cp. '*She is a woman, therefore may be woo'd;*
   She is a woman, therefore may be won.'
                    Titus And., II. i. 82, 83.
   '*She's beautiful, and therefore to be woo'd;*
   She is a woman, therefore to be won.'
                    1 Henry VI., V. iii. 78, 79.

I. ii. 237. '*nothing*'; so Quartos; Folios, '*no Friends.*'

I. iii. 5. '*words*'; so Quartos; Folios read '*eyes.*'

I. iii. 7. '*harm*'; Folios 1, 2, 3, '*harmes.*'

I. iii. 17. '*Here come the lords*'; so Quartos 1, 2; Quartos 3-8, '*Here comes the Lords*'; Folios, '*Here comes the Lord*'; Theobald altered '*Derby*' to '*Stanley,*' as Thomas, Lord Stanley, was not created Earl of Derby till after the accession of Henry VII.

I. iii. 36. '*Madam, we did*'; Folios 1, 2, 3, '*I (i.e. Aye) Madam*'; Quartos, '*Madame we did.*'

I. iii. 43. '*who are they that complain*'; the reading of Quartos; Folios read, '*who is it that complaines.*'

I. iii. 58. '*person*'; so Quartos; Folios, '*Grace.*'

I. iii. 67. '*kindred*'; so Quartos 1, 6, 7, 8; Quartos 2, 3, 4, 5, read '*kinred*'; Folios. '*children.*'

I. iii. 68, 69. '*Makes him to send; that thereby he may gather The ground of your ill-will, and to remove it,*' the reading of Quartos 1-6. (Quarto 6, '*grounds*'); Folios read, '*Makes him to send, that he may learn the ground*'; Pope, '*Makes him to send that he may learn the ground Of your ill-will, and thereby to remove it*'; Capell, '*Hath sent for you; that thereby he may gather The ground of your ill-will, and so remove it,*' &c.

I. iii. 77. '*we*'; so Quartos; Folios, '*I.*'

I. iii. 80. '*whilst many fair promotions*'; the reading of Quartos; Folios, '*while great promotions*'; (evidently to be read as a quadrisyllable).

I. iii. 90. '*cause*'; so Quartos; Folios, '*meane.*'

I. iii. 106. '*With those gross taunts I often have endured*'; so Quartos; Folios read, '*Of those . . . that oft I have e.*'.

I. iii. 109. '*thus taunted, scorn'd, and baited at*'; the reading of Quartos; Folios read, '*so baited, scorn'd, and stormed at.*'

I. iii. 114. Omitted in Folios.

I. iii. 116. Omitted in Quartos.

I. iii. 130. '*Margaret's battle at St. Alban's,*' *i.e.* the second battle of St. Albans, Feb. 17, 1461.

I. iii. 161. '*I being queen*'; so the Quartos; Folios read, '*I am queen.*'

I. iii. 167-169. Omitted in Quartos.

I. iii. 219. '*them,*' *i.e.* '*heaven,*' used in plural sense.

I. iii. 287. '*I'll not believe*'; so Quartos; Folios, '*I will not thinke.*'

I. iii. 321. '*And for your grace; and you, my noble lords*'; Folios,

'And for your Grace, and yours my gracious Lord.'

I. iii. 337. *'old odd ends stolen out'*; so Quartos; Folios, *'odde old ends stolen forth.'*

I. iii. 353. *'Your eyes drop millstones, when fools' eyes drop tears,'* a proverbial expression; *'drop tears'*; the reading of Quartos; Folios, *'fall Teares.'*

I. iv. 3. *'So full of ugly sights, of ghastly dreams'*; so Quartos; Folios, *'So full of fearefull Dreames, of ugly sights.'*

I. iv. 9, 10. *'Methoughts that I had broken from the Tower, And was embark'd to cross to Burgundy'*; so Folios; Quartos read, *'Me thoughts I was imbarkt for Burgundy.'*

I. iv. 25. *'ten thousand'*; so Quartos; Folios, *'a thousand.'*

I. iv. 28. Omitted in Quartos.

I. iv. 36, 37. *'and often . . . ghost'*; omitted in Quartos.

I. iv. 38. *'kept in'*; so Quartos; Folios, *'Stop'd.'*

I. iv. 45. *'who'*; so Quartos; Folios, *'I'*; *'flood,'* river (*'melancholy flood,'* i.e., 'the river Styx').

I. iv. 46. *'grim ferryman'*; i.e. 'Charon'; so Quartos; Folios, *'sowre f.'*

I. iv. 57. *'to your torments'*; so Quartos; Folios, *'unto Torment.'*

I. iv. 59. *'environ'd me about'*; so Quartos; Folios omit *'about.'*

I. iv. 65. *'I promise you, I am afraid to hear you tell it'*; so the Quartos; Folios read, *'I am affraid (me thinks) to hear you tell it.'*

I. iv. 66. *'O Brakenbury'*; Quartos read, *'O Brokenbury'*; Folios, *'Ah Keeper, Keeper!'*; *'those,'* so Quartos; Folios, *'these.'*

I. iv. 69-72. Omitted in Quartos.

I. iv. 72. *'My guiltless wife'*; Clarence's wife died before this date.

I. iv. 73. *'I pray thee, gentle Keeper, stay by me'*; the reading of Quartos; Folios read, *'Keeper, I prythee sit by me a-while.'*

I. iv. 85. *'In God's name what are you, and how came you hither?'*; the reading of Quartos; Folios, *'What would'st thou, Fellow? And how camm'st thou hither?'*

I. iv. 95. *'Here are the keys, there sits the duke asleep'*; so Quartos; Folios read, *'There lies.the Duke asleepe, and there the Keyes.'*

I. iv. 104. *'till the judgement-day'*; so Quartos; Folios, *'til the great judgement-day.'*

I. iv. 112-113. Omitted in Folios.

I. iv. 117. *'my holy humour'*; so Quartos; Folios read, *'this passionate humor of mine.'*

I. iv. 132. *'it . . . thing'*; omitted in Folios.

I. iv. 150. *'shalt we to this gear?'* so Quartos; Folios read, *'shall we fall to worke.'*

I. iv. 152. *'we will chop him in'*; so Quartos; Folios read, *'throw him into.'*

I. iv. 168. Omitted in Quartos.

I. iv. 180. *'call'd forth from out'*; so Quartos; Folios, *'drawne forth among.'*

I. iv. 188. *'to have redemption'*; so Quartos read; Folios, *'for any goodness.'*

I. iv. 189, 236. Omitted in Folios.

I. iv. 206. Omitted in Quartos.

I. iv. 248. *'this world's'*; so Quartos; Folios, *'this earth's.'*

I. iv. 257, 268. *'Relent! 'tis,'* &c.; Folios, *'Relent? no: 'Tis,'* &c.; the text is due to a blending of the readings of Quartos and Folios, first suggested by Tyrwhitt (*vide* Note vii., Camb. ed.).

I. iv. 272. *'like Pilate'*; *cp.* Matthew xxvii. 24.

I. iv. 273. *'grievous guilty murder done'*; so Quartos; Folios, *'grievous murther.'*

I. iv. 281. *'Until the duke take'*; so Quartos; Folios, *'Till that the Duke give.'*

II. i. 5. *'now in peace'*; so Quartos; Folios read, *'more to peace.'*

II. i. 7. *'Rivers and Hastings'*; so Quartos; Folios read, *'Dorset and Rivers.'*

II. i. 33. *'On you or yours'*; the reading of Quartos; Folios read, *'Vpon your Grace.'*

II. i. 40. *'zeal'*; so Quartos; Folios, *'loue.'*

II. i. 44. *'perfect'*; so Quartos; Folios, *'blessed.'*

II. i. 45. *'And in good time, here comes the noble duke'*; so Quartos; Folios read, *'And in good time, Heere comes Sir Richard Ratcliffe, and the Duke.'*

II. i. 56. *'unwittingly'*; so Quartos; Folios read, *'unwillingly.'*

II. i. 66. *'Of you, Lord Rivers, and, Lord Grey, of you'*; so Quartos 1-4; Folios read, *'Of you and you, Lord Riuers and of Dorset.'*

II. i. 67. *'have frown'd on me'*; the reading of Quartos; Folios read, *'have frown'd on me, Of you Lord Wooduill, and Lord Scales of you.'*

II. i. 70-73. Quoted by Milton in *Iconoclastes* by way of illustrating his statement that "the poets, and some English, have been in this point so mindful of decorum, as to put never nine pious words in the mouth of any person, than of a tyrant."

II. i. 99. *'Then speak at once what is it thou demand'st'*; *'speak,'* the reading of Quartos; Folios, *'say'*; *'demand'st,'* the reading of Quartos; Folios, *'requests.'*

II. i. 104. *'that tongue'*; so Folios; Quartos read, *'the same.'*

II. i. 105. *'slew'*; so Quartos; Folios, *'kill'd.'*

II. i. 106. *'cruel'*; Quartos; Folios, *'bitter.'*

II. i. 117. *'his own garments'*; Quartos 6, 7, 8, *'his owne armes'*; Folios, *'his Garments'*; *'gave,'* so Quartos; Folios, *'did give.'*

II. ii. 11. *'sorrow to wail'*; so Folios; Quartos read, *'labour to weepe for.'*

II. ii. 15. *'daily'*; so Quartos; Folios, *'earnest'*; Pope, *'daily earnest,'* omitting *'all to that effect.'*

II. ii. 16. Omitted in Quartos.

II. ii. 46. *'perpetual rest'*; so Quartos; Folios read, *'nere-changing night'*; Collier MS., *'nere-changing light.'*

II. ii. 84-85. *'So do I; I for an Edward weep'*; omitted in Folios.

II. ii. ll. 89-100, 123-140. Omitted in Quartos.

II. ii. 101. *'Madam'*; so Quartos; Folios, *'Sister.'*

II. ii. 144. *'weighty'*; reading of Quartos; Folios omit it.

II. iii. 4. *'Seldom comes the better'*; a proverbial expression; found in Ray's *Proverbs.*

II. iii. 11. *'Woe to that land that's govern'd by a child'*; cp. Ecclesiastes, x. 16.

II. iii. 28. *'sons and brothers haught'*; so Folios; Quartos, *'kindred hauty'*; Capell conjectured, *'kindred hauty are.'*

II. iv. 20. *'if this rule were true'*; so the Cambridge Editors; Quartos 1, 2, *'if this were a true rule'*; Quartos 3-8, *'if this were a rule'*; Folios, *'if his rule were true.'*

II. iv. 62, 63. *'blood against blood, Self,'* &c.; so Quartos; Folios, *'Brother to Brother; Blood to blood, selfe,'* &c.

II. iv. 67. *'Madam, farewell'*; omitted in Quartos.

III. i. 82. *'formal vice, Iniquity'*; Hanmer reads, *'formal wiss antiquary'*; Warburton, *'formal-wise antiquity'*; *'Iniquity'* was no uncommon name of the formal (*i.e.* conventional) comic character, the Vice, of the Morality plays (*cp. e.g. 'The Nice Wanton'*).

III. i. 110, 111; observe this instance of dramatic irony.

III. i. 172-173. Omitted in Quartos.

III. i. 176. *'icy-cold'*; Ingleby's conjecture; Quartos and Folios read, *'icie, cola.'*

III. i. 193. *'Chop off his head, man; somewhat we will do'*; so Quartos; Folios read, *'Chop off his Head: something wee will determine.'*

III. ii. 11. *'razed'*; Quartos 1-4, *'raste'*; Quarto 5, *'Caste'*; Folios 1, 2, *'rased off'*; Folios 3, 4, *'raised off.'* Quoted in Nares *'rashed.' To rase* or *rash* seems to have been an old hunting term used specially for the violence of the boar.

III. ii. 55. *'I will not do it, to the death'*; i.e. 'though death be the consequence.'

III. ii. 105. *'fellow'*; Quartos read, *'Hastings.'*

III. iii. 6, 7. Omitted in Quartos.

III. iii. 14. After this line Folios insert:—*'When she exclaim'd on Hastings, you, and I'*; omitted in Quartos.

III. iii. 23. *'Make haste; the hour of death is expiate'*; so Folio 1; Folios 2-4, *'is now expired'* (*cp. supra* l. 8): *'expiate'* = 'ended, terminated'; Quartos read, *'Come, come, dispatch; the limit of your liues is out'*; Steevens, *'expirate.'*

III. iv. 1. *'My lords, at once'*; so Quartos; Folios, *'Now, Noble Peers.'*

III. iv. 10. *'Who, I, my lord,'* &c., so Quartos; the Folios:—

'*We know each other's Faces; for our Hearts*
He knowes no more of mine, then I of yours,
Or I of his, my Lord, then you of mine.'

III. iv. 74. '*Tellest thou me of "if"*'; so Quartos; Folios, '*Talk'st thou to me of "ifs."*'

III. iv. 81. '*raze his helm*'; Quartos read, '*race his helme*'; Folios 1, 2, '*rowse our Helmes*'; Folios 3, 4, '*Rowze our Helmes*'; Rowe, '*rase our helms*'; (*cp. supra* III. ii. 11).

III. iv. 82. '*But I disdain'd it, and did scorn to fly*'; so Quartos; Folios, '*And I did scorne it, and disdaine to flye.*'

III. iv. 95. '*grace of mortal*'; so Folios; Quartos, '*state of worldly.*'

III. iv. 101-104. Omitted in Quartos.

III. v. 5. '*Tut, I can*'; so Folios; Quartos, '*Tut feare not me, I can.*'

III. v. 7. Omitted in Quartos.

III. v. 10-20. The first Quarto differs in many points from this, the reading of the Folios, especially in making Catesby enter with Hastings' head, though previously Gloster has ordered him '*to overlook the walls.*' A similar discrepancy occurs in Scene IV., ll. 80, 81.

III. v. 51-60. Gloucester's speech given to 'Buckingham' in Folios.

III. v. 69, 70. '*Yet witness . . . farewell*'; so Folios; Quartos read, '*Yet witnesse what we did intend, and so my Lord adue.*'

III. v. 96. '*and . . . adieu*'; 103-105. Omitted in Quartos.

III. v. 100-101. '*I go . . . affords*'; so Folios; Quartos read, '*About three or four a clocke looke to heare What news Guildhall affordeth, and so my Lord farewell.*'

III. vi. 12. '*blind*'; so Quartos; Folios, '*bold.*'

III. vii. 24. '*they spake not a word,*' omitted in Quartos.

III. vii. 25. '*breathing stones,*' *i.e.* they were able to breathe, but without the power of speech; later Quartos, '*breathlesse s.*'

III. vii. ll. 97-98, 118, 125, 142-151, 200, omitted in Quartos.

III. vii. 237. '*Richard, England's royal king*'; so Quartos; Folios, '*King Richard, England's worthie king.*'

IV. i. 7. '*As much to you, good sister! Whither away?*' the reading of Folios; Quartos, which omit ll. 2-6, read, '*Sister, well met, whether awaie so fast?*'

IV. i. 14. '*How doth the prince, and my young son of York?*' so Folios; Quartos read, '*How fares the Prince?*'

IV. i. 15. '*Right well, dear Madam. By your patience*'; the reading of Folios; Quartos read, '*Well Madam, and in health, but by your leave.*'

IV. i. 18. '*why, who's that?*'; the reading of Quartos; Folios, '*who's that?*'

IV. i. 24. *'Then bring me to their sights'*; so Folios; Quartos read, *'Then feare not thou.'*

IV. i. 50. *'To meet you on the way, and welcome you'*; so Quartos; Folios read, *'In your behalfe, to meet you on the way.'*

IV. i. 60. *'red-hot steel'*; Steevens says, "She seems to allude to the ancient mode of punishing a regicide, or any other egregious criminal, viz. by placing a crown of iron, heated red-hot, upon his head."

IV. i. 65. *'Why?'*; so Folios; omitted in Quartos.

IV. i. 75-76. *'As miserable by the death of thee As thou hast made me by my dear lord's death'*; so Quartos; Folios read, *'More miserable by the life of thee, Then,'* &c.; (*cp.* I. ii. 27).

IV. i. 95. *'Eighty odd years'*; the Duchess was actually only sixty-eight at this time.

IV. i. 97-103. Omitted in Quartos.

IV. ii. 16. *'That Edward still should live true noble prince'*; so Quartos and Folios; Theobald, *'That Edward still should live, True noble Prince.'*

IV. ii. 55. *'The boy is foolish'*; *i.e.* Edward Plantagenet, who had been kept imprisoned in the Tower almost from his tenderest years.

IV. ii. 98-115. Omitted in Folios.

IV. iii. 5. *'this ruthless piece of butchery'*; so Quartos 1, 2; Quarto 3, *'thir ruthfull . . . ,'* &c.; Quartos 4-8, *'this ruthfull . . . ,'* &c.; Folios, *'This peece of ruthfull Butchery.'*

IV. iii. 11. *'innocent alabaster'*; so Quarto 8; Quartos 1-7, *'innocent alabaster'*; Folios 1, 2, 3 read *'Alabaster innocent'*; Folio 4, *'Alabaster innocent.'*

IV. iii. 40. *'the Breton Richmond'*; 'after the battle of Tewkesbury he had taken refuge in the court of Francis II., Duke of Bretagne' (Malone).

IV. iv. 17-19, placed after line 34 in Folios.

IV. iv. ll. 20, 21, 28. Omitted in Quartos.

IV. iv. 41. *'Harry'*; Quartos, *'Richard'*; Folios, *'Husband.'*

IV. iv. 52-53. Omitted in Quartos; transposed in Folios.

IV. iv. 72. *'their,'* *i.e.* 'hell's'; (*cp.* the use of 'heaven,' I. iii. 219).

IV. iv. 88-90. The reading of the Quartos is followed in these lines in preference to that of the Folios:—

> *'A dreame of what thou wast, a garish Flagg,*
> *To be the aymne of every dangerous shot;*
> *A sign of dignity, a Breath, a Bubble.'*

IV. iv. ll. 102-104 transposed; l. 103 omitted in Quartos; Folios, *'she'* for *'one.'*

IV. iv. 176. *'Humphrey Hour'*; perhaps a mere personification, as it were, of some particular Hour, formed on the analogy of such phrases as *'Tom Trott,'* &c. According to some, there is an allusion to the phrase *'to dine with Duke Humphrey.'*

IV. iv. 180-183. '*I prithee . . . So!*'; so Folios; Quartos read, '*Du. O hear me speake, for I shall never see thee more.* KING. *Come, come, you are too bitter.*'

IV. iv. 222-235. Omitted in Quartos.

IV. iv. 236-237. '*my enterprise, And dangerous success of bloody wars*'; so Folios; Quartos read, '*my dangerous attempt of hostile armes.*'

IV. iv. 276-277. '*steep'd in Rutland's blood,—A handkerchief*'; so Folios; Quartos read '*a handkercher steept in Rutlands bloud.*'

IV. iv. 277-278, 289-343. Omitted in Quartos.

IV. iv. 325. '*Of ten times*'; Theobald's correction of Folios, '*Oftentimes.*'

IV. iv. 389. '*What canst thou swear by now?*'; omitted in Quartos.

IV. iv. 511-516. So the Folios; the Quartos differ materially in the phraseology of the lines.

V. ii. 17. '*Every man's conscience is a thousand swords*'; Folios, '*men*' for '*swords*'; the words paraphrase '*Conscientia nulle testes.*'

V. iii. 2. '*My Lord of Surrey, why look you so sad?*'; so the Folios; Quarto 1 reads, '*Whie, how now Catesbie, whie lookst thou so bad?*'; the other Quartos, '*Whie . . . so sad?*'

V. iii. 22. '*Sir William Brandon, you shall bear my standard*'; so Folios; Quartos read, '*Where is Sir William Brandon, he shall beare my standerd.*'

V. iii. 23-26. In Quartos these lines are inserted between ll. 43 and 44, and ll. 27, 28, 43 are omitted.

V. iii. 40. '*Good Captain Blunt, bear my good-night to him*'; so Quartos; Folios, '*Sweet Blunt, make some good meanes to speak with him.*'

V. iii. 96. '*tender George*'; George Stanley was at this time already married, though Shakespeare, following Hall and Holinshed, makes him a child.

V. iii. 126. '*By thee was punched full of deadly holes*'; this has been described as one of the worst lines in all Shakespeare, but this is due to the fact that critics have confused (i.) '*punch,*' the technical word for making use of the *puncheon*, a shoemaker's tool for making holes with (Fr. *poinson*, a bodkin, L. *punctionem*), with (ii.) *punch*, to beat, which is a distinct word, and is merely an abbreviation of *punish*.

V. iii. 144. '*Let fall thy lance: despair, and die!*'; Capell reads, '*hurtless lance*'; Collier MS., '*pointless lance*'; but no change is necessary; the line is probably intentionally abrupt, *cp.* 148.

V. iii. 153. '*lead*'; so Quarto 1; all other eds., '*laid.*'

V. iii. 163-164. These lines are Lettsom's conjecture, the true lines being lost.

V. iii. 174. '*I died for hope*'; *i.e.* 'for want of hope,' *cp.* '*dead for hope*' (Greene's *James IV., V., VI.*) = 'dead to hope.' Various unnecessary emendations have been proposed (*v.* Glossary).

V. iii. 181. '*the lights burn blue*,' alluding to the old superstitious belief that when a spirit was present the lights burnt blue.

V. iii. 205-207. '*Methought . . . Richard*'; Johnson proposed to place these lines after line 192.

V. iii. 213-215. 'KING RICH. *O Ratcliff . . ., my lord*,' omitted in Folios.

V. iii. 222. '*eaves-dropper*'; so Folio 4; Quarto 1, '*ease dropper*'; Quarto 2, '*ewse dropper*'; Folios 1, 2, 3, '*Ease-dropper*.'

V. iii. 317. '*Bretons*'; Capell's emendation; Quartos 1, 2, 3, 5, '*Brittains*'; Folios 3, 4, '*Britains*'; Pope, '*Britons*.'

V. iii. 322. '*restrain*'; so Quartos and Folios. Warburton proposed '*distrain*,' and this reading has been adopted by several modern editors.

V. iii. 324. '*mother's cost*,' should be '*brother's cost*'; the error —a mere printer's error—was due to the 2nd edition of Holinshed; *cp.* Hall, '*brought up by my brother's* (*i.e.* Richard's brother-in-law, the Duke of Burgundy) *meanes and mine*.'

V. iii. 345. '*the enemy is past the marsh*'; "There was a large marsh in Bosworth plaine between the two armies, which Richard passed, and arranged his forces so that it protected his right wing. He thus also compelled the enemy to fight with the sun in their faces, a great disadvantage when bows and arrows were in use" (Malone).

V. iv. 22. '*But tell me, is young George Stanley living?*'; so Folios and Quartos; Pope, '*tell me first*'; Keightley, '*tell me, pray*,' &c. There is no need to emend; '*George*' is evidently dissyllabic.

THE FAMOUS HISTORY OF THE LIFE OF KING HENRY VIII

Prol. 3. '*high and working*'; Staunton reads '*and high-working*.'

Prol. 12. '*shilling*'; the usual price for a seat on or next the stage.

Prol. 16. '*a long motley coat*'; the professional garb of the fool or jester.

Prol. 21. The line is either to be taken as a parenthesis, '*that*' referring to '*opinion*' (= reputation); or as following directly on '*opinion*,' *i.e.* 'the reputation we bring of making what we represent strictly in accordance with truth.'

I. i. 6. '*Those suns of glory*'; *i.e.* Francis I., King of France, and Henry VIII., King of England; Folios 3, 4 read '*sons*.'

I. i. 7. '*the vale of Andren. 'Twixt Guynes and Arde*.' Guynes, a town in Picardy belonging to the English; Arde, a town in

Picardy belonging to the French; the vale of Andren between the two towns was the scene of the famous 'Field of the Cloth of Gold.'

I. i. 62, 63. Capell's reading of Folio 1, 'but spider-like, Out of his selfe-drawing web, O gives us note.' Further, Capell and Rowe substituted 'self-drawn' for 'self-drawing.'

I. i. 79, 80. 'The honourable . . . out, . . . him in he papers'; Folios 1, 2, read 'The Council, out . . . him in, he papers,' &c. Pope's explanation of these awkward lines is probably correct:—"His own letter, by his own single authority, and without the concurrence of the council, must fetch him in whom he papers" (i.e. registers on the paper). Various emendations have been proposed; e.g. 'the papers'; 'he paupers.'

I. i. 86. 'minister communication'; Collier MS., 'the consummation'; but the phrase is Holinshed's.

I. i. 90. 'the hideous storm'; "On Mondaie, the eighteenth of June, was such an hideous storme of wind and weather, that manie conjectured it did prognosticate trouble and hatred shortlie after to follow betweene princes" (Holinshed).

I. i. 115. The Duke of Buckingham's surveyor was his cousin, Charles Knevet, or Knyvet, grandson of Humphrey Stafford, First Duke of Buckingham.

I. i. 120. 'venom-mouth'd'; Pope's reading; Folios read 'venom'd-mouth'd.'

I. i. 152. 'Whom from the flow of gall I name not,' &c.; i.e. 'whom I mention, not because I am still angry'; &c.

I. i. 167. 'rinsing,' Pope's unnecessary emendation of the Folio reading 'wrenching,' which is evidently an error for 'renching,' a provincial English cognate of 'rinse,' both words being ultimately derived from the same Scandinavian original, rinse, through the medium of French, rench, a direct borrowing; (Collier MS., 'wrensing').

I. i. 172. 'count-cardinal'; Pope proposed 'court-cardinal.'

I. i. 176. 'Charles the emperor,' viz., Charles V., Emperor of Germany; Katharine was his mother's sister.

I. i. 200. 'Hereford'; Capell's reading; Folios, 'Hertford.'

I. i. 204-206. The meaning of these unsatisfactory lines seems to be, as Johnson explained, 'I am sorry to be present, and an eye-witness of your loss of liberty.'

I. i. 211. 'Abergavenny'; Folios, 'Aburgany,' the usual pronunciation of the name.

I. i. 217. 'Montacute'; Folios read 'Mountacute'; Rowe reads 'Montague.'

I. i. 219. 'chancellor'; Theobald's correction; Folios 1, 2 read 'Councellour.'

I. i. 221. 'Nicholas Hopkins'; Theobald's correction (from

Holinshed) of Folios, *'Michaell'* (probably due to printer's confusion of *'Nich'* with *'Mich'*).

I. ii. 67. *'business'*; Warburton's emendation of Folios, *'baseness.'*

I. ii. 147. *'Henton'*; *i.e.* Nicholas Hopkins, "a monk of an house of the Chartreux Order beside Bristow, called Henton" (Holinshed); there is no need to amend the text.

I. ii. 164. *'confession's seal'*; Theobald's emendation (following Holinshed) of Folios, *'commissions.'*

I. ii. 170. *'To gain'*; the reading of Folio 4; Folios 1, 2, 3, read *'To'*; Collier MS. reads *'To get'*; Grant White, *'To win.'*

I. ii. 179. *'for him'*; Capell's emendation of *'For this'* of the Folios; Collier MS. reads *'From this'*; &c.

I. ii. 190. *'Bulmer'*; Folios read *'Blumer'*; Pope, *'Blomer.'*

I. iii. 13. *'Or springhalt'*; Verplank's (Collier conj.) emendation of Folios, *'A springhalt'*; Pope, *'And springhalt.'*

I. iii. 34. *'wear'*; the reading of Folios 2, 3, 4; Folio 1 reads *'wee'*; Anon. conjecture *'oui.'*

I. iii. 59. *'has wherewithal'*; Folios, *'ha's,'* probably an error for *' 'has,' i.e.* '(he) has.'

I. iv. 6. *'As, first, good company'*; so Folios 1, 2, 3; Folio 4 reads *'As, first good company'*; Theobald, *'as, first-good company'*; Halliwell, *'as far as good company,'* &c.

II. i. 29. *'was either pitied in him or forgotten'*; *i.e.* 'either produced no effect or only ineffectual pity' (Malone).

II. i. 54. *'Sir William Sands'*; Theobald's emendation (from Holinshed) of Folio 1, *'Sir Walter Sands'*; Folios 2, 3, 4, *'Walter Sands.'*

II. i. 86. *'mark'*; Warburton's emendation of Folios, *'make.'*

II. i. 105. *'I now seal it,' i.e.* my truth,—with blood.

II. ii. 83. *'one have-at-him'*; Folio 1, *'one; haue at him'*; Folios 2, 3, 4, *'one heave at him'*; Knight, *'one;—have at him.'*

II. ii. 92. *'Have their free voices,' i.e.* 'have liberty to express their opinions freely'; (Grant White, *'Gave'* for *'Have'*).

II. iii. 14. *'that quarrel, fortune, do'*; Folio 1 reads *'that quarrell. Fortune, do'*; Collier MS., *'that cruel fortune do'*; Keightley, *'that quarrel, by fortune, do'*; Lettsom conjectured *'that fortunes quarrel do'*; Hanmer, *'that quarr'ler, fortune do'*; &c.

II. iii. 46. *'little England'*; Steevens pointed out that Pembrokeshire was known as *'little England'*; and as Anne Bullen was about to be made Marchioness of Pembroke, there may be a special point in the phrase.

II. iii. 93. *'the mud in Egypt,' i.e.* 'the land fertilized by the Nile's overflow.'

II. iv. 60. *'That longer you desire the court,' i.e.* 'desire the court to delay its proceedings'; Folio 4, *'defer'*; Keightley conjectured *'court delay'd.'*

II. iv. 170. '*The Bishop of Bayonne*'; strictly it should be 'the Bishop of Tarbes,' but the mistake was Holinshed's.

II. iv. 172. '*The Duke of Orleans*,' was the second son of Francis I., King of France.

II. iv. 180. '*the bosom of my conscience*'; Holinshed's use of '*secret bottom of my conscience*' justified Theobald's emendation of '*bosom*' to '*bottom*.'

II. iv. 197. '*throe*'; Pope's emendation of Folios, '*throw*.'

II. iv. 202. '*yet not*,' *i.e.* 'not yet.'

II. iv. 223. '*drive*'; Pope's emendation of Folios, '*drives*.'

III. i. 38. '*and that way I am wife in*'; *i.e.* 'concerning my conduct as a wife.' (Rowe proposed '*wise*' for '*wife*.')

III. i. 40. '*Tanta est erga te mentis integritas, regina serenissima*'; 'So great is our integrity of purpose towards thee, most serene princess.'

III. ii. 64. '*He is returned in his opinions*,' *i.e.* 'having sent in advance the opinions he has gathered.'

III. ii. 66. '*Together with all famous colleges*'; Rowe reads, '*Gather'd from all the famous colleges*.'

III. ii. 172. '*been mine so*'; so Folio 1; Folios 2, 3, 4 read '*been so*.'

III. ii. 192. '*that am, have, and will be*,' &c.; the reading of the Folios of these lines, which have taxed the ingenuity of scholars; some two dozen various emendations are recorded in the Cambridge Shakespeare, but probably the text as we have it represents the author's words; the meaning of the passage is clear, and the difficulty is due to the change in construction. Instead of '*that am, have, and will be*,' it has been proposed to read, '*that am your slave, and will be*'; this would get rid of the awkward '*have*' = 'have been,' but probably the line is correct as it stands.

III. ii. 282. '*And dare us with his cap like larks*'; "One of the methods of daring larks was by small mirrors fastened on scarlet cloth, which engaged the attention of these birds while the fowler drew his net over them" (Steevens).

III. ii. 321. '*Cassado*'; so Folios, following Hall and Holinshed; Rowe reads the correct form, '*Cassalis*.'

III. ii. 343. '*Chattels*'; Theobald's emendation of Folios, '*Castles*.'

IV. ii. 58-59. '*Those twins of learning . . . Ipswich and Oxford*'; Wolsey's College, Ipswich, of which the gateway still remains, was founded by Wolsey. Christ Church College, Oxford, was founded by Wolsey: it was first called Cardinal College.

IV. ii. 60. '*the good that did it*'; Pope reads, '*the good he did it*'; Collier MS., '*the good man did it*'; Staunton, '*the good that rear'd it*,' &c. The words, if not corrupt, must mean the 'good man (for the goodness) that caused it, *i.e.* founded it.'

V. i. 34. '*is*'; Theobald, '*he's.*'

V. i. 107. '*you a brother to us,*' *i.e.* 'being a Privy Councillor.'

V. iii. 11-12. '*frail and capable of our flesh*'; Keightley, '*culpable and frail,*' &c.; Pope, '*and capable Of frailty*'; Malone, '*incapable; Of our flesh*'; Mason conj. '*and culpable: Of our flesh,*' &c.

V. iii. 22. '*pace 'em not in their hands*'; *i.e.* 'leading them by the bridle.'

V. iii. 30. '*The upper Germany*'; alluding to Thomas Munzer's insurrection in Saxony (1521-1522), or to the Anabaptist rising in Munster (1535); the passage is from Foxe.

V. iii. 66. '*Lay,*' *i.e.* 'though ye lay.'

V. iii. 85. '*This is too much*'; the Folios give the speech to the Chamberlain, evidently due to confusion of '*Cham.*' and '*Chan.*'

V. iii. 125. '*bare*'; Malone's emendation of Folios, '*base.*'

V. iii. 166. '*You 'ld spare your spoons,*' *i.e.* 'you wish to save your spoons'; alluding to the old custom of giving spoons as christening presents.

V. iv. 25. '*And that I would not for a cow, God save her!*' a proverbial expression still used in the South of England.

V. iv. 58. '*The tribulation of Towerhill, or the limbs of Limehouse.*' There is no evidence for finding in these words the names of Puritan congregations, as commentators have supposed; the alternative phrases are sufficiently expressive without any such supposition, and were perhaps coined for the occasion; they are not found elsewhere.

V. v. 70. '*And your good brethren*'; Thirlby's conjecture, adopted by Theobald; Folios read '*and you good brethren.*'

V. v. 75. '*has*'; *i.e.* 'he has'; Folios, ''*Has.*'

VENUS AND ADONIS

156. '*shouldst*'; Quarto 1, '*should.*'

171. *cp.* Sonnet I.

211. '*lifeless*'; Quartos 1, 2, 3, '*liuelesse.*'

213. '*Statue*'; Quartos 1, 2, 3, '*Statüe*'; *cp.* l. 1013; Quartos 3, 4, '*statües.*'

231; 239; 689. '*deer*'; Quartos 1, 2, 3. '*deare.*'

272. '*stand,*' so Quartos 1-4; the rest '*stands.*'

283. '*stir*'; Quartos 1, 2, 3, '*sturre.*'

304. '*And whether*'; Quartos, '*And where*' (*i.e.* 'wher'er').

334; 402. '*fire*'; Quartos 1, 2, 3, '*fier*; but '*fire,*' l. 494 (rhyming with '*desire*').

353. '*tenderer*'; Quarto 1, '*tendrer*'; the rest, '*tender.*'

362. '*goal*'; Quartos, '*gaile*'; '*Iaile.*'

392. *'master'd'*; Quartos 1, 2, 3, *'maister'd'*; *cp.* l. 114; *'mastering'*; Quartos 1, 2, 3, *'maistring.'*

——, *'rein'*; Quartos 1-10, *'raine.'*

429. *'mermaid's'*; early Quartos, *'marmaides'*; *'marmaids'*; *cp.* l. 777; Quartos 1, 2, 3, *'marmaids'*; Quarto 4, *'mirmaides.'*

434. *'invisible'*; Steevens conjectured *'invincible.'*

454. *'wreck'*; Quartos, *'wracke,' 'wrack'* (*cp.* l. 558).

466. *'bankrupt'*; Quartos, *'bankrout,' 'banckrout,' 'banquerout.'*

466. *'love'*; S. Walker conjectured *'loss.'*

507. *'verdure'*; Quartos 1, 2, 3, *'verdour.'*

529. *'gait'*; Quartos, *'gate.'*

547. *'prey'*; Quartos, *'pray'* (though rhyming with *'obey'*); so *'prayes,'* l. 724, and *'pray'*; (rhyming with *'day'*), l. 1097.

567. *'venturing'*; Quartos, *'ventring.'*

599. *'Tantalus'*; Quartos, *'Tantalus.'*

628. *'venture'*; Quartos, *'venter'* (rhyming with *'enter'*).

632. *'eyes pay'*; Quartos 1, 2, *'eye paies.'*

680. *'overshoot,'* Stevens conjecture; Quartos 1, 2, 3, *'overshut.'*

705. *'doth'*; Quartos 1, 2, 3, *'do.'*

743. *'imposthumes'*; Quartos, *'impostumes.'*

781. *'run'*; Quartos 1, 2, 3, *'ronne'* (rhyming with *'undone'*).

832. *'deeply'*; S. Walker conjectured *'doubly.'*

902. *'together'*; Quartos, *'togither'* (rhyming with *'whither'*); *cp.* l. 971; Quartos 1, 2, 3, *'all together'* (rhyming with *'weather'*); Quarto 4, *'altogither.'*

940. *'random'*; Quartos 1-4, *'randon.'*

993. *'all to nought'* (rhyming with *'wrought'*); Dyce, *'all-to naught'*; Delius, *'all-to naught.'*

1002. *'decease'*; early Quartos, *'decesse'* (rhyming with *'confess'*).

1013-1014. *'stories His'*; Theobald's conjecture; Quartos, *'stories, His.'*

1041. *'ugly'*; Quarto 1, *'oughly.'*

1067. *'limb'*; Quartos, *'lim.'*

1117. *'been'*; Quarto 1, *'bin.'*

1155. *'severe'*; early Quartos, *'seveare'* (rhyming with *'fear'*).

1161. *'servile'*; Quartos 1, 2, *'seruill'*; *cp.* line 392, *'servilely'*; Quartos 1, 2, 3, *'seruilly.'*

THE RAPE OF LUCRECE

8. *'unhappily'*; Quartos 1, 2, 3, *'vnhap'ly.'*

24. *'morning's'*; Quarto 1 (Bodl. 1), *'morning.'*

31. *'apologies'*; Quarto 1 (Bodl. 1), *'appologie.'*

56. *'o'er'*; Quartos 1, 2, 3, *'ore'*; Quarto 4, *'or'e'*; Malone (1780), *'or'* (*i.e.* 'gold').

134-136. Many emendations have been proposed to render clear the meaning of these lines, but no change is necessary: 'the covetous have not, *i.e.* do not possess, that which they possess, longing for the possessions of others'; the second clause of line 135 is in apposition to the first.

195. *'let'*; Schmidt conjectured *'lest.'*

239. *'ay, if'*; early Quartos, *'I, if.'*

637. *i. e.* 'who, in consequence of their own misdeeds, look with indifference on the offences of others' (Schmidt).

649. *'debt'*; early Quartos, *'det'* (rhyming with *'fret'*); similarly l. 696, *'balk'*; Quartos, *'bauk'* (rhyming with *'hawk'*).

782. *'misty'*; Quartos 1, 2, *'mustie.'*

841. *'guilty'*; Malone, *'guiltless,'* but no change is necessary; Lucrece's self-reproach at first assigns the guilt to herself.

930. Perhaps we should read, *'injurious-shifting Time.'*

1134. *'descant'st'*; Quartos, *'descants.'*

1338. *'court'sies'*; Quartos, *'cursies.'*

1662. *'wretched'*; S. Walker conjectured *'wreathed.'*

SONNETS

XII. 4. *'And . . . all'*; so Malone. Quarto, *'And . . . or.'*

XVI. 10. *'this, . . . pen'*; Quarto, *'this (Time's pensel or my pupill pen).'* Massey conjectured *'this time's pencil, or my pupil pen'*; this reading is accepted by several editors, who interpret the first clause to refer either to some particular artist, or to any painter of the time.

XIX. 5. *'fleet'st'*; so Quarto; Dyce, *'fleets'* (rhyming with *'sweets'*); *cp.* VIII. 7.

XX. 7. *'hue, all "hues"'*; Quarto, *'hew all Hews'* (*Hews* in italics).

XXI. 5. *'couplement'*; Quarto, *'coopelment.'*

XXV. 9-11. *'fight . . . quite'*; Malone (Theobald conjectured); Quarto, *'worth . . . quite.'* Theobald conjectured *'worth . . . forth'*; Capell MS., *'might . . . quite.'*

XXVII. 10. *'thy'*; Quarto, *'their'*; a common mistake in the Sonnets, evidently due to the *'y'* being taken for *'e'* with the mark of contraction for *'ir.'*

XXVIII. 13, 14. *'longer . . . strength seem stronger'*; Capell MS. and Collier conjecture; Quarto, *'longer . . . length seeme stronger.'*

XXXI. 8. *'thee'*; Quarto, *'there.'*

XXXIV. 10-12. *'loss . . . cross'*; Quarto, *'losse . . . losse.'*

XXXIV. 13. *'sheds'*; Quarto, *'sheeds'* (rhyming with *'deeds'*).

XXXIX. 12. *'doth'*; Quarto, *'dost.'*

XL. 7. *'thyself'*; Quarto, *'this selfe.'*

XLI. 8. *'she have'*; Tyrwhitt conjectured; Quarto, *'he haue'*; Ewing, *'he has.'*

XLVII. 11. *'not,'* so ed. 1640; Quarto, *'nor.'*

XLIX. 10. *'desert'*; Quarto, *'desart'* (rhyming with *'part'*).

LI. 11. *'neigh—no dull flesh—'* (Malone); Quarto, *'naigh noe dull flesh'*; probably the reading of the Quarto is correct. *'neigh'* = 'neigh after,' 'neigh to,' *cp.* "They were as fed horses in the morning; everyone neighed after his neighbour's wife," Jeremiah v. 8.

LV. 1. *'monuments'*; Quarto, *'monument.'*

LVI. 13. *'Or'*; Tyrwhitt conjecture and Capell MS.; Quarto, *'As'*; Anonymous conjecture, *'Ah!'; 'Else.'*

LVII. 13. *'will'*; Quarto, *'Will'*; Massey conjectured " *'Will.'* "

LXII. 7. *'And for myself,'* i.e. 'and for my own satisfaction,' or perhaps the words merely emphasize the statement.

LXV. 12. *'of'*; Malone; Quarto, *'or'*; Capell MS., *'o'er'*; Gildon, *'on.'*

LXIX. 3. *'that due'*; Capell MS. and Tyrwhitt conjecture; Quarto *'that end'*; Sewell (ed. 2), *'thy due.'*

LXX. 1. *'art,'* ed. 1640; Quarto, *'are.'*

6. *'Thy'*; Capell MS.; Quarto, *'their.'*

LXXIII. 4. *'Bare ruin'd choirs'*; Quarto, *'Bare rn'wd quiers.'*

LXXIV. 14. *'that is this,'* i.e. my spirit is my poetry.

LXXVI. 7. *'tell,'* Capell MS., Quarto, *'fel'*; Lintott, *'fell'*; Nicholson conjectured *'spell.'*

LXXVII. "Probably this sonnet was designed to accompany a present of a book consisting of blank paper" (Steevens).

LXXXV. 3. *'Reserve their'*; Tyler (Anon. conj. MS.), *'Rehearse thy,'* a more plausible reading than *'preserve their,' 'deserve their,'* &c., and other suggestions which have been advanced: there is probably some error in the text as printed.

LXXXVI. 13. *'fill'd'*; Quarto, *'fild'*; Malone, *'fil'd.'*

XCIV. 14. *cp.* Edward III. ii. 1 (printed in 1596):—

> "Poison shows worst in a golden cup;
> Dark night seems darker by the lightning flash;
> Lilies that fester seem far worse than weeds;
> And every glory, that inclines to sin,
> The same is treble by the opposite."

XCV. 12. *'turn'*; Quarto, *'turnes.'*

XCIX. A fifteen-lined sonnet; the first line serves as a sort of introduction, standing outside the sonnet.

XCIX. 15. *'sweet'*; S. Walker conjectured, *'scent.'*

CII. 8. *'her,'* Houseman; Quarto, *'his.'*

CVI. 12. *'skill'*; Tyrwhitt conjecture and Capell MS.; Quarto, *'still.'*

CVII. 8. It has been suggested that this is a possible allusion to the peace completed in 1609, which ended the war between Spain and the United Provinces; but this is merely a random suggestion.

CVIII. 3. *'new . . . new,'* Malone; Quarto, *'new . . . now'*; S. Walker conjectured *'now . . . now.'*

CXII. 8. *'or changes'*; Malone conjectured *'e'er changes'*; Knight conjectured *'so changes.'*

14. *'besides methinks are,'* Capell MS. and Steevens conjecture; Quarto, *'besides me thinkes y'are'*; Dyce, *'besides methinks they're.'*

CXIII. 6. *'latch'*; Quarto, *'lack.'*

14. *'maketh mine untrue'*; so Quarto; Capell MS., and Malone conjecture *'makes mine eye untrue'*; Collier conjectured *'maketh my eyne untrue'*; Malone conjectured *'thy most true mind maketh mine untrue.'*

CXIX. 14. *'ill,'* Malone; Quarto, *'ills.'*

CXX. 6. *'you've'*; Quarto, *'y'haue.'*

CXXIII. 7. *'them,'* i.e. *'what thou dost foist upon us.'*

CXXIV. 13-14. *'The fools of time,'* &c. Tyler sees in these lines a reference to the popular repute of Essex as the "good earl," notwithstanding the "crimes" for which he and certainly his companions were executed; the allusion is probably more general, and perhaps, as Palgrave observes, to "the plotters and political martyrs of the time."

CXXVI. This short poem is of six rhymed couplets; it was evidently not intended to pass as an ordinary sonnet, though after the last line an omission of two lines is marked in the Quarto by two pairs of parentheses. It is the *envoy*, the conclusion of one series of sonnets.

2. *'sickle, hour'*; Quarto, *'sickle, hower'*; perhaps we should read *'sickle hour'*; other suggestions, unsatisfactory for the most part, are, *'fickle mower'*; *'fickle hoar'*; *'sickle hoar'*; &c.

CXXVII. 9-10. *'eyes . . . eyes,'* Quarto; Capell MS., *'eyes . . . hairs'*; S. Walker and Delius conjecture *'hairs . . . eyes'*; Staunton and Brae conjecture *'brows . . . eyes,'* &c.

CXXIX. 11. *'proved, a very,'* Capell MS.; Quarto, *'proud and very.'*

CXXXV. 13. *'no unkind, no'*; Dowden conjectured *'no unkind "No" '*; Rossetti proposed *'skill,'* i.e. *'avail'* instead of *'kill.'*

CXXXVII. cp. PASSIONATE PILGRIM, i.

CXLII. 6-7. cp. EDWARD III. ii. 1:—*'His cheeks put on their scarlet ornaments.'*

CXLIII. 1. *'housewife'*; Quarto, *'huswife.'*

13. *'have thy "Will"'*: *i.e.* Shakespeare's friend Will, not himself.

CXLIV. *cp.* PASSIONATE PILGRIM, ii.

6. *'side,'* so PASSIONATE PILGRIM, and Capell MS.; Quarto, *'sight.'*

9. *'fiend'*; Quarto, *'finde'*; PASSIONATE PILGRIM, *'feend.'*

CXLV. The only sonnet in Shakespeare in eight-syllable verse.

CXLVI. 1-2. *'earth . . . these rebel'*; Quarto, *'earth, My sin-full earth these rebbell'*; Malone, *'earth, Fool'd by those rebel'*; Steevens, *'earth, Starv'd by the rebel'*; Dowden, *'earth [Press'd by] these rebel,'* &c. Probably any one of these readings comes near the original; in this case *array* = clothe. Ingleby renders the word "abuse, afflict, ill-treat"; he reads, *'leagu'd with,'* and takes the participle in close conjunction with *'earth.'* This rendering is ingenious, but very doubtful.

CLII. 13. *'I'*; Quarto, *'eye.'*

A LOVER'S COMPLAINT

12. *'scythed'*; Quarto, *'sithed.'*

37. *'beaded'*; Quarto, *'bedded'* (? = 'imbedded, set').

39. *'weeping margent'*; Malone conjectured *'margent weeping.'*

51. *''gan to tear'*; Quarto, *'gaue to teare'*; Gildon, *'gave a tear.'*

60. *'observed as they flew'*; the clause is probably connected with *'hours'*; "the reverend man had not let the swift hours pass by without gaining some knowledge of the world"; it is possible, however, that *'they'* refers to the torn-up letters.

112. *'manage'*; Quarto, *'mannad'g.'*

118. *'came'*; Sewell's correction; Quarto, *'can'*; Sewell's 2nd ed., *'can for additions get their purpose trim.'*

164. *'woo'*; Quarto, *'vow.'*

182. *'sweets that seem'*; Quarto, *'sweets that seemes'*; Capell MS., *'sweet that seems.'*

228. *'Hallow'd'*; Quarto, *'hollowed'*; Sewell's correction.

241. *'playing the place'*; some error due to the printer has spoilt the line; the first word of the line has been caught up by the compositor's eye from the first of the next line, or *vice versa*: the most ingenious and plausible emendation is *'paling'* for *'playing.'*

260. *'nun'*; Quarto, *'Sunne.'*

261. *'ay'*; Quarto, *'I.'*

271. *'Love's arms are peace'*; so Quarto; Capell MS. and Malone conjecture, *'proof'* for *'peace,'* a plausible change, if any is necessary; other readings are:—*'Love aims at peace'*; *'Love charms our peace'*; *'Love aims a piece'*; &c.

286. *'who glazed with crystal gate'*; Malone, *'who, glaz'd with*

crystal, gate' (*i.e. gate* = 'the ancient perfect tense of the verb *to get*,' *flame* being its object).

308. '*swound*'; Quarto, '*sound*,' *cp.* 305, '*swounding*'; Quarto, '*sounding*.'

THE PASSIONATE PILGRIM

I., II.; *cp.* SONNETS, cxxxviii., cxliv.

III., V.; *cp.* LOVE'S LABOUR'S LOST, IV. iii. 55-68; IV. ii. 102-115.

VIII. 5. John Dowland was one of the most famous of Elizabethan musicians; his song-books appeared in 1597, 1600, and 1603; his '*Pilgrim's Solace*,' 1612. There are many references to him in Elizabethan and later literature, more especially to his '*Lachrymæ, or, Seven Tears figured in seven heavenlie Pavans*' (1605); (*cp.* Bullen's *Lyrics from Elizabethan Song-Books*).

XII. 12. '*stay'st*'; old eds. '*staies*.'

XIII. Two copies of this poem "from a corrected MS." were printed in *Gent. Mag.* xx. 521; xxx. 39; the variants do not improve the poem.

XIV. 20. '*And drives*'; perhaps we should read, '*And daylight drives*' (Anon. conj.). II. *cp.* LOVE'S LABOUR'S LOST, IV. iii. 96-115.

SONNETS TO SUNDRY NOTES
OF MUSIC

III. 5. '*Love's denying*'; Malone's conjecture; old eds., '*Love is dying*'; *England's Helicon*, '*Love is denying*.'

7. '*renying*'; ed. 1599, '*nenying*.'

21. '*Love hath forlorn me*'; Steevens conjectured '*love forlorn I*.'

31-32. '*My sighs . . . Procure to*'; edd. 1599, 1612, '*With sighes . . . procures to*'; the reading of the text is Malone's.

43. '*back peeping*'; edd. 1599, 1612, '*blacke peeping*.'

IV. 4. '*fancy, partial wight*'; Capell MS. and Malone conjecture withdrawn; edd. 1599, 1612, '*fancy (party all might)*'; ed. 1640, '*fancy (partly all might)*'; Malone (from MS. copy), '*fancy, partial like*,' Collier (from MS. copy), '*partial fancy like*'; Steevens conjectured '*fancy, partial tike*'; Furnivall conjectured '*fancy's partial might*.'

45. '*There is no heaven, by holy then*'; the line has been variously emended; Malone reads from an old MS.: —

> *'Here is no heaven; they holy then*
> *Begin, when,'* &c.

No satisfactory emendation has been proposed, and perhaps the original reading may be allowed to stand without the comma after *'heaven'*:—*'there is no heaven by holy then,'* i.e. 'by that holy time'; others suggest, *'be holy then,'* or *'by the holy then,'* &c.

V. 1. *'Live with me, and be my love'*; in *England's Helicon* and other early versions the line runs, *'Come live with me,'* &c., and in this way it is usually quoted. Two verses found in *England's Helicon* are omitted in the present version, but included in the 1640 ed., where *"Love's Answer"* is also in six quatrains; the additional matter was evidently also derived from *England's Helicon*. After l. 12 the following lines are inserted:—

> *'A gown made of the finest wool,*
> *Which from our pretty Lambs we pull.*
> *Fair lined slippers for the cold,*
> *With buckles of the purest gold.'*

The last stanza runs thus:—

> *'The shepherd's swains shall dance and sing,*
> *For thy del'ght each May morning;*
> *If these delights thy mind may move,*
> *Then live with me and be my love.'*

GLOSSARY TO THE HISTORIES
AND POEMS

1H4—King Henry the Fourth. Part I
2H4—King Henry the Fourth. Part II
H5—The Life of King Henry the Fifth
1H6—King Henry the Sixth. Part I
2H6—King Henry the Sixth. Part II
3H6—King Henry the Sixth. Part III
H8—King Henry the Eighth
John—The Life and Death of King John
Lov. C.—A Lover's Complaint
Luc.—The Rape of Lucrece
Pas. P.—The Passionate Pilgrim
Phœn.—The Phœnix and the Turtle
R2—King Richard the Second
R3—King Richard the Third
Son.—Sonnets
Son. to
Music } —Sonnets to Sundry Notes of Music
V. and A.—Venus and Adonis

---

a', he. John i. 1; &c.

abate, blunt. 2H4 i. 1; R3 v. 4

abode, abodements, forebode, forebodings. 3H6 iv. 7; v. 6; H8 i. 1

abrook, endure. 2H6 ii. 4

absey-book, A.B.C. book, primer. John i. 1

accite, arouse, excite. 2H4 ii. 2; v. 2

accomplish, equip, perfect. R2 ii. 1; H5 iv. chor.; get. 3H6 iii. 2

accompt, account, accounts. H5 chor.

account of, make, hold in estimation. R3 iii. 2

achievement,completion.H5 iii. 5

Achilles' spear. Telephus, having been wounded with the point, was healed with the rust of the spear of Achilles. 2H6 v. 1

aconitum,a preparation of aconite sometimes used as a poison. 2H4 iv. 4

act, state. H5 i. 2; put into action. 2H6 v. 1; in act, in the very doing. Son. 152

acture,the process of acting,action. Lov. C. 185

admiral, admiral's ship, carrying lantern at stern. 1H4 iii. 3

admiration, wonder. H5 ii. 2

adsum, I am here. 2H6 i. 4

adulterate,stained by adultery, in origin or conduct. R3 iv. 4; lewd. Son. 121

advance, raise, lift. H5 ii. 2; &c.

advertise, inform.2H6 iv.9;&c.

advertisement, announcement. 1H4 iii. 2; advice. 1H4 iv. 1

advise, bethink. H5 iii. 6

advised, intentional, deliberate. John iv. 2; R2 i. 3; Son. 49; aware, informed. 2H4 i. 1; H5 ii. chor.; careful. 2H6 ii. 4; sedate. 2H6 v. 2

acry, aiery, eagle's nest. John v. 2; eagle's brood. R3 i. 3

affect, resemble. John i. 1; love. 2H4 iv. 5; 1H6 v. 5; aim at. 2H6 iv. 7

affected to, enamoured of. V. & A. 157

affected, stand, is disposed. R3 iii. 1

affection, passion. John v. 2; Luc. 500; inclination. 1H4 iii. 2; 2H4 iv. 4; v. 2

affiance, confidence. H5 ii. 2; 2H6 iii. 1

affy, betroth. 2H6 iv. 1

a-front, abreast. 1H4 ii. 4

after-loss, future grief. Son. 90

against, in anticipation. R2 iii. 4; 2H4 iv. 2; Son. 63

agate, very diminutive person, in allusion to small figures cut in agates for seals. 2H4 i. 2

agazed on, affrighted at. 1H6 i. 1

aiery, see 'aery.'

aim, guess. 3H6 iii. 2

aim, cry, applaud (from archery). John ii. 1

alderliefest, dearest of all. 2H6 i. 1

allay, repress. H8 ii. 1

allegiant, loyal. H8 iii. 2

All-Hallown summer, season of fine weather about Nov. 1 (All Saints' Day); brightness in old age. 1H4 i. 2

all to naught, call, vilify. V. & A. 993

all-too-timeless, most unseasonable. Luc. 44

all-watched, wholly watched through. H5. iv. chor.

amain, with all their strength. 1H6 i. 1; at full speed. 2H6 iii. 1

Amaimon, name of a devil. 1H4 ii. 4

amaze, bewilder, confuse. John iv. 2; R2 v. 2; confound, affright. 1H4 v. 4; &c.; astonish greatly. V. & A. 634

amazement, distraction. John v. 1

amort, all, spiritless, dejected. 1H6 iii. 2

an, an if, if. John i. 1; 2H4 i. 2; &c.

anatomize, lay open, show distinctly. 2H4 Ind.; Luc. 1450

anatomy, Death. John iii. 4

ancient, ensign, bearer of the ensign. 1H4 iv. 2; &c.; old. R3 iii. 1

angel, gold coin, value 10s., stamped with figure of Archangel Michael slaying the dragon. John ii. 1; &c.

annexion, addition. Lov. C. 208

anon, coming! 1H4 ii. 1; &c.

antic, antick, antique, buffoon. R2 iii. 2; H5 iii. 2; 1H6 iv. 7; fantastic shape. Luc. 459

appaid, pleased, content. Luc. 914

appalled, enfeebled. Phœn. 37; made pale. 1H6. i. 2

appeach, impeach. R2 v. 2

appeal, accuse, esp. of treason. R2 i. 1; i. 3; accusation. R2 i. 1; iv. 1

appellant, the accuser. R2 i. 1; i. 3; iv. 1

apple-john, kind of apple said to keep two years, and to be in perfection when shrivelled and withered. 1H4 iii. 3; 2H4 ii. 4

appliance, medical apparatus. 2H4 iii. 1

apprehension, imagination. R2 i. 3; perception. H5 iii. 7; conception of me. 1H6 ii. 4

apprehensive, discerning. 2H4 iv. 3

*approve,*prove.R2 i.3; &c.; confirm. H8 ii. 3; find by experience. Son. 147

apricock, apricot. R2 iii. 4

arbitrement, inquiry. 1H4 iv. 1; decision. H5 iv. 1

argo, blunder for 'ergo,' therefore. 2H6 iv. 2

argosy, a merchant-ship. 3H6 ii. 6

arras, tapestry-hangings. John iv. 1; 1H4 ii. 4

Arthur's show, exhibition of archery by London archers who assumed the names of Arthur and his knights. 2H4 iii. 2

articulate, formulated in articles. 1H4 v. 1

askance, with a side glance. V. & A. 342; Son. 110; turn aside. Luc. 637

*Asmath,*name of evil spirit.2H6 i. 4

aspire, mount up. V. & A. 150

assemblance, appearance. 2H4 iii. 2

assured, betrothed. John ii. 1

astonish, stun. Son. 86

*athwart,*in opposition to the expected course.1H4 i.1; across. H5 v. chor.

atomy, anatomy, skeleton. 2H4 v. 4

atone, reconcile. R2 i. 1

*attach,*arrest.R2 ii.3; &c.; seize, lay hold of. 2H4 ii. 2; H8 i. 1

attainder, stain, taint, disgrace. R2 iv. 1; R3 iii. 5; H8 ii. 1

attaint, ? fatigue. H5 iv. chor.; tainted, disgraced. 1H6 ii. 4; convicted of capital treason.

1H6 ii. 4; 2H6 ii. 4; touched. 1H6 v. 5; infection. V. & A. 741; stain, disgrace. Luc. 825; blame, discredit. Son. 82

attainture, attainder. 2H6 i. 2

attorneyship, proxy. 1H6 v. 5

attribution, praise. 1H4 iv. 1

aunchient, ancient, the bearer of an ensign. H5 iii. 6

avoid, begone. 2H6 i. 4; leave. H8 v. 1

aweless, fearless. John i. 1; not inspiring awe. R3 ii. 4

awful, awe-inspiring. R2 iii. 3; &c.

*awful banks,*respectful bounds, 2H4 iv. 1

awkward, unfair. H5 ii. 4; adverse. 2H6 iii. 2

backsword man, player at single-stick. 2H4 iii. 2

baffle, disgrace a perjured knight with infamy. R2 i. 1; 1H4 i. 2

bait, flap the wings. 1H4 iv. 1; harass. R3 i. 3; fill. H8 v. 4

ban, curse. 1H6 v. 3; &c.

band, bond. R2 i. 1; &c.

ban-dog, dog tied up to guard a house. 2H6 i. 4

bane, ruin. 2H6 v. 1; V. & A. 372

*Barbary hen,*a hen whose feathers are naturally ruffled. 2H4 ii. 4

Barbason, name of a fiend. H5 ii. 1

*barbed,*protected by armour on the breast and flank. R2 iii. 3; R3 i. 1

Bartholomew boar-pig, a pig sold at the fair held in Smithfield on August 24 (St. Bartholomew's Day). 2H4 ii. 4

Bartholomew-tide, the Feast of

St. Bartholomew, August 24.
H5 v. 2

*base,bid a,*challenge to a chase.
V. & A. 303

base court, lower or outer court
of castle. R2 iii. 3

Basilisco-like, the reference is
to a passage in a play called
Soliman and Perseda. John
i. 1

*basilisk,*fabulous serpent whose
mere look was fatal. 2H6 iii.
2; &c.; applied to a kind of
cannon. 1H4 ii. 3; H5 v. 2

bastard, sweet Spanish wine.
1H4 ii. 4

bastinado, cudgelling. John ii. 1

bate, diminish. 1H4 iii. 3; dis-
cord. 2H4 ii. 4; strike off. 2H4
Epil.; flutter as a hawk. H5 iii.
7

bate-breeding, strife-breeding.
V. & A. 655

bateless, keen, that cannot be
blunted. Luc. 9

battalia, army. R3 v. 3

bavin, brushwood. 1H4 iii. 2

bawcock, fine fellow. H5 iii. 2;
iv. 1

beadsman, a pensioner who
prays for the soul of his bene-
factor. R2 iii. 2

bearing-cloth, child's christen-
ing robe. 1H6 i. 3

bear in hand, abuse with false
pretences. 2H4 i. 2

beaver, face-guard of helmet,
the helmet itself. 1H4 iv. 1;
&c.

becoming of, making comely.
Son. 127

*bedlam,*lunatic.John ii.1; mad,
foolish. H5 v. 1; 2H6 iii. 1; v.
1; madhouse (from Hospital
of St. Mary of Bethlehem).
2H6 v. 1

beetle, three-man, rammer re-

quiring three men to lift. 2H4
i. 2

begnaw, gnaw at. R3 i. 3

beholding, beholden, indebted.
John i. 1; R3 ii. 1; H8 i. 4

behoof, benefit. 2H6 iv. 7

beldam, contemptuous term for
old woman. John iv. 2; 2H6 i.
4; grandmother. 1H4 iii. 1;
Luc. 953

belied, ? full of lies. Luc. 1533

bell, book, and candle, ritual of
excommunication, and gener-
ally the pain of spiritual pen-
alties. John iii. 3

bend, aim, point. John ii. 1; H5
v. 2; R3 i. 2

*beshrew, beshrew me, beshrew
my soul,* mild oaths. John v. 4;
&c.

beslubber, besmear. 1H4 ii.
4

bespeak, speak to. R2 v. 2

bested, worse, more hard
pressed. 2H6 ii. 3

bestow, behave. 2H4 ii. 2; re-
pair to your post. H5 iv. 3;
place, lodge, shelter. 1H6 iii.
2; Son. 26

*bestrid,bestride,*defend a fallen
man by standing over his
body. 1H4 v. 1; 2H6 v. 3

betid, happened. R2 v. 1

betide on, happen to. R3 i. 3

*bewray,*betray.3H6 i.1; Son.to
Music, iv.; expose. Luc. 1698

bezonian, raw recruit, beggarly
fellow. 2H4 v. 3; 2H6 iv. 1

bias, originally the weight of
lead let into one side of a bowl
to make it turn towards that
side. John ii. 1; R2 iii. 4

bid, gave. R3 iv. 4

bide, come to, endure. 1H4 iv.
4

biding, dwelling. Luc. 550

*bigamy,*marriage with one who

had been married before. R3
iii. 7

biggin, night-cap. 2H4 iv. 5

bills, halberds. R2 iii. 2; 2H6 iv.
7; promissory notes. 2H6 iv. 7

blank, blank charter, document
with spaces left blank, to be
filled up at the pleasure of the
person to whom it is given. R2
i. 4; ii. 1

blazon, set forth. Lov. C. 217

blench, side-glance. Son. 110

blend, blended. Lov. C. 215

blistered, puffed. H8 i. 3

blue-bottle, nick-name for a
man in a dark-blue uniform,
as a beadle. 2H4 v. 4

blue-cap, Scotchman. 1H4 ii. 4

bob, buffet. R3 v. 3

bodge, do clumsily. 3H6 i. 4

bollen, swollen. Luc. 1417

bolter, piece of cloth used for
sifting. 1H4 iii. 3

bolting-hutch, hutch in which
meal was sifted. 1H4 ii. 4

bombard, leathern jug or bottle
for liquor. 1H4 ii. 4; H8 v. 4

bombast, padding, stuffing. 1H4
ii. 4

bona-roba, wench. 2H4 iii. 2

bones, ten, fingers. 2H6 i. 3

boot, avail. R2 i. 1; iii. 4; 1H6
iv. 6; R3 v. 3; booty. 1H4 ii. 1;
H5 i. 2; put on one's boots.
2H4 v. 3

bore, to trick, cheat. H8 i. 1

bots, parasitical worms in
horses. 1H4 ii. 1

bottled, bloated. R3 i. 3; iv. 4

bottom, ship. John ii. 1; H5 iii.
chor.; low-lying land. 1H4 iii.
1

bound, boundary. John iii. 1;
1H6 i. 2; rebound. R2 i. 2;
cause to leap. H5 v. 2

brabbler, brawler. John v. 2

brach, bitch-hound. 1H4 iii. 1

brain-pan, skull. 2H6 iv. 10

brainsick, foolish, frantic. 1H6
iv. 1

brake, clump of bushes. H8 i.
2; V. & A. 237, 876

brave, bravado. John v. 2; men-
ace, defy. John iv. 2; &c.; fine,
finely appointed, beautiful.
1H4 i. 2; H5 iii. chor.; Son.
12

bravery, splendour. Son. 34

brawn, boar. 1H4 ii. 4; 2H4 i. 1

break, am bankrupt. 2H4 Epil.

breathers, living beings. Son.
81

breathing, beginning of the
word upon a breath. Luc. 1720

brewer's horse, a term of con-
tempt (? a dull-headed beast).
1H4 iii. 3

brief, epitome. John ii. 1; ? ripe,
prevalent. John iv. 3; in short.
John v. 6; letter. 1H4 iv. 4;
speedy. R3 ii. 2

broached, thrust through. H5 v.
chor.; pricked on. 3H6 ii. 2

broken music, music arranged
for different instruments. H5
v. 2

broking pawn, acting as a
broker. R2 ii. 1

brooded, having a brood to
watch over; or, brooding. John
iii. 3

brown bill, halberd, browned to
preserve from rust. 2H6 iv. 10

bruising irons, wounding
swords. R3 v. 3

bubukles, confusion of bubo
(inflamed swellings) and car-
buncle (red pimples). H5 iii.
6

buck, linen for washing. 2H6
iv. 2

buckle, bend under stress. 2H4
i. 1; engage, grapple. 1H6 i.
2; iv. 4; 3H6 i. 4

buckler, shield, defend. 2H6 iii. 2; 3H6 iii. 3

bug, bugbear. 3H6 v. 2

bulk, body. R3 i. 4; Luc. 467

bull-beeves, the flesh of bulls, beef. 1H6 i. 2

bully, fine fellow. H5 iv. 1

bung, pick-pocket. 2H4 ii. 4

burgonet, close-fitting helmet. 2H6 v. 1

burnet, a plant common in meadows. H5 v. 2

burthenwise, as if it were a burthen or refrain. Luc. 1133

busky, bushy. 1H4 v. 1

buss, kiss. John iii. 4; 2H4 ii. 4

by and by, immediately. 2H6 ii. 1

by-drinking, drinking between meals. 1H4 iii. 3

by yea and nay, a mild imprecation. 2H4 iii. 2

cacodemon, evil spirit. R3 i. 3

caddis, worsted yarn, 1H4 ii. 4

cade, small barrel. 2H6 iv. 2

caitiff, vile. R2 i. 2; wretch. R3 iv. 4

caliver, light musket. 1H4 iv. 2; 2H4 iii. 2

callet, callot, low woman, scold. 2H6 i. 3; 3H6 ii. 2

calm, blunder for 'qualm.' 2H4 ii. 4

Cambyses' vein, a ranting style. 1H4 ii. 4

camlet, a name originally for a costly Eastern stuff, afterwards applied to imitations and substitutes. H8 v. 4

can, knows. Phœn. 14

canaries, canary, a light sweet wine from the Canary Islands. 2H4 ii. 4

candle-mine, magazine of tallow. 2H4 ii. 4

canker, corroding evil. John v. 2; dog-rose. 1H4 i. 3; cankerworm. 1H4 iv. 2; &c.

canker-bloom, dog-rose. Son. 54

cankered, venomous, malignant, wicked. John ii. 1; 1H4 i. 3; polluted. 2H4 iv. 5

cannibal, blunder for 'Hannibal.' 2H4 ii. 4

canstick, ? contracted form of 'candlestick.' 1H4 iii. 1

cantle, section, segment. 1H4 iii. 1

canvass, toss in a canvas sheet. 2H4 ii. 4; 1H6 i. 3

cap, a cardinal's hat. 1H6 v. 1

capitulate, draw up articles of agreement. 1H4 iii. 2

captain, chief, principal. Son. 52; 66

captivate, captive. 1H6 ii. 3; take captive. 3H6 i. 4

carbonado, fish, flesh, or fowl scored across, and grilled or broiled upon the coals. 1H4 v. 3

carconet, necklace. Son. 52

card, stir together, mix. 1H4 iii. 2

card, cooling, ? a term of some unknown game; applied to anything that 'cools' a person's passion or enthusiasm. 1H6 v. 3

career, horse's charge in a combat. R2 i. 2

careers, passes, ? indulges in sallies of wit. H5 ii. 1

care-tuned, tuned to care. R2 iii. 2

carnal, carnivorous, bloody, murderous. R3 iv. 4

cart, used for conveying criminals to the gallows and instead of a drop. 1H4 ii. 4

case, put on a mask. 1H4 ii. 2; set of four, as musical instruments. H5 iii. 2; condition.

Son. 108; dress. Lov. C. 116

casque, helmet. R2 i. 3; H5 i. chor.

cast, calculated. 2H4 i. 1

caterpillar, extortioner. 1H4 ii. 2

cates, delicacies. 1H4 iii. 1; 1H6 ii. 3

cautel, crafty device. Lov. C. 303

cavaleiro, gallant. 2H4 v. 3

ceinture, girdle. John iv. 3

censer, *thin man in a*, figure in low relief on the lid of vessels in which perfumes were burned. 2H4 v. 4

censure, judge, estimate. John ii. 1; &c.; judgment, opinion. 1H6 ii. 3; &c.

certes, certainly. H8 i. 1

cess, assessment, estimation. 1H4 ii. 1

chace, term at tennis. H5 i. 2

chafed, enraged. John iii. 1; 3H6 ii. 5; H8 i. 1

chair, throne. R3 iv. 4

challenger, claimant. H5 ii. 4

chamber, province or city directly subject to the king; royal residence. R3 iii. 1

chambers, ordnance used to fire salutes. 2H4 ii. 4; H8 i. 4 (stage direction)

champaign, stretch of open country. Luc. 1247

changing, exchanging. 1H4 i. 3

channel, wear into channels, 1H4 i. 1; gutter. 2H4 ii. 1; 3H6 ii. 2

chaps, jaws. John ii. 1; 2H6 iii. 1; wrinkles. Luc. 1452

characters, written characters. R3 iii. 1; figures. Lov. C. 16

charge, cost, expense. John i. 1; &c.; baggage. 1H4 ii. 1; command. 1H4 ii. 4; R3 v. 3; attack. 2H4 ii. 4; Son. 70; bur-

den. H5 i. 2; blame. Pas. P. xiv.

*charges,be at,*bear the expense. R3 i. 2

Charles' Wain, seven bright stars in Ursa Major. 1H4 ii. 1

charneco, kind of wine. 2H6 ii. 3

cheater, decoy-duck, or other animal used as decoy. 2H4 ii. 4; escheator, officer of exchequer. 2H4 ii. 4

check, reprove. R2 v. 5; 2H4 i. 2; 2H6 i. 2; reproof. 2H4 iv. 3; rebuff. Son. 58

chest, treasury. Son. 65

cheveril,flexible,elastic (as kid-leather). H8 ii. 3

chewet,chough; chatterer.1H4 v. 1

chiding, resounding. H8 iii. 2

chopped, chapped. 2H4 iii. 2; Son. 62

chops, a name for a person with fat or bloated cheeks. 1H4 i. 2

christen, Christian. 1H4 ii. 4

christom, a child in its christening-robe, under a month old. H5 ii. 3

chuck, a familiar term. H5 iii. 2

chuff, churl. 1H4 ii. 2

'cide, decide. Son. 46

cipher, express. Luc. 207, 1396; decipher. Luc. 811

circumstance, details. John ii. 1; 1H6 i. 1; V. & A. 844; ado, detail. 2H6 i. 1; something adventitious or casual. 2H6 v. 2; circumstantial evidence. R3 i. 2

cital, reproof, impeachment. 1H4 v. 2

cite, incite, urge. 2H6 iii. 2; call, bring. R3 i. 4; summon. 3H6 ii. 1; H8 iv. 1

clap i' the clout, hit the mark. 2H4 iii. 2

clap up, settle hastily. John iii. 1; imprison. 2H6 i. 4

clean, cleanly, completely. R2 iii. 1; V. & A. 694

clepe, call by name of. V. & A. 995

climate, region of the sky. John ii. 1; region of the earth. R2 iv. 1

clinquant, glittering. H8 i. 1

clip, clasp, embrace. John v. 2; 2H6 iv. 1; V. & A. 600

clip in, encompass. 1H4 iii. 1

clipper, mutilator of current coin, by fraudulently paring the edges. H5 iv. 1

close, closely, secret, secretly. John iv. 1; &c.; conclusion of musical phrase, theme, or movement. R2 ii. 1; H5 i. 2; grapple, hand-to-hand fight. 1H4 i. 1; make peace. 2H4 ii. 4; strictly confined. R3 iv. 2

closet, private apartment. John iv. 2

closure, limit, circuit. R3 iii. 3; enclosure. V. & A. 782

cloudy, having gloomy looks. 1H4 iii. 2; R3 ii. 2

clout, mark shot at in archery. 2H4 iii. 2

clouted shoon, hob-nailed boots. 2H6 iv. 2

clouts, babe of, rag-doll. John iii. 4

coast, proceed circuitously as a vessel hugging the shore. H8 iii. 2; V. & A. 870

cock and pie, an asseveration, meaning possibly, 'cock,' God, and 'pie,' the ordinal of the R.C. Church. 2H4 v. 1

cockered, pampered, indulged. John v. 1

cock-shut time, twilight (either

when poultry are shut up, or when woodcocks 'shoot,' i.e. fly). R3 v. 3

cog, cheat. R3 i. 3

cognizance, device or mark by which a person is known or distinguished; badge. 1H6 ii. 4

coherence, agreement. 2H4 v.1

coil, fuss, ado. John ii. 1

cold fault, cold or lost scent in hunting. V. & A. 694

collect, conclude, deduce, infer. 2H6 iii. 1

collop, slice of meat. 1H6 v. 4

colour, give a specious appearance to. 1H4 i. 3; excuse. 2H4 i. 2; pretence. 2H4 v. 5; 1H6 ii. 4; pretext. 2H6 iii. 1; H8 i. 1; Luc. 267

colt, befool, cheat, 'take in.' 1H4 ii. 2

come near, touch. 1 H4 i. 2

come o'er, taunt. H5 i. 2

come off, get off, escape. H8 iii. 2

coming in, income. H5 iv. 1

commandments, ten, ten fingernails. 2H6 i. 3

commend, greeting. R2 iii. 1; iii. 3; commit. R2 iii. 3; express to you. H8 ii. 3; present as worthy. Luc. 436

commodity, profit. John ii. 1; 2H4 i. 2; supply. 1H4 i. 2; merchandize. 2H6 iv. 7

community, ordinary occurrence. 1H4 iii. 2

compact, made up of. V. & A. 149

compassed, curved, arched. V. & A. 272

competitor, confederate. R3 iv. 4

compile, compose, especially a work of definite form, as a sonnet. Son. 78

complement, observance. H5 ii. 2

complices, accomplices. R2 ii. 3; 2H4 i. 1

complot, plot. 2H6 iii. 1; R3 iii. 1

compound, agree. John ii. 1; come to terms with. H5 iv. 6

conceit, intelligence, understanding. John iii. 3; 1H6 v. 5; P.P. iv; fancy, invention. R2 ii. 2; 1H6 iv. 1; conception. R3 iii. 4; &c.

conclave, the body of cardinals. H8 ii. 2

conclusion, experiment. Luc. 1160

confederacy, conspiracy. H8 i. 2

confident, sure of your secrecy. H8 ii. 1

confirmity, blunder for 'infirmity.' 2H4 ii. 4

confound, destroy, ruin. John v. 7; &c.; spend, exhaust. 1H4 i. 3; 2H4 iv. 4

confusion, destruction. John ii. 1

congreeing, agree together, accord. H5 i. 2

congreet, greet mutually. H5 v. 2

conjunction, association. 1H4 iv. 1; combination. 2H4 v. 1; union, an astrological term used of two planets in proximity. H8 iii. 2

consent, by my, in my opinion. 1H6 i. 2

consequence, the, that which is to follow. R3 iv. 4

consign, subscribe. 2H4 v. ii; H5 v. 2

consist, be based. 2H4 iv. 1

contemptuous, despicable. 2H6 i. 3

continuantly, blunder for 'continually.' 2H4 ii. 1

contracted, engaged to be married. 1H4 iv. 2; Son. 1

contrariously, diversely. H5 i. 2

control, check, restraint. John i. 1; overpower. Luc. 448, 678

controlling, overpowering. Son. 20

contumeliously, despitefully. 1H6 i. 3

conventicle, secret assembly. 2H6 iii. i.

conversation, behaviour, talk. 2H4 v. 5; connexion. R3 iii. 5

convertite, convert. John v. 1; Luc. 743

convey, carry off. R2 iv. 1; 3H6 iv. 6; pass oneself off. H5 i. 2

conveyance, dishonest practices. 1H6 i. 3; 3H6 iii. 3; riddance. R3 iv. 4

conveyer, thief, cheat. R2 iv. 1

convicted, defeated. John iii. 4

convoy, travelling-money. H5 iv. 3

cony, rabbit. V. & A. 687

cope, encounter. H8 i. 2; V. & A. 888; Luc. 99

copesmate, partner, associate. Luc. 925

coranto, a kind of dance. H5 iii. 5

Corinthian, a wealthy 'man about town.' 1H4 ii. 4

cornet, company of cavalry. 1H6 iv. 3

correctioner, one who administers correction, name applied to a beadle. 2H4 v. 4

corrival, rival. 1H4 i. 3; compeer, partner. 1H4 iv. 4

corroborate, ?a nonsense word. H5 ii. 1

corrosive, fret. 1H6 iii. 3

corsive, remedy causing pain. 2H6 iii. 2

costard, head. R3 i. 4

couch, lie down. 1H4 iii. 1; bow down in submission. H5 iv. 2; cause to cower. Luc. 507

countenance, patronage, favour. 1H4 i. 2; 1H4 iii. 2; bearing, conduct. 1H4 v. 1

court-hand, the style of handwriting used in the English law-courts from the sixteenth to the eighteenth centuries, when it was abolished by statute. 2H6 iv. 2

cousin, a general term of kinship, nephew, grandson, &c. John iii. 1; &c.

covent, convent. H8 iv. 2

cozen, cheat. R3 iv. 4

crack, lively lad. 2H4 iii. 2

cracker, boaster. John ii. 1

crank, twist and turn about. 1H4 iii. 1; V. & A. 682

credent, believing. Lov. C. 279

crescive, growing. H5 i. 1

cresset, basket of iron made to hold fire, flaming stuff. 1H4 iii. 1

crisp, having a surface fretted into minute waves. 1H4 i. 3

cross, thwart. John iii. 1; V. & A. 734; coin stamped with a cross. 2H4 i. 2

cross-row, alphabet. R3 i. 1

crudy, curdy, curded in appearance. 2H4 iv. 3

cry aim, applaud (a term from archery). John ii. 1

cry on, invoke. R3 v. 3

cullion, base fellow. H5 iii. 2; 2H6 i. 3

culverin, a small fire-arm; later, a cannon. 1H4 ii. 3

cure, charge of souls. H8 i. 4

curious, elaborate. 3H6 ii. 5; V. & A. 734; fastidious. Son. 37; careful. Lov. C. 49

currance, current. H5 i. 1

curry, employ flattery towards. 2H4 v. 1

cursorary, cursory. H5 v. 2

curst, ill-tempered, shrewish. 2H6 iii. 2; R3 i. 2; V. & A. 887

curtle-axe, short broad cutting sword. H5 iv. 2

cushes, thigh-pieces. 1H4 iv. 1

Cut, name of a horse. 1H4 ii. 1

cuttle, bully. 2H4 ii. 4

daff, to thrust out of the way. 1H4 iv. 1; P.P. xiv; put off. Lov. C. 297

Daintry, Daventry. 3H6 v. 1

damasked, having the hue of the damask rose. Son. 130

danger, power. V. & A. 639

darnel, rye-grass. H5 v. 2; 1H6 iii. 2

darraign, set in array. 3H6 ii. 2

dash, appearance. 1H6 i. 2; mark of disgrace. Luc. 206

deaf, deafen. John ii. 1

deal, no, not at all. Son. to Music iii

debate, contest. 2H4 iv. 4; Son. 15; 89

deceivable, deceitful. R2 ii. 3

declension, deviation from a standard. R3 iii. 7

decline, go through in order. R3 iv. 4

deep-fet, deep-fetched. 2H6 ii. 4

defeature, defacement. V. & A. 736

defend, forbid. R2 i. 3; 1H4 iv. 3; R3 iii. 7

defunction, death. H5 i. 2

defunctive, suitable to a time of death. Phœn. 14

delve parallels, dig furrows. Son. 60

demise, transmit. R3 iv. 4

denayed, denied. 2H6 i. 3

denier, a small copper French coin. 1H4 iii. 3; R3 i. 2

deputation, appointment as deputy. 1H4 iv. 3

deputy of the ward, police officers. 1H4 iii. 3

deracinate, uproot. H5 v. 2

design, point out by distinctive signs. R2 i. 1

device, heraldic bearing. John i. 1

device in, manner, inclination. V. & A. 789

devoted, holy. R3 i. 2

diapason, bass sounding in concord. Luc. 1132

diet, mode of life. R3 i. 1

diffidence, mistrust. John i. 1; 1H6 iii. 3

diffused, confused, obscure. H5 v. 2; R3 i. 2

digressing, transgressing. R2 v. 3

dint, mark. V. & A. 354

direction, military skill. R3 v. 3

disanimate, deprive of spirit. 1H6 iii. 1

disannul, bring to nothing. 3H6 iii. 3

discomfit, discouragement. 2H6 v. 2

discoverer, scout. 2H4 iv. 1

discuss, make known. H5 iii. 2

disgracious, unpleasing, ungracious. R3 iii. 7; iv. 4

dishabited, dislodged. John ii. 1

dishonest, unchaste. H5 i. 2

dislike, discord. 1H4 v. 1

dismount, lower. Lov. C. 281

dispark, convert park land to other uses. R2 iii. 1

dispense with, compound with. 2H6 v. 1; Luc. 1070; Son. 112

dispiteous, pitiless. John iv. 1

dissentious, seditious. R3 i. 3; V. & A. 657

dissolve, put asunder. R2 ii. 2

distain, stain, defile. R3 v. 3

distemper, mental derangement. H5 ii. 2; perturb. V. & A. 653

distemperature, disorder. 1H4 iii. 1; discomposed appearance. 1H4 v. 1

distrain, take possession of. R2 ii. 3; 1H6 i. 3

distressful, gained by severe toil. H5 iv. 1; distressing. 1H6 v. 4

dive-dapper, a small diving waterfowl. V. & A. 86

division, a florid phrase of melody. 1H4 iii. 1

dogged, cruel. John iv. 1; iv. 3; 2H6 iii. 1

doit, a small Dutch coin = half a farthing. 2H6 iii. 1

dole, pain. 2H4 i. 1

dominations, sovereign rights. John ii. 1

doubt, fear. John iv. 1; &c.; suspect. Son. 75

doubtless, without fear. John iv. 1

dout, extinguish. H5 iv. 2

dowlas, coarse kind of linen. 1H4 iii. 3

down-roping, dripping down. H5 iv. 2

draff, refuse, swine's food. 1H4 iv. 2

drawer, one who draws liquor at a tavern. 1H4 ii. 4

drawn fox, hunted fox and therefore full of cunning. 1H4 iii. 3

drench, draught given to an animal. 1H4 ii. 4; H5 iii. 5

dress, make ready. H5 iv. 1

dressings, presentments. Son. 123

drollery, comic drawing. 2H4 ii. 1

drone, the tone emitted by the bass pipe in a bagpipe. 1H4 i. 2

'due, endue. 1H6 iv. 2

duer, more duly. 2H4 iii. 2

dumb significants, silent signs. 1H6 ii. 4

dump, mournful melody. Luc. 1127

durance, a strong cloth out of which prisoners' clothes were made. 1H4 i. 2

ean, bring forth lambs. 3H6 ii. 5

ear, eare, plough. R2 iii. 2; V. & A. dedic.

earnest, money paid as an instalment to secure a bargain. H5 ii. 2

effect, purport. John iv. 1; suitable manner. 2H4 ii. 1; effectively prove. 2H6 iii. 1; execution R3 i. 2; outward manifestation. Luc. 1555; working efficiency. Son. 36

effectually, actually. Son. 113

effuse, shed. 1H6 v. 4; effusion. 3H6 ii. 6

egally, equally. R3 iii. 7

eisel, vinegar. Son. 111

elvish-marked, marked by fairies. R3 i. 3

emballing, probably used with indelicate sense, or ?investing with the ball as symbol of royalty. H8 ii. 3

embossed, bulging. 1H4 iii. 3

embounded, confined. John iv. 3

embowelled, bowels removed for the purpose of embalming. 1H4 v. 4; disembowelled. R3 v. 2

embracement, embrace. R3 ii. 1; H8 i. 1; V. & A. 312

empery, empire. H5 i. 2; R3 iii. 7

end, saying, phrase. R3 i. 3; at the bottom. H8 ii. 1

endeared to, were, laid importance on. 2H4 ii. 3

enfeoff, hand over as a fief, surrender. 1H4 iii. 2

engaged, detained as a hostage. 1H4 iv. 3; v. 2; bound. 2H4 i. 1

englut, swallow up. H5 iv. 3

engraffed, closely attached. 2H4 ii. 2

engross, amass. 1H4 iii. 2; 2H4 iv. 5; make gross. R3 iii. 7

engrossment, that which has been collected greedily from all quarters. 2H4 iv. 5

enlarge, set at liberty. 1H4 iii. 2; H5 ii. 2; Son. 70; widen. 2H4 i. 1

enlargement, escape. 1H4 iii. 1; release from confinement. 3H6 iv. 6

enow, enough. H5 iv. 1

enpatron me, are my patron saint. Lov. C. 224

ensconce, shelter. Luc. 1515; Son. 49

entertain, maintain. R2 ii. 2; engage. 1H4 v. 1; receive, commence. 1H6 v. 4; keep engaged. R3 i. 2

envy, bear malice. John iii. 4; H8 v. 3; malice, hatred. R2 ii. 1; &c.

Ephesian, boon companion. 2H4 ii. 2

erst, of old. H5 v. 2

esperance, the motto of the Percies. 1H4 ii. 3

espials, spies. 1H6 i. 4; 1H6 iv. 3

estridge, ostrich. 1H4 iv. 1

eternize, make perpetually famous. 2H6 v. 3

even-pleached, smoothly intertwined. H5 v. 2

events, results, ends. R2 ii. 1

ever among, ?continually. 2H4 v. 3

evil, privy. H8 ii. 1

excelling, exquisite. V. & A. 443

exclaim on, cry out against, rail at. V. & A. 930; Luc. 741

exclamation, clamour. 2H4 ii. 1; reproach. H8 i. 2

executor, executioner. H5 i. 2

exempt, remove. 1H6 ii. 4; H8 i. 2

exercise, training. John iv. 2; act of religious devotion. R3 iii. 7; act of preaching, discourse. R3 iii. 2

exhalation, meteor. John iii. 4; 1H4 ii. 4; H8 iii. 2

exhibiters, those who put the case. H5 i. 1

exigent, end. 1H6 ii. 5

exion, blunder for 'action.' 2H4 ii. 1

expense, loss. Son. 30; expenditure, waste. Son. 94

expiate, terminated. R3 iii. 3; bring to an end. Son. 22

extern, external. Son. 125

extinct, extinguished. R2 i. 3

extincture, extinction. Lov. C. 294

extirp, extirpate, uproot. 1H6 iii. 3

extraught, extracted, derived. 3H6 ii. 2

eyne, eyes. V. & A. 633

face, repair a garment with new facings. 1H4 v. 1; outface. H5 iii. 7; act or speak with effrontery. 1H6 v. 3

face-royal, royal face; the stamp on a coin, worth about 10s., called the 'royal.' 2H4 i. 2

factious, given to forming factions. 2H6 v. 1; R3 i. 3

factor, deputy. 1H4 iii. 2; R3 iii. 7

fail, death, to die. H8 i. 2

fain, obliged. 2H4 ii. 1; glad, gladly. H5 i. 1; R3 i. 4

fairly, in respect to beauty. Son. 5

falchion, sword. 3H6 i. 4

fall, be brought forth. John iii. 1; desert. John iii. 1; let fall. R2 iii. 4; R3 v. 3; Luc. 1551; fall away, diminish. H5 v. 2

false esteem, spurious reputation. Son. 127

fame, make famous. Son. 84

familiar, attendant spirit. 1H6 iii. 2; 2H6 iv. 7

famoused, famed. Son. 25

fancy, composition in an impromptu style. 2H4 iii. 2; love. 1H6 v. 3; Luc. 200; Son. to Music iv.; the person loved. Lov. C. 61

fantastic, imaginary. R2 i. 3

farced, stuffed out, pompous. H5 iv. 1

far-fet, far-fetched. 2H6 iii. 1

fast, steadfastly. 2H6 v. 2

fat room, ? vat room. 1H4 ii. 4

fault, loss of scent. V. & A. 694

feast-finding, attending banquets. Luc. 817

feat, neat. Lov. C. 48

fee, pledge. Son. 120

fee-simple, estate belonging to a person without limitation as to the heirs. 2H6 iv. 10

fell, cruel. John iii. 4. &c.

fellow, comrade. 1H4 ii. 2; equal. H8 i. 3

fern-seed, the seed of the fern was supposed to be invisible and to make its possessor also invisible. 1H4 ii. 1

ferret, to hunt (as with ferrets), to worry. H5 iv. 4

fet, fetched. H5 iii. 1

fetch off, 'do for,' get the better of. 2H4 iii. 2

fifteenth, fifteenth part of all a

subject's personal property. 2H6 i. 1

fig, insult by thrusting the thumb between two closed fingers or into the mouth. 2H4 v. 3

fig of Spain, see *fig*. H5 iii. 6

figo, see *fig*. H5 iii. 6; iv. 1

file, list. H8 i. 1; keep pace. H8 iii. 2

fillip, tap, strike. 2H4 i. 2

find, furnish, provide. H5 i. 2

fire-drake, meteor, a man with a fiery nose. H8·v. 4

fire-new, fresh from the mint, brand new. R3 i. 3

firk, beat. H5 iv. 4

fitted, forced by fits or paroxysms. Son. 119

flap-dragon, snap-dragon. 2H4 ii. 4

flap-mouth, mouth with broad hanging lips. V. & A. 920

flats, level ground. John v. 6

flaw, flake (of snow). 2H4 iv. 4; storm. 2H6 iii. 1; make a flaw in, break. H8. i. 1; i. 2; gust of wind. V. & A. 456

fleet, pass away, vanish. John ii. 1; prison of the Fleet. 2H4 v. 5

flesh, make fierce and eager for combat. John v. 1; 2H4 i. 1; fed with flesh like hound trained for chase. H5 ii. 4; hardened in bloodshed. H5 iii. 3; R3 iv. 3; initiate. 1H6 iv. 7

flock, tuft of wool. 1H4 ii. 1

flourish, ornament. R3 i. 3; embellishment. Son. 60

flower-de-luce, fleur de lis, emblem of France. H5 v. 2; 1H6 i. 1; i. 2; 2H6 v. 1

fluxive, flowing. Lov. C. 50

flying at the brook, hawking at waterfowl. 2H6 ii. 1

fobbed, put off, baffled. 1H4 i. 2

foil, gold or silver leaf used as background for transparent gems to set off their lustre. R2 i. 3; &c.; defeat. 1H6 iii. 3; &c.

foin, thrust. 2H4 ii. 1

foison, plentiful harvest. Son. 53

folly, wantonness. Luc. 851

fond, *fondly*, foolish, foolishly. John ii. 1; &c.

foot-boys, boy-attendants. 1H6 iii. 2

footcloth, large ornamental cloth laid over the back of a horse and hanging down to the ground on each side. 2H6 iv. 1; iv. 7; R3 iii. 4

footed, landed. H5 ii. 4

foot land-rakers, vagabond footpads. 1H4 ii. 1

forage, prowl about for prey. John v. 1; H5 i. 2

force of, perforce. Lov. C. 223

force perforce, by very force, in spite of opposition. John iii. 1; 2H4 iv. 1; iv. 4; 2H6 i. 1

forego, put up with. John iii. 1

forehand shaft, arrow for shooting point-blank. 2H4 iii. 2

foreward, vanguard. R3 v. 3

forfend, forbid. R2 iv. 1; 3H6 ii. 1

forgery, deceit. 3H6 iii. 3

forgetive, inventive. 2H4 iv. 3

forslow, delay. 3H6 ii. 3

forspent, worn out. 2H4 i. 1; 3H6 ii. 3

forthcoming, under arrest. 2H6 ii. 1

forward of, eager for. 3H6 iv. 8

forwearied, wearied. John ii. 1

founder, disable, lame. 2H4 iv. 3

foutra, expression of contempt. 2H4 v. 3

fox, broadsword. H5 iv. 4

fracted, broken. H5 ii. 1

frank, sty. 2H4 ii. 2; shut up in a sty. R3 i. 3; iv. 5; liberal. Son. 4

franklin, freeholder; a man of the class next to the gentry. 1H4 ii. 1

frequent, familiar. Son. 117

fret, eat away. R2 iii. 3; H8 iii. 2; V. & A. 767; chafe. 1H4 ii. 2; H5 iv. 7; V. & A. 621; violently agitate. 3H6 ii. 6

frets, stops of a guitar. Luc. 1140

friend, befriend. H5 iv. 5

front, oppose. 1H4 ii. 2; face. H8 i. 2; earliest part. Son. 102

frontier, forehead. 1H4 i. 3; outwork, fortification. 1H4 ii. 3

fubbed off, put off with excuses. 2H4 ii. 1

fuller, one who is employed in cleansing and thickening cloth. H8 i. 2

full-fraught, best accomplished. H5 ii. 2

fulsome, nauseous. John iii. 4; R3 v. 3

furred pack, pack made of skin with the hair outwards. 2H6 iv. 2

fury, inspiration. Son. 100

fustian, worthless, pretentious. 2H4 ii. 4

fustilarian, term of abuse. 2H4 ii. 1

gage, pledge, pawn; especially the glove of a knight thrown down in challenge. R2 i. 1; &c.

gall, injure, annoy. John iv. 3; &c.; harass. H5 i. 2; jest bitterly. H5 v. 1

gallant-springing, growing up in beauty. R3 i. 4

galled, worn away. H5 iii. 1; Luc. 1440; sore with weeping. R3 iv. 4

Gallia, France. 3H6 v. 3

Gallian, French. 1H6 v. 4

galliard, lively dance. H5 i. 2

gallow-glasses, heavy-armed Irish foot-soldiers. 2H6 iv. 9

gan, began. 2H4 i. 1

gaping, shouting. H8 v. 4

garb, style, manner. H5 v. 1

gawd, brightness. John iii. 3

gaze, that which is gazed at. Son. 5

gear, matter, business. 2H6 i. 4; 2H6 iii. 1; R3 i. 4

gelded, deprived. R2 ii. 1

gelding, cutting off from. 1H4 iii. 1

George, the jewel which forms part of the insignia of the Order of the Garter. 2H6 iv. 1; R3 iv. 4

gesture, position, movement. H5 iv. chor.

ghost, corpse. 2H6 iii. 2

gibbet, hang. 2H4 iii. 2

gib cat, old tom-cat. 1H4 i. 2

giglot, wanton. 1H6 iv. 7

gilt, smeared. John ii. 1; gold. H5 ii. chor.

gimmal, double, or made of double rings. H5 iv. 2; contrivance. 1H6 i. 2

gin, spring. 3H6 i. 4

gird, gibe, jeer. 2H4 i. 2; besiege. H5 i. 2; iii. chor.; rebuke. 1H6 iii. 1; invest. 2H6 i. 1

gleek, scoff. H5 v. 1; 1H6 iii. 2

glose, discourse. R2 ii. 1

gloze, interpret. H5 i. 2

gnarling, snarling. R2 i. 3; 2H6 iii. 1

go, pass from your thoughts.

2H6 ii. 3; walk. Son. 51; 130

gobbets, pieces. 2H6 iv. i; v. 2

God before, God being our leader, or ? I swear by God. H5 i. 2; iii. 6

God-den, good evening. H5 iii. 2

good cheap, cheap. 1H4 iii. 3

good den, good evening. John i. 1

good time, in, opportunely. R3 ii. 1

good-year, a meaningless expletive. 2H4 ii. 4

gorbellied, big-bellied. 1H4 ii.2

gossips, godparents, hence of much influence. R3 i. 1; godparents. H8 v. 5

governance, government. 2H6 i. 3

government, self-control. 1H4 i. 2; &c.; command. 1H4 iv. 1

grace, service, honour. 1H4 iii. 1; ornament. H5 ii. prol.

graced, blessed. R3 iv. 4

graff, graft. 2H4 v.3; Luc.1062

grafter, the original tree from which a scion has been taken for grafting. H5 iii. 5

grained, forked. Lov. C. 64

gramercy, many thanks. R3 iii. 2

grate on, oppress, be burdensome to. 2H4 iv. 1

gratulate, congratulate.R3 iv.1

grave, lay in grave. R2 iii. 2; solemn. 1H6 v. 1; engrave, mark. V. & A. 376; Luc. 755

grazing, damage done by a spent ball. H5 iv. 3

greenly, foolishly. H5 v. 2

grind, make sharp. Son. 110

gripe, griffin. Luc. 543

groat, coin worth 4*d.* 2H4 i. 2; H5 v. 1; 2H6 iii. 1

gross, grossly, palpable, palpably, manifestly. H5 ii. 2; Son.

99; stupid, stupidly. John iii. 1; R3 iii. 6; iv. 1

ground, air on which variations are made. R3 iii. 7

guard, trim, ornament. John iv. 2; 2H4 iv. 1; H8 prol.

guardant, guard, sentinel. 1H6 iv. 7

guerdoned, rewarded, recompensed. 2H6 i. 4; 3H6 iii. 3

gulf, whirlpool. H5 ii. 4

gull, bird. 1H4 v. 1; dupe, fool. R3 i. 3

gummed velvet, velvet stiffened with gum. 1H4 ii. 2

gun-stones, stone cannon-balls. H5 i. 2

gust, taste. Son. 114

gyves, fetters. 1H4 iv. 2

habitude, condition of body. Lov. C. 114

haggled, hacked, mangled. H5 iv. 6

hair, nature, texture. 1H4 iv. 1

hale, drag. 2H4 v. 5; 2H6 iv. 1

half-face, thin face. John i. 1

half-faced, thin-faced, poor. 1H4 i. 3; 2H4 iii. 2; with only half the face visible. 2H6 iv. 1

half-faced groat, term applied contemptuously to a thin-faced man. John i. 1

half-kirtle, kirtle about half the usual length. 2H4 v. 4

Half-moon, name of a room in an inn. 1H4 ii. 4

half-sword, at, at close quarters with swords. 1H4 ii. 4

Hallowmas, the Feast of All Saints. R2 v. 1

hand, at, by hand. John v. 2

hand, hold, be on an equality. John ii. 1

hand, out of, at once. 1H6 iii. 2; 3H6 iv. 7

handle, speak of. H5 ii. 3

happily, haply, perhaps. R2 v. 3; 2H6 iii. 1; H8 iv. 2

hardiment, deed of daring. 1H4 i. 3

harness, armour. John v. 2; 1H4 iii. 2

Harry ten shillings, gold piece. 2H4 iii. 2

hatch, half-door. John i. 1; v. 2

hatches, deck. R3 i. 4

haught, haughty. R2 iv. 1; 3H6 ii. 1; R3 ii. 3

haunch, the latter end. 2H4 iv. 4

hautboy, a wooden double-reed wind instrument. 2H4 iii. 2

have-at-him, blow at him. H8 ii. 2

haviour, behaviour. R2 i. 3

havoc, cry, give the order 'havoc' to the army for a sign of general spoliation. John ii. 1

hazard, winning opening in a tennis court. H5 i. 2

head, make, gather an army. 1H4 iii. 1; 2H4 i. 1; 3H6 ii. 1

heavenly-harnessed team, the horses of the sun-god's chariot. 1H4 iii. 1

heavily, heavy, sadly, sad, sorrowful. 2H6 iii. 2; &c.; gloomy, morose. Son. 98; troublesome. V. & A. 156

hedge, creep along by the hedge. H8 iii. 2

helm, helmet. H5 iv. 7; R3 iii. 2

hem, cry, express disapproval by a sharp cough. 1H4 ii. 4

hempen caudle, cant term for hanging. 2H6 iv. 7

herb of grace, rue. R2 iii. 4

hest, behest, determination. 1H4 ii. 3

high-blown, inflated. H8 iii. 2

high-stomached, of high spirit. R2 i. 1

high-swoln, haughty, angry. R3 ii. 2

hild, held. Luc. 1257

hilding, base. 2H4 i. 1; H5 iv.2

hind, boor, peasant. 1H4 ii. 3; 2H6 iii. 2; iv. 2

his, its. John iv. 3; &c.

hive, head-covering. Lov. C. 8

hoise, hoist, heave. 2H6 i. 1; R3 iv. 4

hold hand with, be equal with. John ii. 1

hold in, keep silence. 1H4 ii. 1

holidame, an oath. H8 v. 1

holp, helped. John i. 1; R2 v. 5

home, in full, with a home-thrust. 1H4 i. 3

honesty, chastity. 3H6 iii. 2

honey-seed, blunder for 'homicide.' 2H4 ii. 1

honey-suckle, blunder for 'homicidal.' 2H4 ii. 1

honour-owing, honourable. H5 iv. 6

hose and doublets, in, i.e. without a cloak. 2H6 iv. 7

hound of Crete, ? bloodhound. H5 ii. 1

hull, float at the mercy of the waves. R3 iv. 4; H8 ii. 4

humorous, capricious, quick-tempered. John iii. 1; &c.

humours, dispositions, moods, whims, caprices. John ii. 1; &c.; used without meaning. H5 ii. 1

humours of blood, natural moods. 2H4 ii. 3

hunt-counter, one who hunts counter, or traces the scent backward. 2H4 i. 2

hurly, hurly-burly, tumult, uproar. John iii. 4; 1H4 v. 1; 2H4 iii. 1

husband, husbandman. 2H4 v. iii; H8 iii. 2

huswife, light woman, hussy.

2H4 iii. 2; H5 v. 1

hydra, a many-headed snake, whose heads grew again as fast as they were cut off. 1H4 v. 4; 2H4 iv. 2; H5 i. 1

Iceland dog, shaggy sharp-eared white dog, much imported formerly as ladies' lap-dogs. H5 ii. 1

'ignis fatuus,' will-o'-the-wisp. 1H4 iii. 3

ill-wresting, twisting to a bad sense. Son. 140

imbar, secure. H5 i. 2

imbrue, pierce with weapons. 2H4 ii. 4

immanity, ferocity. 1H6 v. i

immediate, held directly of the sovereign. 2H4 iv. 5

imp, scion, offshoot. 2H4 v. 5; H5 iv. 1; graft new feather's to a falcon's wing. R2 ii. 1

impaint, depict. 1H4 v. 1

impale, circle. 3H6 iii. 3

impawn, pledge. 1H4 iv. 3; put in hazard. H5 i. 2

impleached, interwined. Lov. C. 205

imposthumes, abscess. V. & A. 743

impress, device with a motto. R2 iii. 1; compel to serve. 1H4 i. 1

incapable, unapt to receive impressions. R3 ii. 2

in capite, a feudal term, to hold direct from the sovereign. 2H6 iv. 7

incensed, incited. R3 iii. 1; urge. H8 v. 1

inclusive verge, enclosing edge. R3 iv. 1

income, entrance, advent. Luc. 334

incontinent, immediately. R2 v. 6

increaseful, productive. Luc. 958

indent, enter into an engagement. 1H4 i. 3; indentation. 1H4 iii. 1; twist, turn. V. & A. 704

indentures tripartite, threefold agreement. 1H4 iii. 1

index, prologue. R3 ii. 2; iv. 4

indifferency, absence of bias or favour. John ii. 1; moderation. 2H4 iv. 3

indigest, indigested, formless [mass], shapeless. John v. 7; &c.

indirect, crooked, false. John iii. 1; 1H4 iv. 3

indirection, malpractice. John iii. 1

indite, blunder for 'invite.' 2H4 ii. 1

induction, introduction. 1H4 iii. 1; R3 i. 1; iv. 4

indurance, imprisonment. H8 v. 1

infinitive, blunder for 'infinite.' 2H4 ii. 1

inhabitable, uninhabitable. R2 i. 1

inhearse, bury. Son. 86

inkhorn mate, scribbler. 1H6 iii. 1

inly, inward, inwardly. H5 iv. chor.; 3H6 i. 4

insinewed, inspired with strength. 2H4 iv. 1

instalment, establishment. R3 iii. 1

insulter, assailer. V. & A. 550

insulting, exulting. 1H6 i. 2

insults, glories. Son. 107

intelligence, information brought by spies. John iv. 2; 1H4 iv. 3

intelligencer, secret agent. 2H4 iv. 2; R3 iv. 4

intend, pretend. R3 iii. 5; iii. 7; Luc. 121; direct. Son. 27

intended, intending to march. 1H4 iv. 1; understood. 2H4 iv. 1

intendment, aim. H5 i. 2; design. V. & A. 222

interest, claim. John v. 2; 1H4 iii. 2; Son. 31; property. Son. 74

intermissive, intermittent. 1H6 i. 1

intertissued, interwoven. H5 iv. 1

intervallum, interval. 2H4 v. 1

intituled, having a claim. Luc. 57

invasive, of invasion. John v. 1

investing, showing forth. H5 iv. chor.

investments, vestments. 2H4 iv. 1

invincible, error for 'invisible.' 2H4 iii. 2

invised, ? unseen. Lov. C. 212

inward, intimate. R3 iii. 4; inside, palm. Son. 128

iron-witted, dull-witted. R3 iv. 2

irregular, lawless. 1H4 i. 1

issue, shed tears. H5 iv. 6; descendants. H8 iii. 2

it, he. 2H4 ii. 4

I wis, certainly. R3 i. 3

Jack, term of contempt. 1H4 ii. 4; iii. 3; R3 i. 3; figure which struck bell in old clocks. R2 v. 5; R3 iv. 2

jack-an-apes, monkey, a contemptuous term. H5 v. 2

jacks, keys of virginal. Son. 128

Jack-sauce, saucy Jack. H5 iv. 7

jade, term of pity or contempt for ill-treated or ill-conditioned horse. R2 iii. 3; &c.; treat with contempt. H8 iii. 2

jar, tick. R2 v. 5; quarrel. 1H6 i. 1; iii. 1; V. & A. 100; discord. 2H6 iv. 8

jauncing, ? prancing. R2 v. 5

jealous, apprehensive. V. & A. 321

jennet, Spanish horse. V. & A. 260

jest, amusement, pleasure. R2 i. 3

jet, encroach. R3 ii. 4

Joan, general name for a female rustic. John i. 1

Joan, old, name of a hawk. 2H6 ii. 1

joint-stool, folding chair. 1H4 ii. 4; 2H4 ii. 4

jordan, chamber-pot. 1H4 ii. 1; 2H4 ii. 4

journey-bated, worn with travelling. 1H4 iv. 3

jump, agree. 1H4 i. 2; R3 iii. 1

justling, jostling, busy. 1H4 iv. 1

jutty, project beyond. H5 iii. 1

juvenal, youth. 2H4 i. 2

kecksies, dry hemlock stems. H5 v. 2

keech, roll of tallow. H8 i. 1

kennel, gutter. 2H6 iv. 1

kern, light-armed Irish footsoldier. R2 ii. 1; H5 iii. 7; 2H6 iii. 1

kickshaws, trifle. 2H4 v. 1

Killingworth, Kenilworth. 2H6 iv. 4

kindle, incite. John i. 1

king christen, Christian king. 1H4 ii. 1

kirtle, jacket with petticoat attached. 2H4 ii. 4

knock it, sound, strike up. H8 i. 4

knot, laid-out garden. R2 iii. 4

knot-pated, knotty-pated, block-headed. 1H4 ii. 4

lade, empty, drain. 3H6 iii. 2

lag, late. R3 ii. 1

lag-end, fag-end, last part. 1H4 v. 1; H8 i. 3

lard, enrich, fatten. 1H4 ii. 2; H5 iv. 6

large, at, in full. R2 iii. 1

latch, catch, lay hold of. Son. 113

laund, lawn, glade. 3H6 iii. 1; V. & A. 813

lavolta, waltz-like dance. H5 iii. 5

lay by the heels, imprison. H8 v. 4

lay down, prepare. H5 i. 2

layer up, one who fixes the amount. H5 v. 2

lazar, leper. H5 i. 1

leaping-houses, brothels. 1H4 i. 2

leas, arable land. H5 v. 2

leash, a set of three. 1H4 ii. 4

leather-coats, golden russetings, kind of apple. 2H4 v. 3

leave, give us, courteous form of dismissal. 1H4 iii. 2

leese, lose. Son. 5

leg, bow. R2 iii. 3; 1H4 ii. 4

leman, sweetheart. 2H4 v. 3

lendings, money advanced to soldiers when the regular pay cannot be given. R2 i. 1

let slip, loose hounds from the leash in order to begin the chase. 1H4 i. 3

liefest, dearest. 2H6 iii. 1

lig, lie. H5 iii. 2

liggens, by God's, an oath. 2H4 v. 3

like of, care for. Son. 21

liking, condition. 1H4 iii. 3

limbeck, alembic. Son. 119

Limbo Patrum, slang term for 'prison.' H8 v. 4

lime-twigs, twigs smeared with bird-lime to catch birds. 2H6 iii. 3

limit, appoint. John v. 2; R3 v. 3; appointed time. R2 i. 3; R3 iii. 3

line, strengthen. John iv. 3; &c.; rank. 1H4 iii. 2

link, torch used to light people along the streets. 1H4 iii. 3

linstock, stick holding gunner's match. H5 iii. chor.; 1H6 i. 4 (stage direction)

liquor, moisten with oil. 1H4 ii. 1

lither, yielding. 1H6 iv. 7

livelihood, appearance. R3 iii. 4; vigour, life. V. & A. 26

livery, delivery of a freehold into the possession of its heir. R2 ii. 1; ii. 3; 1H4 iv. 3; dress. Lov. C. 105

lob, hang, drop. H5 iv. 2

lodge, lay flat, beat down. R2 iii. 3; 2H6 iii. 2

lodging, entering into the fold. H5 iii. 7

loggerheads, blockheads. 1H4 ii. 4

long-staff, long cudgel. 1H4 ii. 1

look beyond, misjudge. 2H4 iv. 4

lop, small branch or twig. H8 i. 2

lording, lord. 2H6 i. 1

lout, bumpkin, clown. John ii. 1; make a fool of. 1H6 iv. 3

Love, Venus, queen of love and beauty. V. & A. 328

lubber, blunder for 'leopard.' 2H4 ii. 1

lugged, baited. 1H4 i. 2

Lumbert Street, Lombard Street. 2H4 ii. 1

luxurious, luxury, lascivious, lasciviousness. H5 iii. 5; &c.

madding, becoming mad with love. 2H6 iii. 2

maidenhead, maidenhood. H8 ii. 3

Maid Marian, a character in the morris-dance. 1H4 iii. 3

mailed up, wrapped up. 2H6 ii. 4

main, hand at dice. 1H4 iv. i.; chief point. 2H6 i. 1; maim. 2H6 iv. 2; general. H8 iv. 1; flood. Son. 60

maintenance, bearing. 1H4 v. 4

major, major term of a syllogism. 1H4 ii. 4

makeless, mateless. Son. 9

make tender of, have care for. 1H4 v. 4

makings, symbols. H8 iv. 1

malapert, pert, saucy. 3H6 v. 5; R3 i. 3

male, mate. 3H6 v. 6

malmsey-butt, butt of malmsey, a strong sweet wine. R3 i. 4

malmsey-nose, red-nosed. 2H4 ii. 1

malt worms, beer-drinkers. 1H4 ii. 1; 2H4 ii. 4

mammet, doll. 1H4 ii. 3

mandrake, root supposed to bear human shape, and to shriek when pulled out of the ground, causing madness or death to the hearer. 2H4 i. 2; 2H6 iii. 2

man-queller, murderer. 2H4 ii. 1

marches, borders. H5 i. 2; 3H6 ii. 1

mare, nightmare. 2H4 ii. 1

marish, marsh. 1H6 i. 1

margents, margins. Luc. 102

mark, thirteen shillings and fourpence. John ii. 1; &c.; listen to. 1H4 i. 2; R3 i. 3

marry, interjection = indeed, to be sure, &c. R2 i. 4; &c.

Martlemas, Martinmas, November 11, supposed to be a time of fair weather, applied to a hale old man. 2H4 ii. 2

mate, confound. 2H6 iii. 1; V. & A. 909; match, cope with. H8 iii. 2

maund, basket. Lov. C. 36

maw, stomach. John v. 7; H5 ii. 1

measure, music of stately dance. John iii. 1; stately dance. R2 i. 3; &c.; dancing. H5 v. 2

medicine potable, cordial. 2H4 iv. 5

medicines, love-potions. 1H4 ii. 2

memento mori, reminder of death, such as a skull or other symbolical object. 1H4 iii. 3

mervailous, marvellous. H5 ii. 1

mess, sufficient to make a dish. 2H4 ii. 1; party of four. 3H6 i. 4

mew up, imprison. R3 i. 1

micher, truant. 1H4 ii. 4

mickle, great. H5 ii. 1; 1H6 iv. 6; 2H6 v. 1

Mile-end Green, the usual ground for drill and sports. 2H4 iii. 2

milliner, vendor of fancy wares. 1H4 i. 3

mind, royal, devotion to the king. H8 iv. 1

minion, favourite. John ii. 1; &c.; pert, saucy person. 2H6 i. 3

misdoubt, apprehension. 2H4 iv. 1; mistrust. 2H6 iii. 1; 3H6 v. 6; R3 iii. 2

misprision, misunderstanding, error. 1H4 i. 3; Son. 87

mistreadings, misdeeds. 1H4 iii. 2

mistress-court, chief court, a term in tennis. H5 ii. 4

modern, ordinary, commonplace. John iii. 4; Son. 83

module, counterfeit. John v. 7

moe, more. John v. 4; &c.

moiety, part, share. 1H4 iii. 1; Luc. Dedic.; Son. 46; half. H8 i. 2

moldwarp, mole. 1H4 iii. 1

Monmouth caps, caps made at Monmouth. H5 iv. 7

moon's men, men who rob by night. 1H4 i. 2

Morisco, morris-dancer. 2H6 iii. 1

morris-dance, dance performed by persons in fancy costume. H5 ii. 4

mortal-staring, with a deadly stare. R3 v. 3

mot, motto. Luc. 830

motive, moving limb or organ. R2 i. 1

motley, fool, jester. Son. 110

mought, might. 3H6 v. 2

mould, men of, men of earth, mortal men. H5 iii. 2

mounted, term in falconry. H5 iv. 1

mouse, tear in pieces. John ii. 1

mouth, bark, bay. 1H6 ii. 1

muddy, rascally, dirty. 1H4 ii. 1; 2H4 ii. 4

mure, wall. 2H4 iv. 4

musit, gap in hedge. V. & A. 683

mutine, mutineer. John ii. 1

mysteries, artificial fashions. H8 i. 3

naked, without defence. 3H6 v. 4

narrow ocean, English Channel. H5 i. chor.

naught, call all to, vehemently abuse. V. & A. 993

nave, centre or block of a wheel. 2H4 ii. 4

neaf, hand, fist. 2H4 ii. 4

neck, directly after. 1H4 iv. 3

needs will, is determined to. R3 iii. 1

neif, fist. 2H4 ii. 4

nest of spicery, allusion to the death-pile of the Phœnix, a bird supposed to renew itself from its own ashes. R3 iv. 4

net, sophistry. H5 i. 2

nether-stocks, stockings. 1H4 ii. 4

nice of, make, scruple at. John iii. 4

night crow, night-heron. 3H6 v. 6

nill, will not. Pas. P. xiv.

Nob, Robert. John i. 1

noble, gold coin worth 6s. 8d. R2 i. 1; &c.

noise, band of musicians. 2H4 ii. 4

nonage, minority. R3 ii. 3

nonce, expressly. 1H4 i. 2

nook-shotten, running out into angles. H5 iii. 5

numbers, bands, companies. 2H6 ii. 1

nuthook, catchpole. 2H4 v. 4

nuzzling, nosing. V. & A. 1115

O, anything round. H5 prol.; o', off. H8 v. 4

O, the father, an imprecation. 1H4 ii. 4

ob, a half-penny. 1H4 ii. 4

obedience, obeisance. 2H4 iv. 5

oblation, offering. Son. 125

obstacle, blunder for 'obstinate.' 1H6 v. 4

occasion, necessity, cause. John ii. 1; opportunity. John iv. 2; R3 ii. 2; course of events. John iv. 2

office, service. R2 ii. 2

offices, servants' apartments in a great house, rooms. R2 i. 2; 2H4 i. 3

on ringing, set, started ringing. Luc. 1494

one, score, debt. 2H4 ii. 1

one for that, all's, it does not matter. R3 v. 3

one on another's neck, one immediately after another. Son. 131

oneyers, meaning uncertain, possibly 'great ones.' 1H4 ii. 1

ope, open. John ii. 1

open, in, in public. H8 iii. 2

orb, circuit. 1H4 v. 1

orbed, rounded. Lov. C. 25

order, manner. 2H6 iii. 2; arrange, draw up. R3 v. 3

order, take, take measures, make arrangements. R2 v. 1; &c.

ordinance, ordnance, cannon. John ii. 1

orient, bright. V. & A. 981

orison, prayer. H5 ii. 2

orphans, posthumous children. Son. 97

ort, leaving, refuse. Luc. 985

ostent, show, display. H5 v. chor.

ousel, blackbird. 2H4 iii. 2

outrage, outburst of fury. John iii. 4; R3 ii. 4

out-speak, exceed. H8 iii. 2

outward eye, the opening in a ball for the insertion of the bias or weight. John ii. 1

overscutched, over-whipped. 2H4 iii. 2

overseen, bewitched. Luc. 1206

overshot, beaten in shooting. H5 iii. 7

overween, be arrogant. 2H4 iv. 1

overweening, presumptuous. R2 i. 1

owches, ornaments. 2H4 ii. 4

owse, ooze, mud. H5 i. 2

oyster-wench, girl who sells oysters. R2 i. 4

pack-horse, drudge. R3 i. 3

paction, agreement. H5 v. 2

painted, counterfeit. John iii. 1; R3 i. 3

painted cloth, wall-hangings painted or worked with figures and scenes. 1H4 iv. 2; Luc. 245

pale, enclosure. R2 iii. 4; H8 v. 4; V. & A. 230; enclose. 3H6 i. 4; paleness. V. & A. 589; Luc. 1512

palisadoes, palisades. 1H4 ii. 3

pallet, poor bed. 2H4 iii. 1

palmer, pilgrim. R2 iii. 3; 2H6 v. 1; Luc. 791

paly, pale. H5 iv. chor.; 2H6 iii. 2

pantler, servant in charge of pantry. 2H4 ii. 4

paraquito, parrot. 1H4 ii. 3

Paris-garden, name of a place at Bankside, Southwark, where was a bear-garden. H8 v. 4

parle, parley. John ii. 1; R2 i. 1; H5 iii. 3

parley, exchange of glances. 1H4 iii. 1

parling, speaking. Luc. 100

parmaceti, spermaceti. 1H4 i. 3

Partlet, name of hen in *Reynard the Fox.* 1H4 iii. 3

party-verdict, share in a joint verdict. R2 i. 3

pass, refuse. John ii. 1; passage. H5 ii. chor.; indulge in, as a jest. H5 ii. 1; die. 2H6 iii. 3; care for, regard. 2H6 iv. 2; issue. Son. 103

passenger, wayfarer. R2 v. 3; 2H6 iii. 1; V. & A. 91

pastern, leg. H5 iii. 7

patent, privilege. Son. 87

pauca [verba], in few words. H5 ii. 1

Paul's, St. Paul's Cathedral,

place of general resort for business and amusement. 1H4 ii. 4; 2H4 i. 2; R3 iii. 6

pax, small piece of metal or wood, with figure of Christ on it, offered to laity to kiss; but ? blunder for 'pyx,' box containing the Host. H5 iii. 6

pay, hit, kill. 1H4 ii. 4; v. 3; requite. H5 iv. 1

payment, punishment. H5 iv. 8

peach, turn informer. 1H4 ii. 2

peascod time, the season for peas. 2H4 ii. 4

peevish, wayward. John ii. 1; foolish. H5 iii. 7; silly, childish. 1H6 ii. 4; R3 i. 3; iv. 2

peevish-fond, foolishly perverse. R3 iv. 4

peise, poise, balance. John ii. 1; weigh down. R3 v. 3

pelican, in reference to the fable that the pelican feeds her young with her own blood. R2 ii. 1

pelt, to fling about angry words. Luc. 1418

pelting, insignificant. R2 ii. 1

pencil, paint brush. John iii. 1

pensived, pensive. Lov. C. 219

perdy, par Dieu, by God. H5 ii. 1

periapts, amulets. 1H6 v. 3

perked, dressed. H8 ii. 3

perniciously, to destruction. H8 ii. 1

perpend, consider. H5 iv. 4

pew-fellow, companion. R3 iv. 4

Philip, name formerly given to a sparrow. John i. 1

phœnix, matchless. Lov. C. 93

phraseless, indescribable. Lov. C. 225

pibble pabble, idle talk. H5 iv. 1

pick, pitch. H8 v. 4

picked, refined, punctilious. John i. 1

picking, minute, petty. 2H4 iv. 1

pick-thank, flatterer, talebearer. 1H4 iii. 2

pill, pillage, plunder. R2 ii. 1; R3 i. 3

pinch, vex. 1H4 i. 3

pinnace, small light vessel. 2H6 iv. 1

pioner, pioneer. H5 iii. 2

piping time, time when the pipe is sounded. R3 i. 1

pismires, ants. 1H4 i. 3

pitch, height to which falcon soars, hence height generally. R2 i. 1; &c.

pitch and pay, pay ready money. H5 ii. 3

pith, strength. H5 iii. chor.; V. & A. 26

plain, nothing else but. John ii. 1

plaining, complaint. R2 i. 3; complaining. Luc. 559

plain-song, simple air without variations. H5 iii. 2; H8 i. 3

plated, armed. R2 i. 3

platforms, plans, designs. 1H6 ii. 1

plausibly, with acclamation. Luc. 1854

pleasance, enjoyment. Pas. P. xii

plot, plot of ground, spot. John ii. 1; 2H6 ii. 2

pluck on, bring on. R3 iv. 2

plume-plucked, humbled. R2 iv. 1

point, head of the saddle. 1H4 ii. 1; tagged lace to tie parts of dress. 2H4 i. 1; shoulder-knot or other badge. 2H4 ii. 4; appoint. Luc. 879

pointing, appointing. Son. 14

point of war, trumpet-blast. 2H4 iv. 1

pomegarnet, pomegranate, name of a room in a tavern. 1H4 ii. 4

popinjay, parrot. 1H4 i. 3

*popular,popularity,*vulgar, vulgarity. 1H4 iii. 2; H5 iv. 1

poring, musing, for meditation. H5 iv. chor.

porpentine, porcupine. 2H6 iii. 1

porringer, a cap shaped like a porridge bowl. H8 v. 4

portage, port-hole. H5 iii. 1

posied, inscribed with a posy or motto. Lov. C. 45

postern, little or back door way. R2 v. 5

pot, wooden drinking vessel, bound with hoops. 2H6 iv. 2

potents, potentates. John ii. 1

pottle-pot, tankard holding two quarts. 2H4 ii. 2

poulter, poulterer. 1H4 ii. 4

*pouncet-box,*perfume-box,with perforated lid. 1H4 i. 3

powder, salt. 1H4 v. 4

*powdering-tub,*salting-tub; hot salt-water bath used in treatment of venereal disease. H5 ii. 1

practic, practical. H5 i. 1

practisant, performer in a stratagem. 1H6 iii. 2

precedent, rough draft. John v. 2; R3 iii. 6; proof. R2 ii. 1; sample, example. 1H4 ii. 4; Luc. 1261; indication. V. & A. 26

precept, summons. 2H4 v. 1; H5 iii. 3

precurrer, forerunner. Phœn. 6

pregnancy, ready wit. 2H4 i. 2

premised, sent before the time. 2H6 v. 2

prescription, right derived from immemorial custom. 3H6 iii. 3; direction. H8 i. 1

*presence,*person.John i.1; presence-chamber. R2 i. 3; H8 iii. 1; blunder for 'presents.' 2H6 iv. 7; king's presence. H8 iv. 2

*press,*force into military service. R2 iii. 2; 1H4 iv. 2; commission for pressing soldiers. 1H4 iv. 2; crowd, mob. H8 v. 4

prick, mark. 2H4 ii. 4; Son. 20; put him on the list. 2H4 iii. 2; dial-point. 3H6 i. 4; Luc. 781

primer, more urgent. H8 i. 2

primero, game at cards. H8 v. 1

privity, concurrence. H8 i. 1

prize, estimate. H5 ii. 4; privilege. 3H6 i. 4; 3H6 ii. 1; captive. R3 iii. 7; regard. Son. 143

process, course. R2 ii. 3; story. R3 iv. 3; iv. 4.

procurator, representative. 2H6 i. 1

proditor, traitor. 1H6 i. 3

proface, much good may it do you! 2H4 v. 3

prologue to an egg and butter, grace to an ordinary breakfast. 1H4 i. 2

proud-pied, variously coloured. Son. 98

prune, trim his feathers. 1H4 i. 1

puissance, armed force. John iii. 1; H5 i. chor.; strength, power. R3 v. 3

puke, a kind of woollen cloth. 1H4 ii. 4

pulsidge. blunder for 'pulse.' 2H4 ii. 4

punch, pierce. R3 v. 3

punish by the heels, send to prison. 2H4 i. 2

purl, curl. Luc. 1407

purpled, blood-stained. John ii. 1

pursuivant, officers attendant

upon a herald. 1H6 ii. 5; 2H6 i. 3; R3 iii. 4

putter-on, instigator. H8 i. 2

puttock, kite. 2H6 iii. 2

puzzel, hussy. 1H6 i. 4

pyramis, pyramid. 1H6 i. 6

Pyrenean, Pyrenees. John i. 1

quality, party. 1H4 iv. 3; nature. H8 i. 2

quarter, watch, order. John v. 5

quean, wench, hussy. 2H4 ii. 1

queen it, play the queen. H8 ii. 3

quell, destroy. 1H6 i. 1

quest, inquest, jury. R3 i. 4; Son. 46

question, misgiving. 1H4 iv. 1; discussion. H5 i. 1; converse. Luc. 122

question, in, under trial. 2H4 i. 2

quiddity, subtlety. 1H4 i. 2

quietus, discharge of obligation. Son. 126

quill, in the, ? in form and order. 2H6 i. 3

quillet, tricks in argument, fine points. 1H6 ii. 4; 2H6 iii. 1

quittal, requital. Luc. 236

quitting, setting free. 2H6 iii. 2

quiver, nimble. 2H4 iii. 2

quoif, cap. 2H4 i. 1

quoit, throw. 2H4 ii. 4

quotidian tertian, confusion of quotidian fever, of which the paroxysms return every day, with tertian fever, recurring every third day. H5 ii. 1

rabbit-sucker, sucking rabbit. 1H4 ii. 4

rack, move like vapour. 3H6 ii. 1; cloud, mass of clouds. Son. 33

racked, oppressed, by extortion. 2H6 i. 3

ragged, rugged, rough. R2 v. 5; &c.; beggarly. 2H4 v. 2

raging-wood, raving mad. 1H6 iv. 7

raise head, gather a force, rebel. H8 ii. 1

rampallian, term of abuse. 2H4 ii. 1

ramping, rampant. John iii. 1; 1H4 iii. 1; 3H6 v. 2

rankle, envenom. R2 i. 3; R3 i. 3

rascal, lean deer. 2H4 ii. 4; 1H6 iv. 2

raught, reached. H5 iv. 6; 2H6 ii. 3; 3H6 i. 4

raze, root. 1H4 ii. 1; tear away violently. R3 iii. 2; iii. 4

read, take example. H8 v. 5

reave, deprive. 2H6 v. 1; bereave. V. & A. 766

recomforture, comfort. R3 iv. 4

record, history. Son. 59

recordation to, commemoration of. 2H4 ii. 3

recreant, cowardly, faithless. John iii. 3; R2 i. 1

recure, remedy. R3 iii. 7; V. & A. 465

red lattice, ale-house window. 2H4 ii. 2

redoubted, dreaded. R2 iii. 3; R3 iv. 5

red wheat, late wheat. 2H4 v. 1

re-edified, rebuilt. R3 iii. 1

refuge shame, find a refuge from shame in the fact. R2 v. 5

region, of the upper air. Son. 33

regreet, greeting. John iii. 1; address. R2 i. 3; greet again. R2 i. 3

reguerdon, reward. 1H6 iii. 1; 1H6 iii. 4

rehearse, declare. R2 v. 3

relapse of mortality, deadly rebound. H5 iv. 3

religious house, nunnery. R2 v.1

render, report. 2H4 i. 1; surrender. Son. 126

render, mutual, give and take. Son. 125

rendezvous, last resort, shift. H5 ii. 1

rents, rend, pull apart. 3H6 iii. 2; Lov. C. 55

renying, denying. Son. to Music iii

replication, reply. Lov. C. 122

repugn, oppose. 1H6 iv. 1

resolve, set free from doubt. John ii. 1; dissolve. John v. 4; come to a determination. 1H6 i. 2; 3H6 i. 1; steadfastness. 1H6 v. 5; satisfy, answer. 3H6 iv. 1; R3 iv. 2

resolved correction, chastisement determined upon. 2H4 iv. 1

respite of my wrongs, determined, fixed time to which the punishment of my wrongs is postponed. R3 v. 1

resty, idle. Son. 100

reversion, succession. R2 i. 4; residue. 1H4 iv. 1

rheum, moisture, tears. John iii.1

rheumatic, blunder for 'splenetic.' 2H4 ii. 4; blunder for 'lunatic.' H5 ii. 3; affected or attended with rheum. V. & A. 13

ribs, walls. John ii. 1; R2 iii. 3

ride the wild mare, play at seesaw. 2H4 ii. 4

rids way, gets rid of distance. 3H6 v. 3

right drawn, drawn in a right cause. R2 i. 1

right for right, measure for measure. R3 iv. 4

rigol, circle. 2H4 iv.5; Luc.1745

rim, midriff. H5 iv. 4

rivage, shore. H5 iii. chor.

rive, discharge. 1H6 iv. 2

rivo, Bacchanalian exclamation. 1H4 ii. 4

road, prostitute. 2H4 ii. 2; inroad. H5 i.2; journey. H8 iv.2

roast, rule the, be master. 2H6 i. 1

robustious, violent action. H5 iii. 7

rondure, circle. Son. 21

rood, crucifix. R3 iii. 2

rook, cower. 3H6 v. 6

rope, a derisive cry. 1H6 i. 3

roping, dripping. H5 iii. 5; iv.2

rosed, made rosy. H5 v. 2

rotten, rainy. Son. 34

round, whisper. John ii. 1; surround. R2 iii. 2; R3 iv. 1; plainspoken. H5 iv. 1; circle. V. & A. 368

roundure, circuit. John ii. 1

rout, mob, gang. 2H4 iv. 1; 2H4 iv. 2; disorderly flight. 2H6 v. 2

rowel, small sharp-pointed wheel at the end of a spur. 2H4 i. 1

royal, gold coin worth about 10s.; R2 v. 5; &c.

royal battle, battle for a kingdom. R3 iv. 4

rub, impediment. John iii. 4; &c.

ruffle, stir, bustle. Lov. C. 58

rug-headed, rough-headed. R2 ii. 1

runagate, vagabond. R3 iv. 4

run in, fallen under. H8 i. 2

running banquet, hasty refreshment. H8 i. 4; whipping. H8 v. 4

ruth, pity. R2 iii. 4; Son. 132

ruthful, piteous. 3H6 ii. 5

Saba, the queen of Sheba. H8 v. 5

sack, general name for Spanish white wines. 1H4 i. 2; &c.

sacring bell, bell rung during mass at consecration of the elements. H8 iii. 2

St. *Martin's summer,* days of bright and warm weather coming in November. 1H6 i.2

St. *Nicholas' clerks,* highwaymen. 1H4 ii. 1

sallet, salad. 2H6 iv. 10; close-fitting helmet. 2H6 iv. 10

Samingo, St. Domingo, patron-saint of drinkers. 2H4 v. 3

sanctuary, a church or other sacred place of refuge for fugitives. R3 ii. 4

sand, sand-bank. H5 iv. 1

sarcenet, soft silk material, hence, soft. 1H4 iii. 1

saving your manhoods, apologetic phrase. 2H4 ii. 1

saw, saying, text. 2H6 i.3; Luc. 244; saw each other, met. H8 i. 1

sawn, seen. Lov. C. 91

say, cloth of fine texture resembling serge. 2H6 iv. 7

'sblood, God's blood, an oath. 1H4 i. 2; H5 iv. 8

*scab,*term of contempt.2H4 iii. 2

scaffold, stage. H5 i. chor.

scald, mangy, scabby. H5 v. 1.

scambling, scrambling.H5 i. 1; v. 2

scape, escapade. Luc. 747

scathe, injury. John ii. 1; 2H6 ii. 4; R3 i. 3

scattered stray, stragglers. 2H4 iv. 2

scion, twig, shoot. H5 iii. 5

sconce, fort. H5 iii. 6

scot and lot, pay, thoroughly settle. 1H4 v. 4

scrivener, professional scribe. R3 iii. 6 (stage direction)

scroyles, scabby rascals. John ii. 1

seal, the Great Seal. R3 ii. 4

sear, brand. R3 iv. 1

seated, situated. Luc. 1144

seconds, inferior kind of flour. Son. 125

sect, sex. 2H4 ii. 4

seld, seldom. Pas. P. xiii

self and vain conceit, vain self-conceit. R2 iii. 2

self-born, native. R2 ii. 3

semblable, similar. 2H4 v. 1

seniory, seniority. R3 iv. 4

sennet, set of notes on the trumpet. 3H6 i. 1; R3 iii. 1; H8 ii.4. Stage direction in each case

septentrion, the north. 3H6 i. 4

set, term at cards, as well as at tennis. John v. 2; set out. H5 ii. chor.; sunset. H5 iv. 1; R3 v. 3; sitting. H8 iii. 1; seated. V. & A. 18

*set a match,*planned a robbery. 1H4 i. 2

sets me else, who, who else sets me a stake? a term at dice. R2 iv. 1

setter, one who plans an appointment. 1H4 ii. 2

set to, set, as a broken limb. 1H4 v. 1

seven stars, the Pleiades. 1H4 i. 2; 2H4 ii. 4

shadow, protect. John ii. 1; reflection.John ii. 1;mere names. 2H4 iii. 2

shady stealth, stealthily-moving shadow. Son. 77

shag, shaggy.2H6 iii.1; V. & A. 295

shale, shell. H5 iv. 2

shamefast, shame-faced. R3 i.4

*shape of likelihood,*probability. 1H4 i. 1

shearman, one who shears cloth. 2H6 iv. 2

sheaved, made of straw. Lov. C. 31

sherris, sherris-sack, wine of Xeres, in Spain. 2H4 iv. 3

shog, move, jog. H5 ii. 1; ii. 3

shoon, shoes. 2H6 iv. 2

shot, marksman. 2H4 iii. 2; 1H6 i. 4; H8 v. 4

shot-free, without paying the tavern charge. 1H4 v. 3

shotten, having shed its roe. 1H4 ii. 4

shove-groat shilling, shilling used in game of shove-groat. 2H4 ii. 4

shrift, confession. R3 iii. 4

shriver, confessor. 3H6 iii. 2

shriving work, confession. R3 iii. 2

shroud, sail-rope. John v. 7; 3H6 v. 4; H8 iv. 1; hide oneself. 3H6 iii. 1; iv. 3

Shrove-tide, close of the Carnival, a merry time. 2H4 v. 3

sights, eye-holes in a helmet. 2H4 iv. 1

signal, sign of victory. H5 v. chor.

sign of the leg, bootmaker's sign. 2H4 ii. 4

sign of war, armour, standard, ensign. R2 ii. 2; H5 ii. 2

signory, lordship, estate. R2 iii. 1; iv. 1

silken, effeminate. H5 ii. chor.; R3 i. 3

sinew, knit together. John v. 7; strength. 1H4 iv. 4; nerve. V. & A. 903

sinew together, knit in strength. 3H6 ii. 6

single, simple, silly. 2H4 i. 2; sincere. H8 v. 3

Sir, title of priests. 2H6 i. 2; R3 iii. 2

sirrah, word addressed to inferiors. 1H4 i. 2; 1H6 iii. 1; R3 iii. 2

sistering, neighbouring. Lov. C. 2

sith, since. 3H6 i.1; V. & A.762

skimble-skamble, wild, confused. 1H4 iii. 1

skin-coat, lion's skin. John ii. 1

skirr, move rapidly. H5 iv. 7

slaughter-man, butcher. 3H6 i.4

sleided, untwisted. Lov. C. 48

slept upon, been blinded to the faults of. H8 ii. 2

slips, leash. H5 iii. 1; counterfeit coin. V. & A. 515

slops, loose breeches. 2H4 i. 2

slough, snakeskin. H5 iv. 1; 2H6 iii. 1

slovenry, slovenliness. H5 iv. 3

slug, sluggard. R3 iii. 1

smoke, thrash. John ii. 1

smooth, flatter. 2H6 i. 1; &c.; bland, insinuative. 2H6 iii. 1

smooth-pate, sleek-head. 2H4 i. 2

snatchers, free-booters. H5 i. 2

sneak-cup, one who shirks drinking. 1H4 iii. 3

sneap, snub. 2H4 ii. 1; nipped. Luc. 333

snuff, in, offence at. 1H4 i. 3

soil, explanation. Son. 69

solace, be happy. R3 ii. 3

sonance, sound. H5 iv. 2

sooth, truth. John iv. 1; H5 iii. 6; H8 ii. 3

sophister, one who uses false casuistry. 2H6 v. 1

sore, heavily. R2 ii. 1

sortance, hold, be in accordance. 2H4 iv. 1

sound, proclaim. John iv. 2; H8 v. 2

souse, swoop down on. John v.2

soused gurnet, pickled fish. 1H4 iv. 2

span-counter, boys' game. 2H6 iv. 2

spanned, limited. H8 i. 1

Spanish-pouch, term of contempt. 1H4 ii. 4

spavin, a disease in horses. H8 i. 3

speed, fortune. 1H4 iii. 1

spend their mouths, to give tongue. H5 ii. 4; V. & A. 695

spinster, spinner. H8 i. 2

spital, hospital. H5 ii. 1; v. 1

splitting, that will split the sides of vessels. 2H6 iii. 2

spoil, corruption. 1H4 iii.3; despoil. 2H6 iv. 4; destroy. H8 i. 2

sportive, amorous. Son. 121

spot, disgrace. John v. 2

spotted, polluted. R2 iii. 2

spousal, marriage. H5 v. 2

sprays, branch, twig. H5 iii. 5; 2H6 ii. 3

spright, spirit. V. & A. 181

springhalt, lameness in horses. H8 i. 3

squire, square, rule. 1H4 ii. 2

stain, grow dim. Son. 33

stain to all nymphs, causing them to appear sullied by contrast. V. & A. 9

stale, laughing-stock. 3H6 iii.3

standing tuck, rapier standing on end. 1H4 ii. 4

star, pole-star. Son. 116

starting-hole, refuge, subterfuge. 1H4 ii. 4

statua, statue. R3 iii. 7

statute, security. Son. 134

staves, shafts of lances. R3 v. 3

steeled, hardened. Son. 112

steep-up, precipitous. Son. 7; Pas. P. ix

stelled, fixed. Luc. 1444; Son. 24

stern, place. 1H6 i. 1

sternage of, to, astern of. H5 iii. chor.

stick, hesitate. 2H4 i. 2; Son. to Music iv

stiff-borne, obstinately pursued. 2H4 i. 1

stigmatic, one bearing a brand of deformity. 2H6 v. 1; 3H6 ii. 2

still and anon, now and again. John iv. 1

stillitory, still. V. & A. 443

still lasting, continual. R3 iv. 4

still-pining, ever-longing. Luc. 858

still-slaughtered, ever killed but never dying. Luc. 188

still-stand, standstill. 2H4 ii. 3

stock-fish, dried fish. 1H4 ii. 4

stole, robe. Lov. C. 297

stomach, appetite. 1H4 ii. 3; 2H4 iv. 4; pride. 2H4 i. 1; H8 iv. 2; anger. 1H6 i. 3; 2H6 ii.1

stood, insisted. H5 v. 2

stood to, sided with. H8 ii. 4

stoop, swoop down on the prey. H5 iv. 1

stop, hole in a wind instrument by the opening or closing of which the sounds are produced. 2H4 Ind.

strain courtesy, decline to go first. V. & A. 888

strait, straitly, niggardly. John v. 7; strict, strictly. 1H4 iv. 3; &c.

strangle, extinguish. H8 v. 1; Son. 89

strappado, punishment in which victim was drawn up by his arms strapped behind his back, and suddenly let fall. 1H4 ii. 4

stray, body of stragglers. 2H4 iv. 2; vagrant. 2H6 iv. 10

strength of laws, legal right. Son. 49

strewed, strewn with rushes. R2 i. 3

strict, close. V. & A. 874

strike, strike sail, submit, give way. R2 ii. 1; &c.

striker, dissolute fellow. 1H4 ii. 1

strond, strand. 1H4 i.1; 2H4 i.1

strossers, trowsers. H5 iii. 7

studied, inclined. 2H4 ii. 2

stumbling night, night which causes stumbling. John v. 5

style, list of titles. 2H6 i. 1

suborn, procure. R3 iv. 3

subornation, inciting. 2H6 iii.1; murderous subornation, guilt of underhand murder. 1H4 i. 3

sue his livery, lay claim to his estate. 1H4 iv. 3

suggest, tempt. R2 iii. 4; &c.

sullens, moroseness. R2 ii. 1

sumless, inestimable. H5 i. 2

summered, provided, as cattle with pasture. H5 v. 2

supplies, supply, reserve, reinforcements. 1H4 iv. 3; 2H4 iv. 2

supportance, support. R2 iii. 4

sure card, boon companion. 2H4 iii. 2

surfeit-taking, indulging to excess. Luc. 698

sur-reined, over-ridden.H5 iii.5

suspire, breathe. John iii. 4; 2H4 iv. 5

sutler, provision-seller to the camp. H5 ii. 1

sweep, walk in pomp. 2H6 i. 3

sweeting, term of endearment. 1H6 iii. 3

swelling, angry. R3 ii. 1

swiftest hours, prime of life. Lov. C. 60

swilled, greedily gulped down. H5 iii. 1

swinge, beat. John ii. 1; 2H4 v. 4

swinge-buckler, roysterer. 2H4 iii. 2

sword-and-buckler, common fighter. 1H4 i. 3

sworder, gladiator. 2H6 iv. 1

sworn brother, pledged comrade. R2 v. 1; H5 ii. 1

swound, swoon. Luc. 1486

table, canvas of a picture. John ii. 1; memorandum book. 2H4 ii. 4; Son. 24; 122

tackling, rigging. 3H6 v. 4; R3 iv. 4

tainture, disgrace. 2H6 ii. 1

take head, turn aside. John ii. 1

take it, swear. 1H4 ii. 4

talents, lockets containing hair. Lov. C. 204

tallow-ketch, vessel filled with tallow. 1H4 ii. 4

tally, notched stick for keeping accounts. 2H6 iv. 7; Son. 122

tap for tap, tit for tat. 2H4 ii. 1

tarre, set dogs to fight.John iv.1

tarriance, stay. Pas. P. vi

Tartar, Tartarus, hell. H5 ii. 2

tawny-coats, livery worn by ecclesiastical apparitors.1H6 i.3

teen, grief, vexation, pain. R3 iv. 1; V. & A. 808; Lov. C. 192

temperality, blunder for 'temper.' 2H4 ii. 4

temper with the stars, act and think in conformity with fate. 3H6 iv. 6

tendance, attention. H8 iii. 2

tender, hold dear, take care of, have care for. R2 i. 1; &c.; favour. Luc. 534

termagant, an imaginary Mohammedan deity, represented in the old plays as a most violent character. 1H4 v. 4

termless, indescribable. Lov. C. 94

tertian, a fever of which the paroxysms occur every third day. H5 ii. 1

tester, sixpence. 2H4 iii. 2

tetchy, fretful. R3 iv. 4

theme, business. 2H4 i. 3

theoric, theory. H5 i. 1

thewes, muscles. 2H4 iii. 2

thick-eyed, dim-eyed. 1H4 ii. 3

thick-sighted, short-sighted. V. & A. 136

thrall, slave. R3 iv. 1; enslave. V. & A. 837; slavery. Son. to Music iii.

thralled, held in subjection. Son. 124

threaden, made of thread. H5 iii. chor.; Lov. C. 33

three-farthings, the three-farthing pieces of Elizabeth were thin, and had a rose stamped behind the queen's head. John i. 1

three-man beetle, rammer worked by three men. 2H4 i.2

threne, dirge. Phœn. 49

tickle, unstable. 2H6 i. 1

tickle-brain, strong drink. 1H4 ii. 4

tied, brought into bondage. H8 iv. 2

tike, cur. H5 ii. 1

tilly-fally, expression of contempt. 2H4 ii. 4

time's enemies, the, enemies of the present state of affairs. John iv. 2

times in hope, future times. Son. 60

tire, feed ravenously. 3H6 i. 1; V. & A. 56; make feed ravenously. Luc. 417; head-dress. Son. 53

tired, attired. V. & A. 177

tirrits, ?blunder for 'terrors.' 2H4 ii. 4

toasting-iron, sword. John iv. 3

toasts and butter, effeminate fellows. 1H4 iv. 2

toll, raise a tax. John iii. 1

tongue, English language.1H4 iii. 1

took it on his death, swore by his death. John i. 1

*torn their souls,*perjured themselves. R2 iii. 3

tottering, hanging in rags.John v. 5

touched and tried, tested by the touchstone. John iii. 1

touch, know no, have no skill. R2 i. 3

tower, soar as a bird of prey. John v. 2; &c.

trace, track, follow. 1H4 iii. 1; H8 iii. 2

tract, course. H8 i. 1; Son. 7

trade-fallen, out of employment. 1H4 iv. 2

train, entice, allure, decoy. John iii. 4; 1H4 v. 2; 1H6 ii. 3

tranquillity, gentility. 1H4 ii. 1

travel-tainted, travel-stained. 2H4 iv. 3

treble-dated, living for three ages. Phœn. 17

trench, entrench. 1H4 i. 1; turn into another channel. 1H4 iii. 1; gash. V. & A. 1052

trencher, plate. 2H6 iv. 1

Tribulation of Tower-hill, ?congregation of puritans.H8 v. 4

Trigon, Mars, the third of a planetary triangle. 2H4 ii. 4

trim, ornamental array. 1H4 iv. 1

trimmed in, furnished with. 2H4 i. 3

trip, defeat. 2H4 v. 2

triumph, tournament. R2 v. 2; 1H6 v. 5; public festivity. 1H4 iii. 3

troth, faith. R2 v. 2; Luc. 571

troth-plight, betrothed. H5 ii.1

trow, know, believe. 2H6 iv. 4; H8 i. 1; think. 3H6 v. 1

Troyan, cant name for an evil liver. 1H4 ii. 1

trull, harlot. 3H6 i. 4

truncheon, cudgel. 2H4 ii. 4

tuck, rapier. 1H4 ii. 4

tucket, flourish on trumpet. H5 iv. 2

Turk, Grand Turk, Sultan. 2H4 iii. 2; H5 v. 2

Turk Gregory, Pope Gregory VII. 1H4 v. 3

Turnbull Street, Turnmill Street, Clerkenwell, then of notorious character. 2H4 iii.2

turned, shaped in the turning-lathe. 1H4 iii. 1

tushes, tusks. V. & A. 617

tway, two. H5 iii. 2

twelve score, twelve score yards. 1H4 ii. 4; 2H4 iii. 2

twire, twinkle. Son. 38

umbered, darkened. H5 iv. chor.

unbid, unwelcome. 3H6 v. 1

unbless, neglect to make happy. Son. 3

unblown, unopened. R3 iv. 4

uncoined constancy, which like an unimpressed plain piece of metal has not yet become current coin. H5 v. 2

uncolted, deprived of one's horse. 1H4 ii. 2

uncouple, loose the dogs. V. & A. 673

underbear, endure. John iii. 1; R2 i. 4

underprop, support. John v. 2

underskinker, under-drawer, tapster. 1H4 ii. 4

under-wrought, undermined. John ii. 1

uneared, unploughed. Son. 3

uneath, uneasily, hardly. 2H6 ii. 4

uneven, embarrassing. 1H4 i. 1

unexperient, inexperienced. Lov. C. 318

unfair, deprive of beauty. Son. 5

unfathered, unnaturally produced. 2H4 iv. 4

unfenced, defenceless. John ii.1

unfurnished, untapestried. R2 i. 2; left undefended. H5 i. 2

ungotten, unbegotten. H5 i. 2

unhaired, beardless. John v. 2

unhappied, made unhappy. R2 iii. 1

unjointed, incoherent. 1H4 i. 3

unkind, unnatural. 1H6 iv. 1; childless. V. & A. 204

unkinged, dethroned. R2 iv. 1; v. 5

unkiss, undo by a kiss. R2 v. 1

unlived, dead. Luc. 1754

unowed, without an owner. John iv. 3

unpay, atone by payment for. 2H4 ii. 1

unraised, uninspired. H5 i. chor.

unready, undressed. 1H6 ii. 1

unreverent, irreverent. R2 ii. 1

unset, unplanted. Son. 16

unsorted, unsuitable. 1H4 ii. 3

unstanched, unquenched. 3H6 ii. 6

untainted, unaccused. R3 iii. 6; unblemished. Son. 19

untoward, unmannerly. John i.1

untrimmed, with loose hair, according to bridal custom. John iii. 1

untucked, dishevelled. Lov. C. 31

unwares, unawares. 3H6 ii. 5

unwashed hands, with, immediately. 1H4 iii. 3

upswarmed, raised in swarms. 2H4 iv. 2

up-till, against. Son. to Music vi

urchin-snouted, with snout like hedgehog's. V. & A. 1105

urging, speaking of. R2 iii. 1
urn, grave. H5 i. 2
used myself, behaved. H8 iii. 1
utis, great fun. 2H4 ii. 4

vade, fade. R2 i. 2; &c.
vail, lower. 2H4 i. 1; 1H6 v. 3;
V. & A. 314
*varlet,*knave.2H4 v. 3; servant.
H5 iv. 2
vassal, servile. 1H4 iii. 2
vast, waste, desolate. John iv.
3; R3 i. 4
vaultages, caverns. H5 ii. 4
*vaunt,*exult. R3 v.3; mount up-
wards. Son. 15
*vaward,*vanguard. 2H4 i. 2; H5
iv. 3
*velvet-guard,*person who wears
velvet trimmings. 1H4 iii. 1
verge, compass. R2 ii. 1; 2H6
i. 4; R3 iv. 1
via, let us on. 3H6 ii. 1
vice, grip. 2H4 ii. 1; buffoon in
morality plays. 2H4 iii. 2; R3
iii. 1
vigil, eve. H5 iv. 3
villain, countryman. Luc. 1338
villiago, base coward. 2H6 iv.8
viol, guitar. R2 i. 3
virtuous, essential. 2H4 iv. 5
vizard, mask. 1H4 i. 2; R3 ii. 2
void, vomit. H5 iii. 5; quit. H5
iv. 7; devoid. 2H6 iv. 7
voiding lobby, anteroom. 2H6
iv. 1
Volquessen, Vexin. John ii. 1
vulture, ravenous. V. & A. 551

wafer-cakes, i.e. as easily
broken. H5 ii. 3
wage, hazard. 1H4 iv. 4
walks, wildly, goes to confu-
sion. John iv. 2
wanton, effeminate boy. John
v. 1; luxurious. 1H4 iii. 1;
2H4 i. 1; play. V. & A. 106

ward, posture of defence. 1H4
i. 2; ii. 4; custody. 2H6 v. 1;
guard. R3 v. 3; bolt. Luc. 303
warder, truncheon. R2 i. 3; 2H4
iv. 1
warrantize, security. 1H6 i. 3;
Son. 150
Washford, Wexford. 1H6 iv. 7
wasp-stung, irritable. 1H4 i. 3
wassail candle, festal candle.
2H4 i. 2
*Wat,*name for hare.V. & A. 697
watch, keep awake. R2 ii. 1; V.
& A. 584; stated interval of
time. R2 v. 5; candle which
marked the hours. R3 v. 3;
watchman. Pas. P. xiv.
watch-case, sentry-box. 2H4
iii. 1
watch of woes, divided and
marked only by woes. Luc.
928
water-colours, weak fellows.
1H4 v. 1
water-gall, secondary rainbow.
Luc. 1588
water-work, painting in water-
colours. 2H4 ii. 1
watery moon, i.e. as the tides
are. R3 ii. 2
wean, alienate. 3H6 iv. 4
wear, carry. 1H4 i. 3; wear out.
1H4 ii. 4; V. & A. 506
weed, garment. Luc. 196; Son.
2
ween, suppose, think. 1H6 ii.
5; H8 v. 1
welkin, sky. R3 v. 3
Welsh hook, kind of battle-axe.
1H4 ii. 4
what the good-year, a mild
oath. 2H4 ii. 4
Wheeson, Whitsun. 2H4 ii. 1
whelk, pimple. H5 iii. 6
when, canst tell? expression of
contempt. 1H4 ii. 1
whiffler, one who cleared the

way for a procession. H5 v.
chor.

whipping-cheer, whipping
fare. 2H4 v. 4

whit, jot. R2 ii. 1; R3 iii. 4

white-livered, cowardly. H5
iii. 2; R3 iv. 4

whoreson, bastard. 2H4 i. 2

wight, person, man. H5 ii. 1

wild, weald. 1H4 ii. 1

wilful-opposite, wilfully obsti-
nate. John v. 2

Winchester goose, cant name
for a diseased person. 1H6 i.3

Wincot, Wilmecote near Strat-
ford. 2H4 v. 1

windows, eyelids. R3 v. 3

winked, connived. H5 ii. 2

wink with fulness, close as af-
ter a full meal. Son. 56

wipe, brand, mark of disgrace.
Luc. 537

wistly, wistfully. R2 v. 4; V. &
A. 343; Luc. 1355

witch, bewitch. 1H4 iv. 1;
2H6 iii. 2; 3H6 iii. 2

within a ken, in sight. 2H4 iv.1

witnessed usurpation, traces of
usurpation. 2H4 i. 1

*wittily,*ingeniously.V. & A. 471

witting, knowing. 1H6 ii. 5

woe the while, alas. H5 iv. 7

woman-queller, murderer of
women. 2H4 ii. 1

womby, hollow. H5 ii. 4

wood, mad. V. & A. 740

wooden thing, difficult busi-
ness. 1H6 v. 3

woodman, huntsman. Luc. 580

world, soul. Lov. C. 7

worm, serpent. 2H6 iii. 2; V. &
A. 933

worship, dignity, honour. John
iv. 3; &c.

wo't, wilt thou. 2H4 ii. 1

wrack, ruin. 2H6 i. 3; V. & A.
558

wrangler, adversary. H5 i. 2

wrapped, involved. Luc. 456

wringing, torture. H5 iv. 1

writ, described himself as. 2H4
i. 2; scripture. 2H6 i. 3; R3 i.
3

writhled, wrinkled. 1H6 ii. 3

wrought the mure, worn away
the wall. 2H4 iv. 4

wrung in the withers, pressed
in the shoulders. 1H4 ii. 1

y-clad, clad. 2H6 i. 1

yea-forsooth knave, one who
swears only mild oaths. 2H4
i. 2

yearn, grieve. R2 v. 5; H5 ii. 3;
iv. 3

Yedward, Edward. 1H4 i. 2

yeoman, sheriff's officer. 2H4
ii. 1

yerk, jerk. H5 iv. 7

yoke-fellow, companion. H5 ii.
3; iv. 6

younker, youngster. 1H4 iii. 3;
3H6 ii. 1

'zounds, an imprecation. John
ii. 1